W9-BSJ-463

# McGraw-Hill's
# CHINESE
# DICTIONARY & GUIDE
## *to* 20,000 Essential Words

RECEIVED

OCT 2 0 2010

MINNESOTA STATE UNIVERSITY
MANKATO

Quanyu Huang • Tong Chen • Kuangyan Huang

Mc
Graw
Hill

New York   Chicago   San Francisco   Lisbon   London   Madrid   Mexico City
Milan   New Delhi   San Juan   Seoul   Singapore   Sydney   Toronto

The **McGraw·Hill** Companies

**Library of Congress Cataloging-in-Publication Data**

Huang, Quanyu.
    McGraw-Hill's Chinese dictionary & guide to 20,000 essential words /
Quanyu Huang, Tong Chen, Kuangyan Huang.
        p.  cm.
    In English and Chinese.
    Includes index.
    ISBN 0-07-162924-6 (alk. paper)
    1.  Chinese language—Dictionaries—English.    2.  English language—
Dictionaries—Chinese.   I.  Chen, Tong.   II.  Huang, Kuangyan.   III.  Title.
IV.  Title: McGraw-Hill's Chinese dictionary and guide to 20,000 essential words.
V.  Title: Chinese dictionary & guide to 20,000 essential words.
   PL1455.H7957   2010
   495.1'321—dc22                         2010000227

Ref.
PL
1455
.H7957
2010

Copyright © 2010 by The McGraw-Hill Companies, Inc. All rights reserved.
Printed in the United States of America. Except as permitted under the United States
Copyright Act of 1976, no part of this publication may be reproduced or distributed
in any form or by any means, or stored in a database or retrieval system, without
the prior written permission of the publisher.

1  2  3  4  5  6  7  8  9  10  11  12  13  14  15   WDQ/WDQ   1  9  8  7  6  5  4  3  2  1  0

ISBN   978-0-07-162924-9
MHID     0-07-162924-6

Interior design by Village Bookworks, Inc.

McGraw-Hill books are available at special quantity discounts to use as
premiums and sales promotions or for use in corporate training programs.
To contact a representative, please e-mail us at bulksales@mcgraw-hill.com.

# Contents

汉语断笔码词典
The Chinese Broken Marks Dictionary

# Foreword

Professor Quanyu Huang has done a great favor for students and teachers of Chinese. By introducing his Broken Marks method in *McGraw-Hill's Chinese Dictionary and Guide to 20,000 Essential Words,* Professor Huang has made Chinese characters accessible even to beginning students of the language. Chinese teachers and students are constantly searching for new tools that give learners of Chinese more control over the process of learning characters and reading Chinese. By providing a simple way to look at a Chinese character and count its marks, the Broken Marks method allows even the least experienced learner to find the most complicated character.

This is a time when a Chinese character dictionary for the beginning learner is urgently needed. Beginning learners of Chinese can easily find Chinese materials on the Internet. With this dictionary, they can look up Chinese characters and develop a familiarity with the structure and use of the writing system. The more learners practice with characters, the sooner they are able to distinguish those components that they will later identify as radicals and phonetics. This will permit them to look up characters in standard dictionaries and predict their pronunciation.

To the beginning student of the Chinese language, characters appear as jumbles of strokes. After closely examining and manipulating them for a time, the recurring elements come into focus. The systematic nature of the writing system slowly becomes clear. It *is* a system— just a really *big* system. Even with the most rigorous instruction, the system of radicals and phonetics used in the standard dictionaries emerges slowly. The more exposure learners have to the writing system, the sooner the roles of these recurring elements are detected and put to use.

This dictionary is an intermediate step toward the efficient use of standard Chinese language reference works. I hope my students acquire this tool early in their study of the language and use it to review previously studied characters and to learn new characters. By doing this, they will develop the habit of efficiently referencing a dictionary, and an important element of control and self-management can be built into their Chinese language-learning career.

Galal Walker, Ph.D.
Professor of Chinese Pedagogy
Director of the Chinese Flagship Center
Director of the National East Asian Languages Resource Center
The Ohio State University
Columbus, Ohio  U.S.A.

# Preface

At the dawn of the eighteenth century, Emperor Kangxi of the Qing dynasty ordered a host of scholars and scribes to compile all of the known words under heaven. They assembled a total of 49,030 characters. To organize them, the characters were divided into 214 radical groups, which were then divided into subgroups based on the number of strokes per radical and per character. After six years of intense labor, a massive text spanning 40 volumes was published in 1716. Kangxi had created the very first Chinese dictionary.

Almost all of today's Chinese dictionaries are patterned to a large degree on this original dictionary. This practice has resulted in an unusual phenomenon in the study of Chinese in America and other countries outside China: Very few, if any, Chinese dictionaries are being used by foreign or beginning students of Chinese.

Recently, we conducted a survey of the Chinese classes at Miami University of Ohio. Of the 300-plus students studying Chinese at various levels of proficiency, only two actively used a Chinese dictionary. Why? What could account for the relative uselessness of these dictionaries? What makes them so unappealing to students? How could they be improved?

Traditional Chinese dictionaries today still employ, with minor additions and revisions, the antiquated system constructed three centuries ago by Kangxi's scholars and scribes. That system was intended and designed for use by Chinese people; it was not created with the foreigner in mind. Since the Kangxi model is still in use today, there is no Chinese dictionary designed specifically for use by nonnative beginners.

## What's Wrong with Traditional Chinese Dictionaries?

Why do nonnative students have such difficulty using traditional Chinese dictionaries? Students point to three main problems: (1) radicals, (2) strokes, and (3) related words.

### Radicals

Objectively viewed, the radical system is a rather cumbersome invention and can be confusing and daunting for beginning (and even advanced) Chinese students.

We once asked three native Chinese with Ph.D.s, all of whom have the last name 尹, to find this character in the popular *Xinhua Dictionary with English Translation* (Commercial Press International, 2000). None of them could find it immediately. It took all three of them several attempts, and one almost gave up. Because 尹 is listed not only under the radical 乙 but also under 尸 according to the traditional radical system, our three subjects struggled to perform what should have been a relatively straightforward task: looking up their own surname. If such a system can confuse educated Chinese natives (Ph.D.s, no less), how can one expect a nonnative beginner to be able to use the dictionary with any efficiency or frequency?

### Strokes

It is also difficult for beginners to memorize strokes and count them. Even if one realizes that 尹 belongs to the radical group 乙 or 尸, the next step requires counting the character's strokes. Success relies on an understanding of idiosyncratic traditional strokes. One of the greatest difficulties for nonnative users of Chinese dictionaries is counting strokes. Let us take

尹 as an example. Many American students count five strokes in this character, while some count only three; according to traditional rules, however, the character has four strokes. The culprit is the "linked stroke," an unintuitive but pervasive device that can complicate the search for even the simplest character. The linked stroke is discussed in more detail below.

## Related Words

In English, each word is separated from the words around it by spaces; letters are grouped together to form a word. Imagine how difficult it would be to read English if there were no spaces between words. Unfortunately for nonnative students of Chinese, there are no spaces between words. All Chinese characters (which words are composed of) are set together; spaces are used only to separate clauses and sentences. This creates a monumental problem: Even if one can identify a character's radical, count its strokes correctly, and find the character's meaning in a dictionary (for example, the character 业 in the sentence 他的事业非常成功), one would still have a difficult time figuring out the word in which 业 is used in the sentence. Does it form a word all by itself? Should it be combined with the character to its left (事业) or the one to its right (业非)? Or should it be combined with the two characters to its left (的事业) or the two to its right (业非常)? Or is it the middle character of three (事业非) or even more characters? Each combination is potentially a word with a completely different meaning. Even if one can find the meaning of a particular character in a modern Chinese dictionary, it is useless if one cannot identify the word in which it is being used.

These three problems—radicals, strokes, and related words—have left nonnative students without a tool that students of other languages would consider valuable, if not indispensable.

*McGraw-Hill's Chinese Dictionary and Guide to 20,000 Essential Words* is an elegant solution to these seemingly insoluble problems. Its elegance lies in its simplicity. Emerging from Kangxi's shadow, we offer a brand new dictionary that addresses all three of the problems above, and more: the first Chinese dictionary in history that is entirely innovative, comprehensive, and easy and quick to use.

## Breaking the Linked Stroke

There is no greater example of the kind of esoteric knowledge required to use a Chinese dictionary than the traditional "linked stroke." Derived from the principles of Chinese calligraphy, an art heavily laden with history and custom, the linked stroke is not intuitive.

As an example, let us consider the character 口 ("mouth"). If a beginning student were asked how many strokes are used to construct 口, what would the person say? The obvious answer is "four." If you were to open a dictionary, you could search through the four-stroked characters all day to no avail. You won't find 口 there. The traditional (and correct) answer is that there are only three strokes in 口. The culprit is the linked stroke ㇕, which, according to traditional Chinese calligraphy, is written in one continuous stroke.

This is only a simple example. Some characters contain two, three, or even four linked strokes, each of which can have many forms. They are prevalent enough that searching for a character often becomes a crapshoot, even for those who are fairly familiar with the language.

Chinese people learn to recognize such idiosyncrasies in their early education, as they learn how to write Chinese properly. This takes many years. Even so, many educated Chinese often forget or miscount the number of strokes in even the most popular characters. This reveals the limitations of a dictionary based on counting strokes. To be able to recognize these strokes, one must have studied them extensively. To have studied these strokes extensively, one must know how to write Chinese adeptly. The result is ironic: Knowing how to write Chinese is a prerequisite for using a Chinese dictionary effectively. This is like searching for a match with a torch: What if you don't have a torch? How are beginning students expected to use a dictionary at all?

Our solution was to break the linked stroke, in two senses. Figuratively, we departed from the traditional system, "breaking away" from the method of organizing characters that was established three centuries ago. Our goal was to develop a new method of organization that would provide students with a new and better way to search the dictionary.

In another sense, after much thought and experimentation, we literally broke the linked stroke. Realizing that the linked stroke was one of the main sources of frustration for many dictionary users, we decided that we had to replace it. We realized that each linked stroke could be seen as a composite of distinct, easier-to-recognize "marks." A character could thus be seen as a combination of "broken marks." Most importantly, these marks would be easy to recognize and easy to count for everyone. No additional knowledge (except the ability to count to 20 or so) is required.

## A Step-by-Step Comparison

TRADITIONAL DICTIONARY

- Know 214 different radicals.
- Identify a character's radical.
- Count the radical strokes.
- Find the appropriate index number in the radical index list.
- Count the remaining strokes.
- Find the character from a group of characters according to the remaining strokes.

THE BROKEN MARKS DICTIONARY

- *No comparable step.*
- *No comparable step.*
- *No comparable step.*
- *No comparable step.*

- Count the total marks of the character.
- Identify the first mark.

Using a traditional dictionary, if you make a single mistake in any of the six steps, you will have absolutely no way to find the character you seek. Identifying your error is also frustrating. Most people, even native Chinese, will venture several time-consuming guesses at what could have gone wrong before ultimately finding a character. Many just give up—a common occurrence for even the most experienced Chinese reader or speaker, let alone the beginning student. It is easy to see why more than 99% of beginning students refuse to use a dictionary.

Using the Broken Marks method, there is no need to memorize radicals or be concerned with linked strokes. The Broken Marks method takes much of the pain and guesswork out of what used to be a frustrating, labyrinthine process. The Broken Marks method is faster and more reliable than traditional dictionaries, making it a useful tool for everyone. For the first time, beginning and intermediate students will find themselves using and relying on a Chinese dictionary.

Once you are familiar with the Broken Marks method, you will be able to look up characters in a fraction of the time it would take you with a traditional dictionary. In our testing, a nonnative student using this Broken Marks Chinese dictionary can find a character faster than a native Chinese using a traditional dictionary.

## Four Search Methods

*McGraw-Hill's Chinese Dictionary and Guide to 20,000 Essential Words* comprises 2,000 of the most commonly used characters in modern Mandarin Chinese. By searching for a specific character, a user may quickly and easily find all information related to that character.

In addition to our own Broken Marks method (see Indexes 1 and 2), the dictionary offers three other methods to search for a character. These three methods (Pinyin [Index 3], Radicals and Strokes [Index 4], and English to Chinese [Index 5]) are standard in most dictionaries. In creating our new search method, we have been careful to retain the old, for there is still value in familiarizing oneself with radicals and strokes. Altogether, the four featured methods of searching for a character allow for a great amount of flexibility, so that those who are studying traditional characters or who are familiar with previous systems can also conveniently use this dictionary.

## Other Features

Although our Broken Marks method is extremely fast and efficient, *McGraw-Hill's Chinese Dictionary and Guide to 20,000 Essential Words* is not simply a character finder. It is a comprehensive dictionary and has all of the features of other Chinese dictionaries, even as it introduces several unique features.

1 · While the dictionary has entries for 2,000 of the most frequently used Chinese characters, these characters lead to 20,000 of the most widely used Chinese words and over 5,000 example sentences.

2 · English meanings almost always match the correct Chinese parts of speech. Chinese words often have an asymmetric counterpart in English; alhough the basic meaning is the same, the English expression may not match the original Chinese part of speech. You may have noticed this unusual phenomenon while flipping through other Chinese dictionaries. Using a word correctly as part of a sentence is an important element in learning a language. For this reason, we have endeavored to modify these asymmetric English meanings in order to match the Chinese part of speech.

   Despite our efforts, however, some parts of speech cannot be easily matched by English expressions. For example, 临别, which is considered a verb in Chinese, is best translated as "just before parting" in English—an adverbial prepositional phrase. It is difficult to formulate an English verb expression for this concept. For these more perplexing words, we simply use the best possible translation, leaving the grammatical headache to linguists. Note that the part of speech given always refers to the Chinese word, not to its English meanings.

3 · Secondary meanings are often given to supplement the user's understanding of a word. These meanings add context and are frequently more common in English than the first meaning. For example, 徒劳 is a verb in Chinese. In addition to the first meaning given ("to work to no avail"), we also include a second meaning ("to make a futile effort").

4 · Specific "measure words" are provided for nouns that have them (for example, "a sheet of paper" and "a chunk of meat"). Matching a noun with its proper measure word is one of the most common difficulties faced by students learning Chinese. Few Chinese dictionaries give the measure words for nouns.

5 · The example sentences have been crafted for practicality and frequency of use; many are enriched with unique cultural tidbits about China (for example 中国的右翼是自由派，左翼是保守派；这与美国不同。 *In China, the right wing is liberal but the left is conservative; this is different from America.* By using this dictionary, students can increase their cultural understanding of China.

6 · A single example sentence may contain two or more example words, demonstrating their different meanings and functions and how to use them in a sentence.

7 · An original and colorful personality, ShaGua (昵称), and his family are featured in many of the example sentences. These sentences, many of them witty and humorous, describe their perseverance and hard work, and the difficulties they encounter and success they achieve as immigrants in America.

8 · The dictionary entry for each character includes a comprehensive listing of the most popular related words containing the character, regardless of its position in the word. Students will now be able to look through the list of related words in order to determine the character's usage in a particular sentence.

9 · The hexadecimal Unicode value is given for each of the 2,000 main Chinese characters in this dictionary. This unique feature simplifies keyboard entry for those who need to reproduce the characters on screen and in documents.

# Acknowledgments

We thank the following people and institutions for their roles in bringing this dictionary to publication:

**Christopher Brown**, our publisher, for his vision, openness, and courage in undertaking this massive project.

**Daniel Franklin**, the dictionary's English copy editor, designer, and production manager, for working tirelessly on this project with us, and for being one of a select few who truly understand the joys and pains of compiling, editing, and organizing a dictionary.

Our thanks also extend to **Liu Li**, for copyediting and proofreading the Chinese; to **Ken Lunde** of Adobe Systems Inc., for his valuable suggestions regarding the format of the dictionary; and to **Miguel Sousa** of Adobe Systems Inc., for producing a special version of the pinyin font used in the dictionary.

Professor **Galal Walker**, for lending his expertise and writing a cogent and eloquent Foreword.

Professor **Bob DiDonato**, for introducing this project to McGraw-Hill.

**Miami University** and, in particular, **the Department of German, Russian, and East Asian Languages** and **the Confucius Institute**, for their constant support, services, resources, and assistance.

**Andrew Green** and many other students at Miami University, for moving us with their stories and drawing attention to the need for a new Chinese dictionary system.

We also thank the following people:

Dr. **Lin Xu**, director general of the Beijing-based Confucius Institute headquarters, and **Xueming Liang**, deputy director of Confucius Institute Affairs, for their support.

**Hongbo Zhou**, deputy chief editor of Commercial Press, and **Zhichu Li** and **Mengmeng Duan**, editors of the Chinese edition of this dictionary, for their diligence and hard work.

Deans **Minghua Zhong** and **Bin Wang** of Sun Yat-Sen University, Professor **Gangping Wu** and **Ziheng Zhou** of East China Normal University, Dean **Binxian Zhang** and **Hui Li** of Beijing Normal University, and Dean **Baogui Li** of Liaoning Normal University, for conducting Chinese dictionary usage surveys at their schools, which showed the need for a functional overhaul of the traditional Chinese dictionary.

We also express our gratitude for all the tangible and intangible support that we have received from family members, colleagues, and friends.

# Using the Broken Marks Method

The Broken Marks method of finding a Chinese character consists of two steps:

1. Count the character's Total Marks (TM).
2. Select the character's First Mark (FM) from four options.

The process was designed with ease of use and efficiency in mind. With minimal practice, it should take the user no longer than 60 seconds to find a character's entry in the dictionary.

## Step 1: Count the Character's Total Marks

All Chinese characters can be seen as composites of distinct "marks." Marks are different from the complex traditional Chinese concept of "strokes." (For a description of the difference, refer to Breaking the Linked Stroke on page viii.)

We define *mark* as a part of a character that is separated from other parts by either physical space or a significant change in direction. Marks can be long or short, thick or thin, and straight or slightly curved. A change in direction is considered "significant" if it is about 90 degrees or sharper.

**Example 1** 口 ("mouth") Using the definition of *mark* above, we see that this character is composed of four distinct marks. Each mark is separated by a change in direction.

With one mark on each side, the TM for this character is four.

**Example 2** 飞 ("fly") Count the number of marks in the illustration below.

The horizontal line (1) on top is one mark. It takes a sharp turn into the long, curved right-falling slash (2). The slash ends in the hook at the bottom (3). Two "wings" (4 and 5) protrude from the slash, giving the character a TM of five.

**Example 3** 丝 ("silk") Count the number of marks in the illustration below.

The first four marks (1–4) are separated by sharp directional changes. The identical right side of the character adds another four marks (5–8). The final mark is the horizontal line at the bottom (9). This character has a TM of nine.

If you were able to accurately count the number of total marks in the characters above (and you're feeling adventurous), you may want to begin using the dictionary now.

## Stylistic Variation in Chinese Characters

Because of the differences between printed and handwritten versions of characters, and because of stylized fonts of Chinese characters, the number of total marks for some characters may vary from the number in our indexes. Consider the following examples, in which the characters on the left are from a standard printed font and the ones on the right are from a stylized font.

心 vs. 心    辶 vs. 辶

Since this dictionary counts total marks based on standard printed font styles (such as SimSun [宋体], a common computer font), 心 has six total marks and 辶 has five total marks. If either of these characters is handwritten or set in a stylized font, it may appear to have one fewer mark. Keep this in mind if you are searching for a handwritten character or one set in a stylized font.

In most cases, you will be able to determine the number of total marks for a character you seek. If by chance you do not find the character in the total marks section you expect, you should check the section for one less, or one more, mark. In our experience, this method yields the character you seek with very little time lost.

## Step 2: Select the Character's First Mark

Every character has a First Mark.

1. The first mark of a character is usually the leftmost-highest mark.
2. If a character has no leftmost-highest mark, the first mark is the obviously leftmost mark.
3. If there is no obviously leftmost mark, the first mark is the highest mark.

Once you have identified the First Mark, you must select which of four possible shapes it has.

一    A horizontal line
|    A vertical line
丿    A (straight or slightly curved) left or right falling slash
丶    A dot

The First Mark of every Chinese character must be one of these four.

Let's find the First Mark of some of the characters used above.

The FM here is the leftmost-highest one  : a (straight) falling slash 丿.

Unlike the previous character, this character has no leftmost-highest mark. So we consider the obviously leftmost mark  the First Mark: a dot 丶.

This character has neither a leftmost-highest mark nor an obviously leftmost mark. In this case, the highest mark  is considered the First Mark: a horizontal line 一.

**Additional Tips for Selecting the First Mark**   Some characters may have confusing top sections, making it difficult to select a First Mark. Here are two simple rules to help you determine the First Mark in such a situation.

- The First Mark of a cross formation is the vertical mark. Whenever the highest section of the character is a cross formation, such as 十, the First Mark is the vertical one: 丨. Examples are 土, 由, 上, and 大. Note that the First Mark may be either a vertical line or a left falling slash.

- The First Mark of a right angle is the vertical mark. Whenever the leftmost-highest section of a character meets at a right angle like this 厂, the First Mark is always the vertical one: 丿. This rule applies to both box-type characters and those with a "cape"; 冂 and 风 are examples.

Now that you know how to identify the First Mark of a character, you are ready to use this dictionary.

## Finding the Character Number

Each of the 2,000 characters in this dictionary is assigned a Character Number based on its Total Marks and First Mark. Once you have determined the Total Marks and the First Mark of the character you seek, use Index 1 (Broken Marks of Simplified Chinese Characters) or Index 2 (Broken Marks of Traditional Chinese Characters) to determine its Character Number. Once you know the Character Number, simply turn to the appropriate page to gain access to all the information about that character: pinyin (pronunciation), English meanings, measure words, example sentences, and related words.

## Practice in Finding Characters

Practice searching for each of the following characters by determining its TM and FM. These characters cover almost every type and shape of character you will encounter.

飞　　石　　个　　高　　风　　中

田　　它　　州　　三　　丝　　能

You may check your answers below. FMs are highlighted, and TMs and Character Numbers are given.

| 飞 | 石 | 个 | 高 | 风 | 中 |
|---|---|---|---|---|---|
| TM: 5 | TM: 6 | TM: 3 | TM: 14 | TM: 6 | TM: 5 |
| CN: 81 | CN: 144 | CN: 18 | CN: 1611 | CN: 194 | CN: 86 |

| 田 | 它 | 州 | 三 | 丝 | 能 |
|---|---|---|---|---|---|
| TM: 6 | TM: 8 | TM: 6 | TM: 3 | TM: 9 | TM: 17 |
| CN: 147 | CN: 484 | CN: 233 | CN: 9 | CN: 637 | CN: 1873 |

# Explanatory Chart for Dictionary Entries

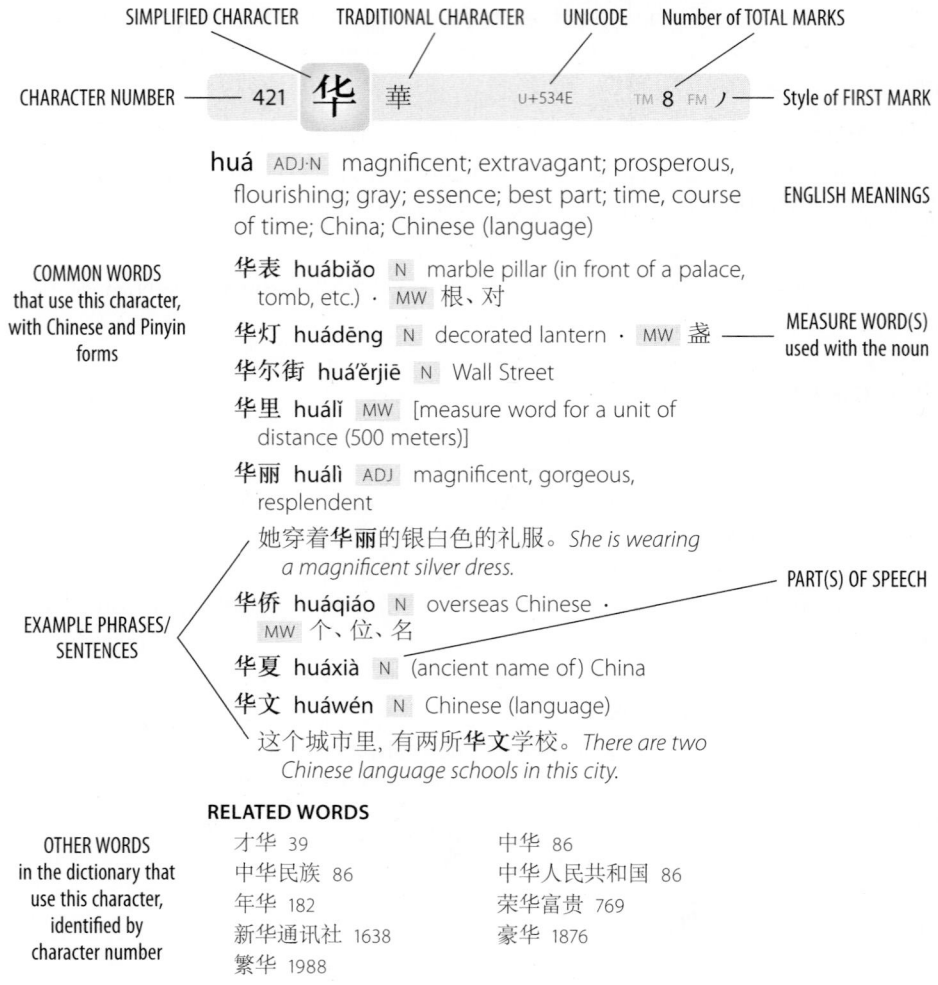

SIMPLIFIED CHARACTER    TRADITIONAL CHARACTER    UNICODE    Number of TOTAL MARKS

CHARACTER NUMBER ——— 421   华   華    U+534E    TM **8** FM ノ ——— Style of FIRST MARK

**huá** ADJ·N magnificent; extravagant; prosperous, flourishing; gray; essence; best part; time, course of time; China; Chinese (language) ——— ENGLISH MEANINGS

COMMON WORDS that use this character, with Chinese and Pinyin forms

华表 **huábiǎo** N marble pillar (in front of a palace, tomb, etc.) · MW 根、对

华灯 **huádēng** N decorated lantern · MW 盏 ——— MEASURE WORD(S) used with the noun

华尔街 **huá'ěrjiē** N Wall Street

华里 **huálǐ** MW [measure word for a unit of distance (500 meters)]

华丽 **huálì** ADJ magnificent, gorgeous, resplendent

她穿着华丽的银白色的礼服。 *She is wearing a magnificent silver dress.*

华侨 **huáqiáo** N overseas Chinese · MW 个、位、名 ——— PART(S) OF SPEECH

EXAMPLE PHRASES/ SENTENCES

华夏 **huáxià** N (ancient name of) China

华文 **huáwén** N Chinese (language)

这个城市里，有两所华文学校。 *There are two Chinese language schools in this city.*

**RELATED WORDS**

OTHER WORDS in the dictionary that use this character, identified by character number

才华 39      中华 86
中华民族 86      中华人民共和国 86
年华 182      荣华富贵 769
新华通讯社 1638      豪华 1876
繁华 1988

# Abbreviations

| | | | | |
|---|---|---|---|---|
| ADJ | adjective | | N | noun |
| ADV | adverb | | NUM | numeral, number |
| AUX | auxiliary | | ONOM | onomatopoeic |
| AV | auxiliary verb | | PFX | prefix |
| CONJ | conjunction | | PREP | preposition |
| EXP | expression | | PRON | pronoun |
| FIG | figurative | | QPRON | interrogative (question) pronoun |
| FM | First Mark (used in the Broken Marks method) | | TM | Total Marks (used in the Broken Marks method) |
| LIT | literally | | V | verb |
| MW | measure word | | | |

# Broken Marks of Simplified Chinese Characters

Use this index to locate the dictionary entry for a Simplified Chinese character (for example, 久).

1. Determine the number of Total Marks (**4**) and the style of the First Mark (丿) of the Simplified Chinese character (久).
2. Using the **TM/FM** column on the left, locate the Simplified Chinese character (久) in the **SIMP CHAR** column.
3. The character number in the last column (**45**) directs you to the correct dictionary entry.

| TM/FM | SIMP CHAR | TRAD CHAR | PINYIN | CHAR NO |
|---|---|---|---|---|
| TM **1** FM 一 | 一 | | yī | 1 |
| TM **2** FM 一 | 二 | | èr | 2 |
| TM **2** FM 丨 | 十 | | shí | 3 |
| TM **2** FM 丿 | 人 | | rén | 4 |
| | 入 | | rù | 5 |
| | 八 | | bā | 6 |
| | 厂 | 厰 | chǎng | 7 |
| TM **3** FM 一 | 丁 | | dīng | 8 |
| | 三 | | sān | 9 |
| | 下 | | xià | 10 |
| | 又 | | yòu | 11 |
| | 工 | | gōng | 12 |
| | 干 | 乾 | gān | 13 |
| | 干 | 幹 | gàn | 13 |
| TM **3** FM 丨 | 上 | | shàng | 14 |
| | 土 | | tǔ | 15 |
| | 士 | | shì | 16 |
| TM **3** FM 丿 | 丈 | | zhàng | 17 |
| | 个 | 個 | gè | 18 |
| | 千 | 韆 | qiān | 19 |
| | 大 | | dà | 20 |
| | 川 | | chuān | 21 |
| TM **3** FM 丶 | 义 | 義 | yì | 22 |
| | 广 | 廣 | guǎng | 23 |
| TM **4** FM 一 | 不 | | bù | 24 |
| | 天 | | tiān | 25 |
| | 开 | 開 | kāi | 26 |
| | 王 | | wáng | 27 |
| | 于 | | yú | 28 |
| | 乙 | | yǐ | 29 |
| | 了 | | le | 30 |
| | 了 | | liǎo | 30 |
| | 刀 | | dāo | 31 |
| | 刁 | | diāo | 32 |
| | 叉 | | chā | 33 |

| TM/FM | SIMP CHAR | TRAD CHAR | PINYIN | CHAR NO |
|---|---|---|---|---|
| TM **4** FM 丨 | 七 | | qī | 34 |
| | 丰 | 豐 | fēng | 35 |
| | 卡 | | kǎ | 36 |
| | 卡 | | qiǎ | 36 |
| | 寸 | | cùn | 37 |
| | 山 | | shān | 38 |
| | 才 | 纔 | cái | 39 |
| | 木 | | mù | 40 |
| | 止 | | zhǐ | 41 |
| | 口 | | kǒu | 42 |
| TM **4** FM 丿 | 儿 | 兒 | ér | 43 |
| | 介 | | jiè | 44 |
| | 久 | | jiǔ | 45 |
| | 么 | 麼 | me | 46 |
| | 升 | | shēng | 47 |
| | 午 | | wǔ | 48 |
| | 夕 | | xī | 49 |
| | 斤 | | jīn | 50 |
| | 牛 | | niú | 51 |
| | 爪 | | zhǎo | 52 |
| | 爪 | | zhuǎ | 52 |
| | 太 | | tài | 53 |
| | 犬 | | quǎn | 54 |
| | 夫 | | fū | 55 |
| | 父 | | fù | 56 |
| | 女 | | nǚ | 57 |
| | 尸 | 屍 | shī | 58 |
| | 力 | | lì | 59 |
| | 井 | | jǐng | 60 |
| | 小 | | xiǎo | 61 |
| | 少 | | shǎo | 62 |
| | 少 | | shào | 62 |
| | 什 | | shén | 63 |
| | 什 | | shí | 63 |
| | 仁 | | rén | 64 |
| | 仆 | 僕 | pú | 65 |
| | 从 | 從 | cóng | 66 |
| TM **4** FM 丶 | 之 | | zhī | 67 |
| | 亡 | | wáng | 68 |

| SIMP CHAR | TRAD CHAR | PINYIN | CHAR NO |
|---|---|---|---|
| 共 | | gòng | 164 |
| 旧 | 舊 | jiù | 165 |
| 归 | 歸 | guī | 166 |
| 叶 | 葉 | yè | 167 |
| 扑 | 撲 | pū | 168 |
| 扒 | | bā | 169 |
| 扒 | | pá | 169 |

**TM 6 FM 丿**

| SIMP CHAR | TRAD CHAR | PINYIN | CHAR NO |
|---|---|---|---|
| 企 | | qǐ | 170 |
| 伞 | 傘 | sǎn | 171 |
| 全 | | quán | 172 |
| 分 | | fēn | 173 |
| 分 | | fèn | 173 |
| 令 | | lìng | 174 |
| 众 | 衆 | zhòng | 175 |
| 白 | | bái | 176 |
| 乞 | | qǐ | 177 |
| 冬 | 鼕 | dōng | 178 |
| 勿 | | wù | 179 |
| 匀 | | yún | 180 |
| 币 | 幣 | bì | 181 |
| 年 | | nián | 182 |
| 毛 | | máo | 183 |
| 朱 | | zhū | 184 |
| 气 | 氣 | qì | 185 |
| 史 | | shǐ | 186 |
| 右 | | yòu | 187 |
| 在 | | zài | 188 |
| 瓜 | | guā | 189 |
| 月 | | yuè | 190 |
| 内 | | nèi | 191 |
| 丸 | | wán | 192 |
| 凡 | | fán | 193 |
| 风 | 風 | fēng | 194 |
| 办 | 辦 | bàn | 195 |
| 央 | | yāng | 196 |
| 夹 | 夾 | jiā | 197 |
| 夹 | 夾 | jiá | 197 |
| 灰 | | huī | 198 |
| 尤 | | yóu | 199 |
| 历 | 歷 | lì | 200 |
| 压 | 壓 | yā | 201 |
| 厌 | 厭 | yàn | 202 |
| 尖 | | jiān | 203 |
| 尘 | 塵 | chén | 204 |
| 亿 | 億 | yì | 205 |
| 付 | | fù | 206 |
| 仙 | | xiān | 207 |
| 代 | | dài | 208 |
| 件 | | jiàn | 209 |
| 价 | 價 | jià | 210 |
| 任 | | rèn | 211 |
| 伏 | | fú | 212 |
| 休 | | xiū | 213 |

| SIMP CHAR | TRAD CHAR | PINYIN | CHAR NO |
|---|---|---|---|
| 伙 | 夥 | huǒ | 214 |
| 化 | | huà | 215 |
| 刊 | | kān | 216 |
| 处 | 處 | chǔ | 217 |
| 处 | 處 | chù | 217 |
| 外 | | wài | 218 |

**TM 6 FM 丶**

| SIMP CHAR | TRAD CHAR | PINYIN | CHAR NO |
|---|---|---|---|
| 产 | 産 | chǎn | 219 |
| 方 | | fāng | 220 |
| 齐 | 齊 | qí | 221 |
| 交 | | jiāo | 222 |
| 为 | 為 | wéi | 223 |
| 为 | 為 | wèi | 223 |
| 关 | 關 | guān | 224 |
| 并 | | bìng | 225 |
| 米 | | mǐ | 226 |
| 羊 | | yáng | 227 |
| 兴 | 興 | xīng | 228 |
| 兴 | 興 | xìng | 228 |
| 庄 | 莊 | zhuāng | 229 |
| 庆 | 慶 | qìng | 230 |
| 穴 | | xué | 231 |
| 心 | | xīn | 232 |
| 州 | | zhōu | 233 |
| 汇 | 匯 彙 | huì | 234 |
| 汉 | 漢 | hàn | 235 |
| 汗 | | hàn | 236 |
| 江 | | jiāng | 237 |
| 壮 | 壯 | zhuàng | 238 |
| 认 | 認 | rèn | 239 |
| 计 | 計 | jì | 240 |

**TM 7 FM 一**

| SIMP CHAR | TRAD CHAR | PINYIN | CHAR NO |
|---|---|---|---|
| 严 | 嚴 | yán | 241 |
| 百 | | bǎi | 242 |
| 可 | | kě | 243 |
| 至 | | zhì | 244 |
| 页 | 頁 | yè | 245 |
| 丙 | | bǐng | 246 |
| 马 | 馬 | mǎ | 247 |
| 买 | 買 | mǎi | 248 |
| 予 | | yú | 249 |
| 予 | | yǔ | 249 |
| 弓 | | gōng | 250 |
| 弄 | | lòng | 251 |
| 弄 | | nòng | 251 |
| 功 | | gōng | 252 |
| 攻 | | gōng | 253 |
| 对 | 對 | duì | 254 |
| 劝 | 勸 | quàn | 255 |
| 刑 | | xíng | 256 |
| 形 | | xíng | 257 |

**TM 7 FM 丨**

| SIMP CHAR | TRAD CHAR | PINYIN | CHAR NO |
|---|---|---|---|
| 出 | 齣 | chū | 258 |
| 吉 | | jí | 259 |

| SIMP CHAR | TRAD CHAR | PINYIN | CHAR NO |
|---|---|---|---|
| TM 7 FM 丨 (continued) | | | |
| 来 | 來 | lái | 260 |
| 皮 | | pí | 261 |
| 虫 | 蟲 | chóng | 262 |
| 电 | 電 | diàn | 263 |
| 书 | 書 | shū | 264 |
| 走 | | zǒu | 265 |
| 步 | | bù | 266 |
| 见 | 見 | jiàn | 267 |
| 早 | | zǎo | 268 |
| 匹 | | pǐ | 269 |
| 因 | | yīn | 270 |
| 四 | | sì | 271 |
| 曲 | 麯 | qū | 272 |
| 曲 | | qǔ | 272 |
| 也 | | yě | 273 |
| 艺 | 藝 | yì | 274 |
| 节 | 節 | jié | 275 |
| 帅 | 帥 | shuài | 276 |
| 切 | | qiē | 277 |
| 切 | | qiè | 277 |
| 北 | | běi | 278 |
| 比 | | bǐ | 279 |
| 坏 | 壞 | huài | 280 |
| 坟 | 墳 | fén | 281 |
| 收 | | shōu | 282 |
| 叫 | | jiào | 283 |
| 叮 | | dīng | 284 |
| 叹 | 嘆 | tàn | 285 |
| 吐 | | tǔ | 286 |
| 吓 | 嚇 | hè | 287 |
| 吓 | 嚇 | xià | 287 |
| 扎 | | zā | 288 |
| 扎 | | zhā | 288 |
| 打 | | dá | 289 |
| 打 | | dǎ | 289 |
| 扛 | | káng | 290 |
| 扩 | 擴 | kuò | 291 |
| 权 | 權 | quán | 292 |
| 杠 | 槓 | gàng | 293 |
| 队 | 隊 | duì | 294 |
| TM 7 FM 丿 | | | |
| 会 | 會 | huì | 295 |
| 合 | | hé | 296 |
| 丢 | | diū | 297 |
| 舌 | | shé | 298 |
| 乐 | 樂 | lè | 299 |
| 乐 | 樂 | yuè | 299 |
| 兵 | | bīng | 300 |
| 台 | 臺檀颱 | tái | 301 |
| 允 | | yǔn | 302 |
| 勾 | | gōu | 303 |
| 匆 | | cōng | 304 |
| 自 | | zì | 305 |
| 血 | | xiě | 306 |

| SIMP CHAR | TRAD CHAR | PINYIN | CHAR NO |
|---|---|---|---|
| 血 | | xuè | 306 |
| 东 | 東 | dōng | 307 |
| 夺 | 奪 | duó | 308 |
| 布 | | bù | 309 |
| 后 | 後 | hòu | 310 |
| 发 | 發 | fā | 311 |
| 发 | 髮 | fà | 311 |
| 尽 | 儘 | jǐn | 312 |
| 尽 | 盡 | jìn | 312 |
| 用 | | yòng | 313 |
| 凤 | 鳳 | fèng | 314 |
| 龙 | 龍 | lóng | 315 |
| 式 | | shì | 316 |
| 杀 | 殺 | shā | 317 |
| 坐 | | zuò | 318 |
| 仇 | | chóu | 319 |
| 伍 | | wǔ | 320 |
| 伴 | | bàn | 321 |
| 似 | | sì | 322 |
| 位 | | wèi | 323 |
| 住 | | zhù | 324 |
| 体 | 體 | tǐ | 325 |
| 作 | | zuō | 326 |
| 作 | | zuò | 326 |
| 行 | | háng | 327 |
| 行 | | xíng | 327 |
| 奴 | | nú | 328 |
| 奸 | | jiān | 329 |
| TM 7 FM 丶 | | | |
| 衣 | | yī | 330 |
| 辛 | | xīn | 331 |
| 市 | | shì | 332 |
| 床 | | chuáng | 333 |
| 应 | 應 | yīng | 334 |
| 应 | 應 | yìng | 334 |
| 当 | 當 | dāng | 335 |
| 当 | 當 | dàng | 335 |
| 宁 | 寧 | níng | 336 |
| 宁 | 寧 | nìng | 336 |
| 闪 | 閃 | shǎn | 337 |
| 必 | | bì | 338 |
| 冲 | 衝 | chōng | 339 |
| 冲 | 衝 | chòng | 339 |
| 决 | | jué | 340 |
| 次 | | cì | 341 |
| 沙 | | shā | 342 |
| 忙 | | máng | 343 |
| 怀 | 懷 | huái | 344 |
| 状 | 狀 | zhuàng | 345 |
| 灯 | 燈 | dēng | 346 |
| 订 | 訂 | dìng | 347 |
| 让 | 讓 | ràng | 348 |
| 议 | 議 | yì | 349 |
| 训 | 訓 | xùn | 350 |

| SIMP CHAR | TRAD CHAR | PINYIN | CHAR NO | | SIMP CHAR | TRAD CHAR | PINYIN | CHAR NO |
|---|---|---|---|---|---|---|---|---|
| **TM 8 FM 一** | | | | | 扫 | 掃 | sào | 402 |
| 而 | | ér | 351 | | 扯 | | chě | 403 |
| 西 | | xī | 352 | | 扶 | | fú | 404 |
| 豆 | | dòu | 353 | | 抄 | | chāo | 405 |
| 再 | | zài | 354 | | 抓 | | zhuā | 406 |
| 更 | | gēng | 355 | | 抖 | | dǒu | 407 |
| 更 | | gèng | 355 | | 折 | | shē | 408 |
| 瓦 | | wǎ | 356 | | 折 | | zhē | 408 |
| 司 | | sī | 357 | | 折 | | zhé | 408 |
| 寻 | 尋 | xún | 358 | | 材 | | cái | 409 |
| 灵 | 靈 | líng | 359 | | 村 | | cūn | 410 |
| 贡 | 貢 | gòng | 360 | | 杯 | | bēi | 411 |
| 召 | | zhào | 361 | | 林 | | lín | 412 |
| 否 | | fǒu | 362 | | 叩 | | kòu | 413 |
| 矛 | | máo | 363 | | 听 | 聽 | tīng | 414 |
| 巧 | | qiǎo | 364 | | 吵 | | chǎo | 415 |
| 戏 | 戲 | xì | 365 | | 此 | | cǐ | 416 |
| 欢 | 歡 | huān | 366 | | 则 | 則 | zé | 417 |
| 邓 | | dèng | 367 | | | | | |
| 列 | | liè | 368 | | **TM 8 FM ノ** | | | |
| 环 | 環 | huán | 369 | | 仓 | 倉 | cāng | 418 |
| 孔 | | kǒng | 370 | | 余 | 餘 | yú | 419 |
| 引 | | yǐn | 371 | | 金 | | jīn | 420 |
| | | | | | 华 | 華 | huá | 421 |
| **TM 8 FM 丨** | | | | | 先 | | xiān | 422 |
| 束 | | shù | 372 | | 农 | 農 | nóng | 423 |
| 幸 | | xìng | 373 | | 句 | | jù | 424 |
| 声 | 聲 | shēng | 374 | | 各 | | gè | 425 |
| 老 | | lǎo | 375 | | 名 | | míng | 426 |
| 求 | | qiú | 376 | | 吞 | | tūn | 427 |
| 杰 | 傑 | jié | 377 | | 告 | | gào | 428 |
| 非 | | fēi | 378 | | 务 | 務 | wù | 429 |
| 其 | | qí | 379 | | 垂 | | chuí | 430 |
| 岁 | 歲 | suì | 380 | | 多 | | duō | 431 |
| 坚 | 堅 | jiān | 381 | | 奔 | | bēn | 432 |
| 兄 | | xiōng | 382 | | 妥 | | tuǒ | 433 |
| 足 | | zú | 383 | | 采 | | cǎi | 434 |
| 呆 | | dāi | 384 | | 负 | 負 | fù | 435 |
| 另 | | lìng | 385 | | 舟 | | zhōu | 436 |
| 里 | 裡 | lǐ | 386 | | 肉 | | ròu | 437 |
| 旱 | | hàn | 387 | | 存 | | cún | 438 |
| 民 | | mín | 388 | | 有 | | yǒu | 439 |
| 医 | 醫 | yī | 389 | | 寿 | 壽 | shòu | 440 |
| 网 | 網 | wǎng | 390 | | 尼 | | ní | 441 |
| 回 | | huí | 391 | | 戒 | | jiè | 442 |
| 团 | 團 糰 | tuán | 392 | | 厄 | | è | 443 |
| 困 | 睏 | kùn | 393 | | 劣 | | liè | 444 |
| 母 | | mǔ | 394 | | 爷 | 爺 | yé | 445 |
| 苹 | 蘋 | píng | 395 | | 谷 | 穀 | gǔ | 446 |
| 师 | 師 | shī | 396 | | 优 | 優 | yōu | 447 |
| 协 | 協 | xié | 397 | | 仍 | | réng | 448 |
| 坪 | | píng | 398 | | 份 | | fèn | 449 |
| 垃 | | lā | 399 | | 仿 | | fǎng | 450 |
| 块 | 塊 | kuài | 400 | | 伟 | 偉 | wěi | 451 |
| 扣 | | kòu | 401 | | 传 | 傳 | chuán | 452 |
| 扫 | 掃 | sǎo | 402 | | | | | |

| | SIMP CHAR | TRAD CHAR | PINYIN | CHAR NO |
|---|---|---|---|---|
| **TM 8 FM 丿** (continued) | 传 | 傳 | zhuàn | 452 |
| | 伤 | 傷 | shāng | 453 |
| | 伪 | 偽 | wěi | 454 |
| | 伯 | | bó | 455 |
| | 估 | | gū | 456 |
| | 伸 | | shēn | 457 |
| | 但 | | dàn | 458 |
| | 供 | | gōng | 459 |
| | 供 | | gòng | 459 |
| | 侨 | 僑 | qiáo | 460 |
| | 往 | | wǎng | 461 |
| | 征 | 徵 | zhēng | 462 |
| | 加 | | jiā | 463 |
| | 如 | | rú | 464 |
| | 妇 | 婦 | fù | 465 |
| | 妖 | | yāo | 466 |
| | 妙 | | miào | 467 |
| | 牧 | | mù | 468 |
| | 狂 | | kuáng | 469 |
| | 印 | | yìn | 470 |
| | 私 | | sī | 471 |
| | 利 | | lì | 472 |
| | 纠 | 糾 | jiū | 473 |
| | 红 | 紅 | hóng | 474 |
| | 幻 | | huàn | 475 |
| | 划 | 劃 | huá | 476 |
| | 划 | 劃 | huà | 476 |
| | 针 | 針 | zhēn | 477 |
| **TM 8 FM 丶** | 言 | | yán | 478 |
| | 吝 | | lìn | 479 |
| | 弃 | 棄 | qì | 480 |
| | 永 | | yǒng | 481 |
| | 库 | | kù | 482 |
| | 灾 | | zāi | 483 |
| | 它 | | tā | 484 |
| | 宇 | | yǔ | 485 |
| | 守 | | shǒu | 486 |
| | 安 | | ān | 487 |
| | 牢 | | láo | 488 |
| | 军 | 軍 | jūn | 489 |
| | 罕 | | hǎn | 490 |
| | 光 | | guāng | 491 |
| | 炎 | | yán | 492 |
| | 冰 | | bīng | 493 |
| | 冷 | | lěng | 494 |
| | 泛 | | fàn | 495 |
| | 注 | | zhù | 496 |
| | 快 | | kuài | 497 |
| | 性 | | xìng | 498 |
| | 炒 | | chǎo | 499 |
| | 讨 | 討 | tǎo | 500 |
| | 讲 | 講 | jiǎng | 501 |
| | 许 | 許 | xǔ | 502 |

| | SIMP CHAR | TRAD CHAR | PINYIN | CHAR NO |
|---|---|---|---|---|
| | 礼 | 禮 | lǐ | 503 |
| | 社 | | shè | 504 |
| | 达 | 達 | dá | 505 |
| | 迁 | 遷 | qiān | 506 |
| | 判 | | pàn | 507 |
| | 补 | 補 | bǔ | 508 |
| **TM 9 FM 一** | 两 | 兩 | liǎng | 509 |
| | 死 | | sǐ | 510 |
| | 歪 | | wāi | 511 |
| | 君 | | jūn | 512 |
| | 武 | | wǔ | 513 |
| | 动 | 動 | dòng | 514 |
| | 珍 | | zhēn | 515 |
| | 改 | | gǎi | 516 |
| | 政 | | zhèng | 517 |
| | 矿 | 礦 | kuàng | 518 |
| | 孙 | 孫 | sūn | 519 |
| | 取 | | qǔ | 520 |
| **TM 9 FM 丨** | 丧 | 喪 | sāng | 521 |
| | 丧 | 喪 | sàng | 521 |
| | 串 | | chuàn | 522 |
| | 卓 | | zhuó | 523 |
| | 卖 | 賣 | mài | 524 |
| | 责 | 責 | zé | 525 |
| | 肃 | 蕭 | sù | 526 |
| | 表 | | biǎo | 527 |
| | 志 | | zhì | 528 |
| | 孝 | | xiào | 529 |
| | 考 | | kǎo | 530 |
| | 者 | | zhě | 531 |
| | 典 | | diǎn | 532 |
| | 具 | | jù | 533 |
| | 昔 | | xī | 534 |
| | 旨 | | zhǐ | 535 |
| | 某 | | mǒu | 536 |
| | 岸 | | àn | 537 |
| | 齿 | 齒 | chǐ | 538 |
| | 异 | | yì | 539 |
| | 毕 | 畢 | bì | 540 |
| | 同 | | tóng | 541 |
| | 国 | 國 | guó | 542 |
| | 县 | 縣 | xiàn | 543 |
| | 果 | | guǒ | 544 |
| | 号 | 號 | háo | 545 |
| | 号 | 號 | hào | 545 |
| | 员 | 員 | yuán | 546 |
| | 吊 | | diào | 547 |
| | 芬 | | fēn | 548 |
| | 花 | | huā | 549 |
| | 芳 | | fāng | 550 |
| | 芽 | | yá | 551 |
| | 苏 | 蘇 | sū | 552 |

| SIMP CHAR | TRAD CHAR | PINYIN | CHAR NO |
|---|---|---|---|
| 苗 | | miáo | 553 |
| 若 | | ruò | 554 |
| 苦 | | kǔ | 555 |
| 英 | | yīng | 556 |
| 茂 | | mào | 557 |
| 均 | | jūn | 558 |
| 吹 | | chuī | 559 |
| 呕 | 嘔 | ǒu | 560 |
| 味 | | wèi | 561 |
| 哎 | | āi | 562 |
| 托 | | tuō | 563 |
| 执 | 執 | zhí | 564 |
| 扭 | | niǔ | 565 |
| 扳 | | bān | 566 |
| 找 | | zhǎo | 567 |
| 技 | | jì | 568 |
| 护 | 護 | hù | 569 |
| 抨 | | pēng | 570 |
| 抹 | | mā | 571 |
| 抹 | | mǒ | 571 |
| 拆 | | chāi | 572 |
| 拉 | | lā | 573 |
| 拌 | | bàn | 574 |
| 拟 | 擬 | nǐ | 575 |
| 拦 | 攔 | lán | 576 |
| 机 | 機 | jī | 577 |
| 朽 | | xiǔ | 578 |
| 松 | 鬆 | sōng | 579 |
| 板 | 闆 | bǎn | 580 |
| 枝 | | zhī | 581 |
| 柑 | | gān | 582 |
| 柱 | | zhù | 583 |
| 栏 | 欄 | lán | 584 |
| 歧 | | qí | 585 |
| 时 | 時 | shí | 586 |
| 旺 | | wàng | 587 |
| 财 | 財 | cái | 588 |
| 败 | 敗 | bài | 589 |
| 阶 | 階 | jiē | 590 |
| 刚 | 剛 | gāng | 591 |

TM **9** FM ノ

| SIMP CHAR | TRAD CHAR | PINYIN | CHAR NO |
|---|---|---|---|
| 含 | | hán | 592 |
| 舍 | 捨 | shě | 593 |
| 舍 | | shè | 593 |
| 委 | | wěi | 594 |
| 争 | | zhēng | 595 |
| 旬 | | xún | 596 |
| 质 | 質 | zhì | 597 |
| 条 | 條 | tiáo | 598 |
| 叁 | | sān | 599 |
| 参 | 參 | cān | 600 |
| 参 | 參 | shēn | 600 |
| 乌 | 烏 | wū | 601 |
| 卑 | | bēi | 602 |

| SIMP CHAR | TRAD CHAR | PINYIN | CHAR NO |
|---|---|---|---|
| 向 | | xiàng | 603 |
| 身 | | shēn | 604 |
| 夸 | 誇 | kuā | 605 |
| 奈 | | nài | 606 |
| 奋 | 奮 | fèn | 607 |
| 奏 | | zòu | 608 |
| 直 | | zhí | 609 |
| 层 | 層 | céng | 610 |
| 成 | | chéng | 611 |
| 甩 | | shuǎi | 612 |
| 希 | | xī | 613 |
| 册 | | cè | 614 |
| 我 | | wǒ | 615 |
| 他 | | tā | 616 |
| 你 | | nǐ | 617 |
| 低 | | dī | 618 |
| 何 | | hé | 619 |
| 仰 | | yǎng | 620 |
| 佣 | 傭 | yōng | 621 |
| 佣 | 傭 | yòng | 621 |
| 佰 | | bǎi | 622 |
| 使 | | shǐ | 623 |
| 侍 | | shì | 624 |
| 依 | | yī | 625 |
| 径 | 徑 | jìng | 626 |
| 好 | | hǎo | 627 |
| 好 | | hào | 627 |
| 妒 | | dù | 628 |
| 妓 | | jì | 629 |
| 妞 | | niǔ | 630 |
| 妹 | | mèi | 631 |
| 姓 | | xìng | 632 |
| 牲 | | shēng | 633 |
| 欣 | | xīn | 634 |
| 拜 | | bài | 635 |
| 邦 | | bāng | 636 |
| 丝 | 絲 | sī | 637 |
| 幼 | | yòu | 638 |
| 纱 | 紗 | shā | 639 |
| 纹 | 紋 | wén | 640 |
| 秋 | 鞦 | qiū | 641 |
| 科 | | kē | 642 |
| 秒 | | miǎo | 643 |
| 和 | | hé | 644 |
| 和 | | huó | 644 |
| 所 | | suǒ | 645 |
| 斩 | 斬 | zhǎn | 646 |
| 知 | | zhī | 647 |
| 肚 | | dù | 648 |
| 肛 | | gāng | 649 |
| 肝 | | gān | 650 |
| 钉 | 釘 | dīng | 651 |
| 钉 | 釘 | dìng | 651 |

| SIMP CHAR | TRAD CHAR | PINYIN | CHAR NO |
|---|---|---|---|
| 充 | | chōng | 652 |
| 变 | 變 | biàn | 653 |
| 夜 | | yè | 654 |
| 忘 | | wàng | 655 |
| 良 | | liáng | 656 |
| 启 | 啓 | qǐ | 657 |
| 店 | | diàn | 658 |
| 庙 | 廟 | miào | 659 |
| 府 | | fǔ | 660 |
| 疗 | 療 | liáo | 661 |
| 疟 | 瘧 | nüè | 662 |
| 写 | 寫 | xiě | 663 |
| 字 | | zì | 664 |
| 宅 | | zhái | 665 |
| 定 | | dìng | 666 |
| 宝 | 寶 | bǎo | 667 |
| 实 | 實 | shí | 668 |
| 空 | | kōng | 669 |
| 空 | | kòng | 669 |
| 养 | 養 | yǎng | 670 |
| 美 | | měi | 671 |
| 单 | 單 | dān | 672 |
| 差 | | chā | 673 |
| 差 | | chà | 673 |
| 差 | | chāi | 673 |
| 举 | 舉 | jǔ | 674 |
| 肖 | | xiào | 675 |
| 类 | 類 | lèi | 676 |
| 闭 | 閉 | bì | 677 |
| 问 | 問 | wèn | 678 |
| 闲 | 閑 | xián | 679 |
| 冻 | 凍 | dòng | 680 |
| 污 | | wū | 681 |
| 汽 | | qì | 682 |
| 油 | | yóu | 683 |
| 沾 | | zhān | 684 |
| 泄 | | xiè | 685 |
| 法 | | fǎ | 686 |
| 洼 | 窪 | wā | 687 |
| 泪 | | lèi | 688 |
| 洋 | | yáng | 689 |
| 洪 | | hóng | 690 |
| 洲 | | zhōu | 691 |
| 浅 | 淺 | qiǎn | 692 |
| 忧 | 憂 | yōu | 693 |
| 怕 | | pà | 694 |
| 怜 | 憐 | lián | 695 |
| 怪 | | guài | 696 |
| 怯 | | qiè | 697 |
| 恢 | | huī | 698 |
| 炉 | 爐 | lú | 699 |
| 炊 | | chuī | 700 |
| 炸 | | zhà | 701 |
| 烂 | 爛 | làn | 702 |
| 讯 | 訊 | xùn | 703 |
| 诀 | 訣 | jué | 704 |
| 证 | 證 | zhèng | 705 |
| 评 | 評 | píng | 706 |
| 诈 | 詐 | zhà | 707 |
| 诉 | 訴 | sù | 708 |
| 诊 | 診 | zhěn | 709 |
| 边 | 邊 | biān | 710 |
| 辽 | 遼 | liáo | 711 |
| 过 | 過 | guò | 712 |
| 进 | 進 | jìn | 713 |
| 还 | 還 | hái | 714 |
| 还 | 還 | huán | 714 |
| 这 | 這 | zhè | 715 |
| 这 | 這 | zhèi | 715 |
| 近 | | jìn | 716 |
| 祈 | | qí | 717 |
| 衫 | | shān | 718 |
| 画 | 畫 | huà | 719 |
| 雨 | | yǔ | 720 |
| 面 | 麵 | miàn | 721 |
| 面 | 麵 | miàn | 721 |
| 录 | 錄 | lù | 722 |
| 型 | | xíng | 723 |
| 顶 | 頂 | dǐng | 724 |
| 项 | 項 | xiàng | 725 |
| 观 | 觀 | guān | 726 |
| 玩 | | wán | 727 |
| 玲 | | líng | 728 |
| 珠 | | zhū | 729 |
| 班 | | bān | 730 |
| 延 | | yán | 731 |
| 羽 | | yǔ | 732 |
| 砂 | | shā | 733 |
| 研 | | yán | 734 |
| 耻 | | chǐ | 735 |
| 劲 | 勁 | jìn | 736 |
| 劲 | 勁 | jìng | 736 |
| 到 | | dào | 737 |
| 克 | | kè | 738 |
| 点 | 點 | diǎn | 739 |
| 青 | | qīng | 740 |
| 查 | | chá | 741 |
| 妻 | | qī | 742 |
| 忠 | | zhōng | 743 |
| 肯 | | kěn | 744 |
| 岗 | 崗 | gǎng | 745 |
| 岩 | | yán | 746 |
| 革 | | gé | 747 |
| 些 | | xiē | 748 |
| 竖 | 竪 | shù | 749 |
| 贤 | 賢 | xián | 750 |
| 导 | 導 | dǎo | 751 |

TM 9 FM 丶

TM 10 FM 一

TM 10 FM 丨

| SIMP CHAR | TRAD CHAR | PINYIN | CHAR NO |
|-----------|-----------|--------|---------|
| 昌 | | chāng | 752 |
| 星 | | xīng | 753 |
| 是 | | shì | 754 |
| 显 | 顯 | xiǎn | 755 |
| 罗 | 羅 | luó | 756 |
| 男 | | nán | 757 |
| 界 | | jiè | 758 |
| 甚 | | shèn | 759 |
| 固 | | gù | 760 |
| 图 | 圖 | tú | 761 |
| 围 | 圍 | wéi | 762 |
| 园 | 園 | yuán | 763 |
| 劳 | 勞 | láo | 764 |
| 芭 | | bā | 765 |
| 茫 | | máng | 766 |
| 茶 | | chá | 767 |
| 草 | | cǎo | 768 |
| 荣 | 榮 | róng | 769 |
| 荧 | 熒 | yíng | 770 |
| 临 | 臨 | lín | 771 |
| 地 | | de | 772 |
| 地 | | dì | 772 |
| 场 | 場 | chǎng | 773 |
| 坑 | | kēng | 774 |
| 坡 | | pō | 775 |
| 吸 | | xī | 776 |
| 吻 | | wěn | 777 |
| 呀 | | yā | 778 |
| 呀 | | ya | 778 |
| 呼 | | hū | 779 |
| 咬 | | yǎo | 780 |
| 哄 | | hōng | 781 |
| 哄 | | hǒng | 781 |
| 哄 | | hòng | 781 |
| 哑 | 啞 | yǎ | 782 |
| 吃 | | chī | 783 |
| 哇 | | wā | 784 |
| 扔 | | rēng | 785 |
| 扮 | | bàn | 786 |
| 押 | | yā | 787 |
| 抽 | | chōu | 788 |
| 担 | 擔 | dān | 789 |
| 拍 | | pāi | 790 |
| 拔 | | bá | 791 |
| 择 | 擇 | zé | 792 |
| 拱 | | gǒng | 793 |
| 拼 | | pīn | 794 |
| 挤 | 擠 | jǐ | 795 |
| 挂 | 掛 | guà | 796 |
| 桂 | | guì | 797 |
| 极 | 極 | jí | 798 |
| 枯 | | kū | 799 |
| 柜 | 櫃 | guì | 800 |
| 标 | 標 | biāo | 801 |

| SIMP CHAR | TRAD CHAR | PINYIN | CHAR NO |
|-----------|-----------|--------|---------|
| 校 | | jiào | 802 |
| 校 | | xiào | 802 |
| 样 | 樣 | yàng | 803 |
| 桥 | 橋 | qiáo | 804 |
| 相 | | xiāng | 805 |
| 相 | | xiàng | 805 |
| 岭 | 嶺 | lǐng | 806 |
| 峡 | 峽 | xiá | 807 |
| 阳 | 陽 | yáng | 808 |
| 阵 | 陣 | zhèn | 809 |
| 昨 | | zuó | 810 |
| 欧 | 歐 | ōu | 811 |
| 账 | 賬 | zhàng | 812 |
| 贩 | 販 | fàn | 813 |
| 贬 | 貶 | biǎn | 814 |
| 封 | | fēng | 815 |
| 故 | | gù | 816 |
| 耕 | | gēng | 817 |
| 助 | | zhù | 818 |
| 劫 | | jié | 819 |
| 却 | | què | 820 |
| 叔 | | shū | 821 |
| 赶 | 趕 | gǎn | 822 |
| 虹 | | hóng | 823 |
| 虾 | 蝦 | xiā | 824 |
| 蚁 | 蟻 | yǐ | 825 |
| 卧 | | wò | 826 |

| SIMP CHAR | TRAD CHAR | PINYIN | CHAR NO |
|-----------|-----------|--------|---------|
| 贪 | 貪 | tān | 827 |
| 态 | 態 | tài | 828 |
| 岔 | | chà | 829 |
| 怎 | | zěn | 830 |
| 色 | | sè | 831 |
| 乖 | | guāi | 832 |
| 秃 | | tū | 833 |
| 香 | | xiāng | 834 |
| 季 | | jì | 835 |
| 包 | | bāo | 836 |
| 每 | | měi | 837 |
| 角 | | jiǎo | 838 |
| 角 | | jué | 838 |
| 重 | | chóng | 839 |
| 重 | | zhòng | 839 |
| 盾 | | dùn | 840 |
| 看 | | kān | 841 |
| 看 | | kàn | 841 |
| 系 | 繫 | jì | 842 |
| 系 | 係 繫 | xì | 842 |
| 鱼 | 魚 | yú | 843 |
| 受 | | shòu | 844 |
| 备 | 備 | bèi | 845 |
| 厕 | 廁 | cè | 846 |
| 厘 | | lí | 847 |
| 尾 | | wěi | 848 |

| SIMP CHAR | TRAD CHAR | PINYIN | CHAR NO | | SIMP CHAR | TRAD CHAR | PINYIN | CHAR NO |
|---|---|---|---|---|---|---|---|---|
| | | | | | 肤 | 膚 | fū | 899 |
| 尿 | | niào | 849 | | 钞 | 鈔 | chāo | 900 |
| 居 | | jū | 850 | | 乱 | 亂 | luàn | 901 |
| 届 | | jiè | 851 | | 刮 | 颳 | guā | 902 |
| 屎 | | shǐ | 852 | | 刽 | 劊 | guì | 903 |
| 牵 | 牽 | qiān | 853 | | 剑 | 劍 | jiàn | 904 |
| 奇 | | jī | 854 | | | | | |
| 奇 | | qí | 854 | | 京 | | jīng | 905 |
| 春 | | chūn | 855 | | 盲 | | máng | 906 |
| 杂 | 雜 | zá | 856 | | 音 | | yīn | 907 |
| 或 | | huò | 857 | | 亲 | 親 | qīn | 908 |
| 皇 | | huáng | 858 | | 完 | | wán | 909 |
| 鸟 | 鳥 | niǎo | 859 | | 宗 | | zōng | 910 |
| 省 | | shěng | 860 | | 审 | 審 | shěn | 911 |
| 省 | | xǐng | 860 | | 穷 | 窮 | qióng | 912 |
| 笑 | | xiào | 861 | | 突 | | tū | 913 |
| 伺 | | cì | 862 | | 间 | 間 | jiān | 914 |
| 伺 | | sì | 862 | | 间 | 間 | jiàn | 914 |
| 例 | | lì | 863 | | 序 | | xù | 915 |
| 侧 | 側 | cè | 864 | | 底 | | dǐ | 916 |
| 便 | | biàn | 865 | | 庞 | 龐 | páng | 917 |
| 促 | | cù | 866 | | 废 | 廢 | fèi | 918 |
| 俗 | | sú | 867 | | 度 | | dù | 919 |
| 保 | | bǎo | 868 | | 座 | | zuò | 920 |
| 信 | | xìn | 869 | | 疹 | | zhěn | 921 |
| 修 | | xiū | 870 | | 疾 | | jí | 922 |
| 彻 | 徹 | chè | 871 | | 症 | 癥 | zhēng | 923 |
| 待 | | dài | 872 | | 症 | 癥 | zhèng | 923 |
| 徒 | | tú | 873 | | 首 | | shǒu | 924 |
| 顺 | 順 | shùn | 874 | | 姜 | 薑 | jiāng | 925 |
| 须 | 須 | xū | 875 | | 券 | | quàn | 926 |
| 约 | 約 | yuē | 876 | | 奖 | 獎 | jiǎng | 927 |
| 娃 | | wá | 877 | | 况 | | kuàng | 928 |
| 奶 | | nǎi | 878 | | 准 | 準 | zhǔn | 929 |
| 妨 | | fáng | 879 | | 恰 | | qià | 930 |
| 姐 | | jiě | 880 | | 恼 | 惱 | nǎo | 931 |
| 姑 | | gū | 881 | | 汤 | 湯 | tāng | 932 |
| 娇 | 嬌 | jiāo | 882 | | 沟 | 溝 | gōu | 933 |
| 物 | | wù | 883 | | 河 | | hé | 934 |
| 犯 | | fàn | 884 | | 治 | | zhì | 935 |
| 狐 | | hú | 885 | | 波 | | bō | 936 |
| 犹 | 猶 | yóu | 886 | | 泼 | 潑 | pō | 937 |
| 绊 | 絆 | bàn | 887 | | 没 | | méi | 938 |
| 轨 | 軌 | guǐ | 888 | | 没 | | mò | 938 |
| 软 | 軟 | ruǎn | 889 | | 池 | | chí | 939 |
| 饥 | 飢 | jī | 890 | | 洁 | 潔 | jié | 940 |
| 饭 | 飯 | fàn | 891 | | 活 | | huó | 941 |
| 饮 | 飲 | yǐn | 892 | | 洽 | | qià | 942 |
| 种 | 種 | zhǒng | 893 | | 浊 | 濁 | zhuó | 943 |
| 种 | 種 | zhòng | 893 | | 涉 | | shè | 944 |
| 秤 | | chèng | 894 | | 派 | | pài | 945 |
| 秩 | | zhì | 895 | | 记 | 記 | jì | 946 |
| 卵 | | luǎn | 896 | | 论 | 論 | lùn | 947 |
| 版 | | bǎn | 897 | | 讽 | 諷 | fěng | 948 |
| 肋 | | lèi | 898 | | | | | |

| SIMP CHAR | TRAD CHAR | PINYIN | CHAR NO |
|---|---|---|---|
| 访 | 訪 | fǎng | 949 |
| 识 | 識 | shí | 950 |
| 译 | 譯 | yì | 951 |
| 详 | 詳 | xiáng | 952 |
| 烘 | | hōng | 953 |
| 迅 | | xùn | 954 |
| 迈 | 邁 | mài | 955 |
| 运 | 運 | yùn | 956 |
| 返 | | fǎn | 957 |
| 连 | 連 | lián | 958 |
| 迟 | 遲 | chí | 959 |
| 叛 | | pàn | 960 |
| 料 | | liào | 961 |
| 衬 | 襯 | chèn | 962 |
| 初 | | chū | 963 |
| 放 | | fàng | 964 |
| 效 | | xiào | 965 |
| 刻 | | kè | 966 |
| 刹 | | chà | 967 |
| 刹 | | shā | 967 |
| 丽 | 麗 | lì | 968 |
| 要 | | yāo | 969 |
| 要 | | yào | 969 |
| 忍 | | rěn | 970 |
| 孕 | | yùn | 971 |
| 承 | | chéng | 972 |
| 艰 | 艱 | jiān | 973 |
| 难 | 難 | nán | 974 |
| 难 | 難 | nàn | 974 |
| 现 | 現 | xiàn | 975 |
| 玻 | | bō | 976 |
| 残 | 殘 | cán | 977 |
| 孤 | | gū | 978 |
| 砍 | | kǎn | 979 |
| 那 | | nà | 980 |
| 邪 | | xié | 981 |
| 致 | 緻 | zhì | 982 |
| 驳 | 駁 | bó | 983 |
| 桌 | | zhuō | 984 |
| 贵 | 貴 | guì | 985 |
| 南 | | nán | 986 |
| 事 | | shì | 987 |
| 畏 | | wèi | 988 |
| 冒 | | mào | 989 |
| 虽 | 雖 | suī | 990 |
| 基 | | jī | 991 |
| 契 | | qì | 992 |
| 盐 | 鹽 | yán | 993 |
| 监 | 監 | jiān | 994 |
| 栽 | | zāi | 995 |
| 苍 | 蒼 | cāng | 996 |
| 荐 | 薦 | jiàn | 997 |
| 荤 | 葷 | hūn | 998 |

| SIMP CHAR | TRAD CHAR | PINYIN | CHAR NO |
|---|---|---|---|
| 莫 | | mò | 999 |
| 获 | 獲 | huò | 1000 |
| 菜 | | cài | 1001 |
| 埋 | | mái | 1002 |
| 埋 | | mán | 1002 |
| 堆 | | duī | 1003 |
| 扬 | 揚 | yáng | 1004 |
| 批 | | pī | 1005 |
| 把 | | bǎ | 1006 |
| 抑 | | yì | 1007 |
| 投 | | tóu | 1008 |
| 抗 | | kàng | 1009 |
| 报 | 報 | bào | 1010 |
| 披 | | pī | 1011 |
| 抬 | | tái | 1012 |
| 拙 | | zhuō | 1013 |
| 拥 | 擁 | yōng | 1014 |
| 拨 | 撥 | bō | 1015 |
| 括 | | kuò | 1016 |
| 拾 | | shí | 1017 |
| 挡 | 擋 | dǎng | 1018 |
| 持 | | chí | 1019 |
| 吗 | 嗎 | má | 1020 |
| 吗 | 嗎 | ma | 1020 |
| 吧 | | bā | 1021 |
| 吧 | | ba | 1021 |
| 吨 | 噸 | dūn | 1022 |
| 咱 | | zán | 1023 |
| 咽 | | yān | 1024 |
| 咽 | | yàn | 1024 |
| 哈 | | hā | 1025 |
| 核 | | hé | 1026 |
| 杨 | 楊 | yáng | 1027 |
| 构 | 構 | gòu | 1028 |
| 柠 | 檸 | níng | 1029 |
| 栋 | 棟 | dòng | 1030 |
| 树 | 樹 | shù | 1031 |
| 档 | 檔 | dàng | 1032 |
| 检 | 檢 | jiǎn | 1033 |
| 帆 | | fān | 1034 |
| 明 | | míng | 1035 |
| 映 | | yìng | 1036 |
| 贱 | 賤 | jiàn | 1037 |
| 贴 | 貼 | tiē | 1038 |
| 赃 | 贓 | zāng | 1039 |
| 防 | | fáng | 1040 |
| 阴 | 陰 | yīn | 1041 |
| 阻 | | zǔ | 1042 |
| 陆 | 陸 | liù | 1043 |
| 陆 | 陸 | lù | 1043 |
| 战 | 戰 | zhàn | 1044 |
| 眨 | | zhǎ | 1045 |
| 邮 | 郵 | yóu | 1046 |
| 即 | | jí | 1047 |

| SIMP CHAR | TRAD CHAR | PINYIN | CHAR NO | | SIMP CHAR | TRAD CHAR | PINYIN | CHAR NO |
|---|---|---|---|---|---|---|---|---|
| 蚊 | | wén | 1048 | | 级 | 級 | jí | 1100 |
| 别 | 别 | bié | 1049 | | 纪 | 紀 | jì | 1101 |
| 别 | 别 弊 | biè | 1049 | | 纷 | 紛 | fēn | 1102 |
| 刺 | | cì | 1050 | | 纸 | 紙 | zhǐ | 1103 |
| | | | | | 纺 | 紡 | fǎng | 1104 |
| 命 | | mìng | 1051 | | 线 | 綫 | xiàn | 1105 |
| 贫 | 貧 | pín | 1052 | | 组 | 組 | zǔ | 1106 |
| 食 | | shí | 1053 | | 细 | 細 | xì | 1107 |
| 念 | | niàn | 1054 | | 织 | 織 | zhī | 1108 |
| 秀 | | xiù | 1055 | | 终 | 終 | zhōng | 1109 |
| 免 | | miǎn | 1056 | | 经 | 經 | jīng | 1110 |
| 危 | | wēi | 1057 | | 转 | 轉 | zhuǎn | 1111 |
| 昏 | | hūn | 1058 | | 转 | 轉 | zhuàn | 1111 |
| 复 | 復 複 | fù | 1059 | | 轮 | 輪 | lún | 1112 |
| 凭 | 憑 | píng | 1060 | | 轻 | 輕 | qīng | 1113 |
| 货 | 貨 | huò | 1061 | | 较 | 較 | jiào | 1114 |
| 贷 | 貸 | dài | 1062 | | 饺 | 餃 | jiǎo | 1115 |
| 努 | | nǔ | 1063 | | 饼 | 餅 | bǐng | 1116 |
| 套 | | tào | 1064 | | 的 | | de | 1117 |
| 轰 | 轟 | hōng | 1065 | | 的 | | dí | 1117 |
| 泰 | | tài | 1066 | | 肌 | | jī | 1118 |
| 眉 | | méi | 1067 | | 肿 | 腫 | zhǒng | 1119 |
| 周 | | zhōu | 1068 | | 胀 | 脹 | zhàng | 1120 |
| 局 | | jú | 1069 | | 胖 | | pàng | 1121 |
| 屁 | | pì | 1070 | | 胜 | 勝 | shèng | 1122 |
| 屈 | | qū | 1071 | | 邻 | 鄰 | lín | 1123 |
| 屋 | | wū | 1072 | | 钓 | 釣 | diào | 1124 |
| 咸 | 鹹 | xián | 1073 | | 钟 | 鍾 | zhōng | 1125 |
| 贰 | 貳 | èr | 1074 | | 铁 | 鐵 | tiě | 1126 |
| 真 | | zhēn | 1075 | | 敌 | 敵 | dí | 1127 |
| 臭 | | chòu | 1076 | | 卸 | | xiè | 1128 |
| 爸 | | bà | 1077 | | 叙 | | xù | 1129 |
| 笋 | | sǔn | 1078 | | 制 | 製 | zhì | 1130 |
| 笨 | | bèn | 1079 | | 创 | 創 | chuàng | 1131 |
| 佛 | | fó | 1080 | | 彩 | | cǎi | 1132 |
| 俊 | | jùn | 1081 | | | | | |
| 俩 | 倆 | liǎ | 1082 | | 育 | | yù | 1133 |
| 俱 | | jù | 1083 | | 哀 | | āi | 1134 |
| 倍 | | bèi | 1084 | | 享 | | xiǎng | 1135 |
| 侃 | | kǎn | 1085 | | 官 | | guān | 1136 |
| 候 | | hòu | 1086 | | 宠 | 寵 | chǒng | 1137 |
| 借 | | jiè | 1087 | | 宣 | | xuān | 1138 |
| 债 | 債 | zhài | 1088 | | 室 | | shì | 1139 |
| 值 | | zhí | 1089 | | 宰 | | zǎi | 1140 |
| 很 | | hěn | 1090 | | 宾 | 賓 | bīn | 1141 |
| 她 | | tā | 1091 | | 究 | | jiū | 1142 |
| 妈 | 媽 | mā | 1092 | | 窄 | | zhǎi | 1143 |
| 姻 | | yīn | 1093 | | 肩 | | jiān | 1144 |
| 特 | | tè | 1094 | | 房 | | fáng | 1145 |
| 独 | 獨 | dú | 1095 | | 麻 | | má | 1146 |
| 租 | | zū | 1096 | | 疯 | 瘋 | fēng | 1147 |
| 积 | 積 | jī | 1097 | | 疼 | | téng | 1148 |
| 规 | 規 | guī | 1098 | | 痒 | 癢 | yǎng | 1149 |
| 爬 | | pá | 1099 | | 闷 | 悶 | mēn | 1150 |

TM 11 FM | (continued)

TM 11 FM 丿

TM 11 FM 丶

| SIMP CHAR | TRAD CHAR | PINYIN | CHAR NO |
|---|---|---|---|
| 闷 | 悶 | mèn | 1150 |
| 闻 | 聞 | wén | 1151 |
| 弟 | | dì | 1152 |
| 益 | | yì | 1153 |
| 羞 | | xiū | 1154 |
| 学 | 學 | xué | 1155 |
| 尚 | | shàng | 1156 |
| 尝 | 嘗 | cháng | 1157 |
| 拳 | | quán | 1158 |
| 净 | | jìng | 1159 |
| 凑 | | còu | 1160 |
| 将 | 將 | jiāng | 1161 |
| 将 | 將 | jiàng | 1161 |
| 柒 | | qī | 1162 |
| 洒 | 灑 | sǎ | 1163 |
| 泥 | | ní | 1164 |
| 沿 | | yán | 1165 |
| 沉 | | chén | 1166 |
| 洗 | | xǐ | 1167 |
| 浓 | 濃 | nóng | 1168 |
| 浩 | | hào | 1169 |
| 浴 | | yù | 1170 |
| 涂 | 塗 | tú | 1171 |
| 淋 | | lín | 1172 |
| 淡 | | dàn | 1173 |
| 恨 | | hèn | 1174 |
| 炖 | 燉 | dùn | 1175 |
| 烛 | 燭 | zhú | 1176 |
| 烟 | | yān | 1177 |
| 烦 | 煩 | fán | 1178 |
| 设 | 設 | shè | 1179 |
| 试 | 試 | shì | 1180 |
| 诗 | 詩 | shī | 1181 |
| 话 | 話 | huà | 1182 |
| 该 | 該 | gāi | 1183 |
| 远 | 遠 | yuǎn | 1184 |
| 违 | 違 | wéi | 1185 |
| 迫 | | pò | 1186 |
| 迷 | | mí | 1187 |
| 送 | | sòng | 1188 |
| 站 | | zhàn | 1189 |
| 祖 | | zǔ | 1190 |
| 神 | | shén | 1191 |
| 祥 | | xiáng | 1192 |
| 袜 | 襪 | wà | 1193 |
| 郊 | | jiāo | 1194 |

| SIMP CHAR | TRAD CHAR | PINYIN | CHAR NO |
|---|---|---|---|
| 夏 | | xià | 1195 |
| 恶 | 惡 | è | 1196 |
| 恶 | 惡 | wù | 1196 |
| 忌 | | jì | 1197 |
| 柔 | | róu | 1198 |
| 球 | | qiú | 1199 |
| 理 | | lǐ | 1200 |

| SIMP CHAR | TRAD CHAR | PINYIN | CHAR NO |
|---|---|---|---|
| 砖 | 磚 | zhuān | 1201 |
| 孩 | | hái | 1202 |
| 建 | | jiàn | 1203 |
| 顽 | 頑 | wán | 1204 |
| 职 | 職 | zhí | 1205 |
| 联 | 聯 | lián | 1206 |
| 驻 | 駐 | zhù | 1207 |
| 张 | 張 | zhāng | 1208 |
| 敢 | | gǎn | 1209 |
| 耐 | | nài | 1210 |

| SIMP CHAR | TRAD CHAR | PINYIN | CHAR NO |
|---|---|---|---|
| 毒 | | dú | 1211 |
| 黄 | | huáng | 1212 |
| 带 | 帶 | dài | 1213 |
| 思 | | sī | 1214 |
| 罢 | 罷 | bà | 1215 |
| 胃 | | wèi | 1216 |
| 梦 | 夢 | mèng | 1217 |
| 载 | 載 | zǎi | 1218 |
| 载 | 載 | zài | 1218 |
| 哲 | | zhé | 1219 |
| 品 | | pǐn | 1220 |
| 哭 | | kū | 1221 |
| 荒 | | huāng | 1222 |
| 著 | | zhù | 1223 |
| 垮 | | kuǎ | 1224 |
| 城 | | chéng | 1225 |
| 堵 | | dǔ | 1226 |
| 呢 | | ne | 1227 |
| 呢 | | ní | 1227 |
| 吼 | | hǒu | 1228 |
| 咖 | | kā | 1229 |
| 抢 | 搶 | qiǎng | 1230 |
| 拘 | | jū | 1231 |
| 招 | | zhāo | 1232 |
| 拣 | 揀 | jiǎn | 1233 |
| 按 | | àn | 1234 |
| 挑 | | tiāo | 1235 |
| 挑 | | tiǎo | 1235 |
| 挥 | 揮 | huī | 1236 |
| 挨 | | āi | 1237 |
| 挨 | | ái | 1237 |
| 振 | | zhèn | 1238 |
| 捉 | | zhuō | 1239 |
| 捧 | | pěng | 1240 |
| 排 | | pái | 1241 |
| 推 | | tuī | 1242 |
| 桃 | | táo | 1243 |
| 枪 | 槍 | qiāng | 1244 |
| 根 | | gēn | 1245 |
| 格 | | gé | 1246 |
| 棒 | | bàng | 1247 |
| 棋 | | qí | 1248 |
| 阿 | | ā | 1249 |

| SIMP CHAR | TRAD CHAR | PINYIN | CHAR NO |
|---|---|---|---|
| 阿 | | ē | 1249 |
| 陈 | 陳 | chén | 1250 |
| 陌 | | mò | 1251 |
| 险 | 險 | xiǎn | 1252 |
| 购 | 購 | gòu | 1253 |
| 贼 | 賊 | zéi | 1254 |
| 盼 | | pàn | 1255 |
| 胡 | 鬍 | hú | 1256 |
| 趁 | | chèn | 1257 |
| 跃 | 躍 | yuè | 1258 |
| 救 | | jiù | 1259 |
| 断 | 斷 | duàn | 1260 |

**TM 12 FM 丿**

| SIMP CHAR | TRAD CHAR | PINYIN | CHAR NO |
|---|---|---|---|
| 盆 | | pén | 1261 |
| 拿 | | ná | 1262 |
| 乘 | | chéng | 1263 |
| 爱 | 愛 | ài | 1264 |
| 焦 | | jiāo | 1265 |
| 售 | | shòu | 1266 |
| 集 | | jí | 1267 |
| 忽 | | hū | 1268 |
| 氧 | | yǎng | 1269 |
| 架 | | jià | 1270 |
| 梨 | | lí | 1271 |
| 厚 | | hòu | 1272 |
| 原 | | yuán | 1273 |
| 展 | | zhǎn | 1274 |
| 泉 | | quán | 1275 |
| 爹 | | diē | 1276 |
| 符 | | fú | 1277 |
| 笔 | 筆 | bǐ | 1278 |
| 笛 | | dí | 1279 |
| 侵 | | qīn | 1280 |
| 倒 | | dǎo | 1281 |
| 倒 | | dào | 1281 |
| 做 | | zuò | 1282 |
| 牺 | 犧 | xī | 1283 |
| 狠 | | hěn | 1284 |
| 狮 | 獅 | shī | 1285 |
| 狱 | 獄 | yù | 1286 |
| 狗 | | gǒu | 1287 |
| 称 | 稱 | chèn | 1288 |
| 称 | 稱 | chēng | 1288 |
| 称 | 稱 | chèng | 1288 |
| 秘 | | mì | 1289 |
| 纯 | 純 | chún | 1290 |
| 结 | 結 | jiē | 1291 |
| 结 | 結 | jié | 1291 |
| 给 | 給 | gěi | 1292 |
| 给 | 給 | jǐ | 1292 |
| 段 | | duàn | 1293 |
| 肺 | | fèi | 1294 |
| 胆 | 膽 | dǎn | 1295 |
| 胶 | 膠 | jiāo | 1296 |

| SIMP CHAR | TRAD CHAR | PINYIN | CHAR NO |
|---|---|---|---|
| 脏 | 髒 | zāng | 1297 |
| 脏 | 臟 | zàng | 1297 |
| 朋 | | péng | 1298 |
| 钢 | 鋼 | gāng | 1299 |
| 钥 | 鑰 | yào | 1300 |
| 钥 | 鑰 | yuè | 1300 |
| 钱 | 錢 | qián | 1301 |
| 钻 | 鑽 | zuān | 1302 |
| 钻 | 鑽 | zuàn | 1302 |
| 铃 | 鈴 | líng | 1303 |
| 铲 | 鏟 | chǎn | 1304 |
| 缺 | | quē | 1305 |
| 甜 | | tián | 1306 |
| 斜 | | xié | 1307 |
| 乳 | | rǔ | 1308 |
| 删 | | shān | 1309 |
| 刷 | | shuā | 1310 |

**TM 12 FM 丶**

| SIMP CHAR | TRAD CHAR | PINYIN | CHAR NO |
|---|---|---|---|
| 章 | | zhāng | 1311 |
| 帝 | | dì | 1312 |
| 衰 | | shuāi | 1313 |
| 恋 | 戀 | liàn | 1314 |
| 家 | 傢 | jiā | 1315 |
| 客 | | kè | 1316 |
| 宪 | 憲 | xiàn | 1317 |
| 宫 | 宮 | gōng | 1318 |
| 害 | | hài | 1319 |
| 容 | | róng | 1320 |
| 案 | | àn | 1321 |
| 穿 | | chuān | 1322 |
| 闹 | 鬧 | nào | 1323 |
| 唐 | | táng | 1324 |
| 席 | | xí | 1325 |
| 庭 | | tíng | 1326 |
| 病 | | bìng | 1327 |
| 疲 | | pí | 1328 |
| 前 | | qián | 1329 |
| 总 | 總 | zǒng | 1330 |
| 盖 | 蓋 | gài | 1331 |
| 着 | | zhāo | 1332 |
| 着 | | zháo | 1332 |
| 着 | | zhe | 1332 |
| 着 | | zhuó | 1332 |
| 卷 | | juǎn | 1333 |
| 卷 | | juàn | 1333 |
| 粪 | 糞 | fèn | 1334 |
| 资 | 資 | zī | 1335 |
| 染 | | rǎn | 1336 |
| 凉 | | liáng | 1337 |
| 凉 | | liàng | 1337 |
| 洞 | | dòng | 1338 |
| 酒 | | jiǔ | 1339 |
| 浇 | 澆 | jiāo | 1340 |
| 浪 | | làng | 1341 |

| SIMP CHAR | TRAD CHAR | PINYIN | CHAR NO |
|---|---|---|---|
| 浮 | | fú | 1342 |
| 消 | | xiāo | 1343 |
| 液 | | yè | 1344 |
| 深 | | shēn | 1345 |
| 添 | | tiān | 1346 |
| 渐 | 漸 | jiàn | 1347 |
| 悄 | | qiǎo | 1348 |
| 悼 | | dào | 1349 |
| 惜 | | xī | 1350 |
| 惧 | 懼 | jù | 1351 |
| 惭 | 慚 | cán | 1352 |
| 词 | 詞 | cí | 1353 |
| 误 | 誤 | wù | 1354 |
| 谁 | 誰 | sheí | 1355 |
| 谁 | 誰 | shuí | 1355 |
| 谈 | 談 | tán | 1356 |
| 炼 | 煉 | liàn | 1357 |
| 适 | 適 | shì | 1358 |
| 逆 | | nì | 1359 |
| 迎 | | yíng | 1360 |
| 袖 | | xiù | 1361 |
| 视 | 視 | shì | 1362 |
| 粉 | | fěn | 1363 |
| 粗 | | cū | 1364 |
| 粘 | | zhān | 1365 |
| 削 | | xiāo | 1366 |
| 削 | | xuē | 1366 |

| SIMP CHAR | TRAD CHAR | PINYIN | CHAR NO |
|---|---|---|---|
| 票 | | piào | 1367 |
| 蛋 | | dàn | 1368 |
| 雪 | | xuě | 1369 |
| 哥 | | gē | 1370 |
| 勇 | | yǒng | 1371 |
| 琴 | | qín | 1372 |
| 鸡 | 鷄 | jī | 1373 |
| 破 | | pò | 1374 |
| 硕 | 碩 | shuò | 1375 |
| 骄 | 驕 | jiāo | 1376 |
| 剥 | | bāo | 1377 |
| 剥 | | bō | 1377 |

| SIMP CHAR | TRAD CHAR | PINYIN | CHAR NO |
|---|---|---|---|
| 素 | | sù | 1378 |
| 虐 | | nüè | 1379 |
| 背 | | bēi | 1380 |
| 背 | | bèi | 1380 |
| 恩 | | ēn | 1381 |
| 辈 | 輩 | bèi | 1382 |
| 崭 | 嶄 | zhǎn | 1383 |
| 晃 | | huǎng | 1384 |
| 晃 | | huàng | 1384 |
| 晕 | 暈 | yūn | 1385 |
| 晕 | 暈 | yùn | 1385 |
| 罚 | 罰 | fá | 1386 |
| 咒 | | zhòu | 1387 |
| 煮 | | zhǔ | 1388 |

| SIMP CHAR | TRAD CHAR | PINYIN | CHAR NO |
|---|---|---|---|
| 黑 | | hēi | 1389 |
| 热 | 熱 | rè | 1390 |
| 圆 | 圓 | yuán | 1391 |
| 药 | 藥 | yào | 1392 |
| 菠 | | bō | 1393 |
| 塔 | | tǎ | 1394 |
| 抛 | | pāo | 1395 |
| 拖 | | tuō | 1396 |
| 指 | | zhǐ | 1397 |
| 挣 | | zhēng | 1398 |
| 挣 | | zhèng | 1398 |
| 捂 | | wǔ | 1399 |
| 捕 | | bǔ | 1400 |
| 损 | 損 | sǔn | 1401 |
| 换 | | huàn | 1402 |
| 掉 | | diào | 1403 |
| 探 | | tàn | 1404 |
| 接 | | jiē | 1405 |
| 控 | | kòng | 1406 |
| 描 | | miáo | 1407 |
| 挺 | | tǐng | 1408 |
| 响 | 響 | xiǎng | 1409 |
| 哨 | | shào | 1410 |
| 啥 | | shá | 1411 |
| 啤 | | pí | 1412 |
| 梅 | | méi | 1413 |
| 棵 | | kē | 1414 |
| 植 | | zhí | 1415 |
| 降 | | jiàng | 1416 |
| 降 | | xiáng | 1416 |
| 限 | | xiàn | 1417 |
| 除 | | chú | 1418 |
| 贿 | 賄 | huì | 1419 |
| 顿 | 頓 | dùn | 1420 |
| 起 | | qǐ | 1421 |
| 跌 | | diē | 1422 |
| 欺 | | qī | 1423 |
| 教 | | jiāo | 1424 |
| 教 | | jiào | 1424 |

| SIMP CHAR | TRAD CHAR | PINYIN | CHAR NO |
|---|---|---|---|
| 盒 | | hé | 1425 |
| 急 | | jí | 1426 |
| 怒 | | nù | 1427 |
| 袋 | | dài | 1428 |
| 贸 | 貿 | mào | 1429 |
| 替 | | tì | 1430 |
| 聋 | 聾 | lóng | 1431 |
| 然 | | rán | 1432 |
| 鬼 | | guǐ | 1433 |
| 岛 | 島 | dǎo | 1434 |
| 奥 | | ào | 1435 |
| 笼 | 籠 | lóng | 1436 |
| 笼 | 籠 | lǒng | 1436 |
| 等 | | děng | 1437 |

| SIMP CHAR | TRAD CHAR | PINYIN | CHAR NO |
|---|---|---|---|
| 答 | | dá | 1438 |
| 签 | 簽 籤 | qiān | 1439 |
| 偿 | 償 | cháng | 1440 |
| 街 | | jiē | 1441 |
| 得 | | dé | 1442 |
| 得 | | děi | 1442 |
| 得 | | de | 1442 |
| 狼 | | láng | 1443 |
| 猎 | 獵 | liè | 1444 |
| 猪 | | zhū | 1445 |
| 猫 | | māo | 1446 |
| 饲 | 飼 | sì | 1447 |
| 娘 | | niáng | 1448 |
| 媒 | | méi | 1449 |
| 移 | | yí | 1450 |
| 程 | | chéng | 1451 |
| 短 | | duǎn | 1452 |
| 练 | 練 | liàn | 1453 |
| 绑 | 綁 | bǎng | 1454 |
| 维 | 維 | wéi | 1455 |
| 股 | | gǔ | 1456 |
| 服 | | fú | 1457 |
| 肠 | 腸 | cháng | 1458 |
| 肥 | | féi | 1459 |
| 脑 | 腦 | nǎo | 1460 |
| 脸 | 臉 | liǎn | 1461 |
| 钙 | 鈣 | gài | 1462 |
| 钩 | 鉤 | gōu | 1463 |
| 铅 | 鉛 | qiān | 1464 |
| 领 | 領 | lǐng | 1465 |
| 欲 | | yù | 1466 |
| 射 | | shè | 1467 |
| 剧 | 劇 | jù | 1468 |

TM 13   FM ㇏

| SIMP CHAR | TRAD CHAR | PINYIN | CHAR NO |
|---|---|---|---|
| 率 | | lǜ | 1469 |
| 率 | | shuài | 1469 |
| 竞 | 競 | jìng | 1470 |
| 童 | | tóng | 1471 |
| 弯 | 彎 | wān | 1472 |
| 旁 | | páng | 1473 |
| 雇 | 僱 | gù | 1474 |
| 盗 | | dào | 1475 |
| 装 | 裝 | zhuāng | 1476 |
| 痘 | | dòu | 1477 |
| 冠 | | guān | 1478 |
| 冠 | | guàn | 1478 |
| 宴 | | yàn | 1479 |
| 宿 | | sù | 1480 |
| 宿 | | xiǔ | 1480 |
| 宿 | | xiù | 1480 |
| 寒 | | hán | 1481 |
| 窃 | 竊 | qiè | 1482 |
| 善 | | shàn | 1483 |
| 普 | | pǔ | 1484 |

| SIMP CHAR | TRAD CHAR | PINYIN | CHAR NO |
|---|---|---|---|
| 觉 | 覺 | jiào | 1485 |
| 觉 | 覺 | jué | 1485 |
| 堂 | | táng | 1486 |
| 减 | | jiǎn | 1487 |
| 悔 | | huǐ | 1488 |
| 惊 | 驚 | jīng | 1489 |
| 愤 | 憤 | fèn | 1490 |
| 情 | | qíng | 1491 |
| 泡 | | pāo | 1492 |
| 泡 | | pào | 1492 |
| 流 | | liú | 1493 |
| 海 | | hǎi | 1494 |
| 清 | | qīng | 1495 |
| 渔 | 漁 | yú | 1496 |
| 渡 | | dù | 1497 |
| 湿 | 濕 | shī | 1498 |
| 诚 | 誠 | chéng | 1499 |
| 询 | 詢 | xún | 1500 |
| 语 | 語 | yǔ | 1501 |
| 读 | 讀 | dú | 1502 |
| 课 | 課 | kè | 1503 |
| 烧 | 燒 | shāo | 1504 |
| 烤 | | kǎo | 1505 |
| 煤 | | méi | 1506 |
| 追 | | zhuī | 1507 |
| 退 | | tuì | 1508 |
| 逃 | | táo | 1509 |
| 选 | 選 | xuǎn | 1510 |
| 途 | | tú | 1511 |
| 逗 | | dòu | 1512 |
| 逛 | | guàng | 1513 |
| 速 | | sù | 1514 |
| 造 | | zào | 1515 |
| 祝 | | zhù | 1516 |
| 被 | | bèi | 1517 |
| 旅 | | lǚ | 1518 |
| 族 | | zú | 1519 |

TM 14   FM 一

| SIMP CHAR | TRAD CHAR | PINYIN | CHAR NO |
|---|---|---|---|
| 费 | 費 | fèi | 1520 |
| 登 | | dēng | 1521 |
| 暂 | 暫 | zàn | 1522 |
| 砸 | | zá | 1523 |
| 硬 | | yìng | 1524 |
| 碎 | | suì | 1525 |
| 碰 | | pèng | 1526 |
| 聊 | | liáo | 1527 |
| 预 | 預 | yù | 1528 |
| 验 | 驗 | yàn | 1529 |

TM 14   FM ｜

| SIMP CHAR | TRAD CHAR | PINYIN | CHAR NO |
|---|---|---|---|
| 壹 | | yī | 1530 |
| 喜 | | xǐ | 1531 |
| 悲 | | bēi | 1532 |
| 虎 | | hǔ | 1533 |
| 虚 | | xū | 1534 |
| 裁 | | cái | 1535 |

| SIMP CHAR | TRAD CHAR | PINYIN | CHAR NO |
|---|---|---|---|
| 禁 | | jìn | 1536 |
| 紧 | 緊 | jǐn | 1537 |
| 幽 | | yōu | 1538 |
| 婴 | 嬰 | yīng | 1539 |
| 暑 | | shǔ | 1540 |
| 最 | | zuì | 1541 |
| 罪 | | zuì | 1542 |
| 骨 | | gǔ | 1543 |
| 量 | | liáng | 1544 |
| 量 | | liàng | 1544 |
| 墓 | | mù | 1545 |
| 营 | 營 | yíng | 1546 |
| 落 | | là | 1547 |
| 落 | | lào | 1547 |
| 落 | | luò | 1547 |
| 蓝 | 藍 | lán | 1548 |
| 博 | | bó | 1549 |
| 填 | | tián | 1550 |
| 挖 | | wā | 1551 |
| 捐 | | juān | 1552 |
| 据 | 據 | jù | 1553 |
| 提 | | tí | 1554 |
| 插 | | chā | 1555 |
| 援 | | yuán | 1556 |
| 搂 | 摟 | lǒu | 1557 |
| 搽 | | chá | 1558 |
| 啃 | | kěn | 1559 |
| 喉 | | hóu | 1560 |
| 哼 | | hēng | 1561 |
| 唱 | | chàng | 1562 |
| 喷 | 噴 | pēn | 1563 |
| 桶 | | tǒng | 1564 |
| 梳 | | shū | 1565 |
| 椅 | | yǐ | 1566 |
| 楼 | 樓 | lóu | 1567 |
| 陪 | | péi | 1568 |
| 赔 | 賠 | péi | 1569 |
| 眼 | | yǎn | 1570 |
| 睡 | | shuì | 1571 |
| 既 | | jì | 1572 |
| 款 | | kuǎn | 1573 |
| 期 | | qī | 1574 |
| 越 | | yuè | 1575 |
| 距 | | jù | 1576 |
| 凯 | 凱 | kǎi | 1577 |
| 都 | | dōu | 1578 |
| 都 | | dū | 1578 |
| 散 | | sǎn | 1579 |
| 散 | | sàn | 1579 |
| TM **14** FM ノ 象 | | xiàng | 1580 |
| 智 | | zhì | 1581 |
| 留 | | liú | 1582 |
| 帮 | 幫 | bāng | 1583 |

| SIMP CHAR | TRAD CHAR | PINYIN | CHAR NO |
|---|---|---|---|
| 厨 | | chú | 1584 |
| 筷 | | kuài | 1585 |
| 假 | | jiǎ | 1586 |
| 假 | | jià | 1586 |
| 偏 | | piān | 1587 |
| 停 | | tíng | 1588 |
| 健 | | jiàn | 1589 |
| 偶 | | ǒu | 1590 |
| 偷 | | tōu | 1591 |
| 催 | | cuī | 1592 |
| 饿 | 餓 | è | 1593 |
| 猜 | | cāi | 1594 |
| 猴 | | hóu | 1595 |
| 姨 | | yí | 1596 |
| 牌 | | pái | 1597 |
| 矮 | | ǎi | 1598 |
| 稀 | | xī | 1599 |
| 稍 | | shāo | 1600 |
| 统 | 統 | tǒng | 1601 |
| 辆 | 輛 | liàng | 1602 |
| 毯 | | tǎn | 1603 |
| 脉 | | mài | 1604 |
| 脓 | 膿 | nóng | 1605 |
| 辞 | 辭 | cí | 1606 |
| 银 | 銀 | yín | 1607 |
| 锁 | 鎖 | suǒ | 1608 |
| 顾 | 顧 | gù | 1609 |
| 敏 | | mǐn | 1610 |
| TM **14** FM ﹨ 高 | | gāo | 1611 |
| 商 | | shāng | 1612 |
| 亮 | | liàng | 1613 |
| 离 | 離 | lí | 1614 |
| 廉 | | lián | 1615 |
| 竟 | | jìng | 1616 |
| 痴 | | chī | 1617 |
| 宽 | 寬 | kuān | 1618 |
| 寄 | | jì | 1619 |
| 塞 | | sāi | 1620 |
| 塞 | | sài | 1620 |
| 窍 | 竅 | qiào | 1621 |
| 望 | | wàng | 1622 |
| 婆 | | pó | 1623 |
| 烫 | 燙 | tàng | 1624 |
| 曾 | | céng | 1625 |
| 曾 | | zēng | 1625 |
| 党 | 黨 | dǎng | 1626 |
| 温 | | wēn | 1627 |
| 淘 | | táo | 1628 |
| 淹 | | yān | 1629 |
| 惯 | 慣 | guàn | 1630 |
| 说 | 說 | shuì | 1631 |
| 说 | 說 | shuō | 1631 |
| 说 | 說 | yuè | 1631 |

| SIMP CHAR | TRAD CHAR | PINYIN | CHAR NO |
|---|---|---|---|
| 阅 | 閱 | yuè | 1727 |
| 阔 | 闊 | kuò | 1728 |
| 冤 | | yuān | 1729 |
| 密 | | mì | 1730 |
| 富 | | fù | 1731 |
| 窗 | | chuāng | 1732 |
| 常 | | cháng | 1733 |
| 掌 | | zhǎng | 1734 |
| 愣 | | lèng | 1735 |
| 慌 | | huāng | 1736 |
| 愉 | | yú | 1737 |
| 涨 | 漲 | zhǎng | 1738 |
| 涨 | 漲 | zhàng | 1738 |
| 混 | | hún | 1739 |
| 混 | | hùn | 1739 |
| 港 | | gǎng | 1740 |
| 湖 | | hú | 1741 |
| 源 | | yuán | 1742 |
| 溪 | | xī | 1743 |
| 溶 | | róng | 1744 |
| 满 | 滿 | mǎn | 1745 |
| 漆 | | qī | 1746 |
| 诡 | 詭 | guǐ | 1747 |
| 诱 | 誘 | yòu | 1748 |
| 调 | 調 | diào | 1749 |
| 调 | 調 | tiáo | 1749 |
| 谜 | 謎 | mí | 1750 |
| 谣 | 謠 | yáo | 1751 |
| 裙 | | qún | 1752 |
| 裸 | | luǒ | 1753 |
| 祸 | 禍 | huò | 1754 |
| 逻 | 邏 | luó | 1755 |
| 道 | | dào | 1756 |
| 通 | | tōng | 1757 |
| 施 | | shī | 1758 |
| 粮 | 糧 | liáng | 1759 |
| 辣 | | là | 1760 |
| 割 | | gē | 1761 |
| TM 16 FM 一 确 | 確 | què | 1762 |
| 弹 | 彈 | dàn | 1763 |
| 弹 | 彈 | tán | 1763 |
| TM 16 FM 丨 喘 | | chuǎn | 1764 |
| 圈 | | juān | 1765 |
| 圈 | | juàn | 1765 |
| 圈 | | quān | 1765 |
| 葡 | | pú | 1766 |
| 幕 | | mù | 1767 |
| 蒸 | | zhēng | 1768 |
| 想 | | xiǎng | 1769 |
| 墙 | 墻 | qiáng | 1770 |
| 揉 | | róu | 1771 |
| 摄 | 攝 | shè | 1772 |
| 摆 | 擺 襬 | bǎi | 1773 |

| SIMP CHAR | TRAD CHAR | PINYIN | CHAR NO |
|---|---|---|---|
| 撕 | | sī | 1774 |
| 横 | | héng | 1775 |
| 横 | | hèng | 1775 |
| 棍 | | gùn | 1776 |
| 幅 | | fú | 1777 |
| 帽 | | mào | 1778 |
| 晚 | | wǎn | 1779 |
| 蜡 | 蠟 | là | 1780 |
| 赚 | 賺 | zhuàn | 1781 |
| 鸭 | 鴨 | yā | 1782 |
| 趣 | | qù | 1783 |
| 跟 | | gēn | 1784 |
| 路 | | lù | 1785 |
| 跳 | | tiào | 1786 |
| 踩 | | cǎi | 1787 |
| 靴 | | xuē | 1788 |
| 鞋 | | xié | 1789 |
| TM 16 FM 丿 舞 | | wǔ | 1790 |
| 靠 | | kào | 1791 |
| 怨 | | yuàn | 1792 |
| 属 | 屬 | shǔ | 1793 |
| 鼻 | | bí | 1794 |
| 舅 | | jiù | 1795 |
| 简 | 簡 | jiǎn | 1796 |
| 箱 | | xiāng | 1797 |
| 嫂 | | sǎo | 1798 |
| 嫁 | | jià | 1799 |
| 嫩 | | nèn | 1800 |
| 绣 | 繡 | xiù | 1801 |
| 脖 | | bó | 1802 |
| 脱 | | tuō | 1803 |
| 脚 | | jiǎo | 1804 |
| 舒 | | shū | 1805 |
| 舔 | | tiǎn | 1806 |
| 锅 | 鍋 | guō | 1807 |
| 够 | 夠 | gòu | 1808 |
| 船 | | chuán | 1809 |
| 毁 | | huǐ | 1810 |
| 鲜 | 鮮 | xiān | 1811 |
| 鲜 | 鮮 | xiǎn | 1811 |
| TM 16 FM 丶 意 | | yì | 1812 |
| 赛 | 賽 | sài | 1813 |
| 酱 | 醬 | jiàng | 1814 |
| 塑 | | sù | 1815 |
| 剪 | | jiǎn | 1816 |
| 懂 | | dǒng | 1817 |
| 游 | | yóu | 1818 |
| 滚 | | gǔn | 1819 |
| 漂 | | piāo | 1820 |
| 漂 | | piǎo | 1820 |
| 漂 | | piào | 1820 |
| 演 | | yǎn | 1821 |
| 渴 | | kě | 1822 |

| | SIMP CHAR | TRAD CHAR | PINYIN | CHAR NO |
|---|---|---|---|---|
| TM 16 FM 丶 (continued) | 漱 | | shù | 1823 |
| | 谎 | 謊 | huǎng | 1824 |
| | 福 | | fú | 1825 |
| | 透 | | tòu | 1826 |
| | 递 | 遞 | dì | 1827 |
| | 逼 | | bī | 1828 |
| | 遗 | 遺 | yí | 1829 |
| | 遥 | | yáo | 1830 |
| | 遮 | | zhē | 1831 |
| | 精 | | jīng | 1832 |
| | 糕 | | gāo | 1833 |
| | 旗 | | qí | 1834 |
| | 颜 | 顏 | yán | 1835 |
| | 就 | | jiù | 1836 |
| TM 17 FM 一 | 雾 | 霧 | wù | 1837 |
| | 需 | | xū | 1838 |
| | 震 | | zhèn | 1839 |
| | 骑 | 騎 | qí | 1840 |
| | 酷 | | kù | 1841 |
| | 醉 | | zuì | 1842 |
| TM 17 FM 丨 | 墨 | | mò | 1843 |
| | 暴 | | bào | 1844 |
| | 整 | | zhěng | 1845 |
| | 照 | | zhào | 1846 |
| | 薪 | | xīn | 1847 |
| | 境 | | jìng | 1848 |
| | 增 | | zēng | 1849 |
| | 搅 | 攪 | jiǎo | 1850 |
| | 揭 | | jiē | 1851 |
| | 摔 | | shuāi | 1852 |
| | 撞 | | zhuàng | 1853 |
| | 喝 | | hē | 1854 |
| | 喝 | | hè | 1854 |
| | 嗓 | | sǎng | 1855 |
| | 障 | | zhàng | 1856 |
| | 跨 | | kuà | 1857 |
| | 题 | 題 | tí | 1858 |
| TM 17 FM 丿 | 鼠 | | shǔ | 1859 |
| | 感 | | gǎn | 1860 |
| | 管 | | guǎn | 1861 |
| | 篮 | 籃 | lán | 1862 |
| | 像 | | xiàng | 1863 |
| | 僵 | | jiāng | 1864 |
| | 绳 | 繩 | shéng | 1865 |
| | 编 | 編 | biān | 1866 |
| | 输 | 輸 | shū | 1867 |
| | 腰 | | yāo | 1868 |
| | 腹 | | fù | 1869 |
| | 腻 | 膩 | nì | 1870 |
| | 锈 | 銹 | xiù | 1871 |
| | 镇 | 鎮 | zhèn | 1872 |
| | 能 | | néng | 1873 |

| | SIMP CHAR | TRAD CHAR | PINYIN | CHAR NO |
|---|---|---|---|---|
| | 躲 | | duǒ | 1874 |
| | 触 | 觸 | chù | 1875 |
| TM 17 FM 丶 | 豪 | | háo | 1876 |
| | 察 | | chá | 1877 |
| | 寝 | 寢 | qǐn | 1878 |
| | 腐 | | fǔ | 1879 |
| | 瘦 | | shòu | 1880 |
| | 憎 | | zēng | 1881 |
| | 慢 | | màn | 1882 |
| | 溜 | | liū | 1883 |
| | 滑 | | huá | 1884 |
| | 滴 | | dī | 1885 |
| | 漏 | | lòu | 1886 |
| | 漫 | | màn | 1887 |
| | 燃 | | rán | 1888 |
| | 端 | | duān | 1889 |
| | 谢 | 謝 | xiè | 1890 |
| | 遇 | | yù | 1891 |
| | 遍 | | biàn | 1892 |
| TM 18 FM 一 | 魂 | | hún | 1893 |
| | 磕 | | kē | 1894 |
| | 聪 | 聰 | cōng | 1895 |
| | 强 | | jiàng | 1896 |
| | 强 | | qiáng | 1896 |
| | 强 | | qiǎng | 1896 |
| | 弱 | | ruò | 1897 |
| | 醋 | | cù | 1898 |
| | 酸 | | suān | 1899 |
| | 歌 | | gē | 1900 |
| TM 18 FM 丨 | 愚 | | yú | 1901 |
| | 薄 | | báo | 1902 |
| | 薄 | | bó | 1902 |
| | 薄 | | bò | 1902 |
| | 塌 | | tā | 1903 |
| | 搞 | | gǎo | 1904 |
| | 携 | 攜 | xié | 1905 |
| | 摘 | | zhāi | 1906 |
| | 撒 | | sā | 1907 |
| | 撒 | | sǎ | 1907 |
| | 概 | | gài | 1908 |
| | 橱 | | chú | 1909 |
| | 隔 | | gé | 1910 |
| | 随 | 隨 | suí | 1911 |
| | 隐 | 隱 | yǐn | 1912 |
| | 瞎 | | xiā | 1913 |
| | 瞒 | 瞞 | mán | 1914 |
| | 瞧 | | qiáo | 1915 |
| | 跑 | | pǎo | 1916 |
| | 疑 | | yí | 1917 |
| | 影 | | yǐng | 1918 |
| TM 18 FM 丿 | 愿 | 願 | yuàn | 1919 |
| | 壁 | | bì | 1920 |

# Broken Marks of Traditional Chinese Characters

Use this index to locate the dictionary entry for a Traditional Chinese character (for example, 訓).

1. Determine the number of Total Marks (**11**) and the style of the First Mark ( 丶 ) of the Traditional Chinese character (訓). Use the Broken Marks method to determine the number of Total Marks.

2. Using the **TM/FM** column on the left, locate the Traditional Chinese character (訓) in the **TRAD CHAR** column.

3. The character number in the last column (**350**) directs you to the correct dictionary entry.

| TM/FM | TRAD CHAR | SIMP CHAR | PINYIN | CHAR NO |
|---|---|---|---|---|
| TM 7 FM ノ | 夾 | 夹 | jiā | 197 |
| | 夾 | 夹 | jiá | 197 |
| TM 8 FM │ | 貝 | 贝 | bèi | 97 |
| | 車 | 车 | chē | 114 |
| | 車 | 车 | jū | 114 |
| | 壯 | 壮 | zhuàng | 238 |
| | 來 | 来 | lái | 260 |
| TM 9 FM │ | 長 | 长 | cháng | 93 |
| | 長 | 长 | zhǎng | 93 |
| | 東 | 东 | dōng | 307 |
| | 狀 | 状 | zhuàng | 345 |
| TM 10 FM 一 | 頁 | 页 | yè | 245 |
| | 兩 | 两 | liǎng | 509 |
| TM 10 FM │ | 見 | 见 | jiàn | 267 |
| | 華 | 华 | huá | 421 |
| TM 10 FM ノ | 針 | 针 | zhēn | 477 |
| TM 10 FM 丶 | 計 | 计 | jì | 240 |
| TM 11 FM 一 | 貢 | 贡 | gòng | 360 |
| TM 11 FM │ | 鬥 | 斗 | dǒu | 71 |
| | 鬥 | 斗 | dòu | 71 |
| | 門 | 门 | mén | 130 |
| | 莊 | 庄 | zhuāng | 229 |
| | 則 | 则 | zé | 417 |
| | 畢 | 毕 | bì | 540 |
| | 峽 | 峡 | xiá | 807 |
| | 別 | 别 | bié | 1049 |
| | 別 | 别 | biè | 1049 |
| TM 11 FM ノ | 兒 | 儿 | ér | 43 |
| | 從 | 从 | cóng | 66 |
| | 隻 | 只 | zhī | 160 |
| | 負 | 负 | fù | 435 |
| | 糾 | 纠 | jiū | 473 |
| | 紅 | 红 | hóng | 474 |
| | 釘 | 钉 | dīng | 651 |
| | 釘 | 钉 | dìng | 651 |

| TM/FM | TRAD CHAR | SIMP CHAR | PINYIN | CHAR NO |
|---|---|---|---|---|
| TM 11 FM 丶 | 産 | 产 | chǎn | 219 |
| | 訂 | 订 | dìng | 347 |
| | 訓 | 训 | xùn | 350 |
| | 庫 | 库 | kù | 482 |
| | 軍 | 军 | jūn | 489 |
| | 凍 | 冻 | dòng | 680 |
| TM 12 FM 一 | 亞 | 亚 | yà | 136 |
| TM 12 FM │ | 馬 | 马 | mǎ | 247 |
| | 書 | 书 | shū | 264 |
| | 責 | 责 | zé | 525 |
| | 員 | 员 | yuán | 546 |
| | 時 | 时 | shí | 586 |
| | 財 | 财 | cái | 588 |
| | 敗 | 败 | bài | 589 |
| | 斬 | 斩 | zhǎn | 646 |
| | 掛 | 挂 | guà | 796 |
| TM 12 FM ノ | 個 | 个 | gè | 18 |
| | 術 | 术 | shù | 91 |
| | 無 | 无 | wú | 139 |
| | 傘 | 伞 | sǎn | 171 |
| | 氣 | 气 | qì | 185 |
| | 風 | 风 | fēng | 194 |
| | 後 | 后 | hòu | 310 |
| | 倉 | 仓 | cāng | 418 |
| | 條 | 条 | tiáo | 598 |
| | 紗 | 纱 | shā | 639 |
| | 紋 | 纹 | wén | 640 |
| | 係 | 系 | xì | 842 |
| | 鈔 | 钞 | chāo | 900 |
| | 倆 | 俩 | liǎ | 1082 |
| TM 12 FM 丶 | 祇 | 只 | zhǐ | 160 |
| | 討 | 讨 | tǎo | 500 |
| | 許 | 许 | xǔ | 502 |
| | 準 | 准 | zhǔn | 929 |
| TM 13 FM 一 | 飛 | 飞 | fēi | 81 |
| | 頂 | 顶 | dǐng | 724 |
| | 項 | 项 | xiàng | 725 |

| TRAD CHAR | SIMP CHAR | PINYIN | CHAR NO |
|---|---|---|---|
| **TM 14 FM 丶** (continued) | | | |
| 達 | 达 | dá | 505 |
| 窪 | 洼 | wā | 687 |
| 牽 | 牵 | qiān | 853 |
| 記 | 记 | jì | 946 |
| 訪 | 访 | fǎng | 949 |
| 詳 | 详 | xiáng | 952 |
| 塗 | 涂 | tú | 1171 |
| 煩 | 烦 | fán | 1178 |
| 煉 | 炼 | liàn | 1357 |
| **TM 15 FM 一** | | | |
| 尋 | 寻 | xún | 358 |
| 孫 | 孙 | sūn | 519 |
| 殘 | 残 | cán | 977 |
| 頑 | 顽 | wán | 1204 |
| 張 | 张 | zhāng | 1208 |
| **TM 15 FM 丨** | | | |
| 乾 | 干 | gān | 13 |
| 萬 | 万 | wàn | 73 |
| 區 | 区 | qū | 99 |
| 槓 | 杠 | gàng | 293 |
| 隊 | 队 | duì | 294 |
| 農 | 农 | nóng | 423 |
| 喪 | 丧 | sāng | 521 |
| 喪 | 丧 | sàng | 521 |
| 單 | 单 | dān | 672 |
| 閉 | 闭 | bì | 677 |
| 問 | 问 | wèn | 678 |
| 閑 | 闲 | xián | 679 |
| 崗 | 岗 | gǎng | 745 |
| 場 | 场 | chǎng | 773 |
| 趕 | 赶 | gǎn | 822 |
| 蒼 | 苍 | cāng | 996 |
| 報 | 报 | bào | 1010 |
| 陰 | 阴 | yīn | 1041 |
| 載 | 载 | zǎi | 1218 |
| 載 | 载 | zài | 1218 |
| 揮 | 挥 | huī | 1236 |
| 賊 | 贼 | zéi | 1254 |
| 蓋 | 盖 | gài | 1331 |
| 裝 | 装 | zhuāng | 1476 |
| **TM 15 FM 丿** | | | |
| 僕 | 仆 | pú | 65 |
| 儀 | 仪 | yí | 122 |
| 會 | 会 | huì | 295 |
| 奪 | 夺 | duó | 308 |
| 爺 | 爷 | yé | 445 |
| 傳 | 传 | chuán | 452 |
| 傳 | 传 | zhuàn | 452 |
| 偽 | 伪 | wěi | 454 |
| 猶 | 犹 | yóu | 886 |
| 飢 | 饥 | jī | 890 |
| 飯 | 饭 | fàn | 891 |
| 飲 | 饮 | yǐn | 892 |
| 種 | 种 | zhǒng | 893 |
| 種 | 种 | zhòng | 893 |

| TRAD CHAR | SIMP CHAR | PINYIN | CHAR NO |
|---|---|---|---|
| 脹 | 胀 | zhàng | 1120 |
| 創 | 创 | chuàng | 1131 |
| 鈣 | 钙 | gài | 1462 |
| 鉛 | 铅 | qiān | 1464 |
| 僱 | 雇 | gù | 1474 |
| **TM 15 FM 丶** | | | |
| 義 | 义 | yì | 22 |
| 廣 | 广 | guǎng | 23 |
| 漢 | 汉 | hàn | 235 |
| 對 | 对 | duì | 254 |
| 補 | 补 | bǔ | 508 |
| 勞 | 劳 | láo | 764 |
| 榮 | 荣 | róng | 769 |
| 熒 | 荧 | yíng | 770 |
| 湯 | 汤 | tāng | 932 |
| 溝 | 沟 | gōu | 933 |
| 設 | 设 | shè | 1179 |
| 試 | 试 | shì | 1180 |
| 詩 | 诗 | shī | 1181 |
| 話 | 话 | huà | 1182 |
| 該 | 该 | gāi | 1183 |
| 資 | 资 | zī | 1335 |
| 漸 | 渐 | jiàn | 1347 |
| 慚 | 惭 | cán | 1352 |
| 視 | 视 | shì | 1362 |
| **TM 16 FM 一** | | | |
| 彙 | 汇 | huì | 234 |
| 務 | 务 | wù | 429 |
| 碩 | 硕 | shuò | 1375 |
| **TM 16 FM 丨** | | | |
| 開 | 开 | kāi | 26 |
| 撲 | 扑 | pū | 168 |
| 墳 | 坟 | fén | 281 |
| 嘆 | 叹 | tàn | 285 |
| 髮 | 发 | fà | 311 |
| 盡 | 尽 | jìn | 312 |
| 掃 | 扫 | sǎo | 402 |
| 掃 | 扫 | sào | 402 |
| 肅 | 肃 | sù | 526 |
| 齒 | 齿 | chǐ | 538 |
| 豎 | 竖 | shù | 749 |
| 圍 | 围 | wéi | 762 |
| 園 | 园 | yuán | 763 |
| 啞 | 哑 | yǎ | 782 |
| 極 | 极 | jí | 798 |
| 賬 | 账 | zhàng | 812 |
| 間 | 间 | jiān | 914 |
| 間 | 间 | jiàn | 914 |
| 駁 | 驳 | bó | 983 |
| 揚 | 扬 | yáng | 1004 |
| 嗎 | 吗 | má | 1020 |
| 嗎 | 吗 | ma | 1020 |
| 楊 | 杨 | yáng | 1027 |
| 構 | 构 | gòu | 1028 |

| TRAD CHAR | SIMP CHAR | PINYIN | CHAR NO |
|---|---|---|---|
| 駐 | 驻 | zhù | 1207 |
| 帶 | 带 | dài | 1213 |
| 夢 | 梦 | mèng | 1217 |
| 搶 | 抢 | qiǎng | 1230 |
| 槍 | 枪 | qiāng | 1244 |
| 輩 | 辈 | bèi | 1382 |
| 嶄 | 崭 | zhǎn | 1383 |
| 暈 | 晕 | yūn | 1385 |
| 暈 | 晕 | yùn | 1385 |
| 圓 | 圆 | yuán | 1391 |
| 損 | 损 | sǔn | 1401 |
| 賄 | 贿 | huì | 1419 |
| 頓 | 顿 | dùn | 1420 |

**TM 16 FM ノ**

| TRAD CHAR | SIMP CHAR | PINYIN | CHAR NO |
|---|---|---|---|
| 與 | 与 | yǔ | 158 |
| 與 | 与 | yù | 158 |
| 歷 | 历 | lì | 200 |
| 傷 | 伤 | shāng | 453 |
| 徵 | 征 | zhēng | 462 |
| 婦 | 妇 | fù | 465 |
| 質 | 质 | zhì | 597 |
| 傭 | 佣 | yōng | 621 |
| 傭 | 佣 | yòng | 621 |
| 媽 | 妈 | mā | 1092 |
| 餃 | 饺 | jiǎo | 1115 |
| 餅 | 饼 | bǐng | 1116 |
| 腫 | 肿 | zhǒng | 1119 |
| 勝 | 胜 | shèng | 1122 |
| 獄 | 狱 | yù | 1286 |
| 稱 | 称 | chèn | 1288 |
| 稱 | 称 | chēng | 1288 |
| 稱 | 称 | chèng | 1288 |
| 貿 | 贸 | mào | 1429 |
| 綁 | 绑 | bǎng | 1454 |
| 維 | 维 | wéi | 1455 |
| 鉤 | 钩 | gōu | 1463 |
| 領 | 领 | lǐng | 1465 |
| 銀 | 银 | yín | 1607 |
| 夠 | 够 | gòu | 1808 |

**TM 16 FM ヽ**

| TRAD CHAR | SIMP CHAR | PINYIN | CHAR NO |
|---|---|---|---|
| 麼 | 么 | me | 46 |
| 齊 | 齐 | qí | 221 |
| 養 | 养 | yǎng | 670 |
| 惱 | 恼 | nǎo | 931 |
| 運 | 运 | yùn | 956 |
| 賓 | 宾 | bīn | 1141 |
| 遠 | 远 | yuǎn | 1184 |
| 詞 | 词 | cí | 1353 |
| 誤 | 误 | wù | 1354 |
| 誰 | 谁 | shéi | 1355 |
| 誰 | 谁 | shuí | 1355 |
| 談 | 谈 | tán | 1356 |
| 憤 | 愤 | fèn | 1490 |
| 漁 | 渔 | yú | 1496 |
| 滿 | 满 | mǎn | 1745 |

**TM 17 FM 一**

| TRAD CHAR | SIMP CHAR | PINYIN | CHAR NO |
|---|---|---|---|
| 電 | 电 | diàn | 263 |
| 預 | 预 | yù | 1528 |
| 確 | 确 | què | 1762 |

**TM 17 FM 丨**

| TRAD CHAR | SIMP CHAR | PINYIN | CHAR NO |
|---|---|---|---|
| 夥 | 伙 | huǒ | 214 |
| 臺 | 台 | tái | 301 |
| 團 | 团 | tuán | 392 |
| 塊 | 块 | kuài | 400 |
| 壽 | 寿 | shòu | 440 |
| 劃 | 划 | huá | 476 |
| 劃 | 划 | huà | 476 |
| 賣 | 卖 | mài | 524 |
| 標 | 标 | biāo | 801 |
| 陽 | 阳 | yáng | 808 |
| 獎 | 奖 | jiǎng | 927 |
| 監 | 监 | jiān | 994 |
| 悶 | 闷 | mēn | 1150 |
| 悶 | 闷 | mèn | 1150 |
| 聞 | 闻 | wén | 1151 |
| 罰 | 罚 | fá | 1386 |
| 熱 | 热 | rè | 1390 |
| 費 | 费 | fèi | 1520 |
| 暫 | 暂 | zàn | 1522 |
| 噴 | 喷 | pēn | 1563 |
| 賠 | 赔 | péi | 1569 |
| 凱 | 凯 | kǎi | 1577 |

**TM 17 FM ノ**

| TRAD CHAR | SIMP CHAR | PINYIN | CHAR NO |
|---|---|---|---|
| 厰 | 厂 | chǎng | 7 |
| 幾 | 几 | jī | 115 |
| 幾 | 几 | jǐ | 115 |
| 厭 | 厌 | yàn | 202 |
| 價 | 价 | jià | 210 |
| 節 | 节 | jié | 275 |
| 衝 | 冲 | chōng | 339 |
| 衝 | 冲 | chòng | 339 |
| 錶 | 表 | biǎo | 527 |
| 奮 | 奋 | fèn | 607 |
| 絲 | 丝 | sī | 637 |
| 劊 | 刽 | guì | 903 |
| 積 | 积 | jī | 1097 |
| 愛 | 爱 | ài | 1264 |
| 統 | 统 | tǒng | 1601 |
| 銅 | 铜 | tóng | 1712 |
| 鋪 | 铺 | pū | 1713 |
| 鋪 | 铺 | pù | 1713 |
| 銷 | 销 | xiāo | 1714 |
| 錯 | 错 | cuò | 1715 |
| 銬 | 铐 | kào | 1716 |

**TM 17 FM ヽ**

| TRAD CHAR | SIMP CHAR | PINYIN | CHAR NO |
|---|---|---|---|
| 幣 | 币 | bì | 181 |
| 當 | 当 | dāng | 335 |
| 當 | 当 | dàng | 335 |
| 誇 | 夸 | kuā | 605 |
| 憐 | 怜 | lián | 695 |
| 審 | 审 | shěn | 911 |

| | TRAD CHAR | SIMP CHAR | PINYIN | CHAR NO |
|---|---|---|---|---|
| **TM 17 FM ヽ** (continued) | 複 | 复 | fù | 1059 |
| | 瘋 | 疯 | fēng | 1147 |
| | 違 | 违 | wéi | 1185 |
| | 澆 | 浇 | jiāo | 1340 |
| | 溼 | 湿 | shī | 1498 |
| | 誠 | 诚 | chéng | 1499 |
| | 詢 | 询 | xún | 1500 |
| | 語 | 语 | yǔ | 1501 |
| | 課 | 课 | kè | 1503 |
| | 慣 | 惯 | guàn | 1630 |
| | 褲 | 裤 | kù | 1634 |
| **TM 18 FM 一** | 頭 | 头 | tóu | 128 |
| | 惡 | 恶 | è | 1196 |
| | 惡 | 恶 | wù | 1196 |
| **TM 18 FM ｜** | 舊 | 旧 | jiù | 165 |
| | 處 | 处 | chǔ | 217 |
| | 處 | 处 | chù | 217 |
| | 穀 | 谷 | gǔ | 446 |
| | 階 | 阶 | jiē | 590 |
| | 麵 | 面 | miàn | 721 |
| | 圖 | 图 | tú | 761 |
| | 擇 | 择 | zé | 792 |
| | 樣 | 样 | yàng | 803 |
| | 薑 | 姜 | jiāng | 925 |
| | 樹 | 树 | shù | 1031 |
| | 賤 | 贱 | jiàn | 1037 |
| | 輪 | 轮 | lún | 1112 |
| | 輕 | 轻 | qīng | 1113 |
| | 鬧 | 闹 | nào | 1323 |
| | 摟 | 搂 | lǒu | 1557 |
| | 樓 | 楼 | lóu | 1567 |
| | 輛 | 辆 | liàng | 1602 |
| | 數 | 数 | shǔ | 1637 |
| | 數 | 数 | shù | 1637 |
| | 墻 | 墙 | qiáng | 1770 |
| **TM 18 FM 丿** | 鄉 | 乡 | xiāng | 117 |
| | 億 | 亿 | yì | 205 |
| | 儘 | 尽 | jǐn | 312 |
| | 餘 | 余 | yú | 419 |
| | 僑 | 侨 | qiáo | 460 |
| | 層 | 层 | céng | 610 |
| | 錄 | 录 | lù | 722 |
| | 徹 | 彻 | chè | 871 |
| | 劍 | 剑 | jiàn | 904 |
| | 獲 | 获 | huò | 1000 |
| | 綫 | 线 | xiàn | 1105 |
| | 經 | 经 | jīng | 1110 |
| | 鍾 | 钟 | zhōng | 1125 |
| | 製 | 制 | zhì | 1130 |
| | 獅 | 狮 | shī | 1285 |
| | 錢 | 钱 | qián | 1301 |
| | 飼 | 饲 | sì | 1447 |

| | TRAD CHAR | SIMP CHAR | PINYIN | CHAR NO |
|---|---|---|---|---|
| | 練 | 练 | liàn | 1453 |
| | 腸 | 肠 | cháng | 1458 |
| | 緩 | 缓 | huǎn | 1708 |
| **TM 18 FM ヽ** | 辦 | 办 | bàn | 195 |
| | 塵 | 尘 | chén | 204 |
| | 寧 | 宁 | níng | 336 |
| | 寧 | 宁 | nìng | 336 |
| | 燈 | 灯 | dēng | 346 |
| | 廟 | 庙 | miào | 659 |
| | 瘧 | 疟 | nüè | 662 |
| | 實 | 实 | shí | 668 |
| | 過 | 过 | guò | 712 |
| | 論 | 论 | lùn | 947 |
| | 遲 | 迟 | chí | 959 |
| | 敵 | 敌 | dí | 1127 |
| | 濃 | 浓 | nóng | 1168 |
| | 糞 | 粪 | fèn | 1334 |
| | 燒 | 烧 | shāo | 1504 |
| | 寬 | 宽 | kuān | 1618 |
| | 說 | 说 | shuì | 1631 |
| | 說 | 说 | shuō | 1631 |
| | 說 | 说 | yuè | 1631 |
| | 請 | 请 | qǐng | 1632 |
| | 懞 | 蒙 | méng | 1654 |
| | 濛 | 蒙 | méng | 1654 |
| | 謠 | 谣 | yáo | 1751 |
| | 禍 | 祸 | huò | 1754 |
| **TM 19 FM 一** | 磚 | 砖 | zhuān | 1201 |
| **TM 19 FM ｜** | 麯 | 曲 | qū | 272 |
| | 擴 | 扩 | kuò | 291 |
| | 嘔 | 呕 | ǒu | 560 |
| | 鞦 | 秋 | qiū | 641 |
| | 點 | 点 | diǎn | 739 |
| | 賢 | 贤 | xián | 750 |
| | 擔 | 担 | dān | 789 |
| | 蝦 | 虾 | xiā | 824 |
| | 雖 | 虽 | suī | 990 |
| | 擁 | 拥 | yōng | 1014 |
| | 檢 | 检 | jiǎn | 1033 |
| | 賺 | 赚 | zhuàn | 1781 |
| | 瞞 | 瞒 | mán | 1914 |
| **TM 19 FM 丿** | 衛 | 卫 | wèi | 82 |
| | 雙 | 双 | shuāng | 146 |
| | 興 | 兴 | xīng | 228 |
| | 興 | 兴 | xìng | 228 |
| | 颱 | 台 | tái | 301 |
| | 鳳 | 凤 | fèng | 314 |
| | 網 | 网 | wǎng | 390 |
| | 舉 | 举 | jǔ | 674 |
| | 颳 | 刮 | guā | 902 |
| | 緻 | 致 | zhì | 982 |
| | 膠 | 胶 | jiāo | 1296 |

| TRAD CHAR | SIMP CHAR | PINYIN | CHAR NO |
|---|---|---|---|
| 鋼 | 钢 | gāng | 1299 |
| 腦 | 脑 | nǎo | 1460 |
| 餓 | 饿 | è | 1593 |
| 鎖 | 锁 | suǒ | 1608 |
| 絕 | 绝 | jué | 1706 |
| 繡 | 绣 | xiù | 1801 |
| 鮮 | 鲜 | xiān | 1811 |
| 鮮 | 鲜 | xiǎn | 1811 |
| 銹 | 锈 | xiù | 1871 |
| 鎮 | 镇 | zhèn | 1872 |
| **TM 19 FM 、** | | | |
| 叢 | 丛 | cóng | 123 |
| 認 | 认 | rèn | 239 |
| 應 | 应 | yīng | 334 |
| 應 | 应 | yìng | 334 |
| 療 | 疗 | liáo | 661 |
| 寫 | 写 | xiě | 663 |
| 類 | 类 | lèi | 676 |
| 遼 | 辽 | liáo | 711 |
| 導 | 导 | dǎo | 751 |
| 雜 | 杂 | zá | 856 |
| 彆 | 别 | biè | 1049 |
| 鄰 | 邻 | lín | 1123 |
| 嘗 | 尝 | cháng | 1157 |
| 燉 | 炖 | dùn | 1175 |
| 適 | 适 | shì | 1358 |
| 營 | 营 | yíng | 1546 |
| 燙 | 烫 | tàng | 1624 |
| 漲 | 涨 | zhǎng | 1738 |
| 漲 | 涨 | zhàng | 1738 |
| 詭 | 诡 | guǐ | 1747 |
| 誘 | 诱 | yòu | 1748 |
| 調 | 调 | diào | 1749 |
| 調 | 调 | tiáo | 1749 |
| 謎 | 谜 | mí | 1750 |
| 賽 | 赛 | sài | 1813 |
| 遺 | 遗 | yí | 1829 |
| 顏 | 颜 | yán | 1835 |
| 寢 | 寝 | qǐn | 1878 |
| **TM 20 FM 一** | | | |
| 發 | 发 | fā | 311 |
| 環 | 环 | huán | 369 |
| 憂 | 忧 | yōu | 693 |
| 職 | 职 | zhí | 1205 |
| **TM 20 FM |** | | | |
| 豐 | 丰 | fēng | 35 |
| 嚇 | 吓 | hè | 287 |
| 嚇 | 吓 | xià | 287 |
| 蘋 | 苹 | píng | 395 |
| 縣 | 县 | xiàn | 543 |
| 鬆 | 松 | sōng | 579 |
| 橋 | 桥 | qiáo | 804 |
| 嶺 | 岭 | lǐng | 806 |
| 歐 | 欧 | ōu | 811 |
| 艱 | 艰 | jiān | 973 |

| TRAD CHAR | SIMP CHAR | PINYIN | CHAR NO |
|---|---|---|---|
| 難 | 难 | nán | 974 |
| 難 | 难 | nàn | 974 |
| 薦 | 荐 | jiàn | 997 |
| 擋 | 挡 | dǎng | 1018 |
| 噸 | 吨 | dūn | 1022 |
| 檔 | 档 | dàng | 1032 |
| 戰 | 战 | zhàn | 1044 |
| 險 | 险 | xiǎn | 1252 |
| 購 | 购 | gòu | 1253 |
| 劇 | 剧 | jù | 1468 |
| 緊 | 紧 | jǐn | 1537 |
| 嬰 | 婴 | yīng | 1539 |
| 藍 | 蓝 | lán | 1548 |
| 罵 | 骂 | mà | 1652 |
| 鴨 | 鸭 | yā | 1782 |
| 題 | 题 | tí | 1858 |
| 輸 | 输 | shū | 1867 |
| **TM 20 FM ノ** | | | |
| 壓 | 压 | yā | 201 |
| 樂 | 乐 | lè | 299 |
| 樂 | 乐 | yuè | 299 |
| 嬌 | 娇 | jiāo | 882 |
| 亂 | 乱 | luàn | 901 |
| 學 | 学 | xué | 1155 |
| 鏟 | 铲 | chǎn | 1304 |
| 償 | 偿 | cháng | 1440 |
| 駕 | 驾 | jià | 1693 |
| 飽 | 饱 | bǎo | 1703 |
| 編 | 编 | biān | 1866 |
| 膩 | 腻 | nì | 1870 |
| 鍵 | 键 | jiàn | 1926 |
| **TM 20 FM 、** | | | |
| 慶 | 庆 | qìng | 230 |
| 講 | 讲 | jiǎng | 501 |
| 禮 | 礼 | lǐ | 503 |
| 親 | 亲 | qīn | 908 |
| 潔 | 洁 | jié | 940 |
| 濁 | 浊 | zhuó | 943 |
| 諷 | 讽 | fěng | 948 |
| 邁 | 迈 | mài | 955 |
| 憑 | 凭 | píng | 1060 |
| 憲 | 宪 | xiàn | 1317 |
| 糧 | 粮 | liáng | 1759 |
| 謊 | 谎 | huǎng | 1824 |
| **TM 21 FM 一** | | | |
| 礦 | 矿 | kuàng | 518 |
| 聰 | 聪 | cōng | 1895 |
| **TM 21 FM |** | | | |
| 鼕 | 冬 | dōng | 178 |
| 蟲 | 虫 | chóng | 262 |
| 藝 | 艺 | yì | 274 |
| 壞 | 坏 | huài | 280 |
| 檯 | 台 | tái | 301 |
| 聲 | 声 | shēng | 374 |
| 蘇 | 苏 | sū | 552 |
| 機 | 机 | jī | 577 |

| | TRAD CHAR | SIMP CHAR | PINYIN | CHAR NO | | TRAD CHAR | SIMP CHAR | PINYIN | CHAR NO |
|---|---|---|---|---|---|---|---|---|---|
| TM 21 FM 丨 (continued) | 擠 | 挤 | jǐ | 795 | TM 22 FM 丶 | 龍 | 龙 | lóng | 315 |
| | 櫃 | 柜 | guì | 800 | | 護 | 护 | hù | 569 |
| | 膚 | 肤 | fū | 899 | | 證 | 证 | zhèng | 705 |
| | 轉 | 转 | zhuǎn | 1111 | | 窮 | 穷 | qióng | 912 |
| | 轉 | 转 | zhuàn | 1111 | | 識 | 识 | shí | 950 |
| | 據 | 据 | jù | 1553 | | 譯 | 译 | yì | 951 |
| | 幫 | 帮 | bāng | 1583 | | 襪 | 袜 | wà | 1193 |
| | 矇 | 蒙 | mēng | 1654 | | 離 | 离 | lí | 1614 |
| | 矇 | 蒙 | méng | 1654 | | 竅 | 窍 | qiào | 1621 |
| | 閱 | 阅 | yuè | 1727 | | 懶 | 懒 | lǎn | 1953 |
| | 闊 | 阔 | kuò | 1728 | | 額 | 额 | é | 1958 |
| | 隨 | 随 | suí | 1911 | TM 23 FM 丨 | 擊 | 击 | jī | 156 |
| TM 21 FM 丿 | 獨 | 独 | dú | 1095 | | 勸 | 劝 | quàn | 255 |
| | 膽 | 胆 | dǎn | 1295 | | 權 | 权 | quán | 292 |
| | 簽 | 签 | qiān | 1439 | | 號 | 号 | háo | 545 |
| | 臉 | 脸 | liǎn | 1461 | | 號 | 号 | hào | 545 |
| | 膿 | 脓 | nóng | 1605 | | 闆 | 板 | bǎn | 580 |
| | 鍋 | 锅 | guō | 1807 | | 檸 | 柠 | níng | 1029 |
| | 縮 | 缩 | suō | 1927 | | 鹹 | 咸 | xián | 1073 |
| TM 21 FM 丶 | 懷 | 怀 | huái | 344 | | 罷 | 罢 | bà | 1215 |
| | 遷 | 迁 | qiān | 506 | | 鬍 | 胡 | hú | 1256 |
| | 還 | 还 | hái | 714 | | 藥 | 药 | yào | 1392 |
| | 還 | 还 | huán | 714 | | 醬 | 酱 | jiàng | 1814 |
| | 癥 | 症 | zhēng | 923 | TM 23 FM 丿 | 態 | 态 | tài | 828 |
| | 癥 | 症 | zhèng | 923 | | 總 | 总 | zǒng | 1330 |
| | 癢 | 痒 | yǎng | 1149 | | 鵝 | 鹅 | é | 1950 |
| | 燭 | 烛 | zhú | 1176 | | 贊 | 赞 | zàn | 1969 |
| | 遞 | 递 | dì | 1827 | TM 23 FM 丶 | 議 | 议 | yì | 349 |
| | 謝 | 谢 | xiè | 1890 | | 糰 | 团 | tuán | 392 |
| TM 22 FM 一 | 醜 | 丑 | chǒu | 85 | | 寶 | 宝 | bǎo | 667 |
| | 聯 | 联 | lián | 1206 | | 廢 | 废 | fèi | 918 |
| | 彈 | 弹 | dàn | 1763 | | 潑 | 泼 | pō | 937 |
| | 彈 | 弹 | tán | 1763 | | 懼 | 惧 | jù | 1351 |
| TM 22 FM 丨 | 嚴 | 严 | yán | 241 | | 選 | 选 | xuǎn | 1510 |
| | 戲 | 戏 | xì | 365 | | 顧 | 顾 | gù | 1609 |
| | 擬 | 拟 | nǐ | 575 | | 黨 | 党 | dǎng | 1626 |
| | 羅 | 罗 | luó | 756 | | 籃 | 篮 | lán | 1862 |
| | 臨 | 临 | lín | 771 | | 辮 | 辫 | biàn | 1957 |
| | 蟻 | 蚁 | yǐ | 825 | TM 24 FM 丨 | 蘭 | 兰 | lán | 126 |
| | 齡 | 龄 | líng | 1687 | | 虧 | 亏 | kuī | 137 |
| | 攝 | 摄 | shè | 1772 | | 齣 | 出 | chū | 258 |
| | 騎 | 骑 | qí | 1840 | | 歡 | 欢 | huān | 366 |
| | 隱 | 隐 | yǐn | 1912 | | 醫 | 医 | yī | 389 |
| | 贈 | 赠 | zèng | 1944 | | 撥 | 拨 | bō | 1015 |
| TM 22 FM 丿 | 優 | 优 | yōu | 447 | | 轟 | 轰 | hōng | 1065 |
| | 織 | 织 | zhī | 1108 | | 躍 | 跃 | yuè | 1258 |
| | 鐵 | 铁 | tiě | 1126 | | 騙 | 骗 | piàn | 1937 |
| | 簡 | 简 | jiǎn | 1796 | TM 24 FM 丿 | 歸 | 归 | guī | 166 |
| | 願 | 愿 | yuàn | 1919 | | 犧 | 牺 | xī | 1283 |
| | 穩 | 稳 | wěn | 1925 | | 籤 | 签 | qiān | 1439 |
| | 鏡 | 镜 | jìng | 1970 | | 辭 | 辞 | cí | 1606 |
| | | | | | | 饅 | 馒 | mán | 1948 |

# Pinyin

Use this index to locate the dictionary entry for a Chinese character based on its pronunciation (for example, the pinyin syllable **bàn**).

1. Locate the pinyin syllable (**bàn**) in the alphabetized PINYIN column on the left. Tone order is as follows:
   - ¯ (flat)
   - ´ (rising)
   - ˇ (falling-rising)
   - ` (falling)
   
   A light or no tone is not marked. Umlaut u (ü) follows u.

2. Within the specific pinyin group, locate the Chinese character you seek (办 or 辦) in the SIMP CHAR or TRAD CHAR column.

3. The character number in the last column (**195**) directs you to the correct dictionary entry. An asterisk indicates that the character has more than one pronunciation.

| PINYIN | SIMP CHAR | TRAD CHAR | CHAR NO | PINYIN | SIMP CHAR | TRAD CHAR | CHAR NO | PINYIN | SIMP CHAR | TRAD CHAR | CHAR NO |
|---|---|---|---|---|---|---|---|---|---|---|---|
| ā | 阿 | | 1249* | bài | 拜 | | 635 | bēi | 悲 | | 1532 |
| āi | 哎 | | 562 | bān | 扳 | | 566 | běi | 北 | | 278 |
| | 哀 | | 1134 | | 班 | | 730 | bèi | 贝 | 貝 | 97 |
| | 挨 | | 1237* | | 般 | | 1718 | | 备 | 備 | 845 |
| ái | 挨 | | 1237* | | 搬 | | 1943 | | 倍 | | 1084 |
| | 癌 | | 1981 | bǎn | 板 | 闆 | 580 | | 背 | | 1380* |
| ǎi | 矮 | | 1598 | | 版 | | 897 | | 辈 | 輩 | 1382 |
| ài | 艾 | | 100 | bàn | 半 | | 127 | | 被 | | 1517 |
| | 爱 | 愛 | 1264 | | 办 | 辦 | 195 | bēn | 奔 | | 432 |
| ān | 安 | | 487 | | 伴 | | 321 | běn | 本 | | 90 |
| àn | 岸 | | 537 | | 拌 | | 574 | bèn | 笨 | | 1079 |
| | 按 | | 1234 | | 扮 | | 786 | bèng | 蹦 | | 1994 |
| | 案 | | 1321 | | 绊 | 絆 | 887 | bī | 逼 | | 1828 |
| | 暗 | | 1676 | bāng | 邦 | | 636 | bí | 鼻 | | 1794 |
| ào | 奥 | | 1435 | | 帮 | 幫 | 1583 | bǐ | 比 | | 279 |
| | | | | bǎng | 绑 | 綁 | 1454 | | 笔 | 筆 | 1278 |
| bā | 八 | | 6 | bàng | 棒 | | 1247 | bì | 币 | 幣 | 181 |
| | 扒 | | 169* | | 傍 | | 1698 | | 必 | | 338 |
| | 芭 | | 765 | | 磅 | | 1936 | | 毕 | 畢 | 540 |
| | 吧 | | 1021* | bāo | 包 | | 836 | | 闭 | 閉 | 677 |
| | 捌 | | 1660 | | 剥 | | 1377* | | 壁 | | 1920 |
| bá | 拔 | | 791 | | 炮 | | 1633* | | 避 | | 1976 |
| bǎ | 把 | | 1006 | báo | 薄 | | 1902* | biān | 边 | 邊 | 710 |
| bà | 爸 | | 1077 | bǎo | 宝 | 寶 | 667 | | 编 | | 1866 |
| | 罢 | 罷 | 1215 | | 保 | | 868 | | 鞭 | | 1967 |
| | 霸 | | 1998 | | 饱 | 飽 | 1703 | biǎn | 贬 | 貶 | 814 |
| ba | 吧 | | 1021* | bào | 报 | 報 | 1010 | biàn | 变 | 變 | 653 |
| bái | 白 | | 176 | | 暴 | | 1844 | | 便 | | 865 |
| bǎi | 百 | | 242 | | 爆 | | 1982 | | 遍 | | 1892 |
| | 佰 | | 622 | bēi | 杯 | | 411 | | 辫 | 辮 | 1957 |
| | 摆 | 擺襬 | 1773 | | 卑 | | 602 | biāo | 标 | 標 | 801 |
| bài | 败 | 敗 | 589 | | 背 | | 1380* | biǎo | 表 | 錶 | 527 |

| PINYIN | SIMP CHAR | TRAD CHAR | CHAR NO |
|---|---|---|---|
| còu | 凑 | | 1160 |
| cū | 粗 | | 1364 |
| cù | 促 | | 866 |
| | 醋 | | 1898 |
| cuī | 催 | | 1592 |
| cūn | 村 | | 410 |
| cún | 存 | | 438 |
| cùn | 寸 | | 37 |
| cuò | 错 | 錯 | 1715 |
| dá | 打 | | 289* |
| | 达 | 達 | 505 |
| | 答 | | 1438 |
| dǎ | 打 | | 289* |
| dà | 大 | | 20 |
| dāi | 呆 | | 384 |
| dǎi | 歹 | | 74 |
| dài | 代 | | 208 |
| | 待 | | 872 |
| | 贷 | 貸 | 1062 |
| | 带 | 帶 | 1213 |
| | 袋 | | 1428 |
| | 戴 | | 1941 |
| dān | 单 | 單 | 672 |
| | 担 | 擔 | 789 |
| dǎn | 胆 | 膽 | 1295 |
| dàn | 但 | | 458 |
| | 淡 | | 1173 |
| | 蛋 | | 1368 |
| | 弹 | 彈 | 1763* |
| dāng | 当 | 當 | 335* |
| dǎng | 挡 | 擋 | 1018 |
| | 党 | 黨 | 1626 |
| dàng | 当 | 當 | 335* |
| | 档 | 檔 | 1032 |
| dāo | 刀 | | 31 |
| dǎo | 导 | 導 | 751 |
| | 倒 | | 1281* |
| | 岛 | 島 | 1434 |
| dào | 到 | | 737 |
| | 倒 | | 1281* |
| | 悼 | | 1349 |
| | 盗 | | 1475 |
| | 道 | | 1756 |
| dé | 得 | | 1442* |
| | 德 | | 1923 |
| de | 地 | | 772* |
| | 的 | | 1117* |
| | 得 | | 1442* |
| děi | 得 | | 1442* |
| dēng | 灯 | 燈 | 346 |
| | 登 | | 1521 |
| děng | 等 | | 1437 |
| dèng | 邓 | | 367 |

| PINYIN | SIMP CHAR | TRAD CHAR | CHAR NO |
|---|---|---|---|
| dèng | 瞪 | | 1966 |
| dī | 低 | | 618 |
| | 滴 | | 1885 |
| dí | 的 | | 1117* |
| | 敌 | 敵 | 1127 |
| | 笛 | | 1279 |
| dǐ | 底 | | 916 |
| dì | 地 | | 772* |
| | 弟 | | 1152 |
| | 帝 | | 1312 |
| | 第 | | 1695 |
| | 递 | 遞 | 1827 |
| diǎn | 典 | | 532 |
| | 点 | 點 | 739 |
| diàn | 电 | 電 | 263 |
| | 店 | | 658 |
| diāo | 刁 | | 32 |
| diào | 吊 | | 547 |
| | 钓 | 釣 | 1124 |
| | 掉 | | 1403 |
| | 调 | 調 | 1749* |
| diē | 爹 | | 1276 |
| | 跌 | | 1422 |
| dīng | 丁 | | 8 |
| | 叮 | | 284 |
| | 钉 | 釘 | 651* |
| dǐng | 顶 | 頂 | 724 |
| dìng | 订 | 訂 | 347 |
| | 钉 | 釘 | 651* |
| | 定 | | 666 |
| diū | 丢 | | 297 |
| dōng | 冬 | | 178 |
| | 东 | 東 | 307 |
| dǒng | 懂 | | 1817 |
| dòng | 动 | 動 | 514 |
| | 冻 | 凍 | 680 |
| | 栋 | 棟 | 1030 |
| | 洞 | | 1338 |
| | 都 | | 1578* |
| dōu | 斗 | 鬥 | 71* |
| dǒu | 抖 | | 407 |
| dòu | 斗 | 鬥 | 71* |
| | 豆 | | 353 |
| | 痘 | | 1477 |
| | 逗 | | 1512 |
| dū | 都 | | 1578* |
| dú | 独 | 獨 | 1095 |
| | 毒 | | 1211 |
| | 读 | 讀 | 1502 |
| dǔ | 堵 | | 1226 |
| dù | 妒 | | 628 |
| | 肚 | | 648 |
| | 度 | | 919 |
| | 渡 | | 1497 |

| PINYIN | SIMP CHAR | TRAD CHAR | CHAR NO |
|---|---|---|---|
| duān | 端 | | 1889 |
| duǎn | 短 | | 1452 |
| duàn | 断 | 斷 | 1260 |
| | 段 | | 1293 |
| duī | 堆 | | 1003 |
| duì | 对 | 對 | 254 |
| | 队 | 隊 | 294 |
| dūn | 吨 | 噸 | 1022 |
| | 蹲 | | 1986 |
| dùn | 盾 | | 840 |
| | 炖 | 燉 | 1175 |
| | 顿 | 頓 | 1420 |
| duō | 多 | | 431 |
| duó | 夺 | 奪 | 308 |
| duǒ | 躲 | | 1874 |
| ē | 阿 | | 1249* |
| é | 鹅 | 鵝 | 1950 |
| | 额 | 額 | 1958 |
| è | 厄 | | 443 |
| | 恶 | 惡 | 1196* |
| | 饿 | 餓 | 1593 |
| | 噩 | | 1960 |
| ēn | 恩 | | 1381 |
| ér | 儿 | 兒 | 43 |
| | 而 | | 351 |
| ěr | 耳 | | 145 |
| èr | 二 | | 2 |
| | 贰 | 貳 | 1074 |
| fā | 发 | 發 | 311* |
| fá | 乏 | | 109 |
| | 罚 | 罰 | 1386 |
| fǎ | 法 | | 686 |
| fà | 发 | 髮 | 311* |
| fān | 帆 | | 1034 |
| | 翻 | | 1989 |
| fán | 凡 | | 193 |
| | 烦 | 煩 | 1178 |
| | 繁 | | 1988 |
| fǎn | 反 | | 111 |
| | 返 | | 957 |
| fàn | 泛 | | 495 |
| | 贩 | 販 | 813 |
| | 犯 | | 884 |
| | 饭 | 飯 | 891 |
| fāng | 方 | | 220 |
| | 芳 | | 550 |
| fáng | 妨 | | 879 |
| | 防 | | 1040 |
| | 房 | | 1145 |
| fǎng | 仿 | | 450 |
| | 访 | 訪 | 949 |
| | 纺 | 紡 | 1104 |

| PINYIN | SIMP CHAR | TRAD CHAR | CHAR NO |
|---|---|---|---|
| hǎo | 好 | | 627* |
| hào | 号 | 號 | 545* |
| | 好 | | 627* |
| | 浩 | | 1169 |
| hē | 喝 | | 1854* |
| hé | 禾 | | 108 |
| | 合 | | 296 |
| | 何 | | 619 |
| | 和 | | 644* |
| | 河 | | 934 |
| | 核 | | 1026 |
| | 盒 | | 1425 |
| hè | 吓 | 嚇 | 287* |
| | 喝 | | 1854* |
| hēi | 黑 | | 1389 |
| hěn | 很 | | 1090 |
| | 狠 | | 1284 |
| hèn | 恨 | | 1174 |
| hēng | 哼 | | 1561 |
| héng | 横 | | 1775* |
| hèng | 横 | | 1775* |
| hōng | 哄 | | 781* |
| | 烘 | | 953 |
| | 轰 | 轟 | 1065 |
| hóng | 红 | 紅 | 474 |
| | 洪 | | 690 |
| | 虹 | | 823 |
| hǒng | 哄 | | 781* |
| hòng | 哄 | | 781* |
| hóu | 喉 | | 1560 |
| | 猴 | | 1595 |
| hǒu | 吼 | | 1228 |
| hòu | 后 | 後 | 310 |
| | 候 | | 1086 |
| | 厚 | | 1272 |
| hū | 呼 | | 779 |
| | 忽 | | 1268 |
| | 糊 | | 1932* |
| hú | 狐 | | 885 |
| | 胡 | 鬍 | 1256 |
| | 湖 | | 1741 |
| | 糊 | | 1932* |
| hǔ | 虎 | | 1533 |
| hù | 户 | | 129 |
| | 互 | | 135 |
| | 护 | 護 | 569 |
| | 糊 | | 1932* |
| huā | 花 | | 549 |
| huá | 华 | 華 | 421 |
| | 划 | 劃 | 476* |
| | 滑 | | 1884 |
| huà | 化 | | 215 |
| | 划 | 劃 | 476* |
| | 画 | 畫 | 719 |

| PINYIN | SIMP CHAR | TRAD CHAR | CHAR NO |
|---|---|---|---|
| huà | 话 | 話 | 1182 |
| huái | 怀 | 懷 | 344 |
| huài | 坏 | 壞 | 280 |
| huān | 欢 | 歡 | 366 |
| huán | 环 | 環 | 369 |
| | 还 | 還 | 714* |
| huǎn | 缓 | 緩 | 1708 |
| huàn | 幻 | | 475 |
| | 换 | | 1402 |
| | 患 | | 1649 |
| huāng | 荒 | | 1222 |
| | 慌 | | 1736 |
| huáng | 皇 | | 858 |
| | 黄 | | 1212 |
| huǎng | 晃 | | 1384* |
| | 谎 | 謊 | 1824 |
| huàng | 晃 | | 1384* |
| huī | 灰 | | 198 |
| | 恢 | | 698 |
| | 挥 | 揮 | 1236 |
| huí | 回 | | 391 |
| huǐ | 悔 | | 1488 |
| | 毁 | | 1810 |
| huì | 汇 | 匯彙 | 234 |
| | 会 | 會 | 295 |
| | 贿 | 賄 | 1419 |
| hūn | 荤 | 葷 | 998 |
| | 昏 | | 1058 |
| | 婚 | | 1701 |
| hún | 混 | | 1739* |
| | 魂 | | 1893 |
| hùn | 混 | | 1739* |
| huó | 和 | | 644 |
| | 活 | | 941* |
| huǒ | 火 | | 72 |
| | 伙 | 夥 | 214 |
| huò | 或 | | 857 |
| | 获 | 獲 | 1000 |
| | 货 | 貨 | 1061 |
| | 祸 | 禍 | 1754 |
| jī | 几 | 幾 | 115* |
| | 击 | 擊 | 156 |
| | 机 | 機 | 577 |
| | 奇 | | 854* |
| | 饥 | 飢 | 890 |
| | 基 | | 991 |
| | 积 | 積 | 1097 |
| | 肌 | | 1118 |
| | 鸡 | 鷄 | 1373 |
| | 激 | | 1955 |
| jí | 及 | | 141 |
| | 吉 | | 259 |
| | 极 | 極 | 798 |

| PINYIN | SIMP CHAR | TRAD CHAR | CHAR NO |
|---|---|---|---|
| jí | 疾 | | 922 |
| | 即 | | 1047 |
| | 级 | 級 | 1100 |
| | 集 | | 1267 |
| | 急 | | 1426 |
| | 籍 | | 1980 |
| jǐ | 几 | 幾 | 115* |
| | 己 | | 132 |
| | 挤 | 擠 | 795 |
| | 给 | 給 | 1292* |
| jì | 计 | 計 | 240 |
| | 技 | | 568 |
| | 妓 | | 629 |
| | 季 | | 835 |
| | 系 | 繫 | 842* |
| | 记 | 記 | 946 |
| | 纪 | 紀 | 1101 |
| | 忌 | | 1197 |
| | 既 | | 1572 |
| | 寄 | | 1619 |
| jiā | 夹 | 夾 | 197* |
| | 加 | | 463 |
| | 家 | 傢 | 1315 |
| jiá | 夹 | 夾 | 197* |
| jiǎ | 甲 | | 149 |
| | 假 | | 1586* |
| jià | 价 | 價 | 210 |
| | 架 | | 1270 |
| | 假 | | 1586* |
| | 驾 | 駕 | 1693 |
| | 嫁 | | 1799 |
| jiān | 尖 | | 203 |
| | 奸 | | 329 |
| | 坚 | 堅 | 381 |
| | 间 | 間 | 914 |
| | 艰 | 艱 | 973 |
| | 监 | 監 | 994 |
| | 肩 | | 1144 |
| jiǎn | 检 | 檢 | 1033 |
| | 拣 | 揀 | 1233 |
| | 减 | | 1487 |
| | 简 | 簡 | 1796 |
| | 剪 | | 1816 |
| jiàn | 件 | | 209 |
| | 见 | 見 | 267 |
| | 剑 | 劍 | 904 |
| | 间 | 間 | 914 |
| | 荐 | 薦 | 997 |
| | 贱 | 賤 | 1037 |
| | 建 | | 1203 |
| | 渐 | 漸 | 1347 |
| | 健 | | 1589 |
| | 箭 | | 1922 |
| | 键 | 鍵 | 1926 |

| PINYIN | SIMP CHAR | TRAD CHAR | CHAR NO |
|---|---|---|---|
| jiāng | 江 | | 237 |
| | 姜 | 薑 | 925 |
| | 将 | 將 | 1161* |
| | 僵 | | 1864 |
| jiǎng | 讲 | 講 | 501 |
| | 奖 | 獎 | 927 |
| jiàng | 将 | 將 | 1161* |
| | 降 | | 1416* |
| | 酱 | 醬 | 1814 |
| | 强 | | 1896* |
| jiāo | 交 | | 222 |
| | 娇 | 嬌 | 882 |
| | 郊 | | 1194 |
| | 焦 | | 1265 |
| | 胶 | 膠 | 1296 |
| | 浇 | 澆 | 1340 |
| | 骄 | 驕 | 1376 |
| | 教 | | 1424* |
| jiáo | 嚼 | | 1999* |
| jiǎo | 角 | | 838* |
| | 饺 | 餃 | 1115 |
| | 脚 | | 1804 |
| | 搅 | 攪 | 1850 |
| jiào | 叫 | | 283 |
| | 校 | | 802* |
| | 较 | 較 | 1114 |
| | 教 | | 1424* |
| | 觉 | 覺 | 1485* |
| jiē | 阶 | 階 | 590 |
| | 结 | 結 | 1291* |
| | 接 | | 1405 |
| | 街 | | 1441 |
| | 揭 | | 1851 |
| jié | 节 | 節 | 275 |
| | 杰 | 傑 | 377 |
| | 劫 | | 819 |
| | 洁 | 潔 | 940 |
| | 结 | 結 | 1291* |
| | 截 | | 1650 |
| jiě | 姐 | | 880 |
| | 解 | | 1928* |
| jiè | 介 | | 44 |
| | 戒 | | 442 |
| | 界 | | 758 |
| | 届 | | 851 |
| | 借 | | 1087 |
| | 解 | | 1928* |
| jīn | 斤 | | 50 |
| | 巾 | | 87 |
| | 今 | | 102 |
| | 金 | | 420 |
| jǐn | 仅 | 僅 | 120* |
| | 尽 | 儘 | 312* |
| | 紧 | 緊 | 1537 |

| PINYIN | SIMP CHAR | TRAD CHAR | CHAR NO |
|---|---|---|---|
| jìn | 尽 | 盡 | 312* |
| | 进 | 進 | 713 |
| | 近 | | 716 |
| | 劲 | 勁 | 736* |
| | 禁 | | 1536 |
| jīng | 京 | | 905 |
| | 经 | 經 | 1110 |
| | 惊 | 驚 | 1489 |
| | 精 | | 1832 |
| jǐng | 井 | | 60 |
| | 警 | | 1987 |
| jìng | 径 | 徑 | 626 |
| | 劲 | 勁 | 736* |
| | 净 | | 1159 |
| | 竞 | 競 | 1470 |
| | 竟 | | 1616 |
| | 敬 | | 1689 |
| | 境 | | 1848 |
| | 静 | | 1947 |
| | 镜 | 鏡 | 1970 |
| jiū | 纠 | 糾 | 473 |
| | 究 | | 1142 |
| jiǔ | 久 | | 45 |
| | 九 | | 116 |
| | 酒 | | 1339 |
| jiù | 旧 | 舊 | 165 |
| | 救 | | 1259 |
| | 舅 | | 1795 |
| | 就 | | 1836 |
| jū | 车 | 車 | 114* |
| | 居 | | 850 |
| | 拘 | | 1231 |
| jú | 局 | | 1069 |
| jǔ | 举 | 舉 | 674 |
| jù | 巨 | | 162 |
| | 句 | | 424 |
| | 具 | | 533 |
| | 俱 | | 1083 |
| | 惧 | 懼 | 1351 |
| | 剧 | 劇 | 1468 |
| | 据 | 據 | 1553 |
| | 距 | | 1576 |
| | 聚 | | 1642 |
| juān | 捐 | | 1552 |
| | 圈 | | 1765* |
| juǎn | 卷 | | 1333* |
| juàn | 卷 | | 1333* |
| | 圈 | | 1765* |
| jué | 决 | | 340 |
| | 诀 | 訣 | 704 |
| | 角 | | 838* |
| | 觉 | 覺 | 1485* |
| | 绝 | 絕 | 1706 |
| | 嚼 | | 1999* |

| PINYIN | SIMP CHAR | TRAD CHAR | CHAR NO |
|---|---|---|---|
| jūn | 军 | 軍 | 489 |
| | 君 | | 512 |
| | 均 | | 558 |
| jùn | 俊 | | 1081 |
| kā | 咖 | | 1229 |
| kǎ | 卡 | | 36* |
| kāi | 开 | 開 | 26 |
| kǎi | 凯 | 凱 | 1577 |
| kān | 刊 | | 216 |
| | 看 | | 841* |
| kǎn | 砍 | | 979 |
| | 侃 | | 1085 |
| kàn | 看 | | 841* |
| káng | 扛 | | 290 |
| kàng | 抗 | | 1009 |
| kǎo | 考 | | 530 |
| | 烤 | | 1505 |
| kào | 铐 | 銬 | 1716 |
| | 靠 | | 1791 |
| kē | 科 | | 642 |
| | 棵 | | 1414 |
| | 磕 | | 1894 |
| kě | 可 | | 243 |
| | 渴 | | 1822 |
| kè | 克 | | 738 |
| | 刻 | | 966 |
| | 客 | | 1316 |
| | 课 | 課 | 1503 |
| kěn | 肯 | | 744 |
| | 啃 | | 1559 |
| kēng | 坑 | | 774 |
| kōng | 空 | | 669* |
| kǒng | 孔 | | 370 |
| | 恐 | | 1644 |
| kòng | 空 | | 669* |
| | 控 | | 1406 |
| kǒu | 口 | | 42 |
| kòu | 扣 | | 401 |
| | 叩 | | 413 |
| kū | 枯 | | 799 |
| | 哭 | | 1221 |
| kǔ | 苦 | | 555 |
| kù | 库 | | 482 |
| | 裤 | 褲 | 1634 |
| | 酷 | | 1841 |
| kuā | 夸 | 誇 | 605 |
| kuǎ | 垮 | | 1224 |
| kuà | 跨 | | 1857 |
| kuài | 块 | 塊 | 400 |
| | 快 | | 497 |
| | 筷 | | 1585 |
| kuān | 宽 | 寬 | 1618 |
| kuǎn | 款 | | 1573 |

| PINYIN | SIMP CHAR | TRAD CHAR | CHAR NO | PINYIN | SIMP CHAR | TRAD CHAR | CHAR NO | PINYIN | SIMP CHAR | TRAD CHAR | CHAR NO |
|---|---|---|---|---|---|---|---|---|---|---|---|
| kuáng | 狂 | | 469 | lián | 联 | 聯 | 1206 | lù | 录 | 錄 | 722 |
| kuàng | 矿 | 礦 | 518 | | 廉 | | 1615 | | 陆 | 陸 | 1043 |
| | 况 | | 928 | liǎn | 脸 | 臉 | 1461 | | 鹿 | | 1724 |
| kuī | 亏 | 虧 | 137 | liàn | 恋 | 戀 | 1314 | | 路 | | 1785 |
| kùn | 困 | 睏 | 393 | | 炼 | 煉 | 1357 | | 露 | | 1997* |
| kuò | 扩 | 擴 | 291 | | 练 | 練 | 1453 | lǚ | 旅 | | 1518 |
| | 括 | | 1016 | liáng | 良 | | 656 | lǜ | 率 | | 1469* |
| | 阔 | 闊 | 1728 | | 凉 | | 1337* | | 绿 | | 1707 |
| | | | | | 量 | | 1544 | luǎn | 卵 | | 896 |
| lā | 垃 | | 399 | | 粮 | 糧 | 1759 | luàn | 乱 | 亂 | 901 |
| | 拉 | | 573 | liǎng | 两 | 兩 | 509 | lún | 轮 | 輪 | 1112 |
| là | 落 | | 1547* | liàng | 凉 | | 1337* | lùn | 论 | 論 | 947 |
| | 辣 | | 1760 | | 量 | | 1544* | luó | 罗 | 羅 | 756 |
| | 蜡 | 蠟 | 1780 | | 辆 | 輛 | 1602 | | 逻 | 邏 | 1755 |
| lái | 来 | 來 | 260 | | 亮 | | 1613 | luǒ | 裸 | | 1753 |
| lán | 兰 | 蘭 | 126 | liáo | 疗 | 療 | 661 | luò | 落 | | 1547* |
| | 拦 | 攔 | 576 | | 辽 | 遼 | 711 | | | | |
| | 栏 | 欄 | 584 | | 聊 | | 1527 | mā | 抹 | | 571* |
| | 蓝 | 藍 | 1548 | liǎo | 了 | | 30* | | 妈 | 媽 | 1092 |
| | 篮 | 籃 | 1862 | liào | 料 | | 961 | má | 吗 | 嗎 | 1020* |
| lǎn | 懒 | 懶 | 1953 | liè | 列 | | 368 | | 麻 | | 1146 |
| làn | 烂 | 爛 | 702 | | 劣 | | 444 | mǎ | 马 | 馬 | 247 |
| láng | 狼 | | 1443 | | 猎 | 獵 | 1444 | mà | 骂 | 罵 | 1652 |
| làng | 浪 | | 1341 | | 裂 | | 1643 | | 吗 | 嗎 | 1020* |
| láo | 牢 | | 488 | lín | 林 | | 412 | mái | 埋 | | 1002* |
| | 劳 | 勞 | 764 | | 临 | 臨 | 771 | mǎi | 买 | 買 | 248 |
| lǎo | 老 | | 375 | | 邻 | 鄰 | 1123 | mài | 卖 | 賣 | 524 |
| lào | 落 | | 1547* | | 淋 | | 1172 | | 迈 | 邁 | 955 |
| lè | 乐 | 樂 | 299* | lìn | 吝 | | 479 | | 脉 | | 1604 |
| le | 了 | | 30* | líng | 灵 | 靈 | 359 | mán | 埋 | | 1002* |
| léi | 雷 | | 1641 | | 玲 | | 728 | | 瞒 | 瞞 | 1914 |
| | 累 | | 1653* | | 铃 | 鈴 | 1303 | | 馒 | 饅 | 1948 |
| lěi | 累 | | 1653* | | 零 | | 1640 | mǎn | 满 | 滿 | 1745 |
| lèi | 类 | 類 | 676 | | 龄 | 齡 | 1687 | màn | 慢 | | 1882 |
| | 泪 | | 688 | lǐng | 岭 | 嶺 | 806 | | 漫 | | 1887 |
| | 肋 | | 898 | | 领 | 領 | 1465 | máng | 忙 | | 343 |
| | 累 | | 1653* | lìng | 令 | | 174 | | 茫 | | 766 |
| lěng | 冷 | | 494 | | 另 | | 385 | | 盲 | | 906 |
| lèng | 愣 | | 1735 | liū | 溜 | | 1883 | māo | 猫 | | 1446 |
| lí | 厘 | | 847 | liú | 流 | | 1493 | máo | 毛 | | 183 |
| | 梨 | | 1271 | | 留 | | 1582 | | 矛 | | 363 |
| | 离 | 離 | 1614 | | 瘤 | | 1951 | mào | 茂 | | 557 |
| lǐ | 里 | 裡 | 386 | liù | 六 | | 69 | | 冒 | | 989 |
| | 礼 | 禮 | 503 | | 陆 | 陸 | 1043* | | 贸 | 貿 | 1429 |
| | 理 | | 1200 | lóng | 龙 | 龍 | 315 | | 帽 | | 1778 |
| lì | 力 | | 59 | | 聋 | 聾 | 1431 | me | 么 | 麼 | 46 |
| | 立 | | 125 | | 笼 | 籠 | 1436* | méi | 没 | | 938* |
| | 历 | 歷 | 200 | lǒng | 笼 | 籠 | 1436* | | 眉 | | 1067 |
| | 利 | | 472 | lòng | 弄 | | 251* | | 梅 | | 1413 |
| | 例 | | 863 | lóu | 楼 | 樓 | 1567 | | 媒 | | 1449 |
| | 丽 | 麗 | 968 | lǒu | 搂 | 摟 | 1557 | | 煤 | | 1506 |
| liǎ | 俩 | 倆 | 1082 | lòu | 漏 | | 1886 | | 霉 | 黴 | 1934 |
| lián | 怜 | 憐 | 695 | | 露 | | 1997* | měi | 美 | | 671 |
| | 连 | 連 | 958 | lú | 炉 | 爐 | 699 | | 每 | | 837 |

| PINYIN | SIMP CHAR | TRAD CHAR | CHAR NO | PINYIN | SIMP CHAR | TRAD CHAR | CHAR NO | PINYIN | SIMP CHAR | TRAD CHAR | CHAR NO |
|---|---|---|---|---|---|---|---|---|---|---|---|
| mèi | 妹 | | 631 | nài | 奈 | | 606 | pái | 牌 | | 1597 |
| mēn | 闷 | 悶 | 1150* | | 耐 | | 1210 | pài | 派 | | 945 |
| mén | 门 | 門 | 130 | nán | 男 | | 757 | pàn | 判 | | 507 |
| mèn | 闷 | 悶 | 1150* | | 难 | 難 | 974* | | 叛 | | 960 |
| mēng | 蒙 | 矇 | 1654* | | 南 | | 986 | | 盼 | | 1255 |
| méng | 蒙 | 矇 濛 懞 | 1654* | nàn | 难 | 難 | 974* | páng | 庞 | 龐 | 917 |
| měng | 蒙 | | 1654* | nǎo | 恼 | 惱 | 931 | | 旁 | | 1473 |
| | 猛 | | 1704 | | 脑 | 腦 | 1460 | pàng | 胖 | | 1121 |
| mèng | 梦 | 夢 | 1217 | nào | 闹 | 鬧 | 1323 | pāo | 抛 | | 1395 |
| mí | 迷 | | 1187 | ne | 呢 | | 1227* | | 泡 | | 1492* |
| | 谜 | 謎 | 1750 | nèi | 内 | | 191 | pǎo | 跑 | | 1916 |
| mǐ | 米 | | 226 | nèn | 嫩 | | 1800 | pào | 泡 | | 1492* |
| mì | 秘 | | 1289 | néng | 能 | | 1873 | | 炮 | | 1633* |
| | 密 | | 1730 | ní | 尼 | | 441 | péi | 陪 | | 1568 |
| | 蜜 | | 1929 | | 泥 | | 1164 | | 赔 | 賠 | 1569 |
| mián | 棉 | | 1670 | | 呢 | | 1227* | pèi | 配 | | 1647 |
| miǎn | 免 | | 1056 | nǐ | 拟 | 擬 | 575 | pēn | 喷 | 噴 | 1563 |
| | 勉 | | 1719 | | 你 | | 617 | pén | 盆 | | 1261 |
| miàn | 面 | 麵 | 721* | nì | 逆 | | 1359 | pēng | 抨 | | 570 |
| | 面 | | 721* | | 腻 | 膩 | 1870 | péng | 朋 | | 1298 |
| miáo | 苗 | | 553 | nián | 年 | | 182 | pěng | 捧 | | 1240 |
| | 描 | | 1407 | niàn | 念 | | 1054 | pèng | 碰 | | 1526 |
| miǎo | 秒 | | 643 | niáng | 娘 | | 1448 | pī | 批 | | 1005 |
| miào | 妙 | | 467 | niǎo | 鸟 | 鳥 | 859 | | 披 | | 1011 |
| | 庙 | 廟 | 659 | niào | 尿 | | 849 | pí | 皮 | | 261 |
| miè | 灭 | 滅 | 75 | nǐn | 您 | | 1692 | | 疲 | | 1328 |
| mín | 民 | | 388 | níng | 宁 | 寧 | 336* | | 啤 | | 1412 |
| mǐn | 敏 | | 1610 | | 柠 | 檸 | 1029 | | 脾 | | 1711 |
| míng | 名 | | 426 | nìng | 宁 | 寧 | 336* | pǐ | 匹 | | 269 |
| | 明 | | 1035 | niū | 妞 | | 630 | pì | 屁 | | 1070 |
| mìng | 命 | | 1051 | niú | 牛 | | 51 | piān | 片 | | 119* |
| mō | 摸 | | 1665 | niǔ | 扭 | | 565 | | 偏 | | 1587 |
| mó | 模 | | 1673* | nóng | 农 | 農 | 423 | | 篇 | | 1921 |
| | 魔 | | 1996 | | 浓 | 濃 | 1168 | piàn | 片 | | 119* |
| mǒ | 抹 | | 571* | | 脓 | 膿 | 1605 | | 骗 | 騙 | 1937 |
| mò | 末 | | 89 | nòng | 弄 | | 251* | piāo | 漂 | | 1820* |
| | 没 | | 938* | nú | 奴 | | 328 | | 飘 | 飄 | 1939 |
| | 莫 | | 999 | nǔ | 努 | | 1063 | piǎo | 漂 | | 1820* |
| | 陌 | | 1251 | nù | 怒 | | 1427 | piào | 票 | | 1367 |
| | 墨 | | 1843 | nuǎn | 暖 | | 1675 | | 漂 | | 1820* |
| mǒu | 某 | | 536 | nuó | 挪 | | 1658 | pīn | 拼 | | 794 |
| mú | 模 | | 1673* | nǚ | 女 | | 57 | pín | 贫 | 貧 | 1052 |
| mǔ | 母 | | 394 | nüè | 疟 | 瘧 | 662 | pǐn | 品 | | 1220 |
| mù | 木 | | 40 | | 虐 | | 1379 | píng | 平 | | 78 |
| | 目 | | 151 | | | | | | 苹 | 蘋 | 395 |
| | 牧 | | 468 | ōu | 欧 | 歐 | 811 | | 坪 | | 398 |
| | 墓 | | 1545 | ǒu | 呕 | 嘔 | 560 | | 评 | 評 | 706 |
| | 幕 | | 1767 | | 偶 | | 1590 | | 凭 | 憑 | 1060 |
| | | | | | | | | | 瓶 | | 1635 |
| ná | 拿 | | 1262 | pá | 扒 | | 169* | pō | 坡 | | 775 |
| nǎ | 哪 | | 1666 | | 爬 | | 1099 | | 泼 | 潑 | 937 |
| nà | 那 | | 980 | pà | 怕 | | 694 | pó | 婆 | | 1623 |
| nǎi | 乃 | | 134 | pāi | 拍 | | 790 | pò | 迫 | | 1186 |
| | 奶 | | 878 | pái | 排 | | 1241 | | 破 | | 1374 |

| PINYIN | SIMP CHAR | TRAD CHAR | CHAR NO |
|---|---|---|---|
| pū | 扑 | 撲 | 168 |
| | 铺 | 鋪 | 1713* |
| pú | 仆 | 僕 | 65 |
| | 葡 | | 1766 |
| pǔ | 普 | | 1484 |
| pù | 铺 | 鋪 | 1713* |
| | 瀑 | | 1974 |
| qī | 七 | | 34 |
| | 妻 | | 742 |
| | 柒 | | 1162 |
| | 欺 | | 1423 |
| | 期 | | 1574 |
| | 漆 | | 1746 |
| qí | 齐 | 齊 | 221 |
| | 其 | | 379 |
| | 歧 | | 585 |
| | 祈 | | 717 |
| | 奇 | | 854* |
| | 棋 | | 1248 |
| | 旗 | | 1834 |
| | 骑 | 騎 | 1840 |
| qǐ | 企 | | 170 |
| | 乞 | | 177 |
| | 启 | 啓 | 657 |
| | 起 | | 1421 |
| qì | 气 | 氣 | 185 |
| | 弃 | 棄 | 480 |
| | 汽 | | 682 |
| | 契 | | 992 |
| | 器 | | 1963 |
| qiǎ | 卡 | | 36* |
| qià | 恰 | | 930 |
| | 洽 | | 942 |
| qiān | 千 | 韆 | 19 |
| | 迁 | 遷 | 506 |
| | 牵 | 牽 | 853 |
| | 签 | 簽 籤 | 1439 |
| | 铅 | 鉛 | 1464 |
| qián | 钱 | 錢 | 1301 |
| | 前 | | 1329 |
| qiǎn | 浅 | 淺 | 692 |
| qiàn | 欠 | | 105 |
| qiāng | 枪 | 槍 | 1244 |
| qiáng | 墙 | 墻 | 1770 |
| | 强 | | 1896* |
| qiǎng | 抢 | 搶 | 1230 |
| | 强 | | 1896* |
| qiāo | 敲 | | 1959 |
| qiáo | 侨 | 僑 | 460 |
| | 桥 | 橋 | 804 |
| | 瞧 | | 1915 |
| qiǎo | 巧 | | 364 |
| | 悄 | | 1348 |

| PINYIN | SIMP CHAR | TRAD CHAR | CHAR NO |
|---|---|---|---|
| qiào | 窍 | 竅 | 1621 |
| qiē | 切 | | 277* |
| qiě | 且 | | 152 |
| qiè | 切 | | 277* |
| | 怯 | | 697 |
| | 窃 | 竊 | 1482 |
| qīn | 亲 | 親 | 908 |
| | 侵 | | 1280 |
| qín | 琴 | | 1372 |
| qǐn | 寝 | 寢 | 1878 |
| qīng | 青 | | 740 |
| | 轻 | 輕 | 1113 |
| | 清 | | 1495 |
| qíng | 情 | | 1491 |
| | 晴 | | 1674 |
| qǐng | 请 | 請 | 1632 |
| qìng | 庆 | 慶 | 230 |
| qióng | 穷 | 窮 | 912 |
| qiū | 秋 | 鞦 | 641 |
| qiú | 囚 | | 161 |
| | 求 | | 376 |
| | 球 | | 1199 |
| qū | 区 | 區 | 99 |
| | 曲 | 麯 | 272* |
| | 屈 | | 1071 |
| qǔ | 曲 | | 272* |
| | 取 | | 520 |
| qù | 去 | | 157 |
| | 趣 | | 1783 |
| | 圈 | | 1765* |
| quán | 全 | | 172 |
| | 权 | 權 | 292 |
| | 拳 | | 1158 |
| | 泉 | | 1275 |
| quǎn | 犬 | | 54 |
| quàn | 劝 | 勸 | 255 |
| | 券 | | 926 |
| quē | 缺 | | 1305 |
| què | 却 | | 820 |
| | 确 | 確 | 1762 |
| qún | 群 | | 1646 |
| | 裙 | | 1752 |
| rán | 然 | | 1432 |
| | 燃 | | 1888 |
| rǎn | 染 | | 1336 |
| | 嚷 | | 1993 |
| ràng | 让 | 讓 | 348 |
| rě | 惹 | | 1657 |
| rè | 热 | 熱 | 1390 |
| rén | 人 | | 4 |
| | 仁 | | 64 |
| rěn | 忍 | | 970 |
| rèn | 任 | | 211 |

| PINYIN | SIMP CHAR | TRAD CHAR | CHAR NO |
|---|---|---|---|
| rèn | 认 | 認 | 239 |
| rēng | 扔 | | 785 |
| réng | 仍 | | 448 |
| rì | 日 | | 96 |
| róng | 荣 | 榮 | 769 |
| | 容 | | 1320 |
| | 溶 | | 1744 |
| róu | 柔 | | 1198 |
| | 揉 | | 1771 |
| ròu | 肉 | | 437 |
| rú | 如 | | 464 |
| rǔ | 乳 | | 1308 |
| rù | 入 | | 5 |
| ruǎn | 软 | 軟 | 889 |
| ruò | 若 | | 554 |
| | 弱 | | 1897 |
| sā | 撒 | | 1907* |
| sǎ | 洒 | 灑 | 1163 |
| | 撒 | | 1907* |
| sāi | 塞 | | 1620* |
| sài | 塞 | | 1620* |
| | 赛 | 賽 | 1813 |
| sān | 三 | | 9 |
| | 叁 | | 599 |
| sǎn | 伞 | 傘 | 171 |
| | 散 | | 1579* |
| sàn | 散 | | 1579* |
| sāng | 丧 | 喪 | 521* |
| sǎng | 嗓 | | 1855 |
| sàng | 丧 | 喪 | 521* |
| sǎo | 扫 | 掃 | 402* |
| | 嫂 | | 1798 |
| sào | 扫 | 掃 | 402* |
| sè | 色 | | 831 |
| shā | 杀 | 殺 | 317 |
| | 沙 | | 342 |
| | 纱 | 紗 | 639 |
| | 砂 | | 733 |
| | 刹 | | 967 |
| shá | 啥 | | 1411 |
| shǎ | 傻 | | 1699 |
| shān | 山 | | 38 |
| | 衫 | | 718 |
| | 删 | | 1309 |
| | 扇 | | 1726* |
| shǎn | 闪 | 閃 | 337 |
| shàn | 善 | | 1483 |
| | 扇 | | 1726* |
| shāng | 伤 | 傷 | 453 |
| | 商 | | 1612 |
| shàng | 上 | | 14 |
| | 尚 | | 1156 |
| shāo | 烧 | 燒 | 1504 |

| PINYIN | SIMP CHAR | TRAD CHAR | CHAR NO | PINYIN | SIMP CHAR | TRAD CHAR | CHAR NO | PINYIN | SIMP CHAR | TRAD CHAR | CHAR NO |
|---|---|---|---|---|---|---|---|---|---|---|---|
| tăng | 躺 | | 1971 | tǔ | 吐 | | 286 | wēn | 温 | | 1627 |
| tàng | 烫 | 燙 | 1624 | tuán | 团 | 團糰 | 392 | wén | 文 | | 70 |
| tāo | 掏 | | 1661 | tuī | 推 | | 1242 | | 纹 | 紋 | 640 |
| táo | 桃 | | 1243 | tuǐ | 腿 | | 1949 | | 蚊 | | 1048 |
| | 逃 | | 1509 | tuì | 退 | | 1508 | | 闻 | 聞 | 1151 |
| | 淘 | | 1628 | tūn | 吞 | | 427 | wěn | 吻 | | 777 |
| tǎo | 讨 | 討 | 500 | tuō | 托 | | 563 | | 稳 | 穩 | 1925 |
| tào | 套 | | 1064 | | 拖 | | 1396 | wèn | 问 | 問 | 678 |
| tè | 特 | | 1094 | | 脱 | | 1803 | wǒ | 我 | | 615 |
| téng | 疼 | | 1148 | tuǒ | 妥 | | 433 | wò | 卧 | | 826 |
| tī | 梯 | | 1669 | | | | | | 握 | | 1662 |
| | 踢 | | 1946 | wā | 洼 | 窪 | 687 | wū | 乌 | 烏 | 601 |
| tí | 提 | | 1554 | | 哇 | | 784 | | 污 | | 681 |
| | 题 | 題 | 1858 | | 挖 | | 1551 | | 屋 | | 1072 |
| tǐ | 体 | 體 | 325 | wá | 娃 | | 877 | wú | 无 | 無 | 139 |
| tì | 替 | | 1430 | wǎ | 瓦 | | 356 | wǔ | 午 | | 48 |
| | 剃 | | 1639 | wà | 袜 | 襪 | 1193 | | 五 | | 79 |
| tiān | 天 | | 25 | wāi | 歪 | | 511 | | 伍 | | 320 |
| | 添 | | 1346 | wài | 外 | | 218 | | 武 | | 513 |
| tián | 田 | | 147 | wān | 弯 | 彎 | 1472 | | 捂 | | 1399 |
| | 甜 | | 1306 | wán | 丸 | | 192 | | 舞 | | 1790 |
| | 填 | | 1550 | | 玩 | | 727 | wù | 勿 | | 179 |
| tiǎn | 舔 | | 1806 | | 完 | | 909 | | 务 | 務 | 429 |
| tiāo | 挑 | | 1235* | | 顽 | 頑 | 1204 | | 物 | | 883 |
| tiáo | 条 | 條 | 598 | wǎn | 挽 | | 1659 | | 恶 | 惡 | 1196* |
| | 调 | 調 | 1749* | | 晚 | | 1779 | | 误 | 誤 | 1354 |
| tiǎo | 挑 | | 1235* | | 碗 | | 1961 | | 雾 | 霧 | 1837 |
| tiào | 跳 | | 1786 | wàn | 万 | 萬 | 73 | xī | 夕 | | 49 |
| tiē | 贴 | 貼 | 1038 | wáng | 王 | | 27 | | 西 | | 352 |
| tiě | 铁 | 鐵 | 1126 | | 亡 | | 68 | | 昔 | | 534 |
| tīng | 厅 | 廳 | 112 | wǎng | 网 | 網 | 390 | | 希 | | 613 |
| | 听 | 聽 | 414 | | 往 | | 461 | | 吸 | | 776 |
| tíng | 庭 | | 1326 | wàng | 旺 | | 587 | | 牺 | 犧 | 1283 |
| | 停 | | 1588 | | 忘 | | 655 | | 惜 | | 1350 |
| tǐng | 挺 | | 1408 | | 望 | | 1622 | | 稀 | | 1599 |
| tōng | 通 | | 1757 | wēi | 危 | | 1057 | | 溪 | | 1743 |
| tóng | 同 | | 541 | | 微 | | 1700 | xí | 习 | 習 | 84 |
| | 童 | | 1471 | wéi | 为 | 為 | 223* | | 席 | | 1325 |
| | 铜 | 銅 | 1712 | | 围 | 圍 | 762 | xǐ | 洗 | | 1167 |
| tǒng | 桶 | | 1564 | | 违 | 違 | 1185 | | 喜 | | 1531 |
| | 统 | 統 | 1601 | | 维 | 維 | 1455 | xì | 戏 | 戲 | 365 |
| | 筒 | | 1696 | wěi | 伟 | 偉 | 451 | | 系 | 係繫 | 842* |
| tòng | 痛 | | 1725 | | 伪 | 偽 | 454 | | 细 | 細 | 1107 |
| tōu | 偷 | | 1591 | | 委 | | 594 | xiā | 虾 | 蝦 | 824 |
| tóu | 头 | 頭 | 128 | | 尾 | | 848 | | 瞎 | | 1913 |
| | 投 | | 1008 | wèi | 卫 | 衛 | 82 | xiá | 峡 | 峽 | 807 |
| tòu | 透 | | 1826 | | 未 | | 88 | | 霞 | | 1977 |
| tū | 秃 | | 833 | | 为 | 為 | 223* | xià | 下 | | 10 |
| | 突 | | 913 | | 位 | | 323 | | 吓 | 嚇 | 287* |
| tú | 图 | 圖 | 761 | | 味 | | 561 | | 夏 | | 1195 |
| | 徒 | | 873 | | 畏 | | 988 | xiān | 仙 | | 207 |
| | 涂 | 塗 | 1171 | | 胃 | | 1216 | | 先 | | 422 |
| | 途 | | 1511 | | 喂 | | 1667 | | 鲜 | 鮮 | 1811* |
| tǔ | 土 | | 15 | | 慰 | | 1968 | | | | |

| PINYIN | SIMP CHAR | TRAD CHAR | CHAR NO | PINYIN | SIMP CHAR | TRAD CHAR | CHAR NO | PINYIN | SIMP CHAR | TRAD CHAR | CHAR NO |
|---|---|---|---|---|---|---|---|---|---|---|---|
| yī | 壹 | | 1530 | yóu | 邮 | 郵 | 1046 | yùn | 孕 | | 971 |
| yí | 仪 | 儀 | 122 | | 游 | | 1818 | | 晕 | 暈 | 1385* |
| | 移 | | 1450 | yǒu | 友 | | 110 | zā | 扎 | | 288* |
| | 姨 | | 1596 | | 有 | | 439 | zá | 杂 | 雜 | 856 |
| | 遗 | 遺 | 1829 | yòu | 又 | | 11 | | 砸 | | 1523 |
| | 疑 | | 1917 | | 右 | | 187 | zāi | 灾 | | 483 |
| yǐ | 乙 | | 29 | | 幼 | | 638 | | 栽 | | 995 |
| | 以 | | 101 | | 诱 | 誘 | 1748 | zǎi | 宰 | | 1140 |
| | 已 | | 133 | yú | 于 | | 28 | | 载 | 載 | 1218* |
| | 蚁 | 蟻 | 825 | | 予 | | 249* | zài | 在 | | 188 |
| | 椅 | | 1566 | | 余 | 餘 | 419 | | 再 | | 354 |
| yì | 义 | 義 | 22 | | 鱼 | 魚 | 843 | | 载 | 載 | 1218* |
| | 亿 | 億 | 205 | | 渔 | 漁 | 1496 | zán | 咱 | | 1023 |
| | 艺 | 藝 | 274 | | 愉 | | 1737 | zàn | 暂 | 暫 | 1522 |
| | 议 | 議 | 349 | | 愚 | | 1901 | | 赞 | 贊 | 1969 |
| | 异 | | 539 | yǔ | 与 | 與 | 158* | zāng | 赃 | 贓 | 1039 |
| | 译 | 譯 | 951 | | 予 | | 249* | | 脏 | 髒 | 1297* |
| | 抑 | | 1007 | | 宇 | | 485 | zàng | 脏 | 臟 | 1297* |
| | 益 | | 1153 | | 雨 | | 720 | | 葬 | | 1656 |
| | 意 | | 1812 | | 羽 | | 732 | | 藏 | | 1978* |
| yīn | 因 | | 270 | | 语 | 語 | 1501 | zāo | 遭 | | 1931 |
| | 音 | | 907 | yù | 玉 | | 77 | | 糟 | | 1956 |
| | 阴 | 陰 | 1041 | | 与 | 與 | 158* | zǎo | 早 | | 268 |
| | 姻 | | 1093 | | 育 | | 1133 | | 澡 | | 1954 |
| yín | 银 | 銀 | 1607 | | 浴 | | 1170 | zào | 造 | | 1515 |
| yǐn | 引 | | 371 | | 狱 | 獄 | 1286 | | 躁 | | 1992 |
| | 饮 | 飲 | 892 | | 欲 | | 1466 | zé | 则 | 則 | 417 |
| | 隐 | 隱 | 1912 | | 预 | 預 | 1528 | | 责 | 責 | 525 |
| yìn | 印 | | 470 | | 遇 | | 1891 | | 择 | 擇 | 792 |
| yīng | 应 | 應 | 334* | yuān | 冤 | | 1729 | zéi | 贼 | 賊 | 1254 |
| | 英 | | 556 | yuán | 元 | | 138 | zěn | 怎 | | 830 |
| | 婴 | 嬰 | 1539 | | 员 | 員 | 546 | zēng | 曾 | | 1625* |
| | 鹰 | 鷹 | 1990 | | 园 | 園 | 763 | | 增 | | 1849 |
| yíng | 荧 | 熒 | 770 | | 原 | | 1273 | | 憎 | | 1881 |
| | 迎 | | 1360 | | 圆 | 圓 | 1391 | zèng | 赠 | 贈 | 1944 |
| | 营 | 營 | 1546 | | 援 | | 1556 | zhā | 扎 | | 288* |
| | 赢 | 贏 | 2000 | | 源 | | 1742 | zhǎ | 眨 | | 1045 |
| yǐng | 影 | | 1918 | yuǎn | 远 | 遠 | 1184 | zhà | 炸 | | 701 |
| yìng | 应 | 應 | 334* | yuàn | 院 | | 1677 | | 诈 | 詐 | 707 |
| | 映 | | 1036 | | 怨 | | 1792 | | 榨 | | 1672 |
| | 硬 | | 1524 | | 愿 | 願 | 1919 | zhāi | 摘 | | 1906 |
| yōng | 佣 | 傭 | 621* | yuē | 约 | 約 | 876 | zhái | 宅 | | 665 |
| | 拥 | 擁 | 1014 | yuè | 月 | | 190 | zhǎi | 窄 | | 1143 |
| yǒng | 永 | | 481 | | 乐 | 樂 | 299* | zhài | 债 | 債 | 1088 |
| | 勇 | | 1371 | | 跃 | 躍 | 1258 | zhān | 占 | | 153* |
| yòng | 用 | | 313 | | 钥 | 鑰 | 1300* | | 沾 | | 684 |
| | 佣 | 傭 | 621* | | 越 | | 1575 | | 粘 | | 1365 |
| yōu | 优 | 優 | 447 | | 说 | 說 | 1631* | zhǎn | 斩 | 斬 | 646 |
| | 忧 | 憂 | 693 | | 阅 | 閱 | 1727 | | 展 | | 1274 |
| | 幽 | | 1538 | yūn | 晕 | 暈 | 1385* | | 崭 | 嶄 | 1383 |
| yóu | 由 | | 148 | yún | 云 | 雲 | 80 | zhàn | 占 | | 153* |
| | 尤 | | 199 | | 匀 | | 180 | | 战 | 戰 | 1044 |
| | 油 | | 683 | yǔn | 允 | | 302 | | 站 | | 1189 |
| | 犹 | 猶 | 886 | yùn | 运 | 運 | 956 | zhāng | 张 | 張 | 1208 |

# Radicals of Chinese Characters

Use this index to find a Chinese character that contains one of the 169 Chinese radicals. This index consists of a Radical Index (page lxi) and a Character Index (pages lxii–lxxxiii).

1. Identify a radical in the character you seek (for example, 木 in 机 or 機).

2. Count the number of strokes (**4**) in the radical (木). The stroke count is based on traditional strokes, not on Broken Marks.

3. In the Radical Index on the opposite page, under the heading for the number of strokes (**4**), locate the radical (木). Radical variants are given in parentheses.

4. Note the radical number (**R68**) in the **RADICAL NUMBER** column on the right.

5. Using the radical key numbers in the running heads of the Character Index that follows, locate the list of characters for the radical number (**R68**).

6. If the character you seek is a Traditional Chinese character (機), scan the **TRAD CHAR** column to locate the character.
   If the character you seek is a Simplified Chinese character (机), either scan the **SIMP CHAR** column to locate the character or count the number of strokes in the character excluding the radical (**2**), then use the **STROKE COUNT** column to locate the character.

7. The character number in the last column (**577**) directs you to the correct dictionary entry.

# RADICAL INDEX

| RADICAL | RADICAL NUMBER |
|---|---|
| **One stroke** | |
| 一 | R1 |
| 丨 | R2 |
| 丿 | R3 |
| 丶 | R4 |
| 乙 (一 乁 乚) | R5 |
| **Two strokes** | |
| 二 | R6 |
| 十 | R7 |
| 厂 | R8 |
| 匚 | R9 |
| 刂 | R10 |
| 卜 | R11 |
| 冂 | R12 |
| 亻 | R13 |
| 八 (丷) | R14 |
| 人 (入) | R15 |
| 勹 | R16 |
| 几 | R17 |
| 儿 | R18 |
| 亠 | R19 |
| 冫 | R20 |
| 冖 | R21 |
| 讠(言) | R22 |
| 卩 | R23 |
| 阝(right) | R24 |
| 阝(left) | R25 |
| 凵 | R26 |
| 刀 | R27 |
| 力 | R28 |
| 厶 | R29 |
| 又 | R30 |
| 廴 | R31 |
| **Three strokes** | |
| 士 | R32 |
| 土 | R33 |
| 工 | R34 |
| 扌 | R35 |
| 艹 | R36 |
| 寸 | R37 |
| 廾 | R38 |
| 大 | R39 |
| 尢 | R40 |
| 小 | R41 |
| 口 | R42 |

| RADICAL | RADICAL NUMBER |
|---|---|
| 口 | R43 |
| 巾 | R44 |
| 山 | R45 |
| 彳 | R46 |
| 彡 | R47 |
| 犭 | R48 |
| 夕 | R49 |
| 夂 | R50 |
| 饣(飠) | R51 |
| 广 | R52 |
| 门 (門) | R53 |
| 氵 | R54 |
| 忄(小) | R55 |
| 宀 | R56 |
| 辶 | R57 |
| 彐(彑) | R58 |
| 尸 | R59 |
| 己 | R60 |
| 弓 | R61 |
| 子 (孑) | R62 |
| 女 | R63 |
| 马 (馬) | R64 |
| 纟(糸) | R65 |
| 幺 | R66 |
| **Four strokes** | |
| 王 | R67 |
| 木 | R68 |
| 犬 | R69 |
| 歹 | R70 |
| 车 (車) | R71 |
| 戈 | R72 |
| 比 | R73 |
| 瓦 | R74 |
| 止 | R75 |
| 支 | R76 |
| 日 | R77 |
| 曰 | R78 |
| 贝 (貝) | R79 |
| 水 | R80 |
| 见 (見) | R81 |
| 牛 (牜) | R82 |
| 手 | R83 |
| 毛 | R84 |
| 气 | R85 |
| 攵 | R86 |
| 片 | R87 |
| 斤 | R88 |

| RADICAL | RADICAL NUMBER |
|---|---|
| 爪 (爫) | R89 |
| 父 | R90 |
| 月 | R91 |
| 欠 | R92 |
| 风 (風) | R93 |
| 殳 | R94 |
| 文 | R95 |
| 方 | R96 |
| 火 | R97 |
| 斗 | R98 |
| 灬 | R99 |
| 户 | R100 |
| 礻 | R101 |
| 心 | R102 |
| 聿 | R103 |
| **Five strokes** | |
| 示 | R104 |
| 石 | R105 |
| 业 | R106 |
| 目 | R107 |
| 田 | R108 |
| 皿 | R109 |
| 罒 | R110 |
| 钅(釒) | R111 |
| 矢 | R112 |
| 禾 | R113 |
| 白 | R114 |
| 瓜 | R115 |
| 鸟 | R116 |
| 疒 | R117 |
| 立 | R118 |
| 穴 | R119 |
| 礻 | R120 |
| 皮 | R121 |
| 矛 | R122 |
| 母 | R123 |
| **Six strokes** | |
| 耒 | R124 |
| 老 | R125 |
| 耳 | R126 |
| 臣 | R127 |
| 西 (覀) | R128 |
| 页 | R129 |
| 虍 | R130 |
| 虫 | R131 |

| RADICAL | RADICAL NUMBER |
|---|---|
| 缶 | R132 |
| 舌 | R133 |
| 竹 (⺮) | R134 |
| 臼 | R135 |
| 自 | R136 |
| 血 | R137 |
| 舟 | R138 |
| 艮 | R139 |
| 衣 | R140 |
| 羊 (羋) | R141 |
| 米 | R142 |
| 羽 | R143 |
| 糸 | R144 |
| **Seven strokes** | |
| 走 | R145 |
| 豆 | R146 |
| 酉 | R147 |
| 豕 | R148 |
| 里 | R149 |
| 足 (⻊) | R150 |
| 身 | R151 |
| 谷 | R152 |
| 角 | R153 |
| 言 | R154 |
| 辛 | R155 |
| **Eight strokes** | |
| 青 | R156 |
| 雨 (⻗) | R157 |
| 齿 (齒) | R158 |
| 隹 | R159 |
| 金 | R160 |
| 鱼 (魚) | R161 |
| **Nine strokes** | |
| 革 | R162 |
| 骨 | R163 |
| 鬼 | R164 |
| 食 | R165 |
| 音 | R166 |
| **Ten or more strokes** | |
| 黑 | R167 |
| 鼠 | R168 |
| 鼻 | R169 |

# CHARACTER INDEX

| SIMP CHAR | TRAD CHAR | STROKE COUNT | PINYIN | CHAR NO |
|---|---|---|---|---|
| **R1 一** | | | | |
| 一 | | | yī | 1 |
| 丁 | | 1 | dīng | 8 |
| 七 | | 1 | qī | 34 |
| 三 | | 2 | sān | 9 |
| 下 | | 2 | xià | 10 |
| 干 | 乾 | 2 | gān | 13 |
| 干 | 幹 | 2 | gàn | 13 |
| 上 | | 2 | shàng | 14 |
| 丈 | | 2 | zhàng | 17 |
| 才 | 纔 | 2 | cái | 39 |
| 万 | 萬 | 2 | wàn | 73 |
| 与 | 與 | 2 | yǔ | 158 |
| 与 | 與 | 2 | yù | 158 |
| 不 | | 3 | bù | 24 |
| 开 | 開 | 3 | kāi | 26 |
| 丑 | 醜 | 3 | chǒu | 85 |
| 无 | 無 | 3 | wú | 139 |
| 牙 | | 3 | yá | 143 |
| 专 | 專 | 3 | zhuān | 155 |
| 正 | | 4 | zhèng | 76 |
| 平 | | 4 | píng | 78 |
| 甘 | | 4 | gān | 95 |
| 且 | | 4 | qiě | 152 |
| 世 | | 4 | shì | 163 |
| 右 | | 4 | yòu | 187 |
| 丙 | | 4 | bǐng | 246 |
| 东 | 東 | 4 | dōng | 307 |
| 丝 | 絲 | 4 | sī | 637 |
| 至 | | 5 | zhì | 244 |
| 而 | | 5 | ér | 351 |
| 死 | | 5 | sǐ | 510 |
| 严 | 嚴 | 6 | yán | 241 |
| 来 | 來 | 6 | lái | 260 |
| 更 | | 6 | gēng | 355 |
| 更 | | 6 | gèng | 355 |
| 求 | | 6 | qiú | 376 |
| 两 | 兩 | 6 | liǎng | 509 |
| 丽 | 麗 | 6 | lì | 968 |
| 表 | 錶 | 7 | biǎo | 527 |
| 事 | | 7 | shì | 987 |
| 歪 | | 8 | wāi | 511 |
| 面 | 麵 | 8 | miàn | 721 |
| 面 | | 8 | miàn | 721 |
| 甚 | | 8 | shèn | 759 |
| 哥 | | 9 | gē | 1370 |
| 噩 | | 15 | è | 1960 |
| **R2 丨** | | | | |
| 丰 | 豐 | 3 | fēng | 35 |
| 中 | | 3 | zhōng | 86 |
| 中 | | 3 | zhòng | 86 |
| 长 | 長 | 3 | cháng | 93 |
| 长 | 長 | 3 | zhǎng | 93 |

| SIMP CHAR | TRAD CHAR | STROKE COUNT | PINYIN | CHAR NO |
|---|---|---|---|---|
| 归 | 歸 | 4 | guī | 166 |
| 史 | | 4 | shǐ | 186 |
| 北 | | 4 | běi | 278 |
| 肉 | | 5 | ròu | 437 |
| 串 | | 6 | chuàn | 522 |
| 非 | | 7 | fēi | 378 |
| 县 | 縣 | 6 | xiàn | 543 |
| 临 | 臨 | 8 | lín | 771 |
| **R3 丿** | | | | |
| 乃 | | 1 | nǎi | 134 |
| 川 | | 2 | chuān | 21 |
| 久 | | 2 | jiǔ | 45 |
| 么 | 麼 | 2 | me | 46 |
| 及 | | 2 | jí | 141 |
| 丸 | | 2 | wán | 192 |
| 乏 | | 3 | fá | 109 |
| 乌 | 烏 | 3 | wū | 601 |
| 生 | | 4 | shēng | 107 |
| 乐 | 樂 | 4 | lè | 299 |
| 乐 | 樂 | 4 | yuè | 299 |
| 用 | | 4 | yòng | 313 |
| 甩 | | 4 | shuǎi | 612 |
| 年 | | 5 | nián | 182 |
| 丢 | | 5 | diū | 297 |
| 色 | | 5 | sè | 831 |
| 危 | | 5 | wēi | 1057 |
| 免 | | 6 | miǎn | 1056 |
| 垂 | | 7 | chuí | 430 |
| 乖 | | 7 | guāi | 832 |
| 拜 | | 8 | bài | 635 |
| 乘 | | 9 | chéng | 1263 |
| 舞 | | 13 | wǔ | 1790 |
| 靠 | | 14 | kào | 1791 |
| **R4 丶** | | | | |
| 义 | 義 | 2 | yì | 22 |
| 之 | | 2 | zhī | 67 |
| 为 | 為 | 3 | wéi | 223 |
| 为 | 為 | 3 | wèi | 223 |
| 主 | | 4 | zhǔ | 124 |
| 永 | | 4 | yǒng | 481 |
| 州 | | 5 | zhōu | 233 |
| 良 | | 5 | liáng | 656 |
| 举 | 舉 | 8 | jǔ | 674 |
| **R5 乙 (乛乁乚)** | 乙 | | yǐ | 29 |
| 了 | | 1 | le | 30 |
| 了 | | 1 | liǎo | 30 |
| 九 | | 1 | jiǔ | 116 |
| 飞 | 飛 | 2 | fēi | 81 |
| 习 | 習 | 2 | xí | 84 |
| 乡 | 鄉 | 2 | xiāng | 117 |
| 乞 | | 2 | qǐ | 177 |

| SIMP CHAR | TRAD CHAR | STROKE COUNT | PINYIN | CHAR NO | | SIMP CHAR | TRAD CHAR | STROKE COUNT | PINYIN | CHAR NO |
|---|---|---|---|---|---|---|---|---|---|---|
| 也 | | 2 | yě | 273 | | 列 | | 4 | liè | 368 |
| 予 | | 3 | yú | 249 | | 则 | 則 | 4 | zé | 417 |
| 予 | | 3 | yǔ | 249 | | 划 | 劃 | 4 | huá | 476 |
| 书 | 書 | 3 | shū | 264 | | 划 | 劃 | 4 | huà | 476 |
| 民 | | 4 | mín | 388 | | 刚 | 剛 | 4 | gāng | 591 |
| 买 | 買 | 5 | mǎi | 248 | | 创 | 創 | 4 | chuàng | 1131 |
| 承 | | 7 | chéng | 972 | | 利 | | 5 | lì | 472 |
| **R6** 二 | | | | | | 判 | | 5 | pàn | 507 |
| 二 | | | èr | 2 | | 别 | 別 | 5 | bié | 1049 |
| 于 | 於 | 1 | yú | 28 | | 别 | 別彆 | 5 | biè | 1049 |
| 亏 | 虧 | 1 | kuī | 137 | | 删 | | 5 | shān | 1309 |
| 井 | | 2 | jǐng | 60 | | 到 | | 6 | dào | 737 |
| 五 | | 2 | wǔ | 79 | | 刮 | 颳 | 6 | guā | 902 |
| 云 | 雲 | 2 | yún | 80 | | 刽 | 劊 | 6 | guì | 903 |
| 互 | | 2 | hù | 135 | | 刻 | | 6 | kè | 966 |
| 亚 | 亞 | 4 | yà | 136 | | 刹 | | 6 | chà | 967 |
| 些 | | 6 | xiē | 748 | | 刹 | | 6 | shā | 967 |
| **R7** 十 | | | | | | 刺 | | 6 | cì | 1050 |
| 十 | | | shí | 3 | | 制 | 製 | 6 | zhì | 1130 |
| 千 | 韆 | 1 | qiān | 19 | | 刷 | | 6 | shuā | 1310 |
| 升 | | 2 | shēng | 47 | | 剑 | 劍 | 7 | jiàn | 904 |
| 午 | | 2 | wǔ | 48 | | 削 | | 7 | xiāo | 1366 |
| 协 | 協 | 4 | xié | 397 | | 削 | | 7 | xuē | 1366 |
| 华 | 華 | 4 | huá | 421 | | 剃 | | 7 | tì | 1639 |
| 毕 | 畢 | 4 | bì | 540 | | 剥 | 剝 | 8 | bāo | 1377 |
| 丧 | 喪 | 6 | sāng | 521 | | 剥 | 剝 | 8 | bō | 1377 |
| 丧 | 喪 | 6 | sàng | 521 | | 剧 | 劇 | 8 | jù | 1468 |
| 卓 | | 6 | zhuó | 523 | | 剩 | | 10 | shèng | 1720 |
| 卖 | 賣 | 6 | mài | 524 | | 割 | | 10 | gē | 1761 |
| 卑 | | 6 | bēi | 602 | | **R11** 卜 | | | | |
| 直 | | 6 | zhí | 609 | | 卡 | | 3 | kǎ | 36 |
| 南 | | 7 | nán | 986 | | 卡 | | 3 | qiǎ | 36 |
| 真 | | 8 | zhēn | 1075 | | 占 | | 3 | zhān | 153 |
| 博 | | 10 | bó | 1549 | | 占 | | 3 | zhàn | 153 |
| **R8** 厂 | | | | | | **R12** 冂 | | | | |
| 厂 | 廠 | | chǎng | 7 | | 内 | | 2 | nèi | 191 |
| 厅 | 廳 | 2 | tīng | 112 | | 册 | 冊 | 3 | cè | 614 |
| 历 | 歷 | 2 | lì | 200 | | 再 | | 4 | zài | 354 |
| 厄 | | 2 | è | 443 | | 网 | 網 | 4 | wǎng | 390 |
| 压 | 壓 | 4 | yā | 201 | | 同 | | 4 | tóng | 541 |
| 厌 | 厭 | 4 | yàn | 202 | | 周 | | 6 | zhōu | 1068 |
| 厕 | | 6 | cè | 846 | | **R13** 亻 | | | | |
| 厘 | | 7 | lí | 847 | | 亿 | 億 | 1 | yì | 205 |
| 厚 | | 7 | hòu | 1272 | | 什 | | 2 | shén | 63 |
| 原 | | 8 | yuán | 1273 | | 什 | | 2 | shí | 63 |
| 厨 | | 10 | chú | 1584 | | 仁 | | 2 | rén | 64 |
| **R9** 匚 | | | | | | 仆 | 僕 | 2 | pú | 65 |
| 区 | 區 | 2 | qū | 99 | | 仅 | 僅 | 2 | jǐn | 120 |
| 巨 | | 2 | jù | 162 | | 仅 | 僅 | 2 | jìn | 120 |
| 匹 | | 2 | pǐ | 269 | | 化 | | 2 | huà | 215 |
| 医 | 醫 | 5 | yī | 389 | | 仇 | | 2 | chóu | 319 |
| **R10** 刂 | | | | | | 仍 | | 2 | réng | 448 |
| 刊 | | 3 | kān | 216 | | 仗 | | 3 | zhàng | 121 |
| 刑 | | 4 | xíng | 256 | | 仪 | 儀 | 3 | yí | 122 |

| | SIMP CHAR | TRAD CHAR | STROKE COUNT | PINYIN | CHAR NO |
|---|---|---|---|---|---|
| R13 亻 (continued) | 付 | | 3 | fù | 206 |
| | 仙 | | 3 | xiān | 207 |
| | 代 | | 3 | dài | 208 |
| | 他 | | 3 | tā | 616 |
| | 件 | | 4 | jiàn | 209 |
| | 价 | 價 | 4 | jià | 210 |
| | 任 | | 4 | rèn | 211 |
| | 伏 | | 4 | fú | 212 |
| | 休 | | 4 | xiū | 213 |
| | 伙 | 夥 | 4 | huǒ | 214 |
| | 伍 | | 4 | wǔ | 320 |
| | 似 | | 4 | sì | 322 |
| | 优 | 優 | 4 | yōu | 447 |
| | 份 | | 4 | fèn | 449 |
| | 仿 | | 4 | fǎng | 450 |
| | 伟 | 偉 | 4 | wěi | 451 |
| | 传 | 傳 | 4 | chuán | 452 |
| | 传 | 傳 | 4 | zhuàn | 452 |
| | 伤 | 傷 | 4 | shāng | 453 |
| | 伪 | 偽 | 4 | wěi | 454 |
| | 仰 | | 4 | yǎng | 620 |
| | 佛 | | 4 | fó | 1080 |
| | 伴 | | 5 | bàn | 321 |
| | 位 | | 5 | wèi | 323 |
| | 住 | | 5 | zhù | 324 |
| | 体 | 體 | 5 | tǐ | 325 |
| | 作 | | 5 | zuō | 326 |
| | 作 | | 5 | zuò | 326 |
| | 伯 | | 5 | bó | 455 |
| | 估 | | 5 | gū | 456 |
| | 伸 | | 5 | shēn | 457 |
| | 但 | | 5 | dàn | 458 |
| | 你 | | 5 | nǐ | 617 |
| | 低 | | 5 | dī | 618 |
| | 何 | | 5 | hé | 619 |
| | 佣 | 傭 | 5 | yōng | 621 |
| | 佣 | 傭 | 5 | yòng | 621 |
| | 伺 | | 5 | cì | 862 |
| | 伺 | | 5 | sì | 862 |
| | 供 | | 6 | gōng | 459 |
| | 供 | | 6 | gòng | 459 |
| | 侨 | 僑 | 6 | qiáo | 460 |
| | 佰 | | 6 | bǎi | 622 |
| | 使 | | 6 | shǐ | 623 |
| | 侍 | | 6 | shì | 624 |
| | 依 | | 6 | yī | 625 |
| | 例 | | 6 | lì | 863 |
| | 侧 | 側 | 6 | cè | 864 |
| | 侃 | | 6 | kǎn | 1085 |
| | 便 | | 7 | biàn | 865 |
| | 促 | | 7 | cù | 866 |
| | 俗 | | 7 | sú | 867 |
| | 保 | | 7 | bǎo | 868 |
| | 信 | | 7 | xìn | 869 |

| | SIMP CHAR | TRAD CHAR | STROKE COUNT | PINYIN | CHAR NO |
|---|---|---|---|---|---|
| | 修 | | 7 | xiū | 870 |
| | 俊 | | 7 | jùn | 1081 |
| | 俩 | 倆 | 7 | liǎ | 1082 |
| | 俱 | | 7 | jù | 1083 |
| | 侵 | | 7 | qīn | 1280 |
| | 倍 | | 8 | bèi | 1084 |
| | 候 | | 8 | hòu | 1086 |
| | 借 | | 8 | jiè | 1087 |
| | 债 | 債 | 28 | zhài | 1088 |
| | 值 | | 8 | zhí | 1089 |
| | 倒 | | 8 | dǎo | 1281 |
| | 倒 | | 8 | dào | 1281 |
| | 做 | | 9 | zuò | 1282 |
| | 偿 | 償 | 9 | cháng | 1440 |
| | 假 | | 9 | jiǎ | 1586 |
| | 假 | | 9 | jià | 1586 |
| | 偏 | | 9 | piān | 1587 |
| | 停 | | 9 | tíng | 1588 |
| | 健 | | 9 | jiàn | 1589 |
| | 偶 | | 9 | ǒu | 1590 |
| | 偷 | | 9 | tōu | 1591 |
| | 催 | | 10 | cuī | 1592 |
| | 傍 | | 10 | bàng | 1698 |
| | 傻 | | 11 | shǎ | 1699 |
| | 像 | | 12 | xiàng | 1863 |
| | 僵 | | 13 | jiāng | 1864 |
| R14 八 (丷) | 八 | | | bā | 6 |
| | 六 | | 2 | liù | 69 |
| | 公 | | 2 | gōng | 103 |
| | 兰 | 蘭 | 3 | lán | 126 |
| | 半 | | 3 | bàn | 127 |
| | 共 | | 4 | gòng | 164 |
| | 关 | 關 | 4 | guān | 224 |
| | 并 | | 4 | bìng | 225 |
| | 兴 | 興 | 4 | xīng | 228 |
| | 兴 | 興 | 4 | xìng | 228 |
| | 兵 | | 5 | bīng | 300 |
| | 其 | | 6 | qí | 379 |
| | 典 | | 6 | diǎn | 532 |
| | 具 | | 6 | jù | 533 |
| | 单 | 單 | 6 | dān | 672 |
| | 首 | | 7 | shǒu | 924 |
| | 前 | | 7 | qián | 1329 |
| | 黄 | | 8 | huáng | 1212 |
| R15 人 (入) | 人 | | | rén | 4 |
| | 入 | | | rù | 5 |
| | 个 | 個 | 1 | gè | 18 |
| | 介 | | 2 | jiè | 44 |
| | 从 | 從 | 2 | cóng | 66 |
| | 以 | | 2 | yǐ | 101 |
| | 今 | | 2 | jīn | 102 |
| | 仓 | 倉 | 2 | cāng | 418 |

| SIMP CHAR | TRAD CHAR | STROKE COUNT | PINYIN | CHAR NO |
|---|---|---|---|---|
| 丛 | 叢 | 3 | cóng | 123 |
| 令 | | 3 | lìng | 174 |
| 企 | | 4 | qǐ | 170 |
| 伞 | 傘 | 4 | sǎn | 171 |
| 全 | | 4 | quán | 172 |
| 众 | 衆 | 4 | zhòng | 175 |
| 会 | 會 | 4 | huì | 295 |
| 余 | 餘 | 5 | yú | 419 |
| 舍 | | 6 | shě | 593 |
| 舍 | 捨 | 6 | shè | 593 |
| 命 | | 6 | mìng | 1051 |
| 舒 | | 10 | shū | 1805 |

**R16 勹**

| SIMP CHAR | TRAD CHAR | STROKE COUNT | PINYIN | CHAR NO |
|---|---|---|---|---|
| 匀 | | 2 | yún | 180 |
| 勾 | | 2 | gōu | 303 |
| 匆 | | 3 | cōng | 304 |
| 勿 | | 3 | wù | 179 |
| 包 | | 3 | bāo | 836 |

**R17 儿**

| SIMP CHAR | TRAD CHAR | STROKE COUNT | PINYIN | CHAR NO |
|---|---|---|---|---|
| 儿 | 兒 | | ér | 43 |
| 元 | | 2 | yuán | 138 |
| 允 | | 2 | yǔn | 302 |
| 兄 | | 3 | xiōng | 382 |
| 先 | | 4 | xiān | 422 |
| 光 | | 4 | guāng | 491 |
| 充 | | 4 | chōng | 652 |
| 克 | | 5 | kè | 738 |
| 党 | 黨 | 8 | dǎng | 1626 |

**R18 几**

| SIMP CHAR | TRAD CHAR | STROKE COUNT | PINYIN | CHAR NO |
|---|---|---|---|---|
| 几 | 幾 | | jī | 115 |
| 几 | 幾 | | jǐ | 115 |
| 凡 | | 1 | fán | 193 |
| 凤 | 鳳 | 2 | fèng | 314 |
| 凭 | 憑 | 6 | píng | 1060 |
| 凯 | 凱 | 6 | kǎi | 1577 |

**R19 亠**

| SIMP CHAR | TRAD CHAR | STROKE COUNT | PINYIN | CHAR NO |
|---|---|---|---|---|
| 亡 | | 1 | wáng | 68 |
| 产 | 産 | 4 | chǎn | 219 |
| 齐 | 齊 | 4 | qí | 221 |
| 交 | | 4 | jiāo | 222 |
| 弃 | 棄 | 5 | qì | 480 |
| 变 | 變 | 6 | biàn | 653 |
| 京 | | 6 | jīng | 905 |
| 享 | | 6 | xiǎng | 1135 |
| 哀 | | 7 | āi | 1134 |
| 亮 | | 7 | liàng | 1613 |
| 高 | | 8 | gāo | 1611 |
| 离 | 離 | 8 | lí | 1614 |
| 率 | | 9 | lǜ | 1469 |
| 率 | | 9 | shuài | 1469 |

**R20 冫**

| SIMP CHAR | TRAD CHAR | STROKE COUNT | PINYIN | CHAR NO |
|---|---|---|---|---|
| 冲 | 衝 | 4 | chōng | 339 |
| 冲 | 衝 | 4 | chòng | 339 |

| SIMP CHAR | TRAD CHAR | STROKE COUNT | PINYIN | CHAR NO |
|---|---|---|---|---|
| 决 | | 4 | jué | 340 |
| 冰 | | 4 | bīng | 493 |
| 冷 | | 5 | lěng | 494 |
| 冻 | 凍 | 5 | dòng | 680 |
| 况 | | 5 | kuàng | 928 |
| 净 | | 6 | jìng | 1159 |
| 准 | | 8 | zhǔn | 929 |
| 凉 | | 8 | liáng | 1337 |
| 凉 | | 8 | liàng | 1337 |
| 凑 | | 9 | còu | 1160 |
| 减 | | 9 | jiǎn | 1487 |

**R21 冖**

| SIMP CHAR | TRAD CHAR | STROKE COUNT | PINYIN | CHAR NO |
|---|---|---|---|---|
| 写 | 寫 | 3 | xiě | 663 |
| 农 | 農 | 4 | nóng | 423 |
| 军 | 軍 | 4 | jūn | 489 |
| 罕 | | 5 | hǎn | 490 |
| 冠 | | 7 | guān | 1478 |
| 冠 | | 7 | guàn | 1478 |
| 冤 | | 9 | yuān | 1729 |

**R22 讠 (言)**

| SIMP CHAR | TRAD CHAR | STROKE COUNT | PINYIN | CHAR NO |
|---|---|---|---|---|
| 认 | 認 | 2 | rèn | 239 |
| 计 | 計 | 2 | jì | 240 |
| 订 | 訂 | 2 | dìng | 347 |
| 让 | 讓 | 3 | ràng | 348 |
| 议 | 議 | 3 | yì | 349 |
| 训 | 訓 | 3 | xùn | 350 |
| 讨 | 討 | 3 | tǎo | 500 |
| 记 | 記 | 3 | jì | 946 |
| 讲 | 講 | 4 | jiǎng | 501 |
| 许 | 許 | 4 | xǔ | 502 |
| 讯 | 訊 | 4 | xùn | 703 |
| 诀 | 訣 | 4 | jué | 704 |
| 论 | 論 | 4 | lùn | 947 |
| 讽 | 諷 | 4 | fěng | 948 |
| 访 | 訪 | 4 | fǎng | 949 |
| 设 | 設 | 4 | shè | 1179 |
| 证 | 證 | 5 | zhèng | 705 |
| 评 | 評 | 5 | píng | 706 |
| 诈 | 詐 | 5 | zhà | 707 |
| 诉 | 訴 | 5 | sù | 708 |
| 诊 | 診 | 5 | zhěn | 709 |
| 识 | 識 | 5 | shí | 950 |
| 译 | 譯 | 5 | yì | 951 |
| 词 | 詞 | 5 | cí | 1353 |
| 详 | 詳 | 6 | xiáng | 952 |
| 试 | 試 | 6 | shì | 1180 |
| 诗 | 詩 | 6 | shī | 1181 |
| 话 | 話 | 6 | huà | 1182 |
| 该 | 該 | 6 | gāi | 1183 |
| 诚 | 誠 | 6 | chèng | 1499 |
| 询 | 詢 | 6 | xún | 1500 |
| 诡 | 詭 | 6 | guǐ | 1747 |
| 误 | 誤 | 7 | wù | 1354 |
| 语 | 語 | 7 | yǔ | 1501 |

| | SIMP CHAR | TRAD CHAR | STROKE COUNT | PINYIN | CHAR NO |
|---|---|---|---|---|---|
| **R22 讠** (continued) | 说 | 説 | 7 | shuì | 1631 |
| | 说 | 説 | 7 | shuō | 1631 |
| | 说 | 説 | 7 | yuè | 1631 |
| | 诱 | 誘 | 7 | yòu | 1748 |
| | 谁 | 誰 | 8 | shéi | 1355 |
| | 谁 | 誰 | 8 | shuí | 1355 |
| | 谈 | 談 | 8 | tán | 1356 |
| | 读 | 讀 | 8 | dú | 1502 |
| | 课 | 課 | 8 | kè | 1503 |
| | 请 | 請 | 8 | qǐng | 1632 |
| | 调 | 調 | 8 | diào | 1749 |
| | 调 | 調 | 8 | tiáo | 1749 |
| | 谜 | 謎 | 9 | mí | 1750 |
| | 谎 | 謊 | 9 | huǎng | 1824 |
| | 谣 | 謠 | 10 | yáo | 1751 |
| | 谢 | 謝 | 10 | xiè | 1890 |
| **R23 卩** | 卫 | 衛 | 1 | wèi | 82 |
| | 印 | | 3 | yìn | 470 |
| | 却 | 郤 | 5 | què | 820 |
| | 卵 | | 5 | luǎn | 896 |
| | 即 | | 5 | jí | 1047 |
| | 卷 | | 6 | juǎn | 1333 |
| | 卷 | | 6 | juàn | 1333 |
| | 卸 | | 7 | xiè | 1128 |
| **R24 阝** (right) | 邓 | | 2 | dèng | 367 |
| | 邦 | | 4 | bāng | 636 |
| | 那 | | 4 | nà | 980 |
| | 邪 | | 4 | xié | 981 |
| | 邮 | 郵 | 5 | yóu | 1046 |
| | 邻 | 鄰 | 5 | lín | 1123 |
| | 郊 | | 6 | jiāo | 1194 |
| | 都 | | 8 | dōu | 1578 |
| | 都 | | 8 | dū | 1578 |
| | 部 | | 8 | bù | 1636 |
| **R25 阝** (left) | 队 | 隊 | 2 | duì | 294 |
| | 阶 | 階 | 4 | jiē | 590 |
| | 阳 | 陽 | 4 | yáng | 808 |
| | 阵 | 陣 | 4 | zhèn | 809 |
| | 防 | | 4 | fáng | 1040 |
| | 阴 | 陰 | 4 | yīn | 1041 |
| | 阻 | | 5 | zǔ | 1042 |
| | 陆 | 陸 | 5 | liù | 1043 |
| | 陆 | 陸 | 5 | lù | 1043 |
| | 阿 | | 5 | ā | 1249 |
| | 阿 | | 5 | ē | 1249 |
| | 陈 | 陳 | 5 | chén | 1250 |
| | 陌 | | 6 | mò | 1251 |
| | 限 | | 6 | xiàn | 1417 |
| | 险 | 險 | 7 | xiǎn | 1252 |
| | 降 | | 7 | jiàng | 1416 |
| | 降 | | 7 | xiáng | 1416 |

| | SIMP CHAR | TRAD CHAR | STROKE COUNT | PINYIN | CHAR NO |
|---|---|---|---|---|---|
| | 除 | | 7 | chú | 1418 |
| | 院 | | 7 | yuàn | 1677 |
| | 陪 | | 8 | péi | 1568 |
| | 陷 | | 8 | xiàn | 1678 |
| | 随 | 隨 | 9 | suí | 1911 |
| | 隐 | 隱 | 9 | yǐn | 1912 |
| | 隔 | | 10 | gé | 1910 |
| | 障 | | 11 | zhàng | 1856 |
| **R26 凵** | 凶 | | 2 | xiōng | 98 |
| | 击 | 擊 | 3 | jī | 156 |
| | 出 | 齣 | 3 | chū | 258 |
| **R27 刀** | 刀 | | | dāo | 31 |
| | 刁 | | | diāo | 32 |
| | 分 | | 2 | fēn | 173 |
| | 分 | | 2 | fèn | 173 |
| | 切 | | 2 | qiē | 277 |
| | 切 | | 2 | qiè | 277 |
| | 争 | | 4 | zhēng | 595 |
| | 券 | | 6 | quàn | 926 |
| | 剪 | | 9 | jiǎn | 1816 |
| **R28 力** | 力 | | | lì | 59 |
| | 办 | 辦 | 2 | bàn | 195 |
| | 劝 | 勸 | 2 | quàn | 255 |
| | 加 | | 3 | jiā | 463 |
| | 劣 | | 4 | liè | 444 |
| | 动 | 動 | 4 | dòng | 514 |
| | 劲 | 勁 | 5 | jìn | 736 |
| | 劲 | 勁 | 5 | jìng | 736 |
| | 劳 | 勞 | 5 | láo | 764 |
| | 助 | | 5 | zhù | 818 |
| | 劫 | | 5 | jié | 819 |
| | 努 | | 5 | nǔ | 1063 |
| | 勇 | | 7 | yǒng | 1371 |
| | 勉 | | 7 | miǎn | 1719 |
| **R29 厶** | 叁 | 參 | 6 | sān | 599 |
| | 参 | 參 | 6 | cān | 600 |
| | 参 | 參 | 6 | shēn | 600 |
| **R30 又** | 又 | | | yòu | 11 |
| | 叉 | | 1 | chā | 33 |
| | 支 | | 2 | zhī | 92 |
| | 友 | | 2 | yǒu | 110 |
| | 反 | | 2 | fǎn | 111 |
| | 双 | 雙 | 2 | shuāng | 146 |
| | 对 | 對 | 3 | duì | 254 |
| | 发 | 發 | 3 | fā | 311 |
| | 发 | 髮 | 3 | fà | 311 |
| | 取 | | 6 | qǔ | 520 |
| | 叔 | | 6 | shū | 821 |

| | SIMP CHAR | TRAD CHAR | STROKE COUNT | PINYIN | CHAR NO | | | SIMP CHAR | TRAD CHAR | STROKE COUNT | PINYIN | CHAR NO |
|---|---|---|---|---|---|---|---|---|---|---|---|---|
| | 叛 | | 7 | pàn | 960 | | | 增 | | 12 | zēng | 1849 |
| | 叙 | | 7 | xù | 1129 | | | 壁 | | 13 | bì | 1920 |
| | 艰 | 艱 | 6 | jiān | 973 | | **R34** 工 | 工 | | | gōng | 12 |
| | 难 | 難 | 8 | nán | 974 | | | 左 | | 2 | zuǒ | 113 |
| | 难 | 難 | 8 | nàn | 974 | | | 功 | | 2 | gōng | 252 |
| | | | | | | | | 巧 | | 2 | qiǎo | 364 |
| **R31** 廴 | 延 | | 5 | yán | 731 | | **R35** 扌 | 扑 | 撲 | 2 | pū | 168 |
| | 建 | | 7 | jiàn | 1203 | | | 扒 | | 2 | bā | 169 |
| | | | | | | | | 扒 | | 2 | pá | 169 |
| **R32** 士 | 士 | | | shì | 16 | | | 扎 | | 2 | zā | 288 |
| | 壮 | 壯 | 3 | zhuàng | 238 | | | 扎 | | 2 | zhā | 288 |
| | 声 | 聲 | 4 | shēng | 374 | | | 打 | | 2 | dá | 289 |
| | 壹 | | 9 | yī | 1530 | | | 打 | | 2 | dǎ | 289 |
| | 鼓 | | 10 | gǔ | 1688 | | | 扔 | | 2 | rēng | 785 |
| | | | | | | | | 扛 | | 3 | káng | 290 |
| **R33** 土 | 土 | | | tǔ | 15 | | | 扩 | 擴 | 3 | kuò | 291 |
| | 圣 | 聖 | 2 | shèng | 142 | | | 扣 | | 3 | kòu | 401 |
| | 去 | | 2 | qù | 157 | | | 扫 | 掃 | 3 | sǎo | 402 |
| | 在 | | 3 | zài | 188 | | | 扫 | 掃 | 3 | sào | 402 |
| | 考 | | 3 | kǎo | 530 | | | 托 | | 3 | tuō | 563 |
| | 地 | | 3 | de | 772 | | | 执 | 執 | 3 | zhí | 564 |
| | 地 | | 3 | dì | 772 | | | 扬 | 揚 | 3 | yáng | 1004 |
| | 场 | 場 | 3 | chǎng | 773 | | | 拨 | 撥 | 3 | bō | 1015 |
| | 坏 | 壞 | 4 | huài | 280 | | | 扯 | | 4 | chě | 403 |
| | 坟 | 墳 | 4 | fén | 281 | | | 扶 | | 4 | fú | 404 |
| | 坐 | | 4 | zuò | 318 | | | 抄 | | 4 | chāo | 405 |
| | 坚 | 堅 | 4 | jiān | 381 | | | 抓 | | 4 | zhuā | 406 |
| | 块 | 塊 | 4 | kuài | 400 | | | 抖 | | 4 | dǒu | 407 |
| | 均 | | 4 | jūn | 558 | | | 折 | | 4 | shē | 408 |
| | 坑 | | 4 | kēng | 774 | | | 折 | | 4 | zhē | 408 |
| | 幸 | | 5 | xìng | 373 | | | 折 | | 4 | zhé | 408 |
| | 坪 | | 5 | píng | 398 | | | 扭 | | 4 | niǔ | 565 |
| | 垃 | | 5 | lā | 399 | | | 扳 | | 4 | bān | 566 |
| | 坡 | | 5 | pō | 775 | | | 找 | | 4 | zhǎo | 567 |
| | 型 | | 6 | xíng | 723 | | | 技 | | 4 | jì | 568 |
| | 垮 | | 6 | kuǎ | 1224 | | | 护 | 護 | 4 | hù | 569 |
| | 城 | | 6 | chéng | 1225 | | | 拟 | 擬 | 4 | nǐ | 575 |
| | 埋 | | 7 | mái | 1002 | | | 扮 | | 4 | bàn | 786 |
| | 埋 | | 7 | mán | 1002 | | | 批 | | 4 | pī | 1005 |
| | 基 | | 8 | jī | 991 | | | 把 | | 4 | bǎ | 1006 |
| | 堆 | | 8 | duī | 1003 | | | 抑 | | 4 | yì | 1007 |
| | 堵 | | 8 | dǔ | 1226 | | | 投 | | 4 | tóu | 1008 |
| | 堂 | | 8 | táng | 1486 | | | 抗 | | 4 | kàng | 1009 |
| | 塔 | | 9 | tǎ | 1394 | | | 报 | 報 | 4 | bào | 1010 |
| | 墓 | | 10 | mù | 1545 | | | 抢 | 搶 | 4 | qiǎng | 1230 |
| | 填 | | 10 | tián | 1550 | | | 抛 | | 4 | pāo | 1395 |
| | 塞 | | 10 | sāi | 1620 | | | 抨 | | 5 | pēng | 570 |
| | 塞 | | 10 | sài | 1620 | | | 抹 | | 5 | mā | 571 |
| | 塑 | | 10 | sù | 1815 | | | 抹 | | 5 | mǒ | 571 |
| | 塌 | | 10 | tā | 1903 | | | 拆 | | 5 | chāi | 572 |
| | 墙 | 墻 | 11 | qiáng | 1770 | | | 拉 | | 5 | lā | 573 |
| | 境 | | 11 | jìng | 1848 | | | 拌 | | 5 | bàn | 574 |
| | 墨 | | 12 | mò | 1843 | | | | | | | |

| SIMP CHAR | TRAD CHAR | STROKE COUNT | PINYIN | CHAR NO |
|---|---|---|---|---|
| **R35** 扌 | | | | |
| (continued) 拦 | 攔 | 5 | lán | 576 |
| 押 | | 5 | yā | 787 |
| 抽 | | 5 | chōu | 788 |
| 担 | 擔 | 5 | dān | 789 |
| 拍 | | 5 | pāi | 790 |
| 拔 | | 5 | bá | 791 |
| 择 | 擇 | 5 | zé | 792 |
| 披 | | 5 | pī | 1011 |
| 抬 | | 5 | tái | 1012 |
| 拙 | | 5 | zhuō | 1013 |
| 拥 | 擁 | 5 | yōng | 1014 |
| 拘 | | 5 | jū | 1231 |
| 招 | | 5 | zhāo | 1232 |
| 拣 | 揀 | 5 | jiǎn | 1233 |
| 拖 | | 5 | tuō | 1396 |
| 拱 | | 6 | gǒng | 793 |
| 拼 | | 6 | pīn | 794 |
| 挤 | 擠 | 6 | jǐ | 795 |
| 挂 | 掛 | 6 | guà | 796 |
| 括 | | 6 | kuò | 1016 |
| 拾 | | 6 | shí | 1017 |
| 挡 | 擋 | 6 | dǎng | 1018 |
| 持 | | 6 | chí | 1019 |
| 按 | | 6 | àn | 1234 |
| 挑 | | 6 | tiāo | 1235 |
| 挑 | | 6 | tiǎo | 1235 |
| 挥 | 揮 | 6 | huī | 1236 |
| 指 | | 6 | zhǐ | 1397 |
| 挣 | | 6 | zhēng | 1398 |
| 挣 | | 6 | zhèng | 1398 |
| 挖 | | 6 | wā | 1551 |
| 挨 | | 7 | āi | 1237 |
| 挨 | | 7 | ái | 1237 |
| 振 | | 7 | zhèn | 1238 |
| 捉 | | 7 | zhuō | 1239 |
| 捂 | | 7 | wǔ | 1399 |
| 捕 | | 7 | bǔ | 1400 |
| 损 | 損 | 7 | sǔn | 1401 |
| 换 | | 7 | huàn | 1402 |
| 挺 | | 7 | tǐng | 1408 |
| 捐 | | 7 | juān | 1552 |
| 挪 | | 7 | nuó | 1658 |
| 挽 | | 7 | wǎn | 1659 |
| 捌 | | 7 | bā | 1660 |
| 捧 | | 8 | pěng | 1240 |
| 排 | | 8 | pái | 1241 |
| 推 | | 8 | tuī | 1242 |
| 掉 | | 8 | diào | 1403 |
| 探 | | 8 | tàn | 1404 |
| 接 | | 8 | jiē | 1405 |
| 控 | | 8 | kòng | 1406 |
| 描 | | 8 | miáo | 1407 |
| 据 | 據 | 8 | jù | 1553 |
| 掏 | | 8 | tāo | 1661 |

| SIMP CHAR | TRAD CHAR | STROKE COUNT | PINYIN | CHAR NO |
|---|---|---|---|---|
| 揉 | | 8 | róu | 1771 |
| 提 | | 9 | tí | 1554 |
| 插 | | 9 | chā | 1555 |
| 援 | | 9 | yuán | 1556 |
| 搂 | 摟 | 9 | lǒu | 1557 |
| 搽 | | 9 | chá | 1558 |
| 握 | | 9 | wò | 1662 |
| 搅 | 攪 | 9 | jiǎo | 1850 |
| 揭 | | 9 | jiē | 1851 |
| 搜 | | 10 | sōu | 1663 |
| 摇 | | 10 | yáo | 1664 |
| 摸 | | 10 | mō | 1665 |
| 摄 | 攝 | 10 | shè | 1772 |
| 摆 | 擺 襬 | 10 | bǎi | 1773 |
| 搞 | | 10 | gǎo | 1904 |
| 携 | 攜 | 10 | xié | 1905 |
| 搬 | | 10 | bān | 1943 |
| 摔 | | 11 | shuāi | 1852 |
| 摘 | | 11 | zhāi | 1906 |
| 撕 | | 12 | sī | 1774 |
| 撞 | | 12 | zhuàng | 1853 |
| 撒 | | 12 | sā | 1907 |
| 撒 | | 12 | sǎ | 1907 |
| 撤 | | 12 | chè | 1942 |
| 操 | | 13 | cāo | 1965 |
| 擦 | | 13 | cā | 1985 |
| **R36** 艹 艺 | 藝 | 1 | yì | 274 |
| 艾 | | 2 | ài | 100 |
| 节 | 節 | 2 | jié | 275 |
| 芬 | | 4 | fēn | 548 |
| 花 | | 4 | huā | 549 |
| 芳 | | 4 | fāng | 550 |
| 芽 | | 4 | yá | 551 |
| 苏 | 蘇 | 4 | sū | 552 |
| 芭 | | 4 | bā | 765 |
| 苍 | 蒼 | 4 | cāng | 996 |
| 苹 | 蘋 | 5 | píng | 395 |
| 苗 | | 5 | miáo | 553 |
| 若 | | 5 | ruò | 554 |
| 苦 | | 5 | kǔ | 555 |
| 英 | | 5 | yīng | 556 |
| 茂 | | 5 | mào | 557 |
| 茫 | | 6 | máng | 766 |
| 茶 | | 6 | chá | 767 |
| 草 | | 6 | cǎo | 768 |
| 荣 | 榮 | 6 | róng | 769 |
| 荧 | 熒 | 6 | yíng | 770 |
| 荐 | 薦 | 6 | jiàn | 997 |
| 荤 | 葷 | 6 | hūn | 998 |
| 荒 | | 6 | huāng | 1222 |
| 药 | 藥 | 6 | yào | 1392 |
| 莫 | | 7 | mò | 999 |
| 获 | 獲 | 7 | huò | 1000 |

| SIMP CHAR | TRAD CHAR | STROKE COUNT | PINYIN | CHAR NO |
|---|---|---|---|---|
| 菜 | | 7 | cài | 1001 |
| 著 | | 8 | zhù | 1223 |
| 菠 | | 8 | bō | 1393 |
| 营 | 營 | 8 | yíng | 1546 |
| 落 | | 9 | là | 1547 |
| 落 | | 9 | lào | 1547 |
| 落 | | 9 | luò | 1547 |
| 葬 | | 9 | zàng | 1656 |
| 葡 | | 9 | pú | 1766 |
| 蓝 | 藍 | 10 | lán | 1548 |
| 蒙 | 矇 | 10 | mēng | 1654 |
| 蒙 | 矇濛懞 | 10 | méng | 1654 |
| 蒙 | | 10 | měng | 1654 |
| 蒜 | | 10 | suàn | 1655 |
| 蔬 | | 12 | shū | 1940 |
| 薪 | | 13 | xīn | 1847 |
| 薄 | | 13 | báo | 1902 |
| 薄 | | 13 | bó | 1902 |
| 薄 | | 13 | bò | 1902 |
| 藏 | | 16 | cáng | 1978 |
| 藏 | | 16 | zàng | 1978 |
| **R37 寸** | | | | |
| 寸 | | | cùn | 37 |
| 寻 | 尋 | 3 | xún | 358 |
| 导 | 導 | 3 | dǎo | 751 |
| 寿 | 壽 | 4 | shòu | 440 |
| 耐 | | 5 | nài | 1210 |
| 封 | | 6 | fēng | 815 |
| 将 | 將 | 6 | jiāng | 1161 |
| 将 | 將 | 6 | jiàng | 1161 |
| 射 | | 7 | shè | 1467 |
| 尊 | | 9 | zūn | 1722 |
| **R38 廾** | | | | |
| 异 | | 3 | yì | 539 |
| 弄 | | 4 | lòng | 251 |
| 弄 | | 4 | nòng | 251 |
| **R39 大** | | | | |
| 大 | | | dà | 20 |
| 天 | | 1 | tiān | 25 |
| 太 | | 1 | tài | 53 |
| 夫 | | 1 | fū | 55 |
| 失 | | 2 | shī | 106 |
| 头 | 頭 | 2 | tóu | 128 |
| 央 | | 2 | yāng | 196 |
| 夹 | 夾 | 3 | jiā | 197 |
| 夹 | 夾 | 3 | jiá | 197 |
| 夺 | 奪 | 3 | duó | 308 |
| 夸 | 誇 | 3 | kuā | 605 |
| 奔 | | 5 | bēn | 432 |
| 奈 | | 5 | nài | 606 |
| 奋 | 奮 | 5 | fèn | 607 |
| 奏 | | 6 | zòu | 608 |
| 奇 | | 5 | jī | 854 |

| SIMP CHAR | TRAD CHAR | STROKE COUNT | PINYIN | CHAR NO |
|---|---|---|---|---|
| 奇 | | 5 | qí | 854 |
| 奖 | 獎 | 6 | jiǎng | 927 |
| 契 | | 6 | qì | 992 |
| 套 | | 7 | tào | 1064 |
| 奥 | | 9 | ào | 1435 |
| **R40 尢** | | | | |
| 尤 | | 1 | yóu | 199 |
| 龙 | 龍 | 2 | lóng | 315 |
| 就 | | 9 | jiù | 1836 |
| **R41 小** | | | | |
| 小 | | | xiǎo | 61 |
| 少 | | 1 | shǎo | 62 |
| 少 | | 1 | shào | 62 |
| 尖 | | 3 | jiān | 203 |
| 尘 | 塵 | 3 | chén | 204 |
| 当 | 當 | 3 | dāng | 335 |
| 当 | 當 | 3 | dàng | 335 |
| 肖 | | 4 | xiào | 675 |
| 尚 | | 5 | shàng | 1156 |
| 尝 | 嘗 | 6 | cháng | 1157 |
| **R42 口** | | | | |
| 口 | | | kǒu | 42 |
| 古 | | 2 | gǔ | 154 |
| 只 | 隻 | 2 | zhī | 160 |
| 只 | 祇 | 2 | zhǐ | 160 |
| 叶 | 葉 | 2 | yè | 167 |
| 可 | | 2 | kě | 243 |
| 叫 | | 2 | jiào | 283 |
| 叮 | | 2 | dīng | 284 |
| 叹 | 嘆 | 2 | tàn | 285 |
| 台 | 臺檯颱 | 2 | tái | 301 |
| 司 | | 2 | sī | 357 |
| 召 | | 2 | zhào | 361 |
| 另 | | 2 | lìng | 385 |
| 叩 | | 2 | kòu | 413 |
| 句 | | 2 | jù | 424 |
| 号 | 號 | 2 | háo | 545 |
| 号 | 號 | 2 | hào | 545 |
| 吉 | | 3 | jí | 259 |
| 吐 | | 3 | tǔ | 286 |
| 吓 | 嚇 | 3 | hè | 287 |
| 吓 | 嚇 | 3 | xià | 287 |
| 合 | | 3 | hé | 296 |
| 后 | 後 | 3 | hòu | 310 |
| 名 | | 3 | míng | 426 |
| 吊 | | 3 | diào | 547 |
| 向 | | 3 | xiàng | 603 |
| 吸 | | 3 | xī | 776 |
| 吃 | | 3 | chī | 783 |
| 吗 | 嗎 | 3 | má | 1020 |
| 吗 | 嗎 | 3 | ma | 1020 |
| 否 | | 4 | fǒu | 362 |
| 呆 | | 4 | dāi | 384 |
| 听 | 聽 | 4 | tīng | 414 |

| SIMP CHAR | TRAD CHAR | STROKE COUNT | PINYIN | CHAR NO | | SIMP CHAR | TRAD CHAR | STROKE COUNT | PINYIN | CHAR NO |
|---|---|---|---|---|---|---|---|---|---|---|
| **R42 口** (continued) 吵 | | 4 | chǎo | 415 | | 嗓 | | 10 | sǎng | 1855 |
| 吞 | | 4 | tūn | 427 | | 嘴 | | 13 | zuǐ | 1984 |
| 告 | | 4 | gào | 428 | | 器 | | 17 | qì | 1963 |
| 吝 | | 4 | lìn | 479 | | 嚷 | | 17 | rǎng | 1993 |
| 君 | | 4 | jūn | 512 | | 嚼 | | 17 | jiáo | 1999 |
| 员 | 員 | 4 | yuán | 546 | | 嚼 | | 17 | jué | 1999 |
| 吹 | | 4 | chuī | 559 | | | | | | |
| 呕 | 嘔 | 4 | ǒu | 560 | | **R43 囗** 囚 | | 2 | qiú | 161 |
| 味 | | 4 | wèi | 561 | | 四 | | 2 | sì | 271 |
| 含 | | 4 | hán | 592 | | 因 | | 3 | yīn | 270 |
| 启 | 啓 | 4 | qǐ | 657 | | 回 | | 3 | huí | 391 |
| 吻 | | 4 | wěn | 777 | | 团 | 團 糰 | 3 | tuán | 392 |
| 呀 | | 4 | yā | 778 | | 困 | 睏 | 4 | kùn | 393 |
| 呀 | | 4 | ya | 778 | | 围 | 圍 | 4 | wéi | 762 |
| 吧 | | 4 | bā | 1021 | | 园 | 園 | 4 | yuán | 763 |
| 吧 | | 4 | ba | 1021 | | 国 | 國 | 5 | guó | 542 |
| 吨 | 噸 | 4 | dūn | 1022 | | 固 | | 5 | gù | 760 |
| 吼 | | 4 | hǒu | 1228 | | 图 | 圖 | 5 | tú | 761 |
| 哎 | | 5 | āi | 562 | | 圆 | 圓 | 7 | yuán | 1391 |
| 呼 | | 5 | hū | 779 | | 圈 | | 8 | juān | 1765 |
| 呢 | | 5 | ne | 1227 | | 圈 | | 8 | juàn | 1765 |
| 呢 | | 5 | ní | 1227 | | 圈 | | 8 | quān | 1765 |
| 咖 | | 5 | kā | 1229 | | | | | | |
| 咒 | | 5 | zhòu | 1387 | | **R44 巾** 巾 | | | jīn | 87 |
| 咬 | | 6 | yǎo | 780 | | 币 | 幣 | 1 | bì | 181 |
| 哄 | | 6 | hōng | 781 | | 帅 | 帥 | 2 | shuài | 276 |
| 哄 | | 6 | hǒng | 781 | | 布 | | 2 | bù | 309 |
| 哄 | | 6 | hòng | 781 | | 市 | | 2 | shì | 332 |
| 哑 | 啞 | 6 | yǎ | 782 | | 师 | 師 | 3 | shī | 396 |
| 哇 | | 6 | wā | 784 | | 帆 | | 3 | fān | 1034 |
| 咱 | | 6 | zán | 1023 | | 希 | | 4 | xī | 613 |
| 咽 | | 6 | yān | 1024 | | 带 | 帶 | 6 | dài | 1213 |
| 咽 | | 6 | yàn | 1024 | | 帝 | | 6 | dì | 1312 |
| 哈 | | 6 | hā | 1025 | | 帮 | 幫 | 6 | bāng | 1583 |
| 品 | | 6 | pǐn | 1220 | | 常 | | 8 | cháng | 1733 |
| 响 | 響 | 6 | xiǎng | 1409 | | 幅 | | 8 | fú | 1777 |
| 哲 | | 7 | zhé | 1219 | | 帽 | | 9 | mào | 1778 |
| 哨 | | 7 | shào | 1410 | | 幕 | | 10 | mù | 1767 |
| 哼 | | 7 | hēng | 1561 | | | | | | |
| 哪 | | 7 | nǎ | 1666 | | **R45 山** 山 | | | shān | 38 |
| 售 | | 8 | shòu | 1266 | | 岁 | 歲 | 3 | suì | 380 |
| 啥 | | 8 | shá | 1411 | | 岗 | 崗 | 4 | gǎng | 745 |
| 啤 | | 8 | pí | 1412 | | 岔 | | 4 | chà | 829 |
| 啃 | | 8 | kěn | 1559 | | 岛 | 島 | 4 | dǎo | 1434 |
| 唱 | | 8 | chàng | 1562 | | 岸 | | 5 | àn | 537 |
| 商 | | 8 | shāng | 1612 | | 岩 | | 5 | yán | 746 |
| 喜 | | 9 | xǐ | 1531 | | 岭 | 嶺 | 5 | lǐng | 806 |
| 喉 | | 9 | hóu | 1560 | | 峡 | 峽 | 6 | xiá | 807 |
| 喷 | 噴 | 9 | pēn | 1563 | | 崭 | 嶄 | 8 | zhǎn | 1383 |
| 喂 | | 9 | wèi | 1667 | | | | | | |
| 喊 | | 9 | hǎn | 1668 | | **R46 彳** 行 | | 3 | háng | 327 |
| 喘 | | 9 | chuǎn | 1764 | | 行 | | 3 | xíng | 327 |
| 喝 | | 9 | hē | 1854 | | 彻 | 徹 | 4 | chè | 871 |
| 喝 | | 9 | hè | 1854 | | 往 | | 5 | wǎng | 461 |

| | SIMP CHAR | TRAD CHAR | STROKE COUNT | PINYIN | CHAR NO |
|---|---|---|---|---|---|
| | 征 | 徵 | 5 | zhēng | 462 |
| | 径 | 徑 | 5 | jìng | 626 |
| | 待 | | 6 | dài | 872 |
| | 很 | | 6 | hěn | 1090 |
| | 徒 | | 7 | tú | 873 |
| | 得 | | 8 | dé | 1442 |
| | 得 | | 8 | de | 1442 |
| | 得 | | 8 | děi | 1442 |
| | 街 | | 9 | jiē | 1441 |
| | 微 | | 11 | wēi | 1700 |
| | 德 | 德 | 12 | dé | 1923 |
| **R47** 彡 | 形 | | 4 | xíng | 257 |
| | 彩 | | 8 | cǎi | 1132 |
| | 影 | | 12 | yǐng | 1918 |
| **R48** 犭 | 犯 | | 2 | fàn | 884 |
| | 狂 | | 4 | kuáng | 469 |
| | 犹 | 猶 | 4 | yóu | 886 |
| | 狐 | | 5 | hú | 885 |
| | 狗 | | 5 | gǒu | 1287 |
| | 独 | 獨 | 6 | dú | 1095 |
| | 狠 | | 6 | hěn | 1284 |
| | 狮 | 獅 | 6 | shī | 1285 |
| | 狱 | 獄 | 6 | yù | 1286 |
| | 狼 | | 7 | láng | 1443 |
| | 猎 | 獵 | 8 | liè | 1444 |
| | 猪 | | 8 | zhū | 1445 |
| | 猫 | | 8 | māo | 1446 |
| | 猜 | | 8 | cāi | 1594 |
| | 猛 | | 8 | měng | 1704 |
| | 猴 | | 9 | hóu | 1595 |
| **R49** 夕 | 夕 | | | xī | 49 |
| | 外 | | 2 | wài | 218 |
| | 多 | | 2 | duō | 431 |
| | 夜 | | 5 | yè | 654 |
| | 梦 | 夢 | 8 | mèng | 1217 |
| | 够 | 夠 | 8 | gòu | 1808 |
| **R50** 夂 | 冬 | 鼕 | 2 | dōng | 178 |
| | 处 | 處 | 2 | chǔ | 217 |
| | 处 | 處 | 2 | chù | 217 |
| | 务 | 務 | 2 | wù | 429 |
| | 各 | | 3 | gè | 425 |
| | 条 | 條 | 4 | tiáo | 598 |
| | 备 | 備 | 5 | bèi | 845 |
| | 复 | 復 複 | 6 | fù | 1059 |
| | 夏 | | 7 | xià | 1195 |
| **R51** 饣 (飠) | 饥 | 飢 | 2 | jī | 890 |
| | 饭 | 飯 | 4 | fàn | 891 |
| | 饮 | 飲 | 4 | yǐn | 892 |
| | 饲 | 飼 | 5 | sì | 1447 |

| | SIMP CHAR | TRAD CHAR | STROKE COUNT | PINYIN | CHAR NO |
|---|---|---|---|---|---|
| | 饱 | 飽 | 5 | bǎo | 1703 |
| | 饺 | 餃 | 6 | jiǎo | 1115 |
| | 饼 | 餅 | 6 | bǐng | 1116 |
| | 饿 | 餓 | 7 | è | 1593 |
| | 馋 | 饞 | 9 | chán | 1924 |
| | 馒 | 饅 | 11 | mán | 1948 |
| **R52** 广 | 广 | 廣 | | guǎng | 23 |
| | 庄 | 莊 | 3 | zhuāng | 229 |
| | 庆 | 慶 | 3 | qìng | 230 |
| | 床 | | 4 | chuáng | 333 |
| | 应 | 應 | 4 | yīng | 334 |
| | 应 | 應 | 4 | yìng | 334 |
| | 库 | 庫 | 4 | kù | 482 |
| | 序 | | 4 | xù | 915 |
| | 店 | | 5 | diàn | 658 |
| | 庙 | 廟 | 5 | miào | 659 |
| | 府 | | 5 | fǔ | 660 |
| | 底 | | 5 | dǐ | 916 |
| | 庞 | 龐 | 5 | páng | 917 |
| | 废 | 廢 | 5 | fèi | 918 |
| | 度 | | 6 | dù | 919 |
| | 庭 | | 6 | tíng | 1326 |
| | 座 | | 7 | zuò | 920 |
| | 唐 | | 7 | táng | 1324 |
| | 席 | | 7 | xí | 1325 |
| | 麻 | | 8 | má | 1146 |
| | 鹿 | | 8 | lù | 1724 |
| | 廉 | | 10 | lián | 1615 |
| | 腐 | | 11 | fǔ | 1879 |
| | 鹰 | 鷹 | 15 | yīng | 1990 |
| **R53** 门 (門) | 门 | 門 | | mén | 130 |
| | 闪 | 閃 | 2 | shǎn | 337 |
| | 闭 | 閉 | 3 | bì | 677 |
| | 问 | 問 | 3 | wèn | 678 |
| | 闲 | 閑 | 4 | xián | 679 |
| | 间 | 間 | 4 | jiān | 914 |
| | 间 | 間 | 4 | jiàn | 914 |
| | 闷 | 悶 | 4 | mēn | 1150 |
| | 闷 | 悶 | 4 | mèn | 1150 |
| | 闻 | 聞 | 6 | wén | 1151 |
| | 闹 | 鬧 | 6 | nào | 1323 |
| | 阅 | 閱 | 7 | yuè | 1727 |
| | 阔 | 闊 | 9 | kuò | 1728 |
| **R54** 氵 | 汁 | | 2 | zhī | 131 |
| | 汇 | 匯彙 | 2 | huì | 234 |
| | 汉 | 漢 | 2 | hàn | 235 |
| | 汗 | | 3 | hàn | 236 |
| | 江 | | 3 | jiāng | 237 |
| | 污 | | 3 | wū | 681 |
| | 汤 | 湯 | 3 | tāng | 932 |
| | 池 | | 3 | chí | 939 |

| SIMP CHAR | TRAD CHAR | STROKE COUNT | PINYIN | CHAR NO | | SIMP CHAR | TRAD CHAR | STROKE COUNT | PINYIN | CHAR NO |
|---|---|---|---|---|---|---|---|---|---|---|
| **R54 氵** (continued) | | | | | | 淹 | | 8 | yān | 1629 |
| 沙 | | 4 | shā | 342 | | 涨 | 漲 | 8 | zhǎng | 1738 |
| 泛 | | 4 | fàn | 495 | | 涨 | 漲 | 8 | zhàng | 1738 |
| 汽 | | 4 | qì | 682 | | 混 | | 8 | hún | 1739 |
| 沟 | 溝 | 4 | gōu | 933 | | 混 | | 8 | hùn | 1739 |
| 没 | | 4 | méi | 938 | | 渡 | | 9 | dù | 1497 |
| 没 | | 4 | mò | 938 | | 湿 | 淫 | 9 | shī | 1498 |
| 沉 | | 4 | chén | 1166 | | 温 | | 9 | wēn | 1627 |
| 注 | | 5 | zhù | 496 | | 港 | | 9 | gǎng | 1740 |
| 油 | | 5 | yóu | 683 | | 湖 | | 9 | hú | 1741 |
| 沾 | | 5 | zhān | 684 | | 游 | | 9 | yóu | 1818 |
| 泄 | | 5 | xiè | 685 | | 渴 | | 9 | kě | 1822 |
| 法 | | 5 | fǎ | 686 | | 源 | | 10 | yuán | 1742 |
| 泪 | | 5 | lèi | 688 | | 溪 | | 10 | xī | 1743 |
| 浅 | 淺 | 5 | qiǎn | 692 | | 溶 | | 10 | róng | 1744 |
| 河 | | 5 | hé | 934 | | 满 | 滿 | 10 | mǎn | 1745 |
| 治 | | 5 | zhì | 935 | | 滚 | | 10 | gǔn | 1819 |
| 波 | | 5 | bō | 936 | | 溜 | | 10 | liū | 1883 |
| 泼 | 潑 | 5 | pō | 937 | | 滑 | | 10 | huá | 1884 |
| 泥 | | 5 | ní | 1164 | | 漆 | | 11 | qī | 1746 |
| 沿 | | 5 | yán | 1165 | | 漂 | | 11 | piāo | 1820 |
| 泡 | | 5 | pāo | 1492 | | 漂 | | 11 | piǎo | 1820 |
| 泡 | | 5 | pào | 1492 | | 漂 | | 11 | piào | 1820 |
| 洼 | 窪 | 6 | wā | 687 | | 演 | | 11 | yǎn | 1821 |
| 洋 | | 6 | yáng | 689 | | 漱 | | 11 | shù | 1823 |
| 洪 | | 6 | hóng | 690 | | 滴 | | 11 | dī | 1885 |
| 洲 | | 6 | zhōu | 691 | | 漏 | | 11 | lòu | 1886 |
| 洁 | 潔 | 6 | jié | 940 | | 漫 | | 11 | màn | 1887 |
| 活 | | 6 | huó | 941 | | 潮 | | 12 | cháo | 1930 |
| 洽 | | 6 | qià | 942 | | 澡 | | 12 | zǎo | 1954 |
| 浊 | 濁 | 6 | zhuó | 943 | | 激 | | 13 | jī | 1955 |
| 派 | | 6 | pài | 945 | | 瀑 | | 15 | pù | 1974 |
| 洒 | 灑 | 6 | sǎ | 1163 | | | | | | |
| 洗 | | 6 | xǐ | 1167 | | **R55 忄** (忄) | 忙 | 3 | máng | 343 |
| 洞 | | 6 | dòng | 1338 | | | 怀 | 懷 | 4 | huái | 344 |
| 浇 | 澆 | 6 | jiāo | 1340 | | 快 | | 4 | kuài | 497 |
| 涉 | | 7 | shè | 944 | | 忧 | 憂 | 4 | yōu | 693 |
| 浓 | 濃 | 7 | nóng | 1168 | | 性 | | 5 | xìng | 498 |
| 浩 | | 7 | hào | 1169 | | 怕 | | 5 | pà | 694 |
| 浴 | | 7 | yù | 1170 | | 怜 | 憐 | 5 | lián | 695 |
| 涂 | 塗 | 7 | tú | 1171 | | 怪 | | 5 | guài | 696 |
| 浪 | | 7 | làng | 1341 | | 怯 | | 5 | qiè | 697 |
| 浮 | | 7 | fú | 1342 | | 恢 | | 6 | huī | 698 |
| 消 | | 7 | xiāo | 1343 | | 恰 | | 6 | qià | 930 |
| 流 | | 7 | liú | 1493 | | 恼 | 惱 | 6 | nǎo | 931 |
| 海 | | 7 | hǎi | 1494 | | 恨 | | 6 | hèn | 1174 |
| 淋 | | 8 | lín | 1172 | | 悄 | | 7 | qiǎo | 1348 |
| 淡 | | 8 | dàn | 1173 | | 悼 | | 8 | dào | 1349 |
| 液 | | 8 | yè | 1344 | | 惜 | | 8 | xī | 1350 |
| 深 | | 8 | shēn | 1345 | | 惧 | 懼 | 8 | jù | 1351 |
| 添 | | 8 | tiān | 1346 | | 惭 | 慚 | 8 | cán | 1352 |
| 渐 | 漸 | 8 | jiàn | 1347 | | 悔 | | 8 | huǐ | 1488 |
| 清 | | 8 | qīng | 1495 | | 惊 | 驚 | 8 | jīng | 1489 |
| 渔 | 漁 | 8 | yú | 1496 | | 情 | | 8 | qíng | 1491 |
| 淘 | | 8 | táo | 1628 | | | | | | |

| SIMP CHAR | TRAD CHAR | STROKE COUNT | PINYIN | CHAR NO |
|---|---|---|---|---|
| 愤 | 憤 | 9 | fèn | 1490 |
| 惯 | 慣 | 9 | guàn | 1630 |
| 愣 | | 9 | lèng | 1735 |
| 慌 | | 9 | huāng | 1736 |
| 愉 | | 9 | yú | 1737 |
| 慢 | | 11 | màn | 1882 |
| 懂 | | 12 | dǒng | 1817 |
| 憎 | | 12 | zēng | 1881 |
| 懒 | 懶 | 13 | lǎn | 1953 |

**R56 宀**

| SIMP CHAR | TRAD CHAR | STROKE COUNT | PINYIN | CHAR NO |
|---|---|---|---|---|
| 宁 | 寧 | 2 | níng | 336 |
| 宁 | 寧 | 2 | nìng | 336 |
| 它 | | 2 | tā | 484 |
| 宇 | | 3 | yǔ | 485 |
| 守 | | 3 | shǒu | 486 |
| 安 | | 3 | ān | 487 |
| 字 | | 3 | zì | 664 |
| 宅 | | 3 | zhái | 665 |
| 牢 | | 4 | láo | 488 |
| 完 | | 4 | wán | 909 |
| 宗 | | 4 | zōng | 910 |
| 定 | | 5 | dìng | 666 |
| 宝 | 寶 | 5 | bǎo | 667 |
| 实 | 實 | 5 | shí | 668 |
| 审 | 審 | 5 | shěn | 911 |
| 官 | | 5 | guān | 1136 |
| 宠 | 寵 | 5 | chǒng | 1137 |
| 宣 | | 6 | xuān | 1138 |
| 室 | | 6 | shì | 1139 |
| 客 | | 6 | kè | 1316 |
| 宪 | 憲 | 6 | xiàn | 1317 |
| 宫 | 宮 | 6 | gōng | 1318 |
| 宰 | | 7 | zǎi | 1140 |
| 宾 | 賓 | 7 | bīn | 1141 |
| 家 | 傢 | 7 | jiā | 1315 |
| 害 | | 7 | hài | 1319 |
| 案 | | 7 | àn | 1321 |
| 宴 | | 7 | yàn | 1479 |
| 宽 | 寬 | 7 | kuān | 1618 |
| 宿 | | 8 | sù | 1480 |
| 宿 | | 8 | xiǔ | 1480 |
| 宿 | | 8 | xiù | 1480 |
| 寄 | | 8 | jì | 1619 |
| 密 | | 8 | mì | 1730 |
| 寒 | | 9 | hán | 1481 |
| 富 | | 9 | fù | 1731 |
| 寝 | 寢 | 10 | qǐn | 1878 |
| 察 | | 11 | chá | 1877 |

**R57 辶**

| SIMP CHAR | TRAD CHAR | STROKE COUNT | PINYIN | CHAR NO |
|---|---|---|---|---|
| 边 | 邊 | 2 | biān | 710 |
| 辽 | 遼 | 2 | liáo | 711 |
| 达 | 達 | 3 | dá | 505 |
| 迁 | 遷 | 3 | qiān | 506 |
| 过 | 過 | 3 | guò | 712 |

| SIMP CHAR | TRAD CHAR | STROKE COUNT | PINYIN | CHAR NO |
|---|---|---|---|---|
| 迅 | | 3 | xùn | 954 |
| 迈 | 邁 | 3 | mài | 955 |
| 进 | 進 | 4 | jìn | 713 |
| 还 | 還 | 4 | hái | 714 |
| 还 | 還 | 4 | huán | 714 |
| 这 | 這 | 4 | zhè | 715 |
| 这 | 這 | 4 | zhèi | 715 |
| 近 | | 4 | jìn | 716 |
| 运 | 運 | 4 | yùn | 956 |
| 返 | | 4 | fǎn | 957 |
| 连 | 連 | 4 | lián | 958 |
| 迟 | 遲 | 4 | chí | 959 |
| 远 | 遠 | 4 | yuǎn | 1184 |
| 违 | 違 | 4 | wéi | 1185 |
| 迎 | | 4 | yíng | 1360 |
| 迫 | | 5 | pò | 1186 |
| 迷 | | 6 | mí | 1187 |
| 送 | | 6 | sòng | 1188 |
| 适 | 適 | 6 | shì | 1358 |
| 逆 | | 6 | nì | 1359 |
| 追 | | 6 | zhuī | 1507 |
| 退 | | 6 | tuì | 1508 |
| 逃 | | 6 | táo | 1509 |
| 选 | 選 | 6 | xuǎn | 1510 |
| 途 | | 7 | tú | 1511 |
| 逗 | | 7 | dòu | 1512 |
| 逛 | | 7 | guàng | 1513 |
| 速 | | 7 | sù | 1514 |
| 造 | | 7 | zào | 1515 |
| 通 | | 7 | tōng | 1757 |
| 透 | | 7 | tòu | 1826 |
| 递 | 遞 | 7 | dì | 1827 |
| 逻 | 邏 | 8 | luó | 1755 |
| 道 | | 9 | dào | 1756 |
| 逼 | | 9 | bī | 1828 |
| 遗 | 遺 | 9 | yí | 1829 |
| 遇 | | 9 | yù | 1891 |
| 遍 | | 9 | biàn | 1892 |
| 遥 | | 10 | yáo | 1830 |
| 遮 | | 11 | zhē | 1831 |
| 遭 | | 11 | zāo | 1931 |
| 遵 | | 12 | zūn | 1975 |
| 避 | | 13 | bì | 1976 |
| 邀 | | 13 | yāo | 1983 |

**R58 彐 (彑)**

| SIMP CHAR | TRAD CHAR | STROKE COUNT | PINYIN | CHAR NO |
|---|---|---|---|---|
| 录 | 錄 | 5 | lù | 722 |

**R59 尸**

| SIMP CHAR | TRAD CHAR | STROKE COUNT | PINYIN | CHAR NO |
|---|---|---|---|---|
| 尸 | 屍 | | shī | 58 |
| 尺 | | 1 | chǐ | 118 |
| 尼 | | 2 | ní | 441 |
| 尽 | 儘 | 3 | jǐn | 312 |
| 尽 | 盡 | 3 | jìn | 312 |
| 层 | 層 | 4 | céng | 610 |

| SIMP CHAR | TRAD CHAR | STROKE COUNT | PINYIN | CHAR NO |
|---|---|---|---|---|
| **R59 尸** (continued) 尾 | 尾 | 4 | wěi | 848 |
| 尿 | | 4 | niào | 849 |
| 局 | | 4 | jú | 1069 |
| 屁 | | 4 | pì | 1070 |
| 居 | | 5 | jū | 850 |
| 届 | | 5 | jiè | 851 |
| 屈 | | 5 | qū | 1071 |
| 屎 | | 6 | shǐ | 852 |
| 屋 | | 6 | wū | 1072 |
| 展 | | 7 | zhǎn | 1274 |
| 属 | 屬 | 8 | shǔ | 1793 |
| **R60 己** 己 | | | jǐ | 132 |
| 已 | | | yǐ | 133 |
| **R61 弓** 弓 | | | gōng | 250 |
| 引 | | 1 | yǐn | 371 |
| 弟 | | 4 | dì | 1152 |
| 张 | 張 | 5 | zhāng | 1208 |
| 弯 | 彎 | 6 | wān | 1472 |
| 弱 | | 7 | ruò | 1897 |
| 弹 | 彈 | 8 | dàn | 1763 |
| 弹 | 彈 | 8 | tán | 1763 |
| 强 | | 8 | jiàng | 1896 |
| 强 | | 8 | qiáng | 1896 |
| 强 | | 8 | qiǎng | 1896 |
| **R62 子** (孑) 子 | | | zǐ | 83 |
| 孔 | | 1 | kǒng | 370 |
| 孕 | | 2 | yùn | 971 |
| 存 | | 3 | cún | 438 |
| 孙 | 孫 | 3 | sūn | 519 |
| 孝 | | 4 | xiào | 529 |
| 孤 | | 5 | gū | 978 |
| 学 | 學 | 5 | xué | 1155 |
| 孩 | | 6 | hái | 1202 |
| **R63 女** 女 | | | nǚ | 57 |
| 奴 | | 2 | nú | 328 |
| 奶 | | 2 | nǎi | 878 |
| 妨 | | 2 | fáng | 879 |
| 奸 | | 3 | jiān | 329 |
| 如 | | 3 | rú | 464 |
| 妇 | 婦 | 3 | fù | 465 |
| 好 | | 3 | hǎo | 627 |
| 好 | | 3 | hào | 627 |
| 她 | | 3 | tā | 1091 |
| 妈 | 媽 | 3 | mā | 1092 |
| 妥 | | 4 | tuǒ | 433 |
| 妖 | | 4 | yāo | 466 |
| 妙 | | 4 | miào | 467 |
| 妒 | | 4 | dù | 628 |
| 妓 | | 4 | jì | 629 |
| 姐 | | 4 | niǔ | 630 |
| 姐 | | 4 | jiě | 880 |
| 委 | | 5 | wěi | 594 |
| 妹 | | 5 | mèi | 631 |
| 姓 | | 5 | xìng | 632 |
| 妻 | | 5 | qī | 742 |
| 姑 | | 5 | gū | 881 |
| 娃 | | 6 | wá | 877 |
| 娇 | 嬌 | 6 | jiāo | 882 |
| 要 | | 6 | yāo | 969 |
| 要 | | 6 | yào | 969 |
| 姻 | | 6 | yīn | 1093 |
| 姨 | | 6 | yí | 1596 |
| 娘 | | 7 | niáng | 1448 |
| 婴 | 嬰 | 8 | yīng | 1539 |
| 婆 | | 8 | pó | 1623 |
| 婚 | | 8 | hūn | 1701 |
| 媒 | | 9 | méi | 1449 |
| 嫌 | | 10 | xián | 1702 |
| 嫂 | | 10 | sǎo | 1798 |
| 嫁 | | 10 | jià | 1799 |
| 嫩 | | 11 | nèn | 1800 |
| **R64 马** (馬) 马 | 馬 | | mǎ | 247 |
| 驳 | 駁 | 4 | bó | 983 |
| 驻 | 駐 | 5 | zhù | 1207 |
| 驾 | 駕 | 5 | jià | 1693 |
| 骄 | 驕 | 6 | jiāo | 1376 |
| 验 | 驗 | 7 | yàn | 1529 |
| 骂 | 罵 | 6 | mà | 1652 |
| 骑 | 騎 | 8 | qí | 1840 |
| 骗 | 騙 | 9 | piàn | 1937 |
| **R65 纟** (糹) 纠 | 糾 | 2 | jiū | 473 |
| 红 | 紅 | 3 | hóng | 474 |
| 约 | 約 | 3 | yuē | 876 |
| 级 | 級 | 3 | jí | 1100 |
| 纪 | 紀 | 3 | jì | 1101 |
| 纱 | 紗 | 4 | shā | 639 |
| 纹 | 紋 | 4 | wén | 640 |
| 纷 | 紛 | 4 | fēn | 1102 |
| 纸 | 紙 | 4 | zhǐ | 1103 |
| 纺 | 紡 | 4 | fǎng | 1104 |
| 纯 | 純 | 4 | chún | 1290 |
| 绊 | 絆 | 5 | bàn | 887 |
| 线 | 綫 | 5 | xiàn | 1105 |
| 组 | 組 | 5 | zǔ | 1106 |
| 细 | 細 | 5 | xì | 1107 |
| 织 | 織 | 5 | zhī | 1108 |
| 终 | 終 | 5 | zhōng | 1109 |
| 经 | 經 | 5 | jīng | 1110 |
| 练 | 練 | 5 | liàn | 1453 |
| 结 | 結 | 6 | jiē | 1291 |
| 结 | 結 | 6 | jié | 1291 |
| 给 | 給 | 6 | gěi | 1292 |

| SIMP CHAR | TRAD CHAR | STROKE COUNT | PINYIN | CHAR NO |
|---|---|---|---|---|
| 给 | 給 | 6 | jǐ | 1292 |
| 绑 | 綁 | 6 | bǎng | 1454 |
| 统 | 統 | 6 | tǒng | 1601 |
| 绝 | 絕 | 6 | jué | 1706 |
| 绣 | 綉 | 7 | xiù | 1801 |
| 维 | 維 | 8 | wéi | 1455 |
| 绿 |  | 8 | lǜ | 1707 |
| 绳 | 繩 | 8 | shéng | 1865 |
| 缓 | 緩 | 9 | huǎn | 1708 |
| 编 | 編 | 9 | biān | 1866 |
| 缩 | 縮 | 11 | suō | 1927 |

**R66 幺**

| SIMP CHAR | TRAD CHAR | STROKE COUNT | PINYIN | CHAR NO |
|---|---|---|---|---|
| 幻 |  | 1 | huàn | 475 |
| 幼 |  | 2 | yòu | 638 |
| 幽 |  | 6 | yōu | 1538 |

**R67 王**

| SIMP CHAR | TRAD CHAR | STROKE COUNT | PINYIN | CHAR NO |
|---|---|---|---|---|
| 王 |  |  | wáng | 27 |
| 玉 |  | 1 | yù | 77 |
| 环 | 環 | 4 | huán | 369 |
| 现 | 現 | 4 | xiàn | 975 |
| 玩 |  | 4 | wán | 727 |
| 珍 |  | 5 | zhēn | 515 |
| 玲 |  | 5 | líng | 728 |
| 玻 |  | 5 | bō | 976 |
| 珠 |  | 6 | zhū | 729 |
| 班 |  | 6 | bān | 730 |
| 球 |  | 6 | qiú | 1199 |
| 理 |  | 7 | lǐ | 1200 |
| 琴 |  | 8 | qín | 1372 |

**R68 木**

| SIMP CHAR | TRAD CHAR | STROKE COUNT | PINYIN | CHAR NO |
|---|---|---|---|---|
| 木 |  |  | mù | 40 |
| 未 |  | 1 | wèi | 88 |
| 末 |  | 1 | mò | 89 |
| 本 |  | 1 | běn | 90 |
| 术 | 術 | 1 | shù | 91 |
| 朱 |  | 2 | zhū | 184 |
| 权 | 權 | 2 | quán | 292 |
| 杀 | 殺 | 2 | shā | 317 |
| 机 | 機 | 2 | jī | 577 |
| 朽 |  | 2 | xiǔ | 578 |
| 杂 | 雜 | 2 | zá | 856 |
| 杠 | 槓 | 3 | gàng | 293 |
| 束 |  | 3 | shù | 372 |
| 材 |  | 3 | cái | 409 |
| 村 |  | 3 | cūn | 410 |
| 极 | 極 | 3 | jí | 798 |
| 杨 | 楊 | 3 | yáng | 1027 |
| 杯 |  | 4 | bēi | 411 |
| 林 |  | 4 | lín | 412 |
| 果 |  | 4 | guǒ | 544 |
| 松 | 鬆 | 4 | sōng | 579 |
| 板 | 闆 | 4 | bǎn | 580 |
| 枝 |  | 4 | zhī | 581 |
| 构 | 構 | 4 | gòu | 1028 |

| SIMP CHAR | TRAD CHAR | STROKE COUNT | PINYIN | CHAR NO |
|---|---|---|---|---|
| 枪 | 槍 | 4 | qiāng | 1244 |
| 某 |  | 5 | mǒu | 536 |
| 柑 |  | 5 | gān | 582 |
| 柱 |  | 5 | zhù | 583 |
| 栏 | 欄 | 5 | lán | 584 |
| 查 |  | 5 | chá | 741 |
| 枯 |  | 5 | kū | 799 |
| 柜 | 櫃 | 5 | guì | 800 |
| 标 | 標 | 5 | biāo | 801 |
| 桌 |  | 5 | zhuō | 984 |
| 柠 | 檸 | 5 | níng | 1029 |
| 栋 | 棟 | 5 | dòng | 1030 |
| 树 | 樹 | 5 | shù | 1031 |
| 柒 |  | 5 | qī | 1162 |
| 柔 |  | 5 | róu | 1198 |
| 架 |  | 5 | jià | 1270 |
| 染 |  | 5 | rǎn | 1336 |
| 桂 |  | 6 | guì | 797 |
| 校 |  | 6 | jiào | 802 |
| 校 |  | 6 | xiào | 802 |
| 样 | 樣 | 6 | yàng | 803 |
| 桥 | 橋 | 6 | qiáo | 804 |
| 核 |  | 6 | hé | 1026 |
| 档 | 檔 | 6 | dàng | 1032 |
| 桃 |  | 6 | táo | 1243 |
| 根 |  | 6 | gēn | 1245 |
| 格 |  | 6 | gé | 1246 |
| 检 | 檢 | 7 | jiǎn | 1033 |
| 梨 |  | 7 | lí | 1271 |
| 梅 |  | 7 | méi | 1413 |
| 桶 |  | 7 | tǒng | 1564 |
| 梳 |  | 7 | shū | 1565 |
| 梯 |  | 7 | tī | 1669 |
| 棒 |  | 8 | bàng | 1247 |
| 棋 |  | 8 | qí | 1248 |
| 集 |  | 8 | jí | 1267 |
| 棵 |  | 8 | kē | 1414 |
| 植 |  | 8 | zhí | 1415 |
| 椅 |  | 8 | yǐ | 1566 |
| 棉 |  | 8 | mián | 1670 |
| 棺 |  | 8 | guān | 1671 |
| 棍 |  | 8 | gùn | 1776 |
| 楼 | 樓 | 9 | lóu | 1567 |
| 概 |  | 9 | gài | 1908 |
| 榨 |  | 10 | zhà | 1672 |
| 模 |  | 10 | mó | 1673 |
| 模 |  | 10 | mú | 1673 |
| 横 |  | 11 | héng | 1775 |
| 横 |  | 11 | hèng | 1775 |
| 橱 |  | 12 | chú | 1909 |

**R69 犬**

| SIMP CHAR | TRAD CHAR | STROKE COUNT | PINYIN | CHAR NO |
|---|---|---|---|---|
| 犬 |  |  | quǎn | 54 |
| 状 | 狀 | 3 | zhuàng | 345 |
| 哭 |  | 6 | kū | 1221 |

| SIMP CHAR | TRAD CHAR | STROKE COUNT | PINYIN | CHAR NO |
|---|---|---|---|---|
| **R70 歹** 歹 | | | dǎi | 74 |
| 残 | 殘 | 5 | cán | 977 |
| **R71 车 (車)** 车 | 車 | | chē | 114 |
| 车 | 車 | | jū | 114 |
| 轨 | 軌 | 2 | guǐ | 888 |
| 软 | 軟 | 4 | ruǎn | 889 |
| 轰 | 轟 | 4 | hōng | 1065 |
| 转 | 轉 | 4 | zhuǎn | 1111 |
| 转 | 轉 | 4 | zhuàn | 1111 |
| 轮 | 輪 | 4 | lún | 1112 |
| 轻 | 輕 | 5 | qīng | 1113 |
| 较 | 較 | 6 | jiào | 1114 |
| 辆 | 輛 | 7 | liàng | 1602 |
| 辈 | 輩 | 8 | bèi | 1382 |
| 输 | 輸 | 9 | shū | 1867 |
| **R72 戈** 戏 | 戲 | 2 | xì | 365 |
| 成 | | 2 | chéng | 611 |
| 式 | | 3 | shì | 316 |
| 戒 | | 3 | jiè | 442 |
| 我 | | 3 | wǒ | 615 |
| 或 | | 4 | huò | 857 |
| 战 | 戰 | 5 | zhàn | 1044 |
| 咸 | 鹹 | 5 | xián | 1073 |
| 载 | 載 | 5 | zǎi | 1218 |
| 载 | 載 | 5 | zài | 1218 |
| 栽 | | 6 | zāi | 995 |
| 截 | | 10 | jié | 1650 |
| 戴 | | 13 | dài | 1941 |
| **R73 比** 比 | | | bǐ | 279 |
| **R74 瓦** 瓦 | | | wǎ | 356 |
| 瓶 | | 6 | píng | 1635 |
| 瓷 | | 6 | cí | 1723 |
| **R75 止** 止 | | | zhǐ | 41 |
| 步 | | 3 | bù | 266 |
| 此 | | 3 | cǐ | 416 |
| 武 | | 4 | wǔ | 513 |
| 歧 | | 4 | qí | 585 |
| **R76 支** 敲 | | 10 | qiāo | 1959 |
| **R77 日** 日 | | | rì | 96 |
| 旧 | 舊 | 1 | jiù | 165 |
| 早 | | 2 | zǎo | 268 |
| 旨 | | 2 | zhǐ | 535 |
| 旬 | | 2 | xún | 596 |
| 旱 | | 3 | hàn | 387 |
| 时 | 時 | 3 | shí | 586 |
| 者 | | 4 | zhě | 531 |
| 昔 | | 4 | xī | 534 |

| SIMP CHAR | TRAD CHAR | STROKE COUNT | PINYIN | CHAR NO |
|---|---|---|---|---|
| 旺 | | 4 | wàng | 587 |
| 昌 | | 4 | chāng | 752 |
| 明 | | 4 | míng | 1035 |
| 昏 | | 4 | hūn | 1058 |
| 星 | | 5 | xīng | 753 |
| 是 | | 5 | shì | 754 |
| 显 | 顯 | 5 | xiǎn | 755 |
| 昨 | | 5 | zuó | 810 |
| 春 | | 5 | chūn | 855 |
| 映 | | 5 | yìng | 1036 |
| 晃 | | 6 | huǎng | 1384 |
| 晃 | | 6 | huàng | 1384 |
| 晕 | 暈 | 6 | yūn | 1385 |
| 晕 | 暈 | 6 | yùn | 1385 |
| 晚 | | 7 | wǎn | 1779 |
| 替 | | 8 | tì | 1430 |
| 普 | | 8 | pǔ | 1484 |
| 暂 | 暫 | 8 | zàn | 1522 |
| 暑 | | 8 | shǔ | 1540 |
| 最 | | 8 | zuì | 1541 |
| 智 | | 8 | zhì | 1581 |
| 曾 | | 8 | céng | 1625 |
| 曾 | | 8 | zēng | 1625 |
| 晴 | | 8 | qíng | 1674 |
| 暗 | | 8 | àn | 1676 |
| 暖 | | 9 | nuǎn | 1675 |
| 暴 | | 9 | bào | 1844 |
| **R78 曰** 曲 | | 2 | qū | 272 |
| 曲 | 麯 | 2 | qū | 272 |
| 冒 | | 5 | mào | 989 |
| **R79 贝 (貝)** 贝 | 貝 | | bèi | 97 |
| 负 | 負 | 2 | fù | 435 |
| 贡 | 貢 | 3 | gòng | 360 |
| 财 | 財 | 3 | cái | 588 |
| 责 | 責 | 4 | zé | 525 |
| 败 | 敗 | 4 | bài | 589 |
| 质 | 質 | 4 | zhì | 597 |
| 贤 | 賢 | 4 | xián | 750 |
| 贩 | 販 | 4 | fàn | 813 |
| 贬 | 貶 | 4 | biǎn | 814 |
| 贪 | 貪 | 4 | tān | 827 |
| 货 | 貨 | 4 | huò | 1061 |
| 购 | 購 | 4 | gòu | 1253 |
| 赔 | 賠 | 4 | péi | 1569 |
| 贵 | 貴 | 5 | guì | 985 |
| 贱 | 賤 | 5 | jiàn | 1037 |
| 贴 | 貼 | 5 | tiē | 1038 |
| 贷 | 貸 | 5 | dài | 1062 |
| 贰 | 貳 | 5 | èr | 1074 |
| 贸 | 貿 | 5 | mào | 1429 |
| 费 | 費 | 5 | fèi | 1520 |
| 账 | 賬 | 6 | zhàng | 812 |

| SIMP CHAR | TRAD CHAR | STROKE COUNT | PINYIN | CHAR NO | | SIMP CHAR | TRAD CHAR | STROKE COUNT | PINYIN | CHAR NO |
|---|---|---|---|---|---|---|---|---|---|---|
| 赃 | 臟 | 6 | zāng | 1039 | | 教 | | 7 | jiào | 1424 |
| 贫 | 貧 | 6 | pín | 1052 | | 敏 | | 7 | mǐn | 1610 |
| 贼 | 賊 | 6 | zéi | 1254 | | 敢 | | 8 | gǎn | 1209 |
| 资 | 資 | 6 | zī | 1335 | | 散 | | 8 | sǎn | 1579 |
| 贿 | 賄 | 6 | huì | 1419 | | 散 | | 8 | sàn | 1579 |
| 赚 | 賺 | 9 | zhuàn | 1781 | | 敬 | | 8 | jìng | 1689 |
| 赛 | 賽 | 10 | sài | 1813 | | 数 | 數 | 9 | shǔ | 1637 |
| 赠 | 贈 | 12 | zèng | 1944 | | 数 | 數 | 9 | shù | 1637 |
| 赞 | 贊 | 12 | zàn | 1969 | | 整 | | 12 | zhěng | 1845 |
| 赢 | 贏 | 13 | yíng | 2000 | | **R87 片** | 片 | | piān | 119 |
| **R80 水** | | | shuǐ | 159 | | | 片 | | piàn | 119 |
| 水 | | | | | | 版 | | 4 | bǎn | 897 |
| 泰 | | 5 | tài | 1066 | | 牌 | | 8 | pái | 1597 |
| 泉 | | 5 | quán | 1275 | | **R88 斤** | 斤 | | jīn | 50 |
| **R81 见** | 见 | 見 | jiàn | 267 | | 所 | | 4 | suǒ | 645 |
| **(見)** | 观 | 觀 | 3 | guān | 726 | | 斩 | 斬 | 4 | zhǎn | 646 |
| | 规 | 規 | 4 | guī | 1098 | | 断 | 斷 | 7 | duàn | 1260 |
| | 视 | 視 | 4 | shì | 1362 | | 新 | | 9 | xīn | 1638 |
| | 觉 | 覺 | 5 | jiào | 1485 | | **R89 爪** | 爪 | | zhǎo | 52 |
| | 觉 | 覺 | 5 | jué | 1485 | | **(⺥)** | 爪 | | zhuǎ | 52 |
| **R82 牛** | 牛 | | niú | 51 | | 采 | | 4 | cǎi | 434 |
| **(⺧)** | 牧 | | 4 | mù | 468 | | 受 | | 4 | shòu | 844 |
| | 牲 | | 5 | shēng | 633 | | 爬 | | 4 | pá | 1099 |
| | 牵 | 牽 | 5 | qiān | 853 | | 爱 | 愛 | 6 | ài | 1264 |
| | 物 | | 4 | wù | 883 | | 乳 | | 4 | rǔ | 1308 |
| | 特 | | 6 | tè | 1094 | | **R90 父** | 父 | | fù | 56 |
| | 牺 | 犧 | 6 | xī | 1283 | | 爷 | 爺 | 2 | yé | 445 |
| **R83 手** | 手 | | shǒu | 104 | | 爸 | | 4 | bà | 1077 |
| | 拳 | | 6 | quán | 1158 | | 爹 | | 6 | diē | 1276 |
| | 拿 | | 6 | ná | 1262 | | **R91 月** | 月 | | yuè | 190 |
| | 掌 | | 8 | zhǎng | 1734 | | 有 | | 2 | yǒu | 439 |
| **R84 毛** | 毛 | | máo | 183 | | 肋 | | 2 | lèi | 898 |
| | 毯 | | 8 | tǎn | 1603 | | 肌 | | 2 | jī | 1118 |
| | 毫 | | 7 | háo | 1721 | | 肚 | | 3 | dù | 648 |
| **R85 气** | 气 | 氣 | | qì | 185 | | 肛 | | 3 | gāng | 649 |
| | 氧 | | 6 | yǎng | 1269 | | 肝 | | 3 | gān | 650 |
| **R86 攵** | 收 | | 2 | shōu | 282 | | 肯 | | 4 | kěn | 744 |
| | 攻 | | 3 | gōng | 253 | | 肤 | 膚 | 4 | fū | 899 |
| | 改 | | 3 | gǎi | 516 | | 肿 | 腫 | 4 | zhǒng | 1119 |
| | 放 | | 4 | fàng | 964 | | 胀 | 脹 | 4 | zhàng | 1120 |
| | 政 | | 5 | zhèng | 517 | | 育 | | 4 | yù | 1133 |
| | 故 | | 5 | gù | 816 | | 肩 | | 4 | jiān | 1144 |
| | 效 | | 6 | xiào | 965 | | 朋 | | 4 | péng | 1298 |
| | 致 | 緻 | 6 | zhì | 982 | | 股 | | 4 | gǔ | 1456 |
| | 敌 | 敵 | 6 | dí | 1127 | | 服 | | 4 | fú | 1457 |
| | 救 | | 7 | jiù | 1259 | | 肠 | 腸 | 4 | cháng | 1458 |
| | 教 | | 7 | jiāo | 1424 | | 肥 | | 4 | féi | 1459 |
| | | | | | | 胖 | | 5 | pàng | 1121 |
| | | | | | | 胜 | 勝 | 5 | shèng | 1122 |

| SIMP CHAR | TRAD CHAR | STROKE COUNT | PINYIN | CHAR NO |
|---|---|---|---|---|
| **R91 月** (continued) | | | | |
| 胃 | | 5 | wèi | 1216 |
| 胡 | 鬍 | 5 | hú | 1256 |
| 肺 | | 5 | fèi | 1294 |
| 胆 | 膽 | 5 | dǎn | 1295 |
| 背 | | 5 | bēi | 1380 |
| 背 | | 5 | bèi | 1380 |
| 胶 | 膠 | 6 | jiāo | 1296 |
| 脏 | 髒 | 6 | zāng | 1297 |
| 脏 | 臟 | 6 | zàng | 1297 |
| 脑 | 腦 | 6 | nǎo | 1460 |
| 脉 | | 6 | mài | 1604 |
| 脓 | 膿 | 6 | nóng | 1605 |
| 胸 | | 6 | xiōng | 1709 |
| 脂 | | 6 | zhī | 1710 |
| 能 | | 6 | néng | 1873 |
| 脸 | 臉 | 7 | liǎn | 1461 |
| 望 | | 7 | wàng | 1622 |
| 脖 | | 7 | bó | 1802 |
| 脱 | | 7 | tuō | 1803 |
| 脚 | | 7 | jiǎo | 1804 |
| 期 | | 8 | qī | 1574 |
| 朝 | | 8 | cháo | 1686 |
| 朝 | | 8 | zhāo | 1686 |
| 脾 | | 8 | pí | 1711 |
| 腰 | | 9 | yāo | 1868 |
| 腹 | | 9 | fù | 1869 |
| 腻 | 膩 | 9 | nì | 1870 |
| 腿 | | 9 | tuǐ | 1949 |
| **R92 欠** | | | | |
| 欠 | | | qiàn | 105 |
| 次 | | 2 | cì | 341 |
| 欢 | 歡 | 2 | huān | 366 |
| 欣 | | 4 | xīn | 634 |
| 欧 | 歐 | 4 | ōu | 811 |
| 欲 | | 7 | yù | 1466 |
| 欺 | | 8 | qī | 1423 |
| 款 | | 8 | kuǎn | 1573 |
| 歌 | | 10 | gē | 1900 |
| **R93 风 (風)** | | | | |
| 风 | 風 | | fēng | 194 |
| 飘 | 飄 | 11 | piāo | 1939 |
| **R94 殳** | | | | |
| 段 | | 5 | duàn | 1293 |
| 毁 | | 9 | huǐ | 1810 |
| **R95 文** | | | | |
| 文 | | | wén | 70 |
| **R96 方** | | | | |
| 方 | | | fāng | 220 |
| 房 | | 4 | fáng | 1145 |
| 施 | | 5 | shī | 1758 |
| 旁 | | 6 | páng | 1473 |
| 旅 | | 6 | lǚ | 1518 |
| 族 | | 7 | zú | 1519 |
| 旗 | | 10 | qí | 1834 |

| SIMP CHAR | TRAD CHAR | STROKE COUNT | PINYIN | CHAR NO |
|---|---|---|---|---|
| **R97 火** | | | | |
| 火 | | | huǒ | 72 |
| 灭 | 滅 | 1 | miè | 75 |
| 灰 | | 2 | huī | 198 |
| 灯 | 燈 | 2 | dēng | 346 |
| 灵 | 靈 | 3 | líng | 359 |
| 灾 | | 3 | zāi | 483 |
| 炎 | | 4 | yán | 492 |
| 炒 | | 4 | chǎo | 499 |
| 炉 | 爐 | 4 | lú | 699 |
| 炊 | | 4 | chuī | 700 |
| 炖 | 燉 | 4 | dùn | 1175 |
| 炸 | | 5 | zhà | 701 |
| 烂 | 爛 | 5 | làn | 702 |
| 炼 | 煉 | 5 | liàn | 1357 |
| 炮 | | 5 | bāo | 1633 |
| 炮 | | 5 | pào | 1633 |
| 烘 | | 6 | hōng | 953 |
| 烛 | 燭 | 6 | zhú | 1176 |
| 烟 | | 6 | yān | 1177 |
| 烦 | 煩 | 6 | fán | 1178 |
| 烧 | 燒 | 6 | shāo | 1504 |
| 烤 | | 6 | kǎo | 1505 |
| 烫 | 燙 | 7 | tàng | 1624 |
| 煤 | | 9 | méi | 1506 |
| 燃 | | 12 | rán | 1888 |
| 爆 | | 15 | bào | 1982 |
| **R98 斗** | | | | |
| 斗 | 鬥 | | dǒu | 71 |
| 斗 | 鬥 | | dòu | 71 |
| 斜 | | 7 | xié | 1307 |
| **R99 灬** | | | | |
| 杰 | 傑 | 4 | jié | 377 |
| 点 | 點 | 5 | diǎn | 739 |
| 焦 | | 8 | jiāo | 1265 |
| 煮 | | 8 | zhǔ | 1388 |
| 热 | 熱 | 6 | rè | 1390 |
| 然 | | 8 | rán | 1432 |
| 熏 | | 10 | xūn | 1690 |
| 蒸 | | 8 | zhēng | 1768 |
| 照 | | 9 | zhào | 1846 |
| 熟 | | 11 | shóu | 1973 |
| 熟 | | 11 | shú | 1973 |
| **R100 户** | | | | |
| 户 | | 1 | hù | 129 |
| 扇 | | 6 | shān | 1726 |
| 雇 | 僱 | 8 | gù | 1474 |
| 扇 | | 6 | shàn | 1726 |
| **R101 礻** | | | | |
| 礼 | 禮 | 1 | lǐ | 503 |
| 社 | | 3 | shè | 504 |
| 祈 | | 4 | qí | 717 |
| 祖 | | 5 | zǔ | 1190 |
| 神 | | 5 | shén | 1191 |
| 祝 | | 5 | zhù | 1516 |

| | SIMP CHAR | TRAD CHAR | STROKE COUNT | PINYIN | CHAR NO |
|---|---|---|---|---|---|
| | 祸 | 禍 | 7 | huò | 1754 |
| | 福 | | 9 | fú | 1825 |
| **R102** 心 | 心 | | | xīn | 232 |
| | 必 | | 1 | bì | 338 |
| | 志 | | 3 | zhì | 528 |
| | 忘 | | 3 | wàng | 655 |
| | 忍 | | 3 | rěn | 970 |
| | 忌 | | 3 | jì | 1197 |
| | 忠 | | 4 | zhōng | 743 |
| | 态 | 態 | 4 | tài | 828 |
| | 念 | | 4 | niàn | 1054 |
| | 忽 | | 4 | hū | 1268 |
| | 怎 | | 5 | zěn | 830 |
| | 思 | | 5 | sī | 1214 |
| | 总 | 總 | 5 | zǒng | 1330 |
| | 急 | | 5 | jí | 1426 |
| | 怒 | | 5 | nù | 1427 |
| | 怨 | | 5 | yuàn | 1792 |
| | 恶 | 惡 | 6 | è | 1196 |
| | 恶 | 惡 | 6 | wù | 1196 |
| | 恋 | 戀 | 6 | liàn | 1314 |
| | 恩 | | 6 | ēn | 1381 |
| | 恐 | | 6 | kǒng | 1644 |
| | 患 | | 7 | huàn | 1649 |
| | 您 | | 7 | nǐn | 1692 |
| | 悲 | | 8 | bēi | 1532 |
| | 惹 | | 8 | rě | 1657 |
| | 愁 | | 9 | chóu | 1691 |
| | 想 | | 9 | xiǎng | 1769 |
| | 意 | | 9 | yì | 1812 |
| | 感 | | 9 | gǎn | 1860 |
| | 愚 | | 9 | yú | 1901 |
| | 慈 | | 9 | cí | 1952 |
| | 愿 | 願 | 10 | yuàn | 1919 |
| | 慰 | | 11 | wèi | 1968 |
| | 憋 | | 11 | biē | 1972 |
| **R103** 聿 | 肃 | 肅 | 4 | sù | 526 |
| | 肆 | | 7 | sì | 1645 |
| **R104** 示 | 示 | | | shì | 140 |
| | 票 | | 6 | piào | 1367 |
| | 禁 | | 8 | jìn | 1536 |
| **R105** 石 | 石 | | | shí | 144 |
| | 矿 | 礦 | 3 | kuàng | 518 |
| | 砖 | 磚 | 3 | zhuān | 1201 |
| | 砂 | | 4 | shā | 733 |
| | 研 | | 4 | yán | 734 |
| | 砍 | | 4 | kǎn | 979 |
| | 破 | | 5 | pò | 1374 |
| | 硕 | 碩 | 6 | shuò | 1375 |
| | 砸 | | 6 | zá | 1523 |

| | SIMP CHAR | TRAD CHAR | STROKE COUNT | PINYIN | CHAR NO |
|---|---|---|---|---|---|
| | 硬 | | 7 | yìng | 1524 |
| | 确 | 確 | 7 | què | 1762 |
| | 碎 | | 8 | suì | 1525 |
| | 碰 | | 8 | pèng | 1526 |
| | 碗 | | 8 | wǎn | 1961 |
| | 磕 | | 10 | kē | 1894 |
| | 磅 | | 10 | bàng | 1936 |
| **R106** 业 | 业 | 業 | | yè | 94 |
| **R107** 目 | 目 | | | mù | 151 |
| | 盲 | | 3 | máng | 906 |
| | 眨 | | 3 | zhǎ | 1045 |
| | 相 | | 4 | xiāng | 805 |
| | 相 | | 4 | xiàng | 805 |
| | 盾 | | 4 | dùn | 840 |
| | 看 | | 4 | kān | 841 |
| | 看 | | 4 | kàn | 841 |
| | 省 | | 4 | shěng | 860 |
| | 省 | | 4 | xǐng | 860 |
| | 眉 | | 4 | méi | 1067 |
| | 盼 | | 4 | pàn | 1255 |
| | 眼 | | 6 | yǎn | 1570 |
| | 睁 | | 6 | zhēng | 1680 |
| | 睡 | | 8 | shuì | 1571 |
| | 瞎 | | 10 | xiā | 1913 |
| | 瞒 | 瞞 | 10 | mán | 1914 |
| | 瞧 | | 12 | qiáo | 1915 |
| | 瞪 | | 12 | dèng | 1966 |
| **R108** 田 | 田 | | | tián | 147 |
| | 由 | | | yóu | 148 |
| | 甲 | | | jiǎ | 149 |
| | 申 | | | shēn | 150 |
| | 电 | 電 | | diàn | 263 |
| | 男 | | 2 | nán | 757 |
| | 界 | | 4 | jiè | 758 |
| | 畏 | | 4 | wèi | 988 |
| | 留 | | 5 | liú | 1582 |
| **R109** 皿 | 盆 | | 4 | pén | 1261 |
| | 盐 | 鹽 | 5 | yán | 993 |
| | 监 | 監 | 5 | jiān | 994 |
| | 益 | | 5 | yì | 1153 |
| | 盒 | | 6 | hé | 1425 |
| | 盗 | | 6 | dào | 1475 |
| | 盛 | | 6 | chéng | 1694 |
| | 盛 | | 6 | shèng | 1694 |
| **R110** 罒 | 罗 | 羅 | 3 | luó | 756 |
| | 罚 | 罰 | 4 | fá | 1386 |
| | 罢 | 罷 | 5 | bà | 1215 |
| | 罪 | | 8 | zuì | 1542 |
| | 置 | | 8 | zhì | 1651 |

| SIMP CHAR | TRAD CHAR | STROKE COUNT | PINYIN | CHAR NO |
|---|---|---|---|---|
| **R111 钅**(金) | | | | |
| 针 | 針 | 2 | zhēn | 477 |
| 钉 | 釘 | 2 | dīng | 651 |
| 钉 | 釘 | 2 | dìng | 651 |
| 钓 | 釣 | 3 | diào | 1124 |
| 钞 | 鈔 | 4 | chāo | 900 |
| 钟 | 鍾 | 4 | zhōng | 1125 |
| 钢 | 鋼 | 4 | gāng | 1299 |
| 钥 | 鑰 | 4 | yào | 1300 |
| 钥 | 鑰 | 4 | yuè | 1300 |
| 钙 | 鈣 | 4 | gài | 1462 |
| 钩 | 鉤 | 4 | gōu | 1463 |
| 铁 | 鐵 | 5 | tiě | 1126 |
| 钱 | 錢 | 5 | qián | 1301 |
| 钻 | 鑽 | 5 | zuān | 1302 |
| 钻 | 鑽 | 5 | zuàn | 1302 |
| 铃 | 鈴 | 5 | líng | 1303 |
| 铅 | 鉛 | 5 | qiān | 1464 |
| 铲 | 鏟 | 6 | chǎn | 1304 |
| 银 | 銀 | 6 | yín | 1607 |
| 铜 | 銅 | 6 | tóng | 1712 |
| 铸 | 鑄 | 6 | kào | 1716 |
| 锁 | 鎖 | 7 | suǒ | 1608 |
| 铺 | 鋪 | 7 | pū | 1713 |
| 铺 | 鋪 | 7 | pù | 1713 |
| 销 | 銷 | 7 | xiāo | 1714 |
| 锅 | 鍋 | 7 | guō | 1807 |
| 锈 | 銹 | 7 | xiù | 1871 |
| 错 | 錯 | 8 | cuò | 1715 |
| 键 | 鍵 | 9 | jiàn | 1926 |
| 镇 | 鎮 | 10 | zhèn | 1872 |
| 镜 | 鏡 | 11 | jìng | 1970 |
| **R112 矢** | | | | |
| 知 | | 3 | zhī | 647 |
| 短 | | 7 | duǎn | 1452 |
| 矮 | | 8 | ǎi | 1598 |
| 疑 | | 9 | yí | 1917 |
| **R113 禾** | | | | |
| 禾 | | | hé | 108 |
| 私 | | 2 | sī | 471 |
| 秃 | | 2 | tū | 833 |
| 秀 | | 2 | xiù | 1055 |
| 和 | | 3 | hé | 644 |
| 和 | | 3 | huó | 644 |
| 季 | | 3 | jì | 835 |
| 秋 | 鞦 | 4 | qiū | 641 |
| 科 | | 4 | kē | 642 |
| 秒 | | 4 | miǎo | 643 |
| 种 | 種 | 4 | zhǒng | 893 |
| 种 | 種 | 4 | zhòng | 893 |
| 香 | | 5 | xiāng | 834 |
| 秤 | | 5 | chéng | 894 |
| 秩 | | 5 | zhì | 895 |
| 租 | | 5 | zū | 1096 |
| 积 | 積 | 5 | jī | 1097 |

| SIMP CHAR | TRAD CHAR | STROKE COUNT | PINYIN | CHAR NO |
|---|---|---|---|---|
| 称 | 稱 | 5 | chèn | 1288 |
| 称 | 稱 | 5 | chēng | 1288 |
| 称 | 稱 | 5 | chèng | 1288 |
| 秘 | | 5 | mì | 1289 |
| 移 | | 6 | yí | 1450 |
| 程 | | 7 | chéng | 1451 |
| 稀 | | 7 | xī | 1599 |
| 稍 | | 7 | shāo | 1600 |
| 税 | | 7 | shuì | 1705 |
| 稳 | 穩 | 10 | wěn | 1925 |
| **R114 白** | | | | |
| 白 | | | bái | 176 |
| 百 | | 1 | bǎi | 242 |
| 的 | | 3 | de | 1117 |
| 的 | | 3 | dí | 1117 |
| 皇 | | 4 | huáng | 858 |
| **R115 瓜** | | | | |
| 瓜 | | | guā | 189 |
| **R116 鸟** | | | | |
| 鸟 | 鳥 | | niǎo | 859 |
| 鸡 | 鷄 | 2 | jī | 1373 |
| 鸭 | 鴨 | 5 | yā | 1782 |
| 鹅 | 鵝 | 7 | é | 1950 |
| **R117 疒** | | | | |
| 疗 | 療 | 2 | liáo | 661 |
| 疟 | 瘧 | 3 | nüè | 662 |
| 疯 | 瘋 | 4 | fēng | 1147 |
| 疹 | | 5 | zhěn | 921 |
| 疾 | | 5 | jí | 922 |
| 症 | 癥 | 5 | zhēng | 923 |
| 症 | 癥 | 5 | zhèng | 923 |
| 疼 | | 5 | téng | 1148 |
| 病 | | 5 | bìng | 1327 |
| 疲 | | 5 | pí | 1328 |
| 痒 | 癢 | 6 | yǎng | 1149 |
| 痘 | | 7 | dòu | 1477 |
| 痛 | | 7 | tòng | 1725 |
| 痴 | | 8 | chī | 1617 |
| 瘦 | | 10 | shòu | 1880 |
| 瘤 | | 10 | liú | 1951 |
| 癌 | | 12 | ái | 1981 |
| **R118 立** | | | | |
| 立 | | | lì | 125 |
| 竖 | 豎 | 4 | shù | 749 |
| 亲 | 親 | 4 | qīn | 908 |
| 站 | | 5 | zhàn | 1189 |
| 竞 | 競 | 5 | jìng | 1470 |
| 竟 | | 5 | jìng | 1616 |
| 章 | | 6 | zhāng | 1311 |
| 童 | | 7 | tóng | 1471 |
| 端 | | 9 | duān | 1889 |
| **R119 穴** | | | | |
| 穴 | | | xué | 231 |
| 穷 | 窮 | 2 | qióng | 912 |

| SIMP CHAR | TRAD CHAR | STROKE COUNT | PINYIN | CHAR NO | | SIMP CHAR | TRAD CHAR | STROKE COUNT | PINYIN | CHAR NO |
|---|---|---|---|---|---|---|---|---|---|---|
| 究 | | 2 | jiū | 1142 | | 须 | 須 | 3 | xū | 875 |
| 空 | | 3 | kōng | 669 | | 顽 | 頑 | 4 | wán | 1204 |
| 空 | | 3 | kòng | 669 | | 顿 | 頓 | 4 | dùn | 1420 |
| 突 | | 4 | tū | 913 | | 预 | 預 | 4 | yù | 1528 |
| 穿 | | 4 | chuān | 1322 | | 顾 | 顧 | 4 | gù | 1609 |
| 窃 | 竊 | 4 | qiè | 1482 | | 领 | 領 | 5 | lǐng | 1465 |
| 窄 | | 5 | zhǎi | 1143 | | 颜 | 顏 | 9 | yán | 1835 |
| 容 | | 5 | róng | 1320 | | 题 | 題 | 9 | tí | 1858 |
| 窍 | 竅 | 5 | qiào | 1621 | | 额 | 額 | 9 | é | 1958 |
| 窗 | | 7 | chuāng | 1732 | | 颤 | 顫 | 13 | chàn | 1991 |
| **R120 衤** | | | | | | **R130 虍** | | | | |
| 补 | 補 | 2 | bǔ | 508 | | 虎 | | 2 | hǔ | 1533 |
| 初 | | 2 | chū | 963 | | 虐 | | 4 | nüè | 1379 |
| 衫 | | 3 | shān | 718 | | 虚 | | 5 | xū | 1534 |
| 衬 | 襯 | 3 | chèn | 962 | | **R131 虫** | | | | |
| 袜 | 襪 | 5 | wà | 1193 | | 虫 | 蟲 | | chóng | 262 |
| 袖 | | 5 | xiù | 1361 | | 虽 | 雖 | 2 | suī | 990 |
| 被 | | 5 | bèi | 1517 | | 虹 | | 3 | hóng | 823 |
| 祥 | | 6 | xiáng | 1192 | | 虾 | 蝦 | 3 | xiā | 824 |
| 裤 | 褲 | 7 | kù | 1634 | | 蚁 | 蟻 | 3 | yǐ | 825 |
| 裙 | | 7 | qún | 1752 | | 蚊 | | 4 | wén | 1048 |
| 裸 | | 8 | luǒ | 1753 | | 蛋 | | 5 | dàn | 1368 |
| | | | | | | 蛇 | | 5 | shé | 1681 |
| **R121 皮** 皮 | | | pí | 261 | | 蜂 | | 7 | fēng | 1682 |
| | | | | | | 蜡 | 蠟 | 8 | là | 1780 |
| **R122 矛** 矛 | | | máo | 363 | | 蜜 | | 8 | mì | 1929 |
| | | | | | | 蠢 | | 15 | chǔn | 1995 |
| **R123 母** 母 | | | mǔ | 394 | | **R132 缶** 缺 | | 4 | quē | 1305 |
| 每 | | 2 | měi | 837 | | **R133 舌** 舌 | | | shé | 298 |
| 毒 | | 4 | dú | 1211 | | 乱 | 亂 | 1 | luàn | 901 |
| **R124 耒** 耕 | | 4 | gēng | 817 | | 甜 | | 5 | tián | 1306 |
| | | | | | | 舔 | | 8 | tiǎn | 1806 |
| **R125 老** 老 | | | lǎo | 375 | | | | | | |
| | | | | | | **R134 竹** (⺮) | | | | |
| **R126 耳** 耳 | | | ěr | 145 | | 笑 | | 4 | xiào | 861 |
| 耻 | | 4 | chǐ | 735 | | 笋 | | 4 | sǔn | 1078 |
| 职 | 職 | 5 | zhí | 1205 | | 笔 | 筆 | 4 | bǐ | 1278 |
| 聋 | 聾 | 5 | lóng | 1431 | | 笨 | | 5 | bèn | 1079 |
| 聊 | | 5 | liáo | 1527 | | 符 | | 5 | fú | 1277 |
| 联 | 聯 | 6 | lián | 1206 | | 笛 | | 5 | dí | 1279 |
| 聪 | 聰 | 9 | cōng | 1895 | | 笼 | 籠 | 5 | lóng | 1436 |
| 聚 | | 12 | jù | 1642 | | 笼 | 籠 | 5 | lǒng | 1436 |
| | | | | | | 第 | | 5 | dì | 1695 |
| **R127 臣** 卧 | | 2 | wò | 826 | | 等 | | 6 | děng | 1437 |
| | | | | | | 答 | | 6 | dá | 1438 |
| **R128 西** 西 (襾) | | | xī | 352 | | 筒 | | 6 | tǒng | 1696 |
| | | | | | | 签 | 簽籤 | 7 | qiān | 1439 |
| **R129 页** 页 | 頁 | | yè | 245 | | 筷 | | 7 | kuài | 1585 |
| 顶 | 頂 | 2 | dǐng | 724 | | 简 | 簡 | 7 | jiǎn | 1796 |
| 项 | 項 | 3 | xiàng | 725 | | 算 | | 8 | suàn | 1697 |
| 顺 | 順 | 3 | shùn | 874 | | 管 | | 8 | guǎn | 1861 |
| | | | | | | 箱 | | 9 | xiāng | 1797 |
| | | | | | | 篇 | | 9 | piān | 1921 |

| | SIMP CHAR | TRAD CHAR | STROKE COUNT | PINYIN | CHAR NO |
|---|---|---|---|---|---|
| **R134 竹** (continued) | 箭 | | 9 | jiàn | 1922 |
| | 篮 | 籃 | 10 | lán | 1862 |
| | 簿 | | 13 | bù | 1979 |
| | 籍 | | 14 | jí | 1980 |
| **R135 臼** | 舅 | | 6 | jiù | 1795 |
| **R136 自** | 自 | | | zì | 305 |
| | 臭 | | 4 | chòu | 1076 |
| **R137 血** | 血 | | | xiě | 306 |
| | 血 | | | xuè | 306 |
| **R138 舟** | 舟 | | | zhōu | 436 |
| | 航 | | 4 | háng | 1717 |
| | 般 | | 4 | bān | 1718 |
| | 船 | | 5 | chuán | 1809 |
| **R139 艮** | 既 | | 4 | jì | 1572 |
| **R140 衣** | 衣 | | | yī | 330 |
| | 衰 | | 5 | shuāi | 1313 |
| | 袋 | | 5 | dài | 1428 |
| | 装 | 裝 | 6 | zhuāng | 1476 |
| | 裁 | | 6 | cái | 1535 |
| | 裂 | | 6 | liè | 1643 |
| **R141 羊** (䒑) | 羊 | | | yáng | 227 |
| | 养 | 養 | 3 | yǎng | 670 |
| | 美 | | 3 | měi | 671 |
| | 差 | | 3 | chā | 673 |
| | 差 | | 3 | chà | 673 |
| | 差 | | 3 | chāi | 673 |
| | 姜 | 薑 | 3 | jiāng | 925 |
| | 羞 | | 4 | xiū | 1154 |
| | 盖 | 蓋 | 5 | gài | 1331 |
| | 着 | | 5 | zhāo | 1332 |
| | 善 | | 6 | shàn | 1483 |
| | 群 | 羣 | 7 | qún | 1646 |
| | 着 | | 9 | zháo | 1332 |
| | 着 | | 9 | zhe | 1332 |
| | 着 | | 9 | zhuó | 1332 |
| **R142 米** | 米 | | | mǐ | 226 |
| | 类 | 類 | 3 | lèi | 676 |
| | 料 | | 4 | liào | 961 |
| | 粉 | | 4 | fěn | 1363 |
| | 粗 | | 5 | cū | 1364 |
| | 粘 | | 5 | zhān | 1365 |
| | 粪 | 糞 | 6 | fèn | 1334 |
| | 粥 | | 6 | zhōu | 1962 |
| | 粮 | 糧 | 7 | liáng | 1759 |
| | 精 | | 8 | jīng | 1832 |
| | 糊 | | 9 | hū | 1932 |
| | 糊 | | 9 | hú | 1932 |
| | 糊 | | 9 | hù | 1932 |
| | 糕 | | 10 | gāo | 1833 |
| | 糖 | | 10 | táng | 1933 |
| | 糟 | | 11 | zāo | 1956 |
| **R143 羽** | 羽 | | | yǔ | 732 |
| | 翅 | | 4 | chì | 1679 |
| | 翻 | | 12 | fān | 1989 |
| **R144 糸** | 系 | 繫 | 1 | jì | 842 |
| | 系 | 係繫 | 1 | xì | 842 |
| | 素 | | 4 | sù | 1378 |
| | 紧 | 緊 | 4 | jǐn | 1537 |
| | 累 | | 5 | léi | 1653 |
| | 累 | | 5 | lěi | 1653 |
| | 累 | | 5 | lèi | 1653 |
| | 繁 | | 11 | fán | 1988 |
| **R145 走** | 走 | | | zǒu | 265 |
| | 赶 | 趕 | 3 | gǎn | 822 |
| | 趁 | | 5 | chèn | 1257 |
| | 起 | | 3 | qǐ | 1421 |
| | 越 | | 5 | yuè | 1575 |
| | 超 | | 5 | chāo | 1684 |
| | 趣 | | 8 | qù | 1783 |
| **R146 豆** | 豆 | | | dòu | 353 |
| | 登 | | 5 | dēng | 1521 |
| **R147 酉** | 酒 | | 3 | jiǔ | 1339 |
| | 配 | | 3 | pèi | 1647 |
| | 酬 | | 6 | chóu | 1648 |
| | 酱 | 醬 | 6 | jiàng | 1814 |
| | 酷 | | 7 | kù | 1841 |
| | 酸 | | 7 | suān | 1899 |
| | 醉 | | 8 | zuì | 1842 |
| | 醋 | | 8 | cù | 1898 |
| | 醒 | | 9 | xǐng | 1938 |
| **R148 豕** | 象 | | 5 | xiàng | 1580 |
| | 豪 | | 7 | háo | 1876 |
| **R149 里** | 里 | 裡 | | lǐ | 386 |
| | 重 | | 2 | chóng | 839 |
| | 重 | | 2 | zhòng | 839 |
| | 野 | | 4 | yě | 1685 |
| | 量 | | 5 | liáng | 1544 |
| | 量 | | 5 | liàng | 1544 |
| **R150 足** (⻊) | 足 | | | zú | 383 |
| | 跃 | 躍 | 4 | yuè | 1258 |
| | 跌 | | 5 | diē | 1422 |
| | 距 | | 5 | jù | 1576 |

| SIMP CHAR | TRAD CHAR | STROKE COUNT | PINYIN | CHAR NO |
|---|---|---|---|---|
| 跑 | | 5 | pǎo | 1916 |
| 跟 | | 6 | gēn | 1784 |
| 路 | | 6 | lù | 1785 |
| 跳 | | 6 | tiào | 1786 |
| 跨 | | 6 | kuà | 1857 |
| 跪 | | 6 | guì | 1945 |
| 踩 | | 8 | cǎi | 1787 |
| 踢 | | 8 | tī | 1946 |
| 蹦 | | 11 | bèng | 1994 |
| 蹲 | | 12 | dūn | 1986 |
| 躁 | | 13 | zào | 1992 |
| R151 身  身 | | | shēn | 604 |
| 躲 | | 6 | duǒ | 1874 |
| 躺 | | 8 | tǎng | 1971 |
| R152 谷  谷 | 穀 | | gǔ | 446 |
| R153 角  角 | | | jiǎo | 838 |
| 角 | | | jué | 838 |
| 触 | 觸 | 6 | chù | 1875 |
| 解 | | 6 | jiě | 1928 |
| 解 | | 6 | jiè | 1928 |
| R154 言  言 | | | yán | 478 |
| 警 | | 12 | jǐng | 1987 |
| R155 辛  辛 | | | xīn | 331 |
| 辞 | 辭 | 6 | cí | 1606 |
| 辣 | | 6 | là | 1760 |
| 辨 | 辯 | 10 | biàn | 1957 |
| R156 青  青 | | | qīng | 740 |
| 静 | | 6 | jìng | 1947 |
| R157 雨 (雩)  雨 | | | yǔ | 720 |
| 雪 | | 3 | xuě | 1369 |
| 零 | | 5 | líng | 1640 |
| 雷 | | 5 | léi | 1641 |
| 雾 | 霧 | 5 | wù | 1837 |
| 需 | | 6 | xū | 1838 |

| SIMP CHAR | TRAD CHAR | STROKE COUNT | PINYIN | CHAR NO |
|---|---|---|---|---|
| 震 | | 7 | zhèn | 1839 |
| 霉 | 黴 | 7 | méi | 1934 |
| 霜 | | 9 | shuāng | 1935 |
| 霞 | | 9 | xiá | 1977 |
| 露 | | 13 | lòu | 1997 |
| 露 | | 13 | lù | 1997 |
| 霸 | | 13 | bà | 1998 |
| R158 齿 (齒)  齿 | 齒 | | chǐ | 538 |
| 龄 | 齡 | 5 | líng | 1687 |
| R159 隹  雌 | | 6 | cí | 1683 |
| R160 金  金 | 金 | | jīn | 420 |
| R161 鱼 (魚)  鱼 | 魚 | | yú | 843 |
| 鲜 | 鮮 | 6 | xiān | 1811 |
| 鲜 | 鮮 | 6 | xiǎn | 1811 |
| R162 革  革 | | | gé | 747 |
| 靴 | | 4 | xuē | 1788 |
| 鞋 | | 6 | xié | 1789 |
| 鞭 | | 9 | biān | 1967 |
| R163 骨  骨 | | | gǔ | 1543 |
| R164 鬼  鬼 | | | guǐ | 1433 |
| 魂 | | 4 | hún | 1893 |
| 魔 | | 11 | mó | 1996 |
| R165 食  食 | | | shí | 1053 |
| 餐 | | 7 | cān | 1964 |
| R166 音  音 | | | yīn | 907 |
| R167 黑  黑 | | | hēi | 1389 |
| R168 鼠  鼠 | | | shǔ | 1859 |
| R169 鼻  鼻 | | | bí | 1794 |

# INDEX 5

# English to Chinese

Use this index to locate the dictionary entry for a Chinese word based on its English meaning(s).

This index contains not only basic English words, but also common English phrases; for example, you can find several Chinese words for "experience" under the entries *experience, to experience,* and *experienced,* but you can also find common phrases that include "experience" under the entries *to gain experience, to know from experience, to learn from experience,* and *life experience.*

Introductory words in italics are disregarded in alphabetizing the entries: these include the articles *a, an,* and *the;* the infinitival *to;* and certain verb phrases, such as *to be, to not be, to become, to do, to get, to go,* and *to take.*

Each Chinese word is followed by the character number under which the word can be found.

all-around person 通才 1757
all-around victory 满堂红 1745
to allege 硬说 1524
to allege falsely 诡称 1747
to be allergic 过敏 712
alley 弄堂 251
alliance 同盟 541, 联盟 1206
allied forces 联军 1206
all-knowing 无所不知 139
to allocate 支配 92, 分配 173,
　划定 476, 配置 1647, 配备
　1647, 调配 1749, 调用 1749
to allocate funds 拨款 1015
allotropy 异型 539
to allow 允许 302, 听凭 414,
　听任 414, 许可 502, 容许 1320
to not allow 不许 24, 不准 24
allowance 补助 508, 补贴 508
to not be allowed 不得 24
alloy 合金 296
all-powerful 万能 73, 全能 172
all-purpose 多功能 431
all-round 全能 172
to allude to 影射 1918
allusion 典故 532
to ally 结盟 1291
alma mater 母校 394
almanac 皇历 858
almost 差点 673, 差不多 673,
　将近 1161
almsgiver 施主 1758
alone 只身 160, 单独 672, 单单
　672, 孤单 978, 独自 1095
to get along 对付 254, 过日子
　712, 投合 1008
along the road 沿途 1165
along the way 沿线 1165, 沿路
　1165
along with 连同 958, 随着 1911
alongside 并肩 225
aloof 超然 1684
already 已然 133, 已经 133,
　都是 1578
to be already so 已然 133
also 并且 225, 加以 463
altar 圣坛 142
to alter 变动 653, 变更 653,
　修改 870, 涂改 1171
to alternate 交替 222, 变换
　653, 轮流 1112
to alternate with 相间 805
alternately 交互 222
alternative name 别名 1049,
　别称 1049
although 虽然 990
altitude 高度 1611
altogether 一共 1, 总共 1330,
　统共 1601
alumna 校友 802
always 一直 1, 从来 66, 历来
　200, 时刻 586, 总是 1330,
　素来 1378
to be always on the go 奔命
　432
to always remember
　念念不忘 1054
to amass 积蓄 1097

amateur 外行 218
to amaze 震惊 1839
amazed 惊奇 1489
to be amazed 哇噻 784
amazing 了不起 30, 惊人 1489
ambassador 大使 20
ambiguity 歧义 585
ambiguous 含混 592
ambition 志向 528, 好强 627,
　远大 1184, 胸襟 1709
to ambush 伏击 212, 埋伏
　1002
to ameliorate 改良 516
to amend 改正 516, 修订 870,
　修改 870
America 美洲 671
American English 美国英语
　671
amiable 随和 1911
amiss 不对 24
ammunition 弹药 1763
ammunition belt 弹袋 1763
ammunition depot 弹药库
　1763
among 其中 379
amount (of money) 金额 420
amount of tax 税额 1705
to amount to 共计 164, 为数
　223, 合计 296, 总计 1330
ample 宽裕 1618
to amuse oneself 消遣 1343,
　解闷 1928
analogy 比方 279, 比喻 279
analysis 分析 173
to analyze 分析 173, 解析 1928,
　解剖 1928
ancestors 先辈 422, 先人 422,
　祖先 1190, 祖辈 1190
ancestral home 祖籍 1190,
　原籍 1273
ancestry 身世 604, 祖宗 1190,
　祖先 1190
ancient 古老 154
ancient and modern
　古今中外 154
ancient book 古书 154, 古籍
　154
ancient building 古迹 154
ancient costume 古装 154
ancient poetry 古诗 154
ancient times 古代 154, 远古
　1184
ancients 古人 154
and 以及 101, 并且 225
and on top of that 而且 351
and so on 什么的 63, 等等
　1437
and what not 什么的 63
and what's more 而且 351
to anesthetize 麻醉 1146
angel 天使 25, 仙女 207
anger 火气 72, 肝火 650, 怒气
　1427, 怒气 1427
to be angered 含怒 592
angina 心绞痛 232
angle 角度 838, 视角 1362
Anglican Church 圣公会 142

angry 气愤 185, 气恼 185,
　红眼 474, 恼火 931
to be angry 愤怒 1490
to get angry 上火 14, 发怒 311,
　发火 311, 惹气 1657
animal 动物 514
animated cartoon 卡通片 36,
　动画片 514
animosity 仇恨 319
annals 史册 186
to annex 合并 296, 吞并 427
to annotate 注释 496, 批注
　1005
to announce 公布 103, 发表
　311, 发布 311, 声明 374, 宣布
　1138, 通告 1757, 揭晓 1851,
　揭示 1851
to announce in advance
　预告 1528
announcement 公告 103,
　启事 657, 通告 1757
to annoy 困扰 393
annoyed 心烦 232, 恼火 931,
　烦恼 1178
annual expenditure 岁出
　380
annual income 年收入 182,
　岁入 380
annual interest 年利 182,
　年息 182
annual meeting 年会 182
annual output 年产量 182
annual report 年报 182
annual salary 年薪 182
annually 年度 182
to annul 废止 918
answer 答案 1438
to answer 对答 254, 应声 334,
　应答 334, 回答 391, 还嘴 714,
　答复 1438, 答话 1438, 解答
　1928
to answer a question 答题
　1438
answer to a riddle 谜底 1750
ant 蚂蚁 825
ant nest 蚁巢 825
antenna 天线 25
anthology 选集 1510
antibiotic 抗菌素 1009,
　抗生素 1009
to anticipate 预想 1528, 意料
　1812
antidiarrhea medication
　止泻药 41
antiques 古董 154, 古玩 154
antiquity 远古 1184
to be antisocial 与世无争 158
antitoxin 抗毒素 1009
antler 鹿角 1724
anxiety 心病 232
anxious 不安心 24, 不安 24,
　心焦 232, 焦急 1265, 着急
　1332, 急于 1426
to be anxious 发愁 311, 担心
　789, 担忧 789
any 任何 211
anyhow 随便 1911

anyway 反正 111, 左不过 113,
　无论如何 139
anywhere 哪儿 1666, 随地 1911,
　随处 1911
to be apart 分开 173
to take apart 拆开 572
to be apart from 距离 1576
apartment 公寓 103
apathetic 淡漠 1173
aphorism 警句 1987
to apologize 赔不是 1569,
　赔礼 1569, 赔罪 1569, 道歉
　1756
apparatus 仪器 122, 用具 313,
　机器 577
apparel 穿戴 1322
apparently 似乎 322, 看来 841
to appeal 上诉 14, 申诉 150,
　号召 545
to appeal to 诉诸 708
to appear 出现 258, 见得 267,
　显露 755
to appear and disappear
　神出鬼没 1191
to appear in court 出庭 258
to appear in public 抛头露面
　1395, 亮相 1613
to appear on stage 上台 14,
　出场 258, 亮相 1613
appearance 长相 93, 仪表 122,
　门面 130, 外观 218, 外形 218,
　形容 257, 状貌 345, 表面 527,
　表象 527, 面目 721, 面貌 721,
　场面 773, 样子 803, 现象 975,
　容貌 1320, 模样 1673
to appease 姑息 881
appetite 胃口 1216
to applaud 欢呼 366, 拍手 790,
　鼓掌 1688
apple 苹果 395
apple jam 苹果酱 395
apple juice 苹果汁 395
appliance(s) 用具 313, 用品
　313
application 用途 313
application (form) 申请 150
to apply 应用 334, 使用 623,
　实施 668, 施行 1758
to apply (ointment, etc.) 外敷
　218
to apply color 着色 1332
to apply for 申请 150
to apply for (a job) 应征 334
to apply makeup 扮装 786,
　涂脂抹粉 1171
to apply mechanically 套用
　1064
to apply paint 涂抹 1171
to apply the brake(s) 制动
　1130
to appoint 任命 211, 任用 211,
　委任 594, 委派 594, 差使 673,
　约定 876, 指定 1397
appointment 约会 876
to appraise 估量 456, 讲评 501,
　定位 666, 评比 706, 评判
　706, 评议 706

*to* appreciate 升值 47, 体味 325, 欣赏 634, 审美 911, 增值 1849, 感激 1860

*to* apprehend (a criminal) 拿获 1262

apprentice 徒弟 873, 徒工 873

approach 来路 260

*to* approach 对待 254, 迫近 1186, 接近 1405, 靠近 1791

appropriate 切合 277, 合适 296, 妥贴 433, 妥当 433, 相当 805, 恰如其分 930, 恰当 930, 适度 1358, 适中 1358, 适宜 1358

*to be* appropriate 对口 254

*to* approve 认证 239, 同意 541, 点头 739, 肯定 744, 准予 929, 批准 1005, 赞成 1969

*to* approve of 认可 239, 赞同 1969

approximate 大概 20

*to* approximate 近似 716

approximately 大约 20

April 四月 271

aptitude 资质 1335

aquatic products 水产 159

Arab 阿拉伯 1249

arbitrarily 任意 211

arbitrary 专断 155, 武断 513

*to* arbitrate 调处 1749

arc 弓形 250, 圆弧 1391

arch 拱形 793

arch over a gateway 门楼 130

archaeology 考古 530

archaism 古语 154

archcriminal 首犯 924

archery target 箭靶 1922

archipelago 群岛 1646

ardent 热烈 1390, 热切 1390, 热心肠 1390

arduous 艰辛 973

area 区域 99, 地段 772, 地区 772, 场地 773, 领域 1465

area untouched by 死角 510

*to* argue 计较 240, 争辩 595, 争论 595, 说理 1631

*to* argue back and forth 扯皮 403

*to* argue noisily 嚷嚷 1993

argument 争论 595, 论据 947, 论点 947

*to* arise 出现 258, 起来 1421

aristocrat 贵族 985

arithmetic 算法 1697, 算术 1697

*to do* arithmetic in one's head 心算 232

arm 手臂 104

arm of the law 法网 686

armaments 军备 489, 武装 513

armband 袖标 1361, 袖章 1361

armchair 靠椅 1791

armed escort 卫队 82

armed forces 兵力 300, 军队 489, 部队 1636

armed guard 卫队 82

armed rebellion 叛乱 960

armored 装甲 1476

armrest 扶手 404

arms 军备 489, 武器 513

arms and ammunition 军火 489

army 队伍 294, 军队 489, 陆海空 1043, 陆军 1043

army and civilian 军民 489

army deserter 逃兵 1509

army provisions 粮草 1759

aroma 香气 834

around 周围 1068

*to go* around 跑遍 1916

*to* arouse 引起 371, 动员 514, 启发 657, 激发 1955, 激起 1955

*to* arrange 支配 92, 处置 217, 布置 309, 安排 487, 摆布 1773, 整理 1845, 编排 1866

*to* arrange an order 编次 1866

*to* arrange temporarily 暂定 1522

arrangement 条理 598

*to* arrest 扣留 401, 拘捕 1231, 拘禁 1231, 拿住 1262

arrest warrant 拘票 1231

*to* arrive 来临 260, 到来 737

*to* arrive (at) 到达 737

*to* arrive late 迟到 959

arrogant 自大 305, 骄傲 1376

*to be* arrogant 目空一切 151

arrow (sign) 箭头 1922

arrow shaft 箭杆 1922

arrowhead 箭头 1922

art 艺术 274, 技艺 568

art exhibition 画展 719

art gallery 画廊 719

art of war 兵法 300

artery 干道 13, 动脉 514

arthritis 关节炎 224

article 条文 598, 论文 947

article (part of speech) 冠词 1478

artificial limb 义肢 22, 假肢 1586

artisan 艺人 274

artist 艺术家 274, 美工 671, 画师 719

artistic 艺术 274

artistic conception 意境 1812

artistic quality 艺术性 274

artistry 技艺 568

arts and crafts 艺术品 274

as 且…且… 152, 既是 1572, 既然 1572

as a matter of fact 其实 379

as a result 于是 28, 以致 101, 因而 270, 结果 1291

as a rule 照例 1846

as above 如上 464

as before 如故 464, 照样 1846

as everyone knows 众所周知 175

as expected 不出所料 24, 果然 544, 果真 544

as far as possible 尽量 312

as follows 如下 464

as for 至于 244

*to not be* as good as 不如 24

as good as assured 十拿九稳 3

as if 仿佛 450, 犹如 886

as it turns out 恰好 930

as large as the heavens 天大 25

as long as 只要 160

as luck would have it 凑巧 1160

as mentioned above 如上 464

as much as one likes 尽情 312

*to do* as one pleases 听便 414

*to be* as one wishes 如愿 464

*to do* as one wishes 随便 1911

as regards 至于 244

as scheduled 如期 464, 准时 929, 按时 1234

as soon as possible 及早 141, 趁早 1257

as soon as … then 一…就 1

as the term suggests 顾名思义 1609

as to 至于 244

as usual 如常 464, 照常 1846, 照例 1846

as well as 以及 101

*to do* as you wish 请便 1632

asbestos 石棉 144

*to* ascend the throne 即位 1047

*to* ascertain 探明 1404

ashamed 羞耻 1154, 羞惭 1154, 惭愧 1352

ashes 灰烬 198, 骨灰 1543

*to go* ashore 下船 10, 上岸 14

Asia 亚洲 136

aside 旁白 1473

*to* ask 发问 311, 问讯 678, 询问 1500, 请求 1632

*to* ask (a guest) to stay 留客 1582

*to* ask a price 要价 969

*to* ask a question 发出 311, 提问 1554

*to* ask about 打听 289

*to* ask earnestly 央告 196, 央求 196

*to* ask for 征求 462

*to* ask for a loan 告贷 428

*to* ask for advice 讨教 500, 领教 1465, 请教 1632

*to* ask for emergency help 告急 428

*to* ask for forgiveness 讨饶 500

*to* ask for help 求人 376, 求援 376, 求救 376, 伸手 457, 搬救兵 1943

*to* ask for leave 请假 1632

*to* ask for leniency 求情 376

*to* ask for time off 请假 1632

*to* ask the price of 询价 1500

*to* ask to see 求见 376

aspect 方面 220, 层面 610, 局面 1069

aspen 杨树 1027

aspiration 志趣 528, 志向 528, 志愿 528

*to* aspire to 渴求 1822

ass 蠢驴 1995

assassin 刺客 1050

*to* assassinate 刺杀 1050

*to* assault 攻击 253, 行凶 327, 冲锋 339, 冲击 339, 进攻 713, 突击 913

*to* assemble 会聚 295, 会合 295, 组装 1106, 组合 1106, 集合 1267, 装配 1476, 调集 1749

*to* assemble and install 组装 1106

assembly hall 礼堂 503

*to* assert 断言 1260, 硬说 1524

*to* assess 权衡 292, 评价 706, 评定 706, 核算 1026

*to* assess the merits of 评功 706

assets 财产 588, 资产 1335

*to* assign 归入 166, 分配 173, 任用 211, 差使 673

*to be* assigned a job 分工 173

assignment 任务 211, 差事 673

*to* assimilate 同化 541, 摄取 1772, 摄入 1772

*to* assist 支援 92, 协助 397, 扶助 404, 帮助 1583, 赞助 1969

*to* assist in a crime 帮凶 1583

*to* assist in managing 帮办 1583

assistance 援助 1556, 帮助 1583

assistant 助手 818, 助教 818, 助理 818, 帮手 1583

*to* associate 联想 1206

*to* associate with 交往 222, 打交道 289, 结交 1291

association 瓜葛 189, 协会 397

assorted 什锦 63

*to* assume 设想 1179, 假设 1586, 假定 1586

*to* assume the office of 担任 789

assurance 保险 868, 把握 1006

*to* assure 保证 868, 保管 868

asthma 气喘 185

astigmatism 散光 1579

*to be* astonished 折服 408

astronomy 天文学 25

astute 精明 1832

at (someone's) invitation 应邀 334

*to be* at a disadvantage 吃亏 783

*to be* at a distance from 距离 1576

at a leisurely pace 慢腾腾 1882

*to be* at a loss 抓瞎 406

at an early date 及早 141

at any time 随时 1911

cha-cha (dance) 恰恰舞 930
chain 连环 958, 连锁 958, 锁链 1608
chair 座椅 920, 椅子 1566
chairperson 主任 124, 主席 124
chalk 粉笔 1363
to challenge 将军 1161, 挑战 1235
champagne 香槟 834
champion 冠军 1478
chance 机会 577, 空子 669, 偶然 1590
to take a chance 碰运气 1526
chancel 圣坛 142
chandelier 吊灯 547
to change 改变 516, 变动 653, 变更 653, 变化 653, 转化 1111, 转变 1111, 转换 1111, 转移 1111
to change (of a shape) 变形 653
to change (of a situation) 变迁 653
to change buses 换车 1402
to change direction 转向 1111
to change into 变成 653
to change irregularly 变幻 653
to change jobs 转业 1111
to change money 换钱 1402
to change shifts 倒班 1281, 换班 1402
to change the date 改期 516
to change trains 换车 1402
channel(s) 沟道 933, 经络 1110, 途径 1511, 航道 1717, 管道 1861
chaos 混沌 1739
chaotic 乱哄哄 901, 乱糟糟 901, 纷乱 1102, 糊涂 1932
chaotic warfare 混战 1739
chapter 章节 1311
character 人格 4, 本色 90, 风格 194, 心地 232, 性格 498, 性质 498, 字符 664, 品质 1220, 品格 1220
characteristic 特征 1094, 特点 1094, 特色 1094, 特有 1094
charge(s) 罪名 1542, 罪状 1542
to charge 收费 282, 冲锋 339, 冲杀 339, 冲击 339
to take charge 挂帅 796
to charge (someone) with 指控 1397
to charge (up) 充电 652
to charge forward 猛冲 1704
to charge to an account 记账 946
to be charged with 担负 789
charitable 慈善 1952
charm 魔力 1996
charming 迷人 1187
chart 图表 761
charter 宪章 1317
to chase 追赶 1507, 追逐 1507
chassis 底盘 916
to chat 交谈 222, 拉扯 573, 闲扯 679, 闲聊 679, 闲谈 679, 谈天 1356, 谈话 1356, 聊天 1527

cheap 低廉 618, 廉价 1615
to cheat 作弊 326, 作假 326, 欺诈 1423, 骗取 1937, 骗钱 1937
to cheat other people 骗人 1937
to be cheated 受骗 844
cheater 骗子 1937
check 方格 220, 账单 812, 格子 1246
to check 考查 530, 考核 530, 查对 741, 校验 802, 审阅 911, 审核 911, 核实 1026, 核对 1026, 检查 1033, 清查 1495
to check (baggage, etc.) 托运 563
to check (chess) 将军 1161
to check a calculation 验算 1529
to check a number 对号 254
to check and accept 验收 1529
to check in 报到 1010, 登记 1521
to check luggage 寄存 1619
to check out (a story) 查证 741
to check residence cards 查户口 741
to check the amount of 查点 741
to check tickets 查票 741
checklist 清单 1495
checkpoint 关卡 224
cheeks 脸蛋 1461
to cheer 欢呼 366
to cheer on 捧场 1240
to cheer (someone) on 加油 463
to cheer up 振作 1238
cheerful 快活 497, 愉快 1737
cheerleader(s) 拉拉队 573
cheers 干杯 13, 碰杯 1526
cheese 奶酪 878
cheetah 猎豹 1444
chef 厨师 1584
chemical fertilizer 化肥 215
chemical industry 化工 215
chemistry 化学 215
to cherish 怀抱 344, 珍爱 515, 珍视 515, 爱惜 1264, 爱护 1264
to cherish the memory of 怀念 344
chess 象棋 1580
chess piece 棋子 1248
chessboard 棋盘 1248
chest 胸膛 1709, 箱子 1797
chest cavity 胸腔 1709
chest measurement 胸围 1709
chest of drawers 五斗柜 79
chest pain 胸闷 1709
to chew out 臭骂 1076
chewing gum 口香糖 42
chicken (meat) 鸡肉 1373
chicken pox 水痘 159
chicken salad 鸡色拉 1373

chicken sandwich 鸡三明治 1373
chicken soup 鸡汤 1373
chief 头子 128, 首领 924
chief commander 主将 124
chief culprit 罪魁祸首 1542, 祸首 1754
chief editor 主编 124
chief examiner 主考 124
chief offender 要犯 969
chieftain 头目 128
child 娃娃 877, 孩子 1202
child laborer 童工 1471
childcare center 托儿所 563
childhood 童年 1471
childhood name 小名 61
childish 幼稚 638
childlike innocence 童心 1471
children 儿童 43, 儿女 43, 子女 83, 子弟 83, 孩子 1202
children's clothing 童装 1471
to chill (down) 冷却 494
chilly 阴冷 1041, 凉飕飕 1337
chimney 烟囱 1177
chimpanzee 黑猩猩 1389
China 中华 86, 中国 86
china bowl 瓷碗 1723
Chinatown 唐人街 1324
chinaware 瓷器 1723
Chinese (language) 中文 86, 汉语 235, 华文 421
Chinese and the West 中西 86
Chinese characters 汉字 235
Chinese chestnut 板栗 580
Chinese food 中餐 86
Chinese herbal medicine 中草药 86
Chinese ink 墨汁 1843
Chinese mainland 中国大陆 86
Chinese nation 中华民族 86
Chinese people 中华民族 86
Chinese-style 中式 86
chitchat 空谈 669
chocolate 巧克力 364
cholesterol 胆固醇 1295
to choose 取舍 520, 挑选 1235, 推举 1242, 选取 1510, 选择 1510
to choose a name for 定名 666
to choose carefully 精选 1832
to choose friends 择交 792
to chop 切碎 277
chopper 砍刀 979
chopsticks 筷子 1585
to be chosen 入选 5
chow mein 炒面 499
to christen 命名 1051
Christmas 圣诞 142
Christmas tree 圣诞树 142
chronic problem 老毛病 375
chronology 年表 182
to chuckle 扑哧 168
church 教堂 1424
to churn 翻腾 1989

cicada 知了 647
cider 苹果汁 395
cigar 雪茄 1369
cigarette 香烟 834, 纸烟 1103, 卷烟 1333
cigarette butt 烟头 1177
cigarette case 烟盒 1177
cinema 电影院 263, 影院 1918
cinnamon 肉桂 437, 桂树 797
circle 环形 369, 圆圈 1391, 圆环 1391, 圈子 1765
circuit 回路 391, 线路 1105
circuitous 弯曲 1472
circular 团圆 392, 通报 1757, 通知 1757
to circulate 周转 1068, 流通 1493, 流传 1493, 通报 1757
circulation 环流 369
circumference 周长 1068, 圆周 1391
circumstances 形势 257, 环境 369, 光景 491, 情景 1491, 境况 1848
circus 马戏 247
cistern 水池 159
citation 引文 371
to cite 引用 371, 援用 1556, 援引 1556
citizen 公民 103, 国民 542
citizenship 国籍 542
citric acid 柠檬酸 1029
citrus 柠檬 1029
citrus fruit 柑果 582
city 城市 1225, 都会 1578
city gate 城门 1225
city proper 市区 332
city residents 市民 332
civil administration 民政 388
civil and military 文武 70
civil aviation 民航 388
civil conflict 内乱 191
civil law 民法 388
civil matter 民事 388
civil police 民警 388
civil rights 民权 388
civil war 内战 191
civilian 平民 78, 老百姓 375, 民用 388
civility 客套 1316
civilization 文化 70, 文明 70
civilized 文明 70
to claim 认领 239, 声称 374
to claim to be 自称 305, 号称 545
clamp 夹板 197, 夹具 197
clan 家族 1315, 部落 1636
to clap one's hands 鼓掌 1688
clappers 拍板 790
clapping 掌声 1734
to clarify 弄清 251, 表白 527
clarinet 黑管 1389
to clash 冲突 339, 撞车 1853
class 类别 676, 种类 893
class monitor 班长 730
classes/grades 班次 730, 班级 730
classical 古典 154, 经典 1110

to drill wells 钻井 1302
drilling rig 钻机 1302
drink 饮料 892
to drink (alcohol) 喝酒 1854
to drink water 喝水 1854
drip 滴答 1885
to drip 滴液 1885
to drip water 滴水 1885
dripping wet 淋漓 1172
drive 劲头 736
to drive 带动 1213, 驾驭 1693
to drive a car 开车 26
to drive a vehicle 行车 327
to drive fast 开快车 26
to drive up (prices) 哄抬 781
to be driven to 迫不得已 1186
driver 司机 357
driver's license 驾照 1693
driving age 驾龄 1693
driving school 驾校 1693
to drool 垂涎 430
to drop 下降 10, 下落 10, 作罢 326, 垂涎 430, 跌落 1422, 脱落 1803
to drop a bomb 投弹 1008
to drop a hint 放空气 964
to drop by parachute 伞投 171
drop of water 水滴 159
to drop off 掉队 1403
to drop out 掉队 1403, 退学 1508
to drop out of school 失学 106, 停学 1588
to drop supplies by air 空投 669
to drop to the ground 卧倒 826
dropper 滴管 1885
drops 点滴 739
drought 旱灾 1107
to drown 淹死 1629
to drug 麻醉 1146
drugs 药剂 1392, 药品 1392, 药物 1392
to take drugs 吸毒 776
drugstore 药房 1392, 药店 1392
to drum up support 游说 1818
drummer 鼓手 1688
drunk 醉醺醺 1842
to be drunk 沉醉 1166
drunkard 酒鬼 1339, 醉汉 1842, 醉鬼 1842
dry 干燥 13
to dry 烘干 953
dry and dull 枯燥 799
dry land 旱地 387
dry season 旱季 387, 寒季 1481
dual 双重 146
dual purpose 两用 509
dualism 二元论 2
dubious 不三不四 24
duck 鸭子 1782
duck (meat) 鸭肉 1782
duck's egg 鸭蛋 1782
duct 管子 1861
to be due 应有 334
to become due 到期 737

due to 由于 148
due to illness 因病 270
duet 二重唱 2
dull 平淡 78, 平板 78, 苍白 996
dull and heavy 枯涩 799
dumbstruck 目瞪口呆 151
to dump 抛售 1395
dumpling 饺子 1115
dunce 蠢货 1995
dung 粪肥 1334
to duplicate 重叠 839, 复写 1059, 复制 1059, 雷同 1641
durable 牢固 488, 耐久 1210, 耐用 1210
dusk 傍晚 1698
dusky 昏暗 1058
dust 灰尘 198, 尘埃 204, 粉尘 1363
to dust 除尘 1418
dust and dirt 尘垢 204
dust particle 尘粒 204
dust shower 尘雨 204
dust storm 尘暴 204
to dust-proof 防尘 1040
dutiful son 孝子 529
duty 义务 22, 责任 525, 职责 1205
obligation 职责 1205
duty-free 免税 1056
dwarf 矮子 1598
to dwell 居住 850
dwelling 住处 324
to dye 染色 1336
to be dying 垂死 430
dynamic 活跃 941, 能动 1873
dynamic state 动态 514
dynasty 王朝 27, 朝代 1686

each 各自 425
each and every one 个个 18
each day 每日 837
each one 各人 425
each other 交互 222, 相互 805
each successive 历次 200
eager 急于 1426
to be eager for 渴求 1822
eagerly 切切 277, 急切 1426
eagle 老鹰 375
ear 耳朵 145
ear canal 耳孔 145
ear pick 耳挖子 145
earl 伯爵 455
earlobe 耳垂 145
early morning 早晨 268, 清晨 1495
early spring 早春 268
early stage 早期 268
early youth 少年 62
earmuffs 耳套 145, 护耳 569
to earn a living 活命 941, 营生 1546
to earn money 挣钱 1398
earnest 认真 239, 热诚 1390
earnestly 切切 277
earnings 收入 282, 收益 282, 所得 645
earphone(s) 耳机 145, 听筒 414

earplug 耳塞 145
earring 耳坠子 145, 耳环 145
earth 大地 20, 泥土 204
Earth 环球 369, 地球 772
earthquake 地震 772
to ease 减轻 1487
to ease pain 镇痛 1872
easily 动不动 514, 轻易 1113
The East 东方 307
east and west 东西 307
eastern Europe 东欧 307
eastern hemisphere 东半球 307
easy 便利 865, 便当 865, 容易 1320
easy job 美差 671
easy to read 顺口 874
easygoing 随和 1911
to eat 吃饭 783, 摄食 1772
eaves 屋檐 1072
to eavesdrop 窃听 1482
to ebb (of the tide) 退潮 1508
eccentric 怪人 696, 乖僻 832
echelon 梯队 1669
echo 反响 111, 回声 391
to echo 回响 391, 呼应 779, 雷同 1641
ecology 生态 107
e-commerce 电子商务 263
to economize 节约 275
economy 经济 1110
economy and trade 经贸 1110
ecstatic 狂喜 469
edge 边沿 710, 边缘 710
to edge out 排挤 1241
to be edible 食用 1053
to edit 剪辑 1816
to edit (large books) 编纂 1866
to edit an original work 改写 516
edition 版本 897
editor 编者 1866, 编辑 1866
editor in chief 主笔 124
to educate 育儿 1133, 教育 1424
to educate (children) 调教 1749
to educate (the young) 启蒙 657
education 文化 70
educational institution 学院 1155
effect 作用 326, 成效 611, 效应 965, 效果 965, 效能 965, 影响 1918
to take effect 生效 107
effective 灵验 359, 管事 1861
to be effective 见效 267, 有效 439
effectiveness 效用 965
efficacy 功效 252
efficiency 功效 252, 效能 965, 效率 965
effluent 废水 918
effort 力气 59
egg 卵子 896, 鸡蛋 1373
egg white 蛋白 1368

egg yolk 卵黄 896
ego 自我 305
egotism 利己主义 472
egotistical 狂妄 469
either … or … 或者 857
either side 两旁 509
elaborate 精心 1832
elasticity 松紧 579
elder 长者 93, 长老 93, 长辈 93
elderly 老年 375, 老龄 375
to elect 推举 1242, 选举 1510
to be elected 当选 335
electorate 选民 1510
electric 电动 263
electric appliance 电器 263
electric circuit 电路 263
electric current 电流 263
electric fan 风扇 194, 电风扇 263
electric iron 电熨斗 263
electric light 电灯 263
electric machinery 电机 263
electric meter 电表 263
electric power 电力 263
to get an electric shock 触电 1875
electric transmission 导电 751
electrician 电工 263
electricity 电气 263
electricity transmission 输电 1867
electrocardiogram 心电图 232
electron 电子 263
to electroplate 电镀 263
elegance 风采 194
elegant 文雅 70, 优美 447, 考究 530, 秀气 1055, 端庄 1889
element 元件 138, 分子 173, 因素 270
elementary 低级 618, 初等 963, 基本 991
elementary course 入门 5
to elevate 升高 47
elevator 升降机 47, 电梯 263
to eliminate 收拾 282, 扫除 402, 埋葬 1002, 排除 1241, 消除 1343
to eliminate illiteracy 扫盲 402
elite 精锐 1832
to elongate 拉长 573, 延伸 731
eloquence 口才 42
emaciated 枯瘦 799, 瘦弱 1880
e-mail 电子邮件 263
to emancipate 解放 1928
embarrassed 难为情 974, 难堪 974
to be embarrassed 作难 326
embassy 使馆 623
to embellish 点缀 739
to embezzle 吞没 427, 克扣 738, 贪污 827, 盗用 1475, 挪用 1658, 舞弊 1790
embittered 愤恨 1490
embodiment 化身 215
to embody 体现 325

kelp 海带 1494

kendo 剑道 904

kerchief 头巾 128

key 门径 130, 关键 224, 声调 374, 重点 839, 按键 1234, 钥匙 1300, 琴键 1372, 锁钥 1608

key document 要件 969

key link 关节 224

key part 要害 969

key point 点子 739

keyboard 键盘 1926

khaki cotton 卡其 36

to kick a ball 踢皮球 1946

kickback 回扣 391

kid 小鬼 61, 羊羔 227

to kidnap (for ransom) 绑票 1454

kidnapper 绑匪 1454

kidney 腰子 1868

to kill 干掉 13, 击毙 156, 杀人 317, 要命 969

to kill and wound 杀伤 317

to kill by beating 虐杀 1379

to kill in revenge 仇杀 319

to kill oneself 自尽 305

to kill the enemy 杀敌 317

to kill unjustifiably 杀害 317

to get killed 丧命 521

to be killed in action 阵亡 809

killer 凶犯 98, 凶手 98

kilogram 公斤 103

kilometer 公里 103

kimono 和服 644

kin 亲戚 908

kind 仁慈 64, 和蔼 644, 和气 644, 种类 893, 厚道 1272

kind and serene 慈祥 1952

kind hospitality 盛情 1694

kindhearted 善良 1483

kindheartedness 仁爱 64

to kindle 燃烧 1888

to kindly accept 笑纳 861

kindness 好意 627, 好心 627, 恩情 1381

kinfolk 亲属 908

king 巨头 162, 君主 512, 国王 542

kingdom 王国 27

to kiss 亲吻 908, 亲嘴 908

kitchen 伙房 214, 厨房 1584

kitchen knife 菜刀 1001

kitchen stove 炉灶 699

kitchen worker 厨工 1584

kite 风筝 194

knack 门路 130, 妙诀 467, 秘诀 1289, 窍门 1621

knapsack 背包 1380

to knead dough 揉面 1771

to kneel down 下跪 10, 跪倒 1945

knickknack 玩意儿 727, 玩具 727

knife 刀子 31

knife and fork 刀叉 31

knife edge 刀刃 31, 刀口 31

knife handle 刀把 31

knight 骑士 1840

to knit 针织 477, 编制 1866, 编织 1866

knitting needle 织针 1108

knitting wool 毛线 183

knob 把手 1006

to knock (on a door) 叩门 413

to knock against 磕碰 1894

to knock at the door 敲门 1959

to knock down 击落 156, 打倒 289

to knock out 磕打 1894

knot 扣子 401

to know 认得 239, 认识 239, 知道 647, 知晓 647, 清楚 1495, 懂得 1817

to not know 不懂 24

to know all about 有数 439

to know by heart 滚瓜烂熟 1819

to know from experience 体会 325

to know how to read 认字 239

to know one's stuff 有两下子 439

to know perfectly well 明知 1035

to know the business 懂行 1817

to know the facts 知情 647

to know the ropes 在行 188, 懂行 1817

to know well 掌握 1734, 熟悉 1973

know-how 门道 130

knowledge 认识 239, 见识 267, 见闻 267, 知识 647, 学问 1155

to be known as 叫做 283, 号称 545

Koran 古兰经 154

Korea 朝鲜 1686

to kowtow 磕头 1894

kung fu 武术 513

label 标记 801, 标签 801, 标号 801

to label unfairly 扣帽子 401

labor 劳方 764, 劳动力 764

to labor 劳动 764

labor and capital 劳资 764

labor and service 劳务 764

labor union 工会 12

laborers 劳工 764

labyrinth 迷宫 1187

lack 欠缺 105

to lack 缺乏 1305, 缺少 1305

to lack ideas 没主意 938

to lack proper etiquette 失礼 106

to lack prospects 没出息 938

lackey 走狗 265, 奴仆 328, 狗腿子 1287

lacquered porcelain 漆器 1746

ladder 扶梯 404, 梯子 1669

ladies' room 女厕所 57

lady 女士 57

to lag behind 退步 1508

lagging behind 后进 310

to be laid up 卧病 826, 病倒 1327

lake 湖泊 1741

lakefront 湖滨 1741

lamb 羊羔 227

to lament 哀叹 1134

lamentable 可悲 243

laminated wood 胶合木 1296

lamp 灯笼 346

lamps and lanterns 灯具 346

land 土地 15, 江山 237, 河山 934, 陆地 1043, 领土 1465

to land 上岸 14, 着陆 1332, 降落 1416, 登陆 1521

land and water 水陆 159

land boundary 地界 772

land force(s) 陆军 1043

land mine 地雷 772

land rent 地租 772

land route 陆路 1043

land under heaven 天下 25

landlord/landlady 地主 772, 房东 1145

landowner 地主 772

landscape 山川 38, 风景 194

language 言语 478, 语文 1501, 语言 1501

lantern 灯笼 346

lantern slide 幻灯 475

lapel (of a jacket) 胸襟 1709

laptop 笔记本电脑 1278

lard 荤油 998, 猪油 1445

large 伟大 451, 肥大 1459

large building 大厦 20

large intestine 大肠 20

large number of 大量 20, 大批 20

large size 大号 20

large-scale 大规模 20, 大型 20, 广大 23

laryngitis 喉炎 1560

larynx 喉咙 1560, 喉咙 1560

laser 激光 1955

to lash 抽打 788

last 最后 1541

to last 历时 200, 延续 731, 持续 1019

to last forever 永存 481

last night 昨晚 810

last part 末尾 89

last ten days of a month 下旬 596

to last until dawn 达旦 505

last year 去年 157

lasting 持久 1019

late 误点 1354

to be late 迟到 959, 晚点 1779

to be late for work 误工 1354, 脱班 1803

latecomers 后来 310

lately 最近 1541

later 之后 67, 以后 101, 后来 310, 后面 310, 底下 916

later development 下文 10

later generations 后人 310, 后代 310

later stage 后期 310

lathe 车床 114

latter half 后半 310

to laugh 发笑 311

to laugh foolishly 傻笑 1699

to launch 开果 26, 发动 311, 发射 311, 创办 1131

to launch a campaign 会战 295

to launch an attack 发起 311

laurel 桂冠 797

lavatory 厕所 846

law 王法 27, 法律 686, 法则 686, 法学 686, 规律 1098

law and order 法纪 686

law of the land 王法 27

to be law-abiding 守法 486

lawn 草地 768, 草坪 768

lawsuit 诉讼 708, 官司 1136, 案件 1321

lax 松懈 579

to lay eggs 产卵 219

to lay out 编排 1866

layer upon layer 层层 610

layman 门外汉 130, 外行 218

layout of a page 版面 897

lazy 懒惰 1953, 懒散 1953, 懒洋洋 1953

to be lazy 偷懒 1591

lazybones 懒汉 1953

to lead 引导 371, 带领 1213, 领先 1465, 领导 1465, 率领 1469, 统帅 1601, 诱导 1748

to lead a conspiracy 主谋 124

to lead a nomadic life 走江湖 265

to lead an idle life 吃闲饭 783

to lead into 引人 371

to lead into a trap 坑害 774

to lead the way 领路 1465

to lead to 导致 751, 致使 982

leader 头脑 128, 首脑 924, 领袖 1465, 领导 1465

leader (of a group) 领队 1465

leadership 领导 1465

leading player 主力 124

leading role 主角 124

to take a leading role 称霸 1288

leaf 叶子 167

leaflet 传单 452

league 同盟 541, 联盟 1206

league games 联赛 1206

leak 漏洞 1886

to leak 泄漏 685, 透漏 1826, 透露 1826, 漏泄 1886

to leak air 漏风 1886

to leak electricity 漏电 1886

to leak gas 漏气 1886

to leak oil 漏油 1886

to leak water 走水 265

to leap 飞跃 81

to leap forward 跃进 1258

to leap up 升腾 47

lung cancer 肺癌 1294
*to* lure 利诱 472, 诱惑 1748
*to* lust for 贪图 827
luster 光彩 491
luxurious 阔气 1728, 豪华 1876
lymph 淋巴 1172
lyric 曲子 272

macaroni 通心粉 1757
machine 机器 577
machine drill 钻床 1302
machine tool 机床 577
machinery 机械 577
mad 疯癫 1147
*to* go mad 发狂 311, 发疯 311
mad dog 疯狗 1147
madman 狂人 469, 疯子 1147
magazine 杂志 856
magic 戏法 365, 幻术 475, 魔术 1996, 魔法 1996
magic power 魔力 1996
magic square 魔方 1996
magical 神奇 1191
magical effect 妙用 467
magnate 巨头 162
magnificent 气壮山河 185, 华丽 421
mahjong 麻将 1146
maid 使女 623, 侍女 624, 娘姨 1448
maiden 处女 217
mail 音信 907, 邮寄 1046, 邮递 1046, 邮件 1046
*to* mail a letter 发信 311, 寄信 1619
mail boat 邮船 1046
mail transfer (of money) 信汇 869
mail vehicle 邮车 1046
mailbox 信筒 869, 信箱 869, 邮筒 1046, 邮箱 1046
main 主要 124, 基本 991
main clause 主句 124
main culprit 主犯 124, 元凶 138
main engine 主机 124
main force 主力军 124
main hall of a building 厅堂 112
main line 干线 13
main point 主旨 124, 重点 839, 症结 923, 要点 969, 要领 969
main road 干道 13
main speaker 主讲 124
main stream (of a river) 主流 124
main street 大街 20
main subject 主课 124
mainland 大陆 20
*to* maintain 支撑 92, 认定 239, 养护 670, 保持 868, 保全 868, 维持 1455, 维修 1455
*to* maintain a foothold 立足 125
*to* maintain a road 养路 670
*to* maintain order 纠察 473
majestic 壮丽 238

major 重大 839
major (in the army) 少校 62
*to* major 主修 124
major social movement 浪潮 1341
majority 大部分 20
majority (of) 多数 431
*to* make 使得 623, 制造 1130
*to* make a concession 让步 348
*to* make a contribution 立功 125
*to* make a copy 抄录 405
*to* make a copy of 复制 1059
*to* make a counteroffer 还价 714
*to* make a decision 裁判 1535
*to* make a false claim 诈称 707
*to* make a fire 生火 107
*to* make a fist 握拳 1662
*to* make a fool of 愚弄 1901
*to* make a fool of oneself 出洋相 258, 出丑 258, 闹笑话 1323
*to* make a fortune 发财 311
*to* make a fresh start 自新 305, 另起炉灶 385
*to* make a futile effort 徒劳 873
*to* make a living 过活 712, 糊口 1932
*to* make a loan 放款 964
*to* make a mistake 失误 106, 弄错 251, 出错 258
*to* make a move 动作 514
*to* make a New Year's call 拜年 635
*to* make a pair 作对 326, 配对 1647
*to* make a penalty shot 罚球 1386
*to* make a policy decision 决策 340
*to* make a printing plate 制版 1130
*to* make a profit 赢利 2000
*to* make a round trip 来回 260, 往复 461
*to* make a sentence 造句 1515
*to* make a sound 发声 311, 做声 1282
*to* make a speech 致辞 982, 演讲 1821, 演说 1821
*to* make a suggestion 出点子 258
*to* make a test flight 试飞 1180
*to* make a turn 转弯 1111
*to* make a video of 录像 722
*to* make allowances (for) 迁就 506
*to* make amends 赔偿 1569
*to* make an appointment 相约 805, 约会 876
*to* make an arbitrary decision 专断 155, 武断 513

*to* make an effort 努力 1063
*to* make an exception (for) 破格 1374, 通融 1757
*to* make an excuse 托词 563, 借故 1087
*to* make an extra effort 加劲 463, 加油 463
*to* make an imitation brand 冒牌 989
*to* make an initial attempt 初试 963
*to* make an inventory 清点 1495
*to* make an overall plan 统筹 1601
*to* make arbitrary decisions 独裁 1095
*to* make arrangements (for) 安置 487, 安顿 487
*to* make better 改善 516
*to* make certain 确保 1762
*to* make clear 交待 222, 交代 222, 弄清 251, 表明 527
*to* make do 对付 254, 将就 1161
*to* make do with 凑数 1160
*to* make excuses 推托 1242
*to* make eyes (at) 挤眉弄眼 795
*to* make friends 交友 222
*to* make friends (with) 相交 805
*to* make full use of 发扬 311
*to* make fun of 开玩笑 26, 寻开心 358, 玩弄 727, 调笑 1749
*to* make green 绿化 1707
*to* make known 揭晓 1851
*to* make love 合欢 296, 性交 498
*to* make money 找钱 567, 赚钱 1781
*to* make more serious 加重 463
*to* make one's way forward 向上 603
*to* make out an invoice 开票 26
*to* make peace 言和 478, 调解 1749
*to* make peace with 讲和 501
*to* make progress 向上 603, 进展 713, 前进 1329
*to* make public 公开 103, 发表 311
*to* make right 拨正 1015
*to* make steel 炼钢 1357
*to* make sure 务使 429, 落实 1547
*to* make tea 泡茶 1492
*to* make the calls 拿主意 1262
*to* make things difficult (for) 刁难 32, 为难 223, 作梗 326
*to* make things easy 作美 326
*to* make toast 烤面包 1505
*to* make trouble 作怪 326
*to* make uniform 找齐 567

*to* make up 装扮 1476, 虚构 1534
*to* make up a deficiency 补足 508
*to* make up a missed lesson 补课 508
*to* make up a prescription 调剂 1749
*to* make up an exam 补考 508
*to* make use of 假借 1586
*to* make war on 讨伐 500
*to* make way for 让路 348
*to* make worse 加剧 463
makeup 结构 1291
malaria 疟疾 662
malaria mosquito 疟蚊 662
male 男子 757
male and female 雌雄 1683
male sex 男性 757
male student 男生 757
malfunction 故障 816
malicious 凶狠 98, 奸险 329, 刻毒 966, 恶毒 1196
malignant 恶性 1196
man 丈夫 17, 爷们 445, 老兄 375, 男性 757, 男子 757
man of virtue 圣贤 142
man on the street 匹夫 269
*to* manage 治理 935, 料理 961, 经营 1110, 管理 1861, 操持 1965
*to* manage a household 当家 335
*to* manage the finances 理财 1200
manager 老板 375, 经理 1110, 管家 1861
Mandarin 国语 542
Mandarin (language) 中国官话 86
*to* maneuver 演习 1821
maniac 狂人 469, 疯子 1147
manic 躁狂 1992
manifest 货单 1061
manifesto 宣言 1138
*to* manipulate 牵线 853
mankind 人类 4
man-machine interaction 人机对话 4
man-made 人工 4, 人造 4
manner 风格 194, 态度 828, 派头 945
manner of speaking 方式 220, 谈吐 1356, 语气 1501
manor 庄园 229
manpower 人力 4, 人工 4, 人手 4
manual 手册 104, 指南 1397
*to* do manual work 人工 4, 做工 1282
*to* manufacture 出产 258, 制造 1130
manufacturing location 产地 219
manure 粪肥 1334, 肥料 1459
manure pit 粪坑 1334

manuscript 文稿 70, 手稿 104
many 许多 502, 好多 627, 好些 627, 繁多 1988
many-sided 多方面 431
Mao Zedong 毛泽东 183
map 地图 772
to map onto 映入 1036
march 步伐 266
March 三月 9
to march 游行 1818
to march (of troops) 行军 327
to march forward bravely 勇往直前 1371
marching order 步调 266
margin 余地 419, 差额 673, 边际 710, 边缘 710
marginal note 注释 496
marital harmony 夫唱妇随 55
mark 标记 801, 记号 946, 符号 1277
to mark 评分 706, 标明 801, 批改 1005
to mark off 划定 476, 划分 476
market 市场 332, 里程碑 386, 集市 1267, 销路 1714
to market 销售 1714
market conditions 行情 327
to market merchandise 推销 1242
market price 市场价格 332
to do a market survey 市场调查 332
market value 市价 332
marketing 市场学 332
marketplace 市场 332
marksman 枪手 1244
marriage 婚嫁 1701, 婚姻 1701
to get married 安家 487
to get married (of a man) 完婚 909
to marry 结婚 1291, 嫁人 1799, 嫁娶 1799
marshal 元帅 138, 纠察 473
martial arts 武术 513
martial law 军法 489
to marvel at 赞叹 1969
marvelous 美妙 671
Marxism 马克思主义 247
Marxism-Leninism 马列主义 247
masculine 阳性 808
mashed (of food) 烂糊 702
mask 面具 721
mass campaign 浪潮 1341
to massage 按摩 1234, 推拿 1242
the masses 大众 20, 民众 388, 群众 1646
master 主子 124, 主人翁 124, 老爷 375, 师傅 396, 名家 426
to master 左右 113, 掌握 1734
master and apprentice 师徒 396
master of ceremonies 司仪 357
masterpiece 杰作 377
master's degree 硕士 1375

mastery 修养 870
match(es) 火柴 72, 比赛 279, 洋火 689, 球赛 1199
to match 匹配 269, 比拟 279, 相符 805, 相称 805, 相当 805, 抗衡 1009, 符合 1277, 配合 1647
to not match 不符 24
to match (up) 配对 1647
matchmaker 媒人 1449
to mate 配种 1647
material 材料 409, 资料 1335
material culture 物质文明 883
material evidence 物证 883
material object 实物 668
material resources 物力 883
materials 器材 1963
maternal 母爱 394
maternal cousin 姨表 1596
maternal grandfather 外公 218, 外祖父 218
maternal grandmother 外婆 218, 外祖母 218
maternal love 母爱 394
maternity hospital 妇产医院 465
mathematics 数学 1637
matrix 模子 1673
matter 物质 883, 事情 987
to matter 算数 1697
to not matter 无所谓 139, 没什么 938, 没关系 938
matter for regret 恨事 1174
mattress 床垫 333
mature 老成 375, 成熟 611
to mature 成长 611, 成年 611, 成熟 611, 到期 737
maturing early 早熟 268
maxim 座右铭 920, 格言 1246
maximum 极大 798, 极限 798, 最大 1541
maximum value 最大值 1541
May 五月 79
may 可以 243
may as well 也好 273
may not 不得 24
may not necessarily 未必 88
maybe 也许 273, 兴许 228, 或者 857, 说不定 1631
maze 迷宫 1187
me 本人 90
meadow 草地 768
meager 微薄 1700
meal 饭菜 891
mean 中数 86, 缺德 1305
to mean 意味着 1812
mean and cowardly 卑怯 602
mean deviation 均差 558
meaning 含义 592, 意义 1812, 意思 1812
meaning of words 语义 1501
meaningful 有意思 439
meaningless 无谓 139
means 办法 195, 方法 220, 路子 1785
meanwhile 同时 541

measles 疹子 921, 麻疹 1146
measure 手段 104, 步骤 266
to measure 丈量 17, 计量 240, 估量 456, 判断 507, 度量 919
to measure up (against) 较量 1114
to measure with the eye 打量 289
measure word 量词 1544
measurement 度量衡 919, 量度 1544
measuring cup 量杯 1544
measuring device 量具 1544
meat 肉食 437
meat and fish 荤腥 998
meat dish 荤菜 998
meat patty 肉饼 437
meat stock 肉汁 437
meatball 肉丸子 437
to mechanically copy 照搬 1846
mechanics 力学 59
mechanism 机构 577, 机关 577
to mechanize 机械化 577
medal 奖章 927
median 中数 86
to mediate 劝架 255, 劝解 255, 排解 1241, 调处 1749, 调和 1749, 调停 1749, 调解 1749
mediator 和事佬 644
medic 救生员 1259
medical affairs 医务 389
medical ethics 医德 389
medical record 病历 1327
medical science 医科 389, 医学 389
medical skill 医术 389
medicinal herbs 药材 1392, 药草 1392
medicine 医学 389, 医药 389, 药剂 1392, 药品 1392, 药物 1392
to take medicine 服药 1457
medicine bottle 药瓶 1392
to meditate 养神 670, 沉思 1166
medium 中等 86
medium-length novel 中篇小说 86
medium-sized 中型 86
to meet 汇合 234, 见面 267, 会见 295, 会面 295, 会合 295, 满足 1745, 遇到 1891, 遇见 1891
to meet (by chance) 相逢 805, 撞见 1853
to meet an attack 应战 334
to meet and discuss 碰头 1526
to meet by appointment 约集 876
to meet unexpectedly 碰见 1526
to meet with 遭遇 1931
to meet with catastrophe 遭劫 1931
meeting 会议 295

meeting place 会场 295
melody 曲调 272, 曲子 272, 调子 1749
melon seeds 瓜子 189
melon vine 瓜藤 189
to melt 溶化 1744
member 会员 295, 成员 611
to become a member of 加入 463
membership dues 会费 295
memorial plaque 牌位 1597
to memorize 熟记 1973
memory 记忆 946
men 男人 757
men and women 男男女女 757, 男女老少 757
men's restroom 男厕 757
to mend 修补 870
menfolk 爷们 445, 男人 757
meningitis 脑膜炎 1460
menses 月经 190
menstrual period 例假 863
mental and physical 身心 604
mental deficiency 低能 618
mental illness 精神病 1832
mental outline 腹稿 1869
to mention 谈起 1356, 提到 1554, 提起 1554
to mention briefly 沾边 684
menu 菜单 1001
merchandise 货物 1061, 制品 1130, 商品 1612
merchandise in stock 现货 975
merciful 仁慈 64
merciless 忍心 970, 残忍 977
mercury (chemical element) 水银 159
Mercury (planet) 水星 159
mercy 慈悲 1952
mere skeleton 空架子 669
merely 左不过 113, 只顾 160, 只管 160, 只不过 160, 只是 160
to merge 打成一片 289, 合并 296, 同盟 541, 混合 1739
to merge into 并入 225
meridian circle 子午圈 83
to merit 值得 1089
merits 功德 252
to mess around 瞎闹 1913
to mess things up 乱套 901, 胡搞 1256, 误事 1354
to mess up 搅乱 1850
message 讯息 703, 信息 869, 音信 907
message written at departure 留言 1582
messenger 来人 260, 使者 623, 信使 869
metal 金属 420
metaphor 比喻 279, 比拟 279, 暗喻 1676, 隐喻 1912
meteor 流星 1493
meteorology 气象 185
meter 公尺 103
method 手段 104, 方法 220

physique 形体 257, 体格 325, 体质 325, 体形 325
piano 钢琴 1299
piano key 琴键 1372
to pick a fight 找事 567
to pick and choose 挑拣 1235
to pick up 拾取 1017, 提取 1554
pickles 泡菜 1492
pickpocket 三只手 9, 扒手 169
picky 挑剔 1235
picnic 野餐 1685
to picnic 野餐 1685
picture 图画 761, 图片 761
to take (a picture) 拍照 790
picture frame 像框 1863
pie in the sky 泡影 1492
to piece together 七拼八凑 34, 拼凑 794, 连贯 958
piercing 刺骨 1050
pigment 颜料 1835
pig's feet 爪尖儿 52
to pile up 归拢 166, 堆积 1003, 堆放 1003
pill 丸药 192, 丸子 192, 药片 1392, 药丸 1392
to pillage 抢劫 1230
pillar 支柱 92, 柱石 583, 柱子 583
pilot 飞行员 81
to pilot 引导 371, 导航 751, 驾驶 1693
to pin down 围困 762
pine (tree) 松树 579, 青松 740
pine nut 松子 579
pineapple 凤梨 314, 菠萝 1393
pink 桃红 1243, 粉红 1363
pink eye 红眼 474
pioneer 尖兵 203, 先锋 422, 先驱 422
to pioneer 首创 924
pioneering work 创举 1131
to do pioneering work 创业 1131
pipe 管子 1861
pipe dream 迷梦 1187
pipeline 管道 1861
to pirate 冒牌 989
pirate ship 贼船 1254
pirated copy (of software) 盗版 1475
pistol 手枪 104
pit of the stomach 心口 232
pitch 音调 907
pitch-black 漆黑 1746
pitched battle 激战 1955
pitfall 陷阱 1678
pitiful 可怜 243, 苦恼 555
pity 遗憾 1829
to pity 可怜 243, 怜悯 695
to take pity on 怜惜 695
pivot point 支点 92
place 位置 323, 位子 323, 所在 645, 地点 772, 地方 772, 场所 773, 部位 1636
place name 地名 772
to place oneself 置身 1651

to place side by side 对照 254
place to go 去处 157
to plagiarize 作弊 326, 抄袭 405
plague of insects 虫灾 262
plain 平原 78, 平川 78, 明了 1035
plain color 素色 1378
plain white cloth 白布 176
plainly 明明 1035
plaintiff 原告 1273
plan 主意 124, 企图 170, 方案 220, 计划 240, 规划 1098, 设计 1179
to plan 计划 240, 计算 240, 打算 289, 有计划 439, 安排 487, 设计 1179
to plan in advance 预谋 1528
to plan secretly 图谋 761
plane (geometry) 平面 78
plane ticket 飞机票 81, 机票 577
planet 行星 327
planetary 行星 327
plank 木板 40
plant 植物 1415
to plant 种植 893, 栽种 995
to plant trees 植树 1415, 绿化 1707
plasma 等离子 1437
plaster 石膏 144
to plaster 抹灰 571
plastic 塑料 1815
plastic cement 塑胶 1815
plate 板块 580, 板材 580
plateau 高原 1611
platform 平台 78, 讲台 501
platform scale 磅秤 1936
play 戏剧 365
to play 玩耍 727
to play a small role 跑龙套 1916
to play a wind instrument 吹奏 559
to play ball 打球 289
to play by the rules 照办 1846
to play hide-and-seek 捉迷藏 1239
to play host 做东 1282
to play in unison 齐奏 221
to play music 奏乐 608
to play the fool 装疯卖傻 1476
to play the leading role 主演 124, 挑大梁 1235
to play the role of 充当 652, 扮演 786
to play tricks 作假 326, 做鬼 1282, 搞鬼 1904
to play tricks on 玩弄 727
to play with fire 玩火 727
to play with one's life 玩命 727
to playact 做戏 1282
playacting 戏院 365
playboy 花花公子 549
player 运动员 956, 选手 1510
player of a stringed instrument 琴师 1372

playground 乐园 299, 操场 1965
playing card 纸牌 1103
playing field 操场 1965
plaything 玩意儿 727, 玩具 727
to plead 央求 196
to plead for 乞求 177
to plead for (someone) 讨情 500
to plead guilty 认罪 239, 服罪 1457
pleasant 愉快 1737, 舒适 1805
pleasant to hear 好听 627
pleasant to the ear 中听 86
pleasantly surprised 惊喜 1489
please don't 请勿 1632
pleased 乐滋滋 299
pleased (with) 快慰 497
pleasing to the ear 动听 514
pleasing to the eye 入眼 5, 中看 86
pleasure 乐趣 299, 乐事 299
pledge 保证 868, 约言 876
to pledge 发誓 311
plentiful 充沛 652, 充裕 652, 充足 652, 富足 1731
plenty 宽裕 1618
pliable 柔软 1198
pliers 夹具 197, 虎钳 1533
plight 处境 217, 地步 772
plot 故事 816, 阴谋 1041, 情节 1491
to plot 图谋 761, 密谋 1730
to plot together 合谋 296
to plow 耕地 817
plug 插头 1555, 塞子 1620
to plug in 插入 1555
plum 梅子 1413
plum blossom 梅花 1413
plum tree 梅树 1413
plumber 水暖工 159
plume 羽毛 732
plump 肥厚 1459
to plunder 劫掠 819, 抢掠 1230
plural 复数 1059
plush 丝绒 637
plutocrat 富豪 1731
pneumatic 气动 185
pneumonia 肺炎 1294
pocket 口袋 42, 袋子 1428, 腰包 1868
pocket money 零花 1640, 零用 1640
pocket watch 怀表 344
pocketknife 小刀 61
pocket-size 袖珍 1361
pockmark 麻子 1146
poem 诗歌 1181
poet 诗人 1181
poetry 诗歌 1181
point 尖端 203, 问题 678
to point at 对准 254
point of a knife 刀尖 31
point of a needle 针尖 477
point of contact 切点 277
point of purchase 销售点 1714

point of the compass 方位 220
point of view 观点 726, 角度 838, 看法 841
to point out 点明 739, 指正 1397, 提示 1554
to point out bluntly 点破 739
to point the way 指引 1397
poison 毒药 1211
to poison 毒化 1211
to take poison 服毒 1457
to poison the mind of 麻醉 1146
poisonous 有毒 439
poisonous snake 毒蛇 1211
poisonous substance 毒物 1211
poker 扑克 168, 纸牌 1103
polar region 极地 798
police 警察 1987
police baton 警棍 1987
police district 管区 1861
police dog 警犬 1987
police substation 派出所 945
police whistle 警车 1987, 警笛 1987
policy 方针 220, 政策 517
policy of benevolence 仁政 64
to polish 修饰 870, 抛光 1395, 擦光 1985, 擦亮 1985
to polish repeatedly 推敲 1242
polished 通顺 1757
polished rod 光杆 491
polite 和气 644, 客气 1316
polite greeting 客套 1316
political circles 政界 517
political comment 政论 517
political opponent 政敌 517
political power 政权 517
political trickery 权术 292
political view 政见 517
politician 政客 517
politics 政治 517
politics and law 政法 517
pollen 花粉 549
to pollute 污染 681, 沾污 684
poly- 多元 431
pond 水池 159, 池塘 939, 池沼 939
pond snail 田螺 147
to ponder 玩味 727, 沉思 1166, 思考 1214, 深思 1345
pool 水池 159, 台球 301, 池塘 939, 池沼 939
poor 困难 393, 穷困 912, 贫困 1052, 贫乏 1052, 贫穷 1052
poor people 穷人 912, 贫民 1052
poor wretch 穷光蛋 912
popcorn 玉米花 77
Pope 教皇 1424
poplar 杨树 1027
poplar and willow 杨柳 1027
poplin (cotton cloth) 府绸 660
popsicle 冰棍 493
popular 吃得开 783, 普及 1484, 通俗 1757

# 汉语断笔码词典

The Chinese Broken Marks Dictionary

1 　**一**　U+4E00　TM **1** FM 一

**一** yī NUM one; single; only; same; a(n); all; whole; each; per

就你一人吗？ *Only yourself?*

他一身汗。 *His whole body is covered with sweat.*

三个中文班, 一班九人 *three Chinese classes with nine students each*

**一般** yībān ADJ the same as, just as; general; common, average

他跟他哥哥一般高。 *He is just as tall as his older brother.*

女性的寿命一般比男性长。 *In general, women live longer than men.*

他的中文说得一般。 *His Chinese is so-so.*

**一半** yībàn NUM one half

**一辈子** yībèizi N lifetime

学中文是一辈子的事情。 *Studying Chinese is a lifelong task.*

**一边** yībiān N·ADV one side; at the same time

他常常一边吃饭一边看电视。 *He often watches TV while eating.*

**一点儿** yīdiǎnr MW [measure word for a bit, a little]

我想吃一点儿饭。 *I'd like just a little bit of rice.*

**一定** yīdìng ADJ·ADV sure, certain; surely, certainly

她一定会通过考试。 *She is sure to pass the exam.*

**一度** yīdù MW·ADV once; for a time

他一度停止学中文。 *He once stopped studying Chinese.*

**一共** yīgòng ADV altogether, in all

一共多少钱? *How much altogether?*

**一哄而散** yīhòng'érsàn EXP to break up in an uproar

**一会儿** yīhuìr MW·ADV in a moment; for a little while

我想和你谈一会儿。 *I'd like to speak to you for a moment.*

**一…就** yī… jiù ADV as soon as … then

他一学中文就想睡觉。 *As soon as he starts studying Chinese, he gets sleepy.*

**一块儿** yīkuàir N·ADV together; in company

我们一块儿练习中文。 *Let us practice Chinese together.*

**一齐** yīqí ADV at the same time

我们一齐读中文第一课。 *Let us read Chinese Lesson One all together.*

**一起** yīqǐ N·ADV the same place; together

我们一起练习中文。 *We all practice Chinese together.*

**一切** yīqiè PRON all; every

一切为了明天的中文考试。 *Everything is focused on tomorrow's Chinese test.*

**一生** yīshēng N all one's life

她的一生都在教中文。 *She has taught Chinese her whole life.*

**一时** yīshí N·ADV period of time; for a short while; temporarily; now … now …

由于我一时疏忽, 输掉了比赛。 *I lost the match because I lost concentration momentarily.*

**一天到晚** yītiān dàowǎn ADV from morning till night, all day long

**一五一十** yīwǔ yīshí EXP to narrate systematically and in full detail

**一下** yīxià MW for a short while; all of a sudden; [measure word for brief, sudden actions]

你进来一下。 *Come in for a minute.*

你看一下, 这是谁的照片? *Have a look; whose photo is this?*

**一向** yīxiàng ADV all along; constantly

**一些** yīxiē NUM some, a few, a little

这个计划有一些小问题。 *There were some minor problems with the program.*

**一心** yīxīn ADJ·ADV of one mind; wholeheartedly

**一样** yīyàng ADJ the same as, just as

弟弟跟哥哥一样高。 *The younger brother is just as tall as the older one.*

**一月** yīyuè N January

**一再** yīzài ADV again and again, repeatedly

同样的问题一再发生。 *The same problems took place again and again.*

**一丈** yīzhàng MW [measure word for a unit of length (= 3⅓ meters)]

**一朝一夕** yīzhāo yīxī EXP overnight; in one day

**1 一 yī** (continued)

一阵 **yīzhèn** MW burst; a while; period of time; [measure word for brief, sudden actions]

她学过一阵中文。 *She once studied Chinese for a while.*

一直 **yīzhí** ADV continuously; always

我们一直是朋友。 *We have been friends the entire time.*

一致 **yīzhì** ADJ unanimous, consistent

一十 **yīshí** NUM ten

一十一 **yīshíyī** NUM eleven

一十二 **yīshí'èr** NUM twelve

一十三 **yīshísān** NUM thirteen

一十四 **yīshísì** NUM fourteen

一十五 **yīshíwǔ** NUM fifteen

一十六 **yīshíliù** NUM sixteen

一十七 **yīshíqī** NUM seventeen

一十八 **yīshíbā** NUM eighteen

一十九 **yīshíjiǔ** NUM nineteen

**RELATED WORDS**

| | | | |
|---|---|---|---|
| 一块钱 | 400 | 十一 | 3 |
| 十一月 | 3 | 六一 | 69 |
| 万一 | 73 | 以一当十 | 101 |
| 专一 | 155 | 吓一跳 | 287 |
| 同一 | 541 | 单一 | 672 |
| 进一步 | 713 | 封一 | 815 |
| 尝一尝 | 1157 | 清一色 | 1495 |
| 统一 | 1601 | 统一战线 | 1601 |
| 数一数二 | 1637 | 第一 | 1695 |
| 第一代 | 1695 | 第一手 | 1695 |
| 第一流 | 1695 | 露一手 | 1997 |
| 二十一 | 2 | 八十一 | 6 |
| 三十一 | 9 | 三合一 | 9 |
| 千篇一律 | 19 | 大吃一惊 | 20 |
| 十一 | 34 | 六十一 | 69 |
| 万无一失 | 73 | 五十一 | 79 |
| 九十一 | 116 | 耳目一新 | 145 |
| 目空一切 | 151 | 四十一 | 271 |
| 打成一片 | 289 | 自成一家 | 305 |
| 首屈一指 | 924 | 孤注一掷 | 978 |
| 别具一格 | 1049 | 天字第一号 | 25 |
| 百里挑一 | 242 | | |

## 2 二 · U+4E8C · TM 2 · FM 一

**èr** NUM·ADJ two; second; different; inferior; disloyal

一二得二。 *One times two equals two.*
傻瓜在二楼。 *ShaGua is on the second floor.*
我对你没有二心。 *I am not disloyal to you.*

**二百五 èrbǎiwǔ** N stupid person; dabbler · MW 个

**二重唱 èrchóngchàng** N duet · MW 首

**二等 èrděng** ADJ second-class, second-rate

**二胡 èrhú** N traditional Chinese instrument · MW 把

**二进制 èrjìnzhì** N binary system

**二郎腿 èrlángtuǐ** EXP cross-legged

我们的中文老师从来不在教室里翘二郎腿。 *Our Chinese teacher never sits cross-legged in the classroom.*

**二流子 èrliúzi** N loafer, idler, hooligan · MW 个

**二手 èrshǒu** ADJ secondhand

我这辆是二手车。 *My car is a used car.*

**二维 èrwéi** ADJ two-dimensional

**二元论 èryuánlùn** N dualism

**二月 èryuè** N February

**二十 èrshí** N twenty

**二十一 èrshíyī** NUM twenty-one

**二十二 èrshí'èr** NUM twenty-two

**二十三 èrshísān** NUM twenty-three

**二十四 èrshísì** NUM twenty-four

**二十五 èrshíwǔ** NUM twenty-five

**二十六 èrshíliù** NUM twenty-six

**二十七 èrshíqī** NUM twenty-seven

**二十八 èrshíbā** NUM twenty-eight

**二十九 èrshíjiǔ** NUM twenty-nine

### RELATED WORDS

## 3 十 · U+5341 · TM 2 · FM 丨

**shí** NUM ten; topmost; perfect

**十二月 shí'èryuè** N December, the twelfth month of the lunar year

**十分 shífēn** ADV very, extremely

见到你十分高兴。 *It is a great pleasure to meet you.*

**十进制 shíjìnzhì** N the decimal system

**十拿九稳 shínájiǔwěn** EXP as good as assured

提前预订才十拿九稳有座位。 *Book early and you'll be assured a seat.*

**十全十美 shíquánshíměi** EXP perfect in every way

**十万火急 shíwànhuǒjí** EXP extremely urgent

**十一月 shíyīyuè** N November, the eleventh month of the lunar year

**十月 shíyuè** N October, the tenth month of the lunar year

**十之八九 shízhībājiǔ** EXP in eight or nine cases out of ten, most likely

他十之八九(十有八九)不学中文了。 *Most likely, he will stop studying Chinese.*

**十字架 shízìjià** N cross, crucifix · MW 个、副

**十字路口 shízìlùkǒu** N intersection; crossroads · MW 个

到下一个十字路口, 向左转。 *At the next intersection, turn left.*

他面对人生的十字路口。 *He is at a crossroads in his life.*

**十足 shízú** ADJ pure, sheer, 100-percent, complete

邻居都说傻瓜是个十足的大好人! *All of ShaGua's neighbors say he is a nice guy through and through!*

**十一 shíyī** NUM eleven

**十二 shí'èr** NUM twelve

**十三 shísān** NUM thirteen

**十四 shísì** NUM fourteen

**十五 shíwǔ** NUM fifteen

**十六 shíliù** NUM sixteen

**十七 shíqī** NUM seventeen

**十八 shíbā** NUM eighteen

**十九 shíjiǔ** NUM nineteen

## 3 十 shí (continued)

**RELATED WORDS**

| | | |
|---|---|---|
| 一十 1 | 一十一 1 | 一十二 1 |
| 一十三 1 | 一十四 1 | 一十五 1 |
| 一十六 1 | 一十七 1 | 一十八 1 |
| 一十九 1 | 二十 2 | 二十一 2 |
| 二十二 2 | 二十三 2 | 二十四 2 |
| 二十五 2 | 二十六 2 | 二十七 2 |
| 二十八 2 | 二十九 2 | 八十 6 |
| 八十一 6 | 八十二 6 | 八十三 6 |
| 八十四 6 | 八十五 6 | 八十六 6 |
| 八十七 6 | 八十八 6 | 八十九 6 |
| 三十 9 | 三十一 9 | 三十二 9 |
| 三十三 9 | 三十四 9 | 三十五 9 |
| 三十六 9 | 三十七 9 | 三十八 9 |
| 三十九 9 | 七十 34 | 七十一 34 |
| 七十二 34 | 七十三 34 | 七十四 34 |
| 七十五 34 | 七十六 34 | 七十七 34 |
| 七十八 34 | 七十九 34 | 七十二行 34 |
| 六十 69 | 六十一 69 | 六十二 69 |
| 六十三 69 | 六十四 69 | 六十五 69 |
| 六十六 69 | 六十七 69 | 六十八 69 |
| 六十九 69 | 五十 79 | 五十一 79 |
| 五十二 79 | 五十三 79 | 五十四 79 |
| 五十五 79 | 五十六 79 | 五十七 79 |
| 五十八 79 | 五十九 79 | 九十 116 |
| 九十一 116 | 九十二 116 | 九十三 116 |
| 九十四 116 | 九十五 116 | 九十六 116 |
| 九十七 116 | 九十八 116 | 九十九 116 |
| 四十 271 | 四十一 271 | 四十二 271 |
| 四十三 271 | 四十四 271 | 四十五 271 |
| 四十六 271 | 四十七 271 | 四十八 271 |
| 四十九 271 | 红十字 474 | 五光十色 79 |
| 一五一十 1 | 以一当十 101 | |

## 4 人    U+4EBA    TM 2 FM 丿

**rén** N person; adult; everybody; others; personality; manpower; hand

三位外国人 *three foreigners*

他已经长大成人。 *He has grown up.*

三组工人 *three groups of workers*

他看不起人。 *He looks down on others.*

傻瓜为人正直。 *ShaGua is honest.*

我们不缺人。 *We are not short on manpower.*

**人本主义 rénběnzhǔyì** N humanism

**人才 réncái** N talented person · MW 个、位

她是一个人才。 *She is a talented person.*

**人次 réncì** MW person time; [measure word for man-hours]

**人大 réndà** N Chinese National People's Congress · MW 届、次

**人道 réndào** N·ADJ humanity, humanitarianism; humane

**人格 réngé** N character, moral quality

认识傻瓜的人都赞赏他的**人格**。 *Many who know ShaGua respect his moral integrity.*

**人工 réngōng** ADJ·N man-made; manual work; manpower

**人海 rénhǎi** N sea of faces, huge crowd of people

**人机对话 rénjīduìhuà** N man-machine interaction

**人家 rénjiā** N household, family; others; oneself · MW 户

我们邻里有九户**人家**。 *There are nine households in our neighborhood.*

**人家**做不到的我们也能做到。 *We can do what others were unable to do.*

**人家**等着你的回答呢！ *I am waiting for your response!*

**人间 rénjiān** N the world

**人口 rénkǒu** N population; number of people

**人类 rénlèi** N mankind; human

**人力 rénlì** N manpower

**人们 rénmen** N people, the public

**人民 rénmín** N the people

**人民币 rénmínbì** N Renminbi (RMB; the official currency of the People's Republic of China) · MW 块、元、毛、角、分

**人情 rénqíng** N human feelings, emotion; favor; human relationship

他不讲**人情**。 *He is unreasonable.*

邻居都欠了傻瓜很多**人情**。 *ShaGua's neighbors owe him many favors.*

**人权 rénquán** N human rights

**人群 rénqún** N crowd; throng · MW 伙

**人参 rénshēn** N ginseng · MW 枝、盒、两

**人生 rénshēng** N life

**人士 rénshì** N personage, public figure · MW 位

各界**人士** *people from various circles*

**人事 rénshì** N personnel matters

**人手 rénshǒu** N manpower

**人事**部门缺少**人手**。 *The Human Resource Department is short on manpower.*

**人寿保险 rénshòubǎoxiǎn** N life insurance

**人物** **rénwù** N figure, personage · MW 个、位、名

他是一位知名**人物**。 *He is a celebrity.*

**人心** **rénxīn** N popular sentiment, will of the people

**人行道** **rénxíngdào** N sidewalk · MW 条

**人行桥** **rénxíngqiáo** N footbridge, pedestrian bridge · MW 座

**人性** **rénxìng** N human nature; humanity

**人造** **rénzào** ADJ man-made

## RELATED WORDS

| | |
|---|---|
| 工人 12 | 土人 15 |
| 丈人 17 | 个人 18 |
| 个人主义 18 | 大人 20 |
| 大人物 20 | 夫人 55 |
| 女人 57 | 小人物 61 |
| 仁人志士 64 | 仆人 65 |
| 文人 70 | 歹人 74 |
| 本人 90 | 生人 107 |
| 友人 110 | 主人 124 |
| 主人公 124 | 主人翁 124 |
| 无人 139 | 圣人 142 |
| 双人 146 | 古人 154 |
| 与人为善 158 | 巨人 162 |
| 众人 175 | 白人 176 |
| 内人 191 | 仙人掌 207 |
| 任人唯亲 211 | 外人 218 |
| 为人 223 | 来人 260 |
| 艺人 274 | 坏人 280 |
| 丢人 297 | 后人 310 |
| 发人深省 311 | 用人 313 |
| 杀人 317 | 仇人 319 |
| 行人 327 | 忙人 343 |
| 引人 371 | 引人入胜 371 |
| 老人 375 | 求人 376 |
| 各人 425 | 名人 426 |
| 伟人 451 | 狂人 469 |
| 私人 471 | 红人 474 |
| 军人 489 | 动人 514 |
| 某人 536 | 拟人 575 |
| 他人 616 | 好人 627 |
| 美人 671 | 单人 672 |
| 类人猿 676 | 闲人 679 |
| 法人 686 | 洋人 689 |
| 怪人 696 | 证人 705 |
| 贤人 750 | 男人 757 |
| 奇人 854 | 待人接物 872 |
| 犯人 884 | 盲人 906 |
| 亲人 908 | 完人 909 |
| 穷人 912 | 恼人 931 |
| 要人 969 | 贱人 1037 |
| 别人 1049 | 真人真事 1075 |
| 敌人 1127 | 疯人院 1147 |

| | |
|---|---|
| 羞人 1154 | 诗人 1181 |
| 迷人 1187 | 送人情 1188 |
| 爱人 1264 | 做人 1282 |
| 恋人 1314 | 客人 1316 |
| 害人虫 1319 | 唐人街 1324 |
| 病人 1327 | 前人 1329 |
| 雪人 1369 | 恩人 1381 |
| 黑人 1389 | 损人利己 1401 |
| 猎人 1444 | 媒人 1449 |
| 旁人 1473 | 惊人 1489 |
| 情人 1491 | 族人 1519 |
| 喜人 1531 | 罪人 1542 |
| 新人 1638 | 骂人 1652 |
| 骂人话 1652 | 超人 1684 |
| 野人 1685 | 路人 1785 |
| 嫁人 1799 | 游人 1818 |
| 能人 1873 | 强人 1896 |
| 骗人 1937 | 熟人 1973 |
| 介绍人 44 | 中华人民共和国 86 |
| 乡下人 117 | 立约人 125 |
| 头面人物 128 | 全国人民 172 |
| 在编人员 188 | 外星人 218 |
| 收件人 282 | 收款人 282 |
| 发言人 311 | 当事人 335 |
| 有心人 439 | 守门人 486 |
| 证婚人 705 | 承租人 972 |
| 局外人 1069 | 候选人 1086 |
| 经纪人 1110 | 制片人 1130 |
| 热心人 1390 | 接班人 1405 |
| 被害人 1517 | 不乏其人 24 |
| 以理服人 101 | 以貌取人 101 |
| 仗势欺人 121 | 目中无人 151 |
| 先发制人 422 | 达官贵人 505 |
| 被保险人 1517 | 怨天尤人 1792 |
| 嫁祸于人 1799 | 广告经纪人 23 |

---

**5　入**　　U+5165　　TM **2**　FM 丿

**rù** V·N to enter; to join; to agree with; income

**入场** **rùchǎng** V to be admitted; to enter

凭票**入场**。 *Admission by ticket only.*

**入场券** **rùchǎngquàn** N admission ticket · MW 张

**入股** **rùgǔ** V to buy a share

**入伙** **rùhuǒ** V to join a gang; to join in a partnership

**入籍** **rùjí** V naturalization

**入境** **rùjìng** V to enter a country

**入境口岸** **rùjìngkǒu'àn** N port of entry · MW 个

**入口** **rùkǒu** N entrance · MW 个

**5 入 rù** (continued)

这条高速公路的入口在哪里？ *Where's the entrance to the highway?*

入库 **rùkù** V to be put in storage

入列 **rùliè** V to take one's place in the ranks

入门 **rùmén** V·N to cross the threshold; elementary course

她的汉语尚未入门。 *She doesn't even know the basics of Chinese yet.*

汉语语法入门 *the basics of Chinese grammar*

入迷 **rùmí** V to be fascinated

傻瓜入迷地读着手中的中文书。 *ShaGua is deeply engrossed in his Chinese book.*

入魔 **rùmó** V to be spellbound

入侵 **rùqīn** V to invade; to intrude

入神 **rùshén** V·ADJ to be enthralled; marvelous

傻瓜看中文电影看得很入神。 *ShaGua was enthralled while watching the Chinese movie.*

入手 **rùshǒu** V to start with, to begin with

学中文要从基本训练入手。 *Study of the Chinese language must begin with training in the basics.*

入选 **rùxuǎn** V to be selected, to be chosen

入学 **rùxué** V to begin school

新生今天入学。 *The new students will begin school today.*

入眼 **rùyǎn** ADJ pleasing to the eye

入狱 **rùyù** V to be put in prison

入账 **rùzhàng** V to enter an item in an account

**RELATED WORDS**

| | | |
|---|---|---|
| 介入 44 | 归入 166 | 并入 225 |
| 买入汇率 248 | 出入 258 | 收入 282 |
| 岁入 380 | 加入 463 | 注入 496 |
| 进入 713 | 吸入 776 | 投入 1008 |
| 映入 1036 | 侵入 1280 | 卷入 1333 |
| 深入 1345 | 插入 1555 | 陷入 1678 |
| 溶入 1744 | 摄入 1772 | 输入 1867 |
| 年收入 182 | 引人入胜 371 | 纯收入 1290 |

**6 八**    U+516B    TM 2   FM 丿

**bā** NUM eight

八成 **bāchéng** MW·ADV eighty percent; most likely

这事情有八成啦。 *We stand a fair chance of success.*

八卦 **bāguà** N set of symbolic signs created in ancient China

八仙 **bāxiān** N Eight Immortals (according to legend)

八月 **bāyuè** N August

八折 **bāzhé** MW twenty-percent discount

这件衣服打八折。 *These clothes are 20 percent off.*

八十 **bāshí** NUM eighty

八十一 **bāshíyī** NUM eighty-one

八十二 **bāshí'èr** NUM eighty-two

八十三 **bāshísān** NUM eighty-three

八十四 **bāshísì** NUM eighty-four

八十五 **bāshíwǔ** NUM eighty-five

八十六 **bāshíliù** NUM eighty-six

八十七 **bāshíqī** NUM eighty-seven

八十八 **bāshíbā** NUM eighty-eight

八十九 **bāshíjiǔ** NUM eighty-nine

**RELATED WORDS**

| | | |
|---|---|---|
| 十八 3 | 王八 27 | 丑八怪 85 |
| 一十八 1 | 二十八 2 | 十之八九 3 |
| 三十八 9 | 七上八下 34 | 七十八 34 |
| 七嘴八舌 34 | 七拼八凑 34 | 七零八落 34 |
| 六十八 69 | 五十八 79 | 五花八门 79 |
| 九十八 116 | 半斤八两 127 | 四十八 271 |
| 四面八方 271 | 乌七八糟 601 | 乱七八糟 901 |

**7 厂 廠**    U+5382    TM 2   FM 丿

**chǎng** N factory, mill, plant

厂房 **chǎngfáng** N building used as a factory · MW 个、间

厂家 **chǎngjiā** N factory · MW 个

厂矿 **chǎngkuàng** N company, firm; mines · MW 个、间、家

厂门 **chǎngmén** N factory gate · MW 个、道

厂商 **chǎngshāng** N firm; contractor · MW 个、名

厂休 **chǎngxiū** N day of rest for factory workers

今天是厂休日，我不用上班。 *I'm not working today because it is our day off.*

厂长 **chǎngzhǎng** N factory director · MW 个、位、名

厂主 **chǎngzhǔ** N factory owner · MW 个、名

厂址 **chǎngzhǐ** N factory address · MW 个

厂子 **chǎngzi** N factory, mill, workshop · MW 个

**RELATED WORDS**

| | | |
|---|---|---|
| 工厂 12 | 水厂 159 | 出厂 258 |
| 药厂 1392 | | |

---

**8** 丁     U+4E01    TM **3** FM 一

**dīng** N man; member of a family; cubed meat

丁当 **dīngdāng** ONOM ding-dong, jingle

丁零当郎 **dīnglingdāngláng** ONOM tinkle; jingle; cling-clang

丁字 **dīngzì** ADJ T-shaped

一直开到丁字路口, 然后向右转。*Drive until the road ends, then turn right.*

**RELATED WORDS**

沙丁鱼 342     补丁 508     园丁 763
尼古丁 441     目不识丁 151

---

**9** 三     U+4E09    TM **3** FM 一

**sān** NUM three; more than two, several; twists and turns

这件事情, 你得三思。*You must think twice about this issue.*

三长两短 **sānchángliǎngduǎn** EXP unexpected misfortune, accident

三重奏 **sānchóngzòu** N trio · MW 段、曲

三等分 **sānděngfèn** N trisection

三度 **sāndù** N three-dimensional

三伏 **sānfú** N·ADJ three ten-day periods of the hot season (summer)

三国 **sānguó** N Three Kingdoms

三合一 **sānhéyī** N three in one

三角 **sānjiǎo** N trigonometry; triangle · MW 个

三轮车 **sānlúnchē** N tricycle · MW 架、辆

三七开 **sānqīkāi** EXP 70-30 ratio

对傻瓜要三七开。*Remember that, on balance, ShaGua is good.*

三思而行 **sānsīérxíng** EXP to think twice (LIT three times) before you act

有些重要的事情, 你要三思而行。*In such an important matter, you should think twice before you act.*

三天两头 **sāntiānliǎngtóu** EXP every other day or so

他三天两头不上中文课。*He skips his Chinese class every other day.*

三心二意 **sānxīnèryì** EXP to be of two minds, to be halfhearted

学中文不能 三心二意。*We must not study Chinese halfheartedly.*

三言两语 **sānyánliǎngyǔ** EXP in a few words

傻瓜上夜校的事, 三言两语说不清。*As for how ShaGua studies in night school, I can't tell you in a few words.*

三月 **sānyuè** N March

三只手 **sānzhǐshǒu** N pickpocket · MW 个

三十 **sānshí** NUM thirty

三十一 **sānshíyī** NUM thirty-one

三十二 **sānshí'èr** NUM thirty-two

三十三 **sānshísān** NUM thirty-three

三十四 **sānshísì** NUM thirty-four

三十五 **sānshíwǔ** NUM thirty-five

三十六 **sānshíliù** NUM thirty-six

三十七 **sānshíqī** NUM thirty-seven

三十八 **sānshíbā** NUM thirty-eight

三十九 **sānshíjiǔ** NUM thirty-nine

**RELATED WORDS**

十三 3     不三不四 24     丢三落四 297
再三 354     低三下四 618     鸡三明治 1373
第三者 1695     一十三 1     二十三 2
八十三 6     七十三 34     六十三 69
五十三 79     九十三 116     四十三 271

---

**10** 下     U+430B    TM **3** FM 一

**xià** N·ADJ·V·MW below, under; inferior, next, lowly; to descend; to get off/out; to fall; to go to; to put in; to take; to make a move; to be less than; [measure word for brief, sudden actions]

地下 *underground*

下个月 *next month*

下车 *to get out of a car*

雨下得很大。*The rain is falling heavily.*

下馆子 *to go to a restaurant*

下功夫 *to make an effort*

**10 下 xià** (continued)

下岗 *unemployment*

不下三天 *no less than three days*

门铃响了五下。 *The doorbell rang five times.*

下班 xiàbān ⓥ to be off duty, to be off work

下半夜 xiàbànyè Ⓝ the time after midnight

下笔 xiàbǐ ⓥ to begin to write

有人说, 写小说最难是下笔。 *Some say the hardest part of writing a novel is just putting pen to paper.*

下边 xiàbian Ⓝ lower level; below, under; next, following

下不为例 xiàbùwéilì EXP not to be repeated

这是个错误, 下不为例。 *This was a mistake that will never happen again.*

下层 xiàcéng Ⓝ lower level

下场 xiàchǎng V·N to go off stage; end, fate

该她下场了。 *She should get off the stage.*

这是坏蛋的下场。 *This is a fitting end for a bad guy.*

下车 xiàchē ⓥ to get off a bus

我应该在哪一站下车? *Which stop do I get off at?*

下船 xiàchuán ⓥ to go ashore, to disembark

下次 xiàcì Ⓝ next time

下等 xiàděng ADJ low-grade, inferior

下放 xiàfàng ⓥ to transfer to a lower level

下飞机 xiàfēijī ⓥ to get off an airplane

下工夫 xiàgōngfu EXP to concentrate one's effort

下跪 xiàguì ⓥ to kneel down

下贱 xiàjiàn ADJ low, contemptible

真下贱。 *What a contemptible and miserable wretch.*

下降 xiàjiàng ⓥ to descend, to drop, to fall; to decline

下酒 xiàjiǔ ⓥ to go with wine

许多人喜欢用花生下酒。 *Many people enjoy having peanuts with wine.*

下课 xiàkè ⓥ to finish class

还有五分钟就下课了。 *The class will be over in five minutes.*

下来 xiàlái ⓥ to come down

他们从楼上下来。 *They are coming downstairs.*

把树上的苹果摘下来 *to pick the apples off the tree*

下列 xiàliè Ⓝ listed below, following

注意下列几个问题。 *Special attention should be paid to the following items.*

下令 xiàlìng ⓥ to give orders

下楼 xiàlóu ⓥ to go downstairs

下落 xiàluò N·V whereabouts; to drop, to fall

我四处打听傻瓜的下落。 *I have been making some inquiries as to ShaGua's whereabouts.*

气球正在下落。 *The balloons are falling.*

下水道 xiàshuǐdào Ⓝ sewer · MW 条

下台 xiàtái ⓥ to step down; to leave office; to fall out of power

下同 xiàtóng ⓥ to be the same below

下文 xiàwén Ⓝ what follows in the passage; later development

傻瓜去中国以后, 就没有下文了。 *Since ShaGua went to China, there has not been any news about him.*

下午 xiàwǔ Ⓝ afternoon · MW 个

下午我们有一节课。 *We will have one class in the afternoon.*

下乡 xiàxiāng ⓥ to go to the countryside

下雨 xiàyǔ ⓥ to rain

下葬 xiàzàng ⓥ to bury

**RELATED WORDS**

**11 又** U+53C8 TM **3** FM 一

**yòu** ADV and; again; besides, too

又… yòu ADV [indicates repetition, continuation]

汽油的价格又提高了。 *The price of oil has gone up again.*

又及 yòují ⓥ to add (another line); postscript

又是 yòushì ADV [indicates an additional idea, an afterthought]

说是一回事, 做又是一回事。 *Saying and doing are two different things.*

他又是老师又是学生。*He is both a teacher and a student.*

又有　**yòuyǒu**　V·ADV　[indicates an additional idea, an afterthought]

她又有了一个男朋友。*She's got another boyfriend.*

又…又…　**yòu… yòu…**　ADV　both … and …

这里的天气又闷又热。*The weather here is both stuffy and humid.*

---

**12 工**　　　U+5DE5　TM **3** FM 一

**gōng**　V·N　to work; worker; labor; project; man day; industry; skill

雇佣童工是非法的。*It is illegal to hire child laborers.*

明天有一个新项目要动工。*We will begin a new project tomorrow.*

这是重工基地。*This is the base of heavy industry.*

工厂　**gōngchǎng**　N　factory · MW 个、家

工场　**gōngchǎng**　N　workshop · MW 个

工潮　**gōngcháo**　N　worker's strike

工程　**gōngchéng**　N　engineering; project · MW 项、个

工程师　**gōngchéngshī**　N　engineer · MW 个、位、名

我的梦想是成为一名工程师。*My dream is to become an engineer.*

工地　**gōngdì**　N　building/construction site · MW 个

工夫　**gōngfu**　N　time; effort; workmanship

虽然大家都说考试很难, 但是他没花什么工夫就考完了。*Although the test was difficult for everyone, he finished it without much effort.*

工会　**gōnghuì**　N　labor union · MW 个

工具　**gōngjù**　N　tool, instrument · MW 个、件、套

语言是交际的工具。*Language is an instrument of communication.*

工龄　**gōnglíng**　N　length of service · MW 年

工农　**gōngnóng**　N　workers and peasants

工钱　**gōngqian**　N　money paid for odd jobs; wages · MW 笔

你一个星期的工钱是多少? *How much do you earn in a week?*

工人　**gōngrén**　N　worker, workman · MW 个、名

工伤　**gōngshāng**　N　injury suffered on the job · MW 次

工商界　**gōngshāngjiè**　N　business circles

工头　**gōngtóu**　N　foreman, boss · MW 个、名

工学院　**gōngxuéyuàn**　N　college of engineering · MW 间、家、所

工资　**gōngzī**　N　wages; pay; income · MW 笔

我们每个星期五发工资。*We get paid every Friday.*

工作　**gōngzuò**　V·N　to work; job · MW 个、项

你做什么工作? *What is your job?*

我在一家大公司工作。*I work at a large company.*

工作服　**gōngzuòfú**　N　work clothes · MW 套、件

### RELATED WORDS

---

**13 干**　乾　　U+5E72　TM **3** FM 一

**gān** (乾)　ADJ·ADV·V　dry; adopted; empty; in vain; to have to do with, to be concerned with

干衣服　*dry clothes*

干女儿　*adopted daughter*

相干　*to be concerned with*

**gàn** (幹)　V·N　to do; to fight; cadre, cell; trunk

干掉他们吧! *Let's get rid of them.*

他是一名高干。*He is a senior official.*

这有一根光秃秃的树干。*There is a stripped tree trunk here.*

干巴巴　**gānbābā**　ADJ　dried up

他的文章干巴巴的。*His articles are dull and dry.*

干杯　**gānbēi**　V　to toast; cheers, bottoms up

为我们的友谊干杯。*I wish to propose a toast to our friendship.*

干瘪　**gānbiě**　ADJ　shriveled

干脆　**gāncuì**　ADJ·ADV　straightforward; simply

**13** 干 **gān/gàn** (continued)

你干脆说"行"还是"不行"。 *Just say yes or no.*

他三天内剪了四次头发，最后干脆理光头。
*He had his hair cut four times in three days, then he finally just shaved it off.*

干瞪眼 **gāndèngyǎn** V to stand by anxiously

干净 **gānjìng** ADJ clean, neat and tidy; completely, totally

这间房很干净。 *The room is meticulously clean.*

干枯 **gānkū** ADJ dried up, withered

干扰 **gānrǎo** V to disturb, to interfere

请不要干扰我的私生活。 *Please don't disturb my privacy.*

干涉 **gānshè** V to interfere, to intervene

请不要干涉我的事情。 *Please don't interfere in my business.*

干燥 **gānzào** ADJ dry, arid; dull, uninteresting

干部 **gànbù** N cadre · MW 个、位、名

干才 **gàncái** N ability, capability

干道 **gàndào** N main road; artery · MW 条

干掉 **gàndiào** V to kill, to get rid of

干活 **gànhuó** V to work, to work on a job

我们干活去吧。 *Let's get to work.*

干劲 **gànjìn** N vigor; enthusiasm · MW 股

干练 **gànliàn** ADJ capable and skillful

干吗 **gànmá** QPRON whatever for!; what to do

傻瓜，你在干吗？ *ShaGua, what are you doing?*

干事 **gànshi** V·N to work; secretary in charge of something · MW 个、名

干线 **gànxiàn** N main line · MW 条

**RELATED WORDS**

| | | |
|---|---|---|
| 才干 39 | 风干 194 | 巧干 364 |
| 若干 554 | 乌干达 601 | 实干 668 |
| 单干 672 | 相干 805 | 烘干 953 |
| 烘干机 953 | 抗干扰 1009 | 树干 1031 |
| 笋干 1078 | 饼干 1116 | 骨干 1543 |
| 愣干 1735 | 精干 1832 | 能干 1873 |
| 鼓足干劲 1688 | 葡萄干 1766 | |

**14** 上    U+4E0A    TM **3** FM |

**shàng** N·V on, previous, upper, upward, higher; better; first (part of); to go up, to get on; to go to; to apply, to put on; to submit; to supply; to appear (in the news); to be engaged

傻瓜在楼上。 *ShaGua is upstairs.*

上个星期 *last week*

你上车吗？ *Are you getting on the bus?*

我明天上北京。 *I will go to Beijing tomorrow.*

该她上场了。 *Let her on the stage.*

请快点儿上菜。 *Could you rush the order?*

她给我上药。 *She is putting medicine on me.*

傻瓜上报啦！ *ShaGua is in the newspaper!*

这栋房子的价钱可能上百万美元。 *The price of this house may be over one million dollars.*

上岸 **shàng'àn** V to go ashore, to land

上班 **shàngbān** V to go to work

上层 **shàngcéng** N upper level

上船 **shàngchuán** V to board a ship

上床 **shàngchuáng** V to go to bed

我晚上十点上床睡觉。 *I go to bed at 10 P.M.*

上蹿下跳 **shàngcuānxiàtiào** EXP to run around on sinister errands; to jump around

上当 **shàngdàng** V to be taken in, to be fooled

当心坏人，不要上当。 *Don't allow yourself to be fooled by evil people.*

上等 **shàngděng** ADJ first-class

上帝 **Shàngdì** N God

上访 **shàngfǎng** V to appeal to the higher authorities for help

上工 **shànggōng** V to go to work

上钩 **shànggōu** V to get hooked, to rise to the bait

上海 **Shànghǎi** N Shanghai

上呼吸道 **shànghūxīdào** N upper respiratory tract

上火 **shànghuǒ** V to get angry

上级 **shàngjí** N higher level; higher authorities · MW 个、位、名

上街 **shàngjiē** V to go out; to go shopping

你今天上街买东西吗？ *Will you go shopping today?*

上课 **shàngkè** V to attend class, to go to class

学校八点半开始上课。 *Classes begin at 8:30.*

上列 **shàngliè** ADJ above; listed above

今天的作业是回答上列三个问题。 *Today's homework is to answer the three questions listed above.*

上流 **shàngliú** N upper class

她正在融入这个城市的上流社会。 *She is moving in fashionable circles in this city.*

上门 **shàngmén** V to deliver goods to the doorstep

我们送货上门。 *We deliver goods to your doorstep.*

**上面 shàngmian** N above; on the surface of; higher authorities; respect, regard

他在汉语上面下了很多功夫。 *He has put a lot of effort into his study of Chinese.*

**上身 shàngshēn** N upper part of the body

**上诉 shàngsù** V to appeal

律师决定向高一级法院上诉。 *The lawyer decided to appeal to a higher court.*

**上台 shàngtái** V to appear on stage; to come to power

**上午 shàngwǔ** N morning · MW 个

他上午十一点才有课。 *He didn't have class until 11 o'clock in the morning.*

我们上午八点钟上班。 *We start work at eight in the morning.*

**上下 shàngxià** N old and young; top to bottom

举国上下一片欢腾。 *The entire nation is very pleased.*

**上学 shàngxué** V to go to school

我今天有点不舒服, 所以没去上学。 *I didn't feel well today, so I didn't go to school.*

**上演 shàngyǎn** V to put on the stage, to perform

**上映 shàngyìng** V to show (a film)

**上涨 shàngzhǎng** V to rise; to go up

在过去三年里, 物价一直在上涨。 *Prices have risen steadily over the past three years.*

**上座 shàngzuò** N seat of honor · MW 个

**RELATED WORDS**

| | | |
|---|---|---|
| 上旬 596 | 七上八下 34 | 以上 101 |
| 占上风 153 | 世上 163 | 至上 244 |
| 马上 247 | 早上 268 | 自上而下 305 |
| 如上 464 | 冰上运动 493 | 向上 603 |
| 身上 604 | 府上 660 | 赶上 822 |
| 看上 841 | 皇上 858 | 座上客 920 |
| 海上 1494 | 楼上 1567 | 掌上明珠 1734 |
| 晚上 1779 | 跟上 1784 | 瞒上欺下 1914 |
| 戴上 1941 | 名义上 426 | 顶头上司 724 |
| 事实上 987 | 谈不上 1356 | 说不上 1631 |
| 至高无上 244 | 青云直上 740 | 蒸蒸日上 1768 |

---

**15 土**    U+571F    TM **3** FM |

**tǔ** N·ADJ soil, earth, land, ground; local, native; unfashionable

**土坝 tǔbà** N earth-filled dam · MW 个、条

**土包子 tǔbāozi** EXP bumpkin, clodhopper · MW 个

有人认为傻瓜是一个土包子。 *Some people think that ShaGua is a simple country bumpkin.*

**土崩瓦解 tǔbēngwǎjiě** EXP to disintegrate, to crumble, to fall apart

**土产 tǔchǎn** N local product

**土地 tǔdì** N land, soil; territory · MW 片

土地国有制 *state ownership of land*

**土豆 tǔdòu** N potato · MW 个、筐、堆

**土方 tǔfāng** N cubic meter of earth; folk remedy

**土匪 tǔfěi** N bandit · MW 个、伙

**土话 tǔhuà** N local dialect · MW 种、类

**土木 tǔmù** N building, construction

**土壤 tǔrǎng** N soil · MW 把、堆

**土著人 tǔzhùrén** N native, aborigine · MW 个、群

**土生土长 tǔshēngtǔzhǎng** EXP locally born and bred

**土特产 tǔtèchǎn** N local specialty · MW 种

这种面条是当地的土特产。 *This type of noodle is a local specialty.*

**土星 tǔxīng** N Saturn (planet)

**土专家 tǔzhuānjiā** N self-taught expert · MW 个、位、名

**RELATED WORDS**

| | | |
|---|---|---|
| 乡土 117 | 水土 159 | 出土 258 |
| 沙土 342 | 冻土 680 | 砂土 733 |
| 故土 816 | 泥土 1164 | 破土 1374 |
| 肥土 1459 | 领土 1465 | 混凝土 1739 |

---

**16 土**    U+58EB    TM **3** FM |

**shì** N scholar; non-commissioned officer; person

**士兵 shìbīng** N rank-and-file soldier · MW 个、队、群

**士气 shìqì** N morale

作为领导, 不能忽视下级的士气。 *As a leader, it is vital to not ignore the morale of your followers.*

**士绅 shìshēn** N gentry · MW 个、位、名

**士卒 shìzú** N soldier, private · MW 个, 名

**RELATED WORDS**

| | | |
|---|---|---|
| 人士 4 | 义士 22 | 女士 57 |
| 卫士 82 | 凡士林 193 | 武士 513 |
| 志士 528 | 护士 569 | 便士 865 |
| 修士 870 | 学士 1155 | 勇士 1371 |
| 硕士 1375 | 教士 1424 | 博士 1549 |
| 院士 1677 | 骑士 1840 | 隐士 1912 |
| 仁人志士 64 | | |

## 17 丈　　　　U+4E08　　TM **3** FM 丿

**zhàng** N husband; man; unit of length (= 3⅓ meters (about 11 feet))

**丈夫** zhàngfu N man; husband ·
MW 个、位、名

你是一个大**丈夫**! *You're the man!*

傻瓜是傻瓜太太的**丈夫**。*ShaGua is Mrs. ShaGua's husband.*

**丈量** zhàngliáng V to measure

**丈母娘** zhàngmǔniáng N wife's mother, mother-in-law · MW 个

**丈人** zhàngrén N wife's father, father-in-law · MW 个

**RELATED WORD**
一丈 1

## 18 个　個　　U+4E2A　　TM **3** FM 丿

**gè** ADJ·MW individual, specific; each; [measure word for things; the most common measure word, used when the measure word specific to a noun is unknown]

你有几**个**朋友? *How many friends do you have?*

三**个**苹果一块钱。*One dollar for three apples.*

**个案** gè'àn N case · MW 个

**个别** gèbié ADJ individual; very few

大多数人都来了, 只有**个别**人请假。*Almost everyone attended; only one or two people asked to be excused.*

**个个** gègè N each and every one, all

晚会上, **个个**都玩得很高兴。*At the party, everybody had a good time.*

**个儿** gèr N size; height

别看她**个儿**不小, 劲儿可不大。*She's big, but she's not so strong.*

**个人** gèrén N individual; personal

**个人**的看法也很重要。*Personal opinion is also important.*

**个人主义** gèrénzhǔyì N individualism

**个体** gètǐ N individual · MW 个

**个性** gèxìng N individuality, personality

我认为傻瓜不会那样做, 那不符合他的**个性**。*I don't think ShaGua would do that; it doesn't fit his personality.*

**个子** gèzi N height, stature

她是个小**个子**女人。*She is a short woman.*

**RELATED WORDS**

几个 115　　几个月 115　　四个现代化 271
自个儿 305　　这个 715　　那个 980
哪个 1666　　整个 1845

## 19 千　韆　　U+5343　　TM **3** FM 丿

**qiān** NUM thousand; many

**千变万化** qiānbiànwànhuà EXP ever-changing; kaleidoscopic

**千方百计** qiānfāngbǎijì EXP by every possible means

她**千方百计**要上中文课。*She tried everything to take the Chinese course.*

**千古** qiāngǔ N for all time, forever and ever

**千金** qiānjīn N lot of money; daughter · MW 个、名

**千里** qiānlǐ N·MW a long distance; [measure word for 1,000 li (unit of length (= ½ kilometer))]

**千篇一律** qiānpiānyīlǜ EXP stereotyped, following the same pattern

他上课总是**千篇一律**。*He always teaches his classes following the same pattern.*

**千万** qiānwàn NUM·ADV ten million; of extreme importance

这事你**千万**记住。*Be sure to bear this in mind.*

**千千万万** qiānqiānwànwàn ADJ thousands and thousands of

**千载难逢** qiānzǎinánféng EXP occurring once in a thousand years, very rare

**RELATED WORDS**

五千 79　　秋千 641

## 20 大　　　　U+5927　　TM **3** FM 丿

**dà** ADJ·N·ADV big, large, great; strong; loud; general, main; old, oldest; size; adult; greatly; fully

**大半** dàbàn N·ADV more than half; very likely

班上**大半**是女生。*Most of the students in class are girls.*

都下午六点了, 他**大半**不会来了。*It is 6 o'clock in the afternoon; most likely he will not come.*

**大本营** dàběnyíng N headquarters, base camp · MW 个、座

**大便** dàbiàn V·N to have a bowel movement; stool, feces · MW 泡、堆

**大伯** dàbó N father's older brother · MW 个、位

**大部分** dàbùfen N greater part, majority

阅读占去了学生**大部分**闲暇时间。*Reading occupies most of a student's free time.*

**大不了** dàbuliǎo ADV at the worst

**大不了**我们再从头开始。*If worse comes to worst, we'll start all over again.*

**大肠** dàcháng N large intestine · MW 条、节

**大潮** dàcháo N spring tide; influential social trend

**大车** dàchē N cart · MW 辆、架

**大吃一惊** dàchīyìjīng EXP to be startled at, to be taken aback

**大打出手** dàdǎchūshǒu EXP to strike violently

**大大** dàdà ADV greatly

他的中文写作水平**大大**提高。*His Chinese composition has greatly improved.*

**大胆** dàdǎn ADJ bold, daring

傻瓜的**大胆**让我吃惊。*I was surprised at ShaGua's boldness.*

**大刀** dàdāo N broadsword · MW 把

**大地** dàdì N earth, mother earth

**大豆** dàdòu N soybean · MW 颗、粒

**大肚子** dàdùzi N big eater; pregnant · MW 个

**大多** dàduō ADV mostly

**大多数** dàduōshù N great majority, most

这个班里**大多数**是二十岁以下的学生。*Most of the students in this class are under 20.*

**大方** dàfāng ADJ generous; natural and poised; in good taste

作为哥哥, 他应该对弟妹们更**大方**些。*As an older brother, he should learn to be more generous to his siblings.*

**大风** dàfēng N fresh gale, strong wind · MW 阵

**大幅度** dàfúdù ADV by a wide margin

**大概** dàgài ADJ·N·ADV approximate; general idea; probably

这仅仅是个**大概**数字。*This is just an approximate number.*

他**大概**走了一个小时。*He left about an hour ago.*

**大哥** dàgē N oldest brother · MW 个、位

**大规模** dàguīmó ADV extensively; large-scale

**大好** dàhǎo ADJ excellent

这是你的**大好**机会! *This is your big chance!*

**大号** dàhào N large size

**大亨** dàhēng N big shot, bigwig · MW 个、位、名

**大话** dàhuà N big talk, boast

他喜欢说**大话**。*He likes to talk big.*

**大伙儿** dàhuǒr PRON we/you all; everybody

宴会后, **大伙儿**都留下来唱卡拉OK。*After the banquet, we all stayed and sang karaoke.*

**大会** dàhuì N conference; general meeting · MW 个

**大家** dàjiā N·PRON all, everybody; great master

里面还有很多空间, **大家**都可以进来。*There's plenty of room for everyone inside.*

**大街** dàjiē N main street · MW 条

**大姐** dàjiě N oldest sister · MW 个、位

**大惊小怪** dàjīngxiǎoguài EXP much ado/fuss about nothing

别**大惊小怪**, 读你的书吧! *Stop fussing and read your book!*

**大局** dàjú N overall situation

**大量** dàliàng ADJ large number of; generous

学生每年都要花**大量**的钱买书。*A large amount of money is spent on books every year.*

**大楼** dàlóu N multistory building · MW 栋、座

**大陆** dàlù N continent; mainland

**大门** dàmén N entrance door; gate · MW 个、道

**大名** dàmíng N surname

**大脑** dànǎo N brain · MW 个

**大批** dàpī ADJ large number/quantity of

**大人** dàren N adult, grown-up · MW 个、位、名

**大人物** dàrénwù N big shot, bigwig · MW 个、位、名

他自以为是个**大人物**, 不过是普通推销员罢了。*He talks as if he's a big shot, but he's just a regular salesman.*

**大厦** dàshà N large building · MW 栋、幢、座

**大使** dàshǐ N ambassador · MW 个、位、名

**大事** dàshì N great event; overall situation · MW 件

**大手大脚** dàshǒudàjiǎo EXP wasteful, extravagant

**大叔** dàshū N uncle · MW 个、位

**大厅** dàtīng N lobby, hall · MW 个

**大同小异** dàtóngxiǎoyì EXP alike except for small differences

**大腿** dàtuǐ N thigh · MW 条

**大雾** dàwù N fog

**大西洋** Dàxīyáng N the Atlantic Ocean

**大写** dàxiě N capitalization

你知道汉字数字的**大写**吗? *Do you know the capital form of a Chinese numeral?*

**大型** dàxíng ADJ large-scale

**大熊猫** dàxióngmāo N giant panda · MW 只、个

**大学** dàxué N college, university · MW 间、所

## 20 大 dà (continued)

**大学生** dàxuéshēng  N  college/university student · MW 个、位、名

傻瓜的大儿子是**大学生**，女儿是高中生，小儿子是小学生。*ShaGua's older son is a college student, his daughter is in high school, and his younger son is in elementary school.*

**大意** dàyì  N·ADJ  general idea; careless

我记得这篇文章的**大意**。*I remember the general idea of this article.*

他做作业时太**大意**了。*He was so careless when he did his homework.*

**大雨** dàyǔ  N  heavy rain, downpour · MW 场

**大院** dàyuàn  N  courtyard · MW 个

**大约** dàyuē  ADV  approximately; probably

他**大约**是去图书馆了。*He has probably gone to the library.*

**大众** dàzhòng  N  the masses, the people

**大自然** dàzìrán  N  nature

### RELATED WORDS

| | | |
|---|---|---|
| 大炮 1633 | 人大 4 | 广大 23 |
| 不大 24 | 天大 25 | 正大 76 |
| 长大 93 | 巨大 162 | 壮大 238 |
| 马大哈 247 | 扩大 291 | 自大 305 |
| 老大 375 | 老大娘 375 | 老大爷 375 |
| 老大难 375 | 伟大 451 | 夸大 605 |
| 夸大其词 605 | 洪大 690 | 极大 798 |
| 重大 839 | 犹大 886 | 庞大 917 |
| 放大 964 | 莫大 999 | 侃大山 1085 |
| 特大 1094 | 浩大 1169 | 远大 1184 |
| 张大 1208 | 挑大梁 1235 | 拿大顶 1262 |
| 胆大 1295 | 短大衣 1452 | 肥大 1459 |
| 最大 1541 | 最大值 1541 | 高大 1611 |
| 宽大 1618 | 说大话 1631 | 盛大 1694 |
| 意大利 1812 | 强大 1896 | 久闻大名 45 |
| 玉皇大帝 77 | 五角大楼 79 | 中国大陆 86 |
| 石沉大海 144 | 世界大战 163 | 代表大会 208 |
| 加拿大 463 | 庞然大物 917 | 船老大 1809 |
| 自高自大 305 | | |

## 21 川 U+5DDD TM 3 FM 丿

**chuān**  N  river

**川流不息** chuānliúbùxī  EXP  flowing past in an endless stream; never-ending

### RELATED WORDS

| | | | |
|---|---|---|---|
| 山川 38 | 平川 78 | 冰川 493 | 河川 934 |

## 22 义 義 U+4E49 TM 3 FM 丶

**yì**  ADJ·N  justice; righteousness; meaning, significance

**义愤** yìfèn  N  righteous indignation

**义卖** yìmài  V  to sell for charity; sale for charity

我们找了些旧衣物准备**义卖**。*We collected some old clothes to sell for charity.*

**义气** yìqi  N  personal loyalty

**义士** yìshì  N  high-minded/righteous person · MW 个、位、名

**义士**不屑于暴行。*A righteous man never resorts to violence.*

**义无反顾** yìwúfǎngù  EXP  honor permits no turning back

**义务** yìwù  N·ADJ  duty, obligation; voluntary

我觉得这是我的**义务**。*I feel it is my duty.*

**义演** yìyǎn  V  to perform for charity, to give a benefit performance

**义正词严** yìzhèngcíyán  EXP  to speak sternly out of a sense of justice

**义肢** yìzhī  N  artificial limb · MW 条

### RELATED WORDS

| | |
|---|---|
| 广义 23 | 仁义道德 64 |
| 正义 76 | 仗义执言 121 |
| 仗义疏财 121 | 主义 124 |
| 尽义务 312 | 名义 426 |
| 名义上 426 | 讲义 501 |
| 同义 541 | 歧义 585 |
| 含义 592 | 定义 666 |
| 贬义 814 | 起义 1421 |
| 语义 1501 | 道义 1756 |
| 意义 1812 | 就义 1836 |
| 疑义 1917 | 仁至义尽 64 |
| 人本主义 4 | 个人主义 18 |
| 天经地义 25 | 共产主义 164 |
| 马列主义 247 | 列宁主义 368 |
| 利己主义 472 | 社会主义 504 |
| 极权主义 798 | 帝国主义 1312 |
| 背信弃义 1380 | 顾名思义 1609 |
| 马克思主义 247 | |

## 23 广 廣 U+5E7F TM 3 FM 丶

**guǎng**  ADJ  wide, vast; numerous

**广播** guǎngbō  V·N  to broadcast; radio

**广播新闻** guǎngbō xīnwén  V·N  to broadcast news; broadcast news · MW 条

广大 **guǎngdà** ADJ wide, vast, large-scale

广东 **Guǎngdōng** N Guangdong Province

广泛 **guǎngfàn** ADJ extensive, wide-ranging

他的兴趣很**广泛**。 *His interests are very wide-ranging.*

广告 **guǎnggào** N advertisement · MW 个、条、则

这个节目的**广告**太多! *This program has too many commercials!*

广告经纪人 **guǎnggàojīngjìrén** N advertising broker · MW 个、名

广开眼界 **guǎngkāiyǎnjiè** EXP field of vision is greatly increased

广阔 **guǎngkuò** ADJ wide, vast, broad

广西 **Guǎngxī** N Guangxi Zhuang Autonomous Region

广义 **guǎngyì** N broad sense

**RELATED WORDS**

做广告 1282        宽广 1618

## 24 不     U+4E0D   TM **4** FM 一

**bù** ADV no; not; [negative prefix]

**不安 bù'ān** ADJ worried, uneasy, anxious
这消息让我十分**不安**。 *The news had me worried.*

**不安全 bù'ānquán** ADJ unsafe, dangerous

**不安心 bù'ānxīn** ADJ unable to settle down, anxious
傻瓜的大儿子把大学申请寄出后，**不安心**了好几个星期。 *After sending out his college applications, ShaGua's older son was anxious for many weeks.*

**不败之地 bùbàizhīdì** EXP invincible/impregnable position

**不比 bùbǐ** V cannot compare with; unlike
他的中文**不比**任何人差。 *His Chinese is as good as anyone's.*

**不必要 bùbìyào** ADV unnecessary
根本**不必要**假装，我知道是你。 *No need to pretend, I know it was you!*

**不变 bùbiàn** V·ADJ don't change; constant, unvarying, fixed

**不便 bùbiàn** ADJ·V inconvenient; short on cash; to be inappropriate
若有**不便**，敬请原谅。 *Please accept our apologies for any inconvenience we have caused.*

**不曾 bùcéng** ADV never
咱俩之间大概从来**不曾**有过好感。 *There was never any love lost between us.*

**不成 bùchéng** V won't do, won't succeed

**不耻下问 bùchǐxiàwèn** EXP to not be ashamed to learn from one's subordinates

**不出所料 bùchūsuǒliào** EXP as expected
**不出所料**，她得了个A。 *As expected, she got an "A."*

**不错 bùcuò** ADJ correct, right; pretty good, not bad
**不错**，他是这么说的。 *Yes, that's what he said.*
这本书真**不错**。 *This book is not bad at all.*

**不大 bùdà** ADV not very, not too; not often

**不但 bùdàn** CONJ not only
他**不但**会说英语，还会说汉语。 *He speaks not only English, but also Chinese.*

**不当 bùdàng** ADJ unsuitable; improper

**不得 bùdé** V must not, may not, to not be allowed
不举手**不得**发言。 *If you don't raise your hand, you don't get to speak.*

**不得不 bùdébù** V·ADV to have to, cannot but
我**不得不**同意你的决定。 *I have no choice but to agree with your decision.*
时间快到了，我**不得不**赶紧走。 *Since time is limited, I must hurry up and go.*

**不得已 bùdéyǐ** ADJ acting against one's will; with no alternative but to
实在**不得已**，她只好请几天假。 *She had no alternative but to ask for a few days' leave.*

**不定 bùdìng** ADJ·ADV uncertain, indefinite; it's not at all certain whether
他明天还**不定**来不来呢。 *It's not at all certain whether he'll come tomorrow.*

**不懂 bùdǒng** V to not know, to not understand

**不断 bùduàn** V·ADV to continue; unceasingly, without interruption, continually
他**不断**地用中文向老师提问。 *He continually asked his teacher questions in Chinese.*

**不对 bùduì** ADJ incorrect, wrong; amiss, abnormal
他学习中文的方法是**不对**的。 *Something's wrong with the way he studies Chinese.*

**不乏其人 bùfáqírén** EXP there is no lack of such people

**不妨 bùfáng** ADV there is no harm in; might as well

**不分彼此 bùfēnbǐcǐ** ADJ making no distinction between what is one's own and what is another's

**不符 bùfú** V to be inconsistent with; to not match

**不敢当 bùgǎndāng** EXP to not deserve (a compliment)

**不公平 bùgōngpíng** ADJ unfair; unjust
生活是**不公平**的。 *Life is unfair.*

**不够 bùgòu** V·ADV to be not enough; inadequately
他觉得这所学校对汉语**不够**重视。 *He feels that there is not enough stress placed on Chinese in school.*

**不顾 bùgù** V to ignore; in spite of
他**不顾**后果硬是要退掉中文课。 *Regardless of the consequences, he wants to drop his Chinese course.*

不管 **bùguǎn** CONJ·V no matter (that/what/who/how); to not care

不管怎么样, 我就是不怕! *It doesn't matter what happens, I'm not scared!*

不规则 **bùguīzé** ADJ irregular, unorthodox

不好意思 **bùhǎoyìsi** EXP to feel embarrassed

她不好意思告诉我, 她中文不及格。 *She was too ashamed to tell me that she had failed her Chinese course.*

不合 **bùhé** V to not conform to, to be unsuited to

不合格 **bùhégé** ADJ disqualified

不会 **bùhuì** V to be unlikely, will not (happen, etc.); to be unable to

她不会来的。 *She will not come.*

她不会说中文。 *She is unable to speak Chinese.*

不及 **bùjí** ADJ not as good as

不见得 **bùjiàndé** ADV not necessarily, not likely

不仅 **bùjǐn** CONJ·ADV not only; not the only one

傻瓜的大儿子不仅是个好学生, 而且还是名优秀的篮球队员。 *ShaGua's older son is not only a good student, but also an excellent basketball player.*

不久 **bùjiǔ** ADJ soon, before long

傻瓜的小儿子问: "多久我才会打篮球?" 傻瓜说: "不久你就会了!" *"How long until I can play basketball?" asked ShaGua's younger son. ShaGua said, "You'll be playing very soon."*

不可 **bùkě** V cannot; must not

不可多得 **bùkěduōdé** EXP rare, hard to get

不客气 **bùkèqi** EXP impolite, rude, blunt

不良 **bùliáng** ADJ out of condition, unhealthy

不灵 **bùlíng** ADJ not working, not effective

不论 **bùlùn** CONJ no matter (what/who/how)

不满 **bùmǎn** ADJ resentful, dissatisfied

不妙 **bùmiào** ADJ far from good; embarrassing

不明 **bùmíng** ADJ·V not clear, unknown; to fail to understand

不能不 **bùnéngbù** V to have to, cannot but

不如 **bùrú** V to not be as good as; had better (do something)

这辆新车耗油太多, 还不如旧的那辆。 *This new car uses too much gas. It's not even as good as the old one.*

不三不四 **bùsānbùsì** EXP dubious; neither one thing nor the other

不识时务 **bùshíshíwù** EXP to show no understanding

不是 **bùshì/bushi** V·N to not be; fault, blame

我不是老师, 是学生。 *I am not a teacher; I am a student.*

这就是你的不是了。 *It's your fault.*

不适应 **bùshìyìng** V to not be in a condition

不死心 **bùsǐxīn** EXP unwilling to give up

不通 **bùtōng** V·ADJ to be blocked up; won't work; illogical

不同 **bùtóng** ADJ unalike, different (from)

不惜 **bùxī** V to not stint, to not spare

不行 **bùxíng** V won't do; to be out of the question

不幸 **bùxìng** ADJ·N unfortunate, sad; misfortune · MW 个

不许 **bùxǔ** V to not allow, must not

不要紧 **bùyàojǐn** ADJ unimportant, not serious

不要脸 **bùyàoliǎn** EXP to have no sense of shame

你这种打扮也敢出去, 真不要脸吗? *You go outside dressed that way? Have you no sense of shame?*

不宜 **bùyí** ADJ not suitable, inadvisable

不用 **bùyòng** ADV need not; do not use; unnecessarily

不在乎 **bùzàihu** V to not mind, to not care

许多人不在乎他们的穿着打扮。 *Many people pay no attention to how they dress.*

不知不觉 **bùzhībùjué** EXP unconsciously, unwittingly

这节中文课在不知不觉中就结束了。 *This Chinese class ended before we even knew it.*

不只 **bùzhǐ** CONJ not only, not merely

不止 **bùzhǐ** V·ADV to continue; continuously, incessantly; more than

不准 **bùzhǔn** V to not allow, to forbid

不足 **bùzú** ADJ not enough, insufficient

**RELATED WORDS**

**24 不 bù** (continued)

| | | | |
|---|---|---|---|
| 差不多 | 673 | 怪不得 | 696 |
| 过不去 | 712 | 吃不下 | 783 |
| 吃不开 | 783 | 吃不消 | 783 |
| 看不惯 | 841 | 犯不着 | 884 |
| 刻不容缓 | 966 | 要不得 | 969 |
| 要不是 | 969 | 忍不住 | 970 |
| 事不宜迟 | 987 | 莫不 | 999 |
| 恨不得 | 1174 | 迫不得已 | 1186 |
| 深不可测 | 1345 | 谈不上 | 1356 |
| 急不可待 | 1426 | 情不自禁 | 1491 |
| 禁不住 | 1536 | 赔不是 | 1569 |
| 说不上 | 1631 | 说不定 | 1631 |
| 说不过去 | 1631 | 数不胜数 | 1637 |
| 摸不透 | 1665 | 睁不开眼 | 1680 |
| 猛不妨 | 1704 | 满不在乎 | 1745 |
| 祸不单行 | 1754 | 想不到 | 1769 |
| 想不开 | 1769 | 靠不住 | 1791 |
| 漫不经心 | 1887 | 弱不禁风 | 1897 |
| 愚不可及 | 1901 | 憋不住 | 1972 |
| 川流不息 | 21 | 片甲不留 | 119 |
| 无微不至 | 139 | 无恶不作 | 139 |
| 无所不知 | 139 | 无所不能 | 139 |
| 与众不同 | 158 | 水泄不通 | 159 |
| 在所不惜 | 188 | 在所不辞 | 188 |
| 自命不凡 | 305 | 坐卧不安 | 318 |
| 坐立不安 | 318 | 非…不可 | 378 |
| 此路不通 | 416 | 执迷不悟 | 564 |
| 美中不足 | 671 | 拾金不昧 | 1017 |
| 念念不忘 | 1054 | 闷声不响 | 1150 |
| 哭笑不得 | 1221 | 视而不见 | 1362 |
| 置之不理 | 1651 | 滴水不漏 | 1885 |
| 风马牛不相及 | 194 | | |

---

**25 天**    U+5929    TM **4** FM 一

**tiān** N·ADJ·MW sky, heaven; day; season; nature; God; overhead; [measure word for days, times, etc.]

**天安门 tiān'ānmén** N Tian An Men (the Gate of Heavenly Peace)

**天边 tiānbiān** N ends of the earth

**天才 tiāncái** N genius, talent · MW 个、位、名
这位钢琴家是真正的**天才**。*He is a master piano player, a true talent.*

**天长日久 tiānchángrìjiǔ** EXP after a considerable period of time

**天大 tiāndà** ADJ as large as the heavens; extremely big

**天敌 tiāndí** N natural enemy · MW 个
狗和猫是**天敌**吗？*Are dogs and cats natural enemies?*

**天地 tiāndì** N heaven and earth; world

**天鹅 tiān'é** N swan · MW 只

**天赋 tiānfù** V·N to be naturally endowed; natural gift, talent

**天花乱坠 tiānhuāluànzhuì** EXP exaggeration (LIT as if it were raining flowers)

**天皇 tiānhuáng** N "Son of Heaven," emperor; emperor of Japan · MW 位

**天经地义 tiānjīngdìyì** EXP unalterable principle; right and proper

**天空 tiānkōng** N sky

**天蓝色 tiānlánsè** N sky blue (color)

**天理 tiānlǐ** N heavenly principle; justice · MW 条
善待他人是一条**天理**。*Being kind to others is a heavenly principle.*

**天南地北 tiānnándìběi** EXP far apart, poles apart

**天气 tiānqì** N weather
今天**天气**不好。*The weather is bad today.*

**天然 tiānrán** ADJ natural
她唱歌的禀赋是**天然**的。*Her talent for singing comes naturally.*

**天然气 tiānránqì** N natural gas

**天生 tiānshēng** ADJ born, innate

**天时 tiānshí** N weather, climate; opportunity · MW 个

**天使 tiānshǐ** N angel · MW 个、名

**天堂 tiāntáng** N heaven

**天天 tiāntiān** ADV every day
傻瓜的小儿子问："我**天天**都得上学吗？"
*"I have to go to school every day?" asked ShaGua's younger son.*

**天文学 tiānwénxué** N astronomy

**天下 tiānxià** N land under heaven, the whole world
傻瓜说："**天下**的人**天天**都得上学。"
*"Everyone in the world has to go to school every day!" ShaGua responded.*

**天线 tiānxiàn** N antenna · MW 条

**天性 tiānxìng** N natural instincts · MW 个

**天真 tiānzhēn** ADJ innocent, simple and unaffected
傻瓜的儿子**天真**地笑着说："你不用！"
*"You don't have to!" his son said, smiling innocently.*

**天子 tiānzǐ** N "Son of Heaven," emperor · MW 个、位、名

天字第一号 **tiānzìdìyīhào** EXP greatest in the world

傻瓜开玩笑说：“知道吧，我天字第一号傻呀！”
*ShaGua joked, "Don't you know I'm the dumbest man in the world!"*

### RELATED WORDS

| | | |
|---|---|---|
| 一天到晚 1 | 三天两头 9 | 开天窗 26 |
| 今天 102 | 几天 115 | 半天 127 |
| 归天 166 | 全天 172 | 白天 176 |
| 冬天 178 | 乐天 299 | 后天 310 |
| 当天 335 | 西天 352 | 老天爷 375 |
| 听天由命 414 | 先天 422 | 成天 611 |
| 秋天 641 | 昨天 810 | 每天 837 |
| 春天 855 | 连天 958 | 苍天 996 |
| 明天 1035 | 阴天 1041 | 夏天 1195 |
| 前天 1329 | 谈天 1356 | 破天荒 1374 |
| 热天 1390 | 聊天 1527 | 暑天 1540 |
| 晴天 1674 | 铺天盖地 1713 | 航天 1717 |
| 航天火箭 1717 | 航天飞机 1717 | 满天 1745 |
| 通天 1757 | 怨天尤人 1792 | 整天 1845 |
| 漫天 1887 | 谢天谢地 1890 | 瞒天过海 1914 |
| 露天 1997 | 半边天 127 | 霉雨天 1934 |
| 无法无天 139 | 狗胆包天 1287 | 热火朝天 1390 |

## 26 开 開    U+5F00    TM 4    FM 一

**kāi** V to open; to open up/out; to start; to set up; to hold; to write out; to drive

开办 **kāibàn** V to open; to set up
在**开办**学校前，我们还有许多事情要做。
*There are still many things to do before we open the school.*

开采 **kāicǎi** V to extract; to exploit

开场 **kāichǎng** V to begin

开车 **kāichē** V to start/drive a car

开除 **kāichú** V to expel, to discharge, to fire

开船 **kāichuán** V to set sail

开裆裤 **kāidāngkù** N open-seat pants (for children) · MW 条

开刀 **kāidāo** V to have an operation
他明天要**开刀**。 *He's going to have surgery tomorrow.*

开发 **kāifā** V to develop, to open up

开放 **kāifàng** V to come into bloom; to lift a ban

开工 **kāigōng** V to start work
这家工厂两年前才**开工**。 *The factory went into operation two years ago.*

开关 **kāiguān** N (power) switch · MW 个

开户 **kāihù** V to open an account

我今天已到银行**开户**。 *I opened an account today at the bank.*

开花 **kāihuā** V to blossom

开会 **kāihuì** V to hold/attend a meeting
作为市长，傻瓜的职责之一是每天主持**开会**。
*One of ShaGua's responsibilities as mayor is to hold daily meetings.*

开火 **kāihuǒ** V to open fire

开卷 **kāijuàn** V to open a book (for examination, etc.)

开快车 **kāikuàichē** V to drive fast; to speed up

开朗 **kāilǎng** ADJ open, clear; cheerful

开幕 **kāimù** V to open/inaugurate (a meeting, etc.); to raise the curtain

开票 **kāipiào** V to make out an invoice

开始 **kāishǐ** V to begin, to start

开市 **kāishì** V to reopen for business

开天窗 **kāitiānchuāng** EXP to open a skylight; to leave a blank (usually in a newspaper)

开庭 **kāitíng** V to open a court session

开头 **kāitóu** N beginning, start · MW 个

开玩笑 **kāiwánxiào** V to crack a joke; to make fun of
傻瓜的孩子们最爱在吃饭的时候跟他**开玩笑**。
*ShaGua's kids love to make fun of him when they eat dinner.*

开销 **kāixiāo** V·N to pay expenses; expenses · MW 笔

开小差 **kāixiǎochāi** V to be absentminded

开心 **kāixīn** ADJ happy
虽然傻瓜假装生气，但看着孩子们**开心**地欢笑，他也**开心**极了。 *Although ShaGua pretends to be angry, watching his kids laugh makes him happy on the inside.*

开业 **kāiyè** V to open a business

开展 **kāizhǎn** V to develop; to launch

开支 **kāizhī** V·N to spend; to pay wages; expenses · MW 笔

### RELATED WORDS

| | | |
|---|---|---|
| 广开眼界 23 | 公开 103 | 公开化 103 |
| 扒开 169 | 分开 173 | 切开 277 |
| 打开 289 | 闪开 337 | 让开 348 |
| 寻开心 358 | 召开 361 | 拆开 572 |
| 拉开 573 | 拨开 1015 | 眉开眼笑 1067 |
| 断开 1260 | 展开 1274 | 散开 1579 |
| 离开 1614 | 裂开 1643 | 错开 1715 |
| 撕开 1774 | 揭开 1851 | 解开 1928 |
| 吃不开 783 | 睁不开眼 1680 | 想不开 1769 |
| 三七开 9 | 左右开弓 113 | 半公开 127 |
| 吃得开 783 | 想得开 1769 | 喜笑颜开 1531 |

## 27 王    U+738B    TM 4   FM 一

**wáng** N king, monarch

王八 **wángba** N tortoise; cuckold; bastard · MW 个、只

王朝 **wángcháo** N dynasty · MW 个
一个**王朝**的消亡意味着另一个**王朝**的产生。
*One dynasty ends and another begins.*

王法 **wángfǎ** N law, law of the land · MW 个、条

王公 **wánggōng** N princes and dukes, nobility · MW 个、名

王宫 **wánggōng** N palace · MW 座

王冠 **wángguān** N crown · MW 顶

王国 **wángguó** N kingdom, realm · MW 个

王后 **wánghòu** N queen · MW 个、位、名

王牌 **wángpái** N trump card · MW 张

王室 **wángshì** N royal family · MW 个

王子 **wángzǐ** N prince · MW 个、名
你以为你是谁？是**王子**吗？ *Who do you think you are? The prince?*

王族 **wángzú** N imperial kinsmen · MW 个、名

### RELATED WORDS

## 28 于    U+4E8E    TM 4   FM 一

**yú** PREP at; in

于今 **yújīn** ADV·N up to the present; today, now

于是 **yúshì** CONJ thereupon; hence, as a result
孩子们要学中文, **于是**, 傻瓜就去买《汉语断笔码词典》。 *ShaGua's kids wanted to study Chinese, so he bought* The Chinese Broken Marks Dictionary.

### RELATED WORDS

## 29 乙    U+4E59    TM 4   FM 一

**yǐ** N second; second of the ten Heavenly Stems

乙等舱 **yǐděngcāng** N second cabin · MW 个

乙等奖 **yǐděngjiǎng** N second prize · MW 个

乙等生 **yǐděngshēng** N grade B student · MW 个、名
我们是极具竞争力的大学, 不接受**乙等生**。 *This is a very competitive university; we do not accept second-tier students.*

## 30 了    U+4E86    TM 4   FM 一

**le** AV [used after a verb/adjective to indicate/confirm the completion of an action or change]; [used at the end of a sentence or at a pause in the middle of a sentence to indicate a change or a new situation]
我吃**了**午饭。 *I did eat lunch.*
我吃午饭**了**。 *I have eaten lunch.*

**liǎo** V·ADV to grasp, to understand; to end, to finish, to settle; can manage; entirely

了不得 **liǎobudé** ADJ terrific, extraordinary

了不起 **liǎobuqǐ** ADJ amazing, extraordinary
他赢了地区联赛的第一名, 自以为**了不起**。 *He won first place at the district tournament, and now he thinks he's something special!*

了得 **liǎode** ADJ how terrible it is, amazing

了解 **liǎojiě** V to understand, to comprehend
傻瓜是唯一**了解**我的人。 *ShaGua is the only one who understands me!*

了却 **liǎoquè** V to settle, to solve

了然 **liǎorán** ADJ understandable, clear

了如指掌 **liǎorúzhǐzhǎng** EXP to know like the palm of one's hand
傻瓜对孩子们说: "我对你们**了如指掌**。" *ShaGua said to his kids, "I know you like I know the palm of my hand."*

了事 **liǎoshì** V to dispose of a matter; to get something over

### RELATED WORDS

## 31 刀    U+5200   TM 4   FM 一

**dāo** N knife; sword

**刀把** dāobà N knife handle · MW 个

**刀背** dāobèi N back of a knife blade

**刀叉** dāochā N knife and fork · MW 把、套、副

**刀割** dāogē V to cut

**刀尖** dāojiān N point of a knife

**刀具** dāojù N cutter; tool · MW 片、套、副

**刀口** dāokǒu N knife edge; crucial point

**刀片** dāopiàn N blade · MW 片

这**刀片**质量真差, 看看**刀口**就知道了! *This knife is of poor quality; just look at its edge!*

**刀刃** dāorèn N knife edge

**刀伤** dāoshāng N incised wound · MW 道

**刀子** dāozi N knife · MW 把

### RELATED WORDS

| | | |
|---|---|---|
| 大刀 20 | 开刀 26 | 小刀 61 |
| 冰刀 493 | 刻刀 966 | 砍刀 979 |
| 菜刀 1001 | 刺刀 1050 | 剃刀 1639 |
| 剪刀 1816 | 刮脸刀 902 | 卷笔刀 1333 |

## 32 刁    U+5201   TM 4   FM 一

**diāo** ADJ tricky, sly

**刁滑** diāohuá ADJ sly, crafty

狐狸的**刁滑**臭名远扬。*The fox is notorious for its cunning.*

**刁难** diāonàn V to create difficulties, to make things difficult

有的老师可能会**刁难**学生。*Some teachers may make things difficult for students.*

## 33 叉    U+53C9   TM 4   FM 一

**chā** N·V fork; hayfork; cross; to fork, to work with a fork; to cross

**叉烧肉** chāshāoròu N barbecued pork · MW 块

**叉腰** chāyāo V to put hands on hips

她双手**叉腰**站在那儿, 看起来很生气。*She looked very angry, standing there with her hands on her hips.*

**叉子** chāzi N fork · MW 把

**打叉** dǎchā V to cross out

你的错误答案, 我都**打叉**了! *I graded your tests and crossed out all of the wrong answers.*

### RELATED WORDS

| | | |
|---|---|---|
| 刀叉 31 | 打叉 33 | 交叉 222 |

## 34 七    U+4E03   TM 4   FM 丨

**qī** NUM seven

**七零八落** qīlíngbāluò EXP scattered here and there

傻瓜不喜欢儿子在修车时把工具丢得**七零八落**。*ShaGua didn't like it that the tools were a mess after his son repaired his car.*

**七拼八凑** qīpīnbācòu EXP to piece together; to rig up

**七巧板** qīqiǎobǎn N tangram (a seven-piece Chinese puzzle) · MW 块

**七窍** qīqiào N the seven orifices in the human head (eyes, ears, nostrils, and mouth)

**七情** qīqíng N the seven human emotions (joy, anger, love, hate, sorrow, fear, and desire)

**七上八下** qīshàngbāxià EXP to be perturbed

傻瓜进行竞选市长的演讲时心里**七上八下**。*When ShaGua gave a speech in the mayoral election, he was nervous and agitated.*

**七十二行** qīshí'èrháng N all sorts of occupations

**七月** qīyuè N July

**七嘴八舌** qīzuǐbāshé EXP everyone talking at once

傻瓜演讲后, 大家**七嘴八舌**地评论, 弄得他心里更是**七上八下**。*After ShaGua's speech, everyone started criticizing him at once, which made him even more agitated.*

**七十** qīshí NUM seventy

**七十一** qīshíyī NUM seventy-one

**七十二** qīshí'èr NUM seventy-two

**七十三** qīshísān NUM seventy-three

**七十四** qīshísì NUM seventy-four

**七十五** qīshíwǔ NUM seventy-five

**七十六** qīshíliù NUM seventy-six

**七十七** qīshíqī NUM seventy-seven

**七十八** qīshíbā NUM seventy-eight

**七十九** qīshíjiǔ NUM seventy-nine

### RELATED WORDS

| | | |
|---|---|---|
| 十七 3 | 三七开 9 | 乌七八糟 601 |
| 乱七八糟 901 | 一十七 1 | 二十七 2 |
| 八十七 6 | 三十七 9 | 六十七 69 |
| 五十七 79 | 九十七 116 | 四十七 271 |

## 35 丰 豐　U+4E30　TM **4** FM |

**fēng** ADJ abundant, plentiful; great; good-looking

丰产 **fēngchǎn** V to have a high yield

丰富 **fēngfù** ADJ·V rich; abundant; to enrich
其实，傻瓜有很**丰富**的生活经验。*In fact, ShaGua's life is full of lots of different experiences.*

丰富多采 **fēngfùduōcǎi** ADJ rich and colorful
傻瓜的演讲内容还是**丰富多采**的。*ShaGua's speech was rich and colorful.*

丰满 **fēngmǎn** ADJ well-developed; fully grown

丰盛 **fēngshèng** ADJ rich; sumptuous

丰收 **fēngshōu** V to have a bountiful harvest

丰硕 **fēngshuò** ADJ rich; plentiful and substantial

丰衣足食 **fēngyīzúshí** EXP to be well-fed and well-clothed
傻瓜刚到美国时非常艰难，但现在可以说是**丰衣足食**了。*ShaGua's first days in America were very hard, but now he and his children are well-fed and well-clothed.*

## 36 卡　U+5361　TM **4** FM |

**kǎ** N card; calorie

**qiǎ** V·N to stick; to hold back; to strangle; clip, fastener; checkpoint

卡宾枪 **kǎbīnqiāng** N carbine rifle · MW 支

卡车 **kǎchē** N truck · MW 辆
傻瓜买了一辆耗油很多的**卡车**。*ShaGua bought a truck that used too much gas.*

卡尺 **kǎchǐ** N calipers · MW 把

卡介苗 **kǎjièmiáo** N BCG (tuberculosis) vaccine · MW 针

卡路里 **kǎlùlǐ** N calorie

卡片 **kǎpiàn** N card · MW 张

卡其 **kǎqí** N khaki cotton · MW 块、匹

卡钳 **kǎqián** N caliber · MW 个、把

卡通片 **kǎtōngpiàn** N animated cartoon · MW 个、部
傻瓜曾经喜欢和孩子们一起看星期六早上播放的**卡通片**。*ShaGua used to watch Saturday morning cartoons with his kids.*

**RELATED WORDS**

关卡 224　　　奥斯卡 1435

## 37 寸　U+5BF8　TM **4** FM |

**cùn** ADJ·MW very small, very short, tiny; inch; [measure word for a unit of length (= 3 centimeters)]

寸步难行 **cùnbùnánxíng** EXP difficult to move even one step

寸金难买 **cùnjīnnánmǎi** EXP money can't buy

寸心 **cùnxīn** N feelings

**RELATED WORDS**

尺寸 118　　　分寸 173　　　鼠目寸光 1859

## 38 山　U+5C71　TM **4** FM |

**shān** N hill, mountain

山川 **shānchuān** N mountains and rivers; landscape · MW 片

山地 **shāndì** N mountainous region, hilly area · MW 片

山顶 **shāndǐng** N mountain summit · MW 个

山东 **Shāndōng** N Shandong Province

山洞 **shāndòng** N cave · MW 个
傻瓜到美国后才有点儿理解柏拉图的**山洞**寓言。*ShaGua did not understand anything about Plato's allegory of the cave until he came to America.*

山峰 **shānfēng** N peak · MW 座

山风 **shānfēng** N mountain breeze · MW 股、阵

山冈 **shāngāng** N low hill · MW 座

山歌 **shāngē** N folk song · MW 首、支
傻瓜喜欢一边干活一边哼**山歌**。*ShaGua likes to hum folk songs to himself while he's working.*

山沟 **shāngōu** N gully, ravine, valley · MW 条

山谷 **shāngǔ** N mountain valley · MW 个、条

山河 **shānhé** N mountains and rivers · MW 片

山洪 **shānhóng** N mountain torrents · MW 场

山岭 **shānlǐng** N mountain ridge/range · MW 个、座

山坡 **shānpō** N mountainside, mountain/hill slope · MW 个
**山坡**上有几块坡田。*There are a few terraces on the hillside.*

山区 **shānqū** N mountainous area · MW 个

山头 **shāntóu** N hilltop, mountaintop · MW 个、座

山西 **Shānxī** N Shanxi Province

山崖 **shānyá** N cliff · MW 个

山羊 **shānyáng** N goat · MW 只、群

山腰 **shānyāo** N halfway up the mountain

山珍海味 **shānzhēnhǎiwèi** N delicacies from land and sea

山庄 **shānzhuāng** N mountain villa · MW 个、座

### RELATED WORDS

| | | |
|---|---|---|
| 小山 61 | 火山 72 | 中山装 86 |
| 江山 237 | 河山 934 | 泰山 1066 |
| 黄山 1212 | 深山 1345 | 移山倒海 1450 |
| 登山 1521 | 假山 1586 | 靠山 1791 |
| 游山玩水 1818 | 翻山越岭 1989 | 气壮山河 185 |
| 侃大山 1085 | 名落孙山 426 | |

---

**39 才** 纔                    U+624D          TM **4** FM |

**cái** N·ADV ability, talent; just now

才干 **cáigàn** N ability, competence

才华 **cáihuá** N literary/artistic talent

傻瓜似乎没有**才华**，但很成功。*ShaGua seems to possess neither literary nor artistic talent, yet he is a success.*

才貌双全 **cáimàoshuāngquán** EXP talented and good-looking

傻瓜的梦想就是**才貌双全**。*Having both good looks and talent is ShaGua's dream.*

才能 **cáinéng** N ability, talent

许多人无法理解：为什么傻瓜没有**才能**也能成功。*Many people could not understand how ShaGua can be successful without any talent.*

才气 **cáiqì** N literary talent

才疏学浅 **cáishūxuéqiǎn** EXP to have little talent and less learning

许多人认为傻瓜**才疏学浅**。*Many people thought ShaGua simple and talentless.*

才思 **cáisī** N power of imagination, creativity

傻瓜常常被小儿子的**才思**吓一跳。*ShaGua was constantly amazed at his younger son's imaginative mind.*

才智 **cáizhì** N ability and wisdom

才子 **cáizǐ** N gifted scholar · MW 个、位、名

### RELATED WORDS

| | | |
|---|---|---|
| 人才 4 | 干才 13 | 天才 25 |
| 口才 42 | 文才 70 | 方才 220 |
| 奴才 328 | 多才多艺 431 | 英才 556 |
| 刚才 591 | 秀才 1055 | 适才 1358 |
| 量才录用 1544 | 通才 1757 | 德才兼备 1923 |

---

**40 木**                    U+6728          TM **4** FM |

**mù** N·ADJ tree; timber, wood; wooden; simple; numb

木板 **mùbǎn** N plank, board · MW 块、条

木材 **mùcái** N wood, timber · MW 块、根

木柴 **mùchái** N firewood · MW 块、根

木耳 **mù'ěr** N fungus · MW 片

木匠 **mùjiang** N carpenter · MW 个、名

耶稣是一名**木匠**。*Jesus was a carpenter.*

木乃伊 **mùnǎiyī** N mummy · MW 个

木偶 **mù'ǒu** N puppet, wooden figure · MW 个、只

木器 **mùqì** N wooden furniture · MW 件

木头 **mùtou** N wood, log · MW 块、条、堆

傻瓜并不笨得像块**木头**。*ShaGua is not as dumb as a piece of wood.*

木箱 **mùxiāng** N wooden trunk · MW 个、只

木星 **mùxīng** N Jupiter (planet)

### RELATED WORDS

| | | |
|---|---|---|
| 土木 15 | 林木 412 | 果木 544 |
| 朽木 578 | 树木 1031 | 独木桥 1095 |
| 积木 1097 | 麻木 1146 | 硬木 1524 |
| 胶合木 1296 | 丛林灌木 123 | |

---

**41 止**                    U+6B62          TM **4** FM |

**zhǐ** V·ADV to stop, to end; only, just

止步 **zhǐbù** V to halt, to stop, to go no farther

请止步！*Please stop here!*

止付 **zhǐfù** V to stop payment

止境 **zhǐjìng** N end, limit

止咳 **zhǐké** V to suppress a cough

止渴 **zhǐkě** V to quench one's thirst

止痛 **zhǐtòng** V to relieve pain

傻瓜告诉孩子：有些药只**止痛**，但不治病。*ShaGua told his kids: Some medicine only relieves pain without curing the ailment.*

止泻药 **zhǐxièyào** N antidiarrhea medication · MW 颗、片、包、剂

止血 **zhǐxuè** V to stop bleeding

止痒 **zhǐyǎng** V to relieve itching

傻瓜告诉孩子：有些药既**止痒**也治病。*ShaGua told his kids: Some medicine relieves itching and also cures the ailment.*

止住 **zhǐzhù** V to stop, to halt, to desist

**41 止 zhǐ** (continued)

**RELATED WORDS**

| | | |
|---|---|---|
| 不止 24 | 中止 86 | 休止 213 |
| 为止 223 | 何止 619 | 举止 674 |
| 废止 918 | 防止 1040 | 阻止 1042 |
| 终止 1109 | 制止 1130 | 禁止 1536 |
| 停止 1588 | 静止 1947 | 望梅止渴 1622 |

---

**42　口**　　U+53E3　　TM **4** FM |

**kǒu** N·MW　mouth; opening, entrance; cut, hole; [measure word for the number of people in a family]

**口岸 kǒu'àn** N　port · MW 个
深圳是中国南部的一个大口岸。*Shenzhen is a large port in southern China.*

**口才 kǒucái** N　eloquence
傻瓜的口才不好。*ShaGua is not eloquent.*

**口吃 kǒuchī** ADJ　stuttering, stammering
傻瓜有点口吃。*ShaGua has always had a slight stutter.*

**口齿 kǒuchǐ** N　enunciation
傻瓜有点儿口齿不清, 但是人们爱听他有个性的演说。*ShaGua cannot enunciate very well, but people enjoy his distinctive speeches.*

**口臭 kǒuchòu** N　bad breath

**口袋 kǒudài** N　pocket · MW 个

**口福 kǒufú** N　luck to get something very nice to eat

**口服 kǒufú** V　to take orally

**口供 kǒugòng** N　confession (by an accused person under examination)

**口号 kǒuhào** N　slogan · MW 个

**口红 kǒuhóng** N　lipstick · MW 支

**口径 kǒujìng** N　bore, caliber (of a rifle); requirements

**口渴 kǒukě** ADJ　thirsty

**口口声声 kǒukǒushēngshēng** EXP　to say again and again

**口令 kǒulìng** N　verbal command; password · MW 个

**口气 kǒuqì** N　tone, manner of speaking
傻瓜当市长后, 讲话的口气还是像傻瓜。*After ShaGua became mayor, his manner of speaking remained ShaGua's.*

**口腔 kǒuqiāng** N　oral cavity, inside of the mouth

**口哨 kǒushào** N　whistle, whistling · MW 声

**口是心非 kǒushìxīnfēi** EXP　to say yes and mean no
傻瓜可能傻, 但是从来不口是心非。*ShaGua might be simple, but he has never said yes when he meant no.*

**口述 kǒushù** V　to state orally

**口水 kǒushuǐ** N　saliva · MW 泡、串

**口头 kǒutóu** N·ADJ　word; oral

**口味 kǒuwèi** N　taste

**口吻 kǒuwěn** N　tone, note
傻瓜的口吻从来不像市长。*ShaGua's tone was never that of a mayor.*

**口香糖 kǒuxiāngtáng** N　chewing gum · MW 颗、包

**口译 kǒuyì** V　to interpret orally

**口音 kǒuyīn** N　voice; accent
傻瓜虽然说英语的时间不短, 但仍有很重的口音。*Although ShaGua has been speaking English for a long time, he still has a strong accent.*

**口语 kǒuyǔ** N　spoken language
傻瓜告诉孩子们: 学中文要练口语。*ShaGua told his kids: The study of Chinese requires practice.*

**口罩 kǒuzhào** N　gauze mask, surgical mask · MW 副

**口子 kǒuzi** N　opening, cut, tear · MW 个、道

**RELATED WORDS**

| | | |
|---|---|---|
| 人口 4 | 入口 5 | 刀口 31 |
| 井口 60 | 失口 106 | 户口 129 |
| 门口 130 | 众口难调 175 | 风口 194 |
| 关口 224 | 心口 232 | 对口 254 |
| 出口 258 | 切口 277 | 合口 296 |
| 伤口 453 | 两口子 509 | 异口同声 539 |
| 夸口 605 | 牲口 633 | 进口 713 |
| 岔口 829 | 顺口 874 | 亲口 908 |
| 借口 1087 | 忌口 1197 | 胃口 1216 |
| 缺口 1305 | 袖口 1361 | 领口 1465 |
| 渡口 1497 | 虎口 1533 | 插口 1555 |
| 搽口红 1558 | 裂口 1643 | 窗口 1732 |
| 港口 1740 | 满口 1745 | 路口 1785 |
| 漱口 1823 | 漱口水 1823 | 漱口杯 1823 |
| 糊口 1932 | 入境口岸 5 | 小两口 61 |
| 目瞪口呆 151 | 吊胃口 547 | 进出口 713 |
| 喷火口 1563 | 祸从口出 1754 | 售票口 1266 |
| 查户口 741 | 报户口 1010 | 十字路口 3 |

---

**43　儿 兒**　　U+513F　　TM **4** FM ノ

**ér** N　child, youngster, youth; son

**儿科 érkē** N　pediatrics

儿女 **érnǚ** N sons and daughters, children · MW 群

傻瓜两口子带**儿女**出去吃饭。*ShaGua and his wife took their sons and daughter out to dinner.*

儿孙 **érsūn** N children and grandchildren; descendants · MW 群

儿童 **értóng** N children · MW 个、名

儿媳妇 **érxífu** N daughter-in-law · MW 个、名

傻瓜说：“先考虑上学的事，以后再给我找**儿媳妇**。”*"Worry about school first," ShaGua said, "then worry about finding me a daughter-in-law!"*

儿戏 **érxì** N trivial matter · MW 场

傻瓜太太说：“找儿媳妇不能**儿戏**。”*Mrs. ShaGua laughed, "Finding a daughter-in-law is not a trivial matter."*

儿子 **érzi** N son · MW 个

傻瓜睡觉时还在想着**儿子**的事。*ShaGua went to bed that night, thinking about his son.*

### RELATED WORDS

| | | |
|---|---|---|
| 个儿 18 | 爪儿 52 | 女儿 57 |
| 生儿育女 107 | 产儿 219 | 吊儿郎当 547 |
| 托儿所 563 | 幼儿 638 | 妻儿老小 742 |
| 鱼儿 843 | 孤儿 978 | 那儿 980 |
| 育儿 1133 | 宠儿 1137 | 乳儿 1308 |
| 哥儿们 1370 | 婴儿 1539 | 哪儿 1666 |
| 一点儿 1 | 一会儿 1 | 一块儿 1 |
| 大伙儿 20 | 爪尖儿 52 | 自个儿 305 |
| 找碴儿 567 | 玩意儿 727 | 新生儿 1638 |
| 混血儿 1739 | 露馅儿 1997 | 小心眼儿 61 |

**44** 介    U+4ECB    TM **4** FM 丿

**jiè** V to be situated between; to take seriously, to mind

介词 **jiècí** N preposition · MW 个

介入 **jièrù** V to get involved, to intervene

介绍 **jièshào** V to introduce, to present; to recommend

介绍人 **jièshàorén** N one who introduces someone · MW 个、名

介意 **jièyì** V to take offense, to mind

傻瓜不**介意**别人说他傻。*ShaGua doesn't mind if others think he's stupid.*

介于 **jièyú** V-N to be situated between; interposition

### RELATED WORDS

| | | |
|---|---|---|
| 卡介苗 36 | 媒介 1449 | 简介 1796 |

**45** 久    U+4E45    TM **4** FM 丿

**jiǔ** ADJ for a long time; long

久病成医 **jiǔbìngchéngyī** EXP A prolonged illness makes a doctor of the patient.

傻瓜从小就病多，结果**久病成医**。*ShaGua had various illnesses when he was young. His prolonged illness has made a doctor of the patient.*

久违 **jiǔwéi** V to not have seen (someone) for ages

久闻大名 **jiǔwéndàmíng** EXP I've been hearing of your great name for a long time.

每个人见到傻瓜时都说：“**久闻大名**！”*Everyone who meets ShaGua says, "I've been hearing of your great name for a long time!"*

久享盛名 **jiǔxiǎngshèngmíng** EXP with a long-standing reputation

傻瓜答：“实在惭愧于‘**久享盛名**’！”*ShaGua responds, "I am very ashamed of this long-standing reputation!"*

久仰 **jiǔyǎng** V to look forward to meeting (someone); I'm pleased to meet you

人们又说：“**久仰，久仰**！”*People say, "I've been looking forward to meeting you!"*

### RELATED WORDS

| | | |
|---|---|---|
| 不久 24 | 长久 93 | 日久 96 |
| 永久 481 | 许久 502 | 持久 1019 |
| 耐久 1210 | 天长日久 25 | 由来已久 148 |

**46** 么 麼    U+4E48    TM **4** FM 丿

**me** QPRON what, why, how

### RELATED WORDS

| | | |
|---|---|---|
| 什么 63 | 什么的 63 | 多么 431 |
| 这么 715 | 怎么 830 | 怎么得了 830 |
| 怎么样 830 | 要么 969 | 那么些 980 |
| 那么 980 | 为什么 223 | 没什么 938 |

**47** 升    U+5347    TM **4** FM 丿

**shēng** V to rise; to go up; to promote

升调 **shēngdiào** N rising tone/note · MW 个

升高 **shēnggāo** V to elevate, to raise

升格 **shēnggé** V to promote; to upgrade

升官发财 **shēngguānfācái** EXP to win a promotion and get rich

升级 **shēngjí** V to go up (one level, one grade, etc.); to escalate

**47 升 shēng** (continued)

**升降机 shēngjiàngjī** N elevator; hoist · MW 台、个

**升旗 shēngqí** V to raise a flag
学校每天都举行**升旗**仪式。 *Before school every day, we must raise the flag.*

**升迁 shēngqiān** V to promote
傻瓜长年默默地、不倦地工作, 因此也从未错失**升迁**机会。 *ShaGua worked quietly and tirelessly at his job for years. He never missed a chance for promotion.*

**升腾 shēngténg** V to leap up, to rise

**升学 shēngxué** V to go to a more advanced school

**升值 shēngzhí** V to appreciate

**RELATED WORDS**

回升 391　　　提升 1554　　　毫升 1721

---

**48 午**　　U+5348　　TM **4** FM 丿

**wǔ** N noon, midday

**午餐 wǔcān** N lunch · MW 个、顿
傻瓜从来不吃**午餐**。 *ShaGua never eats lunch.*

**午饭 wǔfàn** N lunch, midday meal · MW 顿

**午后 wǔhòu** N afternoon

**午前 wǔqián** N morning, before noon, A.M.

**午睡 wǔshuì** N·V afternoon nap; to take a nap after lunch
傻瓜从来不**午睡**。 *ShaGua has also never taken an afternoon nap.*

**午休 wǔxiū** N lunch hour, noon break; midday rest
傻瓜**午休**的时间也总是在干活。 *ShaGua always works during lunch hour.*

**午夜 wǔyè** N midnight
傻瓜常常**午夜**才睡觉。 *ShaGua usually goes to bed at midnight.*

**RELATED WORDS**

下午 10　　　上午 14　　　正午 76　　　子午圈 83
中午 86　　　端午节 1889

---

**49 夕**　　U+5915　　TM **4** FM 丿

**xī** N sunset, dusk; evening, night

**夕阳 xīyáng** N setting sun · MW 片

**夕照 xīzhào** N glow of the setting sun

---

**RELATED WORDS**

前夕 1329　　　除夕 1418　　　一朝一夕 1
只争朝夕 160

---

**50 斤**　　U+65A4　　TM **4** FM 丿

**jīn** MW [measure word for a unit of weight (= 500 grams)]

**斤斤计较 jīnjīnjìjiào** EXP to worry about every little thing, quibble; to be self-centered
傻瓜从来不**斤斤计较**。 *ShaGua has never been self-centered.*

**斤两 jīnliǎng** N weight
他的暗示很有**斤两**。 *What he hinted at couldn't be taken lightly.*

**RELATED WORDS**

公斤 103　　　半斤八两 127

---

**51 牛**　　U+725B　　TM **4** FM 丿

**niú** N ox, cow, bull

**牛车 niúchē** N oxcart · MW 架

**牛痘 niúdòu** N smallpox pustule

**牛粪 niúfèn** N cow manure/dung · MW 堆、泡

**牛角 niújiǎo** N ox horn · MW 只、对

**牛角尖 niújiǎojiān** EXP tip of a horn; insignificant/insoluble problem; deeply engrossed
傻瓜喜欢钻**牛角尖**。 *ShaGua likes to get himself into tight corners.*

**牛劲 niújìn** N tremendous effort; great strength · MW 股

**牛马 niúmǎ** N oxen and horses, beasts of burden · MW 群

**牛毛 niúmáo** N ox hair · MW 根

**牛奶 niúnǎi** N milk · MW 杯、瓶

**牛皮 niúpí** N leather, cowhide · MW 张、块

**牛脾气 niúpíqi** N stubbornness
傻瓜有**牛脾气**。 *ShaGua is quite stubborn.*

**牛肉 niúròu** N beef · MW 块

**牛仔 niúzǎi** N cowboy · MW 个

**牛仔裤 niúzǎikù** N jeans · MW 条
傻瓜总是穿**牛仔裤**。 *ShaGua always wears jeans.*

**RELATED WORDS**

吹牛 559　　　奶牛 878　　　黄牛 1212
乳牛 1308　　　烧牛肉 1504　　　野牛 1685
风马牛不相及 194　　　肉用牛 437

## 52 爪   U+722A   TM 4   FM ノ

**zhǎo** N claw, talon

**zhuǎ** N claw, nail, talon

**爪牙 zhǎoyá** N talon and fang; underling · MW 个、名

你以为你了不起, 你不过是老板的**爪牙**！
*You think you're important, but you're just the boss's lackey!*

**爪尖儿 zhuǎjiānr** N pig's feet

**爪儿 zhuǎr** N paw of a small animal; base of an appliance/tool

**爪子 zhuǎzi** N claw, paw, talon · MW 只、对、副

### RELATED WORDS
钩爪 1463      魔爪 1996

## 53 太   U+592A   TM 4   FM ノ

**tài** ADV highest, greatest; remotest; excessively, too

**太棒了 tàibàngle** EXP excellent

傻瓜对儿子说："**太棒了**！" *ShaGua said to his son, "That's excellent!"*

**太好了 tàihǎole** EXP very good

傻瓜的儿子："**太好了**, 我被大学录取了！"
*"Yes, I've been accepted to college," ShaGua's son said. "This is wonderful!"*

**太极拳 tàijíquán** N tai chi (traditional Chinese shadow boxing) · MW 套

**太空 tàikōng** N firmament, outer space

**太平 tàipíng** ADJ peaceful

**太平洋 Tàipíngyáng** N Pacific Ocean

**太太 tàitai** N wife; Mrs. · MW 个、位、名

傻瓜的**太太**是个家庭主妇。*Mrs. ShaGua is a housewife.*

**太阳 tàiyáng** N sun

**太阳镜 tàiyángjìng** N sunglasses · MW 副

**太阳系 tàiyángxì** N solar system

**太阳穴 tàiyángxué** N temples (of the forehead) · MW 个

**太阴 tàiyīn** N the moon

**太子 tàizǐ** N crown prince · MW 个、名

### RELATED WORDS
老太婆 375    皇太子 858    犹太 886
犹太教 886

## 54 犬   U+72AC   TM 4   FM ノ

**quǎn** N dog

**犬齿 quǎnchǐ** N canine tooth · MW 枚

**犬马之劳 quǎnmǎzhīláo** EXP to serve (someone) faithfully (LIT like a horse)

### RELATED WORDS
狂犬病 469      警犬 1987
牧羊犬 468      丧家之犬 521

## 55 夫   U+592B   TM 4   FM ノ

**fū** N husband; man; manual laborer

**夫唱妇随 fūchàngfùsuí** EXP marital harmony

**夫妇 fūfù** N husband and wife · MW 对

**夫妻 fūqī** N husband and wife · MW 对

傻瓜和傻瓜太太是一对**夫妻**。*ShaGua and Mrs. ShaGua are husband and wife.*

**夫人 fūren** N Mrs.; wife · MW 个、位、名

傻瓜太太是傻瓜的**夫人**。*Mrs. ShaGua is ShaGua's wife.*

### RELATED WORDS
工夫 12      丈夫 17
功夫 252      匹夫 269
奸夫 329      农夫 423
妹夫 631      姐夫 880
姑夫 881      情夫 1491
下工夫 10      抓功夫 406
费工夫 1520      高尔夫 1611

## 56 父   U+7236   TM 4   FM ノ

**fù** N father; older male relative

**父母 fùmǔ** N father and mother, parents · MW 个、位

**父亲 fùqīn** N father · MW 个、位

傻瓜的**父亲**是一个农民。*ShaGua's father was a peasant.*

**父子 fùzǐ** N father and son · MW 对

### RELATED WORDS
伯父 455      叔父 821
祖父 1190      教父 1424
姨父 1596      舅父 1795
生身父母 107      外祖父 218

## 57 女    U+5973    TM **4** FM 丿

**nǔ** N woman, girl, female; daughter

**女厕所 nǚcèsuǒ** N ladies' room, women's lavatory · MW 间

**女儿 nǚ'ér** N daughter; girl · MW 个
傻瓜的**女儿**是高中生。*ShaGua's daughter is a high school student.*

**女方 nǚfāng** N bride's/wife's side (of a family)

**女工 nǚgōng** N female/woman worker · MW 个、名

**女孩 nǚhái** N girl · MW 个、名

**女皇 nǚhuáng** N queen, empress · MW 个、位、名

**女家 nǚjiā** N bride's/wife's family

**女眷 nǚjuàn** N womenfolk of a family · MW 个、名

**女郎 nǚláng** N young woman, girl · MW 个、名

**女人 nǚrén** N woman · MW 个

**女声 nǚshēng** N female voice, female chorus

**女生 nǚshēng** N female student, schoolgirl · MW 个、名

**女士 nǚshì** N Ms.; lady · MW 个、位、名

**女性 nǚxìng** N female sex; woman · MW 个、位、名

**女婿 nǚxù** N son-in-law · MW 个

**女子 nǚzǐ** N woman, female · MW 个、名

### RELATED WORDS

| | |
|---|---|
| 儿女 43 | 少女 62 |
| 子女 83 | 仙女 207 |
| 处女 217 | 妇女 465 |
| 孙女 519 | 使女 623 |
| 侍女 624 | 妓女 629 |
| 男女老少 757 | 修女 870 |
| 舞女 1790 | 男男女女 757 |
| 重孙女 839 | 独生女 1095 |
| 生儿育女 107 | |

## 58 尸 屍    U+5C38    TM **4** FM 丿

**shī** N corpse, dead body, remains

**尸骨 shīgǔ** N skeleton · MW 具、副

**尸体 shītǐ** N corpse, dead body · MW 具

### RELATED WORD

僵尸 1864

## 59 力    U+529B    TM **4** FM 丿

**lì** N·V·ADV power, strength, force; physical strength; ability; to make every effort; energetically

**力不从心 lìbùcóngxīn** EXP inability to perform a task

**力量 lìliàng** N physical strength; power, force · MW 股

**力气 lìqi** N physical strength; effort · MW 股
没有智慧, 只有**力气**是无用的。*Strength is useless without smarts.*

**力求 lìqiú** V to strive; to do one's best

**力所能及 lìsuǒnéngjí** EXP everything in one's power
傻瓜总是做**力所能及**的事。*ShaGua always tries to do everything in his power.*

**力图 lìtú** V to try hard, to strive

**力学 lìxué** N mechanics

**力争 lìzhēng** V to work hard for, to do all one can to
傻瓜总是**力争**把**力所能及**的事做好。*ShaGua always does his best in those things within his power.*

### RELATED WORDS

| | | |
|---|---|---|
| 人力 4 | 火力 72 | 乏力 109 |
| 主力 124 | 主力军 124 | 无力 139 |
| 目力 151 | 水力 159 | 全力 172 |
| 气力 185 | 内力 191 | 风力 194 |
| 压力 201 | 外力 218 | 出力 258 |
| 电力 263 | 权力 292 | 兵力 300 |
| 自力更生 305 | 尽力 312 | 用力 313 |
| 体力 325 | 引力 371 | 协力 397 |
| 听力 414 | 有力 439 | 武力 513 |
| 动力 514 | 卖力 524 | 苦力 555 |
| 财力 588 | 实力 668 | 重力 839 |
| 省力 860 | 物力 883 | 活力 941 |
| 阻力 1042 | 努力 1063 | 张力 1208 |
| 耐力 1210 | 推力 1242 | 着力 1332 |
| 资力 1335 | 视力 1362 | 接力 1405 |
| 脑力 1460 | 费力 1520 | 量力 1544 |
| 眼力 1570 | 智力 1581 | 握力 1662 |
| 猛力 1704 | 通力 1757 | 精力 1832 |
| 暴力 1844 | 能力 1873 | 魔力 1996 |
| 生产力 107 | 年富力强 182 | 巧克力 364 |
| 劳动力 764 | 核动力 1026 | 购买力 1253 |
| 生产能力 107 | | |

## 60 井    U+4E95    TM **4** FM 丿

**jǐng** N·ADV well; [shaped like a well]; neat, orderly

**井底之蛙 jǐngdǐzhīwā** EXP frog in a well; person with a very limited outlook

傻瓜的儿子上大学后, 才发现自己是个**井底之蛙**。 *After ShaGua's son went to college, he felt like the frog who had lived in a well his whole life.*

**井架 jǐngjià** N derrick, wellhead · MW 个

**井井有条 jǐngjǐngyǒutiáo** EXP in perfect order

**井口 jǐngkǒu** N opening of a well; entrance to a mine · MW 个

### RELATED WORDS

水井 159    龙井 315    油井 683
竖井 749    盐井 993    钻井 1302
背井离乡 1380

---

**61 小**    U+5C0F    TM **4** FM ノ

**xiǎo** ADJ small, little, minor; young; a little, for a short time

**小报 xiǎobào** N tabloid newspaper · MW 张、份

这只是当地的一份**小报**, 分量不重。 *It's just a small local newspaper, nothing too big.*

**小辈 xiǎobèi** N younger member (of a family) · MW 个、名

感恩节聚餐时, 长辈坐大桌, **小辈**坐小桌。 *During Thanksgiving dinner, the adults sit at the big table and the kids sit at the smaller one.*

**小便 xiǎobiàn** V·N to urinate; urine · MW 泡

**小辫子 xiǎobiànzi** N short braid · MW 根、条

**小册子 xiǎocèzi** N booklet, pamphlet · MW 本

**小车 xiǎochē** N wheelbarrow, handcart; small car · MW 辆

**小吃 xiǎochī** N snack, refreshment · MW 份

**小丑 xiǎochǒu** N clown · MW 个、名

**小聪明 xiǎocōngmíng** N cleverness in trivial matters; petty trick

傻瓜就是傻瓜, 从来不耍**小聪明**。 *ShaGua is simpleminded and has never played any petty tricks.*

**小刀 xiǎodāo** N small sword; pocketknife · MW 把

**小岛 xiǎodǎo** N isle, small island · MW 个、座

**小道 xiǎodào** N path, trail · MW 条

**小队 xiǎoduì** N team · MW 支

**小姑 xiǎogū** N husband's younger sister · MW 个

**小鬼 xiǎoguǐ** N little devil; kid · MW 个

**小伙子 xiǎohuǒzi** N young fellow · MW 个

怎么你这个**小伙子**也喊腰疼？ *Why is a young man like you complaining about back pain?*

**小结 xiǎojié** V·N to summarize; brief summary · MW 个

**小姐 xiǎojiě** N Miss; young lady · MW 个

请问**小姐**：现在几点？ *Excuse me, Miss. Do you know the time?*

**小舅子 xiǎojiùzi** N wife's younger brother · MW 个

**小考 xiǎokǎo** N midterm exam, quiz · MW 个、次

如果你的**小考**没考好, 你的期末考试得加紧努力！ *If you didn't do well on the midterm, you had better study hard for the final.*

**小两口 xiǎoliǎngkǒu** N young couple · MW 对

**小卖部 xiǎomàibù** N small shop attached to a school, etc. · MW 个、间

**小名 xiǎomíng** N pet name, childhood name · MW 个

不要叫啦, 那是我的**小名**。 *Don't call me that! That's my pet name!*

**小人物 xiǎorénwù** N unimportant person · MW 个、名

我为什么要听你的, 你不过是一个**小人物**罢了。 *I don't need to listen to you; you're just a nobody.*

**小山 xiǎoshān** N hill · MW 座

**小时 xiǎoshí** N hour · MW 个

**小时候 xiǎoshíhou** N in one's childhood

据说, 傻瓜**小时候**有点儿调皮。 *ShaGua was quite naughty when he was a child.*

**小事 xiǎoshì** N trifle, petty thing · MW 件、桩

别想打烂杯子的事了, **小事**一桩。 *Don't worry about the broken glass; it's just a small thing.*

**小市民 xiǎoshìmín** N urban petty bourgeois · MW 个

**小叔子 xiǎoshūzi** N husband's younger brother · MW 个

**小数点 xiǎoshùdiǎn** N decimal · MW 个

**小心 xiǎoxīn** V·ADJ to be careful; careful

**小心眼儿 xiǎoxīnyǎnr** EXP narrow-minded

在聘请优秀老师的事情上, 别耍**小心眼儿**。 *Try not to be narrow-minded about the proposal to hire better teachers.*

**小型 xiǎoxíng** ADJ small-scale, miniature

**小学 xiǎoxué** N primary/elementary school · MW 间、个

**小意思 xiǎoyìsi** N small friendly token

**61** 小 **xiǎo** (continued)

这点儿**小**意思不足以表达我们的谢意。
*Here's a little something we want to give you to say thank you.*

**小组** xiǎozǔ  N  group · MW 个

**RELATED WORDS**

| | | |
|---|---|---|
| 小鹿 1724 | 开小差 26 | 丑小鸭 85 |
| 极小 798 | 每小时 837 | 初小 963 |
| 细小 1107 | 胆小 1295 | 短小 1452 |
| 最小 1541 | 矮小 1598 | 微小 1700 |
| 瘦小 1880 | 弱小 1897 | 缩小 1927 |
| 大惊小怪 20 | 大同小异 20 | 中篇小说 86 |
| 长篇小说 93 | 羊肠小道 227 | 妻儿老小 742 |

---

**62** 少　　U+5C11　　TM **4** FM 丿

**shǎo**  ADJ·V  few, little, less; to lack; to lose; to be missing, to be short

**shào**  ADJ·N  young; son of a rich family, rich kid

**少不了** shǎobuliǎo  V  to be bound to, cannot do (something) without

傻瓜的演说**少不了**"这个，这个…那个，那个…" *ShaGua cannot give a speech without saying, "You know, you know.…"*

**少而精** shǎo'érjīng  EXP  smaller quantity, better quality

吃鱼子酱就是要**少而精**。*When eating caviar, a smaller quantity means better quality.*

**少量** shǎoliàng  ADJ  a small amount, a little, a few

**少数** shǎoshù  ADJ  small number, minority

**少数民族** shǎoshùmínzú  N  minority nationality, ethnic group · MW 个

**少许** shǎoxǔ  N  a little, a few

**少有** shǎoyǒu  ADJ  seldom, rare, exceptional

在这个公司里，**少有**既睿智、风趣，又友善的人。*Smart, funny, and friendly people are few and far between in this company.*

**少妇** shàofù  N  young married woman; young wife · MW 个、名

**少将** shàojiàng  N  major general (in the army) · MW 个、名

**少年** shàonián  N  early youth (ages ten to sixteen) · MW 个、名

**少女** shàonǚ  N  young girl · MW 个、名

**少尉** shàowèi  N  second lieutenant (in the army) · MW 个、名

**少先队** shàoxiānduì  N  Young Pioneers (Communist youth organization) · MW 队

**少校** shàoxiào  N  major (in the army) · MW 个、名

**少爷** shàoye  N  son of a rich family · MW 个、名

**少壮** shàozhuàng  ADJ  young and strong

**RELATED WORDS**

| | | |
|---|---|---|
| 至少 244 | 多少 431 | 青少年 740 |
| 尿少 849 | 缺少 1305 | 短少 1452 |
| 减少 1487 | 稀少 1599 | 阔少 1728 |
| 必不可少 338 | 男女老少 757 | |

---

**63** 什　　U+4EC0　　TM **4** FM 丿

**shén**  QPRON  [used to indicate a question]

**shí**  N  assorted, varied, miscellaneous

**什锦** shíjǐn  ADJ  assorted, mixed

**什物** shíwù  N  sundries, odds and ends

**什么** shénme  QPRON  what, when, etc.

你姓**什么**? *What is your family name?*

你叫**什么**名字? *What is your name?*

你**什么**时候回来? *When are you coming home?*

**什么的** shénmede  EXP  and so on, and what not

太无聊了，这人老是说他的大房子**什么的**。*It was so boring; he spoke on and on about his big house and what not.*

**RELATED WORDS**

| | |
|---|---|
| 为什么 223 | 没什么 938 |

---

**64** 仁　　U+4EC1　　TM **4** FM 丿

**rén**  N·ADJ  benevolence, kindheartedness; humanity; sensitive

**仁爱** rén'ài  N  kindheartedness, charity

**仁爱**是傻瓜的特点之一。*Kindheartedness is one of ShaGua's foremost qualities.*

**仁慈** réncí  ADJ  benevolent, merciful, kind

**仁人志士** rénrénzhìshì  N  people with lofty ideals · MW 个、位、名

**仁义道德** rényìdàodé  N  humanity; justice and virtue; virtue and morality

**仁义道德**是人类社会的脊梁。*The backbone of society is virtue and morality.*

**仁政** rénzhèng  N  policy of benevolence

**仁至义尽** rénzhìyìjìn  V  to do everything required by humanity and duty

**RELATED WORD**

虾仁 824

## 65 仆 僕 U+4EC6 TM 4 FM ノ

**pú** N servant

**仆从 púcóng** N footman; henchman · MW 个、名

**仆人 púrén** N servant · MW 个、名
傻瓜是市长，也是市民的**仆人**。*ShaGua is the mayor, but also a servant to the city residents.*

**RELATED WORDS**

奴仆 328          风尘仆仆 194

## 66 从 從 U+4ECE TM 4 FM ノ

**cóng** PREP·V·N·ADJ·ADV from, through; ever; to join, to be engaged in; to follow, to comply with; follower; secondary; ever, always

**从此 cóngcǐ** CONJ from now on; after that
我从此绝不再喝酒。*From now on, I will never drink again.*

**从…到 cóng… dào** from … to
从今天到下星期，谁都不能喝酒。*From today until next week, no one is allowed to drink.*

**从而 cóng'ér** CONJ thus, thereby

**从简 cóngjiǎn** V to conform to the principle of simplicity

**从今以后 cóngjīnyǐhòu** ADV from now on, henceforth

**从句 cóngjù** N clause · MW 个

**从军 cóngjūn** V to join the army, to enlist

**从来 cónglái** ADV always
傻瓜干活从来不偷懒。*ShaGua has never goofed off on the job.*

**从略 cónglüè** V to be omitted

**从前 cóngqián** N before, formerly

**从容 cóngróng** ADJ calm, unhurried

**从事 cóngshì** V to undertake, to deal with

**从属 cóngshǔ** V to subordinate

**从头 cóngtóu** ADV from the beginning
我没听到故事的开头，请再从头说起。*I didn't hear the first part of the story; please start from the beginning.*

**从中 cóngzhōng** ADV out of, from among

**RELATED WORDS**

仆从 65              主从关系 124
无从 139            听从 414
侍从 624            依从 625
顺从 874            盲从 907
屈从 1071           服从 1457
祸从口出 1754       随从 1911
遵从 1975           力不从心 59
何去何从 619

## 67 之 U+4E4B TM 4 FM ヽ

**zhī** PRON [used to connect a modifier and the word modified]; [used only as object]

**之后 zhīhòu** N later, after, afterward
这个事故发生之后，我会更小心。*After this incident, I will be sure to be more careful.*

**之间 zhījiān** N between, among

**之前 zhīqián** N before, prior to, ago
这个事故发生之前，我的狗从来没有咬过人。*Prior to this incident, my dog never bit anyone!*

**之字路 zhīzìlù** N S curve in a road · MW 条

**RELATED WORDS**

十之八九 3          反之 111
持之以恒 1019       总之 1330
置之不理 1651       不败之地 24
犬马之劳 54         井底之蛙 60
以子之矛，攻子之盾 101    无价之宝 139
众矢之的 175        百分之百 242
当务之急 335        必由之路 338
孔孟之道 370        言外之意 478
丧家之犬 521        丝绸之路 637
鱼米之乡 843        燃眉之急 1888
取而代之 520        总而言之 1330
概而论之 1908

## 68 亡 U+4EA1 TM 4 FM ヽ

**wáng** V·ADJ to die; to escape; to lose; to conquer; deceased

**亡故 wánggù** V to die, to pass away

**亡国 wángguó** V to subjugate a nation; to let a state perish

**亡灵 wánglíng** N soul of a deceased person, departed spirit · MW 个

**亡命 wángmìng** V·ADV to seek refuge, to flee; desperately

**RELATED WORDS**

兴亡 228            存亡 438
伤亡 453            死亡 510
阵亡 809            衰亡 1313
流亡 1493           逃亡 1509

## 69 六   U+516D   TM **4** FM ╲

**liù** NUM six

六边形 **liùbiānxíng** N hexagon · MW 个

六角形 **liùjiǎoxíng** N hexagon · MW 个

六面体 **liùmiàntǐ** N hexahedron, six-sided figure · MW 个

六亲 **liùqīn** N the six relations (father, mother, older brother, younger brother, wife, and sons); all relatives

傻瓜当市长以后，有时候会六亲不认。*After ShaGua became mayor, he wouldn't do any favors for his relatives.*

六一 **liùyī** N International Children's Day (June 1)

六月 **liùyuè** NUM June (month)

六折 **liùzhé** MW forty-percent discount

六十 **liùshí** NUM sixty

六十一 **liùshíyī** NUM sixty-one

六十二 **liùshí'èr** NUM sixty-two

六十三 **liùshísān** NUM sixty-three

六十四 **liùshísì** NUM sixty-four

六十五 **liùshíwǔ** NUM sixty-five

六十六 **liùshíliù** NUM sixty-six

六十七 **liùshíqī** NUM sixty-seven

六十八 **liùshíbā** NUM sixty-eight

六十九 **liùshíjiǔ** NUM sixty-nine

### RELATED WORDS

| | | | | | |
|---|---|---|---|---|---|
| 十六 | 3 | 一十六 | 1 | 二十六 | 2 |
| 八十六 | 6 | 三十六 | 9 | 七十六 | 34 |
| 五十六 | 79 | 九十六 | 116 | 四十六 | 271 |

## 70 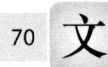   U+6587   TM **4** FM ╲

**wén** N·ADJ·V character; culture, civilization; language; written language; literary language/composition; gentle, refined; to cover up

文本 **wénběn** N text, version · MW 个

文笔 **wénbǐ** N writing style · MW 种

傻瓜的儿子喜欢Carver的朴质简明的文笔。*ShaGua's son liked Carver's writing style because it was simple and sparse.*

文不对题 **wénbùduìtí** EXP beside the point

你的辩驳看来很猛烈，可惜文不对题。*Your argument sounds strong, but is beside the point.*

文才 **wéncái** N literary talent

文采 **wéncǎi** N literary grace/talent

刚看了一眼，还说不上谁有文采。*Let's not call anyone a literary talent based on just one book.*

文法 **wénfǎ** N grammar

文房四宝 **wénfángsìbǎo** N four traditional treasures of study (writing brush, ink stick, ink slab, and paper) · MW 套

电脑是现代版的文房四宝。*A computer is the modern version of the four traditional treasures of study.*

文风 **wénfēng** N writing style · MW 种、类

文稿 **wéngǎo** N manuscript, draft · MW 本、份

文革 **wéngé** N Cultural Revolution · MW 场

文豪 **wénháo** N literary giant/icon, great writer · MW 个、位

文化 **wénhuà** N culture, civilization; education

傻瓜是一个没有文化的市长。*ShaGua is an uneducated mayor.*

文化界 **wénhuàjiè** N cultural circles; cultured people

文化界很尊重这个没有文化的傻瓜市长。*ShaGua, an uneducated mayor, is well-respected and popular in cultural circles.*

文集 **wénjí** N collected works · MW 套

文件 **wénjiàn** N document · MW 份

文教 **wénjiào** N culture and education

文具 **wénjù** N writing materials, stationery · MW 套

文科 **wénkē** N liberal arts, humanities

文盲 **wénmáng** N illiterate · MW 个

傻瓜对儿子说："不要问我，我是一个文盲，不知道谁是文豪。" *ShaGua said to his son, "Don't ask me this question. I am illiterate. I don't know any great writers."*

文明 **wénmíng** N·ADJ civilization, culture; civilized

文凭 **wénpíng** N diploma · MW 个、份

傻瓜非常渴望儿子能拿到毕业文凭。*ShaGua really wanted to see his son graduate and receive a diploma.*

文人 **wénrén** N scholar · MW 个、位、名

傻瓜有时也在心里偷偷地想象：自己是一个毕业于名牌大学的文人。*ShaGua sometimes secretly wished he were a scholar who had graduated from a prestigious university.*

文史 **wénshǐ** N literature and history

文坛 **wéntán** N literary world

文人是要在文坛上舞文弄墨的。*A scholar should write and publish and be part of the literary world.*

文体 **wéntǐ** N style; art and sport, recreation

文武 **wénwǔ** N civil and military

文物 **wénwù** N cultural/historical relic · MW 件

文献 **wénxiàn** N document, literature · MW 份

文学 **wénxué** N literature

文学语言 **wénxuéyǔyán** N literary language

文雅 **wényǎ** ADJ elegant, refined, cultured

没有人认为傻瓜是一个**文雅**的学者。 *No one thought of ShaGua as a cultured or refined scholar.*

文言 **wényán** N classical Chinese

文艺 **wényì** N literature and art

文娱 **wényú** N cultural recreation, entertainment

文摘 **wénzhāi** N abstract, digest · MW 本、则

文章 **wénzhāng** N essay, article · MW 篇

文字 **wénzì** N character; script; writing · MW 篇

**RELATED WORDS**

| | | |
|---|---|---|
| 下文 10 | 天文学 25 | 正文 76 |
| 中文 86 | 本文 90 | 半文盲 127 |
| 古文 154 | 全文 172 | 外文 218 |
| 收文 282 | 作文 326 | 引文 371 |
| 华文 421 | 征文 462 | 英文 556 |
| 条文 598 | 成文 611 | 盲文 906 |
| 论文 947 | 译文 951 | 原文 1273 |
| 短文 1452 | 语文 1501 | 课文 1503 |
| 散文 1579 | 甲骨文 149 | 物质文明 883 |

---

**71 斗** 鬥 U+6597 TM **4** FM ⟍

**dǒu** N·MW [shaped like a cup/dipper]; [measure word for a unit of measure for grain (= 10 liters)]

**dòu** (鬥) V to fight, to struggle against; to denounce

斗胆 **dǒudǎn** V to be bold, to venture

斗笠 **dǒulì** N bamboo hat · MW 顶

有些美国人以为戴**斗笠**是中国人的特征，这是天大的误解。 *Some Americans think that one of the symbols of Chinese people is wearing a bamboo hat, which is a huge mistake.*

斗篷 **dǒupeng** N cape, cloak, mantle · MW 件

斗室 **dǒushì** N small room · MW 间

斗鸡 **dòujī** V·N to have a fighting rooster; cock fighting · MW 只

斗争 **dòuzhēng** V to struggle, to fight; to denounce, to accuse; to strive for

他为了打赢官司进行了不懈的**斗争**。 *He put up a valiant fight against the lawsuit.*

斗志 **dòuzhì** N will to fight

斗智 **dòuzhì** V to engage in a battle of wits

斗嘴 **dòuzuǐ** V to squabble, to quarrel

傻瓜最不喜欢跟傻瓜太太**斗嘴**。 *ShaGua hates to squabble with Mrs. ShaGua.*

**RELATED WORDS**

| | | |
|---|---|---|
| 五斗柜 79 | 争斗 595 | 奋斗 607 |
| 战斗 1044 | 烟斗 1177 | 漏斗 1886 |
| 电熨斗 263 | | |

---

**72 火** U+706B TM **4** FM ⟍

**huǒ** N·ADJ·V fire; anger, temper; fiery, flaming; to get angry, to lose one's temper

这**火**真大。 *This is a very big fire.*

开**火**！ *Open fire!*

他的**火**真大。 *He is very angry.*

火把 **huǒbǎ** N torch · MW 支

点亮**火把**。 *Light a torch.*

火柴 **huǒchái** N match · MW 盒、根

**火柴**慢慢被打火机代替了。 *Matches have been gradually replaced by lighters.*

火车 **huǒchē** N train · MW 列

一列**火车**呼啸着开进站来。 *A train screams as it comes into the station.*

火光 **huǒguāng** N flame, blaze · MW 束、道

**火光**照亮了漆黑的夜晚。 *The flame has illuminated the darkness.*

火红 **huǒhóng** ADJ red as fire, flaming red

火候 **huǒhou** N duration and degree of heating; heating/cooking control

火花 **huǒhuā** N spark · MW 粒

火化 **huǒhuà** V to cremate

火鸡 **huǒjī** N turkey · MW 只

火急 **huǒjí** ADJ urgent, pressing

火箭 **huǒjiàn** N rocket · MW 枚、发

火警 **huǒjǐng** N fire alarm · MW 阵

听到**火警**，大家立即跑出办公室。 *As soon as people hear the fire alarm, they run out of the building.*

火炬 **huǒjù** N torch · MW 支

奥运**火炬**在燃烧。 *The Olympic torches are burning.*

火力 **huǒlì** N firepower; strength of a fire

火炉 **huǒlú** N stove · MW 个、座

火炮 **huǒpào** N cannon, gun · MW 门

火气 **huǒqì** N internal heat; anger, temper

**72 火 huǒ** (continued)

**火热 huǒrè** `ADJ` burning hot, fervent

**火山 huǒshān** `N` volcano · `MW` 座

**火速 huǒsù** `ADV` at top speed

他**火速**赶到现场。 *He ran to the scene at top speed.*

**火腿 huǒtuǐ** `N` ham · `MW` 个、块

**火药 huǒyào** `N` gunpowder · `MW` 箱、包

**火灾 huǒzāi** `N` disastrous fire · `MW` 场

**火葬 huǒzàng** `V` to cremate

**RELATED WORDS**

| | | |
|---|---|---|
| 上火 14 | 开火 26 | 灭火 75 |
| 生火 107 | 走火 265 | 打火机 289 |
| 发火 311 | 灯火 346 | 军火 489 |
| 肝火 650 | 洋火 689 | 过火 712 |
| 玩火 727 | 点火 739 | 香火 834 |
| 恼火 931 | 放火 964 | 核火箭 1026 |
| 防火 1040 | 战火 1044 | 烟火 1177 |
| 趁火打劫 1257 | 救火 1259 | 着火 1332 |
| 热火朝天 1390 | 起火 1421 | 怒火 1427 |
| 烧火 1504 | 烤火 1505 | 喷火口 1563 |
| 惹火烧身 1657 | 隔火墙 1910 | 十万火急 3 |
| 航天火箭 1717 | 万家灯火 73 | |

## 73 万 萬 U+4E07 TM **5** FM 一

**wàn** [NUM·ADV] ten thousand; a very large number; absolutely, definitely

**万般 wànbān** [N·ADV] all the different kinds; extremely

找不到人帮忙，傻瓜**万般**为难。 *ShaGua was in an extremely difficult situation because there was no one to help him.*

**万恶 wàn'è** [ADJ] extremely wicked, absolutely vicious

**万分 wànfēn** [ADV] very much; extremely

在**万分**危机的时刻警察及时赶到。 *In an extremely dangerous situation, the police arrived just in time.*

**万古 wàngǔ** [ADV] forever, eternally

**万家灯火 wànjiādēnghuǒ** [EXP] myriad of twinkling lights

**万金油 wànjīnyóu** [N] balm for treating headaches and other minor ailments; jack of all trades, master of none · [MW] 盒、个

**万里长城 Wànlǐchángchéng** [N] Great Wall (of China)

**万里长征 wànlǐchángzhēng** [N] long march of ten thousand li (one li = about ½ kilometer)

**万能 wànnéng** [ADJ] all-powerful, omnipotent

钱不是**万能**的，但没有钱是万万不能的。 *Money can't do everything, but without money you can't do anything.*

**万无一失 wànwúyīshī** [EXP] perfectly safe; sure to succeed

**万幸 wànxìng** [ADJ] very lucky

**万一 wànyī** [N·CONJ] contingency; just in case, if by any chance

**万一**你不能来，请给我挂电话。 *If by any chance you can't come, please call me.*

**万众 wànzhòng** [N] millions of people

**RELATED WORDS**

## 74 歹 U+6B79 TM **5** FM 一

**dǎi** [ADJ] bad, evil, vicious

**歹毒 dǎidú** [ADJ] vicious

他的话很**歹毒**。 *What he said was very cruel.*

**歹人 dǎirén** [N] bad guy · [MW] 个、名

**歹徒 dǎitú** [N] gangster, thug · [MW] 个、名

他是一个**歹徒**。 *He is a scoundrel.*

**RELATED WORD**

## 75 灭 滅 U+706D TM **5** FM 一

**miè** [V] to go out (of a light, a fire, etc.); to extinguish, to put out; to turn off; to destroy, to wipe out; to die out

**灭火 mièhuǒ** [V] to extinguish / put out a fire

**灭绝 mièjué** [V] to become extinct, to die out

恐龙在地球上**灭绝**了。 *Dinosaurs have become extinct.*

**RELATED WORDS**

## 76 正 U+6B63 TM **5** FM 一

**zhèng** [ADJ·ADV·V] straight; honest; main; sharp; pure; perfect; exactly; precisely; to straighten, to set/put right, to correct

这个门朝**正**南。 *This door faces due south.*

傻瓜这个人很**正**。 *ShaGua is very honest.*

图书馆的**正**门在哪里？ *Where is the main entrance of the library?*

**正**午是12点**正**。 *Noon is 12 o'clock sharp.*

他不是**正**校长，是副校长。 *He is not the president, but the vice president.*

她的普通话不**正**。 *Her Mandarin is not perfect.*

**正本 zhèngběn** [N] original (of a document) · [MW] 份

**76 正 zhèng** (continued)

这个文件的**正本**存放在律师办公室。
*The original copy of this document is kept in my law office.*

**正比 zhèngbǐ** N direct ratio

**正餐 zhèngcān** N dinner · MW 顿

**正常 zhèngcháng** ADJ normal, usual, regular
在中国, 工作日的**正常**上班时间是8小时。
*In China, an ordinary workday is eight hours.*

**正常化 zhèngchánghuà** V to normalize

**正大 zhèngdà** ADJ honest

**正当 zhèngdāng** ADV just when, just as
这件大衣的款式**正当**时令。 *The style of this coat is just in season.*

**正当 zhèngdàng** ADJ proper, appropriate, legitimate
他提出的理由很**正当**。 *He gave a legitimate excuse.*

**正道 zhèngdào** N right way/course · MW 条

**正点 zhèngdiǎn** V to be on schedule (of public transportation)
从纽约来的333号班机**正点**到达。 *Flight 333 from New York will arrive on schedule.*

**正法 zhèngfǎ** V to execute (a criminal)

**正反 zhèngfǎn** ADJ positive and negative

**正方 zhèngfāng** N square; positive side

**正规 zhèngguī** ADJ standard, regular
做这种工作需要经过**正规**的专业训练。 *The job requires formal professional training.*

**正轨 zhèngguǐ** N right track/path · MW 条

**正好 zhènghǎo** ADJ·ADV just in time; just right; fortunately; exactly
你来得**正好**, 我们刚开始上课。 *You came just in time; we have just begun class.*

**正号 zhènghào** N positive sign · MW 个

**正门 zhèngmén** N front door/gate · MW 个、扇、道
人民大会堂的**正门**面对着天安门广场。 *The front of the Great Hall of the People faces Tian'anmen Square.*

**正面 zhèngmiàn** N front, façade · MW 个
明信片的**正面**是我们大学。 *The front of the postcard shows a picture of our university.*

**正派 zhèngpài** ADJ honest, decent
傻瓜是个很**正派**的人。 *ShaGua is a very honest person.*

**正品 zhèngpǐn** N certified product · MW 件

**正气 zhèngqì** N healthy environment

**正巧 zhèngqiǎo** ADV just in time; just happen to
傻瓜路过商店门口, **正巧**看见他女儿从商店出来。 *ShaGua passed by the store and just happened to see his daughter come out.*

**正确 zhèngquè** ADJ right, correct; proper
这个回答**正确**吗? *Is this answer correct?*

**正视 zhèngshì** V to face squarely, to face up to
我们必须**正视**这个问题。 *We must face this problem squarely.*

**正式 zhèngshì** ADJ official, regular
这是一份**正式**文件。 *This is an official document.*

**正是 zhèngshì** V it is
这位不是别人, **正是**我的老朋友傻瓜先生。 *This is none other than my old friend Mr. ShaGua.*

**正题 zhèngtí** N subject/topic (of a talk) · MW 个、道

**正统 zhèngtǒng** ADJ·N orthodox; orthodoxy

**正文 zhèngwén** N text (of a book, etc.)

**正午 zhèngwǔ** N (high) noon

**正误 zhèngwù** V to correct (typographical) errors

**正义 zhèngyì** N·ADJ justice; just, righteous

**正在 zhèngzài** ADV in the process of
傻瓜到我家时, 我**正在**做饭。 *ShaGua arrived at my house while I was cooking.*

**正直 zhèngzhí** ADJ honest, upright

**正中 zhèngzhōng** N right in the middle; center

**正中下怀 zhèngzhòngxiàhuái** EXP exactly what one hopes for

**正宗 zhèngzōng** ADJ·N authentic, genuine; orthodox school

### RELATED WORDS

| | | |
|---|---|---|
| 义正词严 22 | 公正 103 | 反正 111 |
| 立正 125 | 方正 220 | 严正 241 |
| 订正 347 | 非正式 378 | 纠正 473 |
| 改正 516 | 校正 802 | 修正 870 |
| 拨正 1015 | 真正 1075 | 纯正 1290 |
| 指正 1397 | 端正 1889 | 寿终正寝 440 |

**77 玉**  U+7389  TM 5 FM 一

**yù** N·ADJ jade; pure; fair, beautiful, handsome

**玉雕 yùdiāo** N jade carving · MW 个、块

**玉皇大帝 Yùhuángdàdì** N the Jade Emperor (supreme deity of Taoism)

**玉米 yùmǐ** N corn · MW 个、颗

玉米花 yùmǐhuā [N] popcorn · [MW] 颗

中国人爆**玉米花**的方法同美国的不一样。
*The way Chinese make popcorn is different from the American way.*

玉器 yùqì [N] jade article/artifact · [MW] 个、件

中国人喜欢**玉器**。*Chinese people love jade pieces.*

玉石 yùshí [N] jade · [MW] 块

玉玺 yùxǐ [N] imperial jade seal · [MW] 个

**RELATED WORDS**

汉白玉 235　　　抛砖引玉 1395

---

**78 平**　　　U+5E73　　TM **5** FM 一

píng [ADJ·V] flat, level, even; equal, fair;
peaceful, quiet; average, common; to level;
to tie; to calm down; to suppress

地板不**平**。*The floor is not level.*
我感觉不**平**。*I don't feel that this is fair.*
双方打成6**平**。*The two players tied at 6.*

平安 píng'ān [ADJ] safe and sound; quiet and
stable

当傻瓜听说太太**平安**无事时，松了一口气。
*ShaGua heaved a sigh of relief when he heard
that his wife was safe.*

平板 píngbǎn [N·ADJ] flat; dull · [MW] 块

平辈 píngbèi [N] same generation ·
[MW] 个、名

平常 píngcháng [ADJ·ADV] common, ordinary;
usually; in normal times

傻瓜像**平常**一样又提前来了。*ShaGua is early,
as usual.*

平川 píngchuān [N] level land, plain · [MW] 片

平淡 píngdàn [ADJ] flat; dull, ordinary

平等 píngděng [ADJ] equal

平地 píngdì [N] level ground; flat land ·
[MW] 片、块

在这片**平地**上将建一幢大楼。*We will build
a complex on this level ground.*

平定 píngdìng [V] to calm down, to become
tranquil; to suppress, to put down

平凡 píngfán [ADJ] common, ordinary

傻瓜认为自己是一个**平凡**的老百姓。*ShaGua
considers himself an ordinary person.*

平反 píngfǎn [V] to rehabilitate; to overturn
(a sentence)

平方 píngfāng [N·MW] square; [measure word for
squares (square meters, etc.)]

平房 píngfáng [N] one-story house, bungalow ·
[MW] 间、栋

一对医生夫妇曾经住过这栋**平房**。*A doctor and
his wife once lived in this one-story house.*

平分 píngfēn [V] to divide equally, to go fifty-fifty

平和 pínghé [ADJ] gentle, moderate; mild (of
medicine); peaceful

平衡 pínghéng [V·ADJ] to balance; even

中医很强调阴阳**平衡**。*Traditional Chinese
medicine emphasizes the balance between Yin
and Yang.*

平静 píngjìng [ADJ] calm, quiet

他**平静**地叙述了事情的经过。*He described the
entire story calmly.*

平均 píngjūn [V·ADJ] to even, to average; equal

傻瓜的收入低于**平均**水平。*ShaGua's income was
lower than average.*

平面 píngmiàn [N] plane (geometry)

平民 píngmín [N] common people; civilian ·
[MW] 个、位

平权 píngquán [N] equal rights

平生 píngshēng [N] one's whole life

在大儿子过八岁生日时，傻瓜**平生**第一次吃意
大利馅饼。*The first time ShaGua ever ate pizza
was on his older son's eighth birthday.*

平时 píngshí [ADV] usually, ordinarily

他**平时**都是快七点才下班回家。*He usually
comes home from work around 7 P.M.*

平台 píngtái [N] platform · [MW] 个

平坦 píngtǎn [ADJ] level, even, flat

平息 píngxī [V] to quiet down, to subside

平行 píngxíng [ADJ] parallel; concurrent

平原 píngyuán [N] plain, flatlands · [MW] 片

**RELATED WORDS**

| | | |
|---|---|---|
| 太平 53 | 太平洋 53 | 公平 103 |
| 生平 107 | 水平 159 | 水平线 159 |
| 风平浪静 194 | 压平 201 | 和平 644 |
| 持平 1019 | 海平面 1494 | 填平 1550 |
| 不公平 24 | | |

---

**79 五**　　　U+4E94　　TM **5** FM 一

wǔ [NUM] five

五边形 wǔbiānxíng [N] pentagon · [MW] 个

五彩 wǔcǎi [N] multicolored

**五彩**缤纷的气球在天空中飞翔。*Multicolored
balloons were flying in the sky.*

**79 五 wǔ** (continued)

**五重唱 wǔchóngchàng** `N` quintet · `MW` 个、首

**五斗柜 wǔdǒuguì** `N` chest of drawers · `MW` 个

**五谷 wǔgǔ** `N` crops; the five cereals (rice, wheat, beans, and two kinds of millet)

**五官 wǔguān** `N` facial features; the five senses (ears, eyes, lips, nose, and tongue)

**五光十色 wǔguāngshísè** `EXP` multicolored

**五湖四海 wǔhúsìhǎi** `EXP` all corners of the land, all over the country

**五花八门 wǔhuābāmén** `EXP` wide variety

**五角大楼 Wǔjiǎo Dàlóu** `N` pentagon

**五角星 wǔjiǎoxīng** `N` five-pointed star · `MW` 个、颗

中国的国旗上有五个**五角星**。*There are five five-pointed stars on the Chinese national flag.*

**五金 wǔjīn** `N` the five metals (gold, silver, copper, iron, and tin); hardware

**五味 wǔwèi** `N` the five flavors (sweet, sour, bitter, pungent, and salty); all sorts of flavors

**五星红旗 Wǔxīng Hóngqí** `N` Five-Starred Red Flag · `MW` 面

中国的国旗又叫**五星红旗**。*The national flag of the People's Republic of China is called the Five-Starred Red Flag.*

**五月 wǔyuè** `N` May

**五脏 wǔzàng** `N` the five internal organs (heart, liver, spleen, lungs, and kidneys)

**五指 wǔzhǐ** `N` five fingers

**五百 wǔbǎi** `NUM` five hundred

**五千 wǔqiān** `NUM` five thousand

**五万 wǔwàn** `NUM` fifty thousand

**五十 wǔshí** `NUM` fifty

**五十一 wǔshíyī** `NUM` fifty-one

**五十二 wǔshí'èr** `NUM` fifty-two

**五十三 wǔshísān** `NUM` fifty-three

**五十四 wǔshísì** `NUM` fifty-four

**五十五 wǔshíwǔ** `NUM` fifty-five

**五十六 wǔshíliù** `NUM` fifty-six

**五十七 wǔshíqī** `NUM` fifty-seven

**五十八 wǔshíbā** `NUM` fifty-eight

**五十九 wǔshíjiǔ** `NUM` fifty-nine

**RELATED WORDS**

| | | |
|---|---|---|
| 一五一十 1 | 十五 3 | 一十五 1 |
| 二百五 2 | 二十五 2 | 八十五 6 |
| 三十五 9 | 七十五 34 | 六十五 69 |
| 九十五 116 | 四十五 271 | |

---

**80**  云 雲    U+4E91    TM **5** FM 一

**yún** `V·N` to say; cloud

**云彩 yúncǎi** `N` cloud · `MW` 片

云彩把太阳遮住了 *clouds blotting out the sun*

**云层 yúncéng** `N` cloud layer

**云端 yúnduān** `N` place high in the clouds

**云贵高原 YúnGuìgāoyuán** `N` Yunnan-Guizhou Plateau

**云海 yúnhǎi** `N` sea of clouds · `MW` 片

**云集 yúnjí** `V` to gather in a crowd, to swarm, to converge

**云南 Yúnnán** `N` Yunnan Province

**云雀 yúnquè** `N` skylark · `MW` 只

**云雾 yúnwù** `N` clouds and mist, mist; veil · `MW` 片、团

浓密的**云雾**令飞行员难以看清地面上的指示灯。*The clouds and mist were so thick that the pilots could not see the lights on the ground clearly.*

**云霄 yúnxiāo** `N` sky

**云烟 yúnyān** `N` cloud and mist · `MW` 片、团

**RELATED WORDS**

| | | |
|---|---|---|
| 风云 194 | 乌云 601 | 雨云 720 |
| 青云 740 | 青云直上 740 | 星云 753 |
| 阴云 1041 | 疑云 1917 | |

---

**81**  飞 飛    U+98DE    TM **5** FM 一

**fēi** `V·ADJ·ADV` to fly, to flit, to float in the air; unexpected; unfounded; swiftly

**飞驰 fēichí** `V` to speed along

一辆汽车**飞驰**而过。*A car flew past us.*

**飞虫 fēichóng** `N` winged insect · `MW` 只

**飞船 fēichuán** `N` dirigible · `MW` 艘

**飞弹 fēidàn** `N` stray bullet, missile · `MW` 颗、枚

**飞碟 fēidié** `N` UFO (unidentified flying object) · `MW` 个

**飞机 fēijī** `N` aircraft, airplane · `MW` 架

**飞机**将要起飞。*The plane is going to take off.*

**飞机场 fēijīchǎng** `N` airport, airfield · `MW` 个

**飞机票 fēijīpiào** `N` plane ticket · `MW` 张

我想买一张到北京的**飞机票**。*I would like to buy a plane ticket to Beijing.*

**飞行 fēixíng** `V` to fly

飞行航线 **fēixínghángxiàn** N flight route ·
MW 条

飞行员 **fēixíngyuán** N pilot, aviator ·
MW 个、位、名

飞跃 **fēiyuè** V to leap

飞涨 **fēizhǎng** V to soar, to skyrocket (of prices,
etc.)

近几年汽油价格一直在飞涨。*In recent years,
gas prices have skyrocketed.*

**RELATED WORDS**

下飞机 10     突飞猛进 913     试飞 1180
起飞 1421     航天飞机 1717

---

**82** 卫 衛    U+536B    TM **5**   FM —

**wèi** V to protect, to guard, to defend

卫兵 **wèibīng** N guard, bodyguard ·
MW 个、名

卫队 **wèiduì** N armed guard/escort · MW 支

卫生 **wèishēng** N·ADJ hygiene, health; sanitation;
sanitary

农村的卫生状况非常不好。*The sanitation in the
countryside is very poor.*

卫生间 **wèishēngjiān** N restroom, bathroom ·
MW 个、间

请问，卫生间在哪里？*Excuse me. Where is the
bathroom?*

卫生裤 **wèishēngkù** N sweatpants · MW 条

卫生设备 **wèishēngshèbèi** N sanitary
equipment · MW 套

卫生衣 **wèishēngyī** N sweatshirt · MW 件

卫生纸 **wèishēngzhǐ** N toilet paper ·
MW 张、卷

这个厕所不提供卫生纸。*There is no toilet paper
in this bathroom.*

卫士 **wèishì** N bodyguard · MW 个、名

卫星 **wèixīng** N satellite · MW 颗

卫星通信 **wèixīngtōngxìn** N satellite
communication

卫星通信对人们的日常生活影响越来越大。
*Satellite communication influences people's daily
lives more and more.*

**RELATED WORDS**

门卫 130     自卫 305
守卫 486     护卫 569
侍卫 624     保卫 868
防卫 1040     警卫 1987

---

**83** 子    U+5B50    TM **5**   FM —

**zǐ** N·ADJ son; child; person; seed, egg; something
small and hard; copper coin; master [ancient title
of respect for a virtuous man]; young; subsidiary

子弹 **zǐdàn** N bullet · MW 发、颗

这支枪配有五发子弹。*The gun has five bullets.*

子弟 **zǐdì** N sons and younger brothers; children ·
MW 个

这个奖学金是为公司职工子弟设立的。
*This scholarship is only for the children of company
staff.*

子宫 **zǐgōng** N womb, uterus · MW 个

子公司 **zǐgōngsī** N subsidiary company ·
MW 个、家

子女 **zǐnǚ** N sons and daughters, children ·
MW 个

中国的新生代大多是独生子女。*Most of the new
generation of Chinese are only-children.*

子时 **zǐshí** N period from 11 P.M. to 1 A.M.

子孙 **zǐsūn** N children and grandchildren,
descendants · MW 个

虽然傻瓜没上过大学，但他想让子孙们都上
大学。*ShaGua has not gone to college, but he
really wants his children and grandchildren to go
to college.*

子午圈 **zǐwǔquān** N meridian circle (instrument
for observing the stars) · MW 个

子婿 **zǐxù** N son-in-law · MW 个、名

子夜 **zǐyè** N midnight

子音 **zǐyīn** N consonant · MW 个

**RELATED WORDS**

厂子 7     个子 18
天子 25     王子 27
刀子 31     叉子 33
才子 39     口子 42
儿子 43     瓜子 52
太子 53     父子 56
女子 57     中子 86
本子 90     长子 93
日子 96     以子之矛，攻子之盾 101
尺子 118     片子 119
主子 124     头子 128
石子 144     叶子 167
分子 173     分子 173
瓜子 189     丸子 192
夹子 197     尖子 203
方子 220     虫子 262
电子 263     电子商务 263
电子邮件 263     步子 266

## 83 子 zǐ (continued)

| | | | |
|---|---|---|---|
| 曲子 272 | 台子 301 | 量子 1544 | 梳子 1566 |
| 位子 323 | 沙子 342 | 椅子 1566 | 款子 1573 |
| 状子 345 | 豆子 353 | 筷子 1585 | 猴子 1595 |
| 孔子 370 | 老子 375 | 牌子 1597 | 矮子 1598 |
| 老子 375 | 呆子 384 | 毯子 1603 | 银子 1607 |
| 网子 390 | 扣子 401 | 塞子 1620 | 望子成龙 1622 |
| 杯子 411 | 句子 424 | 裤子 1634 | 瓶子 1635 |
| 谷子 446 | 份子 449 | 梯子 1669 | 模子 1673 |
| 性子 498 | 君子 512 | 院子 1677 | 傻子 1699 |
| 孙子 519 | 孝子 529 | 扇子 1726 | 调子 1749 |
| 果子 544 | 松子 579 | 裙子 1752 | 圈子 1765 |
| 板子 580 | 柱子 583 | 棍子 1776 | 棍子 1776 |
| 条子 598 | 册子 614 | 帽子 1778 | 鸭子 1782 |
| 幼子 638 | 肚子 648 | 路子 1785 | 靴子 1788 |
| 钉子 651 | 空子 669 | 鼻子出血 1794 | 鼻子 1794 |
| 炉子 699 | 面子 721 | 箱子 1797 | 嫂子 1798 |
| 珠子 729 | 班子 730 | 脖子 1802 | 锅子 1807 |
| 点子 739 | 妻子 742 | 精子 1832 | 旗子 1834 |
| 男子 757 | 男子汉 757 | 嗓子 1855 | 管子 1861 |
| 拍子 790 | 样子 803 | 篮子 1862 | 绳子 1865 |
| 贩子 813 | 虾子 824 | 腰子 1868 | 瘦子 1880 |
| 岔子 829 | 秃子 833 | 瞎子 1913 | 影子 1918 |
| 包子 836 | 鱼子 843 | 骗子 1937 | 瘤子 1951 |
| 例子 863 | 徒子徒孙 873 | 辫子 1957 | 鞭子 1967 |
| 种子 893 | 卵子 896 | 镜子 1970 | 簿子 1979 |
| 乱子 901 | 刽子手 903 | 一辈子 1 | 二流子 2 |
| 底子 916 | 疹子 921 | 土包子 15 | 大肚子 20 |
| 料子 961 | 桌子 984 | 小辫子 61 | 小册子 61 |
| 核子 1026 | 蚊子 1048 | 小伙子 61 | 小舅子 61 |
| 屋子 1072 | 饺子 1115 | 小叔子 61 | 左撇子 113 |
| 胖子 1121 | 房子 1145 | 半辈子 127 | 耳挖子 145 |
| 麻子 1146 | 疯子 1147 | 耳坠子 145 | 汗珠子 236 |
| 弟子 1152 | 袜子 1193 | 出点子 258 | 出乱子 258 |
| 孩子 1202 | 带子 1213 | 书呆子 264 | 扎猛子 288 |
| 桃子 1243 | 根子 1245 | 打棍子 289 | 丢面子 297 |
| 格子 1246 | 棋子 1248 | 坐月子 318 | 扣帽子 401 |
| 胡子 1256 | 架子 1270 | 抓辫子 406 | 肉丸子 437 |
| 原子能 1273 | 原子弹 1273 | 有路子 439 | 伪君子 454 |
| 原子 1273 | 笛子 1279 | 私生子 471 | 两口子 509 |
| 狮子 1285 | 狮子舞 1285 | 卖关子 524 | 拉肚子 573 |
| 胆子 1295 | 刷子 1310 | 败家子 589 | 舍利子 593 |
| 案子 1321 | 盖子 1331 | 直性子 609 | 好日子 627 |
| 卷子 1333 | 浪子回头 1341 | 夜猫子 654 | 空架子 669 |
| 浪子 1341 | 票子 1367 | 洋嗓子 689 | 洋鬼子 689 |
| 辈子 1382 | 探子 1404 | 烂摊子 702 | 过日子 712 |
| 哨子 1410 | 梅子 1413 | 拔罐子 791 | 乖孩子 832 |
| 盒子 1425 | 袋子 1428 | 皇太子 858 | 穷日子 912 |
| 聋子 1431 | 笼子 1436 | 没法子 938 | 要面子 969 |
| 肠子 1458 | 脑子 1460 | 命根子 1051 | 独生子 1095 |
| 钩子 1463 | 领子 1465 | 哭鼻子 1221 | 爱面子 1264 |
| 童子军 1471 | 弯子 1472 | 狗腿子 1287 | 闹乱子 1323 |
| 被子 1517 | 骨子 1543 | 捂鼻子 1399 | 捂盖子 1399 |
| | | 急性子 1426 | 鬼点子 1433 |
| | | 等离子 1437 | 装样子 1476 |

## 84 习 習　　U+4E60　TM 5 FM 一

**xí** N·V habit, custom, practice; to study, to practice, to review; to be used to

**习惯 xíguàn** N·V habit, custom; to be accustomed/used to · MW 个、种

边听音乐边看书是不是一个好**习惯**？ *Is it a good habit to listen to music while reading?*

**习气 xíqì** N unhealthy/bad habit · MW 个、种

**习俗 xísú** N custom · MW 个、种

吃饺子是中国人过新年的一个**习俗**。*Eating dumplings is a custom of the Chinese New Year.*

**习题 xítí** N exercise (schoolwork) · MW 条、道

对一些人来说，解数学**习题**是件令人愉快的事。*For some people, working on math problems is an enjoyable thing.*

**习性 xíxìng** N behavior, habits · MW 个、种

**习以为常 xíyǐwéicháng** EXP to be accustomed/used to

傻瓜对这里的寒冷气候已**习以为常**。*ShaGua is quite hardened to the cold weather now.*

**习语 xíyǔ** N idiom · MW 条

**习作 xízuò** N sketch; exercise (in composition, drawing, etc.) · MW 幅、篇

### RELATED WORDS

## 85 丑 醜　　U+4E11　TM 5 FM 一

**chǒu** ADJ ugly, unsightly; disgraceful, shameful, scandalous

**丑八怪 chǒubāguài** N very ugly person · MW 个

他是个**丑八怪**。*He is a very ugly person.*

**丑恶 chǒu'è** ADJ ugly, hideous

在这个世界上，**丑恶**的事情到处都有。*Awful events can happen anywhere in the world.*

**丑化 chǒuhuà** V to vilify

**丑剧 chǒujù** N farce · MW 场

**丑事 chǒushì** N scandal · MW 件

好事不出门，**丑事**传千里。*People may not know of the nice things you have done, but your scandals will spread quickly.*

**丑态 chǒutài** N buffoonery · MW 个

**丑闻 chǒuwén** N scandal · MW 件

"水门事件"的**丑闻**使尼克松政府垮台。*The Watergate scandal toppled President Nixon.*

**丑小鸭 chǒuxiǎoyā** N ugly duckling · MW 只

### RELATED WORDS

## 86 中　　U+4E2D　TM 5 FM |

**zhōng** N·ADJ center, middle; China; mid-, medium; intermediary; in progress; all right, suitable

华**中**师大 *Central China Normal University*

**中**美教育比较 *Chinese-American Comparative Education*

我穿**中**号的鞋。*I wear medium-sized shoes.*

在申请过程**中** *in the process of application*

这个方法**中**不**中**？ *Is this way all right?*

**zhòng** V to hit; to fit exactly; to suffer; to fall into

击**中**要害 *to hit home*

她**中**毒了。*She was poisoned.*

他**中**计了。*He has been trapped.*

**中班 zhōngbān** N middle/swing shift; middle class in kindergarten · MW 个

**中部 zhōngbù** N middle/central section

武汉在中国的**中部**。*Wuhan is in the center of China.*

**中餐 zhōngcān** N Chinese meal/food · MW 顿

傻瓜曾经在**中餐**馆打工。*ShaGua once worked at Chinese restaurants.*

**中草药 zhōngcǎoyào** N Chinese herbal medicine · MW 剂、服

**中层 zhōngcéng** N middle level

**中产阶级 zhōngchǎnjiējí** N middle class, bourgeoisie

**中程 zhōngchéng** N intermediate range

**中等 zhōngděng** ADJ medium; secondary

**中东 Zhōngdōng** N the Middle East

**中断 zhōngduàn** V to break off, to suspend

**86 中 zhōng** (continued)

**中饭 zhōngfàn** N lunch · MW 顿、餐

学生们都到饭堂吃**中饭**。*Students eat their lunch in the dining halls.*

**中共中央 Zhōng-Gòng Zhōngyāng** N Central Committee of the Communist Party of China

**中古 zhōnggǔ** N middle antiquity (third to ninth centuries); Middle Ages

**中国 Zhōngguó** N China

**中国大陆 Zhōngguódàlù** N Chinese mainland

**中国共产党 Zhōngguó Gòngchǎndǎng** N Communist Party of China

**中国官话 Zhōngguóguānhuà** N Mandarin (language)

**中国官话**(普通话)在**中国**各地通用。*Mandarin is the national language of China.*

**中国银行 Zhōngguóyínháng** N Bank of China · MW 家

**中华 Zhōnghuá** N China

**中华民族 Zhōnghuámínzú** N Chinese nation/ people

**中华人民共和国 Zhōnghuá Rénmín Gònghéguó** N People's Republic of China

**中间 zhōngjiān** N center, middle; core

他正站在球场**中间**。*He is standing in the middle of the playground.*

**中看 zhōngkàn** ADJ pleasing to the eye, nice-looking

傻瓜的长相不**中看**。*ShaGua is not a good-looking guy.*

**中立 zhōnglì** V to be neutral

**中篇小说 zhōngpiānxiǎoshuō** N novelette, medium-length novel · MW 篇、部

**中秋 zhōngqiū** N the Mid-Autumn Festival (fifteenth day of the eighth lunar month)

**中秋**节是中国传统节日。*Mid-Autumn Festival is a traditional Chinese holiday.*

**中山装 zhōngshānzhuāng** N Chinese tunic suit (commonly referred to as the "Mao jacket," designed by Sun Zhongshan, founder of the Republic of China) · MW 套、件

傻瓜有一套**中山装**。*ShaGua has a Chinese tunic suit.*

**中式 zhōngshì** ADJ Chinese-style

**中山**装是**中式**服装的一种。*The Chinese tunic suit is a Chinese style of dress.*

**中数 zhōngshù** ADJ·N mean; median · MW 个

**中听 zhōngtīng** ADJ pleasant to the ear

**中途 zhōngtú** N halfway, midway

他**中途**下了车。*He got off the bus at the midway point.*

**中外 zhōngwài** N China and foreign countries

他是闻名**中外**的学者。*He is a scholar who is well-known both in China and abroad.*

**中文 Zhōngwén** N Chinese (language)

傻瓜的**中文**不伦不类, 英文不三不四。*ShaGua not only speaks Chinese poorly, but also English.*

**中午 zhōngwǔ** N noon, midday

在中国, 许多人**中午**都睡午觉。*Many people take a nap at noon time.*

**中西 zhōngxī** N Chinese and the West

**中西**文化有很大的不同。*Chinese and Western cultures are very different.*

**中心 zhōngxīn** N center; heart; core, hub · MW 个

市**中心**新建了一个购物**中心**。*A new shopping center has been built downtown.*

**中型 zhōngxíng** ADJ medium-sized

**中性 zhōngxìng** ADJ·N neutral; neuter (grammar)

**中学 zhōngxué** N middle school · MW 间、所

傻瓜的女儿在**中学**读书。*ShaGua's daughter goes to middle school.*

**中央 zhōngyāng** N center, middle; central authorities

纽约的**中央**公园很漂亮。*New York's Central Park is very beautiful.*

**中药 zhōngyào** N traditional Chinese medicine · MW 服、剂、包

**中医 zhōngyī** N traditional Chinese medical science; traditional Chinese medical doctor

很多慢性病人喜欢看**中医**, 吃**中药**。*Many patients with various chronic diseases like to see traditional Chinese medical doctors and take traditional Chinese medicines.*

**中庸 zhōngyōng** N golden mean (of Confucianism)

**中庸**有时很中用。*The golden mean can be very useful.*

**中用 zhōngyòng** V useful

有的东西**中看**不**中用**, 有的东西**中用**不**中看**。*Some things look nice but do not work; some are very useful but may not look nice.*

**中原 zhōngyuán** N central Chinese plains

**中止 zhōngzhǐ** V to suspend, to cease

工作太忙, 傻瓜不得不**中止**夜校的英文学习。*ShaGua was so busy that he could no longer attend night school to learn English.*

**中指 zhōngzhǐ** N middle finger · MW 个

中专 **zhōngzhuān** N special/technical secondary school · MW 间、所

中子 **zhōngzǐ** N neutron · MW 粒

**RELATED WORDS**

| | | |
|---|---|---|
| 中旬 596 | 从中 66 | 正中 76 |
| 正中下怀 76 | 目中无人 151 | 击中 156 |
| 心中有数 232 | 当中 335 | 其中 379 |
| 折中 折衷 408 | 肉中刺 437 | 空中 669 |
| 美中不足 671 | 看中 841 | 初中 963 |
| 集中 1267 | 适中 1358 | 雪中送炭 1369 |
| 眼中钉 1570 | 期中考试 1574 | 高中 1611 |
| 暗中 1676 | 半空中 127 | 古今中外 154 |
| 洋为中用 689 | 购物中心 1253 | |

---

## 87 巾 U+5DFE TM 5 FM |

**jīn** N piece of cloth (a towel, a scarf, etc.) · MW 条

巾帼 **jīnguó** N women · MW 个、位、名

**RELATED WORDS**

| | | |
|---|---|---|
| 手巾 104 | 头巾 128 | 毛巾 183 |
| 围巾 762 | 披巾 1011 | 纸巾 1103 |
| 浴巾 1170 | 领巾 1465 | 餐巾 1964 |
| 红领巾 474 | | |

---

## 88 未 U+672A TM 5 FM |

**wèi** ADV have not; not; no

未必 **wèibì** ADV may not necessarily

叫 "傻瓜" 的**未必**傻。*People named "ShaGua" may not necessarily be stupid.*

未卜先知 **wèibǔxiānzhī** EXP to foresee, to have foresight

傻瓜有时表现出**未卜先知**的能力。*ShaGua sometimes shows foresight.*

未曾 **wèicéng** ADV never, not yet, not before

未尝 **wèicháng** ADV not; not yet

未成年 **wèichéngnián** N underage, not of legal age

未定 **wèidìng** V to be uncertain/undecided

傻瓜想访问中国, 但时间**未定**。*ShaGua wants to visit China, but has not decided on his schedule yet.*

未婚 **wèihūn** V to be unmarried/single

未加工 **wèijiāgōng** V to be crude

未决 **wèijué** V to be unsettled

未来 **wèilái** N future; tomorrow

上大学对孩子的**未来**很有帮助。*Attending college is good for a child's future.*

未了 **wèiliǎo** V to be unfinished

未免 **wèimiǎn** ADV rather, a bit too; truly

为这样的小事吵嘴, **未免**太愚蠢了。*Fighting over a small thing is a bit pointless.*

未能 **wèinéng** V cannot; to fail to

未遂 **wèisuì** V to fail to, to be unable to

未完 **wèiwán** V to be unfinished

未详 **wèixiáng** V to be unknown

未知 **wèizhī** V to be unknown/uncertain

未知数 **wèizhīshù** N unknown number; uncertain · MW 个

傻瓜的英语能不能在夜校得A, 还是个**未知数**。*It is still unknown if ShaGua can get an "A" in English at night school.*

**RELATED WORD**

前所未闻 1329

---

## 89 末 U+672B TM 5 FM |

**mò** N tip, end

末了 **mòliǎo** N finally, last, in the end

末梢 **mòshāo** N tip, end

树枝的**末梢**上站着一只鸟。*There is a bird on the end of the branch.*

末尾 **mòwěi** N end, last part · MW 个

你已读到这本书的**末尾**了吗? *Have you reached the end of the book?*

**RELATED WORDS**

| | | |
|---|---|---|
| 本末倒置 90 | 岁末 380 | 粉末 1363 |

---

## 90 本 U+672C TM 5 FM |

**běn** N·ADJ·ADV·V·MW root; foundation, basis; origin; essence; capital; book; principal, main; original; one's own, native; current, present; originally; according to; to be based on, to follow; [measure word for bound objects (books, magazines, etc.)]

傻瓜以诚信为**本**。*ShaGua's guiding principle is honesty.*

支票**本** checkbook

你是还**本**还是付息。*Do you want to pay back the principal or just interest?*

**90 本 běn** (continued)

傻瓜本不想做市长。*Originally, ShaGua did not want to be the mayor.*

本着这个原则 *according to this principle*

**本地 běndì** N this locality

傻瓜不是**本地**人，但是傻瓜是**本地**足球队的球迷。*ShaGua is not a native of this city, but he is an ardent supporter of the local soccer team.*

**本分 běnfèn** N·ADJ one's duty; dutiful

每人都应尽他的**本分**。*Everyone should do his part.*

**本国 běnguó** N one's own country

**本行 běnháng** N one's profession

**本届 běnjiè** N current, this year's

**本科 běnkē** N undergraduate course

**本来 běnlái** ADJ·ADV original; at first; of course

**本利 běnlì** N principal and interest · MW 笔

**本末倒置 běnmòdàozhì** EXP to confuse cause and effect

**本能 běnnéng** N instinct

下雨时，我们的**本能**反应就是避雨。*Running for shelter is our instinctive reaction when it rains.*

**本年度 běnniándù** N this year

傻瓜被评为本市**本年度**人物。*ShaGua has been selected as this city's person of the year.*

**本人 běnrén** PRON me, myself; oneself

傻瓜说："就**本人**而言，我赞成**本年度**计划。"*ShaGua says, "Personally, I am in favor of the plan for this year."*

**本色 běnsè** N character, true qualities

**本事 běnshi** N skill, ability

傻瓜有时有处变不惊的**本事**。*ShaGua sometimes has the ability to keep calm during emergencies.*

**本题 běntí** N subject under discussion

**本位 běnwèi** N standard

**本文 běnwén** N this text, this article, etc.

**本息 běnxī** N principal and interest · MW 笔

**本性 běnxìng** N nature, instincts · MW 个

这父子俩仅外表相似，**本性**却很不一样。*There is only a superficial likeness between the father and son, for their natures are very different.*

**本意 běnyì** N intention, original idea

那并不是傻瓜的**本意**。*It's not what ShaGua intended.*

**本着 běnzhe** PREP in line/conformity with

**本着**诚信的原则，傻瓜的市长工作干得不错。*In terms of honesty, ShaGua did a good job as mayor.*

**本质 běnzhì** N essence, nature, innate character

**本子 běnzi** N book, notebook · MW 本

**RELATED WORDS**

| | | |
|---|---|---|
| 人本主义 4 | 大本营 20 | 文本 70 |
| 正本 76 | 日本 96 | 亏本 137 |
| 书本 264 | 老本 375 | 成本 61 |
| 还本 714 | 还本付息 714 | 标本 801 |
| 样本 803 | 版本 897 | 译本 951 |
| 连本带利 958 | 基本 991 | 基本功 991 |
| 原本 1273 | 根本 1245 | 秘本 1289 |
| 资本 1335 | 股本 1456 | 剧本 1468 |
| 读本 1502 | 课本 1503 | 蓝本 1548 |
| 赔本 1569 | 脚本 1804 | 够本 1808 |
| 合订本 296 | 笔记本 1278 | 生产成本 107 |
| 产品成本 219 | | |

**91 术 術** U+672F TM **5** FM |

**shù** N art, skill; technique, method, tactic

**术后处理 shùhòuchǔlǐ** N postoperative care

**术语 shùyǔ** N (technical) term, terminology · MW 个

课堂上，老师讲的尽是科学**术语**，让人听不懂。*During class, the teacher is always using complex and scientific terms, which makes it difficult to understand.*

**RELATED WORDS**

| | | |
|---|---|---|
| 手术 104 | 艺术 274 | 艺术家 274 |
| 艺术界 274 | 艺术品 274 | 艺术团 274 |
| 艺术性 274 | 权术 292 | 医术 389 |
| 幻术 475 | 武术 513 | 技术 568 |
| 美术 671 | 剑术 904 | 战术 1044 |
| 学术 1155 | 柔术 1198 | 算术 1697 |
| 骑术 1840 | 骗术 1937 | 魔术 1996 |
| 动手术 514 | | |

**92 支** U+652F TM **5** FM |

**zhī** N·V·MW branch, offshoot; to prop/put up, to raise; to protrude; to support, to sustain; to send away; to pay; [measure word for objects shaped like sticks (pens, chopsticks, candles, etc.)]

天黑了，快**支**起帐篷。*Put up our tent before it gets dark.*

傻瓜谈公务时，常常**支**开傻瓜太太。*ShaGua sends Mrs. ShaGua away when he is discussing official business.*

预**支**房租 *to pay the rent in advance*

**支**部 zhībù　N　branch of the Communist Party of China · MW 个

**支**撑 zhīchēng　V　to support; to maintain

为了**支**撑这个家, 傻瓜不得不努力工作。
*In order to support his family, ShaGua has to work very hard.*

**支**承 zhīchéng　V　to bear weight, to be supporting

**支**持 zhīchí　N·V　support; back; to support; to hold out, to last

傻瓜非常**支**持儿子上大学。 *ShaGua strongly supports his son's eagerness to go to college.*

**支**出 zhīchū　V　to spend, to pay · MW 笔

**支**点 zhīdiǎn　N　fulcrum, pivot point · MW 个

**支**队 zhīduì　N　detachment · MW 个

**支**付 zhīfù　V　to pay

儿子上大学的**支**出超出了傻瓜的**支**付能力。
*His son's college expenses are greater than ShaGua's ability to pay.*

**支**架 zhījià　N　support, stand · MW 个

**支**解 zhījiě　V　to dismember

**支**离 zhīlí　V　to be fragmented/broken

**支**流 zhīliú　N　affluent; branch, tributary; minor aspects · MW 条

**支**配 zhīpèi　V　to arrange, to allocate; to control

傻瓜从不被别人的意见所**支**配。 *ShaGua has never been governed by the opinions of others.*

**支**票 zhīpiào　N　(bank) check · MW 张、本

请在这张**支**票背后签名。 *Please endorse this check.*

**支**气管 zhīqìguǎn　N　bronchus

**支**取 zhīqǔ　V　to withdraw (money)

可以在银行里**支**取多少钱? *How much money can be withdrawn from the bank?*

**支**使 zhīshi　V　to order around; to send away

**支**书 zhīshū　N　secretary of a Party/League branch · MW 个、名

**支**线 zhīxiàn　N　branch line, feeder · MW 条

**支**应 zhīyìng　V　to cope with, to deal with; to supply

**支**援 zhīyuán　V　to support; to assist, to help, to aid

傻瓜主动捐款**支**援这个项目。
*ShaGua volunteered monetary contributions to back this project.*

**支**柱 zhīzhù　N　prop; pillar · MW 个、根

**RELATED WORDS**

开支 26　　　分支 173　　　收支 282
枪支 1244　　党支部 1626　　透支 1826

---

**93　长　長**　　U+957F　　TM **5** FM |

**cháng**　ADJ·N·V·ADV　long; lasting; length; strong point; to be good at; often

长江是中国最**长**的河流。 *The Yangtze River is the longest river in China.*

傻瓜不**长**于演讲。 *ShaGua is not good at giving speeches.*

**zhǎng**　N·V　older, senior; chief, head; to come into being, to grow, to begin to grow, to develop; to acquire; to increase; to enhance

傻瓜是市**长**。 *ShaGua is a mayor.*

他**长**得真快! *He is growing up very fast.*

傻瓜当市**长**以后, **长**了很多见识。 *Being a mayor, ShaGua has gained a lot of experience.*

**长**波 chángbō　N　long wave

**长**城 Chángchéng　N　the Great Wall

**长**处 chángchu　N　strong point · MW 个

傻瓜有很多**长**处。 *ShaGua has many strong points.*

**长**存 chángcún　V　to live forever

**长**笛 chángdí　N　flute · MW 支

**长**度 chángdù　N　length

**长**短 chángduǎn　N　length; accident; good and bad, right and wrong

**长**方体 chángfāngtǐ　N　cube (geometry) · MW 个

**长**方形 chángfāngxíng　N　rectangle · MW 个

**长**江 Chángjiāng　N　Yangtze River

**长**颈鹿 chángjǐnglù　N　giraffe · MW 只

**长**久 chángjiǔ　ADJ　(for a) long time, long-term; permanent

**长**久以来, 有人每年都给傻瓜寄圣诞卡。
*Somebody has sent ShaGua a Christmas card every year for many years.*

**长**距离 chángjùlí　N　long distance

**长**裤 chángkù　N　trousers, pants · MW 条

**长**廊 chángláng　N　covered walk, gallery · MW 条

**长**眠 chángmián　V　to die; to sleep eternally

**长**年 chángnián　ADV　all year long, for a long time

**长**跑 chángpǎo　N　long-distance run

傻瓜**长**年坚持**长**跑。 *ShaGua has stuck with long-distance running for a long time.*

**长**篇小说 chángpiānxiǎoshuō　N　full-length novel · MW 篇、部

**长**期 chángqī　N　long-lasting, longtime

他们是**长**期的合作伙伴。 *They are longtime partners.*

## 93 长 cháng/zhǎng (continued)

**长寿 chángshòu** ADJ long-lived

尽管生活贫穷, 但傻瓜的父母很**长寿**。
*ShaGua's parents lived long lives even though they were very poor.*

**长途 chángtú** N long trip; long distance

**长途电话 chángtúdiànhuà** N long-distance call · MW 个

傻瓜先生, 你有一个**长途电话**。*A long-distance call for you, Mr. ShaGua.*

**长远 chángyuǎn** ADJ long-range; long-term

傻瓜的**长远**计划是在15年内还清房屋贷款。
*ShaGua's long-range plan is to pay off the mortgage within 15 years.*

**长征 chángzhēng** V·N long march; expedition · MW 次

**长辈 zhǎngbèi** N older generation; elder, senior · MW 个、位、名

你应该对**长辈**尊重些。*You should show greater respect for your elders.*

**长大 zhǎngdà** V to grow up, to be brought up

傻瓜的小儿子决心**长大**以后当医生。
*ShaGua's younger son wants to be a doctor when he grows up.*

**长官 zhǎngguān** N senior official · MW 个、位、名

**长见识 zhǎngjiànshi** V to gain experience

**长进 zhǎngjìn** V to progress, to improve

傻瓜的英语**长进**了不少。*ShaGua has made great progress in English.*

**长老 zhǎnglǎo** N elder; senior monk · MW 位、名

**长势 zhǎngshì** N crop growth

**长相 zhǎngxiàng** N looks, features, appearance · MW 个

儿子的**长相**同老子的**长相**差不多。*Father and son look like each other.*

**长者 zhǎngzhě** N elder, senior · MW 个、位、名

**长子 zhǎngzǐ** N oldest son · MW 个、名

### RELATED WORDS

| | | |
|---|---|---|
| 厂长 7 | 三长两短 9 | 天长日久 25 |
| 生长 107 | 车长 114 | 专长 155 |
| 处长 217 | 外长 218 | 州长 233 |
| 队长 294 | 会长 295 | 议长 350 |
| 兄长 382 | 团长 392 | 师长 396 |
| 村长 410 | 伸长 457 | 取长补短 520 |
| 县长 543 | 拉长 573 | 身长 604 |

| | | |
|---|---|---|
| 成长 611 | 科长 642 | 夜长梦多 654 |
| 班长 730 | 延长 731 | 校长 802 |
| 助长 818 | 修长 870 | 首长 924 |
| 周长 1068 | 细长 1107 | 站长 1189 |
| 家长 1315 | 庭长 1326 | 深长 1345 |
| 袖长 1361 | 部长 1636 | 船长 1809 |
| 增长 1849 | 瘦长 1880 | 漫长 1887 |
| 万里长城 73 | 万里征 73 | 与世长辞 158 |
| 土生土长 15 | 语重心长 1501 | 源远流长 1742 |

## 94 业 業 U+4E1A TM 5 FM |

**yè** N·ADV line of business, trade, industry; occupation, profession, employment; course of study; estate, property; cause; already

农业 *agriculture*

毕业 *graduation*

家业 *family property*

业已成功 *to have already been successful*

**业绩 yèjī** N outstanding achievement, accomplishment · MW 个

傻瓜市长的**业绩**不错。*As mayor, ShaGua has made an outstanding achievement.*

**业务 yèwù** N business · MW 个

傻瓜所在的城市已开始增加在亚洲的**业务**。
*ShaGua's city has begun to increase its operations in Asia.*

**业务系统 yèwùxìtǒng** N operations, operational system · MW 个

**业余 yèyú** N spare time, hobby

傻瓜的**业余**爱好是举重。*ShaGua's hobby is weightlifting.*

**业主 yèzhǔ** N owner, proprietor · MW 个、位、名

这家中餐馆的**业主**是傻瓜的朋友。*The owner of this Chinese restaurant is ShaGua's friend.*

### RELATED WORDS

| | | |
|---|---|---|
| 开业 26 | 失业 106 | 专业 155 |
| 企业 170 | 企业管理 170 | 休业 213 |
| 产业 219 | 作业 326 | 行业 327 |
| 林业 412 | 农业 423 | 伟业 451 |
| 毕业 540 | 待业 872 | 事业 987 |
| 转业 1111 | 创业 1131 | 学业 1155 |
| 职业 1205 | 结业 1291 | 渔业 1496 |
| 营业员 1546 | 营业 1546 | 停业 1588 |
| 商业 1612 | 就业 1836 | 半失业 127 |
| 重工业 839 | 轻工业 1113 | 公用事业 103 |

## 95 甘

U+7518 · TM 5 · FM |

**gān** ADJ·V sweet; pleasant; to be willing to

甘拜下风 **gānbàixiàfēng** EXP to throw in the towel, to admit defeat

甘苦 **gānkǔ** N ups and downs, sweetness and bitterness, prosperity and adversity

同甘苦，共患难 *together through thick and thin*

甘露 **gānlù** N sweet dew · MW 滴、粒

甘美 **gānměi** ADJ sweet and refreshing

甘薯 **gānshǔ** N sweet potato · MW 个、块

甘肃 **Gānsù** N Gansu Province

甘心 **gānxīn** V to be willing/satisfied; to be reconciled to

不甘心老是住出租房，傻瓜就贷款买了屋子。 *Not wanting to rent an apartment indefinitely, ShaGua bought a house with a mortgage.*

甘蔗 **gānzhè** N sugarcane · MW 根、节

## 96 日

U+65E5 · TM 5 · FM |

**rì** N·MW sun, daytime, day; daily; [measure word for days]

日出日落 *sunrise and sunset*
多日不见。 *Long time no see.*

日班 **rìbān** N day shift · MW 个
傻瓜在公司里上日班，在餐馆里上夜班。 *ShaGua worked the day shift at his company; he worked the night shift at a Chinese restaurant.*

日报 **rìbào** N daily newspaper · MW 份、张

日本 **Rìběn** N Japan

日产量 **rìchǎnliáng** N daily output/production

日常 **rìcháng** ADJ everyday, day-to-day
傻瓜的日常生活非常简单。 *ShaGua's day-to-day life is very simple.*

日常费用 **rìchángfèiyòng** N continuous assessment · MW 笔

日程 **rìchéng** N program, schedule, agenda; itinerary · MW 个
傻瓜的日程安排得很满。 *ShaGua's schedule is really full.*

日程计划 **rìchéngjìhuà** N schedule planning · MW 个

日光 **rìguāng** N sunlight · MW 束、道

日光灯 **rìguāngdēng** N fluorescent light · MW 盏

日后 **rìhòu** N in the future
为孩子日后读书，傻瓜需要存一大笔钱。 *In order to send his kids to college, ShaGua must save a lot of money.*

日积月累 **rìjīyuèlěi** EXP to accumulate over a long period

日记 **rìjì** N diary, journal · MW 本、篇

日间 **rìjiān** ADV in the daytime, during the day

日渐 **rìjiàn** ADV with each passing day

日久 **rìjiǔ** ADV in the course of time

日历 **rìlì** N calendar · MW 本、张

日期 **rìqī** N date · MW 个
交房租的日期到了。 *The date to pay rent is coming up.*

日前 **rìqián** N the other day, a few days ago

日趋 **rìqū** ADV with each passing day, day to day

日食 **rìshí** N solar eclipse · MW 次

日夜 **rìyè** N day and night
傻瓜日夜工作，连上两个班。 *ShaGua worked two shifts, day and night.*

日益 **rìyì** ADV increasingly; day by day

日用 **rìyòng** N·ADJ daily expenses; for everyday use
我们的日用开支增加了。 *Our daily expenses have increased.*

日语 **Rìyǔ** N Japanese (language)

日照 **rìzhào** N sunshine

日志 **rìzhì** N daily record/journal · MW 本、篇

日子 **rìzi** N day, date; life · MW 个
因为收入太低，傻瓜家的日子不好过。 *Since their income was very low, ShaGua's family struggled.*

**RELATED WORDS**

## 97 贝 贝

U+8D1D · TM 5 · FM |

**bèi** N shellfish

贝雕 **bèidiāo** N scrimshaw, shell carving · MW 件

**97 贝 bèi** (continued)

**贝壳 bèiké** N conch, shell · MW 片

我们在海边捡到这片漂亮的**贝壳**。 *We found this beautiful shell on the beach.*

**贝类 bèilèi** N shellfish, mollusk

**RELATED WORD**

宝贝 667

---

**98 凶** U+51F6 TM 5 FM |

**xiōng** ADJ violent, ferocious, fierce, terrible

**凶暴 xiōngbào** ADJ ferocious

**凶犯 xiōngfàn** N killer, murderer · MW 个、名、伙

警察抓到了杀人**凶犯**。 *The police caught the murderer.*

**凶狠 xiōnghěn** ADJ vicious, malicious

**凶猛 xiōngměng** ADJ ferocious, fierce

**凶器 xiōngqì** N weapon (for committing a crime) · MW 件

警察在树林里找到了作案**凶器**。 *The police found the weapon in the woods.*

**凶手 xiōngshǒu** N murderer, killer · MW 个、名、伙

**凶手**是一名从监狱里逃出来的罪犯。 *The murderer was the one who escaped from prison.*

**凶相 xiōngxiàng** N fierce look · MW 副

**RELATED WORDS**

元凶 138　　　行凶 327　　　帮凶 1583

---

**99 区 區** U+533A TM 5 FM |

**qū** N area, region, district, administrative division

**区别 qūbié** V·N to distinguish, to differentiate; difference · MW 个

你知道这两个词之间的**区别**吗？ *Do you know the difference between the two words?*

**区分 qūfēn** V to make a distinction between, to differentiate

**区分**那些发育不良的幼苗很有必要。 *It is necessary to make a distinction between healthy and unhealthy seedlings.*

**区间 qūjiān** N part of a normal transportation route · MW 个

**区时 qūshí** N time zone · MW 个

中国只有北京时间，没有不同的**区时**。 *China does not have time zones, only Beijing time.*

**区域 qūyù** N region, area · MW 个

今天这个**区域**将有大雨。 *There will be heavy rain in this area today.*

**RELATED WORDS**

| | | |
|---|---|---|
| 山区 38 | 分区 173 | 市区 332 |
| 林区 412 | 灾区 483 | 社区 504 |
| 时区 586 | 地区 772 | 郊区 1194 |
| 险区 1252 | 禁区 1536 | 新区 1638 |
| 港区 1740 | 管区 1861 | 洪泛区 690 |
| 经济特区 1110 | | |

---

**100 艾** U+827E TM 5 FM |

**ài** N wormwood

**艾蒿 àihāo** N wormwood · MW 棵、株

**艾滋病 àizībìng** N acquired immune deficiency syndrome (AIDS)

人们已经注意到**艾滋病**对社会造成的危害。 *People have realized the damage that AIDS has caused to society.*

---

**101 以** U+4EE5 TM 5 FM |

**yǐ** V·PREP·CONJ to use; to take; by, for, according to; in order to, so as to; therefore

**以**其人之道，还治其人之身 *paying someone back in his/her own currency*

**以**抵达先后为序 *in order of arrival*

**以**示尊重 *in order to show one's respect*

**以便 yǐbiàn** CONJ in order to

他打算学中文，**以便**将来到中国工作。 *He is going to study Chinese in order to work in China in the future.*

**以此 yǐcǐ** PREP for this reason; by means of

**以德报怨 yǐdébàoyuàn** EXP to return good for evil

**以毒攻毒 yǐdúgōngdú** EXP to fight poison with poison, to fight fire with fire

**以后 yǐhòu** N after, afterwards, later

傻瓜的儿子上大学**以后**很少回家。 *After ShaGua's son went to college, he hardly ever came home.*

**以及 yǐjí** CONJ as well as; and

**以假乱真 yǐjiǎluànzhēn** EXP to mix the bad with the good

**以来 yǐlái** N since

三年**以来**, 这个学生都在用中文写日记。
*This student has kept a Chinese diary for the past three years.*

**以理服人** yǐlǐfúrén   EXP   to convince by reasoning

**以礼相待** yǐlǐxiāngdài   EXP   to treat with due respect

**以卵击石** yǐluǎnjīshí   EXP   to fight a losing battle (LIT to throw an egg against a rock)

**以貌取人** yǐmàoqǔrén   EXP   to judge people solely by their appearance

**以免** yǐmiǎn   CONJ   in order to avoid, so as not to; in case of

少吃点零食, **以免**长胖。 *Eat fewer snacks so as not to gain weight.*

**以内** yǐnèi   N   within

请在一个星期**以内**还书。 *Please return the books within a week.*

**以前** yǐqián   N   before, previously

很久**以前**, 这里曾经是一个公园。 *There used to be a park here a long time ago.*

**以色列** Yǐsèliè   N   Israel

**以上** yǐshàng   N   more than, above; above-mentioned

请遵守**以上**规则。 *Please obey the regulations above.*

**以身作则** yǐshēnzuòzé   EXP   to set a good example

**以外** yǐwài   N   beyond, outside, other than

除工作**以外**, 傻瓜还有其他特别爱好吗? *Does ShaGua have any special interests other than his job?*

**以往** yǐwǎng   N   before, in the past

**以为** yǐwéi   V   to think, to believe

很多人**以为**中文很难学, 其实并不难。 *Many people consider Chinese a very difficult language, but actually it is not.*

**以下** yǐxià   N   below, under; the following, next

二十一岁**以下**的人不能喝酒。 *Those under 21 may not drink.*

**以一当十** yǐyīdāngshí   EXP   to pit one against ten

**以至** yǐzhì   CONJ   to such an extent, down to, up to

**以致** yǐzhì   CONJ   so that; as a result, consequently

**以子之矛, 攻子之盾** yǐzǐzhīmáo gōngzǐzhīdùn   EXP   to contradict oneself (LIT to thrust your spear through your own shield)

**RELATED WORDS**

| | | |
|---|---|---|
| 习以为常 84 | 可以 243 | 予以 249 |
| 自以为是 305 | 用以 313 | 足以 383 |
| 加以 463 | 所以 645 | 所以然 645 |
| 从今以后 66 | 持之以恒 1019 | |

---

**102**  今    U+4ECA    TM **5**   FM 丿

**jīn**   N   today; this (year); now; the present; until now; from now on

**今后** jīnhòu   N   from now on, in the future

**今天** jīntiān   N   today

她**今天**晚上看不看电视? *Is she going to watch TV tonight?*

**今昔** jīnxī   N   the present and the past

**RELATED WORDS**

| | | |
|---|---|---|
| 于今 28 | 从今以后 66 | 古今中外 154 |
| 至今 244 | 当今 335 | 而今 351 |
| 如今 464 | 现今 975 | 古往今来 154 |
| 古为今用 154 | 厚古薄今 1272 | |

---

**103** 公    U+516C    TM **5**   FM 丿

**gōng**   ADJ·N   public, state-owned; common, general; metric; impartial, fair, just; public affairs; duke (a noble title in feudal China); husband's father, father-in-law; male

**公安** gōng'ān   N   public security

**公报** gōngbào   N   bulletin, public service announcement (PSA) · MW 个

**公布** gōngbù   V   to announce, to publish

协议的细节还没有**公布**。 *The details of the agreement haven't been announced.*

**公差** gōngchā   N   tolerance (engineering)

**公尺** gōngchǐ   N·MW   meter; [measure word for meters]

许多美国人不知道一**公尺**有多长, 但傻瓜很清楚。 *Many Americans don't know how long a meter is, but ShaGua does.*

**公道** gōngdào   N   justice

**公道** gōngdao   ADJ   fair, impartial

傻瓜有点儿笨, 但十分**公道**。 *ShaGua is a little slow, but he is absolutely fair.*

**公敌** gōngdí   N   public enemy · MW 个、名

**公费** gōngfèi   N   public/state expense · MW 笔

**公分** gōngfēn   N·MW   centimeter; [measure word for centimeters]

**公愤** gōngfèn   N   public outcry

凶手的残暴引起**公愤**。 *The murderer's brutal act has caused a public outcry.*

**公告** gōnggào   N·V   announcement, proclamation; to give public notice · MW 个、篇

**103 公 gōng** (continued)

公共 **gōnggòng** ADJ public, common
请保持**公共**场所的安静。*Please be quiet in public.*

公共厕所 **gōnggòngcèsuǒ** N public restroom · MW 间

公共道德 **gōnggòngdàodé** N public morality

公共电话 **gōnggòngdiànhuà** N public/pay telephone · MW 部

公共汽车 **gōnggòngqìchē** N bus · MW 辆

公公 **gōnggong** N husband's father; eunuch · MW 个、位

公海 **gōnghǎi** N open sea

公害 **gōnghài** N public hazard/nuisance, environmental pollution
在**公共**场所抽烟是一种**公害**。*Smoking in public is one type of environmental pollution.*

公函 **gōnghán** N official correspondence · MW 份

公积金 **gōngjījīn** N reserve fund · MW 笔

公家 **gōngjia** N the public; the state

公斤 **gōngjīn** N·MW kilogram; [measure word for kilograms]

公开 **gōngkāi** V·ADJ to make public; open, public
**傻瓜**不喜欢在**公开**场合演讲。*ShaGua doesn't like making speeches in public.*

公开化 **gōngkāihuà** V to come out into the open
政治**公开化**是民主的标志之一。*Politics coming out into the open is a sign of democracy.*

公理 **gōnglǐ** N universal truth · MW 条

公里 **gōnglǐ** N·MW kilometer; [measure word for kilometers]

公立 **gōnglì** ADJ public, government-run
在美国上**公立**大学比较便宜。*Public universities are relatively cheaper in America.*

公历 **gōnglì** N Gregorian calendar

公路 **gōnglù** N highway, road · MW 条

公路桥 **gōnglùqiáo** N highway bridge · MW 座

公论 **gōnglùn** N public opinion · MW 个

公民 **gōngmín** N citizen · MW 个、位、名
每一个**公民**都有责任维护社会公德。*Every citizen is responsible for maintaining societal morality.*

公墓 **gōngmù** N public cemetery · MW 个、片

公平 **gōngpíng** ADJ fair, impartial
每个人都希望得到**公平**的待遇。*Everyone hopes to be treated fairly.*

公婆 **gōngpó** N husband's parents; husband and wife · MW 对

公然 **gōngrán** ADV openly, brazenly

公认 **gōngrèn** V to recognize widely, to acknowledge
**傻瓜**被**公认**是一个工作努力的人。*ShaGua is widely recognized as a hard-working person.*

公式 **gōngshì** N formula · MW 个、道
数学**公式**需要死记。*The math formulas must be memorized.*

公事 **gōngshì** N public affairs, official business · MW 件

公司 **gōngsī** N company, corporation, firm · MW 个、家
**傻瓜**曾给一家很大的**公司**工作。*The company ShaGua once worked for is a very large corporation.*

公议 **gōngyì** V public discussion

公益 **gōngyì** N public welfare

公用事业 **gōngyòngshìyè** N public utility · MW 个

公有 **gōngyǒu** ADJ publicly owned

公寓 **gōngyù** N apartment · MW 所、栋、幢

公元 **gōngyuán** N A.D., C.E. (Common Era)

公园 **gōngyuán** N public park · MW 个
在纽约的中心, 有一个很大的**公园**。*There is a very large park located in the center of New York.*

公约 **gōngyuē** N treaty, pact, joint pledge · MW 个

公债 **gōngzhài** N (government) bond · MW 笔

公章 **gōngzhāng** N official seal · MW 枚
中国**公司**喜欢盖**公章**来保证文件的权威性。*Chinese companies like to show a document's authority by using an official seal.*

公正 **gōngzhèng** ADJ just, impartial

公证 **gōngzhèng** V notarization, authentication
这份文件需要鉴定人做**公证**。*This document needs to be notarized.*

公职 **gōngzhí** N public office/employment · MW 个、份

公制 **gōngzhì** N metric system

公众 **gōngzhòng** N the public

公主 **gōngzhǔ** N princess · MW 个、位、名

**RELATED WORDS**

## 104 手    U+624B    TM 5   FM 丿

**shǒu** N·ADJ hand; expert; in one's hand; handy, convenient

**手背 shǒubèi** N back of the hand
傻瓜的**手背**被邻居的狗咬了一口。 *The back of ShaGua's hand was bitten by the neighbor's dog.*

**手笔 shǒubǐ** N literary skill; handwriting/painting (usually of a famous person); style of living/spending · MW 类

**手臂 shǒubì** N arm; reliable helper · MW 支
他的**手臂**肿了起来。 *His arm was all swollen.*
她是他的得力**手臂**。 *She is one of his most reliable assistants.*

**手表 shǒubiǎo** N (wrist)watch · MW 只

**手册 shǒucè** N handbook, manual · MW 本
学生**手册**可以从网上下载。 *The student handbooks can be downloaded from the website.*

**手段 shǒuduàn** N method, means, tool; measure; trick · MW 个、种
发电子邮件是当今重要的通讯**手段**。 *Today, sending e-mails is an important means of communication.*
她很有**手段**。 *She is good at playing tricks.*

**手法 shǒufǎ** N skill, technique; trick · MW 个、种

**手风琴 shǒufēngqín** N accordion · MW 台、架

**手感 shǒugǎn** N feel, touch · MW 种

**手稿 shǒugǎo** N manuscript, script · MW 本、份
有谁看过傻瓜的小说的**手稿**？ *Who has had a chance to read the manuscript of ShaGua's novel?*

**手工 shǒugōng** N handwork, craft, craftsmanship
这件衣服的**手工**很精细。 *The handwork in this cloth is very fine.*

**手工艺 shǒugōngyì** N handicraft · MW 种

**手脚 shǒujiǎo** N movement of hands/feet, motion; trick · MW 个
傻瓜太太的**手脚**很麻利。 *Mrs. ShaGua's motions are very quick and neat.*
傻瓜太太没有做**手脚**。 *Mrs. ShaGua did not play a trick.*

**手巾 shǒujīn** N towel; handkerchief · MW 条

**手铐 shǒukào** N handcuffs · MW 副

**手帕 shǒupà** N handkerchief · MW 条

**手枪 shǒuqiāng** N pistol, handgun · MW 支

**手巧 shǒuqiǎo** ADJ skillful with one's hands, deft

**手势 shǒushì** N gesture, sign · MW 个
他做了个**手势**表示拒绝。 *He gestured to indicate his refusal.*

**手术 shǒushù** N·V surgical operation; to operate · MW 个、次

**手套 shǒutào** N glove, mitten · MW 对、副

**手提 shǒutí** ADJ portable
**手提**电脑是许多学生的必备学习工具。 *A laptop is a necessary tool for many students.*

**手头 shǒutóu** N on hand

**手推车 shǒutuīchē** N handcart, wheelbarrow · MW 辆、架

**手腕 shǒuwàn** N wrist; trick
她的**手腕**很有力。 *Her wrists are very strong.*
他喜欢耍**手腕**。 *He likes to play tricks.*

**手舞足蹈 shǒuwǔzúdǎo** EXP to dance for joy

**手下 shǒuxià** N subordinate; under the leadership of; on hand · MW 个
这个工头管着几个**手下**。 *There are several workers under this supervisor's management.*

**手写体 shǒuxiětǐ** N handwritten form, script · MW 种

**手心 shǒuxīn** N palm; scope of control

**手续 shǒuxù** N procedure, formality · MW 个
上这所学校需要办注册**手续**。 *To attend this school, one must abide by its registration procedures.*

**手艺 shǒuyì** N craft, skill, workmanship · MW 种

**手语 shǒuyǔ** N sign language · MW 个

**手掌 shǒuzhǎng** N palm · MW 个、对

**手杖 shǒuzhàng** N walking stick, cane; shooting stick · MW 根

**手指 shǒuzhǐ** N finger · MW 根
许多人相信**手指**的运动与大脑的发育有关。 *Many people believe in a link between the movement of the fingers and growth of the brain.*

**手纸 shǒuzhǐ** N toilet paper · MW 张、卷
傻瓜知道中国的厕所没有**手纸**。 *ShaGua knew that there was no toilet paper in the bathrooms in China.*

**手镯 shǒuzhuó** N bracelet · MW 个、对

**手足 shǒuzú** N hands and feet; brother

### RELATED WORDS

| | | |
|---|---|---|
| 二手 2 | 人手 4 | 入手 5 |
| 大手大脚 20 | 凶手 98 | 失手 106 |
| 生手 107 | 左手 113 | 扒手 169 |
| 分手 173 | 白手起家 176 | 右手 187 |
| 对手 254 | 扎手 288 | 住手 324 |

## 104 手 shǒu (continued)

| | | |
|---|---|---|
| 束手无策 372 | 老手 375 | 扶手 404 |
| 伸手 457 | 两手 509 | 动手 514 |
| 动手术 514 | 号手 545 | 扳手 566 |
| 拉手 573 | 身手 604 | 甩手 612 |
| 好手 627 | 举手 674 | 沾手 684 |
| 到手 737 | 拍手 790 | 助手 818 |
| 徒手 873 | 顺手 874 | 亲手 908 |
| 放手 964 | 把手 1006 | 经手 1110 |
| 转手 1111 | 洗手 1167 | 招手 1232 |
| 枪手 1244 | 拿手 1262 | 着手 1332 |
| 袖手旁观 1361 | 指手画脚 1397 | 射手 1467 |
| 选手 1510 | 插手 1555 | 帮手 1583 |
| 高手 1611 | 握手 1662 | 鼓手 1688 |
| 脱手 1803 | 旗手 1834 | 能手 1873 |
| 触手 1875 | 歌手 1900 | 携手 1905 |
| 撒手 1907 | 解手 1928 | 三只手 9 |
| 刽子手 903 | 留后手 1582 | 第二手 1695 |
| 第一手 1695 | 露一手 1997 | 大打出手 20 |

## 105 欠      U+6B20      TM 5   FM 丿

**qiàn** V to owe, to be in debt; to lack, to be short of; to lean forward, to raise the upper part of one's body slightly; to yawn

**欠饱和 qiànbǎohé** V to not be completely saturated

**欠产 qiànchǎn** V to fall short in output
今年天旱, 粮食**欠产**了。 *This year has been so dry that there has been a shortage of grain.*

**欠款 qiànkuǎn** V·N to owe money; debt
当儿子谈到**欠款**时, 傻瓜惊呆了。 *ShaGua froze when his son mentioned his debts.*

**欠缺 qiànquē** V·N to be short of; lack · MW 个

**欠身 qiànshēn** V to lift oneself up

**欠条 qiàntiáo** N IOU (a note acknowledging a debt) · MW 张
傻瓜向朋友借10元钱, 写了张**欠条**。
*ShaGua wrote an IOU to a friend for borrowing ten dollars.*

**欠妥 qiàntuǒ** ADJ improper
他的信在措辞上有些**欠妥**。 *His letter was not very suitably worded.*

**欠账 qiànzhàng** V·N to be in debt; debt · MW 笔

**欠资 qiànzī** V to owe postage

### RELATED WORDS
亏欠 137      哈欠 1025      拖欠 1396

## 106 失      U+5931      TM 5   FM 丿

**shī** V to lose; to miss, to fail to achieve one's end; to lose control; to break (a promise); to get lost

**失败 shībài** V to fail, to lose
红队又**失败**了。 *The red team lost again.*

**失策 shīcè** V to miscalculate, to be unwise

**失察 shīchá** V to neglect one's supervisory duties

**失常 shīcháng** ADJ abnormal, odd

**失宠 shīchǒng** V to fall into disfavor
他本是老板的心腹, 突然**失宠**大家都感到意外。 *He had been the boss's favorite, and his sudden fall from grace surprised everyone.*

**失传 shīchuán** V to be lost, to not be handed down from previous generations; to no longer exist

**失措 shīcuò** V to lose one's head

**失当 shīdàng** ADJ inappropriate, improper
她在晚会上表现**失当**。 *She acted inappropriately at the party.*

**失掉 shīdiào** V to miss, to lose

**失魂落魄 shīhúnluòpò** EXP to be despondent

**失节 shījié** V to be disloyal; to lose one's chastity

**失禁 shījìn** V to be incontinent

**失控 shīkòng** V to be out of control, to lose control

**失口 shīkǒu** EXP slip of the tongue
她**失口**说了句很粗野的话。 *She misspoke and said something offensive.*

**失礼 shīlǐ** V to be rude, to lack proper etiquette
这样做非常**失礼**。 *This is very impolite behavior.*

**失恋 shīliàn** V to be jilted, to lose one's boyfriend/girlfriend

**失落 shīluò** V·ADJ to lose, to be dejected; low-spirited, discouraged

**失眠 shīmián** V to be unable to sleep, to lose sleep

**失明 shīmíng** V to lose one's sight, to go blind

**失陪 shīpéi** EXP excuse my absence
对不起, **失陪**一会儿。 *Sorry, I must excuse myself for a while.*

**失窃 shīqiè** V to have (something) stolen

**失去 shīqù** V to lose; to miss

**失神 shīshén** V to be absentminded/inattentive

**失事 shīshì** V to have an accident
飞机**失事**, 令一百多人丧生。 *The plane accident killed more than 100 people.*

**失势 shīshì** V to lose power/influence

**失手 shīshǒu** V to accidentally drop, to let slip; to blunder

**失算 shīsuàn** V to miscalculate

**失调 shītiáo** V to lose balance; to lack proper care (after an illness, etc.)

**失望 shīwàng** V to lose hope, to be disappointed

那次**失败**令人吃惊, 令人**失望**。*That defeat was a surprise and a disappointment.*

**失误 shīwù** V·N to make a mistake, to slip up; mistake · MW 个、次

**失物 shīwù** V·N to lose an article; lost property

**失物招领 shīwùzhāolǐng** EXP lost-and-found

在**失物招领**处可能会找到你的提包。*You may retrieve your bag at the lost-and-found.*

**失效 shīxiào** V to be no longer valid

这份文件已过期**失效**了。*This document is no longer valid.*

**失信 shīxìn** V to break one's promise

**失学 shīxué** V to drop out of school, to be unable to go to school

**失血 shīxuè** V to lose blood

**失言 shīyán** V to make an indiscreet remark

**失业 shīyè** V to lose one's job, to be out of work

在中国, **失业**又叫做"下岗"。*Unemployment is commonly known as "xiagang" in China.*

**失约 shīyuē** V to fail to keep an appointment, to fail to show up

**失职 shīzhí** V to neglect one's duty

**失踪 shīzōng** V to disappear, to be missing

这只小狗**失踪**了这么久, 十之八九是死了。*The dog has been missing for so long, it is most likely dead.*

**失足 shīzú** V to lose one's footing, to slip; to take a wrong step in life

**RELATED WORDS**

| | | |
|---|---|---|
| 半失业 127 | 走失 265 | 丢失 297 |
| 坐失良机 318 | 丧失 521 | 过失 712 |
| 挂失 796 | 冒失 989 | 报失 1010 |
| 迷失 1187 | 消失 1343 | 损失 1401 |
| 流失 1493 | 散失 1579 | 遗失 1829 |
| 顾此失彼 1609 | 万无一失 73 | 患得患失 1649 |

## 107 生 U+751F TM 5 FM 丿

**shēng** V·N·ADJ·ADV to give birth to, to bear; to grow, to live; to light (a fire); existence, life; living; livelihood; unripe, green, raw, uncooked, unprocessed, unrefined, crude; unfamiliar, strange; very

**生病 shēngbìng** V to be sick

傻瓜今天没来上班, 因为他**生病**了。*ShaGua did not come to work today because he was sick.*

**生产 shēngchǎn** V to produce; to give birth to a child

这家公司**生产**机械刀具。*This firm manufactures machine knives.*

**生产成本 shēngchǎnchéngběn** N production cost · MW 笔

**生产关系 shēngchǎnguānxì** N socioeconomic relations · MW 种

**生产力 shēngchǎnlì** N productivity · MW 种

**生产率 shēngchǎnlǜ** N production rate

**生产能力 shēngchǎnnénglì** N production capacity

**生辰 shēngchén** N birthday

**生成 shēngchéng** V to be born/produced; to form, to grow

**生存 shēngcún** V to survive

由于污染, 人类的**生存**环境越来越糟糕。*Due to pollution, the human survival situation has worsened.*

**生动 shēngdòng** ADJ vivid, lively

他的演讲非常**生动**有趣。*His lecture was very colorful and lively.*

**生儿育女 shēng'éryùnǚ** V to bear sons and daughters

**生根 shēnggēn** V to take root

**生活 shēnghuó** N·V life; to live

傻瓜喜欢城市的热闹**生活**。*ShaGua loves the busy life of the city.*

**生火 shēnghuǒ** V to make a fire

**生姜 shēngjiāng** N ginger · MW 块

**生就 shēngjiù** V to be born/gifted with

**生理 shēnglǐ** N physiology

**生理学 shēnglǐxué** N physiology · MW 门

**生命 shēngmìng** N life · MW 条、个

工作是傻瓜的**生命**。*Work is ShaGua's life.*

**生平 shēngpíng** N ever in one's life

**生气 shēngqì** V to take offense, to get angry

傻瓜太太一**生气**就噘嘴巴。*Mrs. ShaGua pouts whenever she is angry.*

**生前 shēngqián** N during one's lifetime, before one's death

**生人 shēngrén** N stranger · MW 个、名

看见**生人**, 傻瓜的女儿就躲到母亲的身后。*Whenever ShaGua's daughter saw a stranger, she hid behind her mom's back.*

**生日 shēngrì** N birthday

**107** 生 **shēng** (continued)

生身父母 **shēngshēnfùmǔ** N one's own parents · MW 位

生手 **shēngshǒu** N person who is new to a job · MW 个、名

生疏 **shēngshū** ADJ unfamiliar

生水 **shēngshuǐ** N unboiled water · MW 杯
　在中国旅游，切记不要喝**生水**。*Never drink unboiled water when you travel in China.*

生死 **shēngsǐ** N life and death

生态 **shēngtài** N ecology; way of life

生物 **shēngwù** N living being/thing · MW 种、类

生物学 **shēngwùxué** N biology · MW 门

生物钟 **shēngwùzhōng** N biological clock · MW 个

生肖 **shēngxiāo** N animal of the Chinese zodiac (representing the twelve Earthly Branches) · MW 个

生效 **shēngxiào** V to go into effect, to take effect
　这项新法律何时**生效**？*When does the new law go into effect?*

生性 **shēngxìng** N natural disposition

生锈 **shēngxiù** V to get rusty

生涯 **shēngyá** N career, profession

生意 **shēngyì** N business, trade · MW 笔、单
　我从来没有跟她做过**生意**。*I have not conducted any business with her.*

生硬 **shēngyìng** ADJ stiff, rigid; harsh
　傻瓜儿子的中文说得很**生硬**。*ShaGua's son speaks Chinese very stiffly.*

生育 **shēngyù** V to give birth to, to bear; to raise

生长 **shēngzhǎng** V to develop, to grow up

生殖 **shēngzhí** V to procreate, to reproduce

生字 **shēngzì** N new character/word · MW 个
　每天记一个**生字**，积累起来会进步很大。*Memorizing a new character every day will result in great progress.*

**RELATED WORDS**

**108**  禾　　U+79BE　TM **5** FM 丿

**hé** N standing grain (especially rice)

禾场 **héchǎng** N threshing floor · MW 片

禾苗 **hémiáo** N grain seedling; standing grain, rice plant · MW 棵

**109** 乏　　U+4E4F　TM **5** FM 丿

**fá** V·ADJ to lack; tired, weary

乏力 **fálì** ADJ·V fatigued, exhausted; to be incapable of (doing something)
　生病使得她全身**乏力**。*Her illness made her exhausted.*

**RELATED WORDS**

**110** 友　　U+53CB　TM **5** FM 丿

**yǒu** N·ADJ friend; friendly

友爱 **yǒu'ài** ADJ friendly, affectionate; fraternal

友邦 **yǒubāng** N friendly nation · MW 个

友好 **yǒuhǎo** ADJ friendly
　他们对外国人很**友好**。*They are friendly with foreigners.*

友情 **yǒuqíng** N friendship
　同学之间有牢固的**友情**。*There were strong ties between the classmates.*

友人 **yǒurén** N friend · MW 个、位、名

友谊 **yǒuyì** N friendship, fellowship

我提议为我们的**友谊**干杯。 *I wish to propose a toast to our friendship.*

**RELATED WORDS**

| | | |
|---|---|---|
| 交友 222 | 至友 244 | 校友 802 |
| 亲友 908 | 访友 949 | 难友 974 |
| 契友 992 | 战友 1044 | 益友 1153 |
| 朋友 1298 | 密友 1730 | 男朋友 757 |
| 够朋友 1808 | 良师益友 656 | |

---

## 111 反    U+53CD   TM 5 FM 丿

**fǎn** [V·N·ADJ·ADV] to turn over; to return; to revolt; to oppose; counterrevolutionary; in an opposite direction; in reverse; inside out; on the contrary

反客为主。 *A guest switched to being a host.*

反叛 *to rebel*

反问 *to counter with a question*

反其道而行之 *to do exactly the opposite*

穿反衣服 *to wear clothing inside out*

反特 *counterespionage*

**反驳 fǎnbó** [V] to refute

她很尖锐地**反驳**对方。 *She refutes the opposition sharply.*

**反差 fǎnchā** [N] contrast

**反常 fǎncháng** [ADJ] unusual, abnormal

今天傻瓜没有准时上班, 这很**反常**。 *It was very unusual that ShaGua didn't arrive at the office on time today.*

**反动 fǎndòng** [ADJ·N] reactionary; reaction

**反对 fǎnduì** [V] to oppose, to be against

大家上街游行, **反对**增加税收。 *People went to the streets to protest increasing taxes.*

**反而 fǎn'ér** [ADV] on the contrary, instead

游行的队伍不仅没有前进, **反而**后退了。 *Instead of pressing forward, the protesters drew back.*

**反复 fǎnfù** [ADV·V] repeatedly, again and again; to repeat

**反革命 fǎngémìng** [N] counterrevolution · [MW] 个、群

**反光 fǎnguāng** [V·N] to reflect light; reflected light · [MW] 道

**反过来 fǎnguòlái** [EXP] conversely; in turn

**反过来看**, 坏事也可以变好事。 *Conversely, something bad can turn out to be good.*

**反悔 fǎnhuǐ** [V] to go back on one's word

**反馈 fǎnkuì** [V·N] to give feedback; feedback · [MW] 个、份

消费者的**反馈**信息, 可以提高工作质量。 *Consumer feedback will help us improve job quality.*

**反面 fǎnmiàn** [N·ADJ] reverse side; opposite, negative

**反目 fǎnmù** [V] to turn against, to have a dispute

**反派 fǎnpài** [N] villain (in drama, etc.) · [MW] 个、名

**反射 fǎnshè** [V] to reflect; to reverberate; reflex

**反响 fǎnxiǎng** [N] repercussion; echo · [MW] 个

**反向 fǎnxiàng** [V] to reverse; opposite direction

**反省 fǎnxǐng** [V] to question oneself; introspection

**反应 fǎnyìng** [V·N] to react, to respond; reaction, response · [MW] 个

遇到危险时, 人的本能**反应**就是跑开。 *Running away is an instinctive reaction when humans are faced with danger.*

**反映 fǎnyìng** [V] to reflect, to mirror; to report

**反照 fǎnzhào** [V] to reflect light

**反正 fǎnzhèng** [ADV] anyway, in any case

**反正**他从来都不读书, 送书给他有什么用? *He never reads anyway; why send him a book?*

**反证 fǎnzhèng** [V·N] to disprove; counterevidence · [MW] 个

**反之 fǎnzhī** [CONJ] on the contrary, otherwise

**反作用 fǎnzuòyòng** [N] reaction, counteraction · [MW] 个

**RELATED WORDS**

| | | |
|---|---|---|
| 正反 76 | 平反 78 | 相反 805 |
| 违反 1185 | 造反 1515 | 唱反调 1562 |
| 义无反顾 22 | | |

---

## 112 厅 廳    U+5385   TM 5 FM 丿

**tīng** [N] hall, lounge, office; provincial government department

会议厅 *conference hall*

办公厅 *office*

广东省教育厅 *Department of Education of Guangdong Province*

**厅堂 tīngtáng** [N] hall, main hall of a building · [MW] 个

这间房子的**厅堂**很宽敞。 *The main hall of this house is huge.*

**RELATED WORDS**

| | | |
|---|---|---|
| 大厅 20 | 饭厅 891 | 客厅 1316 |
| 餐厅 1964 | 办公厅 195 | 休息厅 213 |
| 自助餐厅 305 | | |

**113** **左**                  U+5DE6    TM **5** FM ノ

**zuǒ** N·ADJ  left, left side; east; left wing; leftist; different, contrary, conflicting

> **左**边 *left side*
> 这个人很**左**。*This person is very leftist.*
> 你们的看法相**左**。*Your ideas are different.*

**左边 zuǒbian** N  left side

> 中国和美国一样, 驾驶员的座位都在车的**左边**。*In both China and America, the driver's seat is on the left.*

**左不过 zuǒbuguò** EXP  anyway; only, merely, just

**左道旁门 zuǒdàopángmén** EXP  heretical sect; unorthodox school; heresy

**左顾右盼 zuógùyòupàn** EXP  to glance left and right

**左面 zuǒmiàn** N  left side

**左撇子 zuǒpiězi** N  left-handed person · MW 个

> 有人认为: **左撇子**比常人聪明。*Some people believe that left-handed people are smarter than right-handed people.*

**左手 zuǒshǒu** N  left hand

**左翼 zuóyì** N  left wing

> 在中国, **左翼**是保守派, 右翼是自由派; 正好与美国相反。*In China, the left is conservative, but the right is liberal. This is different from America.*

**左右 zuǒyòu** N·V·ADV  left and right sides; to master, to control; anyway; more or less

> 现在是三点钟**左右**。*It is about three o'clock now.*
> 你**左右**了她。*You control her.*
> **左右**没事, 咱们就走吧。*We are free anyway; let's go.*

**左右逢源 zuóyòuféngyuán** EXP  to succeed one way or another

**左右开弓 zuóyòukāigōng** EXP  first with one hand, then with the other

**左右为难 zuǒyòuwéinán** EXP  in a dilemma

> 买新车还是二手车, 我**左右为难**。*I'm torn between buying a new or used car.*

**RELATED WORD**

向左 603

---

**车床 chēchuáng** N  lathe · MW 台

**车次 chēcì** N  train/coach number

**车道 chēdào** N  traffic lane · MW 条

**车灯 chēdēng** N  headlight · MW 个、盏、对

**车队 chēduì** N  motorcade · MW 个

**车费 chēfèi** N  fare · MW 笔

**车祸 chēhuò** N  traffic accident · MW 场

**车间 chējiān** N  workshop · MW 个

**车辆 chēliàng** N  vehicle, car · MW 辆

**车轮 chēlún** N  wheel (of a vehicle) · MW 个

**车票 chēpiào** N  train/bus ticket · MW 张

> 我们可以在网上买**车票**。*We can purchase tickets online.*

**车速 chēsù** N  speed (of a vehicle)

> 傻瓜从来没有因为**车速**太快而吃罚单。*ShaGua has never received a speeding ticket.*

**车胎 chētāi** N  tire · MW 个

**车厢 chēxiāng** N  railway carriage, railroad car · MW 节

**车行道 chēxíngdào** N  roadway · MW 条

**车站 chēzhàn** N  railway station, depot, stop · MW 个

**车长 chēzhǎng** N  crew chief · MW 个、位、名

**RELATED WORDS**

| | | |
|---|---|---|
| 下车 10 | 大车 20 | 开车 26 |
| 卡车 36 | 牛车 51 | 小车 61 |
| 火车 72 | 囚车 161 | 风车 194 |
| 出车 258 | 电车 263 | 早车 268 |
| 发车 311 | 行车 327 | 让车道 348 |
| 列车 368 | 舟车 436 | 存车处 438 |
| 快车 497 | 吊车 547 | 机车 577 |
| 夜车 654 | 汽车 682 | 班车 730 |
| 挂车 796 | 卧车 826 | 刹车 967 |
| 邮车 1046 | 货车 1061 | 候车室 1086 |
| 卸车 1128 | 彩车 1132 | 客车 1316 |
| 拖车 1396 | 换车 1402 | 停车 1588 |
| 停车场 1588 | 超车 1684 | 通车 1757 |
| 晚车 1779 | 赛车 1813 | 撞车 1853 |
| 慢车 1882 | 跑车 1916 | 餐车 1964 |
| 警车 1987 | 三轮车 9 | 开快车 26 |
| 手推车 104 | 吉普车 259 | 自行车 305 |
| 自行车道 305 | 洒水车 1163 | 公共汽车 103 |
| 骑自行车 1840 | | |

---

**114** **车**  車                 U+8F66    TM **5** FM ノ

**chē** N  vehicle, automobile; machine/instrument with wheel(s), machine; lathe

**jū** N  chariot; Chinese chess piece

---

**115** **几**  幾                 U+51E0    TM **5** FM ノ

**jī** N·ADV  small table; nearly, almost

> 茶**几** *tea table*
> **几**乎 *almost*

**jǐ** QPRON·ADV how many; a few, several

几点 **jǐdiǎn** QPRON what time

现在几点? *Do you know the time?*

几多钱 **jǐduōqián** QPRON how much money; what is the price

这个玩具要几多钱? *How much does this toy cost?*

几分 **jǐfēn** QPRON·NUM a bit, somewhat; grade, test score

你知道你的考试得了几分吗? *Do you know your test score?*

几个 **jǐgè** QPRON·NUM how many; a few, several

傻瓜常常和几个同事一起去餐馆吃饭。 *ShaGua often ate out with some of his colleagues.*

几个月 **jǐgèyuè** QPRON·NUM how many months; several months

几何 **jǐhé** N·QPRON geometry; how much/many

几件 **jǐjiàn** QPRON·NUM how many items; several items

他只带几件衣服就出差了。 *He only brought a few articles of clothing on his business trip.*

几时 **jǐshí** QPRON when

不知道几时才能加薪? *I have no idea when I'll receive a salary increase.*

几天 **jǐtiān** QPRON·NUM how many days; several days

这几天傻瓜感到身体有些不舒服。 *ShaGua has not felt good for the last few days.*

---

### 116 九　　U+4E5D　　TM 5 FM 丿

**jiǔ** NUM nine; many, numerous

九折 **jiǔzhé** N ten-percent discount

过节后, 商店里的东西都打九折。 *After the holidays, everything in the stores was 10% off.*

九月 **jiǔyuè** N September, the ninth month of the lunar year

九十 **jiǔshí** NUM ninety

九十一 **jiǔshíyī** NUM ninety-one

九十二 **jiǔshí'èr** NUM ninety-two

九十三 **jiǔshísān** NUM ninety-three

九十四 **jiǔshísì** NUM ninety-four

九十五 **jiǔshíwǔ** NUM ninety-five

九十六 **jiǔshíliù** NUM ninety-six

九十七 **jiǔshíqī** NUM ninety-seven

九十八 **jiǔshíbā** NUM ninety-eight

九十九 **jiǔshíjiǔ** NUM ninety-nine

---

**RELATED WORDS**

| | | |
|---|---|---|
| 十九 3 | 一十九 1 | 二十九 2 |
| 十拿九稳 3 | 八十九 6 | 三十九 9 |
| 七十九 34 | 六十九 69 | 五十九 79 |
| 四十九 271 | 十之八九 3 | |

---

### 117 乡 鄉  U+4E61　　TM 5 FM 丿

**xiāng** N country, countryside, rural area; village; hometown

乡巴佬 **xiāngbalǎo** N (country) bumpkin · MW 个、群

如果人家叫你"乡巴佬", 那一定是看不起你。 *If somebody calls you a "country bumpkin," they must feel superior to you.*

乡村 **xiāngcūn** N village; countryside · MW 个

很多人喜欢乡村平和, 宁静的生活。 *Many people like the peace and quiet of country life.*

乡思 **xiāngsī** N homesickness

乡土 **xiāngtǔ** N native land; hometown

乡下 **xiāngxia** N countryside; village

他喜欢乡下生活。 *He preferred country life.*

乡下人 **xiāngxiarén** N country folk · MW 个、群

乡音 **xiāngyīn** N local accent

乡镇 **xiāngzhèn** N village, town · MW 个

中国沿海地区的许多乡镇已开始工业化。 *A number of townships in Chinese coastal areas have begun to industrialize.*

---

**RELATED WORDS**

| | | |
|---|---|---|
| 下乡 10 | 外乡 218 | 老乡 375 |
| 回乡 391 | 异乡 539 | 同乡 541 |
| 他乡 616 | 故乡 816 | 城乡 1225 |
| 鱼米之乡 843 | 背井离乡 1380 | |

---

### 118 尺　　U+5C3A　　TM 5 FM 丿

**chǐ** N·MW rule, ruler; [measure word for a unit of length (= ⅓ meter)]

尺寸 **chǐcùn** N length, size; dimension

你的裤腰的尺寸是多少? *What size waist do you have?*

尺度 **chǐdù** N scale, dimension; standard, yardstick, criterion

衡量一个人成功的尺度是什么? *What is the measure of someone's success?*

尺子 **chǐzi** N ruler · MW 条、个、把

**118 尺 chǐ** (continued)

RELATED WORDS

| | | |
|---|---|---|
| 卡尺 36 | 公尺 103 | 米尺 226 |
| 皮尺 261 | 曲尺 272 | 英尺 556 |
| 标尺 801 | 角尺 838 | 卷尺 1333 |
| 比例尺 279 | | |

---

**119 片**　U+7247　TM **5** FM ノ

**piān** N [used in words to mean photograph, picture, film, etc.]

**piàn** N·V·ADJ·MW flat, thin piece; flake; to cut into slices; brief; incomplete, part of an area; [measure word for flat objects]

**片名 piānmíng** N film title · MW 个

**片头 piāntóu** N film title; first scene (of a film) · MW 个

**片子 piānzi** N movie · MW 个
今天晚上你想看什么**片子**？ *Which movie are you going to watch tonight?*

**片段 piànduàn** N part, fragment, extract · MW 个
傻瓜很吃惊, 他的儿子能背诵莎士比亚剧作的**片段**。 *ShaGua was surprised that his son could recite excerpts from Shakespeare.*

**片甲不留 piànjiǎbùliú** EXP not a single armed warrior remains

**片刻 piànkè** N a short while, a moment
请逗留**片刻**。 *Please stay for a while.*

**片面 piànmiàn** ADJ unilateral, one-sided
傻瓜有时看问题很**片面**。 *Sometimes ShaGua sees things from only one point of view.*

**片言 piànyán** N a few words, a phrase or two

RELATED WORDS

| | | |
|---|---|---|
| 刀片 31 | 卡片 36 | 叶片 167 |
| 切片 277 | 名片 426 | 肉片 437 |
| 图片 761 | 底片 916 | 制片人 1130 |
| 胶片 1296 | 药片 1392 | 钙片 1462 |
| 碎片 1525 | 弹片 1763 | 照片 1846 |
| 像片 1863 | 影片 1918 | 镜片 1970 |
| 卡通片 36 | 只言片语 160 | 动画片 514 |
| 明信片 1035 | 打成一片 289 | |

---

**120 仅 僅**　U+4EC5　TM **5** FM ノ

**jǐn** ADV only, merely

**仅仅 jǐnjǐn** ADV only, barely, just

这**仅仅**是个开头, 好戏还在后面呢。 *This is just the beginning; the best is yet to come.*

**仅有 jǐnyǒu** V to only have
傻瓜刚工作时, 年薪**仅有**两万多美元。 *Initially, ShaGua only made about $20,000 a year.*

**仅是 jǐnshì** V to only/merely be

RELATED WORD

不仅 24

---

**121 仗**　U+4ED7　TM **5** FM ノ

**zhàng** N·V war, battle; weaponry, weapons; guard of honor; to be armed; to rely/depend on

**仗势欺人 zhàngshìqīrén** EXP to rely on force to bully others
有的人就是喜欢**仗势欺人**。 *Some people just like to rely on force to bully people.*

**仗义疏财 zhàngyìshūcái** EXP to be generous to needy people

**仗义执言 zhàngyìzhíyán** EXP to speak out for justice, to take a stand on principle

RELATED WORDS

| | | |
|---|---|---|
| 仪仗 122 | 仪仗队 122 | 打仗 289 |
| 败仗 589 | 仰仗 620 | 依仗 625 |
| 凭仗 1060 | 胜仗 1122 | |

---

**122 仪 儀**　U+4EEA　TM **5** FM ノ

**yí** N appearance, bearing; ceremony, rite; present, gift; apparatus, instrument

**仪表 yíbiǎo** N appearance, bearing, looks; meter, gauge · MW 个、组

**仪器 yíqì** N apparatus, instrument · MW 个、台
医生需要一些精密的**仪器**去诊断病情。 *Doctors need precision instruments to make diagnoses.*

**仪式 yíshì** N ceremony · MW 个
奥运会的开幕**仪式**很精彩。 *The Olympic Opening Ceremony was awesome.*

**仪态 yítài** N bearing, behavior · MW 个

**仪仗 yízhàng** N flags/weapons carried by an honor guard

**仪仗队 yízhàngduì** N honor guard · MW 支
**仪仗队**队员的身高都要求一米八以上。 *Members of the honor guard must be taller than 1.8 meters.*

RELATED WORD

司仪 357

## 123 从 叢  U+4E1B  TM 5 FM ノ

**cóng** [V·N] to crowd together; clump, thicket, grove; crowd; collection

丛刊 **cóngkān** [N] series of books; collection · [MW] 套

丛林 **cónglín** [N] forest, jungle · [MW] 片
建这个新区要砍掉这片**丛林**，真是太可惜了。
*It is a pity to cut down this forest to build a subdivision.*

丛林灌木 **cónglínguànmù** [N] bush · [MW] 片

丛书 **cóngshū** [N] series; collection · [MW] 套

**RELATED WORDS**
花丛 549　　树丛 1031

## 124 主  U+4E3B  TM 5 FM 丶

**zhǔ** [N·ADJ·V] host; owner; master; person concerned; God, Lord; main, primary; to manage, to direct, to be in charge of; to hold a definite view about

今天他是主，我是宾。*He is the host today, and I am a guest.*

他是饭店的主人。*He is the owner of the restaurant.*

今天他是买主，我是卖主。*Today he is the buyer, and I am the seller.*

我的主啊！*My Lord!*

主街道 *main street*

今天他主事。*He is in charge of business today.*

主战 *to advocate war*

主办 **zhǔbàn** [V] to direct; to sponsor; to host

主笔 **zhǔbǐ** [N] editor in chief · [MW] 个、位、名

主编 **zhǔbiān** [N] chief editor · [MW] 个、位、名

主宾席 **zhǔbīnxí** [N] head table, seat of honor · [MW] 个

主持 **zhǔchí** [V] to host; to preside (over)
虽然傻瓜是市长，但他不喜欢**主持**会议。
*Although ShaGua is the mayor, he doesn't like presiding at meetings.*

主词 **zhǔcí** [N] subject · [MW] 个

主次 **zhǔcì** [N] primary and secondary

主从关系 **zhǔcóngguānxì** [N] subordination

主动 **zhǔdòng** [ADJ] full of initiative; voluntary
傻瓜工作积极**主动**，同事们都很尊敬他。
*ShaGua takes a lot of initiative at work; his colleagues have a lot of respect for him.*

主犯 **zhǔfàn** [N] main culprit, principal criminal · [MW] 个、名

主峰 **zhǔfēng** [N] highest peak in a mountain range · [MW] 座

主妇 **zhǔfù** [N] housewife · [MW] 个、名

主观 **zhǔguān** [ADJ] subjective

主管 **zhǔguǎn** [V·N] to be in charge of; person in charge · [MW] 个、位、名

主婚 **zhǔhūn** [V] to officiate at a wedding

主机 **zhǔjī** [N] host computer; main engine · [MW] 个、台

主见 **zhǔjiàn** [N] idea/opinion of one's own · [MW] 个
领导一定要有**主见**。*Leaders must have opinions of their own.*

主讲 **zhǔjiǎng** [V·N] to be the speaker; main speaker · [MW] 个、位、名

主将 **zhǔjiàng** [N] chief commander; key person · [MW] 个、名

主句 **zhǔjù** [N] main clause/sentence · [MW] 个

主角 **zhǔjué** [N] leading role · [MW] 个、位、名
她在这部电影中扮演女**主角**。*She played the leading role in this movie.*

主考 **zhǔkǎo** [V·N] to be in charge of an examination; chief examiner · [MW] 个、位、名

主课 **zhǔkè** [N] main subject, principal course · [MW] 门
读中文专业，我的**主课**应该修什么呢？
*As a Chinese major, what are the main courses I should take?*

主力 **zhǔlì** [N] primary force; leading player · [MW] 支

主力军 **zhǔlìjūn** [N] main force · [MW] 支

主流 **zhǔliú** [N] main stream (of a river); general trend · [MW] 个
什么是当代世界的**主流**？*What's fashionable in today's world?*

主谋 **zhǔmóu** [V·N] to lead a conspiracy; ringleader · [MW] 个、名

主脑 **zhǔnǎo** [N] control center, center of operation

主权 **zhǔquán** [N] sovereign rights; sovereignty

主人 **zhǔrén** [N] host; owner; master · [MW] 个、位、名
这条狗始终忠于它的**主人**。*The dog remained faithful to its master.*

主人公 **zhǔréngōng** [N] leading character (in a story) · [MW] 个、位、名

主人翁 **zhǔrénwēng** [N] master; leading character (in a story) · [MW] 个、位、名

主任 **zhǔrèn** [N] director, chairperson · [MW] 个、名

**124 主 zhǔ** (continued)

**主食 zhǔshí** N staple/main food · MW 个、道

**主题 zhǔtí** N subject/topic (of a speech, document, etc.) · MW 个

**主体 zhǔtǐ** N centerpiece, main part · MW 个

**主席 zhǔxí** N president, chairperson · MW 个、位、名

**主心骨 zhǔxīngǔ** N backbone, mainstay · MW 个、条

**主修 zhǔxiū** V to specialize, to major
傻瓜的儿子在大学曾经**主修**生物学。 *ShaGua's son once majored in Biology.*

**主演 zhǔyǎn** V·N to play the leading role (in a play, a film); main actor

**主要 zhǔyào** ADJ main, principal, major, key, prime
洪水过后, 社会治安成为这个城市的**主要**问题。 *After the flood, public security became a key problem in this city.*

**主义 zhǔyì** N doctrine, theory · MW 个

**主意 zhǔyi** N idea, plan, decision · MW 个
面对这个难题, 傻瓜一下没了**主意**。 *Facing this problem, ShaGua suddenly had no idea what to do.*

**主宰 zhǔzǎi** V to dominate, to dictate

**主张 zhǔzhāng** V·N to advocate, to stand for; proposal, view, standpoint · MW 个

**主旨 zhǔzhǐ** N main point · MW 个

**主治医生 zhǔzhìyīshēng** N physician in charge · MW 个、位、名

**主子 zhǔzi** N master, boss · MW 个、名

### RELATED WORDS

**125** 立    U+7ACB    TM **5** FM 丶

**lì** V·ADJ·ADV to erect, to set up, to establish; to exist, to live; to stand; upright, vertical; immediately, instantaneously

**立案 lì'àn** V to register; to file a case for prosecution

**立场 lìchǎng** N position, stand · MW 个
总统候选人必须表明他们对医疗保险改革所持的**立场**。 *Each of the presidential candidates had to state his position on health insurance reform.*

**立春 lìchūn** N beginning of spring

**立定 lìdìng** V halt!

**立冬 lìdōng** N beginning of winter

**立方 lìfāng** N·MW cube; [measure word for cubic meters] · MW 个

**立竿见影 lìgānjiànyǐng** EXP to produce instant results
这个医疗保险改革方案收到了**立竿见影**的效果。 *This health insurance reform program has produced instant results.*

**立功 lìgōng** V to make a contribution, to render meritorious service

**立柜 lìguì** N clothes closet; wardrobe; cupboard · MW 个

**立户 lìhù** V to register for a household residence card; to open a bank account

**立即 lìjí** ADV immediately
傻瓜要她**立即**离开办公室。 *ShaGua ordered her to leave his office immediately.*

**立刻 lìkè** ADV immediately, promptly
州长请傻瓜**立刻**到办公室商量要事。 *The governor asked ShaGua to come to his office immediately to discuss a matter.*

**立论 lìlùn** V to set forth one's views, to present one's argument

**立秋 lìqiū** N beginning of autumn

**立式 lìshì** ADJ vertical, upright

**立体 lìtǐ** N·ADJ solid; three-dimensional; embracing all aspects

**立体声 lìtǐshēng** N stereo

**立夏 lìxià** N beginning of summer

**立约人 lìyuērén** N contractor · MW 个、名

**立正 lìzhèng** V attention!, freeze!

**立轴 lìzhóu** N vertical scroll painted with calligraphy · MW 根

**立足 lìzú** V to be established, to maintain a foothold; to base oneself on

**立足点 lìzúdiǎn** N foothold; standpoint · MW 个

### RELATED WORDS

| | | | | | |
|---|---|---|---|---|---|
| 创立 | 1131 | 设立 | 1179 | 站立 | 1189 |
| 建立 | 1203 | 倒立 | 1281 | 挺立 | 1408 |
| 起立 | 1421 | 确立 | 1762 | | |

---

**126** 兰 蘭　　　　　U+5170　　　TM **5** FM 丶

**lán** N orchid

兰草 **láncǎo** N fragrant thoroughwort ·
MW 棵、株

兰花 **lánhuā** N cymbidium, orchid · MW 棵、株

**RELATED WORDS**

| | | |
|---|---|---|
| 古兰经 154 | 芬兰 548 | 波兰 936 |
| 苏格兰 552 | 新西兰 1638 | |

---

**127** 半　　　　　　　　U+534A　　　TM **5** FM 丶

**bàn** NUM·ADV half; partly

半…半… **bàn… bàn…** ADV half …, half …

半百 **bànbǎi** NUM fifty (years old)

傻瓜已经年过**半百**, 头发一半白, 一半黑。 *ShaGua is over 50, and his hair is half white, half black.*

半辈子 **bànbèizi** N half a lifetime

半边 **bànbiān** N half of

昨天我们还剩下**半边**匹萨。 *Yesterday, we left half a slice of pizza.*

半边天 **bànbiāntiān** N half of the sky

在中国, 妇女被称为"**半边天**"。 *Women are called "half of the sky" in China.*

半费 **bànfèi** N half the fee

半工半读 **bàngōngbàndú** EXP part work, part study; work-study program

现在越来越多**半工半读**的学生。 *Today, there are more and more students who work part-time and study part-time.*

半公开 **bàngōngkāi** ADJ more or less open

半官方 **bànguānfāng** ADJ semiofficial

半合作 **bànhézuò** ADJ quasipartnership

半价 **bànjià** N half price

圣诞节前, 很多商店的商品以**半价**出售。 *Many stores have half-price sales before Christmas.*

半斤八两 **bànjīnbāliǎng** EXP two of a kind; equal; six of one and half a dozen of the other

论实力, 这两支球队是**半斤八两**。 *In terms of strength, it's an equal match between the two teams.*

半径 **bànjìng** N radius

半空中 **bànkōngzhōng** N in the air, in midair

**半空中**忽然飘起雪花。 *Suddenly, snow is drifting through the air.*

半路 **bànlù** N halfway; along the way

傻瓜在**半路**迷路了。 *ShaGua got lost along the way.*

半路出家 **bànlùchūjiā** EXP to switch to a job for which one is not trained

半票 **bànpiào** N half-price ticket

十二岁以下的孩子可以买**半票**。 *Children under 12 may purchase a half-price ticket.*

半旗 **bànqí** N half-mast

半晌 **bànshǎng** N quite a while

半身像 **bànshēnxiàng** N portrait · MW 张

半失业 **bànshīyè** ADJ employed half-time

半数 **bànshù** N half (the number)

这个班里**半数**的学生考试不及格。 *Half of the students in this class didn't pass the exam.*

半天 **bàntiān** N quite a while

傻瓜在门口等了**半天**, 但还是没见到他想见的人。 *ShaGua had waited for quite a while, but he still didn't see the person with whom he wanted to meet.*

半透明 **bàntòumíng** ADJ semitransparent, translucent

半途 **bàntú** N halfway point, midway

半途而废 **bàntú'érfèi** EXP to give up halfway; to leave (something) unfinished

半文盲 **bànwénmáng** N semiliterate · MW 个、名

半夜 **bànyè** N midnight, middle of the night

半月 **bànyuè** N half-moon; semimonthly

半自动 **bànzìdòng** ADJ semiautomatic

**RELATED WORDS**

| | | |
|---|---|---|
| 一半 1 | 下半夜 10 | 大半 20 |
| 月半 190 | 对半 254 | 东半球 307 |
| 后半 310 | 折半 408 | 各半 425 |
| 多半 431 | 夜半 654 | 南半球 986 |
| 事半功倍 987 | 深更半夜 1345 | |

---

**128** 头 頭　　　　　　U+CDB7　　　TM **5** FM 丶

**tóu** N·ADJ·MW head; hair, hair style; top; end; beginning or end; remnant; chief, head; aspect; first, leading; [measure word for pigs, oxen, bulls, etc.]

头等 **tóuděng** ADJ first-class, first-rate

**128 头 tóu** (continued)

她去旅行总是坐**头**等舱。 *She always travels first class.*

**头顶 tóudǐng** N·V top of the head; to wear/support on one's head

**头发 tóufa** N hair · MW 根、把
傻瓜**头发**已灰白。 *ShaGua's hair is graying.*

**头盖骨 tóugàigǔ** N skullcap · MW 个

**头号 tóuhào** ADJ first-rate, top-quality, number one

**头巾 tóujīn** N scarf, kerchief; headband · MW 条

**头里 tóuli** N ahead, in advance

**头面人物 tóumiànrénwù** N prominent figure, bigwig, big shot · MW 个、位、名
作为市长，傻瓜似乎没有意识到自己已算是这个城市的**头面人物**。 *As mayor, ShaGua doesn't seem to realize that he could be considered a big shot in the city.*

**头目 tóumù** N gang leader; chieftain · MW 个、位、名
他在公司当过个小**头目**。 *He has had a minor leadership role in the business.*

**头脑 tóunǎo** N head, leader, brains · MW 个

**头皮 tóupí** N scalp; dandruff · MW 块

**头疼 tóuténg** ADJ headache
傻瓜**头疼**，吃了两片阿司匹林就好了。 *ShaGua had a headache, but he felt better after taking two aspirin.*

**头条新闻 tóutiáoxīnwén** N top news · MW 条

**头痛 tóutòng** ADJ headache
我可能感冒了，**头痛**得厉害。 *I have a serious headache; I may have the flu.*

**头衔 tóuxián** N official title; academic rank/title · MW 个

**头像 tóuxiàng** N head portrait/sculpture · MW 张

**头油 tóuyóu** N hair oil · MW 瓶

**头晕 tóuyūn** V to be dizzy/giddy
我感到**头晕**，一定是病了。 *I feel horribly dizzy; I must be ill.*

**头重脚轻 tóuzhòngjiǎoqīng** EXP top-heavy

**头子 tóuzi** N boss, chief · MW 个、名

RELATED WORDS

| | | |
|---|---|---|
| 工头 12 | 开头 26 | 山头 38 |
| 木头 40 | 口头 42 | 从头 66 |
| 手头 104 | 片头 119 | 户头 129 |
| 石头 144 | 巨头 162 | 分头 173 |

| | | |
|---|---|---|
| 风头 194 | 尖头 203 | 外头 218 |
| 齐头并进 221 | 关头 224 | 兴头 228 |
| 心头 232 | 对头 254 | 对头 254 |
| 出头 258 | 舌头 298 | 龙头 315 |
| 杀头 317 | 床头 333 | 矛头 363 |
| 老头 375 | 呆头呆脑 384 | 回头路 391 |
| 叩头 413 | 先头 422 | 垂头丧气 430 |
| 光头 491 | 苗头 553 | 苦头 555 |
| 过头 712 | 顶头上司 724 | 劲头 736 |
| 到头 737 | 到头来 737 | 点头 739 |
| 彻头彻尾 871 | 奶头 878 | 没头没脑 938 |
| 派头 945 | 砍头 979 | 埋头 1002 |
| 披头散发 1011 | 抬头 1012 | 念头 1054 |
| 昏头昏脑 1058 | 眉头 1067 | 钟头 1125 |
| 拳头 1158 | 烟头 1177 | 砖头 1201 |
| 带头 1213 | 贼头贼脑 1254 | 焦头烂额 1265 |
| 甜头 1306 | 乳头 1308 | 浪头 1341 |
| 词头 1353 | 迎头 1360 | 晕头转向 1385 |
| 抛头露面 1395 | 掉头 1403 | 探头探脑 1404 |
| 接头 1405 | 笼头 1436 | 街头 1441 |
| 街头巷尾 1441 | 猫头鹰 1446 | 领头 1465 |
| 碰头 1526 | 骨头 1543 | 插头 1555 |
| 猴头 1560 | 喷头 1563 | 剃头 1639 |
| 零头 1640 | 蒜头 1655 | 摇头 1664 |
| 傻头傻脑 1699 | 愣头愣脑 1735 | 愣头青 1735 |
| 源头 1742 | 弹头 1763 | 墙头 1770 |
| 跟头 1784 | 滑头 1884 | 磕头 1894 |
| 箭头 1922 | 馒头 1948 | 额头 1958 |
| 镜头 1970 | 露头 1997 | 水龙头 159 |
| 出风头 258 | 吃苦头 783 | 赶浪头 822 |
| 栽跟头 995 | 贱骨头 1037 | 硬骨头 1524 |
| 摔跟头 1852 | 慢镜头 1882 | 三天两头 9 |
| 浪子回头 1341 | | |

**129 户**      U+6237      TM 5   FM 丶

**hù** N door; household, family; (bank) account

**户籍 hùjí** N resident registration · MW 个
中国实行**户籍**制。 *China employs a resident registration system.*

**户口 hùkǒu** N registered permanent residence · MW 个
在北京上小学，一般来说需要有北京**户口**。 *Generally speaking, you need to be a registered permanent resident to study in a Beijing elementary school.*

**户内 hùnèi** N inside of a house

**户头 hùtóu** N bank account · MW 个

**户外 hùwài** N outdoors; field

**户外运动 hùwàiyùndòng** N outdoor exercise · MW 项

越来越多的人开始注重**户外**运动。*There are more and more people who are starting to be more conscious of outdoor exercise.*

**户主 hùzhǔ** N head of household · MW 个、名

## RELATED WORDS

---

**130　门　門**　U+95E8　TM **5** FM 丶

**mén** N·MW door, gate, entrance; family; sect; class, category; [measure word for academic courses, subjects, majors, etc.]

**门把 ménbà** N doorknob, door handle · MW 个

**门板 ménbǎn** N door shutter · MW 块、副

**门窗 ménchuāng** N door and window · MW 扇

这间房子的**门窗**都关着。*All of the doors and windows of this house are locked.*

**门当户对 méndānghùduì** EXP marriage between families of equal social rank

**门道 méndào** N way to do something, know-how; social connections, contacts · MW 个

傻瓜想不出个**门道**来解决这个难题。*ShaGua could not find a solution to this problem.*

**门第 méndì** N family status

**门房 ménfáng** N gatehouse; gatekeeper · MW 个、名

**门缝 ménfèng** N crack between a door and its frame · MW 条

他没敢开门，只是从**门缝**里向外张望。*He was scared to open the door; he just peered outside through the crack.*

**门岗 méngǎng** N gate sentry

**门户 ménhù** N door, gateway; family status · MW 个

**门警 ménjǐng** N police guard at an entrance · MW 个、名

**门径 ménjìng** N access; key; way · MW 条、个

学习是通向成功的**门径**。*Studying is a key to success.*

**门槛(坎) ménkǎn** N threshold · MW 个、道

**门客 ménkè** N hanger-on (of an aristocrat) · MW 个、名

**门口 ménkǒu** N entrance, doorway · MW 个

迈阿密大学的大**门口**在哪里？*Where is Miami University's main gate?*

**门帘 ménlián** N door curtain · MW 块

**门联 ménlián** N scrolls pasted on either side of a doorway and forming a couplet · MW 对

贴**门联**是中国春节的传统风俗。*Pasted scrolls are a tradition of the Chinese New Year.*

**门楼 ménlóu** N arch over a gateway · MW 个、座

芝加哥中国城的入口处有一座中式的**门楼**。*There is a Chinese-style arch over a gateway in Chicago's Chinatown.*

**门路 ménlù** N knack, way; social connections · MW 个

他的**门路**很广，什么样的人都认识。*He has lots of social connections and knows lots of different people.*

**门面 ménmiàn** N appearance; storefront · MW 个

他的那些书只是装**门面**的——他从来不看。*He only owns those books for show—he never reads them.*

**门牌 ménpái** N house number · MW 个

**门票 ménpiào** N admission ticket · MW 张

北京奥运会开幕式的**门票**很难买到。*It was extremely difficult to purchase a ticket for the Opening Ceremony of the Olympics in Beijing.*

**门庭若市 méntíngruòshì** EXP the courtyard is like a circus

**门外汉 ménwàihàn** N layman · MW 个、名

对于美国法律，傻瓜是个**门外汉**。*ShaGua is a layman when it comes to American law.*

**门卫 ménwèi** N guard, custodian · MW 个、名

**门牙 ményá** N incisor, front tooth · MW 颗、对

他长着一对大**门牙**。*He has a pair of big front teeth.*

**门诊 ménzhěn** N·V outpatient section; to work in an outpatient section

**门诊**时间为上午9时至下午4时。*The outpatient clinic is open from 9 A.M. to 4 P.M.*

## RELATED WORDS

## 130 门 mén (continued)

| | | |
|---|---|---|
| 守门 486 | 守门人 486 | 快门 497 |
| 歪门邪道 511 | 肛门 649 | 宅门 665 |
| 看门 841 | 球门 1199 | 城门 1225 |
| 前门 1329 | 旁门 1473 | 装门面 1476 |
| 登门 1521 | 窍门 1621 | 部门 1636 |
| 摆门面 1773 | 嗓门 1855 | 豪门 1876 |
| 敲门 1959 | 天安门 25 | 走后门 265 |
| 凯旋门 1577 | 五花八门 79 | 左道旁门 113 |

## 131 汁     U+6C41     TM 5 FM 丶

**zhī** N juice

**汁水** zhīshuǐ N juice · MW 杯、瓶

**汁液** zhīyè N juice · MW 杯、瓶

**RELATED WORDS**

| | | | |
|---|---|---|---|
| 肉汁 437 | 果汁 544 | 毒汁 1211 | 乳汁 1308 |
| 榨汁机 1672 | 墨汁 1843 | 苹果汁 395 | |

**132** 己     U+5DF1    TM **6** FM —

**jǐ** PRON self; oneself; one's own

己方 **jǐfāng** N one's own side
己见 **jǐjiàn** N one's own view

**RELATED WORDS**

自己 305     利己主义 472     异己 539
知己 647     你自己 617     身不由己 604
损人利己 1401

**133** 已     U+5DF2    TM **6** FM —

**yǐ** V·ADV to stop, to cease; already; before, previously

已经 **yǐjīng** ADV already
已然 **yǐrán** V·ADV to be already so/true; already
已往 **yǐwǎng** N before, previously

**RELATED WORDS**

早已 268     而已 351     不得已 24
由来已久 148     如此而已 464     迫不得已 1186

**134** 乃     U+4E43    TM **6** FM —

**nǎi** V·ADV·CONJ·PRON to be; that is why, hence, thus; unless; you, your

失败**乃**成功之母。 *Failure is the mother of success.*
**乃**妻 *your wife*

乃是 **nǎishì** V to be; to be indeed
诚信**乃是**傻瓜的做人原则。 *Honesty is an essential aspect of ShaGua's being.*

乃至如此 **nǎizhìrúcǐ** EXP even go so far as to

**RELATED WORD**

木乃伊 40

**135** 互     U+4E92    TM **6** FM —

**hù** ADV mutually, each other, in exchange

互访 **hùfǎng** V to exchange visits
中美两校制定了教授**互访**计划。 *These two Chinese and American universities have created a faculty exchange program.*

互换 **hùhuàn** V to exchange
中美两校制定了学生**互换**计划。 *These two Chinese and American universities have created a student exchange program.*

互惠 **hùhuì** V to reciprocate, to be mutually beneficial

互教互学 **hùjiāohùxué** EXP to teach and learn from each other

互敬互爱 **hùjìnghù'ài** EXP to have mutual respect and love for each other

互利 **hùlì** V to be mutually beneficial
这种交流是**互惠互利**的。 *These exchange programs are mutually beneficial.*

互连 **hùlián** V to interconnect

互联网 **hùliánwǎng** N Internet · MW 个

互谅互让 **hùliànghùràng** EXP mutual understanding and accommodation

互生现象 **hùshēngxiànxiàng** N mutualism

互通有无 **hùtōngyǒuwú** EXP each provides what the other lacks

互为因果 **hùwéiyīnguǒ** EXP interdependency

互相 **hùxiāng** ADV mutually, each other
**互相**帮助是人类的美德之一。 *Helping each other is one of the basic human virtues.*

互助 **hùzhù** V to cooperate, to help each other

**RELATED WORDS**

交互 222     相互 806

**136** 亚 亞     U+4E9A    TM **6** FM —

**yà** ADJ·N inferior, second, sub-; (short name for) Asia

亚军 **yàjūn** N second place, runner-up
这支球队只得**亚军**, 他们感到很遗憾。 *They were disappointed because their team only won second place.*

亚麻 **yàmá** N flax

亚热带 **yàrèdài** N subtropics

**136 亚 yà** (continued)

**亚洲 Yàzhōu** N Asia

中国、日本、南韩都是**亚洲**国家。*China, Japan, and South Korea are all Asian countries.*

**RELATED WORDS**

| | | |
|---|---|---|
| 诺亚方舟 436 | 南亚 986 | 利比亚 472 |
| 肯尼亚 744 | 叙利亚 1129 | 赞比亚 1969 |

---

**137 亏 虧**　　　U+4E8F　　TM **6** FM 一

**kuī** V·ADV·N to lose (money, etc.); to lack, to be short; to treat unfairly; fortunately, luckily; wane (of the moon)

**亏本 kuīběn** V to lose money in business

杀头的买卖有人做, **亏本**的买卖没人做。*Some are willing to engage in deals in which they may lose their heads, but nobody accepts a deal that loses money.*

**亏待 kuīdài** V to treat badly/unfairly

老板认为他没有**亏待**雇员。*The owner didn't think that he treated his employees unfairly.*

**亏得 kuīde** V to be lucky to have

**亏得**朋友的帮忙, 傻瓜才能做好市长的工作。*ShaGua is lucky to have his friends help him do his job well as mayor.*

**亏耗 kuīhào** V to lose (by a natural process)

**亏空 kuīkong** V·N to be in debt; debt, deficit

**亏欠 kuīqiàn** V to have a deficit, to be behind in payment

**亏损 kuīsǔn** V·N to lose; deficit, loss

难怪公司**亏损**, 原来办公室严重超编。*No wonder the firm had losses—the office is terribly overstaffed.*

**亏心 kuīxīn** V·ADJ to feel guilty; guilty

**RELATED WORDS**

| | | |
|---|---|---|
| 幸亏 373 | 多亏 431 | 吃亏 783 |
| 净亏 1159 | 哑巴亏 782 | |

---

**138 元**　　　　U+5143　　TM **6** FM 一

**yuán** N first, primary, basic, fundamental; unit, component, element; [monetary unit of China (= 10 jiao or 100 fen)]

**元宝 yuánbǎo** N shoe-shaped gold/silver ingot · MW 块

**元旦 Yuándàn** N New Year's Day

在中国, 新年的第一天称为 "**元旦**"。*The first day of the year is called "Yuandan" in China.*

**元件 yuánjiàn** N element, component, part · MW 个

电脑是用很多**元件**组装成的。*A computer is assembled from many components.*

**元老 yuánlǎo** N senior leader; founding member · MW 个、位、名

**元年 yuánnián** N first year of an emperor's reign

**元配 yuánpèi** N first wife

**元气 yuánqì** N vitality, vigor, gumption

傻瓜去年生了一场大病, **元气**大损。*ShaGua was seriously ill last year; his vitality suffered a lot.*

**元首 yuánshǒu** N monarch, head of state · MW 个、位、名

**元帅 yuánshuài** N marshal (in the armed forces); commander in chief · MW 个、名

**元素 yuánsù** N essential factor; (chemical) element · MW 个

水是由氢**元素**和氧**元素**组成的。*Water is composed of the elements hydrogen and oxygen.*

**元宵 yuánxiāo** N Lantern Festival (night of the fifteenth day of the first lunar month); sticky rice dumplings · MW 个

**元凶 yuánxiōng** N main culprit · MW 个、名

**元音 yuányīn** N vowel · MW 个

**RELATED WORDS**

| | | |
|---|---|---|
| 二元论 2 | 公元 103 | 状元 345 |
| 多元 431 | 美元 671 | 单元 672 |
| 欧元 811 | 纪元 1101 | 轻元音 1113 |
| 新纪元 1638 | | |

---

**139 无 無**　　　U+65E0　　TM **6** FM 一

**wú** V·N·ADV·CONJ to not have, to be without; there is not; nothing, nil; no, not; regardless, no matter what/whether/etc.

**无比 wúbǐ** V to be unparalleled; incomparably

得到儿子的大学录取通知, 傻瓜**无比**高兴。*ShaGua was incomparably happy when they received news that his older son had been admitted to college.*

**无边无际 wúbiānwújì** EXP boundless, limitless

**无不 wúbù** ADV without exception, invariably

**无产阶级 wúchǎnjiējí** N proletariat, working class

**无偿 wúcháng** ADV freely, gratis

义工们**无偿**地为难民修建临时住房。*The volunteers built houses for the refugees for free.*

无常 **wúcháng** N·V Messenger of Death; to die

无耻 **wúchǐ** ADJ shameless, brazen

无从 **wúcóng** ADV to have no way (of doing something), to not be in a position (to do something)

无地自容 **wúdìzìróng** EXP to have no place to hide from shame

无度 **wúdù** V to be immoderate/excessive

无端 **wúduān** ADV for no reason at all

他**无端**地对自己的同事发火。 *He yelled at his colleagues for no reason at all.*

无恶不作 **wú'èbùzuò** EXP to commit all sorts of crimes

无法无天 **wúfǎwútiān** EXP to be completely lawless, to run wild

无方 **wúfāng** V improper; not knowing how

无妨 **wúfáng** V to be harmless; doesn't matter

无非 **wúfēi** ADV simply, nothing but

无辜 **wúgū** ADJ·N not guilty; innocent person

大家都相信他是**无辜**的。 *Everybody believed that he was innocent.*

无故 **wúgù** ADV without reason/cause

无关 **wúguān** V to be irrelevant, to have nothing to do with

他与这个案件完全**无关**。 *He had nothing to do with this case.*

无家可归 **wújiākěguī** EXP to be homeless

这条可怜的狗**无家可归**。 *This poor dog is homeless.*

无价之宝 **wújiàzhībǎo** EXP priceless treasure

无精打采 **wújīngdǎcǎi** EXP in low spirits, dispirited

无拘束 **wújūshù** V to be unrestrained

无可奈何 **wúkěnàihé** EXP to be helpless, to have no alternative

无愧 **wúkuì** V to have a clear conscience; to be worthy of

无赖 **wúlài** N·ADJ rascal; shameless · MW 个

无礼 **wúlǐ** ADJ rude, impertinent

打断别人说话是很**无礼**的。 *It is rude to interrupt while others are talking.*

无力 **wúlì** ADJ unable, powerless, weak

无聊 **wúliáo** ADJ bored; boring

那节课自始至终十分**无聊**。 *The class was one big yawn from start to finish.*

无论如何 **wúlùnrúhé** ADV anyway, in any case

无名 **wúmíng** ADJ nameless, anonymous

无奈 **wúnài** V·CONJ to have no choice, to be helpless; but, however

面对谣言，傻瓜很**无奈**。 *Regarding rumors, ShaGua felt helpless.*

无能 **wúnéng** ADJ unable, powerless

无情 **wúqíng** ADJ heartless, ruthless

无穷 **wúqióng** ADJ endless, infinite

无权 **wúquán** V to have no right

无人 **wúrén** ADJ unmanned, self-service

无声 **wúshēng** ADJ noiseless, silent, still

无数 **wúshù** ADJ countless, numberless

天上有**无数**的星星。 *There are countless stars in the sky.*

无私 **wúsī** ADJ unselfish, disinterested

无所不能 **wúsuǒbùnéng** EXP omnipotent

无所不知 **wúsuǒbùzhī** EXP all-knowing, omniscient

无所谓 **wúsuǒwèi** V to be indifferent; to not matter

无所用心 **wúsuǒyòngxīn** EXP to not give serious thought to anything

无所作为 **wúsuǒzuòwéi** EXP to attempt nothing and accomplish nothing

无条件 **wútiáojiàn** ADV unconditionally, without preconditions

士兵必须**无条件**地服从指挥。 *Soldiers must follow orders unconditionally.*

无微不至 **wúwēibùzhì** EXP meticulously, in every possible way

无畏 **wúwèi** ADJ fearless

无谓 **wúwèi** ADJ meaningless, pointless

无暇 **wúxiá** V to have no time, to be too busy

傻瓜工作时**无暇**接傻瓜太太的电话。 *When ShaGua is working, he has no time to answer Mrs. ShaGua's phone calls.*

无限 **wúxiàn** ADJ infinite, boundless

傻瓜**无限**的耐心深深地感动了每一个人。 *ShaGua's boundless patience moved everyone deeply.*

无线 **wúxiàn** N wireless

无线电 **wúxiàndiàn** N radio; wireless

无线电话 **wúxiàndiànhuà** N wireless phone · MW 个、部

无效 **wúxiào** V to be invalid/ineffective

无心 **wúxīn** ADV·V unintentionally; to not be in the mood for

无形 **wúxíng** ADJ·ADV intangible; imperceptibly

市场像一只**无形**的手，控制着价格的变动。 *The market is an invisible hand controlling changes in prices.*

无烟 **wúyān** ADJ smokeless

**139 无 wú** (continued)

无疑 **wúyí**   V   to be beyond doubt, to be certain

无异 **wúyì**   V   to be similar; to be the same as

无意识 **wúyìshí**   ADJ   unconscious

无用 **wúyòng**   ADJ   unnecessary; useless

无知 **wúzhī**   ADJ   ignorant

无罪 **wúzuì**   V   to be innocent, to be not guilty

**RELATED WORDS**

| | | |
|---|---|---|
| 义无反顾 22 | 万无一失 73 | 目无法纪 151 |
| 史无前例 186 | 若无其事 554 | 虚无 1534 |
| 毫无 1721 | 漫无边际 1887 | 目中无人 151 |
| 与世无争 158 | 风雨无阻 194 | 至高无上 244 |
| 走投无路 265 | 束手无策 372 | 互通有无 135 |

---

傻瓜的女儿入学考试**及格**了。 *ShaGua's daughter passed the entrance exam.*

及时 **jíshí**   ADJ·ADV   timely; on time, without delay

及物动词 **jíwùdòngcí**   N   transitive verb · MW 个

及早 **jízǎo**   ADV   at an early date, as soon as possible

及至 **jízhì**   PREP   up to, until

**RELATED WORDS**

| | |
|---|---|
| 又及 11 | 不及 24 |
| 以及 101 | 波及 936 |
| 涉及 944 | 论及 947 |
| 普及 1484 | 顾及 1609 |
| 触及 1875 | 遍及 1892 |
| 来不及 260 | 来得及 260 |
| 力所能及 59 | 望尘莫及 1622 |
| 愚不可及 1901 | 风马牛不相及 194 |

---

**140 示**    U+793A    TM **6** FM 一

**shì**   V   to show; to notify; to instruct

示范 **shìfàn**   V   to set an example; to demonstrate

老师给学生**示范**：怎样操作这台仪器？
*The teacher gave the students a demonstration of how the instrument worked.*

示警 **shìjǐng**   V   to warn

示例 **shìlì**   V·N   to give an example / a demonstration; example · MW 个

示威 **shìwēi**   V   to put on a show of force, to march

人们都上街参加**示威**游行了。 *The people have taken to the streets to protest.*

示意 **shìyì**   V   to signal; to hint, to indicate

总统向欢呼的人群挥手**示意**。 *The president is waving his hands to the crowd.*

示众 **shìzhòng**   V   to publicly expose/punish; to publicly denigrate

**RELATED WORDS**

| | | |
|---|---|---|
| 出示 258 | 告示 428 | 表示 527 |
| 启示 657 | 显示 755 | 图示 761 |
| 批示 1005 | 明示 1035 | 展示 1274 |
| 指示 1397 | 预示 1528 | 提示 1554 |
| 请示 1632 | 暗示 1676 | 演示 1821 |
| 揭示 1851 | 液晶显示 1344 | |

---

**141 及**    U+53CA    TM **6** FM 一

**jí**   V·CONJ·PREP   to reach, to come up to; to be as good as; and; to

及格 **jígé**   V   to pass (an exam, etc.)

---

**142 圣 聖**    U+5723    TM **6** FM 一

**shèng**   ADJ·N   holy, sacred; august, imperial; especially talented; sage; saint; genius; emperor

圣餐 **shèngcān**   N   Holy Communion

圣诞 **shèngdàn**   N   Christmas

圣诞树 **shèngdànshù**   N   Christmas tree · MW 棵

圣地 **shèngdì**   N   Holy Land; Holy City

耶路撒冷被看作宗教**圣地**。 *Jerusalem is regarded as the Holy City.*

圣公会 **shènggōnghuì**   N   Episcopal/Anglican Church

圣经 **Shèngjīng**   N   (Holy) Bible · MW 部、本

圣母 **Shèngmǔ**   N   (Blessed) Virgin Mary, Madonna

圣人 **shèngrén**   N   sage; emperor · MW 位

圣坛 **shèngtán**   N   altar; chancel

圣贤 **shèngxián**   N   sage; man of virtue, saint

孔子是中国古代伟大的**圣贤**。 *Confucius was a great sage in ancient China.*

**RELATED WORD**

神圣 1191

---

**143 牙**    U+7259    TM **6** FM 一

**yá**   N   tooth; tooth-like; ivory

牙齿 **yáchǐ**   N   tooth; dental · MW 颗、口、排

傻瓜有一口很不整齐的**牙齿**。 *ShaGua has very crooked teeth.*

牙床 **yáchuáng**   N   gum (oral tissue) · MW 个

牙雕 **yádiāo** [N] ivory carving · [MW] 件

牙缝 **yáfèng** [N] gap between teeth · [MW] 条

牙膏 **yágāo** [N] toothpaste · [MW] 筒

他爱用什麽牌子的**牙膏**？ *Which brand of toothpaste does he prefer?*

牙根 **yágēn** [N] root of a tooth · [MW] 个

牙垢 **yágòu** [N] dental plaque, tartar

牙科 **yákē** [N] dentistry

牙签 **yáqiān** [N] toothpick · [MW] 根

牙刷 **yáshuā** [N] toothbrush · [MW] 把

牙痛 **yátòng** [N] toothache

牙医 **yáyī** [N] dentist · [MW] 个、位、名

牙龈 **yáyín** [N] gum (oral tissue)

牙周炎 **yázhōuyán** [N] periodontitis

### RELATED WORDS

| 爪牙 52 | 门牙 130 | 补牙 508 |
| 咬牙 780 | 拔牙 791 | 奶牙 878 |
| 刷牙 1310 | 假牙 1586 | 西班牙 352 |
| 咬紧牙关 780 | 葡萄牙 1766 | |

---

**144** 石    U+77F3    TM **6** FM 一

**shí** [N] stone, rock

石板 **shíbǎn** [N] slab; slate, flagstone · [MW] 块
客厅的地面是用**石板**铺成的。 *The floor of his living room is slate.*

石沉大海 **shíchéndàhǎi** [EXP] to disappear forever, to receive no response (LIT like a stone dropped into the sea)
寄出的信**石沉大海**。 *The letter was mailed and disappeared forever.*

石雕 **shídiāo** [N] stone carving/sculpture · [MW] 个、件

石膏 **shígāo** [N] plaster · [MW] 块

石灰 **shíhuī** [N] lime · [MW] 桶、袋

石刻 **shíkè** [N] stone carving · [MW] 块

石棉 **shímián** [N] asbestos · [MW] 包

石墨 **shímò** [N] graphite · [MW] 块

石器 **shíqì** [N] stone tool/implement; stone artifact · [MW] 个、件

石头 **shítou** [N] stone; rock · [MW] 块

石英 **shíyīng** [N] quartz · [MW] 块

石油 **shíyóu** [N] petroleum, oil · [MW] 桶

石子 **shízǐ** [N] cobblestone · [MW] 层、粒
路面上铺着一层小**石子**。 *The road is made of cobblestones.*

### RELATED WORDS

| 玉石 77 | 化石 215 | 矿石 518 |
| 柱石 583 | 宝石 667 | 岩石 746 |
| 基石 991 | 钻石 1302 | 碎石 1525 |
| 水滴石穿 159 | 水落石出 159 | 金刚石 420 |
| 红宝石 474 | 绊脚石 887 | 以卵击石 101 |

---

**145** 耳    U+8033    TM **6** FM 一

**ěr** [N] ear

耳边风 **ěrbiānfēng** [EXP] unheeded advice; to turn a deaf ear to
儿子总爱把父亲的话当**耳边风**。 *Sons always like to turn a deaf ear to their fathers.*

耳垂 **ěrchuí** [N] earlobe · [MW] 只、对

耳朵 **ěrduo** [N] ear · [MW] 只、对

耳光 **ěrguāng** [N] slap in the face · [MW] 个、记
她狠狠地打了她男朋友一记**耳光**。 *She gave her boyfriend a stiff slap in the face.*

耳环 **ěrhuán** [N] earring · [MW] 只、对

耳机 **ěrjī** [N] earphones, headset · [MW] 个、副

耳科 **ěrkē** [N] otology

耳孔 **ěrkǒng** [N] ear canal · [MW] 个

耳聋 **ěrlóng** [N] deafness

耳鸣 **ěrmíng** [N] ringing in the ears, tinnitus
中医认为：身体虚弱会引起**耳鸣**。 *According to traditional Chinese medicine, weakness causes ringing in your ears.*

耳目 **ěrmù** [N] ears and eyes; information; informer, spy · [MW] 个、名

耳目一新 **ěrmùyīxīn** [EXP] to find everything fresh and new
傻瓜的市政建设令人**耳目一新**。 *Municipal construction in ShaGua's city makes people feel like everything is fresh and new.*

耳濡目染 **ěrrúmùrǎn** [EXP] to be subtly influenced by what one constantly sees and hears

耳塞 **ěrsāi** [N] earplug · [MW] 副

耳套 **ěrtào** [N] earmuffs · [MW] 副

耳挖子 **ěrwāzi** [N] ear pick · [MW] 枚

耳语 **ěryǔ** [N] to whisper

耳坠子 **ěrzhuìzi** [N] earring · [MW] 个、对
她戴了一对明晃晃的**耳坠子**。 *She wore a pair of shiny earrings.*

### RELATED WORDS

| 木耳 40 | 打耳光 289 | 护耳 569 |
| 咬耳朵 780 | 刺耳 1050 | 逆耳 1359 |
| 面红耳赤 721 | | |

## 146 双 雙    U+53CC    TM 6   FM 一

**shuāng** ADJ·MW two, twin, dual, double, twofold; even; pair; [measure word for objects that come in pairs]

**双胞胎 shuāngbāotāi** N twins · MW 对
她和她姐姐是一对**双胞胎**。 *She and her sister are twins.*

**双边 shuāngbiān** ADJ bilateral, involving two parties
中美两校签定了**双边**协议。 *The Chinese and American universities have signed a bilateral agreement.*

**双层 shuāngcéng** ADJ double-decker; double-tiered

**双重 shuāngchóng** ADJ double, dual, twofold
他有**双重**国籍。 *He has dual nationality.*

**双打 shuāngdǎ** N doubles (sports) · MW 对

**双方 shuāngfāng** N both sides/parties

**双管齐下 shuāngguǎnqíxià** EXP to work on two tasks simultaneously; to work on a problem from two angles (LIT to paint with two brushes)

**双轨 shuāngguǐ** N double track · MW 条

**双号 shuānghào** N even numbers

**双面 shuāngmiàn** ADJ two-sided; double-edged
有人怀疑他是一个**双面**间谍。 *Some people think he is a double agent.*

**双目 shuāngmù** N two eyes
她闭上**双目**，不想再看对方。 *She closed her eyes, not wishing to look at the other person.*

**双亲 shuāngqīn** N parents, father and mother

**双全 shuāngquán** V to have both … and …; to be complete in both respects

**双人 shuāngrén** N two persons; couple

**双日 shuāngrì** N even-numbered days

**双生 shuāngshēng** ADJ twin

**双月刊 shuāngyuèkān** N bimonthly publication · MW 期

**双向 shuāngxiàng** ADJ two-way, bidirectional; interactive
这条街不允许**双向**行车。 *Two-way driving is not permitted on this street.*

**双职工 shuāngzhígōng** N working couple · MW 对

**双周刊 shuāngzhōukān** N biweekly publication · MW 期

**RELATED WORD**

才貌双全 39

## 147 田    U+7530    TM 6   FM 丨

**tián** N field, farmland

**田地 tiándì** N field, farmland; wretched situation, plight · MW 块、片
农民的**田地**被建成了住宅区。 *The farmlands have been used for subdivisions.*
他怎么落到了这个**田地**？ *How has he gotten into such an awful situation?*

**田赋 tiánfù** N feudal land tax

**田埂 tiángěng** N berm between fields · MW 条

**田鸡 tiánjī** N frog · MW 只

**田间 tiánjiān** N field; farm; countryside
公路在**田间**穿过。 *The highways cross the countryside.*

**田径 tiánjìng** N track and field (sports) · MW 条

**田螺 tiánluó** N pond snail · MW 个、只

**田鼠 tiánshǔ** N field vole (rodent) · MW 只

**田野 tiányě** N field, open country/land · MW 片
很多城里人都喜欢乡间的农庄和**田野**。 *Many city people like the farms and fields in the country.*

**田园 tiányuán** N fields and gardens; countryside · MW 片
这条高速公路破坏了农村的**田园**美景。 *The expressway mars the beauty of the countryside.*

**RELATED WORDS**

农田 423      油田 683      坡田 775
种田 893

## 148 由    U+7531    TM 6   FM 丨

**yóu** V·PREP·N to give in to, to let; to be left to (someone) to do, to rest with; to pass through, to go by way of; (done) by; because of, due to; through, by, from; cause, reason

**由不得 yóubude** V to not be up to (someone) to decide
把钱给了她，怎么花就**由不得**你了。 *After you give her money, it is not up to you how to spend it.*

**由此 yóucǐ** PREP from this, thus; therein
傻瓜知道他必须对**由此**产生的一切后果负责。 *ShaGua knew that he had to accept the consequences of his actions.*

**由此可见 yóucǐkějiàn** EXP from this it can be seen that

**由来已久 yóuláiyǐjiǔ** EXP it has been like that for quite some time

**由于 yóuyú** PREP because of, due to, as a result of

由于傻瓜已当了市长，再也不能打两份工了。 *Ever since ShaGua became mayor, he can no longer work two jobs a day.*

**由衷 yóuzhōng** V from the bottom of one's heart, sincere, heartfelt

他**由衷**地感谢朋友对他的支持。 *He sincerely appreciates his friends' support.*

**RELATED WORDS**

| | | |
|---|---|---|
| 来由 260 | 自由 305 | 必由之路 338 |
| 理由 1200 | 根由 1245 | 听天由命 414 |
| 言不由衷 478 | 身不由己 604 | |

---

**149** 甲　　　　　U+7532　　　TM **6** FM |

**jiǎ** N first (in order), grade A; first of the Ten Heavenly Stems; shell; fingernail; armor

盔**甲** *suit of armor*

**甲等 jiǎděng** N first class, grade A

**甲骨文 jiǎgǔwén** N inscriptions on bones/tortoiseshells of the Shang Dynasty

**甲骨文**是目前发现的中国最早的文字。 *"Jiaguwen" are the earliest Chinese characters that have been discovered.*

**甲级 jiǎjí** N first class, grade A

赢了这场比赛，这支球队就要升**甲级**了。 *After this win, the team will advance to Division A.*

**RELATED WORDS**

| | | |
|---|---|---|
| 片甲不留 119 | 马甲 247 | 花甲 549 |
| 指甲 1397 | 装甲 1476 | 脚趾甲 1804 |

---

**150** 申　　　　　U+7533　　　TM **6** FM |

**shēn** V·N to state, to express; (short name for) Shanghai; ninth of the Twelve Earthly Branches

**申报 shēnbào** V to report to a higher body; to declare (dutiable goods)

请书面**申报**你在国外购买的全部商品。 *Please make a written declaration of all the goods you purchased abroad.*

**申辩 shēnbiàn** V to defend oneself, to explain

被告可以请律师为其**申辩**。 *The defendant may hire a lawyer to defend him.*

**申斥 shēnchì** V to rebuke, to reprimand

**申请 shēnqǐng** V·N to apply for; application (form) · MW 份

---

申请奖学金必须先填写**申请表**。 *You must first fill out the application form for the scholarship.*

**申述 shēnshù** V to state, to express, to explain in detail

**申诉 shēnsù** V to appeal, to complain

阅读过律师为你写的**申诉**材料吗？ *Have you read the appeal materials your lawyer wrote?*

**申讨 shēntǎo** V to denounce, to openly condemn

**申谢 shēnxiè** V to thank, to express gratitude

**申冤 shēnyuān** V to get justice

**RELATED WORDS**

| | |
|---|---|
| 引申 371 | 重申 839 |

---

**151** 目　　　　　U+76EE　　　TM **6** FM |

**mù** N·V eye; item; section; list, catalog, table of contents; title; order; to look

**目标 mùbiāo** N target, goal, aim, objective · MW 个

儿子上大学前，傻瓜和他谈过生活**目标**的问题。 *Before ShaGua's older son went to college, ShaGua spoke with him about goals in life.*

**目不识丁 mùbùshídīng** EXP to not know a single word, to be completely illiterate

**目不转睛 mùbùzhuǎnjīng** EXP to be intent; to be all eyes; to gaze/stare fixedly

傻瓜**目不转睛**地看着傻瓜太太的这幅画。 *ShaGua gazed at his wife's picture.*

**目测 mùcè** V to eyeball, to estimate by sight

**目瞪口呆 mùdèngkǒudāi** EXP dumbstruck, stupefied

**目的 mùdì** N purpose; destination · MW 个

傻瓜的女儿的学习**目的**是当一名医生。 *ShaGua's daughter's purpose in her studies is to become a doctor.*

**目光 mùguāng** N view, gaze, look

**目击 mùjī** V to witness, to see with one's own eyes

**目空一切 mùkōngyīqiè** EXP to be arrogant/condescending

**目力 mùlì** N eyesight

**目录 mùlù** N catalog, list, table of contents, directory · MW 个、本

**目前 mùqián** N currently, at present

傻瓜对自己**目前**的状况颇为知足。 *ShaGua is quite content with his present situation.*

**目送 mùsòng** V to watch (someone) go, to gaze after; to see (someone) off

**151** 目 **mù** (continued)

目无法纪 **mùwúfǎjì** EXP to flout the law/rules

目下 **mùxià** N now, at present

目中无人 **mùzhōngwúrén** EXP with one's nose in the air, condescending

傻瓜不喜欢跟**目中无人**的人交朋友。*ShaGua doesn't like to make friends with arrogant people.*

**RELATED WORDS**

| | | |
|---|---|---|
| 反目 111 | 头目 128 | 耳目 145 |
| 耳目一新 145 | 双目 146 | 众目睽睽 175 |
| 价目 210 | 心目 232 | 书目 264 |
| 节目 275 | 名目 426 | 条目 598 |
| 科目 642 | 举目 674 | 过目 712 |
| 面目 721 | 项目 725 | 极目 798 |
| 账目 812 | 侧目 864 | 盲目 906 |
| 明目张胆 1035 | 眉目 1067 | 细目 1107 |
| 品目 1220 | 总目 1330 | 满目 1745 |
| 题目 1858 | 鼠目寸光 1859 | 编目 1866 |
| 篇目 1921 | 醒目 1938 | 耳濡目染 145 |
| 产品目录 219 | 有眉目 439 | |

---

**152** 且      U+4314      TM **6** FM |

**qiě** ADV·CONJ just, for the time being; moreover, both … and …

别着急，**且**听我说完。*Don't worry; just hear me out.*

这种狗既高**且**大。*This breed of dog is both tall and stocky.*

且慢 **qiěmàn** V to wait a moment

在没有查清这个案子之前，**且慢**作任何结论。*Before you've thoroughly investigated this case, please don't jump to any conclusions.*

且…且… **qiě… qiě…** ADV while, as

**RELATED WORDS**

| | | |
|---|---|---|
| 并且 225 | 而且 351 | 姑且 881 |
| 况且 928 | 尚且 1156 | 暂且 1522 |

---

**153** 占 佔      U+5360      TM **6** FM |

**zhān** V·N to divine; divination

**zhàn** (佔) V to occupy, to seize; to hold a certain status

占卜 **zhānbǔ** V to divine; to tell fortunes (using turtleshells, alpine yarrow, etc.)

占卦 **zhānguà** V to divine (using the Eight Diagrams)

---

占课 **zhānkè** V to divine by tossing coins

占星 **zhānxīng** V to divine by astrology

占据 **zhànjù** V to occupy, to hold

这堡垒**占据**了要害地位。*The fort occupies a commanding position.*

占领 **zhànlǐng** V to capture, to seize

军队**占领**了敌国首都。*The army occupied the enemy's capital.*

占便宜 **zhànpiányi** EXP to take advantage

占上风 **zhànshàngfēng** V to gain the upper hand

占先 **zhànxiān** V to take precedence

占线 **zhànxiàn** V to be in use; the line is busy

占用 **zhànyòng** V to occupy, to use

我不想多**占用**你的时间。*I won't take up much of your time.*

占有 **zhànyǒu** V to own, to possess; to occupy; to grasp

**RELATED WORDS**

| | | |
|---|---|---|
| 攻占 253 | 侵占 1280 | 霸占 1998 |

---

**154** 古      U+53E4      TM **6** FM |

**gǔ** ADJ·N ancient, age-old; ancient times

古巴 **Gǔbā** N Cuba

古板 **gǔbǎn** ADJ old-fashioned, inflexible, set in one's ways

傻瓜的孩子认为自己的父亲是一个很**古板**的人。*ShaGua's kids consider their father an inflexible person.*

古代 **gǔdài** N ancient times, antiquity

古典 **gǔdiǎn** ADJ·N classical; classics; classical allusion

古董 **gǔdǒng** N antique · MW 件

古怪 **gǔguài** ADJ odd, strange, bizarre

傻瓜太太认为傻瓜是个很**古怪**的人。*Mrs. ShaGua thinks that her husband is odd.*

古籍 **gǔjí** N ancient book · MW 本、册

古迹 **gǔjì** N historic site; ancient building · MW 处

古今中外 **gǔjīnzhōngwài** EXP ancient and modern, home and abroad; always and everywhere

古兰经 **Gǔlánjīng** N Koran · MW 部、本

古老 **gǔlǎo** ADJ ancient, old

在这个村里有许多**古老**的民宅。*There are many old homesteads in the village.*

古人 **gǔrén** N ancients; forefathers · MW 个、名

古色古香 **gǔsègǔxiāng** EXP antique, quaint

古诗 **gǔshī** N ancient poetry · MW 首

古书 **gǔshū** N ancient book/writing · MW 本

古铜色 **gǔtóngsè** N bronze-colored

古玩 **gǔwán** N antiques, curios · MW 件

北京最大的**古玩**市场是"潘家园"。*"Panjia Yuan" is the biggest antique fair in Beijing.*

古往今来 **gǔwǎngjīnlái** EXP through the ages, since ancient times

古为今用 **gǔwéijīnyòng** EXP to make the past serve the present

古文 **gǔwén** N classical (Chinese) prose · MW 段、篇

古稀 **gǔxī** N seventy years of age

古语 **gǔyǔ** N archaism; old saying

古装 **gǔzhuāng** N ancient costume · MW 件、套

**RELATED WORDS**

| | | | | | |
|---|---|---|---|---|---|
| 千古 | 19 | 万古 | 73 | 中古 | 86 |
| 尼古丁 | 441 | 仿古 | 450 | 考古 | 530 |
| 远古 | 1184 | 厚古薄今 | 1272 | 蒙古 | 1654 |
| 内蒙古 | 191 | | | | |

---

**155** 专 專    U+4E13    TM **6** FM |

**zhuān** V·ADJ·N to monopolize; concentrated; devoted; special; for a particular person, occasion, purpose, etc.; focused on one thing; expert

专案 **zhuān'àn** N special case for investigation · MW 个

专长 **zhuāncháng** N specialty; special skill/knowledge

这个老师的**专长**是中美教育比较。*This teacher's specialty is comparison of the Chinese and American educational systems.*

专程 **zhuānchéng** N special trip

专断 **zhuānduàn** V·ADJ to make an arbitrary decision; arbitrary

专攻 **zhuāngōng** V to specialize in

他喜欢中文，决心**专攻**中国现代文学。*He loves Chinese and has decided to specialize in modern Chinese literature.*

专横 **zhuānhèng** ADJ domineering, imperious; peremptory

专机 **zhuānjī** N private jet · MW 架

"空军一号"是美国总统的**专机**。*Air Force One is the president's private jet.*

专家 **zhuānjiā** N expert, specialist · MW 个、位、名

他是一位知名的教育**专家**。*He is a well-known expert in education.*

专刊 **zhuānkān** N special edition · MW 期

专栏 **zhuānlán** N special column · MW 个

专利 **zhuānlì** N patent · MW 个

专卖 **zhuānmài** V to have exclusive rights to sell

**专卖**店的东西比较贵。*Goods in exclusive stores are expensive.*

专门 **zhuānmén** ADJ·ADV special, specialized; especially

他**专门**研究比较教育。*His specialty is comparing educational systems.*

专心 **zhuānxīn** ADJ single-minded; completely absorbed

除了上课，他还**专心**做课题研究。*In addition to teaching, he also concentrated his attention on research projects.*

专业 **zhuānyè** N·ADJ special field of study, specialty · MW 个、门

他大学的**专业**是国际教育。*He majored in international education in college.*

专一 **zhuānyī** ADJ single-minded

专用 **zhuānyòng** V for a special purpose, dedicated

这个厕所是雇员**专用**的。*This restroom is for employees only.*

专员 **zhuānyuán** N commissioner · MW 个、位、名

专责 **zhuānzé** N specific responsibility

专政 **zhuānzhèng** N dictatorship

专职 **zhuānzhí** N sole duty; full-time job

专制 **zhuānzhì** ADJ autocratic, despotic

专注 **zhuānzhù** V to concentrate on

大家都很欣赏傻瓜对工作的**专注**。*Everyone really appreciates ShaGua's complete absorption in his work.*

专著 **zhuānzhù** N monograph, treatise · MW 本、部、套

**RELATED WORDS**

| | | | |
|---|---|---|---|
| 土专家 | 15 | 中专 | 86 |

---

**156** 击 擊    U+51FB    TM **6** FM |

**jī** V to beat, to hit, to strike; to attack, to assault; to come in contact with, to bump into, to meet

击败 **jībài** V to defeat, to beat

**156 击 jī** (continued)

他**击败**了他的老对手。 *He defeated his old adversary.*

**击毙 jībì** V to shoot dead, to kill

**击沉 jīchén** V to bombard and sink

敌人的军舰被鱼雷**击沉**了。 *The enemy's warship was bombarded and sunk with torpedoes.*

**击穿 jīchuān** V to puncture, to break through

**击发 jīfā** V to ignite; to start; to fire (a gun)

**击毁 jīhuǐ** V to attack and destroy, to smash, to wreck

敌人的坦克被大炮**击毁**了。 *The enemy's tanks have been smashed by our cannons.*

**击剑 jījiàn** V fencing (sports)

**击溃 jīkuì** V to rout, to put to flight

敌军已被全线**击溃**。 *The enemy was routed all along the lines.*

**击落 jīluò** V to knock down, to shoot down

敌人的飞机被火箭**击落**了。 *The enemy's planes were shot down by our missiles.*

**击破 jīpò** V to break up, to destroy

**击球 jīqiú** V to bat, to hit a ball (sports)

**击伤 jīshāng** V to wound (a person); to damage (a plane, ship, etc.)

敌军的指挥官被**击伤**了。 *The enemy's commander was wounded.*

**击退 jītuì** V to beat back, to repel

**击中 jīzhòng** V to hit the point/target

**RELATED WORDS**

| | | |
|---|---|---|
| 目击 151 | 夹击 197 | 伏击 212 |
| 攻击 253 | 打击 289 | 冲击 339 |
| 抨击 570 | 还击 714 | 围击 762 |
| 拍击 790 | 突击 913 | 抗击 1009 |
| 阻击 1042 | 拳击 1158 | 堵击 1226 |
| 射击 1467 | 追击 1507 | 雷击 1641 |
| 截击 1650 | 撞击 1853 | 以卵击石 101 |
| 声东击西 374 | | |

---

**157** **去**      U+53BB      TM **6** FM |

**qù** V·ADJ to go, to leave, to depart; to get rid of, to remove; to cast out, to be apart (from), to lose; to be out of; [used after a verb to indicate movement away from the speaker]; to die; past, last

我们**去**吧！ *Let's go!*

他**去**学校。 *He goes to school.*

---

**去壳** *to remove the shell*

那个同学已经 "**去**" 了。 *That classmate has passed away.*

**去年** *last year*

**去臭 qùchòu** V to deodorize

苏打粉有**去臭**的功能。 *Baking soda can remove odors.*

**去处 qùchù** N whereabouts, site; place to go · MW 个

**去路 qùlù** N way (to), outlet · MW 条

这条狗挡住了窃贼的**去路**。 *The dog blocked the thief's way.*

**去年 qùnián** N last year

**去皮 qùpí** V to peel off

**去声 qùshēng** N falling tone · MW 个

**去世 qùshì** V to die, to pass away

**去伪存真 qùwěicúnzhēn** EXP to discard what's false and retain what's true

**去污 qùwū** V to decontaminate

**去向 qùxiàng** N trace; whereabouts · MW 个

窃贼翻过围墙, 跑得不知**去向**。 *The thief has climbed over the wall and left no trace.*

**RELATED WORDS**

| | | |
|---|---|---|
| 失去 106 | 出去 258 | 夺去 308 |
| 回去 391 | 何去何从 619 | 过去时 712 |
| 过去 712 | 故去 816 | 过得去 712 |
| 过不去 712 | 说不过去 1631 | |

---

**158** **与** **與**      U+4E0E      TM **6** FM |

**yǔ** V·PREP·CONJ to give; to offer, to grant; to get along with; to help, to support; with, together with; and

**yù** V to take part in, to participate in

**与其 yǔqí** CONJ rather than; better than

与其夸夸其谈, 不如埋头苦干。 *It is better to act well than to speak well.*

**与人为善 yǔrénwéishàn** EXP to be friendly and sincere with others

**与日俱增 yǔrìjùzēng** EXP to increase/grow day by day

**与世长辞 yǔshìchángcí** EXP to depart from the world forever, to die

**与世无争 yǔshìwúzhēng** EXP to be aloof/antisocial

**与众不同 yǔzhòngbùtóng** EXP to be different from others, to stand out in the crowd

傻瓜确实与众不同。 *ShaGua is really different from others.*

**与会 yùhuì** V to participate in a meeting/conference

会议结束了，但与会者还围着傻瓜问问题。
*The meeting had finished, but the participants surrounded ShaGua and continued questioning him.*

**与闻 yùwén** V to have a participant's knowledge of

### RELATED WORDS

参与 600     耻与为伍 735     赠与 1944

---

**159 水** U+6C34   TM **6** FM |

**shuǐ** N water; river; [general term for rivers, lakes, seas, etc.]; liquid

**水坝 shuǐbà** N dam, dike · MW 条
三峡水坝是中国最高、最大的水坝。 *Sanxia Dam is the longest and largest dam in China.*

**水泵 shuǐbèng** N water pump · MW 个、台

**水表 shuǐbiǎo** N water meter · MW 个、只

**水兵 shuǐbīng** N sailor, seaman · MW 个、名

**水彩 shuǐcǎi** N watercolor
傻瓜太太的业余爱好是画水彩画。 *Mrs. ShaGua's hobby is painting watercolors.*

**水产 shuǐchǎn** N aquatic products · MW 批

**水厂 shuǐchǎng** N waterworks · MW 家

**水池 shuǐchí** N pond, pool; cistern · MW 个
后院的小水池里养着几条金鱼。 *There are several goldfish in the small ponds in the backyard.*

**水稻 shuǐdào** N paddy; rice planted in a paddy · MW 粒、棵

**水滴 shuǐdī** N drop of water · MW 滴

**水滴石穿 shuǐdīshíchuān** EXP constant effort brings success (LIT dripping water wears through stone)

**水电 shuǐdiàn** N hydroelectric power

**水痘 shuǐdòu** N chicken pox

**水费 shuǐfèi** N water bill · MW 笔

**水分 shuǐfèn** N moisture content; exaggeration
汽油里有水分。 *There is moisture in the gasoline.*
他的报告有水分。 *His report smacks of exaggeration.*

**水管 shuǐguǎn** N water pipe · MW 条

**水果糖 shuǐguǒtáng** N fruit-flavored candy · MW 颗、把

**水晶 shuǐjīng** N crystal
中国的风水认为水晶可以给人带来好运。
*According to Chinese fengshui, crystal can bring good luck.*

**水井 shuǐjǐng** N well · MW 口

**水库 shuǐkù** N reservoir · MW 座

**水利 shuǐlì** N water conservation; irrigation project

**水力 shuǐlì** N waterpower; hydraulic power

**水流 shuǐliú** N river; current, flow · MW 股、条

**水陆 shuǐlù** N land and water, amphibious

**水龙头 shuǐlóngtóu** N faucet, tap, spigot, hydrant · MW 个

**水路 shuǐlù** N waterway, water route · MW 条

**水落石出 shuǐluòshíchū** EXP the truth comes to light; to get to the bottom of (LIT when the water recedes, the rocks emerge)
侦探决心把这个案子搞个水落石出。
*The detective has decided to bring the case to light.*

**水墨画 shuǐmòhuà** N Chinese brush drawing, ink and wash painting · MW 幅

**水泥 shuǐní** N cement · MW 堆

**水暖工 shuǐnuǎngōng** N plumber · MW 个、名

**水泡 shuǐpào** N bubble; blister · MW 个

**水平 shuǐpíng** N standard, level, proficiency; horizontal, parallel with the horizon
傻瓜认为傻瓜太太的绘画水平很糟糕。
*ShaGua thinks that Mrs. ShaGua's paintings are horrible.*

**水平线 shuǐpíngxiàn** N horizontal line · MW 条

**水汽 shuǐqì** N water vapor, steam · MW 股、团

**水深 shuǐshēn** N water depth

**水势 shuǐshì** N water flow

**水塔 shuǐtǎ** N water tower · MW 个

**水桶 shuǐtǒng** N water bucket · MW 个

**水土 shuǐtǔ** N water and land; natural environment, climate

**水位 shuǐwèi** N water level
地震使水井的水位下降。 *The earthquake lowered the water level in the well.*

**水泄不通 shuǐxièbùtōng** EXP to be crowded / densely packed
圣诞节前，商店被购物者挤得水泄不通。
*Right before Christmas, the stores are packed with frantic shoppers.*

**水星 shuǐxīng** N Mercury (planet)

**水锈 shuǐxiù** N water deposit, watermark · MW 块

**159 水 shuǐ** (continued)

水压 **shuǐyā** N water/hydraulic pressure

水银 **shuǐyín** N mercury (chemical element)

水域 **shuǐyù** N river valley; area covered with water · MW 个、片

水运 **shuǐyùn** N water transport

水准 **shuǐzhǔn** N level, standard · MW 个
中文课学生的**水准**不断提高。*Students in the Chinese classes continue to increase the intensity of their studies.*

**RELATED WORDS**

| | | |
|---|---|---|
| 下水道 10 | 口水 42 | 生水 107 |
| 汁水 131 | 走水 265 | 供水 459 |
| 划水 476 | 冷水 494 | 死水 510 |
| 苦水 555 | 污水 681 | 汽水 682 |
| 油水 683 | 泪水 688 | 洪水 690 |
| 雨水 720 | 茶水 767 | 抽水 788 |
| 枯水 799 | 香水 834 | 鱼水 843 |
| 奶水 878 | 废水 918 | 盐水 993 |
| 防水 1040 | 咸水 1073 | 净水 1159 |
| 洒水车 1163 | 洒水机 1163 | 淡水 1173 |
| 泉水 1275 | 胶水 1296 | 甜水 1306 |
| 凉水 1337 | 浇水 1340 | 逆水 1359 |
| 热水 1390 | 药水 1392 | 流水 1493 |
| 海水 1494 | 喷水池 1563 | 停水 1588 |
| 暖水瓶 1675 | 跳水 1786 | 脱水 1803 |
| 墨水 1843 | 薪水 1847 | 喝水 1854 |
| 滴水不漏 1885 | 滴水 1885 | 缩水 1927 |
| 潮水 1930 | 糖水 1933 | 露水 1997 |
| 自来水 305 | 拉下水 573 | 饮用水 892 |
| 泼冷水 937 | 漱口水 1823 | 拖泥带水 1396 |
| 游山玩水 1818 | | |

---

**160** 只 隻 衹    U+53EA    TM **6** FM |

**zhī** (隻) ADV·MW single, one, only; [measure word for dogs, cats, etc.]

**zhǐ** (衹) ADV only, merely

只身 **zhīshēn** ADV alone; by oneself
傻瓜年轻的时候**只身**去过阿拉斯加。*ShaGua went to Alaska by himself when he was young.*

只言片语 **zhīyánpiànyǔ** EXP a word or two, a few isolated words/phrases

只不过 **zhǐbùguò** ADV only, just, merely
别责备他, 他**只不过**开个玩笑。*Don't scold him; it was only a joke.*

只得 **zhǐdé** ADV to have to, to be obliged to

傻瓜一家**只得**住在一套糟糕的小公寓里。*ShaGua's family had to live in a horrid little apartment.*

只顾 **zhǐgù** ADV absorbed (in); simply, merely

只管 **zhǐguǎn** ADV by all means, just, merely
别为我担心, 你**只管**干下去。*Don't worry about me; just go ahead.*

只好 **zhǐhǎo** ADV to have to, to be obliged to
傻瓜的汽车撞坏了, **只好**不要了。*ShaGua's car was damaged in an accident, so he had to do without one.*

只是 **zhǐshì** ADV·CONJ only, just, merely, nothing but; but, however
他的中文学得不错, **只是**发音还不太好。*His Chinese is fine, but his pronunciation isn't too good.*

只要 **zhǐyào** CONJ as long as
我不计较价钱, **只要**车况好就行了。*I don't care about the price, as long as the car is in good condition.*

只有 **zhǐyǒu** CONJ only if, provided that
**只有**时间才能证明你是否正确。*Only time will tell if you are right.*

只争朝夕 **zhǐzhēngzhāoxī** EXP to seize the moment

**RELATED WORDS**

| | |
|---|---|
| 三只手 9 | 不只 24 |

---

**161** 囚    U+56DA    TM **6** FM |

**qiú** V·N to imprison, to jail, to put in jail, to lock up; prisoner, captive, convict

囚车 **qiúchē** N prison van · MW 辆

囚犯 **qiúfàn** N prisoner, convict · MW 个、伙

囚禁 **qiújìn** V to imprison, to put in jail
**囚犯**们被**囚禁**在监狱中。*Prisoners are held in captivity.*

囚牢 **qiúláo** N prison; prison cell · MW 间、座

囚徒 **qiútú** N prisoner, convict · MW 个、伙

---

**162** 巨    U+5DE8    TM **6** FM |

**jù** ADJ huge, tremendous, gigantic

巨大 **jùdà** ADJ huge
她的耳朵上吊着**巨大**的耳环。*Huge earrings dangled from her ears.*

巨额 **jù'é** ADJ enormous amount/sum

巨浪 **jùlàng** [N] enormous wave · [MW] 个
海啸掀起巨浪。*Deep-sea earthquakes created mountainous waves.*

巨流 **jùliú** [N] strong current · [MW] 条

巨人 **jùrén** [N] giant; influential figure · [MW] 个

巨头 **jùtóu** [N] magnate, tycoon, boss; king · [MW] 个

巨型 **jùxíng** [ADJ] giant, enormous

巨著 **jùzhù** [N] (literary) masterpiece, monumental work · [MW] 部

## RELATED WORD

艰巨 973

---

### 163 世　　　　U+4E16　　　TM 6 FM |

**shì** [N] life; lifetime; generation; age, era; world

世代 **shìdài** [N] generation; long period of time
傻瓜家**世代**务农，到了他这一代才开始在城里生活。*ShaGua's ancestors worked on farms for generations. He is the first one in his family to live in the city.*

世故 **shìgu** [N·ADJ] ways of the world; worldly-wise, sophisticated

世纪 **shìjì** [N] century; times · [MW] 个
谁将成为二十一**世纪**最伟大的作家？ *Who will be the greatest writer in the twenty-first century?*

世交 **shìjiāo** [N] family friend; friendship spanning two or more generations

世界 **shìjiè** [N] world
北京是全**世界**最大的城市之一。*Beijing is one of the largest cities in the world.*

世界大战 **shìjièdàzhàn** [N] world war · [MW] 次

世界银行 **shìjièyínháng** [N] World Bank

世界语 **shìjièyǔ** [N] Esperanto (world language)

世面 **shìmiàn** [N] world; facet of life

世上 **shìshàng** [N] in the world, on earth

世事 **shìshì** [N] human affairs, ways of the world
傻瓜的同事认为，傻瓜有些不通**世事**。*ShaGua's colleagues don't think that he understands the ways of the world very well.*

世俗 **shìsú** [N] custom, social convention
傻瓜有时对**世俗**的东西不屑一顾。*Sometimes ShaGua doesn't pay much attention to social conventions.*

世外桃源 **shìwàitáoyuán** [EXP] utopia, place of idyllic beauty · [MW] 个、处

---

世袭 **shìxí** [V·ADJ] to inherit; hereditary

世系 **shìxì** [N] pedigree, bloodline

## RELATED WORDS

| | | |
|---|---|---|
| 去世 157 | 与世无争 158 | 与世长辞 158 |
| 在世 188 | 厌世 202 | 处世 217 |
| 弃世 480 | 永世 481 | 身世 604 |
| 举世 674 | 问世 678 | 乱世 901 |
| 谢世 1890 | | |

---

### 164 共　　　　U+5171　　　TM 6 FM |

**gòng** [V·ADJ·ADV·N] to share; common, general; together, altogether, in all; Communist Party

共产党 **gòngchǎndǎng** [N] Communist Party · [MW] 个

共产主义 **gòngchǎnzhǔyì** [N] communism

共处 **gòngchǔ** [V] to coexist
与其他国家和平**共处**是世界发展的大趋势。*Peaceful coexistence with other countries should be the general direction for world development.*

共存 **gòngcún** [V] to coexist
生物中的**共存**现象很普遍。*Coexistence among living beings is a necessity.*

共和 **gònghé** [N] republic; republicanism

共计 **gòngjì** [V] to amount to, to total
为买这辆车，傻瓜**共计**支出12,000美元。*ShaGua paid a total of $12,000 for this car.*

共勉 **gòngmiǎn** [V] to mutually encourage

共鸣 **gòngmíng** [V·N] to have resonance; sympathy · [MW] 个

共生 **gòngshēng** [V] to grow together and be interdependent, to be symbiotic

共同 **gòngtóng** [ADJ·ADV] common, mutual; jointly, together
绘画是傻瓜太太和儿子的**共同**爱好。*With respect to their love of painting, Mrs. ShaGua and her son have something in common.*

共用 **gòngyòng** [V] to share
两人**共用**一台电脑很不方便。*Two people sharing one computer is very inconvenient.*

共振 **gòngzhèn** [V] to resonate, to vibrate sympathetically

## RELATED WORDS

| | |
|---|---|
| 一共 1 | 中共中央 86 |
| 公共 103 | 公共厕所 103 |
| 公共道德 103 | 公共电话 103 |
| 公共汽车 103 | 总共 1330 |
| 统共 1601 | 中国共产党 86 |
| 中华人民共和国 86 | |

## 165 旧 舊  U+65E7  TM **6** FM |

**jiù** ADJ old; former, past, onetime, bygone; used, worn

**旧地重游** jiùdìchóngyóu EXP to revisit a once-familiar place, to revisit old haunts
回家乡**旧地重游**一直是傻瓜的一个梦想。
*Revisiting familiar places in his hometown is a dream of ShaGua's.*

**旧货** jiùhuò N secondhand/used/pawned goods · MW 批
这张办公桌是他在一家**旧货**店买的。*He picked up that dresser at a pawnshop.*

**旧历** jiùlì N lunar calendar, the old Chinese calendar · MW 本

**旧梦重温** jiùmèngchóngwēn EXP to relive a pleasant experience from one's past

**旧式** jiùshì ADJ old-fashioned; old-style
到香港旅游还可以乘坐**旧式**的有轨电车。
*You can ride on old-fashioned streetcars if you visit Hong Kong.*

**旧约全书** jiùyuēquánshū N Old Testament · MW 部、本

**旧址** jiùzhǐ N old location, former site · MW 个、处

### RELATED WORDS

| | |
|---|---|
| 怀旧 344 | 折旧 408 |
| 仍旧 448 | 守旧 486 |
| 依旧 625 | 故旧 816 |
| 念旧 1054 | 叙旧 1129 |
| 陈旧 1250 | |

## 166 归 歸  U+5F52  TM **6** FM |

**guī** V to return, to go/come back; to give back, to return (something) to (someone); to converge, to come together; to be under the care/charge of; to belong to; to attribute (something) to (someone/something)

**归案** guī'àn V to bring to justice
警察终于把罪犯捉拿**归案**。*The police have brought the criminals to justice.*

**归并** guībìng V to incorporate/merge into

**归档** guīdàng V to file
请把这些旧材料整理**归档**。*Please organize these old materials and file them.*

**归队** guīduì V to rejoin one's unit

**归附** guīfù V to submit to the authority of

**归根结底** guīgēnjiédǐ EXP in the final analysis

**归公** guīgōng V to return/revert to public/state ownership

**归功** guīgōng V to give credit to; to attribute success to

**归国** guīguó V to go home to one's country, to return from abroad

**归航** guīháng V to be going home

**归化** guīhuà V naturalization

**归还** guīhuán V to return, to revert, to give back
星期三之前, 你必须**归还**这两本书给图书馆。
*You must return both books to the library before Wednesday.*

**归结** guījié V to sum up, to conclude, to put in a nutshell

**归咎** guījiù V to blame; to attribute a fault to

**归类** guīlèi V to sort out

**归拢** guīlǒng V to gather, to put together, to pile up

**归谬法** guīmiùfǎ N reductio ad absurdum, taking (something) to a ridiculous extreme

**归纳** guīnà V to conclude, to summarize, to sum up

**归侨** guīqiáo N returnee, Chinese returned from abroad · MW 个、位、名

**归入** guīrù V to classify, to assign

**归属** guīshǔ V to be under the jurisdiction of; to belong to

**归顺** guīshùn V to pledge/swear allegiance to

**归宿** guīsù N final settling place, final destination; end result · MW 个

**归天** guītiān V to die, to pass away

**归途** guītú N journey home, the way back

**归心似箭** guīxīnsìjiàn EXP to be anxious to return home
尚未过节, 他已**归心似箭**。*The holidays were coming; he was anxious to return home.*

**归于** guīyú V to belong to; to be attributed to; to result in

**归罪** guīzuì V to blame

### RELATED WORDS

| | |
|---|---|
| 回归 391 | 划归 476 |
| 叶落归根 167 | 无家可归 139 |
| 宾至如归 1141 | |

## 167 叶 葉  U+53F6  TM **6** FM |

**yè** N leaf, foliage; like a leaf; page; period

叶落归根 **yèluòguīgēn** EXP to return to one's roots

叶片 **yèpiàn** N blade (of a leaf, a propeller, etc.); vane · MW 片

叶子 **yèzi** N foliage, leaf · MW 片
秋季叶子变黄。*The leaves turn yellow in autumn.*

**RELATED WORDS**

百叶窗 242　　枝叶 581　　茶叶 767
树叶 1031　　烟叶 1177　　落叶 1547
绿叶 1707　　霜叶 1935

---

**168　扑　撲**　　U+6251　　TM 6 FM 丨

**pū** V to rush at, to attack, to throw oneself on

扑鼻 **pūbí** V to be pungent
走进她家，一股香味**扑鼻**而来。*Upon entering her house, a fragrance greets you.*

扑哧 **pūchī** V to chuckle; to hiss
看见傻瓜的怪样，傻瓜太太"**扑哧**"一声笑了出来。*Mrs. ShaGua chuckled when she saw how silly ShaGua looked.*

扑打 **pūdǎ** V to beat; to pat

扑粉 **pūfěn** V to put on face powder

扑克 **pūkè** N poker; (deck of) playing cards · MW 张、副

扑空 **pūkōng** V to fail to get what one wants, to come away empty-handed
昨天他去找傻瓜，又**扑空**了。*He went to see ShaGua yesterday, but once again he wasn't home.*

扑灭 **pūmiè** V to extinguish, to put out, to stamp out
山火烧了三天三夜，总算被**扑灭**了。*The wildfire lasted three days and nights, but it has finally been extinguished.*

扑腾 **pūteng** V to thud, to thump; to splash

扑通 **pūtōng** V·ONOM to flop, to plop

**RELATED WORD**

猛扑 1704

---

**169　扒**　　U+6252　　TM 6 FM 丨

**bā** V to cling to, to hold on to; to dig up; to strip/take off; to rake together, to gather up

**pá** V to pick (someone's) pocket, to steal; to rake, to scratch

扒开 **bākāi** V to push aside

扒手 **páshǒu** N pickpocket · MW 个、伙
傻瓜市长跟公共汽车上的**扒手**打了起来。*Mayor ShaGua fought with a pickpocket when he saw him steal things on a bus.*

---

**170　企**　　U+4F01　　TM 6 FM 丿

**qǐ** V to stand on tiptoe; to hope for, to look forward to

企鹅 **qǐ'é** N penguin · MW 只

企求 **qǐqiú** V to seek, to desire
傻瓜最大的**企求**就是小儿子能当医生。*ShaGua's greatest desire is to see his younger son become a doctor.*

企图 **qǐtú** V·N to attempt, to try; to seek; plan, scheme, intention · MW 个
老板**企图**以解雇工人来胁迫他们更卖力地工作。*The boss tried to bully his workers into working harder by threatening them with dismissal.*

企业 **qǐyè** N company, firm, enterprise · MW 个、家
他在一家很大的全国性**企业**工作。*He works at a very large nationwide firm.*

企业管理 **qǐyèguǎnlǐ** N business strategy; business management
傻瓜利用业余时间学习**企业管理**。*ShaGua is now studying business administration in his spare time.*

---

**171　伞　傘**　　U+4F1E　　TM 6 FM 丿

**sǎn** N umbrella; shaped like an umbrella

伞兵 **sǎnbīng** N paratrooper · MW 个、名、群

伞投 **sǎntóu** V to drop by parachute

伞形 **sǎnxíng** N umbrella shape · MW 个

**RELATED WORDS**

雨伞 720　　凉伞 1337　　跳伞 1786
降落伞 1416

---

**172　全**　　U+5168　　TM 6 FM 丿

**quán** ADJ·ADV·V complete, whole, full, total, entire, perfect; completely, entirely; to make perfect/complete; to keep whole/intact
这份名单不**全**。*This roster is incomplete.*

**172** 全 **quán** (continued)

傻瓜全家都爱吃匹萨。*ShaGua's whole family loves pizza.*

这不是傻瓜的全名。*This is not ShaGua's full name.*

傻瓜并不十全十美。*ShaGua is not perfect.*

**全部 quánbù** N whole, entire, complete, total

刚到美国时，傻瓜的**全部**家当不过50美元。*When ShaGua arrived in the States, his family's property was worth about $50.*

**全场 quánchǎng** N whole audience, everyone present

球赛开始前，**全场**观众起立欢迎球队入场。*Before the game started, the whole audience stood up to welcome both teams.*

**全程 quánchéng** N whole journey/distance

**全国 quánguó** N entire nation/country; nationwide

**全国人民 quánguórénmín** N the people; populace

**全国性 quánguóxìng** N nationwide, national

**全集 quánjí** N complete collected works (literature) · MW 套

**全家福 quánjiāfú** N family portrait/photograph · MW 张

**全景 quánjǐng** N full/panoramic view · MW 个

**全局 quánjú** N overall situation, situation as a whole

一个好的副手，不仅能做好自己的工作，还应该有**全局**观念。*As a good associate, he not only performs tough assignments by himself, but he can also see the big picture.*

**全军 quánjūn** N entire army

**全力 quánlì** N everything in one's power; all one's strength

傻瓜正竭尽**全力**解决社会治安问题。*ShaGua is doing everything in his power to resolve the safety issues in his city.*

**全貌 quánmào** N complete picture, full view · MW 个

**全面 quánmiàn** N·ADJ overall, general, comprehensive

傻瓜已**全面**掌握了市长工作的要点。*ShaGua has a comprehensive grasp of the key points of a mayor's job.*

**全民 quánmín** N all the people, entire people

**全能 quánnéng** ADJ all-round; all-powerful, omnipotent

**全年 quánnián** N whole year; all year long

他正在做公司**全年**的生产报表。*He is working on the yearly production report for the company.*

**全盘 quánpán** ADJ overall, complete

**全球 quánqiú** N whole world, entire globe

**全权 quánquán** N full powers

**全然 quánrán** ADV completely, entirely, utterly

**全日制 quánrìzhì** N full-time work

**全身 quánshēn** N whole body; from head to toe

傻瓜在跑完马拉松后，感到**全身**酸痛。*After finishing the marathon, ShaGua ached all over.*

**全神贯注 quánshénguànzhù** EXP to concentrate on, to be entirely absorbed with; with undivided attention

他在**全神贯注**地学中文，竟然没有发现匹萨烤糊了。*He was concentrating so much on studying Chinese that he didn't realize the pizza was burning.*

**全数 quánshù** N whole amount, entire sum, total number

**全速 quánsù** N full/top speed

**全套 quántào** N complete set, full complement

**全体 quántǐ** N everyone, all; entire, whole, total

班上的**全体**同学都喜欢中文。*The entire class showed interest in Chinese.*

**全天 quántiān** N whole day, all day long

他**全天**都在想着那个漂亮的姑娘。*He has been thinking about that pretty girl all day long.*

**全托 quántuō** V to put one's child in a boarding nursery

**全文 quánwén** N full/entire text

老师要求阅读**全文**。*The teacher requested a reading of the full text.*

**全息 quánxī** ADJ holographic

**全线 quánxiàn** N whole front (in a battle); length (of a road, railroad, etc.)

**全休 quánxiū** V to be completely rested/healed (after an illness)

**全自动 quánzìdòng** ADJ automatic

**全组 quánzǔ** N whole group, complete set

这个项目由**全组**成员共同承担。*The whole group is working on this project.*

### RELATED WORDS

## 173 分　U+5206　TM **6** FM 丿

**fēn** V·N·MW  to divide, to separate, to split; to assign, to distribute; to distinguish, to differentiate; branch (of an organization); part, fraction, percent; ingredient, component, element; one tenth [of units of time, length, area, weight, etc.]; [measure word for minutes (of the hour) and for cents/pennies (= ⅟₁₀₀ yuan)]

三十人**分**成三组。*Thirty people are divided into three groups.*

你**分**糖果给孩子。*You are distributing candy to the kids.*

你是非不**分**。*You can't make a distinction between right and wrong.*

这是我们的**分**校。*This is a branch of our school.*

你有十**分**把握吗？*Are you 100% sure?*

一节课一小时五十**分** *one hour and 50 minutes per class*

一元零三**分** *one yuan and three cents*

**fèn** N  component, ingredient; limit

糖**分**太高 *too much sugar content*

你太过**分**了。*You have gone too far.*

**分班** fēnbān V  to divide into classes

**分辨** fēnbiàn V  to distinguish, to differentiate

灯光太暗，傻瓜无法**分辨**路边的标志。*It was so dark that ShaGua could not see the traffic signs.*

**分别** fēnbié V·N·ADV  to split up, to leave; to distinguish; difference; separately, differently

和女朋友**分别**数月，他感到很痛苦。*Having been separated from his ex-girlfriend for several months, he felt a bitter longing.*

**分布** fēnbù V  to be distributed (over an area)

**分层** fēncéng V  to divide into layers, to stratify

**分词** fēncí N  participle · MW 个

**分寸** fēncun N  proper limit for speech/action · MW 个

傻瓜总是告诫孩子，讲话应该注意**分寸**，不可伤人。*ShaGua always warned his kids: "Be careful not to hurt others with your words!"*

**分段** fēnduàn V  to segment

**分发** fēnfā V  to distribute, to hand out

老师把考试卷**分发**给学生。*The teacher distributed the exams to his students.*

**分割** fēngē V  to cut apart, to break up, to partition

**分隔** fēngé V  to separate, to divide, to partition

**分工** fēngōng V  to divide the work; to be assigned a job

傻瓜在公司**分工**搞售后服务。*ShaGua was assigned responsibility for this project.*

**分公司** fēngōngsī N  branch office; subsidiary · MW 个

**分管** fēnguǎn V  to be in charge of

因为工作努力，后来他**分管**售后服务。*Due to his hard work, he was later put in charge of after-sale services.*

**分红** fēnhóng V  to get a bonus, to share profits

**分化** fēnhuà V  to become divided, to break up

**分会** fēnhuì N  branch (of an organization) · MW 个

**分级** fēnjí V  to sort, to classify, to grade

**分家** fēnjiā V  to separate and live apart, to break up

**分解** fēnjiě V  to break down, to separate into parts

**分界** fēnjiè V·N  to divide by boundary; dividing line · MW 条

**分居** fēnjū V  to live apart; to be separated (of a married couple)

他已经跟太太**分居**了，说不定很快就会离婚。*He lived apart from his wife and may divorce her soon.*

**分句** fēnjù N  clause · MW 个

**分开** fēnkāi V  to separate, to be apart

**分类** fēnlèi V  to classify, to sort

**分离** fēnlí V  to separate, to leave

**分裂** fēnliè V  to split, to divide, to break up

**分流** fēnliú V  to bypass (crowds, traffic, etc.)

**分配** fēnpèi V  to assign, to allocate, to distribute

**分批** fēnpī V  to do in batches; to take turns

**分期** fēnqī V  to do in stages/groups/installments

**分歧** fēnqí N  difference, divergence, disagreement · MW 个

他们之间的**分歧**越来越尖锐。*The disagreement between them became greater and greater.*

**分清** fēnqīng V  to make a clear distinction

在黑暗中很难**分清**谁是谁。*It is hard to tell who is who in the dark.*

**分区** fēnqū N·V  district; to divide into districts/zones · MW 个

**分散** fēnsàn V  to divert, to scatter, to decentralize, to disperse

学生三三两两地**分散**在教室里。*The students were dispersed to the corners of the classroom.*

**分手** fēnshǒu V  to break up, to say good-bye

**分摊** fēntān V  to share (expenses), to apportion

**173 分 fēn/fèn** (continued)

分头 **fēntóu** ADV separately

已经计划好了, 大家**分头**去干吧。 *Since our plan has already been decided, please go ahead and do whatever each of you should do.*

分析 **fēnxī** V·N to analyze; analysis · MW 个

请把这个句子的各个成份**分析**一下。 *Please analyze the parts of the sentence.*

分心 **fēnxīn** V to divert, to distract; to pay attention

上课的时候不要**分心**。 *Please pay attention in class.*

分支 **fēnzhī** N subdivision, branch · MW 个

分子 **fēnzǐ** N molecule · MW 个

分组 **fēnzǔ** V to divide into groups

分量 **fènliàng** N weight

虽然这家餐馆的菜价很贵, 但菜的**分量**很足。 *Even though this restaurant is very expensive, the portions are quite filling.*

分内 **fènnèi** N one's job/duty

分外 **fènwài** N not one's duty/responsibility

分子 **fènzǐ** N member; element, part · MW 个、名

**RELATED WORDS**

| | | |
|---|---|---|
| 十分 3 | 不分彼此 24 | 万分 73 |
| 平分 78 | 本分 90 | 区分 99 |
| 公分 103 | 几分 115 | 水分 159 |
| 瓜分 189 | 内分泌 191 | 百分比 242 |
| 百分之百 242 | 百分制 242 | 比分 279 |
| 划分 476 | 均分 558 | 成分 611 |
| 充分 652 | 评分 706 | 过分 712 |
| 每分钟 837 | 记分 946 | 学分 1155 |
| 总分 1330 | 辈分 1382 | 等分 1437 |
| 部分 1636 | 零分 1640 | 满分 1745 |
| 三等分 9 | 大部分 20 | 化学分析 215 |
| 知识分子 647 | 恰如其分 930 | |

**174 令**　　U+4EE4　　TM 6 FM 丿

**lìng** N·V·ADJ order, command; season; to make, to cause; excellent, honorable

**RELATED WORDS**

| | | |
|---|---|---|
| 下令 10 | 口令 42 | 司令 357 |
| 责令 525 | 号令 545 | 时令 586 |
| 条令 598 | 法令 686 | 命令 1051 |
| 夏令 1195 | 指令 1397 | 限令 1417 |
| 禁令 1536 | 调令 1749 | |

**175 众 衆**　　U+4F17　　TM 6 FM 丿

**zhòng** ADJ·N many, numerous; many people, crowd, multitude; the public

众多 **zhòngduō** ADJ numerous

众口难调 **zhòngkǒunántiáo** EXP it's difficult to satisfy everyone, tastes differ

众目睽睽 **zhòngmùkuíkuí** EXP in full view, in broad daylight

**众目睽睽**下, 他竟然在课堂上睡着了。 *He even slept in class where everyone could see.*

众人 **zhòngrén** N everybody

众矢之的 **zhòngshǐzhīdì** EXP target of public criticism

众所周知 **zhòngsuǒzhōuzhī** EXP as everyone knows

**众所周知**, 傻瓜市长没有上过大学。 *It's well known that Mayor ShaGua didn't attend college.*

众议员 **zhòngyìyuán** N U.S. congressman · MW 个、位、名

众议院 **zhòngyìyuàn** N U.S. House of Representatives

**RELATED WORDS**

| | | |
|---|---|---|
| 大众 20 | 万众 73 | 公众 103 |
| 示众 140 | 与众不同 158 | 出众 258 |
| 当众 335 | 民众 388 | 听众 414 |
| 观众 726 | 聚众 1642 | 群众 1646 |

**176 白**　　U+767D　　TM 6 FM 丿

**bái** ADJ·ADV·V white; shiny, bright; plain, pure, blank; incorrectly written, mispronounced; in vain, to no purpose; for nothing, free of charge, gratis; funeral; to state, to explain, to make clear; to look scornfully, to stare coldly

白车 *white car*

东方发白。 *It is bright in the east.*

空白 *blank*

白字 *wrong character*

真相大白。 *The case is clear now.*

他白做了。 *He did it for nothing.*

这是白送的。 *This is a free gift.*

旁白 *an aside*

给你一个白眼 *to give you a scornful look*

白白 **báibái** ADV in vain, for nothing

傻瓜认为买卖股票是**白白**浪费钱。
*ShaGua regards buying and selling stocks as money down the drain.*

**白斑** báibān N white spot · MW 块

**白布** báibù N plain white cloth, calico · MW 块

**白菜** báicài N Chinese cabbage · MW 棵

**白痴** báichī N idiocy; idiot, moron · MW 个、名
真是个**白痴**! *What an idiot!*

**白搭** báidā V to be of no use, to be no good

**白费** báifèi V to waste
老师发现自己在**白费**口舌；学生根本没听懂他说什么。*The teacher saw that he was wasting his breath: The students didn't understand what he was talking about.*

**白骨** báigǔ N bones of the dead · MW 根、块

**白光** báiguāng N white light · MW 道、束

**白脸** báiliǎn N white face (theatrical makeup); villain (in Beijing opera) · MW 张

**白领** báilǐng N white-collar · MW 个、位、名

**白面** báimiàn N (wheat) flour; heroin · MW 团、堆

**白人** báirén N white person, Caucasian · MW 个、位、名

**白日梦** báirìmèng N daydreaming · MW 个

**白色** báisè N white; counterrevolutionary

**白手起家** báishǒuqǐjiā EXP to build up from nothing, to start from scratch
可以说，傻瓜是**白手起家**的。*You could say that ShaGua has built his success out of nothing.*

**白薯** báishǔ N sweet potato · MW 块

**白糖** báitáng N white (refined) sugar · MW 包

**白天** báitiān N day, daytime · MW 个

**RELATED WORDS**

| | | |
|---|---|---|
| 内白 191 | 灰白 198 | 汉白玉 235 |
| 自白 305 | 发白 311 | 红白事 474 |
| 补白 508 | 表白 527 | 空白 669 |
| 洋白菜 689 | 洁白 940 | 苍白 996 |
| 明白 1035 | 独白 1095 | 蛋白 1368 |
| 蛋白质 1368 | 雪白 1369 | 黑白 1389 |
| 旁白 1473 | 清白 1495 | 眼白 1570 |
| 银白色 1607 | 说白 1631 | 漂白 1820 |
| 漂白剂 1820 | 增白剂 1849 | |

---

**177** 乞    U+4E5E    TM **6** FM ノ

qǐ V to beg

**乞丐** qǐgài N beggar · MW 个
他总是怜悯**乞丐**。*He always shows pity for beggars.*

**乞求** qǐqiú V to plead/beg for, to entreat

**乞讨** qǐtǎo V to beg, to mooch
除非万不得已, 谁愿意靠**乞讨**过日子? *Nobody wants to beg unless there is no other choice.*

**RELATED WORDS**

| | |
|---|---|
| 求乞 376 | 讨乞 500 |

---

**178** 冬 鼕    U+51AC    TM **6** FM ノ

dōng N winter

**冬瓜** dōngguā N wax/white gourd, Chinese squash · MW 个

**冬季** dōngjì N winter · MW 个

**冬眠** dōngmián V to hibernate
冬季来临, 蛇进入**冬眠**。*Winter is coming; snakes are beginning to hibernate.*

**冬青** dōngqīng N holly, Chinese ilex · MW 棵

**冬天** dōngtiān N winter · MW 个

**冬衣** dōngyī N winter clothes · MW 件、套

**冬至** dōngzhì N winter solstice

**RELATED WORDS**

| | | |
|---|---|---|
| 立冬 125 | 严冬 241 | 过冬 712 |
| 寒冬腊月 1481 | 越冬 1575 | |

---

**179** 勿    U+52FF    TM **6** FM ノ

wù ADV not; never
请**勿**乱扔垃圾。*Please don't litter.*

**RELATED WORD**

请勿 1632

---

**180** 勻    U+5300    TM **6** FM ノ

yún ADJ-V even, equitable, well-distributed; to even out, to divide evenly, to apportion

**匀称** yúnchèn ADJ well-proportioned, well-balanced
这个姑娘很漂亮, 身材很**匀称**。*She is a pretty girl with a nice figure.*

**匀速** yúnsù N steady pace, uniform speed

**匀整** yúnzhěng ADJ regular, uniform, neat and well-spaced

**RELATED WORDS**

| | |
|---|---|
| 均匀 558 | 拌匀 574 |

**181** **币** 幣    U+5E01    TM **6** FM ノ

**bì** N money, coins, currency

**币值 bìzhí** N currency value

**币制 bìzhì** N monetary standard, currency system · MW 种

### RELATED WORDS

| | | |
|---|---|---|
| 外币 218 | 金币 420 | 货币 1061 |
| 纸币 1103 | 钱币 1301 | 硬币 1524 |
| 银币 1607 | 铜币 1712 | 港币 1740 |
| 人民币 4 | | |

**182** **年**    U+5E74    TM **6** FM ノ

**nián** N·MW year; Spring Festival; age, stage in one's life; era, times; annual harvest; yearly, annual; [measure word for years (of age)]

明**年** *next year*

过**年** *to celebrate the New Year*

童**年** *childhood*

**年**过半百 *over 50 years of age*

清朝末**年** *at the end of the Qing Dynasty*

**年**会 *annual conference*

**年报 niánbào** N annual report · MW 份

公司的**年报**一公布，股票就会上涨。*As soon as the annual report is announced, the company's stocks will go up.*

**年表 niánbiǎo** N chronology · MW 份

**年产量 niánchǎnliàng** N annual output

**年初 niánchū** N beginning of the year

**年代 niándài** N decade; period, time; era · MW 个

傻瓜生于五十**年代**。*ShaGua was born in the '50s.*

**年底 niándǐ** N end of the year

**年初**的工作没有**年底**那么忙。*The beginning of the year is not as busy as the end of the year.*

**年度 niándù** N year (school year, fiscal year, etc.); annual, yearly

**年份 niánfèn** N particular year

**年富力强 niánfùlìqiáng** EXP in the prime of life

**年糕 niángāo** N New Year cake · MW 片、块

**年庚 niángēng** N time of a person's birth

**年关 niánguān** N end of the year · MW 个

**年华 niánhuá** N age, years in one's lifetime; time · MW 个

**年画 niánhuà** N New Year pictures, Spring Festival pictures · MW 张

**年会 niánhuì** N annual meeting · MW 个

**年级 niánjí** N year/grade (in school) · MW 个

傻瓜的女儿上十**年级**。*ShaGua's daughter is in tenth grade.*

**年纪 niánjì** N age

她一点儿也不像她的**年纪**。*She doesn't look her age at all.*

**年鉴 niánjiàn** N yearbook · MW 本、部

**年历 niánlì** N calendar with the entire year printed on one sheet · MW 张

**年利 niánlì** N annual interest · MW 笔

**年龄 niánlíng** N age (of a person, an animal, a plant)

我们问她的**年龄**时，她很不好意思。*She was embarrassed when we asked her her age.*

**年轮 niánlún** N annual growth ring (of a tree) · MW 圈

**年迈 niánmài** N old, aged

**年迈**的老太太头发全白了。*The old lady's hair is all white.*

**年年 niánnián** N every year, year after year

**年青 niánqīng** ADJ young

**年青**人喜欢流行音乐。*The youth like pop music.*

**年轻 niánqīng** ADJ young (usually in the teenage years)

现在我不唱歌了，但我**年轻**时很能唱。*I can't sing anymore, but I could when I was young.*

**年收入 niánshōurù** N annual income · MW 笔

**年岁 niánsuì** N years of age; age

**年息 niánxī** N annual interest · MW 笔

**年薪 niánxīn** N annual salary · MW 份

这个职位的**年薪**是多少？*What is the annual salary for this position?*

**年夜 niányè** N eve of the lunar New Year

**年月 niányue** N years; days

请填写你的出生**年月**。*Please fill in your date of birth.*

**年终 niánzhōng** N end of the year

傻瓜准备用**年终**奖金买一个大屏幕电视。*With his year-end bonus, ShaGua is going to buy a TV with a bigger screen.*

### RELATED WORDS

| | | |
|---|---|---|
| 少年 62 | 本年度 90 | 长年 93 |
| 元年 138 | 去年 157 | 全年 172 |
| 历年 200 | 壮年 238 | 百年 242 |
| 来年 260 | 当年 335 | 当年 335 |
| 老年 375 | 往年 461 | 光年 491 |

**RELATED WORDS**

---

### 183 毛    U+6BDB    TM **6** FM 丿

**máo**  N·ADJ  hair; feather, down; wool; mold, mildew; monetary unit (= 10 cents); semifinished, crude; gross; small, little; careless, rash; alarmed, scared; depreciated (of currency)

脱毛 *to shed hair/fur (of an animal)*

毛毯 *woolen blanket*

食品长毛了。 *The food has grown moldy.*

一块三毛钱 *one yuan and 30 cents*

毛收入 *gross income*

毛小子 *careless boy*

心里发毛 *to feel really scared*

毛笔 **máobǐ**  N  writing brush/pen · MW 支

毛布 **máobù**  N  coarse cotton · MW 匹

毛虫 **máochóng**  N  caterpillar · MW 条
毛虫变成蝴蝶。 *Caterpillars turn into butterflies.*

毛发 **máofà**  N  hair (on the human body) · MW 根

毛纺 **máofǎng**  ADJ  wool spinning

毛巾 **máojīn**  N  towel · MW 条
洗完澡后, 她用毛巾擦干身子。 *After her bath, she dried herself with a towel.*

毛孔 **máokǒng**  N  pore · MW 个

毛利润 **máolìrùn**  N  gross profit · MW 笔

毛料 **máoliào**  N  wool cloth · MW 匹、块

毛驴 **máolǘ**  N  donkey · MW 匹

毛皮 **máopí**  N  fur, pelt · MW 张、块
环保人士反对人们穿毛皮制做的衣服。 *The environmentalist disapproved of people who wear fur.*

毛遂自荐 **máosuìzìjiàn**  EXP  to volunteer one's services

毛细管 **máoxìguǎn**  N  capillary · MW 条

毛线 **máoxiàn**  N  knitting wool, wool yarn · MW 根、团

毛泽东 **Máo Zédōng**  N  Mao Zedong (1893–1976; founder of the People's Republic of China and leader of the Communist Party of China)

毛竹 **máozhú**  N  bamboo · MW 棵

---

### 184 朱    U+6731    TM **6** FM 丿

**zhū**  ADJ·N  bright red; vermilion; cinnabar

朱红色 **zhūhóngsè**  N  vermilion

朱墨 **zhūmò**  N  red and black

---

### 185 气 氣    U+6C14    TM **6** FM 丿

**qì**  N·V  air; gas; weather; smell, odor; flavor; morale, spirits; manner, bearing, air, style; momentum, impetus; anger; vital energy, energy of life; [names of certain symptoms]; to be angry, to make angry, to enrage; to insult; to bully

屋里没空气 *no air in this house*

这人没气了。 *This person isn't breathing.*

气管 *gas line*

傻瓜没有官气。 *ShaGua doesn't put on any bureaucratic airs.*

打气 *to encourage*

生气 *to get angry*

她受气了。 *She was insulted.*

气冲冲 **qìchōngchōng**  EXP  furious, enraged
傻瓜气冲冲地找州长申辩。 *Enraged, ShaGua went to argue with the governor.*

气喘 **qìchuǎn**  V·N  to be short of breath; asthma

气动 **qìdòng**  ADJ  pneumatic

气短 **qìduǎn**  ADJ  breathing hard, short of breath

气氛 **qìfēn**  N  atmosphere

气愤 **qìfèn**  ADJ  angry, furious
他非常气愤。 *He was very angry.*

气概 **qìgài**  N  spirit, mettle

气缸 **qìgāng**  N  cylinder (of an engine) · MW 个

气功 **qìgōng**  N  qigong (a meditative system that uses movement and breathing exercises)
气功在中国有很长的历史, 但许多人不相信它。 *Qigong has a long history in China, but many people today no longer believe in it.*

气管 **qìguǎn**  N  windpipe; air tube · MW 条

## 185 气 qì (continued)

**气候 qìhòu** N climate, weather

今年的气候很反常。 *This year's climate is very abnormal.*

**气力 qìlì** N physical strength; energy

**气量 qìliàng** N tolerance

**气流 qìliú** N air current, airflow · MW 股

**气门 qìmén** N air valve (especially of a tire) · MW 个

**气囊 qìnáng** N air bag/sac · MW 个

**气恼 qìnǎo** ADJ angry, sulky

听了傻瓜的申述后, 州长十分气恼。 *After listening to ShaGua, the governor was furious.*

**气馁 qìněi** ADJ discouraged, despondent

**气泡 qìpào** N bubble; blister (in metal); gas/air pocket · MW 个

**气魄 qìpò** N imposing manner, daring

**气色 qìsè** N complexion; expression, look

**气体 qìtǐ** N gas · MW 股

**气味 qìwèi** N smell, odor; flavor · MW 股

**气温 qìwēn** N air temperature

今天的气温是华氏八十度。 *The temperature today is 80 degrees Fahrenheit.*

**气息 qìxī** N breath; flavor, taste; smell · MW 种

**气象 qìxiàng** N meteorology; weather; atmosphere · MW 派

**气压 qìyā** N barometric/atmospheric pressure

**气质 qìzhì** N disposition, temperament

**气壮山河 qìzhuàngshānhé** EXP magnificent, inspiring

### RELATED WORDS

| | | |
|---|---|---|
| 士气 16 | 义气 22 | 天气 25 |
| 才气 39 | 口气 42 | 力气 59 |
| 火气 72 | 正气 76 | 习气 84 |
| 支气管 92 | 生气 107 | 元气 138 |
| 风气 194 | 压气 201 | 出气 258 |
| 电气 263 | 叹气 285 | 吐气 286 |
| 打气 289 | 杀气 317 | 名气 426 |
| 负气 435 | 冷气 494 | 丧气 521 |
| 志气 528 | 争气 595 | 和气 644 |
| 充气 652 | 空气 669 | 泄气 685 |
| 洋气 689 | 吸气 776 | 抽气 788 |
| 香气 834 | 受气 844 | 娇气 882 |
| 废气 918 | 运气 956 | 忍气吞声 970 |
| 邪气 981 | 秀气 1055 | 臭气 1076 |
| 闷气 1150 | 浩气 1169 | 排气 1241 |
| 氧气 1269 | 客气 1316 | 勇气 1371 |
| 热气 1390 | 怒气 1427 | 服气 1457 |
| 湿气 1498 | 语气 1501 | 喜气洋洋 1531 |
| 骨气 1543 | 喷气 1563 | 喷气式 1563 |
| 淘气 1628 | 惹气 1657 | 暖气 1675 |
| 脾气 1711 | 阔气 1728 | 通气 1757 |
| 喘气 1764 | 怨气 1792 | 意气 1812 |
| 福气 1825 | 透气 1826 | 雾气 1837 |
| 漏气 1886 | 燃气 1888 | 憋气 1972 |
| 不客气 24 | 天然气 25 | 牛脾气 51 |
| 放空气 964 | 碰运气 1526 | 垂头丧气 430 |

## 186 史   U+53F2   TM 6 FM 丿

**shǐ** N history; official historian, official in charge of historical records

**史册 shǐcè** N annals, historical records; history · MW 部

**史迹 shǐjì** N historic site/relics/remains · MW 处

**史料 shǐliào** N historical data/materials · MW 份

**史前 shǐqián** N prehistory

**史诗 shǐshī** N epic · MW 部

**史实 shǐshí** N historical fact/event · MW 个

**史无前例 shǐwúqiánlì** EXP unprecedented in history

**史学 shǐxué** N historiography; science of history

### RELATED WORDS

| | | |
|---|---|---|
| 文史 70 | 历史 200 | 秘史 1289 |

## 187 右   U+53F3   TM 6 FM 丿

**yòu** N·ADJ right (side); right side (in terms of precedence); the Right (politics)

**右边 yòubian** N right (side), on the right

在右边, 你能看到一个学校。 *You'll see a school on your right.*

**右派 yòupài** N the Right (politics); rightist

我的父亲在1957年被划为右派。 *My father was labeled a rightist in 1957.*

**右倾 yòuqīng** N Right deviation (politics)

**右手 yòushǒu** N right-hand (side)

在中国, 不允许左手写字, 所有的人都用右手写字。 *In China, people are not allowed to write with their left hands, so they all use their right hands.*

**右翼 yòuyì** N right wing; the Right (politics)

在中国, 右翼是自由派, 左翼是保守派; 正好与美国相反。 *In China, the right wing is liberal and the left is conservative; this is different from America.*

**RELATED WORDS**

---

## 188 在     U+5728     TM **6** FM 丿

**zài** V·ADV·PREP to exist, to live, to be alive; to be; to stay, to remain; to join / belong to (an organization); to depend on, to rely on; in the process/course of; in, on, at [used to indicate time, place, scope, etc.]

她老人家已经不**在**了。 *The old lady has passed away.*

我**在**里面。 *I am inside.*

"喂, 傻瓜**在**吗?" *"Hello, is ShaGua there?"*

全**在**傻瓜的努力。 *It all depends on ShaGua's efforts.*

傻瓜**在**修车。 *ShaGua is repairing his car.*

**在案 zài'àn** V to be on record

**在编人员 zàibiānrényuán** N permanent staff · MW 个、位、名

**在场 zàichǎng** V to be present, to be on the scene

幸好有证人**在场**, 否则傻瓜就麻烦了。 *Luckily, there were witnesses. Otherwise, ShaGua would have gotten into trouble.*

**在行 zàiháng** ADJ expert (in), good/skillful (at)

**在乎 zàihu** V to care about; to mind [often used in the negative]

傻瓜不**在乎**是否可以得到那个职位。 *ShaGua doesn't care whether or not he gets the position.*

**在家 zàijiā** V to be at home; to be in

周末傻瓜喜欢和孩子们**在家**看电视。 *ShaGua likes to stay at home and watch TV with his kids on the weekend.*

**在理 zàilǐ** ADJ right, reasonable, sensible

**在里面 zàilǐmian** N inside

傻瓜打开提包, 发现车钥匙**在里面**。 *When ShaGua opened his bag, he found his keys inside.*

**在世 zàishì** V to be alive, to exist

**在所不辞 zàisuǒbùcí** EXP without hesitation; will not refuse under any circumstances

**在所不惜 zàisuǒbùxī** EXP will not resent/grudge

**在所难免 zàisuǒnánmiǎn** EXP can hardly be avoided

**在外面 zàiwàimian** N outside

孩子们**在外面**玩儿呢。 *The children are playing outside.*

**在望 zàiwàng** V to be visible, to be in sight/view

**在下 zàixià** PRON I, me

**在先 zàixiān** ADV in the past, before, formerly

**在线 zàixiàn** V to be online

**在押 zàiyā** V to be in detention; to be in prison

**在野 zàiyě** V to be out of office/power

**在意 zàiyì** V to care about, to mind [often used in the negative]

她留还是走, 傻瓜真的不**在意**。 *Whether she stays or goes, ShaGua doesn't really care.*

**在于 zàiyú** V to consist in; to depend on

生命**在于**运动。 *Life depends on exercise.*

**在职 zàizhí** V to be employed; to be at one's post

**在座 zàizuò** V to be present, to be seated at a meeting/banquet

**RELATED WORDS**

---

## 189 瓜     U+74DC     TM **6** FM 丿

**guā** N melon, gourd

**瓜分 guāfēn** V to divide/carve up

他们**瓜**分了胜利果实。 *They divided up the spoils.*

**瓜葛 guāgé** N association, connection

**瓜果 guāguǒ** N fruit (in general) (LIT melons and fruit) · MW 个

**瓜藤 guāténg** N melon vine · MW 条

**瓜子 guāzǐ** N melon seeds · MW 颗

**RELATED WORDS**

---

## 190 月     U+6708     TM **6** FM 丿

**yuè** N moon; month

**月半 yuèbàn** N fifteenth day of a month

**月报 yuèbào** N monthly magazine/report · MW 份、期

**月饼 yuèbǐng** N moon cake · MW 个、块

**190 月 yuè** (continued)

月初 **yuèchū** N beginning of the month

每个月的**月初**有一次考试。*There is a test at the beginning of each month.*

月出 **yuèchū** V moonrise

月度 **yuèdù** N month

月份 **yuèfèn** N month

这里九**月份**的天气最好。*The weather here is best in September.*

月宫 **yuègōng** N moon (LIT palace of the moon) · MW 座

月光 **yuèguāng** N moonlight · MW 道

他们在**月光**下静静地坐着。*They sat quietly in the moonlight.*

月经 **yuèjīng** N menses, period; menstruation

月刊 **yuèkān** N monthly magazine · MW 份、期

月历 **yuèlì** N monthly calendar · MW 份

月亮 **yuèliang** N moon

月票 **yuèpiào** N monthly ticket · MW 张

月球 **yuèqiú** N moon

月食 **yuèshí** N lunar eclipse · MW 次

月台 **yuètái** N railway platform · MW 个

月薪 **yuèxīn** N monthly income/salary · MW 笔

他的**月薪**由公司替他存入银行。*His company deposits his monthly salary into the bank.*

**RELATED WORDS**

---

**191 内 内** U+5185 TM **6** FM 丿

**nèi** N interior, in, inside, inner, internal, within; heart; internal organ; one's wife or her relatives; imperial palace

屋**内** *inside the room*

**内**弟 *my brother-in-law*

大**内** *inner palace*

内凹 **nèi'āo** ADJ indented

内白 **nèibái** N words spoken by an actor offstage · MW 段

内部 **nèibù** N inside, internal, interior, within

他家的**内部**装饰得富丽堂皇。*The interior of his home is magnificent and luxurious.*

内存 **nèicún** N RAM, computer memory

内地 **nèidì** N inland, hinterland, interior (of a country)

内定 **nèidìng** V to be decided at a higher level but not announced (of an official appointment)

内分泌 **nèifēnmì** N endocrine system

内服 **nèifú** V to take orally

这瓶药是**内服**的, 一天三次, 一次两片。*This medicine is to be taken orally, three times a day, two at a time.*

内功 **nèigōng** N neigong (system of building up one's strength through breathing and other exercises of the internal organs)

内行 **nèiháng** N·ADJ expert, specialist; knowledgeable about

傻瓜修车很**内行**。*ShaGua is an expert in car repair.*

内河 **nèihé** N inland river · MW 条

内奸 **nèijiān** N hidden traitor, enemy in the ranks · MW 个、名

内疚 **nèijiù** ADJ guilty; ashamed

提起上次考试, 他露出**内疚**的神情。*When the exam was brought up, his face betrayed his guilt.*

内眷 **nèijuàn** N females in a family, womenfolk · MW 个、名

内科 **nèikē** N internal medicine; medical department

感冒着凉需要看**内科**医生。*You need to see a doctor of internal medicine when you get the flu or catch a cold.*

内裤 **nèikù** N underpants, underwear · MW 条

内力 **nèilì** N internal force · MW 股

内陆 **nèilù** N inland, interior (of a country)

内乱 **nèiluàn** N civil strife/conflict · MW 次

内蒙古 **Nèiměnggǔ** N Inner Mongolia

内幕 **nèimù** N inside story, what goes on behind the scene · MW 个

内勤 **nèiqín** N office staff · MW 个、位、名

内人 **nèirén** N wife

内容 **nèiróng** N content; substance, details, issues

这本书的**内容**很浅白, 一般人都读得懂。*The content of this book is so easy to read, ordinary people can understand it.*

内伤 **nèishāng** N internal injury

他摔了一跤, 没有外伤, 但很可能有**内伤**。*He fell down. Even though he may not have any external injuries, he may have an internal one.*

**内外 nèiwài** N·ADV inside and outside, domestic and foreign; approximately, about

**内务 nèiwù** N internal affairs; domestic/family affairs · MW 件

**内线 nèixiàn** N undercover agent; internal phone line · MW 条

**内详 nèixiáng** V to enclose the name and address of the sender

**内心 nèixīn** N mind, bottom of the heart, innermost world

傻瓜脸部严肃，但**内心**赋有幽默感。*ShaGua has a solemn face, but deep down he is very funny.*

**内省 nèixǐng** V to be introspective

**内衣 nèiyī** N underwear · MW 件

**内因 nèiyīn** N internal cause · MW 个

**内忧外患 nèiyōuwàihuàn** EXP difficulties both domestic and abroad, domestic trouble and foreign invasion

**内在 nèizài** ADJ internal; inherent, intrinsic

**内脏 nèizàng** N internal organs · MW 副

**内战 nèizhàn** N civil war · MW 场

**内政 nèizhèng** N internal affairs (of a country)

**RELATED WORDS**

| | | |
|---|---|---|
| 以内 101 | 户内 129 | 分内 173 |
| 体内 325 | 国内 542 | 室内 1139 |
| 海内 1494 | | |

---

**192 丸** U+4E38   TM **6** FM 丿

**wán** N small ball; pill

**丸药 wányào** N pill (in Chinese medicine) · MW 粒、颗

很多中药被制成**丸药**形状。*Many traditional Chinese medicines are made into pills.*

**丸子 wánzi** N ball; pill; round mass of food (meatball, etc.) · MW 个

**RELATED WORDS**

| | |
|---|---|
| 肉丸子 437 | 药丸 1392 |

---

**193 凡** U+51E1   TM **6** FM 丿

**fán** N·ADJ·ADV mortal world, earth; ordinary, commonplace; every, any, all

凡间 *the earth*

凡人 *ordinary people*

凡事 *anything*

**凡例 fánlì** N notes/guide on how to use a book · MW 篇

**凡是 fánshì** ADV every, any, all; whatever

**凡是**有理智的人都憎恶暴力。*All truly wise people hate violence.*

**凡士林 fánshìlín** N Vaseline · MW 瓶

**RELATED WORDS**

| | | |
|---|---|---|
| 平凡 78 | 非凡 378 | 但凡 458 |
| 自命不凡 305 | | |

---

**194 风 風** U+98CE   TM **6** FM 丿

**fēng** N·V wind; trend, common practice, custom; general mood, attitude, manner, style; news, information; hearsay, rumor; folk songs of the States; [names of certain diseases (epilepsy, etc.)]; to air-dry; to winnow; to be rumored

西风 *west wind*

文风 *style of writing*

风闻 *rumors*

**风暴 fēngbào** N windstorm; crisis · MW 场

夜间起**风暴**了。*A storm arose during the night.*

**风波 fēngbō** N storm; disturbance; crisis · MW 场

**风采 fēngcǎi** N elegance; writing talent

**风车 fēngchē** N windmill · MW 架

**风尘仆仆 fēngchénpúpú** EXP to be travel-weary

**风吹草动 fēngchuīcǎodòng** EXP sign of disturbance/trouble

**风干 fēnggān** V to air-dry

**风格 fēnggé** N personality, character; style, manner · MW 种

我喜欢他的写作**风格**，更喜欢他写的内容。*I like the content more than his style of writing.*

**风景 fēngjǐng** N scenery, landscape, sights · MW 处

那**风景**美丽得无法形容。*The scenery was beautiful beyond description.*

**风镜 fēngjìng** N goggles · MW 副

**风口 fēngkǒu** N drafty place · MW 处

**风浪 fēnglàng** N rough waters; hardships, difficulties

傻瓜经历过许多**风浪**。*ShaGua has experienced many difficulties.*

**风力 fēnglì** N wind power/intensity

**风凉 fēngliáng** ADJ cool

## 194 风 fēng (continued)

**风凉话 fēngliánghuà** EXP irresponsible and sarcastic remark; sarcasm; cynical remark

傻瓜从不对别人说风凉话。 *ShaGua has never said anything irresponsible or sarcastic to others.*

**风马牛不相及 fēngmǎniúbùxiāngjí** EXP to be completely at odds, to be totally unrelated

傻瓜与市长，似乎风马牛不相及。 *ShaGua and the position of mayor seem to be totally unsuited for one another.*

**风貌 fēngmào** N style; scene

**风平浪静 fēngpínglàngjìng** EXP the wind has calmed down and the waves have subsided

**风气 fēngqì** N general mood, atmosphere; common practice · MW 种

**风趣 fēngqù** N·ADJ humor, wit; funny

有时傻瓜有点风趣。 *Sometimes ShaGua is a little funny.*

**风扇 fēngshàn** N electric fan · MW 台

**风声 fēngshēng** N sound of the wind; news; rumor

傻瓜听到了罢工的风声。 *ShaGua has heard rumors of an impending strike.*

**风俗 fēngsú** N custom, mores · MW 个

**风速 fēngsù** N wind speed

**风调雨顺 fēngtiáoyǔshùn** EXP favorable weather/conditions

**风头 fēngtou** N situation, trend; showoff · MW 个

**风险 fēngxiǎn** N danger, risk, hazard · MW 个

**风味 fēngwèi** N distinctive style, flavor, local color · MW 种

这是南方风味的小吃。 *This snack has a uniquely southern flavor.*

**风向 fēngxiàng** N wind direction; situation, the way the wind is blowing · MW 个

**风雨 fēngyǔ** N wind and rain; weather; hardship · MW 场、阵

**风雨无阻 fēngyǔwúzǔ** EXP stopped by neither wind nor rain; regardless of weather conditions

傻瓜上班风雨无阻。 *Neither wind nor rain can stop ShaGua from going to work.*

**风云 fēngyún** N wind and clouds; precarious situation, turmoil

**风疹 fēngzhěn** N rubella

**风筝 fēngzhēng** N kite · MW 只

### RELATED WORDS

## 195 办 辦　U+529E　TM 6　FM 丿

**bàn** V to do, to handle, to manage, to tackle; to attend to, to run; to set up, to get (something) ready, to stage; to punish, to bring to justice

这事让他去办。 *Let him handle this.*

办企业 *to set up a business*

办年货 *New Year shopping*

把这坏蛋办了 *to punish the bad person*

**办案 bàn'àn** V to handle a case

傻瓜办案非常公正。 *ShaGua handles cases very justly.*

**办报 bànbào** V to run a newspaper

**办到 bàndào** V to accomplish, to get (something) done

傻瓜总是说到办到。 *ShaGua always does what he says.*

**办法 bànfǎ** N way, means · MW 个

**办公 bàngōng** V to work, to handle official business

**办公厅 bàngōngtīng** N general office; office building · MW 间

**办理 bànlǐ** V to handle, to conduct, to transact

**办事 bànshì** V to work

傻瓜办事很诚实。 *ShaGua handles affairs very honestly.*

**办学 bànxué** V to run a school

### RELATED WORDS

| | | |
|---|---|---|
| 举办 674 | 法办 686 | 查办 741 |
| 包办 836 | 承办 972 | 创办 1131 |
| 帮办 1583 | 停办 1588 | 置办 1651 |
| 照办 1846 | | |

---

## 196 央    U+592E    TM **6** FM 丿

**yāng** N,V center; to entreat, to beg, to plead; to end, to terminate

**央告 yānggao** V to beg, to ask earnestly

**央求 yāngqiú** V to beg, to plead, to ask earnestly

**央求**傻瓜开后门，往往是徒劳的。
*Begging ShaGua to "open a back door" is usually a useless endeavor.*

### RELATED WORDS

中央 86      中共中央 86

---

## 197 夹 夾    U+5939    TM **6** FM 丿

**jiā** V·N to get hold of; to place in between, to carry under one's arm; to mix, to mingle; clip, clamp; folder

**jiá** ADJ double-layered, lined

**夹板 jiābǎn** N splint; clamp, vise · MW 层

**夹层 jiācéng** N double layer; sandwich · MW 个

**夹带 jiādài** V·N to smuggle, to carry secretly; smuggled note

**夹缝 jiāfèng** N crack, crevice · MW 条

**夹攻 jiāgōng** V to attack from both sides, to flank

今年傻瓜可能要受到两党的**夹攻**。*ShaGua may be attacked by both parties this year.*

**夹击 jiājī** V to attack from both sides, to flank

**夹具 jiājù** N pliers; clamp · MW 副、套

**夹生 jiāshēng** ADJ half-cooked

**夹馅 jiāxiàn** N stuffed with filling (of food)

**夹心 jiāxīn** N sandwich; stuffed with filling

**夹杂 jiāzá** V to be mixed/mingled with

**夹子 jiāzi** N clip, clamp; folder; wallet · MW 个

**夹袄 jiá'ǎo** N lined jacket

### RELATED WORDS

发夹 311      弹夹 1763

---

## 198 灰    U+7070    TM **6** FM 丿

**huī** N·ADJ ash; dust, powder; lime; gray; disheartened, discouraged

**灰暗 huī'àn** ADJ gloomy, murky

天空很**灰暗**，马上要下雨了。*The sky is very gloomy; it will rain soon.*

**灰白 huībái** ADJ grayish white; pale, ashen

**灰尘 huīchén** N dust, dirt

椅子上覆盖了一层**灰尘**。*The chair was coated with dust.*

**灰浆 huījiāng** N mortar (masonry) · MW 团

**灰烬 huījìn** N ashes · MW 堆

**灰冷 huīlěng** ADJ downhearted, discouraged

**灰溜溜 huīliūliū** EXP gloomy, dejected

**灰绿色 huīlǜsè** N grayish green

**灰蒙蒙 huīmēngmēng** EXP overcast; dusky

**灰色 huīsè** N gray; pessimistic, melancholy

**灰心 huīxīn** V to lose heart, to be discouraged

不要**灰心**，每个人都有转运的一天。*Don't lose hope; everyone has his day.*

### RELATED WORDS

| | | |
|---|---|---|
| 石灰 144 | 抹灰 571 | 洋灰 689 |
| 泥灰 1164 | 骨灰 1543 | 银灰 1607 |

---

## 199 尤    U+5C24    TM **6** FM 丿

**yóu** ADJ·ADV·V outstanding; particularly, especially; to complain, to blame others

**尤其 yóuqí** ADV especially, particularly

这个花园很漂亮，**尤其**是春天的时候。
*This garden is very beautiful, especially in spring.*

### RELATED WORD

怨天尤人 1792

---

## 200 历 歷    U+5386    TM **6** FM 丿

**lì** V·ADJ·ADV·N to experience, to undergo, to pass through; previous, past; covering all, one by one; calendar, almanac

**历程 lìchéng** N course, process · MW 个

**历次 lìcì** N each successive, all previous occasions/events

**历代 lìdài** N past generations/dynasties

**200** 历 **lì** (continued)

历法 **lìfǎ** N calendar

历来 **lìlái** ADV always

傻瓜**历来**主张孩子应该接受大学教育。
*ShaGua always believed that kids should go to college.*

历历 **lìlì** ADJ distinct, clear

历年 **lìnián** N over the years

历任 **lìrèn** V to hold jobs successively, to hold jobs one after another

历时 **lìshí** V to last/take (time)

你知道奥林匹克运动会将**历时**多少天吗？
*Do you know how many days the Olympic Games will last?*

历史 **lìshǐ** N history, past records

**RELATED WORDS**

| | | | |
|---|---|---|---|
| 日历 96 | 公历 103 | 旧历 165 | 年历 182 |
| 月历 190 | 来历 260 | 农历 423 | 阳历 808 |
| 皇历 858 | 阴历 1041 | 经历 1110 | 学历 1155 |
| 夏历 1195 | 病历 1327 | 阅历 1727 | 简历 1796 |

**201** 压 壓    U+538B    TM **6** FM 丿

**yā** V to press, to push down; to hold down, to control, to pressure, to pigeonhole

压倒 **yādǎo** V to overwhelm, to overpower, to prevail over

压服 **yāfú** V to force (someone) to submit

压价 **yājià** V to force a price down

压惊 **yājīng** V to help (someone) get over a shock

压境 **yājìng** V to press on the border (of enemy troops)

压垮 **yākuǎ** V to collapse under pressure

快把书包拿下来，它真要把孩子**压垮**了。*Get the bundle off the child's back; it's really weighing him down.*

压力 **yālì** N pressure; burden · MW 股

压裂 **yāliè** V to crack/split open

压平 **yāpíng** V to flatten

压迫 **yāpò** V to oppress; to put pressure on

压气 **yāqì** V to calm (someone's) anger

压强 **yāqiáng** N pressure

压岁钱 **yāsuìqián** N gift of money given to children at the lunar New Year

给孩子**压岁钱**是中国人过年的风俗。
*It is customary to give children money as a lunar New Year gift in China.*

压缩机 **yāsuōjī** N compressor, compactor · MW 台

压抑 **yāyì** V·ADJ to inhibit, to suppress; depressing

低矮的屋顶给人一种**压抑**的感觉。*The room's low ceiling gave a feeling of confinement.*

压榨 **yāzhà** V to press/squeeze (juice, oil, etc.)

压制 **yāzhì** V to suppress, to stifle, to clamp down, to repress

**RELATED WORDS**

| | | |
|---|---|---|
| 水压 159 | 气压 185 | 电压 263 |
| 血压 306 | 扣压 401 | 加压 463 |
| 低压 618 | 挤压 795 | 积压 1097 |
| 黑压压 1389 | 降压 1416 | 欺压 1423 |
| 减压 1487 | 眼压 1570 | 高压 1611 |
| 镇压 1872 | 高血压 1611 | |

**202** 厌 厭    U+538C    TM **6** FM 丿

**yàn** V to be disgusted with, to be fed up with, to detest; to be bored with

厌烦 **yànfán** V to be sick of, to be fed up with

傻瓜太太**厌烦**单调的生活。*Mrs. ShaGua is fed up with the humdrum of daily life.*

厌倦 **yànjuàn** V to be weary/tired of

厌世 **yànshì** V to be world-weary, to be pessimistic

厌恶 **yànwù** V to abhor, to loathe, to be disgusted with; to be allergic to

傻瓜非常**厌恶**那些好吃懒做的人。*ShaGua is disgusted with people who care for nothing but eating.*

**RELATED WORD**

讨厌 500

**203** 尖    U+5C16    TM **6** FM 丿

**jiān** ADJ·N pointed, tapering; sharp, acute, keen; high-pitched, shrill, piercing; acrimonious, caustic, biting; stingy; point; tip; top; best, cream of the crop

她眼睛很**尖**。*Her eyes are very sharp.*

**尖**叫 *scream*

顶**尖** *tip*

拔**尖** *top*

尖兵 **jiānbīng** N pioneer, trailblazer; vanguard · MW 个、名、队

尖端 **jiānduān** N·ADJ point; peak; cutting edge; most advanced

尖角 **jiānjiǎo** N sharp edge · MW 个

尖叫 **jiānjiào** V to scream, to shriek
这女孩痛得尖叫起来。 *The girl was screaming with pain.*

尖刻 **jiānkè** ADJ acrimonious, caustic, biting
他尖刻的话使人哑口无言。 *He silenced others with his biting sarcasm.*

尖锐 **jiānruì** ADJ sharp, penetrating, keen, intense, acute; shrill

尖塔 **jiāntǎ** N steeple, spire · MW 座

尖头 **jiāntóu** N sharp end, pike · MW 个

尖子 **jiānzi** N best · MW 个、名

**RELATED WORDS**

| | | |
|---|---|---|
| 刀尖 31 | 爪尖儿 52 | 舌尖 298 |
| 针尖 477 | 顶尖 724 | 拔尖 791 |
| 冒尖 989 | 眼尖 1570 | 脚尖 1804 |
| 嘴尖 1984 | 牛角尖 51 | |

---

**204** 尘 塵   U+5C18   TM **6** FM 丿

**chén** N dust, dirt; cloud of fine, dry particles; material world; earth

尘土 *dust*

尘世 *this world*

尘埃 **chén'āi** N dust · MW 粒、层

尘暴 **chénbào** N dust devil, dust storm · MW 场

尘垢 **chéngòu** N dust and dirt · MW 层

尘粒 **chénlì** N dust particle · MW 粒、层

尘雨 **chényǔ** N dust shower · MW 阵

**RELATED WORDS**

| | | |
|---|---|---|
| 风尘仆仆 194 | 灰尘 198 | 红尘 474 |
| 砂尘 733 | 吸尘 776 | 吸尘器 776 |
| 防尘 1040 | 烟尘 1177 | 浮尘 1342 |
| 粉尘 1363 | 除尘 1418 | 望尘莫及 1622 |

---

**205** 亿 億   U+4EBF   TM **6** FM 丿

**yì** NUM hundred million

亿万 **yìwàn** NUM hundreds of millions, millions and millions

亿万富翁 **yìwànfùwēng** N multimillionaire, billionaire · MW 个、名

亿万年 **yìwànnián** N eon

---

**206** 付   U+4ED8   TM **6** FM 丿

**fù** V to pay; to hand/turn over, to commit

付方 **fùfāng** N credit side (of a balance sheet)

付款 **fùkuǎn** V to pay, to disburse
我可以用信用卡付款吗？ *May I pay with a credit card?*

付讫 **fùqì** V to be paid off

付钱 **fùqián** V to pay money

付清 **fùqīng** V to pay off, to pay in full
你先付50元，余款月底付清。 *Pay me 50 yuan as a down payment and the rest at the end of the month.*

付息 **fùxī** V to pay interest

付印 **fùyìn** V to submit for publication; to go to press

**RELATED WORDS**

| | | |
|---|---|---|
| 止付 41 | 支付 92 | 交付 222 |
| 对付 254 | 托付 563 | 偿付 1440 |
| 还本付息 714 | | |

---

**207** 仙   U+4ED9   TM **6** FM 丿

**xiān** N immortal; celestial being

仙鹤 **xiānhè** N Siberian white crane · MW 只

仙境 **xiānjìng** N fairyland, fantasyland · MW 处
美丽的桂林山水有如仙境。 *Guilin is so beautiful that it looks like a fairyland.*

仙女 **xiānnǚ** N fairy; angel, female celestial being · MW 个

仙人掌 **xiānrénzhǎng** N cactus · MW 棵

仙逝 **xiānshì** V to die, to pass away

**RELATED WORDS**

| | |
|---|---|
| 八仙 6 | 神仙 1191 |

---

**208** 代   U+4EE3   TM **6** FM 丿

**dài** N·V generation; dynasty; historical period, times, era; to take the place of, to act on behalf of, to act as

代办 **dàibàn** N·V diplomatic representative; to take over, to be an agent, to act for · MW 个、名

代办所 **dàibànsuǒ** N agency · MW 个、间

代表 **dàibiǎo** N·V representative, delegate; to represent, to stand in for · MW 个、位、名

**208 代 dài** (continued)

傻瓜被选为**代表**参加年会。
*ShaGua was selected as a delegate to the annual conference.*

**代表大会 dàibiǎodàhuì** N congress, representative assembly · MW 届、次

**代词 dàicí** N pronoun · MW 个

**代购 dàigòu** V to buy on behalf of

**代号 dàihào** N code name; alias · MW 个

**代换 dàihuàn** V to substitute

**代价 dàijià** N price/cost (of doing something at the expense of something else) · MW 个

**代理 dàilǐ** V·N to be authorized to act on behalf of; representative, agent · MW 个、名

这个**代理**在**代**表他的委托人说话。*The agent spoke on behalf of his boss.*

**代码 dàimǎ** N code · MW 个、组

**代售 dàishòu** V to be commissioned to sell

**代数 dàishù** N algebra

**代替 dàitì** V to substitute for, to take the place of

在这个食谱中, 可用人造黄油**代替**奶油。
*Margarine can be used instead of butter in this recipe.*

**代销 dàixiāo** V to sell as an agent, to sell on commission

**代谢 dàixiè** V to supersede, to replace; to metabolize

**代用 dàiyòng** V to substitute

RELATED WORDS

| | |
|---|---|
| 古代 154 | 世代 163 |
| 年代 182 | 历代 200 |
| 交代 222 | 后代 310 |
| 当代 335 | 取代 520 |
| 时代 586 | 近代 716 |
| 现代化 975 | 现代 975 |
| 替代 1430 | 朝代 1686 |
| 划时代 476 | 取而代之 520 |
| 新陈代谢 1638 | 第一代 1695 |
| 四个现代化 271 | |

RELATED WORDS

| | | |
|---|---|---|
| 文件 70 | 几件 115 | 元件 138 |
| 计件 240 | 收件人 282 | 抄件 405 |
| 条件 598 | 证件 705 | 备件 845 |
| 信件 869 | 软件 889 | 要件 969 |
| 事件 987 | 邮件 1046 | 组件 1106 |
| 案件 1321 | 急件 1426 | 硬件 1524 |
| 部件 1636 | 零件 1640 | 配件 1647 |
| 密件 1730 | 器件 1963 | 无条件 139 |
| 够条件 1808 | 电子邮件 263 | 垃圾邮件 399 |

---

**210 价 價**  U+4EF7　TM 6 FM 丿

**jià** N price; value

**价格 jiàgé** N price · MW 个

那件家具**价格**很低。*The price of that piece of furniture is very low.*

**价款 jiàkuǎn** N cost · MW 笔

**价目 jiàmù** N marked/sticker price · MW 个

**价钱 jiàqian** N price · MW 个

**价值 jiàzhí** N value, worth

RELATED WORDS

| | | |
|---|---|---|
| 半价 127 | 无价之宝 139 | 压价 201 |
| 代价 208 | 计价 240 | 买价 248 |
| 出价 258 | 比价 279 | 作价 326 |
| 市价 332 | 议价 350 | 折价 408 |
| 估价 456 | 讨价还价 500 | 卖价 524 |
| 身价 604 | 定价 666 | 实价 668 |
| 单价 672 | 差价 673 | 评价 706 |
| 还价 714 | 包价 836 | 重价 839 |
| 物价 883 | 底价 916 | 要价 969 |
| 货价 1061 | 特价 1094 | 售价 1266 |
| 原价 1273 | 总价 1330 | 削价 1366 |
| 票价 1367 | 跌价 1422 | 等价 1437 |
| 减价 1487 | 询价 1500 | 虚价 1534 |
| 牌价 1597 | 廉价 1615 | 涨价 1738 |
| 市场价格 332 | 到岸价格 737 | 最低价 1541 |
| 离岸价 1614 | | |

---

**209 件** U+4EF6　TM 6 FM 丿

**jiàn** N·MW correspondence; [measure word for individual matters/items (workpiece, letter, document, etc.)]

傻瓜买了一**件**家具。*ShaGua bought a piece of furniture.*

**件数 jiànshù** N number of pieces

---

**211 任** U+4EFB　TM 6 FM 丿

**rèn** V·N·CONJ to appoint, to assign; to take (a job); to let, to allow; office, official post; term of office; responsibility; no matter

他**任**院长。*He was appointed dean.*

**任**她购买。*Let her buy whatever she wants.*

**任何 rènhé** PRON any; whoever, whatever

有人认为傻瓜傻，有人认为不傻；但**任**何人都说傻瓜诚实。 *Some people think that ShaGua is dumb and some don't, but everyone thinks he is honest.*

**任劳任怨** rènláorènyuàn  EXP  to work hard despite criticism

**任免** rènmiǎn  V  to make appointments and dismissals

**任命** rènmìng  V  to appoint

**任凭** rènpíng  CONJ·V  no matter what/how, despite; to allow

**任期** rènqī  N  term of office, tenure ·  MW  个

**任人唯亲** rènrénwéiqīn  EXP  to appoint (someone) by favoritism

**任务** rènwu  N  task, assignment; quota; mission ·  MW  个

学生的**任务**是学习。 *A student's mission is to learn.*

**任性** rènxìng  ADJ  headstrong, willful, uninhibited

**任意** rènyì  ADV  arbitrarily, at will; randomly

**任用** rènyòng  V  to appoint, to assign

**任职** rènzhí  V  to hold (a position, an office)

**任重道远** rènzhòngdàoyuǎn  EXP  to shoulder a heavy responsibility (LIT a heavy load and a long road)

### RELATED WORDS

| | | |
|---|---|---|
| 主任 124 | 历任 200 | 听任 414 |
| 责任 525 | 责任制 525 | 委任 594 |
| 担任 789 | 重任 839 | 信任 869 |
| 首任 924 | 放任 964 | 现任 975 |
| 接任 1405 | 留任 1582 | 离任 1614 |
| 常任 1733 | 就任 1836 | 班主任 730 |

---

## 212 伏  U+4F0F  TM 6  FM 丿

**fú**  V·N  to bend/lean over; to fall; to subside, to go down; to hide, to conceal; to admit (defeat, guilt); to subdue, to tame; height of summer, hot summer days; volt

**伏笔** fúbǐ  N  hint/foreshadowing (of what is to come in a literary work) ·  MW  个

**伏法** fúfǎ  V  to be executed

**伏击** fújī  V  to ambush

他在一场**伏击**战中死了。 *He died in an ambush.*

**伏暑** fúshǔ  N  hot season ·  MW  个

**伏特** fútè  MW  [measure word for volts]

**伏贴** fútiē  ADJ  obedient, submissive; content

### RELATED WORDS

| | | |
|---|---|---|
| 三伏 9 | 埋伏 1002 | 降伏 1416 | 起伏 1421 |

---

## 213 休  U+4F11  TM 6  FM 丿

**xiū**  V  to stop, to cease; to rest; to divorce one's wife and send her home; don't

**休**想。 *Don't even think about it.*

**休会** xiūhuì  V  to adjourn

**休假** xiūjià  V  to take a vacation

医生竭力劝傻瓜去**休假**。 *The doctor strongly recommended that ShaGua take a vacation.*

**休克** xiūkè  V  to shock

**休眠** xiūmián  V  to be dormant

**休妻** xiūqī  V  to divorce one's wife

**休息厅** xiūxītīng  N  waiting room ·  MW  个、间

**休息** xiūxi  V  to take a breather, to rest

医生告诉傻瓜要好好**休息**。 *The doctor told ShaGua that he was in need of a good rest.*

**休闲** xiūxián  V  to have a leisurely life

**休学** xiūxué  V  to drop out of school

**休养** xiūyǎng  V  to recuperate, to convalesce

**休业** xiūyè  V  to suspend business

**休战** xiūzhàn  V  to call for a truce/cease-fire

**休止** xiūzhǐ  V  to stop, to cease

### RELATED WORDS

| | | | |
|---|---|---|---|
| 厂休 7 | 午休 48 | 全休 172 | 罢休 1215 |
| 退休 1508 | | | |

---

## 214 伙  夥  U+4F19  TM 6  FM 丿

**huǒ**  N·V·MW  meals, board; partner, mate; partnership, company; group, crowd; to combine, to join; [measure word for groups/bands of people, usually with a negative connotation]

**伙伴** huǒbàn  N  companion, partner, associate, buddy ·  MW  个、名、群

傻瓜有个很能干的**伙伴**，把一切打理得井井有条。 *ShaGua has a very able partner who organizes everything for him.*

**伙房** huǒfáng  N  kitchen (in a school, a factory, etc.) ·  MW  间

**伙计** huǒjì  N  partner; shop assistant, clerk; waiter ·  MW  个、名

**伙食** huǒshí  N  food/meals served in a cafeteria/workplace ·  MW  餐、顿

**伙食**费是每人20美元，包三个早餐和两顿晚餐。 *The meal plan is $20 per person for three breakfasts and two suppers.*

**214 伙 huǒ** (continued)

**伙同 huǒtóng** V to be in collusion with

**RELATED WORDS**

| | | |
|---|---|---|
| 入伙 5 | 大伙儿 20 | 小伙子 61 |
| 合伙 296 | 同伙 541 | 拆伙 572 |
| 家伙 1315 | 好家伙 627 | |

---

**215 化**    U+5316    TM **6** FM 丿

**huà** V·N to change, to turn, to transform, to convert; to melt, to dissolve; to burn up; to digest; to civilize; chemistry

**化冻 huàdòng** V to thaw, to defrost
在切牛肉之前, 应该让牛肉**化冻**。 *Before you slice beef, you should defrost it first.*

**化肥 huàféi** N chemical fertilizer · MW 包

**化工 huàgōng** N chemical industry

**化脓 huànóng** V to fester

**化身 huàshēn** N embodiment, personification, incarnation; reincarnation · MW 个

**化石 huàshí** N fossil; remains · MW 块

**化学 huàxué** N chemistry

**化学分析 huàxuéfēnxī** V to conduct a chemical analysis

**化妆 huàzhuāng** V to put on makeup
这个姑娘从来不**化妆**。 *This girl never wears makeup.*

**化装 huàzhuāng** V to dress up, to put on a costume, to disguise oneself

**RELATED WORDS**

| | |
|---|---|
| 文化 70 | 文化界 70 |
| 火化 72 | 丑化 85 |
| 归化 166 | 分化 173 |
| 奴化 328 | 优化 447 |
| 异化 539 | 同化 541 |
| 变化 653 | 美化 671 |
| 进化 713 | 固化 760 |
| 软化 889 | 转化 1111 |
| 净化 1159 | 恶化 1196 |
| 毒化 1211 | 化 1269 |
| 纯化 1290 | 消化 1343 |
| 液化 1344 | 钙化 1462 |
| 退化 1508 | 造化 1515 |
| 硬化 1524 | 量化 1544 |
| 催化 1592 | 催化剂 1592 |
| 矮化 1598 | 绿化 1707 |
| 溶化 1744 | 简化 1796 |
| 简化汉字 1796 | 演化 1821 |
| 僵化 1864 | 腐化 1879 |
| 强化 1896 | 弱化 1897 |
| 激化 1955 | 正常化 76 |
| 公开化 103 | 社会化 504 |
| 机械化 577 | 现代化 975 |
| 数字化 1637 | 简单化 1796 |
| 千变万化 19 | 四个现代化 271 |

---

**216 刊**    U+520A    TM **6** FM 丿

**kān** V·N to publish; to print, to engrave; to correct; publication, periodical

**刊登 kāndēng** V to publish (in a periodical)
他写的小说就**刊登**在这本杂志上。 *The short story he wrote was published by this magazine.*

**刊物 kānwù** N publication, periodical, journal · MW 本

**刊载 kānzǎi** V to publish (in a periodical)

**RELATED WORDS**

| | | |
|---|---|---|
| 丛刊 123 | 专刊 155 | 月刊 190 |
| 书刊 264 | 会刊 295 | 校刊 802 |
| 报刊 1010 | 周刊 1068 | 特刊 1094 |
| 期刊 1574 | 增刊 1849 | 双月刊 146 |
| 双周刊 146 | | |

---

**217 处 處**    U+5904    TM **6** FM 丿

**chǔ** V to get along; to be situated in; to deal with, to manage, to handle; to penalize, to punish

   **相处** *to get along*

**chù** N place, point; department, office

   **处所** *place*

   **人事处** *Human Resources Department*

**处罚 chǔfá** V to penalize, to punish
傻瓜市长违章停车, 受到警察**处罚**。 *Mayor ShaGua was punished by the police for parking in the wrong place.*

**处方 chǔfāng** N prescription · MW 个

**处境 chǔjìng** N plight, unfavorable situation/circumstances · MW 个

**处决 chǔjué** V to put to death, to execute; to decide

**处理 chǔlǐ** V to solve (a problem); to deal with, to handle; to sell at a reduced price; to discipline, to punish; to treat (by a special process)
傻瓜有要事要**处理**, 所以迟到了。 *ShaGua had a matter of importance to deal with, so he was late for an appointment.*

处女 chǔnǚ ⟨N⟩ virgin, maiden · ⟨MW⟩ 个、位、名

处世 chǔshì ⟨V⟩ to conduct oneself, to behave

处死 chǔsǐ ⟨V⟩ to put to death, to execute

处于 chǔyú ⟨V⟩ to be in a position/condition; to stand in

处置 chǔzhì ⟨V⟩ to deal with, to arrange, to handle, to treat; to punish

处处 chùchù ⟨ADV⟩ everywhere, in all aspects
傻瓜在工作中总是试图**处处**领先他人。
*ShaGua always tries to get ahead of others in any way possible in his work.*

处长 chùzhǎng ⟨N⟩ head of a department / an office · ⟨MW⟩ 个、名

### RELATED WORDS

| | | |
|---|---|---|
| 长处 93 | 去处 157 | 共处 164 |
| 出处 258 | 四处 271 | 坏处 280 |
| 用处 313 | 住处 324 | 此处 416 |
| 判处 507 | 苦处 555 | 好处 627 |
| 到处 737 | 相处 805 | 论处 947 |
| 难处 974 | 益处 1153 | 害处 1319 |
| 深处 1345 | 热处理 1390 | 短处 1452 |
| 错处 1715 | 痛处 1725 | 调处 1749 |
| 随处 1911 | 术后处理 91 | 存车处 438 |
| 借书处 1087 | 售票处 1266 | |

---

**218 外**     U+5916    TM **6** FM 丿

wài ⟨N·ADJ·ADV⟩ relative of one's mother; outsider, other; outside, outer, exterior; foreign, abroad; not closely related; unofficial, informal; besides, in addition, outward

见**外** *to consider someone an outsider*

屋**外** *outside the house*

外币 wàibì ⟨N⟩ foreign currency · ⟨MW⟩ 笔

外边 wàibian ⟨N⟩ outside; outer surface, exterior; abroad
他们在图书馆**外边**见面。*They met outside the library.*

外表 wàibiǎo ⟨N⟩ exterior; outward appearance
看**外表**傻瓜有点傻，但实际傻不傻，人们有不同看法。*ShaGua looks a bit dumb on the outside, but people disagree about whether he really is.*

外宾 wàibīn ⟨N⟩ foreign guest/visitor · ⟨MW⟩ 个、位、名

外部 wàibù ⟨N⟩ exterior, external

外地 wàidì ⟨N⟩ other parts of the country

外敷 wàifū ⟨V⟩ to apply (ointment, etc.)

外公 wàigōng ⟨N⟩ maternal grandfather · ⟨MW⟩ 个、位

外观 wàiguān ⟨N⟩ appearance, exterior · ⟨MW⟩ 个

外国 wàiguó ⟨N⟩ foreign country · ⟨MW⟩ 个

外行 wàiháng ⟨N·ADJ⟩ nonprofessional, amateur; layman; nonprofessional, lay · ⟨MW⟩ 个

外号 wàihào ⟨N⟩ nickname · ⟨MW⟩ 个
傻瓜是他的**外号**。*ShaGua is his nickname.*

外汇 wàihuì ⟨N⟩ foreign currency · ⟨MW⟩ 笔

外籍 wàijí ⟨N⟩ foreign nationality

外加 wàijiā ⟨V⟩ to add extra; in addition

外交 wàijiāo ⟨N⟩ diplomacy, foreign affairs

外教 wàijiào ⟨N⟩ foreign teacher

外交关系 wàijiāoguānxì ⟨N⟩ foreign/diplomatic relations · ⟨MW⟩ 个

外交谈判 wàijiāotánpàn ⟨V⟩ to negotiate diplomatically

外界 wàijiè ⟨N⟩ outside world

外景 wàijǐng ⟨N⟩ outdoor scene · ⟨MW⟩ 个、处

外科 wàikē ⟨N⟩ surgery; surgical department

外壳 wàiké ⟨N⟩ envelope; outer covering, shell, case · ⟨MW⟩ 个、片

外来 wàilái ⟨ADJ⟩ outside, external; foreign

外力 wàilì ⟨N⟩ external force · ⟨MW⟩ 股

外卖 wàimài ⟨V·N⟩ to order for takeout · ⟨MW⟩ 个

外贸 wàimào ⟨N⟩ foreign trade

外面 wàimian ⟨N⟩ outside, exterior
傻瓜的家在镇子**外面**。*ShaGua's house is situated just outside of town.*

外婆 wàipó ⟨N⟩ maternal grandmother · ⟨MW⟩ 个、位
傻瓜有两个**外婆**，因为傻瓜的**外公**有两个老婆。*ShaGua has two maternal grandmothers, because his maternal grandfather had two wives.*

外侨 wàiqiáo ⟨N⟩ expatriate · ⟨MW⟩ 个、名

外勤 wàiqín ⟨N⟩ fieldwork, work done outside the office; field personnel · ⟨MW⟩ 个、名

外人 wàirén ⟨N⟩ stranger, outsider; foreigner · ⟨MW⟩ 个、名
只要见过一次傻瓜，你就不会把他当**外人**。*Once you've met ShaGua, you won't consider him a stranger.*

外伤 wàishāng ⟨N⟩ injury, wound · ⟨MW⟩ 处

外甥 wàisheng ⟨N⟩ nephew, sister's son · ⟨MW⟩ 个、名

外事 wàishì ⟨N⟩ foreign affairs · ⟨MW⟩ 件

外孙 wàisūn ⟨N⟩ grandson, daughter's son · ⟨MW⟩ 个、名

外逃 wàitáo ⟨V⟩ to flee abroad, to run away

外套 wàitào ⟨N⟩ coat, overcoat · ⟨MW⟩ 件

**218 外 wài** (continued)

**外头 wàitou** N outside, outdoors

**外围 wàiwéi** N·ADJ periphery; peripheral, surrounding

**外文 wàiwén** N foreign language · MW 种
中文是傻瓜懂的唯一的**外文**。*Chinese is the only foreign language ShaGua knows.*

**外屋 wàiwū** N outer room

**外乡 wàixiāng** N another part of the country

**外销 wàixiāo** V to sell abroad / elsewhere in the country

**外形 wàixíng** N appearance, figure, shape · MW 个
这个岛的**外形**呈三角形。*This island is triangular in shape.*

**外星人 wàixīngrén** N alien, extraterrestrial · MW 个、名

**外因 wàiyīn** N external cause · MW 个

**外用 wàiyòng** ADJ for external use

**外语 wàiyǔ** N foreign language · MW 门、种

**外援 wàiyuán** N foreign aid · MW 批、笔、个

**外在 wàizài** ADJ external, extrinsic

**外债 wàizhài** N foreign debt · MW 笔

**外长 wàizhǎng** N foreign minister, secretary of state · MW 个、位、名

**外罩 wàizhào** N outer garment · MW 件

**外传 wàizhuàn** N unofficial biography

**外资 wàizī** N foreign investment/capital · MW 笔、批

**外族 wàizú** N people not of the same clan · MW 个

**外祖父 wàizǔfù** N maternal grandfather · MW 个、位

**外祖母 wàizǔmǔ** N maternal grandmother · MW 个、位

**RELATED WORDS**

**chǎn** V·N to give birth to, to bear, to breed; to produce, to manufacture, to yield; property, estate; output

助产 *midwife*

房地产 *real estate*

特产 *special products*

**产出 chǎnchū** N output

**产地 chǎndì** N manufacturing location, source (of a product) · MW 个

**产儿 chǎn'ér** N newborn baby · MW 个

**产房 chǎnfáng** N delivery room · MW 间

**产妇 chǎnfù** N woman in labor · MW 个、名

**产后 chǎnhòu** N postnatal, postpartum

**产科 chǎnkē** N obstetrical department

**产粮 chǎnliáng** V to produce grain

**产卵 chǎnluǎn** V to lay eggs

**产品 chǎnpǐn** N product, goods, merchandise · MW 个、件
在世界各地都能看到中国制造的**产品**。*Products that are "made in China" can be found in any country in the world.*

**产品成本 chǎnpǐnchéngběn** N cost of goods · MW 笔

**产品目录 chǎnpǐnmùlù** N product directory · MW 本

**产品设计 chǎnpǐnshèjì** N product design

**产权 chǎnquán** N property rights; title

**产生 chǎnshēng** V to produce; to emerge, to come into being; to cause, to bring about

**产物 chǎnwù** N outcome, result, product · MW 个

**产销 chǎnxiāo** N production and marketing

**产业 chǎnyè** N industry; estate, property · MW 个
中国的旅游业已经成为一个很赚钱的**产业**。*Tourism in China has become a very profitable industry.*

**产值 chǎnzhí** N output value · MW 笔

**RELATED WORDS**

| | |
|---|---|
| 出产 258 | 农产品 423 |
| 估产 456 | 妇产医院 465 |
| 私产 471 | 动产 514 |
| 国产 542 | 财产 588 |
| 低产 618 | 临产 771 |
| 物产 883 | 难产 974 |
| 投产 1008 | 特产 1094 |
| 房产 1145 | 总产值 1330 |
| 总产量 1330 | 资产 1335 |
| 破产 1374 | 减产 1487 |
| 流产 1493 | 停产 1588 |
| 新产品 1638 | 超产 1684 |
| 盛产 1694 | 脱产 1803 |
| 遗产 1829 | 增产 1849 |
| 土特产 15 | 房地产 1145 |
| 总资产 1330 | 中国共产党 86 |

---

## 220　方　U+65B9　TM **6** FM ヽ

**fāng** N·ADJ·ADV·MW　direction; side; place, region; party; method, way; prescription; square; upright; honest; just at the time, only, just; then; [measure word for square objects (square meters, cubic meters, etc.)]

南**方** *the south*

敌**方** *enemy side*

处**方** *prescription*

土**方** *cubic meters*

**方案　fāng'àn** N　scheme, plan; project · MW 个

这两个**方案**，你赞成哪个？*Of the two possible plans, which one do you prefer?*

**方便　fāngbiàn** ADJ·V　convenient; appropriate, suitable; to go to the restroom

在你**方便**的时候，我想跟你谈谈。*When it is convenient, I would like to speak with you.*

她去**方便**了。*She went to the restroom.*

**方才　fāngcái** N　just now

**方程　fāngchéng** N　equation · MW 个

**方法　fāngfǎ** N　method, means, way · MW 个

**方格　fānggé** N　square · MW 个

**方格纸　fānggézhǐ** N　graph paper

**方块　fāngkuài** N　cube, block · MW 个

**方略　fānglüè** N　plan

**方面　fāngmiàn** N　aspect, facet; side; field · MW 个

在工作**方面**，傻瓜绝对是一名优秀的员工。*In terms of work, ShaGua was a truly excellent member of the staff.*

**方式　fāngshì** N　way (of life); pattern, style, manner · MW 个、种

**方位　fāngwèi** N　position; point of the compass · MW 个

**方向　fāngxiàng** N　direction, orientation; the way things stand, trend · MW 个

我们走的**方向**对吗？*Are we going in the right direction?*

**方言　fāngyán** N　dialect · MW 种

据说，中国有80种**方言**，但傻瓜说的是什么**方言**，没有人搞得清楚。*They say there are about 80 dialects of Chinese, but what dialect does ShaGua speak? Nobody knows.*

**方针　fāngzhēn** N　policy, guidelines; guiding principle · MW 个

**方正　fāngzhèng** N　upright character

**方子　fāngzi** N　prescription; formula · MW 个

### RELATED WORDS

| | | |
|---|---|---|
| 土方 15 | 千方百计 19 | 大方 20 |
| 女方 57 | 正方 76 | 平方 78 |
| 长方体 93 | 长方形 93 | 立方 125 |
| 己方 132 | 无方 139 | 双方 146 |
| 付方 206 | 处方 217 | 买方 248 |
| 对方 254 | 四方 271 | 北方 278 |
| 比方 279 | 东方 307 | 后方 310 |
| 西方 352 | 多方面 431 | 卖方 524 |
| 他方 616 | 男方 757 | 劳方 764 |
| 地方 772 | 地方 772 | 南方 986 |
| 复方 1059 | 贷方 1062 | 借方 1087 |
| 官方 1136 | 远方 1184 | 秘方 1289 |
| 前方 1329 | 资方 1335 | 药方 1392 |
| 配方 1647 | 想方设法 1769 | 塌方 1903 |
| 魔方 1996 | 半官方 127 | 非官方 378 |
| 诺亚方舟 436 | 四面八方 271 | |

---

## 221　齐　齊　U+9F50　TM **6** FM ヽ

**qí** ADJ　neat, even, together; on a level with

**齐备　qíbèi** ADJ　ready

所有申请材料都**齐备**了。*The application materials are all ready.*

**齐步走　qíbùzǒu** V　to quick march

**齐唱　qíchàng** V　to be in unison

**齐名　qímíng** V　to be equally famous

**齐全　qíquán** ADJ　complete

这家商店货物**齐全**。*This shop has a fine assortment of goods.*

**齐声　qíshēng** ADV　all together, in chorus

**齐头并进　qítóubìngjìn** EXP　to go forward together, to go hand in hand

**221 齐 qí** (continued)

**齐整 qízhěng** ADJ neat, uniform, even

傻瓜的牙不**齐整**。 *ShaGua's teeth are not even.*

**齐奏 qízòu** V to play in unison

**RELATED WORDS**

| 一齐 1 | 找齐 567 | 看齐 841 |
|---|---|---|
| 整齐 1845 | 双管齐下 146 | |

---

**222 交**    U+4EA4    TM **6** FM 丶

**jiāo** V·N to hand in/over, to give up, to deliver; to associate with, to befriend; to cross, to intersect, to meet, to join (of place or time); to arrive at (an hour, a season, etc.); to contact; to have sexual intercourse, to mate; friendship; relationship; business transaction, deal; boundary; mutually, reciprocally, together, simultaneously

交作业 *to hand in one's homework*

知**交** *best friend*

相**交** *to intersect*

性**交** *sexual intercourse*

成**交** *to have a deal*

滑一**交** *to fall down*

**交班 jiāobān** V to hand over to the next shift

**交叉 jiāochā** V to intersect, to cross, to crisscross

两条路在此**交叉**。 *The two roads intersect here.*

**交错 jiāocuò** V to crisscross, to interlace

**交待 jiāodài** V to explain, to make clear; to come to an unpleasant end

中文考不及格没法向老师**交待**。 *Failing the Chinese test is inexplicable to the teacher.*

**交代 jiāodài** V to hand over; to explain, to make clear; to confess (an error, a crime, etc.)

休假之前，傻瓜把工作**交代**得清清楚楚。 *Before leaving his office for vacation, ShaGua gave clear-cut instructions.*

**交底 jiāodǐ** V to say what one's real intentions are, to lay one's cards on the table

**交点 jiāodiǎn** N intersection · MW 个

**交锋 jiāofēng** V to engage in combat; to compete

**交付 jiāofù** V to pay; to deliver, to consign

**交互 jiāohù** ADV mutually; each other, alternately, in turn

**交换 jiāohuàn** V to exchange, to swap, to trade

他用这本书**交换**那本杂志。 *He traded this book for that magazine.*

**交货 jiāohuò** V to deliver goods

**交际 jiāojì** V to socialize, to interact socially

**交接 jiāojiē** V to hand over; to join, to connect, to associate with

**交界 jiāojiè** V to share a border

**交流 jiāoliú** V·N to exchange; to communicate; give-and-take; alternating current

**交配 jiāopèi** V to mate (especially of animals)

**交涉 jiāoshè** V to negotiate

他进行了必要的**交涉**。 *He has conducted the necessary negotiations.*

**交谈 jiāotán** V to talk, to converse, to chat

**交替 jiāotì** V·ADV to alternate; to replace; one after another, taking turns

**交通 jiāotōng** V·N to communicate; to transport; traffic; underground messenger · MW 个

**交往 jiāowǎng** V to associate with; to have contact with

在国际**交往**中，汉语的使用越来越广泛。 *Chinese is used more and more internationally.*

**交易 jiāoyì** N·V deal, trade, business; to bargain · MW 笔、桩

傻瓜从不做台下的**交易**。 *ShaGua has never conducted any deals "under the table."*

**交易所 jiāoyìsuǒ** N stock exchange · MW 间

**交友 jiāoyǒu** V to make friends

**交战 jiāozhàn** V to be at war; to fight a war

**RELATED WORDS**

| 世交 163 | 外交 218 | 外交谈判 218 |
|---|---|---|
| 打交道 289 | 老交情 375 | 私交 471 |
| 性交 498 | 社交 504 | 成交 611 |
| 邦交 636 | 知交 647 | 择交 792 |
| 相交 805 | 杂交 856 | 转交 1111 |
| 断交 1260 | 结交 1291 | 跌交 1422 |
| 移交 1450 | 提交 1554 | 新交 1638 |
| 绝交 1706 | 忘年交 655 | 难打交道 974 |

---

**223 为** 為    U+4E3A    TM **6** FM 丶

**wéi** V·PREP to be; to become; to serve as, to act as, to do, to act, to perform; to take as; to turn into; to help; to defend, to protect; in the interest of, for the purpose of, for the sake of, because of; by [in the passive voice]; as [in a rhetorical question]

一加一**为**二。 *One plus one equals two.*

为人父 *to become someone's father*
"不能" 或 "不为"。 *"Can't" or "don't."*

**wèi** V·PREP to support, to stand for; for, about

为人着想。 *Think about others.*

为难 **wéinán** V·ADJ to make things difficult for, to create difficulties; embarrassed

傻瓜太太为难傻瓜。 *Mrs. ShaGua has placed ShaGua in a difficult position.*

傻瓜感到为难。 *ShaGua was embarrassed.*

为人 **wéirén** V·N to behave, to conduct oneself; behavior

为时过早 **wéishíguòzǎo** EXP premature, too soon

为首 **wéishǒu** V to be headed by; with (someone) as leader

为数 **wéishù** V to amount to

为止 **wéizhǐ** V to continue up to; until

为主 **wéizhǔ** V to attach the most importance to, to give priority to; to rely mainly on

为此 **wèicǐ** ADV for this reason, to this end, in this respect

傻瓜知道错了，愿为此承担责任。 *ShaGua knows he made a mistake and will take responsibility for it.*

为何 **wèihé** ADV why, for what reason

为了 **wèile** PREP for, for the sake of; in order to

为什么 **wèishénme** ADV why, why/how is it that; for what reason

**RELATED WORDS**

| | | |
|---|---|---|
| 以为 101 | 互为因果 135 | 古为今用 154 |
| 因为 270 | 作为 326 | 行为 327 |
| 有为 439 | 洋为中用 689 | 难为情 974 |
| 难为 974 | 下不为例 10 | 习以为常 84 |
| 左右为难 113 | 与人为善 158 | 自以为是 305 |
| 耻与为伍 735 | 无所作为 139 | |

---

**224 关** 關    U+5173    TM **6** FM 丶

**guān** V·N to shut, to close; to turn off; to lock up, to shut in, to imprison; to close down (a business, etc.); to concern, to involve; to give out / draw (pay); customs; barrier; key part, critical/turning point

她把自己关家里。 *She has locked herself inside her home.*

这家工厂关了。 *This factory has closed down.*

这与你有关吗? *Does this concern you?*

把好质量关。 *Check the quality carefully.*

这是一道难关。 *This is an obstacle.*

关闭 **guānbì** V to close, to shut

关灯 **guāndēng** V to turn off the light

关防 **guānfáng** N official seal; security measures · MW 个

关怀 **guānhuái** V to be concerned about

关键 **guānjiàn** N·ADJ crux, key, crucial point · MW 个

谈判正处于关键的阶段。 *Negotiations were at a crucial stage.*

关节 **guānjié** N joint (skeleton); key/crucial link · MW 个

关节炎 **guānjiéyán** N arthritis · MW 种

关口 **guānkǒu** N critical pass/juncture · MW 个

关联 **guānlián** V to be interrelated; to be linked · MW 个

关门 **guānmén** V to close the doors, to shut down; to refuse discussion/consideration; to refuse to admit others

商店七点半关门。 *The store closes at 7:30.*

关卡 **guānqiǎ** N checkpoint; customs · MW 个

关切 **guānqiè** V to be deeply concerned

关税 **guānshuì** N customs duty · MW 笔

关头 **guāntóu** N critical juncture, turning point · MW 个

关系 **guānxì** N·V relationship, connections; to relate to, to impact on · MW 个

傻瓜在中国有许多关系，但他不太使用。 *ShaGua has lots of connections in China, but he doesn't like to use them.*

关心 **guānxīn** V to care about, to be concerned about; to have on one's mind

关于 **guānyú** PREP concerning, regarding, about

电视正在播放一个关于中国的节目。 *A TV show about China is on right now.*

关照 **guānzhào** V to take care of, to keep an eye on; to notify by word of mouth

傻瓜认为自己是弱者，所以特别关照弱势群体。 *ShaGua considers himself weak, so he takes special care of disadvantaged groups.*

关注 **guānzhù** V to follow (an issue) closely; to pay close attention to

**RELATED WORDS**

| | | |
|---|---|---|
| 开关 26 | 无关 139 | 年关 182 |
| 有关 439 | 卖关子 524 | 拉关系 573 |
| 机关 577 | 过关 712 | 相关 805 |
| 没关系 938 | 难关 974 | 把关 1006 |
| 报关 1010 | 海关 1494 | 验关 1529 |
| 外交关系 218 | 生产关系 107 | 主从关系 124 |
| 裙带关系 1752 | 咬紧牙关 780 | 蒙混过关 1654 |

## 225 并    U+5E76   TM **6** FM 丶

**bìng** [V·ADV·CONJ] to combine, to merge, to bring together, to incorporate; side by side; simultaneously; equally; and

**并发 bìngfā** [V] to develop into; to be complicated by

**并肩 bìngjiān** [V·ADV] to stand side by side; alongside, shoulder to shoulder

**并立 bìnglì** [V] to exist side by side; to exist simultaneously

**并联 bìnglián** [V] to have/make a parallel connection

**并列 bìngliè** [V] to stand side by side; to be juxtaposed; to be equal

**并排 bìngpái** [V] to stand side by side; to lie alongside

**并且 bìngqiě** [CONJ] and; also, in addition; besides, furthermore

他被发现有盗窃行为, **并且**被定了罪。 *He was found to be a thief and was condemned.*

**并入 bìngrù** [V] to merge into

**并行 bìngxíng** [V] to run side by side, to run in parallel

**并重 bìngzhòng** [V] to attach equal importance to, to pay equal attention to

**RELATED WORDS**

归并 166     合并 296     吞并 427
齐头并进 221

## 226 米    U+7C73   TM **6** FM 丶

**mǐ** [N·MW] rice; [measure word for meters (unit of length)]

**米尺 mǐchǐ** [N] meter ruler / tape measure · [MW] 把

**米饭 mǐfàn** [N] cooked rice · [MW] 粒、碗

傻瓜每天要吃一、两碗**米饭**, 否则会感觉浑身乏力。 *ShaGua eats a couple of bowls of rice daily; otherwise he feels lethargic.*

**米粉 mǐfěn** [N] rice noodle · [MW] 团、条、碗

**米酒 mǐjiǔ** [N] rice wine · [MW] 口、杯、瓶

**米色 mǐsè** [N] beige, cream-colored

**米汤 mǐtāng** [N] water in which rice has been cooked · [MW] 口、碗

**RELATED WORDS**

玉米 77     玉米花 77     虾米 824
鱼米之乡 843     厘米 847

## 227 羊    U+7F8A   TM **6** FM 丶

**yáng** [N] sheep; goat

**羊肠小道 yángchángxiǎodào** [N] narrow winding road · [MW] 条

**羊羔 yánggāo** [N] lamb; kid · [MW] 只

**羊毛 yángmáo** [N] fleece, wool · [MW] 团

**羊皮 yángpí** [N] sheepskin · [MW] 张

**羊绒 yángróng** [N] cashmere · [MW] 团

**羊肉 yángròu** [N] mutton · [MW] 块

**RELATED WORDS**

山羊 38     牧羊犬 468     替罪羊 1430

## 228 兴 興    U+5174   TM **6** FM 丶

**xīng** [V] to prosper; to be popular; to get up; to start, to begin

**xìng** [N] mood/desire (to do something); interest; enthusiasm

**兴办 xīngbàn** [V] to initiate, to set up

**兴奋 xīngfèn** [V·N·ADJ] to be excited; excitement; exciting

这个好消息使傻瓜很**兴奋**。 *This piece of good news excited ShaGua.*

**兴建 xīngjiàn** [V] to build, to construct

**兴起 xīngqǐ** [V] to rise, to spring up

**兴盛 xīngshèng** [ADJ] prosperous, flourishing, thriving

**兴亡 xīngwáng** [V] to rise and fall, to flourish and decay

**兴旺 xīngwàng** [ADJ] prosperous, flourishing, thriving

**兴许 xīngxǔ** [ADV] perhaps, maybe

**兴高采烈 xìnggāocǎiliè** [EXP] in high spirits, excited, on top of the world

**兴趣 xìngqù** [N] interest

近来, 中国人对古典音乐的**兴趣**又浓厚起来了。 *Interest in classical music in China has recently been revived.*

**兴头 xìngtóu** [N] enthusiasm, interest

**兴致 xìngzhì** [N] interest; mood to enjoy

傻瓜没有**兴致**打牌。 *ShaGua isn't in the mood to play cards.*

**RELATED WORDS**

扫兴 402     余兴 419     振兴 1238
高兴 1611

## 229 庄 莊 U+5E84 TM 6 FM ⟍

**zhuāng** N village; farm

庄户 **zhuānghù** N peasant household · MW 个、家

庄家 **zhuāngjiā** N banker (in a gambling game) · MW 个、名

庄稼 **zhuāngjia** N crops · MW 片

庄严 **zhuāngyán** ADJ stately, dignified, solemn
会议很庄严。*The conference is very solemn.*

庄园 **zhuāngyuán** N manor · MW 个、座

庄重 **zhuāngzhòng** ADJ serious, solemn
会场很庄重。*The conference hall is very solemn.*

**RELATED WORDS**

山庄 38    村庄 410    端庄 1889

## 230 庆 慶 U+5E86 TM 6 FM ⟍

**qìng** V to celebrate

庆典 **qìngdiǎn** N celebration, festive ceremony · MW 个、次
这个城市正在搞周年庆典。*This city is currently having its anniversary celebration.*

庆贺 **qìnghè** V to celebrate; to congratulate

庆祝 **qìngzhù** V to celebrate
市民举行了盛大的庆祝晚会。*People in the city held a great party to celebrate.*

**RELATED WORDS**

国庆 542    喜庆 1531

## 231 穴 U+7A74 TM 6 FM ⟍

**xué** N cave, den; grave; acupuncture point

穴居 **xuéjū** V to live in a cave

穴位 **xuéwèi** N acupuncture point · MW 个

**RELATED WORDS**

孔穴 370    洞穴 1388    太阳穴 53

## 232 心 U+5FC3 TM 6 FM ⟍

**xīn** N heart; mind; core, center; intelligence; thinking; feeling

心爱 **xīn'ài** ADJ beloved, treasured

他写了一首十四行诗, 献给他心爱的人。
*He wrote a sonnet to his beloved.*

心安理得 **xīn'ānlǐdé** EXP to feel justified, to have a clear conscience

心病 **xīnbìng** N worry, anxiety; secret trouble · MW 个、块

心不在焉 **xīnbùzàiyān** EXP absentminded, inattentive

心肠 **xīncháng** N heart; intention, state of mind, mood

心潮 **xīncháo** N surge of emotion, tidal wave of emotion

心得 **xīndé** N what one has learned (from study/work/etc.) · MW 点、篇
他在日记里写了自己的读书心得。*He wrote his thoughts on the passage in his diary.*

心地 **xīndì** N character, moral nature; mind

心电图 **xīndiàntú** N electrocardiogram · MW 次

心烦 **xīnfán** ADJ irritated, annoyed
最让傻瓜心烦的是读大学的大儿子还没有女朋友, 读小学的小儿子已有女朋友了。
*The thing that irritates ShaGua the most is that his older son in college has not yet had a girlfriend, whereas his younger son in elementary school already has one.*

心服 **xīnfú** V to be definitely convinced

心腹 **xīnfù** N trusted subordinate; henchman · MW 个、名

心肝 **xīngān** N conscience; darling · MW 个

心寒 **xīnhán** ADJ bitterly disappointed

心狠 **xīnhěn** ADJ cruel, ruthless

心怀 **xīnhuái** V·N to harbor, to entertain; intention, purpose; state of mind, mood

心慌 **xīnhuāng** V·ADJ to be nervous; flustered
傻瓜在演讲前, 总是感到心慌。*ShaGua always feels nervous before speeches.*

心肌 **xīnjī** N myocardium (heart muscle)

心急 **xīnjí** ADJ impatient, quick-tempered
心急吃不了热豆腐。*It is difficult to eat hot tofu without patience.*

心计 **xīnjì** N calculation, scheming

心焦 **xīnjiāo** ADJ anxious, worried
他们都在心焦地等待最后的消息。*They are all anxiously awaiting the final result.*

心绞痛 **xīnjiǎotòng** N angina

心境 **xīnjìng** N state of mind, mood · MW 个

心口 **xīnkǒu** N pit of the stomach

心理 **xīnlǐ** N psychology, mentality

**232 心 xīn** (continued)

傻瓜常常不能很好地理解孩子的**心理**。
*ShaGua usually struggles to understand his kids' perspectives.*

**心里 xīnlǐ** N in one's heart/mind, at heart

**心里话 xīnlǐhuà** N one's innermost thoughts and feelings, what's on one's mind · MW 句

青少年往往都不太愿意跟父母说**心里话**。
*Teenagers usually don't want to talk with their parents about their innermost thoughts and feelings.*

**心连心 xīnliánxīn** EXP heart to heart

**心灵 xīnlíng** N mind; soul, spirit

**心满意足 xīnmǎnyìzú** EXP to be perfectly content

**心目 xīnmù** N mood, frame of mind

**心情 xīnqíng** N mood, frame of mind

别来烦我, 我的**心情**不好。*Don't bother me; I'm not in a good mood right now.*

**心软 xīnruǎn** ADJ softhearted

傻瓜看见小狗的可怜样, 又**心软**了, 决定收养这第九只狗。*When ShaGua saw the pitiful little puppy, he became softhearted again and adopted his ninth dog.*

**心神 xīnshén** N mind, state of mind

那只小狗让傻瓜**心神**不定。*The puppy made ShaGua feel uneasy.*

**心事 xīnshì** N preoccupation, load on (someone's) mind; heavy heart · MW 桩

傻瓜**心事**重重地坐在沙发上。*ShaGua sat on the sofa with a heavy heart.*

**心思 xīnsi** N thought, idea; mood

他根本没有**心思**看NBA球赛。*He wasn't in the mood to watch professional basketball at all.*

**心酸 xīnsuān** V·ADJ to grieve; sad

**心算 xīnsuàn** V to do arithmetic in one's head

**心疼 xīnténg** V to love dearly; to feel sorry

**心跳 xīntiào** V to have heart palpitations

**心头 xīntóu** N mind; heart

**心细 xīnxì** ADJ careful; scrupulous

**心胸 xīnxiōng** N broadmindedness

**心虚 xīnxū** ADJ guilty; diffident

**心血 xīnxuè** N painstaking effort · MW 番

不要白费了多年的**心血**。*Don't throw away so many years of painstaking effort.*

**心意 xīnyì** N regard; intention, purpose · MW 个

**心脏 xīnzàng** N heart · MW 颗

**心中有数 xīnzhōngyǒushù** EXP to have a pretty good idea of

必须对事情的进展做到**心中有数**。*We need to have a pretty clear idea of how things are being done.*

**RELATED WORDS**

| | | |
|---|---|---|
| 一心 1 | 人心 4 | 三心二意 9 |
| 开心 26 | 寸心 37 | 小心 61 |
| 小心眼儿 61 | 中心 86 | 甘心 95 |
| 手心 104 | 主心骨 124 | 亏心 137 |
| 无心 139 | 专心 155 | 归心似箭 166 |
| 分心 173 | 内心 191 | 夹心 197 |
| 灰心 198 | 关心 224 | 心中有数 232 |
| 坏心眼 280 | 尽心 312 | 用心 313 |
| 当心 335 | 决心 340 | 欢心 366 |
| 民心 388 | 存心 438 | 有心人 439 |
| 伤心 453 | 安心 487 | 死心 510 |
| 同心 541 | 苦心 555 | 呕心 560 |
| 身心 604 | 好心 627 | 知心 647 |
| 良心 656 | 空心 669 | 忧心 693 |
| 担心 789 | 贪心 827 | 重心 839 |
| 信心 869 | 顺心 874 | 放心 964 |
| 忍心 970 | 核心 1026 | 贴心 1038 |
| 真心 1075 | 违心 1185 | 耐心 1210 |
| 狠心 1284 | 谈心 1356 | 粗心 1364 |
| 背心 1380 | 黑心 1389 | 热心人 1390 |
| 热心 1390 | 热心肠 1390 | 圆心 1391 |
| 狼心狗肺 1443 | 童心 1471 | 寒心 1481 |
| 惊心动魄 1489 | 烧心 1504 | 费心 1520 |
| 留心 1582 | 偏心 1587 | 离心 1614 |
| 痴心 1617 | 宽心 1618 | 野心 1685 |
| 痛心 1725 | 掌心 1734 | 满心 1745 |
| 祸心 1754 | 通心粉 1757 | 精心 1832 |
| 醉心 1842 | 疑心 1917 | 操心 1965 |
| 不安心 24 | 不死心 24 | 口是心非 42 |
| 寻开心 358 | 没良心 938 | 胆战心惊 1295 |
| 语重心长 1501 | 挖空心思 1551 | 力不从心 59 |
| 无所用心 139 | 购物中心 1253 | 漫不经心 1887 |

**233　州**　　　　U+5DDE　　　TM **6** FM 丶

**zhōu** N province; state; autonomous prefecture

**州长 zhōuzhǎng** N governor (of a province, a state) · MW 个、位、名

**RELATED WORD**

贵州 985

**234　汇　匯 彙**　　　U+6C47　　　TM **6** FM 丶

**huì** V·N to converge, to gather together; to transfer; to collect; foreign exchange; foreign currency; collection, assemblage

外**汇** *foreign currency*

汇报 **huìbào** V to report, to give an account of
他正在向上级**汇报**调查结果。 *He was reporting the findings of an investigation to his boss.*

汇编 **huìbiān** V to compile, to collect, to put together

汇成 **huìchéng** V to converge

汇兑 **huìduì** V to remit

汇费 **huìfèi** N remittance fee · MW 笔

汇合 **huìhé** V to come together, to meet, to converge

汇集 **huìjí** V to collect, to compile; to converge, to come together

汇款 **huìkuǎn** V to remit money
请通过银行**汇款**给我方。 *Please wire us the money through a bank.*

汇率 **huìlǜ** N exchange rate

汇票 **huìpiào** N money order, bill of exchange · MW 张

汇钱 **huìqián** V to wire money

汇总 **huìzǒng** V to gather, to collect

**RELATED WORDS**

| | | |
|---|---|---|
| 外汇 218 | 电汇 263 | 侨汇 460 |
| 字汇 664 | 信汇 869 | 词汇 1353 |
| 语汇 1501 | 买入汇率 248 | |

---

**235** 汉 漢 U+6C49 TM 6 FM ヽ

**hàn** N Han nationality; man; Chinese language

汉白玉 **hànbáiyù** N white marble · MW 块

汉堡包 **hànbǎobāo** N hamburger · MW 个

汉奸 **hànjiān** N traitor (to China) · MW 个、名

汉语 **Hànyǔ** N Chinese (language)

汉字 **Hànzì** N Chinese characters · MW 个

汉族 **Hànzú** N Han nationality
除了**汉族**, 中华民族还包括55个少数民族。 *The Chinese nation includes 55 national minorities in addition to the Han.*

**RELATED WORDS**

| | | |
|---|---|---|
| 老汉 375 | 武汉 513 | 好汉 627 |
| 醉汉 1842 | 懒汉 1953 | 门外汉 130 |
| 男子汉 757 | 简化汉字 1796 | |

---

**236** 汗 U+6C57 TM 6 FM ヽ

**hàn** N sweat, perspiration

汗斑 **hànbān** N sweat stain · MW 块

汗臭 **hànchòu** N body odor, unpleasant smell of perspiration · MW 股

汗孔 **hànkǒng** N sweat pore · MW 个

汗毛 **hànmáo** N fine hair (on the human body) · MW 根

汗衫 **hànshān** N undershirt, T-shirt; vest · MW 件
傻瓜穿了件白色的**汗衫**。 *ShaGua wore a white T-shirt.*

汗珠子 **hànzhūzi** N beads of sweat · MW 滴、粒

**RELATED WORDS**

| | | |
|---|---|---|
| 出汗 258 | 血汗 306 | 冷汗 494 | 虚汗 1534 |

---

**237** 江 U+6C5F TM 6 FM ヽ

**jiāng** N river

江岸 **jiāng'àn** N riverbank · MW 条
一排竹子沿**江岸**而生。 *There is a line of bamboo trees growing along the riverbank.*

江湖 **jiānghú** N rivers and lakes; all over the country; an itinerant, wanderer

江山 **jiāngshān** N rivers and mountains; land, country; state power
中国的**江山**很美丽。 *There are beautiful rivers and mountains in China.*

江苏 **Jiāngsū** N Jiangsu Province

江西 **Jiāngxī** N Jiangxi Province

**RELATED WORDS**

| | | |
|---|---|---|
| 长江 93 | 走江湖 265 | 珠江 729 |
| 跑江湖 1916 | | |

---

**238** 壮 壯 U+58EE TM 6 FM ヽ

**zhuàng** ADJ·V·N strong; magnificent; to strengthen, to bolster; Zhuang ethnic group in China

壮大 **zhuàngdà** V·ADJ to expand, to grow in strength; well-built

壮胆 **zhuàngdǎn** V to give courage to, to embolden
他一边走路一边唱歌, 为自己在黑暗中行走**壮胆**。 *He sang to give himself courage while he walked in the dark.*

壮观 **zhuàngguān** ADJ spectacular, magnificent
漫天大雪非常**壮观**。 *Whirling snow is quite magnificent.*

**238 壮 zhuàng** (continued)

壮锦 **zhuàngjǐn** N Zhuang (Chuang) brocade · MW 幅

壮举 **zhuàngjǔ** N brave feat, heroic undertaking · MW 个
傻瓜的**壮举**是在车库摆卖时卖了一辆二手车。
*ShaGua's great feat was to sell his old car at a garage sale.*

壮阔 **zhuàngkuò** ADJ vast, grand

壮丽 **zhuànglì** ADJ majestic, magnificent, glorious

壮烈 **zhuàngliè** ADJ heroic, brave

壮年 **zhuàngnián** N prime of life
傻瓜正当**壮年**。*ShaGua is in the prime of his life.*

壮实 **zhuàngshi** ADJ sturdy, robust
傻瓜长得很**壮实**。*ShaGua is built very sturdy.*

壮志 **zhuàngzhì** N high ideal, great aspiration · MW 个

壮族 **Zhuàngzú** N Zhuang (Chuang) ethnic group in Guangxi Zhuang Autonomous Region

### RELATED WORDS

| | | |
|---|---|---|
| 少壮 62 | 气壮山河 185 | 粗壮 1364 |
| 肥壮 1459 | 健壮 1589 | 强壮 1896 |
| 兵强马壮 300 | | |

---

**239** **认** 認   U+8BA4    TM **6** FM 丶

**rèn** V to know, to recognize, to make out; to admit, to accept

认错 **rèncuò** V to admit a mistake

认得 **rènde** V to be acquainted with, to recognize, to know
傻瓜**认得**她, 但想不起她的名字。
*ShaGua recognized her face, but he couldn't remember her name.*

认定 **rèndìng** V to firmly believe, to maintain; to set one's mind to
傻瓜**认定**了的事情是不会轻易改变的。*As soon as ShaGua sets his mind to something, it becomes very difficult to change.*

认购 **rèngòu** V to buy, to subscribe to, to underwrite (public bonds, etc.)

认可 **rènkě** V to approve of, to endorse, to accept, to confirm; to recognize

认领 **rènlǐng** V to claim; to adopt (a child)
傻瓜一直想到中国去**认领**一个孩子。
*ShaGua has always wanted to adopt a child from China.*

认清 **rènqīng** V to see clearly, to recognize

认生 **rènshēng** V to be shy around strangers
这个孩子**认生**。*This child is shy around strangers.*

认识 **rènshi** V·N to know, to understand, to recognize, to be acquainted with; knowledge, understanding
我昨天**认识**了傻瓜的大儿子。*I got acquainted with ShaGua's older son yesterday.*

认输 **rènshū** V to accept a loss, to admit defeat

认账 **rènzhàng** V to acknowledge (a debt, a fault, etc.); to admit (the truth)

认真 **rènzhēn** ADJ·V serious, earnest; to take seriously, to take to heart
这件事需要我们**认真**对待。*The matter demanded our serious attention.*

认证 **rènzhèng** V to authenticate, to attest, to notarize; to approve

认知 **rènzhī** V to acknowledge, to recognize

认字 **rènzì** V to know/learn how to read

认罪 **rènzuì** V to plead guilty

### RELATED WORDS

| | | | |
|---|---|---|---|
| 公认 103 | 否认 362 | 承认 972 | 确认 1762 |

---

**240** **计** 計   U+8BA1    TM **6** FM 丶

**jì** N·V idea, strategy, plan; to calculate, to compute, to count; to plan, to intend; to give thought to, to give consideration to
傻瓜的**计**谋太差。*ShaGua has very bad ideas.*
忽略不**计**。*Forget it; it doesn't matter.*

计程表 **jìchéngbiǎo** N fare meter (in a taxi) · MW 个

计划 **jìhuà** N·V plan, program; to plan · MW 个
变化常常快于**计划**。*Changes often come faster than we can plan for.*

计价 **jìjià** V to determine the value of

计件 **jìjiàn** V to calculate by the piece

计较 **jìjiào** V to argue, to dispute; to discuss, to deliberate

计量 **jìliàng** V to measure, to calculate

计时 **jìshí** V to calculate by time

计时器 **jìshíqì** N timer; clock · MW 个

计数 **jìshù** V to count, to calculate

计算 **jìsuàn** V to count, to calculate, to compute; to consider; to plan, to plot
**计算**机在核查数据的输入是否正确。
*The computer verified whether the data was loaded correctly or not.*

**计算机** jìsuànjī  N  computer · MW 台
**计算器** jìsuànqì  N  calculator · MW 个

**RELATED WORDS**

| | | |
|---|---|---|
| 心计 232 | 共计 164 | 伙计 214 |
| 合计 296 | 巧计 364 | 有计划 439 |

| | | |
|---|---|---|
| 估计 456 | 妙计 467 | 审计 911 |
| 设计 1179 | 总计 1330 | 预计 1528 |
| 统计 1601 | 统计学 1601 | 累计 1653 |
| 诡计 1747 | 斤斤计较 50 | 日程计划 96 |
| 晴雨计 1674 | 千方百计 19 | 产品设计 219 |

---

| 241 | 严 | 嚴 | U+4E25 | TM **7** FM 一 |

**yán** ADJ strict, stern; tight, close; severe; heavy, extreme; father

严办 **yánbàn** V to deal with severely

严惩 **yánchéng** V to punish severely, to trounce

严冬 **yándōng** N severe winter · MW 个

严防 **yánfáng** V to take strict precautions

严格 **yángé** ADJ strict, rigid, stringent, rigorous
这个老师对学生非常**严格**。*The teacher is very strict with his students.*

严谨 **yánjǐn** ADJ meticulous; careful, precise; well-knit

严禁 **yánjìn** V to strictly prohibit

严酷 **yánkù** ADJ stern; cruel, harsh, brutal, ruthless

严厉 **yánlì** ADJ severe, strict; acrimonious
傻瓜给孩子们制定了**严厉**的家规。*ShaGua has devised strict family rules for his kids.*

严密 **yánmì** ADJ tight; well-conceived

严明 **yánmíng** V·ADJ to strictly enforce; firm but fair, strict and impartial

严肃 **yánsù** ADJ serious, stern, strict, solemn, grave
傻瓜面相**严肃**，但内心却有点儿幽默。*ShaGua has a solemn face, but deep down he is funny.*

严刑 **yánxíng** N cruel punishment

严正 **yánzhèng** ADJ firm but fair; solemn and just

严重 **yánzhòng** ADJ serious, grave, critical
这家公司陷入**严重**的财政危机。*This company was in serious financial difficulty.*

**RELATED WORDS**

| 庄严 229 | 戒严 442 | 尊严 1722 |
| 义正词严 22 | | |

---

| 242 | 百 | | U+767E | TM **7** FM 一 |

**bǎi** NUM·ADJ·ADV hundred; numerous; variety, all kinds of; absolutely

百般 **bǎibān** ADV in every possible way, by every means

傻瓜总是对儿子做事的方式**百般**挑剔。
*ShaGua always finds fault with the way his son does anything.*

百倍 **bǎibèi** N hundredfold, hundred times

百分比 **bǎifēnbǐ** N percentage

百分之百 **bǎifēnzhībǎi** ADV absolutely, one hundred percent

百分制 **bǎifēnzhì** N hundred-mark system (used to quantify assessments)

百货 **bǎihuò** N general merchandise · MW 件、批

百里挑一 **bǎilǐtiāoyī** EXP one in a hundred, very select

百年 **bǎinián** N century, one hundred years; lifetime

百万 **bǎiwàn** NUM million; huge amount

百万富翁 **bǎiwànfùwēng** N millionaire · MW 个、位、名

百姓 **bǎixìng** N common people · MW 个、群
战争的受害者是老**百姓**。*Many atrocities are committed against innocent people in wartime.*

百叶窗 **bǎiyèchuāng** N shutter, blind · MW 扇

**RELATED WORDS**

| 二百五 2 | 五百 79 | 半百 127 |
| 老百姓 375 | 千方百计 19 | |

---

| 243 | 可 | | U+53EF | TM **7** FM 一 |

**kě** ADV·CONJ·V very; but, yet; can, may; to approve; to fit, to suit; to be worth

可爱 **kě'ài** ADJ adorable, lovable, likable; lovely
他的小女儿像天使一样**可爱**。*His little daughter is as lovely as an angel.*

可悲 **kěbēi** ADJ lamentable, deplorable, sad

可变 **kěbiàn** ADJ variable

可耻 **kěchǐ** ADJ disgraceful, shameful, ignominious

可贵 **kěguì** ADJ valuable; admirable, praiseworthy
傻瓜最**可贵**的品质是诚实。*ShaGua's most valuable trait is his honesty.*

可恨 **kěhèn** ADJ detestable, abominable, hateful

可靠 **kěkào** ADJ reliable, dependable; truthful
朋友们都认为傻瓜是一个**可靠**的人。*All of his friends think ShaGua is a reliable man.*

可可 **kěkě** N cocoa

可怜 **kělián** ADJ·V pitiful, wretched; to pity; to have compassion for

可能 **kěnéng** N·ADJ·V probability; possible, likely; maybe, perhaps; may

只要有**可能**, 傻瓜总是设法帮助朋友。
*Whenever possible, ShaGua tries to help his friends.*

傻瓜的反应**可能**有点儿慢, 但不愚蠢。
*ShaGua may be a little slow, but he is not stupid.*

可怕 **kěpà** ADJ frightening, terrible, horrible

可是 **kěshì** CONJ·ADV but, yet, however, nevertheless; indeed, really, definitely

这本书很有意思, **可是**太贵了。*This book is very interesting, but it's too expensive.*

可恶 **kěwù** ADJ detestable, abominable, obnoxious

可惜 **kěxī** ADJ regrettable, unfortunate; what a pity, it's too bad

可喜 **kěxǐ** ADJ heartening, gratifying

可笑 **kěxiào** ADJ ridiculous, absurd; funny, laughable

傻瓜有很多**可笑**的行为。*Much of ShaGua's behavior could be seen as ridiculous.*

可行 **kěxíng** ADJ workable, feasible, practicable

可疑 **kěyí** ADJ suspicious, questionable, doubtful

可以 **kěyǐ** V·ADJ can, may; not bad, passable

我**可以**问一个问题吗？*May I ask a question?*

他的中文还**可以**。*His Chinese is all right.*

可意 **kěyì** ADJ gratifying

**RELATED WORDS**

| | | |
|---|---|---|
| 不可 24 | 不可多得 24 | 无可奈何 139 |
| 认可 239 | 宁可 336 | 许可 502 |
| 许可证 502 | 无家可归 139 | 由此可见 148 |
| 必不可少 338 | 牢不可破 488 | 屈指可数 1071 |
| 深不可测 1345 | 急不可待 1426 | 愚不可及 1901 |
| 非…不可 378 | | |

---

**244** 至 U+81F3 TM **7** FM 一

**zhì** V·ADV·ADJ to arrive; to, until; extremely; most

至宝 **zhìbǎo** N most valuable treasure · MW 个

至诚 **zhìchéng** ADJ sincere

至多 **zhìduō** ADV at most, at best, not more than

他每周**至多**工作四十小时。*He works 40 hours a week at the most.*

至高无上 **zhìgāowúshàng** EXP paramount, supreme; sovereign

至今 **zhìjīn** ADV so far, up to now, to date

---

至上 **zhìshàng** ADJ highest, paramount, supreme; sovereign (in status, power, etc.)

至少 **zhìshǎo** ADV at least

傻瓜每天**至少**要把家里的地板擦洗一次。
*ShaGua has to mop the floor at least once a day.*

至死 **zhìsǐ** ADV unto death

至友 **zhìyǒu** N close/intimate friend · MW 个、位、名

至于 **zhìyú** PREP·V as for, as to, as regards; to go so far as to

他太专心读书, **至于**晚餐, 全忘了。*He was absorbed in reading; as for dinner, he completely forgot.*

**RELATED WORDS**

| | | |
|---|---|---|
| 仁至义尽 64 | 以至 101 | 乃至如此 134 |
| 及至 141 | 冬至 178 | 直至 609 |
| 甚至 759 | 周至 1068 | 宾至如归 1141 |
| 截至 1650 | 无微不至 139 | |

---

**245** 页 頁 U+9875 TM **7** FM 一

**yè** N·MW page, leaf; [measure word for pages]

页码 **yèmǎ** N page number · MW 个

页码印在每页纸的右下方。*The page numbers are printed at the bottom right.*

**RELATED WORDS**

| | |
|---|---|
| 册页 614 | 活页 941 |

---

**246** 丙 U+4E19 TM **7** FM 一

**bǐng** N third; third of the Ten Heavenly Stems

丙等 **bǐngděng** N third grade

丙级 **bǐngjí** N grade C

---

**247** 马 馬 U+9A6C TM **7** FM 一

**mǎ** N horse · MW 匹

马鞍形 **mǎ'ānxíng** N shape of a saddle · MW 个

马不停蹄 **mǎbùtíngtí** EXP nonstop; hurried journey with no stops

马大哈 **mǎdàhā** EXP careless, scatterbrained

中文的"**马大哈**"是指做事既马虎又傻乎乎的人。*"Madaha" in Chinese describes a careless and daft person.*

马到成功 **mǎdàochénggōng** EXP to achieve immediate success

**247 马 mǎ** (continued)

**马后炮 mǎhòupào** EXP belated action; advice given in hindsight

傻瓜最讨厌马后炮。 *What ShaGua hates most is advice given in hindsight.*

**马虎 mǎhu** ADJ careless, negligent, sloppy

**马甲 mǎjiǎ** N vest · MW 件

**马脚 mǎjiǎo** N giveaway; (someone's) hidden character

**马克思主义 Mǎkèsīzhǔyì** N Marxism

**马列主义 Mǎlièzhǔyì** N Marxism-Leninism

**马铃薯 mǎlíngshǔ** N potato · MW 个

**马路 mǎlù** N road, street, avenue · MW 条

**马马虎虎 mǎmǎhūhū** EXP so-so

"你最近怎么样？""马马虎虎!" *"How has it been going?" "Just so-so."*

**马匹 mǎpǐ** N horse · MW 匹

**马上 mǎshàng** ADV right away, immediately

请马上离开这儿! *Please leave immediately!*

**马桶 mǎtǒng** N toilet · MW 个

**马戏 mǎxì** N circus · MW 场

RELATED WORDS

| | |
|---|---|
| 牛马 51 | 犬马之劳 54 |
| 风马牛不相及 194 | 走马灯 265 |
| 走马看花 265 | 兵马 300 |
| 罗马 756 | 拍马屁 790 |
| 河马 934 | 跳马 1786 |
| 赛马 1813 | 跑马 1916 |
| 露马脚 1997 | 兵强马壮 300 |

---

**248 买 買** U+4E70 TM **7** FM 一

**mǎi** V to buy, to purchase

**买办 mǎibàn** N purchasing agent · MW 个、名

**买方 mǎifāng** N buyer · MW 个

**买价 mǎijià** N purchase price · MW 个

**买进 mǎijìn** V to buy up; to buy into

**买卖 mǎimai** N business, buying and selling, deal · MW 笔、单

傻瓜在股票买卖中运气不佳, 赔了很多钱。 *ShaGua was unlucky in his stock dealings, and it cost him a lot of money.*

**买入汇率 mǎirùhuìlǜ** N buying rate

**买通 mǎitōng** V to bribe

钱不能买通傻瓜。 *Money can't bribe ShaGua.*

**买下来 mǎixiàlái** V to finalize a purchase

**买主 mǎizhǔ** N customer, buyer · MW 个、名

---

他那房子找到买主没有？ *Has he found a buyer for his house?*

RELATED WORDS

| | | |
|---|---|---|
| 收买 282 | 购买 1253 | 购买力 1253 |
| 寸金难买 37 | | |

---

**249 予** U+4E88 TM **7** FM 一

**yú** PRON I, me

**yǔ** V to give, to grant

授予 *to confer, to grant, to award*

**予以 yǔyǐ** V to give, to grant

公司予以职工优惠股票的购买权。 *The company allows its employees to buy favorable stocks.*

RELATED WORDS

| | | |
|---|---|---|
| 准予 929 | 给予 1292 | 寄予 1619 |

---

**250 弓** U+5F13 TM **7** FM 一

**gōng** N·V bow; shaped like a bow; arch; to bend; to bow

**弓箭 gōngjiàn** N bow · MW 张

**弓弦 gōngxián** N bowstring · MW 条、根

**弓形 gōngxíng** N arc; bow-shaped · MW 个

RELATED WORD

左右开弓 113

---

**251 弄** U+5F04 TM **7** FM 一

**lòng** N lane

**nòng** V to do, to make; to get; to play/fool with; to play tricks, to manipulate

弄水 *to play in water*

弄菜 *to cook*

弄些酒来 *to get some liquor*

捉弄 *to fool with*

**弄堂 lòngtáng** N alley

**弄错 nòngcuò** V to make a mistake, to err

傻瓜一定是弄错了, 才拿了你的字典。 *ShaGua must have taken your dictionary by mistake.*

**弄好 nònghǎo** V to do well

**弄坏 nònghuài** V to ruin, to spoil, to make a mess of

**弄假成真** nòngjiǎchéngzhēn EXP make-believe comes true

**弄僵** nòngjiāng V to result in a deadlock/ stalemate

**弄清** nòngqīng V to clarify, to make clear

**弄虚作假** nòngxūzuòjiǎ EXP to falsify, to commit fraud

**弄脏** nòngzāng V to smear, to stain

**弄糟** nòngzāo V to spoil, to make a mess of

这个大笨蛋，总是把事情**弄糟**。*He always makes a mess of things; he's a prize idiot.*

**RELATED WORDS**

| | | |
|---|---|---|
| 作弄 326 | 卖弄 524 | 玩弄 727 |
| 拨弄 1015 | 捉弄 1239 | 逗弄 1512 |
| 摆弄 1773 | 愚弄 1901 | 搬弄 1943 |
| 搬弄是非 1943 | 挤眉弄眼 795 | 装神弄鬼 1476 |

---

**252　功**　U+529F　TM **7** FM 一

**gōng** N achievement, success, result; skill, work; contribution; merit

**功臣** gōngchén N hero, person who has rendered outstanding service · MW 个、位、名

**功德** gōngdé N merits; charitable deed

**功夫** gōngfu N skill; skill in Chinese martial arts; attainment; time; leisure/spare time · MW 门

问问傻瓜有没有**功夫**去看**功夫**电影.
*Ask ShaGua whether or not he has time to go to the kung fu movies.*

**功绩** gōngjī N contribution · MW 个

**功课** gōngkè N homework, schoolwork · MW 门

他喜欢在图书馆做**功课**。*He likes to do his homework in the library.*

**功劳** gōngláo N contribution; credit · MW 个

**功利** gōnglì N utility; material gain

**功率** gōnglǜ N power

**功能** gōngnéng N capability; function · MW 个

**功效** gōngxiào N efficiency; efficacy · MW 个

**功用** gōngyòng N function · MW 个

**RELATED WORDS**

| | | |
|---|---|---|
| 立功 125 | 归功 166 | 气功 185 |
| 内功 191 | 用功 313 | 抓功夫 406 |
| 多功能 431 | 有功 439 | 武功 513 |
| 苦功 555 | 肝功能 650 | 评功 706 |
| 奇功 854 | 记功 946 | 练功 1453 |
| 硬功 1524 | 邀功 1983 | 事倍功半 987 |
| 事半功倍 987 | 基本功 991 | 马到成功 247 |

---

**253　攻**　U+653B　TM **7** FM 一

**gōng** V to attack, to assault; to accuse, to charge, to censure; to study, to major/specialize in

**攻击** gōngjī V to attack, to assault

这是对傻瓜的人身**攻击**。*To do this is to launch a personal attack on ShaGua.*

**攻克** gōngkè V to capture, to seize

**攻势** gōngshì N offensive · MW 个

**攻占** gōngzhàn V to attack and occupy

**RELATED WORDS**

| | |
|---|---|
| 专攻 155 | 夹攻 197 |
| 进攻 713 | 围攻 762 |
| 以毒攻毒 101 | 以子之矛，攻子之盾 101 |

---

**254　对　對**　U+5BF9　TM **7** FM 一

**duì** V·PREP·ADJ·MW to answer; to treat; to bring into contact, to fit one into the other; to suit, to agree, to get along; to compare; to identify; to check; to set/adjust (a clock, etc.); to mix/add (liquids); to divide into halves; at, to, toward; with regard to, concerning; opposite, facing; right, correct; normal; [measure word for pairs, couples]

难以言**对** *hard to answer*

针尖**对**麦芒 *needle against an awl; head to head, toe to toe*

这话是**对**着你来的。*These words are directed at you.*

答**对**了 *answered correctly*

**对**味儿 *to like each other's tastes*

**对**答案 *to exchange/compare answers*

**对**点儿糖 *to add a little bit of sugar*

**对**她哭 *to cry to her*

**对半** duìbàn V to divide half and half, to go halves

**对比** duìbǐ V to contrast, to balance

**对不起** duìbuqǐ V to be sorry; I'm sorry, sorry, excuse me

**对不起**, 我忘了你的名字。*I'm sorry, but I've forgotten your name.*

**对策** duìcè N countermeasure, way to deal with a situation · MW 个

傻瓜的**对策**永远是以不变应万变。*The way ShaGua deals with change is always sticking to a fundamental principle.*

**254 对 duì** (continued)

对称 **duìchèn** ADJ symmetrical

对答 **duìdá** V to answer

对待 **duìdài** V to treat, to handle; to approach

对得起 **duìdeqǐ** V to not let (someone) down; to treat fairly

傻瓜做人的原则是**对得起**朋友。
*ShaGua's principle is to treat friends fairly.*

对等 **duìděng** ADJ reciprocity, equity; equality

对方 **duìfāng** N other side/party, opposite side

对付 **duìfu** V to deal/cope with; to make do, to get along

有时候，傻瓜是一个很难**对付**的人。*ShaGua is a very difficult man to deal with sometimes.*

对号 **duìhào** V to check a number (seat number, serial number, etc.)

对话 **duìhuà** V·N to hold talks; dialog, conversation

对焦 **duìjiāo** V to adjust the focus

对抗 **duìkàng** V to confront, to oppose, to resist

对口 **duìkǒu** V to speak/sing alternately (of two performers); to be appropriate, to fit in with one's specialty, to suit one's taste

对立 **duìlì** V to counter, to oppose; to conflict

对流 **duìliú** V convection

对面 **duìmiàn** N opposite

对手 **duìshǒu** N opponent, adversary · MW 个、名

对谈 **duìtán** N dialog

对头 **duìtóu** ADJ correct, on the right track; normal

你学中文的方法不**对头**。*The way you study Chinese is incorrect.*

对头 **duìtou** N enemy, opponent, adversary · MW 个、名

他是你的**对头**。*He is your opponent.*

对外 **duìwài** ADJ·V external, foreign; to resist foreign aggression

对象 **duìxiàng** N object, target; boyfriend, girlfriend, partner · MW 个、名

对应 **duìyìng** V·ADJ to relate to; corresponding, reciprocal

对于 **duìyú** PREP concerning, regarding

对于他来说，喝两瓶酒根本算不了什么。
*Drinking two bottles of wine was nothing to him.*

对照 **duìzhào** V to compare, to place side by side, to contrast

对证 **duìzhèng** V to verify

对准 **duìzhǔn** V to aim/point at

**RELATED WORDS**

不对 24　　　反对 111　　　作对 326
针对 477　　　找对象 567　　成对 611
面对 721　　　面对面 721　　查对 741
校对 802　　　相对 805　　　核对 1026
敌对 1127　　　配对 1647　　　绝对 1706
人机对话 4　　文不对题 70　　门当户对 130

**255 劝** 勸　　　U+529D　　TM **7** FM 一

**quàn** V to encourage, to urge; to persuade; to advise

劝导 **quàndǎo** V to persuade; to advise, to try to convince

劝告 **quàngào** V·N to advise, to counsel; advice · MW 个

他不把傻瓜的**劝告**当回事儿。*He does not care for ShaGua's advice.*

劝架 **quànjià** V to mediate

劝解 **quànjiě** V to mediate; to reassure

劝酒 **quànjiǔ** V to urge (someone) to drink (alcohol)

劝说 **quànshuō** V to persuade; to advise

劝阻 **quànzǔ** V to dissuade (someone) from; to talk (someone) out of

他一心一意想学工科，谁也**劝阻**不了他。
*He's intent on studying engineering, and no one can talk him out of it.*

**RELATED WORD**

规劝 1098

**256 刑**　　　U+5211　　TM **7** FM 一

**xíng** N punishment, penalty, sentence; corporal punishment; torture

刑场 **xíngchǎng** N gallows; execution ground · MW 个

刑罚 **xíngfá** N punishment, penalty · MW 个

刑法 **xíngfǎ** N criminal law, penal code; corporal punishment; torture · MW 个、部

刑律 **xínglǜ** N criminal law · MW 部

刑期 **xíngqī** N prison term · MW 个

刑事 **xíngshì** N criminal · MW 个

刑讯 **xíngxùn** V to interrogate using torture

**RELATED WORDS**

严刑 241　　　死刑 510　　　徒刑 873
服刑 1457　　　酷刑 1841

## 257 形    U+5F62   TM **7** FM 一

**xíng** N·V   form, shape; body; to appear, to look; to compare, to contrast

**形成 xíngchéng** V   to form, to take shape
父母对小孩个性的**形成**有很大影响。
*Parents have a great influence on the formation of a child's character.*

**形迹 xíngjì** N   movements and expression (of a person), bearing

**形容 xíngróng** V·N   to describe; look, appearance, countenance

**形式 xíngshì** N   form, shape, structure · MW 个
孩子的复数**形式**是孩子们。*The plural form of "child" is "children."*

**形势 xíngshì** N   situation, circumstances · MW 个

**形态 xíngtài** N   form, shape; pattern, configuration

**形体 xíngtǐ** N   figure; body; shape (of the body) · MW 个

**形象 xíngxiàng** N·ADJ   image; form, figure; vivid · MW 个

**形状 xíngzhuàng** N   form, shape; appearance; configuration · MW 个

### RELATED WORDS

## 258 出    齣    U+51FA   TM **7** FM |

**chū** V·MW   to go/come out, to exit, to go abroad; to emerge, to appear; to exceed, to go beyond; to bring/take/give out, to produce, to issue, to publish; to show, to put up; to occur, to happen; to pay out, to expend; [measure word for dramatic pieces]

不**出**两天, 她肯定会来。*She must come within two days.*

**出城** *to leave town*

**出家** *to become a monk*

**出介绍信** *to write a letter of recommendation*

**出书** *to publish a book*

**出版 chūbǎn** V   to publish; to come off the press

**出殡 chūbìn** V   to hold a funeral procession

**出操 chūcāo** V   to exercise, to go outside to exercise

**出差 chūchāi** V   to go away on business
下个星期傻瓜将要**出差**。*ShaGua will be away on business next week.*

**出产 chūchǎn** V·N   to produce, to manufacture; output

**出厂 chūchǎng** V   to leave the factory (of products)

**出场 chūchǎng** V   to appear on stage; to enter an arena / a playing field

**出车 chūchē** V   to drive passengers/cargo (to a destination)

**出丑 chūchǒu** V   to make a fool of oneself
别当众**出丑**。*Don't make a fool of yourself in public.*

**出处 chūchù** N   source (of a quotation, allusion), origin · MW 个

**出错 chūcuò** V   to make a mistake

**出点子 chūdiǎnzi** V   to make a suggestion; to express an opinion

**出动 chūdòng** V   to set/start out; to dispatch (troops, etc.)

**出发 chūfā** V   to set out (on a trip); to proceed/ start from

**出风头 chūfēngtou** EXP   to show off, to be in the limelight

**出轨 chūguǐ** V   to derail, to go off the rails

**出汗 chūhàn** V   to sweat, to perspire

**出乎意料 chūhūyìliào** EXP   beyond expectations; unexpected
公司总裁的辞职引起**出乎意料**的反响。
*The resignation of the CEO had unexpected repercussions.*

**出价 chūjià** V   to bid

**出嫁 chūjià** V   to get married (of a woman)

**出境 chūjìng** V   to leave the country/region

**出境检查 chūjìngjiǎnchá** V   emigration control

**出口 chūkǒu** V·N   to export; exit · MW 个

**出来 chūlái** V   to emerge, to come out
雨停了, 太阳**出来**了。*The rain stopped and the sun came out.*

**出力 chūlì** V   to put effort (into), to exert oneself

**出路 chūlù** N   prospects; way out (of difficulty, etc.) · MW 条

**出乱子 chūluànzi** EXP   trouble brewing

**258** 出 chū (continued)

出卖 chūmài　V　to sell, to bring to market; to betray

　　出卖产品 to sell products

　　出卖朋友 to betray one's friends

出毛病 chūmáobìng　EXP　out of order; to go wrong

　　汽车又出毛病。 The car is having issues again.

出门 chūmén　V　to go on a journey; to get married (of a woman)

出面 chūmiàn　V　to act in an official capacity

出名 chūmíng　V·ADJ　to become famous; to be well-known (for)

　　傻瓜现在出名了。 ShaGua is famous now.

出纳 chūnà　N　cashier, teller · MW 个、位、名

出偏差 chūpiānchā　V　to deviate

出气 chūqì　V　to vent one's anger, to air out

出去 chūqù　V　to exit, to go out

出入 chūrù　V·N　to come and go; discrepancy (in numbers, contents, etc.) · MW 个

出生 chūshēng　V　to be born

　　没有人知道傻瓜哪年出生，因为他妈妈只记得是发洪水那年生的。 Nobody knows the exact year that ShaGua was born, because his mom only remembers that year as the year of the great flood.

出示 chūshì　V　to show, to display

出事 chūshì　V　to have an accident; accident

出售 chūshòu　V　to sell

　　2006年以前，中国的法律不禁止向二十一岁以下的人出售酒。 Before 2006 in China, there was no law that forbade the sale of alcohol to people under 21.

出庭 chūtíng　V　to appear in court

出头 chūtóu　V　to get out of a predicament; to take the initiative; to stick out

出土 chūtǔ　V　to be excavated (of historical artifacts/fossils)

出席 chūxí　V　to be present, to attend; to participate

出息 chūxi　N　future prospects

出现 chūxiàn　V　to appear; to emerge, to arise

　　他的车又出现了新问题。 Another problem with his car has surfaced.

出血 chūxuè　V　to bleed, to hemorrhage; to spend money for others

出洋相 chūyángxiàng　EXP　to make a fool of oneself

出于 chūyú　V　to stem/start/proceed from

出院 chūyuàn　V　to leave the hospital, to be discharged

出诊 chūzhěn　V　to visit a patient at home, to make a house call (of a doctor)

出众 chūzhòng　ADJ　outstanding

出走 chūzǒu　V　to run away, to flee (from one's home)

出租 chūzū　V　to rent

　　他暑假将出租他的房子。 He will lease his home in the summer.

**RELATED WORDS**

| | | |
|---|---|---|
| 不出所料 24 | 支出 92 | 月出 190 |
| 产出 219 | 发出 311 | 引出 371 |
| 杰出 377 | 岁出 380 | 迁出 506 |
| 使出 623 | 进出口 713 | 进出 713 |
| 拔出 791 | 看出 841 | 突出 913 |
| 没出息 938 | 派出所 945 | 放出 964 |
| 现出 975 | 神出鬼没 1191 | 展出 1274 |
| 退出 1508 | 提出 1554 | 掏出 1661 |
| 榨出 1672 | 超出 1684 | 演出 1821 |
| 输出 1867 | 大打出手 20 | 半路出家 127 |
| 推陈出新 1242 | 鼻子出血 1794 | 水落石出 159 |
| 挺身而出 1408 | 祸从口出 1754 | |

**259** 吉　　U+5409　　TM **7** FM |

jí　ADJ·N　lucky, auspicious; (short name for) Jilin Province

吉利 jílì　ADJ　lucky, fortunate, auspicious

吉林 Jílín　N　Jilin Province

吉普车 jípǔchē　N　jeep · MW 辆

吉期 jíqī　N　wedding day; lucky day · MW 个

吉它 jítā　N　guitar · MW 把

吉祥 jíxiáng　ADJ　lucky, auspicious

　　北京奥林匹克运动会的吉祥物是福娃。 The mascot of the Beijing Olympics is FuWa.

吉兆 jízhào　N　good/lucky omen

**260** 来　來　　U+6765　　TM **7** FM |

lái　V·N　to come, to arrive; to happen, to take place; future, coming, next

来宾 láibīn　N　guest, visitor · MW 个、位、名

来不及 láibují　V　to be too late to (do something); there is not enough time

　　我们来不及赶火车了。 We didn't have enough time to catch the train.

来到 láidào　V　to come, to arrive

来得及 **láidejí** V to be able to (do something) in time; there's still time

别担心, 还**来得及**赶火车。 *Don't worry, there's still time to catch the train.*

来电 **láidiàn** V·N to inform by telegram; incoming telegram; resumption of power after an outage · MW 封

来犯 **láifàn** V to come to attack

来访 **láifǎng** V to visit

来回 **láihuí** V·N·ADV to make a round-trip; to come and go repeatedly; round-trip; repeatedly, again and again

从家到公司, **来回**要走半小时。 *It takes half an hour to walk from home to the office and back.*

来劲 **láijìn** ADJ exhilarating

来客 **láikè** N visitor, guest · MW 个、位、名

来历 **láilì** N history, past, origin, background; antecedent; source

来临 **láilín** V to come, to arrive; to approach, to come closer

来路 **láilù** N origin, background; approach, incoming road · MW 条

傻瓜的大儿子有些**来路**不明的朋友。 *ShaGua's older son has some friends with shady backgrounds.*

来年 **láinián** N next/coming year

来人 **láirén** N messenger · MW 个

来往 **láiwǎng** V·N to have dealings with; to come and go; communication, dealings

来信 **láixìn** N·V incoming letter; to send a letter here · MW 封

来意 **láiyì** N purpose in coming, reason for coming

来由 **láiyóu** N reason · MW 个

来源 **láiyuán** N·V origin, source; to originate · MW 个

工资是傻瓜收入的主要**来源**。 *ShaGua's salary is his principal source of income.*

**RELATED WORDS**

| | | |
|---|---|---|
| 下来 10 | 从来 66 | 未来 88 |
| 本来 90 | 以来 101 | 由来已久 148 |
| 历来 200 | 外来 218 | 出来 258 |
| 自来水 305 | 后来 310 | 回来 391 |
| 往来 461 | 如来佛 464 | 过来 712 |
| 进来 713 | 近来 716 | 到来 737 |
| 看来 841 | 南来北往 986 | 将来 1161 |
| 原来 1273 | 素来 1378 | 起来 1421 |
| 越来越 1575 | 反过来 111 | 买下来 248 |
| 听起来 414 | 希伯来 613 | 到头来 737 |
| 掉下来 1403 | 塌下来 1903 | 古往今来 154 |
| 礼尚往来 503 | 突如其来 913 | |

---

**261 皮** U+76AE TM 7 FM |

**pí** N·ADJ skin; leather; fur; wrapper; surface; sheet; rubber; naughty; thick-skinned, indifferent; rubbery

皮袄 **pí'ǎo** N fur-lined jacket · MW 件

皮包 **píbāo** N leather handbag, briefcase · MW 个

皮尺 **píchǐ** N tape measure · MW 条

皮带 **pídài** N strap, thong; leather belt; leash · MW 条

要是不系**皮带**, 这小伙子的裤子非掉下来不可。 *The boy's pants only stay up because of a belt.*

皮肤 **pífū** N skin

皮革 **pígé** N leather · MW 块

皮货 **píhuò** N fur, pelt · MW 件

皮毛 **pímáo** N fur; superficial knowledge

皮箱 **píxiāng** N leather suitcase · MW 个

皮衣 **píyī** N fur coat; fur/leather clothing · MW 件

**RELATED WORDS**

| | | |
|---|---|---|
| 牛皮 51 | 头皮 128 | 去皮 157 |
| 毛皮 183 | 羊皮 227 | 扯皮 403 |
| 树皮 1031 | 顽皮 1204 | 鸡皮疙瘩 1373 |
| 剥皮 1377 | 脸皮嫩 1461 | 脸皮 1461 |
| 调皮 1749 | 踢皮球 1946 | 嘴皮子 1984 |
| 厚脸皮 1272 | 鸡毛蒜皮 1373 | |

---

**262 虫** 蟲 U+866B TM 7 FM |

**chóng** N insect; worm

虫害 **chónghài** N pests; insect infestation/blight · MW 只

虫灾 **chóngzāi** N plague of insects · MW 场

虫子 **chóngzi** N insect; worm · MW 只

很多鸟类都吃**虫子**。 *Many birds eat worms.*

**RELATED WORDS**

| | | |
|---|---|---|
| 飞虫 81 | 毛虫 183 | 杀虫剂 317 |
| 臭虫 1076 | 爬虫 1099 | 害虫 1319 |
| 害人虫 1319 | 寄生虫 1619 | |

---

**263 电** 電 U+7535 TM 7 FM |

**diàn** N·V electricity; telegram; to give/get an electric shock; to send a telegram

**263** 电 diàn (continued)

电报 diànbào  N  telegram, cable · MW 份

电表 diànbiǎo  N  electric meter · MW 只

电唱机 diànchàngjī  N  phonograph · MW 台

电车 diànchē  N  streetcar · MW 辆

电池 diànchí  N  battery · MW 个、对

电传 diànchuán  V·N  to telex; telex · MW 封

电灯 diàndēng  N  electric light/lamp · MW 盏
　　电灯开关在哪里？ *Where is the light switch?*

电动 diàndòng  ADJ  electric, power, motor-driven (of machinery)

电镀 diàndù  V  to electroplate, to coat

电风扇 diànfēngshàn  N  electric fan · MW 台

电工 diàngōng  N  electrician; electrical engineering · MW 个、名

电焊 diànhàn  V  to weld

电话 diànhuà  N  telephone; phone call · MW 部、个
　　有空请给我打电话。 *Please call me when you have time.*

电汇 diànhuì  V  to wire money

电机 diànjī  N  electric machinery · MW 台

电缆 diànlǎn  N  (electric) cable · MW 条、根

电力 diànlì  N  electric power, electricity

电流 diànliú  N  electric current · MW 股

电路 diànlù  N  electric circuit; circuitry

电脑 diànnǎo  N  computer · MW 台

电气 diànqì  N  electricity

电器 diànqì  N  electric appliance/device

电视 diànshì  N  television, TV · MW 台
　　你知道中国哪家电视台最大？ *Do you know which television network in China is the biggest?*

电梯 diàntī  N  elevator · MW 个

电线 diànxiàn  N  (electric) wire · MW 条、根

电讯 diànxùn  N  telecommunications

电压 diànyā  N  voltage

电影 diànyǐng  N  film, movie · MW 个、部
　　明天我吃了晚饭去看电影。 *Tomorrow I'll go see a movie after dinner.*

电影院 diànyǐngyuàn  N  cinema, movie theater · MW 家

电熨斗 diànyùdǒu  N  electric iron · MW 个

电源 diànyuán  N  power supply/source · MW 个

电站 diànzhàn  N  power station, electricity-generating plant · MW 个

电子 diànzǐ  N·ADJ  electron; electronic

电子商务 diànzǐshāngwù  N  e-commerce

电子邮件 diànzǐyóujiàn  N  e-mail

**RELATED WORDS**

**264** 书 書   U+4E66   TM **7** FM |

shū  N·V  book; letter; document; handwriting, script, calligraphic style; to write

书包 shūbāo  N  schoolbag, backpack, satchel · MW 个

书报 shūbào  N  books and newspapers

书本 shūběn  N  book · MW 本

书橱 shūchú  N  bookcase · MW 个

书呆子 shūdāizi  EXP  bookworm · MW 个、名

书店 shūdiàn  N  bookstore · MW 家、间

书法 shūfǎ  N  calligraphy · MW 种

书画 shūhuà  N  painting and calligraphy · MW 幅

书籍 shūjí  N  books; literature · MW 本、套

书记 shūji  N  secretary, scribe · MW 个、名

书架 shūjià  N  bookshelf, bookcase; bookstand · MW 个

书刊 shūkān  N  books and periodicals

书目 shūmù  N  catalog, booklist, bibliography · MW 份

书评 shūpíng  N  book review · MW 篇

书写 shūxiě  V  to write

书写体 shūxiětǐ  N  script · MW 种

书信 shūxìn  N  letter, written message · MW 封

书桌 shūzhuō  N  desk · MW 张

**RELATED WORDS**

## 265 走    U+8D70   TM **7** FM |

**zǒu** V to go; to walk; to run; to move; to leave; to visit; to go/pass through; to leak; to escape; to deviate from; to die

**走笔 zǒubǐ** V to write quickly

**走遍 zǒubiàn** V to go everywhere

**走步 zǒubù** V to walk, to step

**走道 zǒudào** N sidewalk; path · MW 条
公园里的**走道**由一块块大青石板铺成。
*The sidewalks in the park are paved with large flagstones.*

**走调 zǒudiào** V to be out of tune

**走动 zǒudòng** V to walk around; to stretch one's legs; to visit each other (of relatives and friends)
天快亮了, 大街上开始有人**走动**了。
*People start to be out and about on the streets at daybreak.*

**走读 zǒudú** V to attend a day school

**走访 zǒufǎng** V to interview; to visit, to go and see

**走风 zǒufēng** V to divulge a secret; to leak

**走狗 zǒugǒu** N lackey, flunky, running dog, stooge · MW 条

**走过场 zǒuguòchǎng** EXP to go through the motions; to make a gesture to give the impression of doing something
这个会开得很马虎, 像**走过场**一样。
*This meeting was so informal that it looked like we were just going through the motions.*

**走后门 zǒuhòumén** V to use "back door" connections to gain an advantage
厌恶 "**走后门**" 的人也想走后门。 *People who most despise "getting in through the back door" are not averse to trying it themselves.*

**走火 zǒuhuǒ** V to discharge / go off accidentally; to overstate

**走江湖 zǒujiānghú** EXP to lead a nomadic life; to wander from place to place and earn a living as a peddler/entertainer

**走廊 zǒuláng** N hall, corridor, passageway · MW 条
我的办公室在那条长**走廊**的尽头。 *My office is at the end of the long corridor.*

**走路 zǒulù** V to walk
**走路**去上班, 既省油又健身。 *By walking to work, not only do you save gasoline, but you get some exercise as well.*

**走马灯 zǒumǎdēng** EXP lantern with a revolving circle of paper horses; merry-go-round

**走马看花 zǒumǎkànhuā** EXP to have a superficial understanding through cursory observation (LIT to view flowers from horseback)

**走南闯北 zǒunánchuǎngběi** EXP to journey north and south; to travel extensively

**走禽 zǒuqín** N flightless birds · MW 只、群

**走失 zǒushī** V to be lost/missing; to wander away

**走水 zǒushuǐ** V to leak water; to catch fire

**走私 zǒusī** V to smuggle
罪犯们**走私**毒品。 *The criminal smuggled drugs.*

**走投无路 zǒutóuwúlù** EXP to have no way out

**走味 zǒuwèi** V to lose flavor

**走向 zǒuxiàng** V·N to move toward, to head for; trend · MW 个

**走样 zǒuyàng** V to lose one's shape, to deviate from

**走运 zǒuyùn** V to be lucky
啊, 真不**走运**! *Oh, bad luck!*

**走着瞧 zǒuzheqiáo** EXP to wait and see
你不相信我会成功? 那我们**走着瞧**吧。 *You don't believe that I will be successful? Then we'll just wait and see.*

### RELATED WORDS

| | | |
|---|---|---|
| 出走 258 | 行走 327 | 奔走 432 |
| 放走 964 | 竞走 1470 | 逃走 1509 |
| 齐步走 221 | | |

## 266 步    U+6B65   TM **7** FM |

**bù** N·V step, pace; stage; step/stage (in a process); condition, state; [part of a place name]; to walk; to march; to tread

**步兵 bùbīng** N infantry; foot soldier · MW 个、名、队

**步步 bùbù** ADV step by step
让我们一**步步**做吧。 *Let's take things one step at a time.*

**步调 bùdiào** N step, pace; marching order · MW 个

**步伐 bùfá** N gait, pace, (measured) step; march · MW 种

**步法 bùfǎ** N footwork · MW 种

**步行 bùxíng** V to walk
汽车抛锚后, 傻瓜冒着雨**步行**去找修车行。 *After his car broke down, ShaGua walked in the rain to find a garage.*

**步骤 bùzhòu** N step; move; measure · MW 个

**步子 bùzi** N step, pace · MW 个

**266 步 bù** (continued)

**RELATED WORDS**

| | | |
|---|---|---|
| 寸步难行 37 | 止步 41 | 齐步走 221 |
| 走步 265 | 让步 348 | 快步 497 |
| 同步 541 | 进步 713 | 地步 772 |
| 却步 820 | 徒步 873 | 狐步舞 885 |
| 迈步 955 | 初步 963 | 退步 1508 |
| 碎步 1525 | 散步 1579 | 留步 1582 |
| 阔步 1728 | 脚步 1804 | 漫步 1887 |
| 跑步 1916 | 稳步 1925 | 进一步 713 |

| | | |
|---|---|---|
| 求见 376 | 足见 383 | 听见 414 |
| 罕见 490 | 政见 517 | 卓见 523 |
| 参见 600 | 成见 611 | 拜见 635 |
| 浅见 692 | 看见 841 | 拙见 1013 |
| 创见 1131 | 远见 1184 | 接见 1405 |
| 短见 1452 | 碰见 1526 | 预见 1528 |
| 偏见 1587 | 高见 1611 | 常见病 1733 |
| 意见 1812 | 撞见 1853 | 遇见 1891 |
| 瞧见 1915 | 立竿见影 125 | 司空见惯 357 |
| 寻短见 358 | 捉襟见肘 1239 | 由此可见 148 |
| 视而不见 1362 | | |

---

**267 见 見** U+89C1 TM 7 FM |

**jiàn** V·N to see, to catch sight of; to meet, to come in contact with, to call on; to be exposed to; to show evidence of, to appear to be; to refer to; opinion, view

**见报 jiànbào** V to be printed in a newspaper; to appear in the news
傻瓜今天又**见报**了。*ShaGua made the news again today.*

**见不得 jiànbudé** V to not be exposed to; to be unfit to be seen, to be unmentionable

**见得 jiànde** V to appear, to seem

**见缝插针 jiànfèngchāzhēn** EXP to take every opportunity

**见鬼 jiànguǐ** EXP fantastic, odd, absurd; go to hell
**见鬼**去吧, 我爱怎么着就怎么着! *Go to hell! I'll do what I please!*

**见解 jiànjiě** N opinion, view; understanding · MW 个

**见面 jiànmiàn** V to see, to meet

**见识 jiànshi** V·N to widen one's knowledge/ experience; knowledge, sense; experience

**见外 jiànwài** ADJ treating (someone) as an outsider

**见闻 jiànwén** N information, knowledge · MW 个

**见习 jiànxí** V to learn on the job; to be on probation

**见效 jiànxiào** V to have the desired effect; to be effective
这个药治感冒很**见效**。*This medicine is very effective against the flu.*

**见证 jiànzhèng** V·N to witness; testimony; proof · MW 个

**RELATED WORDS**

| | | |
|---|---|---|
| 不见得 24 | 长见识 93 | 主见 124 |
| 己见 132 | 会见 295 | 再见 354 |

---

**268 早** U+65E9 TM 7 FM |

**zǎo** N·ADJ·ADV morning; early; former, previous; in advance, beforehand; long ago; as early as

**早安 zǎo'ān** V good morning!

**早班 zǎobān** N morning shift · MW 个

**早餐 zǎocān** N breakfast · MW 份、顿、餐

**早操 zǎocāo** N morning exercises · MW 次

**早场 zǎochǎng** N morning show (theater), matinee

**早车 zǎochē** N morning train/bus · MW 班、趟

**早晨 zǎochén** N early morning
每天**早晨**傻瓜都很早起床。*ShaGua gets up very early every morning.*

**早春 zǎochūn** N early spring · MW 个

**早点 zǎodiǎn** N breakfast; morning snack · MW 份、餐

**早饭 zǎofàn** N breakfast · MW 份、顿、餐

**早期 zǎoqī** N early/initial stage

**早日 zǎorì** ADV soon, shortly, at an early date

**早上 zǎoshang** N morning · MW 个

**早熟 zǎoshú** ADJ maturing/ripening early; precocious

**早晚 zǎowǎn** N·ADV morning and evening; some day, sooner or later
你如果老是迟到, **早晚**要倒霉的。*If you are always late like this, you'll get in trouble sooner or later.*

**早先 zǎoxiān** ADV previously, before

**早已 zǎoyǐ** ADV for a long time; previously; long ago

**RELATED WORDS**

| | | |
|---|---|---|
| 及早 141 | 迟早 959 | 明早 1035 |
| 尚早 1156 | 趁早 1257 | 提早 1554 |
| 为时过早 223 | | |

## 269 匹

U+5339 · TM **7** FM |

**pǐ** V·ADJ·MW to be equal to, to be a match for; single, lone; [measure word for horses, mules, etc. and for bolts of cloth]

**匹敌** pǐdí V to be equal to; to be well-matched

**匹夫** pǐfū N ordinary man, man on the street · MW 个、位

国家兴亡, **匹夫**有责。 *Every man is partly responsible for the fate of his country.*

**匹配** pǐpèi V to match

### RELATED WORDS

马匹 247　　布匹 309　　奥林匹克 1435

## 270 因

U+56E0 · TM **7** FM |

**yīn** CONJ·PREP·N·V because; as a result of, because of, for; reason, cause; to follow; to carry on; to rely on

**因病** yīnbìng PREP due to illness

因病退学 *to leave school due to illness*

**因材施教** yīncáishījiào EXP to teach students according to their abilities

**因此** yīncǐ CONJ so, therefore; that is why

傻瓜的大儿子学习很努力, **因此**通过了考试。 *ShaGua's older son studied very hard, and that is why he passed the exam.*

**因而** yīn'ér CONJ therefore, thus; as a result

**因果** yīnguǒ N cause and effect; karma · MW 个

**因素** yīnsù N factor; element · MW 个

**因特网** yīntèwǎng N Internet · MW 个

**因为** yīnwèi CONJ because

因为傻瓜的大儿子学习努力, 所以成绩还不错。 *ShaGua's older son achieved success because he studied hard.*

### RELATED WORDS

内因 191　　　外因 218　　　成因 611
基因 991　　　原因 1273　　病因 1327
前因后果 1329　起因 1421　　互为因果 135
咖啡因 1229

## 271 四

U+56DB · TM **7** FM |

**sì** NUM four

**四边** sìbiān N four sides

**四边形** sìbiānxíng N quadrilateral · MW 个

**四不象** sìbùxiàng N neither one thing nor the other, nondescript · MW 个

**四重奏** sìchóngzòu N quartet · MW 首

**四处** sìchù N all around, in all directions, everywhere

**四方** sìfāng N all directions, all sides; square, cube

**四个现代化** sìgèxiàndàihuà N Four Modernizations (industry, agriculture, national defense, and science and technology)

**四海** sìhǎi EXP four seas; whole world

**四季** sìjì N four seasons

**四面** sìmiàn N (on) four sides, (on) all sides

**四面八方** sìmiànbāfāng EXP in/from all directions, far and near

人们从**四面八方**拥进纽约这个国际大都会。 *New York is a great international metropolis. People come to New York from every part of the world.*

**四面楚歌** sìmiànchǔgē EXP surrounded on all sides; utterly isolated

**四声** sìshēng N four tones of standard Chinese pronunciation

**四时** sìshí N four seasons

**四月** sìyuè N April, fourth month of the lunar year

**四肢** sìzhī N four limbs, arms and legs

**四十** sìshí NUM forty

**四十一** sìshíyī NUM forty-one

**四十二** sìshí'èr NUM forty-two

**四十三** sìshísān NUM forty-three

**四十四** sìshísì NUM forty-four

**四十五** sìshíwǔ NUM forty-five

**四十六** sìshíliù NUM forty-six

**四十七** sìshíqī NUM forty-seven

**四十八** sìshíbā NUM forty-eight

**四十九** sìshíjiǔ NUM forty-nine

### RELATED WORDS

十四 3　　　　一十四 1　　　二十四 2
八十四 6　　　三十四 9　　　七十四 34
六十四 69　　　文房四宝 70　　五湖四海 79
五十四 79　　　九十四 116　　不三不四 24
丢三落四 297　低三下四 618

## 272 曲 麯

U+66F2 · TM **7** FM |

**qū** (麯) V·ADJ·N to bend; wrong, unjust, unfair; distorted; bend (of a river, etc.); leaven, yeast; song, tune, melody; verse for singing

**272 曲 qū/qǔ** (continued)

**qǔ** N·MW   song, piece of music; [measure word for songs]

**曲别针 qūbiézhēn** N   paper clip · MW 枚

**曲尺 qūchǐ** N   set square, triangle (technical drawing) · MW 把

**曲棍球 qūgùnqiú** N   field hockey · MW 个

**曲解 qūjiě** V   to distort; to misinterpret; to wrench, to twist

傻瓜不善言辞, 所以最讨厌别人**曲解**他的意思。*ShaGua is not good at speaking; what he hates most is somebody misinterpreting his meaning.*

**曲线 qūxiàn** N   curve; curvature · MW 条、道

**曲折 qūzhé** ADJ   winding, tortuous; complicated, intricate

这条路很**曲折**, 沿山边往上延伸。*The road is really tortuous and winds up the side of the mountain.*

**曲调 qǔdiào** N   melody, tune, strain · MW 个、支

**曲剧 qǔjù** N   opera derived from ballad singing · MW 场、幕

**曲艺 qǔyì** N   folk musical theater · MW 个

**曲子 qǔzi** N   tune, melody; lyric · MW 支、首

**RELATED WORDS**

| | | |
|---|---|---|
| 乐曲 299 | 歪曲 511 | 异曲同工 539 |
| 委曲 594 | 委曲求全 594 | 弯曲 1472 |
| 插曲 1555 | 歌曲 1900 | |

---

**273 也**      U+4E5F      TM **7** FM **|**

**yě** ADV   also, too, as well as; either; still, yet

**也好 yěhǎo** ADV   may as well; that's fine; whether … or …

你开车来**也好**, 乘火车来**也好**, 必须准时到达。*Whether you drive or take a train, you must be here on time.*

**也门 Yěmén** N   Yemen

**也许 yěxǔ** ADV   perhaps, maybe, possibly

哦, **也许**我错了。*Oh, maybe I was wrong.*

---

**274 艺 藝**      U+827A      TM **7** FM **|**

**yì** N   skill, craftsmanship; art

**艺妓 yìjì** N   geisha · MW 个、名

**艺名 yìmíng** N   stage name (of an actor) · MW 个

**艺人 yìrén** N   performer, actor, entertainer; artisan, craftsman · MW 个、名、位

**艺术 yìshù** N·ADJ   art; skill, craft; artistic · MW 门

故宫收藏了许多**艺术**珍品。*The Forbidden City has many artistic treasures.*

**艺术家 yìshùjiā** N   artist · MW 个、名、位

**艺术界 yìshùjiè** N   artists' circle

**艺术品 yìshùpǐn** N   work of art; arts and crafts · MW 件

**艺术团 yìshùtuán** N   performing artists' group · MW 个

**艺术性 yìshùxìng** N   artistic quality, artistry

**RELATED WORDS**

| | | |
|---|---|---|
| 文艺 70 | 手艺 104 | 曲艺 272 |
| 技艺 568 | 园艺 763 | 茶艺 767 |
| 手工艺 104 | 多才多艺 431 | |

---

**275 节 節**      U+8282      TM **7** FM **|**

**jié** N·V·MW   festival, holiday; division, part, paragraph; item, matter; moral integrity/fiber, chastity; joint, node, section; to economize, to save; to restrain, to control; to abridge; [measure word for sections/segments (flashlight batteries, class periods, passenger cars of trains, etc.) and for lengths (of bamboo, etc.)]

过**节** *to celebrate a festival*

两**节**课 *two classes*

名**节** *reputation and integrity*

关**节** *joints*

**节**省钱 *to save money*

**节俭 jiéjiǎn** ADJ   frugal, thrifty, economical

**节目 jiémù** N   program; item (on a program) · MW 个

**节日 jiérì** N   festival, traditional holiday; red-letter day · MW 个

春**节**是中国最大的传统**节日**。*The Spring Festival is the most important traditional holiday in China.*

**节省 jiéshěng** V   to conserve, to use sparingly

**节食 jiéshí** V   to eat and drink moderately, to go on a diet

**节余 jiéyú** V·N   to save; surplus, saving

**节育 jiéyù** V   to use contraception, to practice birth control

**节约 jiéyuē** V   to save, to economize

**节制 jiézhì** V   to command, to control

节奏 **jiézòu** N rhythm, tempo, beat; regular pattern · MW 个

**RELATED WORDS**

| | | |
|---|---|---|
| 失节 106 | 关节 224 | 关节炎 224 |
| 环节 369 | 礼节 503 | 枝节 581 |
| 使节 623 | 季节 835 | 春节 855 |
| 音节 907 | 细节 1107 | 删节 1309 |
| 章节 1311 | 情节 1491 | 调节 1749 |
| 端午节 1889 | | |

---

### 276 帅 帥 U+5E05 TM 7 FM |

**shuài** N·ADJ commander in chief; handsome, graceful

**RELATED WORDS**

| | | |
|---|---|---|
| 元帅 138 | 挂帅 796 | 统帅 1601 |

---

### 277 切 U+5207 TM 7 FM |

**qiē** V to cut, to slice, to chop

**qiè** V·ADJ·ADV to correspond to, to conform to/with; to be close to; must, to have to; eager, anxious; definitely

切除 **qiēchú** V to excise, to cut off

切磋 **qiēcuō** V to carve and polish; to compare notes, to learn from group discussion

切点 **qiēdiǎn** N point of contact · MW 个

切断 **qiēduàn** V to break away; to cut off (a supply, etc.)

傻瓜无法**切断**自己的中国文化根。
*ShaGua could not break away from his Chinese cultural roots.*

切开 **qiēkāi** V to incise

切口 **qiēkǒu** N incision; slang · MW 个

切块 **qiēkuài** V to cut into pieces

切片 **qiēpiàn** V·N to cut into slices; section, slice · MW 块、片

切碎 **qiēsuì** V to chop

切削 **qiēxiāo** V to cut

切合 **qièhé** V·ADJ to correspond to, to fit in with; appropriate

切记 **qièjì** V to be sure to keep in mind

切切 **qièqiè** ADJ·ADV sure to; eagerly, earnestly, urgently

切实 **qièshí** ADJ realistic, practical, down-to-earth

大家都认为傻瓜的建议**切实**可行。
*Everybody thinks that ShaGua's proposal is practical and viable.*

切题 **qiètí** V to keep to the point

**RELATED WORDS**

| | | |
|---|---|---|
| 一切 1 | 关切 224 | 亲切 908 |
| 贴切 1038 | 真切 1075 | 迫切 1186 |
| 深切 1345 | 热切 1390 | 急切 1426 |
| 密切 1730 | 确切 1762 | 目空一切 151 |

---

### 278 北 U+5317 TM 7 FM |

**běi** N·V north; to be defeated

北方 **běifāng** N north; China north of the Yellow River

北风 **běifēng** N north wind · MW 阵

北海 **Běihǎi** N North Sea; North Lake Park (in Beijing)

北极 **běijí** N North Pole

北京 **Běijīng** N Beijing

**RELATED WORDS**

| | | |
|---|---|---|
| 台北 301 | 东北 307 | 西北 352 |
| 败北 589 | 河北 934 | 南北 986 |
| 指北针 1397 | 湖北 1741 | 南来北往 986 |
| 天南地北 25 | 走南闯北 265 | |

---

### 279 比 U+6BD4 TM 7 FM |

**bǐ** V·PREP·N to compare, to contrast, to liken to, to draw an analogy; to compete; to copy, to emulate, to model after, to do according to; to be like, to be similar to, to match; to gesture; to depend on; to collude with, to gang up with; than; superior/inferior to; with a score of; close together; next to; by then, by the time; ratio, proportion

他**比**她高。*He is taller than she is.*

傻瓜把狗**比**作忠诚的朋友。*ShaGua sees dogs as loyal friends.*

让我们**比**一**比**。*Let's compete with one another.*

傻瓜**比**着图片给儿子理发。*ShaGua is cutting his older son's hair by following a picture.*

傻瓜说话爱**比**手势。*ShaGua likes to gesture when he talks.*

傻瓜知道自己一年**比**一年老。*ShaGua knows that he is getting older every year.*

正**比** *direct ratio*

**279 比 bǐ** (continued)

比比皆是 **bǐbǐjiēshì** [EXP] ubiquitous; (can be) found everywhere

比方 **bǐfāng** [N·V] analogy; instance; to compare to, to take as an example · [MW] 个

这不过是个**比方**。 *This is only by way of analogy.*

比分 **bǐfēn** [N] score · [MW] 个

比价 **bǐjià** [N·V] price parity; rate of exchange; to compare prices/bids · [MW] 个

比较 **bǐjiào** [V·ADV·PREP] to compare, to contrast; relatively, comparatively; rather

比例 **bǐlì** [N] ratio, proportion · [MW] 个

比例尺 **bǐlìchǐ** [N] scale (architecture) · [MW] 个、把

比利时 **Bǐlìshí** [N] Belgium

比邻 **bǐlín** [N] neighbor

比率 **bǐlǜ** [N] ratio; rate, percentage

比拟 **bǐnǐ** [V·N] to match, to compare, to contrast; metaphor, comparison · [MW] 个

比如 **bǐrú** [CONJ] for example/instance, such as · [MW] 个

她喜欢吃水果，**比如**：苹果、梨子、香蕉等等。 *She likes fruit, such as apples, pears, bananas, etc.*

比赛 **bǐsài** [N·V] game, match; to compete · [MW] 场

比试 **bǐshi** [V] to hold a competition; to measure with one's hand/arm

比喻 **bǐyù** [N·V] analogy; metaphor; to compare, to draw an analogy · [MW] 个

傻瓜喜欢在说话中用**比喻**。 *ShaGua likes to talk in metaphors.*

比翼 **bǐyì** [V] to fly side by side; to help each other

比照 **bǐzhào** [V] to contrast; to base (something) on; according to, in light of

比值 **bǐzhí** [N] ratio; specific gravity

比重 **bǐzhòng** [N] proportion; specific gravity

**RELATED WORDS**

| | | |
|---|---|---|
| 不比 24 | 正比 76 | 无比 139 |
| 对比 254 | 利比亚 472 | 类比 676 |
| 评比 706 | 相比 805 | 按比例 1234 |
| 等比 1437 | 赞比亚 1969 | 百分比 242 |

**280**   **坏**   壞    U+574F    TM **7** FM |

**huài** [V·ADJ·N] to spoil; bad, awful, evil, harmful; extreme; dirty trick

坏处 **huàichu** [N] harm; disadvantage · [MW] 个

坏蛋 **huàidàn** [N] bad egg, evildoer; bastard · [MW] 个、伙

我早晚要跟你算账，你这**坏蛋**！ *I'll get you for that, you bastard!*

坏话 **huàihuà** [N] unpleasant words, vicious talk

坏人 **huàirén** [N] bad person, evildoer · [MW] 个、伙

坏事 **huàishì** [N] bad things · [MW] 件

**坏人做坏事。** *Bad people do bad things.*

坏心眼 **huàixīnyǎn** [N] evil intention · [MW] 个

**RELATED WORDS**

| | | |
|---|---|---|
| 弄坏 251 | 败坏 589 | 破坏 1374 |
| 损坏 1401 | 毁坏 1810 | |

**281**   **坟**   墳    U+575F    TM **7** FM |

**fén** [N] grave, tomb

坟地 **féndì** [N] cemetery, graveyard · [MW] 片

坟墓 **fénmù** [N] grave, tomb · [MW] 个、座

**282**   **收**    U+6536    TM **7** FM |

**shōu** [V·N] to bring/take in, to gather together, to collect; to harvest; to receive, to accept; to put away; to charge; to restrain, to control; to stop, to bring to an end; money received, receipts, income

收作业 *to collect homework*

收稻子 *to harvest rice*

收礼物 *to accept gifts*

这个活动不**收钱**。 *This activity won't cost anything.*

收藏 **shōucáng** [V] to collect; to keep, to store

收场 **shōuchǎng** [V·N] to wind/end up; ending · [MW] 个

收成 **shōuchéng** [N] harvest, crop · [MW] 个

收到 **shōudào** [V] to get, to receive

傻瓜**收到**朋友寄来的圣诞卡。 *ShaGua received Christmas cards from his friends.*

收发 **shōufā** [V·N] to receive and send/transmit; dispatcher · [MW] 个、名

收费 **shōufèi** [V] to collect fees, to charge

收割 **shōugē** [V] to reap, to harvest; to gather in

收工 **shōugōng** [V] to stop work

收回 **shōuhuí** [V] to take back, to withdraw

傻瓜傻在从来不**收回**他说过的话。*ShaGua is dumb for never taking back anything he says.*

**收获** shōuhuò `N·V` harvest; results, gain; to reap, to harvest

**收集** shōují `V` to collect, to gather

**收件人** shōujiànrén `N` recipient (of mail) · `MW` 个、名

**收据** shōujù `N` receipt · `MW` 张

**收款人** shōukuǎnrén `N` payee · `MW` 个、名

**收录** shōulù `V` to record, to include

**收买** shōumǎi `V` to purchase; to bribe, to buy (someone) off

**收盘** shōupán `V` to close, to declare an end to (selling, a chess match, etc.)

**收起** shōuqǐ `V` to pack up

**收讫** shōuqì `V` to have received in full

**收入** shōurù `N·V` income, revenue, earnings; to take in, to include · `MW` 笔

傻瓜只能靠不多的**收入**来养家。*ShaGua had to support his family with his meager income.*

**收拾** shōushi `V` to put in order, to tidy; to clear away, to eliminate; to punish; to repair

**收缩** shōusuō `V` to pull back; to shrink, to contract

**收听** shōutīng `V` to listen to (the radio); to tune in

**收尾** shōuwěi `V·N` to conclude, to wind up; ending · `MW` 个

**收文** shōuwén `N` incoming dispatch · `MW` 份

**收养** shōuyǎng `V` to adopt (a child)

**收益** shōuyì `N` income, profit, earnings · `MW` 笔

**收支** shōuzhī `N` income and expenses; accounts · `MW` 笔

傻瓜的家庭**收支**不平衡。*ShaGua's accounts were not balanced.*

**RELATED WORDS**

| | | |
|---|---|---|
| 丰收 35 | 年收入 182 | 回收 391 |
| 征收 462 | 托收 563 | 查收 741 |
| 吸收 776 | 招收 1232 | 纯收入 1290 |
| 接收 1405 | 签收 1439 | 验收 1529 |
| 税收 1705 | 到货验收 737 | |

---

**283　叫**　U+53EB　TM 7　FM |

**jiào** `V` to shout, to cry; to call; to greet; to order, to hire, to request service; to call (someone) names

**叫唤** jiàohuan `V` to cry/call out; to call

她听到有人**叫唤**。*She heard someone cry out.*

**叫苦** jiàokǔ `V` to grumble, to moan, to complain of hardship

**叫卖** jiàomài `V` to peddle

**叫嚷** jiàorǎng `V` to shout, to rave, to howl

**叫醒** jiàoxǐng `V` to wake (someone) up, to rouse

**叫做** jiàozuò `V` to be called, to be known as

傻瓜不在意被**叫做**"傻瓜"。*ShaGua doesn't mind being called a dummy.*

**RELATED WORDS**

| | | |
|---|---|---|
| 尖叫 203 | 呼叫 779 | 吼叫 1228 |
| 惊叫 1489 | 喊叫 1668 | |

---

**284　叮**　U+53EE　TM 7　FM |

**dīng** `V·ONOM` to sting, to bite (of an insect); to warn, to admonish; to inquire; to say/ask again to make sure; to stick with

**叮当** dīngdāng `ONOM` jingle; ding dong

**叮咛** dīngníng `V` to urge/warn repeatedly

**叮咬** dīngyǎo `V` to sting, to bite (of an insect)

蚊虫特别爱**叮咬**傻瓜。*Mosquitoes really enjoy biting ShaGua.*

**叮嘱** dīngzhǔ `V` to urge/warn again and again

---

**285　叹**　嘆　U+53F9　TM 7　FM |

**tàn** `V` to sigh; to chant, to recite, to intone; to praise, to extol

**叹词** tàncí `N` exclamation, interjection · `MW` 个

**叹服** tànfú `V` to gasp in admiration

**叹气** tànqì `V` to sigh, to heave a sigh

**叹赏** tànshǎng `V` to admire, to express admiration for

**叹息** tànxī `V` to sigh, to heave a sigh

傻瓜发出绝望的**叹息**,转身离去。*With a sigh of despair, ShaGua turned away.*

**RELATED WORDS**

| | | |
|---|---|---|
| 哀叹 1134 | 感叹 1860 | 赞叹 1969 |

---

**286　吐**　U+5410　TM 7　FM |

**tǔ** `V` to spit; to say, to speak

**吐露** tǔlù `V` to reveal, to disclose; to speak one's mind

**286 吐 tǔ** (continued)

她向傻瓜**吐**露了一个秘密。 *She confided in ShaGua.*

**吐气 tǔqì** V to give a sigh of relief, to feel elated and relieved; to exhale

**吐弃 tǔqì** V to reject, to spurn

**吐痰 tǔtán** V to spit

**RELATED WORDS**

吞吐 427       呕吐 560       谈吐 1356
吞吞吐吐 427

---

**287** 吓 嚇    U+5413    TM **7** FM |

**hè** V to threaten, to scare

**xià** V to scare, to frighten

**吓唬 xiàhu** V to scare, to frighten, to intimidate

**吓一跳 xiàyītiào** EXP to be frightened/startled, to be scared out of one's skin

傻瓜被她所说的秘密**吓一跳**。 *ShaGua was frightened by the secret she had confided in him.*

**RELATED WORD**

恐吓 1644

---

**288** 扎    U+624E    TM **7** FM |

**zā** V to bind, to tie

**zhā** V to prick; to stick (with a needle, etc.); to plunge into; to get into

**扎根 zhāgēn** V to take root; to build a foundation

**扎猛子 zhāměngzi** EXP to dive; to swim underwater

**扎实 zhāshí** ADJ sturdy, strong; firm, solid

学习中文需要打下**扎实**的基础。 *Learning Chinese requires laying a strong foundation.*

**扎手 zhāshǒu** V to prick the hand; to be difficult to handle

**扎眼 zhāyǎn** ADJ garish, offensive to the eye

**扎针 zhāzhēn** V to give/have an acupuncture treatment

**RELATED WORD**

挣扎 1398

---

**289** 打    U+6253    TM **7** FM |

**dá** MW [measure word for dozens]

两**打**鸡蛋 *two dozen eggs*

**dǎ** V·PREP to hit, to strike, to beat, to knock; to break, to smash; to fight, to attack; to deal with; to build, to construct; to make, to forge; to buy; to knit, to weave; to mix, to stir, to beat together; to tie up, to pack; to carve, to dig; to lift, to hoist, to raise; to work out, to plan, to calculate; to play; to issue, to send, to dispatch; to receive; to draw; to ladle, to spoon out; to say, to speak; to adopt; to do, to engage in; to turn, to revolve, to rotate; to insert; from, since

打鼓 *to beat a drum*

打破门 *to break the door*

打一道土墙 *to build a wall*

打把剑 *to forge a sword*

打饭 *to buy food*

打围巾 *to knit a scarf*

打果汁 *to make/extract fruit juice*

打洞 *to dig a hole*

打电话 *to make a call*

打稿子 *to write a draft*

打工 *to work*

打球 *to play ball*

打比方 *to give an example*

打问号 *to insert a question mark*

打北京来 *to come from Beijing*

打那以后，我**打**心里爱你。 *From that time on, I have loved you with all my heart.*

**打败 dǎbài** V to defeat, to win over, to beat; to be defeated

**打扮 dǎban** V·N to dress up; style of dress
同学们**打**扮得漂漂亮亮去参加晚会。 *The students dressed up very nicely for the party.*

**打包 dǎbāo** V·N to pack; doggie bag (from a restaurant)

**打包票 dǎbāopiào** EXP to vouch for, to guarantee

**打岔 dǎchà** V to interrupt, to cut in

**打成一片 dǎchéngyīpiàn** EXP to become one; to merge, to integrate

**打倒 dǎdǎo** V to knock down; to overthrow

**打地铺 dǎdìpù** EXP to make a bed on the floor

**打掉 dǎdiào** V to destroy

**打赌 dǎdǔ** V to bet

他敢**打赌**：傻瓜已回家了。*He bet that ShaGua was back home already.*

**打断** dǎduàn V to break (a bone, etc.); to interrupt, to break off

**打盹** dǎdǔn V to doze off

**打耳光** dǎěrguāng V to slap (someone) in the face

**打发** dǎfa V to send; to dismiss, to get rid of; to while away (the time)

**打翻** dǎfān V to overturn; to overthrow

**打嗝** dǎgé V to hiccup; to belch

**打官腔** dǎguānqiāng EXP to talk like a bureaucrat, to talk in official jargon

**打官司** dǎguānsi V to file a lawsuit; to go to court

**打棍子** dǎgùnzi EXP to bludgeon, to hit with a heavy stick

**打鼾** dǎhān V to snore

**打火机** dǎhuǒjī N (cigarette) lighter · MW 个

**打击** dǎjī V to hit, to strike; to attack; to crack down on

**打架** dǎjià V to fight, to scuffle

**打搅** dǎjiǎo V to disturb, to trouble

**打交道** dǎjiāodao V to associate with, to deal with

许多人觉得很容易跟傻瓜**打交道**。*A lot of people think ShaGua is easy to deal with.*

**打劫** dǎjié V to rob

**打开** dǎkāi V to open; to expand; to turn on

**打雷** dǎléi V to thunder

**打量** dǎliang V to size up, to measure with the eye, to look (someone) up and down; to suppose, to think

**打猎** dǎliè V to hunt

**打乱** dǎluàn V to disrupt, to throw into confusion

**打破** dǎpò V to break, to smash

**打气** dǎqì V to inflate, to pump up; to encourage, to bolster

我给车胎**打气**。*I inflated my tires.*

我给她**打气**。*I encouraged her.*

**打球** dǎqiú V to play ball

今天我想去**打球**。*I would like to play ball today.*

**打拳** dǎquán V to box; to do shadow boxing

**打扫** dǎsǎo V to clean, to sweep; to scavenge

**打算** dǎsuan V·N to plan, to calculate, to intend; intention, calculation, consideration · MW 个

你下午**打算**做什么？*What are you going to do this afternoon?*

**打碎** dǎsuì V to break into pieces, to shatter

**打听** dǎting V to ask/inquire about

**打通** dǎtōng V to get through, to establish contact

**打退堂鼓** dǎtuìtánggǔ EXP to back out

**打响** dǎxiǎng V to start shooting, to open fire; to have initial success

**打消** dǎxiāo V to give up on, to cancel; to dispel (a doubt, etc.)

**打仗** dǎzhàng V to fight; to go to war; to fight a battle

**打招呼** dǎzhāohu V to greet, to say hello; to inform, to notify

**打折扣** dǎzhékòu V to give a discount

年底商店的货物大多**打折扣**。*At the end of the year, stores give a discount on most of their merchandise.*

**打针** dǎzhēn V to give/have an injection

**打字** dǎzì V to type (on a typewriter)

### RELATED WORDS

| | | |
|---|---|---|
| 大打出手 20 | 双打 146 | 扑打 168 |
| 武打 513 | 苏打 552 | 扭打 565 |
| 抽打 788 | 拍打 790 | 难打交道 974 |
| 拳打脚踢 1158 | 挨打 1237 | 跌打损伤 1422 |
| 痛打 1725 | 精打细算 1832 | 磕打 1894 |
| 敲打 1959 | 鞭打 1967 | 无精打采 139 |
| 趁火打劫 1257 | | |

**290 扛** U+625B TM 7 FM |

**káng** V to shoulder, to place (something) on one's shoulder

**291 扩** 擴 U+6269 TM 7 FM |

**kuò** V to enlarge, to expand, to extend

**扩充** kuòchōng V to enlarge, to expand, to increase; to strengthen

**扩大** kuòdà V to enlarge, to expand, to increase, to broaden; to aggravate

**扩散** kuòsàn V to spread, to diffuse, to proliferate

**扩展** kuòzhǎn V to expand, to extend, to broaden, to spread

老师希望通过学中文**扩展**学生对中国文化的兴趣。*The teacher hopes students can expand their interest in Chinese culture by studying Chinese.*

**扩张** kuòzhāng V to expand, to extend, to enlarge; to dilate

## 292 权 權　U+6743　TM 7　FM |

**quán** `N·ADV·V` power, authority, might, influence; right, entitlement; initiative; expediency, advisability; tentatively, for the time being; to consider, to weigh, to balance

我有**权**查问你。 *I have the power to question you.*
这是你的发言**权**。 *It is your right to speak.*

**权**衡利弊 *to consider the advantages and disadvantages*

**权贵 quánguì** `N` influential official · `MW` 个、名

**权衡 quánhéng** `V` to consider, to assess, to weigh, to balance

**权力 quánlì** `N` power

**权利 quánlì** `N` right; privilege · `MW` 个
人们有集会和发表言论的**权利**。 *People have the rights of assembly and free speech.*

**权术 quánshù** `N` political trickery · `MW` 个

**权威 quánwēi** `N` authority; authoritativeness · `MW` 个
我的中文老师是语言学**权威**。 *My Chinese teacher is an authority on linguistics.*

**权限 quánxiàn** `N` jurisdiction; limits of power · `MW` 个

**权宜 quányí** `ADJ` expedient

**权益 quányì** `N` rights and interests

### RELATED WORDS

| | | |
|---|---|---|
| 人权 4 | 平权 78 | 主权 124 |
| 无权 139 | 全权 172 | 产权 219 |
| 夺权 308 | 当权 335 | 民权 388 |
| 弃权 480 | 政权 517 | 实权 668 |
| 极权主义 798 | 皇权 858 | 版权 897 |
| 债权 1088 | 特权 1094 | 职权 1205 |
| 掌权 1734 | 霸权 1998 | 优先权 447 |

## 293 杠 槓　U+6760　TM 7　FM |

**gàng** `N·V` thick stick/rod; bar (gymnastics); thick line (to mark mistakes on homework, etc.); certain standard; to cross out, to delete; to dispute

**杠棒 gàngbàng** `N` stout carrying pole · `MW` 根、条

**杠杆 gànggǎn** `N` lever, pry bar; leverage (economic leverage, etc.) · `MW` 根、条

**杠铃 gànglíng** `N` barbell, dumbbell · `MW` 对

### RELATED WORDS

| | |
|---|---|
| 抬杠 1012 | 敲竹杠 1959 |

## 294 队 隊　U+961F　TM 7　FM |

**duì** `N·MW` line/row of people; team; group; squadron; [measure word for troops]

**队列 duìliè** `N` formation; alignment · `MW` 排

**队旗 duìqí** `N` team pennant · `MW` 面

**队伍 duìwu** `N` troops; army, force; formation; team · `MW` 支

**队形 duìxíng** `N` formation · `MW` 个、种

**队员 duìyuán** `N` team member · `MW` 个、名

**队长 duìzhǎng** `N` team leader, captain; conductor · `MW` 个、名

学校乐队排成**队伍**走过街道，**队长**在前面领着**队员**们游行。 *The school band marched through the streets, with the conductor leading the band members.*

### RELATED WORDS

| | | |
|---|---|---|
| 小队 61 | 卫队 82 | 支队 92 |
| 车队 114 | 归队 166 | 乐队 299 |
| 军队 489 | 球队 1199 | 排队 1241 |
| 掉队 1403 | 领队 1465 | 部队 1636 |
| 梯队 1669 | 船队 1809 | 整队 1845 |
| 编队 1866 | 少先队 62 | 仪仗队 122 |
| 拉拉队 573 | | |

## 295 会 會　U+4F1A　TM 7　FM ノ

**huì** `V·N` will; to be possible to; to be able to; to get together, to assemble, to meet; to pay; conference, gathering, party; union, society; temple fair

我**会**去。 *I will go.*
我**会**写中文。 *I am able to write Chinese.*
我有一个**会**。 *I have a meeting.*
我**会**了酒钱。 *I have paid for the wine.*

晚**会** *party*
中文学**会** *Chinese Association*
社**会** *society*
庙**会** *temple fair*

**会餐 huìcān** `V` to dine together

**会场 huìchǎng** `N` meeting place, venue · `MW` 个

**会费 huìfèi** `N` membership dues · `MW` 笔

**会合 huìhé** `V` to meet, to congregate, to assemble, to converge

**会话 huìhuà** `V` to converse, to have a dialog
中文**会话**课非常有趣。 *Conversational Chinese is a really fun class.*

会见 **huìjiàn** [V] to interview; to meet

傻瓜的大儿子渴望那位著名的教授能**会见**他。 *ShaGua's older son is anxious to meet the famous professor.*

会聚 **huìjù** [V] to assemble

会刊 **huìkān** [N] journal (of an association, society, etc.) · [MW] 本、期

会面 **huìmiàn** [V] to meet, to come together

会期 **huìqī** [N] session (of a meeting) · [MW] 个

会商 **huìshāng** [V] to consult, to hold a conference/consultation

会审 **huìshěn** [V] to hold a joint hearing/trial; to review jointly

会师 **huìshī** [V] to join/combine forces

会谈 **huìtán** [V·N] to negotiate, to hold talks; conversation; bilateral/multilateral talks · [MW] 次

他们的**会谈**产生了什么结果？ *What was the outcome of their talks?*

会议 **huìyì** [N] meeting, conference; congress, council · [MW] 个

会员 **huìyuán** [N] member · [MW] 个、名

会战 **huìzhàn** [V] to meet for a decisive battle; to launch a campaign

会长 **huìzhǎng** [N] president (of a club, committee, etc.) · [MW] 个、位、名

会址 **huìzhǐ** [N] conference site · [MW] 个

**RELATED WORDS**

**296 合** U+5408 TM **7** FM 丿

**hé** [V·ADJ·MW] to close, to shut; to join, to combine; to conform to, to suit, to agree; to be equal to, to amount to; whole; [measure word for rounds, bouts, etc.]

**合**上书 *to close a book*

齐心**合**力 *to join forces to work as one*

**合**心意 *suitable for one's thoughts*

一美元**合**七元人民币。 *One dollar is equal to seven yuan RMB.*

合并 **hébìng** [V] to merge, to consolidate; to annex

这两家公司去年**合并**了。 *The two companies merged last year.*

合唱 **héchàng** [V] to sing in a chorus

合成 **héchéng** [V·ADJ] to compose, to synthesize; synthetic

合订本 **hédìngběn** [N] one-volume edition, bound volume · [MW] 个、本

合法 **héfǎ** [ADJ] legal, lawful, legitimate

你应该办理**合法**手续。 *You should go through the legal formalities.*

合格 **hégé** [ADJ·V] qualified; to qualify, to pass, to reach a standard

合乎 **héhū** [V] to conform to/with, to correspond to, to tally with

合欢 **héhuān** [V·N] to make love; to experience sexual bliss; silk tree · [MW] 棵

合伙 **héhuǒ** [V] to collaborate, to form a partnership

合计 **héjì** [V] to amount to, to add up to, to total; to consider, to discuss

合金 **héjīn** [N] alloy

合口 **hékǒu** [V] to heal (of a wound)

合理 **hélǐ** [ADJ] rational, reasonable; equitable

他给了我**合理**的解释。 *He gave me a reasonable explanation.*

合谋 **hémóu** [V] to conspire, to plot together

合拍 **hépāi** [ADJ·V] in time/step/harmony with; to cooperate

合群 **héqún** [ADJ] gregarious, sociable

合身 **héshēn** [ADJ] fit; nice-fitting (of clothes)

合适 **héshì** [ADJ] appropriate, suitable, right; becoming

我们什么时候会面比较**合适**？ *What is a suitable time for us to meet?*

这帽子你戴着很**合适**。 *The hat suits you very well.*

合算 **hésuàn** [ADJ·V] worthwhile; to reckon up

合营 **héyíng** [V] to jointly operate, to co-own

合影 **héyǐng** [N·V] group photo; to take a group photo · [MW] 张

合作 **hézuò** [N·V] cooperation; alliance; to cooperate, to collaborate

**296 合 hé** (continued)

在这个项目上，我需要你的**合作**。 *I need your cooperation in this matter.*

他们决定**合作**开办一家企业。 *They decided to form an alliance.*

**RELATED WORDS**

| | | |
|---|---|---|
| 三合一 9 | 不合 24 | 不合格 24 |
| 半合作 127 | 汇合 234 | 切合 277 |
| 会合 295 | 巧合 364 | 折合 408 |
| 闭合 677 | 场合 773 | 吻合 777 |
| 重合 839 | 投合 1008 | 复合 1059 |
| 组合 1106 | 凑合 1160 | 联合国 1206 |
| 联合 1206 | 集合 1267 | 符合 1277 |
| 结合 1291 | 胶合木 1296 | 适合 1358 |
| 迎合 1360 | 偶合 1590 | 聚合 1642 |
| 配合 1647 | 混合 1739 | 整合 1845 |
| 志同道合 528 | | |

---

**297 丢**     U+4E22     TM **7** FM 丿

**diū** V to lose, to forfeit; to throw away; to toss; to put aside, to leave behind

**丢丑 diūchǒu** V to lose face

**丢掉 diūdiào** V to lose

如果傻瓜**丢掉**工作，有人会高兴。 *If ShaGua loses his job, someone will be happy.*

**丢饭碗 diūfànwǎn** EXP to lose one's job

**丢脸 diūliǎn** V to lose face, to be disgraced

傻瓜不太在意是不是**丢脸**。 *ShaGua doesn't mind losing face.*

**丢面子 diūmiànzi** EXP to lose face

**丢弃 diūqì** V to abandon, to give up; to discard, to scrap

引擎烧掉了，傻瓜不得不**丢弃**那辆车。 *The engine burned up, so ShaGua had to abandon his car.*

**丢人 diūrén** V to lose face, to be disgraced

**丢三落四 diūsānlàsì** EXP forgetful, scatterbrained

**丢失 diūshī** V to lose

**丢下 diūxià** V to throw down, to abandon

---

**298 舌**     U+820C     TM **7** FM 丿

**shé** N tongue; like a tongue

**舌尖 shéjiān** N tip of the tongue

**舌头 shétou** N tongue; ability to talk; enemy soldier captured to get information · MW 个

你的**舌头**真厉害。 *You really can talk!*

今晚去抓一个**舌头**。 *Tonight we will capture an enemy soldier for information.*

**舌战 shézhàn** N to have a heated dispute · MW 场

**RELATED WORDS**

| | | |
|---|---|---|
| 喉舌 1560 | 嚼舌 1999 | 七嘴八舌 34 |

---

**299 乐 樂**     U+4E50     TM **7** FM 丿

**lè** ADJ·V happy, cheerful; to be glad to, to take pleasure in; to laugh

**yuè** N music

**乐得 lèdé** V to be happy to have the chance to

**乐观 lèguān** ADJ optimistic, hopeful, bright

傻瓜很**乐观**，认为自己一定会很快找到工作。 *ShaGua was optimistic that he would soon find a job.*

**乐呵呵 lèhēhē** EXP happy and gay, joyful

**乐极生悲 lèjíshēngbēi** EXP extreme joy can turn into extreme sadness

**乐趣 lèqù** N joy, delight, pleasure, fun · MW 种

**乐事 lèshì** N pleasure · MW 件

**乐天 lètiān** V to be carefree

**乐意 lèyì** V·ADJ to be ready/willing to; to love to; happy, pleased

傻瓜十分**乐意**帮助朋友。 *ShaGua is quite willing to help friends.*

**乐于 lèyú** V to be happy to, to take delight in

**乐园 lèyuán** N playground; paradise · MW 个

**乐滋滋 lèzīzī** ADJ contented, pleased

**乐池 yuèchí** N orchestra · MW 个

**乐队 yuèduì** N band, orchestra · MW 支

**乐谱 yuèpǔ** N musical score, music · MW 本

**乐曲 yuèqǔ** N musical composition, music · MW 首

**乐团 yuètuán** N philharmonic orchestra · MW 个

**RELATED WORDS**

| | | |
|---|---|---|
| 欢乐 366 | 安乐 487 | 快乐 497 |
| 奏乐 608 | 音乐 907 | 俱乐部 1083 |
| 哀乐 1134 | 哀乐 1134 | 享乐 1135 |
| 鼓乐 1688 | 器乐 1963 | 幸灾乐祸 373 |
| 轻音乐 1113 | 摇滚乐 1664 | 管弦乐 1861 |
| 吃喝玩乐 783 | | |

## 300 兵  U+5175  TM 7  FM 丿

**bīng** N soldier; army, troops, force; arms, weapons; military, war-related

**兵法 bīngfǎ** N military strategy, art of war · MW 部

**兵家 bīngjiā** N military commander · MW 个、位

**兵力 bīnglì** N military strength; armed forces, troops

**兵马 bīngmǎ** N military forces (LIT troops and horses) · MW 队、支

**兵强马壮 bīngqiángmǎzhuàng** EXP military might; well-trained and powerful army (LIT strong soldiers and sturdy horses)

**兵团 bīngtuán** N military corps · MW 个

**兵役 bīngyì** N military service

**兵种 bīngzhǒng** N branch of the armed forces · MW 个

### RELATED WORDS

| | | |
|---|---|---|
| 士兵 16 | 卫兵 82 | 水兵 159 |
| 伞兵 171 | 尖兵 203 | 步兵 266 |
| 用兵 313 | 当兵 335 | 列兵 368 |
| 民兵 388 | 伤兵 453 | 征兵 462 |
| 标兵 801 | 救兵 1259 | 宪兵 1317 |
| 哨兵 1410 | 练兵 1453 | 退兵 1508 |
| 逃兵 1509 | 阅兵 1727 | 骑兵 1840 |
| 撤兵 1942 | 搬救兵 1943 | |

## 301 台  臺檯颱  U+53F0  TM 7  FM 丿

**tái** N tower; observatory, deck, terrace; stand, support; stage, platform; like a platform; table; like a table; TV station; typhoon; (short for) Taiwan

站台 *platform*

电视台 *TV station*

台语 *Taiwanese*

**台北 Táiběi** N Taipei

**台词 táicí** N lines (of an actor), script · MW 段、句

**台灯 táidēng** N desk/table lamp; reading lamp · MW 盏

**台风 táifēng** N typhoon, hurricane; stage presence · MW 场

**台阶 táijiē** N step; staircase, flight of steps; way out of an embarrassing situation · MW 级

傻瓜在光滑的**台阶**上摔倒了。 *He slipped on the slippery steps.*

**台球 táiqiú** N pool, billiards; table tennis; Ping-Pong ball

**台湾 Táiwān** N Taiwan

**台子 táizi** N terrace; stage; table · MW 张

### RELATED WORDS

| | | |
|---|---|---|
| 后台 310 | 下台 10 | 上台 14 |
| 平台 78 | 月台 190 | 讲台 501 |
| 拆台 572 | 柜台 800 | 烛台 1176 |
| 站台 1189 | 垮台 1224 | 倒台 1281 |
| 凉台 1337 | 塔台 1394 | 登台 1521 |
| 窗台 1732 | 跳台 1786 | 舞台 1790 |
| 锅台 1807 | 塌台 1903 | 写字台 663 |
| 查号台 741 | | |

## 302 允  U+5141  TM 7  FM 丿

**yǔn** V·ADJ to allow, to permit; to consent; to even up, to divide evenly, to share; fair; suitable, appropriate

**允诺 yǔnnuò** V to promise; to consent

**允许 yǔnxǔ** V to allow, to permit

你知道到中国旅游**允许**携带的款额吗？ *Do you know that there are currency restrictions on the amount of money tourists are allowed to bring into China?*

## 303 勾  U+52FE  TM 7  FM 丿

**gōu** V·N to cross out, to cancel; to take a section from, to strike out; to delineate; to draw, to attract; to collude with, to gang up with

一笔**勾**销 *to write off in a single stroke, to cancel everything*

**勾**起回忆 *evoked memories*

**勾搭 gōudā** V to gang up with

**勾画 gōuhuà** V to sketch, to draw the outline of

**勾结 gōujié** V to collude/collaborate with

警察与黑帮有**勾结**。 *The police were in league with the gangs.*

**勾通 gōutōng** V to join in a plot

**勾销 gōuxiāo** V to expunge, to erase, to remove

**勾引 gōuyǐn** V to entice, to tempt, to seduce

**304** **匆**    U+5306    TM **7** FM 丿

**cōng** ADJ hurried, hasty

匆匆 **cōngcōng** ADJ hasty

匆忙 **cōngmáng** ADJ hurried, hasty, in haste
傻瓜匆匆忙忙赶去邮局。 *ShaGua went to the post office in a hurry.*

**305** **自**    U+81EA    TM **7** FM 丿

**zì** PRON·PREP·ADV oneself, self; from, since; certainly, of course

自爱 **zì'ài** V to have self-respect

自白 **zìbái** V to make one's meaning clear, to vindicate oneself

自卑 **zìbēi** ADJ feeling inferior; low self-esteem

自便 **zìbiàn** V to do at one's convenience

自称 **zìchēng** V to call oneself, to claim to be

自成一家 **zìchéngyìjiā** EXP to have one's own style

自持 **zìchí** V to control oneself

自大 **zìdà** ADJ arrogant, self-important
这个裁缝很自大，自称"天下第一剪"。
*The tailor is really arrogant; he called himself "the Number One tailor in the world."*

自得 **zìdé** ADJ self-satisfied, content

自动 **zìdòng** ADV·ADJ of one's own accord; voluntary; automatic

自发 **zìfā** ADJ spontaneous; unconscious, without thinking
看到傻瓜家有困难，朋友们自发地捐款帮助他。 *Friends spontaneously donated money to ShaGua when they found out his family was having problems.*

自费 **zìfèi** V to pay one's own way

自负 **zìfù** ADJ·V conceited, boastful; to think highly of oneself; to take responsibility
他为人自负。 *He is rather conceited.*
后果自负。 *One should take complete responsibility for the consequences of one's actions.*

自高自大 **zìgāozìdà** EXP self-important
没人喜欢那个自高自大的家伙。 *Nobody likes that pompous fellow.*

自个儿 **zìgěr** N oneself

自供 **zìgòng** V to confess

自豪 **zìháo** ADJ proud; to take pride in

自己 **zìjǐ** PRON oneself; own

能说中文，你不觉得自己很能干吗？
*Do you think you're smart because you can speak Chinese?*

自荐 **zìjiàn** V to recommend oneself

自尽 **zìjìn** V to kill oneself, to commit suicide

自救 **zìjiù** V to save/support oneself

自觉 **zìjué** V·ADJ to be aware of, to realize; conscientious

自控 **zìkòng** V to control oneself; to run automatically

自夸 **zìkuā** V to boast

自来水 **zìláishuǐ** N running water

自力更生 **zìlìgēngshēng** EXP to rely on one's own efforts; self-reliant

自满 **zìmǎn** ADJ self-satisfied, complacent

自命不凡 **zìmìngbùfán** EXP to consider oneself special

自然 **zìrán** N·ADJ·ADV·CONJ nature; natural; normal; naturally, of course

自如 **zìrú** ADJ free, smooth, with ease; self-possessed

自杀 **zìshā** V to commit suicide, to take one's own life

自上而下 **zìshàng'érxià** EXP from top to bottom

自身 **zìshēn** N self, oneself; one's own

自视 **zìshì** V to consider/view oneself

自私 **zìsī** ADJ selfish, self-centered
一个自私的人总是想着自己。 *A selfish person only thinks of him- or herself.*

自卫 **zìwèi** V to defend oneself

自慰 **zìwèi** V to masturbate (LIT to console oneself)

自我 **zìwǒ** PRON·N self; oneself; ego; self-conscious

自习 **zìxí** V to study by oneself

自新 **zìxīn** V to make a fresh start

自信 **zìxìn** V·ADJ to believe in oneself; self-confident
傻瓜最缺少的就是自信。 *What ShaGua lacks most is self-confidence.*

自行 **zìxíng** ADV of one's own accord, voluntarily, by oneself

自行车 **zìxíngchē** N bicycle · MW 辆、架

自行车道 **zìxíngchēdào** N bike path · MW 条

自修 **zìxiū** V to study by oneself, to teach oneself

自学 **zìxué** V to teach oneself

自以为是 **zìyǐwéishì** EXP to believe oneself to be always right

自用 **zìyòng** V to be self-motivated; for private use

自由 zìyóu　N·ADJ　freedom, liberty; free, unrestrained

自愿 zìyuàn　V　to volunteer; to act of one's own free will

慈善事业依靠**自愿**捐赠。*Charities rely on voluntary contributions.*

自在 zìzài　ADJ　free, unrestrained; comfortable, at ease

自责 zìzé　V　to blame oneself

自治 zìzhì　V　to be autonomous; self-government

自主 zìzhǔ　V　to decide for oneself

自助餐厅 zìzhùcāntīng　N　cafeteria · MW 家

自传 zìzhuàn　N　autobiography · MW 本

自尊 zìzūn　V　to have self-respect/self-esteem

自作自受 zìzuòzìshòu　EXP　to suffer as the result of one's own actions

别理他，他是**自作自受**。*Take no notice of him; he is suffering the consequences of his own actions.*

**RELATED WORDS**

| | | |
|---|---|---|
| 大自然 20 | 半自动 127 | 全自动 172 |
| 各自 425 | 私自 471 | 你自己 617 |
| 亲自 908 | 独自 1095 | 超自然 1684 |
| 骑自行车 1840 | 无地自容 139 | 毛遂自荐 183 |
| 听其自然 414 | 沾沾自喜 684 | 洁身自好 940 |
| 情不自禁 1491 | | |

---

**306** 血      U+8840      TM **7** FM ノ

xiě　N　blood

**血**的代价　*price paid in blood*

xuè　N·ADJ　blood; courage; menstrual period, menses; menstruation; related by blood; staunch, unyielding; sincere

血案 xuè'àn　N　murder case · MW 桩

血管 xuèguǎn　N　blood vessel, vein, artery · MW 条

血汗 xuèhàn　N　blood and sweat; hard work · MW 滴

血红 xuèhóng　ADJ　blood red, as red as blood

血迹 xuèjì　N　bloodstain · MW 块

床单上沾满了**血迹**。*The bedsheets are all bloodstained.*

血库 xuèkù　N　blood bank · MW 个

血泪 xuèlèi　N　tears of blood · MW 滴

血球 xuèqiú　N　blood cell · MW 个

血统 xuètǒng　N　blood relationship, bloodline, descent · MW 个

---

血型 xuèxíng　N　blood type · MW 种

血压 xuèyā　N　blood pressure

血液 xuèyè　N　blood · MW 滴、摊

**RELATED WORDS**

| | | |
|---|---|---|
| 止血 41 | 失血 106 | 心血 232 |
| 出血 258 | 呕血 560 | 充血 652 |
| 尿血 849 | 验血 1529 | 高血压 1611 |
| 混血儿 1739 | 鲜血 1811 | 输血 1867 |
| 鼻子出血 1794 | | |

---

**307** 东　東      U+4E1C      TM **7** FM ノ

dōng　N　east; owner, master; host

东半球 dōngbànqiú　N　eastern hemisphere

东北 dōngběi　N　northeast

东道 dōngdào　N　host · MW 个

东方 dōngfāng　N　the East; the Orient

东风 dōngfēng　N　east wind · MW 阵

东海 Dōnghǎi　N　East China Sea

东家 dōngjia　N　form of address formerly used by an employee to his employer · MW 个、位

东南 dōngnán　N　southeast

东欧 Dōng Ōu　N　Eastern Europe

东西 dōngxī　N　east and west; creature, person; thing, stuff · MW 个

你是什么**东西**？*What are you, anyway?*

用完后，请把**东西**放回原处。*Please put everything back when you've finished the work.*

**RELATED WORDS**

| | | |
|---|---|---|
| 广东 23 | 山东 38 | 中东 86 |
| 声东击西 374 | 房东 1145 | 做东 1282 |
| 股东 1456 | 毛泽东 183 | |

---

**308** 夺　奪      U+593A      TM **7** FM ノ

duó　V　to seize, to take by force; to wrest; to compete/contend/strive for; to exceed, to surpass, to outstrip; to deprive

夺标 duóbiāo　V　to win first prize

夺回 duóhuí　V　to recapture

夺取 duóqǔ　V　to capture, to seize; to strive for

部队**夺取**了堡垒。*The army seized the fort.*

夺去 duóqù　V　to snatch, to take away from

他**夺去**她手中的手提袋。*He snatched the handbag from her hands.*

**308 夺 duó** (continued)

夺权 duóquán  V  to seize power

**RELATED WORDS**

争夺 595     劫夺 819     抢夺 1230     剥夺 1377

---

**309**   **布**     U+5E03    TM **7** FM 丿

bù  N·V  cloth; ancient copper coin; to announce, to publicize, to notify; to spread, to diffuse, to extend; to arrange; to decorate

公布 announcement

传布 to spread

布阵 to deploy troops in battle formation

布帛 bùbó  N  cloth and silk; cotton and silk textiles ·  MW  匹、块

布道 bùdào  V  to preach

布店 bùdiàn  N  fabric store ·  MW  个

布告 bùgào  N·V  notice, bulletin ·  MW  个

布告牌 bulletin board

贴布告 to post a notice

布景 bùjǐng  N  (stage) set

布局 bùjú  V  to design, to compose; to begin a chess match

布匹 bùpǐ  N  cloth ·  MW  捆

布衣 bùyī  N  cotton clothes; commoner ·  MW  件、个、介

布置 bùzhì  V  to decorate; to arrange, to fix up

会议的事宜都已布置好了。 *Everything has been arranged for the meeting.*

**RELATED WORDS**

| | | | |
|---|---|---|---|
| 公布 103 | 分布 173 | 白布 176 | 毛布 183 |
| 发布 311 | 纱布 639 | 油布 683 | 砂布 733 |
| 尿布 849 | 桌布 984 | 帆布 1034 | 织布 1108 |
| 宣布 1138 | 麻布 1146 | 胶布 1296 | 散布 1579 |
| 棉布 1670 | 密布 1730 | 幕布 1767 | 摆布 1773 |
| 遍布 1892 | 瀑布 1974 | | |

---

**310**   **后**   後     U+540E    TM **7** FM 丿

hòu  N  rear, back; behind, after, afterwards, later, last; children, offspring, descendant; empress, queen

后半 hòubàn  N  latter half

后备 hòubèi  N  reserve; keeping in reserve

后辈 hòubèi  N  younger generation; offspring ·  MW  个

后代 hòudài  N  later generations; offspring ·  MW  个

后灯 hòudēng  N  backlight ·  MW  盏

后盾 hòudùn  N  backup force; support ·  MW  个

后方 hòufāng  N  rear; far behind the front line ·  MW  个

后顾 hòugù  V  to turn back to take care of, to look back

后果 hòuguǒ  N  aftermath, fallout, consequences ·  MW  个

我将对后果承担全部责任。 *I'll bear full responsibility for the consequences.*

后患 hòuhuàn  N  future trouble ·  MW  个

后悔 hòuhuǐ  V  to regret, to repent

抓住这个机会，否则你会后悔的。 *Seize the opportunity; you'll regret it otherwise.*

后继 hòujì  V  to carry on, to succeed

后脚 hòujiǎo  N  rear foot (in walking)

后进 hòujìn  N·ADJ  juniors, next generation; less advanced; lagging behind ·  MW  名

后来 hòulái  N·ADJ  latecomers; later, afterwards

开始我不同意他的提议，后来我改变了主意。 *I initially disagreed with his proposal, but later I changed my mind.*

后路 hòulù  N  way out; route of retreat ·  MW  条

后妈 hòumā  N  stepmother ·  MW  个

傻瓜有一个后妈。 *ShaGua has a stepmother.*

后门 hòumén  N  back door; under the counter ·  MW  个

午夜时分他打开后门。 *He opened the rear gate at midnight.*

他喜欢开后门。 *He likes backdoor deals.*

后面 hòumian  N  back, rear; behind; later

书的后面 back of the book

孩子落在父母后面。 *The kids trailed behind their parents.*

后脑 hòunǎo  N  hindbrain ·  MW  个

后期 hòuqī  N  later stage/period; behind schedule

后勤 hòuqín  N  logistics

后人 hòurén  N  later generations, descendants ·  MW  个

后事 hòushì  N  what happened next, future event; funeral ·  MW  件

后台 hòutái  N  backstage; behind-the-scenes support ·  MW  个

后天 hòutiān  N  day after tomorrow; postnatal, acquired

**后退** hòutuì  V  to retreat, to draw/fall back

**后退一步, 海阔天空。** *Taking one step back may create endless opportunity.*

**后院** hòuyuàn  N  backyard ·  MW  个

**RELATED WORDS**

| | | |
|---|---|---|
| 王后 27 | 午后 48 | 之后 67 |
| 术后处理 91 | 日后 96 | 以后 101 |
| 今后 102 | 产后 219 | 马后炮 247 |
| 走后门 265 | 而后 351 | 此后 416 |
| 先后 422 | 往后 461 | 向后 603 |
| 身后 604 | 秋后 641 | 过后 712 |
| 事后 987 | 售后服务 1266 | 前后 1329 |
| 背后 1380 | 拖后腿 1396 | 然后 1432 |
| 善后 1483 | 最后 1541 | 落后 1547 |
| 留后手 1582 | 税后 1705 | 幕后 1767 |
| 随后 1911 | 前因后果 1329 | 从今以后 66 |

---

**311**   发   發 髮    U+53D1    TM **7** FM 丿

**fā** (發)  V·MW  to send, to deliver; to hand over, to pay, to spread, to distribute; to express, to convey, to utter; to shoot, to emit; to produce, to generate; to cause; to happen, to occur, to arise, to take place; to expand, to enlarge; to develop, to promote; to get rich, to make a fortune; to feel, to sense, to perceive; to set out, to start a journey; to start (doing); to arouse, to stimulate, to inspire; to enlighten; [measure word for bullets, cartridges, etc.]

**发邮件给朋友** *to send mail to friends*

**给客户发货** *to deliver merchandise to customers*

**老师发问。** *The teacher asks questions.*

**傻瓜发言。** *ShaGua spoke.*

**她发育了。** *She has reached puberty.*

**引发争论** *to cause arguments*

**"文革"爆发。** *The Cultural Revolution erupted.*

**发面** *leaven dough*

**伤口发炎。** *The cut is infected.*

**fà** (髮)  N  hair

**头发** *hair on the head*

**发白** fābái  V  to turn pale; to go white

**发榜** fābǎng  V  to publish a list of successful candidates

**发报** fābào  V  to send a message

**发表** fābiǎo  V  to announce, to make public; to express one's opinion; to publish (an article, etc.) in a periodical

**他发表了不少文章。** *He has published many articles.*

**发病** fābìng  V  to get sick, to fall ill, to break out with (a disease)

**发布** fābù  V  to issue (an order, news, etc.); to release, to announce

**发财** fācái  V  to get rich, to make a fortune

**恭喜发财。** *Congratulations for being so prosperous! (traditional Chinese New Year's greeting)*

**发车** fāchē  V  to depart (of a vehicle)

**发愁** fāchóu  V  to worry, to be anxious

**发出** fāchū  V  to send out, to issue, to deliver; to give out/off; to give an order; to produce (sound, etc.); to ask (a question)

**发达** fādá  ADJ·V  developed; flourishing; to gain fortune and fame

**发呆** fādāi  V  to be in a daze, to stare blankly

**发电** fādiàn  V  to generate electricity

**发动** fādòng  V  to start, to initiate, to launch

**发抖** fādǒu  V  to tremble, to shiver, to shake

**发短信** fāduǎnxìn  V  to text, to send an SMS message

**发疯** fāfēng  V  to go mad/crazy, to become insane

**那个小伙子已经发疯了。** *The young man has already gone mad.*

**发稿** fāgǎo  V  to file a report, to distribute a news dispatch

**发给** fāgěi  V  to issue, to distribute

**把奖品发给优胜者。** *The prizes were distributed to the winners.*

**发光** fāguāng  V  to shine, to give out light

**发还** fāhuán  V  to give back, to return

**发慌** fāhuāng  V  to be nervous

**发挥** fāhuī  V  to bring into play, to give free rein to; to express, to elaborate

**发昏** fāhūn  V  to feel giddy; to faint

**发火** fāhuǒ  V  to lose one's temper, to get angry; to flare up, to catch fire; to draw well (of a stove)

**她很容易发火。** *She angers very easily.*

**发货** fāhuò  V  to deliver merchandise

**发奖** fājiǎng  V  to award prizes

**校长在表彰会上发奖。** *The principal gave away prizes at the ceremony.*

**发掘** fājué  V  to excavate, to unearth

**发觉** fājué  V  to discover, to find

**发狂** fākuáng  V  to go mad/crazy

**发冷** fālěng  V  to feel/catch cold

**发愣** fālèng  V  to stare blankly, to be in a daze

**311 发 fā/fà** (continued)

发麻 **fāmá** V to numb

发霉 **fāméi** V to become moldy/mildewed

发明 **fāmíng** V·N to invent; invention · MW 个

发难 **fānàn** V to revolt

发怒 **fānù** V to get angry

发胖 **fāpàng** V to gain / put on weight; to get fat

发票 **fāpiào** N invoice; receipt · MW 张

发起 **fāqǐ** V to initiate, to sponsor; to start/launch (a war, an attack, etc.)

他是**发起**人之一。 *He is one of the founders.*

发情 **fāqíng** V to rut

发球 **fāqiú** V to serve (a ball)

发热 **fārè** V to run a fever, to have a temperature

发人深省 **fārénshēnxǐng** EXP to set (someone) thinking, to give (someone) food for thought

发烧 **fāshāo** V to have a fever/temperature

她有一点**发烧**。 *She had a slight fever.*

发射 **fāshè** V to launch (a satellite, rocket, etc.)

发声 **fāshēng** V to make/produce a sound, to utter

发生 **fāshēng** V to happen, to occur, to take place

发誓 **fāshì** V to pledge, to vow, to swear

发送 **fāsòng** V to send out, to dispatch (a letter, etc.)

发问 **fāwèn** V to ask; to raise a question

那个人不停地**发问**, 打断傻瓜的发言。 *The man kept interrupting ShaGua's speech with questions.*

发现 **fāxiàn** V·N to discover, to detect; discovery · MW 个

发笑 **fāxiào** V to laugh; to burst out laughing

发信 **fāxìn** V to mail a letter

发行 **fāxíng** V to issue, to publish, to distribute

发芽 **fāyá** V to sprout, to germinate

发言 **fāyán** V·N to speak; speech; statement · MW 个、篇

发言人 **fāyánrén** N spokesperson · MW 个、名

发扬 **fāyáng** V to carry on, to develop, to make full use of

发痒 **fāyǎng** V to itch, to tickle

发音 **fāyīn** V·N to pronounce; pronunciation · MW 个

这两个词拼写不同, 但**发音**相同。 *The two words are spelled differently, but pronounced the same.*

发育 **fāyù** V to develop, to grow

发源 **fāyuán** V to rise, to originate

发展 **fāzhǎn** V·N to develop; to expand; development, growth · MW 个

发胀 **fāzhàng** V to swell

发肿 **fāzhǒng** V to swell

发作 **fāzuò** V to flare up, to break out; to have a fit (of anger)

这人死于心脏病**发作**。 *This man died from a heart attack.*

他有些生气, 但当着大家的面又不好**发作**。 *He was angry, but with everyone present, he kept his temper under control.*

发辫 **fàbiàn** N braid · MW 条、根

发夹 **fàjiā** N hairpin, hair clip · MW 个

发型 **fàxíng** N hairstyle · MW 个、种

发油 **fàyóu** N hair oil · MW 滴、瓶

**RELATED WORDS**

| | | |
|---|---|---|
| 开发 26 | 头发 128 | 击发 156 |
| 分发 173 | 毛发 183 | 并发 225 |
| 出发 258 | 收发 282 | 打发 289 |
| 自发 305 | 沙发 342 | 引发 371 |
| 先发制人 422 | 印发 470 | 补发 508 |
| 奋发 607 | 启发 657 | 待发 872 |
| 须发 875 | 批发 1005 | 转发 1111 |
| 洗发液 1167 | 理发 1200 | 签发 1439 |
| 越发 1575 | 散发 1579 | 假发 1586 |
| 偶发 1590 | 烫发 1624 | 诱发 1748 |
| 蒸发 1768 | 脱发 1803 | 暴发 1844 |
| 照发 1846 | 揭发 1851 | 激发 1955 |
| 爆发 1982 | 升官发财 47 | 披头散发 1011 |
| 容光焕发 1320 | | |

**312**   尽   儘 盡    U+5C3D    TM **7** FM 丿

**jǐn** (儘) ADV·PREP·V as far as possible, to the greatest extent; most; to give priority to

尽快 *as quickly as possible*

**jìn** (盡) V·ADJ to keep on (doing); to exhaust, to use up; to go to extremes, to try one's best; to use to the fullest; to die; complete, all, entire; exhaustive

傻瓜的为人一言难**尽**。 *As a man, ShaGua is hard to describe in just a few words.*

傻瓜做事总是**尽**力而为。 *ShaGua always does his best.*

尽头 *in the end*

钱已**尽**付。 *All the money has been paid.*

尽管 **jǐnguǎn** ADV·CONJ to not hesitate to, unhesitatingly; though, even though

尽管可能会失败, 但他们仍要试一试。
*Though they may all fail, they will try.*

尽量 jǐnliàng  ADV  as far as possible

尽力 jìnlì  V  to do all one can, to try one's best

尽量 jìnliàng  ADV  (to eat/drink) to fullness

尽情 jìnqíng  ADV  to one's heart content, as much as one likes

尽是 jìnshì  V  to be full of
这本书里尽是科学术语。*This book is full of scientific terms.*

尽心 jìnxīn  V  to do one's best; to put one's heart and soul into

尽义务 jìnyìwù  V  to do one's duty, to fulfill one's obligation; to volunteer

尽职 jìnzhí  V  to fulfill one's duty

尽忠 jìnzhōng  V  to be loyal to the end

### RELATED WORDS

---

**313  用**      U+7528    TM **7** FM 丿

yòng  V·N  to use, to employ, to apply; [used in the negative] to need, to have to; expense

用兵 yòngbīng  V  to use military force

用不了 yòngbùliǎo  V  to have more than is needed
用不了三年, 他就可以毕业了。*He will finish school in less than three years.*

用不着 yòngbùzháo  V  to not need

用场 yòngchǎng  N  use, purpose ·  MW  个

用处 yòngchu  N  use, purpose ·  MW  个
抱怨有什么用处？*What's the use in complaining?*
这本参考书对我有用处吗？*Will this reference book be of any use to me?*

用得着 yòngdezháo  V  to find useful

用法 yòngfǎ  N  use, usage ·  MW  个
依照习惯用法 *according to usage*

用费 yòngfèi  N  expense ·  MW  笔
无论用费多少, 都得做。*It will be done at any expense.*

用功 yònggōng  V·ADJ  to study/work hard; hardworking, diligent
傻瓜的大儿子比班上的同学更用功学习。*ShaGua's older son studies harder than anyone else in his class.*

用户 yònghù  N  user, consumer ·  MW  个

用尽 yòngjìn  V  to exhaust, to use up

用劲 yòngjìn  V  to exert oneself (physically)

用具 yòngjù  N  tool, appliance, apparatus ·  MW  套

用力 yònglì  V  to exert oneself

用品 yòngpǐn  N  goods, products; appliances ·  MW  件
这家商店供应各种学习用品。*The store offers a number of items for use by students.*

用人 yòngrén  V·N  to make the best use of personnel; servant ·  MW  个

用途 yòngtú  N  use, application, purpose ·  MW  种
这台机器有多种用途。*There are many uses for this machine.*

用武 yòngwǔ  V  to use force

用心 yòngxīn  ADJ·N  careful, attentive, diligent; intention, purpose
傻瓜在夜校用心学习。*ShaGua really concentrates on his studies in night school.*
这个家伙别有用心。*This guy has ulterior motives.*

用以 yòngyǐ  CONJ  in order to, so as to
略举数例, 用以说明这一原理。*Here are some examples to illustrate this principle.*

用意 yòngyì  N  intention, purpose ·  MW  个

用于 yòngyú  V  to use in/on/for
铝箔用于包装食物。*Aluminum foil can be used for wrapping food.*

用语 yòngyǔ  N  word, term; wording
用语不当 *inappropriate choice of words*
商业用语 *business jargon*

### RELATED WORDS

**313 用 yòng** (continued)

挪用 1658
调用 1749
施用 1758
无所用心 139
古为今用 154
量才录用 1544

常用 1733
通用 1757
反作用 111
日常费用 96
洋为中用 689

---

**314 凤** 鳳　　U+51E4　　TM **7** FM 丿

**fèng** N phoenix

凤凰 **fènghuáng** N phoenix · MW 只

凤梨 **fènglí** N pineapple · MW 个

**RELATED WORD**

龙凤呈祥 315

---

**315 龙** 龍　　U+9F99　　TM **7** FM 丿

**lóng** N dragon (a symbol of royal/imperial authority in feudal times)

龙船 **lóngchuán** N dragon boat · MW 只、艘、条

龙胆 **lóngdǎn** N rough gentian (a flower)

龙灯 **lóngdēng** N dragon lantern · MW 盏

龙凤呈祥 **lóngfèng chéngxiáng** EXP prosperity brought by the dragon and the phoenix

龙骨 **lónggǔ** N bird's sternum; fossil fragment (used in traditional Chinese medicine); keel · MW 条

龙井 **lóngjǐng** N longjing; Dragonwell tea · MW 杯、壶

龙卷风 **lóngjuǎnfēng** N tornado, cyclone; hurricane · MW 阵、场

龙头 **lóngtóu** N tap, faucet; bicycle handlebar; head (of a group, especially of gangsters); beginning (of a queue, etc.) · MW 个

龙王 **lóngwáng** N Dragon King of the Eastern Sea (mythology); god of rain

龙虾 **lóngxiā** N lobster · MW 只

龙眼 **lóngyǎn** N longan; euphoria longan (a fruit tree) · MW 颗

龙舟 **lóngzhōu** N dragon boat, imperial boat · MW 条、艘

**RELATED WORDS**

水龙头 159
乌龙茶 601
跑龙套 1916

尼龙 441
恐龙 1644
望子成龙 1622

---

**316 式**　　U+5F0F　　TM **7** FM 丿

**shì** N style, type; form, pattern, model; ceremony, ritual, formula

式样 **shìyàng** N style, type; design, pattern; fashion · MW 个、种
这件衣服的**式样**真高雅。*This dress is so stylish.*

**RELATED WORDS**

正式 76
公式 103
立式 125
方式 220
样式 803
格式 1246
程式 1451
新式 1638
非正式 378
便携式 865
喷气式 1563

中式 86
仪式 122
旧式 165
形式 257
把式 1006
等式 1437
款式 1573
模式 1673
封闭式 815
落地式 1547

---

**317 杀** 殺　　U+6740　　TM **7** FM 丿

**shā** V to kill, to put to death, to slaughter, to murder; to fight, to go into battle; to reduce, to weaken; to end, to terminate; to cut short, to hold back; [used after a verb] extremely, exceedingly, utterly

**杀**杀对手的威风 *to deflate an opponent's arrogance*

杀虫剂 **shāchóngjì** N insecticide, pesticide · MW 瓶

杀敌 **shādí** V to fight/kill the enemy

杀害 **shāhài** V to murder; to kill unjustifiably
她被恐怖分子**杀害**了。*She was murdered by terrorists.*

杀鸡取卵 **shājīqǔluǎn** EXP to kill the hen that lays the golden eggs

杀菌 **shājūn** V to disinfect

杀气 **shāqì** N murderous look · MW 股

杀人 **shārén** V to kill, to murder

杀伤 **shāshāng** V to inflict casualties on, to kill and wound

杀头 **shātóu** V to behead

**RELATED WORDS**

自杀 305
冲杀 339
残杀 977
枪杀 1244
暗杀 1676

仇杀 319
抹杀 571
刺杀 1050
虐杀 1379
诱杀 1748

## 318 坐　　U+5750　TM 7　FM ノ

**zuò** V·N to sit, to take a seat; to take / travel by (plane, etc.); seat, place

坐标 **zuòbiāo** N coordination · MW 个

坐等 **zuòděng** V to sit back and wait

坐等胜利 *to sit back and wait for a victory*

坐垫 **zuòdiàn** N cushion · MW 个

坐困 **zuòkùn** V to be confined

坐牢 **zuòláo** V to be in prison/jail

如果他继续违法，他会**坐牢**的。 *If he continues to break the law, he will go to prison.*

坐立不安 **zuòlìbù'ān** EXP to be fidgety

坐落 **zuòluò** V to be situated/located (of a building)

坐失良机 **zuòshīliángjī** EXP to let a golden opportunity slip by

坐位 **zuòwèi** N seat · MW 个

我们在餐馆订的**坐位**是背靠背的。 *We had back-to-back seats in the restaurant.*

坐卧不安 **zuòwòbù'ān** EXP to be unable to sit down / sleep easily

坐月子 **zuòyuèzi** EXP month-long confined bedrest after childbirth

**RELATED WORD**

静坐 1947

## 319 仇　　U+4EC7　TM 7　FM ノ

**chóu** N enemy, foe, rival; hatred, enmity, animosity; grudge, feud

仇敌 **chóudí** N enemy, foe · MW 个、名

仇恨 **chóuhèn** V·N to hate bitterly/intensely; animosity, hostility

这种**仇恨**是由种族偏见引起的。 *This hatred was the result of racial prejudice.*

仇人 **chóurén** N personal enemy · MW 个、名

仇杀 **chóushā** V to kill in revenge; vendetta

仇视 **chóushì** V to be hostile to, to regard as an enemy

**RELATED WORDS**

私仇 471　　　　记仇 946

报仇 1010　　　　冤仇 1729

## 320 伍　　U+4F0D　TM 7　FM ノ

**wǔ** NUM·N five (formal variant of the number); army

**RELATED WORDS**

队伍 294　　　　耻与为伍 735

## 321 伴　　U+4F34　TM 7　FM ノ

**bàn** N·V company; companion, partner; to accompany

伴唱 **bànchàng** V to provide vocal accompaniment

伴侣 **bànlǚ** N partner, companon; husband, wife · MW 个、名

伴随 **bànsuí** V to accompany, to follow

伴音 **bànyīn** N sound accompaniment, score · MW 个

伴奏 **bànzòu** V to provide musical accompaniment

**RELATED WORDS**

伙伴 214　　　作伴 326　　　老伴 375

同伴 541　　　相伴 805　　　做伴 1282

结伴 1291　　　旅伴 1518　　　陪伴 1568

舞伴 1790　　　游伴 1818

## 322 似　　U+4F3C　TM 7　FM ノ

**sì** V·ADV·PREP to be similar, to be like, to resemble; to seem, to appear; apparently; as if; than

似乎 **sìhū** ADV apparently; as if

似是而非 **sìshì'érfēi** EXP specious, spurious

**RELATED WORDS**

好似 627　　　类似 676　　　近似 716

相似 805　　　归心似箭 166

## 323 位　　U+4F4D　TM 7　FM ノ

**wèi** N·MW place, location, position; digit; [measure word for respected people]

位次 **wèicì** N precedence, position

位于 **wèiyú** V to be located/situated

人民英雄纪念碑**位**于天安门广场的中心。 *The Monument to the People's Heroes is located in the center of Tian'anmen Square.*

## 323 位 wèi (continued)

**位置** wèizhi   N   location, place; status, position · MW 个

**位子** wèizi   N   seat, place, position · MW 个

这辆车有七个**位子**, 请给客人安排好**位置**。准备开车了。*There are seven seats in this van. Please arrange the seats for our guests; we are ready to go.*

### RELATED WORDS

| | | |
|---|---|---|
| 本位 90 | 水位 159 | 方位 220 |
| 穴位 231 | 坐位 318 | 让位 348 |
| 各位 425 | 定位 666 | 单位 672 |
| 岗位 745 | 地位 772 | 座位 920 |
| 吨位 1022 | 即位 1047 | 学位 1155 |
| 职位 1205 | 品位 1220 | 席位 1325 |
| 牌位 1597 | 部位 1636 | 铺位 1713 |
| 错位 1715 | 就位 1836 | 每单位 837 |

## 324 住   U+4F4F   TM 7 FM 丿

**zhù**   V   to live, to reside, to dwell, to stay; to stop, to cease

**住处** zhùchù   N   residence, dwelling; lodging · MW 个

你知道傻瓜的**住处**吗? *Do you know where ShaGua's house is?*

**住房** zhùfáng   N   housing, lodging

**住户** zhùhù   N   household; resident · MW 个

**住手** zhùshǒu   V   to stop, to stay one's hand

**住宿** zhùsù   V   to stay, to get lodging

**住所** zhùsuǒ   N   dwelling place, residence · MW 个、栋

**住院** zhùyuàn   V   to be hospitalized

听说傻瓜**住院**了。*I've heard that ShaGua has been hospitalized.*

**住宅** zhùzhái   N   house, residence, dwelling · MW 个、栋

**住址** zhùzhǐ   N   address · MW 个

### RELATED WORDS

| | |
|---|---|
| 止住 41 | 抓住 406 |
| 拦住 576 | 顶住 724 |
| 咬住 780 | 居住 850 |
| 记住 946 | 挡住 1018 |
| 站住脚 1189 | 站住 1189 |
| 拿住 1262 | 愣住 1735 |
| 衣食住行 330 | 忍不住 970 |
| 禁不住 1536 | 靠不住 1791 |
| 憋不住 1972 | |

## 325 体 體   U+4F53   TM 7 FM 丿

**tǐ**   N·V   body; part of a body; main part; substance; style; form; system; to experience, to do (something) personally

**体裁** tǐcái   N   genre, type of literature; style · MW 种

**体操** tǐcāo   N   gymnastics · MW 个

**体操馆** tǐcāoguǎn   N   gymnasium · MW 个、座

**体格** tǐgé   N   physical fitness, constitution · MW 种

**体会** tǐhuì   V·N   to know/learn from experience; to realize · MW 个

在中国生活了两个月, 你有什么**体会**? *What have you learned from living in China for two months?*

**体力** tǐlì   N   physical strength

**体谅** tǐliàng   V   to show understanding/sympathy for

**体面** tǐmiàn   N·ADJ   dignity; face; honorable, respectable; good-looking

**体内** tǐnèi   N   internal (to the body); in vivo

**体贴** tǐtiē   V   to show consideration for

傻瓜生病了, 傻瓜太太很**体贴**地照顾他。*ShaGua was ill. Mrs. ShaGua looked after him carefully.*

**体外** tǐwài   ADJ   in vitro

**体味** tǐwèi   V·N   to appreciate, to savor; body odor · MW 种

**体温** tǐwēn   N   body temperature · MW 度

傻瓜发烧了, **体温**达到40度。*ShaGua had a fever of 40 degrees Celsius.*

**体系** tǐxì   N   system; setup · MW 个

**体现** tǐxiàn   V   to embody, to give expression to, to reflect

**体形** tǐxíng   N   physique, build · MW 种

**体验** tǐyàn   V   to learn from experience

**体育** tǐyù   N   sports; physical education

**体制** tǐzhì   N   system; structure, organization · MW 个、种

**体质** tǐzhì   N   physique; constitution · MW 种

**体重** tǐzhòng   N   body weight

### RELATED WORDS

| | | |
|---|---|---|
| 个体 18 | 尸体 58 | 文体 70 |
| 主体 124 | 立体 125 | 立体声 125 |
| 全体 172 | 气体 185 | 形体 257 |
| 团体 392 | 具体 533 | 身体 604 |
| 字体 664 | 固体 760 | 物体 883 |
| 肌体 1118 | 集体 1267 | 总体 1330 |

## 326 作　　　U+4F5C　　TM **7** FM 丿

**zuō** N workshop

**zuò** V·N to do; to rise, to get up; to write, to compose; to pretend; to take (something) as/for, to regard; to feel; to act like, to become; work; writing

**作坊 zuōfang** N workshop · MW 个

**作案 zuò'àn** V to commit a crime

**作罢 zuòbà** V to drop, to give up, to relinquish

**作伴 zuòbàn** V to keep (someone) company, to accompany

**作弊 zuòbì** V to cheat, to practice fraud; to plagiarize

**作对 zuòduì** V to oppose; to make a pair

**作恶 zuò'è** V to do evil

**作法 zuòfǎ** N·V method/way (of doing something); writing technique; to resort to magic · MW 个、种

**作废 zuòfèi** V to become invalid; to cancel, to nullify

**作梗 zuògěng** V to obstruct, to make things difficult

**作怪 zuòguài** V to make trouble/mischief

**作家 zuòjiā** N writer, author · MW 个、名、位

**作假 zuòjiǎ** V to fake, to counterfeit; to cheat, to play tricks

**作价 zuòjià** V to evaluate, to establish a price for

**作践 zuòjian** V to spoil, to waste; to disparage, to run (someone) down

**作客 zuòkè** V to be a guest/visitor; to live away from home

**作料 zuòliao** N condiments; seasoning (often pronounced zuóliao in spoken Chinese) · MW 种

**作乱 zuòluàn** V to stage an armed rebellion

**作美 zuòměi** V to cooperate, to help, to make things easy

**作难 zuònán** V to be embarrassed

**作弄 zuònòng** V to tease; to play a trick on

有人以为傻瓜有点傻，总想**作弄**他。
*Some people think ShaGua is a bit dumb, so they always want to play tricks on him.*

**作为 zuòwéi** N·V·PREP action; accomplishment; to regard (something) as, to take (something) for; to accomplish; as

**作**为一个学生，获得好成绩很重要。
*As a student, achievement is very important.*

**作文 zuòwén** V·N to write a paper; composition, essay

用中文写**作文**有点儿难。*It is not very easy to write a paper in Chinese.*

**作业 zuòyè** N homework, schoolwork; work · MW 次

中文课老师每天都给学生布置**作业**。
*Chinese teachers give their students homework every day.*

**作揖 zuòyī** V to bow with one's hands folded in front

**作用 zuòyòng** N·V action; impact, effect; to act on, to affect · MW 个

**作战 zuòzhàn** V to fight, to do battle

**作者 zuòzhě** N writer, author, artist · MW 个、名、位

**作主 zuòzhǔ** V to decide; to support, to back up

### RELATED WORDS

## 327 行　　　U+884C　　TM **7** FM 丿

**háng** N·MW row, line; profession, line of work; company, firm; birth order; seniority among brothers and sisters; [measure word for things that form a line]

字里**行**间 *between the lines*

同**行** *people in the same profession*

银**行** *banks*

一共有三**行** *three lines altogether*

**xíng** V·ADJ·N to walk; to sail; to drive; to do, to act, to perform, to carry out; to be current; to circulate; all right, okay; capable, competent; travel, trip, journey; behavior, conduct

步**行**街 *pedestrian street*

**327 行 háng/xíng** (continued)

行不行？ *Is that all right?*

行骗 *cheating*

实行 *to carry out*

你真行！ *You are really great!*

流行 *popular*

操行评价 *evaluation of moral conduct*

行程 *travel plan/route*

行帮 hángbāng　N　trade association · MW 个

行当 hángdang　N　profession, line of work; role (especially in traditional Chinese opera) · MW 个

行规 hángguī　N　guild regulation, union rule · MW 个

行话 hánghuà　N　jargon, trade talk · MW 句
　有的医生的**行话**常常把病人弄糊涂了。 *Some doctors often confuse patients with their mindless jargon.*

行列 hángliè　N　ranks; procession · MW 个、队

行情 hángqíng　N　market prices/conditions · MW 个

行业 hángyè　N　industry, business; trade, profession · MW 个
　服务**行业** *service industry*

行不通 xíngbùtōng　V　won't do
　这个想法很好, 但就是**行不通**。 *This idea is very good, but it just won't work.*

行车 xíngchē　V·N　to drive a vehicle; overhead traveling crane · MW 辆

行动 xíngdòng　V·N　to move (around); to take action; mobility; movement; operation · MW 个
　**行动**不便 *having difficulty getting around*
　你必须中断你的**行动**。 *You must put an end to your activities.*
　军事**行动** *military operation*
　实际**行动** *actual deed*

行贿 xínghuì　V　to bribe
　有个商人企图向傻瓜**行贿**。 *A businessman tried to bribe ShaGua.*

行军 xíngjūn　V　to march (of troops)

行李 xíngli　N　luggage, baggage · MW 件

行人 xíngrén　N　pedestrian · MW 个、名

行商 xíngshāng　N　itinerant trade · MW 个、名

行驶 xíngshǐ　V　to go/travel (of a vehicle, ship, etc.)
　超速**行驶** *to drive above the speed limit*

行使 xíngshǐ　V　to exercise (a right, etc.); to perform

行为 xíngwéi　N　behavior, conduct · MW 个
　我悔恨自己的不良**行为**。 *I regret my bad behavior.*

行销 xíngxiāo　V　to be on sale; to sell

行星 xíngxīng　N　planet; planetary · MW 颗

行凶 xíngxiōng　V　to assault; to murder

行医 xíngyī　V　to practice medicine

行政 xíngzhèng　N　administration
　**行政**职能 *administrative function*

行装 xíngzhuāng　N　luggage · MW 套

行踪 xíngzōng　N　whereabouts, location · MW 个

行走 xíngzǒu　V　to walk, to step
　沿着街道**行走** *walking along a street*

**RELATED WORDS**

**328 奴**　　U+5974　TM 7 FM 丿

nú　N·V　slave; to enslave; to treat like a slave

奴才 núcai　N　slave; flunky · MW 个、名

奴化 núhuà　V　to enslave

奴隶 núlì　N　slave; serf · MW 个、名

奴仆 núpú　N　servant; lackey · MW 个、名

奴性 núxìng　N　servility

奴役 núyì　V　to enslave; slavery

**RELATED WORD**

## 329 奸
U+5978    TM **7** FM 丿

**jiān** ADJ·N·V  evil, wicked, wily; treacherous, disloyal to the country; traitor; adultery; to rape

**奸臣 jiānchén** N  treacherous court official · MW 个、名

**奸夫 jiānfū** N  illicit lover, paramour · MW 个、名

**奸妇 jiānfù** N  illicit lover, paramour · MW 个、名

**奸商 jiānshāng** N  unscrupulous businessman, shark · MW 个、名

**奸污 jiānwū** V  to rape

**奸细 jiānxi** N  spy, enemy agent · MW 个、名

**奸险 jiānxiǎn** ADJ  malicious, wicked, wily

**奸淫 jiānyín** V  to rape; to fornicate; to commit adultery

### RELATED WORDS

内奸 191          汉奸 235          强奸 1896

## 330 衣
U+8863    TM **7** FM 丶

**yī** N·V  clothing, clothes, garment; cover; placenta, afterbirth; to wear

**衣橱 yīchú** N  wardrobe · MW 个

**衣服 yīfu** N  clothes · MW 件、套
傻瓜穿的**衣服**总是搭配得不伦不类。
*The clothes ShaGua wears often do not match.*

**衣冠 yīguān** N  hat and clothes · MW 套

**衣柜 yīguì** N  wardrobe · MW 个

**衣架 yījià** N  coat hanger; clothes rack · MW 个

**衣料 yīliào** N  fabric for clothing · MW 块、匹

**衣帽间 yīmàojiān** N  cloakroom · MW 个

**衣裳 yīshang** N  clothes · MW 件、套

**衣食住行 yīshízhùxíng** EXP  food, clothing, housing, and transportation; basic needs

**衣箱 yīxiāng** N  suitcase · MW 个

### RELATED WORDS

丰衣足食 35        冬衣 178        内衣 191
皮衣 261          布衣 309        雨衣 720
衬衣 962          洗衣 1167       浴衣 1170
睡衣 1571         卫生衣 82       羽绒衣 732
短大衣 1452       游泳衣 1818     避弹衣 1976

## 331 辛
U+8F9B    TM **7** FM 丶

**xīn** ADJ  hot, spicy, pungent; strenuous

**辛苦 xīnkǔ** ADJ  strenuous, hard
学中文是件既快乐又**辛苦**的事。
*Studying Chinese is enjoyable, but it's also difficult.*

**辛辣 xīnlà** ADJ  hot, pungent; biting, scathing

**辛劳 xīnláo** ADJ  hard, laborious

**辛勤 xīnqín** ADJ  hardworking, industrious

**辛辛苦苦 xīnxīnkǔkǔ** EXP  to go to a lot of trouble; painstaking

### RELATED WORD

艰辛 973

## 332 市
U+5E02    TM **7** FM 丶

**shì** N·V  city, municipality; market; to buy; to sell

**市场 shìchǎng** N  market, marketplace, bazaar · MW 个
这个农贸**市场**每天都很热闹。*This farmers' market is busy every day.*

**市场调查 shìchǎngdiàochá** V  to do a market survey

**市场价格 shìchǎngjiàgé** N  market price · MW 个

**市场学 shìchǎngxué** N  marketing

**市价 shìjià** N  market value, current price · MW 个

**市郊 shìjiāo** N  suburb, outskirts · MW 个
美国的中产阶级喜欢住在**市郊**, 中国的中产阶级喜欢住在市区。*The American middle class likes to live in suburbs, but the Chinese middle class likes to live in cities.*

**市侩 shìkuài** N  vulgar/boorish person, philistine · MW 个

**市民 shìmín** N  city residents · MW 个、名、位

**市区 shìqū** N  urban area, downtown, city proper · MW 个

**市容 shìróng** N  city's appearance/condition
请保持**市容**整洁。*Please keep the city clean and neat.*

**市委 shìwěi** N  municipal committee · MW 个

**市镇 shìzhèn** N  small town · MW 个

**市政 shìzhèng** N  municipal administration · MW 个

**332 市 shì** (continued)

**RELATED WORDS**

| | | |
|---|---|---|
| 开市 26 | 小市民 61 | 城市 1225 |
| 集市 1267 | 闹市 1323 | 黑市 1389 |
| 都市 1578 | 门庭若市 130 | |

---

**333 床**     U+5E8A    TM **7** FM 丶

**chuáng** [N·MW] bed; shaped like a bed; [measure word for quilts, mattresses, etc.]

床单 **chuángdān** [N] sheet; bedspread, coverlet · [MW] 条

这床单看上去很脏, 我能换一条吗？
*This bedspread looks dirty; may I have another one?*

床垫 **chuángdiàn** [N] mattress · [MW] 个、张

床铺 **chuángpù** [N] bed; bed and bedding · [MW] 张

床头 **chuángtóu** [N] headboard

床罩 **chuángzhào** [N] bedspread · [MW] 个

**RELATED WORDS**

| | | |
|---|---|---|
| 上床 14 | 车床 114 | 牙床 143 |
| 苗床 553 | 机床 577 | 卧床 826 |
| 尿床 849 | 钻床 1302 | 病床 1327 |
| 起床 1421 | 温床 1627 | |

---

**334 应 應**     U+5E94    TM **7** FM 丶

**yīng** [V] should, ought to

**yìng** [V] to answer, to respond, to reply; to permit; to accept, to comply with, to agree to; to handle, to deal/cope with; to correspond to

我回应你。 *I responded to you.*

我没应你这事儿。 *I have not agreed to commit to this.*

应当 **yīngdāng** [V] should, ought to

你们应当坚持你们的意见。 *You should stick to your opinions.*

这样做应当不应当？ *It should be done this way, shouldn't it?*

应得 **yīngdé** [V] to deserve

这是你应得的。 *You deserve it.*

应该 **yīnggāi** [V] should, ought to; to be supposed to, must

我应该首先征得你的同意, 才实施。 *I should have asked for your consent first, and then carried it out.*

应届 **yīngjiè** [N] current, this year's

应有 **yīngyǒu** [V] to be due; ought to have

这是学生对老师应有的尊敬。 *This is an honor due to a teacher from a student.*

应变 **yìngbiàn** [V] to adapt to change; to take emergency measures

应承 **yìngchéng** [V] to agree to

应酬 **yìngchou** [V·N] to socialize with; social engagement · [MW] 个、次

应答 **yìngdá** [V] to answer, to reply

应急 **yìngjí** [V] to respond to an emergency

应景 **yìngjǐng** [V·ADJ] to do (something) for the occasion; timely, appropriate

应考 **yìngkǎo** [V] to take an examination

这次考试使三个应考者落选。 *Three candidates failed the examination.*

应诺 **yìngnuò** [V] to agree to

应聘 **yìngpìn** [V] to accept a job offer

应声 **yìngshēng** [V] to answer, to reply

应邀 **yìngyāo** [V] to be invited; at (someone's) invitation

他应邀在宴会上讲话。 *He was invited to speak at the banquet.*

应用 **yìngyòng** [V] to apply, to use

应战 **yìngzhàn** [V] to meet an attack; to face a challenge

应征 **yìngzhēng** [V] to apply for (a job), to answer a job advertisement; to enlist

**RELATED WORDS**

| | | |
|---|---|---|
| 支应 92 | 反应 111 | 对应 254 |
| 供应 459 | 呼应 779 | 顺应 874 |
| 效应 965 | 适应 1358 | 接应 1405 |
| 响应 1409 | 照应 1846 | 感应 1860 |
| 不适应 24 | | |

---

**335 当 當**     U+5F53    TM **7** FM 丶

**dāng** [V·ADJ·PREP·ONOM] should, ought to; to act/work as, to be; to deserve; to be in charge of, to manage; to match, to equal; in front of, in the presence of; just when; to chime (of a bell); to knock

门当户对 *to be well-matched in socioeconomic status (especially for marriage)*

傻瓜当市长。 *ShaGua serves as mayor.*

当面说清 *to clarify in person*

当说就说。 *You should say whatever it is you ought to say.*

你当得起这个荣誉吗？ *Do you deserve this honor?*

当家作主 *to be the one with power to make decisions*

**dàng** ADJ·V appropriate, proper; to be equal to; to treat as; to assume; to pawn

用人得当 *to choose the right people*

以一当十 *to pit one against ten*

你把朋友当敌人。 *You treated friends as enemies.*

你当我不知？ *You think I don't know?*

当班 **dāngbān** V to work one's shift

当兵 **dāngbīng** V to be a soldier, to serve in the army

当场 **dāngchǎng** ADV then and there, at the scene, on the spot

购物时我习惯当场付现金。 *It is my usual practice when shopping to pay cash on the spot.*

当初 **dāngchū** N in those days; in the beginning, at first

当代 **dāngdài** N present (time); contemporary period

当道 **dāngdào** V·N to hold power; something in the way

当地 **dāngdì** N locality; local

当即 **dāngjí** ADV immediately, right away

他当即给我写了张支票。 *He wrote me a check on the spot.*

当家 **dāngjiā** V to rule the roost, to manage a household

当今 **dāngjīn** N present (time), nowadays

当局 **dāngjú** N authorities

当面 **dāngmiàn** ADV face to face

当年 **dāngnián** N in those days; that very year; prime of life

当前 **dāngqián** V·N to be faced with; present, current

大敌当前 *with a formidable enemy before us*

当权 **dāngquán** V to hold power

当时 **dāngshí** N at the time; right away, then and there

当事人 **dāngshìrén** N person/party involved; litigant · MW 个、名

当务之急 **dāngwùzhījí** EXP vital/urgent matter, top priority

当心 **dāngxīn** V·N to be careful, to look out

当选 **dāngxuǎn** V to be elected

当中 **dāngzhōng** N center; among, of

在我的朋友当中，他看来最年轻。 *Of all of my friends, he looks the youngest.*

当众 **dāngzhòng** ADV publicly

当年 **dàngnián** N that same year

当票 **dàngpiào** N pawn ticket · MW 张

当铺 **dàngpù** N pawnshop · MW 家

当日 **dàngrì** N the same day, that very day

当时 **dàngshí** N right away, then and there

当天 **dàngtiān** N the same day, that very day

当真 **dàngzhēn** V·ADV to take seriously; no kidding, seriously, truly, really

当做 **dàngzuò** V to treat/regard as

**RELATED WORDS**

| | | |
|---|---|---|
| 丁当 8 | 上当 14 | 不当 24 |
| 正当 76 | 正当 76 | 失当 106 |
| 门当户对 130 | 叮当 284 | 行当 327 |
| 妥当 433 | 典当 532 | 充当 652 |
| 押当 787 | 担当 789 | 相当 805 |
| 便当 865 | 恰当 930 | 家当 1315 |
| 适当 1358 | 停当 1588 | 想当然 1769 |
| 稳当 1925 | 丁零当郎 8 | 不敢当 24 |
| 以一当十 101 | 吊儿郎当 547 | 直截了当 609 |

**336 宁** 寧　　U+5B81　　TM **7** FM ╲

**níng** ADJ peaceful, quiet

**nìng** ADV would rather; rather; it would be better

宁静 **níngjìng** ADJ peaceful, quiet, calm; healthy

那是一个宁静，明媚的早晨。 *It was a beautiful morning, calm and serene.*

宁夏 **Níngxià** N Ningxia Hui Autonomous Region

宁可 **nìngkě** ADV would rather; to prefer

我宁可挨饿也不吃那种东西！ *I'd rather go hungry than eat that!*

宁肯 **nìngkěn** ADV would rather

宁愿 **nìngyuàn** ADV would rather; to prefer

我宁愿考不及格，也不作弊。 *I would rather fail than cheat on the exam.*

**RELATED WORDS**

| | | |
|---|---|---|
| 列宁主义 368 | 安宁 487 | 辽宁 711 |

**337 闪** 閃　　U+95EA　　TM **7** FM ╲

**shǎn** V·N to dodge, to get out of the way; to sprain, to twist; to appear suddenly, to flash by; to leave out/behind; lightning; spark, flash

闪电 **shǎndiàn** N lightning · MW 道

**337 闪 shǎn** (continued)

漆黑的夜空中一道**闪**电照亮了天边。 *In the dark sky, a flash of lightning illuminates the horizon.*

**闪光 shǎnguāng** V to flash, to sparkle, to flicker, to dazzle

**闪开 shǎnkāi** V to get out of the way

**闪身 shǎnshēn** V to sidestep, to dodge

**闪烁 shǎnshuò** V to twinkle, to flicker

天空星光**闪烁**。 *The stars twinkle in the sky.*

**闪耀 shǎnyào** V to shine, to glitter; to radiate

**RELATED WORD**

躲闪 1874

---

**338**   **必**      U+5FC5    TM **7** FM 丶

**bì** ADV certainly, surely; necessarily; must, to have to, ought to

**必不可少 bìbùkěshǎo** EXP absolutely necessary, indispensable

**必定 bìdìng** ADV undoubtedly, certainly; to be sure to

他从来不认真学习，考试**必定**不及格。 *He never really studies hard; he will undoubtedly fail his test.*

**必然 bìrán** ADJ·N inevitable, certain; necessity

**必修课 bìxiūkè** N required course · MW 门

**必须 bìxū** V must; to have to

去中国之前，你**必须**好好温习一下中文。 *You must brush up on your Chinese before going to China.*

**必需 bìxū** V·ADJ to need; necessary, essential

**必需品 bìxūpǐn** N necessity · MW 件、批

**必要 bìyào** ADJ necessary, essential, required

**必由之路 bìyóuzhīlù** EXP road one must take, the only way · MW 条

**RELATED WORDS**

不必要 24      未必 88      务必 429
何必 619      想必 1769

---

**339**   **冲**   衝      U+51B2    TM **7** FM 丶

**chōng** V·N to rush forward, to storm; to clash, to collide; important place; thoroughfare; flatland; opposition; to pour boiling water on; to rinse; to offset, to balance; to develop (film, etc.)

**冲**咖啡 *to boil coffee*

要**冲** *important place*

**冲**水 *to flush*

**chòng** ADJ·PREP·V vigorous, powerful; pungent; toward; because of, on the basis of; according to; to punch

有时傻瓜说话很**冲**。 *Sometimes ShaGua speaks very bluntly.*

这酒很**冲**。 *The liquor is very strong.*

她的话是**冲**我来的。 *Her words were aimed at me.*

**冲刺 chōngcì** V to sprint, to dash

**冲淡 chōngdàn** V to dilute

**冲动 chōngdòng** N·ADJ to get excited; to be impulsive

有时傻瓜容易**冲动**。 *Sometimes ShaGua is quite impulsive.*

**冲锋 chōngfēng** V to charge, to assault

**冲服 chōngfú** V to take medicine in solution

**冲击 chōngjī** V to pound; to charge, to assault; to have a big impact on

**冲浪 chōnglàng** V to surf

**冲破 chōngpò** V to break through

狗**冲破**了围栏。 *The dog broke through the fence.*

**冲杀 chōngshā** V to charge, to rush ahead/in

**冲刷 chōngshuā** V to erode, to wash away

**冲突 chōngtū** V·N to conflict; to clash; conflict; contradiction · MW 个、次

**冲洗 chōngxǐ** V to wash; to rinse; to develop (a photograph, etc.)

这地板需要好好**冲洗**一下。 *The floor needs a good scrubbing.*

**冲账 chōngzhàng** V to strike a balance

**RELATED WORDS**

气冲冲 185     脉冲 1604     猛冲 1704
缓冲 1708

---

**340**   **决**      U+51B3    TM **7** FM 丶

**jué** V·ADV to decide, to determine; to execute, to put to death; to burst, to be breached; decisively; definitely, certainly, under any circumstances

处**决** *to put to death*

**决**然 *definitely*

**决**堤。 *The levee was breached.*

**决策 juécè** V to make a policy decision · MW 个

**决策**的重任落在傻瓜肩上。 *The full weight of decision-making falls on ShaGua.*

**决定 juédìng** V·N to decide, to resolve; to determine; decision, resolution · MW 个

他做了英明的**决定**。 *He made a wise decision.*

**决断 juéduàn** V·N to decide, to resolve; resolution · MW 个

**决裂 juéliè** V to rupture, to break; to break relations with

**决赛 juésài** N finals; final/deciding match/competition · MW 场

**决胜 juéshèng** V to decide a battle

**决心 juéxīn** N·V determination, resolve; to make up one's mind to · MW 个

这意外打击没有动摇傻瓜的**决心**。 *The unexpected blow didn't weaken ShaGua's resolve.*

**决议 juéyì** N resolution · MW 个

**决战 juézhàn** N decisive battle · MW 场

**RELATED WORDS**

| | | |
|---|---|---|
| 未决 88 | 处决 217 | 否决 362 |
| 坚决 381 | 先决 422 | 判决 507 |
| 表决 527 | 枪决 1244 | 速决 1514 |
| 裁决 1535 | 解决 1928 | |

---

**341 次** U+6B21 TM 7 FM 丶

**cì** N·ADJ·MW rank, order; second; inferior; [measure word for occurrences, times]

**次货 cìhuò** N inferior products · MW 件、批

**次级 cìjí** N secondary

美国**次级**贷款风暴也影响了中国的股市。 *The explosion of secondary loans in America has also influenced Chinese stocks.*

**次序 cìxù** N order, sequence · MW 个

**次要 cìyào** ADJ secondary, minor, less important

学生首要考虑的是学习，其他都是**次要**的。 *As a student, all other considerations are less important than what you learn.*

**RELATED WORDS**

| | | |
|---|---|---|
| 人次 4 | 下次 10 | 车次 114 |
| 主次 124 | 历次 200 | 位次 323 |
| 再次 354 | 其次 379 | 名次 426 |
| 多次 431 | 层次 610 | 依次 625 |
| 这次 715 | 班次 730 | 场次 773 |
| 顺次 874 | 座次 920 | 首次 924 |
| 初次 963 | 等次 1437 | 编次 1866 |

---

**342 沙** U+6C99 TM 7 FM 丶

**shā** N·ADJ sand; granulated; powdered; paste; hoarse

**沙暴 shābào** N sandstorm · MW 场

**沙场 shāchǎng** N battlefield · MW 个

**沙丁鱼 shādīngyú** N sardine · MW 条

**沙发 shāfā** N sofa, couch · MW 张

**沙锅 shāguō** N casserole (dish); earthenware pot · MW 个

**沙拉 shālā** N salad · MW 盘

**沙粒 shālì** N speck, granule · MW 颗

**沙土 shātǔ** N sandy soil · MW 堆

**沙哑 shāyǎ** ADJ hoarse

**沙子 shāzi** N sand; grit · MW 粒

**RELATED WORDS**

豆沙 353    泥沙 1164

---

**343 忙** U+5FD9 TM 7 FM 丶

**máng** ADJ·V busy, occupied; to be busy with; to hurry

**忙碌 mánglù** ADJ busy, bustling; engrossed in work

他非常**忙碌**。 *He is very busy.*

**忙乱 mángluàn** ADJ rushed, hectic

她在**忙乱**中忘记了告辞。 *Amidst all the rush and confusion, she forgot to say good-bye.*

**忙人 mángrén** N busy person · MW 个、名、位

**忙音 mángyīn** N busy tone (telephone) · MW 阵

**RELATED WORDS**

| | | |
|---|---|---|
| 匆忙 304 | 奔忙 432 | 连忙 958 |
| 急忙 1426 | 帮忙 1583 | 慌忙 1736 |
| 繁忙 1988 | 帮倒忙 1583 | |

---

**344 怀 懷** U+6000 TM 7 FM 丶

**huái** V·N to think of; to keep in mind; to cherish; to become pregnant; bosom, heart; mind, state of mind

**怀抱 huáibào** V·N to embrace; to cherish; bosom; ambition, wish

**怀表 huáibiǎo** N pocket watch · MW 个

**344 怀 huái** (continued)

怀恨 **huáihèn** [V] to nurse a grudge, to harbor resentment

怀旧 **huáijiù** [V] to recall the past, to remember old friends/times

怀念 **huáiniàn** [V] to yearn for, to cherish the memory of

傻瓜常常默默地**怀念**故乡。 *ShaGua often falls silent and thinks of his native land.*

怀胎 **huáitāi** [V] to be pregnant

怀疑 **huáiyí** [V] to suspect, to distrust, to doubt

怀孕 **huáiyùn** [V] to be pregnant

**RELATED WORDS**

| 关怀 224 | 心怀 232 | 忘怀 655 |
| 胸怀 1709 | 满怀 1745 | 正中下怀 76 |

---

**345 状** 狀    U+72B6    TM **7** FM 丶

**zhuàng** [N] shape, form; state, condition; complaint; certificate

状况 **zhuàngkuàng** [N] condition, state (of affairs), situation · [MW] 个

傻瓜的经济**状况**很糟。 *ShaGua's financial affairs were in bad shape.*

状貌 **zhuàngmào** [N] appearance · [MW] 个

状态 **zhuàngtài** [N] condition, state (of affairs), situation · [MW] 个

状语 **zhuàngyǔ** [N] adverb · [MW] 个

状元 **zhuàngyuán** [N] very best; Number One Scholar (title conferred on the person with the best score in the highest imperial examination) · [MW] 个、名、位

状子 **zhuàngzi** [N] written complaint · [MW] 份

**RELATED WORDS**

| 形状 257 | 告状 428 | 诉状 708 |
| 症状 923 | 奖状 927 | 现状 975 |
| 粉状 1363 | 钩状 1463 | 罪状 1542 |
| 奇形怪状 854 | | |

---

**346 灯** 燈    U+706F    TM **7** FM 丶

**dēng** [N] light; lamp, lantern; festoon lighting; burner

灯标 **dēngbiāo** [N] beacon · [MW] 个

灯光 **dēngguāng** [N] light; (stage) lighting · [MW] 束、道

灯火 **dēnghuǒ** [N] lights

灯具 **dēngjù** [N] lighting; lamps and lanterns · [MW] 个、件

灯笼 **dēnglong** [N] lantern, lamp · [MW] 个

灯谜 **dēngmí** [N] riddles (on lanterns) · [MW] 条

灯泡 **dēngpào** [N] lightbulb · [MW] 个

灯塔 **dēngtǎ** [N] lighthouse; beacon · [MW] 座

**灯塔**上的**灯**光在地平线上闪烁着。 *The lights of the lighthouse were blinking on the horizon.*

**RELATED WORDS**

| 车灯 114 | 关灯 224 | 电灯 263 |
| 台灯 301 | 后灯 310 | 龙灯 315 |
| 华灯 421 | 幻灯 475 | 冰灯 493 |
| 吊灯 547 | 花灯 549 | 汽灯 682 |
| 油灯 683 | 点灯 739 | 尾灯 848 |
| 明灯 1035 | 张灯结彩 1208 | 宫灯 1318 |
| 绿灯 1707 | 路灯 1785 | 壁灯 1920 |
| 万家灯火 73 | 日光灯 96 | 走马灯 265 |
| 告警灯 428 | 红绿灯 474 | 信号灯 869 |
| 探照灯 1404 | 聚光灯 1642 | |

---

**347 订** 訂    U+8BA2    TM **7** FM 丶

**dìng** [V] to draw up; to agree on; to order, to subscribe to, to book; to revise, to correct (a textual error); to fasten/staple together, to bind

订单 **dìngdān** [N] purchase order · [MW] 个

公司得到了很多**订单**。 *The company received a lot of orders.*

订费 **dìngfèi** [N] subscription (rate) · [MW] 笔

订购 **dìnggòu** [V] to order, to subscribe to, to book

订户 **dìnghù** [N] subscriber · [MW] 个、名

订婚 **dìnghūn** [V] to get engaged

订货 **dìnghuò** [V] to order goods/products

订正 **dìngzhèng** [V] to correct (a textual error)

**RELATED WORDS**

| 合订本 296 | 拟订 575 | 校订 802 |
| 修订 870 | 制订 1130 | 签订 1439 |
| 装订 1476 | | |

---

**348 让** 讓    U+8BA9    TM **7** FM 丶

**ràng** [V·PREP] to make allowances; to invite; to allow, to let; to have (someone do something); to make way/room for; to transfer, to trade in, to sell; by

让利 *to give profits to*

把朋友让进家 *to invite friends into the house*

傻瓜让大儿子做作业。 *ShaGua asked his older son to do his homework.*

让半价 *to sell for half price*

转让 *to transfer ownership of*

让步 **ràngbù** V to make a concession, to yield

让车道 **ràngchēdào** N passing lane · MW 条

让开 **ràngkāi** V to get out of the way, to step aside

让路 **rànglù** V to make way for

一只狗坐在大门口正中, 不肯让路。 *A dog was sitting in front of the gate and refused to move out of our way.*

让位 **ràngwèi** V to step down, to resign; to give up one's seat

让座 **ràngzuò** V to offer/give one's seat to

**RELATED WORDS**

礼让 503　　忍让 970　　转让 1111
推让 1242　　退让 1508　　割让 1761
互谅互让 135

议价 **yìjià** V·N to bargain; negotiated price · MW 份

议论 **yìlùn** V·N to talk, to discuss; talk, comment, discussion

不要在背后议论别人。 *Don't talk about others behind their backs.*

议事 **yìshì** V to discuss official business

议题 **yìtí** N topic; agenda item · MW 个

议席 **yìxí** N seat in a legislature/parliament · MW 个

议员 **yìyuán** N representative; congressman, congresswoman · MW 个、名、位

议院 **yìyuàn** N legislature, parliament · MW 个

议长 **yìzhǎng** N speaker (of a legislature); president · MW 个、名、位

**RELATED WORDS**

公议 103　　众议员 175　　众议院 175
会议 295　　决议 340　　协议 397
动议 514　　异议 539　　拟议 575
争议 595　　参议员 600　　参议院 600
评议 706　　审议 911　　抗议 1009
建议 1203　　提议 1554　　商议 1612
紧急会议 1537

---

349 议 議 U+8BAE TM 7 FM `

**yì** V·N to discuss, to talk over; comment, remark; opinion, view; proposal

议案 **yì'àn** N proposal; motion · MW 个

议程 **yìchéng** N agenda · MW 个

议定书 **yìdìngshū** N treaty, protocol · MW 份

议和 **yìhé** V to negotiate peace

议会 **yìhuì** N parliament; Congress · MW 个

---

350 训 訓 U+8BAD TM 7 FM `

**xùn** V·N to teach, to instruct; to train, to drill; rule, guideline, standard; explanation of a word

训斥 **xùnchì** V to reprimand

训话 **xùnhuà** V to reprimand (a subordinate)

训练 **xùnliàn** V to train

工作前, 职工将接受一些上岗训练。 *Workers will be trained before they begin work.*

## 351 而 U+800C TM **8** FM 一

**ér** CONJ and, as well as; but, yet

**而后 érhòu** CONJ then, after that

他到了美国，而后又到了中国。 *He went to the United States and then to China.*

**而今 érjīn** N today, now, at present

**而且 érqiě** CONJ not only … but (also) …, and what's more, and on top of that

他会说中文，而且说得很好。 *He speaks Chinese, and on top of that he does so very well.*

**而已 éryǐ** AV that's all, nothing more; nothing but, only

这不过是个笑话而已。 *It is nothing but a joke.*

### RELATED WORDS

| | | |
|---|---|---|
| 少而精 62 | 从而 66 | 反而 111 |
| 因而 270 | 取而代之 520 | 时而 586 |
| 周而复始 1068 | 总而言之 1330 | 视而不见 1362 |
| 然而 1432 | 既而 1572 | 概而论之 1908 |
| 一哄而散 1 | 三思而行 9 | 半途而废 127 |
| 自上而下 305 | 似是而非 322 | 如此而已 464 |
| 侃侃而谈 1085 | 闻风而动 1151 | 背道而驰 1380 |
| 挺身而出 1408 | | |

## 352 西 U+897F TM **8** FM 一

**xī** N west; the West; western

**西安 Xī'ān** N Xi'an (capital city of Shaanxi Province)

**西班牙 Xībānyá** N Spain

**西北 xīběi** N northwest

**西餐 xīcān** N Western-style food · MW 餐、顿

今天我们吃西餐还是吃中餐？ *Should we eat Western or Chinese food today?*

**西方 Xīfāng** N the West; Western Paradise (Buddhism)

**西风 xīfēng** N west wind; Western culture and social mores · MW 阵

**西瓜 xīguā** N watermelon · MW 个、瓣、片、块

**西红柿 xīhóngshì** N tomato · MW 个

**西南 xīnán** N southwest

**西天 xītiān** N India; Western Paradise/Heaven (Buddhism)

**西洋 Xīyáng** N the West, the Western world

**西药 xīyào** N Western medicine · MW 粒、颗、瓶

**西医 xīyī** N Western medicine

**西藏 Xīzàng** N Tibet

**西装 xīzhuāng** N Western-style clothes · MW 套、件

傻瓜穿西装的模样有点儿滑稽。 *When ShaGua wears Western-style clothing, he looks a little funny.*

### RELATED WORDS

| | | |
|---|---|---|
| 大西洋 20 | 广西 23 | 山西 38 |
| 中西 86 | 江西 237 | 东西 307 |
| 新西兰 1638 | 墨西哥 1843 | 声东击西 374 |

## 353 豆 U+8C46 TM **8** FM 一

**dòu** N bean; pea; legume; seed (of a pod-bearing plant); [shaped like a bean]

**豆瓣酱 dòubànjiàng** N thick broad-bean paste · MW 瓶

**豆腐 dòufu** N tofu, bean curd · MW 块

**豆浆 dòujiāng** N soy milk · MW 碗

**豆沙 dòushā** N sweetened black bean paste · MW 团

**豆芽 dòuyá** N bean sprout · MW 根

豆芽有丰富的营养。 *Bean sprouts are rich in nutrients.*

**豆子 dòuzi** N bean; [shaped like a bean]; bead · MW 颗

### RELATED WORDS

| | | |
|---|---|---|
| 土豆 15 | 大豆 20 | 青豆 740 |
| 黄豆 1212 | 绿豆 1707 | |

## 354 再 U+518D TM **8** FM 一

**zài** ADV·V again, more; to a greater extent/degree; still, further; then; forever; besides; even if; to continue; to reappear, to return, to come back

再版 **zàibǎn** [V] to republish; second edition (of a book)

再次 **zàicì** [ADV] once again, one more time
傻瓜从来没有想过会**再次**见到她。*ShaGua never dreamed that he would see her again.*

再会 **zàihuì** [V] to say good-bye

再见 **zàijiàn** [V] to say good-bye; to see (someone) again

再三 **zàisān** [ADV] again and again, over and over
做决定前，傻瓜不得不**再三**考虑。*Before making the decision, ShaGua was forced to reconsider again and again.*

再审 **zàishěn** [V] to examine again, to rehear (a case)

再说 **zàishuō** [V·CONJ] to put off until later; furthermore, besides

**RELATED WORD**
一再 1

---

**355** 更        U+66F4    TM **8** FM 一

**gēng** [V·N] to change, to replace; experience
**gèng** [ADV] more, even more, still more; further

更好 **gènghǎo** [ADV] better; more
这两本书哪一本**更好**？*Which of these two books is better?*

更加 **gèngjiā** [ADV] better; more, even more
我们应该把工作做得**更加**好一些。*We should do our job even better.*

**RELATED WORDS**
变更 653        深更半夜 1345        自力更生 305

---

**356** 瓦        U+74E6    TM **8** FM 一

**wǎ** [N] tile; watt

瓦房 **wǎfáng** [N] tile-roofed house · [MW] 间、栋
瓦特 **wǎtè** [MW] [measure word for watts (a unit of electricity)]

**RELATED WORD**
土崩瓦解 15

---

**357** 司        U+53F8    TM **8** FM 一

**sī** [V·N] to take charge of, to manage, to control; department

司法 **sīfǎ** [N] judiciary

司机 **sījī** [N] driver, chauffeur · [MW] 个、名

司空见惯 **sīkōngjiànguàn** [EXP] common sight/occurrence; to be used to

司令 **sīlìng** [N] commander · [MW] 个、位、名

司药 **sīyào** [N] pharmacist · [MW] 个、名

司仪 **sīyí** [N] master of ceremonies, emcee · [MW] 个、名

**RELATED WORDS**
公司 103        官司 1136        子公司 83
分公司 173      打官司 289      母公司 394
顶头上司 724    跨国公司 1857

---

**358** 寻 尋        U+5BFB    TM **8** FM 一

**xún** [V] to search, to look for, to seek

寻常 **xúncháng** [ADJ] usual, ordinary, common

寻短见 **xúnduǎnjiàn** [EXP] to commit suicide

寻机 **xúnjī** [V] to look for an opportunity

寻开心 **xúnkāixīn** [EXP] to make fun of

寻找 **xúnzhǎo** [V] to look for, to seek
傻瓜在人群中**寻找**她，但就是找不到。*ShaGua looked for her in the crowd, but couldn't find her.*

**RELATED WORDS**
找寻 567        追寻 1507        搜寻 1663
异乎寻常 539

---

**359** 灵 靈        U+7075    TM **8** FM 一

**líng** [ADJ·N] quick, nimble; clever; flexible; effective; mind, intelligence; spirit, soul; deity

灵便 **língbiàn** [ADJ] nimble

灵感 **línggǎn** [N] insight; inspiration · [MW] 个

灵魂 **línghún** [N] soul, spirit

灵活 **línghuó** [ADJ] nimble, agile; flexible
公司采取**灵活**多样的销售方式。*The company executes flexible, diversified sales.*

灵机 **língjī** [N] quick wit, intelligence; sudden inspiration

灵敏 **língmǐn** [ADJ] sensitive; agile

灵巧 **língqiǎo** [ADJ] agile, nimble, deft; skillful, handy
理发师有一双**灵巧**的手。*The hairdresser has skillful hands.*

灵通 **língtōng** [ADJ] well-informed; effective

**359 灵 líng** (continued)

**灵验 língyàn** ADJ effective; accurate (of a prediction)

**灵芝 língzhī** N lingzhi mushroom · MW 棵

**RELATED WORDS**

| | |
|---|---|
| 不灵 24 | 亡灵 68 |
| 心灵 232 | 英灵 556 |
| 机灵 577 | 幽灵 1538 |

---

**360 贡 貢** U+8D21 TM 8 FM 一

**gòng** N·V (object of) tribute; to pay tribute

**贡品 gòngpǐn** N (object of) tribute · MW 件

**贡献 gòngxiàn** V·N to devote, to dedicate; contribution · MW 个

---

**361 召** U+53EC TM 8 FM 一

**zhào** V to summon, to call, to convene

**召开 zhàokāi** V to hold, to convene

今天的会议不大可能**召**开了。*The meeting is not likely to be held today.*

**RELATED WORDS**

| | |
|---|---|
| 征召 462 | 号召 545 |
| 感召 1860 | |

---

**362 否** U+5426 TM 8 FM 一

**fǒu** V·ADV·AV to deny; to denounce; bad, wicked; inferior; no; [used at the end of a question]

**否定 fǒudìng** V·ADJ to negate, to refute; negative

事实**否定**了他的看法。*The facts run counter to his claims.*

**否决 fǒujué** V to veto, to overrule

**否认 fǒurèn** V to deny; to repudiate

**否则 fǒuzé** CONJ otherwise

必须在24小时内提交申请，**否则**不予受理。*The application must be submitted within 24 hours, otherwise it won't be reviewed.*

**RELATED WORD**

是否 754

---

**363 矛** U+77DB TM 8 FM 一

**máo** N spear, lance

**矛盾 máodùn** N·ADJ·V conflict, contradiction (LIT spear and shield); uncertain; contradictory; to conflict · MW 个

他的解释充满**矛盾**。*His explanation is full of contradictions.*

**矛头 máotóu** N barb, spearhead; target · MW 个

**RELATED WORD**

以子之矛，攻子之盾 101

---

**364 巧** U+5DE7 TM 8 FM 一

**qiǎo** ADJ nimble; clever, skillful, ingenious; false, deceitful; coincidental, accidental, opportune

**巧干 qiǎogàn** V to work resourcefully

傻瓜最大的弱点是不会**巧干**。*Not knowing how to work resourcefully is one of ShaGua's weaknesses.*

**巧合 qiǎohé** N coincidence; by chance · MW 个

**巧计 qiǎojì** N clever device · MW 个、则

**巧克力 qiǎokèlì** N chocolate · MW 块、盒

**巧妙 qiǎomiào** ADJ clever, ingenious, smart

他走了一步**巧妙**的棋。*He made a clever move.*

**巧遇 qiǎoyù** V to encounter by chance

**RELATED WORDS**

| | | |
|---|---|---|
| 七巧板 34 | 正巧 76 | 手巧 104 |
| 灵巧 359 | 技巧 568 | 乖巧 832 |
| 恰巧 930 | 轻巧 1113 | 凑巧 1160 |
| 碰巧 1526 | 偏巧 1587 | 花言巧语 549 |
| 熟能生巧 1973 | | |

---

**365 戏 戲** U+620F TM 8 FM 一

**xì** N·V show, play; circus; trick, joke; to play, to have fun; to joke; to tease

**戏法 xìfǎ** N magic · MW 个

**戏剧 xìjù** N theater, drama, play; script (of a play) · MW 场、种

**戏言 xìyán** N joke, joking matter · MW 句

他的一句**戏言**惹火了她。*She was irritated by his joking around.*

**戏院 xìyuàn** N theater; pretending, playacting · MW 个、间、家

**RELATED WORDS**

| | | |
|---|---|---|
| 儿戏 43 | 马戏 247 | 好戏 627 |
| 把戏 1006 | 做戏 1282 | 调戏 1749 |
| 游戏 1818 | 演戏 1821 | 鬼把戏 1433 |
| 填字游戏 1550 | | |

**RELATED WORDS**

| | | |
|---|---|---|
| 入列 5 | 下列 10 | 上列 14 |
| 并列 225 | 马列主义 247 | 队列 294 |
| 行列 327 | 名列前茅 426 | 罗列 756 |
| 系列 842 | 序列 915 | 陈列 1250 |
| 前列腺 1329 | 以色列 101 | |

---

### 366 欢 歡  U+6B22   TM 8   FM 一

**huān** ADJ happy, cheerful; lover, sweetheart; vigorous, in full swing

欢呼 **huānhū** V to cheer, to applaud

欢聚 **huānjù** V to have a joyous get-together

欢乐 **huānlè** ADJ happy, joyful, delighted

欢送 **huānsòng** V to see/send (someone) off

欢喜 **huānxǐ** ADJ·V overjoyed, happy, delighted; to be fond of

儿子上了大学，傻瓜满心欢喜。 *ShaGua was very happy that his son went to college.*

欢心 **huānxīn** N favor; joy

傻瓜当市长后，有些人想博取他的欢心。 *Some people tried to win ShaGua's favor after he became mayor.*

欢迎 **huānyíng** V to welcome, to greet

**RELATED WORDS**

| | | |
|---|---|---|
| 合欢 296 | 狂欢 469 | 空欢喜 669 |
| 喜欢 1531 | | |

---

### 367 邓 U+9093   TM 8   FM 一

**Dèng** N Deng (surname)

邓小平 *Deng Xiaoping (1904–1997; leader of the Communist Party of China)*

---

### 368 列 U+5217   TM 8   FM 一

**liè** V·N to set out, to arrange; list; rank, row; category, kind, sort; (railroad) train; various; each and every

列兵 **lièbīng** N private · MW 个、名

列车 **lièchē** N (railroad) train; trip · MW 节、列

列举 **lièjǔ** V to list; to specify

列宁主义 **lièníngzhǔyì** N Leninism

列席 **lièxí** V to attend as an observer

列传 **lièzhuàn** N historical biography

---

### 369 环 環 U+73AF   TM 8   FM 一

**huán** N·V ring, hoop; element, part; to surround, to encircle

环抱 **huánbào** V to surround

环城 **huánchéng** N around/encircling the city

傻瓜主政后，修了一条环城公路。 *After gaining control of the city government, ShaGua built a highway around the city.*

环顾 **huángù** V to look around, to survey

环节 **huánjié** N segment, link · MW 个

环境 **huánjìng** N environment, circumstances, conditions

环流 **huánliú** N circulation

环路 **huánlù** N beltway · MW 条、道

环球 **huánqiú** N·V the earth, the whole world; global, worldwide; to go around the world

环绕 **huánrǎo** V to surround; to rotate

傻瓜环绕着城市修了一条路。 *The road that ShaGua built encircles the city.*

环视 **huánshì** V to look around

环形 **huánxíng** N shaped like a ring; circle · MW 个

**RELATED WORDS**

| | | |
|---|---|---|
| 耳环 145 | 光环 491 | 吊环 547 |
| 花环 549 | 连环 958 | 圆环 1391 |

---

### 370 孔 U+5B54   TM 8   FM 一

**kǒng** N hole, opening; pit

孔洞 **kǒngdòng** N hole (in a utensil, etc.) · MW 个

孔孟之道 **kǒngmèngzhīdào** N teachings of Confucius and Mencius

孔庙 **kǒngmiào** N temple of Confucius · MW 座

孔雀 **kǒngquè** N peacock · MW 只

孔穴 **kǒngxué** N hole, cavity · MW 个

孔子 **Kǒngzǐ** N Confucius (551–479 B.C.E.)

孔子学院 *the Confucius Institute*

**370 孔 kǒng** (continued)

**RELATED WORDS**

| | | |
|---|---|---|
| 耳孔 145 | 毛孔 183 | 汗孔 236 |
| 面孔 721 | 穿孔 1322 | 鼻孔 1794 |

---

**371 引**    U+5F15    TM **8** FM 一

**yǐn** V to draw; to lead, to guide; to leave, to retreat; to quote, to cite; to cause, to make; to recognize; to attract; to induce

引爆 **yǐnbào** V to ignite, to cause to burn; to detonate

引出 **yǐnchū** V to extract, to draw out

引导 **yǐndǎo** V to lead, to guide; to pilot

引发 **yǐnfā** V to initiate, to trigger

引号 **yǐnhào** N quotation mark · MW 个

引进 **yǐnjìn** V to import (personnel, capital, technology, equipment, etc.); to recommend

引力 **yǐnlì** N attraction; gravitation

引流 **yǐnliú** V drainage

引起 **yǐnqǐ** V to cause; to arouse
他的观点引起了争论。 *His views touched off a debate.*

引人 **yǐnrén** V to lead into

引人入胜 **yǐnrénrùshèng** EXP absorbing, enchanting

引申 **yǐnshēn** V to extend

引文 **yǐnwén** N quotation, citation · MW 段

引言 **yǐnyán** N foreword; introduction · MW 篇

引用 **yǐnyòng** V to quote, to cite
傻瓜没有文化，但喜欢在谈话中引用谚语。 *ShaGua is not educated, but he likes to quote proverbs.*

**RELATED WORDS**

| | | |
|---|---|---|
| 勾引 303 | 吸引 776 | 牵引 853 |
| 指引 1397 | 逗引 1512 | 援引 1556 |
| 摘引 1906 | 抛砖引玉 1395 | |

---

**372 束**    U+675F    TM **8** FM 丨

**shù** V·N·MW to tie (up), to restrain; cluster, bunch, bundle, sheaf; beam (of light); [measure word for bunches, bundles, beams of light, etc.]

束缚 **shùfù** V to tie (up), to restrain, to restrict

束手无策 **shùshǒuwúcè** EXP to be at one's wits' end
他也束手无策，别指望他了。 *He is utterly at a loss for what to do; don't count on him for help.*

**RELATED WORDS**

| | | |
|---|---|---|
| 花束 549 | 约束 876 | 结束 1291 |
| 装束 1476 | 管束 1861 | 无拘束 139 |

---

**373 幸**    U+5E78    TM **8** FM 丨

**xìng** ADJ·N·ADV lucky, fortunate; happy, joyful; receiving imperial favor

幸福 **xìngfú** ADJ·N happy; happiness

幸亏 **xìngkuī** ADV luckily, fortunately
幸亏傻瓜体质好，最近感染的猪流感没有对他造成太大的伤害。 *Fortunately, ShaGua was strong, so he was not affected much by the recent swine flu.*

幸免 **xìngmiǎn** V to survive, to narrowly escape, to land on one's feet

幸运 **xìngyùn** ADJ·N lucky, fortunate; good luck
傻瓜真幸运，能在感染猪流感后痊愈。 *ShaGua sure was lucky to be able to make a full recovery after contracting swine flu.*

幸灾乐祸 **xìngzāilèhuò** EXP to gloat at another's misfortune

**RELATED WORDS**

| | | |
|---|---|---|
| 不幸 24 | 万幸 73 | 荣幸 769 |

---

**374 声 聲**    U+58F0    TM **8** FM 丨

**shēng** N·V sound; voice; tone; reputation; to make a sound; to announce

声波 **shēngbō** N sound wave

声称 **shēngchēng** V to claim, to profess, to state

声带 **shēngdài** N vocal cords · MW 条

声调 **shēngdiào** N note; (Chinese) tone; key · MW 个、种

声东击西 **shēngdōngjīxī** EXP decoy tactics (LIT to feint toward the east and attack in the west)

声明 **shēngmíng** V·N to state, to announce; statement, declaration · MW 篇、份

声势 **shēngshì** N power and influence

声讨 **shēngtǎo** V to condemn; to denounce

声音 **shēngyīn** N voice; sound · MW 个

傻瓜听到远处有个微弱的**声音**。*ShaGua heard a faint sound in the distance.*

**声援** shēngyuán  V  to publicly support

**RELATED WORDS**

| | | |
|---|---|---|
| 女声 57 | 无声 139 | 去声 157 |
| 风声 194 | 齐声 221 | 四声 271 |
| 发声 311 | 应声 334 | 回声 391 |
| 名声 426 | 录声 722 | 放声 964 |
| 轻声 1113 | 闷声不响 1150 | 吼声 1228 |
| 做声 1282 | 铃声 1303 | 响声 1409 |
| 雷声 1641 | 掌声 1734 | 隔声 1910 |
| 口口声声 42 | 立体声 125 | 虚张声势 1534 |
| 异口同声 539 | 忍气吞声 970 | |

## 375 老    U+8001    TM **8**   FM **|**

lǎo  ADJ·ADV·PFX  old, aged; experienced, proven; former; of long standing, dated, antiquated, out of style; overgrown; overcooked, well-done; dark (in color); old people; parents; always; often, regularly; for a long time; very; [prefix used before a surname]

傻瓜太太看起来比傻瓜**老**。*Mrs. ShaGua looks older than ShaGua.*

**老**同学 *former classmates*

**老**式汽车 *old car*

这件衣服的颜色太**老**。*This clothing color is out of style.*

傻瓜**老**是穿颜色太**老**的衣服。*ShaGua always wears clothes with unfashionable colors.*

牛肉炒得太**老**。*The beef is overcooked.*

**老**远就见**老**黄了。*We saw Old Huang quite a ways from here.*

**老百姓** lǎobǎixìng  N  ordinary people; civilian ·  MW  个、名

**老板** lǎobǎn  N  boss, manager ·  MW  个、位、名

傻瓜的**老板**姓吴，是个好人。*ShaGua's boss's family name was Wu; he was very nice.*

**老伴** lǎobàn  N  husband, wife, spouse ·  MW  个、位

**老本** lǎoběn  N  money, capital

**老成** lǎochéng  ADJ  mature, experienced

**老大** lǎodà  N·ADV  oldest child (in a family); Number One; head, leader, captain; very

傻瓜的大儿子是**老大**。*ShaGua's older son is his oldest child.*

傻瓜太太在家里是**老大**。*Mrs. ShaGua wears the pants in the family.*

**老大难** lǎodànán  ADJ  long-standing

**老大娘** lǎodàniáng  N  aunt; grandma ·  MW  个、位

**老大爷** lǎodàyé  N  uncle; grandpa ·  MW  个、位

**老底** lǎodǐ  N  (dubious) past; inheritance

谁都知道傻瓜的**老底**。*Everyone is aware of ShaGua's past.*

**老调** lǎodiào  N  hackneyed theme

**老公** lǎogōng  N  husband ·  MW  个

**老公** lǎogong  N  eunuch ·  MW  个

**老规矩** lǎoguīju  N  old rules and regulations; old customs ·  MW  个、套

**老汉** lǎohàn  N  old man ·  MW  个、名

**老虎** lǎohǔ  N  tiger ·  MW  只

**老家** lǎojiā  N  home; birthplace

**老交情** lǎojiāoqing  N  long-standing friendship ·  MW  段

**老老实实** lǎolao shíshí  EXP  honestly

大家都认为傻瓜是一个**老老实实**的人。*Everybody thinks that ShaGua is an honest person.*

**老练** lǎoliàn  ADJ  experienced, skillful

**老龄** lǎolíng  N  old age; elderly

**老毛病** lǎomáobìng  N  chronic problem; bad habit ·  MW  个

**老年** lǎonián  N  old age; elderly

**老婆** lǎopo  N  wife; old woman ·  MW  个

**老人** lǎorén  N  old people; aged parents/grandparents ·  MW  个、位

**老师** lǎoshī  N  teacher ·  MW  个、位、名

**老实** lǎoshi  ADJ  honest, frank; well-behaved; naive, simple-minded

**老实**说，我不喜欢她。*To be frank, I don't like her.*

你**老实**点！*Behave yourself!*

**老手** lǎoshǒu  N  expert ·  MW  名

**老鼠** lǎoshǔ  N  mouse; rat ·  MW  只

**老太婆** lǎotàipó  N  old woman; grandma ·  MW  个、名

**老天爷** lǎotiānyé  N  God!, heavens!, holy cow!

**老头** lǎotóu  N  old man; father; husband ·  MW  个、名

**老乡** lǎoxiāng  N  fellow villager; country bumpkin; buddy ·  MW  个、位、名

**老兄** lǎoxiōng  N  buddy; brother; man ·  MW  个、位

**老爷** lǎoye  N·ADJ  master, lord, sir; maternal grandpa; old-fashioned, outdated (vehicle, etc.) ·  MW  个、位

**老爷爷** lǎoyéye  N  old man; paternal great-grandpa ·  MW  个、位

**老鹰** lǎoyīng  N  eagle; hawk ·  MW  只

**375 老 lǎo** (continued)

老子 **Lǎozǐ** [N] Laozi (Lao-tzu) (sixth century B.C.E.; philosopher and founder of Taoism)

老子 **lǎozi** [N] father, daddy; I, your father (in anger or contempt); I (in arrogance or fun)

**老子不干了，看你能怎么样!?** *I'm done with this. What can you do about it!?*

**RELATED WORDS**

| | | |
|---|---|---|
| 长老 93 | 元老 138 | 古老 154 |
| 母老虎 394 | 养老 670 | 返老还童 957 |
| 苍老 996 | 衰老 1313 | 敬老院 1689 |
| 阔老 1728 | 船老大 1809 | 妻儿老小 742 |
| 男女老少 757 | 猫哭老鼠 1446 | |

---

**376 求**     U+6C42     TM **8** FM |

**qiú** [V·N] to request, to ask, to beg; to strive; to pursue, to search for; demand

**求成 qiúchéng** [V] to hope for success

**求和 qiúhé** [V] to sue for peace

**求婚 qiúhūn** [V] to propose marriage

**求见 qiújiàn** [V] to ask to see

**求救 qiújiù** [V] to ask/cry for help

　她向傻瓜**求救**。*She cried to ShaGua for help.*

**求乞 qiúqǐ** [V] to beg

**求情 qiúqíng** [V] to ask/beg for leniency/mercy

**求全 qiúquán** [V] to demand perfection

**求饶 qiúráo** [V] to beg for mercy/forgiveness

**求人 qiúrén** [V] to ask for help; to look for talent

**求学 qiúxué** [V] to go to school/college; to study; to seek knowledge

　傻瓜每天到夜校**求学**。*ShaGua goes to night school every night.*

**求援 qiúyuán** [V] to ask for help; to request reinforcements

**求知 qiúzhī** [V] to seek knowledge

　傻瓜上夜校的**求知**行为感动了不少人。 *People have been moved by the fact that ShaGua is attending night school.*

**求助 qiúzhù** [V] to seek help, to ask for help

　如有困难，可**求助**于朋友。*Go to your friends for help if you are in any difficulty.*

**RELATED WORDS**

| | | |
|---|---|---|
| 力求 59 | 企求 170 | 乞求 177 |
| 央求 196 | 供求 459 | 征求 462 |
| 要求 969 | 哀求 1134 | 探求 1404 |

| | | |
|---|---|---|
| 追求 1507 | 请求 1632 | 渴求 1822 |
| 需求 1838 | 吹毛求疵 559 | 委曲求全 594 |
| 实事求是 668 | | |

---

**377 杰 傑**     U+6770     TM **8** FM |

**jié** [ADJ] outstanding, prominent; heroic

**杰出 jiéchū** [ADJ] illustrious, outstanding, remarkable; prominent

　傻瓜是一位**杰出**的市长。*ShaGua is an outstanding mayor.*

**杰作 jiézuò** [N] masterpiece · [MW] 个、部

**RELATED WORD**

豪杰 1876

---

**378 非**     U+975E     TM **8** FM |

**fēi** [V·N·ADJ·ADV] to blame; to run counter to; to insist on; mistake; (short for) Africa; wrong; to have to, simply must; not, un-, non-

**非…不可 fēi… bùkě** [CONJ] to require extra effort; must work even harder

　学习中文**非**得下苦功**不可**。*The study of Chinese requires painstaking effort.*

　你没有必要**非**回答这些问题**不可**。*You are not required to answer these questions.*

**非…非… fēi… fēi…** [V] neither … nor …

　他既**非**学生又**非**老师。*He is neither a teacher nor a student.*

**非常 fēicháng** [ADJ·ADV] exceptional, special, unusual; very, highly, extremely

　傻瓜帮助过的姑娘**非常**感激他。*The girl whom ShaGua had helped was extremely grateful to him.*

**非但 fēidàn** [CONJ] not only

**非法 fēifǎ** [ADJ] illegal, unlawful

**非凡 fēifán** [ADJ] outstanding, extraordinary

**非官方 fēiguānfāng** [ADJ] unofficial

**非难 fēinàn** [V] to censure, to blame

**非正式 fēizhèngshì** [ADJ] unofficial

**非洲 Fēizhōu** [N] Africa

**RELATED WORDS**

| | | |
|---|---|---|
| 无非 139 | 若非 554 | 是非 754 |
| 是非题 754 | 莫非 999 | 除非 1418 |
| 口是心非 42 | 似是而非 322 | 惹事生非 1657 |
| 痛改前非 1725 | 搬弄是非 1943 | |

## 379 其 U+5176 TM 8 FM |

**qí** PRON·ADV he, she, it, they; his, her, its, their; that, such

其次 **qícì** PRON next, second, then
我最喜欢吃桔子，**其次**是香蕉。 *Next to oranges, I like bananas best.*

其间 **qíjiān** N that period/interval; between; among
在校**其间**，我去过他家。 *I went to his home during the school year.*

其实 **qíshí** ADV actually, really, in fact, as a matter of fact
看书似乎很容易，**其实**大有学问。 *Reading seems easy, but it is actually a very intensive activity.*
有人认为学中文很枯燥，**其实**不然。 *Some believe that studying Chinese is boring; in fact, that is not the case.*

其他 **qítā** PRON other; the rest; other than, else
你可以去问**其他**人。 *You can ask someone else.*

其余 **qíyú** PRON other; the rest
**其余**的不用说了。 *The rest is obvious (there is no point in telling it).*

其中 **qízhōng** N among, in, of

### RELATED WORDS

| | | |
|---|---|---|
| 卡其 36 | 与其 158 | 尤其 199 |
| 听其自然 414 | 充其量 652 | 不乏其人 24 |
| 若无其事 554 | 夸大其词 605 | 夸夸其谈 605 |
| 突如其来 913 | 恰如其分 930 | 莫名其妙 999 |

## 380 岁 歲 U+5C81 TM 8 FM |

**suì** N year; time; age

岁出 **suìchū** N annual expenditure

岁末 **suìmò** N end of the year

岁入 **suìrù** N annual income/revenue

岁月 **suìyuè** N years; time
在以后的**岁月**中，她一直记着傻瓜的帮助。 *She remembered ShaGua's help in later years.*

### RELATED WORDS

| | | |
|---|---|---|
| 压岁钱 201 | 守岁 486 | 虚岁 1534 |

## 381 坚 堅 U+575A TM 8 FM |

**jiān** ADJ·N hard, solid; firm, steadfast; stronghold, fortification

坚持 **jiānchí** V to go on, to persist in
傻瓜**坚持**拒收他曾帮过的姑娘给的酬金。 *ShaGua continued to refuse the reward from the young girl he had helped.*

坚定 **jiāndìng** ADJ·V firm, steadfast; to strengthen

坚固 **jiāngù** ADJ firm, solid; sturdy, strong

坚决 **jiānjué** ADJ resolute, determined
傻瓜**坚决**反对这个意见。 *ShaGua resolutely opposed this idea.*

坚强 **jiānqiáng** ADJ·V strong, firm; to strengthen
市里有一个**坚强**的领导班子。 *There is strong leadership in the city.*

坚韧 **jiānrèn** ADJ tenacious; durable

坚实 **jiānshí** ADJ solid, substantial; strong, robust

坚信 **jiānxìn** V to firmly believe; without any doubt

坚硬 **jiānyìng** ADJ hard, solid

## 382 兄 U+5144 TM 8 FM |

**xiōng** N older brother · MW 个

兄弟 **xiōngdì** N brother; brotherhood · MW 个、位
傻瓜和他**兄弟**不太一样，傻瓜富有幽默感。 *Unlike his brother, ShaGua has a sense of humor.*

兄长 **xiōngzhǎng** N older brother; [respectful form of address for one's male friend] · MW 个、位

### RELATED WORDS

| | | |
|---|---|---|
| 老兄 375 | 师兄 396 | 难兄难弟 974 |
| 把兄弟 1006 | 弟兄 1152 | 堂兄 1486 |

## 383 足 U+8D83 TM 8 FM |

**zú** N·ADJ·ADV foot; leg; ample, enough, sufficient; as much as, fully

足够 **zúgòu** V to be enough/sufficient
你有**足够**的时间完成这个工作吗？ *Do you have enough time to finish the job?*

足迹 **zújì** N footprint; track · MW 道

足见 **zújiàn** CONJ it just goes to show

足金 **zújīn** N solid/pure gold

足球 **zúqiú** N soccer · MW 个

足以 **zúyǐ** V to be enough/sufficient
这些事实**足以**证明他是对的。 *These facts are sufficient proof to show he was right.*

**383 足 zú** (continued)

足智多谋 zúzhìduōmóu EXP wise and resourceful
傻瓜不是足智多谋的人。*ShaGua is neither wise nor enterprising.*

### RELATED WORDS

| | | |
|---|---|---|
| 十足 3 | 不足 24 | 手足 104 |
| 失足 106 | 立足 125 | 立足点 125 |
| 补足 508 | 知足 647 | 充足 652 |
| 实足 668 | 远足 1184 | 插足 1555 |
| 鼓足干劲 1688 | 富足 1731 | 满足 1745 |
| 丰衣足食 35 | 手舞足蹈 104 | 心满意足 232 |
| 美中不足 671 | 画蛇添足 719 | |

## 384 呆    U+5446    TM 8 FM |

**dāi** ADJ·V slow-witted, foolish; dumbstruck; to stay

呆板 dāibǎn ADJ stiff, inflexible
傻瓜做事有时有些呆板。*Sometimes ShaGua is inflexible in his business conduct.*

呆头呆脑 dāitóudāinǎo EXP slow-witted
傻瓜看上去有些呆头呆脑。*ShaGua looks a little slow.*

呆账 dāizhàng N bad debt · MW 笔

呆滞 dāizhì ADJ slow; lack of circulation/flow

呆子 dāizi N fool, blockhead, idiot, simpleton · MW 个
傻瓜是个呆子吗? *Is ShaGua an idiot?*

### RELATED WORDS

| | | |
|---|---|---|
| 书呆子 264 | 发呆 311 | 痴呆 1617 |
| 目瞪口呆 151 | | |

## 385 另    U+53E6    TM 8 FM |

**lìng** N·ADV other, another, different; separately

另案 lìng'àn N separate case

另册 lìngcè N other register (as distinct from the regular register; a list of disreputable people maintained in the Qing dynasty; today, a list of people/objects labeled as abnormal)

另类 lìnglèi N·ADV different, special, out of the ordinary · MW 个

另起炉灶 lìngqǐlúzào EXP to make a fresh start; to get one's own way (LIT to set up a separate kitchen)

另外 lìngwài PRON·ADV·CONJ other; separately; moreover, in addition, besides

另行 lìngxíng V to engage in (another activity); separately

另眼看待 lìngyǎnkàndài EXP to treat with special regard/respect

## 386 里 裡    U+91CC    TM 8 FM |

**lǐ** N·MW inside, internal, interior, inner; lining; neighbor; hometown; [measure word for a unit of distance (500 meters)]

里边 lǐbian N inside, interior, within, in
请进, 傻瓜在里边。*Come on in; ShaGua is inside.*

里程 lǐchéng N mileage; course · MW 个、段

里程碑 lǐchéngbēi N milestone, marker · MW 个、座

里里外外 lǐlǐwàiwài EXP inside and out

里面 lǐmiàn N inside, interior, within, in
这个门只能从里面打开。*This door can only be opened from the inside.*

### RELATED WORDS

| | | |
|---|---|---|
| 千里 19 | 万里长城 73 | 万里长征 73 |
| 公里 103 | 头里 128 | 在里面 188 |
| 心里 232 | 心里话 232 | 百里挑一 242 |
| 华里 421 | 表里 527 | 英里 556 |
| 夜里 654 | 这里 715 | 那里 980 |
| 邻里 1123 | 城里 1225 | 胡里胡涂 1256 |
| 稀里糊涂 1599 | 哪里 1666 | 卡路里 36 |
| 暗地里 1676 | | |

## 387 旱    U+65F1    TM 8 FM |

**hàn** ADJ dry; drought; nonirrigated; on land

旱地 hàndì N dry land · MW 块, 片

旱季 hànjì N dry season · MW 个

旱桥 hànqiáo N overpass, viaduct · MW 座

旱灾 hànzāi N drought · MW 场

### RELATED WORD

抗旱 1009

## 388 民    U+6C11    TM 8 FM |

**mín** N the people; person; civilian; folk

民办 mínbàn ADJ nongovernmental, privately run

民兵 **mínbīng** N people's militia; militiaman · MW 个、队

民法 **mínfǎ** N civil law · MW 部

民愤 **mínfèn** N public anger

民风 **mínfēng** N folkways, popular customs · MW 种

民歌 **míngē** N folk song, ballad · MW 首

民工 **míngōng** N (peasant) worker · MW 个、名、队

民航 **mínháng** N civil aviation · MW 家

民间 **mínjiān** N·ADJ folk; nongovernmental; people-to-people

　　民间音乐是一代一代流传下来的。 *Folk music has been passed down from one generation to the next.*

民警 **mínjǐng** N civil police · MW 个、位、名

民情 **mínqíng** N conditions; public opinion

民权 **mínquán** N civil rights · MW 个

民事 **mínshì** ADJ civil case/matter

民俗 **mínsú** N folkways, popular customs · MW 个、种

民心 **mínxīn** N popular sentiment

民谣 **mínyáo** N ballad · MW 首、支

民意 **mínyì** N popular will; public opinion

民用 **mínyòng** ADJ civilian, for civilian use

民政 **mínzhèng** N civil administration

民众 **mínzhòng** N the common people, the masses · MW 群

民主 **mínzhǔ** N·ADJ democracy; democratic

民族 **mínzú** N nationality; ethnic group · MW 个

　　旗袍是中国的一种民族服装。 *The chi-pao [a tight one-piece dress for a woman] is part of Chinese national attire.*

**RELATED WORDS**

| | |
|---|---|
| 人民 4 | 人民币 4 |
| 平民 78 | 公民 103 |
| 全民 172 | 市民 332 |
| 回民 391 | 农民 423 |
| 侨民 460 | 牧民 468 |
| 灾民 483 | 军民 489 |
| 国民 542 | 居民 850 |
| 饥民 890 | 难民 974 |
| 贫民 1052 | 移民 1450 |
| 渔民 1496 | 选民 1510 |
| 游民 1818 | 小市民 61 |
| 少数民族 62 | 中华民族 86 |
| 中华人民共和国 86 | 全国人民 172 |

---

**389 医** 醫 U+533B TM **8** FM |

**yī** N·V (medical) doctor; medicine, medical science; to treat, to cure

医德 **yīdé** N medical ethics

医科 **yīkē** N medical science; medical courses

医疗 **yīliáo** V to treat, to cure

　　并不是所有的工人都有医疗保险。 *Not all of the workers get medical insurance.*

医生 **yīshēng** N doctor, physician · MW 个、位、名

　　你应该去看医生。 *You should see your doctor.*

医师 **yīshī** N certified doctor, physician · MW 个、位、名

医术 **yīshù** N medical skill; art of healing

医务 **yīwù** N medical affairs

医学 **yīxué** N medicine, medical science · MW 门

医药 **yīyào** N medicine, medication

医院 **yīyuàn** N hospital; infirmary · MW 家、间、所

医治 **yīzhì** V to treat, to cure

**RELATED WORDS**

| | |
|---|---|
| 中医 86 | 牙医 143 |
| 行医 327 | 西医 352 |
| 就医 1836 | 主治医生 124 |
| 妇产医院 465 | 久病成医 45 |

---

**390 网** 網 U+7F51 TM **8** FM |

**wǎng** N·V net; like a net; web; network; Internet; to catch with a net

网点 **wǎngdiǎn** N website; branch, outlet · MW 个

网兜 **wǎngdōu** N string bag · MW 个

网罗 **wǎngluó** V to recruit, to headhunt; to bring together

网络 **wǎngluò** N network (economic, computer, social, etc.) · MW 个、张

　　这个公司的服务网络遍布全国。 *This company has a nationwide service network.*

网球 **wǎngqiú** N tennis; tennis ball · MW 个

网校 **wǎngxiào** N Internet school · MW 个、间、所

网站 **wǎngzhàn** N website · MW 个

网址 **wǎngzhǐ** N web address, URL · MW 个

**390** 网 **wǎng** (continued)

你知道中国历史博物馆的**网址**吗？ *Do you know the web address for the Museum of Chinese History?*

**网子 wǎngzi** N net · MW 张

**RELATED WORDS**

| | | |
|---|---|---|
| 法网 686 | 鱼网 843 | 渔网 1496 |
| 漏网 1886 | 互联网 135 | 因特网 270 |

---

## 391 回    U+56DE    TM **8** FM |

**huí** V·N·MW to return, to go back, to turn around; to circle; to answer, to reply; to refuse, to decline; Hui nationality; [measure word for chapters of a book, acts of a play]

**回拜 huíbài** V to pay a return visit

**回报 huíbào** V to report back; to repay; to retaliate

这个投资项目有丰厚的**回报**。 *This investment account has a high rate of return.*

**回避 huíbì** V to avoid, to sidestep

**回程 huíchéng** N return trip · MW 个

**回答 huídá** V·N to answer, to reply; response · MW 个

谁能给我一个**回答**？ *Who can give me an answer?*

**回访 huífǎng** V to pay a return visit

**回顾 huígù** V to look back, to review

**回归 huíguī** V to return, to go back

**回扣 huíkòu** V·N to rebate, to pay a commission; rebate; commission; kickback

美国人讲的"**回扣**"一般指给买方的折扣或佣金；但中国人讲的**回扣**是指卖方所得的酬金。 *When Americans talk about "回扣," they mean a commission for the seller, but when Chinese talk about "回扣," they mean a kickback for the buyer.*

**回来 huílái** V to return, to bring back; back [used after a verb to express the notion of returning]

他很快就把书还**回来**了。 *He returned the book here quickly.*

**回流 huíliú** V to return, to flow back

**回路 huílù** N retreat; circuit · MW 条、个

**回民 huímín** N Hui nationality (a Chinese ethnic minority)

**回去 huíqù** V to return, to go back; back [used after a verb to express the notion of returning]

他很快就把书还**回去**了。 *He quickly returned the book.*

**回声 huíshēng** N echo · MW 声、阵

**回升 huíshēng** V to recover, to pick up; to rise again after a fall

**回收 huíshōu** V to recycle; to retrieve

**回帖 huítiě** N return receipt · MW 个、张

**回头路 huítóulù** N return route · MW 条

**回乡 huíxiāng** V to return home

**回响 huíxiǎng** V·N to echo, to reverberate; to respond; echo

整个大楼**回响**着警报声。 *The whole building reverberated with the siren's warning.*

**回忆 huíyì** V to recall, to recollect

**回执 huízhí** N receipt · MW 张

**RELATED WORDS**

| | | |
|---|---|---|
| 来回 260 | 收回 282 | 夺回 308 |
| 折回 408 | 返回 957 | 驳回 983 |
| 追回 1507 | 退回 1508 | 挽回 1659 |
| 撤回 1942 | 浪子回头 1341 | 起死回生 1421 |

---

## 392 团 團 糰    U+56E2    TM **8** FM |

**tuán** N·V·ADJ·MW ball; shaped like a ball; dumpling; group, society, league; political organization for teenagers; regiment; to roll, to roll into a ball; to unite; round; [measure word for round objects]

面团 *dough*

文工团 *song-and-dance ensemble*

团队精神 *teamwork*

团聚 *conglomerate*

第三团 *Third Regiment*

团成一团 *to roll into a ball*

**团结 tuánjié** V·ADJ to unite; to join forces; to hold a rally; united

**团体 tuántǐ** N organization; team · MW 个

这个慈善**团体**是个非盈利性组织。 *This charity is a nonprofit organization.*

**团圆 tuányuán** V·ADJ to reunite, to have a reunion; round, circular

**团长 tuánzhǎng** N regimental commander; head (of a delegation, troupe, etc.) · MW 个、位、名

**RELATED WORDS**

| | | |
|---|---|---|
| 乐团 299 | 兵团 300 | 社团 504 |
| 党团 1626 | 疑团 1917 | 艺术团 274 |

## 393 困 睏 U+56F0 TM 8 FM |

**kùn** V·N·ADJ to be stricken, to be hard-pressed; to surround, to encircle; to trap, to besiege; sleep; predicament, difficulty; sleepy, tired; exhausted; difficult

**困乏 kùnfá** ADJ tired

**困惑 kùnhuò** ADJ·V confused; to be bewildered
事情太复杂了，我们感到**困惑**。*This issue is too complicated; we're getting confused.*

**困境 kùnjìng** N predicament, difficult position · MW 个

**困苦 kùnkǔ** ADJ hard, difficult, in hardship

**困难 kùnnan** ADJ·N hard, difficult; poor; dire straits; poverty · MW 个

**困扰 kùnrǎo** V to trouble, to perplex; to disturb, to annoy
他被许多**困难**所**困扰**。*He was beset by many problems.*

**困守 kùnshǒu** V to be trapped in a siege, to defend against a siege

### RELATED WORDS

| | |
|---|---|
| 坐困 318 | 围困 762 |
| 穷困 912 | 贫困 1052 |

## 394 母 U+6BCD TM 8 FM |

**mǔ** N mother; female elders; female; origin; parent; nut (for a bolt)

**母爱 mǔ'ài** N maternal love; maternal, motherly · MW 种

**母公司 mǔgōngsī** N parent company · MW 个

**母老虎 mǔlǎohǔ** N tigress · MW 只

**母亲 mǔqīn** N mother · MW 个、位
傻瓜给**母亲**开了一张支票。*ShaGua wrote his mother a check.*

**母校 mǔxiào** N alma mater, old school · MW 个

### RELATED WORDS

| | |
|---|---|
| 丈母娘 17 | 父母 56 |
| 圣母 142 | 伯母 455 |
| 字母 664 | 养母 670 |
| 叔母 821 | 姑母 881 |
| 祖母 1190 | 姨母 1596 |
| 母鹿 1724 | 舅母 1795 |
| 慈母 1952 | 外祖母 218 |
| 生身父母 107 | |

## 395 苹 蘋 U+82F9 TM 8 FM |

**píng** N apple

**苹果 píngguǒ** N apple · MW 个

**苹果酱 píngguǒjiàng** N apple jam · MW 瓶

**苹果汁 píngguǒzhī** N apple juice; cider · MW 杯、瓶
许多孩子喜欢喝**苹果汁**。*Many kids like to drink apple juice.*

## 396 师 師 U+5E08 TM 8 FM |

**shī** V·N to learn; to follow, to imitate; teacher; master, expert; [title of courtesy for a Buddhist monk or Taoist priest]; division, troops, army

**师**其所长 *to learn from his/her strengths*

第四**师** *Fourth Division*

军**师** *adviser*

**师弟 shīdì** N junior (male) fellow apprentice · MW 个、名

**师范 shīfàn** N teacher training; normal school/college/university · MW 个、间

**师傅 shīfu** N master; [respectful form of address for a skilled/qualified worker] · MW 个、位、名

**师姐 shījiě** N senior (female) fellow apprentice · MW 个、位

**师妹 shīmèi** N junior (female) fellow apprentice · MW 个、名

**师生 shīshēng** N teacher and student

**师徒 shītú** N master and apprentice

**师兄 shīxiōng** N senior (male) fellow apprentice · MW 个、位

**师长 shīzhǎng** N teacher; division commander · MW 个、位

**师资 shīzī** N qualified teachers

### RELATED WORDS

| | | |
|---|---|---|
| 会师 295 | 老师 375 | 医师 389 |
| 牧师 468 | 讲师 501 | 良师益友 656 |
| 画师 719 | 导师 751 | 琴师 1372 |
| 教师 1424 | 厨师 1584 | 工程师 12 |

## 397 协 協 U+534F TM 8 FM |

**xié** V·ADJ to assist; to accommodate; joint, common

**协定 xiédìng** N·V agreement, pact; to reach an agreement · MW 个

**397 协 xié** (continued)

**协会 xiéhuì** N association, society ·
MW 个

**协力 xiélì** V to combine efforts, to work as one

**协商 xiéshāng** V to consult, to talk things over;
to negotiate

他们的问题应该通过**协商**解决。
*The trouble between them should be resolved
by discussion.*

**协调 xiétiáo** V·ADJ to coordinate; balanced,
coordinated, harmonious

**协同 xiétóng** V to coordinate (with)

**协议 xiéyì** V·N to negotiate and agree on;
agreement · MW 个

**协助 xiézhù** V to help, to assist

有一组学生**协助**老师做实验。 *A group of
students assisted the teacher in performing
the experiment.*

**协作 xiézuò** V to collaborate

**RELATED WORDS**

妥协 433      政协 517

---

**398 坪**      U+576A      TM 8 FM |

**píng** N level ground; apron

**RELATED WORD**

草坪 768

---

**399 垃**      U+5783      TM 8 FM |

**lā** N garbage

**垃圾 lājī** N garbage, trash, waste · MW 堆

**垃圾袋 lājīdài** N garbage bag · MW 个

**垃圾电邮 lājīdiànyóu** N junk e-mail, spam ·
MW 个、封、件

**垃圾堆 lājīduī** N garbage pile · MW 个

**垃圾食品 lājīshípǐn** N junk food ·
MW 件、种

**垃圾箱 lājīxiāng** N garbage can, wastebasket ·
MW 个

请把**垃圾**放进**垃圾箱**里。 *Please put the garbage
in the wastebasket.*

**垃圾邮件 lājīyóujiàn** N junk mail ·
MW 个、封、件

---

**400 块** 塊      U+5757      TM 8 FM |

**kuài** MW [measure word for pieces, slices, lumps,
chunks, etc.]

一**块**钱 *one dollar*

一**块**砖 *one brick*

一**块**木头 *one piece of wood*

一**块**肉 *one slice of meat*

**RELATED WORDS**

一块儿 1      方块 220      切块 277 板
块 580      姜块 925

---

**401 扣**      U+6263      TM 8 FM |

**kòu** V·N to fasten, to button, to buckle; to tie,
to knot; to turn (something) upside down;
to deduct; to frame; to label; to arrest; to smash/
spike (a ball); button; buckle

钮**扣** *button*

**扣**紧 *straining*

把杯子**扣**过来 *to turn the cup upside down*

**扣**工资 *to deduct part of a salary*

**扣除 kòuchú** V to deduct; to recoup

**扣留 kòuliú** V to detain; to arrest; to confiscate

**扣帽子 kòumàozi** V to label unfairly

傻瓜从不给别人**扣帽子**。 *ShaGua has never
pinned an unfair label on others.*

**扣押 kòuyā** V to detain, to hold

被**扣押**在机场里的人质逃跑了。 *The hostage
being held at the airport escaped.*

**扣压 kòuyā** V to withhold, to hold back

**扣子 kòuzi** N knot; button · MW 颗

**RELATED WORDS**

回扣 391      折扣 408      克扣 738
钩扣 1463      打折扣 289

---

**402 扫** 掃      U+626B      TM 8 FM |

**sǎo** V to sweep; to clear away; to eliminate;
to glance at; to put together

**sào** N broom

**扫除 sǎochú** V to sweep up; to clear away;
to eliminate, to remove

**扫地 sǎodì** V to sweep the floor

扫盲 sǎománg V to eliminate illiteracy

扫描 sǎomiáo V to scan

扫墓 sǎomù V to visit graves to pay respect to the dead

扫清 sǎoqīng V to clear away

扫射 sǎoshè V to strafe, to rake with machine gun fire

扫尾 sǎowěi V to wind up, to finish

扫兴 sǎoxìng V to be disappointed/discouraged

真扫兴！ *How disappointing!*

扫把 sàobǎ N broom · MW 把

扫帚 sàozhou N broom · MW 把

他拿起扫帚帮老人扫地。 *He picked up the broom to help the old man sweep the floor.*

**RELATED WORD**

打扫 289

---

**403 扯** U+626F TM 8 FM |

chě V to pull, to drag; to tear (off), to rip; to chat, to gossip

扯谎 chěhuǎng V to tell a lie

扯皮 chěpí V to wrangle, to argue back and forth, to dispute over trifles

这种扯皮的事很难处理。 *This trifling dispute is very difficult to deal with.*

扯碎 chěsuì V to tear to pieces

**RELATED WORDS**

拉扯 573     闲扯 679     牵扯 853
胡扯 1256     瞎扯 1913

---

**404 扶** U+6276 TM 8 FM |

fú V to steady, to support with the hand; to help up; to assist, to help

扶持 fúchí V to support, to give aid to

政府发放资金来扶持小企业。 *The government helped small businesses with funds.*

扶手 fúshǒu N railing; armrest · MW 个

扶梯 fútī N staircase (with a railing); ladder · MW 个

扶养 fúyǎng V to provide for; to bring up, to foster

扶植 fúzhí V to cultivate; to foster

扶助 fúzhù V to support; to help, to assist

---

**405 抄** U+6284 TM 8 FM |

chāo V to copy, to transcribe; to plagiarize; to raid, to search and confiscate; to grab; to take a shortcut; to fold one's arms

抄书 *to copy a book*

抄家 *to search a house*

抄近路 *to take a shortcut*

抄件 chāojiàn N duplicate, copy · MW 份

抄录 chāolù V to make a copy

抄身 chāoshēn V to search, to frisk

抄送 chāosòng V to send a copy to, to carbon-copy

抄袭 chāoxí V to plagiarize

他因为抄袭别人的论文而受到严厉处罚。 *He was severely punished for plagiarizing someone else's paper.*

抄写 chāoxiě V to copy, to transcribe

**RELATED WORDS**

查抄 741                 照抄 1846
摘抄 1906

---

**406 抓** U+6293 TM 8 FM |

zhuā V to grab, to seize; to scratch; to catch, to arrest; to take control of; to vie; to attract (attention), to fascinate

抓痒 *to scratch an itch*

抓特务 *to arrest a spy*

抓难点 *to pay attention to difficulties*

抓辫子 zhuābiànzi EXP to exploit the shortcomings/mistakes of; to seize on the mistakes of

抓差 zhuāchāi V to draft for a particular task

抓功夫 zhuāgōngfu V to make good use of one's time

抓紧 zhuājǐn V to firmly grasp; to pay close attention to; to make the most of

抓阄 zhuājiū V to draw lots

学生们用抓阄来决定谁为大家查字典。 *Students drew lots to decide who would check the dictionary for everyone.*

抓瞎 zhuāxiā V to be at a loss

抓药 zhuāyào V to fill a prescription (of Chinese herbal medicine)

抓住 zhuāzhù V to grab; to capture, to catch

## 407 抖   U+6296   TM **8** FM |

**dǒu** V to shiver, to shake, to tremble; to bring to light, to expose; to rouse; to gear up; to throw one's weight around

**抖动 dǒudòng** V to shake, to tremble, to vibrate
她的手微微**抖动**。 *Her hands trembled slightly.*

**抖擞 dǒusǒu** V to rouse, to invigorate

### RELATED WORDS

发抖 311      颤抖 1991

## 408 折   U+6298   TM **8** FM |

**shé** V to snap, to break; to lose money

**zhē** V to roll/turn over; to pour back and forth

**zhé** V·N·MW to break, to snap; to lose; to turn back; to convert (something) into; to discount; to defeat; to convince; to fill with admiration; to fold; to unfold; discount; notebook, booklet, folder; [measure word for flat objects (books, pictures, etc.]

**折本 shéběn** V to lose money in business

**折腾 zhēteng** V to do something over and over

**折半 zhébàn** V to reduce by half; to sell at half price

**折叠 zhédié** V to fold
可**折叠**的桌子非常方便。 *The folding table is a great convenience.*

**折断 zhéduàn** V to break

**折兑 zhéduì** V to cash, to exchange for money

**折服 zhéfú** V to be convinced; to be astonished, to be filled with admiration
傻瓜的团队精神让许多人**折服**。 *ShaGua's belief in teamwork has filled many people with admiration.*

**折合 zhéhé** V to convert into

**折回 zhéhuí** V to turn back, to retrace

**折价 zhéjià** V to convert into money
旧车**折价**换新划算吗？ *Did you get a good trade-in price on your old car?*

**折旧 zhéjiù** V to depreciate

**折扣 zhékòu** N discount; rebate

**折磨 zhémó** V to torment, to persecute

**折射 zhéshè** V to reflect, to reveal

**折算 zhésuàn** V to convert (between currencies); conversion factor

**折损 zhésǔn** V to lose

**折椅 zhéyǐ** N folding chair · MW 张、把

**折中／折衷 zhézhōng** V to compromise

### RELATED WORDS

| | | |
|---|---|---|
| 八折 6 | 六折 69 | 九折 116 |
| 曲折 272 | 存折 438 | 波折 936 |
| 转折 1111 | 弯折 1472 | 骨折 1543 |

## 409 材   U+6750   TM **8** FM |

**cái** N material; wood; coffin; talented person

**材料 cáiliào** N material, stuff; data, reference facts; talent
建筑**材料**很贵。 *Building materials are expensive.*

### RELATED WORDS

| | | |
|---|---|---|
| 木材 40 | 因材施教 270 | 取材 520 |
| 板材 580 | 身材 604 | 成材 611 |
| 良材 656 | 废材 918 | 核材料 1026 |
| 钢材 1299 | 素材 1378 | 药材 1392 |
| 教材 1424 | 选材 1510 | 高材生 1611 |
| 棺材 1671 | 题材 1858 | 器材 1963 |
| 蠢材 1995 | | |

## 410 村   U+6751   TM **8** FM |

**cūn** N·ADJ village; rustic

**村寨 cūnzhài** N stockaded village · MW 个

**村长 cūnzhǎng** N village chief/head · MW 个、位、名

**村镇 cūnzhèn** N villages and small towns · MW 个

**村庄 cūnzhuāng** N village · MW 个
这是一个美丽的**村庄**。 *This is a beautiful village.*

### RELATED WORDS

乡村 117      农村 423

## 411 杯   U+676F   TM **8** FM |

**bēi** N·MW cup; glass; drink; trophy; [measure word for drinking vessels]

**杯子 bēizi** N cup; glass · MW 只、个、套

### RELATED WORDS

| | | |
|---|---|---|
| 干杯 13 | 茶杯 767 | 奖杯 927 |
| 酒杯 1339 | 碰杯 1526 | 量杯 1544 |
| 漱口杯 1823 | | |

## 412 林　U+6797　TM 8 FM |

**lín** N woods, forest; forestry; circle, group

森林 *forest, woods*

**林场** línchǎng N tree farm; forestry station · MW 个

**林木** línmù N forest, woods · MW 片

**林区** línqū N region of a forest · MW 个、片

**林业** línyè N forestry, forest industry

**RELATED WORDS**

| | | |
|---|---|---|
| 丛林 123 | 丛林灌木 123 | 吉林 259 |
| 森林 412 | 果林 544 | 园林 763 |
| 树林 1031 | 奥林匹克 1435 | 凡士林 193 |

## 413 叩　U+53E9　TM 8 FM |

**kòu** V to knock; to bow before (to kowtow); to ask, to inquire

**叩门** kòumén V to knock (on a door)

**叩头** kòutóu V to bow before (to kowtow)

100年前, 中国的学生要给老师**叩头**。 *A hundred years ago, students were required to kowtow to their teachers in China.*

**叩诊** kòuzhěn V to tap part of the body as part of a medical examination

## 414 听　聽　U+542C　TM 8 FM |

**tīng** V·MW to listen to, to hear; to obey; to supervise, to administer; to allow, to let; [measure word for cans]

一听罐头 *one can*

**听便** tīngbiàn V to do as one pleases

**听从** tīngcóng V to obey, to comply with

这只狗只**听从**傻瓜的命令。 *This dog only obeys ShaGua's orders.*

**听候** tīnghòu V to wait for

**听话** tīnghuà V·ADJ to obey; obedient

**听见** tīngjiàn V to hear

傻瓜隔着门**听见**儿子在打电话。 *ShaGua heard what his son was saying on the phone through the door.*

**听讲** tīngjiǎng V to attend (a talk, a lecture)

**听觉** tīngjué N (sense of) hearing

**听力** tīnglì N hearing, listening ability

**听命** tīngmìng V to obey an order, to take orders

**听凭** tīngpíng V to allow, to let

**听其自然** tīngqízìrán EXP to let things take their course, to take things as they come

**听起来** tīngqǐlái V to sound (like)

**听起来不错** to sound good

**听取** tīngqǔ V to listen to (an opinion, a report, etc.)

**听任** tīngrèn V to allow, to let

**听说** tīngshuō V to hear (of), to be told

**听说**傻瓜当过厨工。 *They say that ShaGua used to work in a restaurant.*

**听天由命** tīngtiānyóumìng EXP to submit to the will of heaven; to resign oneself to one's fate

**听筒** tīngtǒng N earphone; receiver (of a telephone) · MW 个

**听写** tīngxiě V to dictate

我们的中文课每天都有**听写**。 *We have dictation every day in our Chinese class.*

**听信** tīngxìn V to listen to / get the news; to believe what one hears

**听众** tīngzhòng N audience, listeners · MW 个、位、名

傻瓜不喜欢演讲, 但喜欢回答**听众**的提问。 *What ShaGua hates most is making speeches, but he enjoys answering the audience's questions.*

**RELATED WORDS**

| | | |
|---|---|---|
| 中听 86 | 收听 282 | 打听 289 |
| 动听 514 | 好听 627 | 助听器 818 |
| 监听 994 | 视听 1362 | 探听 1404 |
| 旁听 1473 | 窃听 1482 | |

## 415 吵　U+5435　TM 8 FM |

**chǎo** V to make a racket, to make noise; to disturb (someone) by making noise; to quarrel, to squabble, to argue

**吵架** chǎojià V to quarrel

傻瓜从来不和朋友**吵架**, 但常常和太太**吵架**。 *ShaGua has never quarreled with his friends, but he often quarrels with Mrs. ShaGua.*

**吵闹** chǎonào V·ADJ to bicker; to disturb; noisy

**吵闹**声使我很烦躁。 *The loud noise annoyed me.*

**吵嘴** chǎozuǐ V to bicker, to quarrel, to wrangle

**RELATED WORD**

争吵 595

## 416 此   U+6B64   TM **8** FM |

**cǐ** PRON this, these; here and now; like this

**此岸 cǐ'àn** N here and now, life on earth
(LIT this shore)

**此处 cǐchù** N herein

**此地 cǐdì** N here, this place
傻瓜在**此地**居住多年，已习惯寒冷的气候。
*After living here for years, ShaGua has become numb to the cold climate.*

**此后 cǐhòu** CONJ afterwards, after this, hereafter

**此刻 cǐkè** N now, at present, at the moment
他**此刻**正在吃饭。*He's eating at the moment.*

**此路不通 cǐlùbùtōng** EXP dead end, blind alley
(LIT this road is blocked)

### RELATED WORDS

| | | |
|---|---|---|
| 从此 66 | 以此 101 | 由此 148 |
| 由此可见 148 | 为此 223 | 因此 270 |
| 如此而已 464 | 如此 464 | 依此类推 625 |
| 故此 816 | 顾此失彼 1609 | 不分彼此 24 |
| 乃至如此 134 | | |

## 417 则    U+5219   TM **8** FM |

**zé** N·CONJ·MW standard, norm; rule, regulation, law; then; but; [measure word for written items]

一**则**新闻 *one piece of news*

### RELATED WORDS

| | | |
|---|---|---|
| 否则 362 | 守则 486 | 法则 686 |
| 准则 929 | 细则 1107 | 原则 1273 |
| 然则 1432 | 税则 1705 | 不规则 24 |
| 以身作则 101 | | |

## 418 仓    U+4ED3   TM **8** FM ノ

**cāng** N storehouse; barn; granary; hold (of a ship)

**仓储 cāngchǔ** V to store (grain, goods, etc.)

**仓促 cāngcù** ADJ hasty, hurried, in a hurry
傻瓜做的那个决定太**仓促**，现在倒霉了。
*ShaGua made a rash decision, and now he's suffering for it.*

**仓皇 cānghuáng** ADJ in a panic/flurry

**仓库 cāngkù** N warehouse · MW 个、座

### RELATED WORDS

| | | |
|---|---|---|
| 谷仓 446 | 料仓 961 | 粮仓 1759 |

## 419 余 餘   U+4F59   TM **8** FM ノ

**yú** V·PRON·N to remain, to be left; I, me; surplus; more than, over, extra- (beyond, outside of)

**余波 yúbō** N aftereffects, repercussions · MW 个

**余存 yúcún** N balance · MW 笔

**余党 yúdǎng** N remnants (of a defeated group/coup) · MW 个、伙、帮

**余地 yúdì** N room, leeway, margin · MW 个
没有怀疑的**余地**。*There is no room for doubt.*

**余毒 yúdú** N bad influence

**余额 yú'é** N balance, surplus · MW 笔
傻瓜的银行存款**余额**不多了。*ShaGua's bank balance isn't very large.*

**余悸 yújì** N lingering fear

**余热 yúrè** N lingering heat

**余生 yúshēng** N remainder of one's life, remaining years; survival

**余味 yúwèi** N aftertaste

**余兴 yúxìng** N light entertainment (after a dinner, meeting, etc.); lingering interest

**余音 yúyīn** N lingering sound

### RELATED WORDS

| | | |
|---|---|---|
| 业余 94 | 节余 275 | 其余 379 |
| 多余 431 | 残余 977 | 净余 1159 |
| 结余 1291 | 课余 1503 | 剩余 1720 |
| 赢余 2000 | | |

## 420 金   U+91D1   TM **8** FM ノ

**jīn** N·ADJ gold; metal; money; ancient metal percussion instrument; precious; golden

**金币 jīnbì** N gold coin · MW 枚

**金额 jīn'é** N sum, amount (of money)
刚来美国时，傻瓜户头里的**金额**不到一百美元。
*When ShaGua first came to the States, he had less than $100 in the bank.*

**金刚石 jīngāngshí** N diamond · MW 粒、颗

**金黄色 jīnhuángsè** N golden yellow

**金婚 jīnhūn** N golden wedding

**金库 jīnkù** N (national) treasury · MW 个、座

**金矿 jīnkuàng** N gold mine; gold ore · MW 个、座

**金融 jīnróng** N finance, banking
北京是中国的政治和**金融**中心。*Beijing is the political and financial center of China.*

金属 **jīnshǔ** [N] metal · [MW] 块

金条 **jīntiáo** [N] gold bar · [MW] 根

金字塔 **jīnzìtǎ** [N] pyramid · [MW] 座

**RELATED WORDS**

| | | |
|---|---|---|
| 千金 19 | 寸金难买 37 | 万金油 73 |
| 五金 79 | 合金 296 | 足金 383 |
| 礼金 503 | 佣金 621 | 定金 666 |
| 押金 787 | 包金 836 | 奖金 927 |
| 现金 975 | 基金 991 | 拾金不昧 1017 |
| 租金 1096 | 黄金 1212 | 资金 1335 |
| 罚金 1386 | 股金 1456 | 淘金 1628 |
| 酬金 1648 | 薪金 1847 | 公积金 103 |
| 助学金 818 | | |

---

**421 华** 華　　　U+534E　　TM **8** FM 丿

**huá** [ADJ·N] magnificent; extravagant; prosperous, flourishing; gray; essence; best part; time, course of time; China; Chinese (language)

华表 **huábiǎo** [N] marble pillar (in front of a palace, tomb, etc.) · [MW] 根、对

华灯 **huádēng** [N] decorated lantern · [MW] 盏

华尔街 **huá'ěrjiē** [N] Wall Street

华里 **huálǐ** [MW] [measure word for a unit of distance (500 meters)]

华丽 **huálì** [ADJ] magnificent, gorgeous, resplendent

她穿着**华丽**的银白色的礼服。*She is wearing a magnificent silver dress.*

华侨 **huáqiáo** [N] overseas Chinese · [MW] 个、位、名

华夏 **Huáxià** [N] (ancient name of) China

华文 **huáwén** [N] Chinese (language)

这个城市里，有两所**华文**学校。*There are two Chinese language schools in this city.*

华裔 **huáyì** [N] ethnic Chinese · [MW] 个、位、名

**RELATED WORDS**

| | |
|---|---|
| 才华 39 | 中华 86 |
| 中华民族 86 | 中华人民共和国 86 |
| 年华 182 | 荣华富贵 769 |
| 新华通讯社 1638 | 豪华 1876 |
| 繁华 1988 | |

---

**422 先**　　　U+5148　　TM **8** FM 丿

**xiān** [N·ADV] earlier; past, late, deceased; ancestor; before, in advance

你比他**先**上大学。*You went to college earlier than he did.*

**先**上大学，再工作。*Go to college first, and then work.*

先辈 **xiānbèi** [N] ancestors; older generation · [MW] 个、位、名

先发制人 **xiānfàzhìrén** [EXP] to preempt, to gain the initiative by striking first

先锋 **xiānfēng** [N] pioneer; vanguard · [MW] 个、位、名

先后 **xiānhòu** [N·ADV] priority; seniority; successively, one after another

办事应该有**先后**次序。*Things should be dealt with on a priority basis.*

先进 **xiānjìn** [ADJ·N] advanced, in advance; advanced individual/unit

先决 **xiānjué** [ADJ] prerequisite

先例 **xiānlì** [N] precedent · [MW] 个

先前 **xiānqián** [ADJ] past, previous; before

先驱 **xiānqū** [N] pioneer · [MW] 个、位、名

先人 **xiānrén** [N] ancestors · [MW] 个、位、名

先生 **xiānsheng** [N] Mr., gentleman; teacher; husband · [MW] 个、位、名

先天 **xiāntiān** [ADJ] congenital, innate

他是**先天**性癫痫患者。*He's been epileptic since birth.*

先头 **xiāntóu** [ADJ·N] ahead, in front

先行 **xiānxíng** [V·N] to go ahead; to precede; forerunner; foregoer · [MW] 个、位、名

先兆 **xiānzhào** [N] omen · [MW] 个

先知 **xiānzhī** [N] prophet · [MW] 个、位、名

**RELATED WORDS**

| | | |
|---|---|---|
| 少先队 62 | 占先 153 | 在先 188 |
| 早先 268 | 优先权 447 | 优先 447 |
| 争先 595 | 首先 924 | 祖先 1190 |
| 原先 1273 | 领先 1465 | 率先 1469 |
| 预先 1528 | 未卜先知 88 | |

---

**423 农** 農　　　U+519C　　TM **8** FM 丿

**nóng** [N] agriculture, farming; farmer, peasant

农产品 **nóngchǎnpǐn** [N] produce, agricultural product · [MW] 类、种

农场 **nóngchǎng** [N] farm · [MW] 个、家

农村 **nóngcūn** [N] countryside, rural area · [MW] 个

农夫 **nóngfū** [N] peasant, farmer · [MW] 个、名

农户 **nónghù** [N] peasant household · [MW] 家

**423** 农 **nóng** (continued)

农具 **nóngjù** N farm implement/tool · MW 件、套

农历 **nónglì** N traditional Chinese lunar calendar; agricultural almanac

在中国很多人喜欢看**农历**。 *Many people in China like to check the traditional calendar.*

农民 **nóngmín** N farmer, peasant · MW 个、名

农田 **nóngtián** N farmland · MW 片、块

农药 **nóngyào** N pesticide · MW 种

农业 **nóngyè** N agriculture, farming

现代**农业**正在破坏美丽的**农村**。 *Modern agriculture is destroying the beautiful countryside.*

**RELATED WORD**

工农 12

---

**424** 句    U+53E5    TM **8** FM ノ

**jù** N·MW sentence; [measure word for sentences, lines (of poetry), etc.]

句法 **jùfǎ** N sentence structure, syntax · MW 个、种

句号 **jùhào** N period (punctuation mark) · MW 个

句子 **jùzi** N sentence · MW 个、类

**RELATED WORDS**

| | | |
|---|---|---|
| 从句 66 | 主句 124 | 分句 173 |
| 字句 664 | 例句 863 | 词句 1353 |
| 语句 1501 | 造句 1515 | 警句 1987 |
| 祈使句 717 | | |

---

**425** 各    U+5404    TM **8** FM ノ

**gè** PRON·ADV each, all; different, various; individually, separately, respectively

各半 **gèbàn** ADV half and half; fifty-fifty

各别 **gèbié** ADJ different, distinct, unique

各级 **gèjí** N at different levels

各界 **gèjiè** N all walks of life

各人 **gèrén** N each one, everyone

**各人**有**各人**的想法。 *Everyone has his or her own opinions.*

各位 **gèwèi** N everyone/you-all (form of address)

各自 **gèzì** PRON each; respective

---

**426** 名    U+540D    TM **8** FM ノ

**míng** N·ADJ·V·MW name; reputation, fame; famous, well-known; to describe; to take; to possess; [measure word for persons]

命名 *in the name of*

第一名 *first place*

知名 *well-known*

名册 **míngcè** N register, roll · MW 本

名称 **míngchēng** N name; title · MW 个

名词 **míngcí** N noun · MW 个

名次 **míngcì** N rank, position (in a competition) · MW 个

这名选手在比赛中没有获得**名次**。 *The runner did not place in the race.*

名单 **míngdān** N list of names, roster · MW 个、份

名额 **míng'é** N quota · MW 个

名贵 **míngguì** ADJ rare, priceless; distinguished

他收藏了一些**名贵**的陈年葡萄酒。 *He has some rare vintage wines in his collection.*

名家 **míngjiā** N master, prominent expert; influential family · MW 个、位

名利 **mínglì** N fame and fortune

他们不计个人**名利**。 *They shun personal fame and fortune.*

名列前茅 **mínglièqiánmáo** EXP to come out on top, to rank among the best

名流 **míngliú** N celebrity, distinguished person · MW 个、位

名落孙山 **míngluòsūnshān** EXP to fail an exam; to fail to make the grade

名目 **míngmù** N items, objects; name of (an object) · MW 个

巧立**名目**去赚钱 *to invent all kinds of ways to make money*

名牌 **míngpái** N famous brand, designer; name tag · MW 个

名片 **míngpiàn** N business card · MW 张

名气 **míngqì** N reputation, fame

名人 **míngrén** N celebrity, famous person · MW 个、位

名声 **míngshēng** N reputation, renown · MW 个

名胜 **míngshèng** N tourist/historic site · MW 个、处

名实 **míngshí** N reputation and reality

名堂 **míngtang** N variety; trick; achievement; reason · MW 个

名望 **míngwàng** [N] fame and prestige

他是一位很有**名望**的律师。 *He is a famous lawyer.*

名下 **míngxià** [N] in/under the name of, belonging to

名言 **míngyán** [N] saying; famous remark · [MW] 句、段

名义 **míngyì** [N] in name, nominally · [MW] 个

名义上 **míngyìshàng** [ADV] nominally

名誉 **míngyù** [N] reputation; honorary · [MW] 个

名字 **míngzi** [N] given name · [MW] 个

**RELATED WORDS**

| | | |
|---|---|---|
| 大名 20 | 小名 61 | 片名 119 |
| 无名 139 | 齐名 221 | 出名 258 |
| 艺名 274 | 有名 439 | 具名 533 |
| 同名 541 | 成名 611 | 姓名 632 |
| 知名 647 | 定名 666 | 点名 739 |
| 地名 772 | 挂名 796 | 俗名 867 |
| 奶名 878 | 冒名 989 | 莫名其妙 999 |
| 扬名 1004 | 报名 1010 | 别名 1049 |
| 命名 1051 | 臭名远扬 1076 | 闻名 1151 |
| 恶名 1196 | 联名 1206 | 品名 1220 |
| 著名 1223 | 笔名 1278 | 乳名 1308 |
| 黑名单 1389 | 除名 1418 | 签名 1439 |
| 罪名 1542 | 提名 1554 | 顾名思义 1609 |
| 盛名 1694 | 久闻大名 45 | 久享盛名 45 |

---

### 427 吞　U+541E　TM 8 FM 丿

**tūn** [V] to swallow, to gulp down; to take over, to seize; to take (illegal) possession of, to embezzle

吞并 **tūnbìng** [V] to annex

吞服 **tūnfú** [V] to swallow

有些药需要**吞服**，有些需要饮服。 *Some medicines you swallow whole, others you drink.*

吞没 **tūnmò** [V] to misappropriate; to embezzle

吞没巨款 *to misappropriate a huge sum of money*

吞食 **tūnshí** [V] to devour; to swallow

吞吐 **tūntǔ** [V] to handle (cargo, etc.), to take in and send out (in large quantities); to be hesitant (in speech) (LIT to swallow and spit)

吞吞吐吐 **tūntūntǔtǔ** [EXP] to hem and haw, to be hesitant (in speech)

有话就痛痛快快地说出来，不要**吞吞吐吐**。 *Don't stand around hemming and hawing; speak up.*

吞咽 **tūnyàn** [V] to swallow, to gulp down

**RELATED WORDS**

| | |
|---|---|
| 狼吞虎咽 1443 | 忍气吞声 970 |

---

### 428 告　U+544A　TM 8 FM 丿

**gào** [V] to tell, to inform; to announce, to declare; to file a lawsuit, to accuse; to request

告辞 **gàocí** [V] to take (one's) leave

告贷 **gàodài** [V] to ask for a loan

告急 **gàojí** [V] to be in danger, to report an emergency, to ask for emergency help

洪水猛涨，大坝**告急**。 *The dam was in danger due to the rising water.*

告诫 **gàojiè** [V·N] to warn · [MW] 个

告警 **gàojǐng** [V] to raise the alarm, to report an emergency

指示灯已经**告警**了。 *The indicator light gives a warning.*

告警灯 **gàojǐngdēng** [N] alarm, emergency signal · [MW] 盏

告密 **gàomì** [V] to inform on

傻瓜最讨厌**告密**者。 *ShaGua hates people who snitch on others.*

告示 **gàoshi** [N] notification; official notice, bulletin; poster · [MW] 个

告诉 **gàosu** [V] to tell, to inform

有人**告诉**你了吗？ *Did someone tell you?*

告终 **gàozhōng** [V] to end up

告状 **gàozhuàng** [V] to file a lawsuit; to complain

**RELATED WORDS**

| | | |
|---|---|---|
| 广告 23 | 广告经纪人 23 | 公告 103 |
| 央告 196 | 劝告 255 | 布告 309 |
| 忠告 743 | 报告 1010 | 转告 1111 |
| 宣告 1138 | 原告 1273 | 控告 1406 |
| 被告 1517 | 预告 1528 | 通告 1757 |
| 警告 1987 | 做广告 1282 | |

---

### 429 务 務　U+52A1　TM 8 FM 丿

**wù** [N·V·ADV] business, affairs; to be engaged in; certainly, absolutely, without fail

务必 **wùbì** [ADV] certainly, absolutely, without fail

**务必**在六点之前回家 *to have to come back home before six o'clock*

务使 **wùshǐ** [V] to make sure

务须 **wùxū** [ADV] certainly, definitely

务虚 **wùxū** [V] to discuss principles

**RELATED WORDS**

| | | |
|---|---|---|
| 义务 22 | 业务 94 | 业务系统 94 |
| 内务 191 | 任务 211 | 当务之急 335 |

**429 务 wù** (continued)

| | | |
|---|---|---|
| 医务 389 | 政务 517 | 国务院 542 |
| 时务 586 | 财务 588 | 劳务 764 |
| 事务 987 | 债务 1088 | 特务 1094 |
| 职务 1205 | 乘务员 1263 | 总务 1330 |
| 服务 1457 | 商务 1612 | 税务局 1705 |
| 常务 1733 | 港务局 1740 | 尽义务 312 |
| 不识时务 24 | 电子商务 263 | 售后服务 1266 |

---

**430 垂**   U+5782   TM **8** FM **丿**

**chuí** [V] to hang (down), to dangle; to hand down; to condescend; to be on the verge of

**垂钓 chuídiào** [V] to fish

**垂死 chuísǐ** [V] to be in decline, to be dying

**垂头丧气 chuítóusàngqì** [EXP] to be crestfallen, to be in low spirits
> 即使失败, 傻瓜也不**垂头丧气**。 *Even in failure, ShaGua doesn't get down in the dumps.*

**垂危 chuíwēi** [V] to be critically ill, to be close to death

**垂涎 chuíxián** [V] to drool

**垂直 chuízhí** [V·ADJ] to be perpendicular; vertical

**RELATED WORD**

耳垂 145

---

**431 多**   U+591A   TM **8** FM **丿**

**duō** [ADJ·V·ADV] much, many, a lot (of); more; too much/many, excessive; more than, over; to exceed; how, so; however

**多半 duōbàn** [NUM·ADV] more than half, most; most probably, very likely

**多边 duōbiān** [ADJ] multilateral
> **多边**贸易 *multilateral trade*

**多变 duōbiàn** [ADJ] fickle, changeable

**多才多艺 duōcáiduōyì** [EXP] versatile
> 傻瓜不**多才多艺**。 *ShaGua is not versatile.*

**多层 duōcéng** [ADJ] multilayered, multilevel

**多重 duōchóng** [ADJ] multiple; diverse

**多次 duōcì** [ADJ] repeatedly, again and again

**多方面 duōfāngmiàn** [ADV] many-sided; in several aspects
> 根据实际情况, 我们需要从**多方面**改进我们的工作。 *As a matter of fact, we need to improve in many ways.*

**多功能 duōgōngnéng** [ADJ] multifunction, all-purpose

**多极 duōjí** [N] multistage

**多亏 duōkuī** [V] to be lucky; luckily, thanks to
> **多亏**天气好转, 比赛才能继续进行。 *Thanks to the good weather, the match will continue.*

**多么 duōme** [ADV] how (happy, etc.); what (a great idea, etc.)
> 你无法想象我是**多么**惊讶。 *You can't imagine how surprised I was.*
> 梵高的画**多么**漂亮啊! *How beautiful those van Gogh paintings were!*

**多少 duōshao** [QPRON·ADV·N] how much/many; somewhat, to some extent; certain amount
> 黄教授的班里有**多少**个学生? *How many students are there in Dr. Huang's class?*
> 她**多少**有点失望。 *She was somewhat disappointed.*

**多事 duōshì** [ADJ·V] troublesome; to be eventful/interesting

**多数 duōshù** [N] majority (of), most

**多余 duōyú** [ADJ·V] surplus; redundant, unnecessary; to be left

**多元 duōyuán** [ADJ] multi-, poly-

**多种多样 duōzhǒngduōyàng** [EXP] all sorts (of), varied
> 艺术形式是**多种多样**的。 *The forms of art are many and varied.*

**RELATED WORDS**

| | | |
|---|---|---|
| 大多 20 | 大多数 20 | 几多钱 115 |
| 众多 175 | 至多 244 | 许多 502 |
| 好多 627 | 最多 1541 | 增多 1849 |
| 繁多 1988 | 丰富多采 35 | 不可多得 24 |
| 足智多谋 383 | 差不多 673 | 夜长梦多 654 |

---

**432 奔**   U+5954   TM **8** FM **丿**

**bēn** [V] to speed, to hurry, to rush; to run quickly; to go straight to, to head for; to get close to; to elope

**奔波 bēnbō** [V] to rush around, to hurry back and forth

**奔驰 bēnchí** [V·N] to speed; to run fast; Mercedes Benz (make of automobile)

**奔忙 bēnmáng** [V] to be busy rushing around
> 为了家庭, 傻瓜日夜**奔忙**。 *ShaGua was busy day and night working for his family.*

奔命 **bēnmìng** V to be always on the go;
to be in a desperate hurry

奔跑 **bēnpǎo** V to run, to race

他**奔跑**着追赶公共汽车。*He was running to catch the bus.*

奔腾 **bēnténg** V·N to gallop; to surge (of waves); Pentium (brand of computer chip)

奔走 **bēnzǒu** V to rush around

**RELATED WORDS**

投奔 1008　　　　逃奔 1509

---

**433 妥** U+59A5 TM **8** FM 丿

**tuǒ** ADJ·V appropriate, suitable; ready, settled, resolved, finished

妥当 **tuǒdàng** ADJ appropriate, suitable

你认为怎么**妥**当就怎么办。*Do what you think is right.*

妥贴 **tuǒtiē** ADJ appropriate

妥协 **tuǒxié** V to compromise

**RELATED WORDS**

欠妥 105　　　　稳妥 1925

---

**434 采** U+91C7 TM **8** FM 丿

**cǎi** V·N to pick, to pluck; to collect, to gather; to extract; to select, to choose; to adopt; spirit; complexion; feudal estate

采办 **cǎibàn** V to buy (in large quantities)

采伐 **cǎifá** V to fell, to cut (timber)

采访 **cǎifǎng** V to interview; to gather news/information

知道记者要**采访**，傻瓜躲起来了。
*Knowing reporters wanted to interview him, ShaGua went into hiding.*

采风 **cǎifēng** V to collect folk songs

采购 **cǎigòu** V·N to purchase; purchaser

采集 **cǎijí** V to collect, to gather

采矿 **cǎikuàng** V mining

采取 **cǎiqǔ** V to adopt (a measure, a policy, etc.)

采用 **cǎiyòng** V to adopt (a method, etc.)

**RELATED WORDS**

开采 26　　文采 70　　风采 194
兴高采烈 228　丰富多采 35　无精打采 139

---

**435 负** 負 U+8D1F TM **8** FM 丿

**fù** V·ADJ to carry (on one's back), to bear; to shoulder (responsibility); to suffer, to sustain; to lose (a battle, a game, etc.); to owe, to be in debt; to turn one's back on; to rely on; negative, minus

傻瓜的经济**负**担很重。*ShaGua has a very heavy financial load.*

胜**负** *to win or lose*

**负**重 *to carry heavy stuff*

**负**险抵抗 *to put up a stubborn defense (relying on one's strategic position)*

**负**有盛名 *to have a good reputation*

忘恩**负**义 *to be ungrateful*

**负**数 *negative numbers*

负担 **fùdān** V·N to bear/shoulder (a responsibility, an expense, etc.); burden, load, weight ·
MW 个

傻瓜要**负担**大儿子的学费。*ShaGua is responsible for his older son's tuition.*

负荷 **fùhè** V·N to bear, to shoulder; load

负气 **fùqì** V to do (something) resentfully; to leave in a fit of anger

负伤 **fùshāng** V to be wounded/injured

负载 **fùzài** N load, burden

负责 **fùzé** V·ADJ to be responsible for; to be in charge of; conscientious

我**负责**这个班的教学。*I am in charge of teaching this class.*

他很**负责**。*He is very conscientious.*

他是**负责**人。*He is the person in charge.*

负债 **fùzhài** V·N to be in debt; debt, liabilities ·
MW 笔

**RELATED WORDS**

自负 305　　　　担负 789
重负 839　　　　胜负 1122
欺负 1423

---

**436 舟** U+821F TM **8** FM 丿

**zhōu** N boat

诺亚方**舟** *Noah's Ark*

舟车 **zhōuchē** N journey (LIT boat and vehicle)

**RELATED WORDS**

龙舟 315　　　　破釜沉舟 1374

## 437 肉    U+8089    TM **8** FM 丿

**ròu** [N·ADJ] meat; flesh; pulp/flesh (of fruit); spongy

**肉饼 ròubǐng** [N] meat patty · [MW] 块

**肉店 ròudiàn** [N] butcher shop · [MW] 家

**肉桂 ròuguì** [N] cinnamon

**肉麻 ròumá** [ADJ] disgusting, sickening, nauseating
傻瓜觉得吹捧人很**肉麻**。 *ShaGua thinks that flattering words are nauseating.*

**肉排 ròupái** [N] steak · [MW] 块

**肉片 ròupiàn** [N] slice of meat; sliced meat · [MW] 片

**肉食 ròushí** [N] meat
这人很爱吃肉, 孩子们叫他 "**肉食**动物"。 *This man loves to eat meat, so the kids call him "carnivore."*

**肉丝 ròusī** [N] shredded meat · [MW] 条

**肉丸子 ròuwánzi** [N] meatball · [MW] 个

**肉馅 ròuxiàn** [N] ground meat · [MW] 堆

**肉眼 ròuyǎn** [N] naked eye · [MW] 只、对

**肉用鸡 ròuyòngjī** [N] fryer · [MW] 只

**肉用牛 ròuyòngniú** [N] beef cattle · [MW] 头

**肉汁 ròuzhī** [N] gravy, meat stock · [MW] 勺、滴

**肉中刺 ròuzhōngcì** [N] thorn in the flesh · [MW] 根

**RELATED WORDS**

| | | |
|---|---|---|
| 牛肉 51 | 羊肉 227 | 鱼肉 843 |
| 咸肉 1073 | 肌肉 1118 | 炖肉 1175 |
| 鸡肉 1373 | 猪肉 1445 | 烤肉 1505 |
| 骨肉 1543 | 鸭肉 1782 | 鲜肉 1811 |
| 叉烧肉 33 | 烧牛肉 1504 | |

## 438 存    U+5B58    TM **8** FM 丿

**cún** [V] to exist; to survive; to store, to retain, to save; to deposit, to check in (luggage, etc.); to gather, to accumulate; to harbor, to cherish; to be left with; to be in stock

**存车处 cúnchēchù** [N] parking lot · [MW] 个

**存储 cúnchǔ** [V] to store, to stockpile

**存单 cúndān** [N] deposit receipt · [MW] 张

**存档 cúndàng** [V] to file (a document, etc.)

**存放 cúnfàng** [V] to leave in the care of; to deposit (money, luggage, etc.)

**存根 cúngēn** [N] stub (of a ticket, a check, etc.), counterfoil · [MW] 份

**存户 cúnhù** [N] depositor (banking) · [MW] 个

**存货 cúnhuò** [V·N] to stock merchandise; inventory, stock · [MW] 批

**存款 cúnkuǎn** [V·N] to deposit money; deposit · [MW] 笔
我要**存款**。 *I'd like to deposit some money.*

**存取 cúnqǔ** [V] to access (data)

**存亡 cúnwáng** [N] to live or die; life or death

**存现 cúnxiàn** [V] to deposit cash

**存心 cúnxīn** [V·ADV] to have an intention; deliberately, intentionally

**存在 cúnzài** [V·N] to be, to exist; being, existence
这些东西已经不**存在**了。 *These things no longer exist.*

**存折 cúnzhé** [N] deposit book, passbook (banking) · [MW] 本

**RELATED WORDS**

| | | |
|---|---|---|
| 长存 93 | 生存 107 | 共存 164 |
| 内存 191 | 余存 419 | 永存 481 |
| 库存 482 | 封存 815 | 保存 868 |
| 现存 975 | 残存 977 | 堆存 1003 |
| 寄存 1619 | 去伪存真 157 | |

## 439 有    U+6709    TM **8** FM 丿

**yǒu** [V] to have, to possess; to be, to exist, there is; [to express an estimate, a comparison]; [to express occurrence]; one, some
我**有**钱。 *I have money.*
学校里**有**学生。 *There are students in the school.*
**有**的人 *some people*

**有碍 yǒu'ài** [V] to obstruct

**有的是 yǒudeshì** [EXP] to have plenty of, there is no lack of
别忙, **有的是**时间。 *Don't rush; there's plenty of time.*
里面**有的是**地方。 *There's plenty of room.*

**有底 yǒudǐ** [V] to be fully prepared for what is coming

**有点 yǒudiǎn** [ADV] a bit, a little, somewhat, slightly
他**有点**发烧。 *He is a bit feverish.*
这双鞋**有点**大。 *These shoes are slightly too large.*

**有毒 yǒudú** [ADJ] poisonous

**有功 yǒugōng** [ADJ] having rendered great service

**有关 yǒuguān** [V] to be relevant; to have to do with, to be about, to concern

有关钱的问题，傻瓜总是很小心。*Where money is concerned, ShaGua is always very careful.*

学生收集一切**有关**的信息。*The students absorbed all the relevant information.*

**有害** yǒuhài ADJ harmful, destructive

**有机** yǒujī ADJ organic

**有计划** yǒujìhuà V to plan

**有理** yǒulǐ ADJ reasonable, justified

**有利** yǒulì ADJ favorable, advantageous

**有力** yǒulì ADJ strong, powerful; energetic, vigorous

我们都觉得她的论据很**有力**。*We all felt that her arguments were very powerful.*

他的手臂很**有力**。*He has very strong arms.*

**有两下子** yǒuliǎngxiàzi EXP to know one's stuff, to have real skill

**有路子** yǒulùzi EXP to have powerful friends/connections

**有眉目** yǒuméimù EXP to begin to take shape

**有名** yǒumíng ADJ famous, well-known

**有趣** yǒuqù ADJ interesting, fascinating, amusing

他是一个很**有趣**的人。*He is an interesting person.*

**有时** yǒushí ADV sometimes, now and then

**有事** yǒushì V to have something to do

**有数** yǒushù V·ADJ to know all about; not many, just a few

我心里**有数**。*I know how things stand.*

口袋里只剩**有数**的几块钱了。*There are only a few dollars in my pocket.*

**有所** yǒusuǒ ADV somewhat, to some extent

我必须**有所**作为。*I have to do something.*

**有望** yǒuwàng V to be hopeful/promising

**有为** yǒuwéi V to show promise

**有效** yǒuxiào V·ADJ to be effective / in effect

**有效期** yǒuxiàoqī N period of product viability; expiration date · MW 个

**有些** yǒuxiē ADV some, somewhat, rather

**有心人** yǒuxīnrén N conscientious/resolute person · MW 个

**有益** yǒuyì ADJ useful; profitable

良好的饮食**有益**于健康。*A good diet is conducive to good health.*

**有意** yǒuyì V·ADV to be interested in (doing), to intend (to do); on purpose, intentionally

**有意识** yǒuyìshí ADV consciously

**有意思** yǒuyìsi ADJ significant, meaningful; fascinating, amazing

这个计划很**有意思**。*The plan sounds very interesting.*

**RELATED WORDS**

| | | |
|---|---|---|
| 又有 11 | 少有 62 | 公有 103 |
| 仅有 120 | 占有 153 | 只有 160 |
| 应有 334 | 私有 471 | 具有 533 |
| 所有 645 | 没有 938 | 现有 975 |
| 拥有 1014 | 持有 1019 | 特有 1094 |
| 享有 1135 | 稀有 1599 | 富有 1731 |
| 井井有条 60 | 互通有无 135 | 心中有数 232 |
| 莫须有 999 | | |

**440 寿 壽**     U+5BFF    TM 8 FM 丿

**shòu** N·ADJ longevity; life, lifespan, age; birthday; funeral, burial

**寿辰** shòuchén N birthday (of an old person)

**寿礼** shòulǐ N birthday present (for an old person) · MW 份

**寿面** shòumiàn N noodles eaten on a person's birthday · MW 根、碗

**寿命** shòumìng N lifespan, life; life expectancy

**寿星** shòuxīng N god of longevity · MW 位

**寿终正寝** shòuzhōngzhèngqǐn EXP to die in bed of old age

**RELATED WORDS**

| | | |
|---|---|---|
| 人寿保险 4 | 长寿 93 | 拜寿 635 |
| 做寿 1282 | 高寿 1611 | |

**441 尼**     U+5C3C    TM 8 FM 丿

**ní** N Buddhist nun

**尼泊尔** Níbó'ěr N Nepal

**尼姑** nígū N Buddhist nun · MW 个、位、名

**尼古丁** nígǔdīng N nicotine

**尼龙** nílóng N nylon · MW 块

**尼罗河** Níluóhé N Nile River

**RELATED WORD**

肯尼亚 744

**442 戒**     U+6212    TM 8 FM 丿

**jiè** V·N to guard against; to warn; to give up, to quit; Buddhist religious discipline; (finger) ring

**戒备** jièbèi V to be on the alert; to guard

## 442 戒 jiè (continued)

傻瓜**戒备**地看着记者，不知他们要问什么。
*ShaGua alertly watched the reporters; he wasn't sure what they would ask.*

戒除 jièchú [V] to give up

戒严 jièyán [V] to impose martial law / a curfew

戒指 jièzhi [N] (finger) ring · [MW] 枚

**RELATED WORD**

警戒 1987

---

## 443 厄 U+5384 TM 8 FM 丿

è [N·V] strategic place; disaster, catastrophe; to encounter difficulties, to be in distress

厄运 èyùn [N] misfortune, adversity · [MW] 个

---

## 444 劣 U+52A3 TM 8 FM 丿

liè [ADJ] bad, inferior, of poor quality

劣等 lièděng [ADJ] low-grade, of poor quality

为什么你向我们推销**劣**等产品？ *Why are you trying to sell us such low-grade products?*

劣等品 lièděngpǐn [N] inferior goods · [MW] 个、件

劣等生 lièděngshēng [N] unworthy, considered inferior · [MW] 个、名

劣势 lièshì [N] position of weakness, unfavorable situation · [MW] 个

劣质 lièzhì [ADJ] of poor quality

那个推销员试图把**劣质**产品卖给我们。 *The salesman tried to sell us an inferior brand.*

**RELATED WORDS**

卑劣 602　　低劣 618　　拙劣 1013
恶劣 1196

---

## 445 爷 爺 U+7237 TM 8 FM 丿

yé [N] grandfather; dad's uncle; master; god

爷们 yémen [N] man; menfolk · [MW] 个、位

爷爷 yéye [N] paternal grandpa · [MW] 个、位

**RELATED WORDS**

少爷 62　　老爷爷 375　　老爷 375
姑爷 881　　老天爷 375　　老大爷 375

---

## 446 谷 穀 U+8C37 TM 8 FM 丿

gǔ [N] valley; grain, cereal; millet; unhusked rice

谷仓 gǔcāng [N] barn · [MW] 个、座

谷草 gǔcǎo [N] millet straw · [MW] 堆

谷类 gǔlèi [N] cereal/grain crop

谷物 gǔwù [N] cereal, grain · [MW] 种、堆

谷**物**产品对身体有益。 *Cereal products are good for your health.*

谷种 gǔzhǒng [N] seed grain · [MW] 粒、颗、类

谷子 gǔzi [N] millet; unhusked grain/rice · [MW] 粒、颗

**RELATED WORDS**

山谷 38　　　五谷 79　　　峡谷 807
河谷 934　　幽谷 1538

---

## 447 优 優 U+4F18 TM 8 FM 丿

yōu [ADJ·V] excellent, superior; abundant, ample; to give preferential treatment

优待 yōudài [V] to give preferential treatment

优等 yōuděng [N] first-rate, high-class, superior

优点 yōudiǎn [N] strong point, advantage · [MW] 个

优化 yōuhuà [V] to optimize

优惠 yōuhuì [ADJ] preferential, favorable

优良 yōuliáng [ADJ] fine, good

优美 yōuměi [ADJ] elegant, graceful, exquisite

这个城市的环境很**优美**。 *The city environment is exquisite.*

优胜 yōushèng [ADJ] superior; victorious

优势 yōushì [N] superiority, dominance · [MW] 个

优先 yōuxiān [V] to have priority

优先权 yōuxiānquán [N] priority; preference · [MW] 个

优秀 yōuxiù [ADJ] outstanding, excellent, splendid

傻瓜的大儿子决心成为一名**优秀**的建筑师。 *ShaGua's older son made up his mind to become a top-notch architect.*

优异 yōuyì [ADJ] outstanding, excellent

他在学校取得了**优异**的成绩。 *He got excellent grades in school.*

优越 yōuyuè [ADJ] superior, advantageous

优质 yōuzhì [ADJ] high-/top-quality

**448 仍** U+4ECD TM **8** FM 丿

**réng** V·ADV·CONJ to remain, to stay; to occur frequently; still, yet; hence

**仍旧 réngjiù** V·ADV to continue as before, to remain the same; still

他**仍旧**是十年前的老样子。 *After ten years, he still looked the same.*

**仍然 réngrán** ADV still, yet

**449 份** U+4EFD TM **8** FM 丿

**fèn** N·MW share, portion, part; copy; [measure word for food portions, copies of printed material]

**份额 fèn'é** N share, portion, part

**份子 fènzi** N share (of the price of a gift)

傻瓜结婚时，是朋友们凑**份子**送的礼。
*When ShaGua got married, his friends pooled their money to buy him gifts.*

**RELATED WORDS**

| 年份 182 | 月份 190 | 身份 604 |
|---|---|---|
| 备份 845 | 股份 1456 | |

**450 仿** U+4EFF TM **8** FM 丿

**fǎng** V to imitate, to copy; to resemble, to be like

**仿佛 fǎngfú** V·ADV to be like; similarly; seemingly, as if

我们**仿佛**在哪里见过。 *We seem to have met somewhere.*

**仿古 fǎnggǔ** V to be pseudoclassical, to be in the old style

**仿效 fǎngxiào** V to imitate

**仿造 fǎngzào** V to copy; to counterfeit

**仿真 fǎngzhēn** V to emulate, to simulate

**仿制 fǎngzhì** V to copy, to imitate, to be modeled on; to fake

**RELATED WORDS**

| 相仿 805 | 模仿 1673 |
|---|---|

**451 伟** 偉 U+4F1F TM **8** FM 丿

**wěi** ADJ great, large; beautiful and magnificent

**伟大 wěidà** ADJ great, large; magnificent

**伟绩 wěijī** N great achievements · MW 个

**伟人 wěirén** N great person · MW 个、位、名

谁是中国的**伟人**？ *Who are China's great people?*

**伟业 wěiyè** N exploit, great undertaking

**452 传** 傳 U+4F20 TM **8** FM 丿

**chuán** V to hand down, to pass along, to transfer, to deliver; to spread, to transmit; to conduct; to teach; to express; to summon; to infect; to be contagious

家**传**秘方 *secret prescription handed down in a family*

**传**授秘方 *to pass on a secret recipe*

**zhuàn** N biography; historical novel, tale

自**传** *autobiography*

**传播 chuánbō** V to disseminate, to spread; to transmit, to broadcast

电脑的出现，改变了文化**传播**的方式。
*Computers have changed the way cultures spread.*

**传达 chuándá** V to pass along; to convey

**传单 chuándān** N leaflet, flyer · MW 张

**传导 chuándǎo** V to conduct (heat, electricity, etc.)

**传递 chuándì** V to extend; to transmit, to transfer, to deliver

**传动 chuándòng** V to transmit

**传呼 chuánhū** V to notify (someone) of a phone call

**传话 chuánhuà** V to pass on a message

**传教 chuánjiào** V to do missionary work

**传票 chuánpiào** N (court) summons; voucher · MW 张

**传染 chuánrǎn** V to infect

**传染病 chuánrǎnbìng** N infectious/contagious disease · MW 种

这种**传染病**是由蚊子**传染**的。 *This infectious disease is transmitted through mosquitoes.*

**传授 chuánshòu** V to pass on (knowledge, skill, etc.); to teach

**传说 chuánshuō** V·N people say, it is said; legend · MW 个、种

**传统 chuántǒng** N·ADJ tradition, convention; traditional; conservative · MW 个

许多年轻人希望举办中国**传统**式婚礼。
*Many young people want to have a traditional Chinese wedding.*

**452** 传 **chuán/zhuàn** (continued)

传闻 **chuánwén** [V·N] to hear indirectly; rumor, hearsay · [MW] 个

传真 **chuánzhēn** [N·V] fax (machine); to fax · [MW] 份

传记 **zhuànjì** [N] biography · [MW] 本

**RELATED WORDS**

| | | |
|---|---|---|
| 失传 106 | 外传 218 | 电传 263 |
| 自传 305 | 列传 368 | 评传 706 |
| 宣传 1138 | 祖传 1190 | 流传 1493 |
| 据传 1553 | 谣传 1751 | 遗传 1829 |

---

**453**  傷   U+4F24   TM **8** FM ノ

**shāng** [N·ADJ·V] injury; sad; to injure, to hurt, to harm; to hinder

伤疤 **shāngbā** [N] scar · [MW] 块、道
傻瓜脸上有一道**伤疤**。*ShaGua has a scar on his face.*

伤兵 **shāngbīng** [N] wounded soldier · [MW] 个、群

伤残 **shāngcán** [V·N] to have a permanent disability; disability

伤风 **shāngfēng** [V] to catch a cold

伤感 **shānggǎn** [ADJ] sentimental; sick at heart

伤害 **shānghài** [V] to hurt, to damage
傻瓜不想**伤害**儿子的感情。*ShaGua didn't wish to hurt his son's feelings.*

伤痕 **shānghén** [N] scar; bruise · [MW] 条、道

伤口 **shāngkǒu** [N] wound, cut · [MW] 个、道

伤脑筋 **shāngnǎojīn** [ADJ] bothersome; to be a headache (for)

伤亡 **shāngwáng** [N·V] casualty; to cause casualties

伤心 **shāngxīn** [ADJ] sad, broken-hearted, grieving
儿子出走, 傻瓜极为**伤心**。*ShaGua was heartbroken by his son's refusal to return home.*

**RELATED WORDS**

| | | |
|---|---|---|
| 工伤 12 | 刀伤 31 | 击伤 156 |
| 内伤 191 | 外伤 218 | 杀伤 317 |
| 负伤 435 | 划伤 476 | 扭伤 565 |
| 冻伤 680 | 忧伤 693 | 受伤 844 |
| 哀伤 1134 | 误伤 1354 | 破伤风 1374 |
| 损伤 1401 | 烧伤 1504 | 悲伤 1532 |
| 烫伤 1624 | 撞伤 1853 | 擦伤 1985 |
| 跌打损伤 1422 | | |

---

**454** 伪 偽   U+4F2A   TM **8** FM ノ

**wěi** [ADJ] false, fake, bogus; forged

伪君子 **wěijūnzǐ** [N] hypocrite · [MW] 个、名

伪善 **wěishàn** [ADJ] hypocritical

伪造 **wěizào** [V] to forge, to fake
他**伪造**上司的签字。*He faked his boss's signature.*

伪证 **wěizhèng** [N] perjury, false testimony · [MW] 个

伪装 **wěizhuāng** [V] to disguise; to pretend; to fake
他戴上假发把自己**伪装**起来。*He disguised himself by wearing a wig.*

**RELATED WORDS**

| | |
|---|---|
| 去伪存真 157 | 虚伪 1534 |

---

**455** 伯   U+4F2F   TM **8** FM ノ

**bó** [N] uncle, father's older brother; earl

伯伯 **bóbo** [N] uncle, father's older brother · [MW] 个、位

伯父 **bófù** [N] uncle, father's older brother; [respectful form of address for a man about one's father's age] · [MW] 个、位

伯爵 **bójué** [N] earl, count · [MW] 个、位、名

伯母 **bómǔ** [N] aunt, wife of father's older brother; [respectful form of address for a woman about one's mother's age] · [MW] 个、位

伯仲 **bózhòng** [N] older and younger; about the same, about equal

**RELATED WORDS**

| | | |
|---|---|---|
| 大伯 20 | 希伯来 613 | 阿拉伯 1249 |

---

**456** 估   U+4F30   TM **8** FM ノ

**gū** [V] to guess, to estimate; to evaluate; to reckon

估产 **gūchǎn** [V] to estimate the yield

估定 **gūdìng** [V] to evaluate

估计 **gūjì** [V] to estimate; to reckon · [MW] 个
据保守的**估计**, 他损失达8,000元。*A conservative estimate of the damage was 8,000 yuan.*

估价 **gūjià** [V] to estimate; to evaluate
那辆车他**估价**5,000美元。*He estimated the car to be worth $5,000.*

估量 **gūliàng** [V] to estimate; to appraise, to measure

估值 gūzhí V·N to estimate; estimated value

**RELATED WORD**

低估 618

---

**457 伸** U+4F38 TM **8** FM 丿

shēn V to stretch, to extend; to spread;
to express; to straighten

伸长 shēncháng V to stretch, to extend

伸手 shēnshǒu V to hold out / stretch one's hand;
to ask for help
他伸手到桌子的另一端去拿茶杯。*He reached
across the table for the cup.*

伸缩 shēnsuō V to expand and contract;
to be flexible

伸腿 shēntuǐ V to stretch one's legs

伸腰 shēnyāo V to straighten one's back

伸展 shēnzhǎn V to stretch, to extend
运动之前，伸展一下身体很有必要。
*Before exercise, stretching is very necessary.*

伸张 shēnzhāng V to uphold (justice, etc.);
to promote

**RELATED WORD**

延伸 731

---

**458 但** U+4F46 TM **8** FM 丿

dàn CONJ·ADV but, however; yet, still; only, merely

但凡 dànfán ADV in every case

但是 dànshì CONJ but, however; yet, still
中文很难，但是很有意思。*Chinese is difficult,
but it is very interesting.*

但愿 dànyuàn ADV if only (it were possible to);
I wish
但愿我能精通中文。*I wish I could be a master of
Chinese.*

**RELATED WORDS**

不但 24          非但 378

---

**459 供** U+4F9B TM **8** FM 丿

gōng V to supply, to provide, to furnish

gòng V·N to confess; to give offerings;
confession; sacrificial offering

供电 gōngdiàn V to supply electricity

供给 gōngjǐ V to supply, to provide

供暖 gōngnuǎn V to provide heat

供求 gōngqiú N supply and demand

供热 gōngrè V heat supply
在中国，一般人家里没有中央供热设备。*People
don't have central heating in their houses in China.*

供水 gōngshuǐ V water supply

供销 gōngxiāo N supply and sales; distribution

供养 gōngyǎng V to support (one's parents);
to look after

供应 gōngyìng V·N to supply, to provide; supply
电力供应中断，学校只好关闭。*After the power
outage, the school closed down.*

**RELATED WORDS**

口供 42          自供 305          招供 1232
提供 1554        逼供 1828

---

**460 侨** 僑 U+4FA8 TM **8** FM 丿

qiáo V·N to live abroad; person living abroad,
expatriate

侨胞 qiáobāo N overseas expatriate; national/
countryman living abroad · MW 个、位、名

侨汇 qiáohuì N money sent home by a national
living abroad · MW 笔

侨居 qiáojū V to live abroad; to emigrate

侨眷 qiáojuàn N relatives/dependents of a
national living abroad · MW 个、位、名

侨民 qiáomín N emigrant; national living
abroad · MW 个、位、名

**RELATED WORDS**

归侨 166          外侨 218          华侨 421

---

**461 往** U+5F80 TM **8** FM 丿

wǎng V·PREP·ADJ to go; toward, to; past, former,
previous

往常 wǎngcháng N used to, usually
跟往常一样 *same as always*

往返 wǎngfǎn V to go back and forth

往复 wǎngfù V to go and come back, to make
a round trip

往后 wǎnghòu N from now on, in the future

往来 wǎnglái V to go back and forth; to deal
(with); to contact

**461** 往　**wǎng**　(continued)

往年　**wǎngnián**　N　in earlier years, before

往日　**wǎngrì**　N　in earlier times, formerly

往事　**wǎngshì**　N　past events, the past ·
　MW　件、段

往往　**wǎngwǎng**　ADV　often, frequently; more
often than not
　事故的起因**往往**是粗心。*Accidents often occur
due to carelessness.*

**RELATED WORDS**

| | | |
|---|---|---|
| 以往 101 | 已往 133 | 古往今来 154 |
| 交往 222 | 来往 260 | 向往 603 |
| 过往 712 | 前往 1329 | 勇往直前 1371 |
| 礼尚往来 503 | 南来北往 986 | |

**462**　**征**　徵　U+5F81　TM **8** FM 丿

**zhēng**　V·N　to go on / mount an expedition;
to draft, to recruit; to levy/collect (taxes, etc.);
to ask for, to solicit; symbol; evidence; journey

征兵　**zhēngbīng**　V　to draft, to conscript, to recruit

征调　**zhēngdiào**　V　to draft

征服　**zhēngfú**　V　to conquer, to subjugate
　**征服**人心比武力**征服**难得多。*Conquering by
force is easier than capturing people's minds.*

征购　**zhēnggòu**　V　to procure, to requisition

征集　**zhēngjí**　V　to collect; to draft, to call up,
to recruit
　傻瓜打算**征集**市民对市政建设的建议。
　*ShaGua is going to gather suggestions from the
residents of the city.*

征聘　**zhēngpìn**　V　to invite job applications,
to post job vacancies

征求　**zhēngqiú**　V　to ask for, to solicit

征收　**zhēngshōu**　V　to levy/impose (a tax, a fine,
a tariff, etc.)

征税　**zhēngshuì**　V　to levy a tax

征讨　**zhēngtǎo**　V　to go on a punitive expedition

征途　**zhēngtú**　N　long journey, expedition

征文　**zhēngwén**　V　to solicit articles (for a
publication)

征询　**zhēngxún**　V　to consult, to seek the opinion
of
　公司**征询**用户意见。*The company surveys its
customers.*

征用　**zhēngyòng**　V　to requisition; to commandeer

征召　**zhēngzhào**　V　to draft, to call up, to recruit

**RELATED WORDS**

| | | |
|---|---|---|
| 长征 93 | 应征 334 | 特征 1094 |
| 远征 1184 | 象征 1580 | 万里长征 73 |

**463**　**加**　U+52A0　TM **8** FM 丿

**jiā**　V　to add, to append; to increase; to confer;
plus, more, extra

加班　**jiābān**　V　to work overtime
　上这个新项目，意味着傻瓜又得**加班**加点了。
　*This new project means that ShaGua will be
working overtime again.*

加倍　**jiābèi**　V·ADV　to double/redouble (one's
efforts); doubly

加法　**jiāfǎ**　N　addition · MW　个

加工　**jiāgōng**　V　to process; to rework

加固　**jiāgù**　V　to reinforce, to strengthen

加急　**jiājí**　V　to become more urgent; to handle on
an urgent basis

加紧　**jiājǐn**　V　to speed up; to intensify

加劲　**jiājìn**　V　to make an extra effort

加剧　**jiājù**　V　to aggravate, to make worse, to
exacerbate

加快　**jiākuài**　V　to accelerate, to speed up

加宽　**jiākuān**　V　to widen

加料　**jiāliào**　V　to feed (raw material, supplies, etc.)
to/into

加码　**jiāmǎ**　V　to raise prices; to raise the stakes
(gambling)

加拿大　**Jiānádà**　N　Canada

加强　**jiāqiáng**　V　to strengthen, to reinforce

加热　**jiārè**　V　to heat, to warm

加入　**jiārù**　V　to add/mix into; to join, to become
a member of
　傻瓜的儿子**加入**了大学生俱乐部。*ShaGua's son
joined the university student club.*

加速　**jiāsù**　V　to accelerate, to speed up

加锁　**jiāsuǒ**　V　to lock

加压　**jiāyā**　V　to pressurize

加以　**jiāyǐ**　V·CONJ　to handle, to deal with; also,
in addition, moreover

加油　**jiāyóu**　V　to refuel; to make an extra effort;
to cheer (someone) on, go!, come on!
　**加油**！他们大声地鼓励自己的足球队。
　*"Go!" they screamed for their soccer team.*

加载　**jiāzài**　V　to pick up an additional shipment

加重　**jiāzhòng**　V　to make more serious;
to increase the weight of

你这样做会**加**重学生的思想负担。
*What you are doing will add to the students' worries.*

**RELATED WORDS**

| | | |
|---|---|---|
| 未加工 88 | 外加 218 | 更加 355 |
| 参加 600 | 添加 1346 | 添加剂 1346 |
| 追加 1507 | 施加 1758 | 递加 1827 |
| 增加 1849 | | |

---

**464　如**　　U+5982　TM **8** FM 丿

**rú** `V·PREP·CONJ` to be like; to be as good as, can compare with; such as, like, for example; if

你不**如**她。*You are not as good as she is.*

**如**你所想 *as you thought*

比**如** *for example*

**如**不能上课，请告诉我。*If you can't come to class, please let me know.*

**如常 rúcháng** `ADV` as usual

**如此 rúcǐ** `PRON` like this, in this way, so

真不敢相信，他竟然会**如此**无礼。*I can't believe he's being so rude.*

**如此而已 rúcǐ'éryǐ** `EXP` that's what it all adds up to

**如故 rúgù** `ADV` as before

**如果 rúguǒ** `CONJ` if, in case

**如何 rúhé** `QPRON` how?; what?

比赛结果**如何**？ *How did the competition turn out?*

**如今 rújīn** `N` today, now, nowadays

**如来佛 Rúláifó** `N` Buddha

**如期 rúqī** `ADV` on time, as scheduled

**如若 rúruò** `CONJ` if

**如上 rúshàng** `ADV` as mentioned above, as above

**如实 rúshí** `ADV` accurately; truthfully

请**如实**申报收入税。*Please report your income taxes accurately.*

**如数 rúshù** `ADV` exactly the right amount/number

**如同 rútóng** `V` to be like, to be similar to; same as

**如下 rúxià** `ADV` as follows

**如意 rúyì** `V·N` to be satisfied; according to one's wishes

祝你万事**如意**！ *I wish you good luck in everything!*

**如愿 rúyuàn** `V` to have one's dream come true; to be as one wishes

傻瓜**如愿**了吗？ *Has ShaGua's dream come true?*

---

**RELATED WORDS**

| | | |
|---|---|---|
| 不如 24 | 了如指掌 30 | 比如 279 |
| 自如 305 | 例如 863 | 犹如 886 |
| 突如其来 913 | 恰如其分 930 | 假如 1586 |
| 乃至如此 134 | 无论如何 139 | 宾至如归 1141 |

---

**465　妇**　婦　U+5987　TM **8** FM 丿

**fù** `N` woman; married woman; wife

**妇产医院 fùchǎnyīyuàn** `N` maternity hospital, gynecology/obstetrics hospital · `MW` 家、所

**妇科 fùkē** `N` gynecology

**妇联 fùlián** `N` women's federation/association/league

**妇女 fùnǚ** `N` woman · `MW` 个、位、名

**妇幼 fùyòu** `N` women and children

妇幼保健中心 *health center for women and children*

**RELATED WORDS**

| | | |
|---|---|---|
| 夫妇 55 | 少妇 62 | 主妇 124 |
| 产妇 219 | 奸妇 329 | 泼妇 937 |
| 孕妇 971 | 情妇 1491 | 儿媳妇 43 |
| 夫唱妇随 55 | | |

---

**466　妖**　　U+5996　TM **8** FM 丿

**yāo** `N·ADJ` monster; demon, evil spirit; wicked; bewitching

**妖怪 yāoguài** `N` monster, goblin · `MW` 个、伙

**妖精 yāojing** `N` demon, evil spirit · `MW` 个、伙

**妖魔 yāomó** `N` monster · `MW` 个、伙

**妖娆 yāoráo** `ADJ` fascinating; enchanting

**妖言 yāoyán** `N` heresy · `MW` 个

**妖艳 yāoyàn** `ADJ` coquettish, flirty

---

**467　妙**　　U+5999　TM **8** FM 丿

**miào** `ADJ` wonderful; excellent, fine; exquisite; ingenious, clever; magical

**妙计 miàojì** `N` wonderful idea, brilliant scheme · `MW` 个、则

**妙诀 miàojué** `N` knack, clever way (of doing something) · `MW` 个

**妙龄 miàolíng** `N` young, youthful

**妙用 miàoyòng** `N` magical effect · `MW` 个

**467** 妙 **miào** (continued)

妙语 **miàoyǔ** N clever/witty remark · MW 串
他**妙语**连珠。*His speech was filled with clever remarks.*

RELATED WORDS

| | | |
|---|---|---|
| 不妙 24 | 巧妙 364 | 美妙 671 |
| 奇妙 854 | 奥妙 1435 | 微妙 1700 |
| 绝妙 1706 | 莫名其妙 999 | |

---

**468** 牧    U+7267    TM **8** FM 丿

**mù** V to herd, to shepherd, to tend

牧草 **mùcǎo** N pasture · MW 片

牧场 **mùchǎng** N pasture, grazing land; ranch · MW 个、片

牧民 **mùmín** N herdsman · MW 个、位

牧师 **mùshī** N pastor, priest, minister · MW 个、位、名

牧羊犬 **mùyángquǎn** N sheep/herding dog · MW 条

RELATED WORD

放牧 964

---

**469** 狂    U+72C2    TM **8** FM 丿

**kuáng** ADJ arrogant, overbearing; violent; crazy, maniac; wild

狂暴 **kuángbào** ADJ violent; frantic

狂吠 **kuángfèi** V to howl, to bark furiously

狂风 **kuángfēng** N fierce/gale-force wind · MW 阵

狂欢 **kuánghuān** V to revel, to carouse; to paint the town red
节日**狂欢**通宵达旦。*The festivities went on all night and all day.*

狂犬病 **kuángquǎnbìng** N rabies

狂热 **kuángrè** ADJ crazed, fanatical; feverish, delirious
这种**狂热**正席卷中国。*The craze is sweeping across China.*

狂人 **kuángrén** N maniac, madman, lunatic · MW 个、伙

狂妄 **kuángwàng** ADJ egotistical, arrogant, insolent

狂喜 **kuángxǐ** ADJ ecstatic, exultant

狂言 **kuángyán** N raving
口出**狂言** *to rave*

RELATED WORDS

| | | |
|---|---|---|
| 发狂 311 | 疯狂 1147 | 躁狂 1992 |

---

**470** 印    U+5370    TM **8** FM 丿

**yìn** V·N to print; to stamp; to trace; to conform to, to be in line with; print; stamp

印版 **yìnbǎn** N printing plate · MW 个

印度 **Yìndù** N India

印度洋 **Yìndùyáng** N Indian Ocean

印发 **yìnfā** V to print and distribute

印泥 **yìnní** N red ink paste (used for seals) · MW 块

印染 **yìnrǎn** V to print and dye

印刷 **yìnshuā** V to print
这本字典已经第十次**印刷**了。*The dictionary is in its tenth printing.*

印象 **yìnxiàng** N impression
你对北京的第一**印象**如何？ *What were your first impressions of Beijing?*

印章 **yìnzhāng** N seal, stamp; printed sheet · MW 枚

RELATED WORDS

| | | |
|---|---|---|
| 付印 206 | 封印 815 | 复印 1059 |
| 洗印 1167 | 染印 1336 | 指印 1397 |
| 脚印 1804 | 影印 1918 | |

---

**471** 私    U+79C1    TM **8** FM 丿

**sī** N·ADJ·ADV individual; privacy; property; personal; private, secret; selfish; privately, secretly

私产 **sīchǎn** N private property · MW 笔

私仇 **sīchóu** N personal enmity · MW 笔、桩

私法 **sīfǎ** N private law · MW 部

私房钱 **sīfángqián** N personal savings · MW 笔

私交 **sījiāo** N personal friendship/connections · MW 个

私立 **sīlì** ADJ private, privately run
如果你想送孩子上**私立**学校，你就得付学费。*If you want your child to attend a private school, you must pay tuition.*

私利 **sīlì** N private/selfish interest; personal gain

私了 **sīliǎo** V to settle privately

私情 **sīqíng** N personal relationship; love affair; sexual relations · MW 段

私人 **sīrén** N private, personal; one's own person

私生活 **sīshēnghuó** N personal/private life; privacy

私生子 **sīshēngzǐ** N illegitimate child, bastard · MW 个

私事 **sīshì** N personal affairs/matters; privacy · MW 桩

私通 **sītōng** V to have secret communication with; to commit adultery

私下 **sīxià** ADV in private, secretly

私营 **sīyíng** ADJ privately owned; privately run/operated

私有 **sīyǒu** ADJ privately owned, private

私章 **sīzhāng** N personal seal · MW 枚

私自 **sīzì** ADV secretly; without authorization/permission

图书馆的工具书不得**私自**带出。 *No reference books are to be taken out of the library without permission.*

RELATED WORDS

| | | |
|---|---|---|
| 无私 139 | 走私 265 | 自私 305 |
| 营私 1546 | 隐私 1912 | |

---

472 利     U+2632     TM 8 FM 丿

**lì** N·ADJ·V advantage, benefit; profit, interest; sharp; advantageous, favorable; to benefit, to do good (for); to make use of

利比亚 **Lìbǐyà** N Libya

利弊 **lìbì** N pros and cons; advantages and disadvantages

傻瓜已经考虑过买这辆车的**利弊**。 *ShaGua has considered the pros and cons of having this car.*

利害 **lìhai** ADJ terrible; serious, severe; formidable, tough

利己主义 **lìjǐzhǔyì** N egotism

利率 **lìlǜ** N interest rate

利落 **lìluo** ADJ agile, nimble

利润 **lìrùn** N profit · MW 笔

利息 **lìxī** N interest · MW 笔

百分之五的**利息** *five-percent interest*

利益 **lìyì** N benefit, gain; profit, interest

利用 **lìyòng** V to use; to take advantage of, to exploit

傻瓜告诫儿子要好好**利用**这个机会。 *ShaGua told his son to take advantage of the opportunity.*

---

利诱 **lìyòu** V to entice, to lure

RELATED WORDS

| | | |
|---|---|---|
| 本利 90 | 互利 135 | 专利 155 |
| 水利 159 | 年利 182 | 毛利润 183 |
| 功利 252 | 吉利 259 | 比利时 279 |
| 权利 292 | 名利 426 | 有利 439 |
| 红利 474 | 舍利子 593 | 便利 865 |
| 顺利 874 | 胜利 1122 | 叙利亚 1129 |
| 麻利 1146 | 净利 1159 | 纯利 1290 |
| 流利 1493 | 渔利 1496 | 福利 1825 |
| 暴利 1844 | 赢利 2000 | 损人利己 1401 |
| 既得利益 1572 | 意大利 1812 | 连本带利 958 |

---

473 纠 纠     U+7EA0     TM 8 FM 丿

**jiū** V to correct, to rectify; to supervise; to investigate, to probe; to entangle; to gather together, to assemble

纠察 **jiūchá** V·N to maintain order; steward, marshal · MW 个、名

纠纷 **jiūfēn** N dispute; issue · MW 个、场

傻瓜正全力以赴解决这场**纠纷**。 *ShaGua is doing his best to resolve the dispute.*

纠偏 **jiūpiān** V to correct (an error)

纠正 **jiūzhèng** V to correct (an error); to redress

---

474 红 紅     U+7EA2     TM 8 FM 丿

**hóng** ADJ·N red; popular, in vogue; successful; revolutionary; bonus; dividend

红白事 **hóngbáishì** N weddings and funerals · MW 件

红榜 **hóngbǎng** N honor roll · MW 张

红宝石 **hóngbǎoshí** N ruby · MW 颗、粒

红茶 **hóngchá** N black tea · MW 盒、杯、壶

红尘 **hóngchén** N the world of mortals; human society; worldly affairs

红军 **hóngjūn** N Red Army; Red Army man · MW 个、队

红利 **hónglì** N bonus; dividend (for shareholders) · MW 笔

红脸 **hóngliǎn** V to blush, to turn red · MW 个

红领巾 **hónglǐngjīn** N red scarf; member of the Young Pioneers (Communist youth organization) · MW 个、条

红绿灯 **hónglǜdēng** N traffic signal · MW 盏

**474** 红 **hóng** (continued)

傻瓜在**红绿灯**前睡着了。*ShaGua fell asleep at the traffic light.*

**红旗 hóngqí** N red flag · MW 面

**红人 hóngrén** N rising star; favorite (of someone in power) · MW 个、名

**红色 hóngsè** N·ADJ red (color); revolutionary

**红十字 Hóngshízìhuì** N Red Cross (international humanitarian organization)

**红细胞 hóngxìbāo** N red blood cell · MW 个

**红星 hóngxīng** N five-pointed red star (a symbol of revolution); popular actor/actress · MW 颗、名

**红眼 hóngyǎn** N·V·ADJ pink eye; to see red; angry; jealous · MW 双

她得了**红眼**。*She got pink eye.*

他急**红眼**了。*He is infuriated.*

你得奖，她**红眼**了。*She is jealous of your prize.*

**红运 hóngyùn** N good luck · MW 个

**红肿 hóngzhǒng** ADJ inflamed, red and swollen

**红种人 hóngzhǒngrén** N Native American · MW 个、名、位

**RELATED WORDS**

| | | |
|---|---|---|
| 口红 42 | 火红 72 | 分红 173 |
| 朱红色 184 | 血红 306 | 西红柿 352 |
| 面红耳赤 721 | 桃红 1243 | 粉红 1363 |
| 脸红 1461 | 眼红 1570 | 通红 1757 |
| 鲜红 1811 | 五星红旗 79 | 搽口红 1558 |
| 满堂红 1745 | | |

---

**475** 幻     U+2106     TM **8** FM ノ

**huàn** ADJ unreal, imaginary; magical

**幻灯 huàndēng** N lantern slide; slide show; slide projector · MW 片、台

**幻景 huànjǐng** N illusion · MW 个

**幻境 huànjìng** N fairyland · MW 个

**幻觉 huànjué** N illusion; hallucination; delusion · MW 个

**幻梦 huànmèng** N illusion; dream · MW 个

**幻术 huànshù** N magic · MW 个

**幻想 huànxiǎng** N·V fantasy, illusion; to dream; to imagine · MW 个

孩子常常生活在**幻想**中。*Kids often live in imaginative fantasy worlds.*

**幻象 huànxiàng** N phantom · MW 个

**幻影 huànyǐng** N phantom, mirage · MW 个

**RELATED WORDS**

| | | |
|---|---|---|
| 科幻故事 642 | 变幻 653 | 梦幻 1217 |
| 虚幻 1534 | | |

---

**476** 划 劃     U+2085     TM **8** FM ノ

**huá** V·ADJ to paddle, to row; to scratch; to be worthwhile

**huà** V to delimit, to mark off, to differentiate; to transfer, to assign; to plan

划拨 *to transfer*

计**划** *plan*

**划船 huáchuán** V to row/paddle (a boat), to go boating

**划伤 huáshāng** V to be scratched

**划水 huáshuǐ** V to paddle

**划算 huásuàn** V·ADJ to calculate; good deal

**划定 huàdìng** V to mark off; to allocate

**划分 huàfēn** V to divide; to differentiate, to mark off

在现实生活中，**划分**好人和坏人并不容易。*In real life, it's not so easy to divide people into good and bad.*

**划归 huàguī** V to incorporate, to subsume

**划清 huàqīng** V to make/draw a clear distinction, to distinguish clearly

**划清**是非界限 *to make a clear distinction between right and wrong*

**划时代 huàshídài** ADJ epoch-making, of major importance

**RELATED WORDS**

| | | |
|---|---|---|
| 计划 240 | 规划 1098 | 有计划 439 |
| 日程计划 96 | | |

---

**477** 针 針     U+9488     TM **8** FM ノ

**zhēn** N·MW needle; like a needle; injection, shot; acupuncture; [measure word for stitches, shots, etc.]

**针刺疗法 zhēncìliáofǎ** N acupuncture therapy/ treatment · MW 种

**针刺麻醉 zhēncìmázuì** V to anesthetize through acupuncture

**针对 zhēnduì** V to be aimed/targeted at; to have in mind

傻瓜的言行并不**针对**自己的儿子。*ShaGua's words and actions were not directed at his sons.*

**针尖 zhēnjiān** N point of a needle

**针灸 zhēnjiǔ** N acupuncture and moxibustion (traditional Chinese herbal medicine therapy)

**针织 zhēnzhī** V to knit

**针织物 zhēnzhīwù** N bead netting · MW 件

**RELATED WORDS**

| | | |
|---|---|---|
| 方针 220 | 扎针 288 | 打针 289 |
| 时针 586 | 秒针 643 | 别针 1049 |
| 织针 1108 | 钩针 1463 | 胸针 1709 |
| 撞针 1853 | 曲别针 272 | 逆时针 1359 |
| 指北针 1397 | 见缝插针 267 | |

---

**478　言**　U+8A00　TM **8** FM 丶

**yán** N·V speech; words; characters; to speak, to talk, to say; to describe, to express

**言不由衷** yánbùyóuzhōng EXP to speak tongue in cheek, to not say what one means

傻瓜认为："你看来不那么笨嘛" 往往是别人对他**言不由衷**的恭维话。*ShaGua believes that the sentence "You aren't as big a fool as you look" is a backhanded compliment.*

**言辞** yáncí N words; wording, expression · MW 段

**言和** yánhé V to make peace

**言教** yánjiào N to teach/explain in words

身教胜于**言教**。*Actions speak louder than words. / Teaching by example is better than explaining in words.*

**言论** yánlùn N speech; personal expression/ opinion · MW 个、种

**言谈** yántán V·N to speak, to talk; the way one speaks; what one says

傻瓜的**言谈**举止让人感到他有点笨。*ShaGua's speech and mannerisms made others think he is a bit slow.*

**言外之意** yánwàizhīyì EXP implication; reading between the lines

**言行** yánxíng N words and deeds · MW 种

**言语** yányǔ N·V spoken words, speech; language; to speak, to talk · MW 段

**RELATED WORDS**

| | | |
|---|---|---|
| 三言两语 9 | 文言 70 | 失言 106 |
| 片言 119 | 只言片语 160 | 方言 220 |
| 发言 311 | 发言人 311 | 戏言 365 |
| 引言 371 | 名言 426 | 妖言 466 |
| 狂言 469 | 花言巧语 549 | 直言 609 |
| 导言 751 | 约言 876 | 序言 916 |
| 扬言 1004 | 宣言 1138 | 格言 1246 |
| 断言 1260 | 甜言蜜语 1306 | 前言 1329 |
| 流言 1493 | 语言学 1501 | 语言 1501 |
| 预言 1528 | 留言 1582 | 谣言 1751 |
| 怨言 1792 | 谎言 1824 | 遗言 1829 |
| 察言观色 1877 | 赠言 1944 | 总而言之 1330 |
| 文学语言 70 | 仗义执言 121 | |

---

**479　吝**　U+541D　TM **8** FM 丶

**lìn** ADJ stingy, tight, miserly

**吝啬** lìnsè ADJ stingy

傻瓜对自己很**吝啬**, 对朋友很大方。*ShaGua is very stingy in spending money on himself, but quite generous to his friends.*

**吝惜** lìnxī V to grudge

---

**480　弃**　棄　U+5F03　TM **8** FM 丶

**qì** V to abandon, to discard

**弃权** qìquán V to waive one's right, to abstain (from voting)

**弃世** qìshì V to die

**弃婴** qìyīng N abandoned baby · MW 个

有人说, 傻瓜曾是一个**弃婴**。*Some people have said ShaGua was abandoned as a baby.*

**弃置** qìzhì V to throw away, to discard

那辆车被**弃置**了。*The car has been junked.*

**RELATED WORDS**

| | |
|---|---|
| 吐弃 286 | 丢弃 297 |
| 舍弃 593 | 废弃 918 |
| 放弃 964 | 背弃 1380 |
| 抛弃 1395 | 离弃 1614 |
| 嫌弃 1702 | 遗弃 1829 |
| 背信弃义 1380 | |

---

**481　永**　U+6C38　TM **8** FM 丶

**yǒng** ADV forever, eternally; always

**永不** yǒngbù ADV will never; never

**永存** yǒngcún V to last/endure forever

傻瓜认为, 只有友情是**永存**的, 其他都是暂时的。*ShaGua believes that only friendship can last forever; everything else is temporary.*

**永恒** yǒnghéng ADJ eternal, perpetual, everlasting

**永久** yǒngjiǔ ADJ permanent; eternal, forever

**永久**住址 *permanent address*

只有**永恒**的利益, 没有**永久**的敌人。*There are only everlasting benefits; there are no eternal enemies.*

**永生** yǒngshēng V·N to live forever; eternal life

**永世** yǒngshì ADV forever

**永远** yǒngyuǎn ADV forever, eternally

**482** 库　庫　U+5E93　TM **8** FM 丶

**kù** N warehouse; bank

库藏 **kùcáng** V to store, to have in storage

库存 **kùcún** N stock, inventory; stockpile ·
MW 批

库房 **kùfáng** N warehouse; storeroom ·
MW 间

**RELATED WORDS**

入库 5　　　　水库 159　　　　血库 306
仓库 418　　　金库 420　　　国库 542
宝库 667　　　油库 683　　　数据库 1637
弹药库 1763

**483** 灾　U+707E　TM **8** FM 丶

**zāi** N disaster, catastrophe, calamity; adversity;
(personal) misfortune; bad luck

灾害 **zāihài** N disaster, catastrophe, calamity ·
MW 场

灾荒 **zāihuāng** N famine · MW 场

灾祸 **zāihuò** N disaster; natural/man-made
calamity · MW 场

灾民 **zāimín** N disaster victim · MW 个、群

灾难 **zāinàn** N catastrophe, calamity; suffering ·
MW 场

洪水引起一场大**灾难**。*The flooding caused
a calamity.*

灾情 **zāiqíng** N disaster conditions; calamity

灾区 **zāiqū** N disaster area · MW 个

目前正在给**灾区**空投药品。*Medical supplies are
being dropped into the disaster area.*

**RELATED WORDS**

火灾 72　　　　虫灾 262　　　　幸灾乐祸 373
旱灾 387　　　受灾 844　　　救灾 1259

**484** 它　U+5B83　TM **8** FM 丶

**tā** PRON it

它们 **tāmen** PRON they; them

傻瓜养的三只猫和两条狗老是打架, 他对**它们**
毫无办法。*The two dogs and three cats ShaGua
has fight all the time; he is helpless.*

**RELATED WORD**

吉它 259

**485** 宇　U+5B87　TM **8** FM 丶

**yǔ** N house; room; world; space, universe;
appearance; poise, bearing, manner

宇航 **yǔháng** V to travel through space;
spaceflight

宇宙 **yǔzhòu** N universe, cosmos

宇宙观 **yǔzhòuguān** N worldview ·
MW 个

**RELATED WORD**

庙宇 659

**486** 守　U+5B88　TM **8** FM 丶

**shǒu** V to guard, to defend; to observe,
to abide by; to be close to, to be near

守备 **shǒubèi** V to be on guard duty

守财奴 **shǒucáinú** N scrooge, miser ·
MW 个、名

守法 **shǒufǎ** V to observe the law, to be
law-abiding

守寡 **shǒuguǎ** V to live as a widow

守候 **shǒuhòu** V to keep watch; to wait for

傻瓜太太生病后, 傻瓜每天都**守候**在妻子
身旁。*When Mrs. ShaGua fell ill, ShaGua stayed
at his wife's bedside every day.*

守旧 **shǒujiù** V·ADJ to stick to the old ways;
conservative, reactionary

守门 **shǒumén** V to be on duty at the gate;
to defend the goal (sports)

守门人 **shǒuménrén** N gatekeeper; goalie,
goaltender · MW 个

守岁 **shǒusuì** V to stay up late on New Year's Eve,
to see the new year in

守望 **shǒuwàng** V to keep watch

守卫 **shǒuwèi** V to guard, to defend

狗**守卫**着院子, 不让生人进入。*The dog guarded
the yard against strangers.*

守信 **shǒuxìn** V to keep one's word/promise

守则 **shǒuzé** N rule, regulation ·
MW 条

**RELATED WORDS**

困守 393　　　　　　固守 760
看守 841　　　　　　保守 868
信守 869　　　　　　监守 994
驻守 1207　　　　　墨守成规 1843
镇守 1872　　　　　遵守 1975

## 487 安 | U+5B89 | TM 8 | FM 丶

**ān** ADJ·V·QPRON quiet, calm, at ease; safe; to calm (someone/something) down, to set at ease; to be content/satisfied (with); to put in a suitable place, to find a place for; to install, to set up; where; how

安康 *good health*

身体欠安 *poor health*

安于现状 *to be content with one's current situation*

安罪名 *to bring charges against*

不安好心 *to harbor evil intentions*

安电脑 *to set up a computer*

真理安在? *Where is the truth?*

**安插 ānchā** V to install, to insert; to place (a trusted follower) in a key position

**安定 āndìng** ADJ·V stable, settled; to stabilize

在城里**安定**下来后,傻瓜开始想念自己的家庭。*ShaGua came to miss his family after settling in the city.*

**安顿 āndùn** V·ADJ to settle down; to make arrangements for; peaceful, undisturbed

**安放 ānfàng** V to put (something) where it belongs / in a safe place

**安徽 Ānhuī** N Anhui Province

**安家 ānjiā** V to settle (down); to get married

**安静 ānjìng** ADJ quiet, calm, peaceful

**安乐 ānlè** ADJ comfortable, carefree (LIT peace and happiness)

**安眠 ānmián** V to sleep peacefully

**安宁 ānníng** ADJ calm, peaceful; free from worry, undisturbed

**安排 ānpái** V to arrange, to plan

这对夫妻精心**安排**了退休后的生活。*The couple arranged their retirement wisely.*

**安全 ānquán** ADJ secure, safe

在救人的关头,傻瓜根本无法顾及自身**安全**。*While rescuing someone else, ShaGua completely disregarded his own safety.*

**安慰 ānwèi** V·ADJ to comfort, to console; comforted, reassured

傻瓜太太生病时,傻瓜给了她极大的**安慰**。*ShaGua was a great comfort to Mrs. ShaGua when she was ill.*

**安稳 ānwěn** ADJ steady, smooth; quiet, calm

**安闲 ānxián** ADJ carefree, leisurely

**安心 ānxīn** V to feel at ease; to stop worrying; to keep one's mind on

**安逸 ānyì** ADJ comfortable

**安置 ānzhì** V to make arrangements for

**安装 ānzhuāng** V to install; to mount

### RELATED WORDS

| | | |
|---|---|---|
| 不安 24 | 不安全 24 | 不安心 24 |
| 天安门 25 | 平安 78 | 公安 103 |
| 心安理得 232 | 早安 268 | 西安 352 |
| 问安 678 | 保安 868 | 治安 935 |
| 晚安 1779 | 坐立不安 318 | 坐卧不安 318 |

## 488 牢 | U+7262 | TM 8 | FM 丶

**láo** N·ADJ prison, jail; pen; sacrifice; firm, fast

**牢不可破 láobùkěpò** EXP unbreakable

**牢房 láofáng** N jail; prison cell · MW 间、座

**牢固 láogù** ADJ firm; secure; durable

**牢记 láojì** V to remember clearly, to keep firmly in mind

我们应该**牢记**中国是一个多民族的国家。*We should keep in mind that China is comprised of numerous nationalities.*

**牢靠 láokào** ADJ firm; reliable

**牢笼 láolóng** N cage; trap; shackles · MW 个

**牢骚 láosāo** N·V complaint, grievance; to grumble

这个女孩儿老是发**牢骚**。*This girl always makes complaints.*

**牢狱 láoyù** N prison · MW 座

### RELATED WORDS

| | |
|---|---|
| 囚牢 161 | 坐牢 318 |

## 489 军 軍 | U+519B | TM 8 | FM 丶

**jūn** N army, armed forces; troops; military

**军备 jūnbèi** N arms, armament · MW 批

**军队 jūnduì** N army, armed forces; troops · MW 支

**军阀 jūnfá** N warlord; military junta · MW 个

**军法 jūnfǎ** N martial law · MW 部

**军费 jūnfèi** N military expenditure · MW 笔

**军服 jūnfú** N military/army uniform · MW 套、件

**军官 jūnguān** N (commissioned) officer · MW 个、名

**军火 jūnhuǒ** N arms and ammunition; munitions · MW 批

**军纪 jūnjì** N military discipline · MW 条

**489 军 jūn** (continued)

军阶 **jūnjiē** N military rank · MW 个、级

军民 **jūnmín** N army and civilian, military and civilian

军人 **jūnrén** N soldier · MW 个、名、队
军人必须服从命令。 *Soldiers must obey orders.*

军事 **jūnshì** N military affairs; the military

军衔 **jūnxián** N military rank · MW 个

军需 **jūnxū** N military supplies/matériel · MW 批

军用 **jūnyòng** ADJ military; for military use

**RELATED WORDS**

| | | |
|---|---|---|
| 从军 66 | 亚军 136 | 全军 172 |
| 行军 327 | 红军 474 | 空军 669 |
| 进军 713 | 叛军 960 | 陆军 1043 |
| 敌军 1127 | 将军 1161 | 联军 1206 |
| 冠军 1478 | 海军 1494 | 裁军 1535 |
| 援军 1556 | 主力军 124 | 童子军 1471 |
| 解放军 1928 | | |

---

**490 罕** U+7F55 TM **8** FM 丶

**hǎn** ADJ rare, scarce

罕见 **hǎnjiàn** ADJ rare, seldom seen
这是一起罕见的谋杀。 *This murder is a rare occurrence.*

**RELATED WORD**

希罕 613

---

**491 光** U+5149 TM **8** FM 丶

**guāng** N·ADJ·V·ADV light; brightness; sights, scenery; honor, glory; luster, glint; benefit; smooth, slippery, sleek, polished; bare; used up; to glorify, to bring honor to; only, merely, just

阳光 *sunlight*

这里的风光真好。 *The view here is beautiful.*

沾光 *to benefit from an association with someone else*

时光 *time*

光宗耀祖 *to bring glory to one's ancestors*

光身 *naked*

光头 *shaven head*

吃光用光 *eaten and used up*

光说不干 *words alone without action*

光波 **guāngbō** N light wave · MW 束、道

光彩 **guāngcǎi** N·ADJ luster, radiance, splendor; glorious; brilliant
他在这个事件中扮演了一个极不光彩的角色。 *He played a most shameful part in this event.*

光复 **guāngfù** V to recover (territory, power)

光杆 **guānggān** N polished rod; lonely man · MW 根、个

光滑 **guānghuá** ADJ smooth, glossy, sleek

光环 **guānghuán** N halo; ring of light · MW 个

光辉 **guānghuī** N·ADJ radiance, brilliance; glory; bright; magnificent

光洁 **guāngjié** ADJ bright and clean

光景 **guāngjǐng** N scene; circumstances, situation · MW 个

光亮 **guāngliàng** ADJ·N bright, shiny; light · MW 道

光临 **guānglín** V to be present

光芒 **guāngmáng** N radiance; flashes/rays of light · MW 束、道

光明 **guāngmíng** ADJ·N bright; promising; light · MW 片
看事情的光明面，会使你活得愉快。 *Looking on the bright side of things will help you live happily.*

光年 **guāngnián** N light-year · MW 个

光谱 **guāngpǔ** N spectrum · MW 色

光荣 **guāngróng** ADJ·N glorious, honorable; honor and glory, kudos

光头 **guāngtóu** N bald/shaved head; bald-headed person · MW 个

光秃秃 **guāngtūtū** EXP bare; bleak, barren; bald
可怜的家伙，才30岁头顶已经光秃秃了。 *Poor guy, he is only 30 years old and he is already bald.*

光线 **guāngxiàn** N light; beam, ray · MW 道、束

光耀 **guāngyào** N·V·ADJ glory; to glorify; glorious, honorable, brilliant

光阴 **guāngyīn** N time (available); life

光源 **guāngyuán** N light source · MW 个

光照 **guāngzhào** V to illuminate; to beam, to shine

**RELATED WORDS**

| | | |
|---|---|---|
| 火光 72 | 五光十色 79 | 日光 96 |
| 日光灯 96 | 反光 111 | 耳光 145 |
| 目光 151 | 白光 176 | 月光 190 |
| 发光 311 | 闪光 337 | 灯光 346 |
| 争光 595 | 油光 683 | 沾光 684 |
| 观光 726 | 荧光 770 | 荧光屏 770 |
| 极光 798 | 阳光 808 | 春光 855 |
| 穷光蛋 912 | 烛光 1176 | 柔光 1198 |

| | | |
|---|---|---|
| 容光焕发 1320 | 逆光 1359 | 背光 1380 |
| 抛光 1395 | 验光 1529 | 眼光 1570 |
| 散光 1579 | 亮光 1613 | 聚光灯 1642 |
| 透光 1826 | 遮光 1831 | 增光 1849 |
| 感光 1860 | 激光 1955 | 霞光 1977 |
| 擦光 1985 | 露光 1997 | 打耳光 289 |
| 鼠目寸光 1859 | | |

冰霜 **bīngshuāng**　N　frost; austerity; moral integrity · MW 层

冰糖 **bīngtáng**　N　rock candy · MW 块

冰箱 **bīngxiāng**　N　refrigerator; freezer · MW 个

**RELATED WORDS**

| | | |
|---|---|---|
| 冷冰冰 494 | 结冰 1291 | 溜冰 1883 |
| 滑冰 1884 | | |

---

### 492　炎　U+708E　TM 8　FM ㇏

**yán**　ADJ　scorching, burning hot; inflammation

炎热 **yánrè**　ADJ　scorching/blazing hot
北京的**炎热**天气将持续到九月。*In Beijing, the hot weather will last until September.*

炎暑 **yánshǔ**　N　hot summer · MW 个

炎症 **yánzhèng**　N　inflammation · MW 个

**RELATED WORDS**

| | | |
|---|---|---|
| 肝炎 650 | 咽炎 1024 | 肺炎 1294 |
| 消炎 1343 | 肠炎 1458 | 喉炎 1560 |
| 鼻炎 1794 | 牙周炎 143 | 关节炎 224 |
| 胃肠炎 1216 | 脑膜炎 1460 | |

---

### 493　冰　U+51B0　TM 8　FM ㇏

**bīng**　N·V　ice; like ice; to cool, to put (something) on ice; to feel cold, to be freezing

冰雹 **bīngbáo**　N　hail · MW 颗、场

冰场 **bīngchǎng**　N　skating/ice rink · MW 个

冰川 **bīngchuān**　N　glacier · MW 片

冰刀 **bīngdāo**　N　(ice) skates · MW 把、片

冰灯 **bīngdēng**　N　ice lantern · MW 盏

冰冻 **bīngdòng**　V　to freeze

冰糕 **bīnggāo**　N　ice cream · MW 块、盒

冰棍 **bīnggùn**　N　popsicle · MW 根
街上那个卖**冰棍**的老大娘很可怜。
*The old woman selling popsicles on the street is so pitiful.*

冰河 **bīnghé**　N　glacier (stream) · MW 条

冰冷 **bīnglěng**　ADJ　ice-cold, freezing; indifferent, apathetic

冰凉 **bīngliáng**　ADJ　ice-cold
他的手很**冰凉**。*His hands are ice-cold.*

冰淇淋 **bīngqílín**　N　ice cream · MW 块

冰球 **bīngqiú**　N　ice hockey · MW 个

冰上运动 **bīngshàngyùndòng**　N　ice sports · MW 种

---

### 494　冷　U+51B7　TM 8　FM ㇏

**lěng**　ADJ·V　cold; frosty, cold (in manner); hidden, deserted, out of the way; strange, rare; unpopular, unwelcome; disheartened, disappointed; to cool, to freeze; to ignore

天很**冷**。*The weather is very cold.*
这人怎么**冷冷**的？*Why is his manner so cold?*
这里很**冷**清。*It is deserted here.*
爆**冷**门 *a surprise hit*
打**冷**枪 *to fire a shot (of a sniper)*

冷板凳 **lěngbǎndèng**　N　cold reception; position of no consequence

冷冰冰 **lěngbīngbīng**　ADJ　ice-cold; frosty, cold (in manner)

冷不防 **lěngbufáng**　ADV　suddenly
有人驾车**冷不防**从旁边冲出来，差点儿撞着傻瓜。*A man driving a car suddenly swerved onto the side of the road and nearly hit ShaGua.*

冷餐 **lěngcān**　N　cold meal; buffet · MW 顿、餐

冷藏 **lěngcáng**　V　to refrigerate; to freeze

冷场 **lěngchǎng**　N·V　awkward silence (on stage, at a meeting)

冷淡 **lěngdàn**　ADJ·V　cold, indifferent; to treat coolly, to give the cold shoulder to
不知为啥，她对傻瓜有点儿**冷淡**。*Nobody knew why there was a certain coldness in her attitude toward ShaGua.*

冷冻 **lěngdòng**　V　to refrigerate; to freeze

冷汗 **lěnghàn**　N　cold sweat · MW 阵、身

冷静 **lěngjìng**　ADJ　sober, calm
傻瓜在家常跟傻瓜太太吵架，但在外面很**冷静**。*ShaGua often quarrels with Mrs. ShaGua at home, but he is very cool-headed elsewhere.*

冷酷 **lěngkù**　ADJ　cold-hearted, callous; grim

冷落 **lěngluò**　ADJ·V　deserted, isolated; to leave out in the cold
她冷落傻瓜。*She snubbed ShaGua.*

冷漠 **lěngmò**　ADJ　cold and detached, indifferent

**494 冷 lěng** (continued)

冷暖 **lěngnuǎn** N temperature change (LIT cold and warm)

冷气 **lěngqì** N cold air; air conditioning · MW 股

冷却 **lěngquè** V to cool (off), to chill (down)

冷水 **lěngshuǐ** N cold/unboiled water · MW 盆

冷笑 **lěngxiào** V to sneer; to smile bitterly/ sarcastically

她对傻瓜冷笑一声。*She responded to ShaGua with a sneer.*

冷战 **lěngzhàn** N Cold War · MW 场

**RELATED WORDS**

灰冷 198　　　发冷 311　　　冰冷 493
泼冷水 937　　阴冷 1041　　寒冷 1481

---

**495**  泛 　　　U+6CDB　　TM **8** FM 丶

**fàn** V·ADJ to float; to flood, to overflow; to suffuse; broad, general; superficial

泛称 **fànchēng** N general term · MW 个

泛泛 **fànfàn** ADJ general

泛滥 **fànlàn** V to overflow; to spread unchecked

垃圾邮件泛滥让人头痛。*The flood of junk mail is a real headache.*

泛指 **fànzhǐ** V to make a general reference, to usually indicate

**RELATED WORDS**

广泛 23　　　　洪泛区 690

---

**496** 注 　　　U+6CE8　　TM **8** FM 丶

**zhù** V·N·MW to pour (into); to inject; to concentrate (on); to annotate, to make marginal notes; to record; to register, to enroll; notes; stakes (in gambling); [measure word for business deals]

注册 **zhùcè** V to register, to enroll

请到国际学生办公室注册。*Please go to the International Student Office to register.*

注定 **zhùdìng** V to be destined/doomed

注脚 **zhùjiǎo** N footnote · MW 个、处

注明 **zhùmíng** V to indicate/note clearly

请注明出处。*Please indicate the sources.*

注入 **zhùrù** V to pour/empty (into)

---

注射 **zhùshè** V to inject

注视 **zhùshì** V to stare/gaze at

注释 **zhùshì** V·N to annotate; marginal note · MW 个、处

注销 **zhùxiāo** V to cancel, to write off

注意 **zhùyì** V to pay attention to, to keep one's eyes on; to be careful

请大家注意一下。*May I have your attention, please?*

注音 **zhùyīn** V to write phonetically

注重 **zhùzhòng** V to stress, to emphasize; to pay attention to

**RELATED WORDS**

专注 155　　　关注 224　　　评注 706
备注 845　　　孤注一掷 978　批注 1005
浇注 1340　　　脚注 1804　　　全神贯注 172

---

**497** 快 　　　U+5FEB　　TM **8** FM 丶

**kuài** V·ADJ·ADV to hurry up, to speed; fast, quick, speedy, swift; ingenious, sharp; happy, pleased; quickly; soon

快报 **kuàibào** N bulletin (board) · MW 份

快步 **kuàibù** N quick step

快餐 **kuàicān** N fast food · MW 餐、份

中式快餐不适合我的口味。*Chinese-style fast food doesn't suit my appetite.*

快车 **kuàichē** N express train/bus; hotshot, ace · MW 列、辆

快递 **kuàidì** N express delivery · MW 份、封

快活 **kuàihuo** ADJ happy, cheerful; joyful, delighted

快乐 **kuàilè** ADJ happy, cheerful

祝你生日快乐！*Happy Birthday to you!*

快门 **kuàimén** N camera shutter

快速 **kuàisù** ADJ fast, quick, high-speed

快慰 **kuàiwèi** ADJ pleased (with); taking comfort (from)

快信 **kuàixìn** N express letter · MW 封

快邮 **kuàiyóu** N express mail · MW 封

从中国寄快邮到美国得一个星期左右。*Express mail from China to the States will take around one week to arrive.*

**RELATED WORDS**

开快车 26　　　加快 463　　　赶快 822
明快 1035　　　特快 1094　　　轻快 1113
凉快 1337　　　痛快 1725　　　愉快 1737
嘴快 1984

## 498 性    U+6027   TM **8** FM 乀

**xìng** [N] character, nature, disposition; property, quality; sex; sexuality; gender

**性别 xìngbié** [N] gender, sex

学生登记表上注明了学生的**性别**。 *The student's registration form clearly indicates the student's sex.*

**性病 xìngbìng** [N] sexually transmitted disease (STD) · [MW] 种

**性成熟 xìngchéngshú** [ADJ] sexual maturity

**性感 xìnggǎn** [ADJ] sexy

**性格 xìnggé** [N] character, personality · [MW] 种

傻瓜的**性格**很特别。 *ShaGua is a very unique character.*

**性交 xìngjiāo** [V] to have sex, to make love

**性命 xìngmìng** [N] life · [MW] 条

**性能 xìngnéng** [N] function, performance · [MW] 个

新电视**性能**如何？ *How is the new TV working?*

**性情 xìngqíng** [N] disposition, temperament

**性欲 xìngyù** [N] sexuality; sexual appetite/desire

**性质 xìngzhì** [N] character, nature; quality

**性子 xìngzi** [N] temper · [MW] 个

他是个急**性子**。 *He has a hot temper.*

### RELATED WORDS

| | | |
|---|---|---|
| 人性 4 | 个性 18 | 天性 25 |
| 女性 57 | 习性 84 | 中性 86 |
| 本性 90 | 生性 107 | 任性 211 |
| 奴性 328 | 两性 509 | 异性 539 |
| 同性 541 | 直性子 609 | 良性 656 |
| 定性 666 | 男性 757 | 阳性 808 |
| 线性 1105 | 恶性 1196 | 理性 1200 |
| 毒性 1211 | 品性 1220 | 素性 1378 |
| 急性子 1426 | 急性 1426 | 硬性 1524 |
| 惯性 1630 | 雌性 1683 | 野性 1685 |
| 属性 1793 | 感性 1860 | 慢性 1882 |
| 慢性子 1882 | 酸性 1899 | 全国性 172 |
| 艺术性 274 | 周期性 1068 | 创造性 1131 |

## 499 炒    U+7092   TM **8** FM 乀

**chǎo** [V] to stir-fry, to pan-fry, to sauté

**炒菜 chǎocài** [V] to stir-fry

你想点几个中式**炒菜**吗？ *Do you want to order some Chinese-style stir-fry?*

**炒面 chǎomiàn** [N·V] chow mein, stir-fried noodles; to stir-fry noodles · [MW] 盘、碗

## 500 讨 討    U+8BA8   TM **8** FM 乀

**tǎo** [V·ADJ] to demand; to ask for, to request; to bargain; to discuss; to inquire/probe into; to provoke; to denounce; disagreeable

**讨伐 tǎofá** [V] to make war on

**讨饭 tǎofàn** [V] to beg for food

**讨好 tǎohǎo** [V] to curry favor, to brownnose (LIT to bow and scrape)

傻瓜不喜欢**讨好**他的人。 *ShaGua doesn't like those who brown-nose him.*

**讨还 tǎohuán** [V] to recover, to get back

**讨价还价 tǎojiàhuánjià** [EXP] to bargain, to haggle

傻瓜拒绝**讨价还价**。 *ShaGua refused to bargain over the price.*

**讨教 tǎojiào** [V] to consult, to ask for advice

**讨论 tǎolùn** [V·N] to discuss, to talk over; discussion

让我们来**讨论**这个问题。 *Let's discuss this question.*

**讨便宜 tǎopiányi** [EXP] to seek undue advantage; to look for a bargain

**讨乞 tǎoqǐ** [V] to beg for food/money

**讨情 tǎoqíng** [V] to plead for (someone)

**讨饶 tǎoráo** [V] to beg for mercy; to ask for forgiveness

**讨嫌 tǎoxián** [ADJ] disagreeable, annoying

**讨厌 tǎoyàn** [ADJ·V] disagreeable, nasty, disgusting; to dislike

她总是这样说话，傻瓜很**讨厌**她。 *She always talks in such a way that ShaGua finds her disagreeable.*

### RELATED WORDS

| | | |
|---|---|---|
| 申讨 150 | 乞讨 177 | 声讨 374 |
| 征讨 462 | 研讨 734 | 检讨 1033 |
| 探讨 1404 | | |

## 501 讲 講    U+8BB2   TM **8** FM 乀

**jiǎng** [V·PREP] to speak, to talk, to say; to discuss, to confer, to negotiate; to explain, to interpret; to represent; to emphasize, to stress; as far as (something) is concerned, with regard to, concerning, in terms of

**讲稿 jiǎnggǎo** [N] lecture notes · [MW] 篇

**讲和 jiǎnghé** [V] to make peace with

**讲话 jiǎnghuà** [V·N] to speak, to talk; address, speech · [MW] 个

**501 讲 jiǎng** (continued)

傻瓜心情不好, 不想和任何人**讲话**。 *ShaGua is in a bad mood and doesn't want to speak to anyone.*

**讲解 jiǎngjiě** ⓥ to explain

**讲究 jiǎngjiu** ⓥ·ADJ·ⓝ to pay attention to; to be particular about; exquisite, tasteful; details for consideration

**讲课 jiǎngkè** ⓥ to teach; to lecture

听李老师**讲课**的人已大大增加了。 *Attendance at Professor Li's lectures has increased considerably.*

**讲理 jiǎnglǐ** ⓥ to discuss the merits (of an argument), to reason (with)

**讲评 jiǎngpíng** ⓥ to critique, to appraise

**讲情 jiǎngqíng** ⓥ to intercede/plead for (someone)

**讲师 jiǎngshī** ⓝ lecturer · MW 个、位、名

**讲授 jiǎngshòu** ⓥ to teach; to lecture

**讲台 jiǎngtái** ⓝ platform, stand, dais · MW 个

老师不是神, 但老师的**讲台**是神圣的。 *Teachers are not gods, but their platforms are holy.*

**讲习 jiǎngxí** ⓥ to lecture and study

**讲学 jiǎngxué** ⓥ to give/deliver a lecture

**讲演 jiǎngyǎn** ⓥ to lecture, to give a speech/talk

李教授写完那本书后就到各大学**讲演**。 *After Professor Li finishes writing the book, he will give lectures at various colleges.*

**讲义 jiǎngyì** ⓝ teaching materials; handouts · MW 本

**讲座 jiǎngzuò** ⓝ lecture course · MW 个

**RELATED WORDS**

主讲 124     听讲 414     演讲 1821

---

**502** 许 許 許    U+8BB8     TM **8** FM 丶

**xǔ** ⓥ·ADV to allow, to permit; to promise; to praise, to commend; to agree to marry; maybe, possibly; about, approximately

允**许** *to allow*

也**许** *perhaps*

些**许** *a few*

**许多 xǔduō** NUM much, many; a lot of, lots of

因为水被污染, **许多**鱼类正面临绝种的危险。 *Many fish are disappearing because of water pollution.*

**许婚 xǔhūn** ⓥ to agree to marry

**许久 xǔjiǔ** ADV for ages, for a long time

**许可 xǔkě** ⓥ to allow, to permit

---

**许可证 xǔkězhèng** ⓝ license, permit · MW 份、张

**许诺 xǔnuò** ⓥ to promise

傻瓜不轻易**许诺**。 *ShaGua doesn't make rash promises.*

**许愿 xǔyuàn** ⓥ to vow (to a god); to promise a reward to

政客总是**许愿**, 但从不兑现。 *Politicians always make promises, but they never keep them.*

**RELATED WORDS**

不许 24     少许 62     兴许 228
也许 273     允许 302     或许 857
特许 1094     容许 1320     赞许 1969

---

**503** 礼 禮    U+793C     TM **8** FM 丶

**lǐ** ⓝ·ⓥ gift, present; courtesy, etiquette, manners; ceremony, ritual; to treat with due respect

**礼拜 lǐbài** ⓝ week; day of the week; religious service · MW 个

**礼服 lǐfú** ⓝ ceremonial robe/dress; formal attire · MW 套

**礼花 lǐhuā** ⓝ fireworks · MW 朵

**礼节 lǐjié** ⓝ courtesy, etiquette; protocol · MW 套

宴会的座位是根据**礼节**安排的吗? *Were the seating arrangements for the dinner party according to protocol?*

**礼金 lǐjīn** ⓝ gift of money · MW 笔

**礼貌 lǐmào** ⓝ courtesy, politeness, manners

**礼炮 lǐpào** ⓝ gun salute, salvo · MW 声

**礼品 lǐpǐn** ⓝ gift, present · MW 件

傻瓜不送**礼品**, 也不收**礼品**。 *ShaGua doesn't give gifts to, or accept gifts from, others.*

**礼聘 lǐpìn** ⓥ to cordially enlist the services of

**礼让 lǐràng** ⓥ to give precedence to

**礼尚往来 lǐshàngwǎnglái** EXP courtesy demands reciprocity

**礼堂 lǐtáng** ⓝ assembly hall, auditorium · MW 个、座

**礼物 lǐwù** ⓝ gift, present · MW 个、件

傻瓜送给傻太太一条项链作为周年纪念**礼物**。 *ShaGua gave his wife a necklace as an anniversary gift.*

**礼遇 lǐyù** ⓝ courteous/special treatment

**RELATED WORDS**

以礼相待 101     失礼 106     无礼 139
寿礼 440     典礼 532     夜礼服 654

还礼 714          观礼 726          送礼 1188
赔礼 1569         葬礼 1656         敬礼 1689
婚礼 1701         施礼 1758

## 504 社    U+793E    TM 8 FM 丶

**shè** N organization, agency; society; community

**社会 shèhuì** N society · MW 个
  人类社会 human society

**社会化 shèhuìhuà** V to socialize
孩子必须在同龄人中完成他们的**社会化**，因此私塾不利于孩子的成长。
*Children must complete their socialization among peers, so homeschooling is not good for a child's development.*

**社会科学 shèhuìkēxué** N social sciences

**社会主义 shèhuìzhǔyì** N socialism

**社交 shèjiāo** V social contact

**社论 shèlùn** N (newspaper) editorial; lead article · MW 篇

**社区 shèqū** N community · MW 个

**社团 shètuán** N organization; community · MW 个

### RELATED WORDS

报社 1010                     旅社 1518
新华通讯社 1638

## 505 达 達    U+8FBE    TM 8 FM 丶

**dá** V to reach; to attain; to last; to extend/go to; to understand thoroughly; fluency

**达成 dáchéng** V to reach, to accomplish

**达旦 dádàn** V to last until dawn

**达到 dádào** V to achieve; to reach
水源污染已**达到**危及居民健康的程度。
*Pollution of the water supply reached a level that was harmful to the health of the population.*

**达官贵人 dáguānguìrén** N the great and the good (LIT high officials and noble lords) · MW 名、群

**达意 dáyì** V to express one's ideas/thoughts

### RELATED WORDS

发达 311          传达 452          表达 527
直达 609          到达 737          贤达 750
转达 1111         雷达 1641         溜达 1883
乌干达 601

## 506 迁 遷    U+8FC1    TM 8 FM 丶

**qiān** V to move; to change

**迁出 qiānchū** V to move out

**迁进 qiānjìn** V to move in

**迁就 qiānjiù** V to compromise, to give in; to make allowances (for)
我们绝对不**迁就**他的错误。*We must not ignore his mistakes.*

**迁居 qiānjū** V to move (residence)
为了得到新的工作，傻瓜不得不举家**迁居**外地。*To take the new job, ShaGua's family had to move.*

**迁怒 qiānnù** V to vent one's anger (on)
傻瓜勇于承担责任，不愿**迁怒**于人。*ShaGua is brave in taking on responsibilities and doesn't vent his anger on others.*

**迁徙 qiānxǐ** V to move, to migrate

**迁移 qiānyí** V to move, to migrate; to transfer to shift

### RELATED WORDS

升迁 47                     变迁 653

## 507 判    U+5224    TM 8 FM 丶

**pàn** V·ADV to judge, to pass a verdict, to sentence, to condemn; to decide; to distinguish, to discriminate; to clearly differ; evidently, clearly

**判别 pànbié** V to differentiate, to distinguish

**判处 pànchǔ** V to sentence, to penalize
这名贪污犯被**判处**八年有期徒刑。*The person convicted of graft was sentenced to eight years' imprisonment.*

**判词 pàncí** N (court) verdict · MW 篇

**判定 pàndìng** V to decide, to determine; to judge · MW 个

**判断 pànduàn** V·N to judge; to determine; to measure; judgment · MW 个
傻瓜的**判断**经常出错。*ShaGua's judgment is frequently faulty.*

**判决 pànjué** V to pass judgment on (of a court); to sentence; court decision, judgment

**判罪 pànzuì** V to convict

### RELATED WORDS

改判 516          评判 706          审判 911
批判 1005         宣判 1138         裁判 1535
外交谈判 218

508 **补** 補 U+8865 TM **8** FM 丶

**bǔ** V to mend, to patch, to repair; to fill (a vacancy); to supply; to compensate (for); to add; to nourish

补白 **bǔbái** N·V filler (in a newspaper/magazine); to make up

补偿 **bǔcháng** V to compensate / make up (for)

补充 **bǔchōng** V to supplement, to add; to replenish

运动员喝特殊饮料来**补充**能量。
*Athletes consume special drinks to replenish their energy.*

补丁 **bǔdīng** N patch · MW 个

补发 **bǔfā** V to supply again, to reissue

补给 **bǔjǐ** V to supply

补救 **bǔjiù** V to remedy, to rectify (an error)

补考 **bǔkǎo** V to make up an exam, to take an exam over

傻瓜的大儿子考试不及格，下学期要**补考**。
*ShaGua's older son failed the exam; he had to make it up the following semester.*

补课 **bǔkè** V to make up a missed lesson

补品 **bǔpǐn** N tonic · MW 种

傻瓜太太很喜欢尝试各种各样的**补品**。
*Mrs. ShaGua loves to try various tonics.*

补税 **bǔshuì** V to pay a tax one has evaded; to pay an overdue tax

傻瓜从未被要求**补税**。*ShaGua has never had to pay overdue taxes.*

补贴 **bǔtiē** V·N to help financially, to subsidize; allowance; subsidy · MW 笔

补习 **bǔxí** V to take extra lessons

傻瓜每天上夜校**补习**电脑。*ShaGua attends night school after work to increase his computer knowledge.*

补选 **bǔxuǎn** V to hold a by-election

补牙 **bǔyá** V to fill a tooth

补语 **bǔyǔ** N complement · MW 个

补助 **bǔzhù** V·N to help financially, to subsidize; allowance; subsidy · MW 份

补足 **bǔzú** V to bring up to full strength; to make up a deficiency, to fill (a vacancy, a gap, etc.)

**RELATED WORDS**

| | | |
|---|---|---|
| 修补 870 | 贴补 1038 | 添补 1346 |
| 替补 1430 | 挖补 1551 | 递补 1827 |
| 增补 1849 | 取长补短 520 | |

## 509 两 兩 U+4E24 TM **9** FM 一

**liǎng** NUM·N·MW two; either (side), both (sides); a few; some; [measure word for a unit of weight (50 grams)]

**两倍 liǎngbèi** NUM double
傻瓜的年纪是她的**两倍**。*ShaGua is twice her age.*

**两极 liǎngjí** N·V two poles (of the earth, a magnet, a battery); two extremes; to polarize

**两口子 liǎngkǒuzi** EXP husband and wife, married couple

**两面 liǎngmiàn** N two sides; both sides/aspects

**两难 liǎngnán** ADJ dilemma; predicament; perplexing

**两旁 liǎngpáng** N either side, both sides
路的**两旁**种满了花。*Flowers line both sides of the road.*

**两手 liǎngshǒu** N both hands; dual strategies

**两性 liǎngxìng** N both sexes

**两样 liǎngyàng** ADJ different, distinct
他俩没什么**两样**。*Neither of them is any different.*

**两用 liǎngyòng** ADJ dual purpose

**RELATED WORDS**

| | | |
|---|---|---|
| 斤两 50 | 小两口 61 | 有两下子 439 |
| 三长两短 9 | 三天两头 9 | 三言两语 9 |
| 半斤八两 127 | | |

## 510 死 U+6B7B TM **9** FM 一

**sǐ** V·ADV·ADJ to die, to be dead; to the death, desperately; stubbornly; extremely; dead; deadly; implacable; fixed, rigid, inflexible; inaccessible, closed

**死党 sǐdǎng** N diehard supporters, sworn followers · MW 名、伙、帮

**死敌 sǐdí** N sworn enemy · MW 个、名

**死海 Sǐhǎi** N Dead Sea

**死胡同 sǐhútòng** N impasse, dead end · MW 条
这是一条**死胡同**，没有出口。*This is a dead end; there are no outlets.*

**死缓 sǐhuǎn** N commuted death sentence

**死活 sǐhuó** N·ADV fate, life and death; anyway, simply

**死角 sǐjiǎo** N area untouched by; dead space; blind spot · MW 个
每个人的思维都有一两个**死角**。*Everyone has one or two blind spots in his or her thinking.*

**死路 sǐlù** N dead end; road to ruin · MW 条

**死水 sǐshuǐ** N stagnant water · MW 片

**死亡 sǐwáng** V to die

**死心 sǐxīn** V to give up on (an idea)
第一次盗窃失败后，这个小偷并没有**死心**。*The thief had not given up on the idea of stealing after his first unsuccessful attempt.*

**死刑 sǐxíng** N death penalty, capital punishment · MW 个

**死者 sǐzhě** N the dead/deceased · MW 个、名

**RELATED WORDS**

| | | |
|---|---|---|
| 不死心 24 | 生死 107 | 处死 217 |
| 至死 244 | 垂死 430 | 吊死 547 |
| 找死 567 | 冻死 680 | 怕死 694 |
| 临死 771 | 拼死 794 | 起死回生 1421 |
| 替死鬼 1430 | 淹死 1629 | 贪生怕死 827 |

## 511 歪 U+6B6A TM **9** FM 一

**wāi** ADJ inclined, slanting, askew; devious, crooked

**歪风 wāifēng** N unhealthy trend; contagion · MW 股、阵

**歪门邪道 wāiménxiédào** EXP crooked ways, dishonest means

**歪曲 wāiqū** V to distort, to misrepresent
别**歪曲**我的话。*Stop twisting what I've said.*

**歪斜 wāixié** ADJ crooked
墙上的照片挂得**歪歪斜斜**。*The picture on the wall was hung crooked.*

## 512 君 U+541B TM **9** FM 一

**jūn** N monarch, sovereign, supreme ruler; gentleman, sir, Mr.

**512 君 jūn** (continued)

**君主 jūnzhǔ** N monarch, emperor, king · MW 个、位、名

**君子 jūnzǐ** N gentleman; man of virtue; man of high rank/honor · MW 个、位、名

傻瓜没有**君子**风度, 但没有人不认为他是一个**君子**。 *ShaGua does not have a gentleman's demeanor, but nobody considers him anything else.*

**RELATED WORD**

伪君子 456

---

**513 武** U+6B66 TM **9** FM 一

**wǔ** N·ADJ military, martial; fierce; valiant, brave and powerful

**武打 wǔdǎ** V to perform acrobatic fighting in Chinese opera; to fight using kung fu

**武断 wǔduàn** V·ADJ to make an arbitrary decision; arbitrary; subjective

傻瓜有时有点儿**武断**。 *Sometimes ShaGua can be a little arbitrary.*

**武功 wǔgōng** N military achievements/exploits; martial arts; acrobatic fighting in Chinese opera

**武汉 Wǔhàn** N Wuhan (capital of Hubei Province)

**武力 wǔlì** N force; military strength · MW 种

**武器 wǔqì** N weapon; arms · MW 件、种

核**武器**是对世界和平的威胁。 *Nuclear weapons are a menace to world peace.*

**武士 wǔshì** N warrior · MW 个、名

**武术 wǔshù** N martial arts; kung fu · MW 种

中国**武术**有数千年的历史。 *Chinese martial arts have had several thousand years of history.*

**武装 wǔzhuāng** N·V military equipment, armaments; armed forces; to arm, to equip

**RELATED WORDS**

文武 70　　用武 313　　核武器 1026

---

**514 动 動** U+52A8 TM **9** FM 一

**dòng** V·ADV·N to move, to get moving; to act; to change, to alter; to use; to touch, to affect; to arouse; to tend to; frequently; easily; movement

**动笔 dòngbǐ** V to start writing

**动不动 dòngbudòng** ADV easily; frequently

她**动不动**就感冒。 *She catches colds easily.*

**动产 dòngchǎn** N portable property · MW 笔

**动词 dòngcí** N verb · MW 个

**动荡 dòngdàng** V·ADJ to experience unrest/turmoil/upheaval; turbulent, unstable

**动工 dònggōng** V to begin construction; to build

**动画片 dònghuàpiān** N animated cartoon · MW 部、个

**动机 dòngjī** N motive; motivation, intention · MW 个

傻瓜的**动机**就是多赚钱。 *ShaGua's intention is to make more money.*

**动力 dònglì** N power; strength; impetus, motive · MW 股

傻瓜当市长的真正**动力**是什么? *What is the real motivation behind ShaGua's desire to be mayor?*

**动乱 dòngluàn** V·N to riot; (social) turmoil, unrest, disturbance · MW 场

**动脉 dòngmài** N artery; railway · MW 条

**动人 dòngrén** ADJ moving, touching

这个故事既幽默又**动人**。 *This story is at once humorous and moving.*

**动身 dòngshēn** V to leave, to set out on a journey

**动手 dòngshǒu** V to get to work, to start work

**动手术 dòngshǒushù** V to perform an operation

**动态 dòngtài** N trends, developments; dynamic state · MW 个

**动听 dòngtīng** ADJ pleasing to the ear; persuasive

他唱歌很**动听**。 *His singing is very beautiful.*

**动物 dòngwù** N animal · MW 只、个

**动物园 dòngwùyuán** N zoo · MW 个

**动摇 dòngyáo** V·ADJ to shake; to waver, to vacillate; shaking

**动议 dòngyì** N motion, proposal · MW 个、项

**动用 dòngyòng** V to put to use, to employ; to draw on

傻瓜很少**动用**否决权。 *ShaGua rarely put his veto power to use.*

**动员 dòngyuán** V to mobilize; to arouse

**动作 dòngzuò** N·V movement; action; to act, to make a move · MW 个

体操运动员协调优美的**动作**让人惊叹。 *The fluid movements of the gymnasts took people by surprise.*

**RELATED WORDS**

| | | |
|---|---|---|
| 生动 107 | 反动 111 | 主动 124 |
| 气动 185 | 出动 258 | 电动 263 |
| 走动 265 | 自动 305 | 发动 311 |

行动 327
传动 452
变动 653
哄动 781
盲动 906
运动 956
运动会 956
转动 1111
挑动 1235
推动 1242
起动 1421
流动 1493
摇动 1664
摆动 1773
游动 1818
暴动 1844
能动 1873
激动 1955
半自动 127
惊心动魄 1489
冰上运动 493

冲动 339
机动 577
劳动 764
助动词 818
波动 936
运动员 956
核动力 1026
制动 1130
挥动 1236
浮动 1342
移动 1450
被动 1517
鼓动 1688
跳动 1786
滚动 1819
搅动 1850
触动 1875
颤动 1991
及物动词 141
户外运动 129
闻风而动 1151

抖动 407
松动 579
劳动力 764
牵动 853
活动 941
运动衫 956
轰动 1065
带动 1213
振动 1238
晃动 1384
惊动 1489
挪动 1658
扇动 1726
舞动 1790
震动 1839
感动 1860
滑动 1884
蠢动 1995
全自动 172
风吹草动 194

---

## 515 珍    U+63CD    TM 9 FM —

**zhēn** [N·ADJ·V] treasure; valuable; rare; to value highly

**珍爱 zhēn'ài** [V] to treasure, to cherish
傻瓜**珍爱**太太送给他的表。*ShaGua treasures the watch his wife gave him.*

**珍藏 zhēncáng** [V·N] to collect (valuable books, art treasures, etc.); collection (of valuables) · [MW] 件

**珍贵 zhēnguì** [ADJ] valuable; precious

**珍品 zhēnpǐn** [N] treasure; gem; curio · [MW] 件

**珍视 zhēnshì** [V] to treasure, to cherish, to value
我们应该**珍视**我们之间的友谊。*We should prize our friendship.*

**珍重 zhēnzhòng** [V] to take good care of, to look after; to value highly

**珍珠 zhēnzhū** [N] pearl · [MW] 粒、颗、串

### RELATED WORDS
山珍海味 38      袖珍 1361

---

## 516 改    U+6539    TM 9 FM —

**gǎi** [V] to change, to alter; to transform; to improve; to correct, to revise

---

**改编 gǎibiān** [V] to rearrange, to reorganize; to adapt

**改变 gǎibiàn** [V] to change; to shift; to reform
傻瓜很少**改变**自己的主意。*ShaGua rarely changes his mind.*

**改掉 gǎidiào** [V] to remove; to give up

**改革 gǎigé** [V·N] to reform; transformation · [MW] 个、次

**改行 gǎiháng** [V] to change one's occupation
傻瓜当然是**改行**才当市长的。*Of course, ShaGua had to switch occupations to become mayor.*

**改悔 gǎihuǐ** [V] to repent, to mend one's ways

**改进 gǎijìn** [V·N] to improve; improvement · [MW] 个

**改良 gǎiliáng** [V·N] to improve, to ameliorate; reform · [MW] 个

**改判 gǎipàn** [V] to change (an original sentence)

**改期 gǎiqī** [V] to change the date

**改善 gǎishàn** [V] to improve, to make better
他们之间的关系正在**改善**。*The relationship between them is improving.*

**改写 gǎixiě** [V] to rewrite/revise/edit (an original work)
不是政治家，而是教育工作者能**改写**历史。*Educators, not politicians, are the ones capable of rewriting history.*

**改造 gǎizào** [V] to transform; to reform; to reclaim; to remake

**改正 gǎizhèng** [V] to correct, to amend
我们最好还是帮助他**改正**错误。*We had better help him correct the mistake.*

**改装 gǎizhuāng** [V] to repack; to change one's costume/dress; to remodel

**改组 gǎizǔ** [V] to reorganize; to reshuffle · [MW] 次

### RELATED WORDS
劳改 764    修改 870    批改 1005
涂改 1171    删改 1309    悔改 1488
痛改前非 1725

---

## 517 政    U+653F    TM 9 FM —

**zhèng** [N] politics; political affairs

**政变 zhèngbiàn** [V] to perform a coup d'état; coup

**政策 zhèngcè** [N] policy · [MW] 项
中国政府坚持一胎**政策**。*The Chinese government stood its ground on the one-child policy.*

**政敌 zhèngdí** [N] political opponent · [MW] 个、名

**政法 zhèngfǎ** [N] politics and law

**517 政 zhèng** (continued)

**政府 zhèngfǔ** N government · MW 个

**政见 zhèngjiàn** N political view · MW 项

**政界 zhèngjiè** N political/government circles

**政客 zhèngkè** N politician · MW 个、名

**政论 zhènglùn** N political comment · MW 项

**政权 zhèngquán** N political/state power; regime · MW 个

**政务 zhèngwù** N government affairs/administration

**政协 zhèngxié** N Chinese People's Political Consultative Conference (CPPCC)

**政治 zhèngzhì** N politics; political affairs
傻瓜没有什么**政治**信念。 *ShaGua has no political convictions.*

**RELATED WORDS**

| | | |
|---|---|---|
| 仁政 64 | 专政 155 | 内政 191 |
| 行政 327 | 市政 332 | 民政 388 |
| 执政 564 | 财政 588 | 邮政 1046 |
| 宪政 1317 | 施政 1758 | 摄政 1772 |
| 暴政 1844 | | |

---

**518 矿** 礦    U+77FF    TM **9** FM 一

**kuàng** N mine; ore; mineral

**矿藏 kuàngcáng** N mineral resources · MW 个

**矿工 kuànggōng** N miner, mine worker · MW 个、名

**矿石 kuàngshí** N ore · MW 块

**RELATED WORDS**

| | | |
|---|---|---|
| 厂矿 7 | 金矿 420 | 采矿 434 |
| 油矿 683 | | |

---

**519 孙** 孫    U+5B59    TM **9** FM 一

**sūn** N grandchild; grandson; generations later than that of a grandson

**孙女 sūnnǚ** N granddaughter, son's daughter · MW 个

**孙子 sūnzi** N grandson, son's son · MW 个

**RELATED WORDS**

| | | |
|---|---|---|
| 儿孙 43 | 子孙 83 | 外孙 218 |
| 重孙 839 | 重孙女 839 | 徒孙 873 |
| 名落孙山 426 | 徒子徒孙 873 | |

---

**520 取**    U+53D6    TM **9** FM 一

**qǔ** V to take; to get, to obtain, to gain; to seek; to adopt, to assume; to choose, to select

**取材 qǔcái** V to draw material from; to use as a source (for a book, film, etc.)

**取长补短 qǔchángbǔduǎn** EXP to compensate for each other's deficiencies
多元化的本意就是**取长补短**。 *The original intent of diversity was to make up for one another's deficiencies.*

**取代 qǔdài** V to replace, to substitute; to take over

**取得 qǔdé** V to get, to achieve, to gain
傻瓜为孩子**取得**的成绩感到无比骄傲。 *ShaGua takes great pride in his children's success.*

**取缔 qǔdì** V to prohibit, to ban

**取而代之 qǔérdàizhī** EXP to replace (someone/something); to remove (someone)

**取经 qǔjīng** V to learn from the experience of

**取暖 qǔnuǎn** V to warm oneself (by a fire, etc.); to keep warm

**取舍 qǔshě** V to choose; to accept or reject

**取胜 qǔshèng** V to score a victory (over), to win
傻瓜的**取胜**之道是诚信。 *Honesty is ShaGua's route to victory.*

**取消 qǔxiāo** V to cancel; to abolish
因天气不好, 这次航班不得不**取消**了。 *The scheduled fight had to be canceled because of bad weather.*

**取样 qǔyàng** V to sample

**RELATED WORDS**

| | | |
|---|---|---|
| 支取 92 | 夺取 308 | 听取 414 |
| 采取 434 | 存取 438 | 考取 530 |
| 争取 595 | 进取 713 | 录取 722 |
| 吸取 776 | 获取 1000 | 拾取 1017 |
| 换取 1402 | 猎取 1444 | 领取 1465 |
| 选取 1510 | 博取 1549 | 提取 1554 |
| 榨取 1672 | 摄取 1772 | 骗取 1937 |
| 以貌取人 101 | 杀鸡取卵 317 | |

---

**521 丧** 喪    U+4E27    TM **9** FM |

**sāng** N funeral; mourning

**sàng** V to lose

**丧胆 sàngdǎn** V to be terrified

**丧家之犬 sàngjiāzhīquǎn** EXP stray dog; outcast · MW 条

丧命 sàngmìng [V] to get killed

丧偶 sàng'ǒu [V] to be widowed

丧气 sàngqì [V·ADJ] to feel discouraged/
downhearted; unlucky

傻瓜很少**丧气**。 *ShaGua rarely feels discouraged.*

丧失 sàngshī [V] to lose; to forfeit

**RELATED WORDS**

治丧 935     报丧 1010     垂头丧气 430

---

**522** 串     U+4E32     TM **9** FM |

chuàn [V·MW] to string (together); to pay a visit to,
to drop by; to mix up; to conspire; [measure
word for bunches, strings]

串联 chuànlián [V] to establish ties with; to link up;
to contact

串通 chuàntōng [V] to collaborate; to collude,
to conspire

在考试时, 有些学生**串通**作弊。 *Some students
colluded to cheat on an exam.*

**RELATED WORD**

连串 958

---

**523** 卓     U+5353     TM **9** FM |

zhuó [ADJ] tall and erect; eminent, outstanding,
remarkable

卓见 zhuójiàn [N] excellent opinion · [MW] 项

卓绝 zhuójué [ADJ] unsurpassed; extreme

卓识 zhuóshí [N] good judgment

傻瓜既没有**卓见**也没有**卓识**, 只有傻干。
*ShaGua lacks not only clever ideas but also
judiciousness; he knows only hard work.*

卓越 zhuóyuè [ADJ] outstanding, brilliant

莎士比亚是最**卓越**的戏剧家。 *Shakespeare is
a most brilliant playwright.*

卓著 zhuózhù [ADJ] distinguished, outstanding,
eminent

---

**524** 卖 賣     U+5356     TM **9** FM |

mài [V] to sell; to betray, to sell out; to do the best
one can; to show off

卖方 màifāng [N] seller

卖乖 màiguāi [V] to show off one's cleverness

---

卖关子 màiguānzi [EXP] to keep (someone)
guessing

如果你对傻瓜**卖关子**, 他会急得嗷嗷叫。
*If someone teases ShaGua and keeps him guessing,
he gets impatient.*

卖国 màiguó [V] to betray one's country,
to commit treason

卖价 màijià [N] selling price · [MW] 个

卖劲 màijìn [V] to spend all one's energy, to exert
all one's effort

卖力 màilì [V] to work very hard, to spend all one's
energy

你何必替这种人**卖力**？ *Why should you work so
hard for this kind of person?*

卖弄 màinòng [V] to show off; to flourish,
to brandish

卖主 màizhǔ [N] seller · [MW] 个、名

这是**卖主**签了字的文件。 *This is the document
that the seller has endorsed.*

**RELATED WORDS**

| | | |
|---|---|---|
| 义卖 22 | 小卖部 61 | 专卖 155 |
| 外卖 218 | 买卖 248 | 出卖 258 |
| 叫卖 283 | 甩卖 612 | 拍卖 790 |
| 贩卖 813 | 叛卖 960 | 转卖 1111 |
| 倒卖 1281 | 盗卖 1475 | 零卖 1640 |
| 装疯卖傻 1476 | | |

---

**525** 责 責     U+8D23     TM **9** FM |

zé [N·V] duty, responsibility; to demand, to require;
to cross-examine, to question closely; to blame,
to reproach

责备 zébèi [V] to accuse, to blame

不是傻瓜太太就是傻瓜应该受到**责备**。
*The blame should fall on either Mrs. ShaGua or
ShaGua.*

责成 zéchéng [V] to instruct

责罚 zéfá [V] to punish

责怪 zéguài [V] to blame, to accuse

傻瓜不喜欢**责怪**他人。 *ShaGua doesn't like to
blame others.*

责令 zélìng [V] to order; to instruct (to do)

责骂 zémà [V] to scold, to rebuke

不要**责骂**太多, 他只不过是个傻子。
*Don't scold him too much; after all, he's just
a fool.*

责难 zénàn [V] to blame, to censure

责任 zérèn [N] duty, responsibility, obligation ·
[MW] 个、种

**525** 责 **zé** (continued)

他不能忽视他的**责任**。*He can't ignore his responsibility.*

**责任制** **zérènzhì** N system of job responsibility · MW 个

**责问** **zéwèn** V to call (someone) to account; to question in a reproachful way

**RELATED WORDS**

专责 155     自责 305     负责 435
职责 1205     罪责 1542

---

**526** 肃 肅     U+8083     TM **9** FM |

**sù** ADJ·V respectful; serious, solemn; to eliminate; to clear away, to eradicate

**肃静** **sùjìng** ADJ solemn; silent

**肃立** **sùlì** V to stand (as a mark of respect); to stand at attention

**肃清** **sùqīng** V to clean up, to purge

**RELATED WORDS**

甘肃 95     严肃 241

---

**527** 表 錶     U+8868     TM **9** FM |

**biǎo** N·V watch; meter, gauge; table, form, list; surface, outside, appearance; model, example; to express; to demonstrate; to praise

**表白** **biǎobái** V to vindicate; to explain, to clarify
你必须用中文**表白**自己的心意。*You must explain your intention in Chinese.*

**表报** **biǎobào** N statistical tables and reports · MW 份

**表册** **biǎocè** N statistical forms · MW 份

**表层** **biǎocéng** N surface, top layer · MW 个

**表达** **biǎodá** V to express (an idea, a feeling), to convey
我想知道如何用中文**表达**这个意思。*I want to know how to convey this meaning in Chinese.*

**表格** **biǎogé** N form, table · MW 份、张

**表决** **biǎojué** V to vote

**表里** **biǎolǐ** N outside and inside; outer appearance and inner reality

**表面** **biǎomiàn** N surface, appearance · MW 个

**表明** **biǎomíng** V to make clear; to show, to indicate

他的行为**表明**他是一个好人。*His behavior showed that he was a good man.*

**表亲** **biǎoqīn** N cousin; cousin relationship · MW 个

**表情** **biǎoqíng** N (facial) expression, look · MW 个

**表示** **biǎoshì** V·N to express; to show, to indicate; feelings, attitude · MW 个

**表率** **biǎoshuài** N model, good example · MW 个

**表态** **biǎotài** V to make one's position known
傻瓜拒绝对这个有争议的问题**表态**。*ShaGua refused to commit himself on the controversial subject.*

**表现** **biǎoxiàn** V·N to show, to display; behavior; performance · MW 个

**表象** **biǎoxiàng** N image; presentation; appearance; idea · MW 个

**表扬** **biǎoyáng** V to praise, to commend

**表彰** **biǎozhāng** V to cite (in a report); to commend, to honor

**RELATED WORDS**

手表 104     仪表 122     水表 159
年表 182     代表 208     代表大会 208
外表 218     电表 263     发表 311
怀表 344     华表 421     秒表 643
图表 761     地表 772     姑表 881
报表 1010     钟表 1125     课表 1503
填表 1550     姨表 1596     计程表 240
时刻表 586     检字表 1033     寒暑表 1481

---

**528** 志     U+5FD7     TM **9** FM |

**zhì** N·V will; aspiration, ambition; record; annals; magazine; sign; to remember

**志气** **zhìqi** N drive, ambition, resolve, backbone · MW 种

**志趣** **zhìqù** N aspiration

**志士** **zhìshì** N strong-willed person; person of ideals and integrity · MW 个、位、名

**志同道合** **zhìtóngdàohé** EXP like-minded; to share the same ideals and outlook on life

**志向** **zhìxiàng** N aspiration, ambition, ideal, goal · MW 个

**志愿** **zhìyuàn** N·V aspiration, wish; to volunteer · MW 个
我们大多数是**志愿**人员。*Most of us are volunteers.*

**志愿者** **zhìyuànzhě** N volunteer · MW 个、位、名

## RELATED WORDS

| | | |
|---|---|---|
| 斗志 71 | 日志 96 | 壮志 238 |
| 县志 543 | 标志 801 | 杂志 856 |
| 神志 1191 | 仁人志士 64 | |

---

**529 孝** U+5B5D TM **9** FM |

**xiào** V·N to be dutiful; filial piety; mourning clothes

**孝敬 xiàojìng** V to show filial respect for

**孝顺 xiàoshùn** V·ADJ to show filial piety; filial piety
中国传统文化强调晚辈**孝顺**长辈。
*Traditional Chinese culture emphasizes the filial piety of younger people to their elders.*

**孝子 xiàozǐ** N dutiful son; son in mourning · MW 个、位、名

---

**530 考** U+8003 TM **9** FM |

**kǎo** V·N to give/take an exam, to test/quiz; to check, to inspect; to study; to investigate

**考查 kǎochá** V to examine, to check

**考察 kǎochá** V to inspect; to investigate
没有第一手**考察**资料，傻瓜很难下结论。
*Without firsthand observation, it's difficult for ShaGua to draw a conclusion.*

**考场 kǎochǎng** N exam hall/room · MW 个

**考古 kǎogǔ** V·N to study archaeology; archaeology

**考核 kǎohé** V to examine, to check, to assess (someone's proficiency)

**考究 kǎojiu** V·ADJ to examine closely; to be particular about; tasteful, elegant

**考卷 kǎojuàn** N exam paper · MW 份
请在每一页**考卷**上写上你的名字。*Please write your name on each page of the exam.*

**考虑 kǎolǜ** V to consider, to think over

**考取 kǎoqǔ** V to pass an entrance exam; to be admitted to a school

**考生 kǎoshēng** N candidate for a school entrance exam · MW 个、名

**考试 kǎoshì** N·V exam; to take an exam · MW 个
他宁愿**考试**不及格，也不愿作弊。*He would rather fail the test than cheat.*

**考题 kǎotí** N exam question · MW 道、个

**考问 kǎowèn** V to examine orally, to question

**考验 kǎoyàn** V to test, to put to the test

**考证 kǎozhèng** V to verify, to confirm through research; textual criticism/research

## RELATED WORDS

| | | |
|---|---|---|
| 小考 61 | 主考 124 | 应考 334 |
| 补考 508 | 参考 600 | 查考 741 |
| 备考 845 | 监考 994 | 投考 1008 |
| 报考 1010 | 思考 1214 | 期考 1574 |
| 期终考试 1574 | 期中考试 1574 | |

---

**531 者** U+8005 TM **9** FM |

**zhě** PRON -ist, -er/-or (person); person (who does (something))

## RELATED WORDS

| | | |
|---|---|---|
| 长者 93 | 作者 326 | 死者 510 |
| 使者 623 | 侍者 624 | 或者 858 |
| 记者 946 | 译者 951 | 学者 1155 |
| 笔者 1278 | 前者 1329 | 读者 1502 |
| 患者 1649 | 编者 1866 | 志愿者 528 |
| 第三者 1695 | 新闻记者 1638 | |

---

**532 典** U+5178 TM **9** FM |

**diǎn** N·V standard; standard work; classic; dictionary; law; allusion, literary quotation; ceremony; to be in charge of; to mortgage; to pawn

**典当 diǎndàng** V to mortgage; to pawn

**典范 diǎnfàn** N model, example · MW 个

**典故 diǎngù** N allusion, literary quotation · MW 个
你们知道这个成语的**典故**吗？ *Are you familiar with the allusion in this proverb?*

**典籍 diǎnjí** N canonical text; classical book/record · MW 本、套

**典礼 diǎnlǐ** N ceremony; celebration · MW 个

**典型 diǎnxíng** N·ADJ model; type; typical; representative · MW 个
他是个**典型**的中国人。*He is a typical Chinese person.*

**典押 diǎnyā** V to mortgage; to pawn

**典雅 diǎnyǎ** ADJ refined, elegant

**典章 diǎnzhāng** N institutions; decrees and regulations · MW 部

## RELATED WORDS

| | | |
|---|---|---|
| 古典 154 | 庆典 230 | 字典 664 |
| 法典 686 | 经典 1110 | 词典 1353 |
| 辞典 1606 | 盛典 1694 | |

## 533 具

U+5177　TM **9** FM |

**jù** V·N·MW to possess, to have; to write down; to provide, to furnish; utensil, tool; talent; [measure word for tools, corpses, coffins, etc.]

**具备 jùbèi** V to possess, to have; to be qualified for

他完全不**具备**条件。 *He is absolutely not qualified for this.*

**具名 jùmíng** V to sign, to affix one's signature; to publish with a byline

**具体 jùtǐ** ADJ concrete, specific, particular; detailed

**具有 jùyǒu** V to possess, to have; to be provided with

李老师**具有**丰富的教学经验。 *Teacher Li has a lot of teaching experience.*

**RELATED WORDS**

工具 12　　　刀具 31　　　文具 70
夹具 197　　用具 313　　灯具 346
农具 423　　炊具 700　　面具 721
玩具 727　　茶具 767　　耕具 817
卧具 826　　别具一格 1049　量具 1544
模具 1673　道具 1756　　寝具 1878
器具 1963　餐具 1964

## 534 昔

U+6614　TM **9** FM |

**xī** N the past, old times; yesterday

**昔日 xīrì** N former days/times

**RELATED WORD**

今昔 102

## 535 旨

U+65E8　TM **9** FM |

**zhǐ** N purpose; main point; decree

**旨意 zhǐyì** N design, intent; intention, will · MW 个

**RELATED WORDS**

主旨 124　　　宗旨 910

## 536 某

U+67D0　TM **9** FM |

**mǒu** PRON·N certain; some; [indefinite person/thing]

**某某 mǒumǒu** PRON so-and-so

**某人 mǒurén** PRON someone

关于**某人**或某事 *regard for someone or something*

**某些 mǒuxiē** N some; certain

## 537 岸

U+5CB8　TM **9** FM |

**àn** N (river) bank; shore, coast

**岸线 ànxiàn** N waterfront · MW 条

**RELATED WORDS**

上岸 14　　　口岸 42　　　江岸 237
此岸 416　　　到岸价格 737　河岸 934
沿岸 1165　　海岸 1494　　离岸价 1614
靠岸 1791　　入境口岸 5

## 538 齿 齒

U+9F7F　TM **9** FM |

**chǐ** N tooth; [like a tooth]; protrusion; age

**齿轮 chǐlún** N (machine) gear, gear wheel · MW 个

**齿龈 chǐyín** N gums; gingival

**RELATED WORDS**

口齿 42　　　犬齿 54　　　牙齿 143
启齿 657　　　洁齿 940　　　智齿 1581

## 539 异

U+5F02　TM **9** FM |

**yì** ADJ·N different; other; separate; strange, unusual; surprising; extraordinary surprise

**异常 yìcháng** ADJ·ADV unusual, abnormal; unusually; very, greatly

今年冬天**异常**寒冷。 *This winter is extremely cold.*

**异国 yìguó** N foreign country · MW 个

**异乎寻常 yìhūxúncháng** EXP unusual, exceptional

**异化 yìhuà** V to alienate

**异己 yìjǐ** N alien, outsider; dissident · MW 个、名

**异口同声 yìkǒutóngshēng** EXP with one voice, in unison

大家**异口同声**说傻瓜的好话。 *Everybody praised ShaGua in unison.*

**异曲同工 yìqǔtónggōng** EXP to use different methods with equal success (LIT to render different tunes with equal skill)

**异物 yìwù** N foreign body; ghost; curiosity · MW 个

**异乡 yìxiāng** N foreign/strange land · MW 个

异型 yìxíng  N  allotropy · MW 个

异性 yìxìng  N·ADJ  opposite sex; heterosexual · MW 个、位、名

异议 yìyì  N  objection, dissent · MW 个、项
现在提出**异议**太晚了。 *It is too late now to raise an objection.*

**RELATED WORDS**

| 无异 139 | 优异 447 | 差异 673 |
| 奇异 854 | 特异 1094 | 大同小异 20 |

---

**540  毕  畢**  U+6BD5  TM 9 FM |

bì  V·ADV  to finish, to complete; completely; all

毕竟 bìjìng  ADV  after all, in the final analysis
不要责备他，他**毕竟**是个新手。 *Don't blame him; after all, he is new at this.*

毕生 bìshēng  N  lifetime; all one's life, lifelong
毕生精力 *energy throughout one's life*

毕业 bìyè  V  to graduate, to finish school

**RELATED WORD**

完毕 909

---

**541  同**  U+540C  TM 9 FM |

tóng  V·ADJ·ADV·PREP·CONJ  to be alike; to do together; alike, similar; the same as; in common; with; as … as

同班 tóngbān  V·N  to be in the same class; classmate · MW 个、名

同伴 tóngbàn  N  companion; fellow · MW 个、名

同胞 tóngbāo  N  born of the same parents, brother and sister; compatriots · MW 个、位、名

同辈 tóngbèi  N  same generation · MW 个

同步 tóngbù  V  to sync with, to be in step with

同窗 tóngchuāng  N  schoolmate, classmate · MW 个、位、名

同等 tóngděng  ADJ  of the same class/status/level; equivalent
每个人都将享受**同等**待遇。 *Everybody in here will be treated the same.*

同房 tóngfáng  V  to have sex; to live together

同感 tónggǎn  N  same feeling/impression · MW 个

同行 tóngháng  V·N  to be in the same line of work; people in the same line of work · MW 个、位、名

同化 tónghuà  V  to assimilate
中国传统文化有非常强的**同化**能力。 *Traditional Chinese culture has an extremely strong ability to assimilate other cultures.*

同伙 tónghuǒ  V·N  to conspire with; partner, accomplice · MW 个、名、群

同居 tóngjū  V  to cohabit, to live together

同类 tónglèi  ADJ·N  similar; people/things of the same kind

同僚 tóngliáo  N  colleague · MW 个、位、名

同路 tónglù  V  to go the same way
我们仅仅是**同路**人而已。 *We are just people on the same road.*

同盟 tóngméng  N·V  alliance, league; to merge, to unite · MW 个

同名 tóngmíng  N  of the same name/title

同年 tóngnián  N·V  same year/age; candidates who passed the imperial examinations in the same year; to be a contemporary (of) · MW 个

同期 tóngqī  N  corresponding period; same term/year/class

同情 tóngqíng  V  to sympathize (with), to feel pity (for)
傻瓜**同情**那些无家可归的人。 *ShaGua feels pity for homeless people.*

同时 tóngshí  N·CONJ  at the same time, meanwhile; in addition to, besides

同事 tóngshì  N·V  colleague; to work together · MW 个、位、名

同乡 tóngxiāng  N  person from the same hometown; fellow countryman · MW 个、位、名

同心 tóngxīn  V  to work with a common purpose, to work cooperatively

同性 tóngxìng  ADJ·N  same sex; homosexual

同学 tóngxué  N·V  schoolmate, classmate; to be in the same school · MW 个、位、名
他们是**同班**的**同学**。 *They are classmates.*

同样 tóngyàng  ADJ  same; similar, alike
天天都做**同样**的工作令人难受。 *It is miserable to do the same job every day.*

同一 tóngyī  ADJ  same, identical; unanimous

同义 tóngyì  N  synonym

同意 tóngyì  V  to agree; to approve
我完全**同意**你的观点。 *I couldn't agree with you more.*

**RELATED WORDS**

| 下同 10 | 大同小异 20 | 不同 24 |
| 共同 164 | 伙同 214 | 协同 397 |
| 如同 464 | 志同道合 528 | 相同 805 |
| 连同 958 | 等同 1437 | 陪同 1568 |

**541** 同 tóng (continued)

| | | |
|---|---|---|
| 雷同 1641 | 混同 1739 | 赞同 1969 |
| 死胡同 510 | 异口同声 539 | 异曲同工 539 |
| 与众不同 158 | | |

**542** 国 國　　U+56FD　　TM **9** FM |

guó　N　country, nation, state; national (representing / symbolic of a country)

国宝 guóbǎo　N　national treasure; people who have made special contributions to the country · MW 个

熊猫是中国的**国宝**。*The panda is China's national treasure.*

国宾 guóbīn　N　guest of the state · MW 位

国策 guócè　N　national policy · MW 项

国产 guóchǎn　ADJ　domestic, domestically produced

国防 guófáng　N　national defense

国歌 guógē　N　national anthem · MW 首

国会 guóhuì　N　parliament, Congress (U.S.)

国籍 guójí　N　nationality; citizenship; national identity (of a plane, a ship, etc.)

傻瓜出生在中国, 但现在具有美国**国籍**。 *ShaGua is Chinese by birth but is now a citizen of the United States.*

国际 guójì　ADJ·N　international

我寄了一件**国际**快邮。*I have sent a piece of international express mail.*

国家 guójiā　N　country, nation, state · MW 个

国库 guókù　N　national/state treasury

国民 guómín　N　citizen; national · MW 个

国内 guónèi　ADJ　domestic; interior, internal

现在**国内**的快递服务已经很普遍了。 *Domestic express mail is very popular now.*

国旗 guóqí　N　national flag · MW 面

国情 guóqíng　N　national conditions; state of a country

用**国情**不同来拒绝学习他国文化是错误的。 *It is wrong to use differing national conditions as an excuse to refuse studying other countries' cultures.*

国庆 guóqìng　N　national day

国外 guówài　ADJ　foreign, overseas, abroad

国王 guówáng　N　king · MW 个、位、名

国务院 Guówùyuàn　N　State Council (China); State Department (U.S.)

国宴 guóyàn　N　state banquet · MW 次

国营 guóyíng　ADJ　state-owned, state-run

**国营**经济占中国经济的主要部分。 *The state-owned economy is the main component of the Chinese economy.*

国语 guóyǔ　N　Mandarin; official language of a country

**国语**是中国的官方语言。*Mandarin is the official language of China.*

### RELATED WORDS

| | |
|---|---|
| 三国 9 | 王国 27 |
| 亡国 68 | 中国 86 |
| 中国大陆 86 | 中国共产党 86 |
| 中国官话 86 | 中国银行 86 |
| 本国 90 | 归国 166 |
| 全国 172 | 全国人民 172 |
| 全国性 172 | 外国 218 |
| 卖国 524 | 异国 539 |
| 英国 556 | 美国 671 |
| 美国英语 671 | 举国 674 |
| 法国 686 | 叛国 960 |
| 泰国 1066 | 敌国 1127 |
| 祖国 1190 | 救国 1259 |
| 爱国 1264 | 帝国 1312 |
| 帝国主义 1312 | 岛国 1434 |
| 跨国公司 1857 | 德国 1923 |
| 联合国 1206 | 中华人民共和国 86 |

**543** 县 縣　　U+53BF　　TM **9** FM |

xiàn　N　county

县城 xiànchéng　N　county seat; county town · MW 个

**县城**离这有将近一百里。*The county seat is a hundred li or so away from here.*

县委 xiànwěi　N　county party committee · MW 个

县长 xiànzhǎng　N　county head/magistrate · MW 个、名

县志 xiànzhì　N　county records · MW 本、部

**544** 果　　U+679C　　TM **9** FM |

guǒ　N·ADJ·ADV　fruit; result, outcome, consequence; resolute, determined; surely, truly, as expected

果断 guǒduàn　ADJ　resolute, decisive, firm

果酱 guǒjiàng　N　jam · MW 瓶

果林 **guǒlín** N forest of fruit-bearing trees · MW 片

果木 **guǒmù** N fruit tree · MW 棵

果然 **guǒrán** ADV·CONJ really, as expected

傻瓜说即使下大雪他也来，他**果然**来了。
*ShaGua said he would come, even in heavy snow. Sure enough, he did.*

果实 **guǒshí** N fruit; fruits, gains · MW 个

果树 **guǒshù** N fruit tree · MW 棵、片

果园 **guǒyuán** N orchard · MW 个

果真 **guǒzhēn** ADV·CONJ really, as expected; if indeed/really

果真如此, 我就放心了。*If this is really true, it'll take a load off my mind.*

果汁 **guǒzhī** N fruit juice · MW 杯、瓶

果子 **guǒzi** N fruit · MW 个

### RELATED WORDS

| | | |
|---|---|---|
| 水果糖 159 | 瓜果 189 | 因果 270 |
| 后果 310 | 苹果 395 | 苹果酱 395 |
| 苹果汁 395 | 如果 464 | 柑果 582 |
| 刚果 591 | 成果 611 | 效果 965 |
| 恶果 1196 | 结果 1291 | 硕果 1375 |
| 野果 1685 | 糖果 1933 | 互为因果 135 |
| 前因后果 1329 | | |

---

**545 号 號**   U+53F7   TM **9** FM |

**háo** V to howl; to yell

怒号 *to howl*

**hào** V·N·MW to make a mark; to take the pulse; number (in a series); date; name; firm, business; size; type, kind; order, command; [measure word for days of the month]

序号 *serial number*

今天几号？ *What is today's date?*

名号 *name*

号座位 *to book a seat*

商号 *shop*

大号 *large size*

号称 **hàochēng** V to be known as; to claim to be

号角 **hàojiǎo** N horn, trumpet; bugle call

号令 **hàolìng** N order, verbal command · MW 个

号码 **hàomǎ** N number · MW 个、组

你能告诉我你的电话**号码**吗？ *Would you please tell me your phone number?*

号手 **hàoshǒu** N bugler, trumpeter · MW 个、名

号召 **hàozhào** V to call; to appeal

---

### RELATED WORDS

| | | |
|---|---|---|
| 大号 20 | 口号 42 | 正号 76 |
| 头号 128 | 双号 146 | 代号 208 |
| 外号 218 | 对号 254 | 引号 371 |
| 句号 424 | 字号 664 | 单号 672 |
| 问号 678 | 型号 723 | 查号台 741 |
| 呼号 779 | 挂号 796 | 标号 801 |
| 信号灯 869 | 信号 869 | 记号 946 |
| 冒号 989 | 批号 1005 | 拨号盘 1015 |
| 拨号 1015 | 括号 1016 | 符号 1277 |
| 称号 1288 | 段号 1293 | 病号 1327 |
| 顿号 1420 | 等号 1437 | 逗号 1512 |
| 牌号 1597 | 商号 1612 | 暗号 1676 |
| 编号 1866 | 天字第一号 25 | |

---

**546 员 員**   U+5458   TM **9** FM |

**yuán** N member; -er/-or, -ist, etc.; [person engaged in some field of activity]; personnel

员工 **yuángōng** N staff, personnel; clerk, worker · MW 个、名

公司的**员工**很喜欢新来的经理。*The company's staff likes the new manager very much.*

### RELATED WORDS

| | | |
|---|---|---|
| 专员 155 | 队员 294 | 会员 295 |
| 议员 350 | 动员 514 | 委员 594 |
| 成员 611 | 店员 658 | 定员 666 |
| 译员 951 | 官员 1136 | 教员 1424 |
| 雇员 1474 | 海员 1494 | 党员 1626 |
| 满员 1745 | 幅员 1777 | 船员 1809 |
| 演员 1821 | 随员 1911 | 飞行员 81 |
| 众议员 175 | 参议员 600 | 男演员 757 |
| 运动员 956 | 救生员 1259 | 乘务员 1263 |
| 售票员 1266 | 教职员 1424 | 营业员 1546 |
| 在编人员 188 | | |

---

**547 吊**   U+540A   TM **9** FM |

**diào** V to hang, to suspend; to revoke, to withdraw, to cancel; to raise or lower (with a rope, etc.); to mourn

吊车 **diàochē** N crane; hoist · MW 辆、台

吊灯 **diàodēng** N chandelier · MW 盏

吊儿郎当 **diào'erlángdāng** EXP to fool around

吊环 **diàohuán** N rings (gymnastics) · MW 个、对

吊死 **diàosǐ** V to hang oneself

吊索 **diàosuǒ** N sling · MW 根、条

**547 吊 diào** (continued)

吊胃口 **diàowèikǒu** EXP to tantalize, to whet (someone's) appetite

吊销 **diàoxiāo** V to revoke, to withdraw (an issued certificate)

**RELATED WORD**

塔吊 1394

---

**548 芬** U+82AC TM 9 FM |

**fēn** N fragrance; perfume

芬芳 **fēnfāng** ADJ fragrant, sweet-smelling

芬兰 **Fēnlán** N Finland

---

**549 花** U+82B1 TM 9 FM |

**huā** N·ADJ·V flower, blossom; [like a flower]; fireworks; pattern, design; pretty young woman, beauty; floral; multicolored, variegated; to spend, to expend

开花 *blooming*

火花 *sparks*

挂花 *wound*

棉花 *cotton*

花瓣 **huābàn** N petal · MW 片

花苞 **huābāo** N bud · MW 个

花边 **huābiān** N decorative/floral border · MW 条

花丛 **huācóng** N flowering shrub; cluster of flowers

花灯 **huādēng** N festive lantern · MW 盏

花朵 **huāduǒ** N flower, blossom · MW 束、瓣

花费 **huāfèi** V·N to spend, to pay out; cost, expense · MW 笔

大学四年的**花费**是一笔不小的开支。 *Four years of college is very expensive.*

花粉 **huāfěn** N pollen

傻瓜来美国六年后得了**花粉**过敏症。 *After being in the States for six years, ShaGua developed hay fever.*

花花公子 **huāhuāgōngzǐ** N playboy · MW 个、名

花花绿绿 **huāhuālǜlǜ** EXP colorful, brightly colored

花环 **huāhuán** N garland · MW 个

花卉 **huāhuì** N flowers and plants · MW 束、种

花甲 **huājiǎ** N 60-year cycle · MW 个

他今年正好一个**花甲**。 *He is exactly 60 years old this year.*

花篮 **huālán** N basket of flowers, floral basket · MW 个

花鸟 **huāniǎo** N flowers and birds; traditional Chinese flower-and-bird painting

花钱 **huāqián** V to spend money

花生 **huāshēng** N peanut · MW 粒、颗

傻瓜爱吃**花生**。 *ShaGua loves peanuts.*

花束 **huāshù** N bouquet, bunch of flowers

花纹 **huāwén** N pattern

花絮 **huāxù** N tidbits (of news)

花言巧语 **huāyánqiǎoyǔ** EXP smooth talk (LIT sweet words)

傻瓜最不喜欢**花言巧语**的人。 *ShaGua dislikes smooth-talking people.*

花样 **huāyàng** N variety; decorative pattern; trick · MW 个、种

花招 **huāzhāo** N showy movement (martial arts); trick, game · MW 个、套

别耍**花招**了，好好学习吧。 *Stop relying on your little tricks; please study hard.*

**RELATED WORDS**

| | | |
|---|---|---|
| 天花乱坠 25 | 开花 26 | 火花 72 |
| 五花八门 79 | 兰花 126 | 礼花 503 |
| 泪花 688 | 茶花 767 | 桂花 797 |
| 香花 834 | 种花 893 | 栽花 995 |
| 菜花 1001 | 盆花 1261 | 雪花 1369 |
| 梅花 1413 | 梅花鹿 1413 | 眼花 1570 |
| 零花 1640 | 棉花 1670 | 绣花 1801 |
| 鲜花 1811 | 霜花 1935 | 玉米花 77 |
| 走马看花 265 | | |

---

**550 芳** U+82B3 TM 9 FM |

**fāng** N·ADJ virtue; flowers and grass; good (conduct/reputation), virtuous; fragrant, sweet-smelling

芳香 **fāngxiāng** ADJ·N fragrant, balmy, aromatic (of flowers, grass); fragrance

**RELATED WORD**

芬芳 548

---

**551 芽** U+82BD TM 9 FM |

**yá** N bud, sprout, shoot

**RELATED WORDS**

发芽 311　　　　豆芽 353

## 552 苏 蘇 U+82CF　TM 9 FM |

**sū** [V] to revive, to come to

**苏打 sūdá** [N] soda

**苏格兰 Sūgélán** [N] Scotland

**苏联 Sūlián** [N] Soviet Union

在50年代，**苏联**曾经是许多中国人向往的天堂。 *The Soviet Union was once the heaven that many Chinese yearned for in the '50s.*

**苏醒 sūxǐng** [V] to wake up, to regain consciousness

中国人从鸦片战争的炮声中**苏醒**过来。 *The Chinese people were roused by the thundering booms of the Opium War.*

**苏绣 sūxiù** [N] Suzhou embroidery (one of four traditional Chinese embroidery styles) · [MW] 幅

### RELATED WORD

江苏 237

## 553 苗 U+82D7　TM 9 FM |

**miáo** [N] young plant, seedling; [like a young plant]; offspring, young; descendant; vaccine; ethnic minority

**苗床 miáochuáng** [N] nursery bed · [MW] 个

**苗圃 miáopǔ** [N] nursery garden · [MW] 个

**苗条 miáotiao** [ADJ] slim, willowy, svelte

这个姑娘很**苗条**。 *This girl is very slender.*

**苗头 miáotou** [N] traces/premonition of, first indication of · [MW] 个

一发现不好的**苗头**，就应该进行教育。 *As soon as the first indication of an unhealthy habit is discovered, you should exercise discipline immediately.*

### RELATED WORDS

禾苗 108　　种苗 893　　树苗 1031
痘苗 1477　　蒜苗 1655　　卡介苗 36

## 554 若 U+82E5　TM 9 FM |

**ruò** [V·PRON·CONJ] to be like, to seem; you; as if; if

**若非 ruòfēi** [CONJ] if not

**若非**傻瓜的帮助，那个青少年恐怕早就进监狱了。 *If not for ShaGua's help, that teenager might be in jail already.*

**若干 ruògān** [QPRON] how much/many; certain amount/number; a few, several

**若是 ruòshì** [CONJ] if, supposing, in case

**若无其事 ruòwúqíshì** [EXP] to act as if nothing has happened

你的成绩掉得太多，不能再**若无其事**了。 *Your grades have dropped too much; you can't pretend nothing has happened.*

### RELATED WORDS

如若 464　　假若 1586　　门庭若市 130
受宠若惊 844

## 555 苦 U+82E6　TM 9 FM |

**kǔ** [V·N·ADJ·ADV] to be hard on; to suffer from, to be troubled by; misery, distress; suffering, hardship; bitter, miserable; painful, hard; painstakingly

**苦楚 kǔchǔ** [ADJ] suffering, misery, distress

傻瓜的**苦楚**，只有他自己知道。 *Only ShaGua knows his own troubles.*

**苦处 kǔchù** [N] suffering, hardship · [MW] 个

**苦功 kǔgōng** [N] hard work · [MW] 个

**苦力 kǔlì** [N] hard work · [MW] 个、名

傻瓜曾经干过**苦力**。 *ShaGua was once a manual laborer.*

**苦闷 kǔmèn** [ADJ] depressed, discouraged

**苦闷**的时候，傻瓜会到健身房去举重。 *When he feels depressed, ShaGua lifts weights at the gym.*

**苦难 kǔnàn** [N] suffering, misery, distress

**苦恼 kǔnǎo** [ADJ] distressed, worried; pitiful

**苦水 kǔshuǐ** [N] bitter(-tasting) water; misery; bitterness

**苦头 kǔtóu** [N] suffering, trouble, hardship · [MW] 次

**苦心 kǔxīn** [N] pains (taken)

父母的**苦心**，往往到孩子当父母后才能理解。 *Kids are unable to understand the painstaking effort their parents have gone to until they themselves become parents.*

**苦于 kǔyú** [V] to suffer from, to be afflicted by

**苦衷 kǔzhōng** [N] pain, feeling of pain/embarrassment; predicament · [MW] 个

孩子也有自己的**苦衷**。 *Kids have personal and often painful feelings.*

### RELATED WORDS

甘苦 95　　叫苦 283　　辛苦 331
困苦 393　　何苦 619　　诉苦 708
劳苦 764　　吃苦 783　　吃苦头 783
受苦 844　　穷苦 912　　疾苦 922
刻苦 966　　艰苦 973　　痛苦 1725
辛辛苦苦 331

## 556 英　U+82F1　TM 9 FM |

**yīng** N·ADJ hero, outstanding person; flower; England; English

**英镑 yīngbàng** N pound (sterling) (British monetary unit)

**英才 yīngcái** N talented person, person with outstanding ability/talent · MW 个、位、名

**英尺 yīngchǐ** MW [measure word for feet (a unit of length)]

**英国 Yīngguó** N England, Britain, U.K.

**英俊 yīngjùn** ADJ handsome, good-looking
傻瓜有一个不为人知的妄想：希望能长得**英俊**些。*ShaGua has an unrealistic dream: to be a bit more handsome.*

**英里 yīnglǐ** MW [measure word for miles (a unit of distance)]
别人都用公里，就美国人用**英里**。*Others use kilometers, but Americans use the mile.*

**英灵 yīnglíng** N spirit of the brave departed

**英明 yīngmíng** ADJ wise, brilliant

**英亩 yīngmǔ** MW [measure word for acres (a unit of land area)]

**英文 Yīngwén** N English (language)

**英雄 yīngxióng** N hero · MW 个、位、名
傻瓜在孩子心目中不是一个**英雄**。*ShaGua is not a hero, even in the minds of his kids.*

**英勇 yīngyǒng** ADJ exceptionally brave; heroic

**英语 Yīngyǔ** N English (language)

**英制 yīngzhì** N British system
英国人都不用自己发明的**英制**了，但美国人还死抱不放。*The English don't even use the system they designed, but Americans are still using it.*

**RELATED WORDS**

石英 144　　美国英语 671

## 557 茂　U+8302　TM 9 FM |

**mào** ADJ luxuriant, dense; exuberant; rich and exquisite; splendid

**茂密 màomì** ADJ dense, thick (of vegetation)

**茂盛 màoshèng** ADJ flourishing, thriving, booming
后院的树林很**茂盛**。*The woods in the backyard are very lush.*

## 558 均　U+5747　TM 9 FM |

**jūn** V·ADJ·ADV to divide equally, to even; equal, uniform; without exception, all

**均差 jūnchā** N deviation from the mean

**均等 jūnděng** ADJ equal; fair
机会**均等** *equal opportunity*

**均分 jūnfēn** V to divide equally

**均衡 jūnhéng** ADJ balanced, proportionate, even

**均势 jūnshì** N balance of power

**均匀 jūnyún** ADJ even, well-distributed
把化肥**均匀**地撒在草地里。*Spread the fertilizer on the grass evenly.*

**RELATED WORD**

平均 78

## 559 吹　U+5439　TM 9 FM |

**chuī** V to blow, to puff; to play (a wind instrument); to strike; to boast, to brag; to flatter, to compliment; to break off/up, to fail

**吹吹拍拍 chuīchuīpāipāi** EXP to boast and brown-nose

**吹风 chuīfēng** V to be caught in a draft

**吹毛求疵 chuīmáoqiúcī** EXP to find fault; to criticize unfairly

**吹牛 chuīniú** V to boast, to brag
她喜欢**吹牛**(皮)，什么实际的事都不干。*She talks big, but doesn't actually do anything.*

**吹捧 chuīpěng** V to flatter
她当大家的面**吹捧**上司。*She flatters her boss in front of the others.*

**吹嘘 chuīxū** V to boast, to brag

**吹奏 chuīzòu** V to play (a wind instrument)

**RELATED WORDS**

风吹草动 194　　鼓吹 1688

## 560 呕　嘔　U+5455　TM 9 FM |

**ǒu** V to vomit, to throw up

**呕吐 ǒutù** V to vomit, to throw up
这种病的症状是发烧与**呕吐**。*The symptoms of this disease are fever and vomiting.*

**呕心 ǒuxīn** V to work one's heart out

**呕血 ǒuxuè** V to cough up blood

## 561 味    U+5473   TM **9** FM |

**wèi** V·N to ponder; taste, flavor; smell, odor, fragrance; interest; delicacy

**味道 wèidao** N taste, flavor; smell, odor · MW 种

这盘菜的**味道**非常好。*The dish has a very nice flavor.*

**味精 wèijīng** N monosodium glutamate (MSG) · MW 粒

**味觉 wèijué** N sense of taste · MW 种

### RELATED WORDS

| | | |
|---|---|---|
| 口味 42 | 五味 79 | 气味 185 |
| 风味 194 | 走味 265 | 体味 325 |
| 余味 419 | 美味 671 | 玩味 727 |
| 香味 834 | 咸味 1073 | 甜味 1306 |
| 海味 1494 | 辣味 1760 | 趣味 1783 |
| 意味 1812 | 意味着 1812 | 山珍海味 38 |

## 562 哎    U+54CE   TM **9** FM |

**āi** ONOM oh! (expressing surprise); hey! (expressing disapproval); [interjection expressing disagreement/negation, regret, annoyance]

**哎呀 āiyā** ONOM oh, oh no, oh dear; oops

**哎呀**, 我又犯了愚蠢的错误。*Oh dear, I messed up again.*

**哎哟 āiyō** ONOM oh, oh no; ouch

## 563 托    U+6258   TM **9** FM |

**tuō** V·N to hold in one's palm; to support (from underneath); to set off; to entrust; to rely on; base; support

**托词 tuōcí** N·V to make an excuse, to find a pretext · MW 个

**托儿所 tuō'érsuǒ** N nursery; childcare center · MW 间、家

**托福 tuōfú** V·N to thank; Test of English as a Foreign Language (TOEFL)

**托付 tuōfù** V to entrust; to commit to the care of

**托管 tuōguǎn** V to deposit; to entrust

请问, 这里可以**托管**行李吗? *Excuse me, may I deposit my luggage here for safekeeping?*

**托收 tuōshōu** V to collect

**托运 tuōyùn** V to ship; to check (baggage, etc.)

### RELATED WORDS

| | | |
|---|---|---|
| 全托 172 | 委托 594 | 拜托 635 |
| 重托 839 | 受托 844 | 信托 869 |
| 烘托 953 | 转托 1111 | 推托 1242 |
| 寄托 1619 | | |

## 564 执 執    U+6267   TM **9** FM |

**zhí** V to hold; to grasp, to grip; to catch; to capture; to take charge of, to manage, to direct; to persist in, to stick to; to carry out, to implement

**执笔 zhíbǐ** V to write; to do the actual writing

**执法 zhífǎ** V to enforce the law

**执迷不悟 zhímíbùwù** EXP to refuse to come to one's senses, to stick to one's bad ways

**执行 zhíxíng** V to carry out, to implement, to execute

他正在**执行**一项特殊的使命。*He is carrying out a special mission.*

**执意 zhíyì** ADV stubbornly, obstinately; to insist on

**执掌 zhízhǎng** V to wield; to be in control of

**执照 zhízhào** N license, permit · MW 个

**执政 zhízhèng** V to be in power/office

### RELATED WORDS

| | | |
|---|---|---|
| 回执 391 | 固执 760 | 仗义执言 121 |

## 565 扭    U+626D   TM **9** FM |

**niǔ** V to turn around; to twist, to sprain; to sway, to swing; to grapple/wrestle with; to slant, to skew

**扭打 niǔdǎ** V to wrestle

他们为争夺座位**扭打**起来。*They began to tussle with each other for the seat.*

**扭捏 niǔniē** ADJ bashful, coy

**扭伤 niǔshāng** V to twist, to wrench, to sprain

傻瓜举重时, **扭伤**了手腕。*ShaGua sprained his wrist while he was lifting weights.*

**扭送 niǔsòng** V to seize and turn over

**扭转 niǔzhuǎn** V to turn (something) around; to turn back; to swing

### RELATED WORD

闹别扭 1323

## 566 扳　U+6273　TM 9 FM |

**bān** V to pull/draw (up/out); to turn defeat into victory; to climb up

扳机 **bānjī** N trigger · MW 个

他扣动**扳机**, 但枪哑火, 敌人大摇大摆地走了。
*He pulled the trigger, but the gun jammed and the enemy sauntered away.*

扳手 **bānshou** N wrench · MW 把

## 567 找　U+627E　TM 9 FM |

**zhǎo** V to look for, to seek, to try to find; to give change (to)

找碴儿 **zhǎochár** EXP to find fault; to pick a fight

傻瓜太太真想**找碴儿**同傻瓜吵一架。
*Mrs. ShaGua really wanted to find an excuse to fight with ShaGua.*

找对象 **zhǎoduìxiàng** V to seek a marriage partner

找麻烦 **zhǎomáfan** EXP to look for trouble

跟傻瓜吵架就是在自**找麻烦**。 *Arguing with ShaGua is just inviting trouble!*

找齐 **zhǎoqí** V to make uniform, to even up

找钱 **zhǎoqián** V to give change (to); to make money

找事 **zhǎoshì** V to look for a job; to pick a fight

找死 **zhǎosǐ** V to risk one's life, to court death

找寻 **zhǎoxún** V to look for, to seek

**RELATED WORD**

寻找 358

## 568 技　U+6280　TM 9 FM |

**jì** N skill, ability; technology

技工 **jìgōng** N skilled worker, technician · MW 个、名

技能 **jìnéng** N craftsmanship; technical ability · MW 种、项

技巧 **jìqiǎo** N craftsmanship; technique; acrobatic gymnastics competition · MW 种

修理电脑需要**技巧**。 *Skill is required to fix a computer.*

技术 **jìshù** N skill; technology; technique · MW 个、种、项

这项**技术**还不成熟, 还处于实验阶段。
*This technique is not mature yet, and is still in the experimental stage.*

技艺 **jìyì** N skill; art; artistry · MW 个、种、项

**RELATED WORDS**

科技 642　　杂技 856　　特技 1094
竞技 1470

## 569 护　護　U+62A4　TM 9 FM |

**hù** V to be partial (to), to take sides; to protect, to guard

护短 **hùduǎn** V to cover up (a shortcoming, a fault)

护耳 **hù'ěr** N earmuffs · MW 对

护理 **hùlǐ** V to nurse

护士 **hùshi** N nurse · MW 个、位、名

精神病院有一些男**护士**负责**护理**病人。
*There are some male nurses working in hospitals for the mentally ill.*

护卫 **hùwèi** V·N to protect, to guard; bodyguard · MW 个、名

护养 **hùyǎng** V to cultivate

护照 **hùzhào** N passport · MW 本

这个女孩持美国**护照**。 *The girl holds a United States passport.*

**RELATED WORDS**

养护 670　　看护 841　　保护 868
拥护 1014　　防护 1040　　救护 1259
爱护 1264　　维护 1455　　偏护 1587
调护 1749　　照护 1846

## 570 抨　U+62A8　TM 9 FM |

**pēng** V to attack; to impeach

抨击 **pēngjī** V to attack (in speech, writing)

他并非恶意**抨击**学校。 *His verbal attack on the school was not malicious.*

## 571 抹　U+62B9　TM 9 FM |

**mā** V to wipe

**mǒ** V to apply; to wipe, to smear; to plaster; to erase, to exclude; to strike/blot out

抹除 **mǒchú** V to erase

抹黑 **mǒhēi** V to discredit, to sling mud at
总统候选人互相**抹黑**。*The presidential candidates resorted to mudslinging.*

抹灰 **mǒhuī** V to plaster

抹杀 **mǒshā** V to blot out; to write off
有些人总是想**抹杀**傻瓜的功劳。*Someone always wants to expunge ShaGua's achievements.*

**RELATED WORDS**

涂抹 1171          涂脂抹粉 1171

---

## 572 拆    U+62C6    TM 9 FM |

**chāi** V to tear apart/down/open; to open; to dismantle, to demolish

拆除 **chāichú** V to dismantle; to remove

拆穿 **chāichuān** V to expose
傻瓜不想**拆穿**某些人的把戏。*ShaGua doesn't want to expose others' tricks.*

拆封 **chāifēng** V to seal off

拆毁 **chāihuǐ** V to demolish
这栋楼房被**拆毁**了。*The building was demolished.*

拆伙 **chāihuǒ** V to dissolve (a partnership)

拆开 **chāikāi** V to take apart

拆散 **chāisàn** V to break apart/up
离婚**拆散**了许多家庭。*Divorce breaks up many families.*

拆台 **chāitái** V to undermine

拆卸 **chāixiè** V to dismantle

---

## 573 拉    U+62C9    TM 9 FM |

**lā** V to pull, to drag, to tug; to haul, to transport (by vehicle); to stretch, to extend; to space out; to play (a bowed instrument); to chat; to bring up, to raise

**lá** V to tear; to slit

拉长 **lācháng** V to elongate

拉扯 **lāche** V to pull; to drag/rope in; to chat; to bring up (a child)
我什么都不知道，干吗把我也**拉扯**进去？*I don't know anything; why drag me into it?*

拉倒 **lādǎo** V to forget about it

拉肚子 **lādùzi** V to have diarrhea

拉关系 **lāguānxi** V to try to establish a relationship with; to suck up to, to brownnose

---

拉开 **lākāi** V to pull open

拉拉队 **lāláduì** N cheerleader(s) · MW 支

拉屎 **lāshǐ** V to have a bowel movement

拉手 **lāshǒu** N·V handle; to shake hands · MW 个

拉下脸 **lāxiàliǎn** V to look displeased/irritated
傻瓜太太一不高兴就**拉下脸**来。*As soon as Mrs. ShaGua becomes upset, she immediately begins to look angry.*

拉下水 **lāxiàshuǐ** V to drag into the sewer (FIG)

**RELATED WORDS**

沙拉 342          阿拉伯 1249          拖拉 1396
拖拉机 1396       鸡色拉 1373

---

## 574 拌    U+62CC    TM 9 FM |

**bàn** V to mix (in); to toss (a salad); to quarrel

拌和 **bànhuò** V to mix and stir, to blend

拌匀 **bànyún** V to mix thoroughly
做饼干的关键是把奶油、面粉和水**拌匀**。*The key to making biscuits is to thoroughly mix the butter, flour, and water.*

**RELATED WORD**

搅拌 1850

---

## 575 拟 擬    U+62DF    TM 9 FM |

**nǐ** V to draw up, to draft; to plan, to intend, to be going to; to imitate; to surmise, to infer

拟订 **nǐdìng** V to draw up, to draft, to formulate
她**拟订**了一个度假的计划。*She has worked out a plan for the holidays.*

拟稿 **nǐgǎo** V to draft (a statement, etc.)

拟人 **nǐrén** N personification

拟议 **nǐyì** V to write/draft a proposal/recommendation

**RELATED WORDS**

比拟 279          草拟 768          虚拟 1534
模拟 1673

---

## 576 拦 攔    U+62E6    TM 9 FM |

**lán** V to stop, to block; to hold back, to hinder

拦河坝 **lánhébà** N dam · MW 座、条

拦截 **lánjié** V to intercept

**576 拦 lán** (continued)

**拦路 lánlù** [V] to block the way

> 一条水牛**拦路**，车只好停下来。 *A water buffalo is blocking the way, so the car must stop.*

**拦腰 lányāo** [ADV] by the waist; in half

**拦住 lánzhù** [V] to stop, to hold up

> 那个中国人**拦住**我，问我在哪里学的中文。 *That Chinese person stopped me and asked me where I learned my Chinese.*

**拦阻 lánzǔ** [V] to block, to hinder

**RELATED WORD**

阻拦 1042

---

**577 机 機**    U+673A    TM **9** FM |

**jī** [N] machine, engine; pivot, turning point; opportunity, chance; organic

**机场 jīchǎng** [N] airport · [MW] 个

> 学校已经安排人到**机场**接你。 *The school has arranged for someone to pick you up at the airport.*

**机车 jīchē** [N] locomotive (of a train) · [MW] 辆、台

**机床 jīchuáng** [N] machine tool · [MW] 台

**机动 jīdòng** [ADJ] motorized; flexible; in reserve

**机构 jīgòu** [N] mechanism; organization, structure · [MW] 个

**机关 jīguān** [N] office; department; mechanism · [MW] 个

**机会 jīhuì** [N] opportunity, chance · [MW] 个

> 去中国学习，这可是一生难得的**机会**。 *Studying in a Chinese school is a once-in-a-lifetime chance.*

**机灵 jīling** [ADJ] clever, smart, sharp

**机密 jīmì** [N·ADJ] secret; classified (information) · [MW] 个

**机能 jīnéng** [N] function · [MW] 个

**机票 jīpiào** [N] plane ticket · [MW] 张

> 我已经买好了去中国的往返**机票**。 *I already have a round-trip ticket to China.*

**机器 jīqì** [N] machine, engine; apparatus · [MW] 台

**机械 jīxiè** [N] machinery; mechanism

**机械化 jīxièhuà** [V] to mechanize

**机要 jīyào** [ADJ] confidential

**机遇 jīyù** [N] opportunity; favorable circumstances · [MW] 个

> 不要让**机遇**从你身边溜走。 *Don't let opportunities slip by.*

---

**RELATED WORDS**

| | | |
|---|---|---|
| 人机对话 4 | 飞机 81 | 飞机场 81 |
| 飞机票 81 | 主机 124 | 耳机 145 |
| 专机 155 | 电机 263 | 司机 357 |
| 寻机 358 | 灵机 359 | 有机 439 |
| 动机 514 | 扳机 566 | 时机 586 |
| 良机 656 | 班机 730 | 劫机 819 |
| 伺机 862 | 契机 992 | 投机 1008 |
| 危机 1057 | 候机室 1086 | 转机 1111 |
| 轮机 1112 | 趁机 1257 | 乘机 1263 |
| 钻机 1302 | 客机 1316 | 唱机 1562 |
| 随机 1911 | 下飞机 10 | 升降机 47 |
| 压缩机 201 | 计算机 240 | 电唱机 263 |
| 打火机 289 | 录像机 722 | 录音机 722 |
| 抽风机 788 | 烘干机 953 | 洒水机 1163 |
| 铲运机 1304 | 榨汁机 1672 | 割草机 1761 |
| 摄影机 1772 | 照相机 1846 | 坐失良机 318 |
| 航天飞机 1717 | | |

---

**578 朽**    U+673D    TM **9** FM |

**xiǔ** [V·ADJ] to rot; rotten, decayed

**朽木 xiǔmù** [N] rotten wood/tree · [MW] 根

**RELATED WORD**

腐朽 1879

---

**579 松 鬆**    U+677E    TM **9** FM |

**sōng** [N·ADJ·V] pine tree; loose; soft; light and flaky; to loosen, to untie, to relax, to release

**松绑 sōngbǎng** [V] to untie

**松弛 sōngchí** [ADJ] loose, slack

**松动 sōngdòng** [V] to be loose (of teeth, screws), to be flexible; to become less crowded

> 这孩子的一颗牙开始**松动**了。 *This child's tooth is beginning to loosen.*

**松紧 sōngjǐn** [N] elasticity

**松劲 sōngjìn** [V] to relax one's efforts

**松软 sōngruǎn** [ADJ] soft, spongy; loose

> 新出炉的面包**松软**可口。 *Fresh bread has a nice, light texture.*

**松散 sōngsǎn** [ADJ·V] (structurally) loose; to relax, to take it easy

**松鼠 sōngshǔ** [N] squirrel · [MW] 只

**松树 sōngshù** [N] pine tree · [MW] 棵

**松懈 sōngxiè** [ADJ·V] inattentive, lax; to relax, to slacken

松子 **sōngzǐ** N pine nut · MW 粒、颗

**RELATED WORDS**

青松 740        放松 964        轻松 1113
雪松 1369      稀松 1599

---

580 **板** 闆    U+677F    TM 9 FM |

**bǎn** N·ADJ·V board, plank; blackboard; shutter; blind; boss; shopkeeper, proprietor; stiff, hard; unnatural; to look serious

板材 **bǎncái** N plate · MW 块

板凳 **bǎndèng** N wooden bench/stool · MW 张、条
　屋里摆着两张小**板凳**。*There are two small stools in the room.*

板斧 **bǎnfǔ** N broad ax · MW 把、柄

板块 **bǎnkuài** N plate; slab · MW 块

板栗 **bǎnlì** N Chinese chestnut · MW 颗

板子 **bǎnzi** N board; bamboo/birch for corporal punishment · MW 条、块

**RELATED WORDS**

木板 40        平板 78        门板 130
石板 144       古板 154       夹板 197
老板 375       呆板 384       冷板凳 494
画板 719       地板 772       拍板 790
样板 803       底板 916       刻板 966
挡板 1017      纸板 1103      铁板 1126
钢板 1299      黑板 1389      铺板 1713
跳板 1786      篮板 1862      滑板 1884
隔板 1910      七巧板 34

---

581 **枝**    U+679D    TM 9 FM |

**zhī** N branch, twig; stemmed flower; [long, thin, inflexible object]

枝杈 **zhīchà** N branch, twig · MW 条

枝节 **zhījié** N minor issue; unexpected difficulty (LIT branches and knots) · MW 个

枝叶 **zhīyè** N nonessentials (LIT branches and leaves)
　到了夏天，树的**枝叶**会茂盛起来。
　*The trees and shrubs will be in full bloom in the summer.*
　你说的都是些**枝叶**的东西。*You've only mentioned trivial matters.*

**RELATED WORDS**

修枝 870        树枝 1031

---

582 **柑**    U+67D1    TM 9 FM |

**gān** N mandarin orange; large tangerine

柑果 **gānguǒ** N citrus fruit · MW 个

柑橘 **gānjú** N orange · MW 个
　在中国，你可以买到很多水果，如**柑橘**、香蕉等。*You can buy many kinds of fruit in China, such as oranges and bananas.*

---

583 **柱**    U+67F1    TM 9 FM |

**zhù** N post; upright; pillar, column

柱廊 **zhùláng** N colonnade · MW 条

柱石 **zhùshí** N pillar · MW 根

柱子 **zhùzi** N post; pillar · MW 根
　这是一根大理石**柱子**。*This pillar is made of marble.*

**RELATED WORD**

支柱 92

---

584 **栏** 欄    U+680F    TM 9 FM |

**lán** N fence; railing; hurdle; pen; shed; column

栏杆 **lángān** N railing; banister
　这座房子的外面围着白色的**栏杆**。*A white balustrade circled the house.*

**RELATED WORDS**

专栏 155        跳栏 1786        跨栏赛跑 1857

---

585 **歧**    U+6B67    TM 9 FM |

**qí** ADJ forking, branching (of a road); different; divergent

歧点 **qídiǎn** N fork (of a road) · MW 个

歧路 **qílù** N branching road · MW 条

歧视 **qíshì** V to discriminate (against)
　在很多情况下，我们的社会仍然**歧视**女性。*In many cases, our society still discriminates against women.*

歧义 **qíyì** N ambiguity · MW 个

**RELATED WORD**

分歧 173

**586** 时　時　U+65F6　TM **9** FM |

**shí** N·ADV hour; time; day; season; opportunity, chance; current, present; fashion; now and then, occasionally, from time to time, sometimes … sometimes …

下午六时 *6:00 P.M.*

当时 *at that time*

准时 *on time*

农时 *farming season*

时高时低 *sometimes high and sometimes low*

**时差 shíchā** N time difference; jet lag

每次从中国返回美国, **时差**都使傻瓜感到很难受。 *Jet lag makes ShaGua very uncomfortable every time he returns to the States from China.*

**时常 shícháng** ADV often

**时代 shídài** N times; age, era, epoch · MW 个

**时而 shí'ér** ADV from time to time, sometimes …, sometimes …

**时候 shíhou** N time · MW 个

**时机 shíjī** N opportunity · MW 个

**时机**总是为准备好的人准备的。
*Opportunities await those who are prepared.*

**时间 shíjiān** N time; period of time · MW 个

**时间**就快到了。*It's about time.*

**时刻 shíkè** N·ADV time; moment; always, constantly · MW 个

**时刻表 shíkèbiǎo** N timetable, schedule · MW 张、份

傻瓜心里总有一份紧凑的**时刻表**。
*ShaGua always has a tight schedule in mind.*

**时令 shílìng** N season · MW 个

**时髦 shímáo** ADJ fashionable, stylish

**时期 shíqī** N period in time/history; era · MW 个

这些年是傻瓜一生中最快乐的**时期**。 *These are the happiest years in ShaGua's entire life.*

**时区 shíqū** N time zone · MW 个

**时势 shíshì** N current situation/trend

**时事 shíshì** N current events/affairs

**时态 shítài** N tense · MW 个

傻瓜说英语时常常用错**时态**。*When ShaGua speaks English, he often uses the wrong tense.*

**时务 shíwù** N current affairs · MW 个

**时下 shíxià** ADV at present, currently

**时限 shíxiàn** N time limit · MW 个

**时效 shíxiào** N period of effectiveness/efficacy · MW 个

**时序 shíxù** N time sequence · MW 个

**时运 shíyùn** N luck, fortune · MW 个

**时针 shízhēn** N hour hand · MW 枚

**时钟 shízhōng** N clock · MW 个

**时装 shízhuāng** N fashionable/modern clothing, the latest fashion · MW 件、套

现在中国的**时装**式样变换很快。 *In today's China, fashions change very quickly.*

**RELATED WORDS**

| | | |
|---|---|---|
| 一时 1 | 天时 25 | 小时 61 |
| 小时候 61 | 平时 78 | 子时 83 |
| 区时 99 | 几时 115 | 及时 141 |
| 历时 200 | 为时过早 223 | 计时 240 |
| 计时器 240 | 四时 271 | 当时 335 |
| 有时 439 | 划时代 476 | 同时 541 |
| 定时 666 | 过时 712 | 临时 771 |
| 赶时髦 822 | 每时每刻 837 | 届时 851 |
| 准时 929 | 那时 980 | 即时 1047 |
| 即时通讯 1047 | 学时 1155 | 按时 1234 |
| 适时 1358 | 逆时针 1359 | 顿时 1420 |
| 课时 1503 | 费时 1520 | 暂时 1522 |
| 随时 1911 | 不识时务 24 | 比利时 279 |
| 过去时 712 | 每小时 837 | |

**587** 旺　U+65FA　TM **9** FM |

**wàng** ADJ flourishing, booming; plentiful, bounteous

**旺季 wàngjì** N peak season/period · MW 个

夏天是旅游**旺季**。*Summer is the peak tourist season.*

**旺盛 wàngshèng** ADJ vigorous, exuberant; thriving

**RELATED WORD**

兴旺 228

**588** 财　财　U+8D22　TM **9** FM |

**cái** N money, wealth, riches; property; valuables

**财宝 cáibǎo** N treasure, money and valuables · MW 批

**财产 cáichǎn** N property, possessions, assets · MW 笔

**财富 cáifù** N wealth · MW 笔

他的**财富**比我多百倍, 但他并不快活。
*He is a hundred times richer than I am, but his wealth doesn't bring him happiness.*

**财经 cáijīng** N finance and economics

财力　cáilì　N　financial resources

财贸　cáimào　N　finance and trade

财神　cáishén　N　god of wealth/fortune · MW　个、位、名

财务　cáiwù　N　finance, financial affairs
现在许多大学都面临**财务**上的困难。 *Many universities are facing financial embarrassment right now.*

财政　cáizhèng　N　public finance; fiscal administration

**RELATED WORDS**

| | | |
|---|---|---|
| 发财　311 | 守财奴　486 | 理财　1200 |
| 钱财　1301 | 破财　1374 | 横财　1775 |
| 升官发财　47 | 仗义疏财　121 | |

---

**589　败　败**　U+8D25　TM **9** FM |

bài　V·ADJ　to lose, to be defeated; to destroy, to eliminate, to ruin; shabby, worn-out, dilapidated; withered

败北　bàiběi　V　to be defeated

败坏　bàihuài　V·ADJ　to corrupt; to undermine, to ruin (the mood, the atmosphere, etc.); rotten
他的行为**败坏**了学校的名誉。 *His behavior has ruined his school's reputation.*

败家子　bàijiāzǐ　EXP　spendthrift · MW　个、名

败类　bàilèi　N　scum, lowlife · MW　个、名

败露　bàilù　V　to be exposed (of a plot, etc.)

败落　bàiluò　V　to decline

败诉　bàisù　V　to lose a lawsuit
傻瓜还未**败诉**过。 *ShaGua has not yet lost a lawsuit.*

败仗　bàizhàng　N　losing campaign/battle; defeat · MW　场
他打了**败仗**。 *He has lost the battle.*

**RELATED WORDS**

| | | |
|---|---|---|
| 不败之地　24 | 失败　106 | 击败　156 |
| 打败　289 | 胜败　1122 | 衰败　1313 |
| 腐败　1879 | | |

---

**590　阶　階**　U+9636　TM **9** FM |

jiē　N　step, stair; rank; stage

阶层　jiēcéng　N　stratum; hierarchy · MW　个

阶段　jiēduàn　N　stage, phase, period · MW　个
这门课还没有进入考试**阶段**。 *The class has not yet entered the examination period.*

阶级　jiējí　N　(social) class · MW　个

阶梯　jiētī　N　stairs; ladder; means of advancement
303是一间**阶梯**教室。 *Room 303 is an auditorium.*

**RELATED WORDS**

| | | |
|---|---|---|
| 台阶　301 | 军阶　489 | 中产阶级　86 |
| 无产阶级　139 | | |

---

**591　刚　剛**　U+521A　TM **9** FM |

gāng　ADJ·ADV　firm, strong; just, exactly, barely; only a short while ago

刚才　gāngcái　N　just now
**刚才**你太太给你打电话了。 *Your wife just called you.*

刚刚　gānggāng　ADV　just, just a moment ago

刚果　Gāngguǒ　N　Congo

刚好　gānghǎo　ADV　just, exactly; (just) happen to
傻瓜进门时，**刚好**那人正要离开。 *ShaGua came in just as the man was leaving.*

刚毅　gāngyì　ADJ　resolute, stalwart

刚直　gāngzhí　ADJ　upright and outspoken

**RELATED WORD**

金刚石　420

---

**592　含**　U+542B　TM **9** FM 丿

hán　V　to keep/hold in the mouth; to contain; to nurse; to cherish

含糊　hánhu　ADJ　obscure, vague; careless
她说话**含**含糊糊，傻瓜怎么也听不明白。 *She was so vague that ShaGua couldn't understand her.*

含混　hánhùn　ADJ　ambiguous; vague

含量　hánliàng　N　content

含怒　hánnù　V　to be angered

含笑　hánxiào　V　to smile; with a smile

含羞　hánxiū　V　to be shy

含义　hányì　N　meaning; implication · MW　个
你能解释一下这个词的**含义**吗？ *Would you please explain the meaning of this word?*

含冤　hányuān　V　to be wronged

含怨　hányuàn　V　to bear a grudge

含脂量　hánzhīliáng　N　fat content

**RELATED WORDS**

| | |
|---|---|
| 包含　836 | 暗含　1676 |

## 593 舍 捨　U+820D　TM 9　FM 丿

**shě** (捨) V to give up, to abandon; to give alms

**shè** N house, hut; shed

舍不得 **shěbude** V to hate to (do); to hate to part with
傻瓜很留恋那辆旧车, 一直**舍不得**卖。
*ShaGua has grown very attached to the old car and would hate to sell it.*

舍得 **shěde** V to be willing to part with

舍命 **shěmìng** V to risk one's life

舍弃 **shěqì** V to give up, to abandon
傻瓜决定**舍弃**这份工作, 因为老板歧视工人。
*ShaGua decided to leave this job because the boss discriminated against the workers.*

舍身 **shěshēn** V to give one's life

舍利子 **shèlìzi** N Buddhist bone relics · MW 粒

舍下 **shèxià** N my house

### RELATED WORDS
取舍 520　校舍 802　宿舍 1480
施舍 1758

## 594 委　U+59D4　TM 9

**wěi** V·N·ADV to entrust; to appoint; to throw away, to discard; committee; committee member; indirectly; certainly

委派 **wěipài** V to appoint, to designate, to delegate

委曲 **wěiqū** ADJ·N winding (of a road, a river, etc.); ins and outs, whole story

委曲求全 **wěiqūqiúquán** EXP to stoop to compromise

委屈 **wěiqu** V·ADJ to feel wronged; to be misunderstood; unjustly treated, nursing a grievance
傻瓜工作比别人多, 可拿钱比别人少, 他有时感到有些**委屈**。 *Sometimes, ShaGua felt slightly wronged for getting less money than others despite working much longer.*

委任 **wěirèn** V to appoint

委托 **wěituō** V to entrust, to trust
傻瓜**委托**她把100美元存入银行。 *ShaGua trusted her to deposit a hundred dollars in the bank.*

委婉 **wěiwǎn** ADJ indirect (in speaking); rhythmic (of voice); tactful

委员 **wěiyuán** N committee member · MW 个、位、名

### RELATED WORDS
市委 332　县委 543　省委 860
原委 1273　党委 1626

## 595 争　U+4E89　TM 9　FM 丿

**zhēng** V·ADV to contend, to strive; to argue, to dispute, to debate; to be short of, to lack; how

争霸 **zhēngbà** V to struggle for power

争辩 **zhēngbiàn** V to argue, to debate

争吵 **zhēngchǎo** V to quarrel, to wrangle
傻瓜不愿意为钱的事跟太太**争吵**。
*ShaGua dislikes quarreling with Mrs. ShaGua over money.*

争斗 **zhēngdòu** V to fight, to struggle

争端 **zhēngduān** N dispute; conflict · MW 个、场

争夺 **zhēngduó** V to fight/scramble for

争光 **zhēngguāng** V to win honor for

争论 **zhēnglùn** V·N to argue, to debate; argument · MW 个、场
**争论**是不可避免的, 因为他俩都不喜欢对方。 *An argument was inevitable, because they disliked each other.*

争鸣 **zhēngmíng** V to contend

争气 **zhēngqì** V to try to win credit for (through hard work)

争取 **zhēngqǔ** V to strive/fight for
为**争取**一项合同, 他们展开了竞争。 *They competed with each other for a contract.*

争先 **zhēngxiān** V to try to be the first (to do)

争议 **zhēngyì** V·N to dispute; controversy · MW 个、项
这件事还有**争议**, 先别忙着下结论。 *There's no rush to arrive at a conclusion; this matter is still being debated.*

### RELATED WORDS
力争 59　斗争 71　只争朝夕 160
战争 1044　纷争 1102　竞争 1470
核战争 1026　与世无争 158

## 596 旬　U+65EC　TM 9　FM 丿

**xún** N (period of) ten days

上旬 **shàngxún** N first ten days of a month

下旬 **xiàxún** N last ten days of a month

草莓通常在六月**下旬**上市。*Strawberries usually come to market in late June.*

**中旬** zhōngxún　N　middle ten days of a month

公司每月**中旬**发工资。*The company pays its employees in the middle of each month.*

---

597　质　質　U+8D28　TM 9　FM 丿

zhì　N·ADJ·V　nature, character; quality; substance; pledge; hostage; pawn; simple, plain; to question, to ask

本质　*essence*

人质　*hostage*

朴质　*simple and unadorned*

**质变** zhìbiàn　N　qualitative change

**质地** zhìdì　N　texture

**质量** zhìliàng　N　quality (of a product)

保证**质量** *guarantee of quality*

**质朴** zhìpǔ　ADJ　simple, plain, unaffected

有些人认为傻瓜傻，其实傻瓜是**质朴**。*Some people think that ShaGua is dumb; actually, he is just unpretentious.*

**质问** zhìwèn　V　to question, to interrogate; to query

**质询** zhìxún　V　to question, to inquire; to ask for an explanation

欢迎**质询**产品的**质量**问题。*You are welcome to ask for an explanation about product quality.*

**质疑** zhìyí　V　to query, to call into question

**RELATED WORDS**

| | | |
|---|---|---|
| 本质 90 | 气质 185 | 体质 325 |
| 劣质 444 | 优质 447 | 性质 498 |
| 变质 653 | 实质 668 | 物质文明 883 |
| 物质 883 | 音质 907 | 特质 1094 |
| 品质 1220 | 资质 1335 | 素质 1378 |
| 流质 1493 | 蛋白质 1368 | |

---

598　条　條　U+6761　TM 9　FM 丿

tiáo　N·MW　twig; strip; [long, narrow piece]; item, article; order; [measure word for long, narrow objects (legs, trousers, cigarettes, boats, roads, rivers, etc.), for human lives, and for news items]

**条幅** tiáofú　N　wall scroll; banner · MW 张、条

**条件** tiáojiàn　N　condition; factor, requirement · MW 个

傻瓜做工作，往往都是无**条件**的。*ShaGua often works without conditions.*

**条款** tiáokuǎn　N　clause, article, provision · MW 个、项

**条理** tiáolǐ　N　order, arrangement; orderliness; method

傻瓜的创造性不强，但**条理**性很好。*ShaGua is not creative, but he is well organized.*

**条例** tiáolì　N　regulations, rules, ordinances · MW 个、套

**条令** tiáolìng　N　regulations · MW 个、套

**条目** tiáomù　N　clauses and subclauses (of a document); entry (in a dictionary) · MW 个

**条条框框** tiáotiáokuàngkuàng　N　rules and regulations · MW 个

**条文** tiáowén　N　article, clause · MW 个

**条纹** tiáowén　N　stripe, streak · MW 道

**条约** tiáoyuē　N　treaty, pact · MW 个

这是一个不平等**条约**。*This was an unfair treaty.*

**条子** tiáozi　N　short note; strip (of paper) · MW 张

**RELATED WORDS**

| | | |
|---|---|---|
| 欠条 105 | 头条新闻 128 | 无条件 139 |
| 金条 420 | 苗条 553 | 字条 664 |
| 油条 683 | 面条 721 | 封条 815 |
| 信条 869 | 线条 1105 | 教条 1424 |
| 假条 1586 | 路条 1785 | 够条件 1808 |
| 慢条斯理 1882 | 井井有条 60 | |

---

599　叁　U+53C1　TM 9　FM 丿

sān　NUM　three (capital form of the Chinese numeral)

---

600　参　參　U+53C2　TM 9　FM 丿

cān　V　to join, to participate in, to attend; to refer to, to consult

shēn　N　ginseng

**参观** cānguān　V　to tour

**参加** cānjiā　V　to join, to participate in, to attend

傻瓜不喜欢**参加**开幕式和闭幕式，但喜欢**参加**讨论。*ShaGua doesn't like to attend opening or closing ceremonies, but he likes to participate in discussions.*

**参见** cānjiàn　V　to refer to, to reference; to pay one's respects to

**600 参 cān/shēn** (continued)

参考 **cānkǎo** V·N to consult, to refer to; consultation; reference · MW 个

仅供参考 *for your information (FYI)*

参谋 **cānmóu** N·V adviser, consultant; staff officer; to give advice · MW 个、名

关于这个建议，请参谋参谋。 *Regarding this suggestion, please give your opinion.*

参议员 **cānyìyuán** N senator · MW 个、位、名

傻瓜认识一个参议员。 *ShaGua knows a senator.*

参议院 **cānyìyuàn** N senate · MW 个

参与 **cānyù** V to participate in

参赞 **cānzàn** N diplomatic officer, attaché · MW 个、名

参战 **cānzhàn** V to enter a war; to take part in a battle

参照 **cānzhào** V to act in accordance with; to consult, to refer to · MW 个

**RELATED WORD**

人参 4

---

**601** 乌 烏    U+4E4C    TM **9** FM 丿

**wū** N·ADJ crow; black; dark

乌干达 **Wūgāndá** N Uganda

乌龟 **wūguī** N tortoise, turtle; cuckold · MW 只

乌黑 **wūhēi** ADJ jet-black

傻太太的头发乌黑。 *ShaGua's hair is jet-black.*

乌亮 **wūliàng** ADJ glossy black

乌龙茶 **wūlóngchá** N oolong tea · MW 杯、壶、盒

傻瓜爱喝乌龙茶。 *ShaGua likes to drink oolong tea.*

乌七八糟 **wūqībāzāo** EXP in a horrible mess

乌纱帽 **wūshāmào** EXP official post · MW 顶

乌鸦 **wūyā** N crow · MW 只

乌云 **wūyún** N dark cloud; adverse situation · MW 片

---

**602** 卑    U+5351    TM **9** FM 丿

**bēi** ADJ inferior; of low rank/character; low-lying; humble, modest

卑鄙 **bēibǐ** ADJ dirty; contemptible

卑贱 **bēijiàn** ADJ lowly

卑贱行为 *base behavior*

卑劣 **bēiliè** ADJ dirty; despicable

卑劣勾当 *dirty deal*

卑怯 **bēiqiè** ADJ mean and cowardly

**RELATED WORD**

自卑 305

---

**603** 向    U+5411    TM **9** FM 丿

**xiàng** N·V·ADV·PREP direction; to face, to turn toward; to favor, to side with; against; approaching, near, close to; always; to, toward

向背 **xiàngbèi** V to support or oppose

市民的向背是傻瓜做决策的原则。 *The voices of the city's residents govern ShaGua's actions.*

向导 **xiàngdǎo** N guide · MW 个、名

向后 **xiànghòu** PREP backward

向前 **xiàngqián** PREP·V forward, onward, ahead; to forge ahead

向上 **xiàngshàng** V to make one's way forward; to make progress

向外 **xiàngwài** PREP outward

向往 **xiàngwǎng** V to yearn for, to look forward to

许多人向往美国梦。 *Many people yearn for the American Dream.*

向下 **xiàngxià** PREP downward

向右 **xiàngyòu** PREP toward the right

向右看，你会看到美丽的大海。 *Turn right and you will see the beautiful ocean.*

向着 **xiàngzhe** V to face, to turn toward

向左 **xiàngzuǒ** PREP toward the left

**RELATED WORDS**

| | | |
|---|---|---|
| 一向 1 | 反向 111 | 双向 146 |
| 去向 157 | 风向 194 | 方向 220 |
| 走向 265 | 志向 528 | 定向 666 |
| 单向 672 | 面向 721 | 转向 1111 |
| 偏向 1587 | 朝向 1686 | 航向 1717 |
| 横向 1775 | 欣欣向荣 634 | 晕头转向 1385 |

---

**604** 身    U+8EAB    TM **9** FM 丿

**shēn** N·MW body; life; incarnation; oneself; [measure word for clothes]

身边 **shēnbiān** N nearby, at one's side

身不由己 **shēnbùyóujǐ** EXP involuntarily

作为市长，傻瓜很多时候是**身不由己**的。
*As mayor, ShaGua is often thrown into situations not of his own making.*

**身材 shēncái** N figure; stature, build · MW 个

**身长 shēncháng** N height (of a person)

**身段 shēnduàn** N figure (of a woman); posture/pose (of a dancer) · MW 个

**身份 shēnfen** N identity; status, position · MW 个

傻瓜现在的**身份**，既是移民又是市长。
*ShaGua's current status is as an immigrant but also as a mayor.*

**身高 shēngāo** N height (of a person)

**身故 shēngù** V to die

**身后 shēnhòu** N back/rear (of a person); after one's death

**身价 shēnjià** N social status; one's property/assets

**身教 shēnjiào** V to teach by example

傻瓜不善言辞，**身教**就成了重要手段。
*ShaGua isn't good at speaking, preferring instead to teach by example.*

**身躯 shēnqū** N body; stature · MW 个

**身上 shēnshang** N on one's body/person, with one

**身世 shēnshì** N life experience; ancestry · MW 个

傻瓜的**身世**，知道的人不太多。 *As for ShaGua's ancestry, not many people know about it.*

**身手 shēnshǒu** N skill; talent; agility · MW 个

**身受 shēnshòu** V to experience personally

**身体 shēntǐ** N body; health · MW 个

**身心 shēnxīn** N body and mind; mental and physical

**身孕 shēnyùn** N pregnancy · MW 个

**RELATED WORDS**

---

**605　夸** 誇　U+5938　TM **9** FM ノ

**kuā** V to exaggerate, to overstate; to praise

**夸大 kuādà** V to exaggerate, to overstate

**夸大其词 kuādàqící** V to exaggerate

傻瓜不喜欢**夸大其词**。 *ShaGua doesn't appreciate exaggeration.*

**夸奖 kuājiǎng** V to praise, to commend, to compliment

**夸口 kuākǒu** V to boast, to talk big

**夸夸其谈 kuākuāqítán** EXP to hype, to indulge in exaggeration

傻瓜也不喜欢**夸夸其谈**。 *ShaGua also doesn't like to indulge in exaggeration.*

**夸耀 kuāyào** V to flaunt, to brag about, to show off

**夸张 kuāzhāng** ADJ·V·N exaggerated; to overstate; hyperbole

**RELATED WORD**

---

**606　奈**　U+5948　TM **9** FM ノ

**nài** V·ADJ cannot; helpless; powerless

**奈何 nàihé** V to do (something) to (someone); to be able to handle; to no avail

你能**奈何**她吗？ *Will you be able to handle her?*

**RELATED WORDS**

---

**607　奋** 奮　U+594B　TM **9** FM ノ

**fèn** V to exert oneself; to lift, to raise

**奋斗 fèndòu** V to struggle, to fight; to strive

对傻瓜来说，除了**奋斗**，还是**奋斗**。 *For ShaGua, with respect to working hard, his only answer is to work harder.*

**奋发 fènfā** V to exert oneself, to work hard

**奋勇 fènyǒng** V to act bravely, to summon up one's courage

**奋战 fènzhàn** V to fight bravely

**RELATED WORDS**

## 608 奏　U+594F　TM 9　FM 丿

**zòu** V to play (music); to perform; to achieve, to produce

**奏捷 zòujié** V to win a battle

**奏凯 zòukǎi** V to win a victory

**奏效 zòuxiào** V to prove effective, to have an effect

教育的过程是长期的, 不可能立即**奏效**。
*Education is a long process; its effectiveness can't be immediately proven.*

**奏乐 zòuyuè** V to play music

### RELATED WORDS

| | | |
|---|---|---|
| 齐奏 221 | 节奏 275 | 伴奏 321 |
| 吹奏 559 | 独奏 1095 | 演奏 1821 |
| 三重奏 9 | 四重奏 271 | |

## 609 直　U+76F4　TM 9　FM 丿

**zhí** ADJ·V·ADV straight; vertical; perpendicular; honest, upstanding, frank; to straighten (up), to stretch; directly, straight, simply; continuously

**直播 zhíbō** V to broadcast live

**直达 zhídá** V to go nonstop to

从辛辛那提到北京没有**直达**班机。 *There aren't any direct flights from Cincinnati to Beijing.*

**直到 zhídào** V until, up to

**直观 zhíguān** ADJ directly perceivable

**直接 zhíjiē** ADJ direct, straight; immediate

**直截了当 zhíjiéliǎodàng** ADJ straightforward, blunt

傻瓜喜欢**直截了当**地说话。 *ShaGua likes to speak plainly.*

**直觉 zhíjué** N intuition · MW 个

**直属 zhíshǔ** V·ADJ to be directly subordinate to; directly under

**直率 zhíshuài** ADJ frank, candid

傻瓜是一个很**直率**的人。 *ShaGua is a very frank person.*

**直线 zhíxiàn** N·ADJ straight line; sharp (rise/fall) · MW 条

**直性子 zhíxìngzi** N straightforward/forthright person · MW 个

**直言 zhíyán** V to speak bluntly

**直至 zhízhì** V until, up to

### RELATED WORDS

| | | |
|---|---|---|
| 一直 1 | 正直 76 | 垂直 430 |
| 刚直 591 | 笔直 1278 | 率直 1469 |
| 简直 1796 | 青云直上 740 | 勇往直前 1371 |

## 610 层　層　U+5C42　TM 9　FM 丿

**céng** N·MW floor, story; tier, level; layer; step (in a sequence); [measure word for layers (floors, coats of paint, etc.)]

**层层 céngcéng** ADJ layer upon layer

**层次 céngcì** N arrangement of ideas (in writing, speech); administrative level · MW 个

**层面 céngmiàn** N scope, range; level, surface; aspect · MW 个

### RELATED WORDS

| | | |
|---|---|---|
| 下层 10 | 上层 14 | 云层 80 |
| 中层 86 | 双层 146 | 分层 173 |
| 夹层 197 | 多层 431 | 表层 527 |
| 阶层 590 | 单层 672 | 地层 772 |
| 底层 916 | 基层 991 | 断层 1260 |

## 611 成　U+6210　TM 9　FM 丿

**chéng** V·N·ADJ·MW to accomplish, to succeed (in); to become, to turn into; to ripen; to agree; to approve; achievement; result; fully developed/grown, mature, established; capable, able; [measure word for one tenth]

完**成**任务 *to successfully complete the task*

变**成**一个市长 *to become mayor*

**成**全他人 *to help others accomplish*

这怎么**成**? *How can this be all right?*

傻瓜从来没有**成**就感。 *ShaGua has never felt a sense of accomplishment.*

**成本 chéngběn** N cost (of production, etc.)

**成材 chéngcái** V to become useful; to be a talented person

傻瓜最大的希望是孩子们能**成材**。 *ShaGua's biggest hope is that his children grow up to be talented people.*

**成堆 chéngduī** V to stack, to make a pile

傻瓜每天都要处理**成堆**的文件。 *ShaGua has to deal with piles of documents every day.*

**成对 chéngduì** V to pair

**成分 chéngfen** N composition; identity; status · MW 个

**成规 chéngguī** N conventions, rules · MW 套

**成果 chéngguǒ** N result; achievement · MW 个

**成绩** chéngjì  N  grade, score; success, achievement · MW 个

傻瓜的大儿子学习很努力, 但**成绩**不太好。 *ShaGua's older son studies very hard, but his grades are not very good.*

**成见** chéngjiàn  N  preconceived notion; prejudice · MW 个

傻瓜对任何人都没有**成见**。*ShaGua doesn't have any preconceived notions about anyone.*

**成交** chéngjiāo  V  to strike a bargain, to clinch a deal

**成就** chéngjiù  N·V  success, achievement; to achieve · MW 个

**成立** chénglì  V  to establish, to set up

**成名** chéngmíng  V  to become famous

**成年** chéngnián  V·ADV  to mature, to grow up; to be an adult; all year; year after year

**成批** chéngpī  ADV  group by group

**成熟** chéngshú  V·ADJ  to mature; ripe, mature, full-grown

这人还不**成熟**。*This fellow is not yet mature.*

**成套** chéngtào  V  to form a complete set, to complement one another

**成天** chéngtiān  ADV  all day long; all the time

**成天**叫唤 *to complain all the time*

**成文** chéngwén  N  existing writing

**成问题** chéngwèntí  V  to be a problem

**成效** chéngxiào  N  result, effect · MW 个

**成形** chéngxíng  V  to take shape

**成因** chéngyīn  N  origin; cause, factor · MW 个

**成语** chéngyǔ  N  idiom; proverb · MW 个

傻瓜爱用比喻, 但不太会用**成语**。 *ShaGua loves to use metaphors, but doesn't know how to use idioms very well.*

**成员** chéngyuán  N  member · MW 个、名

**成长** chéngzhǎng  V  to grow up, to mature

**RELATED WORDS**

| | | |
|---|---|---|
| 八成 6 | 不成 24 | 未成年 88 |
| 生成 107 | 汇成 234 | 形成 257 |
| 收成 282 | 打成一片 289 | 合成 296 |
| 自成一家 305 | 老成 375 | 求成 376 |
| 性成熟 498 | 达成 505 | 责成 525 |
| 变成 653 | 看成 841 | 促成 866 |
| 完成 909 | 构成 1028 | 组成 1106 |
| 集成 1267 | 结成 1291 | 速成 1514 |
| 造成 1515 | 落成 1547 | 既成事实 1572 |
| 留成 1582 | 赞成 1969 | 久病成医 45 |
| 生产成本 107 | 产品成本 219 | 马到成功 247 |

| | | |
|---|---|---|
| 弄假成真 251 | 恼羞成怒 931 | 望子成龙 1622 |
| 墨守成规 1843 | | |

**612  甩**   U+7529   TM **9**  FM ノ

**shuǎi**  V  to throw, to toss, to fling; to swing; to leave behind, to throw off

**甩卖** shuǎimài  V  to sell at a reduced price

**甩手** shuǎishǒu  V  to swing one's arms

**613  希**   U+5E0C   TM **9**  FM ノ

**xī**  V·ADJ·N  to hope, to wish; rare, scarce; infrequent; hope, wish

**希伯来** Xībólái  N  Hebrew

**希罕** xīhan  ADJ  rare

这东西我见过, 没什么可**希罕**的。*I've seen this before; it's nothing special.*

**希腊** Xīlà  N  Greece

**希望** xīwàng  V·N  to hope, to dream; to expect; hope, wish · MW 个

总是要有**希望**, 人才能活下去。*A person must have some kind of hope or else he couldn't go on living.*

**614  册**   U+518C   TM **9**  FM ノ

**cè**  N·MW  book, volume; booklet; imperial order to confer a title; [measure word for books]

**册页** cèyè  N  album of paintings/calligraphy · MW 本

**册子** cèzi  N  book, volume; booklet; brochure · MW 本

**RELATED WORDS**

| | | |
|---|---|---|
| 小册子 61 | 手册 104 | 史册 186 |
| 另册 385 | 名册 426 | 注册 496 |
| 表册 527 | 画册 719 | |

**615  我**   U+6211   TM **9**  FM ノ

**wǒ**  PRON  I, me

**我们** wǒmen  PRON  we, us

**RELATED WORDS**

| | | |
|---|---|---|
| 自我 305 | 忘我 655 | 敌我 1127 |

## 616 他    U+4ED6    TM **9**   FM ノ

**tā** PRON he, him; other, another; something/somewhere else

他方 **tāfāng** N the other party

他妈的 **tāmāde** EXP damn it!

他们 **tāmen** PRON they, them

他人 **tārén** PRON others, other people; someone else

为**他人**着想是傻瓜的特点。 *Thinking about others is one of ShaGua's qualities.*

他日 **tārì** N some other time

他乡 **tāxiāng** N place far away from home

**RELATED WORD**

其他 379

## 617 你    U+4F60    TM **9**   FM ノ

**nǐ** PRON you (singular)

你好 **nǐhǎo** V how do you do?; hello, hi

你们 **nǐmen** PRON you (plural)

你自己 **nǐzìjǐ** PRON yourself

## 618 低    U+4F4E    TM **9**   FM ノ

**dī** ADJ·V low; below average; junior, low (in grade/rank); to bend (down), to droop; to lower

低产 **dīchǎn** ADJ low-yield

低潮 **dīcháo** N low tide/ebb · MW 个

低沉 **dīchén** ADJ low, depressed; overcast, gloomy; deep (of a voice)

傻瓜的嗓音很好, 很**低沉**, 但他不爱唱歌。 *ShaGua's singing voice is very deep and very good, but he doesn't like to sing.*

低估 **dīgū** V to underestimate, to underrate

许多人**低估**了傻瓜。 *Many people underestimate ShaGua.*

低级 **dījí** ADJ vulgar; elementary, junior

低贱 **dījiàn** ADJ lowly, humble

低廉 **dīlián** ADJ cheap, inexpensive

低劣 **dīliè** ADJ inferior (in quality), shoddy

低落 **dīluò** ADJ depressed, downcast

低能 **dīnéng** ADJ low energy; mental deficiency; incompetent

如果你真的了解傻瓜, 你会发现他并不**低能**。 *If you really knew ShaGua, you would find that he is not incompetent.*

低年级 **dīniánjí** N primary grades

低三下四 **dīsānxiàsì** EXP lowly, humble

低温 **dīwēn** N low temperature

低息 **dīxī** N low interest

低压 **dīyā** N low pressure

低音 **dīyīn** N bass · MW 个

低于 **dīyú** V to be lower than

实际上, 他的成绩**低于**别人。 *In fact, his grade was lower than the others.*

低脂 **dīzhī** N low fat

傻瓜太太爱喝全脂牛奶, 但傻瓜喜欢**低脂**的。 *Mrs. ShaGua loves to drink 2% milk, but ShaGua likes to drink low-fat milk.*

**RELATED WORDS**

| | | |
|---|---|---|
| 贬低 814 | 降低 1416 | 减低 1487 |
| 最低价 1541 | 最低 1541 | 高低 1611 |

## 619 何    U+4F55    TM **9**   FM ノ

**hé** QPRON who; what; where; when; why; how

何必 **hébì** ADV there is no need; why

你又不去中国, **何必**要学中文? *You aren't going to China, so why are you studying Chinese?*

何不 **hébù** ADV why not

何尝 **hécháng** ADV how can it be that; never

何等 **héděng** ADV·QPRON what kind; what; how

学中文**何等**难啊! *What a struggle it is to study Chinese!*

何妨 **héfáng** ADV why not; might as well

何苦 **hékǔ** ADV why bother; is it worth the trouble to

何况 **hékuàng** CONJ much less, let alone

何去何从 **héqùhécóng** EXP what course to follow

何在 **hézài** V where is (someone/something)?; does (someone/something) exist?

良心**何在**? *Where is your conscience?*

何止 **hézhǐ** V to have far more than

**RELATED WORDS**

| | | |
|---|---|---|
| 几何 115 | 任何 211 | 为何 223 |
| 如何 464 | 奈何 606 | 谈何容易 1356 |
| 无可奈何 139 | 无论如何 139 | |

## 620 仰 U+4EF0 TM 9 FM ノ

**yǎng** V to face upward, to look up; to admire, to respect; to look up to; to rely/depend on; respectfully

**仰望 yǎngwàng** V to look up; to respectfully seek guidance/help from

**仰卧 yǎngwò** V to lie on one's back

**仰泳 yǎngyǒng** N backstroke
傻瓜只会狗刨式, 根本不会**仰泳**。*ShaGua only knows the doggy paddle and doesn't know a thing about the backstroke.*

**仰仗 yǎngzhàng** V to rely on

### RELATED WORDS
久仰 45　　　信仰 869　　　敬仰 1689

## 621 佣 傭 U+4F63 TM 9 FM ノ

**yōng** V·N to hire (a laborer); servant

**yòng** N commission

**佣工 yōnggōng** V to hire (a laborer)

**佣金 yòngjīn** N commission · MW 笔

### RELATED WORD
雇佣 1474

## 622 佰 U+4F70 TM 9 FM ノ

**bǎi** NUM hundred (capital form of the Chinese numeral)

## 623 使 U+4F7F TM 9 FM ノ

**shǐ** V·N·CONJ to use; to apply; to make, to cause, to have (someone) do (something); to send (as an envoy); envoy; if, supposing

指**使** *to tell (someone) to do (something)*

**使**我感动 *it moved me*

纵**使** *even if*

**使不得 shǐbude** V cannot be used; must not

**使出 shǐchū** V to use; to exert

**使得 shǐde** V to make, to cause; can be used; workable, doable

**使馆 shǐguǎn** N embassy · MW 个、间

**使唤 shǐhuan** V to order around, to be bossy

傻瓜不知道怎么**使唤**别人。*ShaGua doesn't even know how to be bossy.*

**使节 shǐjié** N (diplomatic) envoy · MW 个、名

**使劲 shǐjìn** V to exert oneself
别人问傻瓜怎么学中文。他说:"**使劲**学呗!" *Someone asked ShaGua, "How should I study Chinese?" He said, "Buckle down and work hard!"*

**使女 shǐnǚ** N maid · MW 个、名

**使用 shǐyòng** V to use, to employ; to apply

**使者 shǐzhě** N envoy, emissary, messenger · MW 个、名

### RELATED WORDS
大使 20　　　天使 25　　　支使 92
行使 327　　　务使 429　　　好使 627
差使 673　　　祈使句 717　　　促使 866
信使 869　　　致使 982　　　特使 1094
迫使 1186　　　指使 1397　　　假使 1586

## 624 侍 U+4F8D TM 9 FM ノ

**shì** V to wait on, to serve

**侍从 shìcóng** N attendant; retinue · MW 个、名

**侍奉 shìfèng** V to wait on, to look after

**侍女 shìnǚ** N maid · MW 个、名

**侍卫 shìwèi** N·V bodyguard; to protect, to guard · MW 个、名

**侍者 shìzhě** N servant; waiter · MW 个、名
傻瓜当过饭馆儿的**侍者**。*ShaGua was once a waiter in a restaurant.*

### RELATED WORD
服侍 1457

## 625 依 U+4F9D TM 9 FM ノ

**yī** V·CONJ to depend/rely on; to comply with; according to, in light of, judging by

**依此类推 yīcǐlèituī** EXP to use an analogy to make a deduction
读书是愉快的, **依此类推**, 学习也是愉快的。*Reading books brings pleasure, so by deduction, studying should also bring pleasure.*

**依次 yīcì** ADV successively, in proper order

**依从 yīcóng** V to comply with, to yield to
每次傻瓜与太太吵架, 最后总是傻瓜**依从**太太。*Whenever ShaGua and Mrs. ShaGua quarrel, he eventually yields to his wife without fail.*

**依法 yīfǎ** ADV according to law

**625** 依 yī (continued)

依附 yīfù  V  to be attached to

依旧 yījiù  V·ADV  to remain the same; still

依据 yījù  V·N·PREP  to be based on; precedent; according to, on the basis of, judging by ·  MW  个
傻瓜办事总是要有**依据**。 *ShaGua always relies on precedent when conducting business.*

依靠 yīkào  V·N  to rely/depend on; support, backing; dependency ·  MW  个

依赖 yīlài  V  to rely/depend on
谁也不**依赖**谁。 *No one can rely on anyone else.*

依恋 yīliàn  V  to regret leaving, to be reluctant to leave

依然 yīrán  V·ADV  still, as before

依顺 yīshùn  V  to be obedient

依仗 yīzhàng  V  to count on

依照 yīzhào  V·PREP  to be based on; according to, in accordance with

**RELATED WORD**
相依 805

---

**626** 径 徑   U+5F84   TM **9** FM 丿

jìng  N·ADV  path, track, way; means; diameter; directly

径迹 jìngjì  N  path, track ·  MW  条、道

径赛 jìngsài  N  track event/meet ·  MW  场

**RELATED WORDS**

| | | |
|---|---|---|
| 口径 42 | 半径 127 | 门径 130 |
| 田径 147 | 途径 1511 | |

---

**627** 好   U+597D   TM **9** FM 丿

hǎo  ADJ·ADV·V  good, fine; kind, friendly; in order to, so that; very, quite a lot; such, so; to get well, to be in good health; to be easy to

太**好**啦! *Great!*
他看起来**好**极了。 *He looks very healthy.*
吃**好**了? *Have you finished (your food)?*
中文太**好**学了! *Chinese is very easy to learn.*
还是复习吧，明天**好**考试。 *Let's review the textbooks so we can take the exam tomorrow.*
**好**久不见。 *Long time, no see.*

hào  V  to like, to love, to be fond of
他**好**吃。 *He loves to eat.*

好吃 hǎochī  ADJ  tasty, delicious; good to eat
他好吃(hàochī)那些好吃(hǎochī)的东西。 *He loves to eat delicious foods.*

好处 hǎochu  N  benefit, advantage ·  MW  个

好歹 hǎodǎi  N·ADV  good and bad, right and wrong; no matter what, anyhow, in any case
别说了，傻瓜**好歹**也是一个市长。 *Quiet! No matter what, ShaGua is still the mayor.*

好端端 hǎoduānduān  EXP  in perfectly good condition
**好端端**的，哭什么? *Everything is all right; why cry?*

好多 hǎoduō  NUM·QPRON  a lot of, many; how much/many

好感 hǎogǎn  N  favorable impression, attraction ·  MW  个
和傻瓜接触过的人都会对他有**好感**。 *Those who have dealt with ShaGua before have a good impression of him.*

好过 hǎoguò  ADJ·V  having an easy time; to feel well

好汉 hǎohàn  N  brave man; hero ·  MW  个、位、名

好话 hǎohuà  N  word of praise/apology/ persuasion; words to beg for mercy ·  MW  堆、串

好家伙 hǎojiāhuo  EXP  good lord!

好看 hǎokàn  ADJ  good-looking; interesting; embarrassed
她很**好看**。 *She is a good-looking girl.*
有她**好看**的。 *She's in for it!*

好评 hǎopíng  N  favorable comment; high praise ·  MW  个

好球 hǎoqiú  N  good shot (sports) ·  MW  个

好人 hǎorén  N  good person ·  MW  个、位、名
**好人**难做，但傻瓜是一个十足的**好人**。 *It is difficult to be a nice person, but ShaGua is a very nice person.*

好日子 hǎorìzi  N  good days; happy life ·  MW  个

好使 hǎoshǐ  V  to work well

好事 hǎoshì  N  good deed ·  MW  件、桩

好手 hǎoshǒu  N  expert, professional ·  MW  个、位、名

好似 hǎosì  V  to seem, to be like
傻瓜**好似**心事重重。 *ShaGua seems to be burdened by worries.*

好听 hǎotīng  ADJ  pleasant to hear

好戏 hǎoxì  N  good play; really interesting part ·  MW  场

好些 **hǎoxiē** NUM many, quite a lot

好些人不喜欢用字典。 *Many people don't like to use dictionaries.*

好心 **hǎoxīn** N·ADJ kindness, good intention(s); kind

好心不一定有好报。 *Kindness may not necessarily be rewarded.*

他真好心。 *He is very kind.*

好意 **hǎoyì** N kindness, good intention(s)

好在 **hǎozài** ADV fortunately, luckily

好转 **hǎozhuǎn** V to improve, to take a turn for the better

好客 **hàokè** ADJ hospitable, friendly

傻瓜不善言辞，但很好客。 *ShaGua doesn't speak well, but he is very friendly.*

好奇 **hàoqí** ADJ curious, inquisitive

好强 **hàoqiáng** ADJ ambitious, eager to do well in everything

好胜 **hàoshèng** ADJ competitive, having a desire to excel

傻瓜不太爱说话，但很好胜。 *ShaGua doesn't like to talk, but he has a desire to excel.*

傻瓜有三"好"：好客、好胜、好强。 *ShaGua has three traits: friendliness, a desire to win, and an eagerness to excel.*

好恶 **hàowù** N likes and dislikes · MW 个

好战 **hàozhàn** ADJ warlike

**RELATED WORDS**

| | | |
|---|---|---|
| 大好 20 | 不好意思 24 | 太好了 53 |
| 正好 76 | 友好 110 | 只好 160 |
| 弄好 251 | 也好 273 | 更好 355 |
| 讨好 500 | 刚好 591 | 你好 617 |
| 和好 644 | 良好 656 | 美好 671 |
| 问好 678 | 完好 909 | 恰好 930 |
| 要好 969 | 爱好 1264 | 喜好 1531 |
| 最好 1541 | 您好 1692 | 搞好 1904 |
| 洁身自好 940 | | |

---

**628** 妒 　　U+5992　　TM **9** FM 丿

**dù** V to be jealous of, to envy

妒嫉 **dùjì** V to be jealous of

妒忌 **dùjì** V to be jealous of

傻瓜也会妒忌人，有时还挺厉害。 *ShaGua is also jealous of others, and sometimes he is very jealous.*

**RELATED WORD**

忌妒 1197

---

**629** 妓 　　U+5993　　TM **9** FM 丿

**jì** N prostitute

妓女 **jìnǚ** N prostitute, streetwalker · MW 个、名

妓院 **jìyuàn** N brothel · MW 家、间

**RELATED WORD**

艺妓 274

---

**630** 妞 　　U+599E　　TM **9** FM 丿

**niū** N young girl

---

**631** 妹 　　U+59B9　　TM **9** FM 丿

**mèi** N younger sister; younger female cousin; young girl

妹夫 **mèifu** N brother-in-law · MW 个

妹妹 **mèimei** N younger sister · MW 个

你妹妹很漂亮。 *Your younger sister is very pretty.*

**RELATED WORDS**

| | | |
|---|---|---|
| 师妹 396 | 姐妹 880 | 弟妹 1152 |
| 堂妹 1486 | | |

---

**632** 姓 　　U+59D3　　TM **9** FM 丿

**xìng** N·V surname, family name, last name

姓名 **xìngmíng** N full name, family name and given name · MW 个

姓氏 **xìngshì** N surname · MW 个

**RELATED WORDS**

| | | |
|---|---|---|
| 百姓 242 | 种姓 893 | 老百姓 375 |

---

**633** 牲 　　U+7272　　TM **9** FM 丿

**shēng** N domestic animal

牲畜 **shēngchù** N livestock · MW 个

牲口 **shēngkou** N beast of burden, draft animal · MW 个

**RELATED WORD**

牺牲 1283

## 634 欣   U+6B23   TM 9 FM 丿

**xīn** ADJ glad, happy, joyful

**欣赏 xīnshǎng** V to enjoy, to appreciate; to admire

傻瓜不会**欣赏**音乐。*ShaGua doesn't know how to enjoy music.*

**欣悉 xīnxī** V to be glad to learn

**欣喜 xīnxǐ** ADJ glad, happy, joyful

**欣欣向荣 xīnxīnxiàngróng** EXP flourishing, prosperous

现在中国的经济**欣欣向荣**。*Today, the Chinese economy is booming.*

## 635 拜   U+62DC   TM 9 FM 丿

**bài** V·ADV to pay a visit; to pay respect; to enter into a relationship; to congratulate; with respectful formality

**拜别 bàibié** V to take leave of

**拜访 bàifǎng** V to visit, to call on

傻瓜不爱说话，但很爱**拜访**朋友。*ShaGua doesn't like to talk, but he loves to visit his friends.*

**拜会 bàihuì** V to pay an official visit (often of a diplomat)

**拜见 bàijiàn** V to pay a formal visit

**拜年 bàinián** V to make a New Year's call; to wish (someone) a happy new year

**拜寿 bàishòu** V to congratulate an elderly person on his/her birthday

**拜托 bàituō** V to request a favor

朋友**拜托**傻瓜的事远远多过傻瓜**拜托**朋友的事。*Doing favors for his friends is a much more common occurrence than ShaGua requesting a favor of them.*

**RELATED WORDS**

甘拜下风 95    回拜 391    礼拜 503
跪拜 1945

## 636 邦   U+90A6   TM 9 FM 丿

**bāng** N nation, state, country

**邦交 bāngjiāo** N diplomatic relations

**邦联 bānglián** N confederation · MW 个

**RELATED WORDS**

友邦 110    邻邦 1123    联邦 1206

## 637 丝 絲   U+4E1D   TM 9 FM 丿

**sī** N·MW silk; thread; [threadlike]; very small amount; [measure word for a very small specific weight (0.0005 grams) and for a tiny amount]

**丝绸 sīchóu** N silk; silk cloth · MW 匹、段、块

**丝绸之路 sīchóuzhīlù** N Silk Road

**丝带 sīdài** N silk ribbon · MW 条

**丝瓜 sīguā** N luffa (a gourd) · MW 条

**丝毫 sīháo** ADJ a bit; in the slightest amount/degree, in the least

**丝绒 sīróng** N velvet; velour, plush · MW 匹、段、块

**丝竹 sīzhú** N traditional music · MW 曲

**RELATED WORDS**

肉丝 437    真丝 1075    铁丝 1126
钢丝 1299

## 638 幼   U+5E7C   TM 9 FM 丿

**yòu** ADJ·N young, underage; child, infant; children, the young

**幼儿 yòu'ér** N small child, infant · MW 个、名

**幼年 yòunián** N childhood; infancy

傻瓜的**幼年**很艰辛。*ShaGua's childhood was very hard.*

**幼稚 yòuzhì** ADJ young; childish, naive

**幼子 yòuzǐ** N youngest son · MW 个、名

傻瓜的**幼子**还读小学。*ShaGua's younger son is still in elementary school.*

**RELATED WORD**

妇幼 465

## 639 纱 紗   U+7EB1   TM 9 FM 丿

**shā** N yarn; gauze; sheer, curtain fabric

**纱布 shābù** N gauze · MW 块

**纱橱 shāchú** N screened cupboard · MW 个

**纱窗 shāchuāng** N screened window · MW 个

**纱线 shāxiàn** N yarn · MW 条、团

**RELATED WORDS**

乌纱帽 601    棉纱 1670

## 640 纹 紋 U+7EB9 TM 9 FM 丿

**wén** N line; vein; grain (in wood); pattern; design on silk fabric

**纹理 wénlǐ** N vein; grain (in wood) · MW 条、道

**纹路 wénlù** N line · MW 条、道

### RELATED WORDS

| | | |
|---|---|---|
| 花纹 549 | 条纹 598 | 指纹 1397 |
| 裂纹 1643 | 掌纹 1734 | |

## 641 秋 鞦 U+79CB TM 9 FM 丿

**qiū** N autumn, fall; year; (troubled) time; harvest

**秋波 qiūbō** N bright eyes of a woman · MW 个

**秋后 qiūhòu** N after the autumn harvest

**秋季 qiūjì** N autumn, fall · MW 个

**秋千 qiūqiān** N swing · MW 个

**秋天 qiūtiān** N autumn, fall

傻瓜不喜欢**秋天**, 因为落叶使人伤感。
*ShaGua doesn't like fall, because falling leaves make him sad.*

### RELATED WORDS

| | |
|---|---|
| 中秋 86 | 立秋 125 |

## 642 科 U+79D1 TM 9 FM 丿

**kē** N (academic) discipline/branch; (administrative) section/department; branch of medicine; imperial examination; academic training; law

理**科** *the sciences*

内**科** *internal medicine*

销售**科** *sales division/department*

猫**科**动物 *animals of the cat family*

金**科**玉律 *Golden Rule*

**科班 kēbān** N professional training

**科幻故事 kēhuàngùshi** N science fiction, sci-fi · MW 个

**科技 kējì** N science and technology · MW 项

**科目 kēmù** N (academic) subject/course; heading in an accounting ledger · MW 个、门、项

你今年选什么**科目**? *What courses have you taken this year?*

**科学 kēxué** N·ADJ science; scientific; rational · MW 门

**科学院 kēxuéyuàn** N academy of science · MW 间、家

**科研 kēyán** V·N to perform scientific research; scientific research · MW 项

**科长 kēzhǎng** N department head, section chief · MW 个、名

傻瓜连**科长**都没当过, 就当了市长。
*ShaGua had not even served as a department head before, but now he is mayor.*

### RELATED WORDS

| | | |
|---|---|---|
| 儿科 43 | 文科 70 | 本科 90 |
| 牙科 143 | 耳科 145 | 内科 191 |
| 外科 218 | 产科 219 | 医科 389 |
| 妇科 465 | 学科 1155 | 理科 1200 |
| 教科书 1424 | 眼科 1570 | 社会科学 504 |

## 643 秒 U+79D2 TM 9 FM 丿

**miǎo** MW [measure word for seconds (a unit of time)]

**秒表 miǎobiǎo** N stopwatch · MW 个

**秒针 miǎozhēn** N second hand (of a clock, a watch) · MW 枚

### RELATED WORD

毫秒 1721

## 644 和 U+548C TM 9 FM 丿

**hé** V·N·ADJ·CONJ·PREP to join in singing; to compose a poem in reply; to mix, to blend; tie (sports); total, sum; peace; reconciliation; Japan; gentle, mild, moderate; harmonious, on friendly terms; peaceful; and; together with

我**和**你 *you and I*

平**和** *mild*

家庭**和**睦 *harmonious family*

讲**和** *to negotiate peace*

**和**棋 *draw in chess*

**huó** V to mix with liquid

**和**面 *to knead dough*

**和蔼 hé'ǎi** ADJ kind, nice, affable

傻瓜看起来不够**和蔼**。 *ShaGua doesn't look very amiable.*

**和风 héfēng** N soft/gentle/light breeze · MW 阵

**和服 héfú** N kimono · MW 件、套

## 644 和 hé/huó (continued)

和好 **héhǎo** [V] to reconcile (with); to be at peace (with)

傻瓜和太太吵架, 两个月后才**和好**。 *ShaGua and Mrs. ShaGua had an argument and reconciled after two months.*

和缓 **héhuǎn** [ADJ·V] gentle, mild; to relax, to ease up

和解 **héjiě** [V] to reconcile; to settle differences, to compromise

和局 **héjú** [N] tied game · [MW] 个

和睦 **hémù** [ADJ] harmonious, amicable

和平 **hépíng** [N·ADJ] peace; mild, not severe

人类需要**和平**。 *Human beings need their peace.*

和气 **héqi** [ADJ·N] polite; friendly, kind, gentle · [MW] 团

和尚 **héshang** [N] Buddhist monk · [MW] 个、位、名

和事佬 **héshìlǎo** [N] peacemaker, mediator · [MW] 个、名

傻瓜很爱做**和事佬**。 *ShaGua loves to be a peacemaker.*

和谈 **hétán** [N] peace talks · [MW] 次

### RELATED WORDS

| | |
|---|---|
| 平和 78 | 共和 164 |
| 议和 350 | 求和 376 |
| 言和 478 | 讲和 501 |
| 拌和 574 | 祥和 1192 |
| 温和 1627 | 暖和 1675 |
| 饱和 1703 | 缓和 1708 |
| 调和 1749 | 随和 1911 |
| 欠饱和 105 | 中华人民共和国 86 |

---

## 645 所    U+6240    TM **9** FM 丿

**suǒ** [N·MW] place, location; office, bureau; [measure word for buildings (houses, schools, etc.)]

所得 **suǒdé** [N] income; earnings; gains · [MW] 笔

所得税 **suǒdéshuì** [N] income tax · [MW] 笔

所属 **suǒshǔ** [N] subordinate; affiliation

所谓 **suǒwèi** [ADJ] so-called

**所谓**的 "傻瓜", 其实不傻。 *The one called "ShaGua" is not actually dumb.*

所以 **suǒyǐ** [CONJ] so, therefore

因为他学习不努力, **所以**成绩不好。 *He has not studied hard, so his grades are not good.*

---

所以然 **suǒyǐrán** [N] reason why

所有 **suǒyǒu** [ADJ·V·N] all; to own, to have; possession(s)

傻瓜打算承担**所有**的责任。 *ShaGua plans to take all of the blame.*

所在 **suǒzài** [N] place, location

### RELATED WORDS

| | | |
|---|---|---|
| 力所能及 59 | 无所不能 139 | 无所不知 139 |
| 无所谓 139 | 无所用心 139 | 无所作为 139 |
| 众所周知 175 | 在所不辞 188 | 在所不惜 188 |
| 在所难免 188 | 住所 324 | 有所 439 |
| 诊所 709 | 场所 773 | 厕所 846 |
| 前所未闻 1329 | 哨所 1410 | 不出所料 24 |
| 女厕所 57 | 代办所 208 | 交易所 222 |
| 托儿所 563 | 派出所 945 | 公共厕所 103 |

---

## 646 斩 斬    U+65A9    TM **9** FM 丿

**zhǎn** [V] to chop, to cut; to kill; to blackmail, to extort

斩草除根 **zhǎncǎochúgēn** [EXP] to destroy root and branch (LIT to cut the weeds and dig up the roots)

斩钉截铁 **zhǎndīngjiétiě** [EXP] resolutely and decisively, categorically

傻瓜**斩钉截铁**地说："我不傻, 我只不过是诚实。" *ShaGua said decisively, "I am not stupid. I am just honest."*

斩首 **zhǎnshǒu** [V] to behead

---

## 647 知    U+77E5    TM **9** FM 丿

**zhī** [V·N] to know, to be aware of; to inform, to notify; to administer, to be in charge of; knowledge

无所不**知** *to know everything*

通**知** *to inform*

**知**县 *county magistrate*

求**知** *seeking knowledge*

知道 **zhīdào** [V] to know, to be aware of

知己 **zhījǐ** [N·ADJ] bosom/intimate friend; intimate · [MW] 个、位

傻瓜没有红颜**知己**。 *ShaGua doesn't have an intimate female friend.*

知交 **zhījiāo** [N] intimate friend

知觉 **zhījué** [N] perception, sense; consciousness

知了 **zhīliǎo** [N] cicada · [MW] 只

知名 **zhīmíng** ADJ famous, well-known

作为市长，傻瓜在市里很**知名**。*As mayor, ShaGua is famous in the city.*

知情 **zhīqíng** V to know the facts, to be in the know

知识 **zhīshi** N knowledge · MW 种

知识分子 **zhīshifènzǐ** N intellectual; intelligentsia · MW 个、位、名

傻瓜是市长，但不是**知识分子**。*ShaGua is the mayor, but he's not an intellectual.*

知晓 **zhīxiǎo** V to know; to understand

傻瓜**知晓**市里发生的每一件事情。*ShaGua knows everything that has happened in the city.*

知心 **zhīxīn** ADJ intimate, heart-to-heart

傻瓜有一些**知心**朋友。*ShaGua has some intimate friends.*

知音 **zhīyīn** N intimate friend · MW 个、位

知足 **zhīzú** ADJ content with one's lot/situation

人一**知足**，就不会再有进取心。*As long as one is content with one's lot, it is easy to lose motivation to keep forging ahead.*

**RELATED WORDS**

| | | |
|---|---|---|
| 不知不觉 24 | 未知 88 | 未知数 88 |
| 无知 139 | 认知 239 | 求知 376 |
| 先知 422 | 须知 875 | 明知 1035 |
| 真知 1075 | 通知 1757 | 通知书 1757 |
| 未卜先知 88 | 到货通知 737 | |

---

**648 肚** U+809A TM **9** FM ノ

**dù** N belly, stomach, abdomen

肚子 **dǔzi** N stomach · MW 个

**RELATED WORDS**

| | | |
|---|---|---|
| 大肚子 20 | 拉肚子 573 | 鱼肚 843 |

---

**649 肛** U+809B TM **9** FM ノ

**gāng** N anus

肛门 **gāngmén** N anus, anal opening · MW 个

---

**650 肝** U+809D TM **9** FM ノ

**gān** N liver

肝癌 **gān'ái** N liver cancer

---

肝胆 **gāndǎn** N courage; sincerity (LIT liver and gall) · MW 副

傻瓜有一些**肝胆**相照的朋友。*ShaGua has some very trusted and sincere friends.*

肝功能 **gāngōngnéng** N liver function

肝火 **gānhuǒ** N anger, irascibility

肝炎 **gānyán** N hepatitis

肝脏 **gānzàng** N liver · MW 副

傻瓜怀疑自己的**肝脏**有问题。*ShaGua believes he may have liver problems.*

**RELATED WORDS**

| | | |
|---|---|---|
| 心肝 232 | 鱼肝油 843 | 猪肝 1445 |

---

**651 钉** 釘 U+9489 TM **9** FM ノ

**dīng** V·N to follow closely; to gaze at; to nail, to hammer (a nail) into; nail

**dìng** V to nail; to sew on

钉子 **dīngzi** N nail; snag, matter that is difficult to handle; informant, secret agent · MW 枚、个

他在**钉**(dìng)**钉子**(dīngzi)。*He is hammering nails.*

**RELATED WORDS**

| | | |
|---|---|---|
| 斩钉截铁 646 | 碰钉子 1526 | 眼中钉 1570 |

---

**652 充** U+5145 TM **9** FM 丶

**chōng** ADJ·V full; sufficient; to fill (up), to stuff; to assume office; to act/serve as; to disguise as, to pretend to be, to pass off as

冒**充** *to pretend to be*

充当 **chōngdāng** V to serve/act as, to play the role of

实在没有人的话，傻瓜也能**充当**一下足球裁判。*If necessary, ShaGua could serve as a soccer referee.*

充电 **chōngdiàn** V to charge (up)

充分 **chōngfèn** ADJ enough, sufficient; full

充饥 **chōngjī** V to satisfy one's hunger

实在饿了，傻瓜吃两个汉堡包也能**充饥**。*When ShaGua is very hungry, he can eat two hamburgers and be full.*

充满 **chōngmǎn** V to be full of, to be filled with, to be brimming with

充沛 **chōngpèi** ADJ plentiful, abundant

傻瓜有**充沛**的精力。*ShaGua has plenty of energy.*

**652** 充 **chōng** (continued)

充其量 **chōngqíliàng** [ADV] at most, at best; at the worst

傻瓜市长敢做敢当, 即使失败了, **充其量**也就是再回公司当工人。 *As mayor, ShaGua dares to act and bear the responsibilities of his actions. At the worst, he would have to return to his old company as an ordinary worker.*

充气 **chōngqì** [V] to inflate

充数 **chōngshù** [V] to fill places up to a given number, to fill a quota; to function as a stopgap

充血 **chōngxuè** [V] to congest

充裕 **chōngyù** [ADJ] plentiful, abundant

充足 **chōngzú** [ADJ] sufficient, adequate; plentiful

**RELATED WORDS**

| | | |
|---|---|---|
| 扩充 291 | 补充 508 | 冒充 989 |
| 填充 1550 | 假充 1586 | |

---

| | | | | | |
|---|---|---|---|---|---|
| **653** | 变 | 變 | U+53D8 | TM **9** FM 丶 | |

**biàn** [V] to become, to change (into); to transform; to be flexible; to sell off

变成 **biànchéng** [V] to become, to change/turn (into)

要**变成**一个好学生, 不是一朝一夕的事。 *It isn't easy to suddenly transform into a good student.*

变动 **biàndòng** [V] to change, to alter, to modify

变更 **biàngēng** [V] to change, to alter, to modify

变卦 **biànguà** [V] to break an agreement, to go back on one's word

对自己的承诺, 傻瓜从不**变卦**。 *ShaGua has never gone back on his promises.*

变化 **biànhuà** [V] to change, to vary, to transform

变换 **biànhuàn** [V] to vary, to alternate, to convert

变幻 **biànhuàn** [V] to fluctuate, to change irregularly

变迁 **biànqiān** [V] to change (of a situation); changes

变通 **biàntōng** [V] to be flexible; to accommodate/adapt to circumstances

为什么有人说傻瓜傻, 因为他不会**变通**。 *The reason some people think ShaGua is stupid is because he is inflexible.*

变相 **biànxiàng** [ADJ] disguised; covert

变形 **biànxíng** [V] to change (of a shape, a pattern); to be out of shape

变质 **biànzhì** [V] to go bad, to deteriorate; to become morally degenerate

这家商店出售**变质**的牛奶。 *This store sells sour milk.*

**RELATED WORDS**

| | | |
|---|---|---|
| 千变万化 19 | 不变 24 | 可变 243 |
| 应变 334 | 多变 431 | 改变 516 |
| 政变 517 | 质变 597 | 突变 913 |
| 叛变 960 | 转变 1111 | 衰变 1313 |
| 量变 1544 | 演变 1821 | 激变 1955 |

---

| | | | | |
|---|---|---|---|---|
| **654** | 夜 | U+591C | TM **9** FM 丶 | |

**yè** [N] night, evening

夜班 **yèbān** [N] night shift · [MW] 个

因为没人愿上**夜班**, 公司就老安排傻瓜上**夜班**。 *The company always arranged for ShaGua to work the night shift, because nobody else would do it.*

夜半 **yèbàn** [N] midnight

夜长梦多 **yèchángmèngduō** [EXP] a long delay causes lots of complications

夜场 **yèchǎng** [N] evening show · [MW] 个

夜车 **yèchē** [N] night train; turning night into day · [MW] 班、趟

出差时, 为省旅馆费傻瓜常坐**夜车**。 *When ShaGua is on business trips, he often takes a night train to save on hotel bills.*

傻瓜爱开**夜车**。 *ShaGua likes to work deep into the night.*

夜间 **yèjiān** [N] at night, nighttime

夜景 **yèjǐng** [N] night scene, view by night · [MW] 个

坐**夜车**不仅可以节省旅馆费, 还可以欣赏**夜景**。 *On the night train, one can not only save money, but also enjoy the night scenery.*

夜里 **yèlǐ** [N] at night, nighttime

夜礼服 **yèlǐfú** [N] evening dress · [MW] 件、套

夜猫子 **yèmāozi** [N] owl; night owl (person) · [MW] 只

夜晚 **yèwǎn** [N] night, evening · [MW] 个

夜校 **yèxiào** [N] night school · [MW] 间、家

傻瓜上**夜校**学习。 *ShaGua goes to night school.*

夜总会 **yèzǒnghuì** [N] nightclub · [MW] 间、家

傻瓜上夜校, 但上不上**夜总会**? 没人知道。 *ShaGua goes to night school, but nobody knows if he goes to nightclubs.*

**RELATED WORDS**

| | | |
|---|---|---|
| 午夜 48 | 子夜 83 | 日夜 96 |
| 半夜 127 | 年夜 182 | 过夜 712 |
| 连夜 958 | 隔夜 1910 | 下半夜 10 |
| 深更半夜 1345 | | |

## 655 忘

U+5FD8　TM **9** FM 丶

**wàng** [V] to forget

**忘掉 wàngdiào** [V] to forget

许多人想**忘掉**过去, 但他们无法做到。
*Many people wish to forget their past, but they can't.*

**忘怀 wànghuái** [V] to forget

**忘记 wàngjì** [V] to forget

**忘年交 wàngniánjiāo** [N] friendship between generations · [MW] 个

傻瓜的几个**忘年交**都是车行的小工。
*ShaGua has several friends much younger than he who all work as assistants in car garages.*

**忘却 wàngquè** [V] to forget

**忘我 wàngwǒ** [V] to be selfless

**忘形 wàngxíng** [V] to lose one's bearings

得意不**忘形**, 许多有成就的人都做不到。
*Many successful people are unable to remain modest with success.*

### RELATED WORDS

难忘　974　　　　健忘　1589
遗忘　1829　　　　念念不忘　1054

## 656 良

U+826F　TM **9** FM 丶

**liáng** [ADJ·ADV] good, fine; kindhearted; very; much

**良材 liángcái** [N] able person (LIT good timber) · [MW] 个、位

**良策 liángcè** [N] good idea/plan · [MW] 个

傻瓜的**良策**基本都来自基层生活的感受。
*All of ShaGua's good ideas basically come from his simple proletarian intuition.*

**良好 liánghǎo** [ADJ] good, fine; well

**良机 liángjī** [N] good opportunity · [MW] 个

**良机**只是为准备好的人准备的。
*Good opportunities come to those who are prepared.*

**良师益友 liángshīyìyǒu** [EXP] mentor (LIT good teacher and helpful friend) · [MW] 个、位

**良心 liángxīn** [N] conscience

傻瓜说: "我什么都没有, 只有**良心**。"
*ShaGua said, "I have nothing but my conscience."*

**良性 liángxìng** [ADJ] positive (in effect); with satisfactory results; benign

**良缘 liángyuán** [N] good match; good karma · [MW] 个

### RELATED WORDS

不良　24　　　　优良　447
改良　516　　　　没良心　938
善良　1483　　　　坐失良机　318

## 657 启　啓

U+542F　TM **9** FM 丶

**qǐ** [V·N] to open; to guide, to enlighten, to inform; to start, to initiate; note, letter

**启程 qǐchéng** [V] to set out, to begin a journey

**启齿 qǐchǐ** [V] to start to talk about

难以**启齿** *difficulty discussing (something)*

**启发 qǐfā** [V] to arouse, to inspire; to enlighten, to explain

**启发**式教学是一种重要而有效的方法。
*Drawing someone out is an important and effective teaching method.*

**启封 qǐfēng** [V] to unseal

**启航 qǐháng** [V] to set sail

**启蒙 qǐméng** [V] to educate (the young); to impart (basic knowledge), to initiate; to enlighten

**启明星 Qǐmíngxīng** [N] Venus, Morning Star

**启示 qǐshì** [N·V] inspiration; revelation; to enlighten · [MW] 个

移民当选市长的现象给我们什么**启示**?
*What inspiration can people gain from the phenomenon of an immigrant becoming a mayor?*

**启事 qǐshì** [N] notice, announcement · [MW] 则

**启用 qǐyòng** [V] to start using, to put to use

## 658 店

U+5E97　TM **9** FM 丶

**diàn** [N] shop, store; inn, hotel

**店面 diànmiàn** [N] storefront · [MW] 个

**店铺 diànpù** [N] shop, store · [MW] 个、家

**店员 diànyuán** [N] shop assistant, salesperson · [MW] 个、名

**店主 diànzhǔ** [N] shop/store owner · [MW] 个、名

### RELATED WORDS

书店　264　　　　布店　309
肉店　437　　　　饭店　891
客店　1316　　　　酒店　1339
药店　1392　　　　旅店　1518
商店　1612　　　　粮店　1759

**659** **庙** 廟   U+5E99   TM **9** FM ヽ

**miào** N temple; shrine; imperial court

庙会 **miàohuì** N temple fair · MW 个

庙宇 **miàoyǔ** N temple; court · MW 座

**RELATED WORDS**

孔庙 370     宗庙 910

**660** **府**   U+5E9C   TM **9** FM ヽ

**fǔ** N government office; official residence; mansion; prefecture; archive

府绸 **fǔchóu** N poplin (cotton cloth) · MW 段、匹

府上 **fǔshàng** N hometown, native place

**RELATED WORD**

政府 517

**661** **疗** 療   U+7597   TM **9** FM ヽ

**liáo** V to treat, to cure

疗程 **liáochéng** N course of treatment · MW 个

疗法 **liáofǎ** N therapy, treatment · MW 个、种

疗效 **liáoxiào** N treatment efficacy/effect · MW 个

尽管许多西方人怀疑针灸, 但针灸确实有**疗效**。 *Even though many Westerners doubt the efficacy of acupuncture, it has actual curative effects.*

疗养 **liáoyǎng** V to recuperate, to convalesce

**RELATED WORDS**

医疗 389     诊疗 709     治疗 935
针刺疗法 477

**662** **疟** 瘧   U+759F   TM **9** FM ヽ

**nüè** N malaria

疟疾 **nüèjí** N malaria · MW 种

疟蚊 **nüèwén** N malaria mosquito · MW 只、群

**663** **写** 寫   U+5199   TM **9** FM ヽ

**xiě** V to write, to compose; to describe, to depict; to draw, to sketch

写稿 **xiěgǎo** V to write a draft; to write (for a publication)

傻瓜不会**写稿**。 *ShaGua is unable to write for newspapers.*

写生 **xiěshēng** V to paint from life/nature

写真 **xiězhēn** N-V portrait; to describe accurately · MW 份

写字 **xiězì** V to write characters

学中文就得学**写字**。 *To study Chinese, one must learn how to write characters.*

写字台 **xiězìtái** N (writing) desk · MW 张

尽管傻瓜不会**写稿**, 但他的**写字台**很大。 *Although ShaGua is unable to write for newspapers, his desk is very big.*

写作 **xiězuò** V to write, to compose

**RELATED WORDS**

大写 20     手写体 104     书写 264
书写体 264     抄写 405     听写 414
改写 516     拼写 794     复写 1059
特写 1094     描写 1407     速写 1514
填写 1550     简写 1796     编写 1866
缩写 1927

**664** **字**   U+5B57   TM **9** FM ヽ

**zì** N character; script, handwriting style, calligraphy; printing type; receipt, written pledge

字典 **zìdiǎn** N dictionary · MW 本、部

大多数学中文的美国学生不用**字典**。 *Most American students who study Chinese do not use a dictionary.*

字调 **zìdiào** N tone of a Chinese character · MW 个

**字调**是决定一个学汉语的外国人说话是否怪腔怪调的关键。 *The tones of Chinese characters are the reason nonnatives who study Chinese have funny accents.*

字符 **zìfú** N character; letter · MW 个

字号 **zìhào** N font/point size; store/shop name · MW 家、个

字画 **zìhuà** N calligraphy and painting · MW 幅、张

字汇 **zìhuì** N glossary · MW 本

字迹 **zìjī** N handwriting · MW 个、种

傻瓜的**字迹**几乎没人认得出来。 *Hardly anyone could recognize ShaGua's handwriting.*

字句 **zìjù** N (in) writing; words and expressions

字谜 **zìmí** N character/word puzzle · MW 个

**字母** zìmǔ [N] letter (of the alphabet) · [MW] 个、组

**字幕** zìmù [N] caption; subtitle · [MW] 行

**字体** zìtǐ [N] typeface; font; calligraphic style · [MW] 种、类

**字条** zìtiáo [N] brief note · [MW] 张

**字帖** zìtiē [N] copybook · [MW] 本

傻瓜照**字帖**练过字，但他的写字还是太难看。
*ShaGua once used copybooks to practice his calligraphy, but his handwriting is still horrible.*

**字眼** zìyǎn [N] wording; diction · [MW] 个

**字样** zìyàng [N] printed word; model (for a written character) · [MW] 种

**RELATED WORDS**

---

**665 宅**    U+5B85    TM **9** FM 丶

zhái [N] residence, home, house

**宅门** zháimén [N] gate of a mansion · [MW] 个

**宅院** zháiyuàn [N] house with a courtyard · [MW] 个、间

**RELATED WORD**

---

**666 定**    U+5B9A    TM **9** FM 丶

dìng [V·ADJ·ADV] to decide, to set; to fasten, to secure; to settle; to subscribe to, to order, to book; calm; settled, established, arranged; certainly, surely, definitely

固**定** *to fix*

决**定** *to decide*

预**定** *to preorder*

稳**定** *stable*

制**定** *to formulate*

一**定** *certainly*

约**定** *schedule*

**定案** dìng'àn [V·N] to reach a verdict; final decision · [MW] 个

这件事情还没有**定案**。*This is not yet a final decision.*

**定调** dìngdiào [V] to set the tone

**定额** dìng'é [N·V] quota; to have a fixed amount · [MW] 个、份

**定稿** dìnggǎo [N·V] final version; to finalize a manuscript · [MW] 份

**定购** dìnggòu [V] to order (merchandise, etc.)

**定婚** dìnghūn [V] to get engaged

傻瓜和傻瓜太太没有**定婚**就结婚。
*ShaGua and Mrs. ShaGua got married without getting engaged.*

**定货** dìnghuò [V] to order merchandise/products

**定价** dìngjià [N·V] fixed price; to set a price · [MW] 个

**定金** dìngjīn [N] deposit, money up front · [MW] 笔

**定居** dìngjū [V] to settle (down)

**定量** dìngliàng [N·V] ration; fixed quantity; to ration; to quantify

**定名** dìngmíng [V] to name, to choose a name for

**定期** dìngqī [ADJ·V] on a regular basis/schedule; to set a date

傻瓜**定期**向市民报告工作。*ShaGua periodically reports his work to the residents of the city.*

**定然** dìngrán [ADV] certainly

**定时** dìngshí [V·N] at regular intervals; fixed time

**定位** dìngwèi [V·N] to locate, to orient; to evaluate, to appraise

任何人都需要给自己一个恰当的**定位**。
*All people need to find their proper niche in society.*

**定息** dìngxī [N] fixed rate of interest

**定向** dìngxiàng [V] to orient; to determine the direction

**定型** dìngxíng [V] to finalize a design; to fall into a pattern

**定性** dìngxìng [V] to determine (the nature of)

**定义** dìngyì [N·V] definition; to define · [MW] 个

**定语** dìngyǔ [N] attribute · [MW] 个

**定员** dìngyuán [V·N] to have a fixed complement (of staff, etc.); staff(ing) level

**定做** dìngzuò [V] to have (something) made to order

傻瓜的身材有些与众不同，因此他的西服都得**定做**。*ShaGua's build is slightly different from others, so he has to have his suits tailored.*

**666** 定 **dìng** (continued)

**RELATED WORDS**

| | | |
|---|---|---|
| 一定 1 | 不定 24 | 平定 78 |
| 未定 88 | 立定 125 | 内定 191 |
| 认定 239 | 必定 338 | 决定 340 |
| 议定书 350 | 否定 362 | 坚定 381 |
| 协定 397 | 估定 456 | 划定 476 |
| 安定 487 | 注定 496 | 判定 507 |
| 法定 686 | 评定 706 | 肯定 744 |
| 固定 760 | 约定 876 | 审定 911 |
| 特定 1094 | 规定 1098 | 制定 1130 |
| 断定 1260 | 指定 1397 | 限定 1417 |
| 暂定 1522 | 预定 1528 | 裁定 1535 |
| 既定 1572 | 假定 1586 | 锁定 1608 |
| 说定 1631 | 确定 1762 | 镇定 1872 |
| 稳定 1925 | 额定 1958 | 说不定 1631 |

---

**667** 宝 寶    U+5B9D     TM **9** FM ﹨

**bǎo** N·ADJ treasure; jewel; dice; precious

宝宝 **bǎobao** N darling · MW 个

宝贝 **bǎobèi** N treasure; [endearment for a young child] · MW 个

宝贵 **bǎoguì** ADJ valuable; rare

宝剑 **bǎojiàn** N sword · MW 把、柄

宝库 **bǎokù** N treasury; treasure trove · MW 间、座

宝石 **bǎoshí** N precious stone, gem · MW 颗、粒

宝塔 **bǎotǎ** N pagoda · MW 座

宝物 **bǎowù** N treasure · MW 件

宝藏 **bǎozàng** N precious minerals / mineral deposits · MW 批

**RELATED WORDS**

| | | |
|---|---|---|
| 元宝 138 | 至宝 244 | 红宝石 474 |
| 国宝 542 | 财宝 588 | 法宝 686 |
| 珠宝 729 | 活宝 941 | 聚宝盆 1642 |
| 文房四宝 70 | 无价之宝 139 | |

---

**668** 实 實    U+5B9E     TM **9** FM ﹨

**shí** N·ADJ true, actual; solid, substantial; reality, fact; fruit

实干 **shígàn** V to take action

傻瓜是一个**实干**的人。*ShaGua is a person who always takes action.*

实话 **shíhuà** N truth · MW 句

实惠 **shíhuì** N·ADJ real/tangible benefit; solid, tangible

实际 **shíjì** N·ADJ reality; real, actual; practical

实价 **shíjià** N actual price · MW 个

实践 **shíjiàn** N·V practice, to put into practice; to fulfill, to carry out (a promise, etc.)

傻瓜没有文化，但**实践**经验非常丰富。*ShaGua is not educated, but he has many valuable practical experiences.*

实据 **shíjù** N substantial evidence · MW 个

实况 **shíkuàng** N actual situation; live (of a broadcast, etc.)

傻瓜最喜欢看**实况**转播的全国橄榄球决赛。*ShaGua really likes watching the Super Bowl live.*

实力 **shílì** N strength; power

实例 **shílì** N concrete example · MW 个

实情 **shíqíng** N actual situation, true state of affairs

实权 **shíquán** N real power

实施 **shíshī** V to implement, to carry out; to apply

实事 **shíshì** N fact; deed; practical matter; actual thing · MW 件

实事求是 **shíshìqiúshì** EXP to be realistic/practical (LIT to seek the truth from facts)

傻瓜市长的做人原则是**实事求是**。*As mayor, ShaGua's guiding principle is to be pragmatic.*

实物 **shíwù** N real/material object · MW 件

实习 **shíxí** V to practice; to do fieldwork, internship

实现 **shíxiàn** V to achieve, to bring about; to come true

实效 **shíxiào** N actual effect; substantial results

实行 **shíxíng** V to put into practice, to carry out

实验 **shíyàn** V·N to experiment; to test; experimental/laboratory work

实用 **shíyòng** V·ADJ practical; applied

傻瓜是一个强调**实用**的人。*ShaGua is a person who emphasizes pragmatism.*

实质 **shízhì** N substance; essence

实足 **shízú** ADJ full; solid

**RELATED WORDS**

| | | |
|---|---|---|
| 史实 186 | 壮实 238 | 切实 277 |
| 扎实 288 | 老实 375 | 其实 379 |
| 坚实 381 | 名实 426 | 如实 464 |
| 果实 544 | 证实 705 | 忠实 743 |
| 现实 975 | 事实上 987 | 事实 987 |
| 核实 1026 | 真实 1075 | 纪实 1101 |
| 厚实 1272 | 结实 1291 | 诚实 1499 |
| 落实 1547 | 确实 1762 | 老老实实 375 |
| 真凭实据 1075 | 脚踏实地 1804 | 既成事实 1572 |

## 669 空    U+7A7A    TM 9 FM 丶

**kōng** ADJ·N·ADV  empty, hollow; sky, air; for nothing

**kòng** V·ADJ·N  to leave empty/blank; vacant, unoccupied; free time

**空荡荡 kōngdàngdàng** ADJ  (absolutely) empty; deserted; void

**空洞 kōngdòng** N·ADJ  cavity; empty
傻瓜的演讲确实不怎么样, 但绝不**空洞**。 *ShaGua's speeches are really poor, but they're not vacuous.*

**空防 kōngfáng** V  air force (LIT to defend the skies)

**空腹 kōngfù** V  to fast (before a blood test, etc.) (LIT to empty the stomach)

**空话 kōnghuà** N  idle talk; gossip · MW 篇
傻瓜最讨厌说**空话**。 *What ShaGua hates most is idle chitchat.*

**空欢喜 kōnghuānxǐ** EXP  to rejoice too soon

**空架子 kōngjiàzi** EXP  mere skeleton

**空间 kōngjiān** N  space, room; sky, open air · MW 个

**空降 kōngjiàng** V  to parachute

**空军 kōngjūn** N  air force; airman · MW 个、位、名

**空旷 kōngkuàng** ADJ  open, spacious

**空气 kōngqì** N  air; atmosphere

**空前 kōngqián** V  to be unprecedented/unmatched; as never before

**空谈 kōngtán** V·N  to indulge in idle talk; chitchat
傻瓜厌恶**空谈**。 *ShaGua detests indulging in idle chitchat.*

**空投 kōngtóu** V  to drop supplies by air

**空想 kōngxiǎng** N·V  fantasy, daydream; to fantasize, to daydream · MW 个

**空心 kōngxīn** V·ADJ  to be/become hollow; hollow

**空虚 kōngxū** ADJ  empty, hollow, void

**空运 kōngyùn** V  to ship/transport by air; air transport

**空载 kōngzài** V  to be unloaded (of a vehicle)

**空中 kōngzhōng** N·ADJ  in the sky/air; aerial

**空白 kòngbái** N  gap, blank space · MW 片
今天考口语时, 我的脑袋突然一片**空白**。 *When I took the oral quiz, my mind suddenly went blank.*

**空地 kòngdì** N  vacant lot; open space · MW 块

**空额 kòng'é** N  (job) vacancy · MW 个

**空格 kònggé** N  blank space; empty square (indicating an illegible character) · MW 个、行

**空隙 kòngxì** N  gap, empty space; interval, unoccupied time; chance, opening · MW 个、道

**空闲 kòngxián** ADJ·N  free; free/leisure time

**空子 kòngzi** N  space, room; gap; opening, time; chance, opportunity · MW 个
有些人就是喜欢钻**空子**。 *Some people just like to look for loopholes.*

### RELATED WORDS

| | | |
|---|---|---|
| 天空 25 | 太空 53 | 半空中 127 |
| 亏空 137 | 目空一切 151 | 扑空 168 |
| 司空见惯 357 | 闲空 679 | 抽空 788 |
| 放空气 964 | 凭空 1060 | 真空 1075 |
| 趁空 1257 | 填空 1550 | 挖空心思 1551 |
| 留空 1582 | 偷空 1591 | 高空 1611 |
| 晴空 1674 | 航空 1717 | 航空信 1717 |
| 陆海空 1043 | | |

## 670 养 養    U+517B    TM 9 FM 丶

**yǎng** V·ADJ  to support, to provide for; to raise/keep (animals); to grow (plants); to give birth to; to cultivate; to foster; to maintain, to keep in good repair, to look after; to form, to acquire; to rest, to recuperate; adoptive, foster

养儿子 *to give birth to a son*
培养 *to cultivate*
静养 *to rest quietly, to recuperate*

**养病 yǎngbìng** V  to recuperate, to convalesce
他正在**养病**。 *He is recuperating.*

**养护 yǎnghù** V  to maintain, to look after

**养活 yǎnghuó** V  to give birth to; to support; to raise
刚到美国时, 傻瓜要**养活**一家人, 很不容易。 *When ShaGua first arrived in America, it was difficult for him to support his family.*

**养鸡场 yǎngjīchǎng** N  poultry farm · MW 个、家

**养家 yǎngjiā** V  to support one's family

**养老 yǎnglǎo** V  to care for the elderly; to live out one's life in retirement

**养路 yǎnglù** V  to maintain a road/railway

**养母 yǎngmǔ** N  adoptive mother · MW 个、位

**养神 yǎngshén** V  to rest; to meditate
傻瓜常常爱闭目**养神**。 *ShaGua often likes to close his eyes and meditate.*

**养生 yǎngshēng** V  to keep fit, to stay healthy

**养鱼 yǎngyú** V  to raise fish

**养鱼场 yǎngyúchǎng** N  fish farm · MW 个、家

**670 养 yǎng** (continued)

养育 **yǎngyù** 〔V〕 to bring up; to foster

养殖 **yǎngzhí** 〔V〕 to breed; to cultivate (on an aquatic farm)

养猪场 **yǎngzhūchǎng** 〔N〕 hog farm · 〔MW〕 个、家

傻瓜曾经在**养猪场**干活。*ShaGua once worked on a hog farm.*

**RELATED WORDS**

| | | |
|---|---|---|
| 休养 213 | 收养 282 | 扶养 404 |
| 供养 459 | 护养 569 | 疗养 661 |
| 保养 868 | 修养 870 | 给养 1292 |
| 教养 1424 | 笼养 1436 | 饲养 1447 |
| 领养 1465 | 营养 1546 | 喂养 1667 |
| 调养 1749 | 娇生惯养 882 | |

---

**671 美**    U+7F8E    TM **9** FM 丶

**měi** 〔ADJ·N·V〕 beautiful, pretty; satisfactory, good; gratifying; good deed; beautiful object; America; U.S.A.; to beautify; to feel smug; to be pleased (with oneself)

美女 *pretty girl*

完美 *perfect*

美滋滋 *very self-satisfied*

北美 *North America*

美差 **měichāi** 〔N〕 easy/cushy job · 〔MW〕 个、份

美钞 **měichāo** 〔N〕 U.S. currency · 〔MW〕 笔

美称 **měichēng** 〔N〕 honorary title; good name · 〔MW〕 个

美德 **měidé** 〔N〕 virtue, moral excellence · 〔MW〕 个

美感 **měigǎn** 〔N〕 sense of beauty, aesthetic feeling; beautiful impression · 〔MW〕 种

美工 **měigōng** 〔N〕 artist; designer · 〔MW〕 个、名

美观 **měiguān** 〔ADJ〕 beautiful

美国 **Měiguó** 〔N〕 United States of America

美国英语 **Měiguóyīngyǔ** 〔N〕 American English (language)

美好 **měihǎo** 〔ADJ〕 desirable; beautiful; wonderful

现实生活并不像人们想象的那样**美好**。*Real life isn't as wonderful as people imagine.*

美化 **měihuà** 〔V〕 to beautify; to glorify

美丽 **měilì** 〔ADJ〕 beautiful, pretty

这套服装使她更**美丽**了。*The dress makes her look even more beautiful.*

美满 **měimǎn** 〔ADJ〕 perfectly satisfactory; blissful

美梦 **měimèng** 〔N〕 sweet dream · 〔MW〕 个

美妙 **měimiào** 〔ADJ〕 marvelous, wonderful, splendid

她**美妙**的歌声把他们迷住了。*Her marvelous voice fascinated them.*

美人 **měirén** 〔N〕 beautiful woman, beauty · 〔MW〕 个、位、名

美容 **měiróng** 〔V〕 to beautify one's face; to improve one's appearance

美术 **měishù** 〔N〕 fine arts; art; painting

美味 **měiwèi** 〔N〕 delicacy; delicious food

美元 **měiyuán** 〔N〕 (U.S.) dollar · 〔MW〕 块、个

美中不足 **měizhōngbùzú** 〔EXP〕 small blemish/imperfection

美洲 **Měizhōu** 〔N〕 America

**RELATED WORDS**

| | | |
|---|---|---|
| 甘美 95 | 作美 326 | 优美 447 |
| 审美 911 | 南美 986 | 肥美 1459 |
| 健美 1589 | 精美 1832 | 赞美 1969 |
| 真善美 1075 | 十全十美 3 | |

---

**672 单 單**    U+5355    TM **9** FM 丶

**dān** 〔ADJ·ADV·N〕 one, single; odd (number); alone, solitary, by oneself, on one's own; small in number; unlined (of clothing); thin; weak; only; list; sheet; bill

单薄 **dānbó** 〔ADJ〕 thin (of clothing); frail, weak (of a human)

傻瓜的小儿子身体有点**单薄**。*ShaGua's younger son is frail.*

单层 **dāncéng** 〔N〕 single layer; one story

单程 **dānchéng** 〔N〕 one-way

纽约到北京的**单程**机票要600美元。*A one-way ticket from New York to Beijing is $600.*

单纯 **dānchún** 〔ADJ〕 pure, uncomplicated, simple

单词 **dāncí** 〔N〕 word · 〔MW〕 个、组

单单 **dāndān** 〔ADV〕 only, alone

每天**单单**是背单词就得花30分钟。*Just memorizing vocabulary will take 30 minutes a day.*

单调 **dāndiào** 〔ADJ〕 drab; humdrum, monotonous

单独 **dāndú** 〔ADV〕 alone, by oneself, solely; singly

单干 **dāngàn** 〔V〕 to work on one's own

单号 **dānhào** 〔N〕 odd number (of tickets, seats, etc.)

单价 **dānjià** 〔N〕 unit price · 〔MW〕 个

单据 **dānjù** 〔N〕 receipt; invoice, bill · 〔MW〕 张

傻瓜出差, 常常丢失**单**据。 *ShaGua often loses his receipts when he is on business trips.*

**单人** dānrén　N　single person

**单身** dānshēn　N　unmarried/single person · MW 个、位、名

这人都快40了, 还是个**单身**。 *This man is almost 40, but he's still single.*

**单数** dānshù　N　odd number; singular

**单位** dānwèi　N　unit (of measurement); work unit · MW 个

**单向** dānxiàng　N　one-way

**单一** dānyī　ADJ　single, sole; monotonous

**单元** dānyuán　N　unit (of instructional materials); residential unit · MW 个

### RELATED WORDS

| | | |
|---|---|---|
| 床单 333 | 订单 347 | 名单 426 |
| 存单 438 | 传单 452 | 账单 812 |
| 每单位 837 | 保单 868 | 孤单 978 |
| 菜单 1001 | 凭单 1060 | 货单 1061 |
| 清单 1495 | 被单 1517 | 提单 1554 |
| 简单 1796 | 简单化 1796 | 购货单 1253 |
| 黑名单 1389 | 装箱单 1476 | 祸不单行 1754 |

---

### 673　差　U+5DEE　TM 9 FM 丶

**chā**　N　difference; deviation; mistake

**chà**　V·ADJ　to differ from; to be short of; of poor quality; bad; wrong

**chāi**　V·N　to send (on an errand), to dispatch; errand; job

**差别** chābié　N　difference · MW 个

都十几年了, 傻瓜和过去还是没有什么**差别**。 *More than ten years have passed, and ShaGua looks no different.*

**差错** chācuò　N　mistake, error · MW 个

人总是要出些**差错**的, 只有上帝不出错。 *Ordinary people make mistakes; only God never does.*

**差额** chā'é　N　balance (finance); difference; margin · MW 笔

**差价** chājià　N　price difference · MW 个

**差距** chājù　N　disparity, gap, difference · MW 个

人总是有**差距**的, 双胞胎也不能幸免。 *People have their differences; even twins are no exception.*

**差异** chāyì　N　difference, discrepancy

**差不多** chàbùduō　ADJ·ADV　very similar; almost, nearly

**差不多**就可以了, 别那么认真! *Almost is good enough; don't be so serious!*

---

**差点** chàdiǎn　ADV·ADJ　not quite good enough; almost, not quite

**差劲** chàjìn　ADJ　bad, no good

傻瓜的中文很**差劲**。 *ShaGua's Chinese is very poor.*

**差遣** chāiqiǎn　V　to send (on an errand, a mission), to dispatch

**差使** chāishǐ　V·N　to assign, to appoint

**差事** chāishì　N　assignment, commission; errand · MW 份、个

### RELATED WORDS

| | | |
|---|---|---|
| 公差 103 | 反差 111 | 出差 258 |
| 抓差 406 | 均差 558 | 时差 586 |
| 美差 671 | 相差 805 | 误差 1354 |
| 逆差 1359 | 视差 1362 | 偏差 1587 |
| 温差 1627 | 开小差 26 | 出偏差 258 |

---

### 674　举　舉　U+4E3E　TM 9 FM 丶

**jǔ**　V·N·ADJ　to lift, to raise; to choose, to elect; to cite; to start, to initiate; to mobilize, to move; act, deed; whole, entire, all

**举办** jǔbàn　V　to hold, to run, to sponsor

中国在2008年**举办**了奥运会。 *China hosted the Olympic Games in 2008.*

**举国** jǔguó　N　whole nation

中国**举国**上下欢迎奥运会。 *All of China welcomed the Olympics.*

**举例** jǔlì　V　to give an example

**举目** jǔmù　V　to look up

**举世** jǔshì　N　throughout the world

奥林匹克是**举世**瞩目的运动会。 *The Olympics is an event that is the focus of global attention.*

**举手** jǔshǒu　V　to raise one's hand(s) (as a signal)

在中国, 学生必须先**举手**才能回答问题。 *In China, students must raise their hands before answering questions.*

**举行** jǔxíng　V　to hold (a meeting, a contest, etc.)

**举证** jǔzhèng　V　to put to the test

**举止** jǔzhǐ　N　bearing, manner, conduct · MW 个、种

**举重** jǔzhòng　N·V　weightlifting; to lift weights

傻瓜说自己长得矮, 是年轻时练**举重**造成的。 *ShaGua says that he is short because he lifted weights when he was young.*

### RELATED WORDS

| | | |
|---|---|---|
| 壮举 238 | 列举 368 | 荐举 997 |
| 抬举 1012 | 检举 1033 | 创举 1131 |
| 推举 1242 | 选举 1510 | |

## 675 肖   U+8096   TM **9** FM 丶

**xiào** N·V portrait; to resemble, to be like

**肖像 xiàoxiàng** N portrait · MW 个、张

**RELATED WORD**

生肖 107

## 676 类 類   U+7C7B   TM **9** FM 丶

**lèi** N·V·MW kind, type, class, category; genus; to resemble, to be like; [measure word for kinds, types]

**类比 lèibǐ** V to compare

**类别 lèibié** N classification, category, class · MW 个、种

**类人猿 lèirényuán** N hominid · MW 个、只
进化论相信人是**类人猿**进化来的。
*Evolution says that human beings evolved from hominids.*

**类似 lèisì** V to be similar/analogous

**类推 lèituī** V to reason by analogy

**类型 lèixíng** N type, category; typology · MW 个、种
她不是我这种**类型**的人，不可能成为我的女朋友。 *She's not my type, so there's no way she would be my girlfriend.*

**RELATED WORDS**

| | | |
|---|---|---|
| 人类 4 | 贝类 97 | 归类 166 |
| 分类 173 | 另类 385 | 谷类 446 |
| 同类 541 | 败类 589 | 鸟类 859 |
| 种类 893 | 品类 1220 | 词类 1353 |
| 部类 1636 | 依此类推 625 | |

## 677 闭 閉   U+95ED   TM **9** FM 丶

**bì** V to shut, to close; to obstruct, to block; to stop, to put an end to

**闭合 bìhé** V to close

**闭会 bìhuì** V to close/adjourn a meeting

**闭幕 bìmù** V to close, to lower the curtain on (a conference, an exhibition, etc.)
傻瓜不喜欢出席开幕式和**闭幕式**。
*ShaGua doesn't like to attend opening or closing ceremonies.*

**闭塞 bìsè** ADJ out of the way, inaccessible; unenlightened

**RELATED WORDS**

| | | |
|---|---|---|
| 关闭 224 | 封闭 815 | 封闭式 815 |
| 倒闭 1281 | 禁闭 1536 | 密闭 1730 |

## 678 问 問   U+95EE   TM **9** FM 丶

**wèn** V·N to ask, to question, to inquire; to ask/inquire after/about; to hold responsible; to intervene; question

**问安 wèn'ān** V to pay one's respects

**问答 wèndá** V question and answer

**问好 wènhǎo** V to send one's regards to, to say hello to

**问号 wènhào** N question mark · MW 个

**问候 wènhòu** V to send one's regards to, to say hello to
请代我**问候**傻瓜。 *Please send my regards to ShaGua.*

**问卷 wènjuàn** N questionnaire · MW 份

**问世 wènshì** V to be published; to come out (of a book, etc.)

**问题 wèntí** N question; problem; issue, point · MW 个
**问题**比答案重要；因为没有好的**问题**就没有好的答案。 *Questions are more important than answers, because without a good question there will not be a good answer.*

**问讯 wènxùn** V to inquire; to ask

**问罪 wènzuì** V to denounce

**RELATED WORDS**

| | | |
|---|---|---|
| 发问 311 | 责问 525 | 考问 530 |
| 质问 597 | 成问题 611 | 讯问 703 |
| 过问 712 | 查问 741 | 审问 911 |
| 访问 949 | 学问 1155 | 探问 1404 |
| 询问 1500 | 追问 1507 | 提问 1554 |
| 顾问 1609 | 请问 1632 | 疑问 1917 |
| 慰问 1968 | 不耻下问 24 | |

## 679 闲 閑   U+95F2   TM **9** FM 丶

**xián** ADJ·N not busy; idle, not in use; informal; irrelevant; free/spare time, leisure

**闲扯 xiánchě** V to chat
傻瓜不会**闲扯**，只会闷头喝酒。 *ShaGua doesn't know how to chat with others, so he just drinks quietly.*

**闲逛 xiánguàng** V to stroll, to walk around leisurely

闲话 **xiánhuà** N digression; gossip · MW 句、堆

闲空 **xiánkòng** N free/spare time

傻瓜一年到头都很忙，几乎没有**闲空**与傻瓜太太散步。*ShaGua has been busy the entire year, and rarely has free time to take walks with Mrs. ShaGua.*

闲聊 **xiánliáo** V to chat, to engage in chitchat

闲人 **xiánrén** N person with time on his hands, idler · MW 个、名

闲人免进。*No loitering.*

闲散 **xiánsǎn** ADJ idle, free

闲事 **xiánshì** N other people's business

因为傻瓜太太有时爱管**闲事**，傻瓜常常因此与她吵架。*Mrs. ShaGua can be very nosy, which often leads to arguments with ShaGua.*

闲谈 **xiántán** V to chat, to engage in chitchat

闲暇 **xiánxiá** N leisure

**RELATED WORDS**

休闲 213          安闲 487          空闲 669
吃闲饭 783        等闲 1437

---

**680** 冻 凍          U+51BB          TM **9** FM 丶

**dòng** V·N to freeze, to feel very cold, to be frostbitten; jelly; savory food made with juice/gelatin

冻斑 **dòngbān** N frostbite · MW 块

冻疮 **dòngchuāng** N frostbite · MW 个

我今年冬天生**冻疮**了。*I got frostbite this winter.*

冻僵 **dòngjiāng** V to freeze

冻结 **dòngjié** V to congeal; to freeze (a loan, wages, prices)

冻伤 **dòngshāng** N frostbite

冻死 **dòngsǐ** EXP to freeze to death

"今天**冻死**了！"*"Today is horribly cold!"*

冻土 **dòngtǔ** N frozen ground; tundra · MW 块、片

冻雨 **dòngyǔ** N sleet · MW 场、阵、粒

**RELATED WORDS**

化冻 215          冰冻 493          冷冻 494
速冻 1514         解冻 1928         霜冻 1935

---

**681** 污          U+6C61          TM **9** FM 丶

**wū** ADJ·V·N dirty, filthy, foul; corrupt; to get (something) dirty; to smear; sewage; muck

---

污点 **wūdiǎn** N stain, spot · MW 个

谁都会犯错误，只有圣人才没有**污点**。*Anybody can make a mistake; only sages are free of such defects.*

污垢 **wūgòu** N dirt, filth

污秽 **wūhuì** ADJ·N dirty, filthy, foul

污蔑 **wūmiè** V to slander; to vilify; to tarnish

傻瓜常常被人**污蔑**。*ShaGua is slandered quite often.*

污泥 **wūní** N mud · MW 块、团

污染 **wūrǎn** V to pollute, to contaminate

中国的经济发展也带来了环境的**污染**，甚至是道德的**污染**。*While the Chinese economy has developed very fast, it has caused environmental and even moral pollution.*

污辱 **wūrǔ** V to insult, to humiliate; to rape

污水 **wūshuǐ** N wastewater, sewage · MW 滴、摊

污浊 **wūzhuó** ADJ·N dirty, muddy, filthy (of air, water, etc.); dirt, filth

**RELATED WORDS**

去污 157          奸污 329          油污 683
沾污 684          贪污 827          藏垢纳污 1978

---

**682** 汽          U+6C7D          TM **9** FM 丶

**qì** N vapor, steam

汽车 **qìchē** N automobile, car · MW 辆

汽船 **qìchuán** N steamship · MW 条、艘

汽灯 **qìdēng** N gas lamp · MW 盏

汽缸 **qìgāng** N cylinder · MW 个

傻瓜开一辆八个**汽缸**的老式凯迪拉克。*ShaGua drives a vintage eight-cylinder Cadillac.*

汽水 **qìshuǐ** N soft drink, soda · MW 杯、瓶

汽油 **qìyóu** N gas, gasoline · MW 滴、桶、加仑

**汽油**涨价成了人们每天的话题。*The price of gasoline has become a daily topic of conversation.*

**RELATED WORDS**

水汽 159          蒸汽 1768         公共汽车 103

---

**683** 油          U+6CB9          TM **9** FM 丶

**yóu** N·V·ADJ oil, petroleum; fat; to varnish, to paint, to stain; oily; glib, sly

油布 **yóubù** N oilcloth · MW 块

油彩 **yóucǎi** N paint; oil color · MW 块、抹

**683** 油 **yóu** (continued)

油茶 **yóuchá** N tea-oil camellia tree · MW 杯、碗

油灯 **yóudēng** N oil lamp · MW 盏

油罐 **yóuguàn** N oil tank · MW 个

油光 **yóuguāng** ADJ glossy, shiny

油滑 **yóuhuá** ADJ oily; slippery (person)

傻瓜没有一个**油滑**的朋友。*ShaGua doesn't have any devious friends.*

油画 **yóuhuà** N oil painting · MW 幅、张

油迹 **yóujì** N oil stain · MW 块、摊

油井 **yóujǐng** N oil well · MW 口

油库 **yóukù** N fuel depot · MW 个、座

油矿 **yóukuàng** N oil field · MW 个、座

油墨 **yóumò** N printing ink · MW 滴、瓶、摊

油腻 **yóunì** ADJ greasy, fatty, oily

油漆 **yóuqī** N·V paint; to varnish, to paint · MW 滴、摊、桶

油水 **yóushuǐ** N oil; profit · MW 滴

捞油水 *to reap profit*

油田 **yóutián** N oil field · MW 个、片

油条 **yóutiáo** N deep-fried breadstick; slippery person · MW 根

傻瓜最爱吃的早餐是豆浆泡**油条**。*ShaGua's favorite breakfast is fried breadsticks dipped in soy milk.*

傻瓜最不喜欢的是"老油条"。*ShaGua dislikes devious people.*

油污 **yóuwū** N greasy dirt

油炸 **yóuzhà** V to fry, to deep-fry

油脂 **yóuzhī** N grease, oil, fat; profit

**RELATED WORDS**

| | | |
|---|---|---|
| 头油 128 | 石油 144 | 发油 311 |
| 加油 463 | 汽油 682 | 香油 834 |
| 奶油 878 | 荤油 998 | 麻油 1146 |
| 黄油 1212 | 原油 1273 | 炼油 1357 |
| 素油 1378 | 猪油 1445 | 喷油 1563 |
| 蒜油 1655 | 绿油油 1707 | 鞋油 1789 |
| 酱油 1814 | 漏油 1886 | 燃油 1888 |
| 万金油 73 | 鱼肝油 843 | |

---

**684** 沾       U+6CBE     TM **9** FM 丶

**zhān** V to moisten, to soak; to be stained/soiled/covered with; to touch; to benefit/profit from

沾水 *to wet*

沾泥 *covered with mud*

沾便宜 *to gain some benefit*

不**沾**烟酒。*Don't touch cigarettes or alcohol.*

沾边 **zhānbiān** V to touch on lightly, to mention briefly

沾光 **zhānguāng** V to benefit from association with

傻瓜不愿意家人因为他当市长而**沾光**。*ShaGua doesn't want his family to benefit unfairly from his position as mayor.*

沾亲带故 **zhānqīndàigù** EXP to have ties of kinship/friendship

沾染 **zhānrǎn** V to be infected/contaminated with

沾手 **zhānshǒu** V to touch with one's hand; to have a hand in

沾污 **zhānwū** V to pollute, to contaminate

沾沾自喜 **zhānzhānzìxǐ** EXP to feel complacent, to be pleased with oneself, to pat oneself on the back

傻瓜的大儿子中文得了A, 有点**沾沾自喜**。*ShaGua's older son was pleased because he received an "A" in his Chinese class.*

---

**685** 泄       U+6CC4     TM **9** FM 丶

**xiè** V to let out, to discharge, to release; to drain; to leak (news, a secret, etc.); to vent

泄洪 **xièhóng** V to route/release floodwater

泄漏 **xièlòu** V to leak, to disclose, to reveal

傻瓜怕傻瓜太太**泄漏**信息, 所以从来不与她讨论市政府的事情。*ShaGua worries that Mrs. ShaGua might accidentally reveal information, so he has never talked about city government affairs with her.*

泄露 **xièlòu** V to disclose, to reveal

泄密 **xièmì** V to divulge a secret

泄气 **xièqì** V to lose heart, to be disappointed

**RELATED WORDS**

| | | |
|---|---|---|
| 水泄不通 159 | 排泄 1241 | 漏泄 1886 |

---

**686** 法       U+6CD5     TM **9** FM 丶

**fǎ** N·V law, act; method, way; standard, model; magic; Buddhist teaching; to follow, to emulate

法案 **fǎ'àn** N bill, proposed law · MW 个

法办 **fǎbàn** V to bring to justice, to deal with according to law

法宝 **fǎbǎo** N Buddha's doctrine; talisman; magic weapon · MW 个

**法典 fǎdiǎn** N legal code, statutes · MW 部

**法定 fǎdìng** ADJ legal, statutory

**法官 fǎguān** N judge · MW 个、位、名

**法规 fǎguī** N statute · MW 条、部、套

**法国 Fǎguó** N France

傻瓜没有去过**法国**。*ShaGua has not been to France.*

**法纪 fǎjì** N law and order · MW 套

**法警 fǎjǐng** N bailiff · MW 个、名

**法郎 fǎláng** N franc (former monetary unit in Belgium, France, and Luxembourg)

**法理 fǎlǐ** N legal principle · MW 个、条

**法令 fǎlìng** N decree; ordinance · MW 条、部、套

**法律 fǎlǜ** N law, statute · MW 部、条

**法人 fǎrén** N legal/corporate entity · MW 个、名

**法庭 fǎtíng** N (law) court; courtroom · MW 个、间

**法网 fǎwǎng** N arm of the law

**法学 fǎxué** N law; science of law, jurisprudence

**法语 Fǎyǔ** N French (language)

**法院 fǎyuàn** N court of law; court · MW 个、间

**法则 fǎzé** N law; rule; code · MW 条、部、套

**法治 fǎzhì** V rule of law

建立**法治**社会的原因之一是："总统也可能是一个流氓。" *One of the reasons for establishing a society under the rule of law is that "the president could be immoral."*

**法制 fǎzhì** N legal system

**RELATED WORDS**

| | | |
|---|---|---|
| 王法 27 | 文法 70 | 正法 76 |
| 手法 104 | 无法无天 139 | 办法 195 |
| 历法 200 | 伏法 212 | 方法 220 |
| 刑法 256 | 书法 264 | 步法 266 |
| 合法 296 | 兵法 300 | 用法 313 |
| 作法 326 | 司法 357 | 戏法 365 |
| 非法 378 | 民法 388 | 句法 424 |
| 加法 463 | 私法 471 | 守法 486 |
| 军法 489 | 政法 517 | 执法 564 |
| 依法 625 | 疗法 661 | 看法 841 |
| 约法 876 | 犯法 884 | 宗法 910 |
| 没法子 938 | 违法 1185 | 乘法 1263 |
| 笔法 1278 | 做法 1282 | 章法 1311 |
| 宪法 1317 | 除法 1418 | 减法 1487 |
| 语法 1501 | 提法 1554 | 商法 1612 |
| 说法 1631 | 算法 1697 | 税法 1705 |
| 想法 1769 | 解法 1928 | 魔法 1996 |
| 目无法纪 151 | 归谬法 166 | 针刺疗法 477 |
| 想方设法 1769 | | |

---

**687 洼** 窪　U+6D3C　TM **9** FM 丶

**wā** N·ADJ depression, dip, low-lying area; sunken

**洼地 wādì** N depression, low-lying ground · MW 块、片

学生宿舍后面有一块**洼地**。*There is a patch of low-lying ground behind the students' dorm.*

**RELATED WORD**

坑坑洼洼 774

---

**688 泪**　U+6CEA　TM **9** FM 丶

**lèi** N tear, teardrop

**泪痕 lèihén** N tear stain · MW 道

**泪花 lèihuā** N teardrop; tears in one's eyes

**泪水 lèishuǐ** N tear, teardrop · MW 滴

**泪珠 lèizhū** N teardrop · MW 串

**RELATED WORDS**

| | | |
|---|---|---|
| 血泪 306 | 洒泪 1163 | 落泪 1547 |
| 眼泪 1570 | 催泪弹 1592 | |

---

**689 洋**　U+6D0B　TM **9** FM 丶

**yáng** N·ADJ ocean; silver dollar/coin; vast; foreign; modern

*海洋 ocean*

**洋白菜 yángbáicài** N cabbage · MW 棵

**洋葱 yángcōng** N onion · MW 个、头

**洋鬼子 yángguǐzi** EXP foreign devil (term for foreign invaders since the Qing Dynasty) · MW 个

**洋行 yángháng** N foreign company · MW 个、间、家

**洋灰 yánghuī** N cement · MW 堆、袋

**洋火 yánghuǒ** N matches · MW 根、盒

**洋货 yánghuò** N foreign/imported goods · MW 批

**洋气 yángqì** N·ADJ Western style; fashionable

傻瓜再怎么打扮也不**洋气**。*No matter how ShaGua dressed, there just wasn't any trace of Western style in him.*

**洋人 yángrén** N foreigner · MW 个、名

**洋嗓子 yángsǎngzi** N voice trained in Western-style singing

**689** 洋 *yáng* (continued)

洋为中用 *yángwéizhōngyòng* [EXP] to use Western ideas to benefit China (LIT to make foreign things serve China)

洋相 *yángxiàng* [N] awkward behavior; making a spectacle of oneself · [MW] 个

洋洋得意 *yángyángdéyì* [EXP] immensely pleased with oneself

洋溢 *yángyì* [V] to be permeated with; to brim with

**RELATED WORDS**

| 出洋相 258 | 西洋 352 | 远洋 1184 |
| 海洋 1494 | 懒洋洋 1953 | 大西洋 20 |
| 太平洋 53 | 印度洋 470 | 喜气洋洋 1531 |

---

**690** 洪    U+6D2A    TM **9**¹ FM 丶

*hóng* [N·ADJ] flood; big, vast

洪大 *hóngdà* [ADJ] loud

洪泛区 *hóngfànqū* [N] flood plain · [MW] 个、片

洪峰 *hóngfēng* [N] crest (of a flood) · [MW] 个

洪亮 *hóngliàng* [ADJ] loud and clear; sonorous
傻瓜的嗓音很**洪亮**。*ShaGua's voice is very sonorous.*

洪流 *hóngliú* [N] powerful current; flood, onrush · [MW] 条

洪水 *hóngshuǐ* [N] flood; spate, torrent · [MW] 股
去年这里发**洪水**。*There was a flood here last year.*

**RELATED WORDS**

| 山洪 38 | 泄洪 685 | 抗洪 1009 |
| 防洪 1040 | | |

---

**691** 洲    U+6D32    TM **9** FM 丶

*zhōu* [N] continent; island

洲际 *zhōujì* [N] intercontinental

**RELATED WORDS**

| 亚洲 136 | 非洲 378 | 美洲 671 |
| 欧洲 811 | | |

---

**692** 浅 淺    U+6D45    TM **9** FM 丶

*qiǎn* [ADJ] shallow, superficial; simple, easy; not intimate, not close; light (in color); short (in time), for a short while

浅薄 *qiǎnbó* [ADJ] shallow, superficial; shallow and ignorant
傻瓜没有文化, 但不**浅薄**。*ShaGua is uneducated, but he is neither shallow nor ignorant.*

浅见 *qiǎnjiàn* [N] superficial view; humble opinion · [MW] 点

浅陋 *qiǎnlòu* [ADJ] shallow; meager

浅色 *qiǎnsè* [N] light color
傻瓜不喜欢**浅色**的衣服。*ShaGua doesn't like light-colored clothes.*

浅说 *qiǎnshuō* [V] simple introduction

浅易 *qiǎnyì* [ADJ] simple, easy to read and understand

**RELATED WORDS**

| 肤浅 899 | 深浅 1345 | 才疏学浅 39 |

---

**693** 忧 憂    U+5FE7    TM **9** FM 丶

*yōu* [N·V·ADJ] sorrow; anxiety, worry; to be concerned about, to worry about; anxious; sad, depressed

忧愁 *yōuchóu* [ADJ] worried; sad, depressed

忧愤 *yōufèn* [ADJ] worried and indignant

忧虑 *yōulǜ* [V] to be worried/anxious/concerned

忧闷 *yōumèn* [ADJ] depressed

忧伤 *yōushāng* [ADJ] worried, distressed; sad
孩子不听话, 让傻瓜常常感到**忧伤**。*When ShaGua's kids don't listen to him, it often distresses him.*

忧心 *yōuxīn* [V·N] to worry; anxiety

忧郁 *yōuyù* [ADJ] depressed, sullen, in the doldrums

**RELATED WORDS**

| 内忧外患 191 | 担忧 789 |

---

**694** 怕    U+6015    TM **9** FM 丶

*pà* [V·ADV] to fear, to dread; worried, anxious; I'm afraid, perhaps, maybe

怕生 *pàshēng* [V] to be shy around strangers (of a child)

怕事 *pàshì* [V] to be afraid of getting into trouble

怕死 *pàsǐ* [V] to be afraid to die

怕羞 *pàxiū* [V] to be shy/bashful/timid
傻瓜**怕羞**, 但不**怕事**。*ShaGua is timid, but he's not afraid of getting into trouble.*

## RELATED WORDS

| | | |
|---|---|---|
| 可怕 243 | 害怕 1319 | 惧怕 1351 |
| 恐怕 1644 | 哪怕 1666 | 贪生怕死 827 |

---

**695** 怜 憐  U+601C　TM **9** FM ヽ

**lián** [V] to pity, to sympathize with; to love

怜爱 **lián'ài** [V] to love tenderly

怜悯 **liánmǐn** [V] to pity, to express sympathy for

怜惜 **liánxī** [V] to take pity on

傻瓜非常**怜惜**那些辍学的穷孩子。 *ShaGua has pity for all the poor kids who have dropped out of school.*

### RELATED WORD

可怜 243

---

**696** 怪 U+602A　TM **9** FM ヽ

**guài** [ADJ·V·ADV·N] strange, odd; bewildering; to find strange, to be surprised; to blame; quite, really, very; monster, demon

怪不得 **guàibude** [ADV·V] no wonder, so that's why; not to blame

**怪不得**傻瓜怜惜辍学的穷孩子, 因为他也穷过。 *No wonder ShaGua has pity for those poor kids who dropped out of school; he was poor himself.*

怪诞 **guàidàn** [ADJ] weird

怪话 **guàihuà** [N] complaint; snide remark

有什么话好好说, 别说**怪话**。 *Please say what you need to say nicely; don't always make snide remarks.*

怪模怪样 **guàimúguàiyàng** [EXP] grotesque

怪人 **guàirén** [N] eccentric (person) · [MW] 个

怪物 **guàiwù** [N] monster; freak, oddball · [MW] 个

### RELATED WORDS

| | | |
|---|---|---|
| 古怪 154 | 作怪 326 | 妖怪 466 |
| 责怪 525 | 奇怪 854 | 难怪 974 |
| 莫怪 999 | 鬼怪 1433 | 魔怪 1996 |
| 丑八怪 85 | 奇形怪状 854 | 大惊小怪 20 |

---

**697** 怯 U+602F　TM **9** FM ヽ

**qiè** [ADJ·V] timid, cowardly; to have stage fright

怯场 **qièchǎng** [V] to have stage fright

傻瓜对演讲**怯场**。 *ShaGua gets stage fright when he makes speeches.*

怯懦 **qiènuò** [ADJ] fainthearted, timid; cautious

怯生 **qièshēng** [ADJ] shy around strangers

怯阵 **qièzhèn** [V] to have stage fright

### RELATED WORDS

| | | |
|---|---|---|
| 卑怯 602 | 羞怯 1154 | 胆怯 1295 |

---

**698** 恢 U+6062　TM **9** FM ヽ

**huī** [ADJ] extensive, vast

恢复 **huīfù** [V] to recover; to restore; to resume

"文化革命" 后, 中国于1977年**恢复**了高考。 *After the Cultural Revolution, China reinstated the College Entrance Exam in 1977.*

---

**699** 炉 爐 U+7089　TM **9** FM ヽ

**lú** [N] kitchen stove

炉灶 **lúzào** [N] kitchen stove/range · [MW] 个

炉子 **lúzi** [N] stove; oven; furnace · [MW] 个

### RELATED WORDS

| | | |
|---|---|---|
| 火炉 72 | 烘炉 953 | 烤炉 1505 |
| 锅炉 1807 | 壁炉 1920 | 另起炉灶 385 |
| 微波炉 1700 | | |

---

**700** 炊 U+708A　TM **9** FM ヽ

**chuī** [V] to cook (a meal)

炊具 **chuījù** [N] cooking utensil · [MW] 件、套

炊事 **chuīshì** [N] cooking

炊烟 **chuīyān** [N] smoke from a kitchen chimney · [MW] 缕、股

---

**701** 炸 U+70B8　TM **9** FM ヽ

**zhá** [V] to deep-fry

油炸 *to deep-fry*

**zhà** [V·N] to explode, to burst, to blow up; bomb

炸弹 **zhàdàn** [N] bomb; bombshell · [MW] 颗、枚

炸药 **zhàyào** [N] explosive; dynamite · [MW] 包、箱

傻瓜发怒的时候, 像是吃了一肚子**炸药**一样可怕。 *When ShaGua gets very angry, it's like he's full of dynamite.*

**701 炸 zhá/zhà** (continued)

**RELATED WORDS**

油炸 683    轰炸 1065    爆炸 1982
核爆炸 1026

---

**702 烂** 爛   U+70C2   TM **9** FM 丶

**làn** V·ADJ·ADV to be rotten, to spoil; to decay; rotten; tattered, worn-out; overcooked; chaotic, messy; thoroughly, utterly

**烂糊 lànhu** ADJ mashed (of food)

**烂漫 lànmàn** ADJ bright-colored

**烂泥 lànní** N mud; slush; ooze · MW 块、团

**烂熟 lànshú** ADJ overripe; well-cooked; to learn by heart, to know thoroughly

**烂摊子 làntānzi** N awful mess · MW 个

**烂醉 lànzuì** V to be dead/completely drunk

**RELATED WORDS**

破烂 1374    稀烂 1599    腐烂 1879
霉烂 1934    焦头烂额 1265    滚瓜烂熟 1819

---

**703 讯** 訊   U+8BAF   TM **9** FM 丶

**xùn** V·N to ask, to question, to inquire; to interrogate; news; information; message

**讯问 xùnwèn** V to question, to inquire; to interrogate

**讯息 xùnxī** N message · MW 个、条

**RELATED WORDS**

刑讯 256    电讯 263    问讯 678
审讯 911    喜讯 1531    通讯 1757
简讯 1796    即时通讯 1047    新华通讯社 1638

---

**704 诀** 訣   U+8BC0   TM **9** FM 丶

**jué** N mnemonic; knack; trick of the trade

**诀窍 juéqiào** N secret of success; trick of the trade · MW 个

学中文没有**诀窍**，就得勤练。 *There are no secrets of success in studying Chinese except to practice it frequently.*

**RELATED WORDS**

妙诀 467    秘诀 1289

---

**705 证** 證   U+8BC1   TM **9** FM 丶

**zhèng** N·V evidence, proof; certificate, card; to testify; to prove, to demonstrate

**证词 zhèngcí** N testimony · MW 段、篇、份

证人必须提供真实的**证词**。 *Witnesses must provide truthful testimony.*

**证婚人 zhènghūnrén** N chief witness at a wedding · MW 个、位、名

**证件 zhèngjiàn** N certificate; credentials · MW 个、份

**证据 zhèngjù** N evidence, proof; testimony · MW 个、份

让**证据**说话。 *Let the evidence reveal the truth.*

**证明 zhèngmíng** V·N to testify; to prove; evidence; certificate; identification · MW 份、张

**证券 zhèngquàn** N bond, security · MW 张、种

傻瓜有时会买**证卷**，但不买股票。 *ShaGua may sometimes buy bonds, but he never buys stocks.*

**证人 zhèngrén** N witness · MW 个、名

**证实 zhèngshí** V to confirm, to verify

**证书 zhèngshū** N certificate; credentials · MW 种、本

**证物 zhèngwù** N exhibit · MW 个、件

**证物**有时比证人还重要。 *An exhibit might sometimes be more important than a witness.*

**证章 zhèngzhāng** N badge · MW 个、枚

**RELATED WORDS**

公证 103    反证 111    认证 239
对证 254    见证 267    伪证 454
考证 530    举证 674    查证 741
例证 863    保证 868    物证 883
论证 947    凭证 1060    签证 1439
旁证 1473    验证 1529    罪证 1542
确证 1762    许可证 502    借书证 1087
通行证 1757

---

**706 评** 評   U+8BC4   TM **9** FM 丶

**píng** V to judge, to assess; to comment; to criticize, to review

**评比 píngbǐ** V to appraise, to evaluate (using comparison)

**评定 píngdìng** V to assess, to pass judgment on

你对我的**评定**不公平。 *You judged me unfairly.*

**评分 píngfēn** V to grade, to mark, to score

**评功 pínggōng** V to assess the merits of

评级 píngjí  V  to grade products (according to quality)

评价 píngjià  V·N  to assess, to evaluate; evaluation ·  MW  个

评奖 píngjiǎng  V  to determine awards (by discussion)

评理 pínglǐ  V  to judge the rightness/wrongness of

傻瓜太太和傻瓜吵架, 她要邻居给他们**评理**。 *Mrs. ShaGua asked the neighbors to judge the argument between her and ShaGua.*

评论 pínglùn  V·N  to comment on, to discuss; to criticize, to review; article for comment and discussion ·  MW  个、篇

评判 píngpàn  V  to judge, to appraise, to decide

**评判**别人也是在**评判**自己。 *Passing judgment on others is also a judgment on yourself.*

评选 píngxuǎn  V  to choose (using comparison)

评议 píngyì  V  to consult; to appraise (by discussion)

评语 píngyǔ  N  comment, remark ·  MW  个、段

傻瓜最不愿意在文件上写**评语**。 *ShaGua is not willing to write his comments on the document.*

评阅 píngyuè  V  to read and appraise

评注 píngzhù  V  to comment and annotate

评传 píngzhuàn  N  critical biography ·  MW  篇

**RELATED WORDS**

| | | |
|---|---|---|
| 书评 264 | 讲评 501 | 好评 627 |
| 批评 1005 | 品评 1220 | 剧评 1468 |
| 影评 1918 | | |

---

**707** 诈 詐    U+8BC8    TM **9** FM 丶

zhà  V  to cheat, to swindle; to pretend; to bluff

诈称 zhàchēng  V  to make a false claim

诈唬 zhàhu  V  to bluff; to trick

诈骗 zhàpiàn  V  to defraud, to swindle

因为有善良的人, 才会有**诈骗**的人。 *Since there are kindhearted people, there must also be swindlers.*

**RELATED WORDS**

| | |
|---|---|
| 欺诈 1423 | 敲诈 1959 |

---

**708** 诉 訴    U+8BC9    TM **9** FM 丶

sù  V  to tell, to relate; to inform; to accuse; to sue; to appeal

诉苦 sùkǔ  V  to complain, to vent a grievance

诉讼 sùsòng  V  to litigate; lawsuit ·  MW  份

诉冤 sùyuān  V  to inform

诉诸 sùzhū  V  to resort/appeal to

诉状 sùzhuàng  N  indictment ·  MW  个、篇

你什么时候投递这个**诉状**？ *When will you deliver this indictment?*

**RELATED WORDS**

| | | |
|---|---|---|
| 上诉 14 | 申诉 150 | 告诉 428 |
| 败诉 589 | 胜诉 1122 | 哭诉 1221 |
| 原诉 1273 | 控诉 1406 | 起诉 1421 |

---

**709** 诊 診    U+8BCA    TM **9** FM 丶

zhěn  V  to examine, to diagnose (medicine)

诊病 zhěnbìng  V  to diagnose (a disease)

诊察 zhěnchá  V  to examine

诊断 zhěnduàn  V  to diagnose

**诊断**别人容易, **诊断**自己太难。 *It is easy to diagnose others, but difficult to diagnose oneself.*

诊疗 zhěnliáo  V  to diagnose and treat

诊视 zhěnshì  V  to examine (a patient)

诊室 zhěnshì  N  consulting room ·  MW  间

诊所 zhěnsuǒ  N  (medical) clinic ·  MW  个、间、家

诊治 zhěnzhì  V  to diagnose and treat

**RELATED WORDS**

| | | |
|---|---|---|
| 门诊 130 | 出诊 258 | 叩诊 413 |
| 初诊 963 | 候诊 1086 | 急诊 1426 |
| 确诊 1762 | | |

---

**710** 边 邊    U+8FB9    TM **9** FM 丶

biān  N  side, edge; line; verge, brink; periphery; border, boundary, limit; nearby

边防 biānfáng  N  border defense

边际 biānjì  N  limit; margin

边界 biānjiè  N  border, boundary ·  MW  条

边境 biānjìng  N  border ·  MW  条

这是一条和平安宁的**边境**。 *This is a peaceful border.*

边沿 biānyán  N  edge; fringe

边缘 biānyuán  N  edge; margin; verge

边远 biānyuǎn  ADJ  outlying, remote

710 边 biān (continued)

**RELATED WORDS**

| | | |
|---|---|---|
| 一边 1 | 下边 10 | 天边 25 |
| 六边形 69 | 五边形 79 | 左边 113 |
| 半边 127 | 半边天 127 | 无边无际 139 |
| 耳边风 145 | 双边 146 | 右边 187 |
| 外边 218 | 四边 271 | 四边形 271 |
| 里边 386 | 多边 431 | 花边 549 |
| 身边 604 | 沾边 684 | 那边 980 |
| 周边 1068 | 前边 1329 | 等边 1437 |
| 旁边 1473 | 靠边 1791 | 敲边鼓 1959 |
| 漫无边际 1887 | | |

---

**711** 辽　遼　　U+8FBD　TM **9** FM 丶

**liáo** ADJ distant, faraway, remote

辽阔 **liáokuò** ADJ vast, extensive

辽宁 **Liáoníng** N Liaoning Province

辽远 **liáoyuǎn** ADJ distant, faraway, remote

---

**712** 过　過　　U+8FC7　TM **9** FM 丶

**guò** V·AV to cross, to pass through, to go over/through; to spend; to pass (of time); to exceed, to be more than; past, after; [used after a verb to indicate completion of an action]

过磅 **guòbàng** V to weigh (on a scale)

过不去 **guòbuqù** V to be unable to get through/past; to find fault with; to be/feel sorry

你挡在这儿, 我过不去。 *I couldn't get through because you were blocking me.*

你干吗老是跟我过不去? *Why do you pick on me all the time?*

你这样想, 我感到很过不去。 *I am sorry you feel this way.*

过场 **guòchǎng** V·N to cross the stage; interlude

过程 **guòchéng** N process; course · MW 个

过得去 **guòdequ** V·ADJ to be able to get past/through; passable, so-so

傻瓜的英语还过得去。 *ShaGua's English is so-so.*

过冬 **guòdōng** V to pass the winter

过度 **guòdù** ADJ excessive; immoderate

过渡 **guòdù** V to be in transit/transition; interim

过分 **guòfèn** ADJ excessive, undue

过关 **guòguān** V to pass (a barrier, a test, etc.); to go through (an ordeal)

过后 **guòhòu** N afterward, later

过活 **guòhuó** V to make a living

过火 **guòhuǒ** ADJ going too far, going to extremes

过激 **guòjī** ADJ drastic, extreme; extremist

过境 **guòjìng** V to pass through the territory of a country

过来 **guòlái** V to come over/up

过量 **guòliàng** V to be excessive, to be over the top

任何东西过量都不好。 *Anything in excess is not good.*

过路 **guòlù** V to pass by on one's way

过虑 **guòlǜ** V to be overanxious, to worry too much

过敏 **guòmǐn** V to be allergic

过目 **guòmù** V to look over

过年 **guònián** V to celebrate the New Year

小时候盼过年, 过了中年怕过年。 *When you were young, you anticipated the New Year; after passing middle age, you will fear it.*

过期 **guòqī** V to expire; to exceed the time limit

过去 **guòqù** N·V in the past, formerly, previously; to pass by

过去的, 就让它过去吧! *Let bygones be bygones!*

我走过去。 *I went over.*

过去时 **guòqùshí** N past tense · MW 个

过热 **guòrè** V to overheat

过日子 **guòrìzi** V to live; to get along

过剩 **guòshèng** V to be excessive; to have a surplus

过失 **guòshī** N mistake, error · MW 个

就是圣人也会有过失。 *Even sages can make a mistake.*

过时 **guòshí** V·ADJ to be out-of-date; obsolete

过头 **guòtóu** ADJ excessive, too much

过往 **guòwǎng** V to come and go

过问 **guòwèn** V to inquire into, to concern oneself with

亚裔父母总是喜欢过问孩子的事。 *Asian-American parents like to concern themselves with their kids' business.*

过夜 **guòyè** V to stay overnight

过瘾 **guòyǐn** ADJ enjoying oneself to the full, to one's heart's content

过于 **guòyú** ADV too, excessively

**RELATED WORDS**

| | | |
|---|---|---|
| 反过来 111 | 走过场 265 | 好过 627 |
| 记过 946 | 放过 964 | 难过 974 |

莫过于 999    经过 1110    悔过 1488
渡过 1497    罪过 1542    越过 1575
超过 1684    错过 1715    通过 1757
赛过 1813    左不过 113    只不过 160
为时过早 223    说不过去 1631    蒙混过关 1654
瞒天过海 1914

## 713 进 進    U+8FDB    TM 9 FM 丶

**jìn** V to enter, to come/go in; to advance, to move forward/ahead; to bring in; to eat, to drink; to submit, to present

进步 **jìnbù** V·ADJ·N to improve; to pep up; advanced; progress · MW 个
学生的汉语**进步**很大。 *The students have made significant progress in their study of Chinese.*

进场 **jìnchǎng** V to enter an arena (sports)

进程 **jìnchéng** N course, process; progress · MW 个

进出 **jìnchū** V to come and go; ins and outs; turnover (business)

进出口 **jìnchūkǒu** N·V entrance and exit; to import and export

进度 **jìndù** N progress · MW 个

进攻 **jìngōng** V to attack, to assault

进化 **jìnhuà** V to evolve; evolution
你相信**进化**论还是创论论？ *Do you believe in evolution or creationism?*

进军 **jìnjūn** V to advance; to march (of troops)

进口 **jìnkǒu** V·N to import; entrance · MW 个

进来 **jìnlái** V to come in
请**进来**！ *Come in, please!*

进取 **jìnqǔ** V to forge ahead; to be enterprising
**进取**心对一个成功的人来说是必不可少的。 *Ambition is necessary to be a successful person.*

进入 **jìnrù** V to enter, to go into

进退 **jìntuì** V·N to advance and retreat; sense of propriety, knowing when to come and when to go

进行 **jìnxíng** V to carry out, to conduct; to be in progress (of a meeting, etc.)

进修 **jìnxiū** V to engage in advanced study; to take a refresher course
傻瓜想去哈佛**进修**一年。 *ShaGua wants to study at Harvard University for a year.*

进一步 **jìnyíbù** ADV one step further; further

进展 **jìnzhǎn** V to make progress/headway

### RELATED WORDS

二进制 2    十进制 3    长进 93
买进 248    后进 310    引进 371
先进 422    迁进 506    改进 516
迈进 955    跃进 1258    前进 1329
渐进 1347    跟进 1784    增进 1849
跨进 1857    齐头并进 221    突飞猛进 913

## 714 还 還    U+8FD8    TM 9 FM 丶

**hái** ADV still, yet; even more; also, too, as well; fairly, even; really

**huán** V to return, to go/come back, to give back; to repay

还本 **huánběn** V to pay back, to repay

还本付息 **huánběnfùxī** V to repay with interest

还击 **huánjī** V to fight back

还价 **huánjià** V to make a counteroffer

还礼 **huánlǐ** V to give a gift in return
如果傻瓜不得不收别人的礼物，他一定**还礼**。 *If ShaGua has to accept others' gifts, he must present gifts in return.*

还清 **huánqīng** V to pay off, to pay back in full

还原 **huányuán** V to restore, to return (something) to its original condition/shape

还愿 **huányuàn** V to thank God / the gods for answering one's prayers; to fulfill one's promise

还债 **huánzhài** V to settle/repay a debt

还嘴 **huánzuǐ** V to answer/talk back
傻瓜批评孩子时，不允许他们**还嘴**。 *When ShaGua is scolding his kids, he does not allow them to talk back.*

### RELATED WORDS

归还 166    发还 311    讨还 500
送还 1188    偿还 1440    退还 1508
讨价还价 500    返老还童 957

## 715 这 這    U+8FD9    TM 9 FM 丶

**zhè** PRON this; now, right now

**zhèi** PRON this

这般 **zhèbān** PRON so, such, like
傻瓜只有**这般**高。 *ShaGua is only so tall.*

这次 **zhècì** PRON this time; present, now

这个 **zhègè** PRON this (one)

这里 **zhèlǐ** PRON here, over here

**715** 这 zhè/zhèi (continued)

这么 **zhème** | PRON | so, such; this way, like this
傻瓜太太只有**这么**高。 *Mrs. ShaGua is only this tall.*

这些 **zhèxiē** | PRON | these

这样 **zhèyàng** | PRON | so, such; this way, like this

---

**716** 近     U+8FD1    TM **9** FM 丶

**jìn** | ADJ·V | near, close (to); closely related; easy to understand; to approach; to approximate

近程 **jìnchéng** | N | short range

近代 **jìndài** | N | modern times
中国**近代**史很值得研究。 *It is worth it to research modern Chinese history.*

近道 **jìndào** | N | shortcut · MW 条

近海 **jìnhǎi** | N | coastal waters

近郊 **jìnjiāo** | N | suburb(s), outskirts · MW 个
傻瓜最近搬家到**近郊**去了。 *ShaGua recently moved his family to the suburbs.*

近距离 **jìnjùlí** | N | at short range · MW 个

近况 **jìnkuàng** | N | recent developments, the latest

近来 **jìnlái** | ADV | recently, lately
**近来**, 傻瓜的**近况**不太好。 *ShaGua's present situation is not very good.*

近路 **jìnlù** | N | shortcut · MW 条

近期 **jìnqī** | N | in the near future, very soon

---

近亲 **jìnqīn** | N | close relative · MW 个、位

近视 **jìnshì** | N | myopia, nearsightedness
傻瓜不**近视**。 *ShaGua is not nearsighted.*

近似 **jìnsì** | V | to be similar (to); to approximate

**RELATED WORDS**

| | | |
|---|---|---|
| 相近 805 | 亲近 908 | 贴近 1038 |
| 邻近 1123 | 将近 1161 | 远近 1184 |
| 迫近 1186 | 接近 1405 | 最近 1541 |
| 靠近 1791 | 逼近 1828 | 就近 1836 |

---

**717** 祈     U+7948    TM **9** FM 丶

**qí** | V | to pray; to ask for, to request; to wish

祈祷 **qídǎo** | V | to pray
人们总是为明天**祈祷**, 为昨天后悔。 *People always pray for their tomorrows, but regret their yesterdays.*

祈使句 **qíshǐjù** | N | imperative sentence · MW 个、句

祈望 **qíwàng** | V | to hope; to wish

---

**718** 衫     U+886B    TM **9** FM 丶

**shān** | N | shirt

衬衫 **chènshān** | N | shirt · MW 件

**RELATED WORDS**

| | | |
|---|---|---|
| 汗衫 236 | 衬衫 718 | 衬衫 962 |
| 运动衫 956 | | |

## 719 画 畫    U+753B    TM **10** FM 一

**huà** V·N·MW to paint; to draw; picture; stroke (of a Chinese character)

**画板 huàbǎn** N drawing board · MW 块

**画报 huàbào** N illustrated magazine · MW 本、期

**画笔 huàbǐ** N brush; painting brush · MW 支

**画册 huàcè** N photo album · MW 本

**画廊 huàláng** N art gallery · MW 家、间

**画蛇添足 huàshétiānzú** EXP unnecessary (LIT to draw a snake and add feet to it)

**画师 huàshī** N painter; artist · MW 个、位、名

**画室 huàshì** N (art) studio · MW 间

**画像 huàxiàng** V·N to create a portrait; portrait · MW 张

> 傻瓜的办公室里有一张**画像**, 是一位**画师**为他画的。 *There is a portrait in ShaGua's office that was painted by an artist.*

**画展 huàzhǎn** N art exhibition · MW 个

**画纸 huàzhǐ** N drawing paper · MW 张

### RELATED WORDS

| | | |
|---|---|---|
| 年画 182 | 书画 264 | 勾画 303 |
| 动画片 514 | 字画 664 | 油画 683 |
| 图画 761 | 版画 897 | 笔画 1278 |
| 描画 1407 | 漫画 1887 | 壁画 1920 |
| 水墨画 159 | 指手画脚 1397 | |

## 720 雨    U+96E8    TM **10** FM 一

**yǔ** N rain

**雨滴 yǔdī** N raindrop · MW 粒

**雨季 yǔjì** N rainy season · MW 个

> 这个**雨季**不下雨。 *This rainy season is not rainy.*

**雨伞 yǔsǎn** N umbrella · MW 把

> 傻瓜的**雨伞**是那种老式, 带弯把的。
> *ShaGua's umbrella is the old style with a curved handle.*

**雨水 yǔshuǐ** N rainwater; rainfall, rain · MW 滴、粒

**雨鞋 yǔxié** N rubber boots · MW 双、对、只

**雨衣 yǔyī** N raincoat · MW 件

**雨云 yǔyún** N nimbus, rain cloud · MW 团

### RELATED WORDS

| | | |
|---|---|---|
| 下雨 10 | 大雨 20 | 风雨 194 |
| 风雨无阻 194 | 尘雨 204 | 冻雨 680 |
| 阵雨 809 | 阴雨 1041 | 淋雨 1172 |
| 降雨量 1416 | 晴雨计 1674 | 暴雨 1844 |
| 霉雨天 1934 | 风调雨顺 194 | 雷阵雨 1641 |

## 721 面 麵    U+9762    TM **10** FM 一

**miàn** (麵 refers only to flour and flour products) N·V·ADV·MW powder; flour; noodles; soft and floury; face, surface, top, cover; outside; side; aspect; to face; face to face, personally, directly; [measure word for flat, smooth objects (mirrors, flags, etc.)]

**面包 miànbāo** N bread · MW 个、条、块

**面部 miànbù** N facial

> **面部**变化常常反映一个人的内心活动。
> *Facial changes often reflect changes in emotion.*

**面辞 miàncí** V to say good-bye to (in person)

**面对 miànduì** V to face, to encounter

**面对面 miànduìmiàn** V to face each other; opposite, face to face; vis-à-vis

**面额 miàn'é** N forehead; denomination (of currency)

**面红耳赤 miànhóng'ěrchì** EXP to be flushed with anger

> 傻瓜常常与孩子争得**面红耳赤**。 *ShaGua often argues with his kids so ardently that he becomes flushed with anger.*

**面积 miànjī** N (surface) area

**面具 miànjù** N mask · MW 副

> 人们往往让别人看到的是一副**面具**, 而不是他们真实的内心。 *People usually put on a mask for others, hiding their real selves.*

**面孔 miànkǒng** N face; facade · MW 副

**面临 miànlín** V to be faced with, to be up against

**721 面 miàn** (continued)

**面貌 miànmào** N face; looks, appearance · MW 个

**面目 miànmù** N face; features, appearance; sense of shame · MW 副

**面前 miànqián** N in the face of, in front of

**面容 miànróng** N face; features, looks · MW 副

**面色 miànsè** N complexion; facial expression

**面生 miànshēng** ADJ unfamiliar-looking

他很**面生**。 *He looks unfamiliar.*

**面试 miànshì** V·N to interview; to audition; oral quiz · MW 次

**面熟 miànshú** ADJ familiar-looking

昨天在傻瓜办公室里的那个人很**面熟**。 *The person who was in ShaGua's office yesterday looked familiar.*

**面汤 miàntāng** N noodle soup · MW 碗、口

**面条 miàntiáo** N noodles · MW 根、把、碗

**面向 miànxiàng** V to face toward; to be geared to the needs of

**面纸 miànzhǐ** N facial tissue · MW 张、盒

**面子 miànzi** N outside; face, reputation; feelings · MW 个

中国文化特别注重"**面子**"。 *Chinese culture strongly emphasizes saving "face."*

**RELATED WORDS**

**722 录 錄** U+5F55 TM **10** FM 一

**lù** V·N to record, to write down; to copy; to tape-record; to employ, to hire; record; register; collection

**录取 lùqǔ** V to recruit, to enroll; to admit

等待大学的**录取**通知,实在是煎熬人。 *It is very tortuous waiting for admissions information from a college.*

**录声 lùshēng** V to record songs/sound; sound recording

**录像 lùxiàng** V·N to make a video of; videotape · MW 个、段

**录像机 lùxiàngjī** N video recorder · MW 个、台

**录音 lùyīn** V·N to record sound; sound recording, tape · MW 个、段

**录音机 lùyīnjī** N tape/cassette recorder · MW 个

**录用 lùyòng** V to employ, to hire

**RELATED WORDS**

**723 型** U+578B TM **10** FM 一

**xíng** N model, pattern, mould; type; size

**型号 xínghào** N model; type; version · MW 个、种

**RELATED WORDS**

**724 顶 頂** U+9876 TM **10** FM 一

**dǐng** N·V·ADV·MW top, summit, peak; to carry on one's head; to push/lift/prop up; to retort; to cope with, to stand up to; to take the place of, to substitute; very, extremely; most; [measure word for objects with a top (hats, caps, etc.)]

**顶班 dǐngbān** V to take (someone's) shift; to do (someone's) job

傻瓜年轻时经常替别人**顶班**, 特别是大家都不愿上的夜班。 *When ShaGua was young, he often took others' shifts, particularly the night shift, which people didn't like.*

**顶部** dǐngbù　N　top · MW 个

**顶端** dǐngduān　N　top, peak · MW 个

**顶风** dǐngfēng　V　to face into the wind

**顶峰** dǐngfēng　N　peak, crest; peak (of a development, a trend) · MW 个、座

**顶尖** dǐngjiān　N　tops/best (in a certain field); peak, highest point · MW 个

**顶头上司** dǐngtóushàngsi　N　immediate boss · MW 个、位

傻瓜认为市民是他的**顶头上司**。 *ShaGua believes that the residents of the city are his immediate bosses.*

**顶用** dǐngyòng　V　to be of use/help

**顶住** dǐngzhù　V　to withstand

**顶撞** dǐngzhuàng　V　to contradict (a superior, an elder)

**顶嘴** dǐngzuǐ　V　to reply defiantly

傻瓜常**顶撞**上司, 但却不允许自己的孩子**顶嘴**。 *ShaGua often contradicts his bosses, but he doesn't allow his kids to talk back to him.*

**RELATED WORDS**

| | | |
|---|---|---|
| 山顶 38 | 头顶 128 | 到顶 737 |
| 拱顶 793 | 屋顶 1072 | 圆顶 1391 |
| 透顶 1826 | 拿大顶 1262 | |

---

**725 项** 項　U+9879　TM **10** FM 一

**xiàng**　N·MW　item, clause; nape (of the neck); sum (of money)

**项目** xiàngmù　N　item; project; sports event · MW 个

这是我今年最重要的**项目**。 *This is the most important project of the year for me.*

**项圈** xiàngquān　N　necklace · MW 个

**RELATED WORD**

款项 1573

---

**726 观** 觀　U+89C2　TM **10** FM 一

**guān**　N·V　to see, to look at; to watch, to observe

**观测** guāncè　V　to observe

根据你的**观测**, 明天会下雨吗？ *According to your observations, will it rain tomorrow?*

**观察** guānchá　V　to observe, to watch; to survey

**观点** guāndiǎn　N　point of view, opinion · MW 个、种

**观感** guāngǎn　N　impression(s) · MW 个

这样做给人的**观感**不好。 *This won't leave a good impression.*

**观光** guānguāng　V　to go sightseeing

**观看** guānkàn　V　to observe, to view, to watch; to visit

**观礼** guānlǐ　V　to attend a ceremony/celebration (by invitation)

**观念** guānniàn　N　concept, notion, thought; ideology; sense · MW 个、种

傻瓜有些**观念**很保守。 *Some of ShaGua's notions are very conservative.*

**观赏** guānshǎng　V　to view and admire, to enjoy the sight of

**观众** guānzhòng　N　spectator; audience · MW 个、位、名

**RELATED WORDS**

| | | |
|---|---|---|
| 主观 124 | 外观 218 | 壮观 238 |
| 乐观 299 | 参观 600 | 直观 609 |
| 美观 671 | 客观 1316 | 旁观 1473 |
| 悲观 1532 | 微观 1700 | 概观 1908 |
| 宇宙观 485 | 察言观色 1877 | 袖手旁观 1361 |

---

**727 玩** U+73A9　TM **10** FM 一

**wán**　N·V　curio; antique; to play, to enjoy oneself

**玩忽** wánhū　V　to neglect

**玩火** wánhuǒ　V　to play with fire; to trifle with

**玩具** wánjù　N　toy, plaything; knickknack · MW 个、套

孩子把**玩具**当朋友, 大人把朋友当**玩具**。 *Kids treat toys as their friends; adults treat their friends as toys.*

**玩命** wánmìng　V　to take foolish risks, to be reckless; to be extremely driven, to make a great effort

**玩弄** wánnòng　V　to play tricks on, to toy with; to make fun of

有些人就是爱**玩弄**小聪明。 *Some people just enjoy playing petty tricks.*

**玩偶** wán'ǒu　N　doll · MW 个

**玩赏** wánshǎng　V　to enjoy

**玩耍** wánshuǎ　V　to play, to have fun, to enjoy oneself

**玩味** wánwèi　V　to ponder, to contemplate

**727** 玩 **wán** (continued)

玩笑 **wánxiào** N joke; jest · MW 个

不要以为傻瓜是开**玩笑**, 其实, 他的话很值得**玩味**。 *Don't think ShaGua is joking; his words are actually worth thinking about.*

玩意儿 **wányìr** N toy, plaything; knickknack · MW 个

你以为你是什么**玩意儿**? *Who do you think you are?*

**RELATED WORDS**

| | | |
|---|---|---|
| 开玩笑 26 | 古玩 154 | 游玩 1818 |
| 吃喝玩乐 783 | 游山玩水 1818 | |

---

**728** 玲   U+73B2   TM **10** FM 一

**líng** ONOM tinkling of pieces of jade

玲珑 **línglóng** ADJ exquisite (of things); clever and nimble (of people)

---

**729** 珠   U+73E0   TM **10** FM 一

**zhū** N pearl; bead

珠宝 **zhūbǎo** N pearls and jewels; jewelry · MW 颗、粒、件

珠江 **Zhūjiāng** N Zhu River (Pearl River)

珠算 **zhūsuàn** N abacus

傻瓜会来两手**珠算**。 *ShaGua knows how to use the abacus.*

珠子 **zhūzi** N pearl; bead · MW 颗、粒

**RELATED WORDS**

| | | |
|---|---|---|
| 汗珠子 236 | 珍珠 515 | 泪珠 688 |
| 圆珠笔 1391 | 掌上明珠 1734 | |

---

**730** 班   U+73ED   TM **10** FM 一

**bān** N·MW class; team; shift; (theatrical) troupe; [measure word for scheduled transportation services (train service, flight, etc.) and for groups of people (classes, etc.)]

班车 **bānchē** N regular bus (service); shuttle bus · MW 辆、趟

班次 **bāncì** N classes/grades (in school); number of flights/trips/runs/etc. · MW 个

班房 **bānfáng** N jail, prison · MW 个、座

班机 **bānjī** N regular air service; shuttle flight · MW 架、趟

从北京到辛辛那提没有直飞的**班机**。 *There are no direct flights between Beijing and Cincinnati.*

班级 **bānjí** N classes/grades (in school) · MW 个

班长 **bānzhǎng** N class monitor; team leader · MW 个、名

班主任 **bānzhǔrèn** N teacher in charge of a particular class of students · MW 个、位、名

美国的教育体制中没有**班主任**这个概念。 *There is no concept like "banzhuren" in American education.*

班子 **bānzi** N group; troupe · MW 个、套

班组 **bānzǔ** N team/group (in a factory, a school, etc.) · MW 个

**RELATED WORDS**

| | | |
|---|---|---|
| 下班 10 | 上班 14 | 中班 86 |
| 日班 96 | 分班 173 | 交班 222 |
| 早班 268 | 当班 335 | 西班牙 352 |
| 加班 463 | 同班 541 | 科班 642 |
| 夜班 654 | 值班 1089 | 轮班 1112 |
| 倒班 1281 | 换班 1402 | 接班 1405 |
| 接班人 1405 | 领班 1465 | 插班 1555 |
| 航班 1717 | 晚班 1779 | 跟班 1784 |
| 脱班 1803 | | |

---

**731** 延   U+5EF6   TM **10** FM 一

**yán** V to prolong, to extend; to postpone, to put off; to employ

延长 **yáncháng** V to prolong, to extend, to lengthen

你的签证**延长**了吗? *Has your visa been extended?*

延迟 **yánchí** V to delay, to postpone

延缓 **yánhuǎn** V to delay, to postpone; to defer

延聘 **yánpìn** V to employ, to hire; to extend employment (to someone)

延期 **yánqī** V to delay; to postpone, to defer

音乐会**延期**了。 *The concert has been delayed.*

延伸 **yánshēn** V to extend, to stretch, to elongate; to spread

延误 **yánwù** V to delay; to incur loss due to delay

因为大雪的缘故, 班机**延误**了。 *The arriving flight was delayed because of the snow.*

延续 **yánxù** V to continue, to last, to extend

**RELATED WORDS**

| | | |
|---|---|---|
| 顺延 874 | 迟延 959 | 拖延 1396 |

## 732 羽   U+7FBD   TM **10**   FM 一

**yǔ** [N] feather, plume; wing; bird; fifth note of the pentatonic scale

羽毛 **yǔmáo** [N] feather, plume · [MW] 根

羽毛球 **yǔmáoqiú** [N] badminton · [MW] 个

羽绒衣 **yǔróngyī** [N] down-filled coat · [MW] 件

羽翼 **yǔyì** [N] wing · [MW] 对

你应该独立了，不能老是躲在父母的**羽翼**下。 *You should be independent; you can't always be under your parents' wing.*

## 733 砂   U+7802   TM **10**   FM 一

**shā** [N] sand, grit; gravel; granule

砂布 **shābù** [N] abrasive cloth · [MW] 块、片

砂尘 **shāchén** [N] sand dust · [MW] 粒

砂轮 **shālún** [N] grindstone, emery wheel · [MW] 个

砂糖 **shātáng** [N] granulated sugar · [MW] 粒、包

砂土 **shātǔ** [N] sandy/loamy soil · [MW] 堆

砂岩 **shāyán** [N] sandstone · [MW] 块

砂纸 **shāzhǐ** [N] sandpaper · [MW] 张

## 734 研   U+7814   TM **10**   FM 一

**yán** [V] to study, to research; to grind

研究 **yánjiū** [V·N] to study; research · [MW] 个、项

"Graduate student" 翻译成中文叫"**研究生**"，因为过去中国人认为大学生毕业以后才能做**研究**。*The Chinese translation of "graduate student" literally means "research student," because the Chinese used to think that students could not conduct research until they had finished their undergraduate studies.*

研磨 **yánmó** [V] to grind

研讨 **yántǎo** [V] to study and discuss, to deliberate

研制 **yánzhì** [V] to develop; to produce on a trial basis

**RELATED WORD**

科研 642

## 735 耻   U+803B   TM **10**   FM 一

**chǐ** [N·V·ADJ] shame, disgrace, humiliation; to feel shame; to mock; shameful, disgraceful

耻辱 **chǐrǔ** [N] disgrace; ignominy · [MW] 种

耻笑 **chǐxiào** [V] to mock; to sneer at

**耻笑**别人往往使人蒙受**耻辱**。*Sneering at someone often embarrasses him or her.*

耻与为伍 **chǐyǔwéiwǔ** [EXP] to be ashamed to associate with (someone)

**RELATED WORDS**

| | | |
|---|---|---|
| 不耻下问 24 | 无耻 139 | 可耻 243 |
| 羞耻 1154 | 廉耻 1615 | |

## 736 劲 劲   U+52B2   TM **10**   FM 一

**jìn** [N] strength; energy, vigor; spirit, drive, zeal; manner, expression; interest

**jìng** [ADJ] strong; powerful, sturdy

劲头 **jìntóu** [N] strength; energy, vigor; drive, zeal · [MW] 股

劲敌 **jìngdí** [N] formidable opponent/adversary · [MW] 个、名

劲旅 **jìnglǚ** [N] strong contingent · [MW] 支

这是一支**劲旅**，也是我们的**劲敌**。*This is a strong contingent and a formidable adversary.*

**RELATED WORDS**

| | | |
|---|---|---|
| 干劲 13 | 牛劲 51 | 来劲 260 |
| 用劲 313 | 加劲 463 | 卖劲 524 |
| 松劲 579 | 使劲 623 | 差劲 673 |
| 起劲 1421 | 强劲 1896 | 鼓足干劲 1688 |

## 737 到   U+5230   TM **10**   FM 一

**dào** [V·ADJ] to arrive (at), to reach; to leave for; considerate, thoughtful

到岸价格 **dào'ànjiàgé** [N] cost, insurance, and freight (CIF) · [MW] 个

到场 **dàochǎng** [V] to show up; to be present

到处 **dàochù** [ADJ] all around, everywhere

**到处**都有中国餐馆。*There are Chinese restaurants everywhere.*

到达 **dàodá** [V] to arrive (at), to reach, to get (to)

到底 **dàodǐ** [ADV·V] at last; eventually; after all, when all is said and done

**737 到 dào** (continued)

他**到底**是中国人还是日本人？ *Is he Chinese after all, or Japanese?*

**到顶 dàodǐng** V to reach the peak

**到会 dàohuì** V to attend a meeting

**到货通知 dàohuòtōngzhī** N notice of arrival · MW 个

**到货验收 dàohuòyànshōu** V to inspect incoming merchandise

**到家 dàojiā** ADJ·V to reach a very high level; to get home

你真是聪明**到家**了。 *Your intelligence has reached the highest level.*

你**到底**回**到家**了。 *You're finally home!*

**到来 dàolái** V to arrive; to come over

**到期 dàoqī** V to become due (of a loan, etc.); to mature; to expire

你的信用卡**到期**了。 *Your credit card has expired.*

**到手 dàoshǒu** V to be in (someone's) hands/ possession

**到头 dàotóu** V to reach the end

傻瓜当个市长也算走**到头**了。 *Being mayor may be as good as it gets for ShaGua.*

**到头来 dàotóulái** ADV in the end, finally

**RELATED WORDS**

| | | |
|---|---|---|
| 办到 195 | 马到成功 247 | 来到 260 |
| 收到 282 | 达到 505 | 直到 609 |
| 看到 841 | 迟到 959 | 料到 961 |
| 报到 1010 | 周到 1068 | 独到 1095 |
| 做到 1282 | 谈到 1356 | 等到 1437 |
| 签到 1439 | 提到 1554 | 说到底 1631 |
| 驾到 1693 | 遇到 1891 | 遭到 1931 |
| 一天到晚 1 | 从…到 66 | 想不到 1769 |
| 想得到 1769 | | |

---

**738 克**     U+514B     TM **10** FM |

**kè** V·MW can, to be able to; to restrain; to overcome, to subdue, to capture; to digest; to set a time limit; [measure word for grams]

**克服 kèfú** V to overcome, to conquer

傻瓜相信：天下没有**克服**不了的困难。 *ShaGua believes that there are no difficulties on earth that can't be overcome.*

**克复 kèfù** V to retake, to recover

**克扣 kèkòu** V to embezzle

**克隆 kèlóng** V to clone

---

**克制 kèzhì** V to restrain, to control

宗教仇恨和民族情绪是最难**克制**的。 *Religious hatred and national sentiment are extremely difficult to restrain.*

**RELATED WORDS**

| | | |
|---|---|---|
| 扑克 168 | 休克 213 | 马克思主义 247 |
| 攻克 253 | 巧克力 364 | 厘克 847 |
| 毫克 1721 | 奥林匹克 1435 | |

---

**739 点 點**     U+70B9     TM **10** FM |

**diǎn** N·V·MW drop; spot, dot; aspect; point; decimal point; refreshments, pastry, dim sum (type of Chinese cuisine); to nod; to check one by one; to select; to light; to point out; to touch on briefly, to hint; to skim; to embellish; to sow (seeds) in holes; [measure word for ideas (suggestions, opinions, etc.), for small amounts, and for time]

油点 *drop of oil*

特点 *characteristic*

据点 *strong point*

正点 *on time*

一点儿 *little bit*

**点菜 diǎncài** V to order food / a dish

在中国，大家抢着付账，但都不愿**点菜**。 *In China, everyone fights to pay the check, but nobody wants to be the one to order food for everyone.*

**点灯 diǎndēng** V to light a lamp

**点滴 diǎndī** ADJ·N a bit; bits and pieces, odds and ends; drops, droplets

**点火 diǎnhuǒ** V to ignite; to light a fire; to stir up trouble

**点名 diǎnmíng** V to call the roll; to name a person (to do something); to criticize by name

**点明 diǎnmíng** V to point out

**点破 diǎnpò** V to point out bluntly

有些事情，大家心里有数，还是不**点破**的好。 *In some cases, even though people know what is going on, it still isn't good to point out the truth in blunt fashion.*

**点钱 diǎnqián** V to count money

**点头 diǎntóu** V to nod one's head; to approve, to agree

他老爱**点头**。 *He always nods his head.*

他不**点头**，我们没法做。 *We can do nothing without his approval.*

**点缀 diǎnzhuì** V·N to decorate, to embellish; to be purely for show; decoration · MW 个

**点子 diǎnzi** N key point; idea · MW 个

**RELATED WORDS**

| | | |
|---|---|---|
| 一点儿 1 | 正点 76 | 支点 92 |
| 几点 115 | 交点 222 | 出点子 258 |
| 早点 268 | 切点 277 | 网点 390 |
| 有点 439 | 优点 447 | 歧点 585 |
| 差点 673 | 污点 681 | 观点 726 |
| 查点 741 | 茶点 767 | 地点 772 |
| 极点 798 | 标点 801 | 重点 839 |
| 盲点 906 | 准点 929 | 论点 947 |
| 要点 969 | 难点 974 | 基点 991 |
| 检点 1033 | 特点 1094 | 终点 1109 |
| 钟点 1125 | 焦点 1265 | 缺点 1305 |
| 甜点 1306 | 误点 1354 | 指点 1397 |
| 起点 1421 | 鬼点子 1433 | 装点 1476 |
| 清点 1495 | 落点 1547 | 据点 1553 |
| 亮点 1613 | 零点 1640 | 痛点 1725 |
| 晚点 1779 | 糕点 1833 | 端点 1889 |
| 弱点 1897 | 疑点 1917 | 小数点 61 |
| 立足点 125 | 临界点 771 | 销售点 1714 |

---

**740 青** U+9752 TM 10 FM |

**qīng** ADJ·N green; young, youthful; black; green grass; unripe crop

**青菜 qīngcài** N green vegetables; Chinese cabbage · MW 棵、把

**青草 qīngcǎo** N green grass · MW 片、棵、把

**青春 qīngchūn** N youth; youthfulness; spring
青春是无价的。 *Youth is priceless.*

**青豆 qīngdòu** N green soybean · MW 把、粒

**青椒 qīngjiāo** N green pepper · MW 个

**青霉素 qīngméisù** N penicillin · MW 支

**青年 qīngnián** N youth, young people · MW 个、名

**青少年 qīngshàonián** N teenagers, youths · MW 个、名

**青松 qīngsōng** N pine (tree) · MW 棵

**青铜 qīngtóng** N bronze · MW 块

**青蛙 qīngwā** N frog · MW 只

**青虾 qīngxiā** N freshwater shrimp · MW 只

**青鱼 qīngyú** N black carp (fish) · MW 条

**青云 qīngyún** N sky; noble, high in virtue/ position

**青云直上 qīngyúnzhíshàng** EXP rapid promotion, meteoric career

这家伙找了一个好岳父，就青云直上了。
*Look at this guy; after finding a powerful father-in-law, he has had a meteoric career.*

**RELATED WORDS**

| | | |
|---|---|---|
| 冬青 178 | 年青 182 | 鼻青脸肿 1794 |
| 愣头青 1735 | | |

---

**741 查** U+67E5 TM 10 FM |

**chá** V to check, to examine, to investigate; to consult

**查办 chábàn** V to investigate and deal with accordingly

**查抄 cháchāo** V to inventory and confiscate a criminal's possessions

**查点 chádiǎn** V to check the number/amount of

**查对 cháduì** V to check, to verify
答完试卷，一定要查对答案。 *After finishing the exam, you must check your answers again.*

**查封 cháfēng** V to seal up, to close down

**查号台 cháhàotái** N directory inquiries · MW 个

**查户口 cháhùkǒu** V to check residence cards

**查获 cháhuò** V to track down
老师查获了学生作弊的证据。 *The teacher has discovered evidence that the student cheated on the exam.*

**查禁 chájìn** V to ban, to prohibit

**查勘 chákān** V to survey

**查看 chákàn** V to examine (a situation); to look over

**查考 chákǎo** V to examine; to do research on

**查明 chámíng** V to ascertain through investigation; to find out
查明事实真相，才能不冤枉好人，不放过坏人。 *The point of ascertaining facts is to avoid punishing the innocent and setting the guilty free.*

**查票 chápiào** V to check tickets

**查清 cháqīng** V to investigate thoroughly

**查收 cháshōu** V to please find

**查税 cháshuì** V to conduct a tax inspection

**查问 cháwèn** V to question, to interrogate

**查询 cháxún** V to inquire (about); inquiry

**查阅 cháyuè** V to look up; to consult; to read
傻瓜给市图书馆购置具备查阅功能的计算机。 *ShaGua has purchased computers with a search function for the city library.*

**查证 cházhèng** V to check out (a story), to verify

**741 查 chá** (continued)

**RELATED WORDS**

| | | |
|---|---|---|
| 考查 530 | 抽查 788 | 备查 845 |
| 审查 911 | 检查 1033 | 复查 1059 |
| 清查 1495 | 追查 1507 | 搜查 1663 |
| 调查 1749 | 出境检查 258 | 市场调查 332 |

---

**742 妻** U+59BB TM **10** FM |

**qī** N wife; to marry a woman to a man

**妻儿老小 qī'érlǎoxiǎo** EXP married man's entire family

**妻子 qīzi** N wife · MW 个

**RELATED WORDS**

| | | |
|---|---|---|
| 夫妻 55 | 休妻 213 | 前妻 1329 |

---

**743 忠** U+5FE0 TM **10** FM |

**zhōng** ADJ·V·N faithful, loyal; honest; honest and considerate; to be loyal/devoted (to); advice

**忠诚 zhōngchéng** ADJ faithful, loyal

**忠告 zhōnggào** V·N to advise, to admonish; advice · MW 个

**忠厚 zhōnghòu** ADJ honest and considerate

**忠实 zhōngshí** ADJ faithful and trustworthy; true
给朋友的**忠告**必须要**忠实**。 *Advice given to a friend must be true.*

**忠于 zhōngyú** V to be faithful/devoted to
傻瓜是一个**忠厚**的人，虽然常跟傻瓜太太吵架，但非常**忠于**妻子。 *ShaGua is an honest and considerate person who often quarrels with his wife but is still very loyal to her.*

**忠贞 zhōngzhēn** ADJ loyal and dependable

**RELATED WORD**

尽忠 312

---

**744 肯** U+80AF TM **10** FM |

**kěn** ADV·V certainly, definitely; to be ready/willing to; to agree

**肯定 kěndìng** V·ADJ·ADV to affirm; to approve; positive, sure; definitely, undoubtedly

**肯定**别人的长处 *to affirm the strengths of (someone)*

我可以绝对**肯定**(此事)。 *I am 100% positive about it.*

我**肯定**会学中文。 *I am definitely going to study Chinese.*

**肯尼亚 Kěnníyà** N Kenya

**RELATED WORD**

宁肯 336

---

**745 岗** 崗 U+5C97 TM **10** FM |

**gǎng** N mound, ridge; post; sentry, guard

**岗警 gǎngjǐng** N guard on duty · MW 个、名
许多中国大学的大门都有**岗警**。 *There may be a guard posted at the main gate of many Chinese universities.*

**岗哨 gǎngshào** N lookout post · MW 个、名

**岗位 gǎngwèi** N lookout post; station · MW 个

**RELATED WORDS**

| | | |
|---|---|---|
| 门岗 130 | 站岗 1189 | 换岗 1402 |

---

**746 岩** U+5CA9 TM **10** FM |

**yán** N rock; cliff; crag

**岩石 yánshí** N rock · MW 块

**RELATED WORD**

砂岩 733

---

**747 革** U+9769 TM **10** FM |

**gé** V·N to change, to transform; to remove from office, to expel; leather, hide

**革除 géchú** V to abolish, to get rid of

**革命 gémìng** V·N to revolutionize; revolution · MW 场

**革新 géxīn** V·N to innovate, to reform; innovation, renovation · MW 次

**革职 gézhí** V to dismiss, to remove from (a position, an office)
许多搞**革新**的人都被**革职**了，因为并不是每一个人都支持**革新**。 *Because not everyone supports innovations, many who engaged in them were removed from their jobs.*

**RELATED WORDS**

| | | |
|---|---|---|
| 文革 70 | 反革命 111 | 皮革 261 |
| 改革 516 | | |

## 748 些 U+4E9B TM **10** FM |

**xiē** ADJ·MW some; few; several; [measure word for an indefinite amount]

**RELATED WORDS**

| 一些 1 | 有些 439 | 某些 536 |
|---|---|---|
| 好些 627 | 这些 715 | 那些 980 |
| 哪些 1666 | 那么些 980 | |

## 749 竖 竪 U+7AD6 TM **10** FM |

**shù** ADJ·V·N vertical, upright; from top to bottom; to erect, to stand, to set upright; vertical stroke (of a Chinese character); young servant

**竖井 shùjǐng** N pothole; well; (vertical) shaft · MW 口

**竖立 shùlì** V to erect, to stand, to set upright

**竖起 shùqǐ** V to hold up

**竖琴 shùqín** N harp · MW 台

傻瓜爱听教堂里的**竖琴**声。 *ShaGua likes to listen to the harp in church.*

**RELATED WORD**

横竖 1775

## 750 贤 賢 U+8D24 TM **10** FM |

**xián** N·ADJ worthy/virtuous person; virtuous and able, worthy; my dear

**贤达 xiándá** N prominent personage · MW 位

**贤慧 xiánhuì** ADJ virtuous (of a woman)

**贤明 xiánmíng** ADJ wise and able

**贤明**的人不一定娶到**贤慧**的妻子。 *A wise and able man might not necessarily marry a virtuous wife.*

**贤人 xiánrén** N person of virtue · MW 位

**RELATED WORD**

圣贤 142

## 751 导 導 U+5BFC TM **10** FM |

**dǎo** V·N to guide, to channel; to transmit, to conduct; to teach, to direct; adviser; director

**导弹 dǎodàn** N guided missile · MW 枚、发

**导电 dǎodiàn** V electric transmission

**导航 dǎoháng** V to pilot, to navigate

**导师 dǎoshī** N adviser; professor, teacher · MW 个、位、名

**导言 dǎoyán** N introduction (to a written piece) · MW 篇

我请我的**导师**给我的书写一篇**导言**。 *I invited my professor to write an introduction for my book.*

**导演 dǎoyǎn** N·V director; to direct (a play, film, etc.) · MW 个、位、名

人们往往只记得电影的名字，却忘记了**导演**的名字。 *People usually remember only the names of movies, but forget the directors.*

**导致 dǎozhì** V to lead to, to cause, to result in

**RELATED WORDS**

| 劝导 255 | 引导 371 | 传导 452 |
|---|---|---|
| 向导 603 | 推导 1242 | 指导 1397 |
| 教导 1424 | 领导 1465 | 诱导 1748 |
| 编导 1866 | | |

## 752 昌 U+660C TM **10** FM |

**chāng** ADJ prosperous, flourishing

**昌盛 chāngshèng** ADJ prosperous

**RELATED WORD**

繁荣昌盛 1988

## 753 星 U+661F TM **10** FM |

**xīng** N star; satellite; famous/star performer/athlete

**星辰 xīngchén** N star

**星河 xīnghé** N Milky Way (galaxy) · MW 条

**星际 xīngjì** N interplanetary

**星期 xīngqī** N week · MW 个

我们每个**星期**都有中文课。 *We have Chinese classes every week.*

**星球 xīngqiú** N celestial body (planet, satellite, etc.) · MW 个、颗

**星云 xīngyún** N nebula · MW 团

**星座 xīngzuò** N constellation · MW 个

**RELATED WORDS**

| 土星 15 | 木星 40 | 五星红旗 79 |
|---|---|---|
| 卫星 82 | 卫星通信 82 | 占星 153 |
| 水星 159 | 外星人 218 | 行星 327 |
| 寿星 440 | 红星 474 | 明星 1035 |
| 流星 1493 | 零星 1640 | 福星 1825 |
| 五角星 79 | 启明星 657 | |

## 754 是　U+662F　TM **10** FM |

**shì** V·ADJ·ADV·PRON·N to be; to praise; to justify;
right, yes; true; really; certainly; this, that;
major policies

是的，我是学生。 *Yes, I am a student.*

似**是**而非 *seemingly right, but actually wrong*

**是**年 *this year*

国**是** *major policies of the state*

**是的 shìde** V yes; right

**是非 shìfēi** N right and wrong

**是**的，我总**是**和他争论**是非**的问题。
*Yes, I argue with him all the time about what is
right or wrong.*

**是非题 shìfēití** N true or false · MW 道

**是否 shìfǒu** ADV if, whether; whether or not

我想知道：你**是否**做完了**是非题**？
*I would like to know whether or not you have
completed all the true-or-false questions.*

### RELATED WORDS

| | | |
|---|---|---|
| 又是 11 | 不是 24 | 于是 28 |
| 口是心非 42 | 正是 76 | 仅是 120 |
| 乃是 134 | 只是 160 | 凡是 193 |
| 可是 243 | 尽是 312 | 似是而非 322 |
| 但是 458 | 若是 554 | 总是 1330 |
| 既是 1572 | 都是 1578 | 就是 1836 |
| 就是说 1836 | 有的是 439 | 要不是 969 |
| 赔不是 1569 | 搬弄是非 1943 | 比比皆是 279 |
| 自以为是 305 | 实事求是 668 | |

## 755 显　顯　U+663E　TM **10** FM |

**xiǎn** V to show, to display; to be apparent/
obvious/noticeable; prominent, conspicuous;
illustrious and influential

**显赫 xiǎnhè** ADJ illustrious, famous, celebrated;
splendid

**显明 xiǎnmíng** ADJ obvious; distinct

**显露 xiǎnlù** V to appear, to become visible

**显然 xiǎnrán** ADJ clear, obvious, evident

**显然**，**显赫**的人很容易**显露**他们的背景。
*The lives of the famous are very transparent and
easy to follow.*

**显示 xiǎnshì** V to show, to display

**显微镜 xiǎnwēijìng** N microscope · MW 台

**显著 xiǎnzhù** ADJ remarkable, outstanding,
notable

### RELATED WORDS

| | |
|---|---|
| 明显 1035 | 液晶显示 1344 |

## 756 罗　羅　U+7F57　TM **10** FM |

**luó** V·N to display, to spread out; to collect, to
gather together; to sift; net (to catch birds, etc.);
sieve; silk gauze

**罗列 luóliè** V to list, to enumerate; to set out,
to display

**罗马 Luómǎ** N Rome

**罗盘 luópán** N compass · MW 个

中国人用**罗盘**看风水，西方人用中国人发明的
**罗盘**来航海。 *The Chinese used the compass to
practice feng shui; Westerners used the compass,
which the Chinese invented, to make voyages.*

**罗织 luózhī** V to frame, to trump up a charge
against

**罗致 luózhì** V to enlist the services of, to employ,
to recruit

### RELATED WORDS

| | | |
|---|---|---|
| 网罗 390 | 尼罗河 441 | 张罗 1208 |

## 757 男　U+7537　TM **10** FM |

**nán** N male; man; boy; son

**男厕 náncè** N men's restroom · MW 间

**男方 nánfāng** N bridegroom's/husband's side

**男高音 nángāoyīn** N tenor (singing) · MW 个

**男男女女 nánnánnǚnǚ** EXP men and women

**男女老少 nánnǚlǎoshào** EXP men and women;
young and old

候机厅里的**男女老少**都听到**男厕**里传出的
**男高音**。 *Everybody in the boarding area heard
the tenor's voice from the men's bathroom.*

**男朋友 nánpéngyou** N boyfriend; male friend ·
MW 个、位

**男人 nánrén** N men; menfolk · MW 个

**男生 nánshēng** N schoolboy; male student ·
MW 个、名

**男性 nánxìng** N male sex; man · MW 个

**男演员 nányǎnyuán** N actor · MW 个、位、名

**男子 nánzǐ** N male; man · MW 个、名

**男子汉 nánzǐhàn** N real/true man · MW 个、
位、名

**男子**不一定是**男子汉**。 *A male is not necessarily
a man.*

## 758 界 U+754C TM 10 FM |

**jiè** [N] boundary, border; limit; scope, range, extent; circles (groups of people); world; category, division

**界碑 jièbēi** [N] boundary marker/tablet · [MW] 块

**界河 jièhé** [N] boundary river · [MW] 条

**界限 jièxiàn** [N] boundary · [MW] 个

界河边上立着一块界碑，这是国家界限的标志。
*There is a single stone on the bank of the boundary river that marks the nation's border.*

### RELATED WORDS

| | | |
|---|---|---|
| 世界 163 | 世界大战 163 | 世界银行 163 |
| 世界语 163 | 分界 173 | 外界 218 |
| 交界 222 | 各界 425 | 政界 517 |
| 边界 710 | 临界点 771 | 地界 772 |
| 眼界 1570 | 越界 1575 | 商界 1612 |
| 境界 1848 | 工商界 12 | 文化界 70 |
| 艺术界 274 | 影剧界 1918 | 广开眼界 23 |

## 759 甚 U+751A TM 10 FM |

**shèn** [ADV·V·QPRON] very, extremely; to surpass, to be more than; what

甚念 *to miss someone very much*

日甚 *more and more every day*

想甚干甚 *to do whatever you have set your mind to*

**甚至 shènzhì** [ADV·CONJ] even; (to go) so far as to; even to the extent that

傻瓜甚至想过辞职。 *ShaGua even thought about resigning from office.*

## 760 固 U+56FA TM 10 FM |

**gù** [ADJ·ADV·V] solid; firm, stable; undoubtedly, certainly; to defend; to strengthen

**固定 gùdìng** [ADJ·V] fixed; regular; to fix, to set; to regularize

**固化 gùhuà** [V] to solidify

**固然 gùrán** [CONJ] of course, admittedly, undoubtedly

**固守 gùshǒu** [V] to defend tenaciously; to stick/cling to

**固体 gùtǐ** [N] solid (body) · [MW] 个

**固执 gùzhí** [ADJ] stubborn, obstinate

傻瓜这个固执的人，固然要固守他的观点。
*ShaGua is very stubborn, so of course he sticks to his argument.*

### RELATED WORDS

| | | |
|---|---|---|
| 坚固 381 | 加固 463 | 牢固 488 |
| 顽固 1204 | 胆固醇 1295 | 根深蒂固 1245 |

## 761 图 圖 U+56FE TM 10 FM |

**tú** [N·V] picture, drawing; chart, diagram; map; intent, plan, scheme; to paint; to draw; to attempt; to pursue, to seek; to desire

**图案 tú'àn** [N] pattern, design · [MW] 张

**图表 túbiǎo** [N] chart, diagram, table · [MW] 张

**图画 túhuà** [N] picture, painting, drawing · [MW] 张

**图解 tújiě** [V·N] to diagram; graph · [MW] 张

**图景 tújǐng** [N] view, prospect · [MW] 个

**图谋 túmóu** [V·N] to plot, to plan secretly; scheme · [MW] 个

敌人的图谋很阴险。 *Our enemy's plot is very sneaky.*

**图片 túpiàn** [N] picture, photograph · [MW] 张

**图示 túshì** [V·N] to illustrate (with pictures); illustration · [MW] 张

**图书 túshū** [N] books · [MW] 本

**图书馆 túshūguǎn** [N] library · [MW] 间

图书馆里有很多图书、图画、图表、图片……
*There are many books, pictures, charts, and photographs in the library.*

**图形 túxíng** [N] graph; figure; logo · [MW] 个、张

**图样 túyàng** [N] pattern, design · [MW] 个、张

**图章 túzhāng** [N] seal, stamp · [MW] 枚、个

**图纸 túzhǐ** [N] blueprint; drawing · [MW] 张

### RELATED WORDS

| | | |
|---|---|---|
| 力图 59 | 企图 170 | 地图 772 |
| 挂图 796 | 贪图 827 | 版图 897 |
| 描图 1407 | 插图 1555 | 意图 1812 |
| 心电图 232 | | |

## 762 围 圍 U+56F4 TM 10 FM |

**wéi** [V·N] to enclose, to fence off, to surround; circumference, perimeter; girth

**围城 wéichéng** [V] to encircle a city

**762** 围 **wéi** (continued)

围攻 **wéigōng** `V` to besiege; to attack jointly

他遭到一些人的**围攻**。 *He was surrounded and attacked by several people.*

围击 **wéijī** `V` to besiege

围巾 **wéijīn** `N` muffler, scarf · `MW` 条

有个女孩子送了他一条**围巾**。 *A girl gave him a scarf.*

围困 **wéikùn** `V` to besiege; to pin down

这座城市被洪水**围困**了几天。 *The city was boxed in by the flood for a few days.*

围棋 **wéiqí** `N` Go (board game), encirclement chess · `MW` 盘、副

围绕 **wéirǎo** `V` to revolve around; to rotate; to go around (something)

河流**围绕**着这座城，使它看起来像个岛。 *A river surrounds the city, so that the city looks like an island.*

**RELATED WORDS**

| | |
|---|---|
| 外围 218 | 包围 836 |
| 周围 1068 | 胸围 1709 |
| 解围 1928 | |

---

**763** 园 圜    U+56ED    `TM` **10** `FM` |

**yuán** `N` (recreational) park; garden, plot, land for growing vegetables/fruit/trees

园地 **yuándì** `N` garden plot; field; place to organize activities · `MW` 块

园丁 **yuándīng** `N` gardener; teacher · `MW` 个、位、名

中国人把老师比作**园丁**。 *Chinese people liken teachers to gardeners.*

园林 **yuánlín** `N` park; garden; landscape garden · `MW` 个、片

园圃 **yuánpǔ** `N` garden · `MW` 个

园艺 **yuányì** `N` horticulture, gardening; landscaping

摆弄**园艺**成了他新近的爱好。 *Gardening has become her latest hobby.*

**RELATED WORDS**

| | |
|---|---|
| 公园 103 | 田园 147 |
| 庄园 229 | 乐园 299 |
| 果园 544 | 校园 802 |
| 菜园 1001 | 庭园 1326 |
| 游园 1818 | 动物园 514 |

---

**764** 劳 勞    U+52B3    `TM` **10** `FM` |

**láo** `V·N·ADJ` to work, to labor; worker, laborer; toil; achievement, accomplishment; merit, reward; tired, fatigued

劳保 **láobǎo** `N` worker's compensation

劳动 **láodòng** `V` to work, to labor, to do physical labor

经济的发展, 使很多农民离开土地去从事工业**劳动**。 *Economic development has forced many farmers to leave the land to take up industrial work.*

劳动力 **láodònglì** `N` labor, manpower

劳方 **láofāng** `N` labor

劳改 **láogǎi** `V` to reform (criminals) through labor

劳工 **láogōng** `N` workers, laborers · `MW` 个、名

劳驾 **láojià** `V` excuse me

**劳驾**, 能让我过去吗? *Excuse me, can I get through, please?*

劳苦 **láokǔ** `ADJ` toil, hard work

劳累 **láolèi** `ADJ·V` overworked; tired; to cause trouble for

劳碌 **láolù** `ADJ` hardworking

劳神 **láoshén** `V` to bother, to trouble

劳务 **láowù** `N` labor and service

劳役 **láoyì** `N` forced labor

劳资 **láozī** `N` labor and capital; labor and management

**RELATED WORDS**

| | | |
|---|---|---|
| 任劳任怨 211 | 功劳 252 | 辛劳 331 |
| 徒劳 873 | 疲劳 1328 | 酬劳 1648 |
| 操劳 1965 | 慰劳 1968 | 犬马之劳 54 |

---

**765** 芭    U+82AD    `TM` **10** `FM` |

**bā** `N` fragrant plant; herb; banana

芭蕉 **bājiāo** `N` banana · `MW` 条

芭蕉扇 **bājiāoshàn** `N` palm-leaf fan · `MW` 把

芭蕾 **bālěi** `N` ballet

---

**766** 茫    U+832B    `TM` **10** `FM` |

**máng** `ADJ` vast; hazy; boundless and indistinct; ignorant, in the dark, unaware

茫然 **mángrán** `ADJ` oblivious; at a loss

这使他完全**茫然**失措。 *It left him at a complete loss.*

**RELATED WORDS**

苍茫 996     迷茫 1187

---

**767** 茶    U+8336    TM **10** FM |

chá  N  tea

茶杯 chábēi  N  teacup, tea glass · MW 个

茶匙 cháchí  N  teaspoon · MW 个

茶点 chádiǎn  N  tea and cake · MW 件

茶馆 cháguǎn  N  teahouse; cafe · MW 家、间

茶壶 cháhú  N  teapot · MW 个、把

茶花 cháhuā  N  camellia · MW 朵

茶具 chájù  N  tea set · MW 套

茶盘 chápán  N  tea tray · MW 个

茶水 cháshuǐ  N  (boiled) water for tea · MW 杯

茶碗 cháwǎn  N  teacup · MW 个

茶叶 cháyè  N  tea; tea leaves · MW 片、包、盒

茶艺 cháyì  N  skill in serving tea

**RELATED WORDS**

红茶 474    油茶 683    泡茶 1492
绿茶 1707    乌龙茶 601    柠檬茶 1029

---

**768** 草    U+8349    TM **10** FM |

cǎo  N·ADJ·V  grass; straw, hay; draft (of a document); careless; hasty; illegible; cursive; rough, not final (document); to draft, to draw up

草案 cǎo'àn  N  draft (legislation, proposal, etc.) · MW 个

草案准备好了, 你能看一下吗？ *The draft is done; can you take a look?*

草包 cǎobāo  N  straw bag; idiot · MW 个

这是一个**草包**。 *This is a straw bag.*

他是一个**草包**。 *He is an idiot.*

草地 cǎodì  N  lawn; meadow · MW 片

草稿 cǎogǎo  N  draft · MW 份

草料 cǎoliào  N  forage, fodder · MW 堆

草绿 cǎolǜ  ADJ  grass-green

草帽 cǎomào  N  straw hat · MW 顶

草拟 cǎonǐ  V  to draft, to draw up, to prepare

草坪 cǎopíng  N  lawn · MW 片

草率 cǎoshuài  ADJ  careless; sloppy

---

请不要**草率**下结论, 还是先调查一下吧。 *Please don't jump to conclusions; let's investigate first.*

草原 cǎoyuán  N  grassland, prairie · MW 片

草籽 cǎozǐ  N  grass seed · MW 粒

**RELATED WORDS**

中草药 86    兰草 126    谷草 446
牧草 468    斩草除根 646    青草 740
枯草热 799    香草 834    杂草 856
烟草 1177    铲草除根 1304    药草 1392
除草 1418    起草 1421    饲草 1447
野草 1685    粮草 1759    割草机 1761
风吹草动 194

---

**769** 荣 榮    U+8363    TM **10** FM |

róng  N·ADJ  glory; thriving, flourishing (of plants); prosperous; glorious, honorable

荣华富贵 rónghuáfùguì  EXP  glory, splendor; wealth and glory

荣获 rónghuò  V  to be honored with

荣辱 róngrǔ  N  glory and disgrace

荣幸 róngxìng  ADJ  honored; lucky

与您见面感到很**荣幸**。 *I'm honored to meet you.*

荣耀 róngyào  N·ADJ  glory, honor; glorious · MW 个

荣誉 róngyù  N  glory, honor · MW 个

**RELATED WORDS**

光荣 491    虚荣 1534    繁荣 1988
繁荣昌盛 1988    欣欣向荣 634

---

**770** 荧 熒    U+8367    TM **10** FM |

yíng  ADJ·N  glimmering, twinkling; dazzled; screen

荧光 yíngguāng  N  fluorescence

荧光屏 yíngguāngpíng  N  television screen · MW 个

---

**771** 临 臨    U+4E34    TM **10** FM |

lín  V·ADV  to overlook; to face, to confront; to arrive; to be present; to be close to, to be about to; on the point of; just before

临别 línbié  V  just before parting

**771 临 lín** (continued)

读了四年大学, 到**临别**时, 她才说：“我爱你！”
*After four years of college together, she didn't say, "I love you" to the boy until just before they went their separate ways.*

**临产 línchǎn** V to be about to give birth

**临界点 línjièdiǎn** N crisis, critical point · MW 个

**临时 línshí** ADJ·ADV temporary; temporarily

可惜这位非常优异的中文教师是**临时**代课的老师。 *What a pity, this amazing Chinese teacher was only a temporary substitute.*

**临死 línsǐ** V to be facing death, to be on one's deathbed

**临危 línwēi** V to be dying (from illness), to be facing death

**临终 línzhōng** V to be facing death, to be on one's deathbed

RELATED WORDS

| | | |
|---|---|---|
| 来临 260 | 光临 491 | 面临 721 |
| 驾临 1693 | | |

**772 地** U+5730  TM 10  FM |

**de** AV [used after an adjective/phrase to form an adverb before a verb (= English -ly)]

**dì** N Earth; land, fields, soil, ground; floor; prefecture; location, position; situation

**地板 dìbǎn** N floor; field · MW 块

**地表 dìbiǎo** N Earth's surface · MW 层

**地步 dìbù** N condition (usually undesirable), plight; degree, extent · MW 个

**地层 dìcéng** N stratum (geology); layer

**地带 dìdài** N zone, belt, region · MW 个

**地道 dìdào** N tunnel; subway · MW 条

**地道 dìdao** ADJ pure, genuine, authentic; typical; real; well-done

**地点 dìdiǎn** N place, location, locale · MW 个

**地段 dìduàn** N area · MW 个

傻瓜家所处的**地段**不是太好。 *The location of ShaGua's house is not very good.*

**地方 dìfāng** N locality; local administration · MW 个

**地方 dìfang** N place; space, room; part

**地基 dìjī** N foundation, base · MW 个

**地界 dìjiè** N land boundary · MW 个

**地雷 dìléi** N land mine · MW 颗、枚

**地理 dìlǐ** N geography

**地面 dìmiàn** N Earth's surface; ground; floor; (administrative) area

**地名 dìmíng** N place name · MW 个

**地契 dìqì** N title deed (for land) · MW 张、份

**地契**是拥有房地产的证据。 *A title deed is evidence of the ownership of a piece of property.*

**地球 dìqiú** N Earth

**地区 dìqū** N area; district; region · MW 个

**地毯 dìtǎn** N carpet, rug · MW 张、块

**地铁 dìtiě** N subway; subway train · MW 条

**地图 dìtú** N map; atlas · MW 张

在纽约, 有不少人拿着**地图**找**地铁**。 *Quite a few people use maps to locate the subway in New York.*

**地位 dìwèi** N position; status · MW 个

**地下 dìxià** N underground; secret (activity)

**地震 dìzhèn** V·N to shake the earth; earthquake · MW 次

**地址 dìzhǐ** N address; location · MW 个

**地主 dìzhǔ** N landlord; landowner · MW 个

**地租 dìzū** N land rent · MW 笔

RELATED WORDS

| | | |
|---|---|---|
| 工地 12 | 土地 15 | 大地 20 |
| 天地 25 | 山地 38 | 平地 78 |
| 本地 90 | 无地自容 139 | 圣地 142 |
| 田地 147 | 旧地重游 165 | 内地 191 |
| 外地 218 | 产地 219 | 心地 232 |
| 坟地 281 | 打地铺 289 | 当地 335 |
| 旱地 387 | 扫地 402 | 此地 416 |
| 余地 419 | 质地 597 | 空地 669 |
| 洼地 687 | 园地 763 | 草地 768 |
| 场地 773 | 坡地 775 | 极地 798 |
| 阵地 809 | 故地 816 | 耕地 817 |
| 重地 839 | 种地 893 | 基地 991 |
| 菜地 1001 | 陆地 1043 | 特地 1094 |
| 房地产 1145 | 房地契 1145 | 驻地 1207 |
| 荒地 1222 | 盆地 1261 | 席地 1325 |
| 墓地 1545 | 营地 1546 | 落地式 1547 |
| 落地 1547 | 暗地里 1676 | 属地 1793 |
| 就地 1836 | 腹地 1869 | 遍地 1892 |
| 随地 1911 | 天经地义 25 | 天南地北 25 |
| 不败之地 24 | 铺天盖地 1713 | 脚踏实地 1804 |
| 谢天谢地 1890 | | |

## 773 场 場    U+573A    TM **10** FM |

**chǎng** N·MW gathering place; stage; spot; scene; field; game; [measure word for events (sports/cultural events, concerts, etc.)]

场次 **chǎngcì** MW [measure word for the number of times a film has been shown, a play has been performed, etc.]

场地 **chǎngdì** N area; field · MW 个

场合 **chǎnghé** N situation, occasion · MW 个

虽然傻瓜不善言辞, 但讲话很注意**场合**。
*Even though ShaGua is not good at speaking, he is careful to speak appropriately for the occasion.*

场面 **chǎngmiàn** N scene, setting; spectacle; occasion; appearance · MW 个

奥运会开幕式的**场面**很壮观。 *The opening ceremony of the Olympics was just magnificent.*

有些人太讲究**场面**。 *Some people pay too much attention to appearances.*

场所 **chǎngsuǒ** N location, place · MW 个

### RELATED WORDS

| | | |
|---|---|---|
| 入场 5 | 入场券 5 | 下场 10 |
| 工场 12 | 开场 26 | 禾场 108 |
| 立场 125 | 全场 172 | 在场 188 |
| 刑场 256 | 出场 258 | 早场 268 |
| 收场 282 | 会场 295 | 用场 313 |
| 市场 332 | 市场价格 332 | 市场调查 332 |
| 市场学 332 | 当场 335 | 沙场 342 |
| 林场 412 | 农场 423 | 牧场 468 |
| 冰场 493 | 冷场 494 | 考场 530 |
| 机场 577 | 夜场 654 | 怯场 697 |
| 过场 712 | 进场 713 | 到场 737 |
| 包场 836 | 现场 975 | 菜场 1001 |
| 战场 1044 | 终场 1109 | 浴场 1170 |
| 球场 1199 | 捧场 1240 | 猎场 1444 |
| 猪场 1445 | 剧场 1468 | 渔场 1496 |
| 登场 1521 | 散场 1579 | 商场 1612 |
| 晚场 1779 | 舞场 1790 | 操场 1965 |
| 飞机场 81 | 走过场 265 | 养鸡场 670 |
| 养鱼场 670 | 养猪场 670 | 停车场 1588 |

## 774 坑    U+5751    TM **10** FM |

**kēng** N·V hole, pit; tunnel; to trap; to cheat, to defraud; to bury alive

坑道 **kēngdào** N tunnel · MW 条

坑害 **kēnghài** V to lead into a trap

坑坑洼洼 **kēngkēngwāwā** EXP full of bumps and holes, bumpy

### RELATED WORD

粪坑 1334

## 775 坡    U+5761    TM **10** FM |

**pō** N slope; slant, incline

坡地 **pōdì** N hillside field · MW 块、片

坡度 **pōdù** N slope · MW 个

坡田 **pōtián** N sloping field · MW 片、块

### RELATED WORDS

山坡 38      斜坡 1307

## 776 吸    U+5438    TM **10** FM |

**xī** V to inhale, to breathe in; to draw (liquid) into one's body; to absorb; to attract

吸潮器 **xīcháoqì** N dehumidifier · MW 台

吸尘 **xīchén** V to vacuum

吸尘器 **xīchénqì** N vacuum cleaner · MW 台

吸毒 **xīdú** V to take drugs

吸气 **xīqì** V to inhale, to breathe in

吸取 **xīqǔ** V to absorb; to draw

我们必须**吸取**过去的教训。 *We must absorb the lessons of the past.*

吸热 **xīrè** V to absorb heat

吸入 **xīrù** V to inhale; to suck in

吸收 **xīshōu** V to absorb; to suck up; to recruit; to admit

吸收营养 *to absorb nutrients*

吸收入学 *to admit to college*

吸引 **xīyǐn** V to attract; to draw

**吸引**人才方能使社会进步。 *Attracting talented people advances society.*

### RELATED WORDS

呼吸 779      上呼吸道 14      深呼吸 1345

## 777 吻    U+543B    TM **10** FM |

**wěn** V·N to kiss; lips; mouth

吻合 **wěnhé** ADJ·V identical; to coincide

### RELATED WORDS

口吻 42      亲吻 908

## 778 呀    U+5440   TM **10** FM |

**yā** ONOM ah, oh (expressing surprise); to creak, to squeak

**ya** AV [variant of 啊, used after a word ending phonetically in *a, e, i, o,* or *ü*]

**RELATED WORD**

哎呀 562

## 779 呼    U+547C   TM **10** FM |

**hū** V·N·ONOM to exhale, to breathe out; to shout, to cry out; to call; sound of snoring

**呼喊 hūhǎn** V to shout, to yell

**呼号 hūhào** V to wail, to cry out in distress; to radio/call (using letters, Morse code, signs)

**呼唤 hūhuàn** V to call; to shout, to yell · MW 声

中国**呼唤**着教育改革。*China is calling for educational reform.*

**呼叫 hūjiào** V to call; to shout, to yell

**呼救 hūjiù** V to call for help, to send out an SOS

**呼噜 hūlu** N snore, snoring

没有傻瓜惊天动地的**呼噜**，傻瓜太太睡不着觉。 *Without ShaGua's earthshaking snoring, Mrs. ShaGua could not fall asleep.*

**呼吸 hūxī** V to breathe

**呼应 hūyìng** V to echo, to respond (to); to work in concert with

当然，傻瓜太太也惊天动地地**呼应**傻瓜的**呼噜**。 *Of course, Mrs. ShaGua's own snoring echoed ShaGua's and was earthshaking in its own right.*

**RELATED WORDS**

上呼吸道 14    欢呼 366    传呼 452
招呼 1232    称呼 1288    深呼吸 1345
打招呼 289

## 780 咬    U+54AC   TM **10** FM |

**yǎo** V to bite, to snap at; to grip; to pronounce, to articulate; to close in on, to be neck and neck; to corrode (of metal); to irritate (the skin)

叫唤的狗不**咬**人。*Barking dogs seldom bite.*

反**咬**别人 *to make a false countercharge*

**咬**字清晰 *clearly articulating*

**咬**文嚼字 *to fight over every word, to pay excessive attention to wording* (LIT *to bite phrases and chew characters*)

**咬耳朵 yǎo'ěrduo** V to whisper

**咬紧牙关 yǎojǐnyáguān** EXP to grit one's teeth; to bite the bullet (figurative)

**咬牙 yǎoyá** V to clench one's teeth (in hatred/ defiance); to grind one's teeth (in sleep)

再困难也得**咬牙**顶住。*No matter how difficult it is, we must clench our teeth and hold out.*

**咬住 yǎozhù** V to bite (into); to grip, to hold tight, to refuse to let go of

**RELATED WORD**

叮咬 284

## 781 哄    U+54C4   TM **10** FM |

**hōng** ONOM guffaw; roar (of laughter, noise)

**哄**堂大笑 *general outbreak of laughter*

**hǒng** V to fool, to cheat; to coax, to humor, to calm

你**哄**不了傻瓜。*You can't fool ShaGua.*

**hòng** N horseplay; racket, roar (of a crowd)

一**哄**而散 *to scatter/leave with a lot of commotion*

**哄动 hōngdòng** V·ADJ to cause a sensation; stirred up

**哄抬 hōngtái** V to drive up (prices)

**RELATED WORDS**

一哄而散 1    乱哄哄 901    闹哄哄 1323
起哄 1421    瞒哄 1914

## 782 哑 啞    U+54D1   TM **10** FM |

**yǎ** ADJ dumb, mute; speechless; hoarse; husky; unexploded (of a bomb, etc.)

**哑巴 yǎba** N mute person · MW 个、名

**哑巴亏 yǎbakuī** N inability to discuss one's grievances · MW 个

傻瓜吃了很多**哑巴亏**。*ShaGua bears many grievances that he is unable to discuss.*

**RELATED WORDS**

沙哑 342    盲哑教育 906    聋哑 1431
装聋作哑 1476

## 783 吃    U+5403   TM **10** FM |

**chī** V   to eat; to live off/on, to scrounge off;
to absorb, to soak up; to grasp, to understand;
to annihilate, to wipe out, to eradicate;
to endure, to withstand; to take, to suffer;
to exhaust, to be a strain (on); to stammer

吃晚饭 *to eat dinner*

吃手艺 *to make a living (on some skill)*

这种布很吃水。*This kind of cloth absorbs water.*

你吃透了她的话吗？ *Did you really understand
her words?*

吃掉敌人 *to annihilate an enemy*

吃力 *to be a strain*

吃不开 **chībukāi** ADJ   unpopular

有时候，诚信的人反而吃不开。*Oddly, honest
people are sometimes unpopular.*

吃不下 **chībuxià** V   to not feel like eating

吃不消 **chībuxiāo** V   to be unable to stand
(because of exertion, fatigue, etc.)

吃穿 **chīchuān** N   food and clothing

吃醋 **chīcù** EXP   to be jealous (LIT to drink vinegar)

吃得开 **chīdekāi** ADJ   popular

有时候，投机取巧的人反而吃得开。*On the other
hand, sometimes deceitful people are popular.*

吃饭 **chīfàn** V   to eat; to live off/on; to keep
(someone) alive

你想吃饭吗？ *Would you like to eat?*

你靠什么吃饭？ *What keeps you alive?*

也许有人不吃饭，但没有人不吃醋。*There may
be someone who doesn't eat food, but there is no
one who doesn't "drink vinegar" (who isn't jealous).*

吃喝玩乐 **chīhēwánlè** EXP   to eat, drink, and be
merry

吃惊 **chījīng** V   to be surprised/amazed/shocked

吃苦 **chīkǔ** V   to suffer, to put up with hardship

吃苦头 **chīkǔtou** V   to suffer

吃亏 **chīkuī** V   to lose out, to come to grief; to be
at a disadvantage

中国有句名言："吃亏是福。" *There is a famous
Chinese saying: "Suffering a loss can be good luck."*

吃闲饭 **chīxiánfàn** EXP   to lead an idle life;
to be a parasite

吃香 **chīxiāng** EXP   to be very popular

现在中文很吃香。*Today, Chinese is very popular.*

**RELATED WORDS**

大吃一惊 20     口吃 42     小吃 61
好吃 627

## 784 哇    U+54C7   TM **10** FM |

**wā** ONOM   sound of vomiting/crying

哇噻 **wāsāi** ONOM   wow!; to be amazed

## 785 扔    U+6254   TM **10** FM |

**rēng** V   to throw, to toss; to throw away

扔下 **rēngxià** V   to abandon

## 786 扮    U+626E   TM **10** FM |

**bàn** V   to play (the part/role of);
to disguise oneself; to dress up; to put on
(an expression)

扮相 **bànxiàng** N   appearance/look (of an
actor/actress in costume); appearance ·
MW 个

扮演 **bànyǎn** V   to play (the role/part of)

每个人都在社会的舞台上扮演各种角色。
*All people play various roles on society's
stage.*

扮装 **bànzhuāng** V   to apply makeup

**RELATED WORDS**

打扮 289     装扮 1476

## 787 押    U+62BC   TM **10** FM |

**yā** V·N   to detain (in custody); to escort
(a prisoner); to give as security, to mortgage,
to pawn; pledge; signature

押当 **yādàng** V   to pawn

押解 **yājiè** V   to escort (a prisoner)

押金 **yājīn** N   (cash) deposit · MW 笔

傻瓜买房子时，付了一半房价作押金。
*When ShaGua bought his house, he paid 50%
of the sale price as a deposit.*

押韵 **yāyùn** V·ADJ   to rhyme; rhyming

押租 **yāzū** V   to pay a rent deposit

**RELATED WORDS**

在押 188     扣押 401     典押 532
看押 841

## 788 抽　U+62BD　TM **10** FM |

**chōu** V　to take out, to remove; to sprout; to grow up; to absorb; to draw (out); to shrink; to whip, to lash

抽出 *to take out from in between*

抽条 *to put forth*

抽血 *to draw blood*

抽鞭子 *to whip*

抽查 **chōuchá** V　to do a spot-check

抽打 **chōudǎ** V　to whip, to lash

抽风 **chōufēng** V　to cause a draft; to have convulsions

抽风机 **chōufēngjī** N　(ventilating) fan · MW 台

抽筋 **chōujīn** V　to have a cramp

抽空 **chōukòng** V　to find the time

抽泣 **chōuqì** V　to sob

傻瓜的大儿子**抽泣**了。*ShaGua's older son sobbed.*

抽气 **chōuqì** V　to suck/pump air out

抽签 **chōuqiān** V　to draw/cast lots

抽水 **chōushuǐ** V　to pump water

抽税 **chōushuì** V　to levy a tax

抽屉 **chōuti** N　drawer · MW 个

傻瓜的大儿子是从傻瓜的**抽屉**里拿的钱。
*ShaGua's older son took money from ShaGua's drawer.*

抽象 **chōuxiàng** ADJ　abstract

抽烟 **chōuyān** V　to smoke (a cigarette)

傻瓜打过大儿子，因为他偷家里的钱去**抽烟**。
*ShaGua once beat his older son when he stole money from home so that he could get cigarettes to smoke.*

抽样 **chōuyàng** V　to sample · MW 个、份

## 789 担 擔　U+62C5　TM **10** FM |

**dān** V·N　to take on, to undertake; (carrying) pole

担保 **dānbǎo** V　to guarantee, to be responsible for

傻瓜太太**担保**儿子不会再从抽屉里"拿"钱。
*Mrs. ShaGua guaranteed that her older son would not take money from the drawer again.*

担当 **dāndāng** V　to take on, to undertake

担负 **dānfù** V　to bear, to shoulder; to be charged with

担架 **dānjià** N　stretcher · MW 副

担任 **dānrèn** V　to assume the office of; to hold the job of

担心 **dānxīn** V　to worry, to be anxious

傻瓜**担心**儿子再犯错误。*ShaGua worried that his son would make the same mistake again.*

担忧 **dānyōu** V　to worry, to be anxious

傻瓜太太并不**担忧**这个问题。*Mrs. ShaGua, however, wasn't worried.*

### RELATED WORDS

负担 435　　　　承担 972

## 790 拍　U+62CD　TM **10** FM |

**pāi** V·N　to beat; to clap, to pat; to shoot (a photograph, a movie, etc.); to send (a telegram); racket (sports); paddle

拍案 **pāi'àn** V　to slap the table (in anger, surprise, etc.)

傻瓜曾经跟顶头上司**拍案**争吵。*ShaGua once struck his desk in anger in front of his boss.*

拍板 **pāibǎn** V·N　to beat time with clappers; to clinch a deal; to have the final say; clappers · MW 块

拍打 **pāida** V　to beat; to slap, to pat

傻瓜说他没有打孩子，只是轻轻**拍打**他的屁股。
*ShaGua denied beating his older son. He only "lightly patted" him on the rear.*

拍击 **pāijī** V　to beat, to smack

拍马屁 **pāimǎpì** EXP　to flatter, to suck up to

拍卖 **pāimài** V　to auction; to sell merchandise at reduced prices

拍摄 **pāishè** V　to shoot (a photograph, a movie, etc.)

拍手 **pāishǒu** V　to applaud

拍照 **pāizhào** V　to take (a picture); to shoot (a film)

拍子 **pāizi** N　racket; bat; paddle; beat/tempo (music) · MW 个、副

### RELATED WORDS

合拍 296　　　　吹吹拍拍 559

## 791 拔　U+62D4　TM **10** FM |

**bá** V　to pull out/up, to draw out; to suck out; to choose, to select; to lift, to raise; to exceed, to surpass; to capture, to seize

拔出 **báchū** V　to pull/draw out

拔除 **báchú** V to pull out, to remove

傻瓜从腰间**拔出**钳子，**拔除**了钉子。
*ShaGua pulled a pair of pliers from his waistband to remove a nail.*

拔罐子 **báguànzi** V cupping (technique in traditional Chinese medicine)

拔河 **báhé** V tug-of-war (game)

拔尖 **bájiān** ADJ·V outstanding, tip-top, superb; to push oneself to the front

拔牙 **báyá** V to extract a tooth

傻瓜最怕去看牙医，特别怕看牙医给孩子**拔牙**。
*ShaGua was scared to see the dentist, especially watching him extract his children's teeth.*

**RELATED WORDS**

挺拔 1408    海拔 1494    选拔 1510
提拔 1554

虽然他**拼命**地恭维她，但她还是拒绝了他。
*Although he tried desperately to flatter her, she still rejected him.*

不要**拼命**地**拼凑**一些不成为理由的理由来说服我。 *Don't try to put together some unreasonable argument to persuade me.*

拼死 **pīnsǐ** V to risk one's life

拼写 **pīnxiě** V to spell

拼音 **pīnyīn** N·V pinyin (official Chinese romanization system); to combine sounds into syllables · MW 个、组

学会汉语**拼音**是学好中文的第一步。
*Mastering Chinese phonetics is the first step in learning Chinese well.*

**RELATED WORD**

七拼八凑 34

---

**792** 择 擇 U+62E9 TM **10** FM |

**zé** V to choose, to select, to pick

择交 **zéjiāo** V to choose friends

从你**择交**的朋友，就能知道你的未来。
*Depending on your choice of friends, people can guess at how you might turn out.*

**RELATED WORD**

选择 1510

---

**793** 拱 U+62F1 TM **10** FM |

**gǒng** V·N to join one's hands together; to fold one's hands in salute; to surround, to encircle; to arch; arch

拱顶 **gǒngdǐng** N vault; dome · MW 个

拱形 **gǒngxíng** N arch · MW 个

---

**794** 拼 U+62FC TM **10** FM |

**pīn** V to put/piece/join together; to risk one's life; to go all out; to spell

拼凑 **pīncòu** V to put/piece together (pieces, fragments)

拼接 **pīnjiē** V toggle joint

拼命 **pīnmìng** V·ADV to risk one's life; with all one's might; desperately

---

**795** 挤 擠 U+6324 TM **10** FM |

**jǐ** V to squeeze, to press closely together, to crowd; to push one's way, to press; to repel, to reject; to squeeze out, to expel

挤眉弄眼 **jǐméinòngyǎn** EXP to make eyes (at); to wink

挤奶 **jǐnǎi** V to milk (a cow, etc.)

挤压 **jǐyā** V to squeeze, to crowd

他在公共汽车里被**挤压**得喘不过气来。
*There was so little space on the bus that he almost couldn't breathe.*

**RELATED WORDS**

拥挤 1014    排挤 1241

---

**796** 挂 掛 U+6302 TM **10** FM |

**guà** V·N to hang, to put up; to be covered/coated (with); to dial, to call; to hang up; to register (at a hospital, etc.); to hitch (up); to get caught; to worry (about), to be concerned (about)

挂彩 **guàcǎi** V to be wounded in action

挂车 **guàchē** N trailer (vehicle) · MW 辆

挂挡 **guàdǎng** V to put into gear

挂钩 **guàgōu** V to link up with, to establish contact with; coupling (of a railroad car)

挂号 **guàhào** V to register, to take a number (at a hospital, etc.); to send by registered mail

**796** 挂 **guà** (continued)

傻瓜到医院给傻瓜太太**挂号**。*ShaGua went to the hospital to get a number for Mrs. ShaGua.*

傻瓜寄的是**挂号**信，因为里面有重要的材料。 *ShaGua certified the parcel because it contained some important documents.*

挂面 **guàmiàn** N fine dried noodles, pasta · MW 把、碗

挂名 **guàmíng** V titular, in name only

挂念 **guàniàn** V to miss; to be concerned about

傻瓜非常**挂念**他生病的母亲。*ShaGua is very concerned about his sick mother.*

挂牌 **guàpái** V to hang out one's shingle, to open an office / a business; to wear a name tag while on duty

挂失 **guàshī** V to report the loss of

挂帅 **guàshuài** V to be in command, to take charge

挂图 **guàtú** N wall map/chart · MW 张

**RELATED WORDS**

牵挂 853     张挂 1208

---

**797** 桂    U+6842    TM **10** FM |

**guì** N cinnamon; cassia bark tree

桂冠 **guìguān** N laurel, victory garland; contest winner · MW 顶

桂花 **guìhuā** N fragrance; sweet-scented osmanthus · MW 朵

桂树 **guìshù** N cinnamon; cassia bark tree · MW 棵

很多美国人喜欢**桂树**皮味道的饼干。 *Many Americans like doughnuts flavored with cinnamon.*

**RELATED WORD**

肉桂 437

---

**798** 极 極    U+6781    TM **10** FM |

**jí** N·ADV apex; extreme; extremity; to the greatest extent, extremely

极大 **jídà** ADV enormously, (to the) maximum

尽管只演小角色，但她还是感到**极大**的快乐。 *Even though she only has a small role in the play, she is still extremely happy.*

极地 **jídì** N polar region

极点 **jídiǎn** N farthest point, extremity; pole; limit; utmost · MW 个

---

极度 **jídù** N·ADV extreme point; extremely; ultimately

极端 **jíduān** N·ADJ extreme; absolute · MW 个

他从一个**极端**走到另一个**极端**。*He went from one extreme to the other.*

极光 **jíguāng** N aurora, northern/southern (polar) lights · MW 束、道

极目 **jímù** V to look as far as the eye can see

极品 **jípǐn** N highest grade · MW 个

极权主义 **jíquánzhǔyì** N totalitarian

极盛 **jíshèng** ADJ heyday; zenith

极限 **jíxiàn** N limit; maximum · MW 个

天气太冷，居民用电达到**极限**。*The weather was extremely cold, so the residents used up all of the available electricity.*

极小 **jíxiǎo** ADV minimum; least

**RELATED WORDS**

| | | |
|---|---|---|
| 太极拳 53 | 北极 278 | 乐极生悲 299 |
| 多极 431 | 两极 509 | 阳极 808 |
| 南极 986 | 阴极 1041 | 积极 1097 |
| 终极 1109 | 消极 1343 | |

---

**799** 枯    U+67AF    TM **10** FM |

**kū** ADJ withered (of plants, etc.); dried-up (of wells, rivers, etc.); emaciated, shriveled (of the body); dull, uninteresting

枯草热 **kūcǎorè** N hay fever

枯黄 **kūhuáng** ADJ withered and yellow

枯竭 **kūjié** ADJ dried-up; exhausted, spent

她的经济来源**枯竭**了。*Her financial resources have been exhausted.*

枯涩 **kūsè** ADJ dull and heavy

枯瘦 **kūshòu** ADJ emaciated; skinny

枯水 **kūshuǐ** N low water level

枯燥 **kūzào** ADJ dry and dull; bald

不少人觉得傻瓜的演讲**枯燥**乏味。*Many people think ShaGua's speeches are boring.*

**RELATED WORD**

干枯 13

---

**800** 柜 櫃    U+67DC    TM **10** FM |

**guì** N cupboard, cabinet; cashier's (office); shop

柜台 **guìtái** N counter; bar

**RELATED WORDS**

| | | |
|---|---|---|
| 立柜 125 | 衣柜 330 | 钱柜 1301 |
| 五斗柜 79 | | |

---

**801 标 標** U+6807 TM **10** FM |

**biāo** V·N to label, to mark; sign; outward sign, symptom; superficiality; standard, norm; target, quota; prize, award; bid

**标榜 biāobǎng** V to advertise; to boost; to flaunt, to brag about

**标本 biāoběn** N example; sample, specimen · MW 个

**标兵 biāobīng** N model, pacesetter, person/unit that sets an example · MW 个、名、位

不要把自己标榜成标兵。 *Don't flatter yourself by pretending to be a good example.*

**标尺 biāochǐ** N scale · MW 把

**标点 biāodiǎn** N·V punctuation; to punctuate · MW 个

有些大学生尚未学会正确使用标点符号。 *Some college students have not learned how to punctuate correctly.*

**标号 biāohào** N label · MW 个

**标记 biāojì** N label, tab; mark, symbol · MW 个

**标明 biāomíng** V to write a note; to mark, to indicate

在外包装上请标明"小心轻放"字样。 *On the outer packaging, please write "Handle with Care."*

**标签 biāoqiān** N label, tag · MW 个

**标题 biāotí** N title, heading; subject; headline · MW 个

**标语 biāoyǔ** N slogan, catchphrase · MW 条

**标志 biāozhì** N·V sign, symbol; to symbolize; to indicate · MW 个

**标准 biāozhǔn** N·ADJ (official) standard; standard, norm · MW 个

傻瓜给他的孩子定下很高的标准。 *ShaGua sets a very high standard for his children.*

**RELATED WORDS**

| | | |
|---|---|---|
| 目标 151 | 夺标 308 | 坐标 318 |
| 灯标 346 | 音标 907 | 投标 1008 |
| 招标 1232 | 浮标 1342 | 袖标 1361 |
| 指标 1397 | 商标 1612 | 路标 1785 |
| 游标 1818 | 指路标 1397 | |

---

**802 校** U+6821 TM **10** FM |

**jiào** V to check; to proofread; to compare critically; to emend

**xiào** N school; field officer

**校订 jiàodìng** V to check against the authoritative text

**校对 jiàoduì** V·N to proofread; to calibrate; proofreader · MW 个、名

校对工作比较枯燥。 *Proofreading is quite boring.*

**校验 jiàoyàn** V to check; to calibrate

**校正 jiàozhèng** V to proofread and correct; to revise

**校规 xiàoguī** N school regulation · MW 条、套

因为他违反校规，所以被退学了。 *Ever since he broke school regulations, he was expelled from school.*

**校徽 xiàohuī** N school badge/insignia · MW 枚

**校刊 xiàokān** N school magazine · MW 本

**校舍 xiàoshè** N school building; dormitory · MW 栋、幢

中国的校舍不仅包括学生宿舍还包括老师的住房。 *School buildings in China include not only student dormitories but also teachers' housing.*

**校外 xiàowài** N after school; off campus

**校友 xiàoyǒu** N alumnus, alumna · MW 个、名、位

**校园 xiàoyuán** N campus · MW 个

**校长 xiàozhǎng** N principal; president · MW 个、名、位

校长已经做出对那名学生停学处分的决定。 *The principal has decided to suspend the student from school.*

**校址 xiàozhǐ** N school location · MW 个

**RELATED WORDS**

| | | |
|---|---|---|
| 少校 62 | 网校 390 | 母校 394 |
| 夜校 654 | 返校 957 | 学校 1155 |
| 驾校 1693 | | |

---

**803 样 樣** U+6837 TM **10** FM |

**yàng** N appearance; shape; style; sample, model, pattern; kind, type

**样板 yàngbǎn** N sample, model, template; example · MW 个

**样本 yàngběn** N sample book; sample · MW 个、本

## 803 样 yàng (continued)

**样品 yàngpǐn** [N] sample, specimen, swatch · [MW] 个

随函附寄一些**样品**。 *Enclosed are some samples.*

**样式 yàngshì** [N] style, pattern; type · [MW] 个、种

**样样 yàngyàng** [N] every kind, all kinds

别人以为傻瓜**样样**都不会，其实他在夜校学会了用电脑。 *Others think ShaGua knows nothing, but he has learned how to use a computer in night school.*

**样子 yàngzi** [N] appearance, look; expression; shape, figure; sample, pattern

他穿这身衣服的**样子**显得很滑稽。 *His body shape looks very funny in that outfit.*

### RELATED WORDS

| | | |
|---|---|---|
| 一样 1 | 走样 265 | 式样 316 |
| 两样 509 | 取样 520 | 同样 541 |
| 花样 549 | 字样 664 | 这样 715 |
| 图样 761 | 抽样 788 | 怎样 830 |
| 那样 980 | 货样 1061 | 装样子 1476 |
| 选样 1510 | 哪样 1666 | 摆样子 1773 |
| 照样 1846 | 怎么样 830 | 多种多样 431 |
| 怪模怪样 696 | 装模作样 1476 | 模样 1673 |

## 804 桥 橋    U+6865   TM **10** FM |

**qiáo** [N] bridge

**桥洞 qiáodòng** [N] bridge arch · [MW] 个

**桥梁 qiáoliáng** [N] bridge; person/thing that serves as a link · [MW] 座

这个城市因为这座古老的**桥梁**而出名。 *This city is famous for its ancient bridge.*

### RELATED WORDS

| | | |
|---|---|---|
| 旱桥 387 | 人行桥 4 | 公路桥 103 |
| 独木桥 1095 | | |

## 805 相    U+76F8   TM **10** FM |

**xiāng** [ADV·V] each other, mutually; one after another; to evaluate, to see for oneself (whether one likes someone/something)

**xiàng** [N·V] looks, appearance; posture; photograph; phase; minister; prime minister; to look at and appraise, to judge

**相伴 xiāngbàn** [V] to accompany

**相比 xiāngbǐ** [V] to compare with; to contrast

傻瓜太太的中文不错，但与傻瓜**相比**还是差一些。 *Mrs. ShaGua's Chinese is all right, but it is poor compared to ShaGua's.*

**相差 xiāngchà** [V] to differ; discrepancy

**相称 xiāngchèn** [V] to match, to suit

**相持 xiāngchí** [V] to be locked in a stalemate

**相处 xiāngchǔ** [V] to get along (with one another)

**相当 xiāngdāng** [V·ADJ·ADV] to match; to balance; to be equivalent (to); appropriate, suitable; quite

有人认为傻瓜是一个**相当**有耐心的人。 *Some people consider ShaGua quite a patient person.*

**相等 xiāngděng** [V] to be equal

**相对 xiāngduì** [V·ADJ] to be opposite; relative; comparative

**相反 xiāngfǎn** [ADJ·CONJ] opposite; reverse; on the contrary

**相仿 xiāngfǎng** [V] to be similar

**相逢 xiāngféng** [V] to meet (by chance); to come across

**相符 xiāngfú** [V] to conform to, to match

**相干 xiānggān** [V] to have to do with, to be concerned with

**相关 xiāngguān** [V] to be mutually related

失业数字不一定与物价上涨**相关**。 *The unemployment figures are not necessarily related to the rising prices.*

**相互 xiānghù** [ADJ·ADV] reciprocal; mutually, each other

老师发现这两件事情**相互**有联系。 *The teacher discovered that the two events were related to each other.*

**相继 xiāngjì** [ADV] one after another, in succession

**相间 xiāngjiàn** [V] to alternate with

**相交 xiāngjiāo** [V] to intersect, to cross; to make friends (with)

**相近 xiāngjìn** [ADJ] close, near; similar to

**相距 xiāngjù** [V] to be separated by (a distance of); to be away from

**相连 xiānglián** [V] to link, to connect

**相邻 xiānglín** [V] to border on, to be adjacent

**相识 xiāngshí** [V·N] to be acquainted (with each other); acquaintance · [MW] 个

傻瓜太太是在长途火车上与傻瓜**相识**的。 *Mrs. ShaGua first met ShaGua on a long train trip.*

**相思 xiāngsī** [V] to be lovesick; to miss each other

自那以后，傻瓜太太和傻瓜开始**相思**了。 *Since that first meeting, Mrs. ShaGua and ShaGua were pining for each other.*

相似 **xiāngsì** ADJ similar, alike

相通 **xiāngtōng** V to be interlinked/connected

相同 **xiāngtóng** ADJ identical, same

相像 **xiāngxiàng** ADJ alike, similar

相信 **xiāngxìn** V to believe in, to be convinced of, to trust

别**相信**他的话。*Don't believe what he says.*

相依 **xiāngyī** V to depend on each other

相约 **xiāngyuē** V to agree (on a date, meeting place, etc.); to make an appointment

**RELATED WORDS**

| | | |
|---|---|---|
| 长相 93 | 凶相 98 | 互相 135 |
| 变相 653 | 洋相 689 | 扮相 786 |
| 首相 924 | 识相 950 | 真相 1075 |
| 宰相 1140 | 亮相 1613 | 照相 1846 |
| 照相机 1846 | 以礼相待 101 | 出洋相 258 |
| 风马牛不相及 194 | | |

---

**806 岭** 嶺　U+5CAD　TM **10** FM |

**lǐng** N mountain; mountain range; ridge · MW 座

**RELATED WORD**

翻山越岭 1989

---

**807 峡** 峽　U+5CE1　TM **10** FM |

**xiá** N canyon, gorge; strait

峡谷 **xiágǔ** N canyon, gorge; ravine · MW 个

亚利桑那州因那个大**峡谷**而著名。
*Arizona is famous for the Grand Canyon.*

峡湾 **xiáwān** N fiord · MW 个

---

**808 阳** 陽　U+9633　TM **10** FM |

**yáng** N sun; sunlight; male genitals; positive (pole) (electricity); overt, outward; protruding

阳春 **yángchūn** N spring, springtime · MW 个

阳光 **yángguāng** N sunlight, sunshine · MW 道、束

这种植物需要充足的**阳光**。*This plant needs full exposure to the sun.*

阳极 **yángjí** N positive pole · MW 个

阳历 **yánglì** N solar (Western Gregorian) calendar · MW 个

阳性 **yángxìng** N masculine · MW 个

**RELATED WORDS**

| | | |
|---|---|---|
| 夕阳 49 | 太阳 53 | 太阳镜 53 |
| 太阳系 53 | 太阳穴 53 | 阴阳 1041 |
| 斜阳 1307 | | |

---

**809 阵** 陣　U+9635　TM **10** FM |

**zhèn** N·MW period of time, a while; position; front; battle formation; [measure word for events of short duration (a cloudburst, a gust of wind, etc.)]

阵地 **zhèndì** N position; battlefield · MW 个

阵容 **zhènróng** N battle formation; lineup · MW 个

这是一个强大的**阵容**。*This is a strong formation.*

阵亡 **zhènwáng** V to be killed in action/battle

阵线 **zhènxiàn** N front line; ranks; front (political movement) · MW 条

阵雨 **zhènyǔ** N shower · MW 场

明天将偶有**阵雨**。*There will be scattered showers tomorrow.*

**RELATED WORDS**

| | | |
|---|---|---|
| 一阵 1 | 怯阵 697 | 雷阵雨 1641 |

---

**810 昨**　U+6628　TM **10** FM |

**zuó** N yesterday; the past

昨天 **zuótiān** N yesterday

傻瓜**昨**天丢了钱包。*ShaGua lost his wallet yesterday.*

昨晚 **zuówǎn** N yesterday evening; last night

直到**昨晚**傻瓜才发现自己的钱包丢了。*Not until last night did ShaGua realize his wallet was lost.*

---

**811 欧** 歐　U+6B27　TM **10** FM |

**ōu** N Europe

欧洲 **Ōuzhōu** N Europe

欧元 **ōuyuán** N euro (currency) · MW 块

**RELATED WORD**

东欧 307

## 812 账 賬   U+8D26   TM **10** FM |

**zhàng** N account; accounts ledger; debt; credit

**账簿 zhàngbù** N accounts ledger · MW 本

**账单 zhàngdān** N bill, check · MW 个、张

我的**账单**包括服务费了吗？ *Does the bill include a service charge?*

**账户 zhànghù** N account · MW 个

**账款 zhàngkuǎn** N money in an account · MW 笔

请核对**账户**里的**账款**。 *Please check the funds in the account.*

**账目 zhàngmù** N accounting entry · MW 本

### RELATED WORDS

| | | |
|---|---|---|
| 入账 5 | 欠账 105 | 认账 239 |
| 冲账 339 | 呆账 384 | 记账 946 |
| 报账 1010 | 结账 1291 | 清账 1495 |
| 赔账 1569 | 算账 1697 | 销账 1714 |
| 混账 1739 | | |

## 813 贩 販   U+8D29   TM **10** FM |

**fàn** N·V trader; dealer; vendor; peddler; to deal in, to buy to resell

**贩卖 fànmài** V to sell; to peddle

这个人就喜欢**贩卖**他的陈词滥调。 *This guy enjoys constantly peddling his nonsensical thoughts.*

**贩子 fànzi** N dealer · MW 个、名

### RELATED WORD

商贩 1612

## 814 贬 貶   U+8D2C   TM **10** FM |

**biǎn** V to belittle, to disparage; to diminish, to reduce

**贬低 biǎndī** V to belittle; to demote

有人总爱**贬低**傻瓜。 *There's always someone who likes to belittle ShaGua.*

**贬义 biǎnyì** N derogatory expression

**贬值 biǎnzhí** V to depreciate, to devalue

美元在2009年还会继续**贬值**吗？ *Was there a further devaluation of the U.S. dollar in 2009?*

## 815 封   U+5C01   TM **10** FM |

**fēng** V·N·MW to seal/close off/up; envelope; wrapper; [measure word for letters, telegrams]

**封闭 fēngbì** V to seal off/up, to block; to close

请**封闭**这个考场。 *Please seal the exam hall!*

**封闭式 fēngbìshì** N closed/private type (of an event, an operation)

**封存 fēngcún** V to seal up for safekeeping; to freeze (an account, etc.)

**封底 fēngdǐ** N back cover (of a book) · MW 页

**封二 fēng'èr** N inside front cover (of a book) · MW 页

**封建 fēngjiàn** ADJ·N feudal; feudalism

虽然傻瓜生活在美国，但有着不少**封建**观念。 *ShaGua lives in the United States, but he has quite a few feudal ideas.*

**封面 fēngmiàn** N front cover (of a book) · MW 页

请在书的**封面**上签名。 *Please write your name on the front cover of the book.*

**封锁 fēngsuǒ** V to seal off, to block

**封条 fēngtiáo** N paper strip seal · MW 张

**封一 fēngyī** N front cover (of a book) · MW 页

**封印 fēngyìn** N seal · MW 个

### RELATED WORDS

| | | |
|---|---|---|
| 拆封 572 | 启封 657 | 查封 741 |
| 信封 869 | 密封 1730 | |

## 816 故   U+6545   TM **10** FM |

**gù** N·ADJ·V·CONJ incident; reason, cause; friend; acquaintance; original; former; old; deceased; to die; so, therefore; on purpose, deliberately

事**故** accident

何**故**？ *For what reason?*

**故此 gùcǐ** CONJ therefore

**故地 gùdì** N old haunt, once-familiar place · MW 个

**故宫 gùgōng** N Imperial Palace; Forbidden City

**故旧 gùjiù** N old friends

**故居 gùjū** N former residence/home · MW 个

**故去 gùqù** V to die

**故事 gùshi** N story, tale; plot · MW 个

傻瓜的**故事**让人感动。 *People were moved by ShaGua's story.*

故土 **gùtǔ** N native land, homeland; birthplace

故乡 **gùxiāng** N homeland; hometown, birthplace

傻瓜远离**故乡**。 *ShaGua lives a long way from his homeland.*

故意 **gùyì** ADV·N on purpose, intentionally; intention

故障 **gùzhàng** N malfunction, breakdown; fault, error; trouble · MW 个

电脑系统有**故障**。 *There's a bug in the computer system.*

故址 **gùzhǐ** N old site · MW 处

**RELATED WORDS**

| | | |
|---|---|---|
| 亡故 68 | 无故 139 | 世故 163 |
| 如故 464 | 典故 532 | 身故 604 |
| 事故 987 | 借故 1087 | 病故 1327 |
| 掌故 1734 | 科幻故事 642 | 沾亲带故 684 |

---

**817 耕** U+8015 TM **10** FM |

**gēng** V to plow, to till; to make a living

耕畜 **gēngchù** N farm animal · MW 头

耕地 **gēngdì** V·N to plow, to till; cultivated land · MW 片、块

开发商占用**耕地**建住宅区。 *The developers constructed residential buildings on the farmland.*

耕具 **gēngjù** N farm implements · MW 件、套

耕耘 **gēngyún** N·V hard work, diligence; farm work; to plow and weed, to cultivate

一分**耕耘**，一份收获。 *The more plowing and weeding, the better the crop.*

耕作 **gēngzuò** V to farm; to cultivate

---

**818 助** U+52A9 TM **10** FM |

**zhù** V to help, to assist

助词 **zhùcí** N auxiliary word · MW 个

助动词 **zhùdòngcí** N auxiliary verb · MW 个

助教 **zhùjiào** N assistant; teaching assistant · MW 个、名、位

助理 **zhùlǐ** N assistant · MW 个、名

校长**助理** *assistant to the president*

助手 **zhùshǒu** N assistant; aide · MW 个、名

助听器 **zhùtīngqì** N hearing aid · MW 个

助威 **zhùwēi** V to cheer for, to support

助学金 **zhùxuéjīn** N grant-in-aid · MW 笔

傻瓜的儿子有**助学金**，但还打夜工。 *ShaGua's older son supplements his scholarship grant by working in the evenings.*

助长 **zhùzhǎng** V to encourage; to promote, to foster

**RELATED WORDS**

| | | |
|---|---|---|
| 互助 135 | 自助餐厅 305 | 求助 376 |
| 协助 397 | 扶助 404 | 补助 508 |
| 借助 1087 | 救助 1259 | 资助 1335 |
| 捐助 1552 | 援助 1556 | 帮助 1583 |
| 赞助 1969 | | |

---

**819 劫** U+52AB TM **10** FM |

**jié** V·N to rob; to coerce; disaster, misfortune

劫持 **jiéchí** V to hijack

恐怖分子计划**劫持**一架飞机。 *The terrorists planned to hijack a plane.*

劫夺 **jiéduó** V to seize by force, to abduct

劫机 **jiéjī** V to hijack a plane

恐怖分子打算**劫机**。 *The terrorists are going to hijack a plane.*

劫掠 **jiélüè** V to plunder; to loot

**RELATED WORDS**

| | | |
|---|---|---|
| 打劫 289 | 洗劫 1167 | 浩劫 1169 |
| 抢劫 1230 | 遭劫 1931 | 趁火打劫 1257 |

---

**820 却** U+5374 TM **10** FM |

**què** V·ADV to step back; to drive back, to repulse; to reject, to refuse, to decline; but, yet; however

却步 **quèbù** V to shrink back (in fear/disgust/horror)

面对困难，我们不能**却步**。 *We can't back down in the face of hardship.*

**RELATED WORDS**

| | | |
|---|---|---|
| 了却 30 | 冷却 494 | 忘却 655 |
| 退却 1508 | | |

---

**821 叔** U+53D4 TM **10** FM |

**shū** N father's/husband's younger brother

叔父 **shūfù** N uncle, father's younger brother · MW 个

叔母 **shūmǔ** N aunt, wife of father's younger brother · MW 个

**821 叔 shū** (continued)

叔叔 shūshu [N] uncle, father's younger brother ·
[MW] 个

中国人把比自己长一辈的男子叫"叔叔"。
*The Chinese call males one generation older than
themselves "Shushu."*

**RELATED WORDS**

大叔 20　　　　小叔子 61

---

**822 赶 趕** U+8D76 [TM] **10** [FM] |

**gǎn** [V] to catch (up with), to overtake; to run
after, to try to catch; to drive; to drive away/out,
to expel; to encounter, to meet with; to happen
to; until

追赶 *to catch up with*

赶作业 *to rush one's homework*

赶大车 *to drive a carriage/plow*

赶出教室 *to kick someone out of class*

我昨天赶上一场大雪。 *I was caught in heavy
snow yesterday.*

赶集 **gǎnjí** [V] to go to market

赶紧 **gǎnjǐn** [ADV] quickly, hurriedly

我们还是赶紧一点吧。 *We'd better hurry.*

赶快 **gǎnkuài** [ADV] quickly; immediately

赶浪头 **gǎnlàngtou** [V] to follow / go with the
trend

赶上 **gǎnshàng** [V] to catch up with,
to overtake

赶时髦 **gǎnshímáo** [V] to be fashionable

为赶时髦这个姑娘花费了不少钱。
*The girl spends a lot of money to keep up with
current fashions.*

**RELATED WORD**

追赶 1507

---

**823 虹** U+8679 [TM] **10** [FM] |

**hóng** [N] rainbow

虹彩 **hóngcǎi** [N] iridescence; colors of the
rainbow · [MW] 条、道

虹霓 **hóngní** [N] rainbow · [MW] 道、条

---

**824 虾 蝦** U+867E [TM] **10** [FM] |

**xiā** [N] shrimp

虾米 **xiāmi** [N] dried shrimp · [MW] 颗

虾仁 **xiārén** [N] shelled fresh shrimp · [MW] 只

虾子 **xiāzǐ** [N] shrimp eggs · [MW] 个

**RELATED WORDS**

龙虾 315　　　　青虾 740

---

**825 蚁 蟻** U+8681 [TM] **10** [FM] |

**yǐ** [N] ant

蚂蚁 *ant*

蚁巢 **yǐcháo** [N] ant nest · [MW] 个

---

**826 卧** U+5367 [TM] **10** [FM] |

**wò** [V·N] to lie (down); for sleeping; sleeping berth

卧病 **wòbìng** [V] to be laid up / bedridden

卧车 **wòchē** [N] sleeping car · [MW] 辆

卧床 **wòchuáng** [V] to lie/stay in bed

卧倒 **wòdǎo** [V] to drop to the ground

卧房 **wòfáng** [N] bedroom · [MW] 间

傻瓜的房子有三间卧房。 *ShaGua's house has
three bedrooms.*

卧具 **wòjù** [N] bedding · [MW] 套

卧铺 **wòpù** [N] sleeping berth/compartment
(on a train, a boat) · [MW] 个

卧铺票 **wòpùpiào** [N] ticket for a berth · [MW] 张

我想订一张卧铺票。 *I want to book a berth.*

卧室 **wòshì** [N] bedroom · [MW] 间

**RELATED WORDS**

坐卧不安 318　　　　仰卧 620

---

**827 贪 貪** U+8D2A [TM] **10** [FM] ノ

**tān** [V·ADJ] to be greedy for, to covet, to crave;
greedy; corrupt

贪婪 **tānlán** [ADJ] greedy

她的眼睛透出贪婪的神情。 *Her greed showed in
her eyes.*

贪恋 **tānliàn** [V] to cling to, to be reluctant to part
with

贪便宜 **tānpiányi** EXP anxious to get things on the cheap

贪生怕死 **tānshēngpàsǐ** EXP to do anything to save one's neck

贪图 **tāntú** V to lust for, to covet

贪污 **tānwū** V to embezzle; to be corrupt
她因为**贪污**被捕了。 *She was arrested for embezzlement.*

贪心 **tānxīn** ADJ greedy

贪赃 **tānzāng** V to take bribes

贪嘴 **tānzuǐ** V to be gluttonous/greedy (for food)

---

**828**  態    U+6001    TM **10** FM 丿

**tài** N condition; form, posture; manner; voice

态度 **tàidu** N attitude, manner, approach · MW 个

态势 **tàishì** N posture, stance · MW 个

**RELATED WORDS**

| | | |
|---|---|---|
| 丑态 85 | 生态 107 | 仪态 122 |
| 形态 257 | 状态 345 | 动态 514 |
| 表态 527 | 时态 586 | 事态 987 |
| 液态 1344 | 常态 1733 | 静态 1947 |

---

**829** 岔    U+5C94    TM **10** FM 丿

**chà** N·V fork, branch (in a road); accident, mistake; to turn off; to diverge; to be hoarse, to lose one's voice

岔道 *fork in a road*

打**岔** *to interrupt*

岔口 **chàkǒu** N fork in a road, junction · MW 个

岔路 **chàlù** N branching road · MW 条
来到了**岔口**，他不知该走哪一条**岔路**。 *He came to a fork in the road but didn't know which branch to take.*

岔子 **chàzi** N accident; trouble · MW 个
计划出了什么**岔子**？ *What's wrong with the plan?*

**RELATED WORD**

打岔 289

---

**830** 怎    U+600E    TM **10** FM 丿

**zěn** QPRON why; how

怎么 **zěnme** QPRON how, what about [used to ask about the condition, cause, etc. of something]; how [used to ask about the nature, condition, etc. of something]; not so good [used to indicate inadequacy, often in the negative]

怎么了？ *What's wrong?*

你愿意**怎么**办就**怎么**办。 *Do whatever you want.*

不**怎么**好！ *Not so good!*

怎么得了 **zěnmedéliǎo** EXP where will it all end?

怎么样 **zěnmeyàng** QPRON how/what about [used for an unnamed action/condition, in the negative]; not so good
她不**怎么样**！ *She isn't so good!*

怎样 **zěnyàng** QPRON how [used to ask about the nature, condition, etc. of something]
怎样了？ *How is it?*

---

**831**  色    U+8272    TM **10** FM 丿

**sè** N color; scene, scenery; look, expression; feminine charm; lust; quality

色彩 **sècǎi** N color, hue, shade; flavor; tone; appeal
这台电视的**色彩**不是很好。 *This TV's color is not very good.*
这篇小说的文学**色彩**不浓。 *The novel's literary appeal is poor.*

色调 **sèdiào** N hue, shade; tone (of a work of art, a literary work); appeal

色情 **sèqíng** N pornography; eroticism

**RELATED WORDS**

| | | |
|---|---|---|
| 本色 90 | 以色列 101 | 古色古香 154 |
| 白色 176 | 气色 185 | 灰色 198 |
| 米色 226 | 红色 474 | 浅色 692 |
| 面色 721 | 角色 838 | 物色 883 |
| 肤色 899 | 底色 916 | 浊色 943 |
| 难色 974 | 货色 1061 | 套色 1064 |
| 特色 1094 | 彩色 1132 | 淡色 1173 |
| 神色 1191 | 黄色 1212 | 桃色新闻 1243 |
| 原色 1273 | 着色 1332 | 染色 1336 |
| 惧色 1351 | 鸡色拉 1373 | 素色 1378 |
| 黑色 1389 | 掉色 1403 | 起色 1421 |
| 脸色 1461 | 退色 1508 | 蓝色 1548 |
| 眼色 1570 | 暖色 1675 | 暗色 1676 |
| 调色 1749 | 嫩色 1800 | 脱色 1803 |
| 颜色 1835 | 天蓝色 25 | 古铜色 154 |
| 朱红色 184 | 灰绿色 198 | 金黄色 420 |
| 柠檬色 1029 | 清一色 1495 | 银白色 1607 |
| 五光十色 79 | 察言观色 1877 | |

## 832 乖　U+4E56　TM 10　FM 丿

**guāi** ADJ obedient; well-behaved; clever, shrewd

**乖孩子 guāiháizi** N well-behaved child · MW 个、名

**乖戾 guāilì** ADJ twisted, perverse (behavior)

**乖僻 guāipì** ADJ eccentric

**乖巧 guāiqiǎo** ADJ lovable, cute; clever
你的孩子很**乖巧**。*Your child is very cute.*

### RELATED WORD
卖乖 524

## 833 秃　U+79C3　TM 10　FM 丿

**tū** ADJ bald; hairless; bare; barren; blunt; pointless

**秃鹫 tūjiù** N cinereous/black vulture · MW 只

**秃鹰 tūyīng** N condor; bald eagle · MW 只

**秃子 tūzi** N bald head · MW 个
傻瓜还没有变成**秃子**。*ShaGua is not yet bald.*

### RELATED WORD
光秃秃 491

## 834 香　U+9999　TM 10　FM 丿

**xiāng** ADJ·N fragrant; appetizing, delicious; with a good appetite; sound (sleeping); popular; welcome; perfume; spice

睡得**香** *to sleep soundly*

吃得**香** *to be very popular*

烧**香** *to burn incense*

**香槟 xiāngbīn** N champagne · MW 瓶、杯

**香草 xiāngcǎo** N vanilla · MW 根

**香肠 xiāngcháng** N sausage · MW 截
傻瓜喜欢中国式的**香肠**。*ShaGua likes Chinese-style sausage.*

**香醋 xiāngcù** N balsamic vinegar · MW 瓶

**香粉 xiāngfěn** N face/talcum powder · MW 盒

**香港 Xiānggǎng** N Hong Kong

**香菇 xiānggū** N mushroom · MW 枚

**香瓜 xiāngguā** N muskmelon · MW 个

**香花 xiānghuā** N fragrant flower · MW 朵

**香火 xiānghuǒ** N burning incense (at a temple) · MW 支

**香蕉 xiāngjiāo** N banana · MW 根

**香料 xiāngliào** N spice; condiment; perfume · MW 种

**香气 xiāngqì** N fragrance, aroma; incense · MW 股、种

**香水 xiāngshuǐ** N perfume · MW 滴、瓶
她身上的**香水**味很俗气。*Her perfume smells cheap.*

**香甜 xiāngtián** ADJ fragrant; sound (sleeping)

**香味 xiāngwèi** N fragrance, scent · MW 种

**香烟 xiāngyān** N cigarette; incense smoke · MW 根、包

**香油 xiāngyóu** N sesame oil · MW 滴、瓶

**香皂 xiāngzào** N perfumed/scented soap · MW 块

**香脂 xiāngzhī** N face cream · MW 瓶

### RELATED WORDS
口香糖 42　　芳香 550　　吃香 783
烧香 1504　　古色古香 154

## 835 季　U+5B63　TM 10　FM 丿

**jì** N season; time of year; third month of a season; end of a time period; fourth/youngest brother

**季报 jìbào** N quarterly report · MW 份

**季度 jìdù** N quarter (of a year), season · MW 个
天气太冷，这个**季度**的煤气费异常高。*The weather was so cold that this season's gas bill was unusually high.*

**季风 jìfēng** N monsoon

**季节 jìjié** N season · MW 个
春天是一年中最美的**季节**。*Spring is the most beautiful season of the year.*

### RELATED WORDS
冬季 178　　四季 271　　旱季 387
旺季 587　　秋季 641　　雨季 720
春季 855　　淡季 1173　　夏季 1195
寒季 1481

## 836 包　U+5305　TM 10　FM 丿

**bāo** V·N·MW to cover; to wrap; to surround; to include; to contract for; to rent; to charter; to guarantee; to pack; parcel; bag; swelling, lump; tent; [measure word for packs, packages, bundles, etc.]

包伤口 *to wrap a wound*

承包 *contract*

包机 *to charter a plane*

包你喜欢。*I guarantee you will like it.*

背包 *backpack*

邮包 *postal parcel*

长包 *to swell*

两包烟 *two packs of cigarettes*

包办 **bāobàn** V to monopolize; to take sole charge of

包庇 **bāobì** V to shield/harbor (a wrongdoer); to cover up / conceal (an evil deed)

实际上，他在**包庇**他的朋友。*He's actually covering up for his friend.*

包藏 **bāocáng** V to contain; to harbor, to conceal

包场 **bāochǎng** V to book a whole theater

包饭 **bāofàn** V to board, to get/supply meals at a fixed price

包袱 **bāofu** N bundle (wrapped in cloth); burden · MW 个

包工 **bāogōng** V contract

包裹 **bāoguǒ** V·N to wrap; to bundle; package, parcel · MW 个

包涵 **bāohán** V to excuse; to forgive

包含 **bāohán** V to contain; to include

账单中**包含**了小费吗？*Is the tip included in the bill?*

包价 **bāojià** V contract/quoted price

包金 **bāojīn** V to cover with gold leaf, to gild

包括 **bāokuò** V to include; to consist of, to comprise

包揽 **bāolǎn** V to take sole charge of

包围 **bāowéi** V to surround, to encircle

洪水已将城市**包围**。*A flood has surrounded the city.*

包厢 **bāoxiāng** N box · MW 个、节

包销 **bāoxiāo** V to have exclusive selling rights (to), to be the sole agent (for)

包装 **bāozhuāng** V·N to pack (up), to package; packaging; package

包子 **bāozi** N steamed stuffed bun · MW 个

包租 **bāozū** V to rent land / a house for subletting

### RELATED WORDS

### 837 每

**měi** PRON·ADV every, each; frequently, often; whenever

U+6BCF　TM 10　FM 丿

每单位 **měidānwèi** N per unit

每分钟 **měifēnzhōng** N per minute

每每 **měiměi** ADV often

每日 **měirì** N each day

每时每刻 **měishíměikè** ADV all the time

每天 **měitiān** N per day, every day

每天都做同样的工作是很单调的。*It is very dreary to do the same job every day.*

每小时 **měixiǎoshí** N per hour

这辆车的速度可以达到**每小时**两百公里。*This car can reach 200 kilometers per hour.*

### 838 角

**jiǎo** N horn; [shaped like a horn]; bugle; corner; angle; cape, promontory

U+89D2　TM 10　FM 丿

**jué** N·V role; to fight; to quarrel

角尺 **jiǎochǐ** N set square, triangle (technical drawing, engineering) · MW 把

角度 **jiǎodù** N angle; point of view, way of looking at things · MW 个

试从不同的**角度**去看这件事，你可能会得出不同的结论。*To try looking at the affair from a different angle, you may draw a different conclusion.*

角落 **jiǎoluò** N corner; nook · MW 个

角膜 **jiǎomó** N cornea · MW 层

角色 **juésè** N role, part; position · MW 个

她在剧中扮演了一个重要的**角色**。*She had an important role in the play.*

角逐 **juézhú** V to contend; to contest; to compete

### RELATED WORDS

## 839 重    U+91CD   TM **10** FM 丿

**chóng** V·ADV·MW to repeat; to duplicate; to overlap; repeatedly; again, once more; [measure word for layers, tiers]

双重 *double*

**zhòng** V·ADJ·N to stress, to emphasize; heavy; strong, deep; serious; important, momentous; prudent, discreet; weight; heavy industry

病重 *to be seriously ill*

慎重 *discreet*

重版 **chóngbǎn** N republication

重唱 **chóngchàng** N ensemble (of singers) · MW 首

重叠 **chóngdié** V to overlap; to superimpose; to duplicate

重返 **chóngfǎn** V to return (to)

重复 **chóngfù** V to reappear; to repeat
请你再重复一遍。*Please repeat it one more time.*

重合 **chónghé** V to overlap

重建 **chóngjiàn** V to rebuild; to reestablish

重申 **chóngshēn** V to reaffirm; to reiterate, to restate

重孙 **chóngsūn** N great-grandson · MW 个
我再次重申：他是我的重孙。*I'll say it once more: He is my great-grandson.*

重孙女 **chóngsūnnǚ** N great-granddaughter · MW 个

重现 **chóngxiàn** V to reappear

重新 **chóngxīn** ADV once again; re- [verb prefix meaning "again"]
想到还要重新考试，就感到很沮丧。*The thought of having to take the exam again depressed me.*

重组 **chóngzǔ** V to reorganize

重大 **zhòngdà** ADJ great, major; significant, important
加州的大火造成重大损失。*Wildfires in California have caused tremendous losses.*

重地 **zhòngdì** N important location/place · MW 个

重点 **zhòngdiǎn** N main point; key · MW 个
他是一个重点项目的负责人。*He is the leader of a major project.*

重负 **zhòngfù** N heavy load / burden; deadweight

重工业 **zhònggōngyè** N heavy industry

重价 **zhòngjià** N high price · MW 个

重力 **zhònglì** N gravity

重量 **zhòngliàng** N weight; heaviness · MW 个

重任 **zhòngrèn** N important task; heavy responsibility · MW 个
这个重任让他感到肩上的重负。*He was burdened by this important task.*

重赏 **zhòngshǎng** V·N to grant a large award; substantial reward

重视 **zhòngshì** V to attach importance to; to emphasize
我们的中文课非常重视会话技能。*Our Chinese course places great emphasis on conversational skills.*

重托 **zhòngtuō** N great trust · MW 个

重心 **zhòngxīn** N center of gravity; heart, focus, core · MW 个

重型 **zhòngxíng** ADJ heavy, heavy-duty

重要 **zhòngyào** ADJ important, significant; critical, vital, crucial
他是一位重要人物。*He is a VIP.*

重用 **zhòngyòng** V to put (someone) in an important position

### RELATED WORDS

| | | |
|---|---|---|
| 二重唱 2 | 三重奏 9 | 五重唱 79 |
| 头重脚轻 128 | 双重 146 | 任重道远 211 |
| 并重 225 | 庄重 229 | 严重 241 |
| 四重奏 271 | 比重 279 | 体重 325 |
| 多重 431 | 加重 463 | 注重 496 |
| 珍重 515 | 举重 674 | 看重 841 |
| 侧重 864 | 保重 868 | 持重 1019 |
| 笨重 1079 | 轻重 1113 | 净重 1159 |
| 沉重 1166 | 载重 1218 | 着重 1332 |
| 深重 1345 | 湿重 1498 | 语重心长 1501 |
| 偏重 1587 | 超重 1684 | 敬重 1689 |
| 尊重 1722 | 稳重 1925 | 器重 1963 |
| 繁重 1988 | 旧地重游 165 | 旧梦重温 165 |
| 德高望重 1923 | | |

## 840 盾    U+76FE   TM **10** FM 丿

**dùn** N shield

盾牌 **dùnpái** N shield · MW 个、面

### RELATED WORDS

后盾 310
矛盾 363
以子之矛，攻子之盾 101

## 841 看   U+770B   TM **10** FM 丿

**kān** V to look after, to take care of, to tend, to watch over

**kàn** V to look at, to watch; to read; to think, to consider; to visit; to expect; to treat, to regard; to treat (of a doctor)

看电视 *to watch TV*

看书 *to read books*

看问题 *to consider questions*

看朋友 *to visit friends*

全看你了。*Everything depends on you.*

**看管 kānguǎn** V to guard; to look after, to watch; custodian

**看护 kānhù** V to take care of; to nurse (the sick)

**看门 kānmén** V to guard the entrance

**看守 kānshǒu** V·N to guard; jailer · MW 个、名

**看病 kànbìng** V to see/treat a patient (of a doctor); to see a doctor (of a patient)

傻瓜出去看病了。*ShaGua went to see the doctor.*

**看不惯 kànbùguàn** V can't bear to see

傻瓜是个积极肯干的人，**看不惯**别人偷懒。
*ShaGua is a very active person who can't bear to see others idling about.*

**看成 kànchéng** V to look upon as

**看出 kànchū** V to see, to make out

**看穿 kànchuān** V to see through

**看待 kàndài** V to regard, to treat, to look upon

**看到 kàndào** V to catch sight of

**看法 kànfǎ** N point of view, opinion; vision · MW 个

**看见 kànjiàn** V to catch sight of; to see

小偷悄悄地溜出了房子，没人看见他。
*The thief snuck out of the house undetected.*

**看来 kànlái** CONJ apparently; it appears, it seems

**看来**他看穿了我的内心。*Apparently, he read my mind.*

**看齐 kànqí** V to keep up with, to emulate

**看轻 kànqīng** V to underestimate

**看清 kànqīng** V to see clearly

**看热闹 kànrènao** V to enjoy watching a bustling scene

**看上 kànshàng** V to like; to favor

**看透 kàntòu** V to understand thoroughly

**看望 kànwàng** V to visit

傻瓜常在周末去看望他的老母亲。*ShaGua often goes to visit his elderly mother on the weekends.*

**看押 kànyā** V to keep under surveillance

**看涨 kànzhǎng** V to be expected to rise (of market prices)

**看中 kànzhòng** V to fancy, to settle on

傻瓜看中了这辆二手车。*The used car happened to strike ShaGua's fancy.*

**看重 kànzhòng** V to value, to regard as important

**看做 kànzuò** V to regard as, to consider

### RELATED WORDS

| | | |
|---|---|---|
| 中看 86 | 好看 627 | 观看 726 |
| 查看 741 | 难看 974 | 眼看 1570 |
| 照看 1846 | 察看 1877 | 走马看花 265 |
| 另眼看待 385 | | |

## 842 系 係繋   U+7CFB   TM **10** FM 丿

**jì** (繋) V to tie, to fasten, to button; to do up

系鞋带 *to tie shoelaces*

**xì** (係繋) N·V system; academic department; faculty; to relate to, to have to do with; to feel anxious, to be concerned

中文系 *Chinese Department*

联系 *to relate to*

系念 *to be concerned*

**系词 xìcí** N linking verb · MW 个

**系列 xìliè** N series; set · MW 个

环境污染引发了一系列的自然灾害。
*Environmental pollution has triggered a succession of natural disasters.*

**系数 xìshù** N coefficient; factor · MW 个

**系统 xìtǒng** N·ADJ system; methodical, systematic · MW 个

你知道怎么登录这个系统吗？*Do you know how to log in to the system?*

### RELATED WORDS

| | | |
|---|---|---|
| 世系 163 | 关系 224 | 体系 325 |
| 派系 945 | 联系 1206 | 太阳系 53 |
| 业务系统 94 | 拉关系 573 | 没关系 938 |
| 组织系统 1106 | 生产关系 107 | 主从关系 124 |
| 外交关系 218 | 裙带关系 1752 | |

## 843 鱼 魚   U+9C7C   TM **10** FM 丿

**yú** N fish

**鱼翅 yúchì** N shark fin · MW 根

**鱼唇 yúchún** N shark's lip · MW 块

**843 鱼 yú** (continued)

鱼肚 yúdǔ  N  fish maw (as food) · MW 块

鱼儿 yú'ér  N  fish · MW 条

鱼肝油 yúgānyóu  N  cod-liver oil · MW 滴、瓶

鱼缸 yúgāng  N  fishbowl, aquarium · MW 个

鱼钩 yúgōu  N  fishhook · MW 枚

鱼贯 yúguàn  ADV  one after the other, in single file

鱼鳞 yúlín  N  fish scales · MW 片

鱼米之乡 yúmǐzhīxiāng  EXP  land flowing with milk and honey (LIT land of fish and rice)

鱼肉 yúròu  N·V  fish; to cruelly oppress; to victimize

    吃鱼肉 to eat fish

    鱼肉乡里 to cruelly oppress and exploit the common people

鱼水 yúshuǐ  N  close relationship (LIT fish and water)

    这是鱼水之情。 *They go together like fish and water.*

鱼网 yúwǎng  N  fishnet · MW 张

鱼鲜 yúxiān  N  seafood

鱼子 yúzǐ  N  caviar · MW 粒

**RELATED WORDS**

| | | |
|---|---|---|
| 养鱼 670 | 养鱼场 670 | 青鱼 740 |
| 剑鱼 904 | 钓鱼 1124 | 章鱼 1311 |
| 熏鱼 1690 | 鲜鱼 1811 | 墨鱼 1843 |
| 沙丁鱼 342 | | |

---

**844** 受      U+53D7      TM **10** FM 丿

**shòu**  V  to receive, to accept; to suffer, to be subjected to; to endure, to stand; to be pleasant

受潮 shòucháo  V  to be affected by damp/cold

受宠若惊 shòuchǒngruòjīng  EXP  to be overwhelmed by an unexpected favor, to be overwhelmed with gratitude

受挫 shòucuò  V  to be foiled/thwarted, to suffer a setback

受罚 shòufá  V  to be punished

    他因为在学校打架而受罚。 *He was punished for fighting in school.*

受害 shòuhài  V  to suffer injury

受寒 shòuhán  V  to catch a chill

受贿 shòuhuì  V  to accept/take bribes

受奖 shòujiǎng  V  to receive an award

数天前这人还受奖, 今天却因受贿被抓了。 *A few days ago, this man received an award; today, he was arrested for accepting bribes.*

受尽 shòujìn  V  to suffer enough from

受惊 shòujīng  V  to be frightened/startled

受精 shòujīng  V  to be fertilized

受控 shòukòng  V  to be controlled

受苦 shòukǔ  V  to suffer hardship; to have a rough time

    受苦是人生一笔宝贵的财富。 *Suffering hardships is valuable experience.*

受难 shòunàn  V  to suffer a calamity/disaster; to be in distress

受骗 shòupiàn  V  to be cheated/hoodwinked

    傻瓜上当受骗买了那辆汽车。 *ShaGua was tricked into buying that car.*

受气 shòuqì  V  to be bullied/wronged

受辱 shòurǔ  V  to be insulted

受伤 shòushāng  V  to sustain an injury; to be wounded/harmed

    受辱也是一种心灵的受伤。 *Being insulted is a type of psychological injury.*

受审 shòushěn  V  to stand trial

受托 shòutuō  V  to be commissioned

受益 shòuyì  V  to profit by, to benefit from

受用 shòuyong  V  to benefit from

受援 shòuyuán  V  to receive aid

受灾 shòuzāi  V  to be hit by a natural disaster

    洪水过后, 受灾的民众得到政府的救助。 *After the flood, those who suffered from the disaster received aid from the government.*

受罪 shòuzuì  V  to endure (hardship, torture, etc.), to have a hard time

**RELATED WORDS**

| | | |
|---|---|---|
| 身受 604 | 活受罪 941 | 承受 972 |
| 难受 974 | 经受 1110 | 享受 1135 |
| 接受 1405 | 领受 1465 | 蒙受 1654 |
| 够受 1808 | 感受 1860 | 遭受 1931 |
| 自作自受 305 | | |

---

**845** 备 備      U+5907      TM **10** FM 丿

**bèi**  V·ADV  to prepare, to get ready; to have, to possess; to provide against, to prepare for; in every possible way, to the utmost

    准备 to prepare

    防备 to provide for

    具备 to possess

配备 *to be equipped*

备案 bèi'àn V to put on (the) record; to enter in the records

这份资料要存档**备案**。*This material needs to be put on the record.*

备查 bèichá V to be for future reference

备份 bèifèn N backup, spare, extra

备件 bèijiàn N spare parts · MW 个

备考 bèikǎo V·N to prepare (something) for future reference; (reference) notes; appendix

备课 bèikè V to prepare a lesson (of a teacher)

有人以为中文老师不用**备课**，这种想法很无知。*Some people think that Chinese teachers don't need to prepare their lessons, but this is an ignorant notion.*

备料 bèiliào V to prepare animal feed

备用 bèiyòng V to reserve; to have a spare; to have/make a backup

那辆车竟然没有**备用**车轮。*The car doesn't even have a spare tire.*

备注 bèizhù N notes, remarks

**RELATED WORDS**

| | | |
|---|---|---|
| 齐备 221 | 后备 310 | 戒备 442 |
| 守备 486 | 军备 489 | 责备 525 |
| 具备 533 | 完备 909 | 准备 929 |
| 防备 1040 | 设备 1179 | 装备 1476 |
| 预备 1528 | 配备 1647 | 置备 1651 |
| 整备 1845 | 警备 1987 | 卫生设备 82 |
| 德才兼备 1923 | | |

---

**846  厕**  廁     U+5395     TM **10** FM 丿

cè N·V restroom, toilet; to mingle with; to participate in

厕所 cèsuǒ N restroom, lavatory, toilet · MW 间

我要上**厕所**。*I need to go to the bathroom.*

厕纸 cèzhǐ N toilet paper · MW 张、卷

**RELATED WORDS**

| | | |
|---|---|---|
| 女厕所 57 | 男厕 757 | 公共厕所 103 |

---

**847  厘**     U+5398     TM **10** FM 丿

lí MW centi- [measure word for units of length, area, weight, etc. and for interest rates, percentages, etc. (= ¹/₁₀₀)]

厘克 líkè MW centigram

厘米 límǐ MW centimeter

---

**848  尾**     U+5C3E     TM **10** FM 丿

wěi N tail; [like a tail]; end; remainder, remnant; unfinished

狗尾 *dog's tail*

船尾 *stern (of a boat)*

收尾 *winding up, finishing*

尾巴 wěiba N tail; end; person who follows and reports on someone; servile follower · MW 条

尾部 wěibù N back end; tail (of a car)

尾灯 wěidēng N taillight · MW 个

傻瓜买的那辆二手车连**尾灯**都不亮。*The taillights on the used car that ShaGua bought were broken.*

尾随 wěisuí V to follow; to tail

**RELATED WORDS**

| | | |
|---|---|---|
| 末尾 89 | 收尾 282 | 扫尾 402 |
| 首尾 924 | 结尾 1291 | 词尾 1353 |
| 鸡尾酒 1373 | 彻头彻尾 871 | 街头巷尾 1441 |

---

**849  尿**     U+5C3F     TM **10** FM 丿

niào V·N to urinate; urine

尿布 niàobù N diaper · MW 块

尿床 niàochuáng V to wet the bed

傻瓜太太常常跟人说：傻瓜十来岁还**尿床**。*Mrs. ShaGua often tells people that ShaGua wet the bed until he was ten.*

尿道 niàodào N urethra

尿毒症 niàodúzhèng N uremia

尿急 niàojí ADJ urgent urination

尿频 niàopín ADJ frequent urination

尿少 niàoshǎo ADJ oliguria

尿血 niàoxiě V to have blood in one's urine

**RELATED WORDS**

| | | |
|---|---|---|
| 撒尿 1907 | 糖尿病 1933 | 屁滚尿流 1070 |

---

**850  居**     U+5C45     TM **10** FM 丿

jū V·N to live, to reside; to be in / occupy (a position); to claim, to assert; to store up; to stay put, to be at a standstill; house, residence

分居 *to live apart*

居首位 *to be in first place*

自居为汉语专家 *to claim to be a Chinese expert*

**850 居 jū** (continued)

迁居 *to move (residence)*

居留 **júliú** V to reside; to abide

居民 **jūmín** N resident · MW 个、位

居然 **jūrán** ADV unexpectedly; surprisingly

傻瓜太粗心, **居然**连傻瓜太太的生日也忘了。
*It was thoughtless of ShaGua to forget Mrs. ShaGua's birthday.*

居住 **jūzhù** V to live, to reside, to dwell

要想长期在中国**居住**, 你必须申请**居留**证。
*You need to apply for a residency permit if you want to stay in China for a long period of time.*

**RELATED WORDS**

| | | |
|---|---|---|
| 分居 173 | 穴居 231 | 侨居 460 |
| 迁居 506 | 同居 541 | 定居 666 |
| 故居 816 | 邻居 1123 | 客居 1316 |
| 起居 1421 | 散居 1579 | 寄居 1619 |
| 隐居 1912 | | |

---

**851 届** U+5C4A TM **10** FM 丿

**jiè** V·MW to come/fall due; [measure word for the year of a graduating class, an event in a regular series, etc.]

届满 **jièmǎn** V to expire (of a term in office)

届时 **jièshí** ADV at the appointed/scheduled time

**RELATED WORDS**

| | |
|---|---|
| 本届 90 | 应届 334 |

---

**852 屎** U+5C4E TM **10** FM 丿

**shǐ** N excrement, dung; secretion (of the eye, ear, etc.)

**RELATED WORD**

拉屎 573

---

**853 牵** 牽 U+7275 TM **10** FM 丿

**qiān** V to pull, to lead along; to involve; to implicate

牵扯 **qiānchě** V to involve; to implicate

牵动 **qiāndòng** V to touch, to affect; to influence

牵挂 **qiānguà** V to worry, to be deeply concerned

她在中国一切都好, 不用**牵挂**。 *Everything is fine with her in China—no need for you to be concerned.*

牵连 **qiānlián** V to involve (in trouble); to implicate; to be related/connected

这不关我的事, 我可不想**牵连**进去。 *This is not my business; please, I don't want to get involved.*

牵涉 **qiānshè** V to involve; to implicate

他**牵涉**到这起案件。 *He was implicated in this case.*

牵线 **qiānxiàn** V to pull strings, to manipulate

牵引 **qiānyǐn** V to tow, to drag, to draw; to involve (in trouble)

牵制 **qiānzhì** V to pin down (enemy troops, etc.); to contain; to restrain, to restrict

---

**854 奇** U+5947 TM **10** FM 丿

**jī** ADJ odd; fractional amount

奇数 *odd number*

**qí** ADJ·ADV strange, odd; rare; unexpected, unpredictable; surprising; extremely, exceedingly

出奇 *unusually*

惊奇 *surprise*

奇快 *extremely fast*

奇功 **qígōng** N outstanding service · MW 个、件

奇怪 **qíguài** ADJ strange, odd, weird

傻瓜时常提出一些**奇怪**的问题。 *ShaGua raises some strange questions now and then.*

奇景 **qíjǐng** N wonderful view · MW 个、片

奇妙 **qímiào** ADJ wonderful, marvelous, fantastic

中文是一种古老而**奇妙**的语言。 *Chinese is an ancient and wonderful language.*

奇人 **qírén** N special person · MW 个、位

奇谈 **qítán** N strange tale · MW 个、段

奇特 **qítè** ADJ strange, odd, peculiar, unusual

傻瓜太太今天剪了一个很**奇特**的发型。 *Mrs. ShaGua has a very special hairstyle today.*

奇闻 **qíwén** N incredible story · MW 个、则

奇形怪状 **qíxíngguàizhuàng** EXP grotesque (in shape/appearance)

奇异 **qíyì** ADJ strange, odd, bizarre; astonished

**RELATED WORDS**

| | | |
|---|---|---|
| 好奇 627 | 神奇 1191 | 猎奇 1444 |
| 惊奇 1489 | 稀奇 1599 | 离奇 1614 |
| 新奇 1638 | | |

## 855 春　U+6625　TM 10　FM 丿

**chūn** N spring; year; love; vitality; sexual desire

**春风** chūnfēng N spring breeze; happy smiles · MW 股、阵

**春光** chūnguāng N spring scenes; lustful scenes

**春季** chūnjì N spring · MW 个

**春假** chūnjià N spring vacation · MW 个

**春节** Chūnjié N Spring Festival (Chinese New Year)
中国孩子在**春节**时会得到不少"红包"。
*Chinese children receive a lot of "red envelopes" during Spring Festival.*

**春卷** chūnjuǎn N spring roll · MW 个

**春雷** chūnléi N spring thunder · MW 声、阵

**春天** chūntiān N spring, springtime · MW 个

**春游** chūnyóu V spring outing

**春装** chūnzhuāng N spring clothing · MW 件、套

### RELATED WORDS

| | | |
|---|---|---|
| 立春 125 | 早春 268 | 青春 740 |
| 阳春 808 | 迎春 1360 | 新春 1638 |

## 856 杂 雜　U+6742　TM 10　FM 丿

**zá** ADJ·V miscellaneous, sundry; mixed, varied; multicolored; irregular; extra; to mix, to mingle

**杂草** zácǎo N weeds · MW 棵

**杂费** záfèi N miscellaneous expenses · MW 笔
除了车船费，还包括其他**杂费**。
*Besides transportation, all other miscellaneous expenses are included.*

**杂货** záhuò N groceries; miscellaneous items · MW 批
校外有家销售日用**杂货**的商店。
*The store outside the school sells various household products.*

**杂技** zájì N acrobatics

**杂交** zájiāo V to hybridize, to crossbreed

**杂音** záyīn N noise
你的车肯定有问题了，你听听这奇怪的**杂音**！
*There must be something wrong with your car. Just listen to the funny noises!*

**杂志** zázhì N magazine, journal, periodical · MW 本、期

**杂种** zázhǒng EXP hybrid; bastard, son of a bitch (vulgar) · MW 个

### RELATED WORDS

| | | |
|---|---|---|
| 夹杂 197 | 庞杂 917 | 复杂 1059 |
| 混杂 1739 | 错综复杂 1715 | |

## 857 或　U+6216　TM 10　FM 丿

**huò** CONJ·ADV·PRON or; perhaps, maybe; probably; a little; a bit; someone, some person/people

**或然** huòrán ADJ probable

**或许** huòxǔ ADV probably
傻瓜没有按时出现，**或许**他已经改变了主意。
*ShaGua is late; he has probably changed his mind.*

**或者** huòzhě ADV·CONJ perhaps, maybe; or; either … or …
请回答我：是**或者**不是。 *Please answer me: yes or no.*

### RELATED WORD

抑或 1007

## 858 皇　U+7687　TM 10　FM 丿

**huáng** N·ADJ emperor; sovereign; imperial, royal; grand, magnificent

**皇宫** huánggōng N imperial palace · MW 座
故宫是世界上最大的**皇宫**。 *The Forbidden City in Beijing is the world's largest royal palace.*

**皇冠** huángguān N imperial crown · MW 顶

**皇家** huángjiā N imperial family; royalty

**皇历** huánglì N almanac · MW 个

**皇权** huángquán N imperial power

**皇上** huángshang N emperor

**皇室** huángshì N imperial family; royalty

**皇太子** huángtàizǐ N crown prince · MW 个、名

**皇族** huángzú N imperial kin · MW 个、名

### RELATED WORDS

| | | |
|---|---|---|
| 天皇 25 | 女皇 57 | 玉皇大帝 77 |
| 仓皇 418 | 教皇 1424 | 堂皇 1486 |
| 富丽堂皇 1731 | | |

## 859 鸟 鳥　U+9E1F　TM 10　FM 丿

**niǎo** N bird; penis

**鸟粪** niǎofèn N bird droppings · MW 泡、堆

**鸟瞰** niǎokàn V to get/have a bird's-eye view

**859 鸟 niǎo** (continued)

你可以登上景山顶鸟瞰北京。*You can climb to the top of Jing Mountain to get a bird's-eye view of Beijing.*

鸟类 **niǎolèi** N birds · MW 种

鸟笼 **niǎolóng** N birdcage · MW 个

鸟枪 **niǎoqiāng** N fowling piece; air gun · MW 支、杆

**RELATED WORDS**

花鸟 549     候鸟 1086     蜂鸟 1682

---

### 860 省    U+7701   TM **10**   FM ノ

**shěng** N·V province; to save, to economize; to omit, to leave out

**xǐng** V to examine oneself critically, to be introspective; to become conscious; to be aware

省城 **shěngchéng** N provincial capital · MW 个、座

省力 **shěnglì** V to save effort/labor

省略 **shěnglüè** V to omit, to leave out; to delete

最后一段可以省略。*The last paragraph can be omitted.*

省钱 **shěngqián** V to save money

省事 **shěngshì** V to save trouble

在快餐店就餐省事。*It's more convenient to eat at a fast-food restaurant.*

省委 **shěngwěi** N provincial party committee · MW 个

省悟 **xǐngwù** V to realize the truth, to wake up to reality

**RELATED WORDS**

反省 111     内省 191     节省 275
发人深省 311

---

### 861 笑    U+7B11   TM **10**   FM ノ

**xiào** V to smile; to laugh; to ridicule, to laugh at

笑柄 **xiàobǐng** N joke · MW 个

笑话 **xiàohua** N joke · MW 个

傻瓜讲一个老掉牙的笑话，结果大家笑他，没笑笑话。*ShaGua told a very old joke. As a result, no one laughed at the joke, but they did laugh at him.*

笑脸 **xiàoliǎn** N smiling face · MW 张

---

笑眯眯 **xiàomīmī** V to do (something) with a smile on one's face

他讲笑话时，脸上笑眯眯的。*When he told the joke, he had a smile on his face.*

笑纳 **xiàonà** V to kindly accept

笑容 **xiàoróng** N smile · MW 个

**RELATED WORDS**

| | | |
|---|---|---|
| 可笑 243 | 发笑 311 | 冷笑 494 |
| 含笑 592 | 玩笑 727 | 耻笑 735 |
| 哭笑不得 1221 | 闹笑话 1323 | 喜笑颜开 1531 |
| 说笑 1631 | 傻笑 1699 | 微笑 1700 |
| 调笑 1749 | 开玩笑 26 | 眉开眼笑 1067 |

---

### 862 伺    U+5947   TM **10**   FM ノ

**cì** V to wait on

**sì** V to watch; to await

伺候 **cìhou** V to wait on, to serve

伺机 **sìjī** V to watch for one's chance/opportunity

---

### 863 例    U+5947   TM **10**   FM ノ

**lì** N example, instance; precedent, case; rule, regulation; regular, routine

例会 **lìhuì** N regular meeting · MW 个、次

例假 **lìjià** N official holiday; menstrual period · MW 次

例句 **lìjù** N example sentence · MW 个

例如 **lìrú** V to give an example; for instance, such as

你可以在这个商店买日用品，例如，牙膏和香皂。*You can buy household products here—toothpaste and soap, for example.*

例题 **lìtí** N example · MW 道

例外 **lìwài** N exception; irregularity · MW 个

任何规律都有例外。*There is always an exception to any rule.*

例行 **lìxíng** V to be routine

例行公事 **lìxínggōngshì** N routine business · MW 次

例证 **lìzhèng** N illustration, case in point, instance · MW 个

例子 **lìzi** N example, instance, case · MW 个

**RELATED WORDS**

| | | |
|---|---|---|
| 示例 140 | 凡例 193 | 比例 279 |
| 比例尺 279 | 先例 422 | 条例 598 |

| | | |
|---|---|---|
| 实例 668 | 举例 674 | 事例 987 |
| 违例 1185 | 案例 1321 | 病例 1327 |
| 前例 1329 | 惯例 1630 | 照例 1846 |
| 按比例 1234 | 下不为例 10 | 史无前例 186 |

---

## 864 侧 侧    U+5947    TM 10 FM 丿

**cè** [N·V] side; oblique tone; to incline (toward), to lean, to slant

侧面 **cèmiàn** [N] side; flank · [MW] 个

侧目 **cèmù** [V] to glance sideways

侧身 **cèshēn** [V] to one's side; to turn sideways

侧重 **cèzhòng** [V] to emphasize

那个中文班侧重对话和听力。 *That particular Chinese class puts emphasis on dialog and listening skills.*

---

## 865 便    U+5947    TM 10 FM 丿

**biàn** [V·N·ADJ·ADV] to defecate; to urinate; to excrete; stool; urine; convenient, handy; informal, simple; then, in that case; even if

方便 *convenient*

小便 *urine*

即便 *even if*

便秘 **biànbì** [V] to constipate

便池 **biànchí** [N] urinal · [MW] 个

便当 **biàndang** [ADJ·N] convenient, handy; easy; boxed meal · [MW] 盒

便饭 **biànfàn** [N] simple meal, informal banquet · [MW] 顿

便服 **biànfú** [N] casual clothes · [MW] 件、套

参加明天的聚会，穿便服就行了。 *Please dress casually for tomorrow's party.*

便函 **biànhán** [N] informal letter · [MW] 封

便壶 **biànhú** [N] urinal · [MW] 个、把

便笺 **biànjiān** [N] notepaper · [MW] 张

便利 **biànlì** [ADJ] convenient; easy

为便利学生，校外新建了一个百货店。 *A new general store has been built near the school for the students' convenience.*

便士 **biànshì** [N] penny · [MW] 枚

便桶 **biàntǒng** [N] toilet · [MW] 个

便携式 **biànxiéshì** [N] portable

便于 **biànyú** [V] to be convenient

手机变得越来越小，很便于携带。 *Cell phones have become smaller and smaller and are convenient to carry.*

便纸 **biànzhǐ** [N] toilet tissue · [MW] 张、卷、筒

### RELATED WORDS

| | | |
|---|---|---|
| 大便 20 | 不便 24 | 小便 61 |
| 以便 101 | 占便宜 153 | 方便 220 |
| 自便 305 | 灵便 359 | 听便 414 |
| 讨便宜 500 | 贪便宜 827 | 顺便 874 |
| 即便 1047 | 轻便 1113 | 趁便 1257 |
| 请便 1632 | 简便 1796 | 随便 1911 |

---

## 866 促    U+4FC3    TM 10 FM 丿

**cù** [V·ADJ] to urge; to promote; to hurry; urgent; short (of time); hurried; close to, near

促成 **cùchéng** [V] to facilitate

促使 **cùshǐ** [V] to induce; to urge; to promote; to spur, to precipitate

是什么人促使傻瓜做出如此可笑的事？ *Who made ShaGua do such a ridiculous thing?*

### RELATED WORDS

| | | |
|---|---|---|
| 仓促 418 | 局促 1069 | 急促 1426 |
| 短促 1452 | 催促 1592 | |

---

## 867 俗    U+4FD7    TM 10 FM 丿

**sú** [ADJ] popular; common; vulgar

俗名 **súmíng** [N] popular/common name · [MW] 个

俗语 **súyǔ** [N] saying, proverb · [MW] 句

### RELATED WORDS

| | | |
|---|---|---|
| 习俗 84 | 世俗 163 | 风俗 194 |
| 民俗 388 | 粗俗 1364 | 通俗 1757 |

---

## 868 保    U+4FDD    TM 10 FM 丿

**bǎo** [V·N] to protect, to defend; to keep, to maintain; to preserve; to guarantee, to ensure; to insure; guarantor

保安 **bǎo'ān** [N·V] security, security guard/personnel; to ensure public security; to ensure safety · [MW] 个、名

保镖 **bǎobiāo** [N] bodyguard; armed escort · [MW] 个、名

保藏 **bǎocáng** [V] to conserve; to preserve

**868** 保 **bǎo** (continued)

**保持** **bǎochí** [V] to keep, to maintain, to preserve
请**保持**安静。 *Please keep quiet.*

**保存** **bǎocún** [V] to preserve; to conserve

**保单** **bǎodān** [N] warranty; insurance policy · [MW] 份

**保管** **bǎoguǎn** [V·N] to take care of, to safeguard; to assure; warehouse custodian/manager · [MW] 个、名
傻瓜把资料**保管**得很好。 *ShaGua takes good care of the materials.*
傻瓜**保管**能把这件事办好。 *I am sure that ShaGua can get the job done well.*
傻瓜当过**保管**。 *ShaGua used to be a warehouse custodian.*

**保护** **bǎohù** [V] to protect, to safeguard
必须**保护**好计算机里储存的数据。 *Data stored in the computer must be protected.*

**保健** **bǎojiàn** [N] health care

**保留** **bǎoliú** [V] to preserve; to disagree; to retain; to have reservations

**保密** **bǎomì** [V] to keep (something) secret
我们两人之间说的话必须**保密**。 *Whatever is said between us here must be kept confidential.*

**保姆** **bǎomǔ** [N] domestic help; servant; housekeeper; nanny; nurse (in a kindergarten, a nursery) · [MW] 个、名

**保全** **bǎoquán** [V] to save (from damage), to preserve; to maintain

**保守** **bǎoshǒu** [V·ADJ] to guard, to protect; conservative

**保卫** **bǎowèi** [V] to defend, to safeguard

**保温** **bǎowēn** [V] to keep warm; heat conservation

**保险** **bǎoxiǎn** [N·ADJ·V] insurance; assurance; secure, safe; to be bound/sure to
美国学生到中国需要买健康**保险**吗？ *Do American students need to buy health insurance in China?*

**保养** **bǎoyǎng** [V] to take care of one's health; to maintain

**保佑** **bǎoyòu** [V] to bless and protect

**保育** **bǎoyù** [V] to care for a child; to nurse (in general)

**保证** **bǎozhèng** [V·N] to guarantee, to assure; to safeguard; pledge · [MW] 个、项
我**保证**履行我的承诺。 *I assure you that I will do as I said.*

**保重** **bǎozhòng** [V] to express concern about the health of others

**RELATED WORDS**

劳保 764　　担保 789　　准保 929
难保 974　　投保 1008　　被保险人 1517
确保 1762　　人寿保险 4

**869** 信　　U+4FE1　　TM **10** FM ノ

**xìn** [N·V·ADJ] letter, mail; word; information; confidence, trust, faith; proof, evidence; to believe in, to give credence to; to profess faith in; true, sure

书信 *letter*
口信 *oral message*
相信 *to trust*
凭信 *evidence*
引信 *fuse*
信用证 *credit card*
信教 *to profess a religion*

**信贷** **xìndài** [N] credit; credit financing · [MW] 笔

**信封** **xìnfēng** [N] envelope · [MW] 个
他把邮票贴在**信封**上。 *He glued a stamp on the envelope.*

**信奉** **xìnfèng** [V] to believe in; to profess faith in

**信服** **xìnfú** [V] to be convinced

**信鸽** **xìngē** [N] carrier pigeon · [MW] 只

**信号** **xìnhào** [N] signal · [MW] 个

**信号灯** **xìnháodēng** [N] signal light · [MW] 盏

**信汇** **xìnhuì** [N] mail transfer (of money) · [MW] 笔

**信笺** **xìnjiān** [N] writing paper, stationery · [MW] 张

**信件** **xìnjiàn** [N] letter · [MW] 封

**信赖** **xìnlài** [V] to trust, to have faith in, to count on
傻瓜是大家可以**信赖**的人。 *ShaGua is a man on whom everyone can rely.*

**信念** **xìnniàn** [N] conviction; faith, belief · [MW] 个

**信任** **xìnrèn** [V] to trust, to have confidence in

**信使** **xìnshǐ** [N] courier, messenger · [MW] 个、位、名

**信守** **xìnshǒu** [V] to abide/stand by

**信条** **xìntiáo** [N] precept, tenet; creed · [MW] 个

**信筒** **xìntǒng** [N] mailbox · [MW] 个

**信徒** **xìntú** [N] believer, follower · [MW] 个、名

**信托** **xìntuō** [V] to trust; to entrust

**信息** **xìnxī** [N] information; news, message · [MW] 个、条、则
**信息**不准确，结论肯定错。 *If the information is inaccurate, the conclusion will be wrong.*

信箱 xìnxiāng  N  mailbox · MW 个

信心 xìnxīn  N  confidence, faith

信仰 xìnyǎng  N·V  conviction; faith; to believe in (a religion, a political ideology) · MW 个

信用 xìnyòng  N  trustworthiness; credit · MW 个

信誉 xìnyù  N  reputation, prestige · MW 个

信纸 xìnzhǐ  N  writing paper, stationery · MW 张

**RELATED WORDS**

| | | |
|---|---|---|
| 失信 106 | 来信 260 | 书信 264 |
| 自信 305 | 发信 311 | 坚信 381 |
| 听信 414 | 守信 486 | 快信 497 |
| 相信 805 | 音信 907 | 亲信 908 |
| 明信片 1035 | 凭信 1060 | 轻信 1113 |
| 迷信 1187 | 送信 1188 | 背信弃义 1380 |
| 寄信 1619 | 通信 1757 | 确信 1762 |
| 发短信 311 | 航空信 1717 | 卫星通信 82 |

---

**870** 修　　U+4FEE　　TM **10**　FM 丿

xiū  V·N·ADJ  to build; to repair, to mend; to decorate; to trim, to prune; to write; to study; to cultivate; revisionism; long

修桥 *to build a bridge*

修书 *to write a letter*

进修 *advanced study*

修身养性 *to cultivate one's moral character*

修补 xiūbǔ  V  to repair, to mend; retrieval
你能修补这些鞋吗? *Could you have these shoes repaired?*

修长 xiūcháng  ADJ  tall and thin/slender

修订 xiūdìng  V  to amend; to revise (a book, a plan, etc.)

修复 xiūfù  V  to repair; to restore; to renovate

修改 xiūgǎi  V  to amend; to revise; to alter, to modify
公司的预算需要做重大修改。*The company's budget needs drastic revisions.*

修剪 xiūjiǎn  V  to trim, to clip

修建 xiūjiàn  V  to build, to construct

修理 xiūlǐ  V  to repair; to fix; to trim/clip (a tree, a fingernail, etc.); to punish

修面 xiūmiàn  V  to shave

修女 xiūnǚ  N  (Roman Catholic) sister, nun · MW 个、名

修配 xiūpèi  V  to make repairs and supply replacement parts

修身 xiūshēn  V  to cultivate one's moral character

修士 xiūshì  N  (Roman Catholic) brother · MW 个、名

修饰 xiūshì  V  to decorate; to modify; to polish (a written piece)

修养 xiūyǎng  N  accomplishment; training; mastery

修造 xiūzào  V  to build and repair

修整 xiūzhěng  V  to repair and maintain

修正 xiūzhèng  V  to revise; to correct

修枝 xiūzhī  V  to trim, to prune

修筑 xiūzhù  V  to build, to construct
这条新的高速公路正在修筑之中。*The new highway is under construction.*

**RELATED WORDS**

| | | |
|---|---|---|
| 主修 124 | 自修 305 | 必修课 338 |
| 进修 713 | 检修 1033 | 抢修 1230 |
| 维修 1455 | 装修 1476 | 选修 1510 |
| 整修 1845 | 翻修 1989 | |

---

**871** 彻　徹　U+5F7B　　TM **10**　FM 丿

chè  ADJ  thorough, penetrating

彻底 chèdǐ  ADJ  thorough, complete
傻瓜把汽车彻底地检查了一遍。*ShaGua gave the car a thorough inspection.*

彻头彻尾 chètóuchèwěi  EXP  through-and-through, from top to bottom

**RELATED WORDS**

| | | |
|---|---|---|
| 洞彻 1338 | 响彻 1409 | 透彻 1826 |

---

**872** 待　　U+5F85　　TM **10**　FM 丿

dài  V  to wait for; to need; to treat, to deal with; to entertain

待发 dàifā  V  to await orders

待命 dàimìng  V  to await orders

待人接物 dàirénjiēwù  EXP  people skills; way one gets along with people

待续 dàixù  V  to be continued

待业 dàiyè  V  to await a job assignment; to be between jobs

待遇 dàiyù  N  pay; salary and benefits
很多人愿意干这个工作, 因为工资待遇比较好。*Many people like this job because of the salary.*

**872** 待 **dài** (continued)

**RELATED WORDS**

| | | |
|---|---|---|
| 亏待 137 | 交待 222 | 对待 254 |
| 优待 447 | 看待 841 | 招待会 1232 |
| 招待 1232 | 虐待 1379 | 接待 1405 |
| 等待 1437 | 款待 1573 | 期待 1574 |
| 留待 1582 | 宽待 1618 | 以礼相待 101 |
| 另眼看待 385 | 急不可待 1426 | |

---

**873** 徒     U+5F92    TM **10** FM 丿

**tú** N·ADJ·ADV apprentice, pupil, disciple; follower, believer; clique, gang; member; on foot; empty; merely, only; in vain

> 信徒 *believer*
>
> 党徒 *gang members*

**徒步 túbù** ADV on foot

> 徒步旅行正在成为一种时尚。*Traveling on foot is becoming the newest trend.*

**徒弟 túdì** N apprentice, pupil · MW 个、名

**徒工 túgōng** N apprentice · MW 个、名

**徒劳 túláo** V to work to no avail; to make a futile effort

> 你这样学习是徒劳的。*The way you study is useless.*

**徒然 túrán** ADV in vain, to no avail; merely, only

**徒手 túshǒu** ADV bare-handed; unarmed

**徒孙 túsūn** N disciple's disciple · MW 个、名

**徒刑 túxíng** N imprisonment; (prison) sentence

> 这家伙被判五年有期徒刑，这次便宜他了。*The guy was only given a five-year sentence; the court let him off lightly.*

**徒子徒孙 túzǐtúsūn** N disciples and followers · MW 个、名

**RELATED WORDS**

| | | |
|---|---|---|
| 歹徒 74 | 囚徒 161 | 师徒 396 |
| 迁徒 506 | 信徒 869 | 叛徒 960 |
| 暴徒 1844 | | |

---

**874** 顺 顺     U+987A    TM **10** FM 丿

**shùn** ADJ·V·PREP smooth; reasonable; successful; to obey; to arrange, to put in order; to follow, to fall in with; to suit, to agree with; along, (along) with; on the way

> 顺着河流走 *to walk along the river with the current*
>
> 通顺 *coherent*

**顺便 shùnbiàn** ADV conveniently; on the way; by the way

> 顺便问一下，你的太太也一起来吗？*By the way, will your wife come with you?*

**顺次 shùncì** ADV in (proper) order, in sequence

**顺从 shùncó** V to be obedient to

**顺风 shùnfēng** ADJ tail wind (on a journey); fair winds

**顺口 shùnkǒu** ADJ smooth, easy to read; suiting one's taste (of food)

**顺利 shùnlì** ADJ smooth; successful

> 在傻瓜的指导下，这项工作完成得很顺利。*Under ShaGua's guidance, the work was finished smoothly.*

**顺路 shùnlù** ADJ on the way

**顺手 shùnshǒu** ADJ·ADV smooth; handy; conveniently; naturally, in proper order

**顺心 shùnxīn** ADJ satisfactory

**顺序 shùnxù** N order, sequence; in proper order · MW 个

**顺延 shùnyán** V to postpone

**顺眼 shùnyǎn** ADJ nice to look at, pleasing to the eye

**顺应 shùnyìng** V to comply with; to be in tune with

> 顺应历史发展的潮流。*Embrace the current trend.*

**RELATED WORDS**

| | |
|---|---|
| 归顺 166 | 孝顺 529 |
| 依顺 625 | 温顺 1627 |
| 通顺 1757 | 风调雨顺 194 |

---

**875** 须 须     U+987B    TM **10** FM 丿

**xū** V·N must, to have to; to wait; beard; mustache

**须发 xūfà** N hair and beard · MW 根

**须要 xūyào** AV must, to have to

**须知 xūzhī** V·N to notice; one should know that; prerequisites · MW 份、张

> 请你读一读这份旅客须知。*Please read the notice to travelers.*

**RELATED WORDS**

| | |
|---|---|
| 必须 338 | 务须 429 |
| 莫须有 999 | |

## 876 约 約 U+7EA6 TM 10 FM 丿

**yuē** V·ADV·N to arrange; to invite; to restrict; to economize; to reduce; frugally; simply; briefly; about, approximately; agreement, pact; reducing a fraction

约她来办公室 *to ask her to come to the office*
节约钱 *to save money*
制约 *to restrict*
大约 *approximately*

约旦 **Yuēdàn** N Jordan
约定 **yuēdìng** V to agree on; to promise; to appoint · MW 个
约法 **yuēfǎ** V provisional constitution

儿子上大学前，傻瓜跟他**约法**三章：不喝酒，不抽烟，不吸毒。*Before his older son went to college, ShaGua made a three-part covenant with him: "Don't drink, don't smoke, and don't do drugs."*

约会 **yuēhuì** N·V appointment; date; to make an appointment · MW 个
约集 **yuējí** V to meet by appointment; to gather
约略 **yuēlüè** ADV roughly, approximately
约莫 **yuēmo** ADV roughly, approximately
约束 **yuēshù** V to bind; to restrict, to limit (to)
约言 **yuēyán** N promise, pledge · MW 个

**RELATED WORDS**

| | | |
|---|---|---|
| 大约 20 | 公约 103 | 失约 106 |
| 立约人 125 | 旧约全书 165 | 节约 275 |
| 条约 598 | 相约 805 | 契约 992 |
| 特约 1094 | 租约 1096 | 违约 1185 |
| 签约 1439 | 婚约 1701 | 简约 1796 |
| 毁约 1810 | 隐约 1912 | 解约 1927 |

## 877 娃 U+5A03 TM 10 FM 丿

**wá** N baby; child; newborn animal; doll

娃娃 **wáwa** N baby; child; doll · MW 个

## 878 奶 U+5976 TM 10 FM 丿

**nǎi** N·V breast; milk; to breast-feed

奶粉 **nǎifěn** N powdered milk · MW 盒、包
奶酪 **nǎilào** N cheese · MW 块

奶妈 **nǎimā** N wet nurse · MW 个、位、名
奶名 **nǎimíng** N pet name · MW 个

傻瓜有一个连傻瓜太太都不知道的**奶名**。*ShaGua has a nickname that even Mrs. ShaGua doesn't know.*

奶奶 **nǎinai** N grandma; [respectful form of address for an elderly woman] · MW 个、位
奶牛 **nǎiniú** N (milk) cow · MW 头
奶瓶 **nǎipíng** N feeding bottle (for a baby) · MW 个
奶水 **nǎishuǐ** N milk · MW 口、滴
奶糖 **nǎitáng** N toffee · MW 颗、块
奶头 **nǎitóu** N nipple · MW 个
奶牙 **nǎiyá** N milk/baby tooth · MW 只
奶油 **nǎiyóu** N cream; butter · MW 块
奶罩 **nǎizhào** N brassiere · MW 副

**RELATED WORDS**

| | | |
|---|---|---|
| 牛奶 51 | 挤奶 795 | 喂奶 1667 |
| 酸奶 1899 | | |

## 879 妨 U+59A8 TM 10 FM 丿

**fáng** N·V harm; to hinder; to harm

妨碍 **fáng'ài** V to hinder, to obstruct, to block

这场事故**妨碍**了城市交通。*The accident obstructed city traffic.*

妨害 **fánghài** V to jeopardize; to impair; to be harmful to

吸烟**妨害**健康。*Smoking is harmful to your health.*

**RELATED WORDS**

| | | |
|---|---|---|
| 不妨 24 | 无妨 139 | 何妨 619 |
| 猛不妨 1704 | | |

## 880 姐 U+59D0 TM 10 FM 丿

**jiě** N older sister; older female relative; [form of address for a young lady]

姐夫 **jiěfu** N older sister's husband · MW 个、位
姐姐 **jiějie** N older sister · MW 个、位
姐妹 **jiěmèi** N sisters; brothers and sisters; compatriots · MW 个

**RELATED WORDS**

| | | |
|---|---|---|
| 大姐 20 | 小姐 61 | 师姐 396 |

## 881 姑　U+59D1　TM 10　FM 丿

**gū** N·ADV aunt, father's sister; sister-in-law, husband's sister; nun; tentatively, for the time being

**姑表** gūbiǎo N cousinage; relationship between the children of a brother and a sister · MW 个、位

**姑夫** gūfu N uncle, husband of a father's sister · MW 个、位

**姑妈** gūmā N aunt, father's (married) sister · MW 个、位

**姑母** gūmǔ N aunt, father's (married) sister · MW 个、位

**姑娘** gūniang N girl; daughter · MW 个

这个中国**姑娘**长着一双杏眼。 *The Chinese girl has a pair of almond eyes.*

**姑且** gūqiě ADV tentatively, for a/the moment

你**姑且**忍一忍吧。 *Please control yourself for a moment.*

**姑嫂** gūsǎo N sisters-in-law, woman and her brother's wife · MW 个

**姑息** gūxī V to indulge; to appease; to tolerate

绝不能**姑息**这种错误行为。 *We cannot tolerate this inappropriate behavior.*

**姑爷** gūye N son-in-law; [form of address for a man by his wife's family] · MW 个

**RELATED WORDS**
小姑 61
尼姑 441

## 882 娇　嬌　U+5A07　TM 10　FM 丿

**jiāo** ADJ·V lovely; pampered; tender, delicate, frail; to spoil

**娇嫩** jiāonèn ADJ delicate, tender and lovely

**娇气** jiāoqì ADJ whiny, fussy, finicky

那个漂亮女孩一点儿不**娇气**。 *That beautiful girl is not the tiniest bit whiny or finicky.*

**娇生惯养** jiāoshēngguànyǎng EXP pampered since childhood

**娇艳** jiāoyàn ADJ delicate and charming

**RELATED WORD**
撒娇 1907

## 883 物　U+7269　TM 10　FM 丿

**wù** N thing; matter, substance; essence; content; outside world, other people

**物产** wùchǎn N products; produce · MW 批

**物价** wùjià N (commodity) prices

政府提请大家注意，**物价**仍有上涨趋势。 *The government warned everyone of the rise in commodity prices.*

**物理** wùlǐ N physics; laws of nature

**物力** wùlì N material resources

**物色** wùsè V to look for, to seek; to choose (qualified professional people / essentials)

傻瓜在**物色**一个助手。 *ShaGua is looking for an assistant.*

**物体** wùtǐ N body; substance; object · MW 个

你是一个有独立思想的人，而不是一个任人摆布的**物体**。 *You are a human being with independent thought, not a mindless object for others to order around.*

**物证** wùzhèng N material evidence · MW 个

**物质** wùzhì N matter; substance; material things

**物质文明** wùzhìwénmíng ADJ material culture

**物种** wùzhǒng N species · MW 类

**RELATED WORDS**
| | | |
|---|---|---|
| 人物 4 | 什物 63 | 文物 70 |
| 失物 106 | 失物招领 106 | 生物 107 |
| 生物学 107 | 生物钟 107 | 及物动词 141 |
| 刊物 216 | 产物 219 | 谷物 446 |
| 礼物 503 | 动物 514 | 动物园 514 |
| 异物 539 | 宝物 667 | 实物 668 |
| 怪物 696 | 证物 705 | 事物 987 |
| 赃物 1039 | 食物 1053 | 货物 1061 |
| 织物 1108 | 毒物 1211 | 购物中心 1253 |
| 药物 1392 | 植物 1415 | 猎物 1444 |
| 读物 1502 | 博物馆 1549 | 大人物 20 |
| 小人物 61 | 针织物 477 | 头面人物 128 |
| 待人接物 872 | 庞然大物 917 | |

## 884 犯　U+72AF　TM 10　FM 丿

**fàn** V·N to violate; to attack, to invade; criminal, offender

**犯不着** fànbuzháo V to not be worthwhile

在小问题上**犯不着**花这么多时间。 *It isn't worthwhile spending so much time on minor issues.*

**犯得着** fàndezháo V is it worthwhile (often rhetorical)

在小问题上**犯得着**花这么多时间吗？
*Is it worthwhile spending so much time on minor issues?*

**犯法** fànfǎ　V　to break/violate the law

2006年以前，中国青少年喝酒不**犯法**。
*Before 2006, underage drinking was allowed in China.*

**犯规** fànguī　V　to foul (sports); to break the rules

**犯人** fànrén　N　criminal, convict; prisoner · MW 个、名

**犯罪** fànzuì　V　to commit a crime

**RELATED WORDS**

| | | |
|---|---|---|
| 凶犯 98 | 主犯 124 | 囚犯 161 |
| 来犯 260 | 首犯 924 | 要犯 969 |
| 战犯 1044 | 违犯 1185 | 侵犯 1280 |
| 逃犯 1509 | 罪犯 1542 | 惯犯 1630 |
| 触犯 1875 | | |

---

**885　狐**　U+72D0　TM 10 FM 丿

hú　N　fox

**狐步舞** húbùwǔ　N　foxtrot (dance) · MW 个、场

**狐臭** húchòu　N　body odor

**狐狸** húli　N　fox; bewitching woman · MW 只

**狐疑** húyí　V　to doubt

---

**886　犹**　猶　U+72B9　TM 10 FM 丿

yóu　V·ADV　to be like; still, even

**犹大** Yóudà　N　Judas

**犹如** yóurú　V　to be like; as if

美丽的桂林山水**犹如**仙境。*Guilin is so beautiful that it looks like a fantasyland.*

**犹太** Yóutài　N　Jew

**犹太教** Yóutàijiào　N　Judaism

**犹豫** yóuyù　ADJ　hesitant; wavering

傻瓜做事从不**犹豫**。*ShaGua does not waver when conducting business.*

---

**887　绊**　絆　U+7ECA　TM 10 FM 丿

bàn　V　to cause to stumble; to trip, to stumble

**绊倒** bàndǎo　V　to trip, to stumble

小心别**绊倒**了。*Be careful, don't trip.*

---

**绊脚石** bànjiǎoshí　N　stumbling block · MW 个、块

---

**888　轨**　軌　U+8F68　TM 10 FM 丿

guǐ　N　rail; track, course

**轨道** guǐdào　N　railway track; railroad; orbit (of a planet); right track/course · MW 条

**轨迹** guǐjì　N　track; orbit; locus · MW 条、道

**RELATED WORDS**

| | | |
|---|---|---|
| 正轨 76 | 双轨 146 | 出轨 258 |
| 越轨 1575 | | |

---

**889　软**　軟　U+8F6F　TM 10 FM 丿

ruǎn　ADJ　soft; gentle; weak, feeble; easily swayed/influenced

柔**软** *flexible*

心**软** *easily influenced*

**软风** ruǎnfēng　N　light breeze · MW 阵

**软膏** ruǎngāo　N　ointment · MW 支

**软骨** ruǎngǔ　N　cartilage · MW 根、块

**软化** ruǎnhuà　V　to soften

**软件** ruǎnjiàn　N　software · MW 个

我的计算机里装有中文**软件**。*Software for writing in Chinese is installed on my computer.*

**软禁** ruǎnjìn　V　to place under house arrest

**软弱** ruǎnruò　ADJ　weak, feeble

有人认为傻瓜是个**软弱**无能的领导。
*Some people think that ShaGua is a weak leader.*

**软席** ruǎnxí　N　soft seat/berth (first class on a Chinese train) · MW 个

**软组织** ruǎnzǔzhī　N　soft tissue · MW 个、块

**软座** ruǎnzuò　N　soft seat · MW 个

**RELATED WORDS**

| | | |
|---|---|---|
| 心软 232 | 松软 579 | 柔软 1198 |
| 疲软 1328 | | |

---

**890　饥**　飢　U+9965　TM 10 FM 丿

jī　ADJ·N　hungry, starving; famine; crop failure

**饥饿** jī'è　ADJ　hungry, starving

节食让人感到**饥饿**。*Diets make people hungry.*

**饥荒** jīhuāng　N　famine · MW 次、场

 890 饥 jī (continued)

饥民 jīmín　N　famine victim ·　MW　个、名

**RELATED WORD**

充饥 652

---

891　**饭**　飯　U+996D　TM 10　FM 丿

fàn　N　meal; cooked rice/cereal

饭菜 fàncài　N　food; meal ·　MW　份、桌

饭店 fàndiàn　N　restaurant ·　MW　个、家
这家**饭**店除了星期一以外, 每天都营业。
*The restaurant is open every day except Monday.*

饭厅 fàntīng　N　dining hall ·　MW　个

饭桶 fàntǒng　N　rice container; stupid person, imbecile ·　MW　个
蔡先生自以为聪明, 其实是个**饭桶**。
*Mr. Cai is always on his high horse, but he is actually useless.*

**RELATED WORDS**

| | | |
|---|---|---|
| 午饭 48 | 中饭 86 | 米饭 226 |
| 早饭 268 | 丢饭碗 297 | 讨饭 500 |
| 吃饭 783 | 包饭 836 | 便饭 865 |
| 要饭 969 | 煮饭 1388 | 稀饭 1599 |
| 剩饭 1720 | 晚饭 1779 | 吃闲饭 783 |

---

 892　**饮**　飲　U+996E　TM 10　FM 丿

yǐn　V·N　to drink; to harbor, to keep in one's heart; drink, beverage; water

饮料 yǐnliào　N　drink, beverage ·　MW　杯、瓶、罐
你想喝什么**饮料**? *What beverage would you like?*

饮泣 yǐnqì　V　to weep in silence

饮食 yǐnshí　N　diet; food and drink

饮用水 yǐnyòngshuǐ　N　potable water, water for drinking ·　MW　杯、瓶、罐

---

 893　**种**　種　U+79CD　TM 10　FM 丿

zhǒng　N·MW　species; seed; breed; race; courage; [measure word for kinds/types/categories of objects]

zhòng　V　to plant; to grow, to cultivate

种类 zhǒnglèi　N　type, kind, sort; variety; class, category

书店的书籍**种类**繁多。*The bookstore has a variety of books.*

种苗 zhǒngmiáo　N　seeding ·　MW　株、棵

种群 zhǒngqún　N　population; stock ·　MW　个

种姓 zhǒngxìng　N　caste (traditional Indian social division)

种种 zhǒngzhǒng　ADV　all kinds/sorts of, various, a variety of
老师由于**种种**原因迟到了。*The teacher was late for a variety of reasons.*

种子 zhǒngzi　N　seed ·　MW　粒、颗

种族 zhǒngzú　N　race (of people) ·　MW　个

种地 zhòngdì　V　to farm, to work the land
傻瓜的父亲**种地**。*ShaGua's father worked on a farm.*

种痘 zhòngdòu　V　to vaccinate (against smallpox)

种花 zhònghuā　V　to grow flowers

种田 zhòngtián　V　to farm, to be a farmer

种植 zhòngzhí　V　to plant; to grow

**RELATED WORDS**

| | | |
|---|---|---|
| 兵种 300 | 多种多样 431 | 谷种 446 |
| 杂种 856 | 物种 883 | 栽种 995 |
| 特种 1094 | 育种 1133 | 品种 1220 |
| 配种 1647 | | |

---

894　**秤**　U+79E4　TM 10　FM 丿

chèng　N　balance, scale

秤杆 chènggǎn　N　beam (of a scale) ·　MW　根

**RELATED WORD**

磅秤 1936

---

895　**秩**　U+79E9　TM 10　FM 丿

zhì　N　order, sequence; official rank; decade

秩序 zhìxù　N　order, sequence
因为没有老师维持**秩序**, 教室里一片混乱。
*Without a teacher to keep order, the classroom was chaotic.*

---

896　**卵**　U+5375　TM 10　FM 丿

luǎn　N　ovum, egg; testicle; penis; genitals

卵巢 luǎncháo　N　ovary ·　MW　个

卵黄 luǎnhuáng　N　egg yolk · MW 个

卵生 luǎnshēng　ADJ　oviparous, egg-producing

卵子 luǎnzǐ　N　ovum, egg · MW 个

**RELATED WORDS**

以卵击石 101　　产卵 219　　杀鸡取卵 317

## 897 版　U+7248　TM 10 FM 丿

bǎn　N　printing plate/block; edition, version; page

版本 bǎnběn　N　edition, version · MW 个
这个**版本**的书已售完了。*This edition of the book is sold out.*

版画 bǎnhuà　N　picture printed from an engraved plate · MW 幅

版面 bǎnmiàn　N　layout/makeup of a page · MW 个

版权 bǎnquán　N　copyright · MW 个
出版社拥有这本书的**版权**。*The publisher owns the copyright for this book.*

版税 bǎnshuì　N　(author's) royalty · MW 笔

版图 bǎntú　N　territory, domain · MW 个

**RELATED WORDS**

出版 258　　再版 354　　印版 470
重版 839　　刻版 966　　制版 1130
原版 1273　　铜版 1712　　翻版 1989

## 898 肋　U+808B　TM 10 FM 丿

lèi　N　rib

肋骨 lèigǔ　N　rib; ribbing · MW 条、根

## 899 肤　膚　U+80A4　TM 10 FM 丿

fū　N　skin

肤觉 fūjué　N　skin sensation

肤浅 fūqiǎn　ADJ　superficial; skin-deep
傻瓜对经济问题的看法有些**肤浅**。
*ShaGua's understanding of economics is quite superficial.*

肤色 fūsè　N　skin color · MW 种

**RELATED WORDS**

皮肤 261　　肌肤 1118

## 900 钞　钞　U+949E　TM 10 FM 丿

chāo　N　money; paper money

钞票 chāopiào　N　paper money, bill (dollar, etc.) · MW 张、叠
我要两张10美元的**钞票**。*I want two 10-dollar bills.*

**RELATED WORDS**

美钞 671　　现钞 975

## 901 乱　亂　U+4E71　TM 10 FM 丿

luàn　ADJ·N·V　disorderly, confused, in turmoil; chaos; riot, unrest; to mix up, to confuse

乱纷纷 luànfēnfēn　ADV·ADJ　in disarray; disorderly
听见枪声，人们**乱纷纷**地奔跑。
*A gunshot sent the tumultuous crowd running away helter skelter.*

乱哄哄 luànhōnghōng　ADV·ADJ　chaotic, noisy and disorderly

乱伦 luànlún　V　to commit incest

乱蓬蓬 luànpēngpēng　ADJ　disheveled; tangled

乱七八糟 luànqībāzāo　EXP　in a mess
老师来晚了，学生把教室弄得**乱七八糟**。
*The teacher was late and the classroom had been turned upside down by the students.*

乱世 luànshì　N　troubled times · MW 个

乱说 luànshuō　V　to make irresponsible remarks

乱弹琴 luàntánqín　EXP　to talk nonsense
这简直是**乱弹琴**。*That's a lot of nonsense.*

乱套 luàntào　V　to mess things up

乱糟糟 luànzāozāo　ADV·ADJ　chaotic, topsy-turvy; in a mess

乱真 luànzhēn　V　to look genuine (of counterfeit merchandise)

乱子 luànzi　N　disturbance; trouble; disorder · MW 个
你还是老老实实待在家里吧，别出去闹**乱子**了。
*You had better stay at home; don't go out and cause trouble.*

**RELATED WORDS**

内乱 191　　出乱子 258　　打乱 289
作乱 326　　忙乱 343　　动乱 514
叛乱 960　　纷乱 1102　　胡乱 1256
闹乱子 1323　　错乱 1715　　慌乱 1736
暴乱 1844　　搅乱 1850　　天花乱坠 25
以假乱真 101

## 902 刮 颳　U+522E　TM 10 FM 丿

**guā** [V] to scrape; to smear (with paste, etc.); to plunder; to extort; to blow

刮脸 **guāliǎn** [V] to shave

傻瓜每天都**刮脸**。*ShaGua shaves every day.*

刮脸刀 **guāliǎndāo** [N] razor · [MW] 片

刮削 **guāxiāo** [V] to scrape

### RELATED WORD

搜刮 1663

## 903 刽 劊　U+523D　TM 10 FM 丿

**guì** [V] to cut/chop off

刽子手 **guìzishǒu** [N] executioner ·
[MW] 个、名

## 904 剑 劍　U+5251　TM 10 FM 丿

**jiàn** [N] sword, saber; swordplay

剑道 **jiàndào** [N] kendo (swordfighting as a
martial art)

剑客 **jiànkè** [N] swordsman · [MW] 个、位、名

剑术 **jiànshù** [N] (art of) fencing · [MW] 种

剑鱼 **jiànyú** [N] swordfish · [MW] 条

### RELATED WORDS

击剑 156　　　宝剑 667

## 905 京　U+4EAC　TM 10 FM 丶

**jīng** [N] (short name for) Beijing; capital (of a
country)

京城 **jīngchéng** [N] capital (of a country) ·
[MW] 座

京胡 **jīnghú** [N] Chinese bowed string instrument
with a high register · [MW] 把

京剧 **jīngjù** [N] Beijing opera · [MW] 场

**京剧**脸谱具有独特的文化含义。*The makeup
used in Beijing opera has special cultural
significance.*

### RELATED WORDS

北京 278　　　南京 986

## 906 盲　U+76F2　TM 10 FM 丶

**máng** [ADJ·N] blind; undistinguished; impetuous,
rash; ignorant; illiterate

盲从 **mángcóng** [V] to follow blindly, to follow like
sheep

盲点 **mángdiǎn** [N] blind spot · [MW] 个

盲动 **mángdòng** [V] to act rashly

对于如此敏感的事件，他决不会**盲动**。*He will
not act rashly in such a sensitive affair.*

盲目 **mángmù** [ADJ] blind; lacking insight/
understanding

爱情常常是**盲目**的。*Love is often blind.*

盲人 **mángrén** [N] blind person · [MW] 个、位、名

盲文 **mángwén** [N] braille

盲哑教育 **mángyǎjiàoyù** [N] education for the
blind and deaf

### RELATED WORDS

文盲 70　　　扫盲 402　　　半文盲 127

## 907 音　U+97F3　TM 10 FM 丶

**yīn** [N] sound; news; syllable

音标 **yīnbiāo** [N] phonetic symbol · [MW] 个

音波 **yīnbō** [N] sound wave · [MW] 个

音调 **yīndiào** [N] tone; pitch · [MW] 个

音符 **yīnfú** [N] musical note · [MW] 个

音节 **yīnjié** [N] syllable · [MW] 个

音响 **yīnxiǎng** [N] stereo; sound; acoustics ·
[MW] 个

这个教室的**音响**效果很差。*The acoustics in the
classroom are poor.*

音信 **yīnxìn** [N] mail; message · [MW] 个

音乐 **yīnyuè** [N] music · [MW] 段、种

我喜欢流行**音乐**。*I like popular music.*

音质 **yīnzhì** [N] tone/sound quality

### RELATED WORDS

| | | |
|---|---|---|
| 口音 42 | 子音 83 | 乡音 117 |
| 元音 138 | 发音 311 | 伴音 321 |
| 忙音 343 | 声音 374 | 余音 419 |
| 注音 496 | 低音 618 | 知音 647 |
| 录音 722 | 录音机 722 | 拼音 794 |
| 杂音 856 | 浊音 943 | 轻音乐 1113 |
| 话音 1182 | 语音 1501 | 读音 1502 |
| 喉音 1560 | 高音 1611 | 超音速 1684 |
| 鼻音 1794 | 福音 1825 | 嗓音 1855 |
| 隔音 1910 | 颤音 1991 | 男高音 757 |
| 轻元音 1113 | | |

## 908 亲 親　U+4EB2　TM **10** FM ヽ

**qīn** [N·ADJ·ADV·V] parent; relative, kin; marriage; bride; related by blood; intimate; in person, personally; to kiss; to be close to; to touch

亲爱 **qīn'ài** [ADJ] dear, beloved

亲笔 **qīnbǐ** [N·ADV] autograph; personal inscription; in one's own handwriting

亲近 **qīnjìn** [V] to be close to, to be friendly with
学生们都愿意**亲近**这位中文老师。
*The students all want to be friends with this Chinese teacher.*

亲眷 **qīnjuàn** [N] relatives · [MW] 个、名

亲口 **qīnkǒu** [ADV] in one's own words; speaking personally

亲密 **qīnmì** [ADJ] intimate, close
他俩是**亲密**的朋友。*Those two are close friends.*

亲戚 **qīnqi** [N] relative, kin · [MW] 个、位

亲切 **qīnqiè** [ADJ] warm; close

亲热 **qīnrè** [ADJ] affectionate; intimate

亲人 **qīnrén** [N] family member, close relative · [MW] 个、位

亲生 **qīnshēng** [ADJ] one's/natural child/parent

亲手 **qīnshǒu** [ADV] personally; with one's own hands

亲属 **qīnshǔ** [N] relatives, kinfolk · [MW] 个、位

亲王 **qīnwáng** [N] prince; royal highness · [MW] 个、位、名

亲吻 **qīnwěn** [V] to kiss
傻瓜太太是傻瓜**亲吻**的第一个女人。
*Mrs. ShaGua was the first female ShaGua kissed.*

亲信 **qīnxìn** [N] trusted aide/follower · [MW] 个、名

亲眼 **qīnyǎn** [ADV] with one's own eyes; (to witness) personally

亲友 **qīnyǒu** [N] relatives and friends · [MW] 个、位、名

亲自 **qīnzì** [ADV] personally, in person; by oneself
申请签证, 用不着**亲自**去, 邮寄就行了。
*You don't need to go in person to apply for a visa; you can do it by mail.*

亲嘴 **qīnzuǐ** [V] to kiss

### RELATED WORDS

| | | |
|---|---|---|
| 父亲 56 | 六亲 69 | 双亲 146 |
| 母亲 394 | 表亲 527 | 沾亲带故 684 |
| 近亲 716 | 姻亲 1093 | 探亲 1404 |
| 任人唯亲 211 | | |

## 909 完　U+5B8C　TM **10** FM ヽ

**wán** [V·ADJ] to be finished/over, to run out; to complete, to finish; to pay (taxes); entire, whole

完备 **wánbèi** [ADJ] complete, with all the necessary parts/components/steps

完毕 **wánbì** [V] to complete, to finish

完成 **wánchéng** [V] to complete, to accomplish
傻瓜终于**完成**了今年的工作计划。*ShaGua finally fulfilled his goals for work this year.*

完蛋 **wándàn** [EXP] to be finished/doomed; to die

完稿 **wángǎo** [V] to finish a piece of writing

完工 **wángōng** [V] to complete a project; to finish (doing)

完好 **wánhǎo** [ADJ] in perfect condition; intact

完婚 **wánhūn** [V] to get married (of a man)

完结 **wánjié** [V] to finish, to be over, to conclude

完了 **wánliǎo** [V] to be over

完满 **wánmǎn** [ADJ] satisfactory

完全 **wánquán** [ADJ·ADV] complete, whole; totally; entirely
对于傻瓜来说, **完成**这项工作**完全**不成问题。
*ShaGua will have no problem finishing the project.*

完人 **wánrén** [N] perfect person · [MW] 个、位、名

完善 **wánshàn** [ADJ·V] to improve; to perfect

完事 **wánshì** [V] to be settled/done; to finish (doing)

完整 **wánzhěng** [ADJ] complete, thorough; whole, entire

### RELATED WORD

未完 88

## 910 宗　U+5B97　TM **10** FM ヽ

**zōng** [N·MW] ancestor; forefather; clan; sect, faction; aim, purpose; great master

宗法 **zōngfǎ** [N] patriarchal clan system

宗教 **zōngjiào** [N] religion · [MW] 个
她对**宗教**没有任何了解。*She has no knowledge of religion.*

宗庙 **zōngmiào** [N] ancestral temple (of a ruling house) · [MW] 座

宗派 **zōngpài** [N] faction · [MW] 个

宗室 **zōngshì** [N] imperial clan · [MW] 个

宗旨 **zōngzhǐ** [N] aim, purpose · [MW] 个

**910 宗 zōng** (continued)

宗族 **zōngzú** N patriarchal clan · MW 个

在中国的一些农村, **宗族**势力还有很大影响。
*Patriarchal clans still have strong influence in some parts of the Chinese countryside.*

**RELATED WORDS**

正宗 76　　　　祖宗 1190　　　　卷宗 1333

---

**911 审** 審　　U+5BA1　　TM **10** FM 丶

**shěn** V·ADJ to examine, to go over; to interrogate; careful; indeed, really

审查 **shěnchá** V to examine, to inspect; to investigate

审定 **shěndìng** V to examine and approve; to finalize

审核 **shěnhé** V to examine and verify; to check

傻瓜在**审核**2008年的预算。*ShaGua is looking over the 2008 budget.*

审计 **shěnjì** V to audit

审理 **shěnlǐ** V to hear (a case); to bring to trial

审美 **shěnměi** V to appreciate; to make an esthetic judgment

审判 **shěnpàn** V to examine and decide (a case); to sentence

审批 **shěnpī** V to examine and approve

审问 **shěnwèn** V to question; to interrogate

审讯 **shěnxùn** V to interrogate; to hold a trial

**审讯**持续了一个月。*The trial lasted a month.*

审议 **shěnyì** V to examine and discuss; to review, to consider

审阅 **shěnyuè** V to check, to review

**RELATED WORDS**

会审 295　　　再审 354　　　受审 844
初审 963　　　陪审 1568　　　编审 1866

---

**912 穷** 窮　　U+7A77　　TM **10** FM 丶

**qióng** ADJ·N·V·ADV poor, impoverished; end, limit; to exhaust, to use up; thoroughly; extremely

穷光蛋 **qióngguāngdàn** EXP pauper; poor wretch · MW 个

穷尽 **qióngjìn** V to limit; to end

穷苦 **qióngkǔ** ADJ impoverished, poverty-stricken

---

穷困 **qióngkùn** ADJ poor, poverty-stricken

中国不再是一个**穷困**的国家。*China is not a poor country anymore.*

穷人 **qióngrén** N poor people, the poor · MW 个、群

穷日子 **qióngrìzi** N days of poverty · MW 天、段

**RELATED WORDS**

无穷 139　　　　贫穷 1052

---

**913 突**　　U+7A81　　TM **10** FM 丶

**tū** V·ADV to charge; to break out; to stick out, to protrude; suddenly; unexpectedly

突变 **tūbiàn** N·V sudden change; to change suddenly; to mutate · MW 个

突出 **tūchū** ADJ·V outstanding; highlight; obvious, noticeable; protruding; to stress, to highlight

傻瓜个子很矮, 因此在人群中不**突出**。*ShaGua's short stature makes him inconspicuous in a crowd.*

突飞猛进 **tūfēiměngjìn** EXP to advance by leaps and bounds

突击 **tūjī** V to assault; to do a rush job

突破 **tūpò** V to break through

突起 **tūqǐ** V to break out, to erupt

突然 **tūrán** ADJ suddenly; unexpectedly

这场暴雨来得实在太**突然**了。*This storm appeared much too suddenly.*

突如其来 **tūrúqílái** EXP to come all of a sudden

**RELATED WORDS**

冲突 339　　　　唐突 1324

---

**914 间** 間　　U+95F4　　TM **10** FM 丶

**jiān** N·MW between, among; room; within a definite time; [measure word for rooms (offices, bedrooms, etc.)]

**jiàn** N·V space (between); opening; to separate; to sow discord; to thin out (seedlings)

间距 **jiānjù** N distance; interval; separation; space · MW 段

北京和上海之间, 有多少公里**间距**? *How many kilometers separate Beijing and Shanghai?*

**RELATED WORDS**

人间 4　　　　之间 67　　　　中间 86
日间 96　　　　区间 99　　　　车间 114

田间 147    其间 379    民间 388
时间 586    夜间 654    空间 669
相间 805    阴间 1041    房间 1145
期间 1574    离间 1614    晚间 1779
卫生间 82    衣帽间 330

## RELATED WORDS

井底之蛙 60    年底 182    交底 222
老底 375    有底 439    到底 737
封底 815    彻底 871    根底 1245
家底 1315    海底 1494    眼底下 1570
眼底 1570    亮底 1613    摸底 1665
谜底 1750    鞋底 1789    脚底 1804
揭底 1851    说到底 1631    摸清底细 1665
归根结底 166

---

## 915 序    U+5E8F    TM 10 FM 丶

**xù** N·V order, sequence; preface, introduction; to arrange in order

**序列 xùliè** N sequence; alignment, formation · MW 个

**序幕 xùmù** N prelude · MW 个、场
中国于1978年拉开了改革的**序幕**。 *China began its prelude to reform in 1978.*

**序言 xùyán** N foreword, preface, introduction · MW 篇

### RELATED WORDS

次序 341    时序 586    顺序 874
秩序 895    排序 1241    程序 1451

---

## 916 底    U+5E95    TM 10 FM 丶

**dǐ** N bottom; end of a year/month; heart of a matter; ins and outs; record; rough draft; background

**底板 dǐbǎn** N base plate · MW 块

**底层 dǐcéng** N first/ground floor; bottom/lowest rung of society

**底稿 dǐgǎo** N original; draft · MW 篇、份
编辑把文章的**底稿**退还作者。 *The editor returned the manuscript to the author.*

**底价 dǐjià** N minimum/reserve price · MW 个

**底盘 dǐpán** N chassis · MW 个、副

**底片 dǐpiàn** N negative; photographic plate · MW 张

**底色 dǐsè** N undertone · MW 层

**底细 dǐxì** N inside story/information; ins and outs

**底下 dǐxia** N under, below; later, next
我的狗真不中用，一听到打雷就钻到桌子**底下**。 *My dog is easily scared; he always hides under the table when it thunders.*

**底线 dǐxiàn** N baseline (sports); spy · MW 条

**底子 dǐzi** N base, foundation; details; rough draft; background · MW 个

**底座 dǐzuò** N base, foundation, pedestal · MW 个

---

## 917 庞 龐    U+5E9E    TM 10 FM 丶

**páng** ADJ·N very large, huge; innumerable and disordered; face

**庞大 pángdà** ADJ huge
这家大型公司开支**庞大**。 *The giant company operates with an enormous overhead.*

**庞然大物 pángrándàwù** EXP giant, huge monster · MW 个

**庞杂 pángzá** ADJ jumbled up

---

## 918 废 廢    U+5E9F    TM 10 FM 丶

**fèi** V·ADJ to abandon, to give up; to abolish; to depose; to lay waste; disabled, crippled; waste; useless

**废材 fèicái** N wood chip · MW 块、堆

**废除 fèichú** V to abolish; to repeal

**废话 fèihuà** N·V nonsense; to talk nonsense · MW 句、篇、堆
我烦透了这些**废话**！ *I'm tired of this nonsense!*

**废料 fèiliào** N waste (product), scrap; garbage · MW 块、堆

**废品 fèipǐn** N waste (product); reject · MW 件、堆
工厂生产一个**废品**，可以扔了再做；学校出了一个**废品**，社会多了一个包袱。 *A factory can toss out a reject and make the product again; but if a school produces an inferior product, there would just be one more burden.*

**废气 fèiqì** N waste gas; steam

**废弃 fèiqì** V to abandon, to discard
警察在一辆**废弃**的汽车里找到了证据。 *The police found the evidence in an abandoned car.*

**废热 fèirè** N waste heat

**废水 fèishuǐ** N wastewater; effluent

**废止 fèizhǐ** V to abolish, to annul

**918 废 fèi** (continued)

**RELATED WORDS**

| | | |
|---|---|---|
| 作废 326 | 残废 977 | 报废 1010 |
| 荒废 1222 | 偏废 1587 | 半途而废 127 |

---

**919 度**    U+5EA6    TM **10** FM ㇏

**dù** N·V·MW linear measure; degree; extent, degree (of intensity); limit; tolerance; consideration; temperament; attitude; to spend (time); [measure word for degrees (temperature, angle, longitude/latitude, etc.), for kilowatt-hours, and for time]

**度假 dùjià** V to go on vacation

下个月傻瓜可能要去**度假**。 *ShaGua might be going on vacation next month.*

**度量 dùliàng** N·V tolerance; consideration; to measure

**度量衡 dùliànghéng** N measurement; length; capacity and weight

**度蜜月 dùmìyuè** V to enjoy one's honeymoon

**度数 dùshu** N number of degrees (reading)

**RELATED WORDS**

| | | |
|---|---|---|
| 一度 1 | 三度 9 | 长度 93 |
| 尺度 118 | 无度 139 | 年度 182 |
| 月度 190 | 印度洋 470 | 印度 470 |
| 过度 712 | 进度 713 | 坡度 775 |
| 极度 798 | 态度 828 | 季度 835 |
| 角度 838 | 刻度 966 | 难度 974 |
| 制度 1130 | 浓度 1168 | 厚度 1272 |
| 纯度 1290 | 深度 1345 | 适度 1358 |
| 热度 1390 | 限度 1417 | 程度 1451 |
| 湿度 1498 | 速度 1514 | 硬度 1524 |
| 量度 1544 | 高度 1611 | 亮度 1613 |
| 宽度 1618 | 温度 1627 | 零度 1640 |
| 密度 1730 | 调度 1749 | 幅度 1777 |
| 精度 1832 | 强度 1896 | 大幅度 20 |
| 本年度 90 | | |

---

**920 座**    U+5EA7    TM **10** FM ㇏

**zuò** N·MW seat; seat number; stand, base; constellation; [measure word for mountains, buildings, structures, etc.]

**座舱 zuòcāng** N cab/cabin (of a vehicle) · MW 个

**座次 zuòcì** N seating arrangement · MW 个

**座上客 zuòshàngkè** EXP guest of honor · MW 个、位、名

**座谈 zuòtán** V to discuss informally

**座位 zuòwèi** N seat

那个**座位**有人吗？ *Is that seat occupied?*

**座椅 zuòyǐ** N chair, seat · MW 张

**座右铭 zuòyòumíng** N motto, maxim · MW 个、篇

**座钟 zuòzhōng** N desk clock · MW 个

**RELATED WORDS**

| | | |
|---|---|---|
| 上座 14 | 在座 188 | 让座 348 |
| 讲座 501 | 星座 753 | 软座 889 |
| 底座 916 | 插座 1555 | 满座 1745 |
| 就座 1836 | | |

---

**921 疹**    U+75B9    TM **10** FM ㇏

**zhěn** N·V measles; rash

**疹子 zhěnzi** N measles · MW 个、片

**RELATED WORDS**

| | | |
|---|---|---|
| 风疹 194 | 麻疹 1146 | 痒疹 1149 |

---

**922 疾**    U+75BE    TM **10** FM ㇏

**jí** N·V·ADJ disease, illness; suffering, pain; difficulty; to hate, to abhor; fast, rapid, quick

**疾病 jíbìng** N disease, sickness · MW 个

水痘是一种常见的儿童期**疾病**。 *Chicken pox is a common childhood illness.*

**疾风 jífēng** N storm; strong wind · MW 阵、股

**疾苦 jíkǔ** N suffering, hardship, difficulty

**RELATED WORD**

疟疾 662

---

**923 症** 癥    U+75C7    TM **10** FM ㇏

**zhēng/zhèng** N disease; illness

**症候 zhènghòu** N disease; symptom · MW 个

**症结 zhēngjié** N lump in the abdomen; crux, main point · MW 个

**症状 zhèngzhuàng** N symptom · MW 种

这种病的**症状**是发烧与呕吐。 *The symptoms of this disease are fever and vomiting.*

**RELATED WORDS**

| | | |
|---|---|---|
| 炎症 492 | 病症 1327 | 绝症 1706 |
| 癌症 1981 | 尿毒症 849 | |

---

### 924 首    U+9996   TM **10** FM ﹨

**shǒu** N·ADV·MW   head; chief, leader; first, foremost, first of all; [measure word for poems and songs]

首创 **shǒuchuàng** V   to originate, to pioneer

首次 **shǒucì** N   for the first time

首都 **shǒudū** N   capital (of a country) · MW 个

首犯 **shǒufàn** N   ringleader; archcriminal · MW 个、名

首领 **shǒulǐng** N   chief, leader · MW 个、位、名

首脑 **shǒunǎo** N   head (of state); leader · MW 个、位、名

首屈一指 **shǒuqūyīzhǐ** EXP   to come first on the list, to be second to none

首任 **shǒurèn** N   first person to be appointed to a position

首饰 **shǒushì** N   jewelry; head ornament · MW 副、串、套、件

首尾 **shǒuwěi** N   beginning and end; from start to finish

首席 **shǒuxí** N·ADJ   seat of honor; chief (representative, correspondent, etc.); leading (scientist, etc.)

首先 **shǒuxiān** ADV·CONJ   first; above all

我**首先**得把作业交给老师，然后才能去打球。
*I have to give my homework to the teacher first, and then play ball.*

首相 **shǒuxiàng** N   prime minister · MW 个、位

首要 **shǒuyào** ADJ   primary; first; chief

首长 **shǒuzhǎng** N   senior official; commander-in-chief · MW 个、位

**RELATED WORDS**

| | | |
|---|---|---|
| 元首 138 | 为首 223 | 斩首 646 |
| 祸首 1754 | 罪魁祸首 1542 | |

---

### 925 姜 薑    U+59DC   TM **10** FM ﹨

**jiāng** N   ginger

姜块 **jiāngkuài** N   ginger

**RELATED WORD**

生姜 107

---

### 926 券    U+5238   TM **10** FM ﹨

**quàn** N   deed; bond; contract; ticket; certificate

**RELATED WORDS**

| | | |
|---|---|---|
| 证券 705 | 奖券 927 | 债券 1088 |
| 赠券 1944 | 入场券 5 | |

---

### 927 奖 奬    U+5956   TM **10** FM ﹨

**jiǎng** V·N   to reward; to praise, to commend; to encourage; award, prize

奖杯 **jiǎngbēi** N   trophy cup · MW 个

奖罚 **jiǎngfá** V   to reward and punish

奖金 **jiǎngjīn** N   bonus; dividend

工人们因为没有**奖金**而极度不满。
*Workers become very dissatisfied when they don't receive a bonus.*

奖励 **jiǎnglì** V·N   to encourage and reward; award · MW 个

奖品 **jiǎngpǐn** N   award, prize; trophy · MW 个

奖券 **jiǎngquàn** N   lottery ticket · MW 张

奖赏 **jiǎngshǎng** V·N   to reward; to award; reward

傻瓜**奖赏**孩子们。 *ShaGua rewarded his kids.*

奖章 **jiǎngzhāng** N   medal, decoration · MW 枚

奖状 **jiǎngzhuàng** N   certificate of merit · MW 张

**RELATED WORDS**

| | | |
|---|---|---|
| 发奖 311 | 夸奖 605 | 评奖 706 |
| 受奖 844 | 乙等奖 29 | |

---

### 928 况    U+51B5   TM **10** FM ﹨

**kuàng** N·V·CONJ   situation, condition; to compare; moreover, besides, furthermore

况且 **kuàngqiě** CONJ   moreover, besides

现在上饭馆儿太晚了，**况**且又开始下雨了。
*It is too late to go to the restaurant now, and besides, it's beginning to rain.*

**RELATED WORDS**

| | | |
|---|---|---|
| 状况 345 | 何况 619 | 实况 668 |
| 近况 716 | 战况 1044 | 病况 1327 |
| 情况 1491 | 盛况 1694 | 境况 1848 |
| 概况 1908 | | |

## 929 准 準　U+51C6　TM 10　FM 丶

**zhǔn** V·N·ADJ·ADV  to allow, to permit; to follow, to be in accordance with; standard, norm; accurate, exact; quasi-, para-; definitely, certainly

**准保** zhǔnbǎo ADV certainly, for sure

**准备** zhǔnbèi V to prepare, to get ready; to intend, to plan
> 如果考试前不做任何**准备**，你可能会考不及格。
> *Without any preparation before the exam, you may fail.*

**准点** zhǔndiǎn ADJ punctual, on the dot, on time

**准确** zhǔnquè ADJ accurate, exact, precise
> 她的中文发音十分**准确**。*Her Chinese pronunciation is very accurate.*

**准时** zhǔnshí ADJ on time, on schedule

**准予** zhǔnyǔ V to grant, to approve; to permit

**准则** zhǔnzé N standard, norm · MW 条

**RELATED WORDS**

| | | |
|---|---|---|
| 不准 24 | 水准 159 | 对准 254 |
| 标准 801 | 基准 991 | 批准 1005 |
| 核准 1026 | | |

## 930 恰　U+6070　TM 10　FM 丶

**qià** ADJ·ADV  appropriate, proper; exactly, precisely

**恰当** qiàdàng ADJ appropriate, proper

**恰好** qiàhǎo ADV as it turns out; luckily
> 孩子们正在议论《狮王》，**恰好**前几天傻瓜也看了这部片子，因而得以参加讨论。*His kids were talking about* The Lion King. *Coincidentally, ShaGua saw it a few days ago, so he was able to join in the discussion.*

**恰恰** qiàqià ADV just, precisely

**恰恰舞** qiàqiàwǔ N cha-cha (dance) · MW 个

**恰巧** qiàqiǎo ADV by chance, luckily

**恰如其分** qiàrúqífèn EXP appropriate

## 931 恼 惱　U+607C　TM 10　FM 丶

**nǎo** V·ADJ  to be angry/irritated/displeased; to hate; annoyed; upset, unhappy; worried

**恼恨** nǎohèn V to resent; to hate

**恼火** nǎohuǒ ADJ annoyed; angry

> 孩子们不相信傻瓜看过《狮王》，让他很**恼火**。
> *ShaGua was very angry because his kids didn't believe that he had seen* The Lion King.

**恼人** nǎorén ADJ irritated

**恼羞成怒** nǎoxiūchéngnù EXP to fly into a rage out of shame / from an insult

**RELATED WORDS**

| | | |
|---|---|---|
| 气恼 185 | 苦恼 555 | 烦恼 1178 |

## 932 汤 湯　U+6C64　TM 10　FM 丶

**tāng** N  hot/boiling water; soup, broth

**汤包** tāngbāo N steamed dumplings filled with minced meat and gravy · MW 个

**汤匙** tāngchí N soupspoon · MW 个
> 中国传统**汤匙**跟西式**汤匙**很不一样。
> *The traditional Chinese soupspoon is very different from the Western spoon.*

**汤面** tāngmiàn N noodles in soup · MW 碗

**RELATED WORDS**

| | | |
|---|---|---|
| 米汤 226 | 面汤 721 | 鸡汤 1373 |
| 清汤 1495 | 酸辣汤 1899 | |

## 933 沟 溝　U+6C9F　TM 10　FM 丶

**gōu** N  ditch, gully, ravine; trench; groove, rut, furrow

**沟道** gōudào N channel · MW 条

**沟壑** gōuhè N gully · MW 道

**沟渠** gōuqú N irrigation canal/ditch · MW 条

**沟通** gōutōng V to link up; to communicate
> 手机的发明，改变了人们的**沟通**方式。
> *Methods of communication have changed since the invention of the cell phone.*

**RELATED WORDS**

| | | |
|---|---|---|
| 山沟 38 | 河沟 934 | 阴沟 1041 |
| 暗沟 1676 | | |

## 934 河　U+6CB3　TM 10　FM 丶

**hé** N  river; Milky Way (galaxy); Yellow River

**河岸** hé'àn N riverbank · MW 道、条

**河北** Héběi N Hebei Province

**河川** héchuān N river · MW 道、条

**河道** hédào N river course · MW 条

河堤 **hédī** N river levee · MW 道、条

河沟 **hégōu** N brook, stream · MW 道、条

河谷 **hégǔ** N river valley · MW 道、条

河流 **héliú** N river · MW 道、条

长江是世界上最长的**河流**之一。 *The Yangtze River is one of the longest rivers in the world.*

河马 **hémǎ** N hippopotamus · MW 匹

河南 **Hénán** N Henan Province

河山 **héshān** N rivers and mountains; land, territory · MW 片

**RELATED WORDS**

| | | |
|---|---|---|
| 山河 38 | 内河 191 | 冰河 493 |
| 拦河坝 576 | 星河 753 | 界河 758 |
| 拔河 791 | 运河 956 | 黄河 1212 |
| 银河 1607 | 尼罗河 441 | 气壮山河 185 |

---

**935 治**    U+6CBB   TM **10** FM 丶

**zhì** V·N to treat; to cure; to rule, to control; to administer; to conduct research; to punish; to eliminate, to exterminate (pests); stability, peace

治安 **zhì'ān** N public security

治病 **zhìbìng** V to treat an illness

大夫在用某种特制的药给傻瓜**治病**。 *The doctor was treating ShaGua with special medicine.*

治理 **zhìlǐ** V to rule, to govern; to administer, to manage

治疗 **zhìliáo** V to treat; to cure

傻瓜被送到医院**治疗**。 *ShaGua was taken to the hospital to be treated.*

治丧 **zhìsāng** V to make funeral arrangements

治学 **zhìxué** V to conduct scholarly research; to study

治罪 **zhìzuì** V to punish (for a crime)

**RELATED WORDS**

| | | |
|---|---|---|
| 主治医生 124 | 自治 305 | 医治 389 |
| 政治 517 | 法治 686 | 诊治 709 |
| 防治 1040 | 救治 1259 | 统治 1601 |
| 整治 1845 | 鸡三明治 1373 | |

---

**936 波**    U+6CE2   TM **10** FM 丶

**bō** N wave, ripple; storm, surge; unexpected turn of events

波荡 **bōdàng** V to surge, to heave

波动 **bōdòng** V to fluctuate, to rise and fall

从美国到中国的机票在1000 到1500美元之间**波动**。 *The price of a flight from the United States to China fluctuates between $1,000 and $1,500.*

波段 **bōduàn** N wave, wave band (physics) · MW 个

波及 **bōjí** V to involve, to affect

波兰 **Bōlán** N Poland

波浪 **bōlàng** N wave · MW 个、道

波涛 **bōtāo** N great waves, billows · MW 片

波折 **bōzhé** N twists and turns

傻瓜像大多数移民一样，经历过**波折**的生活。 *Like most immigrants, ShaGua has experienced ups and downs in life.*

**RELATED WORDS**

| | | |
|---|---|---|
| 长波 93 | 风波 194 | 声波 374 |
| 余波 419 | 奔波 432 | 光波 491 |
| 秋波 641 | 音波 907 | 短波 1452 |
| 微波 1700 | 微波炉 1700 | 震波 1839 |

---

**937 泼** 潑    U+6CFC   TM **10** FM 丶

**pō** V·ADJ to splash; to sprinkle; rude and unreasonable, shrewish; impetuous

泼妇 **pōfù** N shrew; vixen · MW 个、名

泼辣 **pōla** ADJ pungent; forceful, aggressive; shrewish

泼冷水 **pōlěngshuǐ** EXP to pour cold water on, to dampen (someone's) spirits

不要对他们的热情**泼冷水**。 *Don't spoil their enthusiasm.*

**RELATED WORD**

活泼 941

---

**938 没**    U+6CA1   TM **10** FM 丶

**méi** V·ADV to not have, to be without; there is not; less than; not; never

**mò** V to be inferior to; to sink; to drown; to overflow; to hide, to disappear; to confiscate, to seize; to die

没出息 **méichūxi** V to lack prospects, to have no future

没法子 **méifǎzi** V to be helpless; to be able to do nothing (about)

没关系 **méiguānxi** V to not matter; no problem; don't worry

**938 没 méi/mò** (continued)

听不懂, **没关系**。我再慢慢地说一遍。*If you didn't understand, don't worry. I will say it again slowly.*

没良心 **méiliángxīn** V to go against one's conscience

傻瓜常常干傻事, 但绝不干**没良心**的事。*ShaGua often does stupid things, but never without following his conscience.*

没命 **méimìng** V·ADV to lose one's life; desperately

傻瓜整天**没命**地干活儿。*ShaGua has been desperately working all day long.*

没趣 **méiqù** ADJ to feel snubbed / put out

没什么 **méishénme** V to not matter; never mind

没头没脑 **méitóuméinǎo** EXP illogically, without rhyme or reason

有时傻瓜会干些**没头没脑**的事。*Sometimes, ShaGua may do something without rhyme or reason.*

没有 **méiyǒu** V to not have; there is not; to be not as … as; to be less than

没主意 **méizhǔyi** V to lack ideas

傻瓜常常是有干劲**没主意**。*ShaGua often has enough energy but not enough ideas.*

**RELATED WORDS**

| | | |
|---|---|---|
| 吞没 427 | 埋没 1002 | 沉没 1166 |
| 淹没 1629 | 神出鬼没 1191 | |

---

**939 池** U+6C60 TM **10** FM 丶

**chí** N pond, pool; moat; pit, front part of a theater

池塘 **chítáng** N pond, pool · MW 个

池沼 **chízhǎo** N pond, pool · MW 个

**RELATED WORDS**

| | | |
|---|---|---|
| 水池 159 | 电池 263 | 乐池 299 |
| 便池 865 | 浴池 1170 | 粪池 1334 |
| 喷水池 1563 | | |

---

**940 洁** 潔 U+6D01 TM **10** FM 丶

**jié** ADJ clean

洁白 **jiébái** ADJ pure white

洁白的床单让人感到这家旅馆很干净。*The spotless white sheets made the hotel seem very clean.*

洁齿 **jiéchǐ** V to clean one's teeth

洁身自好 **jiéshēnzìhào** EXP to maintain one's moral integrity, to keep one's hands clean

**RELATED WORDS**

| | | |
|---|---|---|
| 光洁 491 | 清洁 1495 | 廉洁 1615 |
| 简洁 1796 | 整洁 1845 | |

---

**941 活** U+6D3B TM **10** FM 丶

**huó** V·ADJ·ADV·N to live, to be alive; to save, to keep (someone/something) alive; alive; flexible; lively, vivid; exactly; completely; simply; work; product

活宝 **huóbǎo** N clown; buffoon · MW 个

活动 **huódòng** V·N to get exercise; activity; exercise

傻瓜不喜欢户外**活动**。*ShaGua doesn't like outdoor activities.*

活活 **huóhuó** ADV while still alive

活力 **huólì** N vitality, vigor, energy

活命 **huómìng** V·N to survive; to earn a living; life

活泼 **huópo** ADJ lively, vivacious, vivid

这个孩子很**活泼**也很有趣。*This child is very lively and full of fun.*

活期 **huóqī** ADJ current

活受罪 **huóshòuzuì** EXP to suffer a living hell

活页 **huóyè** N loose-leaf (notebook) · MW 张

活跃 **huóyuè** ADJ·V brisk, active, dynamic; to enliven, to invigorate

**RELATED WORDS**

| | | |
|---|---|---|
| 干活 13 | 生活 107 | 灵活 359 |
| 快活 497 | 死活 510 | 养活 670 |
| 过活 712 | 做活 1282 | 零活 1640 |
| 鲜活 1811 | 激活 1955 | 私生活 471 |

---

**942 洽** U+6D3D TM **10** FM 丶

**qià** V·ADJ to consult; to arrange with; harmonious

洽谈 **qiàtán** V to hold talks, to negotiate

**RELATED WORD**

接洽 1405

## 943 浊 濁　U+6D4A　TM 10 FM 丶

**zhuó** ADJ·N  muddy, murky; deep (of voices); confused, chaotic; muddiness, turbidity

浊色 **zhuósè** N  muddy color

浊音 **zhuóyīn** N  voiced consonant (like *b, d, g,* as opposed to *p, t, k*) · MW 个

**RELATED WORDS**

污浊 681　　　混浊 1739

## 944 涉　U+6D89　TM 10 FM 丶

**shè** V  to cross; to wade across; to go through, to experience; to involve

涉及 **shèjí** V  to involve; to touch on (a topic)

涉讼 **shèsòng** V  to be involved in a lawsuit; to sue

涉外 **shèwài** V  to concern foreigners / foreign affairs

**RELATED WORDS**

干涉 13　　　交涉 222　　　牵涉 853

## 945 派　U+6D3E　TM 10 FM 丶

**pài** V·N  to send; to assign; to apportion; group, faction; school

傻瓜太太**派**傻瓜去商店。 *Mrs. ShaGua sent ShaGua to the store.*

委**派** *to appoint*

学**派** *school of thought*

他们是不同的两**派**。 *They are two different groups.*

派别 **pàibié** N  school; group, faction; school of thought · MW 个

派出所 **pàichūsuǒ** N  local police station; police substation · MW 个、间

派遣 **pàiqiǎn** V  to send, to dispatch

派生 **pàishēng** V  to derive

派头 **pàitóu** N  style, manner, air

傻瓜没有什么**派头**。 *ShaGua doesn't put on airs.*

派系 **pàixì** N  faction, clique · MW 个

派驻 **pàizhù** V  to accredit

**RELATED WORDS**

正派 76　　　反派 111　　　右派 187
委派 594　　　宗派 910　　　流派 1493
帮派 1583　　党派 1626

## 946 记 記　U+8BB0　TM 10 FM 丶

**jì** V·N  to remember; to commit to memory; to write down, to record; note, record

记仇 **jìchóu** V  to bear a grudge

记得 **jìde** V  to remember

你**记得**那个姑娘的名字吗？ *Do you remember the girl's name?*

记分 **jìfēn** V  to keep score

记功 **jìgōng** V  to record a merit

记过 **jìguò** V  to record a demerit, to give (someone) a black mark

记号 **jìhao** N  mark; sign · MW 个

记录 **jìlù** V·N  to take notes, to write down; record · MW 个

警察发现这个男子有长期犯罪的**记录**。 *Police found that this man has a long criminal record.*

记事 **jìshì** V  to keep a record; to begin to remember things (of a child); chronicles; record of events

记述 **jìshù** V  to tell, to narrate; to give an account / a description of

记叙 **jìxù** V  to narrate

记忆 **jìyì** V·N  to remember; memory · MW 个

记载 **jìzǎi** V·N  to record, to write down; record · MW 个、篇

记账 **jìzhàng** V  to keep the books; to charge to an account

记者 **jìzhě** N  journalist, reporter · MW 个、名

记住 **jìzhù** V  to bear in mind

**记住**啦，我们乘坐的飞机凌晨起飞。 *Please bear in mind that our plane will take off early in the morning.*

**RELATED WORDS**

日记 96　　　书记 264　　　切记 277
传记 452　　　牢记 488　　　忘记 655
标记 801　　　笔记本 1278　　笔记 1278
速记 1514　　登记 1521　　熟记 1973
簿记 1979　　新闻记者 1638

## 947 论 論　U+8BBA　TM 10 FM 丶

**lùn** V·N·PREP  to discuss; to consider; to decide on, to determine; theory; doctrine; essay; dissertation; in terms of; regarding

论处 **lùnchǔ** V  to punish

论敌 **lùndí** N  debate opponent · MW 个、名

**947** 论 **lùn** (continued)

论点 **lùndiǎn** N argument · MW 个

论断 **lùnduàn** N inference; conclusion · MW 个

论及 **lùnjí** V to touch on

论据 **lùnjù** N argument; basis (of an argument) · MW 个

论理 **lùnlǐ** V·ADV to reason and argue; normally

论述 **lùnshù** V to discuss and analyze
这本书**论述**政治的问题。 *This book discusses political issues.*

论坛 **lùntán** N forum · MW 个

论题 **lùntí** N topic; proposition · MW 个

论文 **lùnwén** N thesis, dissertation; paper, article · MW 篇

论证 **lùnzhèng** V to expound and prove; to demonstrate

论著 **lùnzhù** N research work; book · MW 本、部

**RELATED WORDS**

| | | |
|---|---|---|
| 不论 24 | 公论 103 | 立论 125 |
| 无论如何 139 | 议论 350 | 言论 478 |
| 讨论 500 | 社论 504 | 政论 517 |
| 争论 595 | 评论 706 | 理论 1200 |
| 结论 1291 | 谈论 1356 | 概论 1908 |
| 二元论 2 | 宿命论 1480 | 概而论之 1908 |

**948** 讽 諷   U+8BBD   TM **10** FM ヽ

**fěng** V to mock, to satirize

讽刺 **fěngcì** V·N to satirize; ridicule, satire; irony · MW 个
总的来说, 他谈话的基调是**讽刺**性的。
*Overall, his speaking tone is sarcastic.*

讽喻 **fěngyù** V to relate a satirical allegory

**949** 访 訪   U+8BBF   TM **10** FM ヽ

**fǎng** V to visit, to call on; to investigate

访问 **fǎngwèn** V to visit; to interview
我们正计划六月份**访问**中国。 *We are planning to visit China in June.*

访友 **fǎngyǒu** V to visit a friend

**RELATED WORDS**

| | | |
|---|---|---|
| 上访 14 | 互访 135 | 来访 260 |
| 走访 265 | 回访 391 | 采访 434 |
| 拜访 635 | 家访 1315 | 探访 1404 |
| 察访 1877 | | |

**950** 识 識   U+8BC6   TM **10** FM ヽ

**shí** V·N to know; to recognize; knowledge; learning; insight

识别 **shíbié** V to distinguish; to identify; to recognize
中文的 "人" 字很容易**识别**, 因为它本身就像一个叉开双腿站立的人。 *It is easy to recognize the Chinese character 人, because it looks like a man who is standing with his legs apart.*

识破 **shípò** V to penetrate, to see through

识相 **shíxiàng** V to be sensitive/tactful

识字 **shízì** V to learn to read

**RELATED WORDS**

| | | |
|---|---|---|
| 不识时务 24 | 认识 239 | 见识 267 |
| 卓识 523 | 知识 647 | 知识分子 647 |
| 相识 805 | 结识 1291 | 常识 1733 |
| 意识 1812 | 长见识 93 | 无意识 139 |
| 目不识丁 151 | 有意识 439 | |

**951** 译 譯   U+8BD1   TM **10** FM ヽ

**yì** V to translate; to interpret

译本 **yìběn** N translation · MW 种、部

译码 **yìmǎ** N decoding; interpretation; code · MW 个

译文 **yìwén** N translation · MW 篇
这是**译文**, 原文是中文。 *This is a translation; the original is in Chinese.*

译员 **yìyuán** N interpreter · MW 个、名

译者 **yìzhě** N translator · MW 个、名

**RELATED WORDS**

| | | |
|---|---|---|
| 口译 42 | 笔译 1278 | 编译 1866 |
| 翻译 1989 | | |

**952** 详 詳   U+8BE6   TM **10** FM ヽ

**xiáng** ADJ·V·N detailed; clear; to tell, to explain; to know; details, particulars

详尽 **xiángjìn** ADJ detailed and thorough, exhaustive

详情 **xiángqíng** N detailed information, details · MW 份

详细 **xiángxì** ADJ detailed
傻瓜把**详细**情况告诉警察。 *ShaGua recounted the accident to the police in detail.*

**RELATED WORDS**

未详 88     内详 191     周详 1068

## 953 烘    U+70D8   TM **10** FM ヽ

**hōng** V to dry; to warm; to set off

烘干 **hōnggān** V to dry

烘干机 **hōnggānjī** V clothes dryer

你们有烘干机吗? *Do you have a clothes dryer?*

烘烤 **hōngkǎo** V to roast; to bake

烘炉 **hōnglú** N oven · MW 台

烘托 **hōngtuō** ADJ set off (by contrast)

烘箱 **hōngxiāng** N oven · MW 个

**RELATED WORDS**

乱哄哄 901     臭烘烘 1076     热烘烘 1390

暖烘烘 1675

## 954 迅    U+8FC5   TM **10** FM ヽ

**xùn** ADJ fast, swift, quick

迅即 **xùnjí** ADV immediately

迅猛 **xùnměng** ADJ swift and violent

迅速 **xùnsù** ADJ rapid; prompt

傻瓜**迅速**地回答了警察的提问。
*ShaGua answered the police's questions promptly.*

## 955 迈 邁    U+8FC8   TM **10** FM ヽ

**mài** V·ADJ to step; elderly, aged

迈步 **màibù** V to step; to pace

迈进 **màijìn** V to stride forward

**RELATED WORDS**

年迈 182     豪迈 1876

## 956 运 運    U+8FD0   TM **10** FM ヽ

**yùn** V·N to move; to carry, to transport; to use, to wield; movement, motion; fortune, luck

运动 **yùndòng** V·N to move; sport(s); exercise; movement, campaign · MW 个、种

我喜欢体育运动。*I like sports.*

他喜欢政治运动。*He likes political campaigns.*

运动衫 **yùndòngshān** N sport shirt · MW 个、套、件

运动会 **yùndònghuì** N game (sports) · MW 个

运动员 **yùndòngyuán** N player, athlete · MW 个、名

运费 **yùnfèi** N freight · MW 笔

运河 **yùnhé** N canal · MW 条

运货 **yùnhuò** V to ship cargo

运气 **yùnqì** N fortune, luck · MW 个

运输 **yùnshū** V to transport

运送 **yùnsòng** V to transport, to ship

运算 **yùnsuàn** V to calculate

运行 **yùnxíng** V to move; to run, to operate

傻瓜的管理**运行**还不错，但数学**运算**不行。
*ShaGua is decent at organizational operations, but bad at mathematical calculations.*

运用 **yùnyòng** V to use, to put to use

运载 **yùnzǎi** V to carry (merchandise in a vehicle); to deliver

运转 **yùnzhuàn** V to work; to run, to operate

**RELATED WORDS**

| | | |
|---|---|---|
| 水运 159 | 走运 265 | 幸运 373 |
| 厄运 443 | 红运 474 | 托运 563 |
| 时运 586 | 空运 669 | 命运 1051 |
| 货运 1061 | 转运 1111 | 载运 1218 |
| 铲运机 1304 | 装运 1476 | 碰运气 1526 |
| 营运 1546 | 航运 1717 | 搬运 1943 |
| 户外运动 129 | 冰上运动 493 | |

## 957 返    U+8FD4   TM **10** FM ヽ

**fǎn** V to return, to come/go back

返程 **fǎnchéng** V·N to return; backtracking

返工 **fǎngōng** V to redo (poorly done work)

返航 **fǎnháng** V to return to the point of departure

返回 **fǎnhuí** V to return; to come/go back

返老还童 **fǎnlǎohuántóng** EXP to recover one's youthful vigor, to regain one's youth

返销 **fǎnxiāo** V to resell to the manufacturer

返校 **fǎnxiào** V to return to school (during/after vacation, after graduation)

傻瓜把上夜校叫做"**返校**"，还看做是
"**返老还童**"。*ShaGua referred to going to night school as going "back to school" and also considered it "regaining his youth."*

**RELATED WORDS**

往返 461     重返 839

## 958　连　連　　U+8FDE　TM **10** FM 丶

**lián** [V·ADV·N] to connect, to link; in succession, one after another; repeatedly; including; even; company

连本带利　**liánběndàilì** [EXP] both the principal and the interest

连串　**liánchuàn** [ADJ] consecutive

连词　**liáncí** [N] conjunction (part of speech) ·
[MW] 个

连带　**liándài** [V] to be related (to); to involve

连贯　**liánguàn** [V·ADJ] to piece/string together; consistent

保持**连贯**性是傻瓜做事的特点。
*Consistency is one of ShaGua's traits.*

连环　**liánhuán** [N] chain

连接　**liánjiē** [V] to connect, to link

连累　**liánlěi** [V] to get (someone) into trouble, to implicate

傻瓜敢做敢当，最怕自己**连累**了别人。
*ShaGua isn't afraid to take responsibility for his actions, but he is very afraid of getting others in trouble.*

连忙　**liánmáng** [ADV] hastily; at once

连绵　**liánmián** [V] to be continuous/unbroken

连年　**liánnián** [V] to occur year after year

连日　**liánrì** [V] to occur day after day

连锁　**liánsuǒ** [ADJ] chain

连天　**liántiān** [V] to occur day after day

连同　**liántóng** [CONJ] together with, along with

连续　**liánxù** [V] to continue without stopping

连夜　**liányè** [V·ADV] to occur night after night; all through the night

连用　**liányòng** [V] to continue to use

连载　**liánzǎi** [V] to publish in installments, to serialize

**RELATED WORDS**

互连　135　　　心连心　232　　　相连　805
牵连　853　　　粘连　1365

## 959　迟　遲　　U+8FDF　TM **10** FM 丶

**chí** [ADJ] slow; late, tardy; delayed

迟迟　**chíchí** [ADV] slowly; late

迟到　**chídào** [V] to arrive/be late

迟钝　**chídùn** [ADJ] slow, dull

迟缓　**chíhuǎn** [ADJ] slow, sluggish

迟误　**chíwù** [V] to delay

傻瓜看起来有点**迟钝**，但处理事情从不迟误。
*ShaGua looks a little slow, but he is never slow to respond when it comes to business.*

迟延　**chíyán** [V] to delay

迟早　**chízǎo** [ADV] sooner or later

迟滞　**chízhì** [ADV] slow-moving

**RELATED WORDS**

延迟　731　　　推迟　1242　　　事不宜迟　987

## 960　叛　　U+53DB　TM **10** FM 丶

**pàn** [V] to betray

叛变　**pànbiàn** [V] to betray, to turn traitor

叛匪　**pànfěi** [N] rebel bandit · [MW] 个、伙、帮

叛国　**pànguó** [V] to betray one's country

叛军　**pànjūn** [N] rebel army; rebel · [MW] 队、伙、名

叛乱　**pànluàn** [V] armed rebellion

叛卖　**pànmài** [V] to betray

叛逆　**pànnì** [V·N] to revolt (against); rebel, nonconformist · [MW] 个、名

叛徒　**pàntú** [N] traitor; rebel, insurgent · [MW] 个、名

**RELATED WORD**

背叛　1380

## 961　料　　U+6599　TM **10** FM 丶

**liào** [V·N] to expect; to anticipate; to predict; (raw) material; data; makings; grain feed/fodder

料仓　**liàocāng** [N] feed bin · [MW] 间

料到　**liàodào** [V] to expect; to foresee

料酒　**liàojiǔ** [N] cooking wine · [MW] 瓶

料理　**liàolǐ** [V·N] to manage, to take care of; Japanese cuisine · [MW] 餐

这件事还是你来**料理**吧。*I'll let you take care of this.*

今晚上，我们还是吃日本**料理**吧。*Let's have Japanese cuisine tonight.*

料想　**liàoxiǎng** [V] to expect; to presume

料子　**liàozi** [N] clothing material; wool fabric; good stuff; ability

这是一套**料子**衣。*The clothes are made of wool.*

傻瓜还是有点儿**料子**的。*ShaGua isn't without some ability.*

## RELATED WORDS

| | | |
|---|---|---|
| 毛料 183 | 史料 186 | 作料 326 |
| 衣料 330 | 材料 409 | 加料 463 |
| 草料 768 | 香料 834 | 备料 845 |
| 饮料 892 | 废料 918 | 涂料 1171 |
| 原料 1273 | 资料 1335 | 饲料 1447 |
| 肥料 1459 | 预料 1528 | 填料 1550 |
| 配料 1647 | 调料 1749 | 意料 1812 |
| 塑料 1815 | 颜料 1835 | 照料 1846 |
| 燃料 1888 | 糊料 1932 | 核材料 1026 |
| 不出所料 24 | 出乎意料 258 | 偷工减料 1591 |

---

**962 衬** 襯　　U+886C　　TM **10** FM ＼

**chèn** N·V lining; underwear; to line, to put a lining in; to contrast, to set off

**衬裤 chènkù** N underpants · MW 条

**衬衫 chènshān** N shirt · MW 件

**衬衣 chènyī** N shirt · MW 件

## RELATED WORDS

映衬 1036　　陪衬 1568

---

**963 初**　　U+521D　　TM **10** FM ＼

**chū** ADJ·N first, early, at the beginning of; primary (grade); original

**初步 chūbù** ADJ initial, preliminary

**初次 chūcì** N first time

**初等 chūděng** ADJ elementary, primary

**初稿 chūgǎo** N first draft (of a written piece) · MW 份、篇

**初婚 chūhūn** V to be married for the first time

**初级 chūjí** ADJ primary; junior

**初恋 chūliàn** V to fall in love for the first time; first love

傻瓜从来没有提过他的**初恋**。*ShaGua never mentions his first love.*

**初审 chūshěn** V to be tried/sampled for the first time

**初始 chūshǐ** N initial

**初试 chūshì** V to make an initial attempt; to take a preliminary examination

**初小 chūxiǎo** N lower primary school · MW 间

**初学 chūxué** V to just begin to learn

**初诊 chūzhěn** V to pay an initial visit (to a doctor, a hospital)

**初中 chūzhōng** N junior high school · MW 间

傻瓜的学历到底是**初小**还是**初中**？谁也说不清。*Does ShaGua's educational experience extend through lower primary school or through junior high? Nobody knows for sure.*

## RELATED WORDS

| | | |
|---|---|---|
| 年初 182 | 月初 190 | 当初 335 |
| 起初 1421 | 最初 1541 | |

---

**964 放**　　U+653E　　TM **10** FM ＼

**fàng** V to put, to place; to add; to put/set aside; to release, to set free; to let off; to give way to; to graze, to put out to pasture; to send away, to expel; to light, to fire; to lend (money); to enlarge; to let out (a dress, pants, etc.), to make longer; to bloom; to fell, to cut down

**放出 fàngchū** V to let out/off, to emit

**放大 fàngdà** V to enlarge

**放过 fàngguò** V to let slip

**放火 fànghuǒ** V to set on fire

**放假 fàngjià** V to be on vacation

**放空气 fàngkōngqì** V to drop a hint

**放宽 fàngkuān** V to relax restrictions, to ease

**放款 fàngkuǎn** V to lend, to make a loan

**放牧 fàngmù** V to put out to pasture

**放炮 fàngpào** V to fire a gun; to blow out (of a tire, etc.); to shoot off one's mouth

过节时，傻瓜喜欢**放炮**。*During holidays, ShaGua likes to light firecrackers.*

在会上，傻瓜不喜欢**放炮**。*During meetings, ShaGua doesn't like to talk brashly.*

**放屁 fàngpì** V to pass gas; to talk nonsense

**放弃 fàngqì** V to abandon, to give up

**放任 fàngrèn** V to ignore; to not interfere

**放射 fàngshè** V to radiate, to emit

**放声 fàngshēng** ADV loudly

**放生 fàngshēng** V to free/release captive animals

**放手 fàngshǒu** V to let go

傻瓜总是**放手**让大家干自己的工作。*ShaGua always relinquishes control to allow others to conduct their own business.*

**放肆 fàngsì** ADJ unbridled; wanton

**放松 fàngsōng** V to relax, to loosen

**放下 fàngxià** V to put down, to let go (of)

**放心 fàngxīn** V to be relieved; to set (someone's) mind at rest; to trust

**964 放 fàng** (continued)

这样我就**放心**了。 *If so, I feel relieved.*

我对他很**放心**。 *I believe in him very much.*

**放学 fàngxué** V to finish classes (for the day)

**放映 fàngyìng** V to show/project (a film)

**放纵 fàngzòng** V to indulge, to let (someone) have his own way

**放走 fàngzǒu** V to release, to set free

**RELATED WORDS**

| | | |
|---|---|---|
| 下放 10 | 开放 26 | 存放 438 |
| 安放 487 | 堆放 1003 | 投放 1008 |
| 粗放 1364 | 流放 1493 | 寄放 1619 |
| 施放 1758 | 豪放 1876 | 燃放 1888 |
| 解放 1928 | 解放军 1928 | |

---

**965 效**     U+6548     TM **10**   FM 丶

**xiào** N·V effect; efficacy; efficiency; to imitate; to devote (oneself/something) to

**效果 xiàoguǒ** N effect, result · MW 个

教育的**效果**往往要很久以后才能看出来。
*The effects of education usually don't show until many years later.*

**效率 xiàolǜ** N efficiency; productivity

**效能 xiàonéng** N efficiency; effect · MW 个

**效益 xiàoyì** N benefit; productivity

**效应 xiàoyìng** N effect (greenhouse, etc.), result · MW 个

**效用 xiàoyòng** N usefulness; effectiveness · MW 个

**RELATED WORDS**

| | | |
|---|---|---|
| 失效 106 | 生效 107 | 无效 139 |
| 功效 252 | 见效 267 | 有效期 439 |
| 有效 439 | 仿效 450 | 时效 586 |
| 实效 668 | 成效 611 | 疗效 661 |
| | 特效 1094 | 速效 1514 |

---

**966 刻**     U+523B     TM **10**   FM 丶

**kè** V·N·ADJ to engrave, to carve; engraving; quarter (of an hour); moment; extreme; harsh, unkind

**刻板 kèbǎn** V·ADJ to cut printing blocks; rigid, inflexible

这是**刻板**画。 *This is a picture printed from an engraved block.*

傻瓜常常很**刻板**。 *Sometimes, ShaGua is very stubborn.*

**刻版 kèbǎn** V to cut printing blocks

**刻薄 kèbó** ADJ harsh, unkind

**刻不容缓 kèbùrónghuǎn** EXP to demand immediate action, to be of great urgency

**刻刀 kèdāo** N burin, graver, engraving tools · MW 把

**刻毒 kèdú** ADJ malicious, spiteful

**刻度 kèdù** N graduate; graduated scale · MW 个

**刻苦 kèkǔ** ADJ hardworking

**刻字 kèzì** V to carve characters (on a seal, etc.)

**RELATED WORDS**

| | | |
|---|---|---|
| 片刻 119 | 立刻 125 | 石刻 144 |
| 尖刻 203 | 此刻 416 | 时刻 586 |
| 时刻表 586 | 即刻 1047 | 深刻 1345 |
| 每时每刻 837 | | |

---

**967 刹**     U+5239     TM **10**   FM 丶

**chà** N Buddhist temple

**shā** V to put on the brakes

**刹那 chànà** N instant, split second

**刹车 shāchē** V to put on the brakes; to put a stop to

---

**968** **丽** 麗 　U+4E3D　TM **11**　FM 一

**lì** ADJ beautiful, pretty

**RELATED WORDS**

壮丽 238　　华丽 421　　美丽 671
秀丽 1055　　富丽堂皇 1731

---

**969** **要** 　U+8981　TM **11**　FM 一

**yāo** V to ask for; to demand; to force; to threaten; to invite

**yào** V·ADJ·N·CONJ to want, to wish (to); to be about to; must, should, to need (to); important; essential, vital; if, in case; or; either … or …

**要求 yāoqiú** V·N to request; to require; demand

**要胁 yāoxié** V to force; to threaten

**要不得 yàobude** V to be no good, to be unacceptable/intolerable

**要不是 yàobùshì** CONJ if it were not for

　要不是他改了一下演讲稿，那个演讲还真要不得。 *If he had not revised the draft, that speech would have been no good.*

**要点 yàodiǎn** N essentials, main points · MW 个

**要饭 yàofàn** V to beg for food/money

**要犯 yàofàn** N chief offender, main criminal · MW 个、名

**要害 yàohài** N key part; crucial/strategic point · MW 个

**要好 yàohǎo** ADJ on good terms, close, amicable

**要价 yàojià** V to ask a price

**要件 yàojiàn** N key document; important condition · MW 份、个

　傻瓜半天都抓不住那份**要件**的**要点**。 *ShaGua spent a long time trying, but still could not grasp the main points of the major document.*

**要紧 yàojǐn** ADJ important, serious; essential, vital, critical

**要领 yàolǐng** N essentials, main points · MW 个

**要么 yàome** CONJ or; either … or …

**要面子 yàomiànzi** EXP to be intent on saving face

**要命 yàomìng** V·ADJ to kill; to be incredibly; awful, terrible

**要人 yàorén** N very important person (VIP) · MW 个、位、名

**要闻 yàowén** N important news; headline · MW 条

**RELATED WORDS**

不要紧 24　　不要脸 24　　主要 124
只要 160　　必要 338　　次要 341
机要 577　　重要 839　　须要 875
首要 924　　纪要 1101　　将要 1161
紧要 1537　　提要 1554　　简要 1796
就要 1836　　需要 1838　　摘要 1906
概要 1908　　不必要 24

---

**970** **忍** 　U+5FCD　TM **11**　FM 一

**rěn** V·ADJ to bear, to endure; to hold (oneself) back (from); to have the heart to; cruel, merciless

**忍不住 rěnbuzhù** V can't bear; unbearable; can't help (doing)

**忍耐 rěnnài** V to endure; to show restraint, to control

　记住，**忍耐**的"忍"是"心"上一把"刀"啊，你一定要**忍耐**！ *Remember, "control" in Chinese is a "knife" above your "heart," so you must restrain yourself!*

**忍气吞声 rěnqìtūnshēng** EXP to suffer in silence, to grin and bear it

**忍让 rěnràng** V to hold oneself back; to show patience

**忍痛 rěntòng** V to suffer pain (often unwillingly); very reluctantly

**忍心 rěnxīn** V to bear, to be hardhearted enough to; cruel, merciless

　你**忍心**送你的儿子去中国贫穷的农村体验生活吗？ *Would you be hardhearted enough to send your son to the impoverished Chinese countryside just for the experience?*

**RELATED WORDS**

残忍 977　　容忍 1320

## 971 孕　孕　U+5EF6　TM **11** FM 一

**yùn** V·N to be pregnant; pregnancy

孕妇 **yùnfù** N pregnant woman · MW 个、名

孕期 **yùnqī** N pregnancy; gestation · MW 个

孕育 **yùnyù** V to be pregnant with; to produce offspring, to breed

**RELATED WORDS**

怀孕 344　　　　身孕 604　　　　避孕 1976

## 972 承　U+627F　TM **11** FM 一

**chéng** V to undertake; to support, to bear; to continue, to carry on; to inherit; to be indebted to

承办 **chéngbàn** V to undertake; to sponsor, to host

承包 **chéngbāo** V to enter into a contract

承担 **chéngdān** V to undertake; to bear
勇于**承担**责任是领导人应有的素质。
*Assuming responsibilities with conviction is a characteristic of a leader.*

承接 **chéngjiē** V to undertake; to accept; to continue

承诺 **chéngnuò** V·N to undertake; to promise; undertaking; commitment · MW 个

承认 **chéngrèn** V to recognize, to acknowledge; to give diplomatic recognition to
**承认**别人的长处并不是一件容易的事。*It is not easy to acknowledge the strengths of others.*

承受 **chéngshòu** V to bear, to support; to endure; to inherit

承租人 **chéngzūrén** N tenant · MW 个、名

**RELATED WORDS**

支承 92　　　　应承 334

## 973 艰　艱　U+8270　TM **11** FM 一

**jiān** ADJ difficult, hard

艰巨 **jiānjù** ADJ formidable, difficult and heavy

艰苦 **jiānkǔ** ADJ arduous, difficult; harsh

艰难 **jiānnán** ADJ difficult, hard

艰险 **jiānxiǎn** ADJ hard and dangerous

艰辛 **jiānxīn** ADJ arduous, difficult
傻瓜有过非常**艰辛**的经历。*ShaGua had a very arduous experience.*

## 974 难　難　U+96BE　TM **11** FM 一

**nán** ADJ·V difficult, hard; impossible; disagreeable; to make things difficult for

**nàn** N trouble, adversity; disaster, calamity, tragedy; blame

难保 **nánbǎo** V to not be able to say for sure; to be hard to protect

难产 **nánchǎn** V to be difficult/laborious; to be slow in coming
这个婴儿**难产**。*The labor with this baby was difficult.*
这个方案**难产**。*This proposal is moving along with difficulty.*

难处 **nánchǔ** ADJ·N difficult to get along with · MW 个
这人很**难处**。*It is very difficult to get along with this person.*

难处 **nánchu** ADJ·N trouble; dilemma · MW 个
我有一个**难处**。*I have a dilemma.*

难打交道 **nándǎjiāodao** EXP hard to deal with

难道 **nándào** ADV is it possible that; can it be that
**难道**你不**难打交道**吗？*You don't think you are hard to deal with?*

难得 **nándé** ADJ rare, hard to come by

难点 **nándiǎn** N difficulty, difficult point · MW 个

难懂 **nándǒng** ADJ difficult to understand

难度 **nándù** N (degree of) difficulty

难怪 **nánguài** CONJ·V no wonder; to be understandable; can hardly be blamed
**难怪**她不来上课，原来是生病了。*No wonder she didn't come to class; she has been sick.*
这也**难怪**，她都起不了床，怎么来上课？*She can hardly be blamed. She could not even get out of bed; how could she come to class?*

难关 **nánguān** N crisis · MW 个

难过 **nánguò** ADJ upset; feeling bad

难堪 **nánkān** ADJ embarrassed

难看 **nánkàn** ADJ ugly

难免 **nánmiǎn** ADJ unavoidable; hard to avoid
上大学才学中文，**难免**有些口音。*It is hard to avoid having an accent since you didn't study Chinese until college.*

难色 **nánsè** N sign of embarrassment/reluctance/difficulty

难受 **nánshòu** V to feel unhappy; not to feel well

难说 **nánshuō** V it's hard to say

难题 **nántí** N difficult problem; hot potato · MW 个、道

难忘 **nánwàng** ADJ unforgettable

难为情 **nánwéiqíng** ADJ embarrassed; ashamed

难为 **nánwei** V to put pressure on, to be tough on; thank you for

他不能喝酒，您就别**难为**他了。 *He can't drink; please don't press him.*

**难为**你帮我看孩子。 *Thank you for babysitting my kids!*

难民 **nànmín** N refugee · MW 个、名

难兄难弟 **nànxiōngnàndì** EXP fellow sufferers · MW 个

难友 **nànyǒu** N fellow sufferers · MW 个

### RELATED WORDS

| | | |
|---|---|---|
| 刁难 32 | 为难 223 | 发难 311 |
| 作难 326 | 非难 378 | 困难 393 |
| 灾难 483 | 两难 509 | 责难 525 |
| 苦难 555 | 受难 844 | 艰难 973 |
| 畏难 988 | 危难 1057 | 逃难 1509 |
| 患难 1649 | 蒙难 1654 | 遇难 1891 |
| 疑难 1917 | 避难 1976 | 千载难逢 19 |
| 寸步难行 37 | 寸金难买 37 | 众口难调 175 |
| 在所难免 188 | 老大难 375 | 骑虎难下 1840 |
| 左右为难 113 | | |

---

现任市长是傻瓜。 *The current mayor is ShaGua.*

现实 **xiànshí** N·ADJ reality; real, practical · MW 个

现象 **xiànxiàng** N phenomenon; appearance · MW 个

现行 **xiànxíng** ADJ currently in effect, active

现有 **xiànyǒu** ADJ currently available; existing

现在 **xiànzài** N now, at present; current

现状 **xiànzhuàng** N current situation/condition

### RELATED WORDS

| | | |
|---|---|---|
| 出现 258 | 发现 311 | 体现 325 |
| 存现 438 | 表现 527 | 实现 668 |
| 重现 839 | 互生现象 135 | 四个现代化 271 |

---

## 976 玻 U+73BB TM 11 FM 一

**bō** N glass

玻璃 **bōli** N glass; (glasslike) plastic · MW 块

### RELATED WORD

窗玻璃 1732

---

## 975 现 現 U+73B0 TM 11 FM 一

**xiàn** N·V·ADV current/present (situation); ready money, cash; on hand (of money, etc.); to reveal; to appear; to become visible; in time of need; impromptu

现场 **xiànchǎng** N scene, actual location; on the spot, live

现钞 **xiànchāo** N cash · MW 笔

现出 **xiànchū** V to reveal; to display

现存 **xiàncún** V to be extant; to be available / in stock

现代 **xiàndài** N modern times

现代化 **xiàndàihuà** V modernization

教育的**现代化**是其他**现代化**的基础。 *Educational modernization is a necessary foundation for all other modernizations.*

现货 **xiànhuò** N merchandise in stock · MW 批

现今 **xiànjīn** N nowadays, now

现金 **xiànjīn** N ready money, cash · MW 笔

现款 **xiànkuǎn** N ready money, cash · MW 笔

现任 **xiànrèn** V·ADJ to currently occupy a position; currently in office

---

## 977 残 殘 U+6B8B TM 11 FM 一

**cán** ADJ·V defective, deficient, incomplete; disabled, lame; remaining; cruel, savage; to destroy; to ruin; to injure, to damage; to treat viciously, to abuse

残暴 **cánbào** ADJ cruel, brutal

残存 **cáncún** V to survive

残废 **cánfèi** V·N to be handicapped; disabled person

残害 **cánhài** V to slaughter; to cruelly injure/kill

残酷 **cánkù** ADJ cruel, brutal, ruthless

残留 **cánliú** V to remain, to be left over

残缺 **cánquē** V to be incomplete/deficient, to have parts missing

残忍 **cánrěn** ADJ cruel, merciless

对孩子的错误保持沉默，也是一种**残忍**。 *Disregarding the errors of children is another kind of cruelty.*

残杀 **cánshā** V to murder

残余 **cányú** N survivors; remains; remnants

残渣 **cánzhā** N residue

### RELATED WORD

伤残 453

## 978 孤　U+5B64　TM 11　FM —

**gū** ADJ  alone, solitary; lonely; isolated; orphaned

孤单 **gūdān** ADJ  alone; lonely

孤独 **gūdú** ADJ  solitary; lonely

孤儿 **gū'ér** N  orphan · MW 个、名

孤立 **gūlì** ADJ·V  solitary; isolated; to separate

孤僻 **gūpì** ADJ  unsociable and eccentric

傻瓜曾经是**孤儿**，但他不**孤僻**。
*ShaGua was once an orphan, but he is neither unsociable nor eccentric.*

孤注一掷 **gūzhùyīzhì** EXP  to put all one's eggs in one basket

**RELATED WORD**

遗孤 1829

## 979 砍　U+780D　TM 11　FM —

**kǎn** V  to cut; to chop, to hack; to cut (down); to reduce

砍刀 **kǎndāo** N  chopper · MW 把

砍伐 **kǎnfá** V  to fell (a tree)

砍头 **kǎntóu** V  to behead, to decapitate

## 980 那　U+90A3　TM 11　FM —

**nà** PRON·CONJ  that, those; then, in that case

那边 **nàbiān** PRON  that side; there, over there

那个 **nàgè** PRON  that (one)

那里 **nàli** PRON  that place, there, over there

那么 **nàme** PRON·CONJ  like that, in that way; about, or so; then, such being the case

那么些 **nàmexiē** PRON  so much/many

那么些钱，你怎么花呀？ *How could you ever spend so much money?*

那儿 **nàr** PRON  there, that place; that time

那时 **nàshí** PRON  at that time, then; in those days

打**那时**起，我就学中文了。 *I've been studying Chinese from that moment on.*

那些 **nàxiē** PRON  those

那样 **nàyàng** PRON·ADV  like that, that kind of, such; so, in that case

**RELATED WORD**

刹那 967

## 981 邪　U+90AA　TM 11　FM —

**xié** ADJ  evil, wicked; heretical; irregular, abnormal

邪恶 **xié'è** ADJ  evil, wicked

邪路 **xiélù** N  evil ways · MW 条

邪念 **xiéniàn** N  evil thought, wicked idea · MW 个

邪气 **xiéqì** N  perverse trend; depravity · MW 股

他脑子里有许多**邪念**，所以身上透着一股**邪气**。
*There were so many evil thoughts in his mind that you could feel depravity radiating from his body.*

邪说 **xiéshuō** N  heresy; fallacy · MW 个、种

**RELATED WORD**

歪门邪道 511

## 982 致　緻　U+81F4　TM 11　FM —

**zhì** V·ADJ·N  to send; to devote; to concentrate (on); to achieve, to reach; to cause, to result in; fine, delicate; fascination, interest, appeal

致辞 **zhìcí** V  to make a speech

致敬 **zhìjìng** V  to pay one's respects to, to greet

致命 **zhìmìng** V  fatal, lethal

致使 **zhìshǐ** V  to cause, to result in, to lead to

致谢 **zhìxiè** V  to express thanks/gratitude

向您**致谢**。 *I express my thanks to you.*

致意 **zhìyì** V  to send one's regards

**RELATED WORDS**

| 一致 1 | 以致 101 | 兴致 228 |
| 导致 751 | 罗致 756 | 细致 1107 |
| 招致 1232 | 精致 1832 | |

## 983 驳　駁　U+9A73　TM 11　FM —

**bó** V·ADJ  to contradict, to refute; mixed, variegated; multicolored

驳斥 **bóchì** V  to refute, to rebut

驳船 **bóchuán** N  barge · MW 艘

驳倒 **bódǎo** V  to demolish (an argument, a theory, etc.)

驳回 **bóhuí** V  to reject, to turn down

**RELATED WORDS**

反驳 111　　　　批驳 1005

## 984 桌   U+684C   TM **11** FM |

**zhuō** N table; desk

**桌布 zhuōbù** N tablecloth · MW 块

**桌面 zhuōmiàn** N tabletop; desktop · MW 张

**桌子 zhuōzi** N table; desk · MW 张

### RELATED WORDS

书桌 264     圆桌 1391     课桌 1503

## 985 贵 贵   U+8D35   TM **11** FM |

**guì** ADJ expensive, costly; valuable

**贵宾 guìbīn** N distinguished guest; VIP · MW 个、位、名

**贵州 Guìzhōu** N Guizhou Province

**贵族 guìzú** N aristocrat, nobleman · MW 个、位、名

### RELATED WORDS

| | | |
|---|---|---|
| 云贵高原 80 | 可贵 243 | 权贵 292 |
| 名贵 426 | 珍贵 515 | 宝贵 667 |
| 尊贵 1722 | 达官贵人 505 | 荣华富贵 769 |

## 986 南   U+5357   TM **11** FM |

**nán** N south

**南半球 Nánbànqiú** N Southern Hemisphere

**南北 nánběi** N north and south

**南部 nánbù** N southern part; south

**南方 nánfāng** N the South; region south of the Yangtze River (of China)

**南风 nánfēng** N south wind · MW 阵

**南海 Nánhǎi** N South China Sea

**南极 Nánjí** N South Pole

**南京 Nánjīng** N Nanjing (capital of Jiangsu Province)

**南来北往 nánláiběiwǎng** EXP to be always on the move

**南美 Nánměi** N South America

**南亚 Nányà** N South Asia

### RELATED WORDS

| | | |
|---|---|---|
| 天南地北 25 | 云南 80 | 走南闯北 265 |
| 东南 307 | 西南 352 | 河南 934 |
| 指南 1397 | 越南 1575 | 湖南 1741 |

## 987 事   U+4E8B   TM **11** FM |

**shì** N·V matter, affair, thing; job, work; trouble, problem; accident; responsibility; involvement; to be engaged in; to wait on

**事半功倍 shìbàngōngbèi** EXP to get twice the result with half the effort

**事倍功半 shìbèigōngbàn** EXP to get half the result with twice the effort

**事不宜迟 shìbùyíchí** EXP one must not waste (any more) time

**事端 shìduān** N disturbance, incident · MW 起

**事故 shìgù** N accident; mishap · MW 起

**事后 shìhòu** N after the event, afterwards; in retrospect

**事迹 shìjì** N achievement · MW 个

**事假 shìjià** N leave of absence · MW 次

**事件 shìjiàn** N event, incident · MW 个、起

**事例 shìlì** N example, instance · MW 个

**事前 shìqián** N before the event, in advance

**事情 shìqíng** N matter, affair, thing; business · MW 件

永远没有人知道**事情**的真相。*No one will ever know the truth of the matter.*

**事实 shìshí** N fact; reality · MW 个

**事实上 shìshíshàng** ADV in fact, in reality, actually

**事实上**, 是你们挑起的**事端**; 但是, **事后**你们又不承认。*Truthfully, it was you who caused the incident, but you didn't admit it afterwards.*

**事态 shìtài** N situation, state of affairs

**事物 shìwù** N thing, object · MW 个

**事务 shìwù** N work; affairs (political, economic, etc.)

**事业 shìyè** N undertaking, project; career · MW 个

### RELATED WORDS

| | | |
|---|---|---|
| 人事 4 | 干事 13 | 大事 20 |
| 了事 30 | 小事 61 | 从事 66 |
| 丑事 85 | 本事 90 | 公事 103 |
| 失事 106 | 世事 163 | 办事 195 |
| 外事 218 | 心事 232 | 刑事 256 |
| 出事 258 | 坏事 280 | 乐事 299 |
| 后事 310 | 当事人 335 | 议事 350 |
| 民事 388 | 多事 431 | 有事 439 |
| 往事 461 | 私事 471 | 军事 489 |
| 同事 541 | 找事 567 | 时事 586 |
| 好事 627 | 和事佬 644 | 启事 657 |
| 实事 668 | 实事求是 668 | 差事 673 |

---

**988　畏**　　　U+754F　　TM **11** FM |

**wèi** V·N　to fear, to be afraid of; to respect; fear; admiration

**畏忌　wèijì** V　to have scruples; to fear

**畏惧　wèijù** V　to fear, to dread

**畏难　wèinán** V　to be afraid of difficulty

**畏缩　wèisuō** V　to shrink back (in fear), to flinch

　　傻瓜既不畏难，也不畏缩。 *Not only does ShaGua have no fear of hardship, but he also doesn't flinch when facing it.*

**畏罪　wèizuì** V　to fear punishment for one's crimes

**RELATED WORD**

无畏 139

---

**989　冒**　　　U+5192　　TM **11** FM |

**mào** V·ADV　to emit, to give off; to risk; to pretend to be, to pass for; boldly, rashly; falsely

**冒充　màochōng** V　to pass (oneself/something) off as; to pretend to be

**冒风险　màofēngxiǎn** V　to take risks

　　有人说傻瓜的冒风险是无"知"无畏。
　　*Some people said of ShaGua's risk-taking that "his fearlessness was born of ignorance."*

**冒号　màohào** N　colon (punctuation mark) · MW 个

**冒尖　màojiān** ADJ　outstanding

**冒领　màolǐng** V　to falsely claim as one's own

**冒名　màomíng** V　to assume another's name

**冒牌　màopái** V　to pirate; to make an imitation brand, to produce a counterfeit of a well-known brand

**冒失　màoshi** ADJ　abrupt; rash; indiscreet

**冒险　màoxiǎn** V　to take a risk; to venture

　　在有些情况下，敢于冒险才能脱险。 *In some cases, taking a risk brings peace and safety.*

　　冒险不等于冒失。 *Risk-taking is not the same as acting rashly.*

**冒烟　màoyān** V　smoky, belching smoke

**RELATED WORDS**

假冒 1586　　　感冒 1860

---

**990　虽** 雖　　　U+867D　　TM **11** FM |

**suī** CONJ　although, even if, even though

**虽然　suīrán** CONJ　although, even though

　　虽然冒险和冒失都有一个"冒"字，但那是两个不同的概念。 *Even though both "risk-taking" and "acting rash" use the same Chinese character, "冒," they are two different concepts.*

---

**991　基**　　　U+57FA　　TM **11** FM |

**jī** N·ADJ　base, foundation; primary, fundamental; radical

**基本　jīběn** N·ADJ·ADV　basics; fundamental, elementary; essential, main; on the whole, basically

**基本功　jīběngōng** N　basic skill/training/knowledge · MW 个

　　许多人认为：中国的中小学生的基本功比美国的好；但傻瓜不同意这种看法。 *Many people believe that the basic skills and knowledge of Chinese pupils are better than those of American pupils, but ShaGua doesn't agree.*

**基层　jīcéng** N　grassroots; basic/primary level

**基础　jīchǔ** N　base, foundation; basis · MW 个

**基地　jīdì** N　base · MW 个

**基点　jīdiǎn** N　basic/starting point · MW 个

**基督　Jīdū** N　Jesus

**基金　jījīn** N　reserve/bank fund; endowment · MW 笔

**基石　jīshí** N　cornerstone · MW 块

　　道德的基石铺垫在人的心灵深处。 *The foundation of morality lies deep in people's minds.*

**基因　jīyīn** N　gene · MW 个

**基准　jīzhǔn** N　standard criterion, reference point · MW 个

每个人都有自己的道德**基准**。*Everyone has his or her own moral standard.*

**RELATED WORDS**

地基 772      路基 1785

---

### 992 契    U+5951    TM **11** FM |

**qì** N·V   deed; contract; carved inscription; to agree; to get along; to engrave, to carve

**契机 qìjī** N   turning point, juncture, critical moment · MW 个

每一个人都会面临**契机**, 但并不是每一个人都能抓住**契机**。*Everyone has critical moments, but not everyone can seize those moments.*

**契友 qìyǒu** N   close friend · MW 个、名、位

**契约 qìyuē** N   deed; contract; agreement · MW 份

**RELATED WORDS**

地契 772      房地契 1145

---

### 993 盐 鹽    U+76D0    TM **11** FM |

**yán** N   salt

**盐巴 yánbā** N   salt · MW 粒、颗

**盐湖 yánhú** N   salt lake · MW 个

**盐井 yánjǐng** N   salt well · MW 个、口

**盐水 yánshuǐ** N   saline water, brine · MW 瓶、杯

**RELATED WORD**

咸盐 1073

---

### 994 监 監    U+76D1    TM **11** FM |

**jiān** V·N   to inspect; to supervise; inspector, supervisor; prison, jail

**监测 jiāncè** V   to monitor; to supervise

**监察 jiānchá** V   to supervise; to control

中国需要完善**监察**制度。*China needs to improve its system of checks and balances.*

**监督 jiāndū** V   to supervise; to control

**监工 jiāngōng** V·N   to supervise, to oversee; supervisor, overseer, foreman · MW 个、名

当教师把自己看作**监工**, 他就是失败的教师。*If a teacher considers his role to be that of a supervisor, he will be unsuccessful.*

**监禁 jiānjìn** V   to take into custody, to put in jail

**监考 jiānkǎo** V   to monitor/proctor an exam

学生最高兴的事情是**监考**老师不来**监考**。*What the students like most is when their monitor is absent during an exam.*

**监票 jiānpiào** V   to oversee balloting/voting

**监视 jiānshì** V   to monitor; to oversee; to spy on

**监守 jiānshǒu** V   to have custody of, to guard

**监听 jiāntīng** V   to monitor

**监狱 jiānyù** N   prison, jail · MW 个、座

---

### 995 栽    U+683D    TM **11** FM |

**zāi** V·N   to plant; to grow, to raise; to impose; to force (something) on (someone); to tumble, to fall; to suffer a setback; seedling

**栽花** *to grow flowers*

**栽罪** *to frame, to implicate*

**栽倒 zāidǎo** V   to fall down

**栽跟头 zāigēntou** EXP   to tumble, to fall

**栽培 zāipéi** V   to grow, to cultivate; to foster; to educate; to help (someone) advance in his career

**栽培秧苗** *cultivation of a seedling*

老师**栽培**学生。*Teachers educate students.*

永生难忘您的**栽培**。*I will never forget your patronage.*

**栽赃 zāizāng** V   to frame (someone) (by planting stolen/illegal goods on him)

**栽种 zāizhòng** V   to plant; to grow

**RELATED WORD**

盆栽 1261

---

### 996 苍 蒼    U+82CD    TM **11** FM |

**cāng** ADJ·N   dark green; deep blue; gray, ashen; blue sky; sky above, heaven

**苍白 cāngbái** ADJ   pale, dull, colorless; bland

她的脸色很**苍白**。*Her face is very pale.*

她的解释很**苍白**。*Her explanation is very weak.*

**苍翠 cāngcuì** ADJ   dark green

**苍老 cānglǎo** ADJ   old, aged

**苍茫 cāngmáng** ADJ   vast, boundless

**苍天 cāngtiān** N   sky, firmament; heavens (of celestial powers who determine human fate)

**996** 苍 **cāng** (continued)

英文里没有一个恰当的概念可以翻译中文的"苍天"。*English has no equivalent concept for the Chinese word "苍天."*

苍蝇 **cāngying** N fly; housefly · MW 只

---

**997** 荐 薦 U+8350 TM **11** FM |

**jiàn** V·N to recommend; grass; straw mat

荐举 **jiànjǔ** V to nominate
荐举是科举产生前中国的一种选官制度。*The nomination system was a way of selecting officials before the Imperial Examination was created in China.*

**RELATED WORDS**

自荐 305         推荐 1242
毛遂自荐 183

---

**998** 荤 葷 U+8364 TM **11** FM |

**hūn** N meat

荤菜 **hūncài** N meat dish · MW 道
她吃素菜，不吃荤菜。*She is a vegetarian and doesn't eat dishes that contain meat.*

荤腥 **hūnxīng** N meat and fish
荤油 **hūnyóu** N lard

---

**999** 莫 U+83AB TM **11** FM |

**mò** PRON·ADV no one; nothing; none; no; not; don't

莫不 **mòbù** ADV there is no one (who doesn't)
莫测高深 **mòcègāoshēn** EXP unfathomable, enigmatic
这里的人莫不是莫测高深。*There is no one here who is not unfathomable.*

莫大 **mòdà** ADJ greatest, utmost
莫非 **mòfēi** ADV is it possible that, can it be that
莫非他不是傻瓜？*Is that not ShaGua?*

莫怪 **mòguài** CONJ no wonder that
既然他是傻瓜，就莫怪他要这样干了。*He is "ShaGua" after all; no wonder he wants to do that.*

莫过于 **mòguòyú** ADV nothing is more ... than

---

莫名其妙 **mòmíngqímiào** EXP to be unable to make heads or tails of; without rhyme or reason

莫逆 **mònì** ADJ very friendly; intimate
莫须有 **mòxūyǒu** EXP fabricated; groundless, without basis
这是强加给傻瓜的莫须有罪名。*This is a host of fabricated charges forced on ShaGua.*

**RELATED WORDS**

约莫 876        望尘莫及 1622

---

**1000** 获 獲 U+83B7 TM **11** FM |

**huò** V to capture, to catch; to obtain, to win; to harvest, to reap

获得 **huòdé** V to obtain, to win; to achieve
获取 **huòqǔ** V to obtain, to acquire
获胜 **huòshèng** V to win a victory, to triumph
获悉 **huòxī** V to be informed; to learn of
傻瓜获悉他可能获得一笔贷款。*ShaGua has been informed that he may obtain a loan.*

**RELATED WORDS**

收获 282    查获 741    荣获 769
拿获 1262    破获 1374    捕获 1400
截获 1650

---

**1001** 菜 U+83DC TM **11** FM |

**cài** N vegetable(s), greens; (cooked) dish

菜场 **càichǎng** N food market · MW 个
菜单 **càidān** N menu · MW 份
菜刀 **càidāo** N kitchen/butcher knife · MW 把
傻瓜给傻瓜太太买了一把中式菜刀。*ShaGua bought a Chinese kitchen knife for Mrs. ShaGua.*

菜地 **càidì** N vegetable plot · MW 块、片
菜花 **càihuā** N cauliflower · MW 棵、把
菜摊 **càitān** N vegetable stall · MW 个
刚来美国时，傻瓜也摆过菜摊。*When ShaGua first arrived in the States, he owned a vegetable stall.*

菜肴 **càiyáo** N (cooked) dish · MW 份
菜园 **càiyuán** N vegetable garden · MW 个
菜籽 **càizǐ** N vegetable seeds · MW 颗、粒

**RELATED WORDS**

白菜 176    炒菜 499    点菜 739
青菜 740    饭菜 891    荤菜 998

| | | |
|---|---|---|
| 咸菜 1073 | 凉菜 1337 | 素菜 1378 |
| 菠菜 1393 | 泡菜 1492 | 野菜 1685 |
| 酱菜 1814 | 酸菜 1899 | 蔬菜 1940 |
| 熟菜 1973 | 洋白菜 689 | |

---

**1002　埋**　　U+57CB　　TM **11**　FM |

**mái** V to bury; to hide, to conceal

**mán** V to blame; to complain

埋藏 **máicáng** V to bury; to hide away

埋伏 **máifú** V·N to ambush; to lie in ambush;
to hide · MW 个

埋没 **máimò** V to bury, to cover up; to overlook,
to ignore, to neglect

埋没人才是一种犯罪。 *Neglecting one's talents
is a crime.*

埋头 **máitóu** V to bury/immerse oneself in,
to be engrossed in

埋葬 **máizàng** V to bury; to wreck; to eliminate;
to destroy

埋怨 **mányuàn** V to blame; to complain,
to grumble

傻瓜总是**埋头**苦干，从不**埋怨**。 *ShaGua is
always engrossed in his business and never
complains.*

---

**1003　堆**　　U+5806　　TM **11**　FM |

**duī** V·MW to pile (up); to pack, to crowd;
[measure word for piles (of trash, dirt, etc.)]

堆存 **duīcún** V to store (up)

堆放 **duīfàng** V to pile (up), to stack

堆积 **duījī** V to accumulate; to pile (up)

街道上**堆积**了许多雪。 *A lot of snow was piled on
the streets.*

堆集 **duījí** V to gather (into a mass),
to accumulate

**RELATED WORDS**

成堆 611　　　　　　垃圾堆 399

---

**1004　扬**　揚　　U+626C　　TM **11**　FM |

**yáng** V to raise, to propagate; to scatter,
to spread; to publicize

扬名 **yángmíng** V to become famous

傻瓜当市长，**扬名**各地。 *ShaGua became famous
after he was elected mayor.*

扬言 **yángyán** V to spread about / broadcast
(especially a threat)

**RELATED WORDS**

| | | |
|---|---|---|
| 发扬 311 | 表扬 527 | 飘扬 1939 |
| 赞扬 1969 | 臭名远扬 1076 | |

---

**1005　批**　　U+6279　　TM **11**　FM |

**pī** V·MW to comment, to write comments on;
to criticize; to sell wholesale; [measure word
for groups, batches, and lots (of people,
merchandise, etc.)]

批驳 **pībó** V to refute, to rebut

批发 **pīfā** V to sell wholesale; to sell in bulk

批复 **pīfù** V to respond to; to give an official
written reply

傻瓜**批复**文件很奇特也很简单：要么打叉要么
打勾。 *The official feedback ShaGua gives on
documents is characteristically simple: either
a cross or a check.*

批改 **pīgǎi** V to correct; to mark

老师**批改**作业是一门艺术。 *The correction of
students' homework is an art.*

批号 **pīhào** N lot/batch number · MW 个

批量 **pīliàng** ADV lot, batch

批判 **pīpàn** V to criticize; to repudiate

在"文化大革命"中，许多人受到过**批判**。
*During the Cultural Revolution, many people were
repudiated.*

批评 **pīpíng** V to criticize; to critique; to comment

批示 **pīshì** V·N to comment (on); written
instructions/comments · MW 个、段

批语 **pīyǔ** N criticism; commentary ·
MW 个、段

批阅 **pīyuè** V to read through (official papers);
to evaluate, to referee

批注 **pīzhù** V to annotate, to write comments on

傻瓜不喜欢搞什么**批示**、**批语**、**批阅**或者**批注**什
么的；要么打叉要么打勾。 *ShaGua doesn't
like to write instructions, remarks, comments,
or annotations on documents; he makes either
a cross or a check.*

批准 **pīzhǔn** V to approve, to endorse; to ratify,
to confirm, to certify

**RELATED WORDS**

| | | |
|---|---|---|
| 大批 20 | 分批 173 | 成批 611 |
| 审批 911 | | |

## 1006 把    U+628A    TM **11** FM |

**bǎ** ⟨V·N·MW⟩ to hold; to grasp, to grip; to guard; grip, handle; [measure word for objects with handles (knives, brushes, etc.), for bunches or bundles (flowers, chopsticks, etc.), and for handfuls (of rice, sand, etc.)]

把柄 **bǎbǐng** ⟨N⟩ handle; mistake that can be used against a person · ⟨MW⟩ 个

我手里抓着门的**把柄**。
*I have hold of the door handle.*

小心！我手里抓着你的**把柄**。
*You should be careful! I have evidence that incriminates you.*

把持 **bǎchí** ⟨V⟩ to dominate, to monopolize; to control (feelings, etc.)

把风 **bǎfēng** ⟨V⟩ to be on the lookout

把关 **bǎguān** ⟨V⟩ to guard a pass; to do a final check on; to ensure standards

把式 **bǎshi** ⟨N⟩ skill · ⟨MW⟩ 套

把手 **bǎshou** ⟨N⟩ handle, grip, knob; leadership · ⟨MW⟩ 个

这是门的**把手**。 *This is the doorknob.*

他是学校的第二**把手**。 *He is the second leader of the school.*

把握 **bǎwò** ⟨V·N⟩ to grasp, to seize; certainty (of success), assurance

把戏 **bǎxì** ⟨N⟩ acrobatics; trick · ⟨MW⟩ 个

我有**把握**戳穿他的**把戏**。
*I can expose his trickery.*

把兄弟 **bǎxiōngdì** ⟨N⟩ sworn brothers · ⟨MW⟩ 个、名

**RELATED WORDS**

刀把 31       火把 72
门把 130      扫把 402
拖把 1396     鬼把戏 1433

## 1007 抑    U+6291    TM **11** FM |

**yì** ⟨V·CONJ⟩ to suppress; to repress, to contain; or; but; moreover, besides

抑或 **yìhuò** ⟨CONJ⟩ or

抑郁 **yìyù** ⟨ADJ⟩ depressed, despondent

抑制 **yìzhì** ⟨V⟩ to restrain, to inhibit; to control, to keep down

**RELATED WORD**

压抑 201

## 1008 投    U+6295    TM **11** FM |

**tóu** ⟨V⟩ to throw, to hurl; to toss (toward a goal); to put in; to throw oneself into, to plunge into; to send, to mail; to cast; to project; to seek; to join; to be attracted to; to fit in with, to agree with

投江 *to drown oneself in a river*

投案 **tóu'àn** ⟨V⟩ to surrender (to the police)

投保 **tóubǎo** ⟨V⟩ to buy insurance

投奔 **tóubèn** ⟨V⟩ to seek refuge/shelter

投标 **tóubiāo** ⟨V⟩ to bid, to enter/make a bid

投产 **tóuchǎn** ⟨V⟩ to go into operation/production

投诚 **tóuchéng** ⟨V⟩ to surrender

投弹 **tóudàn** ⟨V⟩ to drop a bomb

投敌 **tóudí** ⟨V⟩ to go over to the enemy

投递 **tóudì** ⟨V⟩ to deliver

投放 **tóufàng** ⟨V⟩ to throw in; to put (money) into circulation, to invest; to put (goods) on the market, to supply

投稿 **tóugǎo** ⟨V⟩ to submit (a manuscript) for publication

投合 **tóuhé** ⟨V⟩ to get along, to agree

**投稿**成不成功，有时也看稿件是不是**投合**编辑的喜好。 *Whether or not your submission is accepted depends in some cases on how much it appeals to the editor's tastes.*

投机 **tóujī** ⟨V·ADJ⟩ to speculate; to seize an opportunity; agreeable, congenial

投寄 **tóujì** ⟨V⟩ to send

投考 **tóukǎo** ⟨V⟩ to sign up for an examination

投靠 **tóukào** ⟨V⟩ to rely on; to seek help from

投篮 **tóulán** ⟨V⟩ to shoot (a basket)

投票 **tóupiào** ⟨V⟩ to vote

投入 **tóurù** ⟨V·N·ADJ⟩ to put/throw into; to throw oneself into; investment; engrossed (in) · ⟨MW⟩ 笔

把选票**投入**投票箱 *to drop a ballot into the ballot box*

他教汉语非常**投入**。 *He is teaching Chinese with great concentration.*

投石问路 **tóushíwènlù** ⟨EXP⟩ to scout ahead, to test the waters (LIT to cast a stone to check the safety of a road)

投降 **tóuxiáng** ⟨V⟩ to surrender, to capitulate

投影 **tóuyǐng** ⟨V⟩ to project; to reflect

投资 **tóuzī** ⟨V·N⟩ to invest; investment · ⟨MW⟩ 笔

**RELATED WORDS**

伞投 171     走投无路 265     空投 669

## 1009 抗

U+6297 TM **11** FM |

**kàng** V to resist; to combat, to fight; to refuse; to defy; to be a match for

抗辩 **kàngbiàn** V to contradict

抗毒素 **kàngdúsù** N antitoxin · MW 剂、粒

抗干扰 **kànggānrǎo** V to stay focused

傻瓜**抗干扰**的能力很强。*ShaGua's ability to stay focused is very strong.*

抗旱 **kànghàn** V to weather a drought; to be drought-resistant

抗衡 **kànghéng** V to contend with/against, to compete; to match

抗洪 **kànghóng** V to fight a flood

今年很不幸，刚**抗旱**，接着又**抗洪**。*This year is bad. We just finished dealing with a drought, and then we had to start fighting a flood.*

抗击 **kàngjī** V to resist, to beat back

抗菌素 **kàngjūnsù** N antibiotic · MW 剂、粒

抗生素 **kàngshēngsù** N antibiotic · MW 剂、粒

抗议 **kàngyì** V to protest

### RELATED WORDS

对抗 254　　违抗 1185　　顽抗 1204

## 1010 报 報

U+62A5 TM **11** FM |

**bào** N·V newspaper; periodical; report; telegram; retribution; to report; to announce; to respond; to reciprocate; to repay; to take revenge

回报 *to repay*

报案 **bào'àn** V to report (to the police)

报表 **bàobiǎo** N report form · MW 份

报仇 **bàochóu** V to take revenge; to avenge

傻瓜说："儿子，打工要'**报酬**'和学功夫要'**报仇**'是不同的词！"*ShaGua said, "Son, getting paid at work is different from learning kung fu to get revenge."*

报酬 **bàochou** N pay; remuneration · MW 笔

报答 **bàodá** V to repay (with action)

傻瓜是一个受人之恩必定**报答**的人。*ShaGua is one who feels he must repay others' favors.*

报道 **bàodào** V·N to report (news); news report (article/broadcast) · MW 则

报到 **bàodào** V to check in, to register; to report for duty

报废 **bàofèi** V to discard, to scrap, to reject

报复 **bàofù** V to retaliate; to avenge

傻瓜为人忠厚，从来没有想过要**报复**任何人。*ShaGua is honest and tolerant and has never thought of retaliating against others.*

报告 **bàogào** V·N to report (to one's superior, to the public); to inform; report · MW 个、场、份

报关 **bàoguān** V to declare (at customs)

报户口 **bàohùkǒu** V to apply for a residence permit

报警 **bàojǐng** V to report to the police; to sound the alarm

报刊 **bàokān** N newspapers and periodicals · MW 期、份

报考 **bàokǎo** V to sign up for an examination; to register

傻瓜去**报考**夜校。*ShaGua signed up for night school.*

报名 **bàomíng** V to sign up (for)

报丧 **bàosāng** V to report a death

报社 **bàoshè** N press, news agency · MW 家、间

报失 **bàoshī** V to report the loss of

报数 **bàoshù** V to count off

报税 **bàoshuì** V to file a tax return; to declare dutiable goods

在中国并不是人人**报税**，月收入上1500元的才**报税**。*Not everyone files a tax return in China. Only those whose monthly income exceeds 1500 yuan need to file a tax return.*

报销 **bàoxiāo** V to submit an expense report; to apply for reimbursement; to write off; to demolish

不管是在中国或美国，出差**报销**都是一件非常麻烦的事。*Regardless of whether you are in China or the U.S., applying for reimbursement is always very inconvenient.*

报账 **bàozhàng** V to submit an expense report

报纸 **bàozhǐ** N newspaper · MW 张

傻瓜不怎么读**报纸**，但每天都看电视，听广播。*ShaGua doesn't really read newspapers, but he watches TV and listens to the radio every day.*

### RELATED WORDS

| | | |
|---|---|---|
| 小报 61 | 日报 96 | 公报 103 |
| 申报 150 | 年报 182 | 月报 190 |
| 办报 195 | 汇报 234 | 电报 263 |
| 书报 264 | 见报 267 | 发报 311 |
| 回报 391 | 快报 497 | 表报 527 |
| 画报 719 | 季报 835 | 周报 1068 |
| 学报 1155 | 情报 1491 | 登报 1521 |
| 预报 1528 | 喜报 1531 | 虚报 1534 |
| 填报 1550 | 酬报 1648 | 通报 1757 |
| 墙报 1770 | 晚报 1779 | 简报 1796 |
| 剪报 1816 | 壁报 1920 | 警报 1987 |
| 以德报怨 101 | | |

## 1011 披   U+62AB   TM **11**   FM |

**pī** V to drape over, to wrap around; to throw on (clothing); to open, to unroll, to spread out; to split open, to crack

**披风 pīfēng** N cloak · MW 件

**披肩 pījiān** N cape; shawl; scarf · MW 块
傻瓜在中国给傻瓜太太买了一块**披肩**。
*ShaGua bought a shawl for Mrs. ShaGua in China.*

**披巾 pījīn** N shawl · MW 块

**披头散发 pītóusànfà** EXP with one's hair in disarray

## 1012 抬   U+62AC   TM **11**   FM |

**tái** V to lift, to raise; to carry (of two or more persons); to quarrel, to bicker

**抬杠 táigàng** V to argue for the sake of arguing

**抬高 táigāo** V to raise

**抬举 táiju** V to favor, to show favor to
你这人怎么不识**抬举**。*Why haven't you learned how to appreciate favors?*

**抬头 táitóu** V to raise one's head; to gain ground, to see the light of day

**RELATED WORD**
哄抬 781

## 1013 拙   U+62D9   TM **11**   FM |

**zhuō** ADJ clumsy, awkward; dull, stupid

**拙笨 zhuōbèn** ADJ clumsy, unskillful

**拙见 zhuōjiàn** N one's humble opinion · MW 点
这是我的**拙见**。*This is my humble opinion.*

**拙劣 zhuōliè** ADJ clumsy; inferior, botched

**RELATED WORDS**
笨拙 1079     愚拙 1901

## 1014 拥 擁   U+62E5   TM **11**   FM |

**yōng** V to embrace, to hold in one's arms; to gather/wrap around; to swarm, to throng; to support

**拥抱 yōngbào** V to embrace, to hug

**拥戴 yōngdài** V to support (as leader)

**拥护 yōnghù** V to support, to endorse
大多数人都**拥护**傻瓜当市长。*Most people endorse ShaGua for mayor.*

**拥挤 yōngjǐ** ADJ·V crowded; to crowd, to push and squeeze

**拥有 yōngyǒu** V to have, to possess, to own

## 1015 拨 撥   U+62E8   TM **11**   FM |

**bō** V·MW to allocate, to assign; to move/adjust/change/dial/poke (with one's hand/foot, a stick, etc.); [measure word for groups and batches (of people, etc.)]

**拨**开 *to move away*

**拨**电话 *to dial a phone number*

调**拨** *to allocate and transfer*

**拨**转 *to turn around*

三**拨**人 *three groups of people*

**拨号 bōhào** V to dial

**拨号盘 bōhàopán** N dial (on a phone) · MW 个

**拨款 bōkuǎn** V·N to allocate funds; appropriation; grant-in-aid; allocation

**拨弄 bōnong** V to fiddle with; to poke around; to stir up
有些人就是爱**拨弄**是非。*Some people just like to stir things up.*

**拨正 bōzhèng** V to correct, to make right

**RELATED WORDS**
挑拨 1235     调拨 1749

## 1016 括   U+62EC   TM **11**   FM |

**kuò** V·N to contract (a muscle, etc.); to include; bracket

**括号 kuòhào** N parenthesis; square bracket; curly brace (punctuation marks) · MW 对

**括弧 kuòhú** N parenthesis (punctuation mark) · MW 对

**RELATED WORDS**
包括 836     简括 1796     概括 1908

## 1017 拾   U+62FE   TM **11**   FM |

**shí** V·NUM to pick up, to put in order; ten (capital form of the Chinese numeral)

拾荒 **shíhuāng** V to eke out a living (LIT to collect scraps)

拾金不昧 **shíjīnbùmèi** EXP to return (something) to its owner, to pick up money and not keep it

他因拾金不昧而得了"傻瓜"之名。 *By not pocketing the wallet he picked up, he earned the name "dummy."*

拾取 **shíqǔ** V to pick up

拾遗 **shíyí** V to expropriate lost property; finders, keepers

**RELATED WORD**

收拾 282

---

**1018** 挡 擋    U+6321    TM **11** FM |

**dǎng** V·N to keep off; to block; to shelter from; fender; blind (of a window, etc.)

挡板 **dǎngbǎn** N barrier; baffle plate; mud flap · MW 块

挡住 **dǎngzhù** V to block, to obstruct

**RELATED WORDS**

挂挡 796        阻挡 1042        换挡 1402
遮挡 1831

---

**1019** 持    U+6301    TM **11** FM |

**chí** V to manage, to direct; to maintain, to support; to hold, to grasp

持股 **chígǔ** V to hold shares; shareholding

持家 **chíjiā** V to run one's home, to keep house

持久 **chíjiǔ** ADJ lasting, enduring; durable; persistent

学中文不是速决战，而是**持久**战。 *Studying Chinese is not a whirlwind campaign, but a long, protracted war.*

持平 **chípíng** ADJ·V unbiased, fair, impartial, just; to keep a balance, to stay level

持续 **chíxù** V to last, to continue

有人想看，傻瓜和对手的争论到底能**持续**多久？ *Some people want to see just how long the argument between ShaGua and his opponent will last.*

持有 **chíyǒu** V to hold, to possess

持之以恒 **chízhīyǐhéng** EXP to persevere; in a persistent way

傻瓜办公室的墙上贴着四个大字：**持之以恒**。 *On the wall in ShaGua's office hang four large Chinese characters that say "Perseverance!"*

---

持重 **chízhòng** ADV prudent, cautious; discreet; dignified

**RELATED WORDS**

| | | |
|---|---|---|
| 支持 92 | 主持 124 | 自持 305 |
| 坚持 381 | 扶持 404 | 相持 805 |
| 劫持 819 | 保持 868 | 把持 1006 |
| 维持 1455 | 僵持 1864 | 操持 1965 |

---

**1020** 吗 嗎    U+5417    TM **11** FM |

**má** QPRON what

**ma** AV [used at the end of a sentence to ask a yes-or-no question or to indicate disagreement; used before a pause in the middle of a sentence to indicate the subject in question]

**RELATED WORD**

干吗 13

---

**1021** 吧    U+5427    TM **11** FM |

**bā** ONOM·N crack, crackling; bar

**ba** AV [used at the end of a sentence (1) to ask for advice, to make a suggestion or request, or to give a mild command; (2) to indicate consent/approval; (3) to indicate doubt or supposition; or (4) to indicate doubt without expecting an answer]

鞭炮"**吧吧**"响。 *The fireworks went "Crack! Crack!"*

酒**吧** *bar*

你还是去**吧**。 *You had better go.*

那就这样**吧**。 *Then this is the way.*

你不会不同意**吧**。 *I doubt that you will disagree.*

好像是这么回事**吧**。 *This seems to be the way.*

讲**吧**，不太好；不讲**吧**，也不太好。 *Whether we speak up or not, it's no good either way.*

**RELATED WORD**

酒吧 1339

---

**1022** 吨 噸    U+5428    TM **11** FM |

**dūn** N·MW ton; [measure word for tons (shipping, etc.)]

吨位 **dūnwèi** N tonnage · MW 个

## 1023 咱 U+54B1 TM **11** FM |

**zán** PRON I, me; we, us

**咱们 zánmen** PRON we, us (including the person spoken to; otherwise "we" or "us" is 我们)

他跟**咱们**不是一路。 *He is not one of us.*

## 1024 咽 嚥 U+54BD TM **11** FM |

**yān** N throat; pharynx

**yàn** (嚥) V to swallow

**咽喉 yānhóu** N throat, pharynx and larynx · MW 条

**咽痛 yāntòng** N pharyngalgia, pain in the pharynx

**咽炎 yānyán** N pharyngitis, inflammation of the pharynx

**咽气 yànqì** V to breathe one's last, to die

### RELATED WORDS

吞咽 427　　　　狼吞虎咽 1443

## 1025 哈 U+54C8 TM **11** FM |

**hā** ONOM·V ha-ha (sound of laughter); to breathe (out); to bend

**哈密瓜 hāmìguā** N Hami melon (muskmelon) · MW 个

**哈欠 hāqian** N yawn · MW 个

**哈腰 hāyāo** V to stoop; to bow; to suck up to

傻瓜不喜欢那些点头**哈腰**的人。 *ShaGua doesn't like suck-ups who bow and nod a lot.*

### RELATED WORDS

马大哈 247　　　　哼哼哈哈 1561

## 1026 核 U+6838 TM **11** FM |

**hé** N·V pit, stone (of fruit); core/heart (of a matter); nucleus; to examine, to check, to investigate

**核爆炸 hébàozhà** V to set off a nuclear explosion

**核材料 hécáiliào** N nuclear material

**核弹 hédàn** N nuclear warhead/bomb · MW 枚、颗

**核动力 hédònglì** N nuclear power

**核弹**和**核动力**电站是战争与和平的分野。 *The difference between nuclear bombs and nuclear power is the dividing line between peace and war.*

**核对 héduì** V to examine, to check

**核火箭 héhuǒjiàn** N nuclear missile · MW 枚

**核能 hénéng** N nuclear energy

**核实 héshí** V to check; to verify

**核算 hésuàn** V to assess, to examine and calculate

经济**核算**也应该**核算**社会效益。 *An economic assessment should take into account social impact.*

**核桃 hétao** N walnut · MW 颗

**核武器 héwǔqì** N nuclear weapon · MW 件

**核心 héxīn** N core; inner circle (political party, government) · MW 个

**核战争 hézhànzhēng** N nuclear war · MW 场

**核战争**将是人类的灾难。 *Any nuclear war would be a catastrophe for humanity.*

**核准 hézhǔn** V to authorize; to examine and approve

**核子 hézǐ** N nucleus; nuclear · MW 个

### RELATED WORDS

考核 530　　　　审核 911　　　　复核 1059

## 1027 杨 楊 U+6768 TM **11** FM |

**yáng** N poplar (tree)

**杨柳 yángliǔ** N poplar and willow; willow · MW 棵、株

**杨树 yángshù** N poplar; aspen · MW 棵、株

## 1028 构 構 U+6784 TM **11** FM |

**gòu** V·N to construct, to build; to form; to compose; to fabricate, to make up; structure; literary composition

**构成 gòuchéng** V to constitute; to form; to compose

**构思 gòusī** V to design

这个小说的**构思**很绝妙。 *The concept of the novel is extremely clever.*

**构型 gòuxíng** N configuration · MW 个

**构造 gòuzào** V·N to build; structure; composition · MW 个

**构筑 gòuzhù** V to construct, to build

## RELATED WORDS

机构 577　　结构 1291　　虚构 1534

---

### 1029 柠 檸 U+67E0 TM **11** FM |

**níng** N lemon

**柠檬** **níngméng** N lemon; citrus · MW 个

**柠檬茶** **níngméngchá** N lemon tea · MW 杯、壶

**柠檬色** **níngméngsè** N lemon yellow

**柠檬酸** **níngméngsuān** N citric acid · MW 种

---

### 1030 栋 棟 U+680B TM **11** FM |

**dòng** N·MW ridgepole, roof/ridge beam; [measure word for buildings (houses, etc.)]

**栋梁** **dòngliáng** N ridge beam · MW 根

---

### 1031 树 樹 U+6811 TM **11** FM |

**shù** N·V tree; to plant; to cultivate; to establish, to set up

**树丛** **shùcóng** N grove; thicket; tufted trees

**树干** **shùgàn** N tree trunk · MW 根

**树立** **shùlì** V to establish, to set up
老师必须在学生中**树立**威信。*Teachers must establish their prestige among their students.*

**树林** **shùlín** N woods, forest; grove · MW 片

**树苗** **shùmiáo** N sapling; transplantable young tree · MW 棵、株

**树木** **shùmù** N trees · MW 棵

**树皮** **shùpí** N (tree) bark · MW 片

**树叶** **shùyè** N (tree) leaves · MW 片

**树枝** **shùzhī** N branch; twig · MW 枝、根

#### RELATED WORDS

| | | |
|---|---|---|
| 果树 544 | 松树 579 | 桂树 797 |
| 杨树 1027 | 桃树 1243 | 梅树 1413 |
| 植树 1415 | 圣诞树 142 | 摇钱树 1664 |

---

### 1032 档 檔 U+6863 TM **11** FM |

**dàng** N file; archive; shelf (for files)

**档案** **dàng'àn** N file; archive; record · MW 份

---

## RELATED WORDS

归档 166　　存档 438　　高档 1611

---

### 1033 检 檢 U+68C0 TM **11** FM |

**jiǎn** (identical to 捡 in the meaning "to pick up, to collect") V to examine, to inspect; to pick up, to collect

**检察** **jiǎnchá** V to prosecute

**检查** **jiǎnchá** V·N to check, to examine, to inspect; self-criticism · MW 份

**检察官** **jiǎncháguān** N prosecutor · MW 个、位、名

**检点** **jiǎndiǎn** ADJ careful/diligent (in examining); cautious, restrained (in speech, actions)
傻瓜看起来有点大大咧咧，其实他很**检点**。
*ShaGua looks a bit careless, but he is actually very cautious.*

**检举** **jiǎnjǔ** V to inform against / accuse (an offender); to report (an offense)
尽管傻瓜很**检点**，但还是有人**检举**他不**检点**。
*Even though ShaGua is very restrained, somebody still faulted him for not being cautious enough.*

**检索** **jiǎnsuǒ** V to research; to look up, to search for; to retrieve

**检讨** **jiǎntǎo** V to engage in self-criticism

**检修** **jiǎnxiū** V to overhaul, to examine and repair

**检验** **jiǎnyàn** V to test, to inspect
实践是**检验**真理的唯一标准。*Practice is the sole criterion for testing truth.*

**检疫** **jiǎnyì** V to quarantine

**检阅** **jiǎnyuè** V to inspect; to review (troops); to look over, to read

**检字表** **jiǎnzìbiǎo** N index (of a Chinese character) · MW 份、张

#### RELATED WORD

出境检查 258

---

### 1034 帆 U+5E06 TM **11** FM |

**fān** N sail; sailboat

**帆布** **fānbù** N canvas; sailcloth · MW 块

**帆船** **fānchuán** N sailboat · MW 艘、只、条

## 1035 明　U+660E　TM **11** FM |

**míng** V·ADJ·ADV to understand; to show, to indicate; to expound; obvious, clear; open; overt, explicit; bright, brilliant; sharp-eyed, perceptive; obviously; plainly, openly

**明白 míngbai** ADJ·V obvious, clear; sensible, reasonable; to understand; to realize; to know
傻瓜是个**明白**人。*ShaGua is a sensible man.*
你不**明白**我的意思。*You don't understand what I mean.*

**明灯 míngdēng** N beacon; bright light · MW 盏

**明晃晃 mínghuǎnghuǎng** ADJ shining, gleaming

**明快 míngkuài** ADJ lucid and lively (of speaking, writing); straightforward

**明朗 mínglǎng** ADJ bright and clear; obvious, clear-cut

**明亮 míngliàng** ADJ·V bright, well-lit; shining; loud and clear; to become clear
那间教室很**明亮**。*That classroom is very bright.*
听了他们的解释，我心里就**明亮**了。*After listening to their explanation, I understand more clearly.*

**明了 míngliǎo** ADJ·V clear, plain; to understand; to be clear about
他的解释很**明了**。*His explanation is very clear.*
我**明了**你的意图。*I understand your intentions.*

**明明 míngmíng** ADV obviously, plainly, undoubtedly

**明目张胆 míngmùzhāngdǎn** EXP brazenly, flagrantly, openly and boldly

**明确 míngquè** ADJ·V clear-cut, explicit, definite; to clarify
他的立场很**明确**。*His stance is very clear.*
你能**明确**你的立场吗？*Could you clarify your stance?*

**明示 míngshì** V to express

**明天 míngtiān** N tomorrow; near future · MW 个

**明显 míngxiǎn** ADJ obvious, clear, evident

**明信片 míngxìnpiàn** N postcard · MW 张

**明星 míngxīng** N star, celebrity · MW 个、位

**明早 míngzǎo** N tomorrow morning

**明知 míngzhī** V to know perfectly well, to be fully aware (of)

**明智 míngzhì** ADJ sensible; sagacious, wise
显然，他的决定是**明智**的。*Obviously, his decision is a wise one.*

### RELATED WORDS

| | | |
|---|---|---|
| 不明 24 | 文明 70 | 失明 106 |
| 严明 241 | 发明 311 | 声明 374 |
| 光明 491 | 注明 496 | 表明 527 |
| 英明 556 | 启明星 657 | 证明 705 |
| 点明 739 | 查明 741 | 贤明 750 |
| 显明 755 | 标明 801 | 指明 1397 |
| 探明 1404 | 高明 1611 | 说明 1631 |
| 简明 1796 | 鲜明 1811 | 透明 1826 |
| 精明 1832 | 照明 1846 | 聪明 1895 |
| 小聪明 61 | 半透明 127 | 鸡三明治 1373 |
| 掌上明珠 1734 | 物质文明 883 | |

## 1036 映　U+6620　TM **11** FM |

**yìng** V to reflect, to mirror; to project; to silhouette

**映衬 yìngchèn** V to set off (by contrast)

**映入 yìngrù** V to map onto

**映射 yìngshè** V to shine on

**映象 yìngxiàng** N image · MW 个

**映照 yìngzhào** V to shine (on)
月亮**映照**在湖面上。*The moon is shining on the lake.*

### RELATED WORDS

| | | |
|---|---|---|
| 上映 14 | 反映 111 | 放映 964 |

## 1037 贱　賤　U+8D31　TM **11** FM |

**jiàn** ADJ inexpensive, cheap; lowly, humble; despicable, contemptible

**贱骨头 jiàngútou** EXP miserable wretch · MW 个

**贱人 jiànrén** N bitch (derogatory), slut, tramp · MW 个

### RELATED WORDS

| | | |
|---|---|---|
| 下贱 10 | 卑贱 602 | 低贱 618 |

## 1038 贴　貼　U+8D34　TM **11** FM |

**tiē** V·N to paste, to glue, to stick; to stay close to; allowance

**贴补 tiēbǔ** V to subsidize

**贴近 tiējìn** V·ADJ to press close to, to snuggle; close, intimate

傻瓜的讲话很**贴近**老百姓的生活。
*ShaGua's speaking mannerisms are very much like those of ordinary people.*

**贴切** tiēqiè  ADJ  suitable, appropriate, apt

**贴身** tiēshēn  ADJ  next to the skin; personal (of a bodyguard, etc.)

**贴心** tiēxīn  ADJ  intimate; confidential

**RELATED WORDS**

| | | |
|---|---|---|
| 伏贴 212 | 体贴 325 | 妥贴 433 |
| 补贴 508 | 张贴 1208 | 粘贴 1365 |
| 服贴 1457 | 剪贴 1816 | |

---

**1039** 赃  臟  U+8D43  TM **11** FM |

**zāng**  N  stolen property, booty

**赃款** zāngkuǎn  N  "dirty" money; bribe money · MW 笔

从省长的房间里搜出一笔**赃款**。*The dirty money was discovered in the governor's house.*

**赃物** zāngwù  N  stolen property; bribe · MW 件

**RELATED WORDS**

| | | |
|---|---|---|
| 贪赃 827 | 栽赃 995 | 贼赃 1254 |
| 销赃 1714 | | |

---

**1040** 防  U+9632  TM **11** FM |

**fáng**  V  to guard/prevent against; to defend; to dam (up)

**防备** fángbèi  V  to guard against

**防尘** fángchén  V  to dust-proof

**防弹** fángdàn  V  to bullet-proof

一个国家的领导人不用坐**防弹**车，这个国家的人民就是和平、幸福的。*If the leader of a nation doesn't need a bulletproof car, the people in the country must be peaceful and happy.*

**防盗** fángdào  V  to guard against theft

**防毒** fángdú  V  to defend against an attack (a biological attack, a computer virus, etc.)

**防腐** fángfǔ  V  to prevent decay

**防洪** fánghóng  V  to prevent flooding

**防护** fánghù  V  to protect; to shelter

**防火** fánghuǒ  V  to fireproof; to prevent fires

这个城市既要**防火**，又要**防洪**。*This city needs to prevent not only fires but also flooding.*

**防水** fángshuǐ  V  to waterproof

**防卫** fángwèi  V  to defend, to protect

**防锈** fángxiù  V  to rust-proof

**防御** fángyù  V  to defend, to guard

**防止** fángzhǐ  V  to prevent

我们要**防止**学生考试作弊。*We should prevent student cheating on the exam.*

**防治** fángzhì  V  to prevent and cure

**RELATED WORDS**

| | | |
|---|---|---|
| 关防 224 | 严防 241 | 国防 542 |
| 空防 669 | 边防 710 | 驻防 1207 |
| 消防 1343 | 预防 1528 | 冷不防 494 |

---

**1041** 阴  陰  U+9634  TM **11** FM |

**yīn**  ADJ·N  overcast, cloudy; sinister; hidden, secret; moon; feminine/negative principle

**阴暗** yīn'àn  ADJ  dark, gloomy; shadowy

这篇小说太**阴暗**。*This novel is too dark.*

**阴沉** yīnchén  ADJ  overcast, cloudy; gloomy

**阴道** yīndào  N  vagina · MW 条

**阴沟** yīngōu  N  sewer · MW 条

**阴极** yīnjí  N  negative pole/electrode · MW 个

**阴间** yīnjiān  N  nether world · MW 个

**阴茎** yīnjīng  N  penis · MW 条

**阴冷** yīnlěng  ADJ  chilly, gloomy and cold

今天有些**阴冷**。*Today is a little bit too gloomy and cold.*

**阴历** yīnlì  N  lunar calendar

**阴凉** yīnliáng  ADJ  shady and cool

**阴谋** yīnmóu  N·V  conspiracy, plot; to conspire, to scheme · MW 个

**阴森** yīnsēn  ADJ  dark, gloomy

**阴天** yīntiān  N  cloudy day; overcast sky · MW 个

**阴险** yīnxiǎn  ADJ  sinister, insidious; treacherous

这个**阴谋**太**阴险**了。*This plot is too insidious.*

**阴阳** yīnyáng  N  yin and yang (in Chinese philosophy, medicine, etc.)

**阴影** yīnyǐng  N  shadow; shadow of doubt · MW 个

这件事在她心里产生了**阴影**。*This matter has caused some doubt in her mind.*

**阴雨** yīnyǔ  N  overcast and rainy · MW 阵

**阴郁** yīnyù  ADJ  gloomy (of weather); not lively (of atmosphere); dismal, depressed

**阴雨**天让人感到**阴郁**。*The overcast and rainy weather makes people feel depressed.*

**阴云** yīnyún  N  dark cloud · MW 团

**RELATED WORDS**

| | | |
|---|---|---|
| 太阴 53 | 光阴 491 | 搞阴谋 1904 |

## 1042 阻 　U+963B　TM 11　FM |

**zǔ** V to prevent, to obstruct; to stop

**阻碍 zǔ'ài** V to obstruct, to block
老师不应该**阻碍**学生的创新思维。
*Teachers should not curb their students' creative thinking.*

**阻挡 zǔdǎng** V to stop; to obstruct

**阻隔 zǔgé** V to separate; to cut off

**阻击 zǔjī** V to block

**阻拦 zǔlán** V to stop; to obstruct, to block, to bar the way

**阻力 zǔlì** N resistance; obstruction · MW 股
在中国，任何改革都会遇到强大的**阻力**。
*Any reform in China would face very strong resistance.*

**阻塞 zǔsè** V to obstruct, to block up

**阻止 zǔzhǐ** V to prevent; to block

**阻滞 zǔzhì** V to clog, to stop up

### RELATED WORDS

劝阻 255　　　拦阻 576　　　风雨无阻 194

## 1043 陆 陸 　U+9646　TM 11　FM |

**liù** NUM six (capital form of the Chinese numeral)

**lù** N land; continent

**陆地 lùdì** N land · MW 片

**陆海空 lùhǎikōng** N army, navy, and air force

**陆军 lùjūn** N land force(s); army · MW 队、支

**陆路 lùlù** N land route · MW 条

**陆续 lùxù** ADV constantly, continually; successively, one after another
一群**陆军**在**陆续**登陆。 *The large army landed ashore, one unit right after another.*

### RELATED WORDS

大陆 20　　　水陆 159　　　内陆 191
着陆 1332　　登陆 1521　　中国大陆 86

## 1044 战 戰 　U+6218　TM 11　FM |

**zhàn** N·V battle; war; warfare; to fight; to shiver, to tremble

**战场 zhànchǎng** N battlefield, battleground · MW 个

**战斗 zhàndòu** V·N to fight, to battle; combat; campaign; militancy · MW 次、场

**战犯 zhànfàn** N war criminal · MW 个、名

**战俘 zhànfú** N prisoner of war (POW) · MW 个、名

**战火 zhànhuǒ** N flames of war · MW 场

**战况 zhànkuàng** N battlefield situation · MW 个

**战略 zhànlüè** N strategy; tactic · MW 个
任何一个**战斗**的失误都可能导致整个**战略**的失败。 *Any mistakes in one battle would cause the entire strategy to fail.*

**战胜 zhànshèng** V to defeat, to triumph over, to conquer

**战术 zhànshù** N tactics; military tactics · MW 个

**战友 zhànyǒu** N comrade-in-arms · MW 个、位

**战争 zhànzhēng** N war; warfare · MW 场
每一场**战争**都会包含许多**战场**和**战斗**，也会产生许多**战犯**和**战俘**。 *Every war has many battlefields and battles, and it creates many war criminals and POWs.*

### RELATED WORDS

内战 191　　　休战 213　　　交战 222
会战 295　　　舌战 298　　　作战 326
应战 334　　　决战 340　　　冷战 494
参战 600　　　奋战 607　　　好战 627
核战争 1026　挑战 1235　　胆战心惊 1295
迎战 1360　　野战 1685　　混战 1739
激战 1955　　统一战线 1601　世界大战 163

## 1045 眨 　U+7728　TM 11　FM |

**zhǎ** V to blink (of an eye); to wink

**眨眼 zhǎyǎn** V to blink; to wink; to twinkle; very short time; in a wink
傻瓜思考问题时，老是喜欢**眨眼**。 *ShaGua always blinks his eyes when he is considering something.*

## 1046 邮 郵 　U+90AE　TM 11　FM |

**yóu** V·N to mail; mail; stamp

**邮包 yóubāo** N parcel post · MW 个

**邮车 yóuchē** N mail vehicle · MW 辆

**邮船 yóuchuán** N mail boat/ship; ocean liner · MW 艘

**邮戳 yóuchuō** N postmark · MW 个、枚

**邮递 yóudì** V to mail, to send by mail

**邮费 yóufèi** N postage · MW 笔

邮购 yóugòu　V　to order by mail

邮寄 yóujì　V　to mail, to send by mail

邮件 yóujiàn　N　mail · MW 封

**邮件**盖三月八日前的**邮戳**才有效。
*Mail postmarked before March 8 is valid.*

邮局 yóujú　N　post office · MW 间

中国的**邮局**星期六也开门。*Post offices are open on Saturday in China.*

邮票 yóupiào　N　stamp · MW 张、枚

邮筒 yóutǒng　N　mailbox · MW 个

邮箱 yóuxiāng　N　mailbox · MW 个

邮政 yóuzhèng　N　postal service

邮资 yóuzī　N　postage · MW 笔

**RELATED WORDS**

| | | |
|---|---|---|
| 快邮 497 | 集邮 1267 | 电子邮件 263 |
| 垃圾邮件 399 | 垃圾电邮 399 | |

---

**1047　即**　U+5373　TM 11 FM |

jí　V·ADJ·ADV·CONJ　to mean, to signify; to approach, to draw near; present, this very, the same; immediately, at once; namely; even if

即便 jíbiàn　CONJ　even if, even though

即将 jíjiāng　ADV　soon; to be about to, to be on the verge of

即刻 jíkè　ADV　immediately

即时 jíshí　ADV　immediately

即使 jíshǐ　CONJ　even if, even

即时通讯 jíshítōngxùn　N　instant messaging (IM)

即位 jíwèi　V　to ascend the throne

**RELATED WORDS**

| | | |
|---|---|---|
| 立即 125 | 当即 335 | 迅即 954 |

---

**1048　蚊**　U+868A　TM 11 FM |

wén　N　mosquito

蚊子 wénzi　N　mosquito · MW 只

**RELATED WORD**

疟蚊 662

---

**1049　别**　别 彆　U+522B　TM 11 FM |

bié　(别)　ADV·V·N·PRON　don't; had better not; to say good-bye; to differentiate; to pin; category; distinction; other, another

---

biè　(别 彆)　ADJ·V　awkward; difficult; uncomfortable; not smooth; to not get along well, to be at odds

别称 biéchēng　N　alternative/other name · MW 个

别管 biéguǎn　CONJ　no matter (who, what, etc.)

别具一格 biéjùyīgé　EXP　to have a unique style

别离 biélí　V　to leave

别名 biémíng　N　alternative/other name · MW 个

傻瓜没有**别名**。*ShaGua doesn't have another name.*

别人 biérén　N·PRON　other people; others; someone else

别墅 biéshù　N　villa · MW 间、栋

这一间**别墅**真是**别具一格**。*This house has a unique style.*

别针 biézhēn　N　safety pin · MW 枚

别字 biézì　N　misspelling; mispronunciation · MW 个

傻瓜常常写**别字**。*ShaGua often writes characters incorrectly.*

别扭 bièniu　N　awkward; difficult; uncomfortable; not smooth

这句子很**别扭**。*This sentence is very awkward.*

真**别扭**！*Very uncomfortable!*

**RELATED WORDS**

| | | |
|---|---|---|
| 个别 18 | 区别 99 | 分别 173 |
| 曲别针 272 | 各别 425 | 性别 498 |
| 判别 507 | 拜别 635 | 差别 673 |
| 类别 676 | 临别 771 | 派别 945 |
| 识别 950 | 特别 1094 | 级别 1100 |
| 叙别 1129 | 话别 1182 | 闹别扭 1323 |
| 惜别 1350 | 辞别 1606 | 离别 1614 |
| 握别 1662 | 错别字 1715 | 阔别 1728 |

---

**1050　刺**　U+523A　TM 11 FM |

cì　N·V　thorn; splinter; sting; to stab, to prick, to pierce; to splinter; to irritate; to assassinate; to spy

刺刀 cìdāo　N　dagger; bayonet · MW 把

刺耳 cì'ěr　ADJ　jarring, ear-piercing, strident

刺骨 cìgǔ　ADJ　piercing, bone-chilling

刺激 cìjī　V·ADJ　to stimulate; to provoke, to incite; exciting; irritating

那种**刺耳**的声音很**刺激**。*That type of ear-piercing noise is very aggravating.*

## 1050 刺 cì (continued)

刺客 **cìkè** [N] assassin · [MW] 个、名

刺杀 **cìshā** [V] to assassinate

刺探 **cìtàn** [V] to spy; to scout

刺客在刺探消息。 *The assassin is scouting out information.*

刺绣 **cìxiù** [V·N] to embroider; embroidery · [MW] 幅

刺眼 **cìyǎn** [ADJ] dazzling, awful-looking

这幅刺绣有点儿刺眼。 *This embroidery is offensive to the eyes.*

### RELATED WORDS

| | |
|---|---|
| 冲刺 339 | 针刺疗法 477 |
| 针刺麻醉 477 | 讽刺 948 |
| 粉刺 1363 | 骨刺 1543 |
| 肉中刺 437 | |

---

**1051** 命      U+547D      TM **11** FM 丿

**mìng** [N·V] life; lifespan; fate, destiny; to order, to command; to assign

命根子 **mìnggēnzi** [EXP] lifeblood · [MW] 条

命令 **mìnglìng** [V·N] to order; command · [MW] 道

命名 **mìngmíng** [V] to name, to christen; to designate; to nominate; to crown

以他的名字命名的试验班开展不太顺利。 *The experimental class in his name has not developed very successfully.*

命题 **mìngtí** [N·V] proposition, statement, thesis; to assign (someone) a topic · [MW] 道

中国学生很善于做命题作文。 *Chinese students are good at producing essays from an assigned topic.*

命运 **mìngyùn** [N] fate, destiny · [MW] 个

### RELATED WORDS

| | |
|---|---|
| 亡命 68 | 生命 107 |
| 任命 211 | 自命不凡 305 |
| 听命 414 | 奔命 432 |
| 寿命 440 | 性命 498 |
| 丧命 521 | 舍命 593 |
| 玩命 727 | 革命 747 |
| 拼命 794 | 待命 872 |
| 没命 938 | 活命 941 |
| 要命 969 | 致命 982 |
| 送命 1188 | 救命 1259 |
| 偿命 1440 | 短命 1452 |
| 宿命论 1480 | 逃命 1509 |
| 算命 1697 | 遵命 1975 |
| 反革命 111 | 听天由命 414 |

---

**1052**  貧      U+8D2B      TM **11** FM 丿

**pín** [ADJ] poor; deficient (in); talkative, loquacious

贫乏 **pínfá** [ADJ] poor, impoverished; lacking/deficient (in)

贫寒 **pínhán** [ADJ] poverty-stricken; hardscrabble

贫困 **pínkùn** [ADJ] poor, impoverished

贫民 **pínmín** [N] poor people, the poor; paupers, indigents · [MW] 个

给贫民传授科技是扶助贫困的好办法。 *Passing on knowledge and technology to the poor is a very good way of helping to eliminate poverty.*

贫穷 **pínqióng** [ADJ] poor, impoverished; needy, destitute

---

**1053** 食      U+98DF      TM **11** FM 丿

**shí** [V·N] to eat; to give food to, to feed; food; animal feed; eclipse (astronomy)

食道 **shídào** [N] esophagus · [MW] 条

食品 **shípǐn** [N] food; provisions · [MW] 种、份

食谱 **shípǔ** [N] recipe; cookbook · [MW] 本、份

食宿 **shísù** [N] room and board

我们负责美国学生在中国的食宿。 *We will pay for the American students' room and board in China.*

食堂 **shítáng** [N] dining room/hall, cafeteria · [MW] 间

食物 **shíwù** [N] food · [MW] 种、份

学生通常不喜欢学校食堂的食物。 *Students usually don't like cafeteria food.*

食用 **shíyòng** [V] to be used for food; to be edible

食指 **shízhǐ** [N] forefinger, index finger · [MW] 根

### RELATED WORDS

| | | |
|---|---|---|
| 日食 96 | 主食 124 | 月食 190 |
| 伙食 214 | 节食 275 | 衣食住行 330 |
| 吞食 427 | 肉食 437 | 饮食 892 |
| 甜食 1306 | 素食 1378 | 煮食 1388 |
| 禁食 1536 | 零食 1640 | 绝食 1706 |
| 粮食 1759 | 摄食 1772 | 熟食 1973 |
| 垃圾食品 399 | 丰衣足食 35 | |

---

**1054** 念      U+5FF5      TM **11** FM 丿

**niàn** [V·N] to read; to study; to attend school; to think of, to miss; thought, idea

念佛 **niànfó** [V] to pray to Buddha

念经 niànjīng  V  to recite Buddhist scripture

念旧 niànjiù  V  to keep old friendships in mind, to be nostalgic

傻瓜是一个念旧的人。 *ShaGua keeps old friendships in mind.*

念念不忘 niànniànbùwàng  EXP  to always remember, to constantly think of

念书 niànshū  V  to read; to recite; to study; to attend school

念头 niàntou  N  thought, idea; intention ·  MW  个

多麼荒谬的念头！ *What a ridiculous idea!*

**RELATED WORDS**

| | | |
|---|---|---|
| 怀念 344 | 观念 726 | 挂念 796 |
| 信念 869 | 邪念 981 | 纪念 1101 |
| 理念 1200 | 思念 1214 | 悼念 1349 |
| 留念 1582 | 想念 1769 | 渴念 1822 |
| 概念 1908 | | |

---

**1055 秀**    U+79C0    TM **11** FM ノ

xiù  ADJ·N  excellent, outstanding; elegant; beautiful; clever, intelligent; talent

秀才 xiùcai  N  scholar; skillful writer ·  MW  个、名
我们公司的这个"秀才"有点迂腐。
*Our company's "scholar" is a little pedantic.*

秀丽 xiùlì  ADJ  beautiful, pretty

秀气 xiùqi  ADJ  delicate; elegant, fine

**RELATED WORDS**

| | | |
|---|---|---|
| 优秀 447 | 俊秀 1081 | 清秀 1495 |

---

**1056 免**    U+514D    TM **11** FM ノ

miǎn  V  to excuse, to exempt; to avoid; to not be allowed, don't

免除 miǎnchú  V  to prevent; to avoid; to discharge, to relieve
他已经被免除了职务。 *He has been removed from office.*

免费 miǎnfèi  V  to be free (of charge)
天下没有免费的午餐。 *There is no such thing as a free lunch in this world.*

免票 miǎnpiào  V  to give a complimentary ticket

免税 miǎnshuì  V  to be exempt from taxation; duty-free, tax-free

免疫 miǎnyì  V  to immunize (from disease)

免职 miǎnzhí  V  to dismiss, to remove from office

他被免职了。 *He was relieved of his post.*

**RELATED WORDS**

| | | |
|---|---|---|
| 未免 88 | 以免 101 | 任免 211 |
| 幸免 373 | 难免 974 | 罢免 1215 |
| 减免 1487 | 避免 1976 | 在所难免 188 |

---

**1057 危**    U+5371    TM **11** FM ノ

wēi  N·V·ADJ  danger; to endanger, to imperil; dangerous

危害 wēihài  V  to jeopardize, to endanger; to harm, to injure
污染是一种公共危害。 *Pollution endangers the public.*

危机 wēijī  N  crisis; critical moment ·  MW  个

危急 wēijí  ADJ  critical
不到十分危急的时候，傻瓜一般不会寻求别人的帮助。 *ShaGua would not ask for help if the situation were not critical.*

危难 wēinàn  N  danger; dire peril; calamity ·  MW  个

危险 wēixiǎn  ADJ  dangerous, risky ·  MW  个

**RELATED WORDS**

| | | |
|---|---|---|
| 垂危 430 | 临危 771 | 病危 1327 |

---

**1058 昏**    U+660F    TM **11** FM ノ

hūn  N·V·ADJ  dusk, twilight; to lose consciousness, to faint; muddled, confused; dark; dim, faint

昏暗 hūn'àn  ADJ  dim; dusky; muddled

昏沉 hūnchén  ADJ  hazy, murky; dazed
教室的灯光很昏暗，让人觉得有点昏沉。 *The classroom was so dim that people became confused and sleepy.*

昏厥 hūnjué  V  to faint

昏迷 hūnmí  V  to lose consciousness, to faint; to be in a coma

昏睡 hūnshuì  V  to sleep lethargically

昏头昏脑 hūntóuhūnnǎo  ADJ  muddleheaded, dizzy
他昏睡了两天，第三天还是昏头昏脑，根本无法考试。 *He slept lethargically for two days, and on the third day he was so muddleheaded, he couldn't take the exam.*

昏眩 hūnxuàn  V  to feel dizzy; to be giddy

**RELATED WORDS**

| | |
|---|---|
| 发昏 311 | 黄昏 1212 |

| 1059 | **复** | 復 複 | U+590D | TM **11** | FM 丿 |

**fù** V to duplicate; to repeat; to recover; to reply to, to respond to; to retaliate

**复辟 fùbì** V to restore (a monarch, a regime) to power

**复查 fùchá** V to reexamine, to check again
许多学生答完试卷后, 往往不愿**复查**答案。
*After finishing an exam, many students are not willing to check their answers.*

**复方 fùfāng** N compound medicine (containing two or more ingredients)

**复合 fùhé** V to compound; to reunite

**复核 fùhé** V to recheck, to reexamine

**复述 fùshù** V to repeat, to retell
让学生**复述**课文, 是汉语教学的方法之一。
*Let students retell the lesson; this is standard pedagogy in teaching Chinese.*

**复数 fùshù** N plural · MW 个

**复习 fùxí** V to review
**复习**对某些学生有作用, 预习对另一些学生起作用; 但有些学生既需要**复习**又需要预习。 *Some students benefit from reviewing lessons; others gain more from previewing lessons; but some need not only to review afterwards, but also to preview beforehand.*

**复写 fùxiě** V to carbon-copy, to duplicate

**复印 fùyìn** V to photocopy, to copy

**复杂 fùzá** ADJ complicated, complex

**复制 fùzhì** V to duplicate, to make a copy of; to clone

**RELATED WORDS**

| 1060 | **凭** | 憑 | U+51ED | TM **11** | FM 丿 |

**píng** V·N·CONJ to lean on/against; to rely/depend on; to use as a basis; evidence, proof; testimony; no matter (what, how, etc.)

**凭单 píngdān** N voucher · MW 张、份

**凭借 píngjiè** V to rely/depend on; by means of
**凭借**老百姓的信任, 傻瓜当上了市长。
*Banking on the trust and support of ordinary people, ShaGua has been elected mayor.*

**凭据 píngjù** N evidence · MW 份

**凭空 píngkōng** ADV without basis; out of thin air

**凭信 píngxìn** V·N to trust; evidence · MW 份

**凭仗 píngzhàng** V to rely on

**凭证 píngzhèng** N evidence, proof; voucher; credentials · MW 张、份
你面对的是法官, 所以不能**凭空**指证, 只能提供**凭据**和**凭证**。 *You are facing a judge, so you can't charge others without grounds; you must provide evidence and proof.*

**RELATED WORDS**

| 1061 | **货** | 貨 | U+8D27 | TM **11** | FM 丿 |

**huò** N goods; commodity; money, currency; idiot

**货币 huòbì** N money, currency · MW 笔

**货车 huòchē** N truck, van; freight train/car · MW 辆
你知道**货车**什么时候到吗? *Do you know when the truck will arrive?*

**货船 huòchuán** N cargo ship, freighter · MW 艘

**货单 huòdān** N manifest; invoice · MW 张、份

**货价 huòjià** N price of goods · MW 个、份

**货款 huòkuǎn** N payment for goods · MW 笔

**货票 huòpiào** N copy of a waybill · MW 张、份

**货品 huòpǐn** N (kinds/types of) goods · MW 件

**货色 huòsè** N goods; stuff; quality of goods; trash, garbage · MW 个
这家商店**货色**齐全。 *Goods of every description are available in this store.*
你是什么**货色**? *What are you made of?*

**货摊 huòtān** N vendor's stall/stand · MW 个

**货物 huòwù** N goods, merchandise; commodity · MW 件

**货样 huòyàng** N sample goods · MW 件

**货源 huòyuán** N source/supply of goods · MW 个

**货运 huòyùn** N freight transport; trucking

**货主 huòzhǔ** N owner of cargo; consignor · MW 个、名

**RELATED WORDS**

| | | |
|---|---|---|
| 卸货 1128 | 送货 1188 | 载货 1218 |
| 购货单 1253 | 售货 1266 | 缺货 1305 |
| 黑货 1389 | 换货 1402 | 提货 1554 |
| 期货 1574 | 通货 1757 | 鲜货 1811 |
| 蠢货 1995 | | |

---

**1062** 贷 貸　　U+8D37　　TM **11** FM ノ

**dài** V　to borrow (money); to lend (money), to loan

贷方 **dàifāng** N　credit; credit side (of a balance sheet)

贷款 **dàikuǎn** V·N　to lend, to loan; loan · MW 笔

**RELATED WORDS**

告贷 428　　　信贷 869　　　借贷 1087

---

**1063** 努　　U+52AA　　TM **11** FM ノ

**nǔ** V　to make an effort; to exert oneself

努力 **nǔlì** V·ADJ　to make an effort, to try hard; hardworking

傻瓜没啥大本事, 只知道傻**努力**。
*ShaGua doesn't have any talent, but he gets down to business and works hard.*

---

**1064** 套　　U+5957　　TM **11** FM ノ

**tào** V·N·MW　to cover, to slip over; to overlap; to interleave; cover; sheath; [measure word for books, clothing, furniture, tools, etc.]

套色 **tàoshǎi** V　to print using process color

套用 **tàoyòng** V　to apply mechanically/by rote

**RELATED WORDS**

| | | |
|---|---|---|
| 手套 104 | 耳套 145 | 全套 172 |
| 外套 218 | 成套 611 | 乱套 901 |
| 客套 1316 | 被套 1517 | 配套 1647 |
| 圈套 1765 | 整套 1845 | 跑龙套 1916 |

---

**1065** 轰 轟　　U+8F70　　TM **11** FM ノ

**hōng** ONOM·V　bang; boom; to rumble; to drive away/off; to attack; to bomb

轰动 **hōngdòng** V　to cause a sensation; to take by storm

傻瓜当选市长, 成为**轰动**一时的新闻。
*ShaGua being elected mayor caused a sensation at the time.*

轰轰烈烈 **hōnghōnglièliè** EXP　vigorous; on a grand and spectacular scale

轰隆 **hōnglōng** ONOM　rumble; roll (of thunder)

轰鸣 **hōngmíng** V　to thunder; to roar

轰炸 **hōngzhà** V　to bomb

---

**1066** 泰　　U+6CF0　　TM **11** FM ノ

**tài** N·ADJ·ADV　(short name for) Thailand; peaceful; safe; most; extreme, too much

泰国 **Tàiguó** N　Thailand

泰然 **tàirán** ADJ　calm, composed

泰山 **Tàishān** N　Mount Tai; father-in-law

---

**1067** 眉　　U+7709　　TM **11** FM ノ

**méi** N　eyebrow, brow; top margin (of a page)

眉笔 **méibǐ** N　eyebrow pencil · MW 支

眉开眼笑 **méikāiyǎnxiào** EXP　to be all smiles, to beam with joy

傻瓜**眉开眼笑**, 因为大儿子的微积分得了C+。
*ShaGua was all smiles because his older son got a C+ in calculus.*

眉毛 **méimao** N　eyebrow, brow · MW 道

眉目 **méimù** N　features, looks (LIT brows and eyes); light at the end of the tunnel

眉头 **méitóu** N　brows · MW 个

**RELATED WORDS**

有眉目 439　　　挤眉弄眼 795　　　燃眉之急 1888

---

**1068** 周　　U+5468　　TM **11** FM ノ

**zhōu** N·V·ADJ·MW　circle; week; to circle; entire, complete; thorough; widespread; thoughtful, attentive; cycle; [measure word for weeks]

圆周 *circumference*

每周一次 *once a week*

绕一周 *to make a circuit*

周三下午 *Wednesday afternoon*

周报 **zhōubào** N　weekly (publication) · MW 期、份

周边 **zhōubiān** N　periphery; circumference

**1068 周 zhōu** (continued)

周长 **zhōucháng** N perimeter; circumference ·
MW 个

周到 **zhōudào** ADJ thorough, attentive;
thoughtful, considerate

周而复始 **zhōu'érfùshǐ** EXP to come full circle

周刊 **zhōukān** N weekly (publication) ·
MW 期、份

周密 **zhōumì** ADJ thorough, meticulous, attentive
to every detail

傻瓜有时考虑事情比较简单, 不够**周密**。
*Sometimes ShaGua thinks about things too simply
and not carefully enough.*

周期 **zhōuqī** N period; cycle; classification of
chemical elements (as in the periodic table) ·
MW 个

这种植物的生长**周期**太长。*The growing cycle
of this plant is too long.*

周期性 **zhōuqīxìng** N periodicity (mathematics,
science)

周全 **zhōuquán** ADJ·V thorough, comprehensive;
to help (someone) attain his/her goal

周身 **zhōushēn** N whole body; from head
to toe

周围 **zhōuwéi** N vicinity; around, surrounding

周详 **zhōuxiáng** ADJ comprehensive, complete

周旋 **zhōuxuán** V to socialize; to deal with

周游 **zhōuyóu** V to travel

周至 **zhōuzhì** ADJ thoughtful

周转 **zhōuzhuǎn** V to turn over, to circulate;
to have enough to meet one's needs

公司的流动资金**周转**不灵。*The company's
circulating funds are insufficient to meet all its
needs.*

**RELATED WORDS**

牙周炎 143　　双周刊 146　　圆周 1391
众所周知 175

---

**1069 局**　　　U+5C40　　TM **11**　FM 丿

**jú** N·V·MW department; office; bureau; shop;
situation; to confine; [measure word for games,
matches, etc.]

局部 **júbù** N part, portion; local; partial ·
MW 个

这只是一个**局部**问题, 不是全局问题。
*This is just a localized problem, not a global one.*

---

局促 **júcù** ADJ narrow, cramped; constrained;
inhibited; short (of time)

局面 **júmiàn** N situation; phase, aspect ·
MW 个

局外人 **júwàirén** N outsider; nonmember ·
MW 个、名

局限 **júxiàn** V·N to limit, to confine; localization ·
MW 个

你不是**局外人**, 你没有**局限**, 应该能打开**局面**。
*You are not an outsider and you don't have any
limitations placed on you; you should be able
to create your own situation.*

**RELATED WORDS**

| | | |
|---|---|---|
| 大局 20 | 全局 172 | 布局 309 |
| 当局 335 | 和局 644 | 邮局 1046 |
| 终局 1109 | 格局 1246 | 结局 1291 |
| 僵局 1864 | 骗局 1937 | 税务局 1705 |
| 港务局 1740 | | |

---

**1070 屁**　　　U+5C41　　TM **11**　FM 丿

**pì** N flatulence; nonsense; useless object;
anything, nothing [used to negate/blame]

屁股 **pìgu** N buttocks, rump; hip · MW 个

屁滚尿流 **pìgǔnniàoliú** EXP to be frightened out
of one's wits

屁话 **pìhuà** N nonsense · MW 通

**RELATED WORDS**

放屁 964　　　狗屁 1287　·　拍马屁 790

---

**1071 屈**　　　U+5C48　　TM **11**　FM 丿

**qū** V·ADJ·N to bend; to bow; to submit, to yield;
to treat unfairly/unjustly; wrong, in the wrong;
injustice

屈从 **qūcóng** V to submit, to give in

屈服 **qūfú** V to submit, to give in, to surrender;
to bow

屈指 **qūzhǐ** V to count on one's fingers

屈指可数 **qūzhǐkěshǔ** EXP very few; can be
counted on one's fingers

傻瓜是**屈指可数**的不愿**屈**从权威的人。
*Very few people are as stubborn and unwilling
to submit to authority as ShaGua is.*

**RELATED WORDS**

委屈 594　　　首屈一指 924　　　冤屈 1729

## 1072 屋　U+5C4B　TM **11** FM 丿

**wū** N house; room

屋顶 **wūdǐng** N roof · MW 个
屋檐 **wūyán** N eaves · MW 个
屋子 **wūzi** N house; room · MW 间

**RELATED WORDS**

外屋 218　　　　房屋 1145

## 1073 咸 鹹 　U+54B8　TM **11** FM 丿

**xián** ADJ·N salted; salty (taste)

咸菜 **xiáncài** N salted vegetables ·
MW 棵、包
咸肉 **xiánròu** N salt-cured meat ·
MW 块、片
咸水 **xiánshuǐ** N salt water · MW 杯
咸味 **xiánwèi** N salty taste
咸盐 **xiányán** N salt · MW 粒、颗、勺

## 1074 贰 貳　U+8D30　TM **11** FM 丿

**èr** NUM two (capital form of the Chinese numeral)

## 1075 真　U+771F　TM **11** FM 丿

**zhēn** N·ADJ·ADV truth; natural state; true, real, genuine; really, truly, indeed

真诚 **zhēnchéng** ADJ sincere, heartfelt
傻瓜可能有很多缺点，但待人**真诚**却是公认的优点。 *ShaGua may have many weaknesses, but treating friends with sincerity is one of his widely recognized strengths.*
真假 **zhēnjiǎ** N true and false; genuine and fake
真空 **zhēnkōng** N vacuum
真凭实据 **zhēnpíngshíjù** N conclusive evidence
控告别人一定要有**真凭实据**。 *Accusing others requires conclusive evidence.*
真切 **zhēnqiè** ADJ clear, vivid; sincere
真情 **zhēnqíng** N real situation; truth; true feelings
真人真事 **zhēnrénzhēnshì** N real people and real events · MW 件

真善美 **zhēnshànměi** ADJ the true, the good, and the beautiful
"**真善美**"的"**真**"讲的是科学；"**善**"讲的是道德；"**美**"讲的是艺术。 *Regarding the three characters "真善美": "True" relates to science, "good" indicates morality, and "beautiful" describes the arts.*
真实 **zhēnshí** ADJ true, real, authentic
真丝 **zhēnsī** N pure silk · MW 块
真相 **zhēnxiàng** N real situation; truth; facts · MW 个
真心 **zhēnxīn** N sincere, heartfelt · MW 片
真真假假 **zhēnzhēnjiǎjiǎ** EXP true mingled with the false
**真相**往往就隐藏在**真真假假**的现象后面。 *The truth is usually tangled with fiction.*
真正 **zhēnzhèng** ADV truly, really
真知 **zhēnzhī** N genuine knowledge

**RELATED WORDS**

| | | |
|---|---|---|
| 天真 25 | 认真 239 | 当真 335 |
| 仿真 450 | 传真 452 | 果真 544 |
| 写真 663 | 乱真 901 | 清真 1495 |
| 逼真 1828 | 以假乱真 101 | 去伪存真 157 |
| 弄假成真 251 | | |

## 1076 臭　U+5C4B　TM **11** FM 丿

**chòu** ADJ smelly, stinky; foul, disgusting; inferior, lousy, poor

臭虫 **chòuchóng** N bedbug · MW 只
臭烘烘 **chòuhōnghōng** EXP stinky, foul-smelling
臭骂 **chòumà** V to curse, to chew out, to give a tongue-lashing to
傻瓜把犯错误的儿子**臭骂**了一顿。 *ShaGua gave his son a tongue-lashing after his son made a mistake.*
臭名远扬 **chòumíngyuǎnyáng** EXP notorious
臭气 **chòuqì** N stench · MW 股
臭氧 **chòuyǎng** N ozone

**RELATED WORDS**

| | | |
|---|---|---|
| 口臭 42 | 去臭 157 | 汗臭 236 |
| 狐臭 885 | 恶臭 1196 | 除臭剂 1418 |
| 铜臭 1712 | 搞臭 1904 | |

## 1077 爸　U+7238　TM **11** FM 丿

**bà** N dad; father

**1078**  笋    U+7B0B    TM **11** FM 丿

**sǔn** N bamboo shoot

竹笋 *bamboo shoots*

笋干 **sǔngān** N dried bamboo shoots ·
MW 片、块

**1079** 笨    U+7B28    TM **11** FM 丿

**bèn** ADJ stupid; silly; clumsy; cumbersome,
awkward

笨蛋 **bèndàn** N fool; idiot · MW 个

笨重 **bènzhòng** ADJ heavy; cumbersome,
unwieldy

笨拙 **bènzhuō** ADJ clumsy, awkward; stupid

这个**笨蛋**的辩解太**笨拙**。*This idiot's explanation
is really stupid.*

**RELATED WORDS**

拙笨 1013     粗笨 1364     愚笨 1901
嘴笨 1984

**1080** 佛    U+4F5B    TM **11** FM 丿

**fó** N Buddha; Buddhism; image/statue of
Buddha

佛教 **fójiào** N Buddhism

佛经 **fójīng** N Buddhist scripture/texts ·
MW 部

佛像 **fóxiàng** N image/figure of Buddha ·
MW 尊

**RELATED WORDS**

仿佛 450     念佛 1054     如来佛 464

**1081** 俊    U+4FCA    TM **11** FM 丿

**jùn** ADJ cute, handsome, pretty, beautiful;
outstanding; talented

他是个**俊**小子。*He is a handsome boy.*

他是一个才**俊**。*He is a talented person.*

俊俏 **jùnqiào** ADJ pretty and charming; elegant

俊秀 **jùnxiù** ADJ pretty and charming; elegant

**RELATED WORD**

英俊 556

**1082**  倆 倆    U+4FE9    TM **11** FM 丿

**liǎ** NUM two; both of us; some, several

**1083** 俱    U+4FF1    TM **11** FM 丿

**jù** ADV all, without exception; completely, entirely

俱乐部 **jùlèbù** N club, organization · MW 家、个

俱全 **jùquán** ADJ every kind; all kinds of; every
variety under the sun

这个**俱乐部**的各种人才一应**俱全**。*There are all
kinds of talented people in this club.*

**RELATED WORD**

与日俱增 158

**1084** 倍    U+500D    TM **11** FM 丿

**bèi** N·MW times, -fold; double; [measure word for
the number of times (something happens / is
done)]

倍减 **bèijiǎn** V to reduce by a factor of

倍率 **bèilǜ** N magnifying power · MW 个

倍数 **bèishù** N multiple · MW 个

**RELATED WORDS**

百倍 242     加倍 463     两倍 509
事倍功半 987     事半功倍 987

**1085** 侃    U+4F83    TM **11** FM 丿

**kǎn** ADJ·V bold and outspoken; to chat

侃大山 **kǎndàshān** EXP to shoot the breeze,
to chew the fat (figurative)

与朋友**侃大山**是一件很惬意的事。*It is very
pleasant to shoot the breeze with friends.*

侃侃而谈 **kǎnkǎn'értán** EXP to speak frankly and
with assurance

**1086**  候    U+5019    TM **11** FM 丿

**hòu** V·N to wait; to inquire after; time; season;
state, condition; symptoms

等**候** *to wait for*

问**候** *to inquire after*

时**候** *time*

火候 *duration and degree of heating (in cooking)*

候车室 **hòuchēshì** N waiting room · MW 间

候机室 **hòujīshì** N airport lounge · MW 间

候鸟 **hòuniǎo** N migratory bird · MW 只

候选人 **hòuxuǎnrén** N candidate (for election) · MW 个、位、名

候诊 **hòuzhěn** V to wait to see the doctor

### RELATED WORDS

| | | |
|---|---|---|
| 火候 72 | 气候 185 | 听候 414 |
| 守候 486 | 时候 586 | 问候 678 |
| 症候 923 | 迎候 1360 | 等候 1437 |
| 小时候 61 | | |

---

**1087** 借     U+501F    TM **11**   FM 丿

**jiè** V to borrow; to lend; to make use of, to take advantage of; to use (something) as a means of

借贷 **jièdài** V·N to borrow money; to lend money; loan · MW 笔

借方 **jièfāng** N debit; debit side (of a balance sheet)

借故 **jiègù** V to make/find an excuse

他总是**借故**不上课。*He always makes excuses for being absent from class.*

借据 **jièjù** N loan receipt, IOU · MW 份

借口 **jièkǒu** V·N to use (something) as an excuse/pretext; excuse, pretext · MW 个

借书处 **jièshūchù** N circulation desk (of a library) · MW 个

借书证 **jièshūzhèng** N library card · MW 个、张

借用 **jièyòng** V to borrow; to have the loan of; to use (something) for another purpose

借债 **jièzhài** V to borrow money

你不能找借口去**借债**。*You can't look for an excuse to borrow money.*

借助 **jièzhù** V to enlist the help of; to fall back on

有些学生能够**借助**字典阅读中文小说。*Some students are able to read Chinese novels with the help of a dictionary.*

### RELATED WORDS

| | | |
|---|---|---|
| 租借 1096 | 凭借 1060 | 假借 1586 |

---

**1088** 债 债     U+503A    TM **11**   FM 丿

**zhài** N debt

债户 **zhàihù** N debtor · MW 个、名

债款 **zhàikuǎn** N loan; debt · MW 笔

债权 **zhàiquán** N creditor's right(s) · MW 个

债券 **zhàiquàn** N bond · MW 笔

债务 **zhàiwù** N debt; liability; indebtedness, financial obligation · MW 笔

债主 **zhàizhǔ** N creditor · MW 个、名

**债户**因为**债务**的问题, 常常躲避**债主**。*Debtors usually avoid seeing their creditors because of their debts.*

### RELATED WORDS

| | | |
|---|---|---|
| 公债 103 | 外债 218 | 负债 435 |
| 还债 714 | 借债 1087 | 逼债 1828 |
| 躲债 1874 | | |

---

**1089** 值     U+503C    TM **11**   FM 丿

**zhí** V·ADJ·N to be worth; to be on duty; to just happen to be; to come upon; worth; worthwhile; value; price

值班 **zhíbān** V to be on duty; to work a shift

值得 **zhíde** V·ADJ to be worth; to merit; worth; deserving

值钱 **zhíqián** ADJ valuable, of great value

值勤 **zhíqín** V to be on duty

值日 **zhírì** V to be on duty for the day

### RELATED WORDS

| | | |
|---|---|---|
| 升值 47 | 币值 181 | 价值 210 |
| 产值 219 | 比值 279 | 估值 456 |
| 贬值 814 | 净值 1159 | 等值 1437 |
| 增值 1849 | 总产值 1330 | 最大值 1541 |

---

**1090** 很     U+5F88    TM **11**   FM 丿

**hěn** ADV very, quite, awfully

---

**1091** 她     U+5979    TM **11**   FM 丿

**tā** PRON she

---

**1092** 妈 媽     U+5988    TM **11**   FM 丿

**mā** N mom; mother

妈妈 **māma** N mom; mother · MW 个、位

傻瓜有一个**妈妈**, 三个姑妈, 六个姨妈。*ShaGua has one mother, three aunts on his father's side, and six aunts on his mother's side.*

1092 妈 mā (continued)

**RELATED WORDS**

后妈 310        他妈的 616        奶妈 878
姑妈 881        姨妈 1596

---

1093    **姻**    U+59FB    TM **11** FM 丿

yīn  N  marriage; relation by marriage

**姻亲 yīnqīn**  N  in-law; relation by marriage ·
MW 个、名

**姻缘 yīnyuán**  N  destiny that brings lovers
together; marriage as a consequence of luck ·
MW 份

傻瓜太太认为是一份说不清的**姻缘**使她跟傻瓜
结合在一起。 *Mrs. ShaGua believes that a
serendipitous turn of events forced her to marry
ShaGua.*

**RELATED WORD**

婚姻 1701

---

1094    **特**    U+7279    TM **11** FM 丿

tè  N·ADJ·ADV  spy, secret agent; special, particular;
unusual, exceptional; for a special purpose,
especially; extremely

**特别 tèbié**  ADJ·ADV  peculiar, unusual; special,
particular; especially, particularly

**特产 tèchǎn**  N  (local/regional) specialty ·
MW 批

所谓"**特产**"就是当地**特别**的物产。
*"Specialties" are unique, locally made products.*

**特大 tèdà**  ADJ  especially/exceptionally large

**特等 tèděng**  N  special grade, top quality

**特地 tèdì**  ADV  for a special purpose, especially

她**特地**送给我这个**特别**的礼物。 *She gave me this
unusual gift for a specific purpose.*

**特点 tèdiǎn**  N  characteristic, distinguishing
feature; peculiarity · MW 个

傻瓜是一个非常有**特点**的市长。
*ShaGua is a mayor with unique traits.*

**特定 tèdìng**  ADJ  specially designated/appointed;
specific, specified

**特工 tègōng**  N  secret service; secret agent ·
MW 个、名

**特惠 tèhuì**  ADJ  most favorable; preferential

**特级 tèjí**  N  special grade, top quality

**特急 tèjí**  ADJ  especially urgent, top priority

**特技 tèjì**  N  stunt; special effect · MW 门

**特价 tèjià**  N  special offer; bargain price · MW 个

**特刊 tèkān**  N  special issue/edition · MW 期

**特快 tèkuài**  N·ADJ  express; very fast · MW 个、件

**特权 tèquán**  N  privilege, prerogative · MW 个

傻瓜有**特权**, 但他不滥用**特权**。
*ShaGua has privileges, but he never abuses them.*

**特色 tèsè**  N  characteristic; special quality ·
MW 个

**特设 tèshè**  V·ADJ  to establish/design (something)
especially for; ad hoc

**特赦 tèshè**  V  to grant a special pardon to

**特使 tèshǐ**  N  special envoy/ambassador ·
MW 个、位、名

**特殊 tèshū**  ADJ  special, unusual, extraordinary

**特务 tèwu**  N  special assignment (military);
special agent, spy · MW 个、名

**特务**就是执行**特殊**任务的人。 *Special agents are
those who carry out special assignments.*

**特效 tèxiào**  N  especially good effect; exceptional
efficacy · MW 个

**特写 tèxiě**  N  feature (article/story); close-up
(in a film) · MW 个、份

**特许 tèxǔ**  V  to give special permission to

**特邀 tèyāo**  V  to invite specially

**特异 tèyì**  ADJ  excellent, exceptionally good;
unique, distinctive

**特意 tèyì**  ADV  for a special purpose, deliberately,
specially

**特有 tèyǒu**  ADJ  special, distinctive; characteristic

**特约 tèyuē**  V  to engage by special arrangement

**特征 tèzhēng**  N  characteristic, feature, trait;
property · MW 个

**特质 tèzhì**  N  special quality; idiosyncrasy ·
MW 种

傻瓜有自己的**特质**。 *ShaGua has his own
idiosyncrasies.*

**特种 tèzhǒng**  ADJ  special, particular

**RELATED WORDS**

独特 1095        土特产 15        伏特 212
因特网 270        瓦特 356        奇特 854
模特 1673        经济特区 1110

---

1095    **独**  獨    U+72EC    TM **11** FM 丿

dú  N·ADJ·ADV  old people without children;
childless; only; single; standoffish; selfish;
intolerant; alone, (all) by oneself, solely

独霸 dúbà  V  to dominate

独白 dúbái  V·N  to deliver a monologue; monologue, soliloquy ·  MW  段

独裁 dúcái  V  to dictate, to make arbitrary decisions; dictatorship, autocratic rule

独裁者也会找到独裁的理由的。
*Dictators find their own autocratic reasons to justify their dictatorships.*

独创 dúchuàng  V  to create the original, to invent by oneself

独到 dúdào  ADJ  original; unique

独立 dúlì  V·ADJ  to declare independence (of a nation/government); to be independent; stand-alone; independent

对许多亚裔孩子来说，思想的独立比经济的独立更重要。 *For many Asian-American kids, thinking independently is more important than economic independence.*

独木桥 dúmùqiáo  N  single-plank bridge; difficult path ·  MW  条

独身 dúshēn  V  to live away from one's home/family; to be unmarried/single

现在许多中国女士选择独身的生活方式。
*Today, many women in China choose to live a single lifestyle.*

独生女 dúshēngnǚ  N  only daughter ·  MW  个、名

独生子 dúshēngzǐ  N  only son ·  MW  个、名

独特 dútè  ADJ  unique, distinctive

独资 dúzī  N  sole proprietorship; wholly owned (company)

独自 dúzì  ADV  alone, by oneself

独奏 dúzòu  V  (vocal/instrumental) solo

RELATED WORDS

单独 672        孤独 978

---

1096  租    U+79DF    TM **11** FM 丿

zū  V·N  to rent; to charter; to lease; to rent out; rent money; land tax

租佃 zūdiàn  V  to rent out land to a tenant (of a landlord)

租户 zūhù  N  tenant ·  MW  个

租借 zūjiè  V  to rent; to lease; to rent out

我打算租借这栋楼来办一所中文学校。
*I am going to rent this building to open a Chinese school.*

租金 zūjīn  N  rent; rental ·  MW  笔

租用 zūyòng  V  to rent; to take on a lease

---

租约 zūyuē  N  lease ·  MW  份

RELATED WORDS

出租 258        地租 772        押租 787
包租 836        承租人 972      转租 1111
房租 1145

---

1097  积  積    U+79EF    TM **11** FM 丿

jī  V·ADJ  to accumulate, to amass; long-standing; indigestion

积极 jījí  ADJ  positive, enthusiastic; active, vigorous

傻瓜想调动一切积极因素来搞市政建设。
*ShaGua wants to mobilize energetically to focus on improving municipal works.*

积聚 jījù  V  to accumulate, to gather

积累 jīlěi  V  to accumulate, to gather

积木 jīmù  N  building blocks; toy bricks ·  MW  块、盒

积蓄 jīxù  V  to save; to accumulate, to amass

别人借傻瓜多年的积蓄去炒股，结果输得一塌糊涂。 *Someone borrowed ShaGua's savings of many years to buy stocks, but it ended up being a complete mess.*

积压 jīyā  V  to overstock; to have a backlog; to put off, to delay

RELATED WORDS

日积月累 96      公积金 103      面积 721
堆积 1003        沉积 1166       容积 1320
聚积 1642        累积 1653

---

1098  规  規    U+89C4    TM **11** FM 丿

guī  V·N  to plan, to devise, to scheme; rule, standard

规程 guīchéng  N  rules, regulations, procedures ·  MW  个、套

规定 guīdìng  N·V  provision, rule, regulation; to specify, to stipulate; to formulate; to regulate ·  MW  个、套

规范 guīfàn  N·V·ADJ  standard, norm; specification; to standardize; standard, normal

规格 guīgé  N  standard, norm; specification, requirement ·  MW  个

规划 guīhuà  N·V  plan; program, project; blueprint; to draw up (a plan) ·  MW  个、套

傻瓜想给市政府的人员规划一套完整的新规章。 *ShaGua is going to draw up a whole new set of regulations for city government employees.*

**1098 规 guī** (continued)

**规矩 guīju** N·ADJ custom, norm, established practice (LIT compass and set square); well-behaved · MW 套

**规律 guīlǜ** N law; regular pattern · MW 个
自然**规律**是不以人的意志为转移的。
*Natural laws are independent of human will.*

**规模 guīmó** N scale, scope, dimensions · MW 个

**规劝 guīquàn** V to advise; to admonish

**规章 guīzhāng** N rule, regulation · MW 个、套

**RELATED WORDS**

| | | |
|---|---|---|
| 大规模 20 | 不规则 24 | 正规 76 |
| 行规 327 | 老规矩 375 | 成规 611 |
| 法规 686 | 校规 802 | 犯规 884 |
| 陈规 1250 | 圆规 1391 | 常规 1733 |
| 墨守成规 1843 | | |

---

**1099 爬** 　U+722C　TM **11** FM 丿

**pá** V to crawl, to creep; to climb; to get/stand up

**爬虫 páchóng** N reptile · MW 条、只

**爬高 págāo** V to climb

**爬行 páxíng** V to crawl, to creep; to trail; to move/work at a snail's pace

---

**1100 级** 级　U+7EA7　TM **11** FM 丿

**jí** N·MW level, rank; course; class, grade, form; step; [measure word for steps, stages, levels, etc.]

**级别 jíbié** N level; rank, grade · MW 个

**RELATED WORDS**

| | | |
|---|---|---|
| 上级 14 | 升级 47 | 甲级 149 |
| 分级 173 | 年级 182 | 丙级 246 |
| 次级 341 | 各级 425 | 多级 431 |
| 阶级 590 | 低级 618 | 评级 706 |
| 班级 730 | 初级 963 | 特级 1094 |
| 品级 1220 | 降级 1416 | 等级 1437 |
| 留级 1582 | 高级 1611 | 超级 1684 |
| 跳级 1786 | 低年级 618 | 中产阶级 86 |
| 无产阶级 139 | | |

---

**1101 纪** 紀　U+7EAA　TM **11** FM 丿

**jì** N discipline; age, epoch, (geological) period

**纪律 jìlǜ** N rule, regulation; discipline · MW 条

**纪年 jìnián** V to record events chronologically

**纪念 jìniàn** V·N to commemorate; souvenir, keepsake · MW 个

**纪实 jìshí** V·N to record actual events; eyewitness account

**纪要 jìyào** N (written) summary; minutes · MW 份
傻瓜没什么文化，因此特别重视别人帮他整理的会议**纪要**。*ShaGua is not educated, so he pays special attention to summaries that others make for him of the main points at conferences.*

**纪元 jìyuán** N beginning of an era · MW 个

**RELATED WORDS**

| | | |
|---|---|---|
| 世纪 163 | 年纪 182 | 军纪 489 |
| 法纪 686 | 经纪人 1110 | 新纪元 1638 |
| 广告经纪人 23 | 目无法纪 151 | |

---

**1102 纷** 紛　U+7EB7　TM **11** FM 丿

**fēn** ADJ confused; numerous; profuse

**纷繁 fēnfán** ADJ numerous and complicated

**纷纷 fēnfēn** ADV one after another; diverse, numerous and confused

**纷乱 fēnluàn** ADJ chaotic, numerous and disorderly

**纷争 fēnzhēng** V to dispute; to quarrel, to wrangle
傻瓜的工作本来就头绪**纷繁**，常常还得处理许多复杂的**纷争**。*ShaGua's work is already wide-ranging and complicated, but he also has to take care of many complex disputes.*

**RELATED WORDS**

| | |
|---|---|
| 纠纷 473 | 乱纷纷 901 |

---

**1103 纸** 紙　U+7EB8　TM **11** FM 丿

**zhǐ** N paper

**纸板 zhǐbǎn** N cardboard · MW 张、块

**纸币 zhǐbì** N paper money/currency, bill, banknote · MW 张

**纸浆 zhǐjiāng** N paper pulp · MW 桶

**纸巾 zhǐjīn** N facial tissue; paper towel · MW 张、盒

**纸牌 zhǐpái** N playing card; poker · MW 张

**纸烟 zhǐyān** N cigarette · MW 支

**纸张 zhǐzhāng** N paper · MW 沓

**RELATED WORDS**

| 手纸 104 | 画纸 719 | 面纸 721 |
| 砂纸 733 | 图纸 761 | 厕纸 846 |
| 便纸 865 | 信纸 869 | 报纸 1010 |
| 宣纸 1138 | 蜡纸 1780 | 剪纸 1816 |
| 壁纸 1920 | 卫生纸 82 | 方格纸 220 |

---

## 1104 纺 紡  U+7EBA TM **11** FM 丿

**fǎng** V·N to spin; thin silk cloth

**纺织 fǎngzhī** V to spin and weave

**RELATED WORDS**

| 毛纺 183 | 棉纺 1670 | 混纺 1739 |

---

## 1105 线 綫 U+7EBF TM **11** FM 丿

**xiàn** N thread; string; wire; cord; line; [shaped like a line]

**线路 xiànlù** N route; line; circuit · MW 条

**线索 xiànsuǒ** N clue, lead; thread; trail · MW 条
这是破案的唯一线索。 *This is the only lead we have in this case.*

**线条 xiàntiáo** N line, outline; streak · MW 根

**线性 xiànxìng** N linear, linearity (mathematics)

**RELATED WORDS**

| 干线 13 | 天线 25 | 支线 92 |
| 无线 139 | 无线电 139 | 无线电话 139 |
| 占线 153 | 全线 172 | 毛线 183 |
| 在线 188 | 内线 191 | 电线 263 |
| 曲线 272 | 光线 491 | 岸线 537 |
| 直线 609 | 纱线 639 | 阵线 809 |
| 牵线 853 | 底线 916 | 经线 1110 |
| 钓线 1124 | 沿线 1165 | 前线 1329 |
| 视线 1362 | 热线 1390 | 射线 1467 |
| 航线 1717 | 路线 1785 | 水平线 159 |
| 飞行航线 81 | 统一战线 1601 | |

---

## 1106 组 組 U+7EC4 TM **11** FM 丿

**zǔ** V·N·MW to organize, to form; group; section; [measure word for series, sets, rows (batteries, etc.)]

**组成 zǔchéng** V to form; to compose

**组合 zǔhé** V·N to constitute, to compose; to assemble, to put/bring together; combination · MW 个

优化**组**合能提高工作效率。 *Organizing labor optimally can promote efficiency.*

**组件 zǔjiàn** N package; module; component · MW 个

**组织 zǔzhī** V·N to organize, to form; organization; system · MW 个
老师经常**组织**学生到中国城去练口语。 *Teachers often organize students to practice Chinese in Chinatown.*

**组织系统 zǔzhīxìtǒng** N organization; system · MW 个、套

**组装 zǔzhuāng** V to assemble, to put together; to assemble and install

**RELATED WORDS**

| 小组 61 | 全组 172 | 分组 173 |
| 改组 516 | 班组 730 | 重组 839 |
| 软组织 889 | 词组 1353 | 党组 1626 |
| 编组 1866 | | |

---

## 1107 细 細 U+7EC6 TM **11** FM 丿

**xì** ADJ thin, fine, slender; narrow; meticulous, careful; detailed; minute, very small

**细胞 xìbāo** N cell · MW 个

**细长 xìcháng** ADJ slender, long and thin

**细节 xìjié** N details, specifics, particulars · MW 个
傻瓜看起来大大咧咧, 但对**细节**特别在意。 *ShaGua looks careless, but he pays close attention to detail.*

**细菌 xìjūn** N germ; bacterium; virus · MW 个

**细密 xìmì** ADJ finely woven; meticulous, careful

**细目 xìmù** N detailed catalog · MW 个

**细腻 xìnì** ADJ exquisite, fine and smooth

**细微 xìwēi** ADJ subtle, fine; sensitive (of gauges, instruments)

**细小 xìxiǎo** ADJ tiny, minute; trivial, petty

**细则 xìzé** N detailed rules and regulations · MW 条
傻瓜对章程的**细则**不太满意。 *ShaGua was not very happy about the detailed rules and regulations.*

**细致 xìzhì** ADJ fastidious, meticulous, scrupulous; precise, intricate

**RELATED WORDS**

| 毛细管 183 | 心细 232 | 奸细 329 |
| 红细胞 474 | 底细 916 | 详细 952 |
| 粗细 1364 | 精细 1832 | 癌细胞 1981 |
| 精打细算 1832 | 摸清底细 1665 | |

## 1108 织 織   U+7EC7   TM 11   FM 丿

**zhī** V to knit; to weave

**织布 zhībù** V to weave (cloth)

**织物 zhīwù** N cloth, fabric; textile · MW 块

**织针 zhīzhēn** N knitting needle · MW 枚

### RELATED WORDS

## 1109 终 終   U+7EC8   TM 11   FM 丿

**zhōng** V·N·ADJ·ADV to die; to end, to finish; death; whole, entire, all; throughout; in the end, eventually; after all

**终场 zhōngchǎng** V end (of a performance, a show, a game, etc.)

**终点 zhōngdiǎn** N end (of a journey); destination; finish line · MW 个

没到达**终点**之前，谁都有希望。
*Before reaching the finish line, everyone has hope.*

**终端 zhōngduān** N terminal · MW 个

**终极 zhōngjí** N final, ultimate · MW 个

**终究 zhōngjiū** ADV eventually, in the end; after all

这**终究**不是解决问题的办法。
*This is not a proper solution after all.*

**终局 zhōngjú** N end; outcome · MW 个

**终了 zhōngliǎo** V to end (of a period)

**终身 zhōngshēn** N one's whole life; for life, lifelong

傻瓜有一些**终身**难忘的朋友。
*ShaGua has some lifelong friends.*

**终生 zhōngshēng** N one's whole life; entire life

**终于 zhōngyú** ADV finally, at last; in the end; eventually, ultimately

**终止 zhōngzhǐ** V to stop, to end, to cease, to conclude

### RELATED WORDS

## 1110 经 經   U+7ECF   TM 11   FM 丿

**jīng** V·N·ADJ to undergo; to endure; to manage, to run; to deal/engage in; scripture; classics; channels; longitude; warp; menses, menstruation; regular; constant

读经 *to read (the) classics*

**经常 jīngcháng** ADV frequently, often; regularly

**经典 jīngdiǎn** N·ADJ classics; religious scripture; classical · MW 个

他**经常**读**经典**著作。 *He often reads the classics.*

**经费 jīngfèi** N expense, outlay, expenditure; funds · MW 笔

**经过 jīngguò** V·N to pass, to go through; experience; course

**经济 jīngjì** N economy; economic

**经济舱 jīngjìcāng** N economy class, coach · MW 个

**经济特区 jīngjìtèqū** N special economic zone (SEZ) · MW 个

**经纪人 jīngjìrén** N broker, middleman, agent · MW 个、名

**经理 jīnglǐ** N manager, director · MW 个、位、名

**经历 jīnglì** V·N to experience, to go through; experience, history; curriculum vitae, career · MW 个

**经络 jīngluò** N channels

**经贸 jīngmào** N economy and trade

**经商 jīngshāng** V to be in business

许多**经商**的**经理**都不坐**经济舱**。 *Many business managers don't sit in coach.*

**经手 jīngshǒu** V to handle / deal with personally

**经受 jīngshòu** V to experience, to undergo; to sustain, to withstand

**经线 jīngxiàn** N meridian, line of longitude

**经验 jīngyàn** N·V to experience, to go through · MW 个

**经营 jīngyíng** V to manage, to run, to operate; to deal in

傻瓜有丰富的**经营**的**经验**。 *ShaGua has extensive management experience.*

### RELATED WORDS

## 1111 转 轉　U+8F6C　TM **11** FM ノ

**zhuǎn** V to turn; to change, to shift; to pass on, to convey, to transfer (objects, letters, opinions, etc.)

**zhuàn** V·MW to turn, to revolve; to rotate; to stroll; [measure word for circles, revolutions, etc.]

**转变 zhuǎnbiàn** V to change, to transform
改革制度可以是一瞬间的事，但**转变**观念则是长期的、痛苦的。*Reforming a system can take only moments, but changing beliefs can be slow and painful.*

**转播 zhuǎnbō** V to relay (a radio/TV broadcast)

**转达 zhuǎndá** V to pass on, to convey

**转动 zhuǎndòng** V to turn (around); to rotate

**转发 zhuǎnfā** V to transmit; to reprint (an article from another publication)

**转告 zhuǎngào** V to transmit, to pass on (a message)

**转化 zhuǎnhuà** V to change, to transform

**转换 zhuǎnhuàn** V to change, to transform; to convert

**转机 zhuǎnjī** N favorable turn of events, turn for the better · MW 个、次
请你**转告**她：**转机**是稍纵即逝的。*Please pass this on to her: The opportunity for change is fleeting.*

**转交 zhuǎnjiāo** V to transmit, to pass on

**转卖 zhuǎnmài** V to resell

**转让 zhuǎnràng** V to transfer (possession)

**转身 zhuǎnshēn** V to turn around

**转手 zhuǎnshǒu** V to resell, to pass on
他**转身**就把刚**转让**得来的车**转手**卖掉了。*He quickly turned around and resold the car that had just been transferred into his possession.*

**转述 zhuǎnshù** V to pass on (a story); as told by another

**转送 zhuǎnsòng** V to transfer, to pass on; to make a present of what one has been given

**转托 zhuǎntuō** V to delegate (a task)

**转弯 zhuǎnwān** V to turn (a corner), to make a turn

**转学 zhuǎnxué** V to transfer to another school (of a student)

**转眼 zhuǎnyǎn** ADV in an instant, in a flash
他**转眼**就把礼物给**转送**掉了。*In a flash, he made a present of what others had just given him.*

**转业 zhuǎnyè** V to change jobs; to transfer to civilian work

**转移 zhuǎnyí** V to transfer, to shift; to divert; to change, to transform

**转运 zhuǎnyùn** V to transfer, to transport; to have a change of luck

**转赠 zhuǎnzèng** V to make a present of what one has been given

**转折 zhuǎnzhé** N turn of events, turning point · MW 个

**转租 zhuǎnzū** V to sublet

**转向 zhuǎnxiàng** V to change direction, to turn (around)

**转悠 zhuànyou** V to turn; to stroll
别再**转悠**了，你面临的是人生重大的**转折**。*Stop meandering; you are facing a critical turning point in your life.*

### RELATED WORDS

| | | |
|---|---|---|
| 扭转 565 | 好转 627 | 运转 956 |
| 拨转 1015 | 周转 1068 | 急转弯 1426 |
| 目不转睛 151 | 晕头转向 1385 | |

## 1112 轮 輪　U+8F6E　TM **11** FM ノ

**lún** V·N·MW to take turns; wheel; [like a wheel]; ring; steamboat; [measure word for large round objects (moons, etc.) and for recurring events (years, etc.)]

**轮班 lúnbān** V (to work) in shifts

**轮船 lúnchuán** N steamboat, steamship · MW 艘

**轮机 lúnjī** N turbine · MW 台

**轮廓 lúnkuò** N contour, outline, profile; rough sketch · MW 个
这就是城市建设规划的大概**轮廓**。*This is a rough sketch of the city's construction plan.*

**轮流 lúnliú** V to take turns, to alternate

**轮胎 lúntāi** N tire · MW 个、对

**轮转 lúnzhuàn** V to rotate

### RELATED WORDS

| | | |
|---|---|---|
| 三轮车 9 | 车轮 114 | 年轮 182 |
| 齿轮 538 | 砂轮 733 | 前轮 1329 |
| 滑轮 1884 | | |

## 1113 轻 輕　U+8F7B　TM **11** FM ノ

**qīng** ADJ·V light (in weight); small (in number, degree, etc.); unimportant, insignificant; relaxed, not serious; gentle, soft; to belittle, to make light of; to slight, to neglect

**1113 轻 qīng** (continued)

轻便 **qīngbiàn** ADJ portable; handy; light

轻薄 **qīngbó** ADJ frivolous; flirtatious, given to philandering

轻敌 **qīngdí** ADJ underestimating the enemy

轻风 **qīngfēng** N light breeze · MW 阵

轻浮 **qīngfú** ADJ frivolous
**轻敌**就是**轻浮**的表现。*Taking your enemy lightly is a sign of your frivolous nature.*

轻工业 **qīnggōngyè** N light industry

轻快 **qīngkuài** ADJ brisk, lively; relaxed, lighthearted

轻蔑 **qīngmiè** V to be scornful/contemptuous

轻巧 **qīngqiǎo** ADJ skillful, handy, dexterous; light and easy, simple

轻生 **qīngshēng** V to commit suicide

轻声 **qīngshēng** ADV softly, in a gentle voice

轻视 **qīngshì** V to despise, to look down on; to take lightly
老师**轻视**学生是不道德的。*Looking down on students as a teacher is immoral.*

轻率 **qīngshuài** ADJ rash, hasty; thoughtless

轻松 **qīngsōng** ADJ relaxed; light

轻微 **qīngwēi** ADJ light, slight; trifling, trivial

轻信 **qīngxìn** V to be credulous

轻易 **qīngyì** ADV rashly; easily, lightly

轻音乐 **qīngyīnyuè** N light music · MW 段、首

轻元音 **qīngyuányīn** N weak vowel (linguistics) · MW 个

轻重 **qīngzhòng** N severity, degree; propriety, seriousness
你这人干事怎么没有一点**轻重**？*How can you handle things so indiscreetly?*

**RELATED WORDS**

年轻 182　　　看轻 841　　　减轻 1487
头重脚轻 128

---

**1114 较 較** U+8F83　TM **11** FM 丿

**jiào** V·ADV to compare; to dispute; to haggle, to quibble; clearly, obviously

较量 **jiàoliàng** V to compete (with); to measure up (against)
我不愿意跟他**较量**中文。*I don't want to put my Chinese up against his.*

**RELATED WORDS**

计较 240　　　比较 279　　　斤斤计较 50

---

**1115 饺 餃** U+997A　TM **11** FM 丿

**jiǎo** N dumpling

饺子 **jiǎozi** N dumpling · MW 个

---

**1116 饼 餅** U+997C　TM **11** FM 丿

**bǐng** N round flat cake; cookie; cake; pastry; [shaped like a cake]

饼干 **bǐnggān** N cookie; cracker · MW 块

**RELATED WORDS**

月饼 190　　　肉饼 437

---

**1117 的** U+7684　TM **11** FM 丿

**de** AUX of [used after a word/phrase to show possession/relation]

**dí** ADV indeed

的确 **díquè** ADV indeed, really, certainly
傻瓜**的确**有点傻。*ShaGua is certainly a little dumb.*

**RELATED WORDS**

目的 151　　　有的是 439　　　是的 754
什么的 63　　　他妈的 616　　　众矢之的 175

---

**1118 肌** U+808C　TM **11** FM 丿

**jī** N flesh; muscle

肌肤 **jīfū** N muscle and skin; close relation

肌肉 **jīròu** N muscle; muscle and flesh · MW 块

肌体 **jītǐ** N (human) body · MW 个

**RELATED WORDS**

心肌 232　　　腹肌 1869

---

**1119 肿 腫** U+80BF　TM **11** FM 丿

**zhǒng** V·N to be swollen, to bloat; tumor

肿瘤 **zhǒngliú** N tumor · MW 个

肿胀 **zhǒngzhàng** V to swell, to be swollen

**RELATED WORDS**

发肿 311　　　红肿 474　　　脓肿 1605
鼻青脸肿 1794

**1120** 胀 脹   U+80C0   TM **11** FM ノ

**zhàng** V to expand, to grow (in size), to swell; to be bloated

胀感 **zhànggǎn** N puffiness

RELATED WORDS

发胀 311      肿胀 1119      腹胀 1869

**1121** 胖   U+80D6   TM **11** FM ノ

**pàng** ADJ fat (of humans), stout, plump

胖子 **pàngzi** N fat person; butterball, fatso · MW 个、名

傻瓜的小儿子是一个小胖子。*ShaGua's younger son is a little fatso.*

RELATED WORDS

发胖 311      肥胖 1459

**1122** 胜 勝   U+80DC   TM **11** FM ノ

**shèng** V·N·ADJ to win; to succeed; to defeat; to be better than; victory; success; superb, wonderful

胜败 **shèngbài** N victory and/or defeat

胜负 **shèngfù** N success and failure; outcome

胜负是兵家常事。*Victory and defeat are commonplace for military commanders.*

胜利 **shènglì** V·N to win, to be victorious; to be successful; victory; success · MW 个

只能胜利不能失败的人是没有出息的。*People who can only face victory but not failure are good-for-nothing.*

胜诉 **shèngsù** V to win a lawsuit

胜仗 **shèngzhàng** N victory, triumph · MW 个

RELATED WORDS

决胜 340     名胜 426     优胜 447
取胜 520     好胜 627     获胜 1000
战胜 1044     制胜 1130     数不胜数 1637
引人入胜 371

**1123** 邻 鄰   U+90BB   TM **11** FM ノ

**lín** N·ADJ neighbor; neighboring; adjacent; close, near

邻邦 **línbāng** N neighboring country · MW 个

邻接 **línjiē** V to border on

邻近 **línjìn** ADJ·N close to, near, nearby, adjacent to; vicinity

邻居 **línjū** N neighbor · MW 个

邻里 **línlǐ** N neighbor; neighborhood · MW 个

傻瓜在邻里很受欢迎。*ShaGua is very popular in his neighborhood.*

RELATED WORDS

比邻 279      相邻 805

**1124** 钓 釣   U+9493   TM **11** FM ノ

**diào** V to fish (with a rod/pole)

钓饵 **diào'ěr** N bait · MW 个

钓竿 **diàogān** N fishing rod · MW 根

钓钩 **diàogōu** N fishhook · MW 枚

钓线 **diàoxiàn** N fishline · MW 根

钓鱼 **diàoyú** V to fish, to go fishing

给我鱼，不如教我钓鱼。*Give me a fish, I will eat today; teach me to fish, I will eat for a lifetime.*

RELATED WORD

垂钓 430

**1125** 钟 鍾   U+949F   TM **11** FM ノ

**zhōng** N clock; time (in hours and minutes); bell

钟爱 **zhōng'ài** V to love; to adore, to cherish (one's offspring, etc.)

钟表 **zhōngbiǎo** N timepieces, clocks and watches · MW 只

钟点 **zhōngdiǎn** N hour · MW 个

钟楼 **zhōnglóu** N bell tower; clock tower · MW 座

钟情 **zhōngqíng** V to fall in love; to be deeply in love

傻瓜太太对傻瓜一见钟情。*Mrs. ShaGua fell in love with ShaGua at first sight.*

钟头 **zhōngtóu** N hour · MW 个

RELATED WORDS

时钟 586     座钟 920     闹钟 1323
警钟 1987     生物钟 107     每分钟 837

## 1126 铁 鐵 U+94C1 TM 11 FM ノ

**tiě** N·ADJ iron; weapon; toughness; ferocity; solid, unalterable

铁板 **tiěbǎn** N hot plate (for cooking) · MW 块

铁道 **tiědào** N railway, railroad · MW 条

铁管 **tiěguǎn** N iron pipe · MW 根

铁匠 **tiějiàng** N blacksmith · MW 个、名

铁路 **tiělù** N railway, railroad · MW 条
> 在中国，**铁路**是经济的大动脉。 *Railways are the big economic arteries of China.*

铁丝 **tiěsī** N wire · MW 根

铁塔 **tiětǎ** N iron tower/pagoda · MW 座

铁锨 **tiěxiān** N shovel · MW 把

**RELATED WORDS**

地铁 772     钢铁 1299     斩钉截铁 646

## 1127 敌 敵 U+654C TM 11 FM ノ

**dí** N·V enemy; to oppose, to resist; to match, to equal

敌对 **díduì** ADJ hostile, antagonistic, belligerent

敌国 **díguó** N enemy state · MW 个
> 多一个**敌国**，少无数朋友。 *Add one enemy state, lose countless friends.*

敌军 **díjūn** N enemy troops, hostile forces · MW 支

敌情 **díqíng** N situation in the enemy camp; intelligence about the enemy · MW 份

敌人 **dírén** N enemy · MW 个
> 只有永久的利益，没有永久的**敌人**。 *Benefits are forever, but not enemies.*

敌我 **díwǒ** N the enemy and us

敌意 **díyì** N hostility, animosity

**RELATED WORDS**

| | | |
|---|---|---|
| 天敌 25 | 公敌 103 | 匹敌 269 |
| 杀敌 317 | 仇敌 319 | 死敌 510 |
| 政敌 517 | 劲敌 736 | 论敌 947 |
| 投敌 1008 | 轻敌 1113 | 情敌 1491 |

## 1128 卸 U+5378 TM 11 FM ノ

**xiè** V to unload; to remove, to take off

卸车 **xièchē** V to unload (goods, etc.) from a vehicle

卸货 **xièhuò** V to unload

**RELATED WORD**

拆卸 572     装卸 1476

## 1129 叙 U+53D9 TM 11 FM ノ

**xù** V to talk, to chat; to narrate, to recount, to relate; to assess, to appraise; to preface

叙别 **xùbié** V to have a farewell talk

叙旧 **xùjiù** V to talk about the old days, to reminisce
> 叙旧往往是快乐的，**叙别**总是伤感的。 *Talking about the past is usually a happy thing, but a farewell is always sad.*

叙利亚 **Xùlìyà** N Syria

叙事 **xùshì** V to narrate, to recount

叙述 **xùshù** V to narrate, to recount, to relate

**RELATED WORD**

记叙 946

## 1130 制 製 U+5236 TM 11 FM ノ

**zhì** V·N to make, to manufacture, to produce; to work out, to formulate; to restrict, to control; to govern; system; institution

中国**制**造 *made in China*

节**制** *to control*

公**制** *metric system*

制版 **zhìbǎn** V to make a printing plate

制裁 **zhìcái** V to impose sanctions against; to punish

制定 **zhìdìng** V to establish, to draw up, to formulate

制订 **zhìdìng** V to establish, to work out, to formulate

制动 **zhìdòng** V to apply the brake(s)

制度 **zhìdù** N (political) system; institution · MW 个、种
> 我们需要**制定**规章**制度**。 *We need to draw up regulations and systems.*

制服 **zhìfú** N·V uniform; to subdue, to bring under control · MW 套
> 中国的许多学校规定学生穿**制服**。 *Many Chinese schools make their students wear uniforms.*
> 傻瓜**制服**了罪犯。 *ShaGua subdued the criminal.*

制片人 **zhìpiànrén** N (movie) producer · MW 个、位、名

制品 **zhìpǐn** N product; merchandise · MW 个

制胜 **zhìshèng** V to win; to subdue

制造 **zhìzào** V to make, to manufacture, to produce; to create

制止 **zhìzhǐ** V to prevent, to restrain, to stop
老师无法**制止**学生的思维。*Teachers are unable to control their students' thoughts.*

制作 **zhìzuò** V to fabricate

**RELATED WORDS**

| 公制 103 | 专制 155 | 币制 181 |
|---|---|---|
| 压制 201 | 节制 275 | 体制 325 |
| 仿制 450 | 英制 556 | 法制 686 |
| 研制 734 | 克制 738 | 牵制 853 |
| 抑制 1007 | 复制 1059 | 创制 1131 |
| 试制 1180 | 控制 1406 | 限制 1417 |
| 熏制 1690 | 税制 1705 | 精制 1832 |
| 管制 1861 | 编制 1866 | 强制 1896 |
| 二进制 2 | 十进制 3 | 全日制 172 |
| 百分制 242 | 先发制人 422 | 责任制 525 |

---

**1131** 创 創    U+521B    TM **11** FM ノ

**chuàng** V to wound, to injure; to cut; to establish, to create; to begin, to initiate

创办 **chuàngbàn** V to establish, to found, to launch

创见 **chuàngjiàn** N original idea, creative thought · MW 个
傻瓜不是一个很有**创见**的人。*ShaGua is not a very creative person.*

创建 **chuàngjiàn** V to establish, to found, to create

创举 **chuàngjǔ** N pioneering work · MW 个

创立 **chuànglì** V to establish, to found, to create, to originate

创始 **chuàngshǐ** V to found, to originate
中国是联合国的**创始**国之一。*China is a founding member of the United Nations.*

创新 **chuàngxīn** V·N to come up with new ideas; creation; innovation · MW 个

创业 **chuàngyè** V to do pioneering work; to carve out a career

创造 **chuàngzào** V to create and produce

创造性 **chuàngzàoxìng** N creativity
不仅要努力工作, 还要有**创造性**。*Besides hard work, creativity is also necessary.*

创制 **chuàngzhì** V to create and produce

**RELATED WORDS**

| 首创 924 | 独创 1095 |
|---|---|

---

**1132** 彩    U+5F69    TM **11** FM ノ

**cǎi** N·V color; lottery prize; winnings (from a game); applause; to cheer, to applaud

彩车 **cǎichē** N float (in a parade) · MW 辆

彩带 **cǎidài** N colored ribbon · MW 条、根

彩绘 **cǎihuì** V·N to paint with colors; colored drawing

彩票 **cǎipiào** N lottery ticket · MW 张
买**彩票**正常, 天天傻等着中彩就不正常了。*It is normal to buy a lottery ticket, but not normal to idly wait for the prize day after day.*

彩色 **cǎisè** N color; multicolored

彩霞 **cǎixiá** N rosy clouds · MW 片

**RELATED WORDS**

| 五彩 79 | 云彩 80 | 水彩 159 |
|---|---|---|
| 光彩 491 | 油彩 683 | 挂彩 796 |
| 虹彩 823 | 色彩 831 | 摸彩 1665 |
| 剪彩 1816 | 精彩 1832 | 张灯结彩 1208 |

---

**1133** 育    U+80B2    TM **11** FM 丶

**yù** V to give birth to; to raise; to educate

育儿 **yù'ér** V to give birth to (children); to educate
国家的未来不在政客手中, 而在那些**育儿**的父母手中。*The country's future is not in the hands of the politicians, but under the control of parents educating their children.*

育种 **yùzhǒng** V to breed (plants, animals)

**RELATED WORDS**

| 生育 107 | 节育 275 | 发育 311 |
|---|---|---|
| 体育 325 | 养育 670 | 保育 868 |
| 孕育 971 | 教育 1424 | 智育 1581 |
| 德育 1923 | 生儿育女 107 | 盲哑教育 906 |

---

**1134** 哀    U+54C0    TM **11** FM 丶

**āi** N·V·ADJ·ADV sorrow, grief; pity; to grieve (for), to mourn; to pity; sad; sorrowfully; pitifully

哀愁 **āichóu** ADJ sad, sorrowful

哀悼 **āidào** V to grieve (for), to mourn

哀乐 **āilè** N grief and joy

哀求 **āiqiú** V to beg, to entreat

哀伤 **āishāng** ADJ sad; heartbroken

哀思 **āisī** N grief

**1134 哀 āi** (continued)

哀叹 **āitàn** V to lament, to sigh

哀求别人、哀叹自己，都不是强者的风范。
*Begging and self-pity are not qualities of a strong person.*

哀乐 **āiyuè** N funeral music · MW 段、曲

**RELATED WORD**

悲哀 1532

---

**1135 享** U+4EAB TM **11** FM 丶

**xiǎng** V to enjoy

享福 **xiǎngfú** V to live comfortably

享乐 **xiǎnglè** V to lead a life of pleasure

享受 **xiǎngshòu** V to enjoy (rights, benefits, etc.)
没有痛苦，就没有享受。*Without suffering, there can be no enjoyment.*

享有 **xiǎngyǒu** V to enjoy (rights, privileges, etc.)

**RELATED WORD**

久享盛名 45

---

**1136 官** U+5B98 TM **11** FM 丶

**guān** N (government) official; officer

官邸 **guāndǐ** N official residence · MW 座

官方 **guānfāng** N official, governmental

官僚 **guānliáo** N bureaucrat · MW 个、名

官司 **guānsi** N lawsuit · MW 场
在中国，很少有官员吃官司。*There are very few government officials who have lawsuits against them in China.*

官衔 **guānxián** N official title · MW 个

官员 **guānyuán** N government official · MW 个、名
官员不一定是官僚，但普通人也可能有官僚主义。*An official may not be a bureaucrat, but ordinary people may be bureaucratic.*

官职 **guānzhí** N government post; official position

**RELATED WORDS**

| | | |
|---|---|---|
| 升官发财 47 | 五官 79 | 长官 93 |
| 半官方 127 | 打官腔 289 | 打官司 289 |
| 非官方 378 | 军官 489 | 达官贵人 505 |
| 法官 686 | 做官 1282 | 感官 1860 |
| 器官 1963 | 中国官话 86 | 检察官 1033 |

---

**1137 宠** 寵 U+5BA0 TM **11** FM 丶

**chǒng** V to dote on, to pamper, to spoil; to favor

宠爱 **chǒng'ài** V to dote on, to pamper

宠儿 **chǒng'ér** N pet; favorite · MW 个
宠儿往往被宠坏了。*The pet has been spoiled rotten.*

**RELATED WORDS**

失宠 106          受宠若惊 844

---

**1138 宣** U+5BA3 TM **11** FM 丶

**xuān** V·N to announce, to declare; to summon to the imperial court (of a king, an emperor); Xuan (rice) paper

宣布 **xuānbù** V to announce, to declare

宣传 **xuānchuán** V to publicize; to disseminate

宣告 **xuāngào** V to declare, to proclaim
这个试验宣告失败。*This experiment has been declared a failure.*

宣判 **xuānpàn** V to pronounce/pass judgment

宣誓 **xuānshì** V to take an oath; to make a vow/pledge

宣言 **xuānyán** N declaration, statement; manifesto · MW 个
他们宣读了一个庄严的独立宣言。*They made a solemn declaration of independence.*

宣纸 **xuānzhǐ** N Xuan paper (made in Xuancheng and used in traditional Chinese painting and calligraphy) · MW 张

---

**1139 室** U+5BA4 TM **11** FM 丶

**shì** N room; house; administrative/working unit

室内 **shìnèi** N indoor; interior

室外 **shìwài** N outdoor; exterior, outside

室温 **shìwēn** N room temperature

**RELATED WORDS**

| | | |
|---|---|---|
| 王室 27 | 斗室 71 | 诊室 709 |
| 画室 719 | 卧室 826 | 皇室 858 |
| 宗室 910 | 教室 1424 | 温室 1627 |
| 寝室 1878 | 候车室 1086 | 候机室 1086 |
| 阅览室 1727 | | |

## 1140 宰 U+5BB0 TM 11 FM ╲

**zǎi** V to slaughter; to overcharge; to govern, to rule

屠宰 *to butcher*
宰相 *prime minister in feudal China*
主宰 *to dominate*

**宰割 zǎigē** V to oppress and exploit

### RELATED WORD

主宰 124

## 1141 宾 賓 U+5BBE TM 11 FM ╲

**bīn** N guest, visitor

**宾馆 bīnguǎn** N hotel · MW 家、间
**宾客 bīnkè** N guest, visitor · MW 个、名
**宾语 bīnyǔ** N object (grammar) · MW 个
**宾至如归 bīnzhìrúguī** EXP to feel at home (in a hotel, etc.)

好的**宾馆**能让**宾客**有**宾至如归**的感觉。
*A good hotel should make its guests feel at home.*

### RELATED WORDS

卡宾枪 36　　主宾席 124　　外宾 218
来宾 260　　国宾 542　　贵宾 985

## 1142 究 U+7A76 TM 11 FM ╲

**jiū** V·ADV to investigate; to study carefully; actually, really; after all

研**究** *to research*
追**究** *to look into*
终**究** *eventually*

**究竟 jiūjìng** N·ADV outcome, result; actually, really; after all

你**究竟**还学不学汉语？ *Are you actually keeping up with your study of Chinese?*

### RELATED WORDS

讲究 501　　考究 530　　研究 734
终究 1109　　探究 1404　　追究 1507

## 1143 窄 U+7A84 TM 11 FM ╲

**zhǎi** ADJ narrow; narrow-minded, petty; hard up, impoverished

**窄道 zhǎidào** N narrow path · MW 条
**窄路 zhǎilù** N narrow road · MW 条

### RELATED WORDS

宽窄 1618　　冤家路窄 1729

## 1144 肩 U+80A9 TM 11 FM ╲

**jiān** N·V shoulder; to undertake; to carry on the shoulder

**肩膀 jiānbǎng** N shoulder · MW 副
傻瓜有一副厚实的**肩膀**。*ShaGua has broad shoulders.*

### RELATED WORDS

并肩 225　　披肩 1011

## 1145 房 U+623F TM 11 FM ╲

**fáng** N house; room; [house-like structure]; branch of a family; shop, store

**房产 fángchǎn** N real estate · MW 处
**房地产 fángdìchǎn** N real estate · MW 处
**房地契 fángdìqì** N title deed · MW 份
**房东 fángdōng** N landlord, landlady · MW 个、名
**房间 fángjiān** N room · MW 个
**房屋 fángwū** N house; building · MW 间
傻瓜是一名**房东**，因为他有一间**房屋**出租给别人。*ShaGua is also a landlord, since he has a house for rent.*
**房主 fángzhǔ** N homeowner · MW 个、名
**房子 fángzi** N house; building · MW 间
**房租 fángzū** N rent · MW 笔

### RELATED WORDS

厂房 7　　　　文房四宝 70
平房 78　　　门房 130
伙房 214　　　产房 219
住房 324　　　瓦房 356
私房钱 471　　库房 482
牢房 488　　　同房 541
班房 730　　　卧房 826
乳房 1308　　客房 1316
病房 1327　　洞房 1338
票房 1367　　药房 1392
楼房 1567　　厨房 1584
新房 1638　　暖房 1675
蜂房 1682　　健身房 1589

## 1146 麻 · U+9EBB · TM **11** FM 丶

**má** V·N·ADJ  to be numb, to tingle; linen; fiber crop, hemp; sesame; anesthesia; numbed, tingling; rough, coarse

**麻痹 mábì** ADJ·V  careless; paralyzed; to lower one's guard

**麻布 mábù** N  sackcloth · MW 块

**麻袋 mádài** N  gunnysack · MW 个

**麻烦 máfan** ADJ·N·V  troublesome, problematic; inconvenient; trouble; to trouble, to bother · MW 个

你**麻烦**大了！ *You got into big trouble!*

不用太**麻烦**你了！ *Don't bother if it's too much trouble.*

**麻将 májiàng** N  mahjong (a game with tiles similar to a card game) · MW 副

**麻利 máli** ADJ  quick and neat

傻瓜太太做事非常**麻利**。 *Mrs. ShaGua is very quick and neat when she does things.*

**麻木 mámù** ADJ  numb; unfeeling

**麻雀 máquè** N  sparrow; mahjong (bird) · MW 只

**麻绳 máshéng** N  hemp rope · MW 条

**麻油 máyóu** N  sesame oil · MW 滴

**麻疹 mázhěn** N  measles

**麻子 mázi** N  pockmark; person with a pockmarked face · MW 颗

傻瓜小时候出过**麻疹**，所以脸上有几颗小**麻子**。 *ShaGua got the measles when he was a child, so there are a few small pockmarks on his face.*

**麻醉 mázuì** V  to anesthetize; to drug; to lull; to poison the mind of

### RELATED WORDS

亚麻 136　　　发麻 311　　　肉麻 437
找麻烦 567　　针刺麻醉 477

## 1147 疯 疯 · U+75AF · TM **11** FM 丶

**fēng** ADJ·V  mad, crazy, insane; wild; to play without inhibition; to spindle (of plants)

**疯癫 fēngdiān** ADJ  mad, insane

**疯狗 fēnggǒu** N  mad/rapid dog · MW 条

别理她，那是一条**疯狗**。 *Don't mind her; she's crazy.*

**疯狂 fēngkuáng** ADJ  crazy; wild

**疯人院 fēngrényuàn** N  insane asylum · MW 间、家

**疯子 fēngzi** N  lunatic, madman, maniac · MW 个

别理他，那是一个**疯子**。 *Forget him; he's a madman.*

### RELATED WORD

发疯 311

## 1148 疼 · U+75BC · TM **11** FM 丶

**téng** V  to hurt, to ache; to love, to be fond of

**疼爱 téng'ài** V  to love dearly

傻瓜太太常常分不清**疼爱**和溺爱的区别。 *Mrs. ShaGua often confuses the difference between loving kids dearly and spoiling them.*

**疼痛 téngtòng** ADJ  sore, achy

### RELATED WORDS

头疼 128　　　心疼 232

## 1149 痒 癢 · U+75D2 · TM **11** FM 丶

**yǎng** ADJ  itch; tickle

**痒疹 yǎngzhěn** N  rash

### RELATED WORDS

止痒 41　　　发痒 311
痛痒 1725

## 1150 闷  · U+95F7 · TM **11** FM 丶

**mēn** ADJ·V  stuffy; to shut oneself/(someone) in(doors); to cover tightly

**mèn** ADJ  low, depressed; muffled (of sound); bored; sealed, tightly closed

**闷气 mēnqì** ADJ  stuffy

**闷热 mēnrè** ADJ  muggy, sultry; hot and stuffy

这是一个**闷热**的季节。 *It was a hot, muggy season.*

**闷声不响 mēnshēngbùxiǎng** EXP  to remain silent

**闷气 mènqì** ADJ  low, depressed

### RELATED WORDS

苦闷 555　　　忧闷 693
沉闷 1166　　愁闷 1691
胸闷 1709　　解闷 1928

## 1151 闻 聞   U+95FB   TM **11** FM 丶

**wén** V·N·ADJ to smell, to sniff at; to hear; news; story; reputation; well-known, famous

**闻风而动 wénfēng'érdòng** EXP to respond immediately to a call; to act at once on hearing the news

**闻名 wénmíng** ADJ·V famous; to know by reputation

傻瓜的新闻太多, 因此远近**闻名**。 *There is often a lot of news concerning ShaGua, so his name is familiar near and far.*

### RELATED WORDS

| | | |
|---|---|---|
| 久闻大名 45 | 丑闻 85 | 与闻 158 |
| 见闻 267 | 传闻 452 | 奇闻 854 |
| 要闻 969 | 新闻 1638 | 新闻记者 1638 |
| 趣闻 1783 | 广播新闻 23 | 头条新闻 128 |
| 桃色新闻 1243 | 前所未闻 1329 | |

## 1152 弟   U+5F1F   TM **11** FM 丶

**dì** N younger brother; younger male cousin/in-law

**弟弟 dìdi** N younger brother; younger male cousin · MW 个

**弟妹 dìmèi** N younger brother's wife; younger brother/sister · MW 个

**弟兄 dìxiong** N brother; friend, companion · MW 个

**弟子 dìzǐ** N disciple; apprentice

中国有不少教授把自己的学生称为 "**弟子**"。 *Quite a few professors improperly refer to their students as "disciples" in China.*

### RELATED WORDS

| | | |
|---|---|---|
| 子弟 83 | 兄弟 382 | 师弟 396 |
| 徒弟 873 | 把兄弟 1006 | 难兄难弟 974 |

## 1153 益   U+76CA   TM **11** FM 丶

**yì** V·N·ADV to benefit, to profit; advantage; increase; increasingly, even more

**益处 yìchù** N benefit, profit, advantage · MW 个

**益友 yìyǒu** N friend and mentor · MW 位

**益友**的最大**益处**是给傻瓜提供无私的忠告。 *The greatest benefit gained by ShaGua from friends and mentors was advice.*

### RELATED WORDS

| | | |
|---|---|---|
| 日益 96 | 公益 103 | 收益 282 |
| 权益 292 | 有益 439 | 利益 472 |
| 受益 844 | 效益 965 | 损益 1401 |
| 良师益友 656 | 既得利益 1572 | 羞惭 1154 |

## 1154 羞   U+7F9E   TM **11** FM 丶

**xiū** V·ADJ·N to shame, to disgrace; shy, bashful; shame, disgrace

**羞惭 xiūcán** ADJ ashamed

**羞耻 xiūchǐ** ADJ ashamed

如果你的一生都没有感到**羞惭**的时候, 不是你太伟大, 而是你不知**羞耻**。 *If you have never felt ashamed of anything in your life, it does not necessarily mean you are great, but that you lack a sense of shame.*

**羞答答 xiūdādā** ADV shyly, coyly

**羞怯 xiūqiè** V to be shy/timid

**羞人 xiūrén** V to feel ashamed/embarrassed

**羞辱 xiūrǔ** V·N to humiliate, to shame, to dishonor; humiliation

### RELATED WORDS

| | | |
|---|---|---|
| 含羞 592 | 怕羞 694 | 恼羞成怒 931 |
| 害羞 1319 | 遮羞 1831 | |

## 1155 学 學   U+5B66   TM **11** FM 丶

**xué** V·N to study, to learn; to imitate, to mimic; learning, knowledge, scholarship; school; science; subject

**学报 xuébào** N academic journal · MW 期

**学费 xuéfèi** N tuition · MW 笔

最近几年, 几乎所有的学校年年涨**学费**。 *In recent years, almost all schools have increased their tuition.*

**学分 xuéfēn** N academic credit · MW 个

**学会 xuéhuì** N·V (learned) society, (scholarly) association; to learn, to master · MW 个

**学籍 xuéjí** N status as a student

**学科 xuékē** N branch of learning, subject, discipline · MW 门

**学历 xuélì** N educational record/level/background · MW 个

没有人知道傻瓜真正的**学历**, 只知道他在上夜校。 *Nobody knows ShaGua's real educational background, but everybody knows that he is attending night school.*

## 1155 学 xué (continued)

学龄 xuélíng   N   school age

学期 xuéqī   N   term, semester · MW 个

学生 xuésheng   N   student, pupil · MW 个、名

学时 xuéshí   N   class/credit hour · MW 个

学士 xuéshì   N   bachelor (degree); scholar · MW 个、名

学术 xuéshù   N   learning; academic

学位 xuéwèi   N   academic degree · MW 个

学问 xuéwen   N   learning, knowledge · MW 门

学习 xuéxí   V   to study, to learn; to imitate, to learn from

学校 xuéxiào   N   school · MW 个、间、所

学业 xuéyè   N   schoolwork, studies

学院 xuéyuàn   N   college; academy; educational institution · MW 个、间、所

学者 xuézhě   N   scholar · MW 个、位、名

傻瓜不是一个**学者**, 但是是一个爱**学习**的人。 *ShaGua is not a scholar, but simply a person who loves to study.*

**RELATED WORDS**

| | | |
|---|---|---|
| 入学 5 | 工学院 12 | 上学 14 |
| 大学 20 | 大学生 20 | 升学 47 |
| 力学 59 | 小学 61 | 文学 70 |
| 文学语言 70 | 中学 86 | 失学 106 |
| 史学 186 | 办学 195 | 休学 213 |
| 化学 215 | 化学分析 215 | 自学 305 |
| 求学 376 | 医学 389 | 讲学 501 |
| 同学 541 | 科学 642 | 科学院 642 |
| 法学 686 | 助学金 818 | 治学 935 |
| 初学 963 | 放学 964 | 转学 1111 |
| 哲学 1219 | 教学 1424 | 退学 1508 |
| 逃学 1509 | 博学 1549 | 留学 1582 |
| 停学 1588 | 商学院 1612 | 数学 1637 |
| 就学 1836 | 天文学 25 | 才疏学浅 39 |
| 生理学 107 | 生物学 107 | 市场学 332 |
| 语言学 1501 | 统计学 1601 | 互教互学 135 |
| 社会科学 504 | | |

## 1156 尚    U+5C1A    TM 11   FM 丶

**shàng**   ADV·CONJ·V   still, yet; rather; to esteem, to value

尚且 shàngqiě   CONJ   still, yet; even

现在谈这个问题, **尚且**太早。 *It is still too early to discuss this issue.*

尚早 shàngzǎo   ADV   still too early

**RELATED WORDS**

礼尚往来 503     和尚 644

## 1157 尝 嘗    U+5C1D    TM 11   FM 丶

**cháng**   V·ADV   to taste; to experience; ever; once

尝试 chángshì   V   to attempt, to try

**尚**未**尝试**, 你怎么知道行不通? *You haven't tried it; how do you know that it doesn't work?*

尝一尝 chángyīcháng   EXP   taste

**RELATED WORDS**

未尝 88     何尝 619     品尝 1220

## 1158 拳    U+62F3    TM 11   FM 丶

**quán**   N·V   fist; boxing; punch; to twist, to curl up

拳打脚踢 quándǎjiǎotī   EXP   to beat up (LIT to punch and kick)

拳击 quánjī   N·V   boxing; to punch

拳头 quántou   N   fist · MW 个

傻瓜学过**拳击**, 因此有人以为傻瓜是被**拳头**打傻的。 *ShaGua used to box, so some believe he is punch-drunk.*

**RELATED WORDS**

打拳 289     猜拳 1594     握拳 1662
太极拳 53

## 1159 净    U+51C0    TM 11   FM 丶

**jìng**   ADJ·ADV·V·N   clean; empty, all gone, with nothing left; net (price, weight, etc.); only, merely, nothing but; to clean; to wash; painted-face role (opera)

净化 jìnghuà   V   to purify; to purge

**净化**环境是中国当前的一个重要任务。 *Cleaning the environment is currently a critical task in China.*

净亏 jìngkuī   N   net loss · MW 笔

净利 jìnglì   N   net profit · MW 笔

净水 jìngshuǐ   N   treated water · MW 杯

净余 jìngyú   N   remainder · MW 笔

净值 jìngzhí   N   net value/worth · MW 笔

这笔生意的**净值**还不到1000美元。 *The net value of this trade is less than $1000.*

净重 jìngzhòng   N   net weight

**RELATED WORDS**

干净 13     清净 1495     擦净 1985

## 1160 凑 U+51D1 TM 11 FM 丶

**còu** V to gather together; to collect; to assemble, to put/come together; to happen by chance; to take advantage of; to approach, to be near to

**凑合 còuhe** V to gather together, to collect; to improvise; to get by, to not be too bad

你们**凑合**在一起弄个乐队吧。*You are getting together to form a band.*

**凑巧 còuqiǎo** ADJ lucky; as luck would have it, by chance

**凑数 còushù** V to make do with

傻瓜的笛子还**凑合**，也就**凑数**吧。*ShaGua's flute playing is not too bad; let's just make do with him as part of the band.*

### RELATED WORDS
拼凑 794　　　紧凑 1537　　　七拼八凑 34

## 1161 将 将 U+5C06 TM 11 FM 丶

**jiāng** ADV·PREP·V·N just, short time ago; with, by, by means of; to take; to handle (a matter); to prod, to provoke; to advance; general

**jiàng** N·V general, commander-in-chief; to command (troops)

将兵 *to command troops*

**将近 jiāngjìn** ADV almost, nearly

**将就 jiāngjiu** V to make do, to put up with, to accept (reluctantly)

乐队有**将近**二十人，至于水平，也就**将就**啦。*The band has nearly 20 members. As for its performance, it was only so-so.*

**将军 jiāngjūn** V·N to check (chess); to challenge; general; high-ranking officer · MW 个、位、名

"**将军！**" *"Check!"*

这是一名**将军**。*This is a general.*

**将来 jiānglái** N future

**将要 jiāngyào** ADV will, to be going to

据说，**将来**乐队**将要**增加到三十人。*They said the band will increase its membership to 30.*

**将领 jiànglǐng** N general · MW 个、位、名

### RELATED WORDS
少将 62　　　主将 124　　　即将 1047
麻将 1146

## 1162 柒 U+67D2 TM 11 FM 丶

**qī** NUM seven (capital form of the Chinese numeral)

## 1163 洒 灑 U+6D12 TM 11 FM 丶

**sǎ** V to sprinkle, to spray; to spill; to scatter; to litter

**洒泪 sǎlèi** V to shed tears

**洒水车 sǎshuǐchē** N sprinkler truck · MW 辆

**洒水机 sǎshuǐjī** N water sprayer · MW 台

### RELATED WORD
飘洒 1939

## 1164 泥 U+6CE5 TM 11 FM 丶

**ní** N mud, soft earth; paste; [like mud (mashed vegetables, fruit, etc.)]

**泥巴 níbā** N mud · MW 块、团

**泥灰 níhuī** N musky coal, marl (loose, crumbly clay) · MW 团

**泥浆 níjiāng** N mud; slurry · MW 团

**泥泞 nínìng** ADJ muddy; boggy

**泥沙 níshā** N silt · MW 堆

**泥土 nítǔ** N earth, soil · MW 堆

### RELATED WORDS
水泥 159　　　印泥 470　　　污泥 681
烂泥 702　　　拖泥带水 1396

## 1165 沿 U+6CBF TM 11 FM 丶

**yán** PREP·V·N along (a river, a road, the edge of something); to follow (a tradition, a pattern, etc.); to trim/border (with tape, ribbon, etc.); edge, border, side

**沿岸 yán'àn** N coastal area, waterfront; bank

**沿海 yánhǎi** N coast, seaboard

**沿路 yánlù** N along the way/road

**沿途 yántú** N along the road; throughout a journey

**沿线 yánxiàn** N along the way/line

**1165** 沿 **yán** (continued)

沿用 **yányòng** V to continue to use (an old method/system, etc.)

沿途看到的农民, 都在**沿用**古老的耕作方法。 *Throughout the journey, all the peasants we saw still employ the old method of tilling the land.*

**RELATED WORD**

边沿 710

---

**1166** 沉     U+6C89     TM **11** FM 丶

**chén** V·ADJ to sink (in water); to submerge, to immerse; to become serious/solemn; to feel heavy/uncomfortable; deep (of degree), profound; heavy

沉淀 **chéndiàn** V·N to settle, to precipitate; sediment

沉积 **chénjī** V to deposit, to silt up

中国文化**沉淀**了不少精华, 也**沉积**了许多糟粕。 *Chinese culture produces many exquisite items, but also leaves behind a lot of soot on the way.*

沉寂 **chénjì** ADJ quiet, still; no news

沉浸 **chénjìn** V to immerse, to soak (in water)

沉闷 **chénmèn** ADJ dreary (of weather, atmosphere, etc.); depressed (of mood)

这部电影有些**沉闷**。 *This movie is a little bit dull.*

沉没 **chénmò** V to sink, to submerge

沉默 **chénmò** ADJ·V quiet, silent; reticent; to keep silent

沉睡 **chénshuì** V to be fast asleep

沉思 **chénsī** V to contemplate, to ponder; to meditate

沉痛 **chéntòng** ADJ deep grief/remorse; severe, grave; bitter

沉重 **chénzhòng** ADJ serious, heavy, somber

傻瓜在**沉思**自己的失误, 看起来既**沉痛**又**沉重**。 *ShaGua pondered the lessons, and looked to be in profound grief.*

沉着 **chénzhuó** ADJ calm, coolheaded

沉醉 **chénzuì** V to become intoxicated; to be drunk

大家都**沉醉**在节日的欢乐之中, 只有傻瓜在**沉思**一些问题。 *Everybody has become intoxicated in the happy holiday atmosphere; only ShaGua ruminates by himself over some unknown questions.*

**RELATED WORDS**

| | | |
|---|---|---|
| 石沉大海 144 | 击沉 156 | 低沉 618 |
| 阴沉 1041 | 昏沉 1058 | 浮沉 1342 |
| 消沉 1343 | 深沉 1345 | 破釜沉舟 1374 |

---

**1167** 洗     U+6D17     TM **11** FM 丶

**xǐ** V to wash, to bathe; to develop (film); to wipe; to clear away, to eliminate; to devastate; to erase (a recording); to shuffle (playing cards); to baptize

洗涤 **xǐdí** V to wash; to rinse

洗发液 **xǐfàyè** N shampoo · MW 瓶

洗劫 **xǐjié** V to loot

上星期六, 有一家商店被**洗劫**。 *A store was looted last Saturday.*

洗脸盆 **xǐliǎnpén** N washbowl, washbasin · MW 个

洗手 **xǐshǒu** V to wash one's hands; to quit one's job

洗刷 **xǐshuā** V to scrub; to clear oneself of

她在**洗刷**地板。 *She is scrubbing the floor.*

她在**洗刷**自己的罪名。 *She is clearing her criminal record.*

洗衣 **xǐyī** V to wash clothes

洗印 **xǐyìn** V to develop and print (film)

洗澡 **xǐzǎo** V to take a bath/shower

**RELATED WORDS**

| | | |
|---|---|---|
| 冲洗 339 | 刷洗 1310 | 清洗 1495 |
| 梳洗 1565 | 淘洗 1628 | |

---

**1168** 浓 濃     U+6D53     TM **11** FM 丶

**nóng** ADJ dense, thick; strong; great, keen

浓度 **nóngdù** N concentration; strength; density, thickness

浓厚 **nónghòu** ADJ great/strong/intense (of interest)

浓缩 **nóngsuō** V to concentrate

这本书**浓缩**了作者的思想。 *This book has concentrated the author's thoughts.*

浓雾 **nóngwù** N smog; thick fog · MW 团

浓烟 **nóngyān** N thick smoke · MW 股

浓郁 **nóngyù** ADJ dense (of a forest, etc.); rich (in color, fragrance, etc.)

## 1169 浩 U+6D69 TM **11** FM ヽ

**hào** ADJ great, vast, grand; much, many

浩大 **hàodà** ADJ huge; vast

浩荡 **hàodàng** ADJ vast and mighty, broad and powerful

浩繁 **hàofán** ADJ vast; many and varied

浩劫 **hàojié** N catastrophe, great calamity · MW 场

"文化大革命"是中国的一场**浩劫**。
*The "Great Cultural Revolution" was a great calamity in China.*

浩气 **hàoqì** N noble spirit · MW 股

## 1170 浴 U+6D74 TM **11** FM ヽ

**yù** N·V bath; to bathe

浴场 **yùchǎng** N public beach; outdoor swimming pool · MW 个

傻瓜不喜欢到**浴场**游泳，但傻瓜太太喜欢。
*ShaGua doesn't like swimming at public beaches, but Mrs. ShaGua does.*

浴池 **yùchí** N public bathhouse · MW 个

浴缸 **yùgāng** N bathtub · MW 个

浴巾 **yùjīn** N bath towel · MW 条

浴盆 **yùpén** N bathtub · MW 个

浴衣 **yùyī** N bathrobe · MW 件

**RELATED WORDS**

淋浴 1172          盆浴 1261

## 1171 涂 塗 U+6D82 TM **11** FM ヽ

**tú** V to spread, to smear, to apply; to cross out, to erase; to scribble, to scrawl

涂改 **túgǎi** V to alter

傻瓜的大儿子喜欢**涂改**作业。*ShaGua's older son constantly erases and rewrites his homework.*

涂料 **túliào** N paint

涂抹 **túmǒ** V to apply paint

涂鸦 **túyā** V to have poor handwriting, to scrawl

涂脂抹粉 **túzhīmǒfěn** EXP to apply makeup

傻瓜太太喜欢在脸上**涂脂抹粉**。*Mrs. ShaGua enjoys applying makeup to her face.*

**RELATED WORDS**

糊涂 1932     胡里胡涂 1256     稀里糊涂 1599

## 1172 淋 U+6DCB TM **11** FM ヽ

**lín** V to drench, to pour; to sprinkle, to splash; to strain, to filter

淋巴 **línbā** N lymph · MW 个

淋漓 **línlí** ADJ dripping wet; uninhibited

淋湿 **línshī** V to get soaked

淋雨 **línyǔ** V to get wet in the rain

傻瓜心烦的时候，喜欢出去**淋雨**。*When ShaGua gets frustrated, he likes to go out and stand in the rain.*

淋浴 **línyù** V to take a shower

**RELATED WORD**

冰淇淋 493

## 1173 淡 U+6DE1 TM **11** FM ヽ

**dàn** ADJ tasteless, bland (of food); weak (of an alcoholic beverage); light (in color); thin (of a liquid, a gas); sluggish (of business); lacking interest, indifferent

淡薄 **dànbó** ADJ thin, light, dim, flagging

他对中文的兴趣渐渐**淡薄**了。*His interest in Chinese has been gradually flagging.*

淡季 **dànjì** N off-season (of business) · MW 个

**淡季**的机票特别便宜。*Airline tickets are very cheap in the off-season.*

淡漠 **dànmò** ADJ indifferent, apathetic; faint, dim

淡色 **dànsè** N pale/light color

淡水 **dànshuǐ** N fresh/potable water

**RELATED WORDS**

平淡 78          冲淡 339          冷淡 494
暗淡 1676

## 1174 恨 U+6068 TM **11** FM ヽ

**hèn** V to hate, to have a grudge against; to regret

恨不得 **hènbude** V to wish one could; to desire strongly; can't wait for

老师教得太差，学生**恨不得**马上下课。
*The students wished the class would end immediately, because the teacher was lousy.*

恨事 **hènshì** N matter for regret · MW 件

**1174 恨 hèn** (continued)

**RELATED WORDS**

| | | |
|---|---|---|
| 可恨 243 | 仇恨 319 | 怀恨 344 |
| 恼恨 931 | 愤恨 1490 | 怨恨 1792 |
| 遗恨 1829 | 憎恨 1881 | |

---

## 1175 炖 燉   U+7096   TM **11** FM 丶

**dùn** [V] to stew slowly, to braise, to simmer; to warm

**炖肉 dùnròu** [V·N] to stew; braised meat
傻瓜太太最爱吃**炖肉**。 *Mrs. ShaGua loves braised meat.*

**RELATED WORD**

清炖 1495

---

## 1176 烛 燭   U+70DB   TM **11** FM 丶

**zhú** [N] candle; to illuminate, to light up

**烛光 zhúguāng** [N] candlelight
傻瓜太太喜欢在**烛光**下吃炖肉, 傻瓜无法欣赏这种罗曼蒂克。 *Mrs. ShaGua likes to eat braised meat in candlelight, but ShaGua doesn't enjoy this type of romance.*

**烛台 zhútái** [N] candlestick · [MW] 个

**RELATED WORD**

蜡烛 1780

---

## 1177 烟   U+70DF   TM **11** FM 丶

**yān** [N·V] tobacco; cigarette; opium; smoke; to be irritated by smoke

**烟草 yāncǎo** [N] tobacco

**烟尘 yānchén** [N] air pollution (LIT smoke and dust)

**烟囱 yāncōng** [N] chimney; stovepipe · [MW] 个

**烟斗 yāndǒu** [N] tobacco/opium pipe · [MW] 个

**烟盒 yānhé** [N] cigarette case · [MW] 个

**烟火 yānhuǒ** [N] smoke and fire; fireworks; cooked food

**烟头 yāntóu** [N] cigarette butt · [MW] 个
傻瓜收集自己吸剩的**烟头**, 再放到**烟斗**里抽。 *ShaGua collected his cigarette butts and smoked them in a pipe.*

**烟雾 yānwù** [N] smoke; mist; smog · [MW] 团

**烟叶 yānyè** [N] tobacco leaf · [MW] 片

---

**RELATED WORDS**

| | | |
|---|---|---|
| 云烟 80 | 无烟 139 | 炊烟 700 |
| 抽烟 788 | 香烟 834 | 冒烟 989 |
| 纸烟 1103 | 浓烟 1168 | 卷烟 1333 |
| 烤烟 1505 | 禁烟 1536 | |

---

## 1178 烦 煩   U+70E6   TM **11** FM 丶

**fán** [ADJ·V] irritated, annoyed, upset; fed up; to trouble, to bother

**烦恼 fánnǎo** [ADJ] worried; annoyed
没有**烦恼**就没有欢乐。 *Without agony, there would be no happiness.*

**烦琐 fánsuǒ** [ADJ] overelaborate, tedious, loaded down with trivial details

**烦躁 fánzào** [ADJ] agitated, fretful, irritable and restless
考试的时候, 学生一定要控制**烦躁**情绪。 *Students must control their anxiety when they take exams.*

**RELATED WORDS**

| | | |
|---|---|---|
| 厌烦 202 | 心烦 232 | 麻烦 1146 |
| 腻烦 1870 | 找麻烦 567 | |

---

## 1179 设 設   U+8BBE   TM **11** FM 丶

**shè** [V·CONJ] to set up; to plan; to suppose; given, if, in case

**设备 shèbèi** [N] equipment; facilities · [MW] 台、套

**设计 shèjì** [V·N] to design, to plan, to scheme; plan; project · [MW] 个

**设立 shèlì** [V] to establish, to set up, to found

**设施 shèshī** [N] facilities; installation · [MW] 个、套

**设想 shèxiǎng** [V·N] to imagine; to assume, to presume; tentative/preliminary plan · [MW] 个
这套**设备**是根据傻瓜的**设想**来**设计**的。 *This equipment was designed according to ShaGua's preliminary plans.*

**设宴 shèyàn** [V] to give a banquet
傻瓜**设宴**招待远方的客人。 *ShaGua gave a banquet for his friends from afar.*

**设置 shèzhì** [V] to set up; to install; to customize; setting

**RELATED WORDS**

| | | |
|---|---|---|
| 特设 1094 | 建设 1203 | 架设 1270 |
| 虚设 1534 | 假设 1586 | 铺设 1713 |
| 常设 1733 | 摆设 1773 | 卫生设备 82 |
| 产品设计 219 | 想方设法 1769 | |

## 1180 试 試 U+88D5 TM 11 FM 丶

**shì** V·N to try; to test; examination

**试飞** shìfēi V to make a test flight

**试管** shìguǎn N test tube · MW 个、只

**试卷** shìjuàn N exam paper · MW 张

**试探** shìtàn V to probe/explore (a question); to sound/try out

**试题** shìtí N test questions · MW 道、条

有些学生总是喜欢**试探**关于**试卷**或**试题**的内容。 *Some students always like to inquire about the questions on the exam.*

**试行** shìxíng V to try out, to test

**试验** shìyàn V·N to test, to experiment; trial; experimentation · MW 个、次

**试用** shìyòng V to try out; on trial

**试制** shìzhì V to create a prototype

请**试用**一下我们**试制**的设备。 *Please try out our prototype model.*

### RELATED WORDS

| | | |
|---|---|---|
| 比试 279 | 考试 530 | 面试 721 |
| 初试 963 | 尝试 1157 | 笔试 1278 |
| 调试 1749 | 期终考试 1574 | 期中考试 1574 |

## 1181 诗 詩 U+88D7 TM 11 FM 丶

**shī** N poetry, verse; poem

**诗歌** shīgē N poetry; poem · MW 首

**诗集** shījí N collection of poems; poetry anthology · MW 本

**诗人** shīrén N poet · MW 个、位、名

傻瓜小时候的梦想是发表一首**诗歌**，出版一本**诗集**，当一名**诗人**。 *ShaGua's childhood dream was to write a poem, publish a poetry anthology, and be a poet.*

### RELATED WORDS

| | |
|---|---|
| 古诗 154 | 史诗 186 |

## 1182 话 話 U+88DD TM 11 FM 丶

**huà** N·V speech, talk, conversation; words; sayings; story; dialect; to talk/speak about

**话别** huàbié V to say good-bye

**话剧** huàjù N stage play; modern drama · MW 场、幕

**话题** huàtí N topic of conversation · MW 个

**话**别的**话题**总是那么沉重。 *Saying good-bye is always such a heavy matter.*

**话筒** huàtǒng N microphone · MW 个

**话音** huàyīn N voice; tone · MW 声

### RELATED WORDS

| | | |
|---|---|---|
| 土话 15 | 大话 20 | 对话 254 |
| 电话 263 | 坏话 280 | 会话 295 |
| 行话 327 | 训话 349 | 听话 414 |
| 传话 452 | 讲话 501 | 好话 627 |
| 实话 668 | 空话 669 | 闲话 679 |
| 怪话 696 | 笑话 861 | 废话 918 |
| 屁话 1070 | 神话 1191 | 梦话 1217 |
| 谈话 1356 | 粗话 1364 | 鬼话 1433 |
| 答话 1438 | 童话 1471 | 插话 1555 |
| 留话 1582 | 假话 1586 | 说话 1631 |
| 谎话 1824 | 风凉话 194 | 心里话 232 |
| 闹笑话 1323 | 说大话 1631 | 骂人话 1652 |
| 人机对话 4 | 中国官话 86 | 长途电话 93 |
| 公共电话 103 | 无线电话 139 | |

## 1183 该 該 U+88E5 TM 11 FM 丶

**gāi** V·PRON ought to, should; to deserve, it serves (someone) right; most likely, probably; to owe; this, that; the above-mentioned

应**该** *should*

她**该**骂。 *She deserves a good scolding.*

你**该**钱。 *You owe money.*

**该**人 *that person*

她又**该**迟到了。 *She most likely will be late.*

### RELATED WORD

应该 334

## 1184 远 遠 U+8FDC TM 11 FM 丶

**yuǎn** ADJ·V distant, remote; far, by a great deal; to keep away from

**远程** yuǎnchéng ADJ long-distance; long-range; remote

傻瓜在夜校修一些**远程**教育的课程。 *ShaGua is taking some online courses in night school.*

**远大** yuǎndà ADJ long-range; broad, ambitious, far-reaching

**远道** yuǎndào N long way

**远方** yuǎnfāng N distant place; afar

**1184 远 yuǎn** (continued)

孔子说："有朋自**远**方来不亦乐乎？"
*Confucius said, "Is it not delightful to have friends coming from afar?"*

**远古 yuǎngǔ** [N] antiquity, ancient times

**远见 yuǎnjiàn** [N] foresight, farsightedness · [MW] 个

傻瓜提了一些很有**远见**的主张。
*ShaGua advocated some ideas that show very good foresight.*

**远郊 yuǎnjiāo** [N] outer suburbs · [MW] 个

**远近 yuǎnjìn** [ADV] everywhere, far and near; distance

**远距离 yuǎnjùlí** [N] long distance

**远洋 yuǎnyáng** [N] ocean

**远征 yuǎnzhēng** [V] to go on an expedition

**远足 yuǎnzú** [N] hike

傻瓜喜欢在雨中**远足**。*ShaGua likes to hike in the rain.*

**RELATED WORDS**

| | | |
|---|---|---|
| 长远 93 | 永远 481 | 边远 710 |
| 辽远 711 | 望远镜 1622 | 源远流长 1742 |
| 跳远 1786 | 遥远 1830 | 臭名远扬 1076 |
| 任重道远 211 | | |

---

**1185 违 違** U+8FDD TM **11** FM 丶

**wéi** [V] to disobey, to violate, to break; to be separated; to depart

**违背 wéibèi** [V] to violate, to go against

**违法 wéifǎ** [V] to break the law; to be illegal

2006年前，任何年纪的人在中国喝酒都不**违法**。
*Before 2006 in China, it was legal for anyone to drink regardless of age.*

**违反 wéifǎn** [V] to violate (a rule, a regulation, etc.), to run counter to

**违反**规章制度 *to violate regulations*

**违犯 wéifàn** [V] to violate

**违犯**法令 *to violate the law*

**违禁 wéijìn** [V] to violate (a ban, a prohibition)

**违抗 wéikàng** [V] to disobey; to defy

**违例 wéilì** [V] to violate/break the rules

**违心 wéixīn** [V] to be against one's conscience

人常常不得不做一些**违心**的事。*People often have to do things against their conscience.*

**违约 wéiyuē** [V] to break a contract; to break a promise; to violate a treaty

---

**违章 wéizhāng** [V] to violate/break the rules

**RELATED WORD**

久违 45

---

**1186 迫** U+8FEB TM **11** FM 丶

**pò** [V] to force, to compel

**迫不得已 pòbùdéyǐ** [EXP] to be forced/driven to, to have no alternative

**迫害 pòhài** [V] to persecute

"文革"的残酷在于许多人**迫不得已**去**迫害**他人甚至自己的亲人。*The ruthlessness of the "Cultural Revolution" drove many people to persecute others, including their own family members.*

**迫近 pòjìn** [V] to approach, to get close to

**迫切 pòqiè** [ADJ] pressing, urgent, imperative

**迫使 pòshǐ** [V] to force, to compel; to necessitate

**RELATED WORDS**

| | |
|---|---|
| 压迫 201 | 被迫 1517 |

---

**1187 迷** U+8FF7 TM **11** FM 丶

**mí** [V·N] to be lost; to be fascinated by, to become obsessed with; to be confused/deluded; fan, enthusiast

沉**迷** *to be fascinated by*

球**迷** *fans*

**迷宫 mígōng** [N] labyrinth, maze · [MW] 座

人生就像一座**迷宫**。*Life is like a labyrinth.*

**迷航 míháng** [V] to get lost

**迷糊 míhu** [ADJ] confused

**迷惑 míhuò** [V] to confuse, to puzzle; to mislead

傻瓜有时对人生感到**迷惑**。*Sometimes, life puzzles ShaGua.*

**迷恋 míliàn** [V] to be obsessed/infatuated with

**迷路 mílù** [V] to lose one's way, to get lost

**迷茫 mímáng** [ADJ] confused

**迷梦 mímèng** [N] pipe dream · [MW] 个

**迷人 mírén** [ADJ] enchanting, charming; attractive

**迷失 míshī** [V] to lose (one's way, etc.); to be off track

**迷途 mítú** [V] to lose one's way

迷惘 **míwǎng** `ADJ` perplexed

迷雾 **míwù** `N` dense fog

在**迷雾**中**迷路**的感觉, 就像进入**迷梦**一样。
*When you lose your way in a dense fog, you may feel as if you're in a dream.*

迷信 **míxìn** `V·ADJ` to have blind faith in; superstitious

大部分中国人不信教, 但**迷信**。*Most Chinese people are not religious; instead, they're superstitious.*

### RELATED WORDS

| | | |
|---|---|---|
| 入迷 5 | 执迷不悟 564 | 昏迷 1058 |
| 球迷 1199 | 捉迷藏 1239 | 着迷 1332 |
| 影迷 1918 | | |

---

### 1188 送 U+9001 TM 11 FM 丶

**sòng** `V` to deliver; to give; to give (as a present); to see (someone) off/out; to accompany, to escort

送殡 **sòngbìn** `V` to attend a funeral

送电 **sòngdiàn** `V` to deliver electric power

送还 **sònghuán** `V` to give back

西方人讲: "世间没有免费的午餐"; 中国文化讲**送还**人情。*Westerners say, "There is no such thing as a free lunch!" Chinese culture tells us to "repay favors."*

送货 **sònghuò** `V` to deliver merchandise

送客 **sòngkè** `V` to see (someone) off/out

送礼 **sònglǐ** `V` to give a present to

送命 **sòngmìng** `V` to lose one's life

送人情 **sòngrénqíng** `V` to do a favor at no cost to oneself

"**送人情**"是中国文化的一个特点。
*Doing favors for others (but expecting reciprocation) is a characteristic of Chinese culture.*

送信 **sòngxìn** `V` to deliver a letter

送行 **sòngxíng** `V` to see (someone) off, to say good-bye to (someone)

送葬 **sòngzàng** `V` to attend a funeral

送终 **sòngzhōng** `V` to bury a parent

在中国, 送礼不能送钟, 因为"送钟"与"送终"同音。*You can't give someone a clock as a gift in China, because "give a clock" in Chinese sounds similar to "bury a parent."*

### RELATED WORDS

| | | |
|---|---|---|
| 目送 151 | 发送 311 | 欢送 366 |
| 抄送 405 | 扭送 565 | 运送 956 |

---

| | | |
|---|---|---|
| 转送 1111 | 葬送 1656 | 递送 1827 |
| 输送 1867 | 赠送 1944 | 雪中送炭 1369 |

### 1189 站 U+7AD9 TM 11 FM 丶

**zhàn** `V·N` to stand, to be on one's feet; to take a stand; to stop, to halt; station; stop; center where a service is provided

站岗 **zhàngǎng** `V` to stand guard

站立 **zhànlì** `V` to stand

站票 **zhànpiào** `N` standing-room-only ticket · `MW` 张

站台 **zhàntái** `N` (railway) platform · `MW` 个

站稳 **zhànwěn** `V` to stand firm

你不要变来变去, 要**站稳**立场。*You should not waver; you must keep a firm stance.*

站长 **zhànzhǎng** `N` stationmaster · `MW` 个、名

站住 **zhànzhù** `V` to stop, to halt; to stand firm; to be tenable

"**站住**, 不许动!" *"Stop, don't move!"*

你刚来, **站住**再说。*You are new, so stand your ground first before speaking.*

站住脚 **zhànzhùjiǎo** `V` to stand firm; to be tenable

新校长**站住脚**了吗? *Has the new president gained his footing?*

你的观点**站**不**住脚**。*Your argument doesn't hold water.*

### RELATED WORDS

| | | |
|---|---|---|
| 车站 114 | 电站 263 | 网站 390 |
| 粮站 1759 | | |

---

### 1190 祖 U+7956 TM 11 FM 丶

**zǔ** `N` grandparent; ancestor; founder, originator

祖辈 **zǔbèi** `N` ancestor · `MW` 位

祖传 **zǔchuán** `V` to be handed down from one's ancestors

傻瓜所学的功夫是**祖传**的。*The kung fu that ShaGua learned was handed down from his ancestors.*

祖父 **zǔfù** `N` (paternal) grandfather · `MW` 位

祖国 **zǔguó** `N` native land, motherland

傻瓜的**祖国**是中国。*ShaGua's motherland is China.*

祖籍 **zǔjí** `N` family/ancestral home

**1190 祖 zǔ** (continued)

祖母 **zǔmǔ** N (paternal) grandmother · MW 位

祖先 **zǔxiān** N ancestry; ancestors · MW 位

祖宗 **zǔzōng** N ancestry; ancestors

祖祖辈辈 **zǔzǔbèibèi** N for generations

这是黄家**祖祖辈辈**的梦想。 *This is an ancestral dream of the Huang family.*

**RELATED WORDS**

外祖父 218       外祖母 218

---

**1191 神**    U+795E    TM **11** FM 丶

**shén** N·ADJ god, deity, divinity; spirit; mind; expression, look; supernatural; amazing; magical; smart, clever

神出鬼没 **shénchūguǐmò** EXP to come and go, to appear and disappear

神甫 **shénfu** N (Catholic) priest · MW 个、名

神话 **shénhuà** N myth; fairy tale; preposterous nonsense · MW 个

这是一个古老而美丽的**神话**。 *This is an ancient but beautiful myth.*

这是一个他吹出来的**神话**。 *This is preposterous nonsense he has made up.*

神经 **shénjīng** N·ADJ nerve; out of one's mind · MW 条

这是**神经**外科医生。 *This is a neurosurgeon.*

你发**神经**啦? *Are you crazy?*

神秘 **shénmì** ADJ mysterious; mystical

神奇 **shénqí** ADJ magical; mystical; miraculous

神色 **shénsè** N expression, look

今天傻瓜的**神色**不对，有点**神秘**兮兮的。 *ShaGua doesn't look right today; he seems a little mysterious.*

神圣 **shénshèng** ADJ sacred, holy

神仙 **shénxiān** N supernatural/celestial being; immortal · MW 个、位

---

神志 **shénzhì** N mind; state of mind, consciousness

**RELATED WORDS**

| | | |
|---|---|---|
| 入神 5 | 失神 106 | 全神贯注 172 |
| 心神 232 | 财神 588 | 养神 670 |
| 劳神 764 | 鬼神 1433 | 脑神经 1460 |
| 装神弄鬼 1476 | 眼神 1570 | 精神 1832 |
| 精神病 1832 | 疑神疑鬼 1917 | 聚精会神 1642 |

---

**1192 祥**    U+7965    TM **11** FM 丶

**xiáng** ADJ lucky; auspicious, propitious

祥和 **xiánghé** ADJ auspicious and peaceful/ harmonious

**RELATED WORDS**

吉祥 259       慈祥 1952       龙凤呈祥 315

---

**1193 袜** 襪    U+889C    TM **11** FM 丶

**wà** N socks; stockings

袜子 **wàzi** N socks · MW 只、对

傻瓜有时两边脚穿两只不同的**袜子**。 *Sometimes, ShaGua wears two different socks on his feet.*

**RELATED WORD**

短袜 1452

---

**1194 郊**    U+90CA    TM **11** FM 丶

**jiāo** N suburbs, outskirts

郊区 **jiāoqū** N suburbs, outskirts

傻瓜住在**郊区**。 *ShaGua lives in the suburbs.*

**RELATED WORDS**

市郊 332       近郊 716       远郊 1184
城郊 1225

## 1195 夏 U+590F TM **12** FM 一

**xià** [N] summer

夏季 **xiàjì** [N] summer · [MW] 个
夏历 **xiàlì** [N] lunar (traditional Chinese) calendar
夏令 **xiàlìng** [N] summertime
夏天 **xiàtiān** [N] summer · [MW] 个
夏威夷 **Xiàwēiyí** [N] Hawaii
　　夏威夷的夏季很热。 *Hawaii is hot in the summer.*

**RELATED WORDS**

立夏 125　　宁夏 336　　华夏 421
盛夏 1694

## 1196 恶 惡 U+6076 TM **12** FM 一

**è** [ADJ·N] fierce, ferocious; bad, evil, wicked; wickedness

**wù** [V] to dislike; to hate, to loathe

恶霸 **èbà** [N] local bully · [MW] 个、名
恶臭 **èchòu** [N] stench, offensive odor · [MW] 股、阵
恶毒 **èdú** [ADJ] malicious, venomous, vicious
恶感 **ègǎn** [N] bad impression, ill feeling
恶果 **èguǒ** [N] disastrous result · [MW] 个
恶狠狠 **èhěnhěn** [ADV] fiercely, ferociously
恶化 **èhuà** [V] to deteriorate, to worsen
恶劣 **èliè** [ADJ] bad; vile
恶梦 **èmèng** [N] nightmare · [MW] 个
　　我对她没有恶感, 只不过见面后做了个恶梦。
　　*I don't have any ill feelings toward her; it was only that I had a nightmare after meeting her.*
恶名 **èmíng** [N] bad reputation · [MW] 个
恶魔 **èmó** [N] evil spirit, demon, devil · [MW] 个、名
恶习 **èxí** [N] vice, bad habit · [MW] 个
恶性 **èxìng** [ADJ] malignant; vicious, horrific
恶作剧 **èzuòjù** [N] trick, prank; practical joke · [MW] 个
　　这个家伙的恶名就是爱搞恶作剧。
　　*This guy has a bad reputation because he likes to play practical jokes.*

**RELATED WORDS**

万恶 73　　丑恶 85　　无恶不作 139
厌恶 202　　可恶 243　　作恶 326
好恶 627　　邪恶 981　　险恶 1252
深恶痛绝 1345　　善恶 1483　　罪恶 1542
嫌恶 1702　　痛恶 1725　　憎恶 1881

## 1197 忌 U+5FCC TM **12** FM 一

**jì** [V] to be jealous of, to envy; to fear, to dread; to avoid; to give up, to abstain from, to quit

忌辰 **jìchén** [N] anniversary of a parent's death · [MW] 个
忌妒 **jídù** [V] to be jealous of, to envy
忌讳 **jìhuì** [V·N] to be superstitious about; to avoid; taboo · [MW] 个
　　学中文最忌讳三天打鱼两天晒网。
　　*The biggest taboo in studying Chinese is to fail to practice it daily.*
忌口 **jìkǒu** [V] to avoid certain food(s)

**RELATED WORDS**

妒忌 628　　畏忌 988　　禁忌 1536
猜忌 1594　　顾忌 1609

## 1198 柔 U+67D4 TM **12** FM 一

**róu** [ADJ] soft, supple; gentle

柔道 **róudào** [N] judo
柔光 **róuguāng** [N] subdued light · [MW] 束、道
柔媚 **róumèi** [ADJ] gentle and lovely
柔嫩 **róunèn** [ADJ] tender and delicate
柔软 **róuruǎn** [ADJ] soft, pliable; lithe
柔术 **róushù** [N] jujitsu
　　日本的柔道和巴西的柔术是不同的武术。
　　*Japanese judo and Brazilian jujitsu are two different martial arts.*

**RELATED WORD**

温柔 1627

## 1199 球 U+7403 TM **12** FM 一

qiú  N  ball; ball game; globe, Earth, world; sphere; [shaped like a sphere]

**球场 qiúchǎng** N (sports/playing) field · MW 个

**球队 qiúduì** N (ball) team · MW 支

**球门 qiúmén** N goal · MW 个

**球迷 qiúmí** N fan · MW 个、名

**球赛 qiúsài** N ball game; match; tournament · MW 场

球场边上的球迷在等待两支球队进行球赛。
*A crowd of fans awaits the ball game between the two teams.*

**球形 qiúxíng** ADJ spherical

### RELATED WORDS

| | | |
|---|---|---|
| 击球 156 | 全球 172 | 月球 190 |
| 打球 289 | 台球 301 | 血球 306 |
| 发球 311 | 环球 369 | 足球 383 |
| 网球 390 | 冰球 493 | 好球 627 |
| 星球 753 | 地球 772 | 排球 1241 |
| 棒球 1247 | 罚球 1386 | 练球 1453 |
| 眼球 1570 | 篮球 1862 | 曲棍球 272 |
| 东半球 307 | 羽毛球 732 | 南半球 986 |
| 滚雪球 1819 | 踢皮球 1946 | |

## 1200 理 U+7406 TM **12** FM 一

lǐ  V·N  to manage, to run; to put in order, to tidy up; to acknowledge; reason, logic; natural science (especially physics)

管理 *to manage*

整理 *to put in order*

道理 *reason*

合理 *logic*

**理财 lǐcái** V to manage the finances

**理睬 lǐcǎi** V to pay attention to; to show interest in

**理发 lǐfà** V to get a haircut

傻瓜从来不上理发店，都是傻瓜太太帮他理发。
*ShaGua has never been to a barber shop; Mrs. ShaGua cuts his hair.*

**理会 lǐhuì** V to notice; to understand

我不理会她。*I don't take any notice of her.*
我理会他的意思。*I understood his meaning.*

**理解 lǐjiě** V to understand, to comprehend

**理科 lǐkē** N science (as a subject); science (department)

**理论 lǐlùn** N·V theory; principle; -ism; debate; to argue · MW 个

关于这个理论，他要跟她理论。*He wants to debate this theory with her.*

**理念 lǐniàn** N idea; principle · MW 个

**理事 lǐshì** N council member · MW 个、名

**理想 lǐxiǎng** N·ADJ ideal, aspiration; ideal · MW 个

**理性 lǐxìng** N·ADJ reason; rationality; reasonable

**理由 lǐyóu** N reason, grounds, justification · MW 个、条

**理智 lǐzhì** N·ADJ intellect; reason; wise; rational

你应该理智地想一想，你没有理由不去追求这个理想。*You should think about it logically. You don't have any reason not to pursue this ideal.*

### RELATED WORDS

| | | |
|---|---|---|
| 天理 25 | 以理服人 101 | 公理 103 |
| 生理 107 | 生理学 107 | 在理 188 |
| 办理 195 | 代理 208 | 处理 217 |
| 心理 232 | 合理 296 | 有理 439 |
| 讲理 501 | 护理 569 | 条理 598 |
| 纹理 640 | 法理 686 | 评理 706 |
| 地理 772 | 助理 818 | 修理 870 |
| 物理 883 | 审理 911 | 治理 935 |
| 论理 947 | 料理 961 | 经理 1110 |
| 哲理 1219 | 按理 1234 | 推理 1242 |
| 原理 1273 | 总理 1330 | 情理 1491 |
| 清理 1495 | 梳理 1565 | 说理 1631 |
| 调理 1749 | 道理 1756 | 整理 1845 |
| 管理 1861 | 心安理得 232 | 热处理 1390 |
| 术后处理 91 | 企业管理 170 | 置之不理 1651 |
| 慢条斯理 1882 | | |

## 1201 砖 砖 U+7816 TM **12** FM 一

zhuān  N  brick; [shaped like a brick]

**砖头 zhuāntou** N brick · MW 块

### RELATED WORDS

抛砖引玉 1395　　瓷砖 1723

## 1202 孩 U+5B69 TM **12** FM 一

hái  N  child

**孩子 háizi** N child; children; son, daughter · MW 个

### RELATED WORDS

女孩 57　　乖孩子 832

## 1203 建    U+5EFA    TM **12** FM 一

**jiàn** V to build, to construct, to erect; to establish, to found; to propose, to advocate

**建立 jiànlì** V to build; to establish, to set up

**建设 jiànshè** V·N to build, to construct; construction · MW 个、项

**建议 jiànyì** V·N to propose, to suggest; proposal, suggestion · MW 个、条

**建造 jiànzào** V to build, to construct

**建筑 jiànzhù** V·N to build, to construct; building, structure · MW 个、栋

我的**建议**是**建造**一栋独特的**建筑**。
*My suggestion is to build a truly unique building.*

### RELATED WORDS

| | | |
|---|---|---|
| 兴建 228 | 封建 815 | 重建 839 |
| 修建 870 | 创建 1131 | 营建 1546 |
| 福建 1825 | | |

## 1204 顽 顽    U+987D    TM **12** FM 一

**wán** ADJ stupid, foolish; stubborn, obstinate; naughty, mischievous

**顽固 wángù** ADJ stubborn, obstinate; persistent, diehard

有时候傻瓜很**顽固**。*Sometimes, ShaGua is very stubborn.*

**顽抗 wánkàng** V to stubbornly resist

**顽皮 wánpí** ADJ naughty, mischievous

**顽强 wánqiáng** ADJ tenacious; hard to defeat

傻瓜是一个**顽强**的人。*ShaGua is a tough guy.*

**顽童 wántóng** N urchin, very naughty boy, young menace · MW 个

傻瓜小时候虽然不是**顽童**，但比较**顽皮**。
*ShaGua was not a menace as a child, but he was still quite naughty.*

## 1205 职 職    U+804C    TM **12** FM 一

**zhí** N·V duty, job; position, post; office; to administer

**职称 zhíchēng** N professional title · MW 个

**职工 zhígōng** N staff · MW 个、名

**职权 zhíquán** N authority; (official) power

**职位 zhíwèi** N position, post · MW 个

**职务 zhíwù** N position, post · MW 个

虽然傻瓜的**职务**是市长，但他没有专业**职称**。
*ShaGua's position is that of mayor, but he doesn't have a professional title.*

**职业 zhíyè** N occupation, profession; career · MW 个

**职责 zhízé** N responsibility, duty, obligation · MW 个

作为市长，傻瓜有很多**职权**，也有许多**职责**。
*As mayor, ShaGua has a lot of official powers, but also responsibilities.*

### RELATED WORDS

| | | |
|---|---|---|
| 公职 103 | 失职 106 | 双职工 146 |
| 专职 155 | 在职 188 | 任职 211 |
| 尽职 312 | 革职 747 | 免职 1056 |
| 官职 1136 | 教职员 1424 | 退职 1508 |
| 停职 1588 | 辞职 1606 | 离职 1614 |
| 就职 1836 | 解职 1927 | 撤职 1942 |

## 1206 联 聯    U+8054    TM **12** FM 一

**lián** V·N to unite; to join, to ally oneself with; couplet

**联邦 liánbāng** N federation · MW 个

**联合 liánhé** V·ADJ to unite; to join; to form an alliance / a union / a coalition; joint; combined

**联合国 Liánhéguó** N United Nations (U.N.)

**联结 liánjié** V to join; to connect, to link; to bind

民众**联名**要求把各州**联结**成一个松散的**联邦**。
*People signed their names to build a loose federation.*

**联军 liánjūn** N allied forces/troops; united army · MW 支、队

**联络 liánluò** V to contact; to keep in contact/touch

让我们保持**联络**吧。*Let's keep in touch.*

**联盟 liánméng** N alliance, coalition, league, union · MW 个

**联名 liánmíng** V jointly (declared/sponsored/signed)

**联赛 liánsài** N league games/matches · MW 次、轮

**联系 liánxì** V to relate; to connect, to link; to get in touch with, to contact

**联想 liánxiǎng** V to associate, to connect in one's mind

你的名字让我**联想**到我的初恋情人。
*Your name reminds me of my first love.*

**1206 联 lián** (continued)

**RELATED WORDS**

| | | |
|---|---|---|
| 门联 130 | 互联网 135 | 关联 224 |
| 并联 225 | 妇联 465 | 串联 522 |
| 苏联 552 | 邦联 636 | |

## 1207 驻 駐 U+9A7B TM **12** FM 一

**zhù** V to be stationed (of troops/personnel); to stop; to stay

中国**驻**美国大使 *ambassador of the People's Republic of China to the U.S.*

**驻地 zhùdì** N camp, place where troops, etc. are stationed; administrative seat · MW 个

**驻防 zhùfáng** V to be on garrison duty

**驻守 zhùshǒu** V to garrison; to defend

**RELATED WORDS**

派驻 945      常驻 1733

## 1208 张 張 U+5F20 TM **12** FM 一

**zhāng** V·MW to open; to spread, to stretch; to exaggerate; to open a new business; to lay out, to display; to look, to glance; [measure word for paper, tables, and faces]

**张弛 zhāngchí** V to tense and relax

**张大 zhāngdà** V to open wide; to exaggerate

**张灯结彩 zhāngdēngjiécǎi** EXP to be decorated with lanterns and streamers

**张挂 zhāngguà** V to hang up (a picture, a curtain, etc.)

**张力 zhānglì** N tension (physics) · MW 股

**张罗 zhāngluo** V to attend to

人们在**张罗**着新商店的开张。 *People are making arrangements for the opening ceremony of the new store.*

**张贴 zhāngtiē** V to post, to put up (a notice, a poster, etc.)

**张望 zhāngwàng** V to peep (through a crack); to look around

一些人**张**大嘴巴在**张望**新商店的开张。 *Some people are looking around with their mouths open at the grand opening of the new store.*

**张嘴 zhāngzuǐ** V to open one's mouth (to say something); to ask for a favor

**RELATED WORDS**

| | | |
|---|---|---|
| 主张 124 | 扩张 291 | 伸张 457 |
| 夸张 605 | 纸张 1103 | 虚张声势 1534 |
| 紧张 1537 | 铺张 1713 | 慌张 1736 |
| 舒张 1805 | 明目张胆 1035 | |

## 1209 敢 U+6562 TM **12** FM 一

**gǎn** V·ADJ·ADV to dare, to have courage to; to be certain/sure; to venture; courageous, daring; probably; perhaps

**敢于 gǎnyú** V to dare

傻瓜**敢于**改革。 *ShaGua is not afraid of reform.*

**RELATED WORDS**

不敢当 24      胆敢 1295      勇敢 1371

## 1210 耐 U+8010 TM **12** FM 一

**nài** V·ADJ to be resistant; to endure; durable

**耐久 nàijiǔ** ADJ durable, long-lasting

**耐力 nàilì** N endurance, stamina

**耐心 nàixīn** N·ADJ patience; endurance; patient

傻瓜没有**耐心**钓鱼，但练举重却很有**耐力**。 *ShaGua doesn't have the patience to fish, but he does have the endurance to lift weights.*

**耐用 nàiyòng** ADJ durable

**RELATED WORDS**

忍耐 970      能耐 1873

## 1211 毒 U+6BD2 TM **12** FM 丨

**dú** N·ADJ·V poison, toxin; narcotics; [something harmful to the brain]; poisonous; noxious; to kill with poison

**毒害 dúhài** V·N to poison (someone's mind); to harm (someone's health) with narcotics; bad/pernicious influence

你在**毒害**青少年。 *You are poisoning young people.*
我们必须清除种族主义的**毒害**。 *We must purge the pernicious influence of racism.*

**毒化 dúhuà** V to poison; to spoil

**毒蛇 dúshé** N poisonous snake · MW 条

**毒物 dúwù** N poisonous substance · MW 个

**毒性 dúxìng** N toxicity; virulence · MW 种

毒药 **dúyào** N poison · MW 片、包

毒汁 **dúzhī** N venom · MW 滴

**RELATED WORDS**

| | | |
|---|---|---|
| 歹毒 74 | 以毒攻毒 101 | 余毒 419 |
| 有毒 439 | 吸毒 776 | 尿毒症 849 |
| 刻毒 966 | 抗毒素 1009 | 防毒 1040 |
| 恶毒 1196 | 狠毒 1284 | 病毒 1327 |
| 消毒 1343 | 服毒 1457 | 流毒 1493 |
| 蛇毒 1681 | 蜂毒 1682 | 遗毒 1829 |
| 解毒 1928 | | |

---

### 1212 黄    U+9EC4    TM **12**   FM |

**huáng** ADJ·N·V yellow; gold; to fizzle out, to fall through

树叶**黄**了。 *The leaves have turned yellow.*

计划**黄**了。 *The plan has failed.*

黄豆 **huángdòu** N soybean · MW 颗、粒

黄瓜 **huángguā** N cucumber · MW 条

黄河 **Huánghé** N Yellow River

黄昏 **huánghūn** N dusk; evening · MW 个

黄金 **huángjīn** N gold · MW 块、条

黄牛 **huángniú** N ox; cattle · MW 头

**黄昏**时分，**黄河**边上有几头**黄牛**在悠荡。
*A few cattle wander slowly on the bank of the Yellow River at dusk.*

黄色 **huángsè** N yellow; pornographic

黄山 **Huángshān** N Mount Huang

黄油 **huángyóu** N butter · MW 块

**RELATED WORDS**

| | | |
|---|---|---|
| 金黄色 420 | 枯黄 799 | 卵黄 896 |
| 蛋黄 1368 | | |

---

### 1213 带 帶    U+5E26    TM **12**   FM |

**dài** V·N to take, to bring; to lead; to direct;
to raise, to bring up; to do (something
incidental); to have, to contain; to reveal;
to wear; to come with, to be included;
to inspire; to promote; strap, belt, band, girdle;
tire; zone; area

忘了**带**钱。 *I forgot to bring money.*

**带**路 *to lead the way*

**带**孩子 *to look after (children)*

头发**带**点水 *drops of water on hair*

录像**带** *videocassette tape*

热带 *burning zone*

带动 **dàidòng** V to spur on; to drive, to power

带领 **dàilǐng** V to guide, to lead

带头 **dàitóu** V to be the first; to take the lead

你**带头**吧。 *Please lead.*

带子 **dàizi** N strap, belt; audiotape; videotape ·
MW 条、盘

**RELATED WORDS**

| | | |
|---|---|---|
| 夹带 197 | 皮带 261 | 声带 374 |
| 丝带 637 | 地带 772 | 连带 958 |
| 彩带 1132 | 热带 1390 | 拖带 1396 |
| 领带 1465 | 海带 1494 | 温带 1627 |
| 裤带 1634 | 裙带关系 1752 | 鞋带 1789 |
| 腰带 1868 | 携带 1905 | 飘带 1939 |
| 亚热带 136 | 沾亲带故 684 | 连本带利 958 |
| 拖泥带水 1396 | | |

---

### 1214 思    U+601D    TM **12**   FM |

**sī** V·N to think, to consider, to deliberate,
to meditate; to miss, to long for; reasoning

思潮 **sīcháo** N trend of thought · MW 股、种

思考 **sīkǎo** V to think deeply, to ponder;
to reason

思路 **sīlù** N train of thought; thinking, reasoning ·
MW 个

**傻瓜**的**思路**还是比较清晰的。 *ShaGua's thoughts
are quite clear.*

思虑 **sīlǜ** V to consider carefully

思念 **sīniàn** V to think of; to miss, to long for

思维 **sīwéi** N thought; thinking · MW 种

思想 **sīxiǎng** N thought; thinking; idea;
ideology

**RELATED WORDS**

| | | |
|---|---|---|
| 三思而行 9 | 才思 39 | 乡思 117 |
| 心思 232 | 相思 805 | 构思 1028 |
| 哀思 1134 | 沉思 1166 | 深思 1345 |
| 意思 1812 | 小意思 61 | 马克思主义 247 |
| 有意思 439 | 顾名思义 1609 | 不好意思 24 |
| 挖空心思 1551 | | |

---

### 1215 罢 罷    U+7F62    TM **12**   FM |

**bà** V to stop, to cease; to dismiss; to end,
to finish

罢黜 **bàchù** V to dismiss (from office); to reject

罢工 **bàgōng** V to go on strike

**1215 罢 bà** (continued)

**罢免 bàmiǎn** V to dismiss/remove (from office); to recall

人们**罢工**, 要求**罢免**市长。 *People are going on strike in order to have the mayor dismissed.*

**罢休 bàxiū** V to give up, to abandon (a goal, etc.)

他们不达目的, 绝不**罢休**。 *They will not give up until they have reached their goal.*

**RELATED WORD**

作罢 326

---

**1216 胃**     U+80C3    TM **12** FM |

**wèi** N stomach

**胃病 wèibìng** N stomach trouble/illness

**胃肠炎 wèichángyán** N gastroenteritis

**胃口 wèikǒu** N appetite; liking

**胃痛 wèitòng** N stomachache

傻瓜常常**胃痛**。 *ShaGua often has stomachaches.*

**RELATED WORDS**

吊胃口 547     肠胃 1458

---

**1217 梦 夢**     U+68A6    TM **12** FM |

**mèng** N·V dream; to dream, to fancy

**梦话 mènghuà** N talking in one's sleep; nonsense

我昨晚听到你说**梦话**。 *I heard you talking in your sleep last night.*

你是在说**梦话**。 *What you are saying is nonsense.*

**梦幻 mènghuàn** N illusion, dream · MW 个

**梦境 mèngjìng** N dreamworld, dreamland · MW 个

**梦想 mèngxiǎng** V·N to dream; illusion; daydream

**梦想**也可以成为一种动力。 *Dreams can be a type of motivation.*

这是不可能的, 你别白日**梦想**了。 *It's impossible! Stop daydreaming.*

**RELATED WORDS**

旧梦重温 165    幻梦 475    美梦 671
迷梦 1187     恶梦 1196    做梦 1282
睡梦 1571     白日梦 176   夜长梦多 654

---

**1218 载 載**     U+8F7D    TM **12** FM |

**zǎi** N·V year; to record, to write down; to publish; to reprint

**zài** V·CONJ to carry; to hold, to be full of; and, as well as; while

**载货 zàihuò** V to carry freight/cargo

**载运 zàiyùn** V to transport (by vehicle)

**载重 zàizhòng** V to load; carrying/weight capacity

**RELATED WORDS**

千载难逢 19     刊载 216     负载 435
加载 463      空载 669     记载 946
运载 956      连载 958     满载 1745

---

**1219 哲**     U+54F2    TM **12** FM |

**zhé** N·ADJ wise man, sage; wise, intelligent

**哲理 zhélǐ** N philosophical theory

**哲学 zhéxué** N philosophy

---

**1220 品**     U+54C1    TM **12** FM |

**pǐn** V·N to sample; to taste, to savor; article, product; grade, class, quality; type, kind; character

**品尝 pǐncháng** V to taste, to savor

你来品尝一下这瓶葡萄酒。 *Please taste this wine.*

**品德 pǐndé** N moral character, morality

**品格 pǐngé** N character; quality and style (of literary/artistic works)

傻瓜的**品格**得到人们的赞扬。 *People praise ShaGua's character.*

**品级 pǐnjí** N grade (of a product, etc.); workmanship

**品类 pǐnlèi** N category, class

**品名 pǐnmíng** N name of a product, brand name · MW 个

**品目 pǐnmù** N item; list of items · MW 个

**品评 pǐnpíng** V to judge; to comment on

请品评这部小说。 *Please comment on this novel.*

**品位 pǐnwèi** N grade, rank, quality; personal status

**品性 pǐnxìng** N moral character

**品质 pǐnzhì** N character; quality · MW 种

**品种 pǐnzhǒng** N breed; species; variety/kind (of products) · MW 个

## RELATED WORDS

---

### 1221 哭 　U+54ED　TM 12 FM |

**kū** V to cry, to weep

**哭鼻子 kūbízi** EXP to sniffle, to snivel

**哭哭啼啼 kūkutítí** EXP to cry one's eyes out, to wail

**哭泣 kūqì** V to weep, to sob

**哭诉 kūsù** V to complain tearfully

**哭笑不得 kūxiàobùdé** EXP to not know whether to laugh or cry

傻瓜讲的一些笑话，让人**哭笑不得**。 *People didn't know whether to laugh or cry at ShaGua's jokes.*

#### RELATED WORD

---

### 1222 荒 　U+8352　TM 12 FM |

**huāng** ADJ·N·V desolate; out of practice; unreasonable, ridiculous; famine; lean year; wasteland; shortage; to waste; to neglect

**荒诞 huāngdàn** ADJ absurd

**荒地 huāngdì** N wasteland; uncultivated land · MW 片、块

**荒废 huāngfèi** V to leave uncultivated; to neglect; to be out of practice

这块地**荒废**了。 *This piece of land was left uncultivated.*

因为长期不使用，傻瓜的中文几乎**荒废**了。 *Since ShaGua had not used Chinese for a long time, he was out of practice.*

**荒凉 huāngliáng** ADJ bleak and desolate

**荒谬 huāngmiù** ADJ ridiculous, absurd

**荒唐 huāngtáng** ADJ absurd, preposterous

这个观点**荒谬**，论证也**荒唐**。 *This thesis is absurd, and the proof is ridiculous.*

---

**荒野 huāngyě** N wilds · MW 片

**荒原 huāngyuán** N wasteland · MW 片

#### RELATED WORDS

---

### 1223 著 　U+8457　TM 12 FM |

**zhù** ADJ·V·N outstanding, notable; to show, to prove; to write; work

**著称 zhùchēng** ADJ celebrated, famous

**著名 zhùmíng** ADJ famous

**著述 zhùshù** V to write; to compile

**著作 zhùzuò** N work · MW 部、本

他是**著名**的教育家，出版过很多**著作**。 *He is a very famous educator with many influential publications to his credit.*

#### RELATED WORDS

---

### 1224 垮 　U+57AE　TM 12 FM |

**kuǎ** V to collapse, to fail; to break/wear down

**垮台 kuǎtái** V to fall from power; to collapse

#### RELATED WORDS

---

### 1225 城 　U+57CE　TM 12 FM |

**chéng** N city, urban area; town; within the city wall

**城堡 chéngbǎo** N castle · MW 座

**城郊 chéngjiāo** N suburbs, outskirts

**城里 chéngli** N inside the city

傻瓜想好好治理一下**城里**的治安。 *ShaGua is intent on improving public security in the city.*

**城门 chéngmén** N city gate · MW 个、扇、道

**城市 chéngshì** N city; town · MW 个

**城乡 chéngxiāng** N town and country (LIT city and countryside)

**城镇 chéngzhèn** N town · MW 个

**1225 城 chéng** (continued)

**RELATED WORDS**

| | | |
|---|---|---|
| 长城 93 | 环城 369 | 县城 543 |
| 围城 762 | 省城 860 | 京城 905 |
| 都城 1578 | 万里长城 73 | |

---

**1226 堵**     U+5835    TM **12** FM |

**dǔ** V·ADJ to stop up, to block up; stifled; suffocated; oppressed

堵击 **dǔjī** V to intercept and attack

堵塞 **dǔsè** V to block up
傻瓜想好好治理一下城市交通**堵塞**的问题。
*ShaGua is intent on improving traffic in the city.*

---

**1227 呢**     U+5462    TM **12** FM |

**ne** AV [used at the end of a sentence (1) to indicate a question, (2) to indicate strong agreement or an exaggerated effect, or (3) to indicate a continued state/action]

我学中文，你**呢**？ *I study Chinese; how about you?*
他不这样做，那才怪**呢**！ *It would be strange if he didn't do so.*
还要学好些年**呢**。 *There are still several years to continue studying.*

**ní** N wool cloth

呢料子 **níliàozi** N wool material · MW 块

呢绒 **níróng** N wool fabric · MW 块

---

**1228 吼**     U+543C    TM **12** FM |

**hǒu** V·N to roar; to growl; to shout; to shriek (of winds, sirens, etc.); loud noise

吼叫 **hǒujiào** V to roar; to howl; to shout

吼声 **hǒushēng** N roar, roaring · MW 声
傻瓜的**吼**声把一个小流氓吓跑了。 *ShaGua scared off a thug by bellowing at him.*

---

**1229 咖**     U+5496    TM **12** FM |

**kā** N coffee

咖啡 **kāfēi** N coffee (drink/grounds) · MW 杯

咖啡壶 **kāfēihú** N coffeepot · MW 把

咖啡因 **kāfēiyīn** N caffeine
因为咖啡里有**咖啡因**，所以傻瓜不喝**咖啡**。
*ShaGua doesn't drink coffee because of the caffeine.*

---

**1230 抢 搶**     U+62A2    TM **12** FM |

**qiǎng** V to rob, to loot; to snatch, to grab; to rush (a harvest, emergency measures, etc.); to touch; to knock

抢夺 **qiǎngduó** V to seize, to grab

抢购 **qiǎnggòu** V to buy in a panic, to rush to buy

抢劫 **qiǎngjié** V to rob; to pillage

抢救 **qiǎngjiù** V to rescue, to save; to salvage
抢救病人 *to rescue a patient*

抢掠 **qiǎnglüè** V to loot; to plunder
**抢劫**他人10元钱是罪犯，**抢掠**他国资源是总统。
*Robbing $10 from others is the act of a criminal; taking other countries' resources is the act of a president.*

抢修 **qiǎngxiū** V to rush to repair, to make an urgent repair
抢修公路 *to rush to repair the highway*

---

**1231 拘**     U+62D8    TM **12** FM |

**jū** V to arrest; to restrain; to restrict, to limit

拘捕 **jūbǔ** V to capture; to arrest

拘谨 **jūjǐn** ADJ overly cautious; reserved
傻瓜是一个很**拘谨**的人。 *ShaGua is an overly cautious person.*

拘禁 **jūjìn** V to restrain; to take into custody; to arrest

拘留 **jūliú** V to detain

拘票 **jūpiào** N arrest warrant · MW 张
警察带拘票来**拘捕**嫌疑犯。 *Police use arrest warrants to arrest criminals.*

**RELATED WORD**

无拘束 139

---

**1232 招**     U+62DB    TM **12** FM |

**zhāo** V·N to beckon; to enlist; to recruit; to attract; to provoke, to tease; to confess; to be contagious, to infect; to trick; device, move

招标 **zhāobiāo** V　to invite bids

招待 **zhāodài** V　to entertain (guests); to serve

招待会 **zhāodàihuì** N　(press) conference ·
MW 次、个

招供 **zhāogòng** V　to confess, to admit
罪犯**招供**了他的罪行。 *The criminal confessed
his crime.*

招呼 **zhāohu** V　to call; to greet; to notify, to tell;
to look after, to take care of
打**招呼** *to greet*
**招呼**她回家 *to tell her to go home*
**招呼**来访者 *to take care of visitors*

招领 **zhāolǐng** V　to post a "found" notice,
to announce that lost property has been found

招聘 **zhāopìn** V　to advertise a job opening,
to invite applications for a job
学校要**招聘**一位中文教师。 *The school is going
to hire a Chinese teacher.*

招惹 **zhāorě** V　to provoke; to cause

招生 **zhāoshēng** V　to enroll students

招收 **zhāoshōu** V　to recruit; to hire

招手 **zhāoshǒu** V　to wave (one's hand)

招致 **zhāozhì** V　to result in, to lead to
傻瓜从事的改革**招致**许多批评。 *The reforms
ShaGua has been enacting have brought a lot
of criticism.*

**RELATED WORDS**

打招呼　289　　　花招　549　　　绝招　1706
失物招领　106

---

1233　拣　揀　　U+62E3　　TM 12 FM |

**jiǎn** V　to select, to choose; to collect, to gather

拣选 **jiǎnxuǎn** V　to select, to choose

**RELATED WORD**

挑拣　1235

---

1234　按　　U+6309　　TM 12 FM |

**àn** V·PREP·N　to press (with one's finger/hand),
to push down; to shelve, to put aside; to restrain,
to control; according to; on the basis of; note
**按**下这个方案 *to set this proposal aside for a while*
**按**住怒火 *to control my anger*
**按**枪等待 *to keep my hand on the gun and wait*
**按**质论价 *to discuss prices on the basis of quality*

按比例 **ànbǐlì** ADV　in proportion

按键 **ànjiàn** V·N　to press (a key, a button);
key, button · MW 个

按理 **ànlǐ** ADV　according to reason; normally,
in the normal course of events
**按理**说，她应该到了。 *According to the schedule,
she should have been here.*

按摩 **ànmó** V　to massage

按钮 **ànniǔ** N　push button · MW 个

按期 **ànqī** ADV　on schedule

按时 **ànshí** ADV　on time, on schedule

按照 **ànzhào** ADV　according to; in light of
**按照**合同，他得**按期**付款。 *According to the terms
of the contract, he must pay his money on
schedule.*

---

1235　挑　　U+6311　　TM 12 FM |

**tiāo** V·N　to select, to choose, to pick; to nitpick,
to be hypercritical; to carry (something) on
a carrying pole; to shoulder; carrying pole
(and its load)

**tiǎo** V　to raise, to lift (up); to poke, to prick;
to incite, to stir up

挑错 **tiāocuò** V　to find fault

挑拣 **tiāojiǎn** V　to pick and choose, to be
particular

挑剔 **tiāotì** V·ADJ　to nitpick, to be hypercritical;
fastidious, picky

挑选 **tiāoxuǎn** V　to select, to choose

挑字眼 **tiāozìyǎn** V　to find fault with a choice of
words
这个老师就是爱**挑字眼**。 *This teacher just likes to
find fault with your choice of words.*

挑拨 **tiǎobō** V　to incite, to instigate
傻瓜最讨厌**挑拨**是非的人。 *ShaGua hates people
who stir up trouble.*

挑大梁 **tiǎodàliáng** EXP　to play the leading role;
to be the backbone
我们就是要**挑选**能**挑大梁**的人。 *We just want
to select people who will be able to play the
leading role.*

挑动 **tiǎodòng** V　to provoke, to stir up

挑逗 **tiǎodòu** V　to provoke, to tease; to entice,
to tantalize

挑唆 **tiǎosuō** V　to incite, to instigate

挑战 **tiǎozhàn** V　to challenge
傻瓜乐于迎接**挑战**。 *ShaGua is a person who likes
a challenge.*

**RELATED WORD**

百里挑一　242

## 1236 挥 挥   U+6325   TM 12 FM |

**huī** V to wave, to brandish; to wipe away/off; to command (an army); to direct; to scatter, to disperse

**挥动 huīdòng** V to wave, to brandish

**挥霍 huīhuò** V to squander; to spend extravagantly

有些人喜欢**挥霍**纳税人的钱。 *Some people like to squander the taxpayers' money.*

**挥舞 huīwǔ** V to wave, to brandish

### RELATED WORDS

发挥 311      指挥 1397      瞎指挥 1913

## 1237 挨   U+6328   TM 12 FM |

**āi** V to follow in sequence; to be next to; to get close to

> 挨个点名 *to call the roll*
>
> 他**挨**着我坐。 *She sits next to me.*

**ái** V to suffer, to put up with, to endure; to drag out, to delay

> 挨饿 *to suffer from hunger*
>
> 上课**挨**时间 *to kill time in class*

**挨打 áidǎ** V to suffer a beating

傻瓜的儿子因为打架**挨**(爸爸)**打**了。 *ShaGua had to beat his older son because he fought with someone at school.*

## 1238 振   U+632F   TM 12 FM |

**zhèn** V to rouse oneself; to boost; to shake, to vibrate; to activate

**振动 zhèndòng** V to vibrate

发这个音你要**振动**声带。 *Your vocal cords must vibrate to produce this sound.*

**振奋 zhènfèn** V·ADJ to inspire, to stimulate; exciting

**振兴 zhènxīng** V to revitalize; to promote

**振作 zhènzuò** V to pull oneself together; to cheer up

你不能整天上课挨时间, 要**振作**起来。 *You can't keep wasting your time in class; you have to perk up.*

### RELATED WORDS

共振 164      颤振 1991

## 1239 捉   U+6349   TM 12 FM |

**zhuō** V to catch, to capture; to hold, to grasp

**捉襟见肘 zhuōjīnjiànzhǒu** EXP to have more problems than one can cope with

**捉迷藏 zhuōmícáng** V to play hide-and-seek

**捉摸 zhuōmō** V to predict (with difficulty); to ascertain

这个人不可**捉摸**, 整天像在**捉迷藏**。 *This person is difficult to understand; it's like he's playing hide-and-seek all the time.*

**捉弄 zhuōnòng** V to tease, to make fun of

### RELATED WORDS

捕捉 1400      贼喊捉贼 1254      捕风捉影 1400

## 1240 捧   U+6367   TM 12 FM |

**pěng** V·MW to hold in both hands; to boost; to flatter; [measure word for a (double) handful of peanuts, etc.]

**捧场 pěngchǎng** V to boost, to encourage; to cheer on

晚上傻瓜有一个演讲, 他的朋友都准备去给他**捧场**。 *ShaGua has a speech in the evening. His friends plan to cheer him on.*

**捧腹 pěngfù** V to shake with laughter (LIT to hold one's belly with both hands)

### RELATED WORD

吹捧 559

## 1241 排   U+6392   TM 12 FM |

**pái** V·N·MW to arrange; to put in order; to rehearse (a play, etc.); to push open; row, line, lineup; platoon; raft; [measure word for seats, rows, buildings, etc.]

**排斥 páichì** V to reject, to exclude, to remove

不能**排斥**异己。 *You can't exclude those who hold different views from you.*

**排除 páichú** V to eliminate, to get rid of; to rule out

**排队 páiduì** V to line up

**排骨 páigǔ** N chop, cutlet, rib (cut of meat); skinny person · MW 根

**排行 páiháng** V to rank (in seniority, birth order, etc.)

排挤 **páijǐ** 〔V〕 to edge/sqeeze out
不能**排挤**他人。 *You can't squeeze others out.*

排解 **páijiě** 〔V〕 to mediate, to reconcile

排练 **páiliàn** 〔V〕 to rehearse
今晚**排练**小品。 *We will rehearse the skit tonight.*

排气 **páiqì** 〔V〕 to exhaust, to ventilate

排球 **páiqiú** 〔N〕 volleyball · 〔MW〕 个

排泄 **páixiè** 〔V〕 to drain; to excrete (body waste)

排序 **páixù** 〔V〕 to sequence

排字 **páizì** 〔V〕 to typeset, to compose

**RELATED WORDS**

并排 225　　　肉排 437　　　安排 487
编排 1866

---

**1242 推** U+63A8　TM **12** FM |

**tuī** 〔V〕 to push, to shove; to delay, to postpone; to shift; to push away; to recommend; to choose, to elect; to hold in esteem; to push forward, to promote, to advance; to deduce, to infer; to consider all aspects of; to scrape; to cut, to pare; to mow

推测 **tuīcè** 〔V〕 to infer, to surmise
你的**推测**不正确。 *Your guess is incorrect.*

推陈出新 **tuīchénchūxīn** 〔EXP〕 to innovate, to push out the old and bring in the new

推迟 **tuīchí** 〔V〕 to delay, to postpone
傻瓜的大儿子**推迟**一年上大学, 到车行去打工。
*ShaGua's older son deferred college for one year and worked in a garage.*

推崇 **tuīchóng** 〔V〕 to hold in esteem, to praise highly

推辞 **tuīcí** 〔V〕 to refuse/decline (an appointment, an invitation, etc.)

推导 **tuīdǎo** 〔V〕 to infer, to deduce

推倒 **tuīdǎo** 〔V〕 to overturn, to push over

推动 **tuīdòng** 〔V〕 to promote, to encourage, to motivate

推断 **tuīduàn** 〔V〕 to infer, to deduce; to extrapolate

推翻 **tuīfān** 〔V〕 to overthrow, to overturn

推荐 **tuījiàn** 〔V〕 to recommend

推举 **tuījǔ** 〔V〕 to choose, to elect

推理 **tuīlǐ** 〔V〕 to infer; to reason
他的**推断**和**推理**, **推翻**了老师的假设。
*His deduction and reasoning disproved the teacher's hypothesis.*

推力 **tuīlì** 〔N〕 thrust · 〔MW〕 股

推拿 **tuīná** 〔V〕 to massage

推敲 **tuīqiāo** 〔V〕 to polish/refine repeatedly; to scrutinze closely

推让 **tuīràng** 〔V〕 to decline (a position, a favor, etc. out of modesty)

推算 **tuīsuàn** 〔V〕 to calculate, to estimate, to reckon

推托 **tuītuō** 〔V〕 to make excuses
请不要再**推托**了, 你的老师强力**推荐**你。
*Please don't make any more excuses; your teacher has strongly recommended you.*

推想 **tuīxiǎng** 〔V〕 to imagine, to guess

推销 **tuīxiāo** 〔V〕 to market/promote (merchandise)

推行 **tuīxíng** 〔V〕 to carry out, to implement

**RELATED WORDS**

手推车 104　　　类推 676　　　依此类推 625

---

**1243 桃** U+6843　TM **12** FM |

**táo** 〔N〕 peach; [shaped like a peach]; walnut

桃红 **táohóng** 〔N〕 pink

桃李 **táolǐ** 〔N〕 peaches and plums; student
黄老师**桃李**满天下。 *Teacher Huang has students all over the country.*

桃色新闻 **táosèxīnwén** 〔N〕 (news of a) sex scandal · 〔MW〕 条

桃树 **táoshù** 〔N〕 peach tree · 〔MW〕 棵

桃子 **táozi** 〔N〕 peach · 〔MW〕 个

**RELATED WORDS**

核桃 1026　　　世外桃源 163

---

**1244 枪** 槍 U+67AA　TM **12** FM |

**qiāng** 〔N·V〕 rifle; gun, firearm; [shaped like a gun]; spear; to knock

枪弹 **qiāngdàn** 〔N〕 bullet · 〔MW〕 颗

枪决 **qiāngjué** 〔V〕 to execute by firing squad

枪杀 **qiāngshā** 〔V〕 to shoot dead

枪手 **qiāngshǒu** 〔N〕 marksman; gunman · 〔MW〕 个、名

枪替 **qiāngtì** 〔V〕 to fraudulently take an exam for (someone else)

枪支 **qiāngzhī** 〔N〕 firearms, guns · 〔MW〕 捆、批
是人在**枪杀**人, 还是**枪支**在**枪杀**人? *Do people kill people, or do guns kill people?*

**1244 枪 qiāng** (continued)

**RELATED WORDS**

| | | |
|---|---|---|
| 手枪 104 | 鸟枪 859 | 猎枪 1444 |
| 卡宾枪 36 | | |

---

**1245 根** U+6839 TM 12 FM |

**gēn** N·ADV·MW root (of a plant); base, foundation; origin, source; offspring, progeny; solution (of an algebraic equation); thoroughly, completely; [measure word for long, thin objects (rope, straw, needles, etc.)]

一根面条 *noodle*

树根 *roots of a tree*

祸根 *root of trouble*

扎根 *to take root*

**根本 gēnběn** N·ADJ·ADV base, foundation; basic, fundamental, essential; at all; thoroughly · MW 个

这是事情的根本。 *This is the root of the affair.*

她根本不知道事情的根本。 *She doesn't know a thing about the fundamentals of the situation.*

**根除 gēnchú** V to root out

**根底 gēndǐ** N foundation · MW 个

**根据 gēnjù** N·PREP basis, grounds; according to; in light of · MW 个

**根绝 gēnjué** V to root/stamp out; to eradicate

**根深蒂固 gēnshēndìgù** EXP deep-rooted

**根由 gēnyóu** N cause · MW 个

**根源 gēnyuán** N source, origin, cause · MW 个

**根子 gēnzi** N root; origin · MW 个

**RELATED WORDS**

| | | |
|---|---|---|
| 生根 107 | 牙根 143 | 归根结底 166 |
| 扎根 288 | 存根 438 | 命根子 1051 |
| 祸根 1754 | 墙根 1770 | 叶落归根 167 |
| 斩草除根 646 | 铲草除根 1304 | |

---

**1246 格** U+683C TM 12 FM |

**gé** N·V check, pattern of squares; standard, pattern; style; character; (legal) case; probe; to fight

**格调 gédiào** N (literary/artistic) style; character · MW 个

我不喜欢这部小说的格调。 *I don't like the style of this novel.*

**格局 géjú** N pattern, setup, structure · MW 个

**格式 géshì** N form, pattern · MW 种

**格外 géwài** ADV especially, particularly

写这种信是有一定格式的, 你要格外注意。 *There is a specific format for a letter of this kind to which you should pay particular attention.*

**格言 géyán** N maxim; motto · MW 句

傻瓜很喜爱某些特定的格言。 *ShaGua likes following particular maxims.*

**格子 gézi** N check, pattern of squares · MW 个

**RELATED WORDS**

| | | |
|---|---|---|
| 人格 4 | 升格 47 | 及格 141 |
| 风格 194 | 价格 210 | 方格纸 220 |
| 方格 220 | 严格 241 | 合格 296 |
| 体格 325 | 性格 498 | 表格 527 |
| 苏格兰 552 | 空格 669 | 规格 1098 |
| 品格 1220 | 资格 1335 | 破格 1374 |
| 够格 1808 | 不合格 24 | 市场价格 332 |
| 到岸价格 737 | 别具一格 1049 | |

---

**1247 棒** U+68D2 TM 12 FM |

**bàng** N·ADJ stick; club, cudgel; great; capable

**棒球 bàngqiú** N baseball · MW 个

**RELATED WORDS**

| | | |
|---|---|---|
| 太棒了 53 | 杠棒 293 | 棍棒 1776 |

---

**1248 棋** U+68CB TM 12 FM |

**qí** N chess; board game; chessman

**棋盘 qípán** N chessboard · MW 副

**棋子 qízǐ** N chess piece, chessman · MW 颗、副

社会像一副棋盘, 人就像上面的棋子。 *Society is like a chessboard, and people are like the pieces on the board.*

**RELATED WORDS**

| | |
|---|---|
| 围棋 762 | 象棋 1580 |

---

**1249 阿** U+963F TM 12 FM |

**ā** PFX [prefix for names of people]; [used before kinship terms]

**ē** V to pander to

阿拉伯 **Ālābó** N Arab

阿姨 **āyí** N aunt, mother's sister; [form of address for a woman of one's parents' age who is not related to one's family]; [form of address for a childcare worker or female housekeeper] · MW 个、位

中国人通常把长一辈的女性叫"阿姨"。
*Chinese people usually call females one generation older than them "aunt."*

---

**1250 陈** 陳     U+9648     TM **12** FM |

**chén** V·ADJ to exhibit, to lay/set out, to arrange; to narrate, to tell; old; stale

陈醋 **chéncù** N black (aged) vinegar · MW 瓶

陈腐 **chénfǔ** ADJ dated (LIT old and decayed)

陈规 **chénguī** N stereotyped · MW 个、套

陈旧 **chénjiù** ADJ outdated, out-of-date

陈列 **chénliè** V to display, to exhibit

陈述 **chénshù** V to state; to explain; to enunciate

请不要再**陈述**那些**陈腐**的**陈规**了。*Please don't repeat that old stereotype anymore.*

**RELATED WORDS**

推陈出新 1242     新陈代谢 1638

---

**1251 陌**     U+964C     TM **12** FM |

**mò** N·ADJ footpath; path between fields; strange

陌生 **mòshēng** ADJ strange, unfamiliar

我对你还是有些**陌生**。*You are still unfamiliar to me.*

---

**1252 险** 險     U+9669     TM **12** FM |

**xiǎn** N·ADJ·ADV place difficult to access, narrow pass; danger, risk; dangerous, perilous; vicious; nearly, almost

天险 *extremely dangerous barrier*

脱险 *to be out of danger*

危险 *dangerous*

阴险 *sinister*

险遭不测 *to come within an inch of death*

险恶 **xiǎn'è** ADJ dangerous; vicious

险境 **xiǎnjìng** N dangerous situation · MW 个

险区 **xiǎnqū** N danger zone · MW 个

---

**RELATED WORDS**

| | | |
|---|---|---|
| 风险 194 | 奸险 329 | 保险 868 |
| 艰险 973 | 冒险 989 | 阴险 1041 |
| 危险 1057 | 探险 1404 | 惊险 1489 |
| 脱险 1803 | 遇险 1891 | 冒风险 989 |
| 被保险人 1517 | 人寿保险 4 | |

---

**1253 购** 購     U+8D2D     TM **12** FM |

**gòu** V to buy, to purchase

购货单 **gòuhuòdān** N order form · MW 份、张

购买 **gòumǎi** V to buy, to purchase

购买力 **gòumǎilì** N purchasing power

购物中心 **gòuwùzhōngxīn** N shopping center/mall · MW 个

傻瓜常常拿着傻瓜太太写的**购货单**到**购物中心**去**购买**东西。*ShaGua often buys things at the mall from a list that Mrs. ShaGua gives him.*

**RELATED WORDS**

| | | |
|---|---|---|
| 代购 208 | 认购 239 | 订购 347 |
| 采购 434 | 征购 462 | 定购 666 |
| 邮购 1046 | 抢购 1230 | 选购 1510 |
| 预购 1528 | | |

---

**1254 贼** 賊     U+8D3C     TM **12** FM |

**zéi** N·ADJ·ADV thief; traitor; enemy; evil, wicked; cunning, sly; extremely; especially

贼船 **zéichuán** N pirate ship · MW 只、条

贼喊捉贼 **zéihǎnzhuōzéi** EXP thief crying "Stop, thief!"

贼头贼脑 **zéitóuzéinǎo** EXP to behave furtively/stealthily

明明是你考试时**贼头贼脑**地作弊，你却**贼喊捉贼**。*Obviously, it was you who cheated on the test, but you're pointing your finger at others.*

贼赃 **zéizāng** N stolen goods · MW 批

**RELATED WORDS**

盗贼 1475     窃贼 1482

---

**1255 盼**     U+76FC     TM **12** FM |

**pàn** V to yearn/long/hope (for); to look

盼望 **pànwàng** V to yearn/long/hope (for); to look forward to

**1255 盼 pàn** (continued)

**RELATED WORD**

渴盼 1822　　　　左顾右盼 113

---

**1256 胡** 鬍　U+80E1°　TM **12** FM |

**hú** N·ADV mustache; beard; recklessly; outrageously

胡扯 **húchě** V to talk nonsense

胡搞 **húgǎo** V to mess things up

胡椒 **hújiāo** N pepper · MW 颗、粒

胡里胡涂 **húlihútu** EXP confused, muddleheaded, in a daze

胡乱 **húluàn** ADV carelessly; casually
你这样**胡乱**地放**胡椒**，面条还能吃吗？
*You carelessly added too much pepper; are the noodles even edible?*

胡萝卜 **húluóbo** N carrot · MW 条、根

胡闹 **húnào** V to run wild; to be mischievous

胡说 **húshuō** V·N to talk drivel; nonsense

胡子 **húzi** N mustache; beard; bandit · MW 根
傻瓜的大儿子长**胡子**了。*ShaGua's older son has grown a beard.*
别**胡说**，他不是**胡子**！ *Don't talk nonsense; he's not a bandit.*

**RELATED WORDS**

二胡 2　　　　死胡同 510　　　　京胡 905
剃胡子 1639

---

**1257 趁** U+8D81　TM **12** FM |

**chèn** V·PREP to avail oneself of, to take advantage of; to possess; to pursue, to run after; to catch up with, to overtake; while

趁便 **chènbiàn** ADV when it is convenient

趁火打劫 **chènhuǒdǎjié** EXP to profit from another person's misfortune (LIT to loot a burning house)

趁机 **chènjī** V to seize an opportunity; to take advantage of a situation

趁空 **chènkòng** V to use one's spare time

趁早 **chènzǎo** ADV as soon as possible; before it's too late
他**趁火打劫**后，又**趁早**溜掉了。*He robbed the owner while the house was on fire and then ran away as quickly as possible.*

---

**1258 跃** 躍　U+8DC3　TM **12** FM |

**yuè** V to leap, to jump, to spring

跃进 **yuèjìn** V to leap forward
中国在*1958*年曾经搞过一次"大**跃进**"。
*There was a "Great Leap Forward" in China in 1958.*

**RELATED WORDS**

飞跃 81　　　　活跃 941　　　　跳跃 1786

---

**1259 救** U+6551　TM **12** FM |

**jiù** V to rescue, to save; to salvage; to help, to relieve

救兵 **jiùbīng** N reinforcements, relief troops · MW 支、队

救国 **jiùguó** V to save the country
科教**救国**。*Save the country with science and education.*

救护 **jiùhù** V to give first aid to; to rescue

救火 **jiùhuǒ** V to fight a fire

救济 **jiùjì** V to relieve
**救济**灾区 *to extend relief to a disaster area*

救命 **jiùmìng** V to save a life; Help!, Save me!

救生 **jiùshēng** V to save a life

救生员 **jiùshēngyuán** N medic · MW 个、名

救灾 **jiùzāi** V to provide disaster relief

救治 **jiùzhì** V to treat and cure
**救生员**在**救治**伤员。*The medic is treating the wounded.*

救助 **jiùzhù** V to help (someone) in danger/trouble

**RELATED WORDS**

| | | |
|---|---|---|
| 自救 305 | 求救 376 | 补救 508 |
| 呼救 779 | 抢救 1230 | 急救 1426 |
| 营救 1546 | 援救 1556 | 挽救 1659 |
| 遇救 1891 | 解救 1928 | 搬救兵 1943 |

---

**1260 断** 斷　U+65AD　TM **12** FM |

**duàn** V·ADV to break, to snap; to break off, to stop; to give up, to abstain from; to judge, to decide; absolutely; decidedly [in negative constructions]

断层 **duàncéng** N (geological) fault; gap (in talent, intellect) · MW 个

断电 **duàndiàn** V to have a power failure/outage

断定 **duàndìng** V to conclude, to determine

断交 **duànjiāo** V to sever diplomatic relations; to fall out, to break off a friendship

现在还不能**断定**两国是否已经**断交**。*It is still too early to decide whether or not the two countries have severed diplomatic relations.*

断绝 **duànjué** V to sever, to break/cut off

断开 **duànkāi** V to break/cut off

断裂 **duànliè** V to crack, to break apart

断然 **duànrán** ADV absolutely, flatly, categorically

断言 **duànyán** V·N to assert, to state with certainty; judgment, conclusion

你现在能**断然**地**断言**傻瓜不能当州长吗? *Now, are you absolutely sure that ShaGua cannot be governor?*

**RELATED WORDS**

| | | |
|---|---|---|
| 不断 24 | 中断 86 | 专断 155 |
| 切断 277 | 打断 289 | 决断 340 |
| 折断 408 | 判断 507 | 武断 513 |
| 果断 544 | 诊断 709 | 论断 947 |
| 推断 1242 | 裁断 1535 | 截断 1650 |
| 割断 1761 | 隔断 1910 | |

---

**1261** 盆 U+76C6 TM **12** FM 丿

**pén** N basin; pot; tub

盆地 **péndì** N basin · MW 个、块

盆花 **pénhuā** N potted flower · MW 蔟、朵

盆景 **pénjǐng** N bonsai; landscape in a pot · MW 个

盆浴 **pényù** V to bathe (in a tub)

盆栽 **pénzāi** V growing plants in pots; bonsai

有些家长用制做"**盆栽**"的方式来培养孩子, 非常不利于孩子的健康成长。*Some parents raise their children and control their development like bonsai trees; this is very bad for a child's development.*

**RELATED WORDS**

| | | |
|---|---|---|
| 浴盆 1170 | 脸盆 1461 | 澡盆 1954 |
| 洗脸盆 1167 | 聚宝盆 1642 | |

---

**1262** 拿 U+62FF TM **12** FM 丿

**ná** V to hold; to capture, to catch, to take; to get, to obtain

拿大顶 **nádàdǐng** V to perform a handstand

拿得起 **nádeqǐ** V to be able/competent

傻瓜**拿得起**市长的工作。*ShaGua can handle his job as mayor.*

拿获 **náhuò** V to apprehend (a criminal)

拿手 **náshǒu** ADJ adept; good at

这是他的**拿手**好戏。*This is what he is very good at.*

拿主意 **názhǔyi** V to make the calls, to be in charge

在市政府里, 傻瓜**拿主意**; 在家里傻瓜太太**拿主意**。*ShaGua makes the calls at City Hall; Mrs. ShaGua makes the calls at home.*

拿住 **názhù** V to hold firmly; to arrest

**RELATED WORDS**

| | | |
|---|---|---|
| 十拿九稳 3 | 加拿大 463 | 推拿 1242 |

---

**1263** 乘 U+4E58 TM **12** FM 丿

**chéng** V·N to ride, to travel by; to make use of, to take advantage of; to multiply; vehicle

乘船 **chéngchuán** V to be on a ship; to travel by ship

乘法 **chéngfǎ** N multiplication · MW 个

乘机 **chéngjī** ADV to seize the chance

他**乘机**去了一次中国。*He seized the opportunity to go to China.*

乘客 **chéngkè** N passenger · MW 个、名、位

乘务员 **chéngwùyuán** N crew member, attendant; conductor · MW 个、名

**RELATED WORD**

被乘数 1517

---

**1264** 爱 愛 U+7231 TM **12** FM 丿

**ài** V·ADJ to love, to like; to cherish, to treasure; to enjoy; to tend to, to be apt to, to be in the habit of; loved; beloved; favorite

爱戴 **àidài** V to love and esteem

爱国 **àiguó** V·ADJ to love one's country; patriotic

爱好 **àihào** V·N to be fond of; hobby · MW 个

他唯一的**爱好**是当一个"沙发土豆"。*His sole hobby is being a "couch potato."*

爱护 **àihù** V to cherish; to treasure

爱面子 **àimiànzi** EXP to worry about losing face, to be sensitive about one's reputation

"**爱面子**"是中国人的一个特点。*"Being sensitive about one's reputation" is a characteristic of Chinese people.*

1264 爱 ài (continued)

爱情 àiqíng  N  love (between a man and a woman)

爱人 àiren  N  spouse, husband, wife (in China) · MW 个、位

爱惜 àixī  V  to cherish, to love dearly; to value

在中国，配偶都称为"**爱人**"，至于是不是有**爱情**则另当别论。*All spouses are called "爱人" in China; as for whether or not they love each other, that's another question altogether.*

爱憎 àizēng  V  to love and hate

**RELATED WORDS**

| | | |
|---|---|---|
| 仁爱 64 | 友爱 110 | 心爱 232 |
| 可爱 243 | 自爱 305 | 母爱 394 |
| 珍爱 515 | 怜爱 695 | 亲爱 908 |
| 钟爱 1125 | 宠爱 1137 | 疼爱 1148 |
| 恋爱 1314 | 惜爱 1350 | 恩爱 1381 |
| 热爱 1390 | 喜爱 1531 | 博爱 1549 |
| 偏爱 1587 | 敬爱 1689 | 割爱 1761 |
| 慈爱 1952 | 互敬互爱 135 | |

**1265  焦    U+7126    TM 12  FM 丿**

jiāo  ADJ·N  burnt, scorched; dry, parched; worried, anxious; coke (processed coal)

焦点 jiāodiǎn  N  focal point, central issue · MW 个

焦急 jiāojí  ADJ  worried, anxious

焦距 jiāojù  N  focal length

找不到**焦点**，就无法对**焦距**。*If you can't find the focal point, then you won't be able to adjust the focal length.*

焦煤 jiāoméi  N  coking coal · MW 块、吨

焦头烂额 jiāotóulàn'é  EXP  in bad shape, in a terrible fix

焦躁 jiāozào  ADJ  restless, impatient

**RELATED WORDS**

| | | |
|---|---|---|
| 心焦 232 | 对焦 254 | 聚焦 1642 |

**1266  售    U+552E    TM 12  FM 丿**

shòu  V  to sell

售后服务 shòuhòufúwù  N  after-sales service

这种电脑没有**售后服务**。*There is no after-sales service for this type of computer.*

售货 shòuhuò  V  to sell goods

售价 shòujià  N  selling price · MW 个

售票处 shòupiàochù  N  ticket office · MW 个

售票口 shòupiàokǒu  N  ticket window · MW 个

售票员 shòupiàoyuán  N  ticket seller (for a bus, a train, etc.) · MW 个、名

**RELATED WORDS**

| | | |
|---|---|---|
| 代售 208 | 出售 258 | 抛售 1395 |
| 零售 1640 | 销售 1714 | 销售点 1714 |
| 销售额 1714 | 销售税 1714 | |

**1267  集    U+96C6    TM 12  FM 丿**

jí  V·N  to gather, to collect; market; anthology

集成 jíchéng  V  integrated

集合 jíhé  V  to gather, to assemble

集结 jíjié  V  to concentrate, to build up

集市 jíshì  N  market; country fair · MW 个

集体 jítǐ  N  collective; community; team · MW 个

傻瓜总是尊重**集体**的决定。*ShaGua always respects team decisions.*

集邮 jíyóu  V  to collect stamps

集中 jízhōng  V  to concentrate, to centralize

傻瓜不得不**集中**全市最优秀的人才来完成城市的改造方案。*ShaGua has to bring together all of the talented people of the city to work on restructuring the city.*

集装箱 jízhuāngxiāng  N  (shipping) container · MW 个

集资 jízī  V  to raise funds

**RELATED WORDS**

| | | |
|---|---|---|
| 文集 70 | 云集 80 | 全集 172 |
| 汇集 234 | 收集 282 | 采集 434 |
| 征集 462 | 赶集 822 | 约集 876 |
| 堆集 1003 | 诗集 1181 | 选集 1510 |
| 聚集 1642 | 群集 1646 | 搜集 1663 |
| 密集 1730 | 调集 1749 | 影集 1918 |
| 邀集 1983 | | |

**1268  忽    U+5FFD    TM 12  FM 丿**

hū  ADV·V  suddenly; to neglect, to overlook, to ignore

忽…忽… hū… hū…  ADV  now … now …

今天**忽**冷**忽**热。*Today's weather is cold one minute and hot the next.*

忽略 **hūlüè** V to neglect, to overlook, to ignore

忽然 **hūrán** ADV suddenly, all at once, quickly and unexpectedly

忽视 **hūshì** V to neglect, to overlook, to ignore

老师绝不能忽视学生的自尊。 *Teachers should never neglect students' self-esteem.*

**RELATED WORDS**

玩忽 727　　　飘忽 1939

---

**1269 氧** U+6C27 TM **12** FM ノ

**yǎng** N oxygen

氧化 **yǎnghuà** V to oxidize

氧气 **yǎngqì** N oxygen · MW 瓶

**RELATED WORD**

臭氧 1088

---

**1270 架** U+67B6 TM **12** FM ノ

**jià** V·N·MW to erect; to support, to prop (up); to ward off, to withstand; frame, rack; [measure word for planes, pianos, cameras, etc.]

架设 **jiàshè** V to erect (on posts, etc.)

架子 **jiàzi** N air; haughty manner; frame, rack, stand; structure, outline

傻瓜不喜欢摆架子。 *ShaGua doesn't like to put on an air of importance.*

这个电视需要一个架子。 *This TV needs a stand.*

文章的架子已搭好。 *The outline of the article has been created.*

**RELATED WORDS**

井架 60　　　　支架 92　　　　劝架 255
书架 264　　　打架 289　　　衣架 330
吵架 415　　　空架子 669　　担架 789
骨架 1543　　散架 1579　　摆架子 1773
十字架 3

---

**1271 梨** U+68A8 TM **12** FM ノ

**lí** N pear

**RELATED WORD**

凤梨 314

---

**1272 厚** U+539A TM **12** FM ノ

**hòu** ADJ·V thick; deep; profound; generous, magnanimous; rich/strong (in flavor); rich (in family wealth); to favor; to stress

厚钢板 *thick steel plate*

深厚友谊 *deep friendship*

傻瓜很忠厚。 *ShaGua is generous.*

利润丰厚。 *Profits are strong.*

家底深厚 *great family wealth*

厚古薄今 *to stress the past, not the present*

厚薄 **hòubó** N thickness

厚道 **hòudào** ADJ kind, generous

傻瓜很厚道。 *ShaGua is very generous.*

厚度 **hòudù** N thickness

厚脸皮 **hòuliǎnpí** EXP thick-skinned, defiant

她很厚脸皮。 *She is really thick-skinned.*

厚实 **hòushi** ADJ rich; abundant; solid

**RELATED WORDS**

忠厚 743　　　浓厚 1168　　　肥厚 1459
宽厚 1618　　温厚 1627

---

**1273 原** U+539F TM **12** FM ノ

**yuán** ADJ·V·N original; primary; unprocessed, raw; to excuse, to pardon, to forgive; open country, plain

原版 **yuánbǎn** N original edition; original cassette/videotape

原本 **yuánběn** N·ADV original manuscript; original version; originally; formerly · MW 份

这是一份原本。 *This is an original manuscript.*

原稿 **yuángǎo** N original manuscript · MW 份

原告 **yuángào** N plaintiff · MW 个、名

原本这位原告不想来，但最后还是来了。 *Originally, the plaintiff did not want to come, but he finally did.*

原籍 **yuánjí** N ancestral home, native place

原价 **yuánjià** N original price

原来 **yuánlái** N·ADJ·ADV original; former; originally; it turns out, all along

他原来不是老师。 *He wasn't always a teacher.*

我知道了，原来她是一位老师。 *I see, it turns out that she is a teacher.*

原理 **yuánlǐ** N principle; theory · MW 个

原谅 **yuánliàng** V to forgive, to excuse

**1273 原 yuán** (continued)

原料 **yuánliào** [N] raw material; ingredient

原色 **yuánsè** [N] primary color

原始 **yuánshǐ** [ADJ] original, first; primitive, undeveloped

原诉 **yuánsù** [N] original lawsuit · [MW] 个

原委 **yuánwěi** [N] whole story; full details

原文 **yuánwén** [N] original text · [MW] 份

她告诉我事情的**原委**，并让我看了我**原文**，我就**原谅**了她。 *She related the entire story to me and let me read the original document, so I forgave her.*

原先 **yuánxiān** [N] original; former

原意 **yuànyì** [N] original meaning

原因 **yuányīn** [N] cause, reason · [MW] 个

原油 **yuányóu** [N] crude oil

原则 **yuánzé** [N] principle; in general · [MW] 个

**原则**上说，我不能放弃我**原先**的**原则**，但愿意寻求新的解决办法。 *In general, I am unwilling to abandon my basic principles, but I am willing to find a new solution.*

原著 **yuánzhù** [N] original work · [MW] 部

原子 **yuánzǐ** [N] atom · [MW] 个

原子弹 **yuánzǐdàn** [N] atomic bomb · [MW] 颗、枚

原子能 **yuánzǐnéng** [N] atomic/nuclear energy

**RELATED WORDS**

| | | |
|---|---|---|
| 平原 78 | 中原 86 | 还原 714 |
| 草原 768 | 荒原 1222 | 高原 1611 |
| 露原形 1997 | 云贵高原 80 | |

---

**1274 展**　　U+5C55　TM **12** FM 丿

**zhǎn** [V·N] to open up, to spread out; to give free rein to; to exhibit, to show; to postpone, to delay; exhibition

展翅 **zhǎnchì** [V] to spread one's wings

展出 **zhǎnchū** [V] to exhibit, to put on display

展开 **zhǎnkāi** [V] to open up; to spread out; to carry out

展览 **zhǎnlǎn** [V] to exhibit, to show

展品 **zhǎnpǐn** [N] exhibit; item on display · [MW] 件

展示 **zhǎnshì** [V] to reveal, to show

学生要**展示**自己的个性和能力。 *Students ought to reveal their own characters and talents.*

展望 **zhǎnwàng** [V] to look ahead; to forecast

展销 **zhǎnxiāo** [V] to display for sale

---

**RELATED WORDS**

| | | |
|---|---|---|
| 开展 26 | 扩展 291 | 发展 311 |
| 伸展 457 | 进展 713 | 画展 719 |
| 施展 1758 | 舒展 1805 | |

---

**1275 泉**　　U+6CC9　TM **12** FM 丿

**quán** [N] spring; mouth of a spring

泉水 **quánshuǐ** [N] spring · [MW] 汪、眼

泉眼 **quányǎn** [N] mouth of a spring · [MW] 个

泉源 **quányuán** [N] fountainhead · [MW] 个

饮水不忘**泉源**。 *When you drink water, you should not forget its source. (Never forget those who have helped you.)*

**RELATED WORDS**

| | | |
|---|---|---|
| 喷泉 1563 | 温泉 1627 | 源泉 1742 |

---

**1276 爹**　　U+7239　TM **12** FM 丿

**diē** [N] dad, father

爹爹 **diēdie** [N] dad, father · [MW] 个

---

**1277 符**　　U+7B26　TM **12** FM 丿

**fú** [N·V] symbol, mark; talisman; to accord with, to be in keeping with

符号 **fúhào** [N] symbol, mark, sign · [MW] 个

文字是表达特定意思的**符号**。 *Written characters are symbols that indicate certain meanings.*

符合 **fúhé** [V] to accord with, to match

傻瓜的言行**符合**他的性格。 *ShaGua's words and deeds are in accord with his nature.*

**RELATED WORDS**

| | | |
|---|---|---|
| 不符 24 | 字符 664 | 相符 805 |
| 音符 907 | | |

---

**1278 笔 筆**　　U+7B14　TM **12** FM 丿

**bǐ** [N·MW] pen; pencil; brush; calligraphy, drawing; calligraphic technique, handwriting; (brush) stroke (of a Chinese character); [measure word for sums of money and for business deals]

笔调 **bǐdiào** N tone/style (of writing) · MW 种

笔法 **bǐfǎ** N calligraphic/artistic technique; calligraphy, drawing · MW 种

笔画 **bǐhuà** N stroke · MW 个

断笔码字典的最大特点就是对传统**笔画**的革新。 *The main feature of the Broken Marks Dictionary is an innovation of the traditional strokes system.*

笔记 **bǐjì** N·V notes; type of literature consisting of short sketches; to take down (in writing)

笔记本 **bǐjìběn** N notebook · MW 本

笔记本电脑 **bǐjìběndiànnǎo** N laptop, notebook computer · MW 本

笔名 **bǐmíng** N pen name · MW 个

笔墨 **bǐmò** N pen and ink; writing; article

笔试 **bǐshì** N·V written exam; to take a written exam · MW 次

笔译 **bǐyì** V to translate (in writing)

笔者 **bǐzhě** N this writer/author · MW 个、名

这篇文章的**笔者**有个很奇怪的**笔名**，写作的**笔调**也很独特。 *The author of this article has a very unique writing style and a very strange pen name.*

笔直 **bǐzhí** ADJ perfectly straight

### RELATED WORDS

| | | |
|---|---|---|
| 下笔 10 | 文笔 70 | 手笔 104 |
| 主笔 124 | 毛笔 183 | 伏笔 212 |
| 走笔 265 | 动笔 514 | 执笔 564 |
| 画笔 719 | 亲笔 908 | 眉笔 1067 |
| 钢笔 1299 | 着笔 1332 | 卷笔刀 1333 |
| 粉笔 1363 | 铅笔 1464 | 落笔 1547 |
| 蜡笔 1780 | 随笔 1911 | 圆珠笔 1391 |

---

**1279** 笛    U+7B1B    TM **12** FM 丿

**dí** N bamboo flute

笛子 **dízi** N bamboo flute; flute · MW 支

### RELATED WORDS

长笛 93      警笛 1987

---

**1280** 侵    U+4FB5    TM **12** FM 丿

**qīn** V to invade; to infringe/encroach on; to approach, to get near to

侵犯 **qīnfàn** V to infringe/encroach on

侵犯人权 *to infringe on (someone's) human rights*

侵害 **qīnhài** V to violate

侵略 **qīnlüè** V to invade

侵入 **qīnrù** V to invade; to violate

侵蚀 **qīnshí** V to corrode, to erode

侵蚀思想 *corrosive ideologies*

侵占 **qīnzhàn** V to invade and occupy, to seize

侵占他国 *to invade and occupy another country*

### RELATED WORD

入侵 5

---

**1281** 倒    U+5012    TM **12** FM 丿

**dǎo** V to fall, to collapse; to fail, to go bankrupt; to overthrow (a government, a political leader); to transfer, to change; to offer for sale

摔倒 *to fall*

倒手 *to change hands*

倒开身 *to move around*

倒卖 *to resell at a profit*

**dào** V·ADJ·ADV to dump, to pour; to move backwards, to reverse; upside down; but, on the contrary, instead

倒车 *to back a car up*

倒茶 *to pour tea*

反倒 *upside down*

倒班 **dǎobān** V to change shifts

倒闭 **dǎobì** V to go bankrupt

工厂倒闭。 *The factory closed down.*

倒换 **dǎohuàn** V to rotate

倒塌 **dǎotā** V to collapse (of a building)

房屋倒塌。 *The house collapsed.*

倒台 **dǎotái** V to fall from power

政府倒台。 *The government has fallen from power.*

倒酒 **dàojiǔ** V to pour wine

倒立 **dàolì** V to be upside down

### RELATED WORDS

| | | |
|---|---|---|
| 压倒 201 | 打倒 289 | 拉倒 573 |
| 卧倒 826 | 绊倒 887 | 驳倒 983 |
| 栽倒 995 | 推倒 1242 | 病倒 1327 |
| 晕倒 1385 | 跌倒 1422 | 帮倒忙 1583 |
| 跪倒 1945 | 本末倒置 90 | 移山倒海 1450 |

## 1282 做　U+505A　TM 12　FM 丿

**zuò** [V] to make, to produce; to cook; to write; to do, to engage in; to be; to become; to be used as; to form a relationship; to hold/ have (a family celebration); to pretend

做衣服 *to make clothes*

做饭 *to cook food*

做文章 *to write a paper*

做买卖 *to engage in trade*

做老师 *to be a teacher*

做朋友 *to become friends with*

做假 *to pretend*

做伴 **zuòbàn** [V] to keep (someone) company

做到 **zuòdào** [V] to accomplish, to achieve

傻瓜总是说到**做到**。 *ShaGua has always been as good as his word.*

做东 **zuòdōng** [V] to play host

做法 **zuòfǎ** [N] method/way (of doing something) · [MW] 个、种

做工 **zuògōng** [V] to do manual work; to act (in traditional opera)

做官 **zuòguān** [V] to be an official

傻瓜从**做工**到**做官**, 走了很长一段路。 *From doing manual work to being an officeholder, ShaGua has come a long way.*

做广告 **zuòguǎnggào** [V] to advertise

做鬼 **zuòguǐ** [V] to play tricks

做活 **zuòhuó** [V] to work

做客 **zuòkè** [V] to be a guest

今天我**做东**, 你**做客**。 *Today, I am the host and you are the guest.*

做梦 **zuòmèng** [V] to dream; to daydream

做人 **zuòrén** [V] to conduct oneself; to behave with integrity

做声 **zuòshēng** [V] to make a sound

做事 **zuòshì** [V] to do work; to handle affairs

做寿 **zuòshòu** [V] to celebrate a birthday (usually of elderly people)

做戏 **zuòxì** [V] to act in a play; to put on a play; to playact

做主 **zuòzhǔ** [V] to decide; to back up, to support

这个事情我**做主**。 *I will make a decision regarding this issue.*

这个事情我给你**做主**。 *I will back you up on this issue.*

做作 **zuòzuò** [ADJ] affected

### RELATED WORDS

叫做 283　　　当做 335　　　定做 666
看做 841

## 1283 牺 犧　U+727A　TM 12　FM 丿

**xī** [V] to sacrifice, to give up

牺牲 **xīshēng** [V·N] to give one's life for; to sacrifice · [MW] 个

## 1284 狠　U+72E0　TM 12　FM 丿

**hěn** [V·ADJ·ADV] to harden; ruthless, fierce; resolute, relentless; firmly, sternly

狠毒 **hěndú** [ADJ] vicious, cruel

狠心 **hěnxīn** [ADJ·V] heartless; to harden one's heart

做父母的, 有时需要对孩子"**狠心**"一些。 *As parents, you may sometimes have to make a painful decision.*

### RELATED WORDS

凶狠 98　　　心狠 232　　　恶狠狠 1196

## 1285 狮 獅　U+72EE　TM 12　FM 丿

**shī** [N] lion

狮子 **shīzi** [N] lion · [MW] 头

狮子舞 **shīzǐwǔ** [N] lion dance (a traditional Chinese dance mimicking a lion's movements) · [MW] 个

## 1286 狱 獄　U+72F1　TM 12　FM 丿

**yù** [N] prison, jail; lawsuit, case

狱吏 **yùlì** [N] prison official · [MW] 个、名

### RELATED WORDS

入狱 5　　　牢狱 488　　　监狱 994
冤狱 1729

## 1287 狗　U+72D7　TM 12　FM 丿

**gǒu** [N] dog

狗胆包天 **gǒudǎnbāotiān** [EXP] monstrous audacity

狗屁 **gǒupì** EXP nonsense

狗腿子 **gǒutuǐzi** EXP hired thug, lackey, henchman · MW 个

狗熊 **gǒuxióng** N black bear · MW 只

**RELATED WORDS**

| | | |
|---|---|---|
| 走狗 265 | 疯狗 1147 | 热狗 1390 |
| 狼狗 1443 | 猎狗 1444 | 赛狗 1813 |
| 狼心狗肺 1443 | | |

---

**1288** 称 稱   U+79F0   TM **12** FM 丿

**chēng** V·N to call, to name; to say, to express; to commend, to praise; to weigh; name; title

**chèn** V to match, to suit, to balance

**chèng** N lever/platform balance/scale · MW 杆、台

称霸 **chēngbà** V to take a leading role

称号 **chēnghào** N name; title · MW 个

称呼 **chēnghu** V·N to call, to address as, to name; form of address · MW 个

在中国，**称呼**人是很有学问的。 *Addressing others in China requires a lot of work.*

称量 **chēngliáng** V to weigh

称谓 **chēngwèi** N form of address; title indicating relationship · MW 个

称赞 **chēngzàn** V to praise

**RELATED WORDS**

| | | |
|---|---|---|
| 匀称 180 | 对称 254 | 自称 305 |
| 声称 374 | 名称 426 | 泛称 495 |
| 号称 545 | 美称 671 | 诈称 707 |
| 相称 805 | 别称 1049 | 职称 1205 |
| 著称 1223 | 统称 1601 | 尊称 1722 |
| 诡称 1747 | 通称 1757 | 简称 1796 |

---

**1289** 秘   U+79D8   TM **12** FM 丿

**mì** ADJ secret; mysterious

秘本 **mìběn** N treasured, privately owned rare book · MW 本

秘方 **mìfāng** N secret recipe/formula · MW 个

秘诀 **mìjué** N secret of success; knack; trade secret · MW 个

秘密 **mìmì** ADJ·N secret, confidential; secrecy · MW 个

秘史 **mìshǐ** N secret history · MW 部

秘书 **mìshū** N secretary · MW 个、名

---

**RELATED WORDS**

| | | |
|---|---|---|
| 便秘 865 | 神秘 1191 | 奥秘 1435 |
| 隐秘 1912 | | |

---

**1290** 纯 純   U+7EAF   TM **12** FM 丿

**chún** ADJ·ADV pure; genuine; net; skillful; entirely

纯粹 **chúncuì** ADJ·ADV pure; only; completely, purely

纯度 **chúndù** N purity

纯化 **chúnhuà** V to purify

纯利 **chúnlì** N net profit · MW 笔

纯收入 **chúnshōurù** N net income · MW 笔

纯正 **chúnzhèng** ADJ pure

他说一口流利而**纯正**的汉语。 *He speaks fluent and pure Chinese.*

**RELATED WORDS**

| | |
|---|---|
| 单纯 672 | 提纯 1554 |

---

**1291** 结 結   U+7ED3   TM **12** FM 丿

**jiē** V to bear (fruit); to produce

**jié** V·N to forge; to join together, to unite; to settle, to conclude; to tie; to knit; knot; written guarantee/pledge; receipt

结巴 **jiēbā** V·N to stammer; stutterer

结实 **jiēshi** ADJ strong, sturdy; solid

傻瓜长得很**结实**，但说话有点儿**结巴**。 *ShaGua is very sturdy, but he stammers a little bit.*

结伴 **jiébàn** V to go with; to form groups

结冰 **jiébīng** V to freeze, to ice up/over

结肠 **jiécháng** N colon, large intestine · MW 根、条

结成 **jiéchéng** V to form, to forge (an alliance, etc.)

结构 **jiégòu** N·V structure, construction; composition, makeup; to organize · MW 个

这间房子的**结构**很独特。 *The structure of this house is very unique.*

结果 **jiéguǒ** CONJ·N·V as a result; in the end; result, outcome; to kill · MW 个

结合 **jiéhé** V to combine, to integrate; to become a couple

结婚 **jiéhūn** V to marry

结交 **jiéjiāo** V to become friends with, to associate with

**1291 结 jiē/jié (continued)**

结晶 jiéjīng N·V crystal; crystallization; precious result; to crystallize · MW 个

十多年前，傻瓜和傻瓜太太结婚了。他们结合的结晶是生了二子一女。 *More than 10 years ago, ShaGua and Mrs. ShaGua were married. The precious results of their union are two sons and one daughter.*

结局 jiéjú N outcome, final result, ending · MW 个

结论 jiélùn N conclusion; verdict · MW 个

结盟 jiéméng V to ally, to align

结清 jiéqīng V to settle, to square up

结识 jiéshí V to get to know

结束 jiéshù V to end, to finish

结算 jiésuàn V to settle up

结尾 jiéwěi N·V end, ending; to wind up, to finish · MW 个

结业 jiéyè V to complete a course; to finish one's studies

结余 jiéyú V·N to have a cash surplus; balance

结账 jiézhàng V to settle up

你如果结识了傻瓜，每次吃饭他都会抢着结账。 *Once ShaGua gets to know you, he rushes to pay the bill whenever you go to a restaurant together.*

**RELATED WORDS**

| | | |
|---|---|---|
| 小结 61 | 归结 166 | 勾结 303 |
| 团结 392 | 冻结 680 | 完结 909 |
| 症结 923 | 联结 1206 | 集结 1267 |
| 总结 1330 | 领结 1465 | 硬结 1524 |
| 归根结底 166 | 张灯结彩 1208 | |

**1292 给 給** U+7ED9　TM **12** FM 丿

gěi V·PREP to give, to grant; to pass, to hand [after a verb]; to let, to allow; for; to; for the benefit of; by [in a passive construction]

给钱 *to give money*

还给她 *to return to her*

不给她去。 *Don't allow her to go.*

jǐ V·ADJ to supply, to provide; to be well provided for; sufficient; ample

补给 *to supply*

给养 jǐyǎng N provisions

给予 jǐyǔ V to give, to render

**RELATED WORDS**

| | | |
|---|---|---|
| 发给 311 | 供给 459 | 补给 508 |

**1293 段** U+6BB5　TM **12** FM 丿

duàn N·MW section, segment, part; paragraph; passage; [measure word for sections (a stretch of road, etc.), periods (of time), and parts (of writing, speeches), etc.]

段落 duànluò N paragraph; phase, stage · MW 个

这也是人生的一个段落。 *This is also a stage of life.*

**RELATED WORDS**

| | |
|---|---|
| 手段 104 | 片段 119 |
| 分段 173 | 阶段 590 |
| 身段 604 | 地段 772 |
| 波段 936 | |

**1294 肺** U+80BA　TM **12** FM 丿

fèi N lung

肺癌 fèi'ái N lung cancer

肺炎 fèiyán N pneumonia

**RELATED WORD**

狼心狗肺 1443

**1295 胆 膽** U+80C6　TM **12** FM 丿

dǎn N·V courage, bravery, audacity; gallbladder; liner (of a container); to dare

胆大 dǎndà ADJ bold, audacious

傻瓜很胆大。 *ShaGua is very bold.*

胆敢 dǎngǎn V to dare, to have the gall

胆固醇 dǎngùchún N cholesterol

胆量 dǎnliàng N courage, guts

胆怯 dǎnqiè ADJ shy, timid

胆小 dǎnxiǎo ADJ timid; cowardly

傻瓜的女儿很胆小。 *ShaGua's daughter is very timid.*

胆战心惊 dǎnzhànxīnjīng EXP to be scared out of one's wits

胆子 dǎnzi N courage, guts

**RELATED WORDS**

| | |
|---|---|
| 大胆 20 | 斗胆 71 |
| 壮胆 238 | 龙胆 315 |
| 丧胆 521 | 肝胆 650 |
| 狗胆包天 1287 | 明目张胆 1035 |

## 1296 胶 膠 U+80F6 TM 12 FM 丿

**jiāo** N·V·ADJ glue; rubber; to fasten with glue; adhesive; sticky; viscous

胶布 **jiāobù** N adhesive plaster · MW 块、卷
胶合木 **jiāohémù** N laminated wood · MW 块
胶卷 **jiāojuǎn** N film · MW 卷
胶囊 **jiāonáng** N capsule · MW 颗、粒
胶片 **jiāopiàn** N film · MW 卷
胶水 **jiāoshuǐ** N glue · MW 滴、瓶

**RELATED WORD**
塑胶 1815

## 1297 脏 髒 臟 U+810F TM 12 FM 丿

**zāng** (髒) ADJ dirty; filthy

**zàng** (臟) N internal organ (of the body)

脏字 **zāngzì** N dirty word · MW 个
无论什么语言，最容易学的就是脏字。
*No matter what language it is, dirty words are the easiest ones to learn.*
脏器 **zàngqì** N internal organ (of the body) · MW 个

**RELATED WORDS**

| | | |
|---|---|---|
| 五脏 79 | 内脏 191 | 心脏 232 |
| 弄脏 251 | 肝脏 650 | 脾脏 1711 |

## 1298 朋 U+670B TM 12 FM 丿

**péng** N·V friend; to gang up

朋党 **péngdǎng** N clique · MW 个
朋友 **péngyou** N friend · MW 个、位
孩子把玩具当朋友，成人把朋友当玩具。
*Kids treat their toys like friends; adults treat their friends like toys.*

**RELATED WORDS**
男朋友 757      够朋友 1808

## 1299 钢 鋼 U+94A2 TM 12 FM 丿

**gāng** N·V steel; to sharpen

钢板 **gāngbǎn** N steel plate · MW 块
钢笔 **gāngbǐ** N pen · MW 支
钢材 **gāngcái** N steel, steel products · MW 吨

钢管 **gāngguǎn** N steel pipe · MW 根、条
钢琴 **gāngqín** N piano · MW 台
钢丝 **gāngsī** N steel wire · MW 根、条
钢铁 **gāngtiě** N·ADJ iron and steel; strong, unbreakable · MW 吨

**RELATED WORD**
炼钢 1357

## 1300 钥 鑰 U+80F6 TM 12 FM 丿

**yào**/yuè N key

钥匙 **yàoshi** N key · MW 把
什么是开启心灵的钥匙？ *What is the key to unlocking people's minds?*

**RELATED WORD**
锁钥 1608

## 1301 钱 錢 U+80F6 TM 12 FM 丿

**qián** N money; riches; copper coin; [like a coin]

钱包 **qiánbāo** N purse; wallet · MW 个
钱币 **qiánbì** N coin · MW 个、枚
钱财 **qiáncái** N money; wealth · MW 笔
与亲人谈钱财伤感情，与情人谈感情伤钱财。
*Discussing money with relatives will hurt relationships; discussing love with lovers (dating) will hurt your wallet.*
钱柜 **qiánguì** N money box · MW 个
钱款 **qiánkuǎn** N money · MW 笔

**RELATED WORDS**

| | | |
|---|---|---|
| 工钱 12 | 付钱 206 | 价钱 210 |
| 汇钱 234 | 花钱 549 | 找钱 567 |
| 点钱 739 | 省钱 860 | 值钱 1089 |
| 挣钱 1398 | 换钱 1402 | 费钱 1520 |
| 零钱 1640 | 摇钱树 1664 | 骗钱 1937 |
| 几多钱 115 | 压岁钱 201 | 一块钱 400 |
| 私房钱 471 | | |

## 1302 钻 鑽 U+80F6 TM 12 FM 丿

**zuān** V to drill; to penetrate; to study intensively; to dig into

**zuàn** V·N to drill; drill; diamond; jewel

钻床 **zuànchuáng** N machine drill · MW 台
钻机 **zuànjī** N drilling rig · MW 台

**1302** 钻 **zuān/zuàn** (continued)

钻井 **zuànjǐng** [V·N] to drill wells; well drilling · [MW] 口

钻石 **zuànshí** [N] diamond; precious gem · [MW] 颗、粒

---

**1303**  鈴    U+80F6    TM **12**   FM 丿

**líng** [N] bell; [shaped like a bell]

铃铛 **língdāng** [N] small bell · [MW] 个

铃声 **língshēng** [N] tinkling/ringing (of a bell) · [MW] 阵

**RELATED WORDS**

马铃薯 247     杠铃 293     警铃 1987

---

**1304** 铲 鏟    U+80F6    TM **12**   FM 丿

**chǎn** [N·V] shovel, spade; to level off; to root up

铲草除根 **chǎncǎochúgēn** [EXP] to eradicate (LIT to pull the weeds and dig up the roots)

铲除 **chǎnchú** [V] to root out, to eradicate
铲除种族主义的流毒。*Root out the pernicious influence of racism.*

铲运机 **chǎnyùnjī** [N] bulldozer · [MW] 台

---

**1305** 缺    U+80F6    TM **12**   FM 丿

**quē** [V·ADJ·N] to lack, to be short of; to be absent; broken; incomplete; imperfect; vacancy, opening

缺德 **quēdé** [ADJ] mean; wicked

缺点 **quēdiǎn** [N] defect, shortcoming, weakness · [MW] 个
固执既是傻瓜的**缺点**也是他的优点。
*ShaGua's stubbornness is a defect, but also a virtue.*

缺额 **quē'é** [N] vacancy · [MW] 个

缺乏 **quēfá** [V] to lack, to be short of

缺货 **quēhuò** [V] to be out of stock

缺课 **quēkè** [V] to miss a class
父母缴学费, 学生**缺课**, 说得通吗?
*Does it make any sense for students to miss classes while their parents are paying tuition?*

缺口 **quēkǒu** [N] gap · [MW] 个

缺勤 **quēqín** [V] to be absent from duty

缺少 **quēshǎo** [V] to lack, to be short of

缺席 **quēxí** [V] to miss, to be absent

缺陷 **quēxiàn** [N] defect; downside · [MW] 个

**RELATED WORDS**

欠缺 105     残缺 977     暂缺 1522

---

**1306**  甜    U+80F6    TM **12**   FM 丿

**tián** [ADJ] sweet; happy, pleasant

甜点 **tiándiǎn** [N] dessert · [MW] 块
傻瓜太太十分爱吃**甜点**。*Mrs. ShaGua loves dessert a lot.*

甜酒 **tiánjiǔ** [N] sweet wine · [MW] 杯

甜蜜 **tiánmì** [ADJ] sweet; happy

甜食 **tiánshí** [N] sweet food; dessert · [MW] 份

甜水 **tiánshuǐ** [N] fresh water

甜头 **tiántou** [N] sweet taste; pleasant flavor; benefit
让他尝一尝**甜头**。*Let him enjoy the benefit for now.*

甜味 **tiánwèi** [N] sweet taste

甜言蜜语 **tiányánmìyǔ** [EXP] sweet nothings (LIT sweet words and honeyed phrases), meaningless words
傻瓜不会跟傻瓜太太**甜言蜜语**。*ShaGua doesn't know how to whisper sweet nothings to Mrs. ShaGua.*

**RELATED WORDS**

香甜 834     嘴甜 1984

---

**1307** 斜    U+659C    TM **12**   FM 丿

**xié** [ADJ] slanting, inclined, tilted

斜角 **xiéjiǎo** [N] oblique angle · [MW] 个

斜面 **xiémiàn** [N] inclined plane · [MW] 个

斜坡 **xiépō** [N] slope · [MW] 个

斜阳 **xiéyáng** [N] setting sun · [MW] 个
傻瓜坐在**斜坡**上看着**斜阳**。*ShaGua is sitting on a slope and watching the setting sun.*

**RELATED WORD**

歪斜 511

---

**1308**  乳    U+4E73    TM **12**   FM 丿

**rǔ** [N·ADJ] breast; milk; newborn (animal); sucking

乳儿 rǔ'ér　N　nursing infant · MW 个

乳房 rǔfáng　N　breast · MW 个、对

乳名 rǔmíng　N　pet name · MW 个

没有人知道傻瓜的**乳名**是什么？ *Nobody knows what ShaGua's pet name was.*

乳牛 rǔniú　N　milk cow; dairy cattle · MW 头

乳品 rǔpǐn　N　dairy · MW 件

乳头 rǔtóu　N　nipple · MW 个

乳汁 rǔzhī　N　milk · MW 滴、杯

亚洲某国提出一个口号："一杯**乳汁**救一个民族。" *An Asian country came up with the slogan "A cup of milk will rescue a nation."*

乳脂 rǔzhī　N　butterfat · MW 块

**RELATED WORD**

腐乳 1879

---

**1309 删**　U+5220　TM **12** FM ノ

shān　V　to delete, to omit

删除 shānchú　V　to delete, to cross out

删改 shāngǎi　V　to revise, to edit

我**删改**了他的文章。 *I have revised his paper.*

删节 shānjié　V　to abridge, to cut

---

**1310 刷**　U+5237　TM **12** FM ノ

shuā　V·N·ONOM　to brush; to scrub; to clean; to wash; to eliminate, to remove; to rustle; brush; swish

刷洗 shuāxǐ　V　to scrub; to wash

傻瓜曾经在餐馆**刷洗**过盘子。 *ShaGua once washed dishes in restaurants.*

刷新 shuāxīn　V　to break

刷新纪录 *to break a record*

刷牙 shuāyá　V　to brush one's teeth

傻瓜问儿子："某人一边**刷牙**，一边吹口哨，可能吗？"儿子答："可以！刷他的假牙。" *ShaGua asked his son, "Is it possible for someone to brush their teeth while whistling?" His son answered, "Yes, they can brush their dentures!"*

刷子 shuāzi　N　brush · MW 把

**RELATED WORDS**

牙刷 143　　冲刷 339　　印刷 470
洗刷 1167　　粉刷 1363

---

**1311 章**　U+7AE0　TM **12** FM 丶

zhāng　N·V·MW　article; chapter; section; rule, regulation, clause; constitution; seal, stamp; badge, medal; to order

篇章 *chapter*

违章 *to break the rules and regulations*

宪章 *constitution*

奏章 *memorial to the throne*

图章 *stamp*

袖章 *armband*

章程 zhāngchéng　N　regulation; constitution · MW 个

章法 zhāngfǎ　N　structure (of a written piece); art of composition · MW 个

章节 zhāngjié　N　chapter; section · MW 个

章鱼 zhāngyú　N　octopus · MW 条

**RELATED WORDS**

文章 70　　公章 103　　印章 470
私章 471　　典章 532　　证章 705
图章 761　　奖章 927　　规章 1098
违章 1185　　宪章 1317　　盖章 1331
袖章 1361　　简章 1796　　像章 1863

---

**1312 帝**　U+5E1D　TM **12** FM 丶

dì　N　emperor; supreme being; God; imperialism

帝国 dìguó　N　empire · MW 个

帝国主义 dìguózhǔyì　N　imperialism

帝王 dìwáng　N　emperor, monarch · MW 个

**RELATED WORDS**

上帝 14　　玉皇大帝 77

---

**1313 衰**　U+8870　TM **12** FM 丶

shuāi　V·ADJ　to decline, to wane; declining; weak, feeble

衰败 shuāibài　V　to decline

衰变 shuāibiàn　V　to decay

衰减 shuāijiǎn　V　to weaken

衰老 shuāilǎo　ADJ　old and feeble; decrepit

衰落 shuāiluò　V　to decline, to go downhill

衰弱 shuāiruò　ADJ　weak, feeble

**1313 衰 shuāi** (continued)

衰退 **shuāituì** V to decline, to falter (of the body, spirit, will, capability, etc.); to be failing, to deteriorate (of a country's political/economic situation)

记忆力**衰退**是一个人开始**衰老**的象征。 *A decline in memory is a sign of old age and feebleness.*

衰亡 **shuāiwáng** V to become feeble and die; to die out

---

**1314**  戀    U+604B    TM **12** FM ╲

**liàn** V to love; to long for, to miss

恋爱 **liàn'ài** V·N to love; mutual love between a man and a woman

婚姻是**恋爱**的坟墓, 还是**恋爱**的开始? *Is marriage love's grave or just its beginning?*

恋人 **liànrén** N lover, sweetheart, girlfriend/ boyfriend · MW 个、位

**RELATED WORDS**

| | | |
|---|---|---|
| 失恋 106 | 依恋 625 | 贪恋 827 |
| 初恋 963 | 迷恋 1187 | 热恋 1390 |
| 留恋 1582 | | |

---

**1315** 家 傢    U+5BB6    TM **12** FM ╲

**jiā** N·MW family; home, household; workplace; school of thought; -ary/-er/-ian/-ist [suffix for a specialist in an area]; [measure word for families and businesses (stores, restaurants, hotels, etc.)]

家常 **jiācháng** N daily life of a family; domestic affairs

家畜 **jiāchù** N livestock; cattle · MW 个、头

家当 **jiādàng** N family property/possessions · MW 笔

傻瓜没有多少**家当**。 *ShaGua doesn't own much family property.*

家底 **jiādǐ** N family property

家访 **jiāfǎng** V to visit students' families

**家访**是中国教育的一个特色。 *Teachers visiting students' families is typical of Chinese education.*

家伙 **jiāhuo** N tool; weapon; fellow, guy · MW 个、帮

家家户户 **jiājiāhùhù** EXP every family; every household

家教 **jiājiào** N upbringing; family education; private tutor

---

家眷 **jiājuàn** N wife and children · MW 个

家婆 **jiāpó** N mother-in-law · MW 个

家谱 **jiāpǔ** N family history/tree · MW 本

傻瓜珍藏了一本**家谱**。 *ShaGua keeps a careful journal of the family history.*

家禽 **jiāqín** N poultry · MW 个、只

家庭 **jiātíng** N family; household · MW 个

家用 **jiāyòng** N·ADJ family/living expenses; for home use, domestic, household, home · MW 笔

家长 **jiāzhǎng** N head of a family; parent/ guardian · MW 个、位、名

老师拜访学生的**家庭**, 跟**家长**谈**家教**、聊**家常**, 就是所谓的 **"家访"**。 *When a teacher visits a student's family to talk about family education and domestic life, it is called "visiting family."*

家族 **jiāzú** N clan; family · MW 个

**RELATED WORDS**

| | | |
|---|---|---|
| 人家 4 | 厂家 7 | 大家 20 |
| 女家 57 | 万家灯火 73 | 公家 103 |
| 无家可归 139 | 专家 155 | 全家福 172 |
| 分家 173 | 在家 188 | 庄家 229 |
| 兵家 300 | 东家 307 | 作家 326 |
| 当家 335 | 老家 375 | 名家 426 |
| 安家 487 | 丧家之犬 521 | 国家 542 |
| 败家子 589 | 好家伙 627 | 养家 670 |
| 到家 737 | 皇家 858 | 持家 1019 |
| 酒家 1339 | 起家 1421 | 娘家 1448 |
| 冤家 1729 | 冤家路窄 1729 | 管家 1861 |
| 搬家 1943 | 土专家 15 | 艺术家 274 |
| 剧作家 1468 | 慈善家 1952 | 半路出家 127 |
| 白手起家 176 | 自成一家 305 | |

---

**1316** 客    U+5BA2    TM **12** FM ╲

**kè** N·V visitor, guest; traveler; customer; to settle/live in a strange place; to be a stranger

贵**客** *distinguished guest*

旅**客** *traveler*

顾**客** *customer*

政**客** *politician*

**客**居 *to live abroad*

客车 **kèchē** N passenger train; bus · MW 辆、列

客店 **kèdiàn** N hotel, inn · MW 家

客房 **kèfáng** N guest room; hotel room · MW 间

客观 **kèguān** ADJ objective, unbiased

客户 **kèhù** N customer, client; tenant farmer family · MW 个、名、位

客机 **kèjī** N passenger plane · MW 架

客满 **kèmǎn** V to be sold out (of hotel rooms, theater seats, etc.)

客票 **kèpiào** N passenger ticket · MW 张

客气 **kèqi** ADJ·V polite, courteous; to speak/behave deferentially
你不要跟他**客气**，还是**客观**地告诉他实情吧。
*You shouldn't be so deferential with him; it's better to give it to him straight.*

客人 **kèrén** N visitor, guest · MW 个、位、名
**客店**里来了很多**客人**，所以**客房**都住满了。
*There are a lot of guests in the hotel currently, and all of the rooms are sold out.*

客商 **kèshāng** N business people · MW 个、名

客套 **kètào** N·V polite greeting; courtesy, civility; to exchange greetings

客厅 **kètīng** N living room; reception room · MW 间

**RELATED WORDS**

---

**1317** 宪 憲 U+5BAA TM **12** FM 丶

**xiàn** N law, statute; constitution

宪兵 **xiànbīng** N military police · MW 个、名

宪法 **xiànfǎ** N constitution (of a country) · MW 部

宪章 **xiànzhāng** N charter; decrees and regulations · MW 部

宪政 **xiànzhèng** N constitutional government
这是依据**宪法**建构的**宪政**。 *This is a constitutional government that is structured by a constitution.*

---

**1318** 宫 宮 U+5BAB TM **12** FM 丶

**gōng** N club, place for cultural activities and recreation; palace; temple; uterus; home of supernatural beings

宫灯 **gōngdēng** N palace lantern · MW 盏

宫殿 **gōngdiàn** N palace · MW 座
故宫是世界上最大的**宫殿**。 *The Forbidden City is the largest royal palace in the world.*

宫廷 **gōngtíng** N royal court · MW 座

**RELATED WORDS**

---

**1319** 害 U+5BB3 TM **12** FM 丶

**hài** N·V disadvantage; disaster; to harm, to injure; to kill, to murder; to contract / suffer from (an illness); to feel uneasy

伤害 *harm*

灾害 *disaster*

杀害 *to kill*

害病 *to be ill*

害虫 **hàichóng** N pest, destructive insect · MW 只、群

害处 **hàichu** N harm; evil · MW 个

害怕 **hàipà** V to be scared

害人虫 **hàirénchóng** N evil creature · MW 个
别**害怕**那个**害人虫**。 *Don't be afraid of that pest!*

害羞 **hàixiū** V to be bashful/shy

**RELATED WORDS**

---

**1320** 容 U+5BB9 TM **12** FM 丶

**róng** V·N·ADV to hold, to contain, to fit; to tolerate; to allow; facial expression; looks, appearance; probably; perhaps

容光焕发 **róngguānghuànfā** EXP glowing with health

容积 **róngjī** N volume

容量 **róngliàng** N capacity; volume

容貌 **róngmào** N looks, appearance · MW 个

容纳 **róngnà** V to tolerate; to hold, to fit

容器 **róngqì** N container · MW 个

容忍 **róngrěn** V to tolerate; to condone
能**容忍**他人的错误，这是傻瓜市长的一大特点。
*Tolerating the mistakes of others is one of ShaGua's chief qualities as mayor.*

## 1320 容 róng (continued)

容许 róngxǔ [V] to permit, to allow; to tolerate

容易 róngyì [ADJ] easy

汉语的"好**容易**"和"好不**容易**"都表达"很难"的意思。*In Chinese, "好容易" and "好不容易" have the same meaning: "very difficult."*

**RELATED WORDS**

| | | |
|---|---|---|
| 从容 66 | 内容 191 | 形容 257 |
| 市容 332 | 美容 671 | 面容 721 |
| 阵容 809 | 笑容 861 | 宽容 1618 |
| 愁容 1691 | 整容 1845 | 刻不容缓 966 |
| 谈何容易 1356 | 无地自容 139 | |

## 1321 案    U+6848    TM **12** FM 丶

àn [N] lawsuit, case; record, file; plan, proposal

案件 ànjiàn [N] lawsuit, case · [MW] 个

案例 ànlì [N] case · [MW] 个

案情 ànqíng [N] details of a case · [MW] 个

案子 ànzi [N] case · [MW] 个

**RELATED WORDS**

| | | |
|---|---|---|
| 个案 18 | 立案 125 | 专案 155 |
| 归案 166 | 在案 188 | 办案 195 |
| 方案 220 | 血案 306 | 作案 326 |
| 议案 350 | 另案 385 | 定案 666 |
| 法案 686 | 图案 761 | 草案 768 |
| 拍案 790 | 备案 845 | 投案 1008 |
| 报案 1010 | 档案 1032 | 破案 1374 |
| 教案 1424 | 答案 1438 | 提案 1554 |
| 假案 1586 | 疑案 1917 | 翻案 1989 |

## 1322 穿    U+7A7F    TM **12** FM 丶

chuān [V·ADV] to put on, to wear; to go/pass through, to cross; to pierce, to penetrate; to string/piece together; through

穿插 chuānchā [V] to weave in; to insert

黄老师喜欢在上课中**穿插**一些笑话。*Professor Huang likes to spice things up with some jokes when he teaches.*

中国军队喜欢打**穿插**战。*Chinese troops like to use infiltration in their battles.*

穿戴 chuāndài [V·N] to dress, to wear (clothes); apparel · [MW] 身

傻瓜的**穿戴**往往有些过时。*ShaGua's clothing is usually a little outdated.*

穿孔 chuānkǒng [V] to bore a hole

穿梭 chuānsuō [V] to shuttle back and forth

穿越 chuānyuè [V] to pass through, to cross

**RELATED WORDS**

| | | |
|---|---|---|
| 击穿 156 | 拆穿 572 | 吃穿 783 |
| 看穿 841 | 烧穿 1504 | 说穿 1631 |
| 揭穿 1851 | 水滴石穿 159 | |

## 1323 闹 鬧    U+95F9    TM **12** FM 丶

nào [V·ADJ] to make noise; to vent (feelings, etc.); to fall ill; to suffer from; to go in for (an activity); noisy

闹别扭 nàobièniu [EXP] to fall out with, to be at odds with

闹翻 nàofān [V] to fall out with

傻瓜的大儿子开始只是和女朋友**闹别扭**；最后，还真**闹翻**了。*In the beginning, ShaGua's older son had difficulties with his girlfriend until finally he broke up with her.*

闹鬼 nàoguǐ [V] to be haunted

闹哄哄 nàohōnghōng [ADJ] noisy

闹剧 nàojù [N] farce; slapstick comedy · [MW] 场

闹乱子 nàoluànzi [V] disturbance, trouble

闹市 nàoshì [N] busy shopping district · [MW] 个

闹事 nàoshì [V] to create a disturbance, to cause trouble

有些人在**闹市**里**闹事**。*Some people instigated a massive riot downtown.*

闹笑话 nàoxiàohua [V] to make a fool of oneself

闹钟 nàozhōng [N] alarm clock · [MW] 个

**RELATED WORDS**

| | | |
|---|---|---|
| 吵闹 415 | 胡闹 1256 | 热闹 1390 |
| 瞎闹 1913 | 看热闹 841 | |

## 1324 唐    U+5510    TM **12** FM 丶

táng [N·ADJ] Tang Dynasty (618–907 C.E.); [surname]; boastful; exaggerated; in vain, for nothing

唐人街 tángrénjiē [N] Chinatown · [MW] 个

唐突 tángtū [ADJ] brusque, rude

**RELATED WORD**

荒唐 1222

## 1325 席

**xí** N·MW　mat; seat; seat in parliament; banquet, feast; [measure word for speech and talk]

**席地 xídì** V to sit on the ground

**席卷 xíjuǎn** V to sweep, to engulf; to roll up (like a mat)

*1992年后, 市场经济席卷了中国。The market economy swept through China after 1992.*

**席位 xíwèi** N seat (at an assembly, a gathering) · MW 个

### RELATED WORDS

| | | |
|---|---|---|
| 主席 124 | 出席 258 | 议席 350 |
| 列席 368 | 软席 889 | 首席 924 |
| 缺席 1305 | 凉席 1337 | 宴席 1479 |
| 硬席 1524 | 主宾席 124 | |

## 1326 庭

**tíng** N　hall; law court; front courtyard; front yard

**庭园 tíngyuán** N flower garden; grounds · MW 个

**庭院 tíngyuàn** N courtyard · MW 个

**庭长 tíngzhǎng** N presiding judge · MW 个、位、名

*庭长在法庭上宣判了案子。The presiding judge ruled in the court case.*

### RELATED WORDS

| | | |
|---|---|---|
| 开庭 26 | 门庭若市 130 | 出庭 258 |
| 法庭 686 | 家庭 1315 | |

## 1327 病

**bìng** N·V　illness, disease; fault, defect; to be ill

**病床 bìngchuáng** N hospital bed · MW 张

**病倒 bìngdǎo** V to be laid up, to be down with an illness

**病毒 bìngdú** N virus · MW 种

**病房 bìngfáng** N hospital ward · MW 间

**病故 bìnggù** V to die of an illness

**病号 bìnghào** N patient · MW 个

*那个病号躺在6号病房的3号病床上。The patient lay on sickbed No. 3 in ward No. 6.*

**病假 bìngjià** N sick leave · MW 天

**病菌 bìngjūn** N bacteria, germs · MW 种

**病况 bìngkuàng** N (patient's) condition

**病历 bìnglì** N medical record · MW 份

**病例 bìnglì** N (medical) case · MW 个

**病情 bìngqíng** N (patient's) condition

**病人 bìngrén** N patient · MW 个、位、名

**病痛 bìngtòng** N slight illness

**病危 bìngwēi** ADJ to be critically ill

*病人的病情很严重, 已经到了病危的程度。The patient's condition is so serious that he is now in critical condition.*

**病因 bìngyīn** N cause of disease, pathogen · MW 个

**病愈 bìngyù** V to recover (from an illness)

**病症 bìngzhèng** N illness, disease · MW 个、种

### RELATED WORDS

| | | |
|---|---|---|
| 久病成医 45 | 生病 107 | 心病 232 |
| 因病 270 | 发病 311 | 性病 498 |
| 养病 670 | 诊病 709 | 卧病 826 |
| 看病 841 | 疾病 922 | 治病 935 |
| 胃病 1216 | 害病 1319 | 染病 1336 |
| 患病 1649 | 暴病 1844 | 霉病 1934 |
| 艾滋病 100 | 出毛病 258 | 老毛病 375 |
| 传染病 452 | 狂犬病 469 | 流行病 1493 |
| 常见病 1733 | 精神病 1832 | 糖尿病 1933 |

## 1328 疲

**pí** ADJ　tired, weary, exhausted

**疲惫 píbèi** ADJ weary, exhausted

**疲乏 pífá** ADJ weary, fatigued

**疲倦 píjuàn** ADJ tired and sleepy

**疲劳 píláo** ADJ weary, tired

**疲软 píruǎn** ADJ tired and feeble; weak (of demand for commodities)

*傻瓜感觉疲软。ShaGua feels fatigued.*

*市场疲软。The market is weakening.*

## 1329 前

**qián** N·PREP　front, forward, forefront; first; former, earlier; future, prospect; prior to

**前辈 qiánbèi** N older generation; senior; forefather · MW 个、位、名

**前臂 qiánbì** N forearm · MW 只

## 1329 前 qián (continued)

前边 qiánbian  N  in front; ahead

前程 qiánchéng  N  future; journey ahead ·  MW  个

前方 qiánfāng  N  ahead; (battle)front ·  MW  个

前后 qiánhòu  N  front and back; from beginning to end (in time); around

傻瓜准备春节**前后**访问中国。*ShaGua is going to visit China around the Chinese New Year.*

前进 qiánjìn  V  to go forward, to advance; to forge ahead, to make progress

前景 qiánjǐng  N  foreground; future (prospects) ·  MW  个

前例 qiánlì  N  precedent ·  MW  个

前列腺 qiánlièxiàn  N  prostate ·  MW  个

前轮 qiánlún  N  front wheel ·  MW  个

前门 qiánmén  N  front door ·  MW  个

前面 qiánmian  N  in the front, at the head

前妻 qiánqī  N  ex-wife ·  MW  个

前人 qiánrén  N  forefathers; predecessors ·  MW  个、位、名

前所未闻 qiánsuǒwèiwén  EXP  unprecedented

前提 qiántí  N  premise; precondition ·  MW  个

前天 qiántiān  N  day before yesterday

前途 qiántú  N  future; career ·  MW  个

前往 qiánwǎng  V  to leave for, to be bound for

前夕 qiánxī  N  eve; moment before (something) is going to happen

前线 qiánxiàn  N  front line, battlefront ·  MW  条

前言 qiányán  N  foreword; preface; introduction ·  MW  篇

**前天**他同意给那书写**前言**，但**前提**是必须在五月份看到书稿。*The day before yesterday, he agreed to write a preface for the book, but the precondition was to finish the manuscript in May.*

前因后果 qiányīnhòuguǒ  EXP  from cause to effect

前者 qiánzhě  N  former

### RELATED WORDS

## 1330 总 總   U+603B   TM **12** FM 丶

zǒng  V·ADJ·ADV  to assemble, to gather; to sum up; total; head; general; always, invariably; anyway, after all; inevitably, sooner or later

汇总 *to assemble*

总的形势 *overall situation*

总经理 *general manager*

你**总**得有个说法吧。*You had still better explain it.*

总产量 zǒngchǎnliàng  N  total output

总产值 zǒngchǎnzhí  N  total output value

总得 zǒngděi  ADV  must, to have to

总额 zǒng'é  N  total amount/value

总而言之 zǒng'éryánzhī  EXP  in short, in a word

**总而言之**，今年的**总产值**比去年高。*To sum up, this year's total output is higher than last year's.*

总分 zǒngfēn  N  total points, overall score

总纲 zǒnggāng  N  general program ·  MW  个、份

总共 zǒnggòng  ADV  altogether, in all

总计 zǒngjì  V  to amount to, to total

总价 zǒngjià  N  grand total

总结 zǒngjié  V·N  to sum up, to summarize; summary ·  MW  个

总理 zǒnglǐ  N  premier, prime minister ·  MW  位

总领事 zǒnglǐngshì  N  consul general ·  MW  个、位、名

**总领事**向**总理**提交了一份**总结**。*The consul general submitted a summary to the prime minister.*

总目 zǒngmù  N  comprehensive table of contents ·  MW  个

总是 zǒngshì  ADV  always

总数 zǒngshù  N  (sum) total

总体 zǒngtǐ  N  overall, general

总统 zǒngtǒng  N  president ·  MW  位

总务 zǒngwù  N  general affairs/services; general manager ·  MW  个、位、名

总之 zǒngzhī  CONJ  in short, in a word

**总之**，傻瓜是个大好人。*All in all, ShaGua is a very nice guy.*

总资产 zǒngzīchǎn  N  total assets ·  MW  笔

**总统**拥有的**总资产**不计其数。*The total assets of the president are unlimited.*

### RELATED WORDS

## 1331 盖 蓋    U+76D6    TM 12 FM 丶

**gài**  V·N  to cover; to seal, to stamp; to surpass, to prevail over; to block out; to build, to construct; lid, cover

**盖章 gàizhāng**  V  to seal, to stamp

**盖子 gàizi**  N  lid, cover, cap, top · MW 个

### RELATED WORDS

头盖骨 128        捂盖子 1399        瓶盖 1635
铺盖 1713        遮盖 1831        铺天盖地 1713

## 1332 着    U+7740    TM 12 FM 丶

**zhāo**  N  move; tactic

**zháo**  V  to touch, to feel; to burn, to be lit; to be affected by (cold, etc.)

**zhe**  AV  [used to indicate continuing progress]; [used to emphasize a command]

**zhuó**  V  to wear (clothes); to apply, to use; to send

**着慌 zháohuāng**  V  to become flustered

**着火 zháohuǒ**  V  to be on fire

**着急 zháojí**  ADJ  worried, anxious

大楼一**着火**, 大家都**着急**、**着慌**。
*As the building caught fire, people became worried and alarmed.*

**着凉 zháoliáng**  V  to catch cold

**着迷 zháomí**  V  to be fascinated, to be fanatical

**着魔 zháomó**  V  to be possessed/obsessed

**着笔 zhuóbǐ**  V  to put pen to paper

**着力 zhuólì**  V  to put effort into; to exert oneself

**着陆 zhuólù**  V  to land

**着落 zhuóluò**  N·V  whereabouts; result; source; to rest with · MW 个

**着色 zhuósè**  V  to apply color

**着手 zhuóshǒu**  V  to begin, to set about

**着想 zhuóxiǎng**  V  to consider, to think about

至今这个计划的预算还没有**着落**, 现在必须**着手**落实资金问题, 否则就晚了。
*There haven't been any financial results from this program. We must get to work on the funding right now; otherwise, it will be too late.*

**着眼 zhuóyǎn**  V  to keep in mind; to consider (a certain aspect)

**着重 zhuózhòng**  V  to emphasize; to underline

### RELATED WORDS

本着 90        走着瞧 265        向着 603
沉着 1166        睡着 1571        随着 1911
用不着 313        用得着 313        犯不着 884
犯得着 884        意味着 1812

## 1333 卷    U+5377    TM 12 FM 丶

**juǎn**  V·N·MW  to roll up; to sweep away/up; roll; spool; reel; [measure word for small rolled objects (scrolls, rolls of toilet paper, etc.)]

**juàn**  N  exam paper; book; document; volume

**卷笔刀 juǎnbǐdāo**  N  pencil sharpener · MW 把

**卷尺 juǎnchǐ**  N  tape measure · MW 个

**卷入 juǎnrù**  V  to be involved in

**卷烟 juǎnyān**  N  cigarette · MW 支

**卷子 juànzi**  N  exam paper · MW 份

他一边抽着**卷烟**, 一边准备**卷子**。*He was preparing his exam paper while smoking a cigarette.*

**卷宗 juànzōng**  N  file; folder · MW 份

### RELATED WORDS

开卷 26        龙卷风 315        考卷 530
问卷 678        春卷 855        试卷 1180
胶卷 1296        席卷 1325

## 1334 粪 糞    U+7CAA    TM 12 FM 丶

**fèn**  N  excrement, feces; dung

大**粪** *excrement*

**粪池 fènchí**  N  cesspool · MW 个

**粪肥 fènféi**  N  manure, dung · MW 堆

**粪坑 fènkēng**  N  manure pit · MW 个

### RELATED WORDS

牛粪 51        鸟粪 859

## 1335 资 資    U+8D44    TM 12 FM 丶

**zī**  N·V  money; expenses; (natural) ability; qualifications; record of service; to subsidize, to support; to provide, to supply

**资本 zīběn**  N  capital · MW 笔

**资产 zīchǎn**  N  property; assets · MW 笔

**资方 zīfāng**  N  employer · MW 个

**1335 资 zī** (continued)

**资格 zīgé** N qualifications; seniority

你根本没有**资格**讨论这个问题。 *You are not even qualified to discuss this question.*

**资金 zījīn** N funds; capital · MW 笔

**资力 zīlì** N financial strength

**资料 zīliào** N data; material · MW 批

**资源 zīyuán** N resources · MW 个

**资质 zīzhì** N natural endowment, aptitude; intelligence

**资助 zīzhù** V·N to subsidize; financial aid · MW 笔

谁能**资助**她上大学？ *Who will be able to provide her financial aid for college?*

RELATED WORDS

| | | |
|---|---|---|
| 工资 12 | 欠资 105 | 外资 218 |
| 师资 396 | 劳资 764 | 投资 1008 |
| 邮资 1046 | 独资 1095 | 集资 1267 |
| 总资产 1330 | | |

---

**1336 染**     U+67D3     TM **12** FM 丶

**rǎn** V to dye; to contract (a disease)

**染病 rǎnbìng** V to catch a disease

这孩子**染病**了。 *This kid has caught a disease.*

**染色 rǎnsè** V to dye

**染印 rǎnyìn** V to print pigments/colors

RELATED WORDS

| | | |
|---|---|---|
| 传染病 452 | 传染 452 | 印染 470 |
| 污染 681 | 沾染 684 | 感染 1860 |
| 耳濡目染 145 | | |

---

**1337 凉**     U+51C9     TM **12** FM 丶

**liáng** ADJ·V cool; cold; discouraged, disappointed; to make cool

**liàng** V to let cool

**凉菜 liángcài** N cold dish · MW 碟

**凉快 liángkuai** ADJ nice and cool

**凉伞 liángsǎn** N shade · MW 把

**凉爽 liángshuǎng** ADJ cool

今天真**凉爽**。 *Today is pleasantly cool.*

**凉水 liángshuǐ** N cool (unboiled) water · MW 杯

---

**凉飕飕 liángsōusōu** ADJ chilly

**凉台 liángtái** N balcony · MW 个

**凉亭 liángtíng** N pavilion · MW 个

**凉席 liángxí** N summer sleeping mat · MW 张

**凉鞋 liángxié** N sandal · MW 双、对

RELATED WORDS

| | | |
|---|---|---|
| 风凉 194 | 风凉话 194 | 冰凉 493 |
| 阴凉 1041 | 荒凉 1222 | 着凉 1332 |
| 清凉 1495 | | |

---

**1338 洞**     U+6D1E     TM **12** FM 丶

**dòng** N hole; cavity; cave

**洞察 dòngchá** V to see clearly

**洞彻 dòngchè** V to understand thoroughly

**洞房 dòngfáng** N bridal chamber · MW 间

**洞穴 dòngxué** N cave, cavern · MW 个

RELATED WORDS

| | | |
|---|---|---|
| 山洞 38 | 孔洞 370 | 空洞 669 |
| 桥洞 804 | 黑洞 1389 | 漏洞 1886 |

---

**1339 酒**     U+9152     TM **12** FM 丶

**jiǔ** N alcohol, liquor, spirits; wine

**酒吧 jiǔbā** N bar; taproom · MW 间、家

傻瓜不喝酒，从来没有去过**酒吧**。 *ShaGua doesn't drink any alcohol, and he has never been to a bar.*

**酒杯 jiǔbēi** N wine cup/glass · MW 个

**酒店 jiǔdiàn** N wine shop; bar; restaurant; hotel · MW 家、间

**酒鬼 jiǔguǐ** N drunkard · MW 个、名

**酒会 jiǔhuì** N (cocktail) party · MW 个

这个**酒鬼**，逢酒会必去。 *This boozer would go to any open cocktail party.*

**酒家 jiǔjiā** N wine shop; restaurant · MW 家、间

**酒精 jiǔjīng** N alcohol; ethanol · MW 瓶

RELATED WORDS

| | | |
|---|---|---|
| 下酒 10 | 米酒 226 | 劝酒 255 |
| 料酒 961 | 倒酒 1281 | 甜酒 1306 |
| 啤酒 1412 | 烧酒 1504 | 祝酒 1516 |
| 喝酒 1854 | 餐酒 1964 | 鸡尾酒 1373 |
| 葡萄酒 1766 | | |

## 1340 浇 浇 U+6D47 TM 12 FM 丶

**jiāo** V to water; to irrigate; to soak; to cast, to mould

**浇灌** jiāoguàn V to water; to irrigate; to pour

**浇水** jiāoshuǐ V to water; to pour
傻瓜最喜欢黄昏时分给花草**浇水**。*The most enjoyable thing for ShaGua is to water his flowers and grass at dusk.*

**浇注** jiāozhù V to pour

**浇铸** jiāozhù V to cast, to mould

## 1341 浪 U+6D6A TM 12 FM 丶

**làng** N·ADJ·V wave; unrestrained; wasteful; to stroll; to wander, to roam

**浪潮** làngcháo N tide; major social movement; mass campaign · MW 个
反战的**浪潮**席卷全国。*Waves of antiwar protests have swept the entire country.*

**浪荡** làngdàng V to loaf around

**浪费** làngfèi V to waste, to squander

**浪漫** làngmàn ADJ romantic
傻瓜太太老是抱怨傻瓜不懂得什么叫"**浪漫**"。*Mrs. ShaGua often complains that ShaGua doesn't understand what "romance" is.*

**浪头** làngtou N tide; wave; trend · MW 个

**浪子** làngzǐ N spendthrift; loafer · MW 个

**浪子回头** làngzǐhuítóu EXP return of the prodigal son

### RELATED WORDS
巨浪 162    风浪 194    冲浪 339
赶浪头 822    波浪 936    热浪 1390
流浪 1493    风平浪静 194

## 1342 浮 U+6D6E TM 12 FM 丶

**fú** V·ADJ to float; to swim; to exceed, to overflow; superficial, frivolous; inflated; temporary; movable

**浮标** fúbiāo N buoy · MW 个

**浮尘** fúchén N surface dust

**浮沉** fúchén V to drift along

**浮动** fúdòng V to float; to fluctuate
最近股市**浮动**太大。*Recently, stocks have fluctuated too much.*

### RELATED WORDS
轻浮 1113    漂浮 1820

## 1343 消 U+6D88 TM 12 FM 丶

**xiāo** V·N to disappear, to vanish; to eliminate, to remove; to pass/spend (time); to take (a certain amount of time); news

**消沉** xiāochén ADJ depressed, downhearted

**消除** xiāochú V to eliminate, to remove

**消毒** xiāodú V to disinfect, to sanitize

**消防** xiāofáng V to fight/control a fire

**消费** xiāofèi V·N to consume; consumption · MW 笔

**消耗** xiāohào V to consume, to use up

**消化** xiāohuà V to digest; to understand and absorb (knowledge, learning)
我需要**消化消化**刚吃的东西。*I need to digest what I've eaten.*
我需要**消化消化**你说的东西。*I need some time to digest what you've said.*

**消极** xiāojí ADV negative, pessimistic
你的想法太**消极**了! 不能那么**消沉**! *Your thoughts are too negative; you shouldn't be so despondent.*

**消灭** xiāomiè V to perish, to die out; to eradicate

**消遣** xiāoqiǎn V to amuse oneself; to while away the time
你这是在**消遣**我, 难道不是吗? *You're playing a joke on me, aren't you?*

**消散** xiāosàn V to dissipate

**消失** xiāoshī V to disappear, to vanish

**消息** xiāoxi N news; information · MW 条

**消炎** xiāoyán V to reduce fever/inflammation

### RELATED WORDS
打消 289    取消 520    吃不消 783

## 1344 液 U+6DB2 TM 12 FM 丶

**yè** N liquid, fluid; juice

**液化** yèhuà V to liquefy

**液晶** yèjīng N liquid crystal

**液晶显示** yèjīngxiǎnshì N liquid crystal display (LCD)

**液态** yètài N liquid (state)

**液体** yètǐ N liquid

1344 液 yè (continued)

**RELATED WORDS**

| | | |
|---|---|---|
| 汁液 131 | 血液 306 | 溶液 1744 |
| 滴液 1885 | 洗发液 1167 | |

---

**1345 深** U+6DF1   TM **12** FM 丶

**shēn** ADJ·N·ADV deep; dark (in color); remote; profound, difficult; close, intimate (of relations/feelings); late (at night); depth; very, greatly, deeply

深奥 **shēn'ào** ADJ profound, difficult to understand

深不可测 **shēnbùkěcè** EXP to have no bottom; incomprehensible, unfathomable

有人认为傻瓜傻, 也有人认为他**深不可测**。 *Some people think that ShaGua is really dumb; others believe that he is too deep to fathom.*

深长 **shēncháng** ADJ profound

深沉 **shēnchén** ADJ deep; profound

在浮躁的社会里, 傻瓜的单纯让人以为是**深沉**。 *ShaGua's simplicity makes people in this impulsive society think he is profoundly deep.*

深处 **shēnchù** N profundity; abyss

深度 **shēndù** N depth

深更半夜 **shēngēngbànyè** EXP in the dead of night

深呼吸 **shēnhūxī** V deep breath

深刻 **shēnkè** ADJ deep; profound

学生们都佩服陈老师思考问题**深刻**。 *All of the students admired Professor Chen's profound insights.*

深浅 **shēnqiǎn** N depth; sense of propriety

深切 **shēnqiè** ADV sincerely, in a heartfelt manner, deeply

深情 **shēnqíng** ADJ deep feelings/affection

深入 **shēnrù** V·ADV to penetrate; deeply, thoroughly

深山 **shēnshān** N remote mountains · MW 座

深深 **shēnshēn** ADJ profoundly

深思 **shēnsī** V to ponder, to reflect on

深恶痛绝 **shēnwùtòngjué** EXP to hate bitterly, to detest

深重 **shēnzhòng** ADJ very grave; extremely serious

深入地**深思**应试教育的问题, 你才会感到危机的**深重**。 *Ponder deeply exam-oriented education, and you may notice the serious nature of its problems.*

**RELATED WORDS**

| | | |
|---|---|---|
| 水深 159 | 根深蒂固 1245 | 高深 1611 |
| 发人深省 311 | 莫测高深 999 | |

---

**1346 添** U+6DFB   TM **12** FM 丶

**tiān** V to add; to increase

添补 **tiānbu** V to replenish; to fill a gap

添加 **tiānjiā** V to add; to increase

添加剂 **tiānjiājì** N additive · MW 瓶

添置 **tiānzhì** V to acquire, to add (something) to one's possessions

学校图书馆最近**添置**了大批图书。 *The school library recently added a lot of books.*

**RELATED WORD**

画蛇添足 719

---

**1347 渐** 渐 U+6E10   TM **12** FM 丶

**jiàn** ADV gradually, by degrees

渐渐 **jiànjiàn** ADV gradually, little by little

月亮**渐渐**地消失在海面上。 *The moon gradually sank into the sea.*

渐进 **jiànjìn** V to advance gradually, to progress step by step

**RELATED WORD**

日渐 96

---

**1348 悄** U+6084   TM **12** FM 丶

**qiǎo** ADV quietly, silently; secretly

悄悄 **qiāoqiāo** ADV silently, noiselessly; secretly

月亮**悄悄**地消失在海面上。 *The moon quietly sank into the sea.*

**RELATED WORD**

静悄悄 1947

---

**1349 悼** U+60BC   TM **12** FM 丶

**dào** V to mourn (for), to lament

悼词 **dàocí** N eulogy · MW 篇

悼念 **dàoniàn** V to mourn (for), to grieve (over)

**RELATED WORDS**

哀悼 1134　　　　追悼 1507

---

## 1350 惜 U+60DC TM **12** FM 丶

**xī** V to cherish, to value, to treasure; to spare, to use sparingly; to pity; to regret, to begrudge

**惜爱 xī'ài** V to be in love

**惜别 xībié** V to be reluctant to part, to hate to see (someone/something) go

**惜别**2010, 迎来了2011。 *Hate to see 2010 go, but looking forward to 2011.*

**RELATED WORDS**

| | | |
|---|---|---|
| 不惜 24 | 可惜 243 | 吝惜 479 |
| 怜惜 695 | 爱惜 1264 | 痛惜 1725 |
| 在所不惜 188 | | |

---

## 1351 惧 懼 U+60E7 TM **12** FM 丶

**jù** V to fear, to dread

**惧怕 jùpà** V to fear, to dread

**惧色 jùsè** N look of fear

对于考试, 他面有**惧色**。 *Facing the exam, he looks scared.*

**RELATED WORDS**

畏惧 988　　　　恐惧 1644　　　　疑惧 1917

---

## 1352 惭 慚 U+60ED TM **12** FM 丶

**cán** ADJ ashamed

**惭愧 cánkuì** ADJ ashamed

试没考好, 傻瓜的儿子感到很**惭愧**。 *ShaGua's son felt ashamed because he didn't test well.*

**RELATED WORD**

羞惭 1154

---

## 1353 词 詞 U+88CD TM **12** FM 丶

**cí** N words; classical Chinese poetry with a set pattern

**词典 cídiǎn** N dictionary · MW 本、部

**词汇 cíhuì** N vocabulary · MW 个

有人觉得中文的**词汇**难记; 有人觉得语法难学。 *Some people feel that Chinese vocabulary is difficult to remember; others feel that the grammar is more difficult.*

**词句 cíjù** N expression; words and sentences · MW 个

**词类 cílèi** N parts of speech · MW 种

**词头 cítóu** N prefix · MW 个

**词尾 cíwěi** N suffix · MW 个

**词组 cízǔ** N phrase · MW 个

**RELATED WORDS**

| | | |
|---|---|---|
| 介词 44 | 主词 124 | 分词 173 |
| 代词 208 | 叹词 285 | 台词 301 |
| 名词 426 | 判词 507 | 动词 514 |
| 托词 563 | 单词 672 | 证词 705 |
| 助词 818 | 系词 842 | 连词 958 |
| 答词 1438 | 冠词 1478 | 语词 1501 |
| 祝词 1516 | 虚词 1534 | 量词 1544 |
| 唱词 1562 | 数词 1637 | 题词 1858 |
| 谢词 1890 | 歌词 1900 | 义正词严 22 |
| 助动词 818 | 及物动词 141 | 夸大其词 605 |

---

## 1354 误 誤 U+8BEF TM **12** FM 丶

**wù** N·V·ADV mistake, error; to miss; to harm, to damage; by mistake, by accident

**误差 wùchā** N error · MW 个

**误点 wùdiǎn** V late, behind schedule

**误工 wùgōng** V to be late for work

**误会 wùhuì** V·N to misunderstand; misunderstanding · MW 个

**误解 wùjiě** V·N to misread; misunderstanding · MW 个

**误伤 wùshāng** V to injure accidentally

**误事 wùshì** V to delay work/business; to mess things up

对不起, 我**误会**了你的意思, 希望没有**误事**。 *Sorry, I misunderstood you. Hopefully, it has not caused any loss to the business.*

**RELATED WORDS**

| | | |
|---|---|---|
| 正误 76 | 失误 106 | 延误 731 |
| 迟误 959 | 错误 1715 | |

---

## 1355 谁 誰 U+8C01 TM **12** FM 丶

**shéi/shuí** QPRON who; someone; anyone

## 1356 谈 談 U+8C08 TM 12 FM 丶

**tán** V·N to talk, to converse; to discuss; conversation

谈不上 **tánbushàng** EXP out of the question
傻瓜**谈不上**是一个优秀的政治家。 *ShaGua is far from being an outstanding politician.*

谈到 **tándào** V to talk about, to refer to

谈何容易 **tánhéróngyì** EXP easier said than done

谈话 **tánhuà** V·N to chat; to discuss; statement · MW 番

谈论 **tánlùn** V to talk about, to discuss

谈起 **tánqǐ** V to mention, to speak of

谈天 **tántiān** V to chat

谈吐 **tántǔ** N way of talking, manner of speaking
这个教授的**谈吐**真好！ *This professor's delivery is excellent!*

谈心 **tánxīn** V to have a heart-to-heart talk
要和她**谈心**？**谈何容易**！ *Having a heart-to-heart talk with her is easer said than done.*

### RELATED WORDS

| | | |
|---|---|---|
| 交谈 222 | 对谈 254 | 会谈 295 |
| 言谈 478 | 和谈 644 | 空谈 669 |
| 闲谈 679 | 奇谈 854 | 座谈 920 |
| 洽谈 942 | 商谈 1612 | 漫谈 1887 |
| 外交谈判 218 | 夸夸其谈 605 | 侃侃而谈 1085 |

## 1357 炼 煉 U+70BC TM 12 FM 丶

**liàn** V to smelt; to refine; to polish, to improve

炼钢 **liàngāng** V to make steel

炼油 **liànyóu** V to refine oil

### RELATED WORDS

| | |
|---|---|
| 提炼 1554 | 精炼 1832 |

## 1358 适 適 U+9002 TM 12 FM 丶

**shì** ADJ·V suitable, proper; comfortable, well; right, opportune; to follow, to pursue

适才 **shìcái** ADV just now

适当 **shìdàng** ADJ suitable, proper

适度 **shìdù** ADJ appropriate

适合 **shìhé** V·ADJ to fit, to suit; suitable

适龄 **shìlíng** N right age

适时 **shìshí** ADV at the right moment
刚才你见到傻瓜时，应该**适时**地提出那些**适当**的建议。 *You just met ShaGua. You should take the opportunity to make your suggestions now.*

适宜 **shìyí** ADJ appropriate; favorable

适意 **shìyì** ADJ agreeable

适应 **shìyìng** V to adapt to, to get used to
**适应**新的变化，是成功的必要条件。 *Adapting to change is a necessary condition for success.*

适用 **shìyòng** ADJ suitable; applicable

适中 **shìzhōng** ADJ appropriate, just right

### RELATED WORDS

| | | |
|---|---|---|
| 不适应 24 | 合适 296 | 舒适 1805 |

## 1359 逆 U+9006 TM 12 FM 丶

**nì** ADJ·V·N adverse, contrary; to go against, to disobey, to defy; rebel; traitor

逆差 **nìchā** N trade deficit · MW 个

逆耳 **nì'ěr** V to grate on the ear
忠言**逆耳**利于行。 *Frank words are unpleasant to hear, but are good for improving one's conduct.*

逆风 **nìfēng** V·N to head into the wind; headwind

逆光 **nìguāng** V to be looking into the light

逆境 **nìjìng** N adversity
**逆境**是成功者的舞台。 *Adverse situations are a stage for successful people.*

逆流 **nìliú** V·N to go against the current/trend; countercurrent; unhealthy trend · MW 股

逆时针 **nìshízhēn** V to move in a counterclockwise direction

逆水 **nìshuǐ** V to go against the current
**逆水**行舟，不进则退。 *When moving against the current, if you're not advancing, you're going backwards.*

逆行 **nìxíng** V to go the wrong way down a one-way street

### RELATED WORDS

| | |
|---|---|
| 叛逆 960 | 莫逆 999 |

## 1360 迎 U+8FCE TM 12 FM 丶

**yíng** V to welcome, to greet; to meet; to face; to move against/toward

迎春 **yíngchūn** V to greet the new year

迎风 **yíngfēng** V to face the wind

迎合 **yínghé** V to cater to, to pander to

傻瓜最恨无原则地**迎合**上司的人。 *ShaGua hates those who cater to their bosses by abandoning their own principles.*

迎候 **yínghòu** V to await the arrival of

迎接 **yíngjiē** V to welcome

惜别2010，**迎接**2011。 *Hate to see 2010 go, but looking forward to 2011.*

迎面 **yíngmiàn** ADV·V head-on, face to face; to step forward; to confront directly

迎头 **yíngtóu** ADV head-on, directly

迎新 **yíngxīn** V to see in the new year

迎战 **yíngzhàn** V to meet head-on (an enemy, an opposing team, etc.)

**RELATED WORD**

欢迎 366

---

**xiù** N·V sleeve; cuff (of a sleeve); to tuck inside a sleeve

袖标 **xiùbiāo** N armband · MW 个

袖长 **xiùcháng** N outer sleeve

袖口 **xiùkǒu** N cuff · MW 个

袖手旁观 **xiùshǒupángguān** EXP to stand by and do nothing

如果你有困难，我绝不**袖手旁观**。 *If you have difficulties, I will not stand by and do nothing.*

袖筒 **xiùtǒng** N sleeve · MW 根

袖章 **xiùzhāng** N armband · MW 个

袖珍 **xiùzhēn** ADJ pocket-size

**RELATED WORD**

领袖 1465

---

**shì** V·N to look at, to watch; to regard; to inspect; vision; attention; perspective

视差 **shìchā** N parallax · MW 个

视察 **shìchá** V to inspect; to observe

视程 **shìchéng** N visual range · MW 个

视而不见 **shì'érbùjiàn** EXP to turn a blind eye to

---

有些官员所谓的"**视察**"，对问题是**视**而不见。 *Some officials do inspections by looking and intentionally not seeing problems.*

视角 **shìjiǎo** N angle, perspective · MW 个

审视同样的问题，由于**视角**不同，可能会得出不同的结论。 *Viewing the same problem from different perspectives may lead to different conclusions.*

视觉 **shìjué** N vision, (sense of) sight

视力 **shìlì** N vision, sight

视频 **shìpín** N video frequency; video capability (of a phone, a computer, etc.)

视听 **shìtīng** N seeing and hearing; audiovisual

视线 **shìxiàn** N line of vision; attention

视野 **shìyě** N field of vision; perspective; worldview

你的**视野**不够开阔。 *Your worldview is not very broad.*

**RELATED WORDS**

| | | |
|---|---|---|
| 正视 76 | 电视 263 | 自视 305 |
| 仇视 319 | 环视 369 | 注视 496 |
| 珍视 515 | 歧视 585 | 诊视 709 |
| 近视 716 | 重视 839 | 监视 994 |
| 轻视 1113 | 忽视 1268 | 探视 1404 |
| 怒视 1427 | 虎视眈眈 1533 | 透视 1826 |

---

**fěn** N·V powder; to crumble, to crush; to pulverize

粉笔 **fěnbǐ** N chalk · MW 支

老师就像**粉笔**，不断地消耗自己去书写别人的蓝图。 *A teacher is similar to a piece of chalk— continuously expending itself to draw blueprints for others.*

粉尘 **fěnchén** N powder; dust · MW 粒

粉刺 **fěncì** N acne · MW 颗

粉盒 **fěnhé** N powder box · MW 个

粉红 **fěnhóng** ADJ pink

粉末 **fěnmò** N powder · MW 层、堆

粉刷 **fěnshuā** V to paint; to whitewash

粉碎 **fěnsuì** V to smash, to break into pieces

粉状 **fěnzhuàng** ADJ powdery

**RELATED WORDS**

| | | |
|---|---|---|
| 扑粉 168 | 米粉 226 | 花粉 549 |
| 香粉 834 | 奶粉 878 | 搽粉 1558 |
| 脂粉 1710 | 通心粉 1757 | 涂脂抹粉 1171 |

## 1364 粗 　U+7C97　TM **12** FM 丶

**cū** [ADJ·ADV] thick; coarse; crude; rough, unfinished; careless; rude, vulgar; roughly

粗暴　**cūbào**　[ADJ]　crude, rough

粗笨　**cūbèn**　[ADJ]　clumsy

粗鄙　**cūbǐ**　[ADJ]　vulgar

粗糙　**cūcāo**　[ADJ]　coarse, rough

粗放　**cūfàng**　[ADJ]　extensive

粗话　**cūhuà**　[N]　vulgar/obscene language · [MW] 句

　　无论那种语言，**粗话**最容易学。*No matter the language, vulgar words are the easiest to learn.*

粗鲁　**cūlǔ**　[ADJ]　rude, impolite

粗俗　**cūsú**　[ADJ]　vulgar, coarse

粗细　**cūxì**　[N]　(degree of) finish, quality of work (LIT coarse and fine)

粗心　**cūxīn**　[ADJ]　careless; thoughtless

粗野　**cūyě**　[ADJ]　crude; rude; boorish

粗壮　**cūzhuàng**　[ADJ]　sturdy; strong

　　这个人身体不**粗壮**，但语言**粗鲁**，行为**粗野**。*He is not a physically strong person, but his speech and behavior are crude.*

## 1365 粘 　U+7C98　TM **12** FM 丶

**zhān** [V·ADJ] to stick/cling to; to be joined to; sticky

粘接　**zhānjiē**　[V]　to splice

粘连　**zhānlián**　[V]　to adhere

粘贴　**zhāntiē**　[V]　to paste; to stick

　　粘贴广告 *to paste up / post flyers*

## 1366 削 　U+524A　TM **12** FM 丶

**xiāo** [V] to cut

**xuē** [V] to peel

削价　**xuējià**　[V]　to cut prices

　　圣诞节前后，所有商店都在**削价**出售商品。*Around Christmas, all the stores were cutting prices to offer special sales.*

削弱　**xuēruò**　[V]　to weaken

**RELATED WORDS**

切削 277　　　刮削 902　　　剥削 1377

## 1367 票 · U+7968 · TM **13** · FM 一

**piào** N ticket; receipt; banknote; bill; ballot; stamp; hostage; amateur opera performance

**票房 piàofáng** N ticket office · MW 间

**票价 piàojià** N ticket price, admission fee
航空公司在旅游旺季都提高**票价**。
*During the peak tourist season, the airlines raise their ticket prices.*

**票据 piàojù** N bill; receipt; voucher · MW 张

**票子 piàozi** N paper money, banknote; ticket · MW 张

### RELATED WORDS

| | | |
|---|---|---|
| 开票 26 | 支票 92 | 车票 114 |
| 半票 127 | 门票 130 | 月票 190 |
| 汇票 234 | 发票 311 | 当票 335 |
| 传票 452 | 机票 577 | 查票 741 |
| 钞票 900 | 监票 994 | 投票 1008 |
| 邮票 1046 | 免票 1056 | 货票 1061 |
| 彩票 1132 | 站票 1189 | 拘票 1231 |
| 售票处 1266 | 售票口 1266 | 售票员 1266 |
| 客票 1316 | 绑票 1454 | 股票 1456 |
| 退票 1508 | 选票 1510 | 粮票 1759 |
| 船票 1809 | 飞机票 81 | 打包票 289 |
| 卧铺票 826 | | |

## 1368 蛋 · U+86CB · TM **13** · FM 一

**dàn** N egg; [shaped like an egg]; insulting words

**蛋白 dànbái** N albumen, egg white · MW 个

**蛋白质 dànbáizhì** N protein

**蛋糕 dàngāo** N cake · MW 块

**蛋黄 dànhuáng** N yolk · MW 个

### RELATED WORDS

| | | |
|---|---|---|
| 坏蛋 280 | 完蛋 909 | 笨蛋 1079 |
| 鸡蛋 1373 | 脸蛋 1461 | 鸭蛋 1782 |
| 滚蛋 1819 | 穷光蛋 912 | |

## 1369 雪 · U+96EA · TM **13** · FM 一

**xuě** N·ADJ·V snow; bright; snow-white; to avenge

**雪白 xuěbái** ADJ snow-white

**雪暴 xuěbào** N snowstorm · MW 场

**雪崩 xuěbēng** N avalanche · MW 场

**雪糕 xuěgāo** N ice cream · MW 块

**雪花 xuěhuā** N snowflake · MW 片
雪花在天空中飞舞。*Snowflakes are dancing in the air.*

**雪茄 xuějiā** N cigar · MW 根、支

**雪亮 xuěliàng** ADJ bright (as snow), shiny

**雪人 xuěrén** N snowman · MW 个

**雪松 xuěsōng** N cedar (tree) · MW 棵

**雪中送炭 xuězhōngsòngtàn** EXP to help when it is most needed (LIT to send coal in snowy weather)
这个时候你来帮忙, 那真是雪中送炭啊!
*Your providing help at this moment is like sending coal in snowy weather.*

### RELATED WORDS

| | | |
|---|---|---|
| 滚雪球 1819 | 滑雪 1884 | 暴风雪 1844 |

## 1370 哥 · U+54E5 · TM **13** · FM 一

**gē** N brother; older brother; male cousin

**哥哥 gēge** N older brother · MW 个

**哥儿们 gērmen** N brothers; pals, buddies · MW 个
咱们是**哥儿们**。*We are buddies.*

**哥嫂 gēsǎo** N older brother and his wife · MW 个、位

### RELATED WORDS

| | |
|---|---|
| 大哥 20 | 墨西哥 1843 |

## 1371 勇 · U+52C7 · TM **13** · FM 一

**yǒng** ADJ brave, valiant, courageous; conscript

**勇敢 yǒnggǎn** ADJ brave, courageous

**勇猛 yǒngměng** ADJ valiant, brave and fierce

**勇气 yǒngqì** N courage; nerve
我们要有**勇气**去尝试新的变化。*We ought to have courage to attempt change.*

## 1371 勇 yǒng (continued)

**勇士 yǒngshì** N warrior; brave man · MW 个、名

**勇往直前 yǒngwǎngzhíqián** EXP to march forward bravely

**勇于 yǒngyú** V to dare to, to have the courage to

傻瓜**勇于**改革。 *ShaGua bravely supports reform.*

**RELATED WORDS**

英勇 556　　　　　奋勇 607

---

## 1372 琴  U+7434　TM **13** FM 一

**qín** N (stringed) musical instrument; piano

**琴键 qínjiàn** N key (of a musical instrument); piano key · MW 个

**琴师 qínshī** N musician; player of a stringed instrument · MW 个、位、名

**琴弦 qínxián** N string (of a musical instrument) · MW 根、条

**RELATED WORDS**

竖琴 749　　　　　钢琴 1299
提琴 1554　　　　　手风琴 104
乱弹琴 901

---

## 1373 鸡 鷄 U+9E21　TM **13** FM 一

**jī** N chicken; prostitute

**鸡蛋 jīdàn** N egg · MW 个

**鸡毛蒜皮 jīmáosuànpí** EXP trifle, trivial matter
傻瓜太太特别爱管**鸡毛蒜皮**的小事。
*Mrs. ShaGua especially likes to take care of trivial matters.*

**鸡皮疙瘩 jīpígēda** EXP goosepimples

**鸡肉 jīròu** N chicken (meat) · MW 块

**鸡三明治 jīsānmíngzhì** N chicken sandwich · MW 块

**鸡色拉 jīsèlā** N chicken salad · MW 碟

**鸡汤 jītāng** N chicken soup · MW 碗

**鸡尾酒 jīwěijiǔ** N cocktail · MW 杯

**RELATED WORDS**

斗鸡 71　　　　　火鸡 72
田鸡 147　　　　　杀鸡取卵 317
养鸡场 670　　　　肉用鸡 437

---

## 1374 破 U+7834　TM **13** FM 一

**pò** ADJ·V damaged, broken; lousy, inferior, poor; to cut; to break; to defeat; to capture (a city); to spend; to expose; to crack/solve (a case)

**破案 pò'àn** V to solve a case

**破财 pòcái** V to suffer a financial loss

**破产 pòchǎn** V to go bankrupt; to fall through

**破除 pòchú** V to get rid of, to do away with

**破费 pòfèi** V to spend money
不必**破费**！ *You needn't go to the expense!*

**破釜沉舟 pòfǔchénzhōu** EXP to decide to fight to the death; to burn one's bridges (LIT to break the cauldrons and sink the boats)

**破格 pògé** V to make an exception; to break a rule
他被**破格**提拔为教授。 *An exception was made, and he was promoted to full professor.*

**破坏 pòhuài** V to destroy; to break, to violate; to damage
**破坏**旧世界，建设新世界。 *Destroy the old world and build a new one.*

**破获 pòhuò** V to crack (a case) and capture (a criminal)

**破烂 pòlàn** ADJ tattered, ragged

**破裂 pòliè** V to burst; to split, to break up
他们的关系**破裂**了。 *Their relationship has ended.*

**破落 pòluò** V to decline (in wealth, position)

**破灭 pòmiè** V to perish; to be shattered; to vanish
理想绝对不能**破灭**。 *The ideal must not disappear.*

**破伤风 pòshāngfēng** N tetanus

**破碎 pòsuì** V to smash, to break into pieces

**破损 pòsǔn** V to be damaged/worn

**破天荒 pòtiānhuāng** EXP to be unprecedented

**破土 pòtǔ** V to break ground (for a building project, etc.)
学校的实验室**破土**动工了。 *They broke ground for the school laboratory.*

**破晓 pòxiǎo** V to dawn

**破鞋 pòxié** N torn shoe; promiscuous woman · MW 个

**破绽 pòzhàn** N flaw, weak spot (LIT burst seam) · MW 个

**RELATED WORDS**

击破 156　　　　　打破 289
冲破 339　　　　　点破 739
突破 913　　　　　识破 950
爆破 1982　　　　　牢不可破 488

## 1375 硕 碩　U+7855　TM **13** FM 一

**shuò** ADJ·N　very large; master's degree

硕果 **shuòguǒ** N　achievement; success · MW 个

硕士 **shuòshì** N　master's degree · MW 个、名

**RELATED WORD**

丰硕 35

## 1376 骄 驕　U+9A84　TM **13** FM 一

**jiāo** ADJ　arrogant, conceited; severe, intense

骄傲 **jiāo'ào** ADJ·N　arrogant; proud; pride

我们为你**骄傲**。*We are proud of you.*

## 1377 剥　U+5265　TM **13** FM 一

**bāo/bō** V　to shell; to peel; to skin

剥皮 **bāopí** V　to peel off the skin

剥夺 **bōduó** V　to strip (someone) of, to deprive (by law)

许多人被**剥夺**了人身自由。*Many people have been deprived of their personal liberty.*

剥离 **bōlí** V　to come off

剥落 **bōluò** V　to peel off

剥削 **bōxuē** V　to exploit

谁**剥削**谁? 这是一个很有意思的问题。*Who exploited whom? This is a very interesting question.*

## 1378 素　U+7D20　TM **13** FM |

**sù** ADJ·N·ADV　plain, simple; native, original; white; vegetarian; vegetable; basic element; usually, habitually; always

吃**素** *vegetarian*

元**素** *element*

平**素** *always*

素材 **sùcái** N　source material (in literature, art)

他在搜集写作的**素材**。*He is gathering material for his writing.*

素菜 **sùcài** N　vegetable dish · MW 道

素绸 **sùchóu** N　white silk · MW 块、匹

素来 **sùlái** ADV　always; usually

素描 **sùmiáo** N　sketch; literary sketch · MW 张

素色 **sùsè** N　plain color

素食 **sùshí** N　vegetarian food/diet

他是**素食**者, 素来只吃素菜。*He is a vegetarian who always eats vegetable dishes.*

素性 **sùxìng** N　nature

素雅 **sùyǎ** ADJ　simple but elegant

她的穿着很**素雅**。*Her clothing is very simple but elegant.*

素油 **sùyóu** N　vegetable oil

素质 **sùzhì** N　quality; essence; character

中国要实行**素质**教育。*China wants to institute quality education.*

**RELATED WORDS**

| | | |
|---|---|---|
| 元素 138 | 因素 270 | 激素 1955 |
| 青霉素 740 | 抗生素 1009 | 抗菌素 1009 |
| 抗毒素 1009 | 维生素 1455 | |

## 1379 虐　U+8650　TM **13** FM |

**nüè** ADJ·V·N　cruel; tyrannical; to abuse; disaster, catastrophe

虐待 **nüèdài** V　to abuse, to mistreat

中国父母一般不把打孩子看作**虐待**孩子。*Chinese parents usually don't regard beating children as abusing them.*

虐杀 **nüèshā** V　to kill (someone) by beating him/her

**RELATED WORD**

暴虐 1844

## 1380 背　U+80CC　TM **13** FM |

**bēi** V·N　to carry on one's back; to take on (a responsibility, etc.); knapsack

**背**书包 *to carry a schoolbag*

**bèi** N·V·ADJ　back (of a person, of an object); to have one's back toward; to recite (from memory); to leave, to go away; to violate, to break; to hide (something) from; (to do something) behind (someone's) back; unlucky; hard of hearing

牛**背** *back of a cow*

**背**墙而立 *to stand with one's back toward a wall*

**背**着人说话 *to talk behind (someone's) back*

## 1380 背 bēi/bèi (continued)

背包 bēibāo   N   knapsack ·   MW   个

背部 bèibù   N   back; instep

背道而驰 bèidào'érchí   EXP   to go in the opposite direction

背风 bèifēng   ADJ   out of the wind

背光 bèiguāng   V   to be in poor light; to stand in one's own light

背后 bèihòu   N   behind; at the back, in the rear

背景 bèijǐng   N   background ·   MW   个

    傻瓜的**背景**很简单。*ShaGua's background is very simple.*

背井离乡 bèijǐnglíxiāng   EXP   to leave one's hometown

背离 bèilí   V   to depart/deviate from

背面 bèimiàn   N   back; reverse side

背叛 bèipàn   V   to betray

背弃 bèiqì   V   to abandon, to forsake

背书 bèishū   V   to recite a lesson from memory; to endorse (a check, a proposal, etc.)

    傻瓜最怕**背书**。*ShaGua was afraid to recite the lessons from memory.*

    傻瓜常常得给一些项目**背书**。*ShaGua has to endorse proposals quite often.*

背诵 bèisòng   V   to recite (from memory)

背心 bèixīn   N   sleeveless garment ·   MW   件

背信弃义 bèixìnqìyì   EXP   to break faith with

背影 bèiyǐng   N   view of the back of (someone/something) ·   MW   个

### RELATED WORDS

| | | |
|---|---|---|
| 刀背 31 | 手背 104 | 向背 603 |
| 违背 1185 | 靠背 1791 | |

## 1381 恩   U+6069   TM 13   FM |

ēn   N   kindness, favor

恩爱 ēn'ài   ADJ   affectionate

恩惠 ēnhuì   N   favor

    傻瓜总是在心里记住别人的**恩惠**。 *ShaGua always keeps the favors of others in mind.*

恩情 ēnqíng   N   profound kindness

恩人 ēnrén   N   benefactor, patron ·   MW   个、位

恩怨 ēnyuàn   N   mixture of gratitude and resentment

### RELATED WORD

感恩 1860

## 1382 辈 輩   U+8F88   TM 13   FM |

bèi   N   generation; lifetime; contemporaries; rank/position in the generational hierarchy of a family/clan

辈分 bèifen   N   seniority; position in the family hierarchy

辈子 bèizi   N   lifetime; one's whole life

### RELATED WORDS

| | | |
|---|---|---|
| 一辈子 1 | 小辈 61 | 平辈 78 |
| 长辈 93 | 半辈子 127 | 后辈 310 |
| 先辈 422 | 同辈 541 | 祖辈 1190 |
| 前辈 1329 | 晚辈 1779 | 祖祖辈辈 1190 |

## 1383 崭 嶄   U+5D2D   TM 13   FM |

zhǎn   ADJ   fine; swell

崭新 zhǎnxīn   ADJ   brand-new

    傻瓜给傻瓜太太买了一辆**崭新**的车, 但他自己却开二手车。*ShaGua bought a brand new car for Mrs. ShaGua, but he drives a used car.*

## 1384 晃   U+6643   TM 13   FM |

huǎng   V   to flash past; to dazzle

huàng   V   to shake; to rock; to sway

晃荡 huàngdàng   V   to shake; to rock; to sway

晃动 huàngdòng   V   to shake; to rock; to sway

### RELATED WORDS

| | |
|---|---|
| 明晃晃 1035 | 摇晃 1664 |

## 1385 晕 暈   U+6655   TM 13   FM |

yūn/yùn   ADJ·V   dizzy; giddy; to feel dizzy/giddy; to swoon

晕倒 yūndǎo   V   to faint, to pass out

晕厥 yūnjué   V   to faint, to pass out

晕头转向 yūntóuzhuànxiàng   EXP   confused and disoriented

晕晕乎乎 yūnyunhūhū   ADJ   dizzy; giddy

    傻瓜一上游船就**晕晕乎乎**, **晕头转向**。 *As soon as ShaGua gets on a cruise ship, he becomes dizzy, confused, and disoriented.*

### RELATED WORD

头晕 128

## 1386 罚 罰 U+7F5A   TM 13 FM |

**fá** V·N to punish, to penalize, to discipline; punishment, penalty

**罚金 fájīn** N fine · MW 笔

**罚款 fákuǎn** V·N to fine, to impose a fine · MW 笔

傻瓜当市长后还因为停车停错地方被警察**罚款**。 *ShaGua was given a parking ticket after he became mayor.*

**罚球 fáqiú** V to make a penalty shot/kick (sports)

**RELATED WORDS**

处罚 217          刑罚 256          责罚 525
受罚 844          奖罚 927

## 1387 咒 U+5492   TM 13 FM |

**zhòu** V·N to curse, to swear, to damn; to put a curse on; incantation

**咒骂 zhòumà** V to swear at, to curse

**咒语 zhòuyǔ** N incantation · MW 通

## 1388 煮 U+716E   TM 13 FM |

**zhǔ** V to cook; to boil; to stew

**煮饭 zhǔfàn** V to cook

在家里，总是傻瓜太太**煮饭**。 *Mrs. ShaGua cooks at home all the time.*

**煮食 zhǔshí** V to cook

## 1389 黑 U+9ED1   TM 13 FM |

**hēi** ADJ·N black; dark; wicked; secret; illegal; reactionary

**黑白 hēibái** N black and white; right and wrong

**黑斑 hēibān** N black spot · MW 块

傻瓜脸上有一块**黑斑**。 *There is a black spot on ShaGua's face.*

**黑板 hēibǎn** N blackboard · MW 块

**黑洞 hēidòng** N black hole (astronomy) · MW 个

**黑管 hēiguǎn** N clarinet · MW 支

傻瓜很喜欢听**黑管**，但不会吹。 *ShaGua likes to listen to the clarinet, but he doesn't know how to play one.*

**黑货 hēihuò** N smuggled goods · MW 批

**黑面包 hēimiànbāo** N black bread · MW 块、条

傻瓜很喜欢吃**黑面包**。 *ShaGua loves black bread.*

**黑名单 hēimíngdān** N blacklist · MW 份

**黑幕 hēimù** N inside story (of a plot, a shady deal, etc.) · MW 块

**黑人 hēirén** N black people · MW 个、位、名

**黑色 hēisè** N black

**黑市 hēishì** N black market · MW 个

**黑心 hēixīn** N evil mind · MW 颗

**黑猩猩 hēixīngxing** N chimpanzee · MW 个

**黑熊 hēixióng** N black bear · MW 个

**黑压压 hēiyāyā** EXP dense/dark mass of; sunless

**RELATED WORDS**

抹黑 571          乌黑 601          漆黑 1746

## 1390 热 熱 U+70ED   TM 13 FM |

**rè** ADJ·N·V hot; warm; popular; heat (in cooking); fever; fad, craze; to envy; to heat/warm up

**热门货** *popular goods*

**汉语热** *Chinese fever*

**发热** *to have a fever*

**眼热** *to envy*

**热热菜** *to warm up the dishes*

**热爱 rè'ài** V to love deeply

只有**热爱**教育事业的人才能当好老师。 *Only those who love education deeply are able to be good teachers.*

**热潮 rècháo** N craze · MW 个

**热诚 rèchéng** ADJ earnest; warm and sincere

**热处理 rèchǔlǐ** V to treat with heat

**热带 rèdài** N tropics

**热度 rèdù** N temperature

**热风 rèfēng** N hot wind/air · MW 阵

**热狗 règǒu** N hot dog · MW 条

**热烘烘 rèhōnghōng** EXP quite warm

**热乎乎 rèhūhū** EXP warm

傻瓜爱吃**热乎乎**的**热狗**。 *ShaGua likes to eat warm hot dogs.*

**热火朝天 rèhuǒcháotiān** EXP to be in full swing

**热浪 rèlàng** N heat wave · MW 阵

**热恋 rèliàn** V to be passionately in love

**热烈 rèliè** ADJ ardent, enthusiastic; heated

**1390 热 rè** (continued)

热闹 **rènao** ADJ·V   buzzing with excitement, lively; to liven up

傻瓜不喜欢**热闹**的场合。 *ShaGua doesn't like lively occasions.*

热能 **rènéng** N   thermal energy

热气 **rèqì** N   steam; hot air; seething with activity · MW 股

热切 **rèqiè** ADV   ardent; earnest

热情 **rèqíng** ADJ·N   enthusiastic, passionate; zeal, passion · MW 股

傻瓜**热情**地请在**热恋**中的傻瓜太太吃**热狗**。 *ShaGua enthusiastically invited Mrs. ShaGua, who was head over heels in love with him, to eat a hot dog.*

热水 **rèshuǐ** N   hot water · MW 杯、壶、桶

热天 **rètiān** N   summer; hot season/weather

热线 **rèxiàn** N   (telephone) hotline · MW 条

傻瓜给市民开通**热线**电话后, 每天都有许多民众**热切**地给他打电话。 *ShaGua has opened a hotline for the residents of the city. As a result, many people make fervent phone calls to the mayor every day.*

热心 **rèxīn** ADJ   enthusiastic; warm-hearted

热心肠 **rèxīncháng** N   ardent · MW 副

热心人 **rèxīnrén** N   enthusiast · MW 个、位、名

**RELATED WORDS**

| | | |
|---|---|---|
| 火热 72 | 亚热带 136 | 发热 311 |
| 余热 419 | 供热 459 | 加热 463 |
| 狂热 469 | 炎热 492 | 过热 712 |
| 吸热 776 | 看热闹 841 | 亲热 908 |
| 废热 918 | 闷热 1150 | 散热 1579 |
| 绝热 1706 | 酷热 1841 | 隔热 1910 |
| 枯草热 799 | | |

**1391 圆 圆**   U+5706   TM **13** FM |

**yuán** ADJ·N·V   round, circular; spherical; satisfactory; tactful; circle; ring; to justify, to make plausible

圆顶 **yuándǐng** N   dome · MW 个

圆规 **yuánguī** N   compass (drafting) · MW 个

圆弧 **yuánhú** N   arc · MW 个

圆滑 **yuánhuá** ADJ   sly, smooth and evasive

他很**圆滑**, 他不会做出任何承诺的。 *He is very evasive, so he won't make any commitments.*

圆环 **yuánhuán** N   circle; ring · MW 个

圆满 **yuánmǎn** ADJ   satisfactory; perfect

她的解释并不**圆满**。 *Her explanation was not very satisfactory.*

圆圈 **yuánquān** N   circle; ring · MW 个

圆心 **yuánxīn** N   center of a circle · MW 个

圆形 **yuánxíng** N   circular shape; round · MW 个

圆周 **yuánzhōu** N   circumference · MW 个

圆珠笔 **yuánzhūbǐ** N   ballpoint pen · MW 支

圆桌 **yuánzhuō** N   round table · MW 张

**圆桌**上有一支**圆珠笔**。 *There is a ballpoint pen on the round table.*

**RELATED WORDS**

| | |
|---|---|
| 团圆 392 | 滚圆 1819 |

**1392 药 藥**   U+836F   TM **13** FM |

**yào** N·V   medicine; drug; poison; to kill with poison; to cure with medicine

药材 **yàocái** N   medicinal herbs · MW 种

药草 **yàocǎo** N   medicinal herbs · MW 种

药厂 **yàochǎng** N   pharmaceutical factory · MW 间、家

药店 **yàodiàn** N   drugstore, pharmacy · MW 间、家

药方 **yàofāng** N   prescription · MW 个

她的病在心里, 你怎么开**药方**？ *The real problem is in her mind; what can you prescribe for her?*

药房 **yàofáng** N   drugstore, pharmacy · MW 间

药剂 **yàojì** N   medicine; drug · MW 服

药棉 **yàomián** N   absorbent cotton · MW 团

药片 **yàopiàn** N   pill, tablet · MW 片

药品 **yàopǐn** N   drugs; medicine · MW 种

中国人有一个说法：世界上什么**药品**都有, 就是没有后悔药。 *A Chinese saying: There are numerous medicines in the world, but no medicine for regret.*

药瓶 **yàopíng** N   medicine bottle · MW 个

药水 **yàoshuǐ** N   liquid medicine · MW 瓶

药丸 **yàowán** N   pill · MW 粒、颗

药物 **yàowù** N   drugs; medicine · MW 种

**RELATED WORDS**

| | | |
|---|---|---|
| 火药 72 | 中药 86 | 丸药 192 |
| 西药 352 | 司药 357 | 医药 389 |
| 抓药 406 | 农药 423 | 炸药 701 |
| 毒药 1211 | 服药 1457 | 弹药 1763 |
| 弹药库 1763 | 止泻药 41 | 中草药 86 |

## 1393 菠 U+83E0 TM 13 FM |

**bō** N spinach; pineapple

菠菜 **bōcài** N spinach · MW 棵

菠萝 **bōluó** N pineapple · MW 个

## 1394 塔 U+5854 TM 13 FM |

**tǎ** N pagoda; tower; [shaped like a pagoda]

塔吊 **tǎdiào** N tower crane · MW 台

塔台 **tǎtái** N control tower · MW 个

### RELATED WORDS

| 水塔 | 159 | 尖塔 | 203 | 灯塔 | 346 |
| 宝塔 | 667 | 铁塔 | 1126 | 金字塔 | 420 |

## 1395 抛 U+629B TM 13 FM |

**pāo** V to throw; to leave behind, to abandon; to sell in large quantities; to dispose of; to expose, to show

抛光 **pāoguāng** V to polish

抛锚 **pāomáo** V to break down

抛弃 **pāoqì** V to abandon, to desert

抛售 **pāoshòu** V to dispose of (by selling cheaply), to dump

抛头露面 **pāotóulùmiàn** EXP to appear in public, to show one's face in public

傻瓜太太喜欢**抛头露面**, 但傻瓜不喜欢。 *Mrs. ShaGua likes to show her face in public, but ShaGua doesn't.*

抛掷 **pāozhì** V to throw

抛砖引玉 **pāozhuānyǐnyù** EXP to get the ball rolling, to offer humble remarks to prompt others to speak (LIT to throw a brick to attract jade)

每次开会, 傻瓜都说: "还是我来**抛砖引玉**吧……" *ShaGua begins each meeting in the same way: "I guess I had better get the ball rolling…."*

## 1396 拖 U+62D6 TM 13 FM |

**tuō** V to pull; to trail (along behind); to delay, to postpone

拖把 **tuōbǎ** N mop · MW 把

拖车 **tuōchē** N trailer (pulled by a vehicle) · MW 辆

拖船 **tuōchuán** N tugboat · MW 艘

拖带 **tuōdài** V to tow

拖后腿 **tuōhòutuǐ** V to hold (someone) back, to impede

傻瓜太太从不拖傻瓜的**后腿**。 *Mrs. ShaGua has never held ShaGua back.*

拖拉 **tuōlā** ADJ dilatory; stalling

拖拉机 **tuōlājī** N tractor · MW 台

拖累 **tuōlěi** V to encumber, to be a burden to/on; to implicate

拖泥带水 **tuōnídàishuǐ** EXP to be hurried and careless

傻瓜办事很干脆, 从不**拖泥带水**。 *ShaGua does things very simply, not sloppily.*

拖欠 **tuōqiàn** V to be behind in payments

拖沓 **tuōtà** ADJ dilatory; sluggish

拖鞋 **tuōxié** N slippers; sandals · MW 双、对、只

拖延 **tuōyán** V to delay, to put off

由于她办事拖沓, 使得这个项目**拖延**了很长时间, 也**拖欠**了许多款项。 *Due to her sluggish handling of things, this project has been delayed for a long time and the funding that was lost cannot be recovered.*

## 1397 指 U+629B TM 13 FM |

**zhǐ** V·N to point at/to; to give directions; to point out; to refer to; to depend on; finger

指北针 **zhǐběizhēn** N compass · MW 个

指标 **zhǐbiāo** N target; quota · MW 个

指斥 **zhǐchì** V to denounce, to rebuke

指导 **zhǐdǎo** V to direct, to guide, to coach, to instruct

指点 **zhǐdiǎn** V to give directions, to show how; to talk behind (someone's) back

你的中文说得那么地道, 能不能**指点**一下? *You speak perfect Chinese; could you give me some pointers?*

指定 **zhǐdìng** V to appoint, to designate

他被**指定**为**指导**这个项目的负责人。 *He was appointed leader of the project.*

指挥 **zhǐhuī** V·N to command; direction, command

指甲 **zhǐjiǎ** N fingernail · MW 片

指教 **zhǐjiào** V to give advice

请多多**指教**。 *Kindly give me your advice.*

## 1397 指 zhǐ (continued)

指靠 zhǐkào   V   to depend on

指控 zhǐkòng   V   to accuse (someone) of, to charge (someone) with

有人企图**指控**傻瓜歧视妇女。*Somebody tried to charge ShaGua with discrimination against women.*

指令 zhǐlìng   N   order, command; direction ·   MW   道

指路标 zhǐlùbiāo   N   fingerpost, guidepost for travelers ·   MW   个

指明 zhǐmíng   V   to show clearly, to indicate

指南 zhǐnán   N   guide, manual ·   MW   本

指使 zhǐshǐ   V   to incite, to provoke

你不能**指使**孩子去干这种事。*You can't provoke kids to act like this.*

指示 zhǐshì   N·V   instruction; to give directions; to order ·   MW   个、道

指手画脚 zhǐshǒuhuàjiǎo   EXP   to gesticulate; to criticize indiscriminately

你能不能少**指手画脚**，多干些实事！*Could you stop making these meaningless gestures and get down to business!*

指数 zhǐshù   N   (numerical/statistical) index/indicator ·   MW   个

指纹 zhǐwén   N   fingerprint ·   MW   道、条

指引 zhǐyǐn   V   to point the way, to guide

指印 zhǐyìn   N   fingerprint ·   MW   个

指正 zhǐzhèng   V   to point out

### RELATED WORDS

| | |
|---|---|
| 五指 79 | 中指 86 |
| 手指 104 | 戒指 442 |
| 泛指 495 | 食指 1053 |
| 屈指 1071 | 屈指可数 1071 |
| 瞎指挥 1913 | 了如指掌 30 |
| 首屈一指 924 | |

## 1398 挣    U+629B    TM 13 FM |

zhēng   V   to struggle

zhèng   V   to earn; to get/break free

挣扎 zhēngzhá   V   to struggle

垂死**挣扎** *to put up a dying struggle*

挣钱 zhèngqián   V   to earn money

美国人是**挣钱**致富，中国人是省钱致富。*Americans try to make money to be rich; Chinese try to save money to be rich.*

## 1399 捂    U+6342    TM 13 FM |

wǔ   V   to cover, to seal; to muffle; to wrap up

捂鼻子 wǔbízi   V   to cover one's nose with one's hand

捂盖子 wǔgàizi   V   to cover up the truth

我们要知道真相，不要**捂盖子**！*Don't hide the truth from us!*

## 1400 捕    U+6355    TM 13 FM |

bǔ   V   to catch, to seize; to capture; to arrest

捕风捉影 bǔfēngzhuōyǐng   EXP   to act on hearsay (LIT to chase the wind and clutch at shadows)

有人老是对傻瓜的绯闻**捕风捉影**。*Some people are chasing shadows by investigating ShaGua's supposed affair.*

捕俘 bǔfú   V   to capture enemy personnel (for intelligence purposes)

捕获 bǔhuò   V   to catch, to capture

捕捉 bǔzhuō   V   to seize, to capture

### RELATED WORDS

| | |
|---|---|
| 拘捕 1231 | 追捕 1507 |
| 诱捕 1748 | |

## 1401 损 损    U+635F    TM 13 FM |

sǔn   V·ADJ   to lose; to damage (an object); to speak sarcastically; to make fun of; mean

损害 sǔnhài   V   to harm, to injure

损耗 sǔnhào   V   to cause wear and tear; to waste

你的行为，既**损耗**自己的精力，又**损害**社区的利益。*Your actions not only were a waste of energy, but also damaged community property.*

损坏 sǔnhuài   V   to damage (an object)

损人利己 sǔnrénlìjǐ   EXP   to harm others to benefit oneself

损伤 sǔnshāng   V   to damage, to harm

损失 sǔnshī   V·N   to lose; loss ·   MW   个

时间的**损失**是一种无法弥补的**损失**。*Losing time is an irreparable loss.*

损益 sǔnyì   V   to increase and decrease; profit and loss

### RELATED WORDS

| | |
|---|---|
| 亏损 137 | 折损 408 |
| 破损 1374 | 毁损 1810 |
| 跌打损伤 1422 | |

## 1402 换

U+6362    TM **13** FM |

**huàn** V  to trade, to exchange; to change, to replace

换班 **huànbān** V  to change shifts

换车 **huànchē** V  to change trains/buses

换挡 **huàndǎng** V  to shift gears

傻瓜对孩子说："你们在学习上应该'换挡'——加速！" *ShaGua said to his kids, "You should 'shift gears' in your studies—pick up the pace!"*

换岗 **huàngǎng** V  to relieve a sentry

换货 **huànhuò** V  to exchange goods

换钱 **huànqián** V  to change money

换取 **huànqǔ** V  to exchange (something) for; to get in return

她用这种方式来**换取**上司的信任。*She used this tactic to gain her boss's trust.*

换算 **huànsuàn** V  to convert (currency)

### RELATED WORDS

| | | |
|---|---|---|
| 互换 135 | 代换 208 | 交换 222 |
| 变换 653 | 转换 1111 | 倒换 1281 |
| 掉换 1403 | 替换 1430 | 退换 1508 |
| 置换 1651 | 调换 1749 | 撤换 1942 |

## 1403 掉

U+6389    TM **13** FM |

**diào** V  to fall, to drop; to fall behind; to lose; to reduce; to turn (something) around; to change, to substitute, to swap

掉队 **diàoduì** V  to drop out/off

不努力学习，就会**掉队**。*You will lag behind if you don't study hard.*

掉换 **diàohuàn** V  to exchange, to swap

掉色 **diàoshǎi** V  to fade, to lose color

掉头 **diàotóu** V  to turn around

我们在前面的路口**掉头**。*We will turn around at the next intersection.*

掉下来 **diàoxiàlái** V  to fall down

### RELATED WORDS

| | | |
|---|---|---|
| 干掉 13 | 失掉 106 | 打掉 289 |
| 丢掉 297 | 改掉 516 | 忘掉 655 |

## 1404 探

U+63A2    TM **13** FM |

**tàn** V  to explore; to visit; to stick (something) out; to look/inquire into; to scout, to spy

探测 **tàncè** V  to explore, to probe

探访 **tànfǎng** V  to visit, to call on

探戈 **tàngē** N  tango · MW 个

探究 **tànjiū** V  to probe/inquire into, to investigate

培养孩子的**探究**精神是教育的一项重要任务。*Fostering an inquisitive nature in children is a critical task of education.*

探明 **tànmíng** V  to ascertain, to verify

探亲 **tànqīn** V  to go home; to visit one's family

探求 **tànqiú** V  to search for, to seek

探视 **tànshì** V  to visit

探索 **tànsuǒ** V  to explore; to probe

探讨 **tàntǎo** V  to inquire into; to investigate

老师应该引导学生从不同的角度去**探讨**问题。*Teachers should show students how to approach a subject from different perspectives.*

探听 **tàntīng** V  to try to find out

傻瓜不允许傻瓜太太**探听**市政府的事情。*ShaGua doesn't allow Mrs. ShaGua to fish for information about the city government.*

探头探脑 **tàntóutànnǎo** EXP  to stick one's head in and look around

探望 **tànwàng** V  to visit; to look around

探问 **tànwèn** V  to make cautious inquiries about

探险 **tànxiǎn** V  to explore

探照灯 **tànzhàodēng** N  searchlight · MW 盏

探子 **tànzi** N  scout, spy · MW 个、名

### RELATED WORDS

| | |
|---|---|
| 刺探 1050 | 试探 1180 |

## 1405 接

U+63A5    TM **13** FM |

**jiē** V  to approach; to get in touch with; to connect, to link; to receive; to catch; to meet; to take over

接班 **jiēbān** V  to begin/work one's shift

接班人 **jiēbānrén** N  successor · MW 个、位、名

接触 **jiēchù** V  to get in touch with, to come into contact with

真正**接触**傻瓜后，你会觉得傻瓜好像并不傻。*After getting to know ShaGua, you might not feel that he is dumb anymore.*

接待 **jiēdài** V  to receive (a visitor)

接见 **jiējiàn** V  to interview

作为一个市长，傻瓜经常要**接见**和**接待**客人。*As mayor, ShaGua often has to interview and receive visitors.*

**1405 接 jiē** (continued)

接近 **jiējìn** V to approach

接力 **jiēlì** V to relay, to work/operate in relays

接洽 **jiēqià** V to take up a matter with

接任 **jiērèn** V to take over (a job, etc.); to replace

接生 **jiēshēng** V to deliver (a child)

接收 **jiēshōu** V to receive; to admit; to take over

接受 **jiēshòu** V to accept; to take on

在**接见**或**接待**客人时，傻瓜只**接收**文件，不**接受**礼物。 *When ShaGua interviews or receives visitors, he only gets documents and never accepts gifts.*

接替 **jiētì** V to take over (a job, etc.); to replace

接头 **jiētóu** V to contact, to get in touch with; to link up

接应 **jiēyìng** V to coordinate with; to back (someone) up

**RELATED WORDS**

交接 222     直接 609     拼接 794
连接 958     承接 972     邻接 1123
迎接 1360    粘接 1365    嫁接 1799
待人接物 872

---

**1406 控** U+63A7 TM **13** FM |

**kòng** V to control; to accuse, to charge; to turn (a container) upside down; to drain, to pour out

控告 **kònggào** V to accuse; to complain

控诉 **kòngsù** V to accuse; to denounce

控制 **kòngzhì** V to control, to dominate

当我们面对一些无法**控制**的事情，我们只能**控制**自己。 *When we are faced with situations we are unable to control, then we have to control ourselves.*

**RELATED WORDS**

失控 106     自控 305     受控 844
指控 1397    数控 1637    遥控 1830

---

**1407 描** U+63CF TM **13** FM |

**miáo** V to trace, to copy; to touch up, to retouch

描画 **miáohuà** V to draw

描绘 **miáohuì** V to draw; to describe

傻瓜太太无法**描绘**傻瓜。 *Mrs. ShaGua is unable to describe ShaGua.*

---

描述 **miáoshù** V to describe, to characterize

描图 **miáotú** V to trace

描写 **miáoxiě** V to depict, to describe

报纸上对傻瓜的**描写**，都有些失真。 *The depictions of ShaGua in the newspapers tend to be inaccurate.*

**RELATED WORDS**

扫描 402     素描 1378

---

**1408 挺** U+633A TM **13** FM |

**tǐng** V·ADJ·ADV to straighten; to stick out; to endure; hard and straight, erect, stiff; outstanding, extraordinary; very

挺拔 **tǐngbá** ADJ tall and straight

挺立 **tǐnglì** V to stand upright

挺身而出 **tǐngshēn'érchū** EXP to step forward boldly

---

**1409 响 響** U+54CD TM **13** FM |

**xiǎng** V·N·ADJ to sound; to ring; to resound; to echo; noise, sound; loud, noisy

响彻 **xiǎngchè** V to reverberate, to resound

响亮 **xiǎngliàng** ADJ loud and clear

响声 **xiǎngshēng** N noise, sound

响应 **xiǎngyìng** V to respond (to)

大家踊跃地**响应**捐款的倡议。 *People have responded enthusiastically to appeals for donations.*

**RELATED WORDS**

反响 111     打响 289     回响 391
音响 907     影响 1918    闷声不响 1150

---

**1410 哨** U+54E8 TM **13** FM |

**shào** N·V post; patrol; to reconnoiter; to whistle

哨兵 **shàobīng** N sentry · MW 个、名

哨所 **shàosuǒ** N sentry post · MW 个

哨子 **shàozi** N whistle · MW  只

**RELATED WORDS**

口哨 42     岗哨 745

## 1411 啥 U+5565 TM 13 FM |

**shá** QPRON　what

你要干啥？ *What do you want to do?*

## 1412 啤 U+5564 TM 13 FM |

**pí** N　beer

啤酒 **píjiǔ** N　beer ・ MW 杯、瓶

## 1413 梅 U+6885 TM 13 FM |

**méi** N　plum

梅花 **méihuā** N　plum blossom ・ MW 朵
梅花鹿 **méihuālù** N　deer ・ MW 只
梅树 **méishù** N　plum tree ・ MW 棵
梅子 **méizi** N　plum ・ MW 个

### RELATED WORD

望梅止渴 1622

## 1414 棵 U+68F5 TM 13 FM |

**kē** MW　[measure word for plants (trees, vegetables, grass, flowers, etc.)]

## 1415 植 U+690D TM 13 FM |

**zhí** V·N　to plant; to grow; to establish; botany; flora; vegetation

植树 **zhíshù** V　to plant trees
植物 **zhíwù** N　plant; vegetation ・ MW 种

### RELATED WORDS

扶植 404　　种植 893　　移植 1450

## 1416 降 U+964D TM 13 FM |

**jiàng** V　to fall, to drop; to reduce, to lower

**xiáng** V　to surrender, to capitulate; to control, to tame

投降 *to surrender*
降低 **jiàngdī** V　to reduce

降级 **jiàngjí** V　to reduce to a lower rank, to degrade
降落 **jiàngluò** V　to land; to descend
降落伞 **jiàngluòsǎn** N　parachute ・ MW 个
降旗 **jiàngqí** V　to lower a flag
降温 **jiàngwēn** V　to cool off; to decline in enthusiasm, to wane

中文热至今没有**降温**的迹象。 *There has been no sign of decline in "Chinese fever."*

降压 **jiàngyā** V　to reduce pressure, to decompress
降雨量 **jiàngyǔliàng** N　rainfall, precipitation
降伏 **xiángfú** V　to vanquish, to tame

### RELATED WORDS

下降 10　　升降机 47　　空降 669
投降 1008

## 1417 限 U+9650 TM 13 FM |

**xiàn** N·V　limit; confines; to limit, to restrict

限定 **xiàndìng** V　to limit, to restrict
限度 **xiàndù** N　limitation ・ MW 个
限额 **xiàn'é** N　quota; ration ・ MW 个
限量 **xiànliàng** N　to limit (the quantity of) ・ MW 个
限令 **xiànlìng** N　to order (someone) to do (something) within a certain time period ・ MW 道
限期 **xiànqī** N　deadline, time limit ・ MW 个
限速 **xiànsù** N　speed limit ・ MW 个

这条高速公路的**限速**是每小时45英里。 *The speed limit for this highway is 45 miles per hour.*

限于 **xiànyú** V　to be confined to
限制 **xiànzhì** V　to limit, to restrict

学生的思维不应该受到**限制**。 *A student's thoughts should not be stifled.*

### RELATED WORDS

无限 139　　权限 292　　时限 586
界限 758　　极限 798　　局限 1069
期限 1574

## 1418 除 U+9664 TM 13 FM |

**chú** V·PREP　to get rid of, to eliminate; to divide; except, besides

除草 **chúcǎo** V　to weed

**1418 除 chú** (continued)

除尘 **chúchén** V to dust

除臭剂 **chúchòujì** N deodorant · MW 瓶

除法 **chúfǎ** N division

除非 **chúfēi** CONJ unless

> 她不可能不来上课，**除非**她病了。*She will surely come to class, unless she is sick.*

除了 **chúle** PREP except, besides

> 除了中文以外，他还学日文。*In addition to Chinese, he also studies Japanese.*

> 除了他以外，我们都学中文。*We all study Chinese except him.*

除名 **chúmíng** V to remove (from a roll/list)

除外 **chúwài** V to exclude

除夕 **chúxī** N New Year's Eve

**RELATED WORDS**

| | | |
|---|---|---|
| 开除 26 | 切除 277 | 扣除 401 |
| 扫除 402 | 戒除 442 | 抹除 571 |
| 拆除 572 | 革除 747 | 拔除 791 |
| 废除 918 | 免除 1056 | 排除 1241 |
| 根除 1245 | 铲除 1304 | 删除 1309 |
| 消除 1343 | 破除 1374 | 被除数 1517 |
| 割除 1761 | 摘除 1906 | 解除 1928 |
| 撤除 1942 | 斩草除根 646 | 铲草除根 1304 |

---

**1419** 贿　贿　　U+8D3F　　TM **13** FM |

**huì** V·N to bribe; bribe; bribery

贿赂 **huìlù** V·N to bribe; bribe; bribery

> 在中国，现在**贿赂**的现象很普遍。*Bribes are very common in China now.*

贿选 **huìxuǎn** V to get elected through bribery

**RELATED WORDS**

| | |
|---|---|
| 行贿 327 | 受贿 844 |

---

**1420** 顿　顿　　U+987F　　TM **13** FM |

**dùn** V·ADJ·ADV·MW to pause; to arrange; to bow as a sign of respect, to kowtow; tired, fatigued; suddenly; immediately; [measure word for meals and for actions that occur without repetition (a criticism, a reprimand, a beating, etc.)]

顿挫 **dùncuò** V pause and transition in rhythm/melody

顿号 **dùnhào** N enumerative (serial) comma (punctuation mark in Chinese) · MW 个

顿时 **dùnshí** ADV immediately

> 他一讲话大家**顿时**笑起来。*As he began to speak, everybody immediately began laughing.*

**RELATED WORDS**

| | | |
|---|---|---|
| 安顿 487 | 停顿 1588 | 整顿 1845 |

---

**1421** 起　　U+8D77　　TM **13** FM |

**qǐ** V·MW to get/stand up; to remove; to grow, to form; to become; to draft, to draw up; to establish, to initiate; [used after a verb to indicate upward movement], up; [measure word for unpredictable events (accidents, fires, etc.)]

起草 **qǐcǎo** V to draft, to draw up

起程 **qǐchéng** V to leave, to set out

起初 **qǐchū** ADV at first, originally

> 起初傻瓜不愿意竞选市长，后来被市民的热情所感动，才参加竞选。*Originally, ShaGua didn't want to run for mayor; later, he was encouraged by city residents and decided to run.*

起床 **qǐchuáng** V to get up

起点 **qǐdiǎn** N starting point · MW 个

> 对傻瓜来说，当市长是他人生的一个新**起点**。*Being mayor is a new point of departure for ShaGua.*

起动 **qǐdòng** V to start

起飞 **qǐfēi** V to take off (of/in an airplane); to begin to develop rapidly

> 中国的经济已经开始**起飞**。*The Chinese economy has taken off quickly.*

起伏 **qǐfú** V to undulate, to rise and fall; to fluctuate

起哄 **qǐhòng** V to heckle; to stir up trouble

起火 **qǐhuǒ** V to start a fire (for cooking); to catch fire; to get angry

> 你能给壁炉**起火**吗？*Could you start a fire in the fireplace?*

> 房子**起火**了！*The house is on fire!*

> 你别**起火**，我们慢慢说。*Don't get angry; let's talk calmly.*

起家 **qǐjiā** V to build up (fame, a fortune, etc.)

> 傻瓜的美国梦是白手**起家**的。*ShaGua's American dream was to start with nothing.*

起劲 **qǐjìn** ADV energetically, enthusiastically

起居 **qǐjū** N daily/everyday life

起来 **qǐlái** V to get up, to arise

起立 **qǐlì** V to stand up, to rise

起落 **qǐluò** V to rise and fall

起码 qǐmǎ [ADV] minimum; at least

这是最起码的要求。 *This is the bare minimum requirement.*

起跑 qǐpǎo [V] to start a race

起色 qǐsè [N] improvement; sign of recovery

傻瓜的大儿子的成绩开始有起色了。 *ShaGua's older son's grades have gotten better.*

起身 qǐshēn [V] to leave, to set out, to start (a journey)

起始 qǐshǐ [V·N] to originate, to initiate; origin

起死回生 qǐsǐhuíshēng [EXP] to rise from the dead

起诉 qǐsù [V] to sue, to bring a lawsuit against

起义 qǐyì [V] to revolt

起因 qǐyīn [N] cause, origin · [MW] 个

他们吵架的起因是什么？ *What caused their quarrel?*

起源 qǐyuán [V·N] to originate; to stem from; origin; genesis · [MW] 个

**RELATED WORDS**

| | | |
|---|---|---|
| 一起 1 | 兴起 228 | 收起 282 |
| 发起 311 | 引起 371 | 另起炉灶 385 |
| 听起来 414 | 竖起 749 | 突起 913 |
| 谈起 1356 | 提起 1554 | 想起 1769 |
| 激起 1955 | 了不起 30 | 白手起家 176 |
| 对不起 254 | 对得起 254 | 拿得起 1262 |
| 禁得起 1536 | | |

---

**1422 跌** U+8DCC [TM] **13** [FM] |

diē [V] to tumble, to fall (down); to plummet

跌打损伤 diēdǎsǔnshāng [EXP] injury from a fall

跌倒 diēdǎo [V] to fall

跌价 diējià [V] to decrease in price

傻瓜太太问傻瓜："什么时候汽油才跌价？" *Mrs. ShaGua asked ShaGua, "When will gasoline prices go down?"*

跌交 diējiāo [V] to trip and fall

跌落 diēluò [V] to fall (of an object); to fall, to drop (of prices, yields, etc.)

**RELATED WORD**

暴跌 1844

---

**1423 欺** U+6B3A [TM] **13** [FM] |

qī [V] to deceive; to cheat; to bully

欺负 qīfu [V] to bully

傻瓜的大儿子在学校老是被人欺负。 *ShaGua's older son was bullied in school.*

欺瞒 qīmán [V] to fool

欺骗 qīpiàn [V] to deceive, to trick

欺压 qīyā [V] to bully, to push around; to oppress

欺诈 qīzhà [V] to cheat, to swindle

**RELATED WORDS**

仗势欺人 121　　　瞒上欺下 1914

---

**1424 教** U+6559 [TM] **13** [FM] |

jiāo [V] to teach

jiào [V·N] to teach, to educate, to tutor; religion

教书 jiāoshū [V] to teach

教学 jiāoxué [V] to teach; to teach and learn

教案 jiào'àn [N] lesson plan · [MW] 份

教材 jiàocái [N] teaching materials · [MW] 本

教导 jiàodǎo [V] to instruct

教父 jiàofù [N] godfather · [MW] 个、位、名

教皇 jiàohuáng [N] Pope

教诲 jiàohuì [V] to teach

教会 jiàohuì [N] (Christian) church/religion · [MW] 个

教科书 jiàokēshū [N] textbook · [MW] 本

教练 jiàoliàn [N] coach · [MW] 个、位、名

下班后，傻瓜是一名武术教练。 *ShaGua also coaches martial arts after work.*

教师 jiàoshī [N] teacher, instructor · [MW] 个、位、名

傻瓜太太的梦想是当一名教师。 *Mrs. ShaGua's dream is to be a teacher.*

教室 jiàoshì [N] classroom · [MW] 间

教士 jiàoshì [N] clergy(man) · [MW] 个、名

教授 jiàoshòu [N·V] professor; to teach, to instruct · [MW] 个、位、名

教唆 jiàosuō [V] to instigate, to incite

教堂 jiàotáng [N] church; temple · [MW] 间

教条 jiàotiáo [N·ADJ] dogma, doctrine, creed; dogmatic

傻瓜有时很教条。 *Sometimes, ShaGua is very dogmatic.*

教学 jiàoxué [N] schooling, education

教养 jiàoyǎng [N·V] breeding; upbringing; to bring up; to educate

教育 jiàoyù [V·N] to educate; education

教员 jiàoyuán [N] teacher, instructor · [MW] 个、位、名

## 1424 教 jiāo/jiào (continued)

教职员 jiàozhíyuán N teaching and administrative staff · MW 个、位、名

**RELATED WORDS**

| | | |
|---|---|---|
| 文教 70 | 互教互学 135 | 外教 218 |
| 传教 452 | 言教 478 | 讨教 500 |
| 身教 604 | 助教 818 | 宗教 910 |
| 佛教 1080 | 家教 1315 | 指教 1397 |
| 领教 1465 | 请教 1632 | 调教 1749 |
| 道教 1756 | 犹太教 886 | 盲哑教育 906 |
| 因材施教 270 | | |

---

## 1425 盒  U+76D2   TM **13**   FM ノ

hé N·MW box (especially a small box); [measure word for (small) boxes and cases]

盒子 hézi N box; case · MW 个

**RELATED WORDS**

| | | |
|---|---|---|
| 烟盒 1177 | 粉盒 1363 | 墨盒 1843 |

---

## 1426 急 U+6025   TM **13**   FM ノ

jí N·ADJ·V emergency; priority; anxious; impatient, quick-tempered; rapid, fast; violent; urgent; to be eager to help; to worry; to make anxious

急不可待 jíbùkědài EXP too impatient to wait, extremely anxious

急促 jícù ADV hastily, rapidly

急件 jíjiàn N urgent document · MW 份

急救 jíjiù V to have/give first aid / emergency treatment

急剧 jíjù ADV rapidly; suddenly

急流 jíliú N torrent; whitewater, rapids · MW 条

急忙 jímáng ADV hurriedly, hastily

收到**急件**后，傻瓜**急忙**采取了**急救**措施。
*After receiving the urgent documents, ShaGua has quickly taken emergency measures.*

急切 jíqiè ADV eagerly; urgently

急性 jíxìng ADJ acute (of a disease); impetuous

急性子 jíxìngzi N impetuous person, hothead · MW 个

急需 jíxū V to be badly in need of, to urgently need

急于 jíyú ADJ anxious, eager

急躁 jízào ADJ impetuous, impatient

急诊 jízhěn N emergency treatment · MW 个

---

傻瓜太太可能得了**急性**阑尾炎，傻瓜这个**急性子**，**急不可待**地等**急诊**的结果。
*Mrs. ShaGua had acute appendicitis. ShaGua is an impetuous person and was very impatient while waiting for the results of the emergency procedure.*

急转弯 jízhuǎnwān N sharp/sudden turn · MW 个

**RELATED WORDS**

| | | |
|---|---|---|
| 火急 72 | 心急 232 | 应急 334 |
| 告急 428 | 加急 463 | 尿急 849 |
| 危急 1057 | 特急 1094 | 焦急 1265 |
| 着急 1332 | 紧急会议 1537 | 紧急 1537 |
| 缓急 1708 | 躁急 1992 | 十万火急 3 |
| 当务之急 335 | 燃眉之急 1888 | |

---

## 1427 怒  U+6012   TM **13**   FM ノ

nù N·ADJ anger, rage; angry, furious; forceful, powerful, vigorous, dynamic

怒斥 nùchì V to reproach, to rebuke angrily

怒火 nùhuǒ N anger, fury · MW 团、股

怒气 nùqì N anger, rage · MW 股

怒视 nùshì V to glare at

傻瓜满腔**怒火**，他**怒视**着记者，**怒斥**她的胡编乱造。*ShaGua was filled with fury. He glared at the reporter and angrily rebuked her for the misleading article.*

**RELATED WORDS**

| | | |
|---|---|---|
| 发怒 311 | 迁怒 506 | 含怒 592 |
| 愤怒 1490 | 盛怒 1694 | 激怒 1955 |
| 恼羞成怒 931 | | |

---

## 1428 袋 U+888B   TM **13**   FM ノ

dài N·MW bag, sack, pouch; pocket; [measure word for bags, bagfuls, pocketfuls, etc.]

袋鼠 dàishǔ N kangaroo · MW 只

袋装 dàizhuāng N in bags, bagged

袋子 dàizi N bag; pocket · MW 个

**RELATED WORDS**

| | | |
|---|---|---|
| 口袋 42 | 麻袋 1146 | 脑袋 1460 |
| 弹袋 1763 | 垃圾袋 399 | |

---

## 1429 贸 貿  U+8D38   TM **13**   FM ノ

mào N transaction; trade, commerce

贸然 màorán ADV rashly, hastily

你不应该**贸然**地给傻瓜下结论。*You shouldn't draw a hasty conclusion about ShaGua.*

**贸易** **màoyì** N trade, commercial activity

**RELATED WORDS**

外贸 218     财贸 588     经贸 1110

---

### 1430 替

U+66FF   TM **13**   FM 丿

**tì** V·PREP to replace, to substitute for; to decline; for, on behalf of

**替补** **tìbǔ** V to substitute for

**替代** **tìdài** V to replace

**替工** **tìgōng** V to be a replacement worker, to be a substitute

**替换** **tìhuàn** V to replace, to substitute for
我能用那双鞋**替换**这双吗？*May I trade this pair of shoes for that pair?*

**替身** **tìshēn** N substitute, replacement; stuntman · MW 个

**替死鬼** **tìsǐguǐ** N scapegoat · MW 个、名

**替罪羊** **tìzuìyáng** N scapegoat · MW 个

**RELATED WORDS**

代替 208     交替 222     接替 1405

---

### 1431 聋 聾

U+804B   TM **13**   FM 丿

**lóng** ADJ deaf; hard of hearing

**聋哑** **lóngyǎ** N deaf and mute

**聋子** **lóngzi** N deaf person · MW 个

**RELATED WORD**

耳聋 145

---

### 1432 然

U+7136   TM **13**   FM 丿

**rán** ADJ·PRON·CONJ·ADV correct; so, like that; but, however; suddenly; [adverb/adjective suffix]

**然而** **rán'ér** CONJ yet, however
虽然中文很难学；**然而**，学起来却很有意思。*The Chinese language is very difficult to learn, but learning Chinese is very interesting.*

**然后** **ránhòu** CONJ afterwards; next
他先学中文，**然后**学日文。*He studied Chinese first, and then Japanese.*

**然则** **ránzé** ADV then, after that

**RELATED WORDS**

| | | |
|---|---|---|
| 了然 30 | 公然 103 | 已然 133 |
| 全然 172 | 自然 305 | 必然 338 |
| 仍然 448 | 果然 544 | 依然 625 |
| 定然 666 | 显然 755 | 固然 760 |
| 茫然 766 | 居然 850 | 或然 857 |
| 徒然 873 | 突然 913 | 庞然大物 917 |
| 虽然 990 | 泰然 1066 | 断然 1260 |
| 忽然 1268 | 诚然 1499 | 既然 1572 |
| 偶然 1590 | 竟然 1616 | 截然 1650 |
| 超然 1684 | 猛然 1704 | 飘然 1939 |
| 大自然 20 | 所以然 645 | 超自然 1684 |
| 想当然 1769 | 飘飘然 1939 | 听其自然 414 |

---

### 1433 鬼

U+9B3C   TM **13**   FM 丿

**guǐ** N·ADJ ghost, spirit; dirty trick; sensitive, surreptitious; clever; terrible, bad

**鬼把戏** **guǐbǎxì** N dirty trick · MW 出

**鬼点子** **guǐdiǎnzi** N wicked idea · MW 个
傻瓜有时喜欢**鬼点子**，但从来都讨厌**鬼把戏**。*ShaGua may sometimes enjoy wicked ideas, but he always disapproves of dirty tricks.*

**鬼怪** **guǐguài** N·ADJ forces of evil (LIT ghosts and monsters); strange · MW 个

**鬼话** **guǐhuà** N lie, falsehood; nonsense · MW 篇、通

**鬼魂** **guǐhún** N ghost, spirit · MW 个
傻瓜不相信**鬼魂**。*ShaGua doesn't believe in ghosts.*

**鬼脸** **guǐliǎn** N funny face; grimace; mask used as a toy · MW 个、张

**鬼神** **guǐshén** N supernatural beings (LIT ghosts and deities) · MW 个

**RELATED WORDS**

| | | |
|---|---|---|
| 小鬼 61 | 见鬼 267 | 洋鬼子 689 |
| 做鬼 1282 | 闹鬼 1323 | 酒鬼 1339 |
| 醉鬼 1842 | 搞鬼 1904 | 魔鬼 1996 |
| 神出鬼没 1191 | 装神弄鬼 1476 | 疑神疑鬼 1917 |

---

### 1434 岛 島

U+5C9B   TM **13**   FM 丿

**dǎo** N island, isle

**岛港** **dǎogǎng** N island harbor · MW 个

**岛国** **dǎoguó** N island country · MW 个
岛国不一定导致岛国心态。*An island country may not necessarily lead to an island state of mind.*

**岛屿** **dǎoyǔ** N islands · MW 个

**1434 岛 dǎo** (continued)

RELATED WORDS

小岛 61　　　　海岛 1494　　　　群岛 1646

---

**1435 奥**　　U+5965　　TM **13**　FM 丿

**ào** ADJ profound, unfathomable; obscure, mysterious

**奥林匹克 Àolínpǐkè** N Olympics

**奥秘 àomì** N mystery; secret · MW 个

傻瓜的成功并没有什么**奥秘**。*There is no mystery to ShaGua's success.*

**奥妙 àomiào** ADJ profound; subtle; mysterious

**奥斯卡 Àosīkǎ** N Oscar (Academy Award)

RELATED WORD

深奥 1345

---

**1436 笼** 籠　　U+7B3C　　TM **13**　FM 丿

**lóng** N cage, coop; food steamer; basket

**lǒng** V·N to cover; to envelop; bamboo trunk/case

**笼头 lóngtóu** N halter (headgear for animals) · MW 个

**笼养 lóngyǎng** V to be raised in a cage

**笼子 lóngzi** N cage, coop · MW 个

RELATED WORDS

灯笼 346　　　　牢笼 488　　　　鸟笼 859
蒸笼 1768

---

**1437 等**　　U+7B49　　TM **13**　FM 丿

**děng** V·PREP·MW to wait; to be equal; namely; and so on, and so forth; etc.; by the time, when; [measure word for class, grade, or rank, and for kind, sort, etc.]

**等比 děngbǐ** N geometric ratio · MW 个

**等边 děngbiān** N equilateral · MW 条

**等次 děngcì** N position in a series; grade

**等待 děngdài** V to wait (for)

**等到 děngdào** PREP·V by the time, when; to wait until

**等到**她下课，我们就一起回家。*When class ends, we're going home.*

我愿意**等待**她**等到**头发白。*I will wait for her until my hair turns white.*

**等等 děngděng** ADV and so on; etc.; to wait a minute

**等分 děngfēn** V to divide into equal parts

**等号 děnghào** N equals sign · MW 个

**等候 děnghòu** V to wait (for); to expect

**等级 děngjí** N grade, rank; social status · MW 个

**等价 děngjià** N equal (in) value; equivalence

**等距 děngjù** N equal distance · MW 个

**等离子 děnglízǐ** N plasma

**等式 děngshì** N equality · MW 个

**等同 děngtóng** V to equate; to be equal

**等外 děngwài** ADJ substandard

**等闲 děngxián** ADJ ordinary; unimportant

有人认为：傻瓜不是**等闲**之辈。*Some people think that ShaGua is an odd person.*

**等于 děngyú** V to be equal/equivalent to, to be the same as

**等值 děngzhí** N equal value; equivalence

RELATED WORDS

| | | |
|---|---|---|
| 二等 2 | 三等分 9 | 下等 10 |
| 上等 14 | 乙等舱 29 | 乙等奖 29 |
| 乙等生 29 | 平等 78 | 中等 86 |
| 头等 128 | 甲等 149 | 丙等 246 |
| 对等 254 | 坐等 318 | 劣等 444 |
| 劣等品 444 | 劣等生 444 | 优等 447 |
| 同等 541 | 均等 558 | 何等 619 |
| 相等 805 | 初等 963 | 特等 1094 |
| 高等 1611 | | |

---

**1438 答**　　U+7B54　　TM **13**　FM 丿

**dá** V to answer, to respond (to); to reciprocate; to repay

**答案 dá'àn** N answer; solution · MW 个

好的问题有时比好的**答案**更有价值。*Sometimes, a good question is more valuable than a good answer.*

**答辩 dábiàn** V to reply; to defend (a thesis/dissertation, a charge in court, etc.)

**答词 dácí** N thank-you/acceptance speech · MW 篇

**答复 dáfù** V to answer, to reply

**答话 dáhuà** V to answer, to reply

答题 **dátí** [V] to answer a question

答谢 **dáxiè** [V] to express one's thanks/appreciation

**RELATED WORDS**

| | | |
|---|---|---|
| 对答 254 | 应答 334 | 回答 391 |
| 问答 678 | 报答 1010 | 羞答答 1154 |
| 选答题 1510 | 滴答 1885 | 解答 1928 |
| 赠答 1944 | | |

---

**1439** 签 簽 籤 U+7B7E TM **13** FM ノ

**qiān** [V·N] to sign; to endorse; to write brief comments on a document; label; (small sharp-pointed) stick; toothpick

签到 **qiāndào** [V] to sign in

签订 **qiāndìng** [V] to agree to and sign (a treaty, a contract, etc.)

签发 **qiānfā** [V] to sign and issue (a document, etc.)

签名 **qiānmíng** [V·N] to sign (one's name); signature · [MW] 个

签收 **qiānshōu** [V] to sign (a delivery confirmation)

签署 **qiānshǔ** [V] to sign officially

签约 **qiānyuē** [V] to sign (a contract)

签证 **qiānzhèng** [N] visa · [MW] 个

傻瓜**签收**了有他的中国**签证**的挂号邮件。
*ShaGua signed his name upon receiving the certified letter containing his Chinese visa.*

签字 **qiānzì** [V·N] to sign (one's name), to endorse; signature · [MW] 个

**RELATED WORDS**

| | | |
|---|---|---|
| 牙签 143 | 抽签 788 | 标签 801 |

---

**1440** 偿 償 U+507F TM **13** FM ノ

**cháng** [V] to compensate, to repay; to fulfill, to satisfy

偿付 **chángfù** [V] to pay (back)

偿还 **chánghuán** [V] to repay, to pay back

有时候，别人给你一个面子，你是需要**偿还**的。
*At times, you need to pay back the favors others have done for you.*

偿命 **chángmìng** [V] to pay with one's life

偿清 **chángqīng** [V] to pay off (a debt)

**RELATED WORDS**

| | | |
|---|---|---|
| 无偿 139 | 补偿 508 | 赔偿 1569 |

---

**1441** 街 U+8857 TM **13** FM ノ

**jiē** [N] street; downtown street; market; country fair

街道 **jiēdào** [N] street; neighborhood · [MW] 条

街头 **jiētóu** [N] street corner

街头巷尾 **jiētóuxiàngwěi** [EXP] everywhere; all over town (LIT streets and lanes)

在中国的**街头巷尾**都能看到这本书。*You can find this book everywhere in China.*

**RELATED WORDS**

| | | |
|---|---|---|
| 上街 14 | 大街 20 | 逛街 1513 |
| 骂街 1652 | 华尔街 421 | 唐人街 1324 |

---

**1442** 得 U+5F97 TM **13** FM ノ

**dé** [V·ADJ·AV] to get; to catch; to be suitable; to equal; to be finished/ready; glad; satisfied; comfortable, cozy; [used between a verb and its complement to indicate possibility]; [used after a verb/adjective to introduce a complement of result]; [used directly after certain verbs to indicate possibility]

傻瓜的儿子**得**到好成绩。*ShaGua's son got a high score.*

她说话**得**体。*She speaks appropriately.*

工资快**得**了。*The paycheck will be ready soon.*

**得**意 *satisfied*

**děi** [V] to need; must, to have to, should

我**得**去上课。*I must go to class.*

快吃药吧，不然你**得**生病。*Please take the medicine; otherwise, you will get sick.*

**RELATED WORDS**

| | | |
|---|---|---|
| 不得 24 | 不得不 24 | 不得已 24 |
| 了得 30 | 亏得 137 | 只得 160 |
| 心得 232 | 认得 239 | 对得起 254 |
| 来得及 260 | 见得 267 | 乐得 299 |
| 自得 305 | 用得着 313 | 应得 334 |
| 取得 520 | 舍得 593 | 使得 623 |
| 所得 645 | 所得税 645 | 过得去 712 |
| 吃得开 783 | 犯得着 884 | 记得 946 |
| 难得 974 | 获得 1000 | 值得 1089 |
| 拿得起 1262 | 总得 1330 | 觉得 1485 |
| 禁得起 1536 | 博得 1549 | 既得利益 1572 |
| 患得患失 1649 | 想得到 1769 | 想得开 1769 |
| 懂得 1817 | 懒得 1953 | 赢得 2000 |
| 不见得 24 | 了不得 30 | 由不得 148 |
| 见不得 267 | 舍不得 593 | 使不得 623 |

**1442 得 dé/děi** (continued)

| | | |
|---|---|---|
| 洋洋得意 689 | 怪不得 696 | 怎么得了 830 |
| 要不得 969 | 恨不得 1174 | 迫不得已 1186 |
| 不可多得 24 | 心安理得 232 | 哭笑不得 1221 |

---

**1443 狼**   U+72FC   TM **13** FM 丿

**láng** N   wolf

狼狗 **lánggǒu** N   wolfhound · MW 只, 条

狼吞虎咽 **lángtūnhǔyàn** EXP   to gobble up, to wolf down (food)

狼心狗肺 **lángxīngǒufèi** EXP   ungrateful

---

**1444 猎** 獵   U+730E   TM **13** FM 丿

**liè** V·N   to hunt; to pursue, to seek; hunting; hunter

猎豹 **lièbào** N   cheetah · MW 只

猎场 **lièchǎng** N   hunting ground · MW 个

猎狗 **liègǒu** N   hunting dog · MW 只、条

   傻瓜家养了两条**猎狗**。 *ShaGua's family has two hunting dogs.*

猎户 **lièhù** N   hunter · MW 个、名

猎奇 **lièqí** V   to seek novelty

   孩子好奇，成人**猎奇**。 *Kids are curious; adults seek novelty.*

猎枪 **lièqiāng** N   shotgun; hunting rifle; sporting gun · MW 支

猎取 **lièqǔ** V   to hunt; to pursue, to seek

猎人 **lièrén** N   hunter; huntsman · MW 个、名

猎物 **lièwù** N   prey, quarry · MW 个

**RELATED WORD**

打猎 289

---

**1445 猪**   U+732A   TM **13** FM 丿

**zhū** N   pig; hog; swine

猪场 **zhūchǎng** N   hog farm · MW 个

猪肝 **zhūgān** N   pork liver · MW 个

猪流感 **zhūliúgǎn** N   swine flu, H1N1 virus

猪肉 **zhūròu** N   pork · MW 块

   我们要尊重穆斯林不吃**猪肉**的习俗。 *We ought to respect the Muslim custom of not eating pork.*

---

猪油 **zhūyóu** N   lard · MW 滴、块

**RELATED WORDS**

| | | |
|---|---|---|
| 养猪场 670 | 野猪 1685 | 蠢猪 1995 |

---

**1446 猫**   U+732B   TM **13** FM 丿

**māo** N·V   cat; to hide (oneself)

猫哭老鼠 **māokūlǎoshǔ** EXP   to shed crocodile tears (LIT the cat weeps for the dead mouse)

猫头鹰 **māotóuyīng** N   owl · MW 只

猫熊 **māoxióng** N   panda · MW 只

猫眼 **māoyǎn** N   cat's eye · MW 个、只

**RELATED WORDS**

| | | |
|---|---|---|
| 夜猫子 654 | 野猫 1685 | 馋猫 1924 |
| 大熊猫 20 | | |

---

**1447 饲** 飼   U+9972   TM **13** FM 丿

**sì** V·N   to raise, to rear (animals); to feed; forage, fodder

饲草 **sìcǎo** N   forage grass · MW 堆

饲料 **sìliào** N   forage, fodder, feed · MW 堆

饲养 **sìyǎng** V   to raise, to rear (animals); to feed

---

**1448 娘**   U+5A18   TM **13** FM 丿

**niáng** N   mom, mother; auntie, elderly married woman

娘家 **niángjia** N   married woman's parents' home

娘舅 **niángjiù** N   (maternal) uncle · MW 个、位

娘胎 **niángtāi** N   (mother's) womb

   我还在**娘胎**里就知道你不是一个好人。 *I have known that you were a bad guy for a long time.*

娘姨 **niángyí** N   maid, female servant · MW 个

**RELATED WORDS**

| | | |
|---|---|---|
| 姑娘 881 | 新娘 1638 | 丈母娘 17 |
| 老大娘 375 | | |

---

**1449 媒**   U+5A92   TM **13** FM 丿

**méi** N   matchmaker; go-between, intermediary

媒介 **méijiè** N   intermediary · MW 个

媒人 **méiren** 　N　matchmaker ·　MW　个、名

媒体 **méitǐ** 　N　(news) media ·　MW　个

傻瓜不喜欢**媒体**的纠缠。*ShaGua doesn't like the media bothering him.*

---

### 1450 移 　U+79FB　TM **13**　FM ノ

**yí** 　V·N　to move, to shift; to change, to alter; to immigrate; immigration

移动 **yídòng** 　V　to move, to shift

移交 **yíjiāo** 　V　to transfer, to hand over

移民 **yímín** 　V·N　to emigrate/immigrate; settler, immigrant ·　MW　个、名

从某种意义上说，美国人都是**移民**。*In a sense, all Americans are immigrants or descendants of immigrants.*

移山倒海 **yíshāndǎohǎi** 　EXP　to make a massive, powerful transformation (LIT to remove mountains and drain seas)

移植 **yízhí** 　V　to transplant

#### RELATED WORDS

迁移 506　　转移 1111

---

### 1451 程 　U+7A0B　TM **13**　FM ノ

**chéng** 　N　journey; road; distance; procedure, course, sequence; schedule; rule, regulation

程度 **chéngdù** 　N　level, standard, degree; extent

程式 **chéngshì** 　N　pattern, formula ·　MW　个

程序 **chéngxù** 　N　procedure; program ·　MW　个

傻瓜在夜校学电脑**程序**常识。*ShaGua studied the basics of computer programming in night school.*

#### RELATED WORDS

| | | |
|---|---|---|
| 工程 12 | 工程师 12 | 中程 86 |
| 日程 96 | 日程计划 96 | 专程 155 |
| 全程 172 | 历程 200 | 方程 220 |
| 计程表 240 | 议程 350 | 里程 386 |
| 里程碑 386 | 回程 391 | 启程 657 |
| 疗程 661 | 单程 672 | 过程 712 |
| 进程 713 | 近程 716 | 返程 957 |
| 规程 1098 | 远程 1184 | 章程 1311 |
| 前程 1329 | 视程 1362 | 起程 1421 |
| 课程 1503 | 旅程 1518 | 航程 1717 |
| 路程 1785 | | |

---

### 1452 短 　U+77ED　TM **13**　FM ノ

**duǎn** 　ADJ·V·N　short, brief (in space, time, etc.); to lack; to owe; weakness

短波 **duǎnbō** 　N　short-wave (radio)

短处 **duǎnchu** 　N　fault; weakness

傻瓜的一些**短处**，如憨厚等，也正是他的长处。*Some of ShaGua's weaknesses are also his strengths, such as simplicity and honesty, etc.*

短促 **duǎncù** 　ADJ　very brief

短大衣 **duǎndàyī** 　N　short overcoat ·　MW　件

短见 **duǎnjiàn** 　N　shortsighted view; suicide ·　MW　个

她说的都是**短见**之言。*Everything she said was shortsighted.*

她要寻**短见**。*She wanted to commit suicide.*

短裤 **duǎnkù** 　N　shorts; (short) underwear ·　MW　条

短命 **duǎnmìng** 　ADJ　short-lived

短跑 **duǎnpǎo** 　N　dash, sprint (race)

短期 **duǎnqī** 　N　short-term

短少 **duǎnshǎo** 　V　to lack, to miss, to be short of/on

短袜 **duǎnwà** 　N　sock ·　MW　对

短文 **duǎnwén** 　N　short article; essay ·　MW　篇

这篇**短文**真棒！*This essay is marvelous!*

短小 **duǎnxiǎo** 　ADJ　short, concise

短暂 **duǎnzàn** 　ADJ　short, brief; transient

#### RELATED WORDS

| | | |
|---|---|---|
| 长短 93 | 气短 185 | 发短信 311 |
| 寻短见 358 | 护短 569 | 简短 1796 |
| 缩短 1927 | 三长两短 9 | 取长补短 520 |

---

### 1453 练 練 　U+7EC3　TM **13**　FM ノ

**liàn** 　V·ADJ　to practice; to train, to drill; skilled; experienced

练兵 **liànbīng** 　V　to drill troops; to train professionally

练功 **liàngōng** 　V　to do exercises

练球 **liànqiú** 　V　to practice (a sport involving a ball)

练习 **liànxí** 　V·N　to practice; to exercise ·　MW　个

傻瓜常常**练习**武术。*ShaGua practices martial arts quite often.*

**1453 练 liàn** (continued)

RELATED WORDS

| | | |
|---|---|---|
| 干练 13 | 训练 349 | 老练 375 |
| 排练 1241 | 教练 1424 | 简练 1796 |
| 演练 1821 | 操练 1965 | 熟练 1973 |

**1454 绑** 綁    U+7ED1    TM **13** FM 丿

**bǎng** V to tie (up)

绑匪 **bǎngfěi** N kidnapper · MW 个、名

绑紧 **bǎngjǐn** V to tie (something) tight

绑票 **bǎngpiào** V to kidnap (for ransom)

RELATED WORD

松绑 579

**1455 维** 維    U+7EF4    TM **13** FM 丿

**wéi** V·N to keep, to maintain; to hold together; thought; dimension

维持 **wéichí** V to maintain; to support

维护 **wéihù** V to protect, to safeguard

维生素 **wéishēngsù** N vitamin · MW 粒、瓶

维新 **wéixīn** V to reform

中国历史上搞**维新**的人几乎都没有好的结局。 *Those who have attempted political renewal in Chinese history have not had happy endings.*

维修 **wéixiū** V to maintain (equipment, etc.)

RELATED WORDS

| | |
|---|---|
| 二维 2 | 思维 1214 |

**1456 股**    U+80A1    TM **13** FM 丿

**gǔ** N·MW department (of a business); thigh; strand, ply; share (of company stock); [measure word for air currents, smells, electric current, and spirals; for string-shaped objects (skeins of yarn, etc.); for groups of (bad) people; and for one of several equal parts]

股本 **gǔběn** N capital stock; capitalization

股东 **gǔdōng** N shareholder, stockholder · MW 个、位、名

股份 **gǔfèn** N share; stock

股金 **gǔjīn** N share price · MW 笔

股票 **gǔpiào** N share; stock

傻瓜对**股票**不感兴趣。*ShaGua is not interested in stocks.*

股息 **gǔxī** N dividend · MW 笔

RELATED WORDS

| | | |
|---|---|---|
| 入股 5 | 持股 1019 | 屁股 1070 |

**1457 服**    U+670D    TM **13** FM 丿

**fú** V·N to take (medicine); to serve (a sentence, as an officeholder, in the army, etc.); to comply with, to obey; to convince; to adapt to, to become accustomed to; to wear; clothes

信服 *to be convinced*

说服 *to persuade*

水土不服 *not accustomed to the climate, not acclimated*

衣服 *clothes*

**fù** MW [measure word for doses of medicine]

服从 **fúcóng** V to obey

服毒 **fúdú** V to take poison

服气 **fúqì** V to be convinced, to be won over, to accept

服饰 **fúshì** N dress; attire · MW 种

服侍 **fúshì** V to nurse; to wait on; to look after

服输 **fúshū** V to admit defeat, to concede

傻瓜从来不**服输**。*ShaGua has never admitted defeat.*

服贴 **fútiē** ADJ docile, submissive; proper, fitting

服务 **fúwù** V to serve

服刑 **fúxíng** V to serve a (prison) sentence

他对**服刑**不**服气**。*He doesn't agree with the sentence he must serve.*

服药 **fúyào** V to take medicine

服装 **fúzhuāng** N clothing, dress · MW 件、套

服罪 **fúzuì** V to plead guilty

RELATED WORDS

| | | |
|---|---|---|
| 口服 42 | 内服 191 | 压服 201 |
| 心服 232 | 叹服 285 | 衣服 330 |
| 冲服 339 | 折服 408 | 吞服 427 |
| 征服 462 | 军服 489 | 礼服 503 |
| 和服 644 | 克服 738 | 便服 865 |
| 信服 869 | 屈服 1071 | 制服 1130 |
| 说服 1631 | 舒服 1805 | 工作服 12 |
| 以理服人 101 | 夜礼服 654 | 售后服务 1266 |

## 1458 肠 腸   U+80A0   TM 13   FM 丿

**cháng** N intestines; sausage; heart

**肠道 chángdào** N intestines · MW 条

**肠胃 chángwèi** N stomach and intestines

**肠炎 chángyán** N enteritis

**肠子 chángzi** N intestines · MW 条

### RELATED WORDS

大肠 20    羊肠小道 227    心肠 232
香肠 834    胃肠炎 1216    结肠 1291
热心肠 1390

## 1459 肥   U+80A5   TM 13   FM 丿

**féi** N·ADJ·V fertilizer, manure; fat; fertile; profitable, lucrative; loose; to fertilize; to get rich

**肥大 féidà** ADJ loose, large, baggy (of clothing)
傻瓜穿的衣服都很**肥大**。 *All the clothes ShaGua wears are loose.*

**肥厚 féihòu** ADJ plump; fleshy

**肥料 féiliào** N fertilizer, manure · MW 堆

**肥美 féiměi** ADJ fertile; rich

**肥胖 féipàng** ADJ fat, overweight

**肥土 féitǔ** N fertile soil · MW 片

**肥沃 féiwò** ADJ fertile
这片土地多**肥沃**啊！ *What a piece of fertile land this is!*

**肥皂 féizào** N soap · MW 块

**肥壮 féizhuàng** ADJ stout and strong

### RELATED WORDS

化肥 215    粪肥 1334    减肥 1487
施肥 1758

## 1460 脑 腦   U+8111   TM 13   FM 丿

**nǎo** N brain; mind; head

**脑袋 nǎodai** N brain; mind; head · MW 个

**脑海 nǎohǎi** N brain; mind

**脑浆 nǎojiāng** N brains

**脑筋 nǎojīn** N mind · MW 个
你这个死**脑筋**！ *This was your stupid idea!*

**脑壳 nǎoké** N skull · MW 个

**脑力 nǎolì** N brains, brain power, intellect

**脑膜炎 nǎomóyán** N meningitis

**脑神经 nǎoshénjīng** N cranial nerve

**脑子 nǎozi** N brain; mind · MW 个
你真是没有**脑子**。 *You're brain-dead.*

### RELATED WORDS

大脑 20    主脑 124    头脑 128
电脑 263    后脑 310    伤脑筋 453
首脑 924    满脑子 1745    呆头呆脑 384
没头没脑 938    昏头昏脑 1058    贼头贼脑 1254
探头探脑 1404    傻头傻脑 1699    愣头愣脑 1735

## 1461 脸 臉   U+8138   TM 13   FM 丿

**liǎn** N face; facial expression; front

**脸蛋 liǎndàn** N cheeks; face · MW 张

**脸红 liǎnhóng** V to blush with shame

**脸面 liǎnmiàn** N face; feelings; self-respect · MW 个

**脸盆 liǎnpén** N washbowl, washbasin · MW 个

**脸皮 liǎnpí** N face; feelings; sense of shame · MW 张

**脸皮嫩 liǎnpínèn** EXP bashful, shy

**脸色 liǎnsè** N complexion; facial expression · MW 个
她的**脸色**不好。 *She doesn't look well.*
她的**脸色**很难看。 *Her facial expression is very bad.*

### RELATED WORDS

白脸 176    丢脸 297    红脸 474
笑脸 861    刮脸 902    刮脸刀 902
洗脸盆 1167    厚脸皮 1272    鬼脸 1433
满脸 1745    嘴脸 1984    翻脸 1989
不要脸 24    拉下脸 573    鼻青脸肿 1794

## 1462 钙 鈣   U+9499   TM 13   FM 丿

**gài** N calcium

**钙化 gàihuà** V to calcify

**钙片 gàipiàn** N calcium · MW 片

## 1463 钩 鉤   U+94A9   TM 13   FM 丿

**gōu** N·V hook; to crochet; to make a checkmark, to check off

**钩扣 gōukòu** N fastener · MW 个

**钩爪 gōuzhǎo** N finger · MW 个

**1463 钩 gōu** (continued)

钩针 **gōuzhēn** N crochet hook · MW 枚

钩状 **gōuzhuàng** N hooklike

钩子 **gōuzi** N hook · MW 个

**RELATED WORDS**

上钩 14    挂钩 796    鱼钩 843
钓钩 1124

**1464 铅** 鉛   U+94C5   TM **13** FM ノ

**qiān** N lead

铅笔 **qiānbǐ** N pencil · MW 支

铅字 **qiānzì** N letter, type (typography) · MW 个、枚

**1465 领** 領   U+9886   TM **13** FM ノ

**lǐng** V·N to lead; to get, to receive; to accept; to understand; to adopt; to possess; to occupy; collar; neck; outline; main point

领班 **lǐngbān** N foreman, supervisor · MW 个、名

领带 **lǐngdài** N necktie; tie · MW 条
傻瓜至今不会打**领带**。 *ShaGua still does not know how to properly tie a tie.*

领导 **lǐngdǎo** V·N to lead, to guide; leadership; leader · MW 个、位、名

领队 **lǐngduì** N leader (of a group) · MW 个、位、名

领工 **lǐnggōng** N foreman (of a gang of workers) · MW 个、名

领会 **lǐnghuì** V to understand
傻瓜不善言辞，但能很快**领会**问题的要领。 *ShaGua is not good at speaking, but he is able to quickly grasp the essentials of any problem.*

领教 **lǐngjiào** V to experience; to ask for advice; thanks

领结 **lǐngjié** N bow tie · MW 个

领巾 **lǐngjīn** N scarf · MW 条

领口 **lǐngkǒu** N neckband · MW 个

领款 **lǐngkuǎn** V to withdraw money

领路 **lǐnglù** V to lead the way

领情 **lǐngqíng** V to be grateful
傻瓜是个很**领情**的人，他不会忘记你给他的帮助。 *ShaGua is someone who feels grateful to anybody who has helped him.*

领取 **lǐngqǔ** V to get

领事 **lǐngshì** N consul · MW 个、名

领受 **lǐngshòu** V to accept; to receive

领头 **lǐngtóu** V to take the lead

领土 **lǐngtǔ** N territory; land · MW 片、块

领先 **lǐngxiān** V to lead, to be in the lead

领袖 **lǐngxiù** N leader; model (LIT collar and sleeves) · MW 个、位、名

领养 **lǐngyǎng** V to adopt
傻瓜和傻瓜太太打算**领养**一个中国孤儿。 *ShaGua and Mrs. ShaGua are going to adopt an orphan from China.*

领域 **lǐngyù** N field, area; realm; territory, district · MW 个

领子 **lǐngzi** N collar · MW 个

**RELATED WORDS**

占领 153   白领 176   认领 239
红领巾 474   首领 924   要领 969
冒领 989   将领 1161   带领 1213
招领 1232   总领事 1330   率领 1469
蓝领 1548   失物招领 106

**1466 欲**   U+6B32   TM **13** FM ノ

**yù** V·ADV to want, to wish, to desire; to demand; about to, on the verge of

欲望 **yùwàng** N wish, desire · MW 个
我有一个很强烈的**欲望**，就是到中国去学中文。 *I have a very strong desire: to go to China to study Chinese.*

**RELATED WORD**

性欲 498

**1467 射**   U+5C04   TM **13** FM ノ

**shè** V to shoot, to fire; to spout; to emit (light, heat, etc.); to allude to, to insinuate

射击 **shèjī** V to shoot, to fire

射箭 **shèjiàn** V to shoot arrows

射手 **shèshǒu** N shooter · MW 个、名

射线 **shèxiàn** N ray; straight line · MW 条

射影 **shèyǐng** N projection (geometry) · MW 个

**RELATED WORDS**

反射 111   发射 311   扫射 402
折射 408   注射 496   放射 964
映射 1036   速射 1514   喷射 1563
照射 1846   影射 1918

## 1468 剧 劇   U+5267   TM **13**   FM ㇓

**jù** N drama, play; opera; show

**剧本 jùběn** N script; screenplay · MW 本
如果一个人能事先偷看自己的人生**剧本**, 不知会怎么样？ *If a person could steal a glance at the drama of his or her future life in advance, what would happen?*

**剧场 jùchǎng** N theater · MW 个

**剧烈 jùliè** ADJ severe; violent, fierce

**剧评 jùpíng** N drama review; dramatic criticism · MW 篇

**剧院 jùyuàn** N theater · MW 个、家

**剧作家 jùzuòjiā** N dramatist, playwright · MW 个、位、名
在西方人眼里, 人生**剧本**的**剧作家**只能是上帝。 *In the eyes of Westerners, the playwright of all life is God.*

### RELATED WORDS

| | | |
|---|---|---|
| 丑剧 | 85 | 曲剧 | 272 |
| 戏剧 | 365 | 加剧 | 463 |
| 京剧 | 905 | 话剧 | 1182 |
| 闹剧 | 1323 | 急剧 | 1426 |
| 喜剧 | 1531 | 悲剧 | 1532 |
| 舞剧 | 1790 | 歌剧 | 1900 |
| 影剧界 | 1918 | 恶作剧 | 1196 |

## 1469  率   U+7387   TM **13**   FM ㇏

**lǜ** N rate; proportion; ratio

比率 *ratio*

**shuài** V·N·ADJ·ADV to lead; to command; model; frank, straightforward; rash, hasty; generally, usually

**率领 shuàilǐng** V to lead, to head

**率先 shuàixiān** V to take the lead in; to initiate
这所大学**率先**在俄亥俄州开设中文课。
*This university took the lead in offering Chinese programs in the state of Ohio.*

**率直 shuàizhí** ADJ frank, blunt

### RELATED WORDS

| | | |
|---|---|---|
| 汇率 | 234 | 功率 | 252 |
| 比率 | 279 | 利率 | 472 |
| 表率 | 527 | 直率 | 609 |
| 草率 | 768 | 效率 | 965 |
| 倍率 | 1084 | 轻率 | 1113 |
| 统率 | 1601 | 税率 | 1705 |
| 概率 | 1908 | 生产率 | 107 |
| 买入汇率 | 248 | | |

## 1470 竞 競   U+7ADE   TM **13**   FM ㇏

**jìng** V to compete; to contend

**竞技 jìngjì** N sports, athletics · MW 个

**竞赛 jìngsài** N contest, competition; race · MW 场

**竞选 jìngxuǎn** V to run for (office)
傻瓜**竞选**市长, 傻瓜的儿子也想**竞选**学生会主席。 *ShaGua was elected mayor. His older son also wants to be elected student body president at his school.*

**竞争 jìngzhēng** V to compete

**竞走 jìngzǒu** N walking race

## 1471 童   U+7AE5   TM **13**   FM ㇏

**tóng** N child; boy; children

**童工 tónggōng** N child laborer · MW 个、名

**童话 tónghuà** N fairy tales · MW 个

**童年 tóngnián** N childhood · MW 个
傻瓜做过**童工**, 他的**童年**非常艰辛。 *ShaGua was a child laborer; his childhood was very hard.*

**童心 tóngxīn** N childlike innocence · MW 颗
只有**童心**才能理解**童话**的意境。 *Only those with childlike innocence can understand the meaning of fairy tales.*

**童谣 tóngyáo** N nursery rhymes · MW 首

**童装 tóngzhuāng** N children's clothing · MW 件、套

**童子军 Tóngzǐjūn** N Boy Scout · MW 队

### RELATED WORDS

| | | |
|---|---|---|
| 儿童 43 | 顽童 1204 | 返老还童 957 |

## 1472 弯 彎   U+5F2F   TM **13**   FM ㇏

**wān** V·N·ADJ to bend; to curl; to curve; to pull (a bow); turn; curve; bend; winding, curved; bent; crooked

**弯路 wānlù** N winding/crooked road · MW 条
人生没有不走**弯路**的。 *There is not a single person who has not hit a detour in his or her life.*

**弯曲 wānqū** ADJ winding, curving; circuitous; wavy

**弯折 wānzhé** V to bend; to buckle

**弯子 wānzi** N turn; bend · MW 个

### RELATED WORDS

| | |
|---|---|
| 转弯 1111 | 急转弯 1426 |

| 1473 | **旁** | | U+65C1 | TM **13** FM 丶 |

**páng** N side; edge; other, else

旁白 **pángbái** N aside, narrator's comment (in a play) · MW 段

旁边 **pángbiān** N side; beside; nearby

旁观 **pángguān** V to look on

旁观者清。 *A bystander is always clearheaded.*

旁门 **pángmén** N side door · MW 扇

旁人 **pángrén** N someone else; others; outsiders · MW 个

旁听 **pángtīng** V to sit in on; to audit (a class)

傻瓜想旁听管理学。 *ShaGua wants to audit a management class.*

旁证 **pángzhèng** N circumstantial evidence · MW 个

**RELATED WORDS**

两旁 509      左道旁门 113      袖手旁观 1361

| 1474 | **雇** | 僱 | U+96C7 | TM **13** FM 丶 |

**gù** V to hire, to employ

雇工 **gùgōng** V·N to hire labor; hired worker · MW 个、名

雇佣 **gùyōng** V to hire, to employ

雇员 **gùyuán** N employee · MW 个、名

雇主 **gùzhǔ** N employer · MW 个、名

雇主要雇佣一些雇员和雇工。 *Employers hire employees and laborers.*

**RELATED WORD**

解雇 1928

| 1475 | **盗** | | U+76D7 | TM **13** FM 丶 |

**dào** V·N to steal; to rob; to burglarize; robber; pirate

盗版 **dàobǎn** N pirated copy (of software, etc.)

盗伐 **dàofá** V to fell trees illegally

盗匪 **dàofěi** N robber, bandit · MW 个、名

盗卖 **dàomài** V to steal and sell

盗窃 **dàoqiè** V to steal; to burglarize

盗用 **dàoyòng** V to embezzle, to misappropriate

盗贼 **dàozéi** N robber, thief · MW 个、名

有个盗贼去盗窃了商店的东西。 *A thief went to steal from a store.*

**RELATED WORDS**

防盗 1040      偷盗 1591      强盗 1896

| 1476 | **装** | 裝 | U+88C5 | TM **13** FM 丶 |

**zhuāng** N·V to load; to install; to dress up; to pretend; clothing; luggage

装扮 **zhuāngbàn** V to dress up; to disguise

装备 **zhuāngbèi** N·V equipment; to equip, to furnish · MW 套

装裱 **zhuāngbiǎo** V to mount (a picture, etc.)

装点 **zhuāngdiǎn** V to decorate, to adorn

装订 **zhuāngdìng** V to bind

装疯卖傻 **zhuāngfēngmàishǎ** EXP to play the fool

装潢 **zhuānghuáng** V·N to mount (a picture, etc.); decoration

装甲 **zhuāngjiǎ** ADJ·N armored; plate armor

装假 **zhuāngjiǎ** V to pretend

装聋作哑 **zhuānglóngzuòyǎ** EXP to pretend to be deaf and mute; to feign ignorance

装门面 **zhuāngménmiàn** EXP to put up a facade/ front, to keep up appearances

傻瓜不主张做那些装门面的事情。 *ShaGua does not advocate putting up a false front.*

装模作样 **zhuāngmúzuòyàng** EXP to put on an act

装配 **zhuāngpèi** V to assemble, to put/fit together

装腔作势 **zhuāngqiāngzuòshì** EXP to strike a pose, to be pretentious

装神弄鬼 **zhuāngshénnòngguǐ** EXP to disguise oneself as a ghost/deity; to be deliberately mystifying

装饰 **zhuāngshì** N·V ornament; to decorate · MW 种

装束 **zhuāngshù** N·V dress, clothing, outfit; to pack for a journey/trip · MW 种

装蒜 **zhuāngsuàn** V to pretend not to know, to play dumb

别装蒜了，你心里清楚得很。 *Don't pretend you don't know anything; you actually know everything.*

装箱单 **zhuāngxiāngdān** N packing list · MW 份

装卸 **zhuāngxiè** V to load and unload

装修 **zhuāngxiū** V to fix up, to renovate (a house, etc.)

装样子 **zhuāngyàngzi** EXP to put on an act

装运 **zhuāngyùn** V to load and ship/transport

装置 **zhuāngzhì** N·V installation; equipment; to install; to equip

**RELATED WORDS**

| | | |
|---|---|---|
| 古装 154 | 化装 215 | 行装 327 |
| 西装 352 | 伪装 454 | 安装 487 |
| 武装 513 | 改装 516 | 时装 586 |
| 扮装 786 | 包装 836 | 春装 855 |
| 组装 1106 | 集装箱 1267 | 袋装 1428 |
| 服装 1457 | 桶装 1564 | 散装 1579 |
| 假装 1586 | 瓶装 1635 | 盛装 1694 |
| 精装 1832 | 中山装 86 | |

---

**1477** 痘 U+75D8 TM **13** FM 丶

**dòu** N smallpox

痘苗 **dòumiáo** N vaccine · MW 针

**RELATED WORDS**

| | | |
|---|---|---|
| 牛痘 51 | 水痘 159 | 种痘 893 |

---

**1478** 冠 U+51A0 TM **13** FM 丶

**guān** N hat; cap; crown; crest

**guàn** N·V crown; champion; to put on a hat; to precede; to crown with

冠词 **guàncí** N article (part of speech) · MW 个

冠军 **guànjūn** N champion · MW 个

**RELATED WORDS**

| | | |
|---|---|---|
| 王冠 27 | 衣冠 330 | 桂冠 797 |
| 皇冠 858 | | |

---

**1479** 宴 U+5BB4 TM **13** FM 丶

**yàn** V·N to give/host a dinner; banquet

宴会 **yànhuì** N banquet; feast · MW 个

宴请 **yànqǐng** V to invite to a banquet
傻瓜常常宴请客人。*ShaGua often invites guests to banquets.*

宴席 **yànxí** N banquet; feast · MW 桌

**RELATED WORDS**

| | | |
|---|---|---|
| 国宴 542 | 设宴 1179 | 盛宴 1694 |

---

**1480** 宿 U+5BBF TM **13** FM 丶

**sù** V·ADJ to stay overnight; long-standing; veteran

**xiǔ** MW [measure word for nights]

**xiù** N constellation (ancient term)

宿命论 **sùmìnglùn** N fatalism

宿舍 **sùshè** N dormitory · MW 间

宿营 **sùyíng** V to encamp (of troops)

宿愿 **sùyuàn** N long-cherished ambition · MW 个

傻瓜不相信**宿命论**，但是没有人知道他的**宿愿**。
*ShaGua doesn't believe in fatalism, but nobody knows his most cherished wish.*

**RELATED WORDS**

| | | |
|---|---|---|
| 归宿 166 | 住宿 324 | 食宿 1053 |
| 留宿 1582 | 寄宿 1619 | |

---

**1481** 寒 U+5BD2 TM **13** FM 丶

**hán** ADJ·V cold; poor, needy; to tremble with fear

寒潮 **háncháo** N cold wave · MW 个
今年的**寒潮**来得很早。*The cold wave arrived very early this year.*

寒冬腊月 **hándōnglàyuè** EXP severe winter

寒风 **hánfēng** N cold wind · MW 阵

寒季 **hánjì** N dry season · MW 个

寒假 **hánjià** N winter vacation · MW 个

寒冷 **hánlěng** ADJ cold, frigid

寒流 **hánliú** N cold spell · MW 股

寒暑表 **hánshǔbiǎo** N thermometer · MW 个

寒酸 **hánsuān** ADJ poverty-stricken, wretched; shabby
你的这一身打扮有点儿**寒酸**。*Your clothes are a bit shabby.*

寒心 **hánxīn** ADJ disillusioned; bitterly disappointed

**RELATED WORDS**

| | | |
|---|---|---|
| 心寒 232 | 受寒 844 | 贫寒 1052 |

---

**1482** 窃  竊 U+7A83 TM **13** FM 丶

**qiè** V·ADV to steal; secretly, furtively

窃据 **qièjù** V to usurp; to unjustly occupy

窃听 **qiètīng** V to eavesdrop; to wiretap

**1482 窃 qiè** (continued)

**窃贼 qièzéi** N burglar; thief · MW 个、名
盗窃一分钱的是**窃贼**, **窃**据一个国家的是总统。
*A man who steals a penny is a thief; one who usurps a country is a president.*

**RELATED WORDS**

失窃 106     盗窃 1475     偷窃 1591

---

**1483 善** U+5584   TM **13** FM 丶

**shàn** N·ADJ·V·ADV goodness; good; wise; satisfactory; kind, friendly; to do well, to be an expert at; to be apt/prone to; properly, well

**善恶 shàn'è** ADJ good and evil
**善后 shànhòu** V to deal with the aftermath; to make funeral arrangements
**善良 shànliáng** ADJ kindhearted
**善意 shànyì** N good will/intention(s) · MW 个
**善于 shànyú** V to be good at
这位先生很**善于**处理那些棘手的**善后**工作。
*This gentleman is very adept at handling the aftermath of difficult situations.*
**善终 shànzhōng** V to die a natural death

**RELATED WORDS**

伪善 454     改善 516     完善 909
真善美 1075     慈善 1952     慈善家 1952
与人为善 158

---

**1484 普** U+666E   TM **13** FM 丶

**pǔ** ADJ general; universal; popular

**普遍 pǔbiàn** ADJ general, common; universal
**普及 pǔjí** V·ADJ to spread; to popularize; universal; popular
**普**及汉语已经成为美国的一项重要国策。
*Expanding the study of Chinese has been an important policy in the States.*
**普通 pǔtōng** ADJ common, ordinary
**普选 pǔxuǎn** V to conduct a general election

**RELATED WORD**

吉普车 259

---

**1485 觉** 覺 U+89C9   TM **13** FM 丶

**jiào** N sleep

---

**jué** V·N to feel; to wake up; to become aware of; sense

**觉察 juéchá** V to sense, to detect, to realize
**觉得 juéde** V to feel; to think
她**觉得**他**觉察**了她的问题。 *She felt that he had figured out her problem.*
**觉悟 juéwù** V·N to become aware of; awareness

**RELATED WORDS**

自觉 305     发觉 311     听觉 414
幻觉 475     味觉 561     直觉 609
知觉 647     肤觉 899     视觉 1362
睡觉 1571     痛觉 1725     感觉 1860
触觉 1875     察觉 1877     不知不觉 24

---

**1486 堂** U+5802   TM **13** FM 丶

**táng** N·MW hall (for a specific purpose); main room (of a house); court of law; [used to indicate the relationship between cousins, etc. with the same paternal grandfather/great-grandfather]; [measure word for school classes and periods]

**堂皇 tánghuáng** ADJ grand, stately
他的家很富丽**堂皇**。 *His house is very beautiful and grand.*
**堂妹 tángmèi** N younger female cousin · MW 个、名
**堂堂 tángtáng** ADJ imposing; dignified
**堂兄 tángxiōng** N older male cousin · MW 个、名

**RELATED WORDS**

天堂 25     厅堂 112     弄堂 251
名堂 426     礼堂 503     食堂 1053
教堂 1424     课堂 1503     亮堂 1613
满堂红 1745     澡堂 1954     打退堂鼓 289
富丽堂皇 1731

---

**1487 减** U+51CF   TM **13** FM 丶

**jiǎn** V to subtract, to deduct; to reduce; to decrease, to lessen, to diminish

**减产 jiǎnchǎn** V to reduce output/production
**减低 jiǎndī** V to reduce, to lower
**减法 jiǎnfǎ** N subtraction
**减肥 jiǎnféi** V to lose weight, to slim down
傻瓜的大儿子打算放暑假后实行**减肥**计划。
*ShaGua's older son is going to stick with his weight-loss plan during summer break.*

减缓 jiǎnhuǎn [V] to retard, to slow down

减价 jiǎnjià [V] to reduce (a price), to discount

减免 jiǎnmiǎn [V] to reduce or exempt from (tuition, taxation, etc.); to mitigate or nullify (punishment, etc.)

减轻 jiǎnqīng [V] to lighten, to ease

减弱 jiǎnruò [V] to weaken, to abate

减少 jiǎnshǎo [V] to reduce

老师用**减少**作业来**减轻**学生的负担。 *Teachers try to reduce homework to lighten students' load.*

减速 jiǎnsù [V] to slow down, to reduce speed

减退 jiǎntuì [V] to decline, to drop, to go down

减压 jiǎnyā [V] to reduce pressure, to relax

**RELATED WORDS**

倍减 1084　　衰减 1313　　递减 1827
缩减 1927　　偷工减料 1591

---

**1488 悔** 悔　　U+6094　　TM **13** FM 丶

huǐ [V] to regret; to repent

悔改 huǐgǎi [V] to repent and mend one's ways

悔过 huǐguò [V] to repent

**悔过**是容易的，**悔改**就困难了。
*Repenting an error isn't very difficult, but mending it on top of repenting is.*

悔悟 huǐwù [V] to realize and repent one's error

**RELATED WORDS**

反悔 111　　后悔 310　　改悔 516
追悔 1507

---

**1489 惊** 驚　　U+60CA　　TM **13** FM 丶

jīng [V] to be frightened/startled; to surprise, to startle; to alarm; to stampede

惊动 jīngdòng [V] to alarm; to alert; to disturb

惊慌 jīnghuāng [ADJ] alarmed, scared

惊叫 jīngjiào [V] to cry out (in fear)

惊奇 jīngqí [ADJ] surprised, amazed

惊人 jīngrén [ADJ] amazing; alarming

惊喜 jīngxǐ [ADJ] pleasantly surprised

她因为得了让她**惊喜**的成绩而**惊叫**起来。
*She screamed in pleasant surprise when she saw her grade.*

惊险 jīngxiǎn [ADJ] alarmingly dangerous, thrilling

惊心动魄 jīngxīndòngpò [EXP] horrifying; breathtaking

那个**惊心动魄**的电影让我有点儿**惊慌**。
*The hair-raising movie scared me a little.*

**RELATED WORDS**

大惊小怪 20　　压惊 201　　吃惊 783
受惊 844　　虚惊 1534　　震惊 1839
大吃一惊 20　　受宠若惊 844　　胆战心惊 1295

---

**1490 愤** 憤　　U+6124　　TM **13** FM 丶

fèn [ADJ] angry, furious; indignant; resentful

愤恨 fènhèn [ADJ] indignantly resentful, embittered

愤慨 fènkǎi [ADJ] indignant

愤怒 fènnù [V] to be angry/indignant

老师判分不公平，引起学生的**愤怒**。 *The teacher didn't grade the students fairly, and it angered them.*

**RELATED WORDS**

义愤 22　　公愤 103　　气愤 185
民愤 388　　忧愤 693　　悲愤 1532
怨愤 1792

---

**1491 情** 情　　U+60C5　　TM **13** FM 丶

qíng [N] feeling; kindness; affection; love; passion; sexual desire; state, condition

情报 qíngbào [N] intelligence (report); information · [MW] 份

情不自禁 qíngbùzìjīn [EXP] cannot contain oneself, cannot refrain from, can't help but

情操 qíngcāo [N] sentiment

情敌 qíngdí [N] rival in love · [MW] 个、名

情调 qíngdiào [N] sentiment; taste; mood, atmosphere · [MW] 种

这不是一种健康的**情调**。 *This is not a healthy sentiment.*

这家咖啡馆的**情调**很不错。 *The atmosphere in this cafe is not bad at all.*

情夫 qíngfū [N] male lover (of a married woman) · [MW] 个、名

情妇 qíngfù [N] female lover (of a married man) · [MW] 个、名

情感 qínggǎn [N] emotion, feeling; friendship · [MW] 种

情节 qíngjié [N] plot; case · [MW] 个

情景 qíngjǐng [N] scene; sight; circumstances · [MW] 个

**1491 情 qíng** (continued)

**情况 qíngkuàng** N situation, condition; case; (military) development · MW 个

**情理 qínglǐ** N sense; reason

**情侣 qínglǚ** N sweethearts, lovers · MW 个、位、名

**情面 qíngmiàn** N feelings · MW 个

中国人很讲**情面**。*Chinese people are very sensitive about saving face.*

**情趣 qíngqù** N temperament and interests

**情人 qíngrén** N sweetheart, lover; intimate friend · MW 个、名

**情书 qíngshū** N love letter · MW 封

在许多**情况**下，**情人**是不需要写**情书**的。*In many cases, lovers don't need to write each other love letters.*

**情形 qíngxing** N situation, condition

**情绪 qíngxù** N emotions, feelings; mood

在这种**情形**下，不应该有这种**情绪**。*You shouldn't have these feelings in such a situation.*

**情意 qíngyì** N affection; goodwill

**情谊 qíngyì** N friendship

**情愿 qíngyuàn** V to be willing to; to prefer, would rather

她不**情愿**表露自己的**情感**。*She is not willing to show her true feelings.*

**RELATED WORDS**

**1492 泡**      U+6CE1      TM **13** FM ㇏

**pāo** N·MW puffy and soft, spongy; small lake; [measure word for feces/excrement and urine]

**pào** V·N to soak; to infuse; to dawdle; bubble; [shaped like a bubble]

**泡菜 pàocài** N pickles · MW 坛

**泡茶 pàochá** V to make tea

傻瓜喜欢**泡茶**喝。*ShaGua enjoys making tea to drink.*

**泡蘑菇 pàomógu** EXP to procrastinate, to use delaying tactics

**泡沫 pàomò** N foam; bubble · MW 个

**泡影 pàoyǐng** N visionary idea/plan, pie in the sky (LIT soap bubble) · MW 个

**RELATED WORDS**

**1493 流**      U+6D41      TM **13** FM ㇏

**liú** V·N to flow; to spread, to circulate; to change for the worse; to banish; current (of water); class, grade

**流鼻涕 liúbítì** V to have a runny nose

**流产 liúchǎn** V to have an abortion; to miscarry; to fall through

**流传 liúchuán** V to hand down; to spread, to circulate

**流动 liúdòng** V to flow; to move; to go from place to place

**流毒 liúdú** V·N to exert an evil influence; harmful/evil effect

种族主义的**流毒**曾经**流传**甚广。*The harmful effects of racism were widespread.*

**流放 liúfàng** V to banish; to float logs downstream

**流感 liúgǎn** N flu

**流浪 liúlàng** V to wander; to roam around

傻瓜收养了三条**流浪**狗。*ShaGua has adopted three homeless dogs.*

**流利 liúlì** ADJ fluent; smoothly written

傻瓜的英语说得不**流利**。*ShaGua can't speak English fluently.*

**流露 liúlù** V to reveal; to show unintentionally

**流氓 liúmáng** N hooligan, rogue; immoral/indecent behavior; indecency · MW 个

**流派 liúpài** N school (of thought); sect · MW 个

**流失 liúshī** V to erode, to run off

**流水 liúshuǐ** N running water · MW 条

**流通 liútōng** V to circulate

**流亡 liúwáng** V to go into exile

流星 liúxīng N meteor, shooting star · MW 颗

流行 liúxíng V·ADJ to be popular; prevalent; fashionable

今年**流行**这种发式。*This is this year's fashionable hairstyle.*

流行病 liúxíngbìng N epidemic disease · MW 种

流言 liúyán N rumor; gossip · MW 个

流域 liúyù N valley; river basin

流质 liúzhì N fluid

**RELATED WORDS**

| | | |
|---|---|---|
| 二流子 2 | 上流 14 | 川流不息 21 |
| 支流 92 | 主流 124 | 水流 159 |
| 巨流 162 | 分流 173 | 气流 185 |
| 交流 222 | 对流 254 | 电流 263 |
| 环流 369 | 引流 371 | 回流 391 |
| 名流 426 | 洪流 690 | 河流 934 |
| 轮流 1112 | 逆流 1359 | 急流 1426 |
| 寒流 1481 | 暖流 1675 | 源流 1742 |
| 溪流 1743 | 漂流 1820 | 潮流 1930 |
| 激流 1955 | 第一流 1695 | 源远流长 1742 |
| 屁滚尿流 1070 | | |

---

## 1494 海

U+6D77　　TM **13** FM 丶

hǎi N·ADJ·ADV ocean; sea; lake; huge group (of people/things); extra large; countless; randomly; everywhere

海岸 hǎi'àn N seacoast; beach, shore · MW 个

海拔 hǎibá N elevation (above sea level)

海滨 hǎibīn N seashore, seaside, beach · MW 个

海带 hǎidài N kelp · MW 条

海岛 hǎidǎo N island · MW 个

海底 hǎidǐ N seabed, seafloor · MW 个

海风 hǎifēng N sea breeze/wind · MW 阵

海港 hǎigǎng N seaport; harbor · MW 个

海关 hǎiguān N customs · MW 个

海景 hǎijǐng N seascape · MW 个

在这个**海岛**上可以看到美丽的**海景**。*You can view very beautiful seascapes from this island.*

海军 hǎijūn N navy · MW 队

海绵 hǎimián N sponge (marine animal) · MW 块

海内 hǎinèi N whole world; throughout the country

海平面 hǎipíngmiàn N sea level · MW 个

海上 hǎishang N at sea, maritime

---

海水 hǎishuǐ N seawater; sea

海外 hǎiwài N overseas; abroad

海味 hǎiwèi N seafood

海鲜 hǎixiān N seafood

傻瓜住在**海滨**城市，但他不喜欢吃**海鲜**。*Although ShaGua lives in an oceanfront city, he doesn't like seafood.*

海啸 hǎixiào N tsunami

海洋 hǎiyáng N ocean

海员 hǎiyuán N seaman, sailor · MW 个、名

**RELATED WORDS**

| | | |
|---|---|---|
| 人海 4 | 上海 14 | 云海 80 |
| 公海 103 | 四海 271 | 北海 278 |
| 东海 307 | 死海 510 | 近海 716 |
| 南海 986 | 陆海空 1043 | 沿海 1165 |
| 脑海 1460 | 航海 1717 | 山珍海味 38 |
| 五湖四海 79 | 石沉大海 144 | 移山倒海 1450 |
| 瞒天过海 1914 | | |

---

## 1495 清

U+6E05　　TM **13** FM 丶

qīng ADJ·V pure, clean; clear, distinct; fresh; quiet; impartial, honest; simple, plain; to clean up; to be settled (of a debt, an account, etc.)

清白 qīngbái ADJ pure, clean; innocent

清查 qīngchá V to investigate, to check

清晨 qīngchén N early morning · MW 个

清楚 qīngchu ADJ·V clear, distinct; to know, to be aware of

傻瓜说话不太**清楚**。*ShaGua doesn't speak very clearly.*

傻瓜对这个案子很**清楚**。*ShaGua knew this case well.*

清脆 qīngcuì ADJ clear and melodious (of sound)

清单 qīngdān N checklist; list of items · MW 份

清点 qīngdiǎn V to make an inventory

清炖 qīngdùn V to boil/stew in broth

清洁 qīngjié ADJ clean, spotless

清净 qīngjìng ADJ peace and quiet

清理 qīnglǐ V to sort out; to tidy up

清凉 qīngliáng ADJ cool and refreshing

清算 qīngsuàn V to settle, to resolve; to expose and criticize

每月**清算**帐目 *to balance your account monthly*

**清算**他的罪行 *to expose and criticize her crimes*

清汤 qīngtāng N clear soup, broth

清晰 qīngxī ADJ clear, distinct

## 1495 清 qīng (continued)

清洗 qīngxǐ [V] to clean; to wash, to rinse; to get rid of
　清洗地板 to wash the floor
　清洗内奸 to weed out the traitor

清醒 qīngxǐng [ADJ] wide-awake; clearheaded

清秀 qīngxiù [ADJ] delicate and pretty

清一色 qīngyīsè [ADJ] all of the same color, monotone; identical

清帐 qīngzhàng [V] to settle an account

清真 Qīngzhēn [N] Islamic; Muslim

清蒸 qīngzhēng [V] to steam in broth

### RELATED WORDS

| | |
|---|---|
| 分清 173 | 付清 206 |
| 认清 239 | 弄清 251 |
| 扫清 402 | 划清 476 |
| 肃清 526 | 还清 714 |
| 查清 741 | 看清 841 |
| 结清 1291 | 偿清 1440 |
| 摸清底细 1665 | |

## 1496 渔 漁 U+6E14 TM 13 FM 丶

yú [N·V] fishing; fishery; to fish; to steal; to usurp
　授人以鱼, 不如授人以渔。 Give me a fish and I will eat today; teach me to fish and I will eat for a lifetime.

渔场 yúchǎng [N] fishing ground · [MW] 个

渔船 yúchuán [N] fishing boat · [MW] 艘

渔港 yúgǎng [N] fishing port · [MW] 个

渔利 yúlì [V] to profiteer, to reap unfair profits
　你这样渔利很不道德。 Your reaping unfair profits is very immoral.

渔民 yúmín [N] fisherman · [MW] 个

渔网 yúwǎng [N] fishnet · [MW] 张

渔业 yúyè [N] fishery; fishing industry

## 1497 渡 U+6E21 TM 13 FM 丶

dù [V·N] to cross (a body of water); to ferry (people, goods, etc.) across; ferry

渡船 dùchuán [N] ferry, ferryboat · [MW] 艘

渡过 dùguò [V] to cross over; to pass through
　傻瓜渡过了许多困难和危机。 ShaGua has survived many difficulties and crises.

渡海 dùhǎi [V] to sail across a sea

渡口 dùkǒu [N] ferry crossing · [MW] 个

### RELATED WORD

过渡 712

## 1498 湿 溼 U+6E7F TM 13 FM 丶

shī [ADJ] wet, damp, moist, humid; moistness

湿度 shīdù [N] humidity

湿气 shīqì [N] moisture

湿润 shīrùn [ADJ] damp, moist

湿透 shītòu [V] to wet through

湿重 shīzhòng [N] weight when wet

### RELATED WORDS

| | |
|---|---|
| 淋湿 1172 | 潮湿 1930 |

## 1499 诚 誠 U+88DA TM 13 FM 丶

chéng [ADJ·ADV·CONJ] honest; sincere; true, real; honestly; really, indeed

诚恳 chéngkěn [ADJ] sincere

诚然 chéngrán [ADV·CONJ] truly; to be sure, certainly

诚实 chéngshí [ADJ] honest, truthful
　诚然, 傻瓜是一名官员, 但他很诚实。 To be sure, ShaGua is a political official, but he is nonetheless very honest.

诚意 chéngyì [N] sincerity; good faith

诚挚 chéngzhì [ADJ] sincere; cordial

### RELATED WORDS

| | |
|---|---|
| 至诚 244 | 忠诚 743 |
| 投诚 1008 | 真诚 1075 |
| 热诚 1390 | |

## 1500 询 詢 U+88E2 TM 13 FM 丶

xún [V] to ask; to inquire

询价 xúnjià [V] to ask the price (of)

询问 xúnwèn [V] to ask, to inquire; to question
　老师询问学生的学习情况。 The teacher asked about his students' studies.

### RELATED WORDS

| | |
|---|---|
| 征询 462 | 质询 597 |
| 查询 741 | |

## 1501 语 語 U+88ED TM 13 FM 丶

**yǔ** N·V language; words; proverb; vernacular; speech; to speak; to talk; to tell, to inform

语词 yǔcí N words and phrases · MW 个

语调 yǔdiào N tone; intonation · MW 个

语法 yǔfǎ N grammar

语汇 yǔhuì N vocabulary · MW 个

语句 yǔjù N sentence · MW 个

语录 yǔlù N quotation · MW 段

语气 yǔqì N tone of voice; manner of speaking · MW 种

语文 yǔwén N language; Chinese (language); language and literature

语言 yǔyán N language · MW 种

中文是一种很难学的**语言**, 其**语音**、**语调**、**语词**和**语法**都很难学。 Chinese is a very difficult language to learn: Its pronunciation, tones, words and phrases, and grammar are all difficult.

语言学 yǔyánxué N linguistics · MW 门

语义 yǔyì N meaning of words; semantics · MW 个

信不信由你, 狗能从你的**语气**中理解你的**语义**。 Believe it or not, dogs can understand the meaning of your words from your tone of voice.

语音 yǔyīn N pronunciation · MW 个

语重心长 yǔzhòngxīncháng EXP to speak sincerely

### RELATED WORDS

| | | |
|---|---|---|
| 口语 42 | 习语 84 | 术语 91 |
| 日语 96 | 手语 104 | 耳语 145 |
| 古语 154 | 外语 218 | 汉语 235 |
| 用语 313 | 状语 345 | 妙语 467 |
| 言语 478 | 补语 508 | 国语 542 |
| 英语 556 | 成语 611 | 定语 666 |
| 法语 686 | 评语 706 | 标语 801 |
| 俗语 867 | 批语 1005 | 宾语 1141 |
| 咒语 1387 | 谜语 1750 | 文学语言 70 |
| 世界语 163 | 三言两语 9 | 只言片语 160 |
| 花言巧语 549 | 美国英语 671 | 甜言蜜语 1306 |

## 1502 读 讀 U+8BFB TM 13 FM 丶

**dú** V to read; to attend school; to pronounce

读本 dúběn N textbook · MW 本

读书 dúshū V to read (a book, etc.); to study; to attend school

傻瓜在**读书**。 ShaGua is reading a book.

傻瓜到夜校**读书**。 ShaGua attends night school.

读物 dúwù N reading material · MW 种

读音 dúyīn N pronunciation · MW 个

读者 dúzhě N reader (person) · MW 个、位、名

### RELATED WORDS

| | | |
|---|---|---|
| 走读 265 | 选读 1510 | 阅读 1727 |
| 精读 1832 | 半工半读 127 | |

## 1503 课 課 U+8BFE TM 13 FM 丶

**kè** N·V subject; course; class; lesson; to tax

课本 kèběn N textbook · MW 种、本

课表 kèbiǎo N class schedule; syllabus · MW 份

课程 kèchéng N course; curriculum · MW 门

课时 kèshí N credit hour · MW 个

课堂 kètáng N classroom · MW 个

课外 kèwài N extracurricular; after school

课文 kèwén N text; lesson · MW 篇

课余 kèyú N after school

**课余**, 学生拿着**课本**和**课表**去找老师商谈**课时**的问题。 After school, students brought their textbooks and class schedules to discuss their credit hours with their teacher.

课桌 kèzhuō N desk · MW 张

### RELATED WORDS

| | | |
|---|---|---|
| 下课 10 | 上课 14 | 主课 124 |
| 占课 153 | 功课 252 | 讲课 501 |
| 补课 508 | 备课 845 | 缺课 1305 |
| 选课 1510 | 停课 1588 | 必修课 338 |

## 1504 烧 燒 U+70E7 TM 13 FM 丶

**shāo** V·N to burn; to heat; to cook; to bake; to roast; to braise; to have a temperature; fever

烧穿 shāochuān V to burn out

烧毁 shāohuǐ V to burn down/up, to destroy by fire

烧火 shāohuǒ V to light a fire

烧酒 shāojiǔ N strong white liquor · MW 杯、瓶

烧烤 shāokǎo N·V barbecue; to roast

烧牛肉 shāoniúròu N·V roast beef; to cook beef

烧伤 shāoshāng V to burn (of medicine)

烧香 shāoxiāng V to burn incense (before an idol)

**1504 烧 shāo** (continued)

烧心 **shāoxīn** V heartburn

喝**烧**酒会感到**烧心**。 *Drinking liquor will give you heartburn.*

RELATED WORDS

叉烧肉 33      发烧 311      退烧 1508
高烧 1611      燃烧 1888      惹火烧身 1657

---

**1505 烤**      U+70E4    TM **13** FM 丶

**kǎo** V to bake; to roast; to toast; to broil; to warm oneself

烤火 **kǎohuǒ** V to warm oneself by a fire

烤炉 **kǎolú** N oven · MW 个

烤面包 **kǎomiànbāo** V-N to make toast; toast · MW 个、条

烤肉 **kǎoròu** V-N to roast; barbecue · MW 块

烤箱 **kǎoxiāng** N oven · MW 个

烤鸭 **kǎoyā** N roast duck · MW 只

烤烟 **kǎoyān** N flue-cured tobacco · MW 片

RELATED WORDS

烘烤 953      烧烤 1504

---

**1506 煤**      U+7164    TM **13** FM 丶

**méi** N coal

煤炭 **méitàn** N coal · MW 块、吨

RELATED WORD

焦煤 1265

---

**1507 追**      U+8FFD    TM **13** FM 丶

**zhuī** V to run after, to chase; to investigate; to trace; to seek; to reminisce

追捕 **zhuībǔ** V to pursue and capture

追查 **zhuīchá** V to investigate; to trace

追悼 **zhuīdào** V to mourn

追赶 **zhuīgǎn** V to chase, to pursue

追回 **zhuīhuí** V to recover, to retrieve

追悔 **zhuīhuǐ** V to regret; to repent

你可以**追悔**虚度时光，但你无法**追回**时光。 *You can regret wasting time, but you cannot recover it.*

追击 **zhuījī** V to pursue and attack

追加 **zhuījiā** V to add, to supplement

追究 **zhuījiū** V to investigate

追求 **zhuīqiú** V to seek; to pursue, to woo

老师要培养学生**追求**真理的精神。 *Teachers should foster student interest in seeking truth.*

傻瓜的大儿子想**追求**一个女孩子。 *ShaGua's older son wants to woo a girl.*

追溯 **zhuīsù** V to trace back to

追随 **zhuīsuí** V to follow, to adhere to

追问 **zhuīwèn** V to question closely; to inquire

在中国的学校，**追问**的气氛不浓厚。 *Chinese classrooms do not have a very strong climate of open intellectual inquiry.*

追寻 **zhuīxún** V to search (for); to track down

追忆 **zhuīyì** V to recall, to recollect

追逐 **zhuīzhú** V to pursue, to chase

追踪 **zhuīzōng** V to follow the trail of, to trace, to track

---

**1508 退**      U+9000    TM **13** FM 丶

**tuì** V to retreat; to remove; to quit; to withdraw/retire from; to decline, to fade; to recede; to return, to refund; to cancel

退避 **tuìbì** V to withdraw and stay away

退兵 **tuìbīng** V to retreat

退步 **tuìbù** V to lag/fall behind

退潮 **tuìcháo** V to ebb (of the tide)

退出 **tuìchū** V to withdraw from; to quit

退化 **tuìhuà** V to become worse

一个人的**退化**是从心态开始的，而不是从体力开始的。 *A person's decline begins with his state of mind, not physical strength.*

退还 **tuìhuán** V to return, to give/send back

退换 **tuìhuàn** V to exchange a purchase

退回 **tuìhuí** V to return; to give back; to go back

中国已无法**退回**到原来的老路。 *It would be impossible for China to return to its former state.*

退款 **tuìkuǎn** V to refund

退路 **tuìlù** N line of retreat · MW 条

退票 **tuìpiào** V to return a ticket; to bounce (a check)

退却 **tuìquè** V to retreat, to back down

退让 **tuìràng** [V] to concede; to step back/aside

傻瓜从来不会**退却**, 但必要时会做出一定的**退让**。 *ShaGua has never backed down, but he may be willing to step aside if necessary.*

退色 **tuìsè** [V] to fade

退烧 **tuìshāo** [V] to bring down a fever

退缩 **tuìsuō** [V] to shrink/hold back; to balk

对于那个疑难大案, 傻瓜还没有**退缩**。 *In pursuing the suspicious case, ShaGua has not cowered yet.*

退休 **tuìxiū** [V] to retire

退学 **tuìxué** [V] to quit school, to drop out

退职 **tuìzhí** [V] to resign from office

**RELATED WORDS**

| 击退 | 156 | 打退堂鼓 | 289 | 后退 | 310 |
| 进退 | 713 | 衰退 | 1313 | 减退 | 1487 |
| 辞退 | 1606 | 隐退 | 1912 | 撤退 | 1942 |

---

**1509 逃** U+9003　　TM **13** FM 丶

**táo** [V] to escape, to flee; to run away; to evade, to dodge; to shirk

逃奔 **táobèn** [V] to run away to (a place)

逃避 **táobì** [V] to escape; to evade

逃兵 **táobīng** [N] army deserter · [MW] 个、群

不能当改革的**逃兵**。 *You shouldn't desert the revolution.*

逃窜 **táocuàn** [V] to run away, to flee (in disorder)

逃犯 **táofàn** [N] escapee, fugitive · [MW] 个

逃荒 **táohuāng** [V] to flee from famine

傻瓜是在父母**逃荒**时出生的。 *ShaGua was born when his parents were fleeing from famine.*

逃命 **táomìng** [V] to run for one's life

逃难 **táonàn** [V] to flee from disaster

逃跑 **táopǎo** [V] to run away, to escape

逃生 **táoshēng** [V] to run for one's life

逃税 **táoshuì** [V] to evade taxes

逃脱 **táotuō** [V] to escape; to evade

逃亡 **táowáng** [V] to go into exile, to flee from one's home/country

逃学 **táoxué** [V] to cut class

世上有从未**逃学**的学生吗? *Are there any students who have never cut classes?*

逃走 **táozǒu** [V] to escape, to flee

**RELATED WORD**

外逃 218

---

**1510 选 選** U+9009　　TM **13** FM 丶

**xuǎn** [V·N] to select, to choose; to vote; to elect; selection (person/thing); collection, anthology

选拔 **xuǎnbá** [V] to select (the best)

选材 **xuǎncái** [V] to select talent; to select material

选答题 **xuǎndátí** [N] multiple choice · [MW] 道

你做完**选答题**了吗? *Have you finished the multiple-choice section?*

选读 **xuǎndú** [V] to select passages to read; selected readings

选购 **xuǎngòu** [V] to select and buy

选集 **xuǎnjí** [N] anthology · [MW] 本、套

选举 **xuǎnjǔ** [V] to elect

选课 **xuǎnkè** [V] to select courses

选民 **xuǎnmín** [N] voter; electorate · [MW] 个、位

选票 **xuǎnpiào** [N] vote, ballot · [MW] 张

**选举**不一定能**选拔**出最优秀的人才, 因为**选民**的**选票**不一定投给最优秀的人才。 *The most talented people may not be chosen in an election because voters may not vote for the most gifted ones.*

选取 **xuǎnqǔ** [V] to select, to choose

选手 **xuǎnshǒu** [N] contestant, player · [MW] 个、名

选题 **xuǎntí** [N] selection of a topic · [MW] 个

选修 **xuǎnxiū** [V] to take as an elective course

这个学期你**选修**什么课? *What courses will you take this semester?*

选样 **xuǎnyàng** [V·N] to sample; sampling

选择 **xuǎnzé** [V] to select, to choose, to pick

**RELATED WORDS**

| 入选 | 5 | 当选 | 335 | 补选 | 508 |
| 评选 | 706 | 候选人 | 1086 | 拣选 | 1233 |
| 挑选 | 1235 | 贿选 | 1419 | 竞选 | 1470 |
| 普选 | 1484 | 落选 | 1547 | 精选 | 1832 |

---

**1511 途** U+9014　　TM **13** FM 丶

**tú** [N] way; route; road; path

途经 **tújīng** [V] by way of, via

途径 **tújìng** [N] way, channel; road · [MW] 条

成功没有便捷的**途径**。 *There are no shortcuts to success.*

**1511 途 tú** (continued)

**RELATED WORDS**

| | | |
|---|---|---|
| 中途 86 | 长途 93 | 长途电话 93 |
| 半途 127 | 半途而废 127 | 归途 166 |
| 用途 313 | 征途 462 | 沿途 1165 |
| 迷途 1187 | 前途 1329 | 旅途 1518 |
| 通途 1757 | 路途 1785 | |

---

**1512** 逗 　U+9017　TM **13** FM 丶

**dòu** V·ADJ to tease; to stay; to stop, to pause; funny, amusing

逗号 **dòuhào** N comma · MW 个

逗留 **dòuliú** V to stay; to stop

逗弄 **dòunong** V to tease, to make fun of
傻瓜小的时候，常常被人**逗弄**。 *When ShaGua was young, he was teased quite a bit.*

逗引 **dòuyǐn** V to tease

**RELATED WORD**

挑逗 1235

---

**1513** 逛 　U+901B　TM **13** FM 丶

**guàng** V to stroll, to go for a walk/stroll; to roam

逛街 **guàngjiē** V to take a walk, to stroll down the streets
傻瓜太太最爱**逛街**，说是女人不**逛街**就有病了。 *Mrs. ShaGua loves strolling down the streets; she believes any woman that doesn't must be sick.*

**RELATED WORDS**

| | |
|---|---|
| 闲逛 679 | 游逛 1818 |

---

**1514** 速 　U+901F　TM **13** FM 丶

**sù** ADJ·N·V fast, quick; speed, velocity; to invite

速成 **sùchéng** V to speed up; to take a crash course
学中文不是吃快餐；因而无法**速成**。 *Studying Chinese is not like eating fast food; there is no way to speed it up.*

速冻 **sùdòng** V to fast freeze

速度 **sùdù** N speed

速记 **sùjì** V to take notes in shorthand

速决 **sùjué** V to decide quickly

速射 **sùshè** V to fire rapidly

速效 **sùxiào** N quick results

速写 **sùxiě** N (quick) sketch; literary sketch · MW 篇

**RELATED WORDS**

| | | |
|---|---|---|
| 火速 72 | 车速 114 | 全速 172 |
| 匀速 180 | 风速 194 | 加速 463 |
| 快速 497 | 迅速 954 | 限速 1417 |
| 减速 1487 | 高速 1611 | 超速 1684 |
| 超音速 1684 | | |

---

**1515** 造 　U+9020　TM **13** FM 丶

**zào** V to make, to create; to invent, to concoct; to go to, to arrive at; to achieve, to accomplish; to train

造成 **zàochéng** V to cause, to bring about

造船 **zàochuán** V to build ships

造反 **zàofǎn** V to rebel, to revolt

造福 **zàofú** V to benefit (someone)

造化 **zàohuà** N Mother Nature, nature; Creator; good luck

造就 **zàojiù** V·N to cultivate; achievements
"文革"**造就**了一批思想者。 *The Cultural Revolution created a bunch of thinkers.*
他是一位很有**造就**的作家。 *He is a very accomplished writer.*

造句 **zàojù** V to make/create a sentence
请用中文**造句**。 *Please use Chinese to create a sentence.*

造型 **zàoxíng** V·N to model, to mold; modeling, moldmaking · MW 个

造谣 **zàoyáo** V to start a rumor
有人总是爱给傻瓜**造谣**。 *Some people always like to start rumors about ShaGua.*

造诣 **zàoyì** N accomplishments, achievements

**RELATED WORDS**

| | | |
|---|---|---|
| 人造 4 | 仿造 450 | 伪造 454 |
| 改造 516 | 修造 870 | 构造 1028 |
| 制造 1130 | 创造性 1131 | 创造 1131 |
| 建造 1203 | 假造 1586 | 塑造 1815 |
| 编造 1866 | | |

---

**1516** 祝 　U+795D　TM **13** FM 丶

**zhù** V to wish, to express good wishes; to cut off

祝词 **zhùcí** N congratulatory speech · MW 篇

祝福 zhùfú V to wish happiness/luck to

祝贺 zhùhè V to congratulate

祝贺你的成功！ *Congratulations on your success!*

祝捷 zhùjié V to celebrate victory

祝酒 zhùjiǔ V to toast, to drink a toast

祝颂 zhùsòng V to express good wishes

祝愿 zhùyuàn V to wish

祝愿你永远快乐。 *I wish you eternal happiness.*

**RELATED WORDS**

庆祝 230    预祝 1528

---

**1517** 被 U+88AB TM **13** FM 丶

bèi PREP·V·N by [indicates agency in a passive sentence]; [used before a verb to make it passive]; to cover; quilt

被保险人 bèibǎoxiǎnrén N insured (person) · MW 个、名

被乘数 bèichéngshù N multiplicand · MW 个

被除数 bèichúshù N dividend · MW 个

被单 bèidān N (bed) sheet · MW 床

被动 bèidòng ADJ passive; disadvantageous

我们一定要化被动为主动。 *We must regain the initiative.*

被告 bèigào N defendant · MW 个、名

被害人 bèihàirén N victim; injured party · MW 个、名

被告有时也是被害人。 *The defendant can sometimes be the victim.*

被迫 bèipò V to be forced/compelled

被套 bèitào N quilt cover · MW 床

被子 bèizi N quilt · MW 床

---

**RELATED WORD**

棉被 1670

---

**1518** 旅 U+65C5 TM **13** FM 丶

lǚ V·N to travel; trip; brigade; troops

旅伴 lǚbàn N traveling companion · MW 个、名

旅程 lǚchéng N itinerary; journey · MW 段

旅店 lǚdiàn N hotel, motel, inn · MW 家

旅费 lǚfèi N travel expenses · MW 笔

旅馆 lǚguǎn N hotel, inn · MW 间

旅客 lǚkè N hotel guest; tourist; passenger · MW 个、位、名

旅社 lǚshè N hotel · MW 家

旅途 lǚtú N journey, trip · MW 个

旅行 lǚxíng V to travel; to journey; to tour

这是旅行社给你们订的旅馆。 *This is the hotel that your travel agent booked for you.*

旅游 lǚyóu V to travel; to tour

**RELATED WORD**

劲旅 736

---

**1519** 族 U+65CF TM **13** FM 丶

zú N clan; nationality; group (of people/things); family death penalty

族人 zúrén N clan members · MW 个、名

**RELATED WORDS**

王族 27  外族 218  汉族 235

壮族 238  民族 388  皇族 858

种族 893  宗族 910  贵族 985

家族 1315  藏族 1978  少数民族 62

中华民族 86

## 1520 费 費　U+8D39　TM **14** FM 一

**fèi** N·V·ADJ　fee; expenses; to spend; to charge; to cost; to expend; wasteful; expensive

**费工夫 fèigōngfu** V to take time and energy

**费解 fèijiě** ADJ hard to understand

如果学中文不**费工夫**, 那就令人**费解**了。
*It would be incomprehensible if the study of Chinese didn't take time and energy.*

**费力 fèilì** V to take a lot of effort

**费钱 fèiqián** V to cost a lot

**费时 fèishí** V to be time-consuming

**费事 fèishì** V·ADJ to take a lot of trouble; troublesome; difficult

**费心 fèixīn** V to devote a lot of care

这件事让您**费心**了。 *Sorry this matter gave you so much trouble.*

**费用 fèiyòng** N cost, expense; charge; expenditure · MW 笔

### RELATED WORDS

## 1521 登　U+767B　TM **14** FM 一

**dēng** V　to climb, to go up; to pedal; to step up on(to); to put on, to wear (shoes, etc.); to publish; to record; to harvest

**登报 dēngbào** V to publish in the newspaper

傻瓜的新闻又**登报**了。 *News about ShaGua has been published in the newspaper again.*

**登场 dēngchǎng** V to go on stage; to enter

**登高 dēnggāo** V to climb up; to climb up a mountain on the Double Ninth Festival (ancient custom)

**登记 dēngjì** V to register, to check in

**登陆 dēnglù** V to land, to come ashore

**登门 dēngmén** V to visit, to call on

傻瓜经常**登门**拜访贫民窟的朋友。
*ShaGua often visits his friends living in the slums.*

**登山 dēngshān** V to climb a mountain

**登台 dēngtái** V to go on stage; to enter politics

### RELATED WORD

## 1522 暂 暫　U+6682　TM **14** FM 一

**zàn** ADJ·ADV　temporary; brief, momentary; transient; temporarily

**暂定 zàndìng** V to arrange temporarily

**暂缓 zànhuǎn** V to postpone, to defer

**暂且 zànqiě** ADV for the moment, temporarily

请**暂且**对这个分数保密。 *Please keep this score confidential for now.*

**暂缺 zànquē** V to be currently vacant (of a job); to be temporarily out of stock (of a product)

**暂时 zànshí** N temporary, for the moment; transient

**暂停 zàntíng** V to suspend, to stop for the time being; to have a time-out (sports)

**暂行 zànxíng** ADJ provisional; temporary, interim (of laws, rules and regulations)

让我们**暂时**实行这个**暂行**规定吧。
*For the time being, let's implement this interim regulation.*

### RELATED WORD

## 1523 砸　U+7838　TM **14** FM 一

**zá** V　to pound, to tamp; to smash, to break; to fail

**砸碎 zásuì** V to break into pieces

## 1524 硬    U+786C    TM **14** FM —

**yìng** ADJ·ADV   hard; firm, tough; obstinate; good-quality; doggedly; reluctantly

硬币 **yìngbì** N   coin · MW 枚

硬度 **yìngdù** N   hardness

硬功 **yìnggōng** N   great proficiency · MW 个

硬骨头 **yìnggǔtou** N   dauntless/unyielding person; difficult and stubborn person · MW 块、个

傻瓜有时候是一块难啃的**硬骨头**。
*ShaGua sometimes is a difficult, stubborn person.*

硬化 **yìnghuà** V   to harden, to stiffen

硬件 **yìngjiàn** N   hardware; equipment · MW 个

硬结 **yìngjié** N·V   hardened (mass); to harden · MW 个

硬木 **yìngmù** N   hardwood · MW 条、块

傻瓜自己铺家里的**硬木**地板。*ShaGua installed the hardwood floor in his house by himself.*

硬说 **yìngshuō** V   to assert, to allege

硬席 **yìngxí** N   hard seat (on a train, etc.) · MW 张

硬性 **yìngxìng** N   rigid; stiff; inflexible

**RELATED WORDS**

生硬 107     坚硬 381     僵硬 1864
强硬 1896     嘴硬 1984

## 1525 碎    U+788E    TM **14** FM —

**suì** V·ADJ   to break into pieces, to smash; broken; talkative

碎步 **suìbù** N   short step

碎片 **suìpiàn** N   fragment; chip · MW 块

碎石 **suìshí** N   gravel, crushed stone · MW 块

**RELATED WORDS**

切碎 277     打碎 289     扯碎 403
粉碎 1363     破碎 1374     零碎 1640
嘴碎 1984

## 1526 碰    U+78B0    TM **14** FM —

**pèng** V   to touch, to bump; to meet, to run into; to take a chance

碰杯 **pèngbēi** V   to clink glasses; cheers

碰壁 **pèngbì** V   to encounter difficulties; to hit a brick wall

碰钉子 **pèngdīngzi** V   to be rebuffed

谁都愿碰杯, 不愿碰钉子(碰壁)。*Everybody loves to offer a toast, but no one enjoys being rebuffed (hitting a brick wall).*

碰见 **pèngjiàn** V   to meet unexpectedly, to run into

碰巧 **pèngqiǎo** ADV   accidentally

碰巧我碰见她。*I ran into her by accident.*

碰头 **pèngtóu** V   to meet and discuss, to put (their) heads together; to see each other

碰运气 **pèngyùnqì** V   to take a chance, to try one's luck

碰撞 **pèngzhuàng** V   to crash, to collide

**RELATED WORD**

磕碰 1894

## 1527 聊    U+804A    TM **14** FM —

**liáo** V·ADV   to chat; to rely on; just; slightly, barely

聊天 **liáotiān** V   to chat

傻瓜太太喜欢**聊天**儿, 傻瓜不喜欢。
*Mrs. ShaGua loves to chat, but ShaGua doesn't.*

**RELATED WORDS**

无聊 139     闲聊 679

## 1528 预 預    U+9884    TM **14** FM —

**yù** V·ADV   to participate in; to intervene; in advance, beforehand

预报 **yùbào** V   to forecast, to predict

傻瓜每天都要看电视的天气**预报**。
*ShaGua watches the weather forecast on TV every day.*

预备 **yùbèi** V   to prepare, to get ready

预测 **yùcè** V   to predict, to foresee

预定 **yùdìng** V   to book, to schedule in advance

预防 **yùfáng** V   to prevent

预感 **yùgǎn** V·N   to have a presentiment (of); premonition · MW 个

预告 **yùgào** V·N   to announce in advance; to give advance warning (of); foretelling · MW 个

预购 **yùgòu** V   to purchase in advance

预计 **yùjì** V   to estimate; to predict

**1528 预 yù** (continued)

预见 **yùjiàn** N·V foresight; to predict, to foresee · MW 个

预料 **yùliào** V to expect; to predict

许多事情无法**预料**，但许多事情可以**预计**。
*Many things are unpredictable, but many can be planned for in advance.*

预谋 **yùmóu** N·V premeditation; to plan in advance · MW 个

预期 **yùqī** V to expect; to predict

预赛 **yùsài** N preliminary contest/heat · MW 场

预示 **yùshì** V to foretell; to portend

预算 **yùsuàn** N·V budget; to calculate in advance · MW 个

预习 **yùxí** V to prepare a lesson by previewing it

**预习**是学中文的一个好方法。
*Preparing a lesson by previewing it is a good way to study Chinese.*

预先 **yùxiān** ADV in advance, beforehand

预想 **yùxiǎng** V·N to expect, to anticipate; preconception · MW 个

预言 **yùyán** V·N to predict, to foretell; prediction · MW 个

预兆 **yùzhào** N premonition; omen · MW 个

预祝 **yùzhù** V to congratulate beforehand

---

**1529** 验 驗    U+9A8C    TM **14** FM 一

**yàn** V·N to inspect, to examine; to prove effective; desired result

验关 **yànguān** V to inspect (at customs)

验光 **yànguāng** V to have an eye examination

验收 **yànshōu** V to check and accept

傻瓜没有**验收**这个工程。*ShaGua has not checked and accepted this project.*

验算 **yànsuàn** V to check a calculation

验血 **yànxuè** V to have a blood test

验证 **yànzhèng** V to verify, to validate

你应该**验证**她的报告。*You should verify her report.*

**RELATED WORDS**

| | | |
|---|---|---|
| 体验 325 | 灵验 359 | 考验 530 |
| 实验 668 | 校验 802 | 检验 1033 |
| 经验 1110 | 试验 1180 | 到货验收 737 |

---

**1530** 壹    U+58F9    TM **14** FM |

**yī** NUM one (capital form of the Chinese numeral)

---

**1531** 喜    U+559C    TM **14** FM |

**xǐ** V·N to be happy; to like; to be pregnant; happy event; red-letter (day)

喜爱 **xǐ'ài** V to like, to be fond of

喜报 **xǐbào** N announcement of joyful news · MW 个

喜好 **xǐhào** V to like, to be fond of

他这人就**喜好**这些玩意儿。*He is the kind of person who loves this stuff.*

喜欢 **xǐhuan** V·ADJ to like; to love; happy

喜剧 **xǐjù** N comedy · MW 场

傻瓜**喜欢**看**喜剧**。*ShaGua likes to watch comedies.*

喜气洋洋 **xǐqìyángyáng** EXP jubilant, joyful, full of joy

喜庆 **xǐqìng** ADJ·N·V joyous; happy event; to celebrate

喜人 **xǐrén** ADJ delightful; heartening

喜事 **xǐshì** N happy event; wedding · MW 件

喜笑颜开 **xǐxiàoyánkāi** EXP to light up (with pleasure)

喜讯 **xǐxùn** N happy/good news · MW 个

傻瓜**喜笑颜开**，一定是孩子有什么**喜讯**。*ShaGua is lit up with pleasure; he must have some good news from his kids.*

喜悦 **xǐyuè** ADJ happy; joyous

**RELATED WORDS**

| | | |
|---|---|---|
| 可喜 243 | 欢喜 366 | 狂喜 469 |
| 欣喜 634 | 惊喜 1489 | 道喜 1756 |
| 空欢喜 669 | 沾沾自喜 684 | |

---

**1532** 悲    U+60B2    TM **14** FM |

**bēi** ADJ·N sad; pity, compassion; sadness; grief

悲哀 **bēi'āi** ADJ sad, sorrowful

悲惨 **bēicǎn** ADJ miserable; tragic

悲愤 **bēifèn** ADJ grief and anger

悲观 **bēiguān** ADJ pessimistic

悲剧 **bēijù** N tragedy · MW 个、场

悲伤 **bēishāng** ADJ sad, sorrowful

傻瓜有不少**悲伤**的故事，但他从不悲观。
*ShaGua has quite a few sad stories, but he has never been pessimistic.*

**悲痛 bēitòng** ADJ sorrowful; grieved

**RELATED WORDS**

可悲 243　　慈悲 1952　　乐极生悲 299

---

### 1533 虎

U+864E　TM **14** FM |

**hǔ** N tiger

**虎口 hǔkǒu** N jaws of death (tiger's mouth); part of the hand between the thumb and index finger · MW 个

**虎钳 hǔqián** N pliers · MW 台

**虎视眈眈 hǔshìdāndān** EXP to glare like a tiger ready to pounce on its prey

**RELATED WORDS**

马虎 247　　老虎 375　　骑虎难下 1840
壁虎 1920　　马马虎虎 247　　母老虎 394
狼吞虎咽 1443

---

### 1534 虚 虚

U+865A　TM **14** FM |

**xū** N·ADJ·ADV void; emptiness; empty; false; timid; humble, modest; weak, in poor health; in vain

**虚报 xūbào** V to misreport, to report fraudulently

**虚词 xūcí** N function word · MW 个

**虚构 xūgòu** V to fabricate, to make up

**虚汗 xūhàn** N night sweat · MW 身

**虚幻 xūhuàn** ADJ unreal, illusory

**虚假 xūjiǎ** ADJ false, phony
别整天**虚构**那些**虚假**的东西了！*Stop making up those phony lies all the time.*

**虚价 xūjià** N nominal price · MW 个

**虚惊 xūjīng** N false alarm · MW 场

**虚拟 xūnǐ** V·ADJ to be invented; fictitious; theoretical

**虚荣 xūróng** N·ADJ vanity; vain
这个人很爱**虚荣**，为人也很**虚假**。*This person loves vanity and is quite phony.*

**虚弱 xūruò** ADJ weak, in poor health

**虚设 xūshè** ADJ nominal, in name only

**虚岁 xūsuì** N nominal age (counting one year old at birth)
中国人讲**虚岁**，美国人不讲。*Chinese usually use nominal ages, but not Americans.*

---

**虚脱 xūtuō** N·V exhaustion; to collapse

**虚伪 xūwěi** ADJ deceptive; hypocritical

**虚无 xūwú** ADJ nonexistent

**虚张声势 xūzhāngshēngshì** EXP to bluff and bluster, to make an empty show of strength
别**虚张声势**了，谁不知道你**虚弱**！*Don't bluff and bluster; everybody knows you're weak.*

**RELATED WORDS**

心虚 232　　弄虚作假 251　　务虚 429
空虚 669

---

### 1535 裁

U+88C1　TM **14** FM |

**cái** V to cut (paper, cloth, etc. with a knife, a scissors); to reduce, to pare, to lessen; to judge; to decide; to sanction

**裁定 cáidìng** V to judge, to pass judgment on

**裁断 cáiduàn** V to consider and decide

**裁缝 cáifeng** N·V tailor, dressmaker; to tailor · MW 个、名
这个**裁缝**自称"天下第一剪"。*The tailor referred to himself as "the Number One tailor in the world."*

**裁剪 cáijiǎn** V to cut out

**裁决 cáijué** V to judge, to adjudicate

**裁军 cáijūn** V to disarm, to engage in disarmament

**裁判 cáipàn** V·N to judge; to make a decision; referee, umpire, judge · MW 个、位、名
这个结果应该由**裁判**来**裁定**。*The referee should determine the result.*

**RELATED WORDS**

体裁 325　　独裁 1095　　制裁 1130
剪裁 1816

---

### 1536 禁

U+7981　TM **14** FM |

**jìn** V to prohibit, to forbid; to imprison; to contain oneself

**禁闭 jìnbì** V to confine, to lock up

**禁不住 jìnbuzhù** V to be unable to endure

**禁得起 jìndeqǐ** V to be able to endure
傻瓜**禁得起**别人的攻击。*ShaGua is able to put up with attacks from others.*

**禁忌 jìnjì** N·V taboo; to avoid · MW 个

**禁令 jìnlìng** N prohibition, ban · MW 道

**1536 禁 jìn** (continued)

**禁区 jìnqū** N restricted zone; penalty box (sports) · MW 个、块

这些议题都不能触及，因为是**禁区**。 *These topics cannot be touched, because they are off limits.*

**禁食 jìnshí** V to fast, to refrain from eating

**禁烟 jìnyān** V to refrain from smoking

**禁止 jìnzhǐ** V to prohibit, to forbid

**RELATED WORDS**

| | | |
|---|---|---|
| 失禁 106 | 囚禁 161 | 严禁 241 |
| 查禁 741 | 软禁 889 | 监禁 994 |
| 违禁 1185 | 拘禁 1231 | 弱不禁风 1897 |
| 情不自禁 1491 | | |

**1537 紧** 紧   U+7D27   TM **14** FM |

**jǐn** ADJ·V tight; secure; close; small; urgent, pressing; tense; strict; short of money; to tighten

**紧逼 jǐnbī** V to press hard, to close in (on)

**紧凑 jǐncòu** ADJ fast-paced and on point; compact; terse

这一节课很**紧凑**。 *This class is very fast-paced and on point.*

**紧跟 jǐngēn** V to follow closely, to keep in step with; to comply with

**紧急 jǐnjí** ADJ urgent, pressing

**紧急会议 jǐnjíhuìyì** N emergency meeting · MW 个

傻瓜接到一个**紧急**电话，连夜开了一个**紧急会议**。 *ShaGua received an urgent call, so he held an emergency meeting late at night.*

**紧密 jǐnmì** ADJ close together; dense; inseparable

**紧握 jǐnwò** V to hold firmly, to not let go; to control

**紧要 jǐnyào** ADJ critical, crucial

**紧张 jǐnzhāng** ADJ nervous; intense; in short supply

傻瓜演讲时总是很**紧张**。 *ShaGua is always nervous when he makes speeches.*

越来越多美国人学中文以致中文教材供应**紧张**。 *More and more Americans have begun studying Chinese, with the result that Chinese teaching materials are in short supply.*

**RELATED WORDS**

| | | |
|---|---|---|
| 抓紧 406 | 加紧 463 | 松紧 579 |
| 咬紧牙关 780 | 赶紧 822 | 要紧 969 |
| 绑紧 1454 | 锁紧 1608 | 嘴紧 1984 |
| 不要紧 24 | | |

**1538 幽**   U+5E7D   TM **14** FM |

**yōu** ADJ remote, secluded; secret, hidden; of the nether world

**幽暗 yōu'àn** ADJ dim; gloomy

**幽谷 yōugǔ** N deep and secluded valley · MW 个

**幽会 yōuhuì** N secret meeting of lovers; date · MW 次

**幽魂 yōuhún** N ghost · MW 个

**幽静 yōujìng** ADJ quiet and secluded, peaceful

这里很**幽静**。 *It is very peaceful here.*

**幽灵 yōulíng** N ghost, spirit · MW 个

**幽默 yōumò** ADJ humorous

**幽雅 yōuyǎ** ADJ quiet and elegant; refined

由于酒店的环境很**幽雅**，不少人来这里**幽会**。 *Since the restaurant is quiet and elegant, quite a few couples like to secretly meet up here.*

**1539 婴** 嬰   U+5A74   TM **14** FM |

**yīng** N baby, infant

**婴儿 yīng'ér** N baby, infant · MW 个

**RELATED WORD**

弃婴 480

**1540 暑**   U+6691   TM **14** FM |

**shǔ** N heat; hot weather; midsummer

**暑假 shǔjià** N summer break/vacation · MW 个

学生做梦都想着放**暑假**。 *Students always dream about summer break.*

**暑期 shǔqī** N summertime; summer vacation · MW 个

**暑天 shǔtiān** N hot (summer) day

**RELATED WORDS**

| | | |
|---|---|---|
| 伏暑 212 | 炎暑 492 | 寒暑表 1481 |
| 盛暑 1694 | 酷暑 1841 | 避暑 1976 |

**1541 最**    U+6700   TM **14** FM |

**zuì** ADV most; least; best; in first place; incomparably

**最初 zuìchū** ADV at first, initially

最大 zuìdà ADV biggest; maximum

最大值 zuìdàzhí N maximum value

最低 zuìdī ADV lowest; minimum

最低价 zuìdījià N minimum price · MW 个

最多 zuìduō ADV most

最高 zuìgāo ADV highest; tallest; supreme

最好 zuìhǎo ADV best; had better, it would be best

你是班里**最好**的学生。 *You are the best student in the class.*

你**最好**把作业做完。 *You had better finish your homework.*

最后 zuìhòu ADV last, finally

最佳 zuìjiā ADV best, first-rate, top

**最后**双方制定了**最佳**的合作方案。 *The two parties finally formulated the best collaborative plan possible.*

最近 zuìjìn N lately, recently; soon, in the next few days

最小 zuìxiǎo ADV least

最终 zuìzhōng N final, ultimate, last

---

### 1542 罪 U+7F6A TM 14 FM |

zuì N·V crime; suffering, hardship; fault, blame; punishment; to blame

罪恶 zuì'è N crime; evil · MW 个

罪犯 zuìfàn N criminal, offender · MW 个、名

罪过 zuìguò N fault; offense · MW 个

罪魁祸首 zuìkuíhuòshǒu N chief culprit · MW 个、名

罪名 zuìmíng N charge, accusation · MW 个

罪孽 zuìniè N sin · MW 个

罪人 zuìrén N criminal; sinner · MW 个、名

罪行 zuìxíng N crime, criminal act; offense · MW 桩

罪责 zuìzé N guilt; responsibility for an offense · MW 个

罪证 zuìzhèng N evidence of a crime · MW 个

罪状 zuìzhuàng N charges/facts about a crime; nature of an offense · MW 个

他是一个历史的**罪人**，有很多**罪名**和**罪状**。 *He was an infamous criminal who committed many offenses and has many charges against him.*

#### RELATED WORDS

| | | | | | |
|---|---|---|---|---|---|
| 无罪 | 139 | 归罪 | 166 | 认罪 | 239 |
| 判罪 | 507 | 问罪 | 678 | 受罪 | 844 |
| 犯罪 | 884 | 治罪 | 935 | 畏罪 | 988 |
| 栽罪 | 995 | 替罪羊 | 1430 | 服罪 | 1457 |
| 赔罪 | 1569 | 活受罪 | 941 | | |

---

### 1543 骨 U+9AA8 TM 14 FM |

gǔ N bone; skeleton; framework; quality; character; spirit

骨刺 gǔcì N spur, bony growth

骨干 gǔgàn N backbone · MW 个、名

骨骼 gǔgé N skeleton; cadre · MW 副

骨灰 gǔhuī N ashes, remains (after cremation) · MW 堆

骨架 gǔjià N skeleton; framework · MW 副

骨气 gǔqì N strength of character; (moral) integrity

傻瓜很有**骨气**。 *ShaGua has moral integrity.*

骨肉 gǔròu N flesh and blood, kin, blood/close relation

骨髓 gǔsuǐ N bone marrow

骨头 gǔtou N bone; sting · MW 块

狗爱啃**骨头**。 *Dogs love to eat bones.*

这人讲话有**骨头**。 *There was bitterness in the words he spoke.*

骨折 gǔzhé V to fracture

骨子 gǔzi N ribs; frame

#### RELATED WORDS

| | | | | | |
|---|---|---|---|---|---|
| 尸骨 | 58 | 甲骨文 | 149 | 白骨 | 176 |
| 龙骨 | 315 | 软骨 | 889 | 肋骨 | 898 |
| 贱骨头 | 1037 | 刺骨 | 1050 | 排骨 | 1241 |
| 硬骨头 | 1524 | 主心骨 | 124 | 头盖骨 | 128 |

---

### 1544 量 U+91CF TM 14 FM |

liáng V to measure

liàng V·N to measure; to consider; to appraise, to assess, to estimate; quantity, volume; capacity

量杯 liángbēi N measuring cup · MW 个

量度 liángdù N measurement

量具 liángjù N measuring device · MW 件

量变 liàngbiàn N quantitative change

从**量变**到质变 *from quantitative to qualitative change*

量才录用 liàngcáilùyòng EXP to assign jobs to people according to their abilities

**1544 量 liáng/liàng** (continued)

量才录用是傻瓜的原则。 *One of the principles on which ShaGua operates is to assign jobs to people according to their abilities.*

**量词 liàngcí** N measure word · MW 个

搭配量词是外国人学中文的一大难题。 *Measure words are a big problem for foreigners studying Chinese.*

**量化 liànghuà** V to quantify

**量力 liànglì** V to estimate one's own strength/ability

**量子 liàngzǐ** N quantum · MW 个

**RELATED WORDS**

| | | |
|---|---|---|
| 丈量 17 | 大量 20 | 力量 59 |
| 少量 62 | 分量 173 | 气量 185 |
| 计量 240 | 打量 289 | 尽量 312 |
| 尽量 312 | 估量 456 | 含量 592 |
| 质量 597 | 定量 666 | 过量 712 |
| 重量 839 | 度量 919 | 度量衡 919 |
| 批量 1005 | 较量 1114 | 称量 1288 |
| 胆量 1295 | 容量 1320 | 限量 1417 |
| 商量 1612 | 数量 1637 | 微量 1700 |
| 能量 1873 | 日产量 96 | 年产量 182 |
| 含脂量 592 | 充其量 652 | 总产量 1330 |
| 降雨量 1416 | | |

---

**1545 墓**     U+5893     TM **14** FM |

**mù** N grave, tomb

**墓碑 mùbēi** N tombstone, gravestone · MW 块

**墓地 mùdì** N cemetery, graveyard · MW 块

傻瓜给自己选好了墓地，还做好了墓碑。 *ShaGua has selected his graveyard, and even made his own tombstone.*

**墓葬 mùzàng** V to bury (in a grave)

**RELATED WORDS**

| | | |
|---|---|---|
| 公墓 103 | 坟墓 281 | 扫墓 402 |

---

**1546 营** 營     U+8425     TM **14** FM |

**yíng** N·V battalion; barracks; camp; to operate, to run; to seek

**营地 yíngdì** N camp, encampment · MW 块、片

**营建 yíngjiàn** V to construct, to build

**营救 yíngjiù** V to rescue, to save

**营生 yíngshēng** V to earn a living

---

**营私 yíngsī** V to engage in graft; to feather one's nest

**营养 yíngyǎng** N nutrition; nourishment

他缺乏营养。 *He lacks nutrition.*

**营业 yíngyè** V to do business; to trade

**营业员 yíngyèyuán** N clerk, salesperson · MW 个、名

**营运 yíngyùn** V to operate, to run

学校营建的汉语学习中心下学期开始营运。 *The Chinese Study Center that the school just built will begin operation next semester.*

**营帐 yíngzhàng** N tent · MW 座

**RELATED WORDS**

| | | |
|---|---|---|
| 合营 296 | 私营 471 | 国营 542 |
| 经营 1110 | 宿营 1480 | 野营 1685 |
| 露营 1997 | 大本营 20 | |

---

**1547 落**     U+843D     TM **14** FM |

**là** V to leave (out); to be missing; to leave behind; to fall behind

我把钱包落在教室了。 *I left my wallet in the classroom.*

**lào** V to fall; to go down; to fall behind; to get

**luò** V to fall; to go down; to set; to lower; to fall behind; to decline; to belong to, to fall to; to stay

**落枕 làozhěn** V to have a stiff neck (from sleeping)

**落笔 luòbǐ** V to start writing/drawing, to put pen to paper

这篇文章从哪里落笔？ *Where should we begin this article?*

**落成 luòchéng** V to be completed (of a building)

**落地 luòdì** V to fall to the ground; to be born (of a baby)

**落地式 luòdìshì** N type of floor

**落点 luòdiǎn** N placement/spotting (of a ball) (sports) · MW 个

**落后 luòhòu** V·ADJ to fall/drop behind; backward

**落泪 luòlèi** V to shed tears, to weep

傻瓜太太从未见过傻瓜落泪。 *Mrs. ShaGua has never seen ShaGua weep.*

**落日 luòrì** N setting sun

**落实 luòshí** V·ADJ to carry out, to implement; to make sure; to feel at ease

做计划难，落实计划更难。 *It is difficult to formulate a plan, but more difficult to carry out a plan.*

我感觉心里**落**实了许多。 *My mind is much more at ease.*

**落选** luòxuǎn　V　to lose an election/competition

**落叶** luòyè　N　fallen/dead leaves ・　MW　片

**落枕** làozhěn　V　to have a stiff neck (from sleeping)

### RELATED WORDS

| | | |
|---|---|---|
| 下落 10 | 失落 106 | 击落 156 |
| 水落石出 159 | 叶落归根 167 | 坐落 318 |
| 名落孙山 426 | 利落 472 | 冷落 494 |
| 败落 589 | 低落 618 | 角落 838 |
| 段落 1293 | 衰落 1313 | 着落 1332 |
| 破落 1374 | 剥落 1377 | 降落伞 1416 |
| 降落 1416 | 起落 1421 | 跌落 1422 |
| 部落 1636 | 群落 1646 | 陷落 1678 |
| 涨落 1738 | 脱落 1803 | 失魂落魄 106 |
| 丢三落四 297 | 七零八落 34 | |

---

**1548　蓝**　藍　U+84DD　TM **14** FM |

**lán**　N　blue; azure; indigo plant

**蓝本** lánběn　N　original version ・　MW　个

这个规划的**蓝本**在哪儿？ *Where is the original version of this program?*

**蓝领** lánlǐng　N　blue-collar worker ・　MW　个、名

**蓝色** lánsè　N　blue (color)

### RELATED WORD

天蓝色 25

---

**1549　博**　U+535A　TM **14** FM |

**bó**　ADJ·V·N　abundant; erudite, well-informed; to win, to gain; ancient chess game; gambling

**博爱** bó'ài　N　universal love

人应该有**博爱**精神。 *Humans should have universal love.*

**博得** bódé　V　to win, to gain (favor, sympathy, etc.)

**博览** bólǎn　V　to read widely

**博览会** bólǎnhuì　N　exhibition, fair, exposition ・　MW　个、届

**博取** bóqǔ　V　to win, to gain

**博士** bóshì　N　doctor; Ph.D. ・　MW　个、位、名

傻瓜有一个连傻瓜太太都不知道的梦想，就是获得哈佛的**博士**学位。 *ShaGua has a dream that even Mrs. ShaGua doesn't know about: to get a doctoral degree from Harvard.*

**博物馆** bówùguǎn　N　museum ・　MW　间

**博学** bóxué　ADJ　erudite, learned

---

**1550　填**　U+586B　TM **14** FM |

**tián**　V　to fill; to fill in; to complete; to replenish; to supplement

**填报** tiánbào　V　to complete and submit

**填表** tiánbiǎo　V　to fill in a form

傻瓜最恨**填表**，特别是税表。 *What ShaGua hates most is to fill out forms, particularly tax return forms.*

**填充** tiánchōng　V　to fill up, to stuff

**填空** tiánkòng　V　to fill in the blanks

**填料** tiánliào　N　filler

**填平** tiánpíng　V　to fill and level

**填写** tiánxiě　V　to fill in; to write (data in a box)

请**填写**这份表格。 *Please fill out this form.*

**填字游戏** tiánzìyóuxì　N　crossword puzzle ・　MW　个

---

**1551　挖**　U+6316　TM **14** FM |

**wā**　V　to dig, to scoop out; to explore, to probe

**挖补** wābǔ　V　to repair by replacing a damaged part

**挖掘** wājué　V　to dig, to excavate

**挖空心思** wākōngxīnsī　EXP　to rack one's brains (for one's own advantage)

这人就爱**挖空心思**打别人的主意。 *This guy likes racking his brains to take advantage of others.*

### RELATED WORD

耳挖子 145

---

**1552　捐**　U+6350　TM **14** FM |

**juān**　V·N　to donate, to contribute; to relinquish, to abandon; tax

**捐款** juānkuǎn　V·N　to contribute; donation ・　MW　笔

在中国，**捐款**还不是很流行。 *Making donations has not been very popular in China.*

**捐献** juānxiàn　V　to donate, to contribute

**捐赠** juānzèng　V　to donate, to contribute ・　MW　批、笔

**1552 捐 juān** (continued)

捐助 **juānzhù** V to offer assistance; to contribute · MW 批、笔

傻瓜悄悄**捐助**了三个中国孤儿。
*ShaGua made a quiet contribution to three Chinese orphans.*

---

**1553 据** 據 U+636E TM **14** FM |

**jù** V·N·PREP to occupy; to seize; evidence; according to

据传 **jùchuán** V rumor has it that

据传，傻瓜有个红颜知己。*Rumor has it that ShaGua has an intimate female friend.*

据点 **jùdiǎn** N stronghold · MW 个

据悉 **jùxī** V it is reported; according to reports

**RELATED WORDS**

| | | |
|---|---|---|
| 占据 153 | 收据 282 | 依据 625 |
| 实据 668 | 单据 672 | 证据 705 |
| 论据 947 | 凭据 1060 | 借据 1087 |
| 根据 1245 | 票据 1367 | 窃据 1482 |
| 数据 1637 | 数据库 1637 | 真凭实据 1075 |

---

**1554 提** U+63D0 TM **14** FM |

**tí** V to carry; to put forward, to advance, to raise; to mention; to move to an earlier date; to collect; to extract

提案 **tí'àn** N proposal; motion · MW 个

提拔 **tíba** V to promote

提包 **tíbāo** N bag, handbag · MW 个

提倡 **tíchàng** V to promote, to encourage

提出 **tíchū** V to put forward, to raise

提纯 **tíchún** V to purify

提单 **tídān** N bill of lading · MW 份

提到 **tídào** V to mention, to refer to

提法 **tífǎ** N wording, formulation · MW 个、种

他的**提法**很独特。*The wording he proposed is quite unique.*

提纲 **tígāng** N outline; synopsis · MW 个

提高 **tígāo** V to raise; to increase; to improve

提供 **tígōng** V to supply, to offer (advice, accommodations, etc.)

提货 **tíhuò** V to take delivery of goods

提交 **tíjiāo** V to submit

你的想法很好，为什么不**提交**一个**提案**呢？
*Your idea is very good; why not submit a proposal?*

提款 **tíkuǎn** V to withdraw money

提炼 **tíliàn** V to refine, to process, to purify

提名 **tímíng** V to nominate

提起 **tíqǐ** V to mention; to raise (a topic, a fist, spirits, etc.)

提前 **tíqián** V to advance, to move to an earlier time

提琴 **tíqín** N violin family · MW 把

提取 **tíqǔ** V to pick up, to collect; to draw

提升 **tíshēng** V to promote; to upgrade

提示 **tíshì** V to point out

提问 **tíwèn** V to ask a question · MW 个

请**提示**一下什么时候我们才可以**提问**。
*Please point out when we can ask questions.*

提箱 **tíxiāng** N suitcase · MW 个

提携 **tíxié** V to promote; to guide and support

他能有今天(的成就)，全靠您的**提携**。
*His achievements today should be completely credited to your guidance and support.*

提醒 **tíxǐng** V to remind; to warn

提要 **tíyào** N summary; synopsis, abstract · MW 个、篇

提议 **tíyì** V·N to propose; suggestion; motion · MW 个

你应该**提前提出**你的**提议**。*You ought to propose your suggestions earlier.*

提早 **tízǎo** V to move to an earlier date

**RELATED WORDS**

| | |
|---|---|
| 手提 104 | 前提 1329 |

---

**1555 插** U+63D2 TM **14** FM |

**chā** V to insert, to stick in; to pierce

插班 **chābān** V to enroll late in a class

插话 **chāhuà** V to interrupt

插口 **chākǒu** N outlet, socket · MW 个

插曲 **chāqǔ** N episode; interlude · MW 段、个

插入 **chārù** V to insert, to plug in

插手 **chāshǒu** V to get involved in

你不要**插手**我的事情。*You shouldn't involve yourself in my business.*

插头 **chātóu** N plug · MW 个

插图 **chātú** N illustration; diagram · MW 张、页

插足 **chāzú** V to participate in; to involve oneself in

你不要**插足**这个肮脏的政治交易。
*You shouldn't get involved in this dirty political deal.*

插嘴 **chāzuǐ** V to interrupt, to break in

傻瓜不爱说话，但傻瓜太太很爱**插嘴**。
*ShaGua doesn't like to talk, but Mrs. ShaGua loves to jump into others' conversations.*

插座 **chāzuò** N outlet, socket · MW 个

**RELATED WORDS**

安插 487　　穿插 1322　　见缝插针 267

---

**1556 援** U+63F4 TM **14** FM |

**yuán** V to aid, to help; to rescue; to quote, to cite; to pull (by hand)

援救 **yuánjiù** V to rescue, to save

援军 **yuánjūn** N reinforcements · MW 队

援引 **yuányǐn** V to quote, to cite

你**援引**的这段话真精彩。*Your quote was wonderful.*

援用 **yuányòng** V to quote, to cite

援助 **yuánzhù** V·N to help; support, assistance

**RELATED WORDS**

支援 92　　外援 218　　声援 374
求援 376　　受援 844

---

**1557 搂** 摟 U+6402 TM **14** FM |

**lǒu** V to embrace

---

**1558 搽** U+643D TM **14** FM |

**chá** V to put on, to apply (powder, makeup, lotion, etc.)

搽粉 **cháfěn** V to powder

搽口红 **chákǒuhóng** V to put on lipstick

傻瓜太太每天都**搽粉**，**搽口红**。*Mrs. ShaGua puts on powder and lipstick every day.*

---

**1559 啃** U+5543 TM **14** FM |

**kěn** V to bite; to gnaw

---

**1560 喉** U+5589 TM **14** FM |

**hóu** N throat; larynx

喉咙 **hóulóng** N throat; larynx · MW 条

喉舌 **hóushé** N mouthpiece · MW 个

你不是他的**喉舌**，你是一个独立的人。*You are not his mouthpiece, but an independent person.*

猴头 **hóutóu** N larynx

喉炎 **hóuyán** N laryngitis

喉音 **hóuyīn** N fauces (passage between the mouth and pharynx) · MW 个

**RELATED WORD**

咽喉 1024

---

**1561 哼** U+54FC TM **14** FM |

**hēng** V·ONOM to moan, to groan; humph (expressing disapproval/suspicion); to hum

哼哼哈哈 **hēnghenghāhā** EXP to hem and haw

---

**1562 唱** U+5531 TM **14** FM |

**chàng** V to sing, to chant; to call loudly, to cry

唱词 **chàngcí** N ballad lyrics · MW 段

唱反调 **chàngfǎndiào** V to express a contrary opinion (LIT to sing a different tune)

唱高调 **chànggāodiào** V to use high-sounding words, to talk big

你这个人不是**唱高调**，就是**唱反调**。
*You're always either talking big or being negative.*

唱歌 **chànggē** V to sing (a song)

唱机 **chàngjī** N phonograph; gramophone · MW 台

**RELATED WORDS**

夫唱妇随 55　　齐唱 221　　电唱机 263
合唱 296　　伴唱 321　　重唱 839
演唱 1821　　歌唱 1900　　二重唱 2
五重唱 79

---

**1563 喷** 噴 U+55B7 TM **14** FM |

**pēn** V to spurt, to gush, to spray

喷火口 **pēnhuǒkǒu** N crater · MW 个

喷漆 **pēnqī** V to spray paint

**1563** 喷 **pēn** (continued)

喷气 **pēnqì** [V] to blast (with compressed air)

喷气式 **pēnqìshì** [N] jet propulsion

喷泉 **pēnquán** [N] fountain; spring · [MW] 个

喷射 **pēnshè** [V] to spurt, to spray

喷水池 **pēnshuǐchí** [N] fountain · [MW] 个

喷嚏 **pēntì** [N] sneeze · [MW] 个

中国民间有一个说法, 打**喷嚏**是有人在谈论你。
*There is a Chinese saying that claims when you sneeze, it means someone is talking about you.*

喷头 **pēntóu** [N] showerhead · [MW] 个

喷雾 **pēnwù** [V] to spray; to spit

喷雾器 **pēnwùqì** [N] spray, atomizer · [MW] 个

喷油 **pēnyóu** [V] to gush oil

喷嘴 **pēnzuǐ** [N] nozzle · [MW] 个

---

**1564** 桶     U+6876    TM **14** FM |

**tǒng** [N·MW] bucket; barrel; keg; tub

桶装 **tǒngzhuāng** [ADJ] barreled

**RELATED WORDS**

水桶 159     马桶 247     便桶 865
饭桶 891

---

**1565** 梳     U+68B3    TM **14** FM |

**shū** [V·N] to comb; comb

梳理 **shūlǐ** [V] to comb (one's hair)

梳洗 **shūxǐ** [V] to comb one's hair and wash up

梳妆 **shūzhuāng** [V] to get dressed up, to dress and apply makeup

梳妆是傻瓜太太每天的必修课。 *Mrs. ShaGua must dress and apply makeup every day.*

梳子 **shūzi** [N] comb · [MW] 把

---

**1566** 椅     U+6905    TM **14** FM |

**yǐ** [N] chair

椅子 **yǐzi** [N] chair · [MW] 把

**RELATED WORDS**

折椅 408     座椅 920     摇椅 1664
靠椅 1791     躺椅 1971

---

**1567** 楼 樓     U+697C    TM **14** FM |

**lóu** [N] building with two or more stories; floor, level; attic; tower

楼道 **lóudào** [N] corridor, passageway, hallway · [MW] 条

楼房 **lóufáng** [N] building with two or more stories · [MW] 座

楼上 **lóushàng** [N] upstairs

楼梯 **lóutī** [N] stairs · [MW] 个

上**楼梯**后, 往右转, 我的房间在**楼道**的尽头。 *After you go up the stairs, turn right; my room is at the end of the hall.*

楼下 **lóuxià** [N] downstairs

**RELATED WORDS**

下楼 10     大楼 20     门楼 130
钟楼 1125     牌楼 1597     五角大楼 79

---

**1568** 陪     U+966A    TM **14** FM |

**péi** [V] to keep (someone) company; to accompany; to help, to assist

陪伴 **péibàn** [V] to keep (someone) company; to accompany

陪衬 **péichèn** [V·N] to set off, to enhance (by contrast); foil · [MW] 个

你以为你是什么? 你不过是一个**陪衬**。 *Who do you think you are? You're just a foil.*

陪客 **péikè** [V] to keep guests company; to service clients (of a prostitute)

陪审 **péishěn** [V] to serve on a jury

有些华人不愿意做**陪审**工作。 *Some Chinese people are unwilling to serve on a jury.*

陪同 **péitóng** [V] to accompany, to be together with; to guide

陪葬 **péizàng** [V] to be buried with the dead (of funerary objects)

**RELATED WORD**

失陪 106

---

**1569** 赔 賠     U+8D54    TM **14** FM |

**péi** [V] to compensate, to make good; to apologize

赔本 **péiběn** [V] to sustain a business loss

赔不是 **péibùshi** [V] to apologize

赔偿 **péicháng** [V] to compensate; to make amends, to atone

赔款 **péikuǎn** [V·N] to pay reparations; reparations · [MW] 笔

赔礼 **péilǐ** [V] to apologize

光赔款还不行，还得赔礼、赔不是。 *Reparations will not be enough; you also have to apologize.*

赔账 **péizhàng** [V] to pay for the loss of (cash, goods, etc.)

赔罪 **péizuì** [V] to apologize

## 1570 眼    U+773C    TM **14**   FM |

**yǎn** [N·MW] eye; small hole; key point, crux; sight, vision; [measure word for wells, cave dwellings, etc.]

眼巴巴 **yǎnbābā** [EXP] eagerly expecting/awaiting; feeling helpless (while something bad happens)

傻瓜太太眼巴巴地盼着儿子带个女朋友回家。 *Mrs. ShaGua is eagerly looking forward to her older son bringing a girlfriend home.*

他们眼巴巴地看着房子被水淹没了。 *They are watching helplessly as their houses are flooded.*

眼白 **yǎnbái** [N] white of the eye

眼馋 **yǎnchán** [ADJ] envious

眼底 **yǎndǐ** [N] at the moment, now

眼底下 **yǎndǐxia** [EXP] right before one's eyes

眼福 **yǎnfú** [N] feast for the eyes, good fortune (of seeing someone/something)

昨天傻瓜没有眼福见到总统。 *ShaGua didn't have the good fortune of seeing the president yesterday.*

眼光 **yǎnguāng** [N] sight, vision; perspective

眼红 **yǎnhóng** [ADJ] envious

眼花 **yǎnhuā** [ADJ] with blurred/dim vision

眼尖 **yǎnjiān** [ADJ] sharp-eyed

眼界 **yǎnjiè** [N] perspective; horizons

你的眼界很宽。 *Your perspective is very broad.*

眼镜 **yǎnjìng** [N] glasses · [MW] 副

眼睛 **yǎnjing** [N] eye · [MW] 只、双

眼看 **yǎnkàn** [V·ADV] to watch helplessly; soon, in a moment

眼科 **yǎnkē** [N] ophthalmology

眼泪 **yǎnlèi** [N] tears; crying · [MW] 滴

眼力 **yǎnlì** [N] eyesight; judgment

傻瓜没有什么文化，但很有眼力。 *ShaGua was not well educated, but his judgment is sharp.*

眼帘 **yǎnlián** [N] eyes

眼前 **yǎnqián** [N] before one's eyes; at the moment

眼球 **yǎnqiú** [N] eyeball · [MW] 个

眼圈 **yǎnquān** [N] eye socket · [MW] 个

眼色 **yǎnsè** [N] wink; meaningful look/glance

学生在课堂上互相看眼色。 *The students are exchanging glances in class.*

你不能老是看你的老板的眼色行事。 *You shouldn't always take cues from your boss.*

眼神 **yǎnshén** [N] expression (in one's eyes)

眼生 **yǎnshēng** [ADJ] strange, unfamiliar

眼熟 **yǎnshú** [ADJ] familiar

眼下 **yǎnxià** [N] at the moment

眼压 **yǎnyā** [N] intraocular pressure

眼睁睁 **yǎnzhēngzhēng** [ADV] (watching) helplessly

眼中钉 **yǎnzhōngdīng** [EXP] thorn in one's side · [MW] 颗

### RELATED WORDS

| | | |
|---|---|---|
| 入眼 5 | 扎眼 288 | 龙眼 315 |
| 另眼看待 385 | 肉眼 437 | 红眼 474 |
| 字眼 664 | 顺眼 874 | 亲眼 908 |
| 眨眼 1045 | 刺眼 1050 | 转眼 1111 |
| 泉眼 1275 | 着眼 1332 | 猫眼 1446 |
| 睁眼 1680 | 醉眼 1842 | 瞎眼 1913 |
| 瞪眼 1966 | 干瞪眼 13 | 广开眼界 23 |
| 小心眼儿 61 | 坏心眼 280 | 眉开眼笑 1067 |
| 挑字眼 1235 | 挤眉弄眼 795 | 睁不开眼 1680 |

## 1571 睡    U+7761    TM **14**   FM |

**shuì** [V] to sleep

睡觉 **shuìjiào** [V] to sleep; to go to bed

睡帽 **shuìmào** [N] nightcap (cloth cap) · [MW] 顶

睡梦 **shuìmèng** [V] to dream; to slumber

睡眠 **shuìmián** [N] sleep, slumber

傻瓜总是睡眠不足。 *ShaGua never gets enough sleep.*

睡醒 **shuìxǐng** [V] to wake up

睡衣 **shuìyī** [N] night clothes, pajamas · [MW] 件

睡意 **shuìyì** [N] sleepiness, drowsiness

都半夜三更了，傻瓜还是没有睡意。 *It is past midnight and ShaGua is still not drowsy.*

睡着 **shuìzháo** [V] to sleep

### RELATED WORDS

| | | |
|---|---|---|
| 午睡 48 | 昏睡 1058 | 沉睡 1166 |
| 熟睡 1973 | | |

**1572 既**    U+65E2    TM **14** FM |

**jì** CONJ·ADV both … and …, as well as; since; already

**既成事实 jìchéngshìshí** EXP fait accompli, irreversible fact

**既得利益 jìdélìyì** EXP vested interest

**既定 jìdìng** ADJ fixed, established

**既而 jì'ér** CONJ afterwards, then

**既然 jìrán** CONJ since, as; now that

既然你说了，就要做到。 *Since you said it, you should do it.*

既然这是既定方针，又是既成事实；那我们就照着做吧。 *Since this is an established policy and that's the fact of the matter, we ought to follow its example.*

**既是 jìshì** CONJ since, as; now that

**1573 款**    U+6B3E    TM **14** FM |

**kuǎn** N·V·MW sum of money; signature (in an inscription); style; item, section, clause; person of wealth; to entertain; [measure word for the type, kind, or style of clothing, etc., and for the section of an article in a legal document, etc.]

**款待 kuǎndài** V to entertain; to treat cordially

**款式 kuǎnshì** N style; design · MW 个、种

**款项 kuǎnxiàng** N sum of money, funds; item, clause · MW 笔、条

这个合同能带来一大笔款项。 *This contract can bring in a lot of money.*

这个合同有这一条款项吗？ *Does the contract contain this clause?*

**款子 kuǎnzi** N sum of money, funds · MW 笔

**RELATED WORDS**

| | | | |
|---|---|---|---|
| 欠款 | 105 | 付款 | 206 |
| 价款 | 210 | 汇款 | 234 |
| 收款人 | 282 | 存款 | 438 |
| 条款 | 598 | 账款 | 812 |
| 放款 | 964 | 现款 | 975 |
| 拨款 | 1015 | 赃款 | 1039 |
| 货款 | 1061 | 贷款 | 1062 |
| 债款 | 1088 | 钱款 | 1301 |
| 罚款 | 1386 | 领款 | 1465 |
| 退款 | 1508 | 捐款 | 1552 |
| 提款 | 1554 | 税款 | 1705 |
| 赠款 | 1944 | | |

**1574 期**    U+671F    TM **14** FM |

**qī** N·V·ADV·MW scheduled time; time period; time limit; to appoint; to expect; to hope; yearly; monthly; completely; [measure word for issues of periodicals and for classes and courses]

**期待 qīdài** V to await; to expect

**期货 qīhuò** N futures (of a commodity) · MW 批

**期间 qījiān** N time (period); course

**期刊 qīkān** N periodical · MW 本、期

他期待着期刊的出版。 *He looks forward to the periodical being published.*

**期考 qīkǎo** N end-of-term/final exam · MW 次

**期望 qīwàng** V to expect; to hope · MW 个

**期限 qīxiàn** N deadline; time limit · MW 个

**期中考试 qīzhōngkǎoshì** N midterm exam · MW 次

傻瓜的大儿子非常期望自己能考好期中考试。 *ShaGua's older son really expected his midterm to go well.*

**期终考试 qīzhōngkǎoshì** N end-of-term/final exam · MW 次

**RELATED WORDS**

| | | | |
|---|---|---|---|
| 长期 | 93 | 日期 | 96 |
| 分期 | 173 | 任期 | 211 |
| 刑期 | 256 | 吉期 | 259 |
| 早期 | 268 | 会期 | 295 |
| 后期 | 310 | 如期 | 464 |
| 改期 | 516 | 同期 | 541 |
| 时期 | 586 | 定期 | 666 |
| 过期 | 712 | 近期 | 716 |
| 延期 | 731 | 到期 | 737 |
| 星期 | 753 | 活期 | 941 |
| 孕期 | 971 | 周期性 | 1068 |
| 周期 | 1068 | 学期 | 1155 |
| 按期 | 1234 | 限期 | 1417 |
| 短期 | 1452 | 预期 | 1528 |
| 暑期 | 1540 | 假期 | 1586 |
| 缓期 | 1708 | 晚期 | 1779 |
| 脱期 | 1803 | 霜期 | 1935 |
| 有效期 | 439 | | |

**1575 越**    U+8D8A    TM **14** FM |

**yuè** V·ADV to jump over; to exceed; to be in high spirits; increasingly; more and more

**越冬 yuèdōng** V to survive the winter

**越发 yuèfā** ADV increasingly; the more … the more …

越轨 yuèguǐ V to overstep the bounds

越过 yuèguò V to cross; to go beyond, to rise above

越界 yuèjiè V to overstep the bounds

越境 yuèjìng V to cross the border illegally

越来越 yuèláiyuè ADV more and more

有人认为，傻瓜越来越傻了。*Some people believe that ShaGua has gotten dumber and dumber.*

越南 Yuènán N Vietnam

越野 yuèyě V to go cross-country; to go a great distance

**RELATED WORDS**

| | | | |
|---|---|---|---|
| 优越 | 447 | 卓越 | 523 |
| 穿越 | 1322 | 超越 | 1684 |
| 跨越 | 1857 | 翻山越岭 | 1989 |

---

**1576 距** U+8DDD TM **14** FM |

jù V·N to be apart from; distance; at a distance of

距离 jùlí V·N to be apart from, to be at a distance from; (spatial) distance; time interval

现实与理想往往存在一些距离。*There is usually a gap between reality and the ideal.*

**RELATED WORDS**

| | | | |
|---|---|---|---|
| 长距离 | 93 | 差距 | 673 |
| 近距离 | 716 | 相距 | 805 |
| 间距 | 914 | 远距离 | 1184 |
| 焦距 | 1265 | 等距 | 1437 |

---

**1577 凯** 凯 U+51EF TM **14** FM |

kǎi N triumph, victory

凯歌 kǎigē N victory song · MW 首

凯旋 kǎixuán V to return in triumph

凯旋门 kǎixuánmén N triumphal arch · MW 座

**RELATED WORD**

奏凯 608

---

**1578 都** U+90FD TM **14** FM |

dōu ADV all; already

dū N capital city; big city

都是 dōushì ADV all; every; both; already

都城 dūchéng N capital city · MW 座

都会 dūhuì N city; metropolis · MW 个

都市 dūshì N big city; metropolis · MW 个

都市和都会应该都是一个意思。*"Big city" and "metropolis" should mean the same thing.*

**RELATED WORD**

首都 924

---

**1579 散** U+6563 TM **14** FM |

sǎn V·ADJ·N to loosen, to come loose; loose; scattered; medicinal powder

sàn V to distribute; to separate; to break up; to let out; to dispel

散光 sǎnguāng N astigmatism

散架 sǎnjià V to fall apart

散居 sǎnjū V to live scattered

散漫 sǎnmàn ADJ unorganized, careless and sloppy

这个学生很散漫。*This student is very undisciplined.*

散文 sǎnwén N prose; essay · MW 篇

散装 sǎnzhuāng ADJ loose, packed loosely (of goods)

散播 sànbō V to spread

散布 sànbù V to disseminate; to scatter, to diffuse

有人喜欢散布傻瓜的谣言。*Somebody likes spreading rumors about ShaGua.*

散步 sànbù V to take a walk

散场 sànchǎng V to be over, to let out (of a performance, etc.)

散发 sànfā V to give off (a scent, etc.); to send out, to distribute

散会 sànhuì V to be over (of a meeting)

散会了，还有很多人在围着傻瓜。*The conference has ended, but there are many people still surrounding ShaGua.*

散开 sànkāi V to spread out/apart; to disperse

散热 sànrè V to dissipate heat

散失 sànshī V to lose; to evaporate; to scatter and disappear

傻瓜找到了一些散失多年的朋友。*ShaGua has located some friends who had scattered and disappeared a long time ago.*

**RELATED WORDS**

| | | | |
|---|---|---|---|
| 分散 | 173 | 扩散 | 291 |
| 拆散 | 572 | 松散 | 579 |
| 闲散 | 679 | 消散 | 1343 |
| 离散 | 1614 | 解散 | 1928 |
| 懒散 | 1953 | 披头散发 | 1011 |
| 一哄而散 | 1 | | |

## 1580 象　U+8C61　TM **14** FM 丿

**xiàng** N elephant; appearance; shape; image

象棋 **xiàngqí** N chess; Chinese chess · MW 副

傻瓜不会下**象棋**。 *ShaGua doesn't know how to play chess.*

象征 **xiàngzhēng** N symbol; token · MW 个

### RELATED WORDS

| | | |
|---|---|---|
| 气象 185 | 对象 254 | 形象 257 |
| 印象 470 | 幻象 475 | 表象 527 |
| 抽象 788 | 现象 975 | 映象 1036 |
| 假象 1586 | 想象 1769 | 四不象 271 |
| 找对象 567 | 互生现象 135 | |

## 1581 智　U+667A　TM **14** FM 丿

**zhì** N·ADJ wisdom; wit; intelligence; brainpower; insight; wise

智齿 **zhìchǐ** N wisdom tooth · MW 颗

智慧 **zhìhuì** N wisdom; intelligence

智力 **zhìlì** N intelligence; intellect

智谋 **zhìmóu** N wisdom and resourcefulness

智能 **zhìnéng** N intelligence, brainpower

智商 **zhìshāng** N intelligence quotient (IQ)

傻瓜说虽然自己有几颗**智齿**，但就是**智商**不高，**智谋**不多，**智力**不足，**智慧**不够。 *ShaGua said that even though he had several wisdom teeth, his IQ was low, his intelligent ideas were few, and his brightness and wisdom were lacking.*

智育 **zhìyù** N intellectual education

### RELATED WORDS

| | | |
|---|---|---|
| 才智 39 | 斗智 71 | 足智多谋 383 |
| 明智 1035 | 理智 1200 | 德智体 1923 |

## 1582 留　U+7559　TM **14** FM 丿

**liú** V to remain, to stay; to study abroad; to ask (someone) to stay; to keep, to save; to accept, to take; to leave behind

留步 **liúbù** V to stop here, to not bother to go any farther

留成 **liúchéng** V to preserve, to keep

留待 **liúdài** V to postpone, to leave (something) for later

留后手 **liúhòushǒu** V to leave room for maneuver

傻瓜做事不喜欢**留后手**。 *ShaGua doesn't like to leave loopholes when he conducts business.*

留话 **liúhuà** V to leave word / a message

留级 **liújí** V to fail admission to next year's course; to repeat a year (in school)

傻瓜读书时曾**留级**。 *ShaGua was held back in school.*

留客 **liúkè** V to ask (a guest) to stay

留空 **liúkōng** V to leave blank space (in writing)

留恋 **liúliàn** V can't bear to part from; to be reluctant to leave

留念 **liúniàn** V to keep as a souvenir/memento

留任 **liúrèn** V to remain in office

许多人希望傻瓜**留任**。 *Many people hoped that ShaGua would remain in office.*

留宿 **liúsù** V to put (someone) up for the night

留心 **liúxīn** V to be careful; to keep one's eyes open

留学 **liúxué** V to study abroad

留言 **liúyán** V·N to leave a message; message written at departure · MW 个、段

留意 **liúyì** V to be careful; to look out, to keep one's eyes open

傻瓜的中国朋友请他**留意**他们的孩子在美国**留学**的情况。 *ShaGua's Chinese friends asked him to keep an eye out for their kids studying in America.*

留影 **liúyǐng** V to take a photograph as a memento

留用 **liúyòng** V to continue to employ

### RELATED WORDS

| | | |
|---|---|---|
| 扣留 401 | 居留 850 | 保留 868 |
| 残留 977 | 拘留 1231 | 逗留 1512 |
| 停留 1588 | 挽留 1659 | 遗留 1829 |
| 片甲不留 119 | | |

## 1583 帮　幫　U+5E2E　TM **14** FM 丿

**bāng** V·N·MW to help; to be hired; side; gang; [measure word for groups (of people)]

帮办 **bāngbàn** V·N to assist in managing; deputy · MW 个、名

帮倒忙 **bāngdàománg** EXP to be more of a hindrance than a help

你这样做实际上是在**帮倒忙**。 *The way you acted was actually more of a hindrance than a help.*

帮工 **bānggōng** N helper · MW 个、名

帮会 **bānghuì** N secret society · MW 个

帮忙 **bāngmáng** V to help; to do a favor for

帮派 **bāngpài** N gang; faction · MW 个

帮手 **bāngshou** N helper; assistant · MW 个、名

帮凶 **bāngxiōng** V·N to be an accomplice, to assist in a crime; accomplice, accessory · MW 个、名

帮助 **bāngzhù** V·N to help, to assist, to aid; assistance · MW 个

她给我无私的**帮助**。*She gave me unselfish assistance.*

**RELATED WORD**

行帮 327

---

### 1584 厨　U+53A8　TM 14 FM 丿

**chú** N kitchen; cook

厨房 **chúfáng** N kitchen · MW 间

厨工 **chúgōng** N kitchen worker · MW 个、名
傻瓜在许多餐馆儿当过**厨工**。*ShaGua used to be a kitchen worker in several restaurants.*

厨师 **chúshī** N cook; chef · MW 个、名

---

### 1585 筷　U+7B77　TM 14 FM 丿

**kuài** N chopsticks

筷子 **kuàizi** N chopsticks · MW 双、对

---

### 1586 假　U+5047　TM 14 FM 丿

**jiǎ** ADJ·N·CONJ false; artificial; fake, phony; if, supposing

**jià** N holiday; vacation

请假 *to ask for time off*

假案 **jiǎ'àn** N frame-up, fabricated case · MW 桩

假充 **jiǎchōng** V to pretend to be

假定 **jiǎdìng** V·N to suppose; to assume; (scientific) hypothesis · MW 个

假发 **jiǎfà** N wig · MW 副、顶

假话 **jiǎhuà** N lie · MW 个

假借 **jiǎjiè** V to make use of

假冒 **jiǎmào** V to pose as; to pass (a fake) off as (genuine)

假如 **jiǎrú** CONJ if, in case

**假如**你要讲**假话**, 一定要**假定**对方是笨蛋。 *If you want to lie, you must assume the other person to be an idiot.*

假若 **jiǎruò** CONJ if, supposing, in case

假山 **jiǎshān** N rock garden · MW 座

假设 **jiǎshè** CONJ·V·N if; to assume; hypothesis · MW 个

**假设**他是正确的, 结果会是什么呢？ *Assuming he is correct, what is the result?*
这不过是一个**假设**而已。 *This is just a hypothesis.*

假使 **jiǎshǐ** CONJ if, in the event that

假说 **jiǎshuō** N hypothesis · MW 个

假想 **jiǎxiǎng** N imagination; hypothesis · MW 个

傻瓜心里从来没有**假想**敌。 *ShaGua has never had an imaginary enemy.*

假象 **jiǎxiàng** N false/deceptive appearance · MW 个

假牙 **jiǎyá** N false teeth, dentures · MW 颗、副

假意 **jiǎyì** N·ADV hypocrisy; hypocritically; insincerely

假造 **jiǎzào** V to forge, to counterfeit

假肢 **jiǎzhī** N artificial limb · MW 个

假装 **jiǎzhuāng** V to pretend

假期 **jiàqī** N vacation · MW 个

假日 **jiàrì** N holiday; day off · MW 个

假条 **jiàtiáo** N leave permit · MW 张

如果你缺课, 必须要**请假**, 要有**假条**。 *If you are to be absent, you must request a leave permit.*

**RELATED WORDS**

---

### 1587 偏　U+504F　TM 14 FM 丿

**piān** V·ADJ·ADV to move to one side; inclined; biased; stubbornly; on the contrary

偏爱 **piān'ài** V to favor, to show partiality to · MW 个

傻瓜太太**偏爱**小儿子。 *Mrs. ShaGua favors her younger son.*

偏差 **piānchā** N deviation; error · MW 个

偏废 **piānfèi** V to give unequal emphasis to

**1587 偏 piān** (continued)

偏护 **piānhù** V to be partial to

偏激 **piānjī** ADJ extreme (of an opinion, a proposition, etc.); radical

偏见 **piānjiàn** N bias, prejudice · MW 个

傻瓜不**偏激**，对人也没有**偏见**。*ShaGua is not radical in his opinions, and he doesn't have any bias toward people.*

偏离 **piānlí** V to deviate, to diverge

偏僻 **piānpì** ADJ remote, out-of-the-way

偏偏 **piānpiān** ADV persistently; just, only; contrary to expectations

偏巧 **piānqiǎo** ADV by chance, as luck would have it

偏袒 **piāntǎn** V to side with

偏题 **piāntí** N trick question · MW 道

这次考试，老师**偏偏**出了**偏题**。*The teacher, contrary to expectations, put some trick questions on this written exam.*

偏向 **piānxiàng** V·N to favor, to be partial to; deviation · MW 个

偏心 **piānxīn** ADJ bias, partiality

傻瓜有些**偏心**大儿子，但绝不**偏袒**他的错误。*ShaGua is partial to his older son, but he has never approved of his mistakes.*

偏重 **piānzhòng** V to emphasize

**RELATED WORDS**

出偏差 258      纠偏 473

---

**1588** 停      U+505C      TM **14** FM 丿

**tíng** V to stop; to pause; to stop off/over, to stay; to park

停办 **tíngbàn** V to close down, to discontinue

停产 **tíngchǎn** V to stop production

停车 **tíngchē** V to stop (of a vehicle); to park

停车场 **tíngchēchǎng** N parking lot/area · MW 个

停当 **tíngdang** ADJ ready; settled

什么都准备**停当**，就等你的命令了。*All set, and awaiting your order.*

停电 **tíngdiàn** V to cut electricity; to cause a power outage

停顿 **tíngdùn** V to stop; to pause · MW 个

停工 **tínggōng** V to stop work, to shut down

停航 **tíngháng** V to suspend (flights, service)

停靠 **tíngkào** V to stop at (of a train, a ship, a plane, etc.)

停课 **tíngkè** V to suspend classes; to be suspended from class

停留 **tíngliú** V to stay temporarily, to stop over

停水 **tíngshuǐ** V to cut off the water supply

停歇 **tíngxiē** V to stop doing business; to stop for a rest

停学 **tíngxué** V to drop out of school; to expel from school

**停课**是警告；**停学**是处分。*Suspension from class is a warning, but expulsion is a punishment.*

停业 **tíngyè** V to close (a business)

经济危机引发商店**停业**，工厂**停产**，企业**停工**……*The economic crisis has caused many stores to close, factories to stop production, and businesses to shut down….*

停职 **tíngzhí** V to be suspended (from one's duties)

停止 **tíngzhǐ** V to stop, to halt

停滞 **tíngzhì** V to stagnate; to bog down

**RELATED WORDS**

暂停 1522      调停 1749      马不停蹄 247

---

**1589** 健      U+5065      TM **14** FM 丿

**jiàn** ADJ·V healthy; strong; to strengthen; to be good at

健康 **jiànkāng** ADJ in good health

学生不但需要生理的**健康**，还需要心理的**健康**。*Students need not only health of body but also health of mind.*

健美 **jiànměi** ADJ·N healthy and fit; bodybuilding

健全 **jiànquán** ADJ·V perfect; complete; sound; to strengthen

健身操 **jiànshēncāo** N fitness/bodybuilding exercise · MW 套

健身房 **jiànshēnfáng** N gymnasium; fitness room · MW 间

健忘 **jiànwàng** ADJ forgetful

健壮 **jiànzhuàng** ADJ healthy and strong; robust

傻瓜经常去**健身房**，所以身体很**健壮**。*ShaGua goes to the gym often, so he is very healthy.*

**RELATED WORDS**

保健 868      强健 1896      稳健 1925

## 1590 偶 U+5076 TM **14** FM 丿

**ǒu** N·ADV idol; image; even number; spouse; in pairs; by chance; casually

**偶尔 ǒu'ěr** ADV·ADJ occasionally; by chance; accidental

**偶发 ǒufā** ADJ accidental, chance

**偶合 ǒuhé** V to coincide

**偶然 ǒurán** ADJ·ADV accidental, chance; casual; accidentally, by chance
这种**偶合**是**偶然**发生的。 *Coincidences like these happen by chance.*

### RELATED WORDS

木偶 40    丧偶 521    玩偶 727
配偶 1647

## 1591 偷 U+5077 TM **14** FM 丿

**tōu** V·N·ADV to steal; to find time; to take time (off); to muddle through; thief; secretly, stealthily

**偷盗 tōudào** V to steal

**偷工减料 tōugōngjiǎnliào** EXP to take shortcuts and use less/shoddy material
学中文有方法，但**偷工减料**绝不是办法。
*There are some wise ways to study Chinese, but skimping on hard work or taking shortcuts is absolutely not the way.*

**偷空 tōukòng** V to take time off

**偷懒 tōulǎn** V to be lazy

**偷窃 tōuqiè** V to steal; to burglarize
**偷盗**一分钱是小偷，**偷窃**一个国家是总统。
*Someone who steals a penny is a thief; someone who steals a country is a president.*

**偷情 tōuqíng** V to have a secret affair with

**偷生 tōushēng** V to live without purpose

**偷税 tōushuì** V to evade taxes
傻瓜从不**偷税**。 *ShaGua has never evaded taxes.*

**偷偷 tōutōu** ADV secretly, stealthily

**偷偷摸摸 tōutōumōmō** EXP surreptitiously, on the sly

## 1592 催 U+50AC TM **14** FM 丿

**cuī** V to urge (someone) to do (something); to hurry, to speed up

**催促 cuīcù** V to urge; to press

傻瓜**催促**傻瓜太太学英文。 *ShaGua is pushing Mrs. ShaGua to study English.*

**催化 cuīhuà** V to catalyze (chemistry)

**催化剂 cuīhuàjì** N catalyst

**催泪弹 cuīlèidàn** N tear-gas grenade · MW 颗

**催眠 cuīmián** V to hypnotize; to lull to sleep
傻瓜太太说："学英文就是**催眠**。"
*Mrs. ShaGua says, "Studying English puts me to sleep."*

## 1593 饿 餓 U+997F TM **14** FM 丿

**è** ADJ·V hungry; to starve

### RELATED WORD

饥饿 890

## 1594 猜 U+731C TM **14** FM 丿

**cāi** V to guess; to suspect, to have doubts about

**猜测 cāicè** V to guess, to speculate

**猜忌 cāijì** V to be suspicious/jealous of

**猜谜 cāimí** V to guess a riddle
傻瓜最讨厌的就是**猜谜**。 *What ShaGua hates most is answering riddles.*

**猜拳 cāiquán** V to play a finger-guessing game

**猜想 cāixiǎng** V to suppose, to guess

**猜疑 cāiyí** V to suspect, to be suspicious of
你可以**猜测**别人，但不应该**猜疑**别人。
*You can speculate about others, but you shouldn't be suspicious of them without reason.*

## 1595 猴 U+7334 TM **14** FM 丿

**hóu** N·ADJ monkey; clever, smart; naughty and impish

**猴子 hóuzi** N monkey · MW 个、只

## 1596 姨 U+59E8 TM **14** FM 丿

**yí** N maternal aunt, mother's sister; wife's sister

**姨表 yíbiǎo** N maternal cousin · MW 个

**姨父 yífù** N maternal uncle, aunt's husband · MW 个、位

**1596 姨 yí** (continued)

**姨妈 yímā** N (married) maternal aunt ·
MW 个、位

**姨母 yímǔ** N (married) maternal aunt ·
MW 个、位

**RELATED WORDS**

阿姨 1249　　　　娘姨 1448

**1597 牌** U+724C TM **14** FM 丿

**pái** N bulletin board; plaque, sign; brand (name);
game pieces (playing cards, dominos, etc.)

**牌号 páihào** N store name · MW 个

**牌价 páijià** N list price · MW 个

**牌楼 páilou** N ceremonial gateway, decorated
archway · MW 个、座

**牌位 páiwèi** N memorial tablet/plaque · MW 个

**牌照 páizhào** N license plate · MW 个

**牌子 páizi** N tag; sign; brand, trademark ·
MW 张

**RELATED WORDS**

| 王牌 | 27 | 门牌 | 130 | 名牌 | 426 |
|---|---|---|---|---|---|
| 挂牌 | 796 | 盾牌 | 840 | 冒牌 | 989 |
| 纸牌 | 1103 | 路牌 | 1785 | | |

**1598 矮** U+77EE TM **14** FM 丿

**ǎi** ADJ short (in stature); low; of low rank/grade

**矮化 ǎihuà** V to belittle
有些人就是喜欢**矮化**傻瓜。 *Some people just like
to belittle ShaGua.*

**矮小 ǎixiǎo** ADJ short; low

**矮子 ǎizi** N short person; dwarf · MW 个

**RELATED WORD**

高矮 1611

**1599 稀** U+7A00 TM **14** FM 丿

**xī** ADJ rare; sparse; thin; watery

**稀薄 xībó** ADJ thin

**稀饭 xīfàn** N porridge, rice/millet gruel · MW 碗

**稀客 xīkè** N infrequent visitor · MW 位、名

**稀烂 xīlàn** ADJ completely mashed

**稀里糊涂 xīlihútú** EXP muddleheaded
别以为傻瓜**稀里糊涂**地当市长，他心里清楚
得很。 *Don't think that ShaGua is muddleheaded
as a mayor; everything is very clear in his mind.*

**稀奇 xīqí** ADJ strange; curious

**稀少 xīshǎo** ADJ few; scarce, sparse

**稀释 xīshì** V to dilute

**稀疏 xīshū** ADJ few and scattered

**稀松 xīsōng** ADJ sloppy

**稀有 xīyǒu** ADJ rare, unusual
十年前中文在美国还是一种**稀有**语种，
学习的人很**稀少**。 *Ten years ago, Chinese was
a rare language in America and few people
studied it.*

**RELATED WORD**

古稀 154

**1600 稍** U+7A0D TM **14** FM 丿

**shāo** ADV a little, slightly, somewhat

**稍微 shāowēi** ADV a little, slightly
你学中文能不能**稍微**努力一点儿？ *Do you think
you could study Chinese with a little more
concentration?*

**1601 统 統** U+7EDF TM **14** FM 丿

**tǒng** V·N·ADV to unite; to command; system;
[tube-shaped part of an object, clothing, etc.];
all; entirely

**统称 tǒngchēng** V·N to be collectively known as;
general term · MW 个
中华民族是中国境内56个民族的**统称**。
*The Chinese nationality is an umbrella term for
the 56 different ethnic groups in China.*

**统筹 tǒngchóu** V to make an overall plan,
to plan (a project) as a whole

**统共 tǒnggòng** ADV altogether, in all

**统计 tǒngjì** V·N to add up, to count; statistics;
census

**统计学 tǒngjìxué** N statistics · MW 门

**统帅 tǒngshuài** V·N to command; to lead;
commander in chief · MW 个、位、名
总统是三军的**统帅**。 *The president is the
commander in chief of the three armed services.*

**统率 tǒngshuài** V to command

**统统 tǒngtǒng** ADV completely, entirely, totally

统一 **tǒngyī** V·ADJ to unite; to integrate; unified

统一战线 **tǒngyīzhànxiàn** N united front

统治 **tǒngzhì** V to rule; to dominate; to run a country/area politically

少数民族曾数次**统治**了中国, 但最后都被中国文化同化了。 *Several times throughout history ethnic minorities ruled China, but they were finally assimilated into Chinese culture.*

**RELATED WORDS**

正统 76　　　　　血统 306
传统 452　　　　系统 842
总统 1330　　　　业务系统 94
组织系统 1106

---

**1602　辆** 輛　　U+8F86　TM **14** FM 丿

**liàng** MW [measure word for vehicles (bicycles, cars, trucks, etc.)]

**RELATED WORD**

车辆 114

---

**1603　毯**　　U+6BEF　TM **14** FM 丿

**tǎn** N rug; carpet; blanket

毯子 **tǎnzi** N carpet; blanket · MW 张、床

**RELATED WORD**

地毯 772

---

**1604　脉**　　U+8109　TM **14** FM 丿

**mài** N blood vessels; pulse; vein (of a leaf, an insect wing, etc.)

脉搏 **màibó** N pulse

摸一摸社会的**脉搏** *to have one's finger on the pulse of society*

脉冲 **màichōng** N pulse

**RELATED WORDS**

动脉 514　　　　静脉 1947

---

**1605　脓** 膿　　U+8113　TM **14** FM 丿

**nóng** N pus

脓包 **nóngbāo** N pustule, boil; worthless fellow · MW 个

这是一个**脓包**。 *This is a boil.*

他是一个**脓包**。 *He is a worthless fellow.*

脓疮 **nóngchuāng** N running sore · MW 个

脓肿 **nóngzhǒng** N abscess · MW 块

**RELATED WORD**

化脓 215

---

**1606　辞** 辭　　U+8F9E　TM **14** FM 丿

**cí** N·V diction, speech; to depart; to resign; to lay off, to dismiss

辞别 **cíbié** V to say good-bye

辞呈 **cíchéng** N letter of resignation · MW 份

傻瓜写好了**辞呈**, 准备**辞别**自己的同事。 *ShaGua has written his letter of resignation and is going to say good-bye to his colleagues.*

辞典 **cídiǎn** N dictionary · MW 本、部

辞书 **císhū** N dictionary · MW 部

辞退 **cítuì** V to dismiss, to fire

辞职 **cízhí** V to resign

我们昨天已经**辞退**你, 你今天再**辞职**就没有意义了。 *We fired you yesterday, so it doesn't make any sense for you to resign today.*

**RELATED WORDS**

告辞 428　　　　言辞 478
面辞 721　　　　致辞 982
推辞 1242　　　与世长辞 158
在所不辞 188

---

**1607　银** 銀　　U+94F6　TM **14** FM 丿

**yín** N silver (metal); money; silver (color)

银白色 **yínbáisè** N silver-white

银币 **yínbì** N silver coin · MW 枚

银行 **yínháng** N bank · MW 家

银河 **yínhé** N Milky Way · MW 条

银灰 **yínhuī** ADJ silver-gray

傻瓜已经有一些**银灰色**的头发。 *ShaGua has some silver-gray hairs.*

银子 **yínzi** N money; silver · MW 锭

**RELATED WORDS**

水银 159　　　　中国银行 86
世界银行 163

## 1608 锁 鎖  U+9501  TM **14** FM 丿

**suǒ** N·V lock; [like a lock]; chain; to lock (up); to knit

**锁定 suǒdìng** V to lock in/up

**锁紧 suǒjǐn** V to lock

**锁链 suǒliàn** N chain · MW 串

**锁钥 suǒyuè** N key · MW 个

学习中文是了解中国文化的一个重要**锁钥**。
*Studying Chinese is one key to understanding Chinese culture.*

### RELATED WORDS
加锁 463     封锁 815     连锁 958

## 1609 顾 顧  U+987E  TM **14** FM 丿

**gù** V·ADV·CONJ to turn around and look at; to look after, to attend to; to visit; to shop at; on the contrary; however, but

**顾此失彼 gùcǐshībǐ** EXP to attend to one thing and lose sight of another; to let things slip

你学中文又学日文，有点**顾此失彼**。
*Your studying Chinese and Japanese at the same time seems like you might be learning one at the expense of the other.*

**顾及 gùjí** V to take into account, to consider

**顾忌 gùjì** V to have scruples/misgivings

傻瓜干事情没有什么**顾忌**。*ShaGua doesn't have any misgivings about conducting business.*

**顾客 gùkè** N customer; client · MW 个、位、名

**顾虑 gùlǜ** N·V misgivings; apprehension; to worry

**顾名思义 gùmíngsīyì** EXP as the term suggests

**顾名思义**，傻瓜就是有点傻。*As the name implies, ShaGua is a little dumb.*

**顾全 gùquán** V to consider fully

**顾问 gùwèn** N adviser; consultant · MW 个、位、名

### RELATED WORDS
不顾 24        左顾右盼 113    只顾 160
后顾 310       环顾 369       回顾 391
照顾 1846      义无反顾 22

## 1610  敏  U+654F  TM **14** FM 丿

**mǐn** ADJ quick, agile; clever, quick-witted

**敏感 mǐngǎn** ADJ sensitive

**敏捷 mǐnjié** ADJ quick, agile, nimble

傻瓜不够**敏感**；但因练武，动作比较**敏捷**。
*ShaGua is not very sensitive, but due to his practice of martial arts, his movements are quite quick.*

**敏锐 mǐnruì** ADJ quick; sharp, acute, keen (of the senses)

### RELATED WORDS
灵敏 359        过敏 712

## 1611 高  U+9AD8  TM **14** FM 丶

**gāo** ADJ·N tall; high; above-average; loud; high-priced; height; altitude

**高矮 gāo'ǎi** N height

**高昂 gāo'áng** ADJ·V high (of voice, mood); to hold (one's head, etc.) high

**高材生 gāocáishēng** N brilliant student · MW 个、位、名

**高潮 gāocháo** N high tide; climax · MW 个

**高大 gāodà** ADJ huge, tall and big

**高档 gāodàng** ADJ high-end; top-quality

**高等 gāoděng** ADJ higher; advanced, high-ranking

**高低 gāodī** N·ADV height; sense of propriety, appropriateness; simply

有时傻瓜就是爱与人争**高低**。*Sometimes, ShaGua just likes to compete with others.*

傻瓜**高低**不听别人阻劝。*ShaGua simply refused to listen to others' advice no matter what.*

**高调 gāodiào** N big talk, bombast

**高度 gāodù** N height; altitude · MW 个

**高尔夫 gāo'ěrfū** N golf; golf ball

**高峰 gāofēng** N peak; height · MW 个、座

**高级 gāojí** ADJ senior; advanced, high-level

傻瓜从不打**高尔夫**，对他来说这种娱乐太**高级**了。*ShaGua has never played golf before; it's too high-class for him.*

**高见 gāojiàn** N your brilliant idea · MW 个

**高空 gāokōng** N high altitude

**高龄 gāolíng** N advanced/old age

**高明 gāomíng** ADJ·N brilliant; wise person, expert

你的主意真**高明**。*Your idea is really brilliant.*

你认为不行，就另请**高明**吧。*If you don't think it will work, then go find another expert.*

**高烧 gāoshāo** N high fever

**高深 gāoshēn** ADJ advanced; profound

**高手 gāoshǒu** N expert · MW 个、位、名

他是一名谈判**高手**。*He is an expert negotiator.*

**高寿** gāoshòu ADJ·N age; longevity

**高速** gāosù ADJ high-speed

**高温** gāowēn N high temperature

**高兴** gāoxìng ADJ·V glad; to be happy to, to enjoy

**高血压** gāoxuèyā N high blood pressure

傻瓜有时有点**高血压**。*Sometimes, ShaGua's blood pressure is a bit high.*

**高压** gāoyā N high pressure; high voltage

**高音** gāoyīn N high tone/register · MW 个

**高于** gāoyú ADV higher/greater than

他认为他的成绩**高于**班上的同学。*He believed his grade was higher than those of his classmates.*

**高原** gāoyuán N plateau · MW 个

**高中** gāozhōng N high school · MW 间、所

**RELATED WORDS**

| | | |
|---|---|---|
| 升高 47 | 兴高采烈 228 | 至高无上 244 |
| 自高自大 305 | 身高 604 | 男高音 757 |
| 抬高 1012 | 爬高 1099 | 登高 1521 |
| 最高 1541 | 提高 1554 | 唱高调 1562 |
| 德高望重 1923 | 云贵高原 80 | 莫测高深 999 |

---

**1612 商** U+5546 TM **14** FM 丶

**shāng** V·N to discuss; to consult; trade, commerce, business; trader; businessperson; quotient; second class of initials (ancient Chinese phonology)

**商标** shāngbiāo N trademark; brand; logo · MW 个

**商场** shāngchǎng N shopping center; commercial district/area · MW 家

这是这一带最大的**商场**。*This is the biggest mall in the area.*

他是**商场**的高手。*He is an expert in the business world.*

**商店** shāngdiàn N store, shop · MW 家

**商法** shāngfǎ N commercial law · MW 部

**商贩** shāngfàn N small retailer · MW 个、名

**商号** shānghào N store, shop (old business term) · MW 个

**商界** shāngjiè N business/commercial circles

**商量** shāngliáng V to discuss; to consult

**商品** shāngpǐn N commodity; merchandise · MW 个、种

**商谈** shāngtán V to discuss; to negotiate

**商务** shāngwù N business affairs

---

**商学院** shāngxuéyuàn N business college · MW 家

**商业** shāngyè N commerce, business

**商议** shāngyì V to discuss; to confer

**商学院**的教授们在**商议**修订**商法**的问题。*The professors at the business college are discussing revisions to commercial law.*

**RELATED WORDS**

| | | |
|---|---|---|
| 厂商 7 | 工商界 12 | 会商 295 |
| 行商 327 | 奸商 329 | 协商 397 |
| 经商 1110 | 客商 1316 | 智商 1581 |
| 通商 1757 | 电子商务 263 | |

---

**1613 亮** U+4EAE TM **14** FM 丶

**liàng** ADJ·V·N bright; loud and clear; enlightened; to shine; flash; show

**亮底** liàngdǐ V to reveal one's plan, position, etc.

你就**亮底**吧，别磨磨蹭蹭了。*Please tell us your position—no more dawdling.*

**亮点** liàngdiǎn N bright spot · MW 个

**亮度** liàngdù N brightness

**亮光** liàngguāng N light; beam/shaft of light · MW 道、束

**亮晶晶** liàngjīngjīng ADJ glittering, sparkling

**亮堂** liàngtang ADJ bright; enlightened

**亮相** liàngxiàng V to appear on stage / in public; to strike a stage pose; to declare one's position/views

你的**亮相**没什么**亮点**。*There were no bright spots in the announcement of your position.*

**RELATED WORDS**

| | | |
|---|---|---|
| 月亮 190 | 光亮 491 | 乌亮 601 |
| 洪亮 690 | 明亮 1035 | 雪亮 1369 |
| 响亮 1409 | 漂亮 1820 | 透亮 1826 |
| 擦亮 1985 | | |

---

**1614 离** 離 U+79BB TM **14** FM 丶

**lí** V to leave; to be away from; to do without; to defy; to violate

**离岸价** lí'ànjià N free on board (FOB) · MW 个

**离别** líbié V to leave; to be away from

**离婚** líhūn V to divorce

**离间** líjiàn V to alienate, to sow discord

**离解** líjiě V to dissociate

**1614 离 lí** (continued)

离境 **líjìng** V to leave (a country, a place)

离开 **líkāi** V to leave

傻瓜十来岁时**离开**中国。*ShaGua left China when he was about ten.*

离奇 **líqí** ADJ strange, odd

傻瓜的经历有些**离奇**。*ShaGua's autobiography is quite odd.*

离弃 **líqì** V to abandon, to desert

离任 **lírèn** V to leave one's post/job

有人希望傻瓜**离任**。*Some people hope that ShaGua will leave his position.*

离散 **lísàn** V to be dispersed/scattered/separated

离心 **líxīn** V to be at odds with the organization/leadership

离职 **lízhí** V to leave one's post/job

她是因为**离婚**才**离职**的。*She left her job because of the divorce.*

**RELATED WORDS**

| | | |
|---|---|---|
| 支离 92 | 分离 173 | 别离 1049 |
| 剥离 1377 | 背离 1380 | 等离子 1437 |
| 距离 1576 | 偏离 1587 | 脱离 1803 |
| 游离 1818 | 隔离 1910 | 撤离 1942 |
| 长距离 93 | 近距离 716 | 远距离 1184 |
| 背井离乡 1380 | | |

**1615** 廉    U+5EC9    TM **14** FM ＼

**lián** ADJ honest; incorruptible; cheap

廉耻 **liánchǐ** N integrity, sense of honor/shame

廉价 **liánjià** N cheap/inexpensive (goods)

廉洁 **liánjié** ADJ honest; incorruptible

有些人认为, 傻瓜之所以**廉洁**是因为他太傻。*Some people think ShaGua is incorruptible because of his stupidity.*

**RELATED WORD**

低廉 618

**1616** 竟    U+7ADF    TM **14** FM ＼

**jìng** V·ADJ·ADV to finish, to complete; throughout, whole; actually; eventually, in the end

竟然 **jìngrán** ADV unexpectedly, surprisingly

傻瓜**竟然**不会打领带。*Surprisingly, ShaGua still does not know how to tie a tie properly.*

**RELATED WORDS**

毕竟 540      究竟 1142

**1617** 痴    U+75F4    TM **14** FM ＼

**chī** ADJ·V silly; sentimental; idiotic; to be crazy/insane

痴呆 **chīdāi** ADJ dim-witted; stupid

痴情 **chīqíng** N·ADJ passion, infatuation; passionate, infatuated

痴心 **chīxīn** N·ADJ blind passion, infatuation; infatuated

据说, 有女子对傻瓜**痴情**(**痴心**)。*They say that some girls are infatuated with ShaGua.*

**RELATED WORD**

白痴 176

**1618** 宽 寬    U+5BBD    TM **14** FM ＼

**kuān** ADJ·N·V wide; broad; lenient; comfortable, well-off; width; to relax, to relieve; to extend

宽畅 **kuānchàng** ADJ worry-free

宽敞 **kuānchang** ADJ spacious, roomy

宽大 **kuāndà** ADJ spacious, wide; lenient

客厅很**宽大**。*The living room is very spacious.*

对敌人要**宽大** *to be merciful to the enemy*

宽待 **kuāndài** V to treat with leniency

宽度 **kuāndù** N width; breadth

宽广 **kuānguǎng** ADJ broad, extensive, vast

宽厚 **kuānhòu** ADJ muscular; generous

傻瓜心胸**宽广**, 待人**宽厚**。*ShaGua is kindhearted and treats people generously.*

宽阔 **kuānkuò** ADJ broad; spacious; open-minded

宽容 **kuānróng** ADJ·V tolerant; lenient; to forgive

宽恕 **kuānshù** V to forgive

傻瓜很能**宽容**、**宽恕**他人。*ShaGua is glad to be lenient and forgive others.*

宽慰 **kuānwèi** V to comfort, to console; to be relieved

宽心 **kuānxīn** V to feel relieved

宽裕 **kuānyù** ADJ well-off; plenty, ample

宽窄 **kuānzhǎi** N width

**RELATED WORDS**

加宽 463      放宽 964

## 1619 寄   U+5BC4   TM 14   FM ヽ

**jì** V to mail; to deposit; to place; to depend on

**寄存 jìcún** V to check/deposit (luggage, etc.)

**寄放 jìfàng** V to leave

我可以**寄放**行李在这儿吗？ *May I leave my luggage here?*

**寄居 jìjū** V to live (away from home)

**寄生 jìshēng** V to be a parasite

**寄生虫 jìshēngchóng** N parasite · MW 条

这是一条**寄生虫**。 *This is a parasite.*

这是社会的**寄生虫**。 *This is a parasite on our society.*

**寄宿 jìsù** V to lodge, to stay

**寄托 jìtuō** V to entrust to; to place/pin (one's hopes, feelings, etc.) on

**寄信 jìxìn** V to mail a letter

**寄予 jìyǔ** V to place/pin (one's hopes, feelings, etc.) on; to express

傻瓜把希望**寄托**在大儿子身上，傻瓜太太把理想**寄予**小儿子。 *ShaGua places his hopes on his older son, but Mrs. ShaGua places hers on her younger son.*

### RELATED WORDS

投寄 1008      邮寄 1046

## 1620 塞   U+585E   TM 14   FM ヽ

**sāi** V to stuff (something) into; to plug; to cork

**sài** N strategic location

要**塞** *fortification; fort*

**塞子 sāizi** N cork, stopper, plug · MW 个

### RELATED WORDS

耳塞 145      闭塞 677      阻塞 1042
堵塞 1226      鼻塞 1794

## 1621 窍 窾   U+7A8D   TM 14   FM ヽ

**qiào** N hole, aperture; crux, key

**窍门 qiàomén** N knack; secret (to doing something successfully) · MW 个

学中文的**窍门**就是更加努力地学习。 *The trick to studying Chinese is to study harder.*

### RELATED WORDS

七窍 34      诀窍 704

## 1622 望   U+671B   TM 14   FM ヽ

**wàng** V·N·PREP to gaze into the distance; to watch; to hope; hope; at; to

**望尘莫及 wàngchénmòjí** EXP too far behind to catch up; too late to do

他的中文太棒了，我**望尘莫及**。 *His Chinese is marvelous, and I am too far behind to catch up.*

**望风 wàngfēng** V to be on the lookout

**望梅止渴 wàngméizhǐkě** EXP to console oneself with false hopes

**望远镜 wàngyuǎnjìng** N telescope; binoculars · MW 副

**望子成龙 wàngzǐchénglóng** EXP to have high expectations for one's son(s)

### RELATED WORDS

失望 106    在望 188    名望 426
有望 439    守望 486    希望 613
仰望 620    祈望 717    看望 841
张望 1208    盼望 1255    展望 1274
探望 1404    欲望 1466    期望 1574
绝望 1706    渴望 1822    遥望 1830
愿望 1919    德高望重 1923

## 1623 婆   U+5A46   TM 14   FM ヽ

**pó** N old woman; mother-in-law, husband's mother

媒**婆** *female matchmaker*

**婆婆 pópo** N mother-in-law, husband's mother; maternal grandmother · MW 个、位、名

### RELATED WORDS

公婆 103    外婆 218    老婆 375
家婆 1315    媒婆 1623    老太婆 375

## 1624 烫 燙   U+70EB   TM 14   FM ヽ

**tàng** ADJ·V hot; scalding; to scald, to burn; to heat; to perm

**烫发 tàngfà** V to get/give a permanent; to perm

傻瓜太太喜欢**烫发**。 *Mrs. ShaGua likes to perm her hair.*

**烫伤 tàngshāng** N scald (injury)

### RELATED WORD

滚烫 1819

## 1625 曾　　U+66FE　TM **14** FM 丶

**céng** ADV once; ever

**zēng** N relationship between great-grandchildren and great-grandparents

**曾经 céngjīng** ADV once; ever
傻瓜**曾经**在许多家餐馆儿当过厨工。
*ShaGua once worked as a kitchen worker in several different restaurants.*

**RELATED WORDS**

不曾 24　　　　未曾 88

## 1626 党　黨　　U+515A　TM **14** FM 丶

**dǎng** N political party; Communist Party (in China); faction; clan

**党派 dǎngpài** N party; faction, clique · MW 个
傻瓜不属于任何**党派**。*ShaGua doesn't belong to any political parties.*

**党团 dǎngtuán** N Communist Party and Communist Youth League; parties and other organizations

**党委 dǎngwěi** N party committee · MW 个

**党员 dǎngyuán** N party member · MW 个、名

**党支部 dǎngzhībù** N party branch · MW 个

**党组 dǎngzǔ** N leading party group · MW 个

**RELATED WORDS**

余党 419　　　死党 510　　　朋党 1298
共产党 164　　中国共产党 86

## 1627 温　　U+6E29　TM **14** FM 丶

**wēn** N·ADJ·V temperature; warm; mild; tender; to warm up (leftovers, etc.); to review

**温饱 wēnbǎo** N adequate food and clothing

**温差 wēnchā** N temperature difference · MW 个
这里四季的**温差**不大。*The temperature difference between seasons is small here.*

**温床 wēnchuáng** N hotbed; garden frame · MW 个

**温带 wēndài** N temperate zone · MW 片

**温度 wēndù** N temperature

**温和 wēnhé** ADJ temperate (of climate); moderate; gentle/mild (of disposition, manner, speech, etc.)

温带的天气很**温和**。*The weather in temperate zones is mild.*
这人说话很**温和**。*This man's voice is very gentle.*

**温厚 wēnhòu** ADJ gentle, good-natured

**温暖 wēnnuǎn** ADJ·V warm; to warm

**温情 wēnqíng** N warmheartedness; tenderness

**温泉 wēnquán** N hot spring · MW 个

**温柔 wēnróu** ADJ gentle; tender

**温室 wēnshì** N greenhouse · MW 间
不要把孩子培养成**温室**里的花朵。*Don't raise kids to be flowers in a greenhouse (overprotected and sheltered).*

**温顺 wēnshùn** ADJ docile, meek

**温习 wēnxí** V to review
每天花一定的时间**温习**中文, 是学汉语的好方法。*Using a specific time to review Chinese every day is a good way to study Chinese.*

**RELATED WORDS**

气温 185　　　体温 325　　　低温 618
保温 868　　　室温 1139　　降温 1416
高温 1611　　旧梦重温 165

## 1628 淘　　U+6DD8　TM **14** FM 丶

**táo** V·ADJ to wash, to rinse; to dredge, to pan (for gold, etc.); to clean out; to consume; naughty

**淘金 táojīn** V·N to pan (for gold, etc.); panning (for gold, etc.)

**淘气 táoqì** ADJ naughty; mischievous
**淘气**的孩子将来可能反而有出息。*Naughty kids may have a bright future.*

**淘汰 táotài** V to eliminate (through selection/competition)

**淘洗 táoxǐ** V to wash

## 1629 淹　　U+6DF9　TM **14** FM 丶

**yān** V to flood; to tingle (from sweat); to delay

**淹没 yānmò** V to submerge, to flood

**淹死 yānsǐ** V to drown

## 1630 惯　慣　　U+60EF　TM **14** FM 丶

**guàn** ADJ·V habitual; to be used to, to be in the habit of; to indulge, to spoil

惯犯 **guànfàn** [N] habitual offender ·
[MW] 个、名

惯例 **guànlì** [N] convention; usual practice ·
[MW] 个

惯性 **guànxìng** [N] inertia

惯用 **guànyòng** [V] to consistently use/practice
这是那个**惯犯**的**惯用**手法。*This is a common tactic of an habitual offender.*

**RELATED WORDS**

习惯 84　　　看不惯 841　　　娇生惯养 882
司空见惯 357

---

**1631　说　說**　　U+8BF4　TM **14** FM 丶

**shuì** [V] to persuade

**shuō** [V·N] to say, to speak; to explain; to scold;
theory; doctrine

**yuè** [ADJ] happy

说白 **shuōbái** [N] spoken part (in an opera)

说不定 **shuōbudìng** [ADV] perhaps, maybe

说不过去 **shuōbuguòqù** [V] cannot be justified /
explained away

说不上 **shuōbushàng** [V] cannot say/tell

说穿 **shuōchuān** [V] to reveal, to tell what
(something) really is

说大话 **shuōdàhuà** [V] to brag, to boast
**说穿**了，你就是在**说大话**。*The truth is, you are just bragging about yourself.*

说到底 **shuōdàodǐ** [EXP] in the final analysis

说定 **shuōdìng** [V] to settle, to agree on

说法 **shuōfa** [N] version; wording; opinion;
justification · [MW] 个
他这样做总得有个**说法**吧。*He must give an explanation for what he has done.*

说服 **shuōfú** [V] to persuade, to convince
往往只有自己才能**说服**自己。*Very often, a man can only be convinced by himself.*

说话 **shuōhuà** [V·N] to speak, to talk; speech;
conversation
傻瓜**说话**有点儿口吃。*ShaGua speaks with a slight stutter.*

说谎 **shuōhuǎng** [V] to lie, to tell a lie

说理 **shuōlǐ** [V] to argue; to reason things out

说明 **shuōmíng** [V·N] to explain; to prove;
explanation · [MW] 个

说情 **shuōqíng** [V] to plead for (mercy, etc.) for;
to intercede for

说情是中国文化的一大社会现象。
*Interceding on someone's behalf is a popular social custom in Chinese culture.*

说笑 **shuōxiào** [V] to joke around

**RELATED WORDS**

劝说 255　　　再说 354　　　听说 414
传说 452　　　浅说 692　　　乱说 901
难说 974　　　邪说 981　　　胡说 1256
硬说 1524　　　假说 1586　　　游说 1818
演说 1821　　　能说会道 1873　　瞎说 1913
解说 1928　　　就是说 1836　　中篇小说 86
长篇小说 93

---

**1632　请　請**　　U+8BF7　TM **14** FM 丶

**qǐng** [V] to request, to ask; to invite; to engage;
please

请便 **qǐngbiàn** [V] to go ahead, to do as you wish

请假 **qǐngjià** [V] to ask for leave / time off
如果你不想学中文，**请便**！不要不**请假**就不来上课。*If you don't want to study Chinese, do as you wish! But don't miss class without asking for permission.*

请柬 **qǐngjiǎn** [N] written invitation · [MW] 张

请教 **qǐngjiào** [V] to consult, to ask for (someone's)
advice/opinion; please enlighten me

请客 **qǐngkè** [V] to entertain; to treat
**请客**也是中国文化的一大社会现象。
*Inviting others to dinner is also a popular social custom in Chinese culture.*

请求 **qǐngqiú** [V·N] to ask; request · [MW] 个
请您考虑我的这个**请求**。*Please consider my request.*

请示 **qǐngshì** [V] to request information; to ask for
instructions

请帖 **qǐngtiě** [N] written invitation · [MW] 张

请问 **qǐngwèn** [V] excuse me; may I ask

请勿 **qǐngwù** [V] please don't

请愿 **qǐngyuàn** [V] to petition (for action to be
taken); to ask the gods

**RELATED WORDS**

申请 150　　　宴请 1479　　　邀请 1983

---

**1633　炮**　　U+70AE　TM **14** FM 丶

**bāo** [V] to sauté

**pào** [N] cannon; firecracker

**1633** 炮  bāo/pào  (continued)

大炮  *cannon; one who talks big; blunt speaker*
这个家伙是个**大炮**。 *This guy is a big talker.*

**RELATED WORDS**

火炮 72　　　　礼炮 503　　　　放炮 964
鞭炮 1967　　　马后炮 247

---

**1634**   裤　褲　　　U+88E4　　TM **14**  FM 丶

kù  N  trousers, pants

**裤衩 kùchǎ**  N  underpants ・ MW 条

**裤带 kùdài**  N  belt ・ MW 条、根

**裤兜 kùdōu**  N  pants pocket ・ MW 个

**裤腰 kùyāo**  N  waistband (of trousers)

**裤子 kùzi**  N  trousers, pants ・ MW 条

这条**裤子**没有**裤兜**。 *These pants don't have any pockets.*

**RELATED WORDS**

长裤 93　　　内裤 191　　　衬裤 962
短裤 1452　　棉裤 1670　　开裆裤 26
牛仔裤 51　　卫生裤 82　　棉毛裤 1670

---

**1635**  瓶　　　U+74F6　　TM **14**  FM 丶

píng  N・MW  bottle; vase; jar; [measure word for wine, water, etc.]

**瓶盖 pínggài**  N  capsule ・ MW 个

**瓶颈 píngjǐng**  N  bottleneck ・ MW 个

这个**瓶颈**很奇特。 *The neck on this bottle is very odd.*

学中文的**瓶颈**是没有适用的字典。 *The bottleneck in studying Chinese is the lack of a proper Chinese dictionary.*

**瓶装 píngzhuāng**  ADJ  bottled

**瓶子 píngzi**  N  bottle; vase; jar ・ MW 个

**RELATED WORDS**

奶瓶 878　　　药瓶 1392　　　暖水瓶 1675

---

**1636**  部　　　U+90E8　　TM **14**  FM 丶

bù  N・V・MW  part; department; office; headquarters; troops; to preside; to command; [measure word for books, films, machines, etc.]

**部队 bùduì**  N  armed forces; army; troops ・ MW 支

**部分 bùfen**  N  part; section; (individual) share ・ MW 个

**部件 bùjiàn**  N  parts, components ・ MW 个

**部类 bùlèi**  N  category ・ MW 个

**部落 bùluò**  N  tribe; clan ・ MW 个

**部门 bùmén**  N  department; branch ・ MW 个

**部署 bùshǔ**  V  to deploy; to organize

学中文是美国政府的一个战略**部署**。 *The study of Chinese has become a strategic imperative of the United States government.*

**部属 bùshǔ**  N  subordinate; troops under one's command ・ MW 个

**部位 bùwèi**  N  position, place, location ・ MW 个

**部下 bùxià**  N  subordinate; troops under one's command ・ MW 个、名

**部长 bùzhǎng**  N  head (of a department) ・ MW 个、位、名

这个**部门**的**部长**没有几个**部下**。 *The head of this department doesn't have many subordinates.*

**RELATED WORDS**

干部 13　　　大部分 20　　　中部 86
支部 92　　　全部 172　　　内部 191
外部 218　　　面部 721　　　顶部 724
尾部 848　　　南部 986　　　局部 1069
背部 1380　　小卖部 61　　　俱乐部 1083
党支部 1626

---

**1637**   数　數　　　U+6570　　TM **14**  FM 丶

shǔ  V  to count; to rank; to be uppermost; to list, to enumerate; to blame

数(shǔ)数(shù) *to count numbers*
他数第一。 *He is considered Number One.*
历数罪状 *to air one's grievances*

shù  N・NUM  figure, number; fate; several

数(shǔ)数(shù) *to count numbers*
岁数 *ages*
劫数 *fate*
数次 *several times*

**数不胜数 shǔbùshèngshǔ**  EXP  innumerable

**数一数二 shǔyīshǔ'èr**  EXP  to count as one of the best; top one or two

他的中文在班里**数一数二**。 *His Chinese is among the best in the class.*

**数词 shùcí**  N  numeral ・ MW 个

数据 shùjù N data · MW 个

数据库 shùjùkù N database · MW 个

数控 shùkòng ADJ computer numerical controlled (CNC)

这家工厂有**数**不胜**数**的**数**控机床。 *There are countless computer numerical controlled machines in this factory.*

数量 shùliàng N quantity, amount

数码 shùmǎ N numeral; digital

数学 shùxué N mathematics

数字 shùzì N number, figure, digit · MW 个

数字化 shùzìhuà V to digitize

## RELATED WORDS

| | | |
|---|---|---|
| 小数点 61 | 少数 62 | 少数民族 62 |
| 中数 86 | 半数 127 | 无数 139 |
| 全数 172 | 代数 208 | 件数 209 |
| 为数 223 | 计数 240 | 多数 431 |
| 有数 439 | 如数 464 | 充数 652 |
| 单数 672 | 系数 842 | 度数 919 |
| 报数 1010 | 复数 1059 | 倍数 1084 |
| 凑数 1160 | 总数 1330 | 指数 1397 |
| 算数 1697 | 整数 1845 | 大多数 20 |
| 未知数 88 | 被除数 1517 | 被乘数 1517 |
| 心中有数 232 | 屈指可数 1071 | |

---

**1638 新**    U+65B0    TM **14** FM 丶

xīn N·V·ADJ·ADV new (people/things); to renew; new, up-to-date; brand new; newly married; newly

新产品 xīnchǎnpǐn N new product · MW 个

新陈代谢 xīnchéndàixiè EXP the old gives way to the new; metabolism

这个**新**产品是**新**陈代谢的结果。 *This new product is a result of the old giving way to the new.*

新春 xīnchūn N days following Chinese New Year's Day

新房 xīnfáng N bridal chamber; new house · MW 间

新华通讯社 Xīnhuá tōngxùnshè N Xin Hua News Agency

新婚 xīnhūn V to be newly wed

新纪元 xīnjìyuán N new era · MW 个

新疆 Xīnjiāng N Xinjiang Autonomous Region

新交 xīnjiāo V·N to be newly acquainted; new friend · MW 个

新郎 xīnláng N bridegroom · MW 个、位、名

新年 xīnnián N New Year

许多中国人喜欢在**新年**或**新春**时举办**新婚**典礼。 *Many Chinese like to be married on New Year's Day or on the lunar New Year's Day.*

新娘 xīnniáng N bride · MW 个、位、名

新奇 xīnqí ADJ novel; strange

新区 xīnqū N newly developed area · MW 个、片

新人 xīnrén N newly married couple, bride and bridegroom; newcomer; new talent · MW 个

新生 xīnshēng N freshman; new life; rebirth · MW 个

他是一名**新生**。 *He is a freshman.*

傻瓜在美国获得了**新生**。 *ShaGua started a new life in America.*

新生儿 xīnshēng'ér N newborn baby · MW 个

新式 xīnshì ADJ in the latest style; up-to-date

新闻 xīnwén N news · MW 条、则

新闻记者 xīnwénjìzhě N reporter, journalist · MW 个、位、名

新西兰 Xīnxīlán N New Zealand

新型 xīnxíng ADJ new type of, new-style

新颖 xīnyǐng ADJ new and original; novel

傻瓜不喜欢**新颖**或者**新奇**的东西。 *ShaGua doesn't like anything novel or original.*

## RELATED WORDS

| | | |
|---|---|---|
| 自新 305 | 革新 747 | 重新 839 |
| 创新 1131 | 刷新 1310 | 迎新 1360 |
| 崭新 1383 | 维新 1455 | 翻新 1989 |
| 广播新闻 23 | 头条新闻 128 | 桃色新闻 1243 |
| 耳目一新 145 | 推陈出新 1242 | |

---

**1639 剃**    U+5243    TM **14** FM 丶

tì V to shave

剃刀 tìdāo N razor · MW 把

剃胡子 tìhúzi V to shave

傻瓜每天用**剃刀**来**剃胡子**。 *ShaGua shaves with a razor every day.*

剃头 tìtóu V to have one's head shaved

## 1640 零 — U+96F6 · TM **15** · FM 一

**líng** [NUM·ADJ·V] zero; part; odd; spare, little extra; to wither

零点 **língdiǎn** [N] midnight; zero point

零度 **língdù** [N] zero

零分 **língfēn** [N] zero · [MW] 个

又考了一个零分 *another zero on a test*

零工 **línggōng** [N] odd job; part-time job · [MW] 个

零花 **línghuā** [V·N] to pay incidental expenses; pocket/spending money · [MW] 点

打点儿零工, 挣些零花。 *Do odd jobs to make some spending money.*

这些给你零花吧。 *Here's some spending money.*

零活 **línghuó** [N] odd job · [MW] 个

零件 **língjiàn** [N] spare parts · [MW] 个

零卖 **língmài** [V] to (sell) retail

零钱 **língqián** [N] small change; pocket money

零食 **língshí** [N] snack · [MW] 种

傻瓜不喜欢吃零食。 *ShaGua doesn't like snacks.*

零售 **língshòu** [V] to (sell) retail

零碎 **língsuì** [ADJ·N] fragmentary, piecemeal; odds and ends

零头 **língtóu** [N] small change

零星 **língxīng** [ADJ] odd; fragmentary; scattered

零用 **língyòng** [V·N] to spend money on minor purchases; pocket money

**RELATED WORDS**

丁零当郎 8　　七零八落 34

## 1641 雷 — U+96F7 · TM **15** · FM 一

**léi** [N] thunder

雷暴 **léibào** [N] thunderstorm · [MW] 阵、场

雷达 **léidá** [N] radar · [MW] 部、台

雷电 **léidiàn** [N] thunder and lightning; thunderbolt · [MW] 阵

雷击 **léijī** [V] to be struck by lightning

雷厉风行 **léilìfēngxíng** [EXP] at lightning speed

傻瓜太太做事从来都是**雷厉风行**, 傻瓜则常常思前想后。 *Mrs. ShaGua always finishes her work lickety-split, but ShaGua is prudent and deliberate.*

雷鸣 **léimíng** [N] roll of thunder; very loud sounds · [MW] 阵

雷声 **léishēng** [N] thunderclap; thunder · [MW] 阵

雷同 **léitóng** [V] to echo; to duplicate; identical

雷阵雨 **léizhènyǔ** [N] thundershower · [MW] 场

**RELATED WORDS**

打雷 289　　地雷 772　　春雷 855

## 1642 聚 — U+805A · TM **15** · FM 一

**jù** [V] to assemble, to get together; to amass, to accumulate

聚宝盆 **jùbǎopén** [N] treasure trove · [MW] 个

聚餐 **jùcān** [V] to have a dinner party; to dine together

汉语角的活动应该改为**聚餐**闲聊的形式。 *The activity of Chinese Corner should be changed to a conversational dinner party.*

聚光灯 **jùguāngdēng** [N] spotlight · [MW] 盏

聚合 **jùhé** [V] to get together

聚会 **jùhuì** [V·N] to get together; party; social gathering · [MW] 个

周末到了, 大家都忙**聚会**。 *The weekend is coming and people are busy preparing for parties.*

聚积 **jùjī** [V] to accumulate; to build up

她需要要**聚积**精力学中文！ *She must build up her energy to study Chinese.*

聚集 **jùjí** [V] to convene, to gather

聚焦 **jùjiāo** [V] to focus

聚精会神 **jùjīnghuìshén** [EXP] to focus all one's attention (on)

学中文必须**聚精会神**。 *You must concentrate when you study Chinese.*

聚众 **jùzhòng** [V] to gather a crowd

**RELATED WORDS**

会聚 295　　欢聚 366　　积聚 1097

## 1643 裂    U+88C2    TM **15** FM 一

**liè** V·N to crack, to break open, to split; breach; gap; split

裂缝 **lièfèng** N crack; crevice · MW 条、道

裂痕 **lièhén** N crack; fissure · MW 道
> 心灵上的**裂痕**是很难弥合的。 *A cleft in the heart is very difficult to close.*

裂开 **lièkāi** V to split open

裂口 **lièkǒu** N breach; gap; split · MW 条、道

裂纹 **lièwén** N crack; flaw · MW 条、道
> 杯子上有一道**裂纹**。 *There is a crack in the cup.*

**RELATED WORDS**

| | | |
|---|---|---|
| 分裂 173 | 压裂 201 | 决裂 340 |
| 断裂 1260 | 破裂 1374 | 割裂 1761 |
| 撕裂痛 1774 | 爆裂 1982 | |

## 1644 恐    U+6050    TM **15** FM 一

**kǒng** V·ADJ·ADV to threaten; panicky; probably

恐怖 **kǒngbù** ADJ fearful; horrible

恐吓 **kǒnghè** V to terrify; to threaten

恐慌 **kǒnghuāng** ADJ panicky; frightened, scared

恐惧 **kǒngjù** ADJ horrifying; fearsome

恐龙 **kǒnglóng** N dinosaur · MW 个、只

恐怕 **kǒngpà** V·ADV to fear, to dread; I'm afraid; probably
> 你这样学中文，**恐怕**不行。 *I'm afraid your way of studying Chinese won't work.*
> **恐怕**傻瓜收到的是**恐吓**信。 *I'm afraid the letter ShaGua received may have been a threatening one.*

## 1645 肆    U+8086    TM **15** FM 一

**sì** NUM four (capital form of the Chinese numeral)

**RELATED WORD**

放肆 964

## 1646 群    U+7FA4    TM **15** FM 一

**qún** N·MW crowd; group; [measure word for people, birds, bees, cows, etc.]

群岛 **qúndǎo** N group of islands, archipelago · MW 个

群集 **qúnjí** V to flock together, to swarm

群落 **qúnluò** N community · MW 个

群情 **qúnqíng** N public sentiment

群体 **qúntǐ** N community; colony; group · MW 个

群众 **qúnzhòng** N the masses; non-Party members · MW 批

**RELATED WORDS**

| | | |
|---|---|---|
| 人群 4 | 合群 296 | 种群 893 |
| 超群 1684 | | |

## 1647 配    U+914D    TM **15** FM 一

**pèi** V·N to marry (of a couple); to mate; to mix; to measure up to, to be worthy of; to allocate; to fit; to match; spouse

配备 **pèibèi** V·N to allocate; to provide; equipment

配对 **pèiduì** V to match (up), to make a pair
> 傻瓜和傻瓜太太正好**配对**。 *ShaGua and Mrs. ShaGua are a match.*

配方 **pèifāng** N prescription · MW 个

配合 **pèihé** V to coordinate; to complement, to match; to fit

配件 **pèijiàn** N accessories; spare parts · MW 个

配角 **pèijué** N supporting role · MW 个
> 傻瓜认为：市长是一个为各个部门提供各种支持的**配角**。 *ShaGua believes that the mayor's role is one of support, providing assistance to every department.*

配料 **pèiliào** V·N to combine ingredients; ingredients (in a recipe)

配偶 **pèiǒu** N spouse, husband, wife · MW 个

配套 **pèitào** V to form a (complete) set

配置 **pèizhì** V·N to allocate; to deploy (forces); configuration

配种 **pèizhǒng** V to mate; to breed

**RELATED WORDS**

| | | |
|---|---|---|
| 支配 92 | 元配 138 | 分配 173 |
| 交配 222 | 匹配 269 | 修配 870 |
| 装配 1476 | 调配 1749 | 调配 1749 |

## 1648 酬    U+916C    TM **15** FM 一

**chóu** N·V payment; to repay a favor; to reward; to socialize (with); to fulfill

酬报 **chóubào** V to reward

**1648 酬 chóu** (continued)

**酬金 chóujīn** [N] monetary reward; remuneration · [MW] 笔

**酬劳 chóuláo** [V·N] to thank (someone) with a gift; to repay; reward · [MW] 笔

这是你加班的**酬劳**。 *This is your reward for working overtime.*

**酬谢 chóuxiè** [V] to thank (someone) with a gift; to repay

**RELATED WORDS**

应酬 334     报酬 1010

---

**1649 患**     U+60A3     TM **15** FM |

**huàn** [V·N] to contract (an illness); to suffer from; to worry; peril; disaster

**患病 huànbìng** [V] to get sick

**患得患失 huàndéhuànshī** [EXP] to worry about personal gains and losses

**患难 huànnàn** [N] trials and tribulations, adversity

共**患难**容易, 共富贵难。 *It is easy to suffer together, but difficult to share riches and honor with one another.*

**患者 huànzhě** [N] sufferer; patient · [MW] 个、名

**RELATED WORDS**

后患 310     隐患 1912     内忧外患 191

---

**1650 截**     U+622A     TM **15** FM |

**jié** [V·MW] to cut, to sever; to chop; to stop, to block; [measure word for pieces/sections/lengths of objects (branches, wood, chalk, etc.)]

**截断 jiéduàn** [V] to cut off

**截获 jiéhuò** [V] to intercept, to cut off and capture

**截击 jiéjī** [V] to intercept

**截然 jiérán** [ADV] sharply; completely

我们两人的看法**截然**相反。 *The two of us have completely different ideas.*

**截至 jiézhì** [V] until, up to; by

**截**至这个学期, 他还没有女朋友。 *Until this semester, he never had a girlfriend.*

**RELATED WORDS**

拦截 576     直截了当 609     斩钉截铁 646

---

**1651 置**     U+7F6E     TM **15** FM |

**zhì** [V] to put; to set up, to establish; to buy

**置办 zhìbàn** [V] to buy, to purchase

**置备 zhìbèi** [V] to purchase (equipment, furniture, etc.)

**置备**办公用具 *to purchase office equipment*

**置换 zhìhuàn** [V] to displace (chemistry); to replace

**置身 zhìshēn** [V] to place oneself, to take up a position

**置疑 zhìyí** [V] to doubt

傻瓜做出决定后, 就不容别人**置疑**。 *After ShaGua makes a decision, he does not allow others to doubt him.*

**置之不理 zhìzhībùlǐ** [EXP] to ignore; to wave/brush aside

**RELATED WORDS**

处置 217     布置 309     位置 323
弃置 480     安置 487     设置 1179
添置 1346     装置 1476     配置 1647
本末倒置 90

---

**1652 骂** 罵     U+9A82     TM **15** FM |

**mà** [V] to abuse; to insult, to curse; to scold

**骂街 màjiē** [V] to shout and scream in public

**骂人 màrén** [V] to swear (at people)

傻瓜打过人, 但从不**骂人**。 *ShaGua has hit others before, but he's never sworn at people.*

**骂人话 màrénhuà** [N] abusive language; swearword · [MW] 句

**RELATED WORDS**

责骂 525     臭骂 1076     咒骂 1387
痛骂 1725     谩骂 1887

---

**1653 累**     U+7D2F     TM **15** FM |

**léi** [ADJ] haggard; clusters of; wordy

**lěi** [V·ADV] to accumulate; to involve; to implicate; repeatedly; continuously

**lèi** [ADJ·V] tired, weary; to tire; to wear out; to work hard

**累累 léiléi** [ADJ] clusters/heaps of; countless

果实**累累** *fruit growing in clusters*

**累赘 léizhuì** [N·V·ADJ] nuisance; to burden; cumbersome

累积 **lěijī** V to accumulate

累计 **lěijì** V to add up; to accumulate

累计一共三块钱。 *It is three dollars altogether.*

累累 **lěilěi** ADJ·ADV countless; again and again

罪行累累 *to have a long criminal record*

**RELATED WORDS**

劳累 764          连累 958          积累 1097
拖累 1396         日积月累 96

---

**1654 蒙** 矇濛懞 U+8499          TM **15** FM |

**mēng** (矇) V·ADJ to cheat, to deceive; to make a wild guess; unconscious

**méng** (矇濛懞) V·N to cover; to encounter; to receive; ignorance

**Měng** N Mongolian

蒙蔽 **méngbì** V to deceive, to fool

蒙混 **ménghùn** V to deceive, to mislead

蒙混过关 **ménghùnguòguān** EXP to slip by; to gloss over one's faults

你的口试老师已录音，你不可能蒙混过关。 *Your teacher recorded your oral quiz, so you won't be able to trick her.*

蒙昧 **méngmèi** ADJ uncivilized; ignorant

蒙难 **méngnàn** V to be confronted by danger; to meet with disaster

蒙受 **méngshòu** V to suffer, to sustain, to incur

蒙古 **Měnggǔ** N Mongolia

傻瓜一直想去看看蒙古的大草原。 *ShaGua has been thinking about visiting the Mongolian steppes.*

**RELATED WORDS**

内蒙古 191          灰蒙蒙 198          启蒙 657

---

**1655 蒜** U+849C          TM **15** FM |

**suàn** N garlic

蒜瓣 **suànbàn** N garlic clove · MW 片

蒜苗 **suànmiáo** N garlic sprouts · MW 棵

蒜头 **suàntóu** N garlic bulb · MW 个

据说，吃蒜头对身体有好处。 *They say garlic is good for your health.*

蒜油 **suànyóu** N garlic oil · MW 瓶

**RELATED WORD**

装蒜 1476          鸡毛蒜皮 1373

---

**1656 葬** U+846C          TM **15** FM |

**zàng** V to bury

葬礼 **zànglǐ** N funeral ceremony; burial rites

葬身 **zàngshēn** V to be buried

葬送 **zàngsòng** V to ruin; to put an end to

不要葬送了自己的未来。 *Don't ruin your own future.*

**RELATED WORDS**

下葬 10          火葬 72          埋葬 1002
送葬 1188        墓葬 1545        陪葬 1568

---

**1657 惹** U+60F9          TM **15** FM |

**rě** V to cause (trouble, a problem); to stir up, to provoke; to bring upon oneself, to incur

惹火烧身 **rěhuǒshāoshēn** EXP to court disaster; to be asking for trouble

惹祸 **rěhuò** V to court disaster; to stir up trouble

你老是惹祸！ *You're always stirring up trouble.*

惹气 **rěqì** V to get angry

惹事 **rěshì** V to stir up trouble

惹事生非 **rěshìshēngfēi** EXP to stir up trouble, to provoke a dispute

你老是这样惹事生非，必然会惹火烧身。 *You always provoke disputes; you must be asking for trouble.*

**RELATED WORD**

招惹 1232

---

**1658 挪** U+632A          TM **15** FM |

**nuó** V to move, to shift

挪动 **nuódòng** V to move, to shift

傻瓜的汽车停在禁停区，警察让他把车挪动一下。 *ShaGua parked his car in a no-parking zone and the police asked him to move.*

挪威 **Nuówēi** N Norway

挪用 **nuóyòng** V to embezzle/divert (funds)

---

**1659 挽** U+633D          TM **15** FM |

**wǎn** V to draw; to pull (a cart, etc.); to hold; to roll up; to lament the death of

挽歌 **wǎngē** N dirge; elegy · MW 首、曲

**1659** 挽 **wǎn** (continued)

挽回 **wǎnhuí** [V] to retrieve/redeem
(an unfavorable situation)

我们需要做些事情去**挽回**面子。 *We must do
something to save face.*

挽救 **wǎnjiù** [V] to save, to rescue

挽留 **wǎnliú** [V] to persuade (someone) to stay

学生们都想**挽留**那个代课老师。 *Students want
that substitute teacher to stay.*

---

**1660** 捌      U+634C      TM **15** FM |

**bā** [NUM] eight (capital form of the Chinese
numeral)

---

**1661** 掏      U+638F      TM **15** FM |

**tāo** [V] to pull/take out (with the hand); to dig,
to scoop out

掏出 **tāochū** [V] to draw out; to hollow out

掏腰包 **tāoyāobāo** [V] to pick (someone's) pocket;
to pay out of one's own pocket

这次我得**掏腰包**请客了。 *This time, I have to foot
the bill for my guests.*

---

**1662** 握      U+63E1      TM **15** FM |

**wò** [V] to hold, to grasp; to shake (hands)

握别 **wòbié** [V] to shake hands at parting

握力 **wòlì** [N] (strength of one's) grip

握拳 **wòquán** [V] to make a fist

握手 **wòshǒu** [V] to shake hands

在中国，**握手**不一定表示成交，喝酒反而可能
成交。 *In China, a handshake may not necessarily
close a deal, whereas drinking may actually be
more effective.*

**RELATED WORDS**

把握 1006      紧握 1537      掌握 1734

---

**1663** 搜      U+641C      TM **15** FM |

**sōu** [V] to look for, to search; to rummage

搜查 **sōuchá** [V] to search; to ransack

---

搜刮 **sōuguā** [V] to extort

搜集 **sōují** [V] to collect, to gather

傻瓜**搜集**李小龙的电影。 *ShaGua has been
collecting Bruce Lee movies.*

搜身 **sōushēn** [V] to conduct a body search

搜索 **sōusuǒ** [V] to search/hunt for

搜寻 **sōuxún** [V] to hunt for, to seek

学生在网上**搜寻**研究资料。 *Students are
searching for research materials online.*

---

**1664** 摇      U+6447      TM **15** FM |

**yáo** [V] to shake; to rock

摇摆 **yáobǎi** [V] to sway, to swing; to wave

摇臂 **yáobì** [N] rocker arm (machinery)

摇动 **yáodòng** [V] to wave; to shake

摇滚乐 **yáogǔnyuè** [N] rock and roll

傻瓜一听到**摇滚乐**就**摇头**。 *Whenever ShaGua
hears rock and roll music, he shakes his head.*

摇晃 **yáohuàng** [V] to rock, to sway

摇篮 **yáolán** [N] cradle, place of origin · [MW] 个

傻瓜是个弃婴，没有母亲边唱儿歌，
边摇**摇篮**的经历。 *ShaGua was abandoned as
a baby; his mother never sang to him while rocking
his cradle.*

摇钱树 **yáoqiánshù** [N] ready source of money ·
[MW] 棵

摇头 **yáotóu** [V] to shake one's head

摇椅 **yáoyǐ** [N] rocking chair · [MW] 张

**RELATED WORD**

动摇 514

---

**1665** 摸      U+6478      TM **15** FM |

**mō** [V] to touch, to stroke; to fish out; to feel/find
one's way

摸不透 **mōbutòu** [V] to wonder; to be puzzled

傻瓜看起来很简单，但又让人**摸不透**。
*ShaGua looks very simple, but he is a puzzle
to some people.*

摸彩 **mōcǎi** [V] to draw numbers/tickets to
determine the prize winners in a raffle/lottery

摸底 **mōdǐ** [V] to sound (someone) out; to know
the real situation

明天要有一次**摸底**考试。 *There will be an
assessment test tomorrow.*

摸清底细 **mōqīngdǐxì** V to get to the bottom of the story

摸索 **mōsuǒ** V to grope, to fumble; to do things slowly

**RELATED WORDS**

捉摸 1239                    触摸 1875
偷偷摸摸 1591

---

**1666** 哪        U+54EA        TM **15** FM |

**nǎ** QPRON which, what; how can/could

哪个 **nǎgè** QPRON which

哪里 **nǎli** QPRON where; wherever

哪能 **nǎnéng** QPRON how can

你哪能学中文不学汉字呢？ *How can you study Chinese without studying characters?*

哪怕 **nǎpà** CONJ even; even if/though; no matter how

哪怕再晚，你也得做完作业。 *No matter how late it is, you must finish your homework.*

哪儿 **nǎr** QPRON where; anywhere

哪些 **nǎxiē** QPRON who; which, what

搬家前你必须想好：哪些东西放在哪里？ *Before you move, you have to consider which things will go where.*

哪样 **nǎyàng** QPRON what kind (of); whatever

---

**1667** 喂        U+5582        TM **15** FM |

**wèi** ONOM·V hello; hey; to feed

喂奶 **wèinǎi** V to breast-feed

喂养 **wèiyǎng** V to feed; to raise

母乳喂养的孩子更健康。 *Children who are breast-fed will be healthier.*

---

**1668** 喊        U+55A8        TM **15** FM |

**hǎn** V to shout, to yell; to call (someone); to address (someone)

喊叫 **hǎnjiào** V to shout; to cry out

喊冤 **hǎnyuān** V to cry out a grievance

你别喊冤了，你的中文只能得B。 *Don't come crying to me; your Chinese only deserves a "B."*

**RELATED WORDS**

呼喊 779                    贼喊捉贼 1254

---

**1669** 梯        U+68AF        TM **15** FM |

**tī** N ladder; steps; stairs

梯队 **tīduì** N echelon · MW 支

梯形 **tīxíng** N trapezoid · MW 个

108是梯形教室。 *Room 108 is a trapezoid-shaped classroom.*

梯子 **tīzi** N ladder; stepladder · MW 架

我需要一架梯子。 *I need a ladder.*

**RELATED WORDS**

电梯 263        扶梯 404        阶梯 590
楼梯 1567      滑梯 1884

---

**1670** 棉        U+68C9        TM **15** FM |

**mián** N cotton; cotton floss

棉袄 **mián'ǎo** N cotton-padded jacket · MW 件

棉被 **miánbèi** N cotton-padded quilt, comforter · MW 床

棉布 **miánbù** N cotton; cotton cloth · MW 块、匹

许多人喜欢穿纯棉的棉布衣服。 *Many people like to wear 100% cotton clothes.*

棉纺 **miánfǎng** N cotton spinning · MW 锭

棉花 **miánhua** N cotton; raw cotton · MW 朵、团

棉裤 **miánkù** N cotton-padded trousers/pants · MW 条

棉毛裤 **miánmáokù** N cotton trousers (worn as underwear) · MW 条

棉纱 **miánshā** N cotton yarn · MW 锭

棉絮 **miánxù** N cotton fiber/batting · MW 团

棉织品 **miánzhīpǐn** N cotton goods · MW 件

**RELATED WORDS**

石棉 144                    药棉 1392

---

**1671** 棺        U+68FA        TM **15** FM |

**guān** N coffin

棺材 **guāncai** N coffin · MW 副

---

**1672** 榨        U+69A8        TM **15** FM |

**zhà** V to press; to extract

榨出 **zhàchū** V to squeeze out

**1672 榨 zhà** (continued)

**榨取 zhàqǔ** V to squeeze; to swindle, to defraud

**榨汁机 zhàzhījī** N juicer · MW 个

傻瓜太太用**榨汁机**来**榨取**果汁。
*Mrs. ShaGua is using a juicer to squeeze juice.*

**RELATED WORD**

压榨 201

---

**1673　模**　　　U+6A21　　TM **15** FM |

**mó** N·V model; pattern; to imitate

**mú** N mold; pattern

**模范 mófàn** N model; fine example · MW 个、位、名

**模仿 mófǎng** V to imitate; to model oneself on

学汉语要**模仿**中国人说话，减少怪腔怪调。
*You should mimic Chinese people speaking Chinese to minimize your funny accent.*

**模糊 móhu** ADJ·V blurred; dim; to blur; to confuse

**模拟 mónǐ** V to imitate; to simulate

我的**模拟**考试没考好。*I didn't do well on my simulated practice test.*

**模式 móshì** N model; pattern · MW 个

**模特 mótè** N model · MW 个、名

**模型 móxíng** N model; pattern · MW 个

**模具 mújù** N mold; pattern · MW 个、副、套

**模样 múyàng** N·ADV look, appearance; trend; approximately, about

**模子 múzi** N matrix, mold, pattern

**RELATED WORDS**

| | |
|---|---|
| 怪模怪样 696 | 规模 1098 |
| 装模作样 1476 | 大规模 20 |

---

**1674　晴**　　　U+6674　　TM **15** FM |

**qíng** ADJ sunny, clear; fine

**晴空 qíngkōng** N clear sky

**晴朗 qínglǎng** ADJ sunny

**晴天 qíngtiān** N sunny day · MW 个

今天是大**晴天**。*Today is a very sunny day.*

**晴雨计 qíngyǔjì** N barometer · MW 个

---

**1675　暖**　　　U+6696　　TM **15** FM |

**nuǎn** ADJ warm

**暖房 nuǎnfáng** N greenhouse · MW 间

**暖烘烘 nuǎnhōnghōng** ADJ nice and warm

**暖壶 nuǎnhú** N thermos bottle · MW 只

**暖和 nuǎnhuo** ADJ·V warm; to warm up

今天是晴天，很**暖和**。*Today is a sunny day and very warm.*

**暖流 nuǎnliú** N warm current · MW 股

**暖气 nuǎnqì** N central heating; warm air

傻瓜曾经给人修过**暖气**。*ShaGua was once a heating system repairman.*

**暖色 nuǎnsè** N warm color

**暖水瓶 nuǎnshuǐpíng** N thermos bottle · MW 只

**RELATED WORDS**

| | | |
|---|---|---|
| 水暖工 159 | 供暖 459 | 冷暖 494 |
| 取暖 520 | 温暖 1627 | |

---

**1676　暗**　　　U+6697　　TM **15** FM |

**àn** ADJ dark; dim; underhand; secret, clandestine

**暗暗 àn'àn** ADV secretly; inwardly

**暗藏 àncáng** V to hide, to conceal

**暗娼 ànchāng** N unlicensed prostitute · MW 个、名

**暗淡 àndàn** ADJ dim, faint; dismal, depressing

色彩**暗淡**。*The color is faint.*

生活**暗淡**。*Life is hopeless.*

**暗地里 àndìli** ADV secretly

他**暗地里**学了三年中文。*He has secretly studied Chinese for three years.*

**暗沟 àngōu** N underground drain · MW 条

**暗害 ànhài** V to murder; to stab in the back

**暗含 ànhán** V to imply

**暗号 ànhào** N secret signal · MW 个

**暗礁 ànjiāo** N submerged reef · MW 块

**暗色 ànsè** N dark color

**暗杀 ànshā** V to murder in a premeditated fashion; to assassinate

**暗示 ànshì** V·N to hint; suggestion, hint · MW 个

傻瓜常常不能领会**暗示**，所以最好把话挑明了。
*ShaGua doesn't usually take a hint; you had better speak directly.*

暗影 **ànyǐng** N shadow · MW 个
暗喻 **ànyù** N metaphor · MW 个
暗中 **ànzhōng** N·ADV dark; secretly, surreptitiously

**RELATED WORDS**

灰暗 198          阴暗 1041          昏暗 1058
幽暗 1538

---

**1677 院**          U+9662          TM **15** FM |

**yuàn** N yard; courtyard; public institution; college; academy; hospital

院士 **yuànshì** N academician · MW 个、位、名
院子 **yuànzi** N courtyard · MW 个

**RELATED WORDS**

| | | |
|---|---|---|
| 大院 20 | 出院 258 | 后院 310 |
| 住院 324 | 议院 350 | 戏院 365 |
| 医院 389 | 妓院 629 | 宅院 665 |
| 法院 686 | 学院 1155 | 庭院 1326 |
| 剧院 1468 | 影院 1918 | 工学院 12 |
| 众议院 175 | 电影院 263 | 国务院 542 |
| 参议院 600 | 科学院 642 | 疯人院 1147 |
| 商学院 1612 | 敬老院 1689 | 妇产医院 465 |

---

**1678 陷**          U+9677          TM **15** FM |

**xiàn** V·N to sink; to cave in; to frame (on a false charge); to be captured (of a city, etc.); trap; defect, fault

陷害 **xiànhài** V to frame (on a false charge)
陷阱 **xiànjǐng** N trap; pitfall · MW 个
文化的差异可能成为人们交往的**陷阱**。 *Cultural differences can create pitfalls during interaction.*
陷落 **xiànluò** V to sink, to subside
陷入 **xiànrù** V to sink/fall into; to get bogged down (in)

**RELATED WORDS**

缺陷 1305          塌陷 1903

---

**1679 翅**          U+7FC5          TM **15** FM |

**chì** N wing; fin; [like a wing]

翅膀 **chìbǎng** N wing; [like a wing] · MW 对
想象力是创造的**翅膀**。 *Imagination constitutes the wings of creativity.*

---

**RELATED WORDS**

鱼翅 843          展翅 1274

---

**1680 睁**          U+7741          TM **15** FM |

**zhēng** V to open (one's eyes)

睁不开眼 **zhēngbùkāiyǎn** EXP to hardly open one's eyes
阳光让人**睁不开眼**。 *Sunshine makes it hard for people to open their eyes.*
睁眼 **zhēngyǎn** V to open one's eyes

**RELATED WORD**

眼睁睁 1570

---

**1681 蛇**          U+86C7          TM **15** FM |

**shé** N snake; smuggler

蛇毒 **shédú** N snake venom
**蛇毒**也可以成为中药。 *Even venom can be used in traditional Chinese medicine.*
蛇蝎 **shéxiē** N vicious people (LIT snakes and scorpions)
蛇形 **shéxíng** ADJ snakelike; S-shaped

**RELATED WORDS**

画蛇添足 719          毒蛇 1211

---

**1682 蜂**          U+8702          TM **15** FM |

**fēng** N·ADV bee; wasp; in swarms

蜂巢 **fēngcháo** N honeycomb · MW 个
蜂毒 **fēngdú** N bee poison
蜂房 **fēngfáng** N beehive · MW 个
蜂蜡 **fēnglà** N beeswax · MW 块
蜂蜜 **fēngmì** N honey · MW 瓶
中医把**蜂蜜**、**蜂蜡**, 甚至**蜂巢**都当成可治病的药。 *Honey, beeswax, and even honeycomb are all considered to be traditional Chinese medicine.*
蜂鸟 **fēngniǎo** N hummingbird · MW 只
蜂王 **fēngwáng** N queen bee · MW 只
蜂窝 **fēngwō** N honeycomb · MW 个

**RELATED WORD**

蜜蜂 1929

## 1683 雌   U+96CC   TM 15   FM |

**cí** N female

**雌雄 cíxióng** N male and female

决一**雌雄** to determine the winners and losers
(LIT to discern who is a male and who is a female)

**雌性 cíxìng** N female

## 1684 超   U+8D85   TM 15   FM |

**chāo** V·ADJ to exceed; to overtake, to surpass; to transcend; ultra-; super-; extra-

**超产 chāochǎn** V to exceed a production goal

**超车 chāochē** V to overtake (another car)

**超出 chāochū** V to exceed; to overstep

**超额 chāo'é** V to exceed a quota

**超过 chāoguò** V to exceed; more than

**超级 chāojí** ADJ super-; extraordinary

**超假 chāojià** V to overstay one's leave / time off

这个学生又**超假**了。 This student overstayed her time off again.

**超龄 chāolíng** V to be overage / too old

**超前 chāoqián** ADJ ahead of one's time; advanced; in the lead

**超群 chāoqún** V to be head and shoulders above the rest

**超然 chāorán** ADJ aloof; taking neither side

在政治上，傻瓜比较**超然**，既不是共和党也不是民主党。 Regarding politics, ShaGua takes neither a Republican nor a Democratic point of view.

**超人 chāorén** N superman · MW 个

**超速 chāosù** V to exceed the speed limit

**超音速 chāoyīnsù** N supersonic speed

**超越 chāoyuè** V to exceed; to surpass

**超重 chāozhòng** V to overload

**超自然 chāozìrán** ADJ supernatural

对中国人来说，"天" 是一个**超自然**的概念。 "The Heavens" is a supernatural concept for Chinese people.

## 1685 野   U+91CE   TM 15   FM |

**yě** N·ADJ open country; border; out of power; wild, uncultivated; untamed; rude; unruly

田**野** open country

分**野** line of demarcation

在**野**党 party not in power

粗**野** rude

孩子心玩**野**了 child who plays so much that he/she can't concentrate on studying

**野菜 yěcài** N (edible) wild herb · MW 棵、把

**野餐 yěcān** V·N to picnic; picnic · MW 次

**野草 yěcǎo** N weeds · MW 棵

**野果 yěguǒ** N wild fruit · MW 个

**野花 yěhuā** N wildflowers · MW 朵

**野蛮 yěmán** ADJ uncivilized; cruel, brutal

**野猫 yěmāo** N wildcat · MW 只

**野牛 yěniú** N wild ox · MW 头

**野人 yěrén** N savage person · MW 个

**野生 yěshēng** ADJ wild; uncultivated

**野兽 yěshòu** N wild animal · MW 个

**野兔 yětù** N hare · MW 只

**野外 yěwài** N open country; field

傻瓜太太很喜欢到**野外**去**野餐**。 Mrs. ShaGua loves to picnic in the country.

**野心 yěxīn** N wild ambition/scheme · MW 个

**野性 yěxìng** N wild nature; savagery

**野营 yěyíng** V to camp

傻瓜不理解：为什么有些人放着好好的房子不住，跑到**野外**去**野营**？ ShaGua doesn't understand: Why do some people choose not to live in their wonderful homes, but race to camp in the wilderness?

**野战 yězhàn** V to fight on a battlefield

**野猪 yězhū** N wild boar · MW 只、头

### RELATED WORDS

| | | |
|---|---|---|
| 田野 147 | 在野 188 | 荒野 1222 |
| 视野 1362 | 粗野 1364 | 越野 1575 |
| 朝野 1686 | 撒野 1907 | |

## 1686 朝   U+671D   TM 15   FM |

**cháo** V·N·PREP to face; to have an audience with the emperor; to make a pilgrimage to; imperial court; dynasty; reign; government; toward

**zhāo** N day; morning; dawn

**朝代 cháodài** N dynasty · MW 个

**朝廷 cháotíng** N royal/imperial court; imperial government · MW 个

**朝鲜 Cháoxiǎn** N Korea

**朝向 cháoxiàng** N exposure · MW 个

中国人认为, 坐南朝北的**朝向**的房子风水好。
*Chinese believe that a house facing north with its back to the south is good feng shui.*

**朝野** cháoyě　N　government and the people

RELATED WORDS

一朝一夕 1　　　王朝 27　　　只争朝夕 160
热火朝天 1390

---

**1687**　**龄**　龄　　U+9F84　TM **15** FM 丨

líng　N　age; years; duration

RELATED WORDS

老龄 375　　　妙龄 467　　　学龄 1155
适龄 1358　　　高龄 1611　　　超龄 1684
驾龄 1693

---

**1688**　**鼓**　　U+9F13　TM **15** FM 丨

gǔ　N·V　drum; [like a drum]; to rouse;
to swell, to bulge; to beat, to strike; to sound;
to blow (with bellows, etc.)

**鼓吹** gǔchuī　V　to advocate; to brag, to boast

**鼓动** gǔdòng　V　to rouse, to agitate

**鼓励** gǔlì　V　to encourage, to urge

傻瓜喜欢**鼓励**别人, 不喜欢**鼓吹**自己。
*ShaGua loves to encourage others, but dislikes bragging about himself.*

**鼓手** gǔshǒu　N　drummer · MW 个、名

**鼓舞** gǔwǔ　V　to inspire; to encourage

**鼓乐** gǔyuè　N　music accompanied by drums ·
MW 段

**鼓掌** gǔzhǎng　V　to clap one's hands, to applaud

观众拼命**鼓掌**, **鼓励**歌手再接再厉。
*The audience is applauding loudly to show appreciation for the singer.*

**鼓足干劲** gǔzúgànjìn　V　to go all out

RELATED WORDS

铜鼓 1712　　　腰鼓 1868　　　敲边鼓 1959
打退堂鼓 289

---

**1689**　**敬**　　U+656C　TM **15** FM 丨

jìng　V·ADV　to respect; to offer (food, drink, etc.)
politely; respectfully

**敬爱** jìng'ài　V　to revere, to respect and love

---

**敬贺** jìnghè　V　to congratulate respectfully

**敬老院** jìnglǎoyuàn　N　nursing home (LIT home of respect for the aged) · MW 家、间

**敬礼** jìnglǐ　V　to salute; respectfully yours (letter closing)

**敬佩** jìngpèi　V　to admire, to esteem

我很**敬佩**我的中文老师。*I admire my Chinese teacher very much.*

**敬仰** jìngyǎng　V　to revere; to venerate

**敬意** jìngyì　N　respect; tribute

对您的不同意见, 我表示**敬意**。*I respect your conflicting opinion.*

**敬赠** jìngzèng　V　to offer respectfully

**敬重** jìngzhòng　V　to respect highly, to have high regard for

RELATED WORDS

互敬互爱 135　　　孝敬 529　　　致敬 982
尊敬 1722

---

**1690**　**熏**　　U+718F　TM **15** FM 丿

xūn　V　to smoke; to fumigate; to cure (meat, fish, etc.) with smoke

**熏鱼** xūnyú　N　smoked fish · MW 条

**熏蒸** xūnzhēng　V　to stifle; to suffocate

**熏制** xūnzhì　V　to cure with smoke

傻瓜劝人戒烟: "抽烟就像**熏制**肉品, 可能好吃但不健康。" *ShaGua persuaded others to quit smoking: "Smoking is just like smoke-curing meat; it may taste good, but it's unhealthy."*

---

**1691**　**愁**　　U+6101　TM **15** FM 丿

chóu　V·ADJ·N　to worry, to be anxious; sad;
sorrow

**愁闷** chóumèn　ADJ　gloomy, in low spirits

**愁容** chóuróng　N　worried look · MW 副

RELATED WORDS

发愁 311　　　忧愁 693　　　哀愁 1134

---

**1692**　**您**　　U+60A8　TM **15** FM 丿

nín　PRON　you (polite form of address)

**您好** nínhǎo　V　how are you?

## 1693 驾 駕   U+9A7E   TM **15**   FM 丿

**jià** V to drive

- 驾到 **jiàdào** V to arrive (of a respected visitor)
- 驾临 **jiàlín** V (to have) your esteemed presence (honorific)
- 驾龄 **jiàlíng** N driving age · MW 年
- 驾驶 **jiàshǐ** V to drive; to pilot, to steer
- 驾校 **jiàxiào** N driving school · MW 间
- 驾驭 **jiàyù** V to control; to drive
- 驾照 **jiàzhào** N driver's license · MW 个

**RELATED WORD**

劳驾 764

## 1694 盛   U+76DB   TM **15**   FM 丿

**chéng** V to fill, to ladle out; to hold, to contain

    盛酒 *to fill a bowl with wine*

**shèng** ADJ·ADV flourishing; intense; grand; abundant; popular; greatly, deeply

- 盛产 **shèngchǎn** V to be rich in, to abound in
- 盛大 **shèngdà** ADJ grand, magnificent
- 盛典 **shèngdiǎn** N grand ceremony · MW 个
- 盛会 **shènghuì** N grand assembly; pageant · MW 次
- 盛况 **shèngkuàng** N grand occasion/affair
- 盛名 **shèngmíng** N great reputation · MW 个
- 盛怒 **shèngnù** V to rage, to be in a rage
- 盛情 **shèngqíng** N boundless generosity; kind hospitality

    感谢您的**盛情**！ *Thanks for your boundless generosity!*

- 盛暑 **shèngshǔ** N height of summer
- 盛夏 **shèngxià** N midsummer, peak of summer
- 盛行 **shèngxíng** V to be very popular; to be in fashion

    现在美国**盛行**学中文。 *Studying Chinese is now very popular in the States.*

- 盛宴 **shèngyàn** N grand banquet; feast · MW 个

    **盛典**以后，举行**盛宴**，真是**盛况**空前。 *After the grand ceremony, a magnificent banquet was held; the grand occasion was wonderful.*

- 盛装 **shèngzhuāng** N splendid attire; best clothes · MW 套

**RELATED WORDS**

| | | |
|---|---|---|
| 丰盛 35 | 兴盛 228 | 茂盛 557 |
| 旺盛 587 | 昌盛 752 | 极盛 798 |
| 强盛 1896 | 久享盛名 45 | 繁荣昌盛 1988 |

## 1695 第   U+7B2C   TM **15**   FM 丿

**dì** PFX·N [used as a prefix to indicate an ordinal number]; grading in the imperial examinations; mansion; residence

- 第二手 **dì'èrshǒu** N secondhand
- 第三者 **dìsānzhě** N third party; person who has sexual relations with a married person · MW 个

    有人说她是傻瓜的**第三者**。 *Some claim she was the third party in ShaGua's marriage.*

- 第一 **dìyī** N first; most important; Number One
- 第一代 **dìyīdài** N first generation
- 第一流 **dìyīliú** N five stars; first class, tops
- 第一手 **dìyīshǒu** N firsthand

    他总是想获得**第一手**资料，而不是**第二手**资料。 *He always wants to get his information firsthand, not secondhand.*

**RELATED WORDS**

| | |
|---|---|
| 门第 130 | 天字第一号 25 |

## 1696 筒   U+7B52   TM **15**   FM 丿

**tǒng** N bamboo tube; [tube-shaped]

**RELATED WORDS**

| | | |
|---|---|---|
| 听筒 414 | 信筒 869 | 邮筒 1046 |
| 话筒 1182 | 袖筒 1361 | 滚筒 1819 |

## 1697 算   U+7B97   TM **15**   FM 丿

**suàn** V·ADV to calculate; to count; to consider; to plan; to suppose, to guess; to include; let it be; finally

- 算法 **suànfǎ** N arithmetic; algorithm · MW 种
- 算命 **suànmìng** V to tell (someone's) fortune
- 算盘 **suànpán** N abacus; scheme · MW 个

    这个**算盘**真漂亮。 *This abacus is very beautiful.*
    你的**算盘**打得很精。 *The plan you formulated is quite ingenious.*

- 算术 **suànshù** N arithmetic · MW 门
- 算数 **suànshù** V to count, to matter

算账 **suànzhàng** `V` to do one's accounting; to get even with

他每天晚上都算账。 *He does his accounting every night.*

放心吧，有人会找你算账的。 *Don't worry, someone will try to get even with you.*

**RELATED WORDS**

| | | |
|---|---|---|
| 失算 106 | 心算 232 | 计算 240 |
| 计算机 240 | 计算器 240 | 打算 289 |
| 合算 296 | 折算 408 | 划算 476 |
| 珠算 729 | 运算 956 | 核算 1026 |
| 推算 1242 | 结算 1291 | 换算 1402 |
| 清算 1495 | 预算 1528 | 验算 1529 |
| 演算 1821 | 精打细算 1832 | |

---

**1698** 傍  U+508D   TM **15**   FM 丿

**bàng** `V` to be close to; to depend on

傍晚 **bàngwǎn** `N` toward evening, at dusk

---

**1699** 傻 U+50BB   TM **15**   FM 丿

**shǎ** `ADJ` stupid, foolish; inflexible

傻瓜 **shǎguā** `N` fool · `MW` 个

这本词典的主人翁就是傻瓜。 *The main character in this dictionary is ShaGua.*

傻头傻脑 **shǎtóushǎnǎo** `EXP` to be muddleheaded; to look foolish

傻笑 **shǎxiào** `V` to giggle; to laugh foolishly

傻子 **shǎzi** `N` fool; simpleton · `MW` 个

傻瓜不是人们所想的傻子。 *ShaGua is not a simpleton like people think.*

**RELATED WORD**

装疯卖傻 1476

---

**1700** 微  U+5FAE   TM **15**   FM 丿

**wēi** `ADJ·ADV` tiny; micro-; slightly

微波 **wēibō** `N` ripple; microwave (physics)

微波炉 **wēibōlú** `N` microwave oven · `MW` 个

微薄 **wēibó** `ADJ` meager, scanty

微风 **wēifēng** `N` gentle breeze; breathing · `MW` 阵

微风轻拂。 *A gentle breeze is softly blowing.*

微观 **wēiguān** `ADJ` microscopic

---

微量 **wēiliàng** `ADJ` minute quantity of

微妙 **wēimiào** `ADJ` delicate; subtle

很多微妙的问题，傻瓜认为不微妙。 *Many subtle questions are not so to ShaGua.*

微弱 **wēiruò** `ADJ` faint; feeble, frail, weak

微微 **wēiwēi** `ADV` slightly

微小 **wēixiǎo** `ADJ` small, little, tiny

没有微小，就没有巨大。 *Without the infinitesimal, there would not be the astronomical.*

微笑 **wēixiào** `V·N` to smile; to laugh quietly

微型 **wēixíng** `ADJ` tiny; mini-

**RELATED WORDS**

| | | |
|---|---|---|
| 无微不至 139 | 显微镜 755 | 细微 1107 |
| 轻微 1113 | 稍微 1600 | |

---

**1701** 婚 U+5A5A   TM **15**   FM 丿

**hūn** `V·N` to wed, to marry; marriage; wedding

婚嫁 **hūnjià** `N` marriage

婚礼 **hūnlǐ** `N` wedding (ceremony) · `MW` 个

傻瓜和傻瓜太太没有举行婚礼。 *ShaGua and Mrs. ShaGua did not have a wedding ceremony.*

婚姻 **hūnyīn** `N` marriage; wedlock · `MW` 个

婚约 **hūnyuē** `N` engagement; marriage contract · `MW` 个

**RELATED WORDS**

| | | |
|---|---|---|
| 未婚 88 | 主婚 124 | 订婚 347 |
| 求婚 376 | 金婚 420 | 许婚 502 |
| 定婚 666 | 证婚人 705 | 完婚 909 |
| 初婚 963 | 结婚 1291 | 离婚 1614 |
| 新婚 1638 | | |

---

**1702** 嫌 U+5ACC   TM **15**   FM 丿

**xián** `V` to dislike; to mind; suspicion; resentment, grudge

嫌弃 **xiánqì** `V` to give (someone) the cold shoulder (`LIT` to dislike and avoid)

许多孩子长大后嫌弃父母，但父母永远不嫌弃儿女。 *Many children will dislike and avoid their parents when they grow up, but parents would never do this to their children.*

嫌恶 **xiánwù** `V` to detest, to loathe

嫌疑 **xiányí** `N` suspicion; suspected (of)

**RELATED WORDS**

讨嫌 500        避嫌 1976

## 1703 饱 饱 · U+9971   TM **15** FM 丿

**bǎo** V·ADJ·ADV   to eat until full; to satisfy; full; fully

饱和 **bǎohé** V   to saturate; to fill to capacity

饱满 **bǎomǎn** ADJ   full; plump; vigorous

### RELATED WORDS

欠饱和 105      温饱 1627

## 1704 猛   U+731B   TM **15** FM 丿

**měng** ADJ·ADV   fierce; brave; suddenly, abruptly; fiercely

猛不防 **měngbufáng** ADV   by surprise

猛冲 **měngchōng** V   to charge forward

猛不防，有人向傻瓜**猛冲**过去。*Someone rushed ShaGua by surprise.*

猛力 **měnglì** ADV   vigorously; violently

猛烈 **měngliè** ADJ   fierce; violent; drastic

猛扑 **měngpū** V   to pounce on

猛然 **měngrán** ADV   suddenly, abruptly

傻瓜**猛然**意识到：他的亲生父母可能会到他被遗弃的地方找他。*ShaGua suddenly realized that his biological parents might return to look for him at the place where he was abandoned.*

猛兽 **měngshòu** N   beast of prey · MW 头

猛醒 **měngxǐng** V   to suddenly realize, to wake up (to the truth)

### RELATED WORDS

凶猛 98      扎猛子 288      迅猛 954
勇猛 1371      突飞猛进 913

## 1705 税  U+7A0E   TM **15** FM 丿

**shuì** N   tax; duty

税额 **shuì'é** N   amount of tax

税法 **shuìfǎ** N   tax law · MW 部

虽然傻瓜是市长，但他不太懂**税法**。*Although ShaGua is mayor, he isn't really familiar with tax law.*

税后 **shuìhòu** N   after taxes

税款 **shuìkuǎn** N   tax payment; taxation · MW 笔

税率 **shuìlǜ** N   tax rate · MW 个

税收 **shuìshōu** N   tax revenue · MW 笔

税务局 **shuìwùjú** N   tax office · MW 个

税则 **shuìzé** N   tax regulation · MW 条

傻瓜总是忠实地根据**税则**向**税局**缴纳**税款**。*ShaGua has always honestly paid his taxes to the IRS according to tax regulations.*

税制 **shuìzhì** N   tax system · MW 个

### RELATED WORDS

| | | |
|---|---|---|
| 关税 224 | 征税 462 | 补税 508 |
| 查税 741 | 抽税 788 | 版税 897 |
| 报税 1010 | 免税 1056 | 逃税 1509 |
| 偷税 1591 | 避税 1976 | 所得税 645 |
| 销售税 1714 | | |

## 1706 绝 绝   U+7EDD   TM **15** FM 丿

**jué** V·ADJ·ADV   to cut off; to exhaust; to have no descendants; to die; finished; hopeless; extremely; absolutely

绝对 **juéduì** ADJ·ADV   absolute; unconditional; definitely

绝迹 **juéjì** V   to be eradicated; to vanish

绝交 **juéjiāo** V   to break off relations; to break up

绝路 **juélù** N   blind alley; impasse · MW 条

绝密 **juémì** ADJ   top-secret; confidential

绝妙 **juémiào** ADJ   extremely clever; exquisite

傻瓜的炒菜堪称**绝妙**。*ShaGua's cooking is exquisite.*

绝热 **juérè** V   to insulate from heat

绝食 **juéshí** V   to fast; to go on a hunger strike

绝望 **juéwàng** V·ADJ   to give up all hope; to feel desperate; hopeless

绝缘 **juéyuán** V   to be cut off / isolated from; to insulate

为了准备汉语水平考试，他打算与朋友**绝缘**一个月。*In order to prepare for the HSK test, he is going into isolation from his friends for a month.*

这种材料是**绝缘**的。*This is electrical insulating material.*

绝招 **juézhāo** N   unique skill · MW 个

学中文**绝对**没有**绝招**；如果有，那就是更努力地学习。*There is absolutely no unique skill for studying Chinese. If there were, it would be to study harder.*

绝症 **juézhèng** N   terminal illness, incurable disease · MW 个

### RELATED WORDS

| | | |
|---|---|---|
| 灭绝 75 | 卓绝 523 | 根绝 1245 |
| 断绝 1260 | 谢绝 1890 | 隔绝 1910 |
| 深恶痛绝 1345 | | |

## 1707 绿 U+7EFF TM 15 FM 丿

lǜ ADJ green

绿茶 lǜchá N green tea · MW 杯、包、盒

绿灯 lǜdēng N green light; go-ahead, permission (to do something) · MW 盏

绿灯亮了才能开车。 *Only when it's a green light can you go.*

学校给学汉语大开绿灯。 *The school is providing all sorts of resources for studying Chinese.*

绿豆 lǜdòu N mung bean · MW 颗、粒

绿化 lǜhuà V to make green; to plant trees

绿叶 lǜyè N green leaves · MW 片

绿油油 lǜyōuyōu ADJ green

山下是绿油油的田野。 *There are green fields at the foot of the hill.*

**RELATED WORDS**

灰绿色 198　　红绿灯 474　　草绿 768
墨绿 1843　　花花绿绿 549

## 1708 缓 緩 U+7F13 TM 15 FM 丿

huǎn V·ADJ to delay; to revive; slow; relaxed

缓冲 huǎnchōng V to buffer

缓和 huǎnhé V·ADJ to relax; relaxed

缓急 huǎnjí N degree of urgency

缓慢 huǎnmàn ADJ slow; tardy

学中文学到一定程度，速度会缓慢下来。 *When you study Chinese at a certain level, your improvement will slow.*

缓期 huǎnqī V to postpone, to defer

**RELATED WORDS**

死缓 510　　和缓 644　　延缓 731
迟缓 959　　减缓 1487　　暂缓 1522
刻不容缓 966

## 1709 胸 U+80F8 TM 15 FM 丿

xiōng N chest; breast; heart; mind

胸怀 xiōnghuái N·V heart; mind; to have/keep in mind

胸襟 xiōngjīn N ambition; broadmindedness; lapel (of a jacket)

傻瓜的胸襟很宽广。 *The breadth of ShaGua's mind is tremendous.*

胸闷 xiōngmèn ADJ chest pain

胸腔 xiōngqiāng N chest cavity

胸膛 xiōngtáng N chest; breast

胸围 xiōngwéi N chest measurement; bust

胸罩 xiōngzhào N bra · MW 副

胸针 xiōngzhēn N brooch · MW 枚

**RELATED WORD**

心胸 232

## 1710 脂 U+8102 TM 15 FM 丿

zhī N fat, grease; rouge

脂肪 zhīfáng N fat; fattiness

越来越多的人喝低脂肪牛奶。 *More and more people like to drink low-fat milk.*

脂粉 zhīfěn N cosmetics (LIT rouge and powder) · MW 层

**RELATED WORDS**

含脂量 592　　低脂 618　　油脂 683
香脂 834　　涂脂抹粉 1171　　乳脂 1308
脱脂 1803

## 1711 脾 U+813E TM 15 FM 丿

pí N spleen

脾气 píqi N mood, temper; temperament

傻瓜的脾气很不好。 *ShaGua has a very bad temper.*

脾脏 pízàng N spleen · MW 个

**RELATED WORD**

牛脾气 51

## 1712 铜 銅 U+94DC TM 15 FM 丿

tóng N copper

铜版 tóngbǎn N copperplate (printing) · MW 块

铜币 tóngbì N copper coin · MW 枚

铜臭 tóngchòu N stink of money

散发出铜臭味的金钱让许多人丧失理智。 *The stink of money has made many lose all reason.*

铜鼓 tónggǔ N bronze drum · MW 个

铜器 tóngqì N bronze · MW 件

**RELATED WORDS**

古铜色 154　　青铜 740

## 1713 铺 鋪　　U+94FA　TM **15** FM 丿

**pū** V·N　to spread, to extend; to pave; to lay

**pù** N　store, shop; plank bed

**铺盖 pūgài** V·N　to cover, to spread (evenly) over; bedding; bedclothes · MW 卷、套、床

**铺路 pūlù** V　to pave (a road, etc.)
傻瓜喜欢给城市**铺路**。*ShaGua loves to pave roads for his city.*

**铺设 pūshè** V　to lay (a road, railway, wiring, etc.)

**铺天盖地 pūtiāngàidì** EXP　swarming and pervasive (LIT to blot out the sky and cover up the earth)

**铺张 pūzhāng** ADJ　extravagant; wasteful
傻瓜做事不**铺张**。*ShaGua is not wasteful in conducting business.*

**铺板 pùbǎn** N　bed board · MW 块

**铺面 pùmiàn** N　shop front · MW 个

**铺位 pùwèi** N　bunk; berth · MW 个

### RELATED WORDS

| | | |
|---|---|---|
| 床铺 333 | 当铺 335 | 店铺 658 |
| 卧铺 826 | 卧铺票 826 | 打地铺 289 |

## 1714 销 銷　　U+9500　TM **15** FM 丿

**xiāo** V·N　to sell; to spend; to cancel; to melt (of metal); pin; peg

滞**销** *to be unsalable/unmarketable*
这个商店有许多**滞销**产品。*There are lots of products in this store that are unfit to be sold.*

**销毁 xiāohuǐ** V　to destroy by burning

**销路 xiāolù** N　market; sales channel · MW 个
这本汉语教材的**销路**不好。*There is no market for this Chinese textbook.*

**销售 xiāoshòu** V　to sell; to market

**销售点 xiāoshòudiǎn** N　point of purchase · MW 个

**销售额 xiāoshòu'é** N　sales volume; sales quota · MW 笔

**销售税 xiāoshòushuì** N　sales tax · MW 笔

**销赃 xiāozāng** V　to dispose of stolen goods

**销账 xiāozhàng** V　to cancel / write off an account

### RELATED WORDS

| | | |
|---|---|---|
| 开销 26 | 代销 208 | 外销 218 |
| 产销 219 | 勾销 303 | 行销 327 |
| 供销 459 | 注销 496 | 吊销 547 |

| | | |
|---|---|---|
| 包销 836 | 返销 957 | 报销 1010 |
| 推销 1242 | 展销 1274 | 滞销 1714 |
| 脱销 1803 | 撤销 1942 | |

## 1715 错 錯　　U+9519　TM **15** FM 丿

**cuò** V·ADJ·N　to miss; to alternate; to grind; incorrect; bad; complex; fault; mistake

**错别字 cuòbiézì** N　misspelled/mispronounced character · MW 个
在中国，老师是不允许写**错别字**的。*Teachers in China are not allowed to misspell or mispronounce characters.*

**错处 cuòchù** N　fault · MW 个

**错过 cuòguò** V　to miss
傻瓜迟到，**错过**了航班。*ShaGua was late and he missed the flight.*

**错开 cuòkāi** V　to stagger, to alternate

**错乱 cuòluàn** ADJ　in disorder; cluttered

**错位 cuòwèi** V　to misplace; to displace

**错误 cuòwù** N·ADJ　mistake, error; wrong, incorrect · MW 个
老师不能有**错误**，是把老师和神**错位**了。*A teacher can't make any mistakes, for they have been falsely identified as gods.*

**错综复杂 cuòzōngfùzá** EXP　intricate, complex

### RELATED WORDS

| | | |
|---|---|---|
| 不错 24 | 交错 222 | 认错 239 |
| 弄错 251 | 出错 258 | 差错 673 |
| 挑错 1235 | | |

## 1716 铐 銬　　U+94D0　TM **15** FM 丿

**kào** V·N　to handcuff; handcuffs

### RELATED WORD

手铐 104

## 1717 航　　U+822A　TM **15** FM 丿

**háng** V·N　to sail, to navigate; to fly; boat; ship

**航班 hángbān** N　(scheduled) flight · MW 个
从辛辛那提到北京没有直达**航班**。*There is no direct flight from Cincinnati to Beijing.*

**航程 hángchéng** N　voyage; air/sea distance · MW 段

航船 **hángchuán** [N] boat; ship · [MW] 艘

航道 **hángdào** [N] channel; course; sea lane · [MW] 条

航海 **hánghǎi** [V] to sail, to navigate

航迹 **hángjì** [N] flight path · [MW] 条

航空 **hángkōng** [V] to fly (an airplane)

航空信 **hángkōngxìn** [N] airmail letter · [MW] 封
寄一封**航空信**到中国需要十天。 *It takes ten days to send airmail to China.*

航路 **hánglù** [N] air/sea route · [MW] 条

航天 **hángtiān** [V] space flight; aerospace

航天飞机 **hángtiānfēijī** [N] space shuttle · [MW] 架
据说，从**航天飞机**上可以看到长城。 *They say you can see the Great Wall from the space shuttle.*

航天火箭 **hángtiānhuǒjiàn** [N] space rocket · [MW] 枚

航线 **hángxiàn** [N] path; air/sea route · [MW] 条

航向 **hángxiàng** [N] course

航行 **hángxíng** [V] to sail, to navigate; to fly

航运 **hángyùn** [V] to ship/transport by sea

**RELATED WORDS**

| | | |
|---|---|---|
| 归航 166 | 民航 388 | 宇航 485 |
| 启航 657 | 导航 751 | 返航 957 |
| 迷航 1187 | 停航 1588 | 飞行航线 81 |

---

**1718** 般          U+822C    TM **15** FM ノ

**bān** [N·ADJ] sort, kind, type; as; alike (in); so-so

**RELATED WORDS**

| | | |
|---|---|---|
| 一般 1 | 万般 73 | 百般 242 |
| 这般 715 | | |

---

**1719** 勉          U+52C9    TM **15** FM ノ

**miǎn** [V] to strive; to encourage; to force (someone) to (continue doing something)

勉励 **miǎnlì** [V] to encourage, to urge

勉强 **miǎnqiǎng** [V·ADJ·ADV] to force (someone) to (do something); to do with difficulty; strained; barely enough
**勉强**别人，不如**勉励**别人。 *It is better to encourage others than to force them.*
他**勉强**同意了。 *He barely agreed.*

**RELATED WORD**
共勉 164

---

**1720** 剩          U+5269    TM **15** FM ノ

**shèng** [V] to be left (over), to remain

剩饭 **shèngfàn** [N] leftover
傻瓜总要把**剩饭**吃完，才煮新饭。 *ShaGua always finishes leftovers before preparing a new dish.*

剩下 **shèngxià** [V] to be left (over), to remain

剩余 **shèngyú** [V] to be left (over), to remain

**RELATED WORD**
过剩 712

---

**1721** 毫          U+6BEB    TM **15** FM 丶

**háo** [N] fine long hair; writing brush; in the least, at all

毫克 **háokè** [MW] milligram

毫毛 **háomáo** [N] soft hair on the body · [MW] 根

毫秒 **háomiǎo** [MW] millisecond

毫升 **háoshēng** [MW] milliliter

毫无 **háowú** [ADV] completely without; not in the least
我对这个人和这件事都**毫无**兴趣。 *I am not at all interested in this person or this affair.*

**RELATED WORD**
丝毫 637

---

**1722** 尊          U+5C0A    TM **15** FM 丶

**zūn** [V·N·MW] to respect; to honor; senior; [measure word for statues and images of deities]

尊称 **zūnchēng** [N·V] honorific title; to address respectfully · [MW] 个
中国人在姓前面或后面加个"老"字，就成了**尊称**。 *Chinese people add a "老" before or after your family name as a sign of respect.*

尊贵 **zūnguì** [ADJ] respected; honorable

尊敬 **zūnjìng** [V·ADJ] to respect; distinguished

尊严 **zūnyán** [N] dignity; honor

尊重 **zūnzhòng** [V] to respect; to value
我厌恶你的发言，但我**尊重**你的发言权。 *I hate what you said, but I respect your right to say it.*

**RELATED WORD**
自尊 305

## 1723 瓷 · U+74F7 · TM 15 FM 〵

**cí** N porcelain; chinaware, china

瓷器 **cíqì** N porcelain; chinaware · MW 件

瓷碗 **cíwǎn** N china bowl · MW 个

瓷砖 **cízhuān** N ceramic tile · MW 块

## 1724 鹿 · U+9E7F · TM 15 FM 〵

**lù** N deer

公鹿 *stag, buck*

母鹿 *doe*

小鹿 *fawn*

鹿角 **lùjiǎo** N antler · MW 对

鹿茸 **lùróng** N young deer antler (before ossification)

鹿茸是一种很名贵的妇科中药。
*The antler of a young stag is a rare Chinese traditional medicine used in gynecology.*

**RELATED WORDS**

长颈鹿 93　　梅花鹿 1413

## 1725 痛 · U+75DB · TM 15 FM 〵

**tòng** V·N·ADJ·ADV to ache; to grieve; suffering; sadness; painful; deeply, bitterly

痛斥 **tòngchì** V to attack bitterly (with words)

痛处 **tòngchù** N sore/tender spot · MW 个

痛打 **tòngdǎ** V to beat soundly

痛点 **tòngdiǎn** N sore spot · MW 个

痛恶 **tòng'è** V to detest bitterly

痛改前非 **tònggǎiqiánfēi** EXP to make a clean break with the past

痛感 **tònggǎn** V·N to feel keenly; (sense of) pain

痛觉 **tòngjué** N pain sensation

痛苦 **tòngkǔ** ADJ painful; agonizing

学中文既痛苦又有趣。*Studying Chinese is painful, but also interesting.*

痛快 **tòngkuai** ADJ happy, joyful; forthright

我感觉很痛快。*I feel very happy.*

你办事真痛快。*Your conduct is quite up-front.*

痛骂 **tòngmà** V to scold severely

痛惜 **tòngxī** V to regret deeply

痛心 **tòngxīn** ADJ distressed; sad

---

她放弃学中文，让老师感到很痛心。*Her giving up on studying Chinese distressed her teacher.*

痛痒 **tòngyǎng** N suffering; difficulties

**RELATED WORDS**

| | | |
|---|---|---|
| 止痛 41 | 头痛 128 | 牙痛 143 |
| 忍痛 970 | 咽痛 1024 | 疼痛 1148 |
| 沉痛 1166 | 胃痛 1216 | 病痛 1327 |
| 悲痛 1532 | 腰痛 1868 | 腹痛 1869 |
| 镇痛 1872 | 触痛 1875 | 心绞痛 232 |
| 深恶痛绝 1345 | 撕裂痛 1774 | |

## 1726 扇 · U+6247 · TM 15 FM 〵

**shān** V to incite, to stir up; to slap

**shàn** N·MW fan; leaf; [measure word for doors, windows, etc.]

扇动 **shāndòng** V to incite; to provoke

这篇小说很能扇动人的情绪。*This novel can really stir the reader's emotions.*

扇形 **shànxíng** N fan-shaped; sector (mathematics) · MW 个

扇子 **shànzi** N fan · MW 把

**RELATED WORDS**

风扇 194　　电风扇 263　　芭蕉扇 765

## 1727 阅 閱 · U+9605 · TM 15 FM 〵

**yuè** V to read, to scan; to review; to inspect; to undergo, to experience

阅兵 **yuèbīng** V to review/inspect troops

阅读 **yuèdú** V to read

阅览 **yuèlǎn** V to read

阅览室 **yuèlǎnshì** N reading room · MW 间

阅历 **yuèlì** N·V experience; to experience

虽然傻瓜没阅读过什么书籍，但他的人生阅历很丰富。*Although ShaGua has not read many books, his life experience is very rich.*

**RELATED WORDS**

| | | |
|---|---|---|
| 评阅 706 | 查阅 741 | 审阅 911 |
| 批阅 1005 | 检阅 1033 | 翻阅 1989 |

## 1728 阔  闊 · U+9614 · TM 15 FM 〵

**kuò** ADJ wide, broad; vast; rich, wealthy

阔别 **kuòbié** V to be separated for a long time

傻瓜**阔**别家乡有二十多年了。 *ShaGua has been away from his hometown for over 20 years.*

**阔步** kuòbù  V  to take great strides

**阔绰** kuòchuò  ADJ  ostentatious; extravagant

**阔老** kuòlǎo  N  rich man · MW 个、名

**阔气** kuòqi  ADJ  luxurious; extravagant, lavish
这女人真**阔气**。 *This lady is very fancy.*

**阔少** kuòshào  N  son of a rich family ·
MW 个、名

**RELATED WORDS**

广阔 23　　　　壮阔 238　　　　辽阔 711
宽阔 1618　　　摆阔 1773

---

### 1729 冤  U+51A4  TM **15** FM ＼

yuān  N·ADJ·V  injustice; grievance; hatred, enmity; bad luck; to dupe, to fool

**冤仇** yuānchóu  N  enmity, rancor · MW 笔

**冤家** yuānjia  N  enemy, foe; sweetheart (in opera) · MW 个

**冤家路窄** yuānjiālùzhǎi  EXP  Enemies are bound to meet on a narrow road.

**冤屈** yuānqū  N  unfair treatment; injustice ·
MW 个

**冤枉** yuānwang  V·ADJ  to be treated unfairly; to be falsely charged; not worthwhile, in vain, for nothing
我被**冤枉**了。 *I was treated unfairly.*
你这样学中文，是在走**冤枉**路。 *The way you studied Chinese has all been in vain.*

**冤狱** yuānyù  N  unjust charge/verdict · MW 起

**RELATED WORDS**

申冤 150　　　含冤 592　　　诉冤 708
喊冤 1668

---

### 1730 密  U+5BC6  TM **15** FM ＼

mì  ADJ·N  dense, thick; close; meticulous; secret

**密闭** mìbì  ADJ  airtight

**密布** mìbù  V  to be densely covered; to be full of

**密度** mìdù  N  density; thickness

**密封** mìfēng  V  to seal tightly

**密集** mìjí  ADJ  concentrated; crowded together

**密件** mìjiàn  N  confidential letter/document ·
MW 份

**密码** mìmǎ  N  secret code; password · MW 组

---

这是一封用**密码**写成的**密封**起来的**密件**。 *This is a sealed confidential letter written in a secret code.*

**密谋** mìmóu  V  to plot, to conspire

**密切** mìqiè  ADJ·ADV·V  close, intimate; carefully; to build close relations (between two parties)
**密切**注意他们的**密切**关系。 *Pay careful attention to their close relationship.*

**密友** mìyǒu  N  close friend · MW 个、位

**RELATED WORDS**

严密 241　　　告密 428　　　茂密 557
机密 577　　　泄密 685　　　保密 868
亲密 908　　　哈密瓜 1025　　周密 1068
细密 1107　　　秘密 1289　　　紧密 1537
绝密 1706　　　精密 1832

---

### 1731 富  U+5BCC  TM **15** FM ＼

fù  ADJ  rich, wealthy; abundant; enriching

**富豪** fùháo  N  rich and powerful person; plutocrat · MW 个、名

**富丽堂皇** fùlìtánghuáng  ADJ  sumptuous; splendid

**富强** fùqiáng  ADJ  rich and powerful (of a country)

**富有** fùyǒu  ADJ·V  rich, wealthy; to be rich in, to be full of

**富于** fùyú  V  to be rich in, to be full of

**富裕** fùyù  ADJ·V  well-to-do, prosperous; to enrich, to make prosperous

**富足** fùzú  ADJ  rich, affluent; plentiful, abundant
金钱**富足**并不等于知识**富有**。 *Wealth does not equal being rich in knowledge.*

**RELATED WORDS**

丰富 35　　　　丰富多采 35　　　年富力强 182
财富 588　　　豪富 1876　　　亿万富翁 205
百万富翁 242　荣华富贵 769

---

### 1732 窗  U+7A97  TM **15** FM ＼

chuāng  N  window; shutter

**窗玻璃** chuāngbōli  N  windowpane · MW 块

**窗户** chuānghu  N  window; casement · MW 扇

**窗口** chuāngkǒu  N  window · MW 个、扇
眼睛是心灵的**窗口**。 *The eyes are a window on the soul.*

**窗框** chuāngkuàng  N  window frame ·
MW 个

**1732 窗 chuāng** (continued)

窗帘 chuānglián　N　window curtains · MW 块

窗台 chuāngtái　N　windowsill · MW 个

**RELATED WORDS**

| | | |
|---|---|---|
| 门窗 130 | 同窗 541 | 纱窗 639 |
| 橱窗 1909 | 开天窗 26 | 百叶窗 242 |

---

## 1733 常　U+5E38　TM 15 FM 丶

**cháng**　N·ADJ·ADV　morality; normal, common; constant; often; usually

常常 chángcháng　ADV　frequently; usually

常规 chángguī　N　convention; routine · MW 个
创造的第一步就是打破**常规**。*The first step in creation is to break free from convention.*

常会 chánghuì　N　regular meeting; ordinary session · MW 次

常见病 chángjiànbìng　N　common disease · MW 种
用错量词是外国人学中文的"**常见病**"。
*Using the wrong measure word is a "common disease" among nonnative students of Chinese.*

常任 chángrèn　ADJ　permanent; standing

常设 chángshè　V　standing

常识 chángshí　N　general knowledge; common sense · MW 个
这是**常识**,不是什么深奥的理论。*This is just common sense; it's not a difficult theory.*

常态 chángtài　N　normal state (of affairs)

常务 chángwù　ADJ　day-to-day, routine; standing

常用 chángyòng　ADJ　in common use

常驻 chángzhù　ADJ　resident; permanent

**RELATED WORDS**

| | | |
|---|---|---|
| 正常 76 | 正常化 76 | 平常 78 |
| 日常 96 | 日常费用 96 | 失常 106 |
| 反常 111 | 无常 139 | 寻常 358 |
| 非常 378 | 往常 461 | 如常 464 |
| 异常 539 | 时常 586 | 经常 1110 |
| 家常 1315 | 通常 1757 | 照常 1846 |
| 习以为常 84 | 异乎寻常 539 | |

---

## 1734 掌　U+638C　TM 15 FM 丶

**zhǎng**　N·V　palm; sole; pad; horseshoe; to control, to be in charge of; to slap

掌舵 zhǎngduò　V　to be at the helm

掌故 zhǎnggù　N　(historical) anecdotes; tales · MW 个
傻瓜知道一些清朝皇帝的**掌故**。*ShaGua knows a few stories about the emperors of the Qing Dynasty.*

掌管 zhǎngguǎn　V　to control, to be in charge of
在家里,傻瓜太太**掌管**财政。*Mrs. ShaGua is in charge of the family budget.*

掌权 zhǎngquán　V　to be in power; to exercise control

掌上明珠 zhǎngshàngmíngzhū　EXP　to be the apple of (someone's) eye (LIT the pearl in (someone's) palm)

掌声 zhǎngshēng　N　clapping, applause · MW 阵

掌纹 zhǎngwén　N　palm print · MW 条

掌握 zhǎngwò　V　to be in charge of; to master, to know well
老师**掌握**了课堂。*The class is under the teacher's control.*
我**掌握**了汉语语法。*I know Chinese grammar well.*

掌心 zhǎngxīn　N　hollow of the palm; sphere of control

**RELATED WORDS**

| | | |
|---|---|---|
| 手掌 104 | 执掌 564 | 鼓掌 1688 |
| 脚掌 1804 | 魔掌 1996 | 仙人掌 207 |
| 了如指掌 30 | | |

---

## 1735 愣　U+6123　TM 15 FM 丶

**lèng**　V·ADJ·ADV　to stare blankly; to be stupefied; rash, reckless; rashly, recklessly

愣干 lènggàn　V　to do things recklessly
傻瓜有时候会不顾后果地**愣干**。*Sometimes, ShaGua does things rashly.*

愣头愣脑 lèngtóulèngnǎo　EXP　rash, reckless

愣头青 lèngtóuqīng　N　blunderer; knucklehead · MW 个、名

愣住 lèngzhù　V　to be taken aback
看见狗冲过来,他**愣住**了。*He was taken aback when a dog rushed at him.*

---

## 1736 慌　U+614C　TM 15 FM 丶

**huāng**　ADJ　nervous; flustered, confused

慌乱 huāngluàn　ADJ　flustered, bewildered

考完试要检查, 不能**慌乱**。 *You must check your exam after you're done; don't rush through it in a frenzy.*

**慌忙** huāngmáng  ADJ  hurried, in a great rush

**慌张** huāngzhāng  ADJ  nervous; flustered

傻瓜刚学开车时, 一上高速就**慌张**。
*When ShaGua was first learning to drive, he would become flustered as soon as he got on the highway.*

### RELATED WORDS

心慌 232          发慌 311          着慌 1332
惊慌 1489          恐慌 1644

---

**1737**  **愉**  U+6109  TM **15** FM 丶

yú  ADJ  happy, joyful

**愉快** yúkuài  ADJ  cheerful; delightful, pleasant

祝你旅途**愉快**。 *Have a good time on your trip!*

---

**1738**  **涨** 漲  U+6DA8  TM **15** FM 丶

zhǎng  V  to rise (of water, prices, etc.)

zhàng  V  to expand, to swell; to flush

**涨潮** zhǎngcháo  V  high tide; rising tide

**涨价** zhǎngjià  V  to increase in price

**涨落** zhǎngluò  V  to rise and fall

傻瓜承受不了股票的**涨落**, 所以不敢玩股票。
*ShaGua couldn't stand the rise and fall of the stock market, so he doesn't play the stocks anymore.*

### RELATED WORDS

上涨 14          飞涨 81          看涨 841
暴涨 1844

---

**1739**  **混**  U+6DF7  TM **15** FM 丶

hún  ADJ  muddy; murky; foolish

**混蛋** *scoundrel*

hùn  V·ADV  to mix; to confuse; to pass (something) off as; to drift, to muddle along; to get along with; aimlessly; thoughtlessly

**混沌** hùndùn  N·ADJ  chaos; muddleheaded; innocent as a child

**混纺** hùnfǎng  V·N  to mix, to blend; mix, blend

**混合** hùnhé  V  to mix, to mingle, to merge

---

把中文和英文**混合**来讲, 在中国叫做 "洋泾浜", 在美国叫做 "Chinglish"。 *Mixing Chinese with English is called "pidgin" in China, and "Chinglish" in America.*

**混凝土** hùnníngtǔ  N  concrete · MW 包、袋

**混同** hùntóng  V  to confuse, to mix up

**混淆** hùnxiáo  V  to confuse, to garble, to mix up

中国文化**混淆**了老师和圣人的关系。
*Chinese culture has mixed up the idea of the teacher with that of the sage.*

**混血儿** hùnxuè'ér  N  person of mixed race · MW 个、名

**混杂** hùnzá  V  to mix, to mingle

**混战** hùnzhàn  V·N  to engage in a shifting battle; chaotic warfare · MW 场

**混账** hùnzhàng  ADJ  scoundrel; bastard

**混浊** hùnzhuó  ADJ  muddy; murky

### RELATED WORDS

含混 592          蒙混 1654          蒙混过关 1654

---

**1740**  **港**  U+6E2F  TM **15** FM 丶

gǎng  N  harbor; airport; (short name for) Hong Kong

**港币** gǎngbì  N  Hong Kong dollar

现在一个人民币兑换不了一个**港币**。
*Presently, one yuan RMB is not worth as much as one HK dollar.*

**港口** gǎngkǒu  N  port; harbor · MW 个

**港区** gǎngqū  N  port area · MW 个

**港湾** gǎngwān  N  harbor · MW 个

**港务局** gǎngwùjú  N  port authority · MW 个

### RELATED WORDS

香港 834          岛港 1434          海港 1494
渔港 1496

---

**1741**  **湖**  U+6E56  TM **15** FM 丶

hú  N  lake

**湖北** Húběi  N  Hubei Province

**湖滨** húbīn  N  lakefront

**湖南** Húnán  N  Hunan Province

在美国有很多**湖南**餐馆, 但没见过一家**湖北**餐馆。 *There are many Hunan restaurants in America, but no Hubei restaurants.*

**湖泊** húpō  N  lake · MW 个

**1741** 湖 **hú** (continued)

**RELATED WORDS**

五湖四海 79     江湖 237       盐湖 993
走江湖 265       跑江湖 1916

---

**1742** 源      U+6E90      TM **15** FM ＼

**yuán** N source (of a river); fountainhead; source, cause, root

源流 **yuánliú** N source and course (of a river, etc.); origin and development

源泉 **yuánquán** N source; fountainhead, wellspring

没有任何力量可以切断文化的**源泉**。
*No force can cut off one's cultural roots.*

源头 **yuántóu** N source · MW 个

饮水不忘**源头**。 *When you drink water, you must not forget where it comes from.*

源源 **yuányuán** ADV in a steady stream, continuously

源远流长 **yuányuǎnliúcháng** EXP time-honored; to have a long history (LIT distant source and long river)

**RELATED WORDS**

来源 260     电源 263     发源 311
光源 491     货源 1061     根源 1245
泉源 1275     资源 1335     起源 1421
能源 1873     左右逢源 113     世外桃源 163

---

**1743** 溪      U+6EAA      TM **15** FM ＼

**xī** N small stream, brook, creek

溪涧 **xījiàn** N mountain stream · MW 条

溪流 **xīliú** N brook, stream · MW 条

我们家门前有一条弯弯曲曲的**溪流**。
*There is a winding brook in front of our house.*

---

**1744** 溶      U+6EB6      TM **15** FM ＼

**róng** V to dissolve

溶化 **rónghuà** V to dissolve; to melt, to thaw

在阳光下，积雪开始**溶化**。 *The snow is beginning to melt in the sunshine.*

溶解 **róngjiě** V to dissolve; to thaw

溶入 **róngrù** V to dissolve in

溶液 **róngyè** N solution (chemistry)

---

**1745** 满 滿      U+6EE1      TM **15** FM ＼

**mǎn** V·ADJ·ADV·N to fill; to be satisfied; to expire; full; complete; completely; Man nationality

满不在乎 **mǎnbùzàihu** EXP to not worry at all, couldn't care less

满额 **mǎn'é** V to fulfill a quota

满分 **mǎnfēn** N perfect score · MW 个

美国学生学中文很难得**满分**，因为写字常常漏笔画。 *American students find it difficult to get a perfect score studying Chinese because they often miss strokes.*

满腹 **mǎnfù** V to have one's mind filled with

满怀 **mǎnhuái** V to have one's heart filled with, to be filled with

满口 **mǎnkǒu** N·ADV mouth full of (lies, compliments, false teeth, etc.); fluently (language); unreservedly (LIT full mouth)

这姑娘**满口**中文。 *This girl speaks Chinese all the time.*

满脸 **mǎnliǎn** V to have one's face covered with, across one's whole face

满面 **mǎnmiàn** V to have one's face covered with, across one's whole face

满目 **mǎnmù** V to fill the eyes (with beautiful scenery, etc.)

满脑子 **mǎnnǎozi** V to have one's head/mind filled/stuffed with

这学生**满脑子**都是中文。 *This student's mind is stuffed with Chinese.*

满身 **mǎnshēn** V to have one's body covered with, covered all over with

满堂红 **mǎntánghóng** EXP all-around victory, success across the board

满天 **mǎntiān** V to be all across the sky

满心 **mǎnxīn** ADV from the bottom of one's heart

满员 **mǎnyuán** V to be full

这个中文老师的课堂**满员**了。 *This Chinese teacher's classroom is full.*

满月 **mǎnyuè** N one month old (of a baby); full moon

满载 **mǎnzài** V to be full to capacity

满足 **mǎnzú** V·ADJ to satisfy, to meet; content, satisfied

满座 **mǎnzuò** V to have a capacity audience, to be at capacity

**RELATED WORDS**

| | | |
|---|---|---|
| 不满 24 | 丰满 35 | 心满意足 232 |
| 自满 305 | 充满 652 | 美满 671 |
| 届满 851 | 完满 909 | 客满 1316 |
| 圆满 1391 | 饱满 1703 | |

---

**1746　漆**　　U+6F06　　TM **15** FM 丶

**qī** N·V lacquer; paint; to coat with lacquer/paint

漆黑 **qīhēi** ADJ pitch-black; inky

漆黑的夜晚，没有一丝星光。 *There were no stars in the ink-black sky.*

漆器 **qīqì** N lacquered porcelain · MW 件、套

**RELATED WORDS**

油漆 683　　　喷漆 1563

---

**1747　诡 詭**　　U+8BE1　　TM **15** FM 丶

**guǐ** ADJ deceitful; tricky; scheming

诡辩 **guǐbiàn** V to quibble

诡称 **guǐchēng** V to allege falsely; to pretend

诡计 **guǐjì** N intrigue; trick · MW 个

这个家伙既喜欢**诡辩**，又喜欢玩**诡计**。 *This guy not only likes to quibble when speaking, but he also enjoys playing tricks.*

---

**1748　诱 誘**　　U+8BF1　　TM **15** FM 丶

**yòu** V to guide; to lure, to entice, to tempt

诱捕 **yòubǔ** V to trap

诱导 **yòudǎo** V to guide, to lead; to induce

诱饵 **yòu'ěr** N bait · MW 个

诱发 **yòufā** V to bring out, to cause (a disease, etc.); to induce

花粉**诱发**过敏。 *Pollen causes allergies.*

诱惑 **yòuhuò** V·N to lure, to entice; temptation · MW 个

这个世界充满了**诱惑**。 *There are too many temptations in this world.*

诱骗 **yòupiàn** V to trap; to trick

诱杀 **yòushā** V to trap and kill

**RELATED WORD**

利诱 472

---

**1749　调 調**　　U+8C03　　TM **15** FM 丶

**diào** V·N to shift, to transfer; accent; tune, melody; key, pitch; tone; intonation

**tiáo** V to mix, to blend; to harmonize; to mediate; to recuperate; to tease, to provoke; to regulate

调拨 **diàobō** V to allocate and transfer (goods, funds, etc.); to send

调查 **diàochá** V·N to investigate; inquiry

调查先于发言。 *Research should come before making a speech.*

调度 **diàodù** V·N to organize and dispatch (people, trains, buses, etc.); dispatcher · MW 个、名

调换 **diàohuàn** V to exchange

调换一下思维角度，你可能更容易理解别人的想法或处境。 *Exchanging points of view may help you understand others' situations better.*

调集 **diàojí** V to assemble; to muster

调令 **diàolìng** N transfer order · MW 个

调配 **diàopèi** V to allocate; to deploy

调用 **diàoyòng** V to allocate; to transfer

调子 **diàozi** N melody, tune; note; mood/tone (of a speech, etc.); view · MW 个

这个音乐的**调子**不错。 *The tone of this music is very nice.*

他的文章还是那个老**调子**。 *His article still holds the same view.*

调处 **tiáochù** V to mediate; to arbitrate

调和 **tiáohé** V·ADJ to mediate; to compromise; harmonious

调护 **tiáohù** V to nurse a convalescing patient

调剂 **tiáojì** V to adjust; to equalize; to make up a prescription

调教 **tiáojiào** V to educate (children); to train (animals)

调节 **tiáojié** V to adjust, to regulate

调节温度 *to adjust the temperature*

调解 **tiáojiě** V to mediate; to make peace

调理 **tiáolǐ** V to recuperate; to take care of

调料 **tiáoliào** N condiment; seasoning

调配 **tiáopèi** V to mix, to blend

调皮 **tiáopí** ADJ naughty; disobedient

**调皮**的孩子不一定没有出息。 *Naughty kids are not necessarily hopeless or without a future.*

调频 **tiáopín** V to adjust the frequency

调情 **tiáoqíng** V to flirt

**1749** 调 diào/tiáo (continued)

调色 tiáosè   V   to mix colors/paints

调试 tiáoshì   V   to test-run (equipment, etc.); to debug (a computer program)

调停 tiáotíng   V   to mediate; to intervene

调戏 tiáoxì   V   to molest (a woman)

调笑 tiáoxiào   V   to make fun of, to tease

调养 tiáoyǎng   V   to take good care of oneself (after illness)

调整 tiáozhěng   V   to adjust, to regulate; to restructure; to balance

调整心态 *to adjust your state of mind*

**RELATED WORDS**

| | | |
|---|---|---|
| 升调 47 | 失调 106 | 风调雨顺 194 |
| 走调 265 | 步调 266 | 曲调 272 |
| 声调 374 | 老调 375 | 协调 397 |
| 征调 462 | 字调 664 | 定调 666 |
| 单调 672 | 色调 831 | 音调 907 |
| 格调 1246 | 笔调 1278 | 情调 1491 |
| 语调 1501 | 高调 1611 | 强调 1896 |
| 市场调查 332 | 唱反调 1562 | 唱高调 1562 |
| 众口难调 175 | | |

---

**1750** 谜 谜   U+8C1C   TM **15** FM 丶

mí   N   riddle; mystery

谜底 mídǐ   N   answer to a riddle; truth of the matter ·   MW   个

谜语 míyǔ   N   riddle; conundrum ·   MW   个

人生就像一个**谜语**，没有人知道**谜底**。*Life is just like a riddle to which no one knows the answer.*

**RELATED WORDS**

| | | |
|---|---|---|
| 灯谜 350 | 字谜 671 | 猜谜 1610 |
| 解谜 1932 | | |

---

**1751** 谣 謠   U+8C23   TM **15** FM 丶

yáo   N   ballad, folk song; rumor

谣传 yáochuán   V·N   to be rumored, rumor has it that; rumor ·   MW   个

谣言 yáoyán   N   rumor, hearsay ·   MW   个

谣言不一定不真实。*A rumor may not always be false.*

**RELATED WORDS**

| | | |
|---|---|---|
| 民谣 388 | 童谣 1471 | 造谣 1515 |
| 歌谣 1900 | | |

---

**1752** 裙   U+88D9   TM **15** FM 丶

qún   N   skirt; apron

裙带关系 qúndàiguānxì   N   nepotism ·   MW   个

美国人说的**裙带关系**就是中国人说的走后门。*Nepotism in America is called "opening the back door" in China.*

裙子 qúnzi   N   skirt ·   MW   条

---

**1753** 裸   U+88F8   TM **15** FM 丶

luǒ   V   to be naked; to expose

裸露 luǒlù   V   to be naked

裸体 luǒtǐ   V·N   to be naked; nudity, nakedness

---

**1754** 祸 禍   U+7978   TM **15** FM 丶

huò   N·V   misfortune; to harm

祸不单行 huòbùdānxíng   EXP   when it rains, it pours

祸从口出 huòcóngkǒuchū   EXP   a loose tongue causes a lot of trouble

祸根 huògēn   N   root of the trouble ·   MW   条

我们必须铲除**祸根**。*We must root out the source of the trouble.*

祸害 huòhai   N·V   disaster; to damage; to destroy ·   MW   个

祸事 huòshì   N   disaster ·   MW   桩

祸首 huòshǒu   N   chief culprit ·   MW   个、名

我们一定要逮住**祸首**。*We must arrest the chief culprit.*

祸心 huòxīn   N   evil intent ·   MW   颗

**祸**不从口出，**祸根**出自**祸心**。*Disaster doesn't come from careless talk; the root of the trouble is evil intent.*

**RELATED WORDS**

| | |
|---|---|
| 车祸 114 | 灾祸 483 |
| 惹祸 1657 | 横祸 1775 |
| 嫁祸于人 1799 | 罪魁祸首 1542 |
| 幸灾乐祸 373 | |

---

**1755** 逻 邏   U+903B   TM **15** FM 丶

luó   N   patrol

逻辑 luójí   N   logic ·   MW   个

## 1756 道　U+9053　TM 15 FM ＼

**dào** N·V·MW  road; journey; way; channel; course; principle; morals; line; Taoism; Taoist; secret society; to speak, to say; [measure word for objects in the shape of a line (rivers, roads, wrinkles, etc.), for courses of a meal; for walls; and for questions, orders, etc.]

道德 **dàodé** N  morals; morality; ethics

道教 **dàojiào** N  Taoism (a Chinese religion)

道具 **dàojù** N  stage property; prop · MW 个
学生不是老师表演的**道具**。 *Students are not props for their teachers' performance.*

道理 **dàoli** N  truth; principle; reason; sense; method · MW 个、条

道路 **dàolù** N  road; way · MW 条
**道路**是人走出来的。 *Paths are created by people walking.*

道歉 **dàoqiàn** V  to apologize
他向她**道歉**。 *He apologized to her.*

道喜 **dàoxǐ** V  to congratulate on a happy occasion

道谢 **dàoxiè** V  to thank

道义 **dàoyì** N  morality and justice

### RELATED WORDS

| | |
|---|---|
| 人道 4 | 干道 13 |
| 小道 61 | 正道 76 |
| 公道 103 | 公道 103 |
| 左道旁门 113 | 车道 114 |
| 门道 130 | 走道 265 |
| 东道 307 | 布道 309 |
| 当道 335 | 味道 561 |
| 知道 647 | 近道 716 |
| 地道 772 | 地道 772 |
| 坑道 774 | 尿道 849 |
| 轨道 888 | 剑道 904 |
| 沟道 933 | 河道 934 |
| 难道 974 | 报道 1010 |
| 阴道 1041 | 食道 1053 |
| 铁道 1126 | 窄道 1143 |
| 远道 1184 | 柔道 1198 |
| 厚道 1272 | 背道而驰 1380 |
| 街道 1441 | 肠道 1458 |
| 楼道 1567 | 航道 1717 |
| 弹道 1763 | 管道 1861 |
| 跑道 1916 | 霸道 1998 |
| 人行道 4 | 下水道 10 |
| 仁义道德 64 | 公共道德 103 |
| 车行道 114 | 任重道远 211 |
| 打交道 289 | 让车道 348 |
| 志同道合 528 | 上呼吸道 14 |

| | |
|---|---|
| 羊肠小道 227 | 自行车道 305 |
| 孔孟之道 370 | 歪门邪道 511 |
| 难打交道 974 | 能说会道 1873 |

## 1757 通　U+901A　TM 15 FM ＼

**tōng** V·ADJ·N  to lead to, to connect with; to inform; to understand; to know; open; logical; ordinary; overall; expert

通报 **tōngbào** V·N  to inform; to circulate; circular, bulletin · MW 个

通才 **tōngcái** N  all-around person · MW 个、位、名

通常 **tōngcháng** ADV  usually, ordinarily
他**通常**上午学中文。 *He usually studies Chinese in the morning.*

通畅 **tōngchàng** ADJ  clear, unobstructed

通车 **tōngchē** V  to be open to traffic

通称 **tōngchēng** V·N  to be generally known as; common term · MW 个

通道 **tōngdào** N  route; passageway; (communications) channel · MW 条

通电 **tōngdiàn** V  to switch on (an electrical device); to electrify; to send a telegram

通风 **tōngfēng** V  to ventilate; to disclose information
这个建筑的**通风**很好。 *This building is well ventilated.*
你不能给她**通风**报信。 *You can't tip her off.*

通告 **tōnggào** V·N  to announce; public notice, announcement · MW 个

通过 **tōngguò** V·PREP  to adopt (a bill, etc.); to pass; by means of; by way of
**通过**一年的学习，学生们的中文进步很大。 *Students have made great progress after one year of studying Chinese.*

通红 **tōnghóng** ADJ  bright red

通货 **tōnghuò** N  currency · MW 笔

通缉 **tōngjī** V  to place on a wanted list

通力 **tōnglì** ADV  with a concerted effort

通路 **tōnglù** N  access; thoroughfare · MW 条

通气 **tōngqì** V·ADJ  to ventilate; to stay in touch; sensible

通融 **tōngróng** V  to stretch the rules (for), to make an exception (for)
**通融**也是中国文化的一个特点。 *Bending the rules for someone is also a characteristic of Chinese culture.*

**1757 通 tōng** (continued)

通商 **tōngshāng** V to have trade relations

通顺 **tōngshùn** ADJ coherent; smooth, polished

通俗 **tōngsú** ADJ popular; common

通天 **tōngtiān** V to have direct access to the highest authorities

通途 **tōngtú** N thoroughfare · MW 条

通宵 **tōngxiāo** N all night; overnight · MW 个

为了准备考试, 学生常常**通宵**学中文。
*Students often study Chinese all night in order to prepare for a test.*

通晓 **tōngxiǎo** V to understand thoroughly

通心粉 **tōngxīnfěn** N macaroni · MW 盘

通信 **tōngxìn** V to communicate by letter, to correspond

通行 **tōngxíng** V to pass through; to be in common use

通行证 **tōngxíngzhèng** N pass; permit · MW 张

学好中文是走向世界的"**通行证**"。
*Studying Chinese is a pass to the world arena.*

通讯 **tōngxùn** V·N to communicate; news report/ dispatch; correspondence · MW 篇

通用 **tōngyòng** V to be in common use

通知 **tōngzhī** V·N to notify, to inform; notice, circular · MW 个

通知书 **tōngzhīshū** N notice · MW 份

**RELATED WORDS**

| | |
|---|---|
| 不通 24 | 卡通片 36 |
| 互通有无 135 | 扑通 168 |
| 交通 222 | 买通 248 |
| 打通 289 | 勾通 303 |
| 灵通 359 | 私通 471 |
| 串通 522 | 变通 653 |
| 相通 805 | 沟通 933 |
| 普通 1484 | 流通 1493 |
| 想通 1769 | 精通 1832 |
| 卫星通信 82 | 行不通 327 |
| 到货通知 737 | 即时通讯 1047 |
| 新华通讯社 1638 | 水泄不通 159 |
| 此路不通 416 | |

**1758 施** U+65BD TM **15** FM 丶

**shī** V to carry out; to exert; to apply, to use

施放 **shīfàng** V to discharge, to fire

施肥 **shīféi** V to spread manure, to fertilize

施工 **shīgōng** V to construct

正在**施工**的工地又脏又乱。 *The construction site is messy and dirty.*

施加 **shījiā** V to exert (pressure, influence, etc.); to impose

施礼 **shīlǐ** V to salute

施舍 **shīshě** V to give alms

教育不是一种**施舍**, 而是一种奉献。
*Education is not the giving of alms, but devoted servitude.*

施行 **shīxíng** V to put in force, to implement; to apply

施用 **shīyòng** V to use, to employ

施展 **shīzhǎn** V to put to good use

老师应该给学生**施展**才能的机会。
*Teachers should provide their students with opportunities to display their talents.*

施政 **shīzhèng** V to govern; to administer

施主 **shīzhǔ** N almsgiver; benefactor · MW 个、位、名

教师不是一位**施主**, 而是一个"仆人"。
*An educator is not an alms giver, but a servant.*

**RELATED WORDS**

| | | |
|---|---|---|
| 实施 668 | 设施 1179 | 因材施教 270 |

**1759 粮 糧** U+7CAE TM **15** FM 丶

**liáng** N grain; food; provisions

粮仓 **liángcāng** N granary; barn · MW 座

粮草 **liángcǎo** N army provisions · MW 堆

粮店 **liángdiàn** N grain shop · MW 家

粮票 **liángpiào** N food coupon · MW 张

粮食 **liángshi** N cereals; food

二十年前, 人们(在中国)还要用**粮票**到**粮店**去买**粮食**。 *Twenty years ago in China, people bought grain from grain shops with food coupons.*

粮站 **liángzhàn** N grain distribution station · MW 个

**RELATED WORD**

产粮 219

**1760 辣** U+8FA3 TM **15** FM 丶

**là** ADJ·N hot, sharp, spicy; vicious, ruthless

辣酱 **làjiàng** N thick chili sauce · MW 瓶

辣椒 **làjiāo** N hot pepper · MW 个

辣味 làwèi  N  spicy taste

四川菜的**辣味**同湖南菜的**辣味**不一样。
*The spicy taste of Sichuan food is different from the spiciness of Hunan.*

**RELATED WORDS**

辛辣 331          泼辣 937          酸辣汤 1899

1761  **割**                    U+5272          TM **15**  FM ﹨

gē  V  to cut; to cut apart, to divide

割爱 gē'ài  V  to give up what one treasures

既然您喜欢它，我只好**割**爱了。*Since you love it so much, I will have to give up what I also treasure.*

割草机 gēcǎojī  N  mower ·  MW  台

割除 gēchú  V  to cut off

割断 gēduàn  V  to cut off, to sever

我们不应该**割断**文化的根。*We shouldn't cut off our cultural roots.*

割裂 gēliè  V  to cut apart, to separate

割让 gēràng  V  to cede (territory, etc.)

**RELATED WORDS**

刀割 31          分割 173          收割 282
宰割 1140

## 1762 确 確 U+786E TM **16** FM 一

**què** V·ADJ·ADV to ensure; true; reliable; authentic; firmly; indeed, truly, really

确保 **quèbǎo** V to ensure, to make certain

确定 **quèdìng** V·ADJ to confirm; definite, certain

确立 **quèlì** V to set up, to establish

确切 **quèqiè** ADJ definite; reliable; exact, precise
傻瓜有确切的证据去确定这件事是违法的。
*ShaGua has reliable evidence to prove that this is illegal.*

确认 **quèrèn** V to confirm; to acknowledge

确实 **quèshí** ADJ·ADV true; reliable; really, certainly

确信 **quèxìn** V to firmly believe; to be completely convinced
我们确信他能确保学生的安全。
*We firmly believe that he can guarantee his students' safety.*

确凿 **quèzáo** ADJ conclusive, undeniable

确诊 **quèzhěn** V to confirm a diagnosis
医生已经确诊他得了阑尾炎。*The doctor has confirmed that he has appendicitis.*

确证 **quèzhèng** V·N to prove, to confirm; ironclad proof, conclusive evidence · MW 个

**RELATED WORDS**

| 正确 76 | 准确 929 | 明确 1035 |
| 的确 1117 | 精确 1832 | |

## 1763 弹 彈 U+5F39 TM **16** FM 一

**dàn** N pellet; bullet; cannonball; bomb

**tán** V to play, to pluck (a musical instrument); to flick; to flip; to spring

弹袋 **dàndài** N ammunition belt · MW 条

弹道 **dàndào** N trajectory · MW 条

弹夹 **dànjiā** N clip; magazine · MW 个

弹壳 **dànké** N shell/cartridge case · MW 个、枚

弹片 **dànpiàn** N shell fragment · MW 枚、块

弹头 **dàntóu** N bullet; warhead · MW 个、颗
核弹头威胁世界和平。*Atomic bombs have threatened world peace.*

弹药 **dànyào** N ammunition · MW 批

弹药库 **dànyàokù** N ammunition depot · MW 个、间、座

**RELATED WORDS**

| 飞弹 81 | 子弹 83 | 炸弹 701 |
| 导弹 751 | 乱弹琴 901 | 投弹 1008 |
| 核弹 1026 | 防弹 1040 | 枪弹 1244 |
| 避弹衣 1976 | 原子弹 1273 | 催泪弹 1592 |

## 1764 喘 U+5598 TM **16** FM |

**chuǎn** V·N to gasp; to breathe rapidly, to pant; asthma

哮喘 *asthma*

喘气 **chuǎnqì** V to breathe deeply; to take a breather
他忙得连喘气的机会都没有。*He is so busy that he can't even take a breather.*

喘息 **chuǎnxī** V to pant; to take a breather

**RELATED WORD**

气喘 185

## 1765 圈 U+5708 TM **16** FM |

**juān** V to pen (in); to confine; to put in jail

**juàn** N corral, sty, fold (for sheep)

**quān** N·V circle; group, clique; to circle; to encircle; to mark with a circle

圈套 **quāntào** N snare, trap · MW 个

圈子 **quānzi** N circle, clique · MW 个
有人喜欢在同事中搞小圈子。*Some people like to create cliques among colleagues.*

**RELATED WORDS**

| 项圈 725 | 圆圈 1391 | 眼圈 1570 |
| 子午圈 83 | | |

## 1766 葡 U+8461 TM **16** FM |

**pú** N grape

葡萄　pútáo　N　grape　·　MW　颗、串

葡萄干　pútáogān　N　raisin　·　MW　颗、盒

葡萄酒　pútáojiǔ　N　(grape) wine　·　MW　杯、瓶

你喜欢红**葡萄酒**还是白**葡萄酒**？*Do you like white or red wine?*

葡萄糖　pútáotáng　N　glucose　·　MW　包

葡萄牙　Pútáoyá　N　Portugal

---

### 1767　幕　U+5E55　TM **16** FM |

mù　N　curtain; tent; office of the commanding officer; act

幕布　mùbù　N　curtain　·　MW　块

幕后　mùhòu　N　behind the scenes; backstage

傻瓜不知道是谁在**幕后**操纵这件事。
*ShaGua doesn't know who is in control behind the scenes.*

幕僚　mùliáo　N　aides and staff　·　MW　个、名

**RELATED WORDS**

| 开幕 26 | 内幕 191 | 字幕 664 |
| 闭幕 677 | 序幕 915 | 黑幕 1389 |
| 揭幕 1851 | 谢幕 1890 | |

---

### 1768　蒸　U+84B8　TM **16** FM |

zhēng　V　to evaporate; to steam; to braise

蒸发　zhēngfā　V　to evaporate

蒸锅　zhēngguō　N　food steamer　·　MW　个

蒸馏　zhēngliú　V　to distill

蒸笼　zhēnglóng　N　food steamer　·　MW　个

蒸汽　zhēngqì　N　steam　·　MW　团、股

水**蒸汽**覆盖了浴室的镜子。*Moisture from the steam has covered the mirror in the bathroom.*

蒸蒸日上　zhēngzhēngrìshàng　EXP　becoming more prosperous every day

**RELATED WORDS**

| 清蒸 1495 | 熏蒸 1690 |

---

### 1769　想　U+60F3　TM **16** FM |

xiǎng　V　to think; would like to; to miss, to long for

想必　xiǎngbì　ADV　most probably, most likely

想不到　xiǎngbudào　V　to not expect

想不开　xiǎngbukāi　V　to take to heart; to take things too seriously

想当然　xiǎngdāngrán　V　to take for granted

想得到　xiǎngdédào　V　to think; to expect

想得开　xiǎngdekāi　V·ADJ　to not take to heart; to look on the bright side of things; lighthearted

想法　xiǎngfa　N　idea; opinion　·　MW　个

你**想**得到她会有这种**想法**吗？*Can you believe she came up with this idea?*

想方设法　xiǎngfāngshèfǎ　EXP　to do everything possible; to move heaven and earth

想念　xiǎngniàn　V　to miss, to long for

**想**必你**想**不到她会**想念**你。*Most likely, you didn't expect that she would miss you.*

想起　xiǎngqǐ　V　to recall, to think of

想通　xiǎngtōng　V　to think things through; to become convinced

他**想通**以后，就**想方设法**竞选市长。
*Once he thought it through, he tried every means possible to be elected mayor.*

想象　xiǎngxiàng　V·N　to imagine; to visualize; imagination　·　MW　个

**RELATED WORDS**

| 休想 213 | 幻想 475 | 空想 669 |
| 料想 961 | 设想 1179 | 理想 1200 |
| 联想 1206 | 思想 1214 | 梦想 1217 |
| 推想 1242 | 着想 1332 | 预想 1528 |
| 假想 1586 | 猜想 1594 | 意想 1812 |
| 感想 1860 | | |

---

### 1770　墙　墙　U+5899　TM **16** FM |

qiáng　N　wall; [like a wall]

墙报　qiángbào　N　wall newspaper (displayed and read in public places)　·　MW　版

墙壁　qiángbì　N　wall　·　MW　面

傻瓜办公室的**墙壁**上挂着一幅中国水墨画。
*There is a traditional Chinese painting hanging on a wall in ShaGua's office.*

墙根　qiánggēn　N　foot/base of a wall/fence

墙角　qiángjiǎo　N　corner (of a room, etc.)　·　MW　个

**墙角**放着一对中国青花瓷瓶。*There are two Chinese vases in the corners.*

墙脚　qiángjiǎo　N　foot/base of a wall/fence

墙头　qiángtóu　N　top of a wall

**RELATED WORD**

隔火墙 1910

## 1771 揉 U+63C9 TM 16 FM |

**róu** V to knead; to rub; to caress; to cause (something) to bend

**揉搓 róucuō** V to rub; to torment

**揉面 róumiàn** V to knead dough
学生在学怎么**揉面**包饺子。
*Students are learning how to knead dough for dumplings.*

## 1772 摄 攝 U+6444 TM 16 FM |

**shè** V to absorb, to assimilate; to take a photograph; to act for

**摄取 shèqǔ** V to absorb, to assimilate
学中文也是在**摄取**多元文化的营养。
*Studying Chinese is another way to absorb the substance of cultural diversity.*

**摄入 shèrù** V to absorb; to assimilate

**摄食 shèshí** V to eat, to consume (of animals)
有的动物喜欢在夜里**摄食**。*Some animals like to eat at night.*

**摄影 shèyǐng** V to shoot a film; to take a photograph

**摄影机 shèyǐngjī** N (movie) camera · MW 台、部

**摄政 shèzhèng** V to act as regent/governor

**RELATED WORD**
拍摄　790

## 1773 摆 擺 襬 U+6446 TM 16 FM |

**bǎi** V·N to put, to place; to arrange; to display; to wave; to talk about; pendulum; hem (of a gown, a jacket, a skirt, etc.)

**摆布 bǎibù** V to arrange; to order around, to control

**摆动 bǎidòng** V to swing; to sway

**摆架子 bǎijiàzi** V to put on airs
甭**摆架子**了，谁不知道你呀？*Don't put on airs; who doesn't know who you are?*

**摆阔 bǎikuò** V to be ostentatious; to parade one's wealth

**摆门面 bǎiménmiàn** V to keep up appearances

**摆弄 bǎinòng** V to move back and forth; to fiddle with

**摆设 bǎishe** V·N to furnish and decorate (a room); decorations · MW 个、套
你家**摆设**很讲究。*Your house is elaborately decorated.*
你不是一个**摆设**，而是一个领导。*You are not just a poster boy, but one of the leaders.*

**摆摊子 bǎitānzi** V to set up a booth/stall; to maintain a large organization

**摆脱 bǎituō** V to shake off, to cast away (old ideas, etc.)

**摆样子 bǎiyàngzi** V to do (something) for show
学中文不是为了**摆样子**。
*The study of Chinese should not be done for show.*

**RELATED WORD**
摇摆　1664

## 1774 撕 U+6495 TM 16 FM |

**sī** V to tear, to rip

**撕毁 sīhuǐ** V to tear up

**撕开 sīkāi** V to tear, to rip
她急急忙忙地**撕开**信封。*She tore the letter open in a hurry.*

**撕裂痛 sīliètòng** N tearing pain

## 1775 横 U+6A2A TM 16 FM |

**héng** ADJ·ADV·V·N horizontal; across; sideways; violently; flagrantly; to move/turn crosswise; horizontal stroke (of a Chinese character)

**hèng** ADJ harsh; unreasonable; unexpected

**横竖 héngshù** ADV in any case, anyway
中文是必修课，**横竖**你都得学。
*Chinese is a required course; you have to take it regardless.*

**横向 héngxiàng** ADJ horizontal; lateral

**横行 héngxíng** V to run wild

**横暴 hèngbào** ADJ perverse; violent; cruel

**横财 hèngcái** N ill-gotten gains · MW 笔
有些整天人只想着发**横财**。*Some only think of realizing ill-gotten gains.*

**横祸 hènghuò** N unexpected disaster

**RELATED WORD**
专横　155

## 1776 棍

U+68CD · TM **16** FM |

**gùn** N stick, rod; scoundrel, rascal

**棍棒 gùnbàng** N club, cudgel · MW 条、根

**棍子 gùnzi** N stick; long, slender piece of wood/bamboo · MW 条、根

### RELATED WORDS

曲棍球 272　　　打棍子 289　　　冰棍 493
警棍 1987

## 1777 幅

U+5E45 · TM **16** FM |

**fú** N·MW width; breadth; size; [measure word for paintings, calligraphic works, maps, etc.]

**幅度 fúdù** N range, scope, extent

她的中文成绩有很大**幅度**的提高。
*She has made considerable progress in her Chinese.*

**幅员 fúyuán** N size; area

### RELATED WORDS

大幅度 20　　　条幅 598　　　篇幅 1921

## 1778 帽

U+5E3D · TM **16** FM |

**mào** N hat; cap; caplike cover

**帽徽 màohuī** N insignia on a cap · MW 枚

**帽盔 màokuī** N helmet · MW 顶

**帽檐 màoyán** N brim of a hat · MW 个

**帽子 màozi** N hat; cap; label · MW 顶

无论春夏秋冬，傻瓜从来不戴**帽子**。*No matter how hot or cold it is, ShaGua never wears a hat in any season.*

### RELATED WORDS

衣帽间 330　　　扣帽子 401　　　草帽 768
睡帽 1571　　　脱帽 1803　　　戴帽子 1941
乌纱帽 601

## 1779 晚

U+665A · TM **16** FM |

**wǎn** N·ADJ evening; night; late; belated; delayed, behind; later, succeeding

**晚安 wǎn'ān** V to say good night

**晚班 wǎnbān** N night shift · MW 个

**晚报 wǎnbào** N evening paper · MW 份、张

**晚辈 wǎnbèi** N younger generation; juniors · MW 个、名

**晚餐 wǎncān** N dinner, supper · MW 顿

**晚餐**时间是六点钟。*Dinner is at 6 o'clock.*

**晚场 wǎnchǎng** N evening show · MW 次

**晚车 wǎnchē** N night train · MW 趟

**晚点 wǎndiǎn** V to be late, to be behind schedule

从北京来的飞机**晚点**了一个小时。
*The flight from Beijing is one hour late.*

**晚饭 wǎnfàn** N dinner, supper · MW 餐、顿

傻瓜都是在吃**晚饭**的时候读**晚报**。
*ShaGua always reads the evening newspaper while he eats dinner.*

**晚会 wǎnhuì** N (evening) party · MW 个

**晚间 wǎnjiān** N evening; night

**晚年 wǎnnián** N old age · MW 个

**晚期 wǎnqī** N late period (of an artist, a writer)

**晚上 wǎnshang** N evening; night · MW 个

**晚上**傻瓜上夜校。*ShaGua goes to night school in the evening.*

### RELATED WORDS

早晚 268　　　夜晚 654　　　昨晚 810
傍晚 1698　　　一天到晚 1

## 1780 蜡 蠟

U+8721 · TM **16** FM |

**là** N wax; candle

**蜡笔 làbǐ** N crayon · MW 根、支、盒

盒子里有十二支不同颜色的**蜡笔**。*There are twelve different-colored crayons in the box.*

**蜡像 làxiàng** N wax image · MW 尊

**蜡纸 làzhǐ** N wax paper · MW 张

**蜡烛 làzhú** N candle · MW 根

老师像一根**蜡烛**，燃烧自己，照亮别人。
*A teacher is like a candle that burns itself to give off light for others.*

### RELATED WORD

蜂蜡 1682

## 1781 赚 賺

U+8D5A · TM **16** FM |

**zhuàn** V to earn money; to make a profit

**赚钱 zhuànqián** V to make money / a profit

很多学中文的学生想去中国打工**赚钱**。
*Many students who study Chinese want to work and make money in China.*

## 1782 鸭 鸭 U+9E2D TM 16 FM |

**yā** N duck; duckling

**鸭蛋** yādàn N duck's egg · MW 个

**鸭绒** yāróng N down; eiderdown · MW 团

**鸭肉** yāròu N duck (meat) · MW 块

**鸭子** yāzi N duck · MW 只

### RELATED WORDS

烤鸭 1505　　丑小鸭 85

## 1783 趣 U+8DA3 TM 16 FM |

**qù** N·ADJ interest; inclination; interesting, entertaining

**趣味** qùwèi N interest; taste; delight
学中文很有**趣味**。*Studying Chinese is a delight.*

**趣闻** qùwén N interesting news · MW 个
傻瓜有很多**趣闻**。*There is a lot of interesting news about ShaGua.*

### RELATED WORDS

风趣 194　　兴趣 228　　乐趣 299
有趣 439　　志趣 528　　没趣 938
情趣 1491

## 1784 跟 U+8DDF TM 16 FM |

**gēn** PREP·CONJ·V·N with; to; toward; from; same as; and; to follow, to go with; to marry (of a woman); heel

**跟班** gēnbān V to join a regular shift/class

**跟进** gēnjìn V to follow; to follow up

**跟前** gēnqián N closeness; approach; in front of
傻瓜把孩子们叫到**跟前**，告诉他们学中文的重要性。*ShaGua asked his kids to gather around him, and told them all of the importance of studying Chinese.*

**跟上** gēnshàng V to keep pace with; to catch up with

**跟随** gēnsuí V to follow, to go after
学生**跟随**着老师大声读课文。*Students follow along as their teachers read the lesson aloud.*

**跟头** gēntou N tumble; fall · MW 个

**跟踪** gēnzōng V to track, to tail
他企图**跟踪**别人，结果自己摔了一个**跟头**。*He tried to tail someone, but he took a tumble himself.*

### RELATED WORDS

栽跟头 995　　紧跟 1537　　鞋跟 1789
脚跟 1804　　摔跟头 1852

## 1785 路 U+8DEF TM 16 FM |

**lù** N road; path; route; way; journey; distance; means; line; sequence

**路标** lùbiāo N road sign · MW 个

**路程** lùchéng N distance traveled · MW 段
从美国到中国**路程**很遥远。*There is a huge distance between China and the U.S.*

**路灯** lùdēng N streetlight · MW 盏

**路基** lùjī N roadbed · MW 层

**路口** lùkǒu N intersection, crossing · MW 个
怎么面对人生的**路口**？*How should one face a crossroads in life?*

**路面** lùmiàn N road surface · MW 层

**路牌** lùpái N street sign · MW 个
在中国，**路牌**上只写汉字，没有拼音。*In China, there are street signs with Chinese characters, but no pinyin.*

**路人** lùrén N passerby; stranger · MW 个、名

**路条** lùtiáo N travel permit; pass · MW 张

**路途** lùtú N road; way; journey · MW 段

**路线** lùxiàn N itinerary; route; line; (political) course · MW 条

**路障** lùzhàng N roadblock, barricade · MW 个

**路子** lùzi N way; means; personal connections
这个家伙有很多**路子**。*This guy has a lot of minor resources and personal connections to deal with situations.*

### RELATED WORDS

| | | |
|---|---|---|
| 卡路里 36 | 公路 103 | 公路桥 103 |
| 半路 127 | 半路出家 127 | 门路 130 |
| 去路 157 | 水路 159 | 马路 247 |
| 出路 258 | 来路 260 | 电路 263 |
| 走路 265 | 后路 310 | 让路 348 |
| 环路 369 | 回路 391 | 此路不通 416 |
| 有路子 439 | 死路 510 | 同路 541 |
| 拦路 576 | 歧路 585 | 纹路 640 |
| 养路 670 | 过路 712 | 近路 716 |
| 岔路 829 | 顺路 874 | 邪路 981 |
| 陆路 1043 | 线路 1105 | 铁路 1126 |
| 窄路 1143 | 沿路 1165 | 迷路 1187 |
| 思路 1214 | 指路标 1397 | 领路 1465 |
| 弯路 1472 | 退路 1508 | 绝路 1706 |
| 铺路 1713 | 销路 1714 | 航路 1717 |

道路 1756  通路 1757  十字路口 3
之字路 67  回头路 391  冤家路窄 1729
走投无路 265  必由之路 338  丝绸之路 637

---

**1786 跳** U+8DF3 TM **16** FM |

**tiào** V to jump, to leap; to hop; to bounce; to beat; to skip

跳板 **tiàobǎn** N diving board · MW 块

跳动 **tiàodòng** V to beat, to pulse
演讲就要开始了，傻瓜的心脏剧烈地**跳动**起来。 *When it was almost time for the speech, ShaGua's heart began to pump powerfully.*

跳级 **tiàojí** V to skip a grade

跳栏 **tiàolán** N hurdle race · MW 个

跳马 **tiàomǎ** N horse-vaulting (gymnastics) · MW 个

跳伞 **tiàosǎn** V to parachute; to bale out

跳绳 **tiàoshéng** V·N to skip rope; jump/skip rope · MW 根

跳水 **tiàoshuǐ** V to dive; to commit suicide by jumping into water and drowning

跳台 **tiàotái** N diving tower/platform · MW 个

跳舞 **tiàowǔ** V to dance
傻瓜的女儿喜欢**跳舞**，特别是红绸舞。 *ShaGua's daughter likes to dance, particularly the Chinese Red Silk Dance.*

跳远 **tiàoyuǎn** V to perform the long jump

跳跃 **tiàoyuè** V to jump; to bound; to hop (for joy)

跳蚤 **tiàozǎo** N flea · MW 只

跳闸 **tiàozhá** V to trip (a circuit breaker)

**RELATED WORDS**

心跳 232  吓一跳 287  蹦蹦跳跳 1994
上蹿下跳 14

---

**1787 踩** U+8E29 TM **16** FM |

**cǎi** V to step on; to trample

---

**1788 靴** U+9774 TM **16** FM |

**xuē** N boot

靴子 **xuēzi** N boot · MW 对、双

---

**1789 鞋** U+978B TM **16** FM |

**xié** N shoe

鞋带 **xiédài** N shoelace · MW 根
**鞋带**松了，请系上。 *Your shoelace is loose; please tie it.*

鞋底 **xiédǐ** N sole (of a shoe) · MW 个

鞋垫 **xiédiàn** N insole · MW 对

鞋跟 **xiégēn** N heel (of a shoe) · MW 个

鞋油 **xiéyóu** N shoe polish · MW 点、盒
傻瓜从来不擦**鞋油**。 *ShaGua never polishes his shoes.*

**RELATED WORDS**

雨鞋 720  凉鞋 1337  破鞋 1374
拖鞋 1396  跑鞋 1916

---

**1790 舞** U+821E TM **16** FM 丿

**wǔ** N·V dance; to dance; to flutter; to wave, to brandish; to play with

舞伴 **wǔbàn** N dance partner · MW 个、位、名

舞弊 **wǔbì** V to embezzle

舞场 **wǔchǎng** N dance hall, ballroom · MW 个

舞蹈 **wǔdǎo** N dance · MW 个

舞动 **wǔdòng** V to wave, to brandish

舞会 **wǔhuì** N dance; ball; dance party · MW 场
今晚上有一场**舞会**，你参加吗？ *Will you attend the ball tonight?*

舞剧 **wǔjù** N ballet · MW 场

舞女 **wǔnǚ** N dancing girl; taxi dancer · MW 个、名

舞台 **wǔtái** N stage · MW 个
社会是人生的大**舞台**。 *Society is a huge stage for life.*

**RELATED WORDS**

手舞足蹈 104  挥舞 1236  鼓舞 1688
跳舞 1786  歌舞 1900  狐步舞 885
恰恰舞 930  狮子舞 1285  踢踏舞 1946

---

**1791 靠** U+9760 TM **16** FM 丿

**kào** V·PREP to lean (on/against); to keep to; to rely on; to trust; by

靠岸 **kào'àn** V to draw alongside; to reach shore

靠背 **kàobèi** N back of a chair

## 1791 靠 kào (continued)

**靠边 kàobiān** V to keep to the side

劳驾，请靠边站一站。 *Excuse me, please keep to the side.*

**靠不住 kàobuzhù** V to be unreliable

**靠近 kàojìn** V to be nearby / close to; to approach

**靠山 kàoshān** N backer, sponsor, patron; backing, sponsorship · MW 个

有时候，靠山也是靠不住的。 *A sponsor may sometimes be unreliable.*

**靠椅 kàoyǐ** N armchair · MW 张

### RELATED WORDS

| | | |
|---|---|---|
| 可靠 243 | 牢靠 488 | 依靠 625 |
| 投靠 1008 | 指靠 1397 | 停靠 1588 |

## 1792 怨  U+6028　　TM **16** FM 丿

**yuàn** V·N to blame; resentment; hatred

**怨愤 yuànfèn** N resentment and indignation

**怨恨 yuànhèn** V·N to resent; to hate; resentment

**怨气 yuànqì** N grievance, complaint; resentment · MW 股

你哪来那么多怨气？ *Where did you get so much resentment?*

**怨天尤人 yuàntiānyóurén** EXP to blame everyone but oneself (LIT to blame God and man)

**怨言 yuànyán** N complaint

一旦决定去做了，傻瓜绝无怨言。 *As long as a decision has been made, ShaGua will never complain.*

### RELATED WORDS

| | | |
|---|---|---|
| 含怨 592 | 埋怨 1002 | 恩怨 1381 |
| 以德报怨 101 | 任劳任怨 211 | |

## 1793 属 屬 U+5C5E　　TM **16** FM 丿

**shǔ** V to be affiliated with, to belong to; to be subordinate to, to be under

**属地 shǔdì** N possession (of territory); dependency · MW 个

**属性 shǔxìng** N property; attribute · MW 个

**属于 shǔyú** V to belong to, to be owned by; to be part of

傻瓜属于沉默寡言的人。 *ShaGua is a person of few words.*

### RELATED WORDS

| | | |
|---|---|---|
| 从属 66 | 归属 166 | 金属 420 |
| 直属 609 | 所属 645 | 亲属 908 |
| 部属 1636 | | |

## 1794 鼻 U+9F3B　　TM **16** FM 丿

**bí** N nose

**鼻孔 bíkǒng** N nostril · MW 个

**鼻梁 bíliáng** N bridge (of the nose)

**鼻毛 bímáo** N nose hair · MW 根

傻瓜不剪鼻毛，说是剪了股票要跌。 *ShaGua refused to cut his nose hairs, because he believed that doing so would make his stock drop.*

**鼻腔 bíqiāng** N nasal cavity

**鼻青脸肿 bíqīngliǎnzhǒng** ADJ badly battered (LIT bloody nose and swollen face)

**鼻塞 bísāi** V to have a stuffy nose

**鼻炎 bíyán** N rhinitis

**鼻音 bíyīn** N nasal sound · MW 个

**鼻子 bízi** N nose · MW 个

**鼻子出血 bízichūxuè** V to have a nosebleed

### RELATED WORDS

| | | |
|---|---|---|
| 扑鼻 168 | 哭鼻子 1221 | 捂鼻子 1399 |
| 流鼻涕 1493 | 塌鼻子 1903 | |

## 1795 舅 U+8205　　TM **16** FM 丿

**jiù** N maternal uncle; brother-in-law, wife's brother

**舅父 jiùfù** N maternal uncle, mother's brother · MW 个、位

**舅舅 jiùjiu** N maternal uncle, mother's brother · MW 个、位

**舅母 jiùmu** N wife of mother's brother · MW 个、位

### RELATED WORDS

| | |
|---|---|
| 小舅子 61 | 娘舅 1448 |

## 1796 简  簡 U+7B80　　TM **16** FM 丿

**jiǎn** ADJ·N simple; brief; simplified; letter; bamboo slips (for writing)

**简报 jiǎnbào** N bulletin; briefing · MW 份

简便 jiǎnbiàn ADJ convenient, handy

简称 jiǎnchēng V·N to call (someone/something) for short; short form; abbreviation · MW 个

简单 jiǎndān ADJ simple; ordinary; casual, careless

傻瓜头脑简单。*ShaGua's mind is simple.*

这个人不简单。*This person is unusual.*

简单化 jiǎndānhuà V to oversimplify

简短 jiǎnduǎn ADJ brief, succinct

简化 jiǎnhuà V to simplify

简化汉字 jiǎnhuàhànzì N simplified Chinese characters

现在大多数学中文的美国学生都学简化汉字。
*Now, most American students who study Chinese learn simplified Chinese characters.*

简洁 jiǎnjié ADJ succinct, concise (of speech, writing, etc.)

简介 jiǎnjiè N brief introduction; synopsis · MW 份

简括 jiǎnkuò V to briefly summarize

简历 jiǎnlì N résumé · MW 份

傻瓜的简历不简单。*ShaGua's résumé is not simple.*

简练 jiǎnliàn ADJ succinct, concise

简陋 jiǎnlòu ADJ crude (of a house, a facility, etc.)

简明 jiǎnmíng ADJ simple and clear, concise

简谱 jiǎnpǔ N numerical musical notation (as opposed to Western staff-based musical notation) · MW 份

傻瓜不识简谱。*ShaGua can't read numerical sheet music.*

简朴 jiǎnpǔ ADJ simple and unadorned; plain

简体 jiǎntǐ N simplified style of Chinese characters

简写 jiǎnxiě V·N to write simplified characters; to write simply; simplified Chinese characters (as opposed to traditional characters)

简讯 jiǎnxùn N news in brief · MW 份

简要 jiǎnyào ADJ brief, concise

简易 jiǎnyì ADJ simple and easy; simply constructed

简约 jiǎnyuē ADJ brief, concise; sketchy

简章 jiǎnzhāng N general regulations; briefing · MW 份

简直 jiǎnzhí ADV simply; at all

傻瓜说话很简短，有时简直是不成句。
*ShaGua speaks very briefly; sometimes he doesn't finish sentences at all.*

**RELATED WORDS**

从简 66      精简 1832

---

| 1797 | 箱 | | U+7BB1 | TM **16** | FM 丿 |

xiāng N box; trunk; case; [shaped like a box]

箱子 xiāngzi N box; case; chest · MW 个、只

**RELATED WORDS**

| | | |
|---|---|---|
| 木箱 40 | 皮箱 261 | 衣箱 330 |
| 冰箱 493 | 信箱 869 | 烘箱 953 |
| 邮箱 1046 | 装箱单 1476 | 烤箱 1505 |
| 提箱 1554 | 垃圾箱 399 | 集装箱 1267 |

---

| 1798 | 嫂 | | U+5AC2 | TM **16** | FM 丿 |

sǎo N sister-in-law, older brother's wife; form of address for a friend's wife or married woman about one's own age

嫂嫂 sǎosao N sister-in-law, older brother's wife · MW 个、位

嫂子 sǎozi N sister-in-law, older brother's wife · MW 个、位

**RELATED WORDS**

姑嫂 881      哥嫂 1370

---

| 1799 | 嫁 | | U+5AC1 | TM **16** | FM 丿 |

jià V to marry (of a woman); to shift/transfer (the blame, the loss, the burden, etc.) to

嫁祸于人 jiàhuòyúrén V to shift the blame to

嫁接 jiàjiē V to graft (botany)

嫁娶 jiàqǔ V to marry

嫁人 jiàrén V to marry

这个姑娘还读高中时就开始想嫁人的事了。
*This girl has been thinking about marriage since high school.*

嫁妆 jiàzhuang N dowry

傻瓜太太已为上小学的女儿准备好了嫁妆。
*Mrs. ShaGua has already prepared a dowry for her daughter, who is still in elementary school.*

**RELATED WORDS**

出嫁 258      婚嫁 1701

---

| 1800 | 嫩 | | U+5AE9 | TM **16** | FM 丿 |

nèn ADJ tender; rare (of meat); light (in color); green, immature, inexperienced

嫩色 nènsè N light color

**1800 嫩 nèn** (continued)

嫩稚 **nènzhì** ADJ tender

**RELATED WORDS**

娇嫩 882　　　柔嫩 1198　　　鲜嫩 1811
脸皮嫩 1461

---

**1801 绣** 綉　　U+7EE3　　TM **16** FM ノ

**xiù** V·N to embroider; embroidery

湘**绣** Hunan embroidery

绣花 **xiùhuā** V to embroider

绣像 **xiùxiàng** N embroidered portrait ·
MW 幅

**RELATED WORDS**

苏绣 552　　　　　　刺绣 1050

---

**1802 脖**　　U+8116　　TM **16** FM ノ

**bó** N neck; [shaped like a neck]

脖子 **bózi** N neck · MW 条
纽约的饭店也卖"北京烤鸭"，但鸭**脖子**
特别长。 There are some stores that sell Beijing
Roast Duck in New York, but the ducks' necks
are exceptionally long.

---

**1803 脱**　　U+8131　　TM **16** FM ノ

**tuō** V to shed, to lose (skin, hair, etc.);
to fall out (of hair); to take off; to escape (from);
to miss

脱班 **tuōbān** V to be late for work

脱产 **tuōchǎn** V to be released from one's regular
work

脱发 **tuōfà** V to lose one's hair
傻瓜已**脱发**。 ShaGua is balding.

脱离 **tuōlí** V to break off (relations, etc.);
to get away from

脱漏 **tuōlòu** V to be left out / omitted

脱落 **tuōluò** V to drop, to come / fall off

脱毛 **tuōmáo** V to shed hair/fur (of animals)

脱帽 **tuōmào** V to take off one's hat

脱期 **tuōqī** V to fail to come out on time,
to miss a deadline (of a periodical)

脱色 **tuōsè** V to fade

傻瓜的牛仔裤已**脱色**。 ShaGua's jeans have
faded.

脱身 **tuōshēn** V to get away/free

脱手 **tuōshǒu** V to let slip (out of one's hands);
to get rid of (goods)

脱水 **tuōshuǐ** V to be dehydrated

脱险 **tuōxiǎn** V to escape danger; to be out of
danger

脱销 **tuōxiāo** V to run out of (goods); to be out
of stock
这本中文教材**脱销**至少半年了。 This Chinese
textbook has been sold out for at least half
a year.

脱脂 **tuōzhī** V to remove fat (from)

**RELATED WORDS**

逃脱 1509　　　　　　虚脱 1534
摆脱 1773　　　　　　解脱 1928

---

**1804 脚**　　U+811A　　TM **16** FM ノ

**jiǎo** N foot; base; role, part, character

脚本 **jiǎoběn** N script; scenario · MW 本
人生的**脚本**谁也不敢预先偷看。
Nobody would dare steal a glimpse at the script
of his or her future life.

脚步 **jiǎobù** N step; footstep; pace · MW 个

脚底 **jiǎodǐ** N sole (of the foot) · MW 个

脚跟 **jiǎogēn** N heel; footing · MW 个

脚尖 **jiǎojiān** N tiptoe; tip of the toe ·
MW 个

脚踏实地 **jiǎotàshídì** EXP down-to-earth
傻瓜总是**脚踏实地**地工作。 ShaGua always works
in an unpretentious manner.

脚印 **jiǎoyìn** N footprint; track · MW 个

脚掌 **jiǎozhǎng** N sole (of the foot) · MW 个

脚趾 **jiǎozhǐ** N toe · MW 个

脚趾甲 **jiǎozhǐjia** N toenail · MW 片

脚注 **jiǎozhù** N footnote · MW 处
诚信是傻瓜的人生**脚注**。 Honesty is one of the
many footnotes to ShaGua's character.

**RELATED WORDS**

手脚 104　　　　　　马脚 247
后脚 310　　　　　　注脚 496
绊脚石 887　　　　　墙脚 1770
腿脚 1949　　　　　　头重脚轻 128
拳打脚踢 1158　　　　站住脚 1189
露马脚 1997　　　　　大手大脚 20
指手画脚 1397

## 1805 舒  U+8212  TM **16**  FM 丿

shū  V·ADJ  to spread; to stretch (out); to relax; easy; leisurely

舒畅  shūchàng  ADJ  happy; carefree

舒服  shūfu  ADJ  comfortable

舒适  shūshì  ADJ  cozy, snug; pleasant
傻瓜的生活已很**舒适**, 但他总忘不了艰辛的岁月。 *ShaGua has had a comfortable life, but he has never forgotten the hardships of his past.*

舒展  shūzhǎn  V·ADJ  to spread; to stretch (out); comfortable, pleasant

舒张  shūzhāng  ADJ  diastole (of the heart)

## 1806 舔  U+8214  TM **16**  FM 丿

tiǎn  V  to lick; to lap

## 1807 锅 鍋  U+9505  TM **16**  FM 丿

guō  N  pot; pan; wok; boiler

锅巴  guōbā  N  crust of cooked rice · MW 块
傻瓜会用**锅巴**烧一道很好吃的菜。 *ShaGua knows how to use the crust of cooked rice to make a very delicious dish.*

锅炉  guōlú  N  boiler · MW 台

锅台  guōtái  N  stove top · MW 个

锅子  guōzi  N  pot; pan · MW 个

**RELATED WORDS**

沙锅 342          蒸锅 1768

## 1808 够 夠  U+591F  TM **16**  FM 丿

gòu  V·ADJ·ADV  to reach (a certain point, a standard, etc.), to come up to; to reach with one's hand, to get hold of; enough, sufficient; really, quite

够本  gòuběn  V  to break even

够格  gòugé  V  to be qualified

够朋友  gòupéngyou  EXP  to deserve to be called a true friend
跟傻瓜打过交道的人, 都说傻瓜**够朋友**。 *Those who have come in contact with ShaGua all say that ShaGua is a good friend.*

够呛  gòuqiàng  ADJ  unbearable; terrible
她的中文**够呛**。 *Her Chinese is terrible.*

够受  gòushòu  ADJ  hard to bear; quite an ordeal

够条件  gòutiáojiàn  V  to be qualified

**RELATED WORDS**

不够 24          足够 383          能够 1873

## 1809 船  U+8239  TM **16**  FM 丿

chuán  N  boat; ship; shipboard

船舶  chuánbó  N  shipping; watercraft · MW 艘

船舱  chuáncāng  N  ship's hold; cabin · MW 间

船队  chuánduì  N  fleet; flotilla · MW 支

船工  chuángōng  N  deckhand · MW 个、名

船老大  chuánlǎodà  N  chief crewman of a wooden boat · MW 个、名

船票  chuánpiào  N  passenger ticket (on a boat) · MW 张

船员  chuányuán  N  crew (of a ship); sailor · MW 个、名
傻瓜曾经想当一名**船员**。 *ShaGua once wanted to be a sailor.*

船长  chuánzhǎng  N  captain; shipmaster · MW 个、位、名

船主  chuánzhǔ  N  ship owner · MW 个、名

**RELATED WORDS**

| | | |
|---|---|---|
| 下船 10 | 上船 14 | 开船 26 |
| 飞船 81 | 龙船 315 | 划船 476 |
| 汽船 682 | 驳船 983 | 帆船 1034 |
| 邮船 1046 | 货船 1061 | 轮船 1112 |
| 贼船 1254 | 乘船 1263 | 拖船 1396 |
| 渔船 1496 | 渡船 1497 | 造船 1515 |
| 航船 1717 | | |

## 1810 毁  U+9BC1  TM **16**  FM 丿

huǐ  V  to damage; to ruin, to destroy; to burn down; to defame, to slander

毁谤  huǐbàng  V  to slander
总是有一些人**毁谤**傻瓜。 *Someone is always slandering ShaGua.*

毁坏  huǐhuài  V  to damage; to ruin, to destroy

毁灭  huǐmiè  V  to destroy; to exterminate
**毁灭**也意味着新生。 *Destruction also means a new beginning.*

毁损  huǐsǔn  V  to damage

**1810 毁 huǐ** (continued)

**毁誉 huǐyù** V to blame or praise

**毁约 huǐyuē** V to break one's promise

傻瓜从不**毁约**。 *ShaGua has never gone back on his word.*

**RELATED WORDS**

| 击毁 156 | 拆毁 572 | 烧毁 1504 |
| 销毁 1714 | 撕毁 1774 | |

---

**1811** 鲜 鲜    U+9C9C    TM **16** FM 丿

**xiān** ADJ·N fresh; unfading (of flowers); bright, bright-colored; delicious, tasty; delicacy; seafood

**xiǎn** ADJ little; rare

**鲜红 xiānhóng** ADJ bright red; scarlet

**鲜花 xiānhuā** N (fresh) flowers · MW 朵、支

**鲜活 xiānhuó** ADJ live

**鲜货 xiānhuò** N fresh produce; fresh seafood · MW 批

**鲜明 xiānmíng** ADJ bright; distinct

傻瓜旗帜**鲜明**地支持市政改革。 *ShaGua is taking a clear-cut stand in reforming the municipal administration.*

**鲜嫩 xiānnèn** ADJ fresh and tender

**鲜肉 xiānròu** N fresh meat · MW 块

**鲜血 xiānxuè** N blood; lifeblood · MW 滴

**鲜艳 xiānyàn** ADJ bright-colored

**鲜鱼 xiānyú** N fresh fish · MW 条

傻瓜的拿手菜是红烧**鲜鱼**。 *ShaGua's favorite dish is braised fresh fish.*

**RELATED WORDS**

| 鱼鲜 843 | 海鲜 1494 | 朝鲜 1686 |

---

**1812** 意    U+610F    TM **16** FM 丶

**yì** N·V meaning; idea; wish; to expect

**意大利 Yìdàlì** N Italy

**意会 yìhuì** V to sense; to sense intuitively

**意见 yìjian** N view; opinion · MW 条

**意境 yìjìng** N artistic conception; creative concept · MW 个

汉语的**意境**，有时只能**意会**不能言传。 *Some Chinese concepts can only be sensed intuitively and cannot be described in words.*

---

**意料 yìliào** V to anticipate, to expect

**意气 yìqì** N spirit; temperament

**意识 yìshí** N·V consciousness, awareness; to be conscious of, to realize

**意思 yìsi** N·V meaning; idea; opinion; wish; interest; to mean

我不懂你的**意思**。 *I don't understand your meaning.*

我麻烦你太多了, 得送些东西**意思意思**。 *I must give you something as a token of my appreciation.*

**意图 yìtú** N intention · MW 个

**意外 yìwài** ADJ unexpected, unforeseen

他的**意图**, 让人感到**意外**。 *His intention surprised everybody.*

**意味 yìwèi** N significance; implication; flavor

**意味着 yìwèizhe** V to signify, to mean; to imply

**意想 yìxiǎng** V to intend; to expect

**意义 yìyì** N meaning, significance · MW 个

你的话毫无**意义**。 *Your words are nonsense.*

**RELATED WORDS**

| 大意 20 | 介意 44 | 小意思 61 |
| 本意 90 | 生意 107 | 主意 124 |
| 无意识 139 | 示意 140 | 在意 188 |
| 任意 211 | 心意 232 | 可意 243 |
| 来意 260 | 乐意 299 | 用意 313 |
| 民意 388 | 有意思 439 | 有意识 439 |
| 有意 439 | 如意 464 | 注意 496 |
| 达意 505 | 旨意 535 | 同意 541 |
| 执意 564 | 好意 627 | 玩意儿 727 |
| 故意 816 | 致意 982 | 特意 1094 |
| 敌意 1127 | 原意 1273 | 适意 1358 |
| 善意 1483 | 情意 1491 | 诚意 1499 |
| 睡意 1571 | 留意 1582 | 假意 1586 |
| 敬意 1689 | 醉意 1842 | 谢意 1890 |
| 随意 1911 | 愿意 1919 | 不好意思 24 |
| 心满意足 232 | 出乎意料 258 | 没主意 938 |
| 拿主意 1262 | 三心二意 9 | 言外之意 478 |
| 洋洋得意 689 | | |

---

**1813** 赛 赛    U+8D5B    TM **16** FM 丶

**sài** V·N to compete; to surpass, to outdo; competition; contest, game, match

**赛车 sàichē** V·N to race cars; race car · MW 辆

**赛狗 sàigǒu** V to race dogs

**赛过 sàiguò** V to overtake; to surpass

**赛马 sàimǎ** V to race horses

据说, 中国将来可能允许**赛马**。 *They say that horse racing might be allowed in China in the near future.*

**赛跑** sàipǎo  V  to race

**赛艇** sàitǐng  V·N  to row (sports); racing boat ·  MW  艘

**RELATED WORDS**

| | | |
|---|---|---|
| 比赛 279 | 决赛 340 | 径赛 626 |
| 球赛 1199 | 联赛 1206 | 竞赛 1470 |
| 预赛 1528 | 跨栏赛跑 1857 | |

---

**1814** 酱 醬    U+9171    TM **16** FM 丶

jiàng  N  thick soybean sauce; paste; jam

**酱菜** jiàngcài  N  vegetables pickled in soy sauce ·  MW  瓶、坛

**酱油** jiàngyóu  N  soy sauce ·  MW  瓶

**RELATED WORDS**

| | | |
|---|---|---|
| 果酱 544 | 辣酱 1760 | 豆瓣酱 353 |
| 苹果酱 395 | | |

---

**1815** 塑    U+5851    TM **16** FM 丶

sù  V·N  to model, to mold; plastic

**塑胶** sùjiāo  N  plastic cement; synthetic resin ·  MW  块

**塑料** sùliào  N  plastic ·  MW  块

这是一个**塑料**杯子。 *This is a plastic cup.*

**塑像** sùxiàng  N  statue ·  MW  个、尊

**塑造** sùzào  V  to model, to mold, to shape

---

**1816** 剪    U+526A    TM **16** FM 丶

jiǎn  V·N  to cut (with scissors); to clip, to trim; to eliminate, to exterminate; scissors; [shaped like scissors]

**剪报** jiǎnbào  V·N  to clip a news item from a newspaper; newspaper clipping ·  MW  份、张

**剪裁** jiǎncái  V  to cut out (a garment); to tailor; to edit out, to cut (writing)

傻瓜会**剪裁**衣服, 但不会**剪裁**文章。 *ShaGua can tailor clothing, but he can't edit an article carefully.*

**剪彩** jiǎncǎi  V  to cut a ribbon (in a ceremony)

**剪刀** jiǎndāo  N  scissors; shears ·  MW  把

**剪辑** jiǎnjí  V  to edit; to cut and paste (a newspaper item); to cut and edit (a film)

**剪贴** jiǎntiē  V  to clip (out of a newspaper, etc.) and paste (in a scrapbook, on cards, etc.)

傻瓜**剪辑**、**剪贴**了许多重要的市政新闻。 *ShaGua has cut and pasted many important news articles about the municipal administration.*

**剪影** jiǎnyǐng  N  paper-cut silhouette; outline, sketch ·  MW  个、张

**剪纸** jiǎnzhǐ  N·V  paper-cut/scissors-cut art; to cut paper ·  MW  张

**RELATED WORDS**

| | |
|---|---|
| 修剪 870 | 裁剪 1535 |

---

**1817** 懂    U+61C2    TM **16** FM 丶

dǒng  V  to understand; to know

**懂得** dǒngde  V  to understand; to know

**懂行** dǒngháng  V  to know the business; to know the ropes

**懂事** dǒngshì  V·ADJ  to be sensible/thoughtful; sensitive to the needs/concerns of others

傻瓜很希望自己的孩子**懂事**。 *ShaGua really wants his kids to be sensitive to the needs of others.*

**RELATED WORDS**

| | |
|---|---|
| 不懂 24 | 难懂 974 |

---

**1818** 游    U+6E38    TM **16** FM 丶

yóu  V·ADJ·N  to swim; to travel, to tour; to rove; to stroll; roving; one of three sections of a river (up, middle, and down)

**游伴** yóubàn  N  travel companion ·  MW  个、名

**游标** yóubiāo  N  cursor (machinery) ·  MW  个

**游荡** yóudàng  V  to loaf, to loiter; to wander

**游动** yóudòng  V  to move about; to go from place to place

一群海豚在海中**游动**。 *A pod of dolphins is moving about in the sea.*

**游逛** yóuguàng  V  to go sightseeing; to stroll around

**游客** yóukè  N  traveler, tourist; visitor ·  MW  个、名

有些学中文的学生爱找中国**游客**练汉语。 *Some students who study Chinese enjoy practicing their Chinese with Chinese tourists.*

**游览** yóulǎn  V  to go sightseeing, to tour; to visit

**1818** 游　**yóu** (continued)

游离　**yóulí**　V　to drift away; to leave (a group)

游民　**yóumín**　N　vagrant, vagabond · MW 个、名

游人　**yóurén**　N　tourist, sightseer; visitor · MW 个、名

游山玩水　**yóushānwánshuǐ**　EXP　to go on a scenic tour

游说　**yóushuì**　V　to lobby; to drum up support

游玩　**yóuwán**　V　to go sightseeing; to stroll around

游戏　**yóuxì**　N　recreation; game · MW 个

玩**游戏**就必须遵守**游戏**的规则。*One must follow the rules of the game if one is to play.*

游行　**yóuxíng**　V　to march; to parade

游泳　**yóuyǒng**　V　to swim

游泳衣　**yóuyǒngyī**　N　swimsuit · MW 件

游园　**yóuyuán**　V　to visit a park

RELATED WORDS

春游 855　　周游 1068　　旅游 1518
漫游 1887　　填字游戏 1550　　旧地重游 165

---

**1819** 滚　　U+6EDA　　TM **16** FM 乀

**gǔn**　V·ADJ·N　to roll; to boil; to roll to make bigger by increasing layers; to get out, to scram; rolling; boiling; sewing method

滚蛋　**gǔndàn**　V　to get out, to scram, to go to hell (as a command)

滚动　**gǔndòng**　V　to roll; to tumble

滚翻　**gǔnfān**　V　to roll

滚瓜烂熟　**gǔnguālànshú**　EXP　to know by heart; to recite fluently

有些学生把课文背得**滚瓜烂熟**。*Some students recited the text fluently.*

滚滚　**gǔngǔn**　ADJ·ADV　rolling; continuously

滚烫　**gǔntàng**　ADJ　boiling hot

滚筒　**gǔntǒng**　N　cylinder; roller; drum · MW 个

滚雪球　**gǔnxuěqiú**　V　to snowball

滚圆　**gǔnyuán**　ADJ　very round; round as a ball; rotund

RELATED WORDS

屁滚尿流 1082　　摇滚乐 1675　　翻滚 1989

---

**1820** 漂　　U+6F02　　TM **16** FM 乀

**piāo**　V　to drift; to float

---

**piǎo**　V　to bleach; to rinse

**piào**　ADJ　good-looking, pretty, beautiful

漂泊　**piāobó**　V　to drift aimlessly; to have no steady profession/lifestyle

漂浮　**piāofú**　V　to float; to be superficial; to be showy (of artistic style)

漂流　**piāoliú**　V　to drift; to wander

河面上**漂流**着一条无人的小船。*A small empty boat is drifting about in the river.*

漂白　**piǎobái**　V　to bleach

漂白剂　**piǎobáijì**　N　bleach · MW 瓶

漂亮　**piàoliang**　ADJ　pretty, beautiful; wonderful

---

**1821** 演　　U+6F14　　TM **16** FM 乀

**yǎn**　V　to perform; to exercise; to follow a routine; to develop, to evolve

演变　**yǎnbiàn**　V　to develop, to evolve

演唱　**yǎnchàng**　V　to sing (in a performance)

演出　**yǎnchū**　V　to perform

演化　**yǎnhuà**　V　to evolve

傻瓜太太问傻瓜：如果人是猴子**演化**的，为啥那么多猴子还是猴子, 没**演化**成人？*Mrs. ShaGua asked ShaGua: If human beings evolved from monkeys, why are there so many monkeys who are still monkeys and not yet evolved into humans?*

演讲　**yǎnjiǎng**　V　to make/give a speech; to lecture

演练　**yǎnliàn**　V　to drill, to practice

**演练**是学汉语的一个好方法。*Drilling is a good way to study Chinese.*

演示　**yǎnshì**　V　to demonstrate

演说　**yǎnshuō**　V·N　to make/give a speech; to speak; speech

演算　**yǎnsuàn**　V　to calculate, to work out (mathematics)

演习　**yǎnxí**　V　to maneuver; to exercise; to practice

演戏　**yǎnxì**　V　to act in a play; to pretend

用中文**演说**、用中文**演戏**, 都是学汉语的好方法。*Giving speeches in Chinese and acting in a Chinese play are both good ways to study Chinese.*

演员　**yǎnyuán**　N　actor, actress · MW 个、名

演奏　**yǎnzòu**　V　to play a musical instrument; to perform music

RELATED WORDS

上演 14　　义演 22　　主演 124
讲演 501　　导演 751　　男演员 757
扮演 786

## 1822 渴

U+6E34　　TM **16** FM ヽ

**kě** [ADJ] thirsty

口渴 *thirsty*

饥渴 *hunger and thirst*

渴念 **kěniàn** [V] to miss (someone/something) very much

渴盼 **kěpàn** [V] to wish (for) eagerly; to thirst for

渴求 **kěqiú** [V] to aspire to; to be eager/hungry for

渴望 **kěwàng** [V] to yearn/long for

**RELATED WORDS**

止渴 41　　　口渴 42　　　解渴 1928
望梅止渴 1622

## 1823 漱

U+6F31　　TM **16** FM ヽ

**shù** [V] to gargle; to rinse

漱口 **shùkǒu** [V] to gargle; to rinse (one's mouth)

漱口杯 **shùkǒubēi** [N] rinsing cup (for brushing teeth) · [MW] 个

漱口水 **shùkǒushuǐ** [N] mouthwash · [MW] 瓶、杯

## 1824 谎 謊

U+8C0E　　TM **16** FM ヽ

**huǎng** [N·V] lie, falsehood; to tell a lie

谎话 **huǎnghuà** [N] lie, falsehood · [MW] 个

谎言 **huǎngyán** [N] falsehood · [MW] 个

谎话重复一千遍还是谎言，成不了真理。
*Repeating a lie a thousand times will not make it true.*

**RELATED WORDS**

扯谎 403　　　说谎 1631　　　撒谎 1907

## 1825 福

U+798F　　TM **16** FM ヽ

**fú** [N] good fortune; happiness

福建 **Fújiàn** [N] Fujian Province

福利 **fúlì** [N] benefits; welfare

当市长后，傻瓜认识到完善社会福利很不容易。
*After becoming mayor, ShaGua realized that it is not easy to provide perfect social welfare.*

福气 **fúqi** [N] good fortune

福星 **fúxīng** [N] lucky star · [MW] 个

福音 **fúyīn** [N] Gospel (Christian); good news · [MW] 个

**RELATED WORDS**

口福 42　　　幸福 373　　　托福 563
享福 1135　　造福 1515　　祝福 1516
眼福 1570　　全家福 172

## 1826 透

U+900F　　TM **16** FM ヽ

**tòu** [V·ADJ·ADV] to penetrate; to pass through; to tell secretly; to leak (out); to appear; thorough; complete; thoroughly; fully

透彻 **tòuchè** [ADJ] penetrating, incisive

透顶 **tòudǐng** [ADJ] thoroughly

透风 **tòufēng** [V] to ventilate, to let air in; to divulge a secret

透光 **tòuguāng** [V] to be transparent

透亮 **tòuliàng** [V] to be bright; to be clear

透漏 **tòulòu** [V] to leak; to divulge

透露 **tòulù** [V] to leak; to reveal, to disclose

你这样透漏来透露去，还不如透彻地说个明白。
*You are leaking information all over the place; you might as well just disclose everything.*

透明 **tòumíng** [ADJ] transparent; open (not secret)

透气 **tòuqì** [V] to ventilate

透视 **tòushì** [N·V] X-ray; to grasp the essence of

透支 **tòuzhī** [V] to overdraw

傻瓜从来没有透支过存款。*ShaGua has never overdrawn his bank account.*

**RELATED WORDS**

半透明 127　　看透 841　　　湿透 1498
摸不透 1665

## 1827 递 遞

U+9012　　TM **16** FM ヽ

**dì** [V·ADV] to hand over, to pass; progressively, in succession

递补 **dìbǔ** [V] to fill vacancies in the proper order

递加 **dìjiā** [V] to increase progressively/cumulatively

递减 **dìjiǎn** [V] to decrease progressively

知识递加，愚昧递减。*When knowledge is progressively increased, ignorance will be progressively decreased.*

递解 **dìjiè** [V] to escort a criminal from one place to another

递送 **dìsòng** [V] to deliver (a package, etc.)

**1827 递 dì** (continued)

递增 dìzēng  V  to increase progressively/cumulatively

全世界学中文的人数每年都在**递增**。
*The number of people in the world who study Chinese increases progressively each year.*

**RELATED WORDS**

传递 452    快递 497    投递 1008
邮递 1046

---

**1828 逼**    U+903C    TM **16** FM 丶

**bī**  V  to close in on; to force, to compel; to press for

逼供 bīgòng  V  to extract a confession

逼近 bījìn  V  to press on toward; to approach

金融风暴的危机在**逼近**傻瓜管理的城市。
*An economic crisis was bearing down on ShaGua's city.*

逼债 bīzhài  V  to press for repayment of a debt

逼真 bīzhēn  ADJ  lifelike, true to life

**RELATED WORD**

紧逼 1537

---

**1829 遗 遗**    U+9057    TM **16** FM 丶

**yí**  V  to omit, to leave out; to lose; to leave behind, to bequeath, to hand down; to give, to make a present of; to ejaculate

遗产 yíchǎn  N  legacy; cultural/material wealth passed down  ·  MW 笔

遗传 yíchuán  N·V  heredity; to pass down; to inherit

物质的**遗产**可以继承, 精神的**遗产**不容易**遗传**。
*Material inheritance can be passed on to the next generation, but it is difficult to do so with spiritual heritage.*

遗毒 yídú  N  evil legacy

遗孤 yígū  N  orphan  ·  MW 个

遗骸 yíhái  N  remains (of a dead person)  ·  MW 副

遗憾 yíhàn  ADJ·N  regretful; pity  ·  MW 个

傻瓜并不**遗憾**当了市长。*ShaGua doesn't regret being mayor.*

遗恨 yíhèn  N  eternal regret  ·  MW 个

傻瓜最大的**遗恨**是没有上大学。
*ShaGua's greatest regret is not going to college.*

---

遗迹 yíjì  N  historical remains; traces  ·  MW 个、处

遗精 yíjīng  V  to ejaculate involuntarily

遗留 yíliú  V  to leave behind, to hand down

遗弃 yíqì  V  to abandon; to desert (one's wife and children)

这个孩子被亲生母亲**遗弃**在一家医院里。
*This child was abandoned in a hospital by his biological mother.*

遗失 yíshī  V  to lose

遗书 yíshū  N  last letter (of a dying person)  ·  MW 封、份

遗孀 yíshuāng  N  widow  ·  MW 个、名

遗体 yítǐ  N  remains (of a dead person)  ·  MW 具

遗忘 yíwàng  V  to forget

**遗忘**也是人的一种自我保护。*Forgetting is also a form of human self-protection.*

遗言 yíyán  N  last words (of a dying person)  ·  MW 份

遗愿 yíyuàn  N  last wish (of a dying person)  ·  MW 个

遗址 yízhǐ  N  ruins; relics  ·  MW 个

遗嘱 yízhǔ  N  will  ·  MW 份

**RELATED WORD**

拾遗 1017

---

**1830 遥**    U+9065    TM **16** FM 丶

**yáo**  ADJ  distant, remote; far away

遥测 yáocè  V  to monitor/measure remotely

遥感 yáogǎn  V  to sense remotely

遥控 yáokòng  V  to control remotely

电视**遥控**器被小狗咬坏了。*The remote control for the TV was chewed up by the little dog.*

遥望 yáowàng  V  to gaze into the distance

傻瓜有时**遥望**夜空, 沉默不语。
*ShaGua sometimes looked quietly into the sky at night.*

遥遥 yáoyáo  ADJ  distant, far away

遥远 yáoyuǎn  ADJ  distant, remote

---

**1831 遮**    U+906E    TM **16** FM 丶

**zhē**  V  to conceal; to cover up, to obstruct, to screen

遮蔽 zhēbì  V  to hide from view; to cover up

遮藏 zhēcáng　V　to conceal; to cover up

遮丑 zhēchǒu　V　to gloss over (one's faults)

遮挡 zhēdǎng　V　to shelter oneself from; to keep out

遮盖 zhēgài　V　to hide

　谎言终究无法**遮盖**真理。 *The truth can never be covered up by lies.*

遮光 zhēguāng　V　to shade; to screen

遮羞 zhēxiū　V　to hush up a scandal

　你没有什么好**遮羞**的！ *You have nothing to hide!*

遮掩 zhēyǎn　V　to hide; to block

---

## 1832　精　U+7CBE　TM 16　FM 丶

**jīng**　ADJ·N　refined; excellent; precise; smart, clever; skilled, proficient; essence; energy; sperm

精彩 jīngcǎi　ADJ　brilliant, wonderful

精打细算 jīngdǎxìsuàn　EXP　to budget carefully

　面对金融危机，傻瓜必须**精打细算**。 *Facing the economic crisis, ShaGua must budget carefully.*

精读 jīngdú　V　to read carefully and thoroughly

　**精读**也是学中文的好方法。 *Intensive reading is also good for studying Chinese.*

精度 jīngdù　N　accuracy, precision

精干 jīnggàn　ADJ　competent; crack

精简 jīngjiǎn　V　to retrench; to reduce (spending, etc.)

精力 jīnglì　N　energy, vigor

精炼 jīngliàn　V　to refine, to purify (chemistry)

精美 jīngměi　ADJ　exquisite; delicate

精密 jīngmì　ADJ　accurate, precise

精明 jīngmíng　ADJ　astute, shrewd

精确 jīngquè　ADJ　accurate; precise, exact

　你的计算非常**精确**。 *Your calculations are accurate.*

精锐 jīngruì　ADJ　crack; elite

精神 jīngshén　N　spirit; essence, gist

　**精神**财富 *spiritual wealth*

精神病 jīngshénbìng　N　mental illness; psychosis

精神 jīngshen　ADJ　spirited; vigorous

精通 jīngtōng　V·ADJ　to be proficient in; expert at

精细 jīngxì　ADJ　meticulous; fine

精心 jīngxīn　ADV　meticulous; elaborate

精选 jīngxuǎn　V　to choose carefully

　中文教材必须**精选**。 *Chinese teaching materials must be chosen carefully.*

---

精制 jīngzhì　V　to refine; to make with extra care

精致 jīngzhì　ADJ　exquisite; delicate

精装 jīngzhuāng　ADJ　clothbound, hardcover (of a book)

　我喜爱这本**精装**的词典。 *I love this hardbound dictionary.*

精子 jīngzǐ　N　sperm · MW 个

### RELATED WORDS

| | | |
|---|---|---|
| 无精打采 139 | 妖精 466 | 味精 561 |
| 受精 844 | 酒精 1339 | 聚精会神 1642 |
| 遗精 1829 | 少而精 62 | |

---

## 1833　糕　U+7CD5　TM 16　FM 丶

**gāo**　N　cake; pudding

糕点 gāodiǎn　N　cakes; pastries · MW 块、件

　中国人不喜欢在**糕点**里放太多糖。 *Chinese don't like to put too much sugar in their cakes.*

### RELATED WORDS

| | | |
|---|---|---|
| 年糕 182 | 冰糕 493 | 蛋糕 1368 |
| 雪糕 1369 | 糟糕 1956 | |

---

## 1834　旗　U+65D7　TM 16　FM 丶

**qí**　N　flag; banner

　锦**旗** *silk banner (as an award)*

旗袍 qípáo　N　chi-pao, cheongsam (long gown worn by a woman) · MW 件

　**旗袍**是中国的民族服装。 *The cheongsam is part of the Chinese national costume.*

旗手 qíshǒu　N　standard-bearer · MW 个、位、名

旗帜 qízhì　N　flag; banner · MW 面

旗子 qízi　N　flag; banner · MW 面

　**旗子**飘扬。 *Flags are waving.*

### RELATED WORDS

| | | |
|---|---|---|
| 升旗 47 | 半旗 127 | 队旗 294 |
| 红旗 474 | 国旗 542 | 降旗 1416 |
| 锦旗 1834 | 五星红旗 79 | |

---

## 1835　颜　颜　U+989C　TM 16　FM 丶

**yán**　N　face; countenance; color

颜料 yánliào　N　pigment; coloring; paint

**颜色 yánsè** N facial expression; color; revenge

这件衣服的**颜色**很好。*The color of this piece of clothing is very nice.*

给他一点**颜色**瞧瞧。*Let's teach him a lesson.*

**RELATED WORD**

喜笑颜开 1531

---

**1836 就** U+5C31 TM **16** FM 丶

**jiù** V·ADV·CONJ·PREP to come near; to accomplish; to go with; to eat (something) with; at once; already, as early as; as much/many as; only; exactly; then; even if/though; with regard to, on, about

**就地 jiùdì** ADV on the spot

**就近 jiùjìn** ADV nearby, close at hand

你应该**就近**找一个中文辅导老师。*You should find a Chinese tutor nearby.*

**就寝 jiùqǐn** V to sleep

深夜了，**就寝**吧。*It is midnight: time to sleep.*

**就任 jiùrèn** V to take office

**就是 jiùshì** ADV·CONJ·AV exactly, quite right; only, just; even, even if; [often used with 了 at the end of a sentence to indicate affirmation]

**就是说 jiùshìshuō** CONJ that is to say, in other words

**就位 jiùwèi** V to take one's place, to be in place

**就绪 jiùxù** V to be in order, to be ready

**就学 jiùxué** V to attend school

你还是**就地就学**吧。*It's best if you attend school locally.*

**就要 jiùyào** ADV to be about to, to be on the verge of

**就业 jiùyè** V to get a job

作为市长，傻瓜不得不思考明年市里的**就业**问题。*As mayor, ShaGua has to consider the question of city employment for next year.*

**就医 jiùyī** V to go to the doctor, to seek medical treatment

**就义 jiùyì** V to die a martyr; to be executed for championing a cause

**就职 jiùzhí** V to assume/take office

**就座 jiùzuò** V to take one's seat, to be seated

**就是说**，现在请各位**就座**。*That is to say, please take your seats.*

**RELATED WORDS**

| | |
|---|---|
| 生就 107 | 迁就 506 |
| 成就 611 | 将就 1161 |
| 造就 1515 | 一···就 1 |

| 1837 | 雾 | 霧 | U+96FE | TM **17** FM — |

**wù** N fog; mist; fine spray of water

**雾气 wùqì** N fog; mist · MW 团

**雾凇 wùsōng** N soft rime (surface ice formed by freezing fog/mist) · MW 层

**RELATED WORDS**

| 大雾 20 | 云雾 80 | 浓雾 1168 |
| 烟雾 1177 | 迷雾 1187 | 喷雾 1563 |
| 喷雾器 1563 | | |

| 1838 | 需 | | U+9700 | TM **17** FM — |

**xū** V·N to need, to require; necessities, needs

**需求 xūqiú** N requirement; demand

满足**需求** to meet the demand

**需要 xūyào** V·N to need; to require; to demand; necessities, needs

**RELATED WORDS**

| 必需 338 | 必需品 338 | 军需 489 |
| 急需 1426 | | |

| 1839 | 震 | | U+9707 | TM **17** FM — |

**zhèn** V·N to shake; to vibrate; to quake; to be excited; earthquake

**震波 zhènbō** N seismic wave · MW 阵

**震颤 zhènchàn** V to tremble, to quiver

**震荡 zhèndàng** V to shake; to quake

每人都必须面对金融危机的**震荡**。 *Everybody must face the aftershock of the economic crisis.*

**震动 zhèndòng** V to shake; to quake

**震撼 zhènhàn** V to shake; to vibrate

**震惊 zhènjīng** V·ADJ to shock, to amaze; surprised, stunned

**震惊**世界 *to shock the whole world*

**震慑 zhènshè** V to awe; to frighten

**RELATED WORD**

地震 772

| 1840 | 骑 | 騎 | U+9A91 | TM **17** FM — |

**qí** V·N to ride; to straddle; cavalry; rider

**骑兵 qíbīng** N cavalry; cavalryman · MW 名、队

**骑虎难下 qíhǔnánxià** EXP impossible to stop halfway (LIT if you're riding a tiger, it's hard to get off)

凡是对学中文感到**骑虎难下**的, 都是一些不够努力的学生。 *The students who feel as if they are riding a tiger and can't get off are not studying Chinese hard enough to be effective.*

**骑士 qíshì** N knight · MW 个、名

**骑术 qíshù** N horsemanship, equestrian skill

**骑自行车 qízìxíngchē** V to ride a bicycle

| 1841 | 酷 | | U+9177 | TM **17** FM — |

**kù** ADJ·ADV cruel, ruthless; cool; very, extremely

**酷热 kùrè** ADJ extremely hot (of weather)

**酷暑 kùshǔ** N intense heat of summer · MW 个

**酷刑 kùxíng** N cruel punishment · MW 种

**RELATED WORDS**

| 严酷 241 | 冷酷 494 | 残酷 977 |

| 1842 | 醉 | | U+9189 | TM **17** FM — |

**zuì** N·V drunkard; to be intoxicated

**醉鬼 zuìguǐ** N drunkard · MW 个、名

**醉鬼**最爱说的一句话是"我没有醉!" *All drunkards have a favorite saying: "I am not drunk!"*

**醉汉 zuìhàn** N drunkard · MW 个、名

**醉心 zuìxīn** V to be engrossed in

他**醉心**于中文学习。 *He's deeply engrossed in the study of Chinese.*

**醉醺醺 zuìxūnxūn** EXP drunk

**1842** 醉 **zuì** (continued)

"醉醺醺的，你怎么能开车？" *"You are so drunk, how can you drive?"*

醉眼 **zuìyǎn** N pie-eyed look (effect of alcohol consumption on the eyes) · MW 双

醉意 **zuìyì** N signs/sensation of getting drunk

**RELATED WORDS**

烂醉 702      麻醉 1146      沉醉 1166
针刺麻醉 477

---

**1843** 墨    U+58A8    TM **17** FM |

**mò** N ink; calligraphy and painting; learning; black; dark; corrupt; (short name for Mexico)

墨盒 **mòhé** N ink box · MW 只

墨迹 **mòjì** N ink mark; (someone's) handwriting/painting

墨镜 **mòjìng** N sunglasses · MW 副
孩子们说傻瓜装"酷"，从此他不再戴墨镜。 *Ever since ShaGua's kids teased him for trying to be "cool" by wearing sunglasses, he never wore them again.*

墨绿 **mòlǜ** N dark green (color)

墨守成规 **mòshǒuchéngguī** EXP to stick to established practice; to be a stickler for routine

墨水 **mòshuǐ** N ink; book learning · MW 滴、瓶
这个人有点儿墨水。 *This person is educated.*

墨西哥 **Mòxīgē** N Mexico

墨鱼 **mòyú** N sepia; inkfish · MW 条

墨汁 **mòzhī** N Chinese ink · MW 滴、瓶

**RELATED WORDS**

石墨 144     水墨画 159     朱墨 184
油墨 683     笔墨 1278

---

**1844** 暴    U+66B4    TM **17** FM |

**bào** V·ADJ·ADV·N to bulge, to stick out; to expose, to reveal; to ruin; violent; cruel; vicious; hot-tempered; suddenly and fiercely; violence; ruthless person

暴病 **bàobìng** N acute onset (of a serious illness)

暴跌 **bàodiē** V to slump, to fall steeply (of prices, etc.)

暴动 **bàodòng** V to rebel; to riot

暴发 **bàofā** V to break out

---

暴风 **bàofēng** N gale, windstorm · MW 场
1966年"文化革命"爆发，像一场暴风席卷了中国。 *In 1966, the "Cultural Revolution" erupted and swept across China like a windstorm.*

暴风雪 **bàofēngxuě** N snowstorm; blizzard · MW 场

暴力 **bàolì** N violence; force/violence exercised by the government

暴利 **bàolì** N enormous profits; sudden huge profits · MW 笔

暴露 **bàolù** V to expose, to reveal
金融危机暴露了许多问题。 *The economic crisis has exposed many problems.*

暴乱 **bàoluàn** N·V rebellion; to riot · MW 场

暴虐 **bàonüè** ADJ brutal, cruel

暴徒 **bàotú** N ruffian, thug · MW 个、群

暴行 **bàoxíng** N outrage; atrocity · MW 个

暴雨 **bàoyǔ** N torrential rain; rainstorm · MW 场

暴躁 **bàozào** ADJ irritable; hot-tempered

暴涨 **bàozhǎng** V to rise suddenly and sharply (of floods, prices, etc.)
油价暴涨又暴跌。 *The price of oil has soared and also slumped.*

暴政 **bàozhèng** N tyranny; despotism · MW 个

**RELATED WORDS**

凶暴 98     风暴 194     尘暴 204
沙暴 342     狂暴 469     残暴 977
粗暴 1364     雪暴 1369     雷暴 1641
横暴 1775

---

**1845** 整    U+6574    TM **17** FM |

**zhěng** ADJ·V whole, complete; neat, tidy; to put in order; to repair; to punish

整备 **zhěngbèi** V to reorganize and outfit (troops)

整编 **zhěngbiān** V to reorganize (troops)

整队 **zhěngduì** V to line up (of troops)

整顿 **zhěngdùn** V to reorganize
整顿金融体系刻不容缓。 *Reorganizing the financial system can't be delayed for even a moment.*

整风 **zhěngfēng** V to rectify incorrect styles of work/thinking (Maoist slogan)

整个 **zhěnggè** ADJ whole, entire

整合 **zhěnghé** V to integrate; to conform

整洁 **zhěngjié** ADJ clean and tidy
别人是整洁，傻瓜是洁而不整。 *Others are clean and tidy; ShaGua is clean but not tidy.*

整理 zhěnglǐ　V　to put in order, to arrange

整齐 zhěngqí　ADJ　neat, orderly

整容 zhěngróng　V　to have/perform plastic surgery

整数 zhěngshù　N　integer, whole number ·　MW　个

整套 zhěngtào　N　complete set (of)

整体 zhěngtǐ　N　whole, entirety ·　MW　个

整天 zhěngtiān　ADV　whole day; all day long ·　MW　个

　　傻瓜整天忙忙碌碌地工作。*ShaGua is busy working all day long.*

整形 zhěngxíng　V　to have/perform plastic surgery

整修 zhěngxiū　V　to repair; to renovate

整整 zhěngzhěng　ADV　wholly, fully

整治 zhěngzhì　V　to repair; to dredge (a river, etc.); to punish

　　傻瓜决定整治市容。*ShaGua decided to renew the appearance of the city.*

　　整治一下那个坏家伙。*That bad guy needs to be punished.*

**RELATED WORDS**

| | | |
|---|---|---|
| 匀整 180 | 齐整 221 | 修整 870 |
| 完整 909 | 调整 1749 | |

照看 zhàokàn　V　to look after, to watch

照例 zhàolì　ADV　as usual, as a rule

照料 zhàoliào　V　to take care of, to tend

　　为了照料孩子, 傻瓜太太不得不当全职家庭主妇。*In order to take care of their kids, Mrs. ShaGua has to be a full-time housewife.*

照明 zhàomíng　V　to light up

照片 zhàopiàn　N　photograph ·　MW　张

照射 zhàoshè　V　to light up, to illuminate

照相 zhàoxiàng　V　to take a photograph

　　傻瓜不喜欢照相, 但喜欢看照片。*ShaGua doesn't like to take pictures, but he enjoys looking at them.*

照相机 zhàoxiàngjī　N　camera ·　MW　个、架、台

照样 zhàoyàng　V·ADV　as before, as usual; according to the example, in the same style

　　傻瓜星期天照样工作。*ShaGua works as usual, even on Sunday.*

照应 zhàoyìng　V　to look after; to coordinate

**RELATED WORDS**

| | | |
|---|---|---|
| 夕照 49 | 日照 96 | 反照 111 |
| 关照 224 | 对照 254 | 比照 279 |
| 光照 491 | 执照 564 | 护照 569 |
| 参照 600 | 依照 625 | 拍照 790 |
| 映照 1036 | 按照 1234 | 探照灯 1404 |
| 牌照 1597 | 驾照 1693 | 遵照 1975 |

---

**1846　照**　　U+7167　　TM 17 FM |

zhào　V·PREP　to shine; to light up; to reflect; to take a photograph; to take care of, to look after; to contrast; to inform; to understand; according to; in the direction of

照搬 zhàobān　V　to imitate, to mechanically copy

照办 zhàobàn　V　to act accordingly; to play by the rules

照常 zhàocháng　ADV　as usual

照抄 zhàochāo　V　to copy word for word

　　我们要培养能独立思考的学生, 而不是照抄老师讲稿的复印机。*We must promote the development of students with independent thinking, not copy machines.*

照发 zhàofā　V　to issue/provide as before

照顾 zhàogù　V　to care for; to show consideration to

照管 zhàoguǎn　V　to look after, to provide for

照护 zhàohù　V　to look after (patients, etc.)

照会 zhàohuì　V·N　to deliver a note to; note ·　MW　份

---

**1847　薪**　　U+85AA　　TM 17 FM |

xīn　N　salary; firewood; fuel

薪俸 xīnfèng　N　salary; wages; stipend ·　MW　笔

薪金 xīnjīn　N　salary; wages; stipend ·　MW　笔

薪水 xīnshuǐ　N　salary; wages; stipend ·　MW　笔

　　当市长的薪水不是很高, 但责任却很大。*A mayor's salary is not very large, yet he has a lot of responsibilities.*

**RELATED WORDS**

年薪 186　　月薪 194

---

**1848　境**　　U+5883　　TM 17 FM |

jìng　N　border; place, area, territory; situation

境界 jìngjiè　N　boundary; level ·　MW　个

境况 jìngkuàng　N　condition; circumstances ·　MW　个

　　傻瓜经济境况并不是很好。*ShaGua's financial situation is not very good.*

**RELATED WORDS**

| | | |
|---|---|---|
| 入境 5 | 入境口岸 5 | 止境 41 |
| 压境 201 | 仙境 207 | 处境 217 |
| 心境 232 | 出境 258 | 出境检查 258 |
| 环境 369 | 困境 393 | 幻境 475 |
| 边境 710 | 过境 712 | 梦境 1217 |
| 险境 1252 | 逆境 1359 | 越境 1575 |
| 离境 1614 | 意境 1812 | |

---

**1849 增** U+589E TM **17** FM |

**zēng** V to increase, to add (to); to enhance; to gain

**增白剂 zēngbáijì** N whitener (laundry agent) · MW 瓶

**增补 zēngbǔ** V to supplement

**增产 zēngchǎn** V to increase production/output

**增多 zēngduō** V to increase, to grow in number

**增光 zēngguāng** V to add glory to; to do (someone) credit

**增加 zēngjiā** V to increase, to raise

**增进 zēngjìn** V to enhance; to promote

**增刊 zēngkān** N supplement (of a newspaper/periodical) · MW 期

报刊的**增刊**往往特别有意思。
*Special supplements of magazines are usually more interesting.*

**增强 zēngqiáng** V to strengthen; to enhance

**增援 zēngyuán** V to reinforce

**增长 zēngzhǎng** V to increase, to rise, to grow

金融危机使经济**增长**变缓。*The economic crisis has slowed down economic growth.*

这些年, 工资**增加**不多, 通货膨胀倒**增长**不少。
*These last few years, salaries have not increased much, but inflation has grown faster.*

**增殖 zēngzhí** V to increase, to grow

**增值 zēngzhí** V to rise in value, to appreciate

**RELATED WORDS**

| | | |
|---|---|---|
| 递增 1827 | 激增 1955 | 与日俱增 158 |

---

**1850 搅** 攪 U+6405 TM **17** FM |

**jiǎo** V to stir, to mix; to disturb, to upset

**搅拌 jiǎobàn** V to stir, to mix

**搅动 jiǎodòng** V to stir, to mix; to agitate

**搅乱 jiǎoluàn** V to disturb, to upset, to mess up

傻瓜临时改变议程, **搅乱**了整个安排。
*ShaGua's change in schedule messed up all of the arrangements.*

**RELATED WORD**

打搅 289

---

**1851 揭** U+63ED TM **17** FM |

**jiē** V to take down/off, to remove; to uncover; to expose; to raise, to hoist

**揭穿 jiēchuān** V to expose; to disclose

证人的证词**揭穿**了被告的谎言。*The witness's testimony exposed the defendant's lie.*

**揭底 jiēdǐ** V to reveal the inside story

**揭发 jiēfā** V to expose, to bring to light

**揭开 jiēkāi** V to uncover; to open

**揭开**学习中文的新篇章。*Open a new chapter in the study of Chinese.*

**揭露 jiēlù** V to expose, to reveal

**揭幕 jiēmù** V to unveil; to open (of an important event); to raise the curtain

**揭示 jiēshì** V to reveal; to announce

**揭晓 jiēxiǎo** V to announce, to make known

傻瓜焦急地等待选举结果的**揭晓**。
*ShaGua was anxious as he awaited the election announcement.*

---

**1852 摔** U+6454 TM **17** FM |

**shuāi** V to fall, to tumble; to fall out (of); to fall and break; to throw; to beat

**摔跟头 shuāigēntou** V to tumble; to trip and fall

**摔跤 shuāijiāo** V to fall over; to blunder; to wrestle

他在溜冰场上不停地**摔跤**。*He fell repeatedly at the skating rink.*

---

**1853 撞** U+649E TM **17** FM |

**zhuàng** V to bump into; to collide; to meet by chance; to dash

**撞车 zhuàngchē** V to collide (of vehicles); to clash

**撞击 zhuàngjī** V to run into, to collide (with)

**撞见 zhuàngjiàn** V to meet by chance

傻瓜在饭店门口**撞见**了多年未见的朋友。
*ShaGua ran into some friends that he hadn't seen in years.*

**撞伤 zhuàngshāng** V to be injured in a collision
很多人在75号公路发生的**撞车**事故中被**撞伤**。
*Many people were crushed and injured in the traffic collision on I-75.*

**撞针 zhuàngzhēn** N firing pin · MW 枚

**RELATED WORDS**

顶撞 724　　　　碰撞 1526

---

1854　喝　　　U+559D　　TM **17** FM |

**hē** V to drink; to drink alcohol

**hè** V·ADV to shout; loudly

**喝酒 hējiǔ** V to drink (alcohol)
2006年以前，在中国是没有**喝酒**的年龄限制的。
*Before 2006, there was no drinking age restriction in China.*

**喝水 hēshuǐ** V to drink water

**RELATED WORD**

吃喝玩乐 783

---

1855　嗓　　　U+55D3　　TM **17** FM |

**sǎng** N throat; voice

**嗓门 sǎngmén** N throat; voice

**嗓音 sǎngyīn** N voice
傻瓜太太的**嗓音**很糟糕。*Mrs. ShaGua's voice is horrible.*

**嗓子 sǎngzi** N throat; voice

**RELATED WORD**

洋嗓子 689

---

1856　障　　　U+969C　　TM **17** FM |

**zhàng** N·V screen; barrier; to hinder, to obstruct

**障碍 zhàng'ài** N·V barrier; obstacle; obstruction; to hinder · MW 个
辨认方块字是外国人学中文最大的**障碍**。
*One of the biggest obstacles in studying Chinese for nonnative learners is recognizing Chinese characters.*

**障蔽 zhàngbì** V to block, to obstruct · MW 个

---

**RELATED WORDS**

故障 816　　　　路障 1785

---

1857　跨　　　U+8DE8　　TM **17** FM |

**kuà** V to step, to stride; to ride; to surpass, to go beyond

**跨国公司 kuàguógōngsī** N multinational corporation · MW 个
他曾在一家**跨国公司**工作。*He once worked for a multinational corporation.*

**跨进 kuàjìn** V to step, to stride

**跨栏赛跑 kuàlánsàipǎo** N hurdle race · MW 场

**跨越 kuàyuè** V to step across; to leap over; to go beyond

---

1858　题 题　　　U+9898　　TM **17** FM |

**tí** N topic, subject; title; problem; inscription

**题材 tícái** N subject matter, theme · MW 个、种

**题词 tící** V·N to write a dedication / an inscription; foreword; dedication · MW 个

**题解 tíjiě** N note explaining the title/background of a book; exercise key · MW 道、本

**题目 tímù** N title; topic; (exercise/exam) question · MW 个、道
今天讲演的**题目**是什么？*What is the topic of the speech today?*

**RELATED WORDS**

| | | |
|---|---|---|
| 正题 76 | 习题 84 | 本题 90 |
| 主题 124 | 切题 277 | 议题 350 |
| 考题 530 | 问题 678 | 标题 801 |
| 例题 863 | 论题 947 | 难题 974 |
| 命题 1051 | 试题 1180 | 话题 1182 |
| 答题 1438 | 选题 1510 | 偏题 1587 |
| 成问题 611 | 是非题 754 | 选答题 1510 |
| 文不对题 70 | | |

---

1859　鼠　　　U+9F20　　TM **17** FM 丿

**shǔ** N mouse; rat

**鼠目寸光 shǔmùcùnguāng** EXP shortsighted; to see only what is under one's nose

**RELATED WORDS**

| | | |
|---|---|---|
| 田鼠 147 | 老鼠 375 | 松鼠 579 |
| 袋鼠 1428 | 猫哭老鼠 1446 | |

## 1860 感    U+611F   TM **17** FM 丿

**gǎn** V·N to feel, to sense; to be grateful; to be moved/touched; to be sensitive (to light; of film, blueprint paper, etc.); to be affected by (cold, etc.); to catch cold; feeling, sentiment

**感动 gǎndòng** V to be moved/touched

**感恩 gǎn'ēn** V to be grateful/thankful
傻瓜是一个知道**感恩**的人。*ShaGua is someone who is always grateful.*

**感官 gǎnguān** N sense organ

**感光 gǎnguāng** V to be light-sensitive

**感激 gǎnjī** V to be indebted/grateful/thankful (for), to appreciate
我很**感激**您的帮助。*I appreciate your help.*

**感觉 gǎnjué** V·N to feel, to perceive; to sense; perception; sensation

**感慨 gǎnkǎi** V to sigh

**感冒 gǎnmào** N·V flu; to catch cold
傻瓜很少**感冒**。*ShaGua rarely gets the flu.*

**感情 gǎnqíng** N feeling, emotion · MW 种、点

**感染 gǎnrǎn** V to infect; to influence; to affect

**感受 gǎnshòu** N·V experience; impression; to feel; to be affected by · MW 种、点

**感叹 gǎntàn** V to sigh
傻瓜常常**感叹**自己的人生变化。*ShaGua often sighs deeply over the changes in his life.*

**感想 gǎnxiǎng** N impressions; reflections · MW 个

**感谢 gǎnxiè** V to thank, to be grateful to

**感性 gǎnxìng** N perception

**感应 gǎnyìng** V to induce; to respond, to react

**感召 gǎnzhào** V to inspire

**RELATED WORDS**

| | | |
|---|---|---|
| 手感 104 | 灵感 359 | 伤感 453 |
| 性感 498 | 同感 541 | 好感 627 |
| 美感 671 | 观感 726 | 胀感 1120 |
| 恶感 1196 | 情感 1491 | 流感 1493 |
| 预感 1528 | 敏感 1610 | 痛感 1725 |
| 遥感 1830 | | |

## 1861 管    U+7BA1   TM **17** FM 丿

**guǎn** V·N·CONJ to manage, to be in charge of, to administer; to discipline; to guarantee; to provide; pipe; tube; duct; wind instrument; no matter (what, how, etc.)

**管道 guǎndào** N pipeline; channel

**管家 guǎnjiā** N manager; housekeeper · MW 个、名
在中国，**管家**正在成为一个受青睐的职业。*Housekeeping has become a popular career in China.*

**管理 guǎnlǐ** V to supervise, to manage, to run

**管区 guǎnqū** N administrative district; police district · MW 个

**管事 guǎnshì** V·ADJ to be in charge; useful; effective
在我们这里傻瓜**管事**。*ShaGua is in charge here.*
傻瓜的话在这里挺**管事**。*ShaGua's words are very effective here.*

**管束 guǎnshù** V to restrain, to control

**管辖 guǎnxiá** V to administer, to have jurisdiction over

**管弦乐 guǎnxiányuè** N orchestral music · MW 首

**管制 guǎnzhì** V to control; to place under surveillance

**管子 guǎnzi** N pipe; tube; duct · MW 条

**RELATED WORDS**

| | | |
|---|---|---|
| 不管 24 | 主管 124 | 双管齐下 146 |
| 水管 159 | 只管 160 | 分管 173 |
| 气管 185 | 血管 306 | 尽管 312 |
| 托管 563 | 看管 841 | 保管 868 |
| 别管 1049 | 铁管 1126 | 试管 1180 |
| 钢管 1299 | 黑管 1389 | 掌管 1734 |
| 照管 1846 | 滴管 1885 | 支气管 92 |
| 企业管理 170 | 毛细管 183 | |

## 1862  篮    U+7BEE   TM **17** FM 丿

**lán** N basket; basketball

**篮板 lánbǎn** N backboard · MW 块

**篮球 lánqiú** N basketball · MW 个、只
姚明是一位世界知名的**篮球**明星。*Yao Ming is a well-known international basketball star.*

**篮子 lánzi** N basket · MW 个、只

**RELATED WORDS**

| | | |
|---|---|---|
| 花篮 549 | 投篮 1008 | 摇篮 1664 |

## 1863  像    U+50CF   TM **17** FM 丿

**xiàng** V·N·PREP to resemble, to look like; to look as if, to seem; portrait; such as, as if

像框 **xiàngkuāng** N picture frame · MW 个

像片 **xiàngpiàn** N photograph; image · MW 张

像章 **xiàngzhāng** N badge with someone's portrait on it · MW 枚

RELATED WORDS

| | | |
|---|---|---|
| 头像 128 | 肖像 675 | 画像 719 |
| 录像 722 | 录像机 722 | 相像 805 |
| 佛像 1080 | 蜡像 1780 | 绣像 1801 |
| 塑像 1815 | 影像 1918 | 半身像 127 |

---

**1864 僵**  U+50F5  TM **17** FM 丿

**jiāng** ADJ stiff, rigid; deadlocked

僵持 **jiāngchí** V to be in a stalemate, to be deadlocked

僵化 **jiānghuà** V to become rigid

僵局 **jiāngjú** N deadlock, impasse · MW 个
打破僵局 to break a deadlock

僵尸 **jiāngshī** N corpse · MW 具

僵硬 **jiāngyìng** ADJ stiff; rigid, inflexible

RELATED WORDS

弄僵 251          冻僵 680

---

**1865 绳 繩**  U+7EF3  TM **17** FM 丿

**shéng** N·V rope; string; guideline; to restrain; to continue; to measure

绳索 **shéngsuǒ** N rope; cord · MW 条、根

绳子 **shéngzi** N rope; string; cord · MW 条、根

RELATED WORDS

麻绳 1146          跳绳 1786

---

**1866 编 编**  U+7F16  TM **17** FM 丿

**biān** V to weave; to organize; to edit; to write (lyrics, a play, etc.); to compose (a song, etc.); to fabricate; book (used as part of a book's title); authorized organizational structure

编次 **biāncì** V·N to arrange an order; order of arrangement

编导 **biāndǎo** N·V writer-director; to write and direct · MW 个、位、名

傻瓜记得很多电影名字, 但不知道任何**编导**的名字。 *ShaGua remembers the names of many movies, but he doesn't know the names of any writers or directors.*

编队 **biānduì** V to form into columns; to organize into teams

编号 **biānhào** V·N to number; serial number · MW 个

编辑 **biānjí** N·V editor; to edit · MW 个、位、名
**编辑**在**编辑**词典。 *The editor is editing a dictionary.*

编码 **biānmǎ** V·N to code; to encode; coding · MW 个、组

编目 **biānmù** V·N to catalog; catalog

编排 **biānpái** V to arrange, to lay out

编审 **biānshěn** V·N to read and edit; copy editor · MW 个、位、名

编写 **biānxiě** V to compile
**编写**中文教材 *to compile Chinese teaching materials*

编译 **biānyì** V·N to translate and edit; translator-editor · MW 个、位、名

编造 **biānzào** V to compile, to draw up; to fabricate, to invent
她**编造**预算。 *She drew up a budget.*
他**编造**谎言。 *He fabricated lies.*

编者 **biānzhě** N editor; compiler · MW 个、位、名

编织 **biānzhī** V to weave; to knit; to braid

编制 **biānzhì** V to weave; to knit

编著 **biānzhù** V to compile

编组 **biānzǔ** V to organize (people, vehicles, etc.) into groups

编纂 **biānzuǎn** V to compile, to edit (large books)

RELATED WORDS

| | | |
|---|---|---|
| 主编 124 | 在编人员 188 | 汇编 234 |
| 改编 516 | 整编 1845 | 摘编 1906 |

---

**1867 输 輸**  U+8F93  TM **17** FM 丿

**shū** V to lose, to be defeated; to transport, to convey; to contribute, to donate

输出 **shūchū** V to send out, to emit (a signal, etc.); to export

输电 **shūdiàn** V electricity transmission

输入 **shūrù** V to enter (data, etc.); to introduce; to import

输送 **shūsòng** V to transfer, to convey

输血 **shūxuè** V to transfuse blood

**1867** 输 shū (continued)

输赢 shūyíng [N] victory or defeat

傻瓜很在乎**输赢**。 *ShaGua is quite concerned with winning and losing.*

**RELATED WORDS**

认输 239      运输 956      服输 1457

---

**1868** 腰     U+8170     TM **17** FM 丿

yāo [N] waist (of the body, clothing, etc.); pocket; middle (part)

腰包 yāobāo [N] pocket; purse; wallet · [MW] 个

傻瓜经常自己掏**腰包**请客。 *ShaGua often treats guests with his own money.*

腰带 yāodài [N] waistband; belt · [MW] 个

腰鼓 yāogǔ [N] waist drum (worn and played in the Ansai Waist Drum Dance) · [MW] 个

腰身 yāoshēn [N] waistline; girth

腰痛 yāotòng [N] backache

腰椎 yāozhuī [N] lumbar vertebra · [MW] 节

傻瓜常常**腰痛**，因为**腰椎**有问题。 *ShaGua often has backaches because he has problems with his lower back.*

腰子 yāozi [N] kidney · [MW] 个、对

**RELATED WORDS**

叉腰 33      山腰 38      伸腰 457
拦腰 576      哈腰 1025      裤腰 1634
掏腰包 1661

---

**1869** 腹     U+8179     TM **17** FM 丿

fù [N] stomach, belly; abdomen; front; mind; rounded cavity of a vessel/bottle

腹地 fùdì [N] hinterland · [MW] 个

腹稿 fùgǎo [N] mental outline · [MW] 份

傻瓜都是先打好**腹稿**才演讲。 *ShaGua always prepares a draft in his mind before making a speech.*

腹肌 fùjī [N] abdominal muscle · [MW] 条

腹痛 fùtòng [V] to have abdominal pain

腹泻 fùxiè [V] to have diarrhea

腹胀 fùzhàng [V] to have abdominal bloating

他告诉医生，他感到有些**腹胀**和**腹痛**。 *He told his doctor that he felt some abdominal bloating and pain.*

---

**RELATED WORDS**

心腹 232      空腹 669      捧腹 1240
满腹 1745

---

**1870** 腻 腻     U+817B     TM **17** FM 丿

nì [ADJ·V] oily, greasy; meticulous; dirty, filthy; to be bored (with)

腻烦 nìfán [ADJ] to be bored / fed up (with)

**RELATED WORDS**

油腻 683      细腻 1107      滑腻 1884

---

**1871** 锈 锈     U+9508     TM **17** FM 丿

xiù [N·V] rust; to become rusty

锈斑 xiùbān [N] rust spot · [MW] 块

**RELATED WORDS**

生锈 107      水锈 159      防锈 1040

---

**1872** 镇 镇     U+9547     TM **17** FM 丿

zhèn [N·V·ADJ] town; trading center; garrison; to guard; to suppress; to cool (with water, ice); to calm; tranquil, calm

镇定 zhèndìng [ADJ·V] calm, cool, composed; to calm down

考试一定要**镇定**。 *You must calm yourself when taking an exam.*

镇静 zhènjìng [ADJ·V] calm, cool, composed; to calm down

镇守 zhènshǒu [V] to guard

镇痛 zhèntòng [V] to ease pain

镇压 zhènyā [V] to suppress, to put down

**RELATED WORDS**

乡镇 117      市镇 332      村镇 410
城镇 1225

---

**1873** 能     U+80FD     TM **17** FM 丿

néng [V·N] can, to be able to; talent, ability; energy

能动 néngdòng [ADJ] active; dynamic

能干 nénggàn [ADJ] able, capable

能够 nénggòu [V] can, to be able to

能力 **nénglì** N ability; competence

能量 **néngliàng** N energy; capacity

能耐 **néngnài** N capability; skill

傻瓜是否**能干**？有没有**能力**？有没有**能耐**？
人们的看法不同。 *Is ShaGua able? Is he
competent? Is he skillful? Thoughts differ.*

能人 **néngrén** N talented/gifted person ·
MW 个、位、名

大家都认为傻瓜不是一个**能人**。*People don't
think ShaGua is a gifted person.*

能手 **néngshǒu** N expert · MW 个、位、名

能说会道 **néngshuōhuìdào** EXP good at
speaking

傻瓜不是**能说会道**的人。*ShaGua doesn't speak
well.*

能源 **néngyuán** N energy/power source

### RELATED WORDS

| | | |
|---|---|---|
| 不能不 24 | 才能 39 | 万能 73 |
| 未能 88 | 本能 90 | 无能 139 |
| 全能 172 | 可能 243 | 功能 252 |
| 性能 498 | 技能 568 | 机能 577 |
| 低能 618 | 效能 965 | 核能 1026 |
| 热能 1390 | 智能 1581 | 哪能 1666 |
| 熟能生巧 1973 | 力所能及 59 | 生产能力 107 |
| 多功能 431 | 肝功能 650 | 原子能 1273 |
| 无所不能 139 | | |

---

**1874 躲** U+8EB2 TM **17** FM ノ

**duǒ** V to hide (oneself); to avoid, to dodge

躲避 **duǒbì** V to hide (oneself); to avoid

傻瓜说：“我从来没有**躲避**过什么人。”
*ShaGua said, "I have never avoided anybody."*

躲藏 **duǒcáng** V to hide (oneself); to go into
hiding

躲闪 **duǒshǎn** V to dodge, to evade

躲债 **duǒzhài** V to avoid a creditor

傻瓜太太对傻瓜说：“你年轻时有过一次
**躲债**……” *Mrs. ShaGua said, "You once avoided
a creditor when you were young...."*

---

**1875 触** 觸 U+89E6 TM **17** FM ノ

**chù** V to touch, to come into contact (with)

触电 **chùdiàn** V to get an electric shock

触动 **chùdòng** V to touch; to collide (with)

触犯 **chùfàn** V to offend; to violate

触及 **chùjí** V to touch

触觉 **chùjué** V·N to touch; (sense of) touch ·
MW 个

触摸 **chùmō** V to touch

触手 **chùshǒu** N tentacle

触痛 **chùtòng** V to touch a tender spot

任何改革都会**触动**、**触痛**，甚至**触犯**一些人。
*Any serious reform will collide with certain
interests or step on some toes, and maybe
even offend.*

### RELATED WORD

接触 1405

---

**1876 豪** U+8C6A TM **17** FM 丶

**háo** ADJ hero, outstanding person; forthright;
despotic; arrogant

豪放 **háofàng** ADJ uninhibited; bold and
unrestrained

豪富 **háofù** ADJ powerful and wealthy

豪华 **háohuá** ADJ luxurious; extravagant

中国一些地方政府的办公楼装修得非常**豪华**。
*Some local government office buildings are very
luxurious in China.*

豪杰 **háojié** N hero; demigod

豪迈 **háomài** ADJ heroic

豪门 **háomén** N rich and powerful clan;
dynasty

豪情 **háoqíng** N lofty sentiment

豪爽 **háoshuǎng** ADJ straightforward,
forthright

傻瓜生性**豪爽**。*ShaGua is forthright.*

### RELATED WORDS

| | | |
|---|---|---|
| 文豪 70 | 自豪 305 | 富豪 1731 |

---

**1877 察** U+5BDF TM **17** FM 丶

**chá** V to observe; to examine, to scrutinize;
to look into

察访 **cháfǎng** V to investigate by making the
rounds

察觉 **chájué** V to be conscious of; to become
aware of

傻瓜老是不能**察觉**别人的暗示。*ShaGua is never
able to take a hint from others.*

察看 **chákàn** V to watch, to observe; to examine,
to look carefully at

**1877 察 chá** (continued)

察言观色 **cháyánguānsè** EXP   to carefully weigh others' words and closely watch their expressions, to read people

傻瓜很不善于**察言观色**。 *ShaGua is very poor at taking cues from others' words and facial expressions.*

**RELATED WORDS**

| | | |
|---|---|---|
| 失察 106 | 纠察 473 | 考察 530 |
| 诊察 709 | 观察 726 | 监察 994 |
| 检察 1033 | 检察官 1033 | 洞察 1338 |
| 视察 1362 | 觉察 1485 | 警察 1987 |

---

**1878**  寝    U+5BDD    TM **17** FM ㇏

**qǐn** V·N   to sleep; bedroom; imperial tomb

寝具 **qǐnjù** N   bedding · MW 套

寝室 **qǐnshì** N   bedroom; dormitory · MW 间

**RELATED WORDS**

就寝 1836     寿终正寝 440

---

**1879** 腐    U+8150    TM **17** FM ㇏

**fǔ** V·ADJ·N   to decay, to rot; rotten; tofu, bean curd

腐败 **fǔbài** V·ADJ   to rot; to degenerate (of behavior, a system, an organization, etc.); to corrupt

**腐败**现象是中国的改革必须正视的严重问题。 *Corruption is a serious problem that reform movements must face in China.*

腐化 **fǔhuà** V   to degenerate; to corrupt

腐烂 **fǔlàn** V   to corrupt; to rot, to decompose

腐乳 **fǔrǔ** N   fermented bean curd · MW 块

腐蚀 **fǔshí** V   to corrode; to corrupt

腐朽 **fǔxiǔ** V·ADJ   to rot; rotten, decayed; decadent

一堆**腐朽**的木头堆放在屋檐下。 *A pile of rotten wood is located under the eave.*

腐竹 **fǔzhú** N   dried cream of soy milk · MW 块

**RELATED WORDS**

豆腐 353     防腐 1040     陈腐 1250

---

**1880** 瘦    U+7626    TM **17** FM ㇏

**shòu** ADJ   thin; lean; tight; not fertile

瘦长 **shòucháng** ADJ   tall and thin, lanky

瘦弱 **shòuruò** ADJ   thin and weak, emaciated

瘦小 **shòuxiǎo** ADJ   thin and small, scrawny

傻瓜家的人都不**瘦小**。 *None of ShaGua's family members are scrawny.*

瘦子 **shòuzi** N   lean/thin person · MW 个、名

**RELATED WORD**

枯瘦 799

---

**1881** 憎    U+618E    TM **17** FM ㇏

**zēng** V   to hate, to detest, to abhor

憎恨 **zēnghèn** V   to hate, to detest

傻瓜**憎恨**那些使用不道德的手段欺骗公众的政客。 *ShaGua hates politicians who use immoral means to trick the public.*

憎恶 **zēngwù** V   to abhor, to loathe

**RELATED WORD**

爱憎 1247

---

**1882** 慢    U+6162    TM **17** FM ㇏

**màn** ADJ·ADV   slow; indifferent; rude; gradually

慢车 **mànchē** N   slow train · MW 列

慢镜头 **mànjìngtóu** N   slow motion · MW 个、组

傻瓜是急性子，你从来看不到他**慢腾腾**的**慢镜头**。 *ShaGua is a hotheaded fellow; you won't ever see him in slow motion.*

慢慢 **mànmān/mànmàn** ADV   slowly; gradually

时间**慢慢**流逝，但事情还是没有进展。 *Time has passed slowly, but there hasn't been any progress on the project.*

慢跑 **mànpǎo** V   to jog

慢腾腾 **màntēngtēng** ADV   at a leisurely pace

慢条斯理 **màntiáosīlī** EXP   deliberately, slowly and methodically

慢性 **mànxìng** ADJ   slow; chronic (of a disease)

慢性子 **mànxìngzi** N   unemotional temperament · MW 个

**RELATED WORDS**

且慢 152     缓慢 1708

---

**1883**  溜    U+6E9C    TM **17** FM ㇏

**liū** V·ADJ   to skate; to slide; to sneak off; smooth

溜冰　liūbīng　V　to skate

溜达　liūda　V　to go for a walk

**RELATED WORD**

灰溜溜　198

---

### 1884 滑　　U+6ED1　　TM **17** FM 丶

huá　ADJ·V　slippery; smooth; cunning; to slip, to slide

滑板　huábǎn　N　skateboard · MW 块

滑冰　huábīng　V　to skate

滑动　huádòng　V　to slide

滑轮　huálún　N　pulley · MW 个

滑腻　huánì　ADJ　velvety, silky-smooth (of the skin)

滑润　huárùn　ADJ　smooth

滑梯　huátī　N　(children's) slide · MW 个

滑头　huátóu　ADJ　slippery, cunning, foxy

这个家伙真**滑头**。*This guy is a sly old fox.*

滑翔　huáxiáng　V　to glide

飞机在天空中**滑翔**。*A plane is gliding across the sky.*

滑行　huáxíng　V　to skid; to slip, to slide

滑雪　huáxuě　V　to ski

傻瓜不爱溜冰，也不爱**滑雪**。*ShaGua likes neither skating nor skiing.*

**RELATED WORDS**

刁滑　32　　　　光滑　491　　　　油滑　683
圆滑　1391

---

### 1885 滴　　U+6EF4　　TM **17** FM 丶

dī　V·MW　to drip; [measure word for drops (of water, blood, etc.)]

滴答　dīdā　ONOM　drip; ticktock (of a clock)

滴管　dīguǎn　N　dropper · MW 支

滴水　dīshuǐ　V　to drip water

滴水不漏　dīshuǐbùlòu　EXP　watertight; with no loophole

律师的辩解**滴水不漏**。*The lawyer's defense was extremely tight.*

滴液　dīyè　V　to drip

**RELATED WORDS**

水滴　159　　　水滴石穿　159　　　雨滴　720
点滴　739

---

### 1886 漏　　U+6F0F　　TM **17** FM 丶

lòu　V·N　to leak; to divulge; to miss; to leave out; waterclock; hourglass

水管**漏**水。*The water pipe is leaking.*

她**漏**了飞机。*She has missed her plane.*

漏电　lòudiàn　V　to leak electricity

漏洞　lòudòng　N　leak; loophole · MW 个

傻瓜很善于发现各种管子上的**漏洞**。*ShaGua has a knack for finding leaks in pipes.*

傻瓜有时不能发现自己说话的**漏洞**。*Sometimes, ShaGua can't see the loopholes in his own arguments.*

漏斗　lòudǒu　N　funnel · MW 个

漏风　lòufēng　V　to leak air

漏气　lòuqì　V　to leak gas

漏网　lòuwǎng　V　to slip through the net

这是一个**漏网**的坏蛋。*This is an elusive bad guy.*

漏泄　lòuxiè　V　to leak (of chemicals, etc.)

漏油　lòuyóu　V　to leak oil

**RELATED WORDS**

泄漏　685　　　脱漏　1803　　　透漏　1826
滴水不漏　1885

---

### 1887 漫　　U+6F2B　　TM **17** FM 丶

màn　V·ADJ　to overflow; to flood; all over (the place), everywhere; extensive

漫步　mànbù　V　to stroll; to ramble

傻瓜太太抱怨傻瓜，从未和她在黄昏中**漫步**。*Mrs. ShaGua often complains that ShaGua has never taken her for a romantic stroll at dusk.*

漫不经心　mànbùjīngxīn　EXP　absentminded; careless; negligent

傻瓜做事从来不会**漫不经心**。*ShaGua is never careless when it comes to business.*

漫长　màncháng　ADJ　extensive; endless

漫画　mànhuà　N　cartoon; comic strip · MW 张、副

漫漫　mànmàn　ADJ　very long; boundless; all over the place

漫谈　màntán　V　to discuss informally

傻瓜只会谈正事，不知道如何与人**漫谈**。*ShaGua only knows how to talk business; he doesn't know how to have an informal discussion with others.*

**1887 漫 màn** (continued)

漫天 **màntiān** V·ADV  to be all over the sky, to fill the sky; boundlessly; outrageously

漫无边际 **mànwúbiānjì** ADV  boundlessly; on a tangent

傻瓜绝对不**漫无边际**地胡扯。 *ShaGua would never ramble on endlessly.*

漫游 **mànyóu** V  to wander; to travel around

**RELATED WORDS**

烂漫 702

散漫 1579

浪漫 1341

---

**1888  燃**  U+71C3  TM **17** FM 丶

**rán** V  to burn; to light, to ignite

燃放 **ránfàng** V  to set off (fireworks, etc.)

燃料 **ránliào** N  fuel · MW 批

燃眉之急 **ránméizhījí** N  matter of extreme urgency · MW 个

现在的**燃眉之急**是整顿金融秩序。 *Right now, a matter of extreme urgency is to reorganize the financial system.*

燃气 **ránqì** N  fuel gas · MW 种、类

燃烧 **ránshāo** V  to burn; to kindle

燃油 **rányóu** N  fuel oil · MW 滴、桶

金融风暴来临，**燃油**价格一路猛跌。 *When the economic crisis hit, fuel prices dropped rapidly.*

---

**1889  端**  U+7AEF  TM **17** FM 丶

**duān** V·ADJ·N  to hold (something) level; to carry; upright; proper; end; beginning; cause, reason; aspect

端点 **duāndiǎn** N  end point · MW 个

端午节 **Duānwǔjié** N  Dragon Boat Festival

端正 **duānzhèng** ADJ·V  upright; proper; correct; to rectify

端庄 **duānzhuāng** ADJ  elegant; dignified

这个女士真**端**庄。 *This lady is very elegant.*

**RELATED WORDS**

云端 80

尖端 203

好端端 627

极端 798

终端 1109

无端 139

争端 595

顶端 724

事端 987

---

**1890  谢 謝**  U+8C22  TM **17** FM 丶

**xiè** V  to thank; to apologize; to excuse oneself

谢词 **xiècí** N  thank-you speech

傻瓜市长的**谢词**总是很简单："谢谢！" *As mayor, ShaGua's thank-you speech is always simple: "Thanks!"*

谢绝 **xièjué** V  to refuse, to decline, to turn down

傻瓜最不喜欢应酬，**谢绝**了许多宴请。 *ShaGua doesn't like parties; he has refused a lot of invitations.*

谢幕 **xièmù** V  to take a curtain call

谢世 **xièshì** V  to die

谢天谢地 **xiètiānxièdì** EXP  thank goodness; thank heaven

谢谢 **xièxie** V  to thank; to say thank you

谢意 **xièyì** N  gratitude; thanks · MW 番

**RELATED WORDS**

申谢 150

答谢 1438

感谢 1860

代谢 208

酬谢 1648

新陈代谢 1638

致谢 982

道谢 1756

---

**1891  遇**  U+9047  TM **17** FM 丶

**yù** V·N  to meet (with), to encounter; to treat; opportunity

遇到 **yùdào** V  to run into, to encounter, to meet

傻瓜的孩子都不知道当年爸爸是怎么**遇到**妈妈的。 *ShaGua's kids don't even know how their dad met their mom.*

遇害 **yùhài** V  to be murdered

遇见 **yùjiàn** V  to run into, to encounter, to meet

遇救 **yùjiù** V  to be rescued/saved

遇难 **yùnàn** V  to die in an accident; to be tortured to death

遇事 **yùshì** V  to be faced with an emerging situation

遇险 **yùxiǎn** V  to run into danger

**RELATED WORDS**

巧遇 364

待遇 872

礼遇 503

遭遇 1931

机遇 577

---

**1892  遍**  U+904D  TM **17** FM 丶

**biàn** ADJ·MW  all over, everywhere; [measure word for the number of times an action occurs]

傻瓜开车走**遍**了49个大陆州。*ShaGua has driven all over the 49 continental states.*

傻瓜读过九**遍**《圣经》。*ShaGua has read the Bible from cover to cover nine times.*

**遍布** biànbù   V   to be found everywhere, to be all over

**遍地** biàndì   ADV   everywhere, all over the place

**遍及** biànjí   V   to spread all over

傻瓜的朋友**遍及**全美国。*ShaGua's friends are spread all across the U.S.*

**RELATED WORDS**

走遍 265         普遍 1484         跑遍 1916

---

**1893** 魂    U+9B42    TM **18**   FM 一

**hún** N soul; spirit; mood

魂魄 **húnpò** N soul; psyche

**RELATED WORDS**

失魂落魄 106    灵魂 359    鬼魂 1433
幽魂 1538

---

**1894** 磕    U+78D5    TM **18**   FM 一

**kē** V to knock (hard against); to bump; to bow before, to kowtow

磕打 **kēda** V to knock (something) out (of)

磕碰 **kēpèng** V to knock/bump against

磕头 **kētóu** V to bow before, to kowtow

很久以前，中国学生要给老师磕头。
*A long time ago, Chinese students had to kowtow to their teachers.*

---

**1895** 聪 聰    U+806A    TM **18**   FM 一

**cōng** ADJ wise, clever; (sense of) hearing

聪慧 **cōnghuì** ADJ smart, bright

聪明 **cōngming** ADJ clever, bright

聪明不等于智慧。*Being clever is not the same as intelligence.*

**RELATED WORD**

小聪明 61

---

**1896** 强    U+5F3A    TM **18**   FM 一

**jiàng** ADJ stubborn

倔强 *unbending*

**qiáng** V·ADJ·ADV to force; to strengthen, to enhance; strong; better; extra, slightly more than; by force

**qiǎng** V to make an effort; to strive

勉强 *to strive*

强大 **qiángdà** ADJ powerful, mighty

---

强盗 **qiángdào** N robber, bandit; hijacker ·
MW 个、伙

强调 **qiángdiào** V to stress, to emphasize

傻瓜的演讲最爱强调"诚信"二字。
*ShaGua usually likes to emphasize "honesty" in his speeches.*

强度 **qiángdù** N intensity, strength

强风 **qiángfēng** N strong breeze · MW 股、阵

强化 **qiánghuà** V to consolidate; to intensify, to strengthen

强奸 **qiángjiān** V to rape; to assault sexually

强健 **qiángjiàn** ADJ strong; sturdy

强劲 **qiángjìn** ADJ powerful; vigorous

强烈 **qiángliè** ADJ strong; keen; sharp, intense

强人 **qiángrén** N robber; intrepid person ·
MW 个、位、伙

他是一个强人！*He's a robber!*

在家里，傻瓜太太是一个强人。*Mrs. ShaGua is a powerful person in their family.*

强盛 **qiángshèng** ADJ powerful and prosperous (often of a country)

强行 **qiángxíng** V to force

强硬 **qiángyìng** ADJ tough; intransigent

强制 **qiángzhì** V to force, to compel

强壮 **qiángzhuàng** ADJ strong; sturdy

**RELATED WORDS**

| | | |
|---|---|---|
| 压强 201 | 兵强马壮 300 | 坚强 381 |
| 加强 463 | 好强 627 | 顽强 1204 |
| 勉强 1719 | 富强 1731 | 增强 1849 |
| 年富力强 182 | | |

---

**1897** 弱    U+5F31    TM **18**   FM 一

**ruò** ADJ weak, feeble; inferior; young

弱不禁风 **ruòbùjīnfēng** ADJ fragile, extremely delicate (LIT too weak to stand a gust of wind)

弱点 **ruòdiǎn** N shortcoming; weakness ·
MW 个、堆

傻瓜看起来有一大堆弱点，但那些弱点加起来又变成了他的优点。*ShaGua seems to have a lot of weaknesses, but by putting those weaknesses together, they become a strength.*

弱化 ruòhuà [V] to weaken

弱小 ruòxiǎo [ADJ] small and weak

**RELATED WORDS**

| | | |
|---|---|---|
| 软弱 889 | 衰弱 1313 | 削弱 1366 |
| 减弱 1487 | 虚弱 1534 | 微弱 1700 |
| 瘦弱 1534 | | |

---

**1898 醋**    U+918B    TM **18**   FM 一

cù [N] vinegar; jealousy (as in a love affair)

醋酸 cùsuān [N] acetic acid

**RELATED WORDS**

| | | |
|---|---|---|
| 吃醋 783 | 香醋 834 | 陈醋 1250 |
| 酸醋 1899 | 糖醋 1933 | |

---

**1899 酸**    U+9178    TM **18**   FM 一

suān [ADJ·N] sour, tart; sad; grieved; pedantic; acid; tingle; ache

酸菜 suāncài [N] pickled Chinese cabbage · [MW] 棵、片、坛

酸醋 suāncù [N] vinegar · [MW] 瓶

酸辣汤 suānlàtāng [N] hot and sour soup · [MW] 碗

流行于美国中餐馆的**酸辣汤**，在中国并没有什么名气。*Hot and sour soup, which is popular in Chinese restaurants in the States, is not well-known in China.*

酸奶 suānnǎi [N] yogurt · [MW] 瓶、盒

酸性 suānxìng [N] acidity

**RELATED WORDS**

| | | |
|---|---|---|
| 心酸 232 | 寒酸 1481 | 柠檬酸 1029 |
| 醋酸 1898 | | |

---

**1900 歌**    U+6B4C    TM **18**   FM 一

gē [V·N] to sing; song

歌唱 gēchàng [V] to sing

歌词 gēcí [N] song lyrics · [MW] 首

歌剧 gējù [N] opera · [MW] 场

歌谱 gēpǔ [N] song melody · [MW] 曲

歌曲 gēqǔ [N] tune · [MW] 首

歌手 gēshǒu [N] singer · [MW] 个、位、名

歌颂 gēsòng [V] to sing the praises of, to extol

歌舞 gēwǔ [N] song and dance

歌谣 gēyáo [N] ballad, folk song · [MW] 首

傻瓜酷爱民族**歌谣**，但就是记不住歌词。*ShaGua really loves folk songs, but he can't remember the words.*

歌咏 gēyǒng [V] to sing

**RELATED WORDS**

| | | |
|---|---|---|
| 山歌 38 | 民歌 388 | 国歌 542 |
| 诗歌 1181 | 唱歌 1562 | 凯歌 1577 |
| 挽歌 1659 | 赞歌 1969 | 四面楚歌 271 |

---

**1901 愚**    U+611A    TM **18**   FM |

yú [V·ADJ] to fool; foolish; stupid

愚笨 yúbèn [ADJ] foolish; stupid

愚不可及 yúbùkějí [ADJ] foolish to the nth degree

愚蠢 yúchǔn [ADJ] foolish, silly

傻瓜**愚蠢**吗？有的说蠢，有的说不蠢，有的说又蠢又不蠢。*Is ShaGua stupid? Some say "yes," some say "no," some say "yes and no."*

愚钝 yúdùn [ADJ] slow-witted

愚昧 yúmèi [ADJ] ignorant

愚弄 yúnòng [V] to deceive; to ridicule, to make a fool of

愚拙 yúzhuō [ADJ] clumsy and stupid

---

**1902 薄**    U+8584    TM **18**   FM |

báo [ADJ] thin; cold; weak; infertile

bó [ADJ·V] weak; meager; mean, unkind; frivolous; to look down on, to belittle

bò [N] peppermint

薄脆 báocuì [ADJ] thin and crisp (cooking style)

薄荷 bòhe [N] peppermint

**RELATED WORDS**

| | | |
|---|---|---|
| 单薄 672 | 浅薄 692 | 刻薄 966 |
| 轻薄 1113 | 淡薄 1173 | 厚薄 1272 |
| 稀薄 1599 | 微薄 1700 | 厚古薄今 1272 |

---

**1903 塌**    U+584C    TM **18**   FM |

tā [V] to collapse, to fall down; to sink, to slump; to settle/calm down

塌鼻子 tābízi [N] flat nose · [MW] 个

**1903 塌 tā** (continued)

这家伙有一个**塌**鼻子。*This guy has a flat nose.*

**塌方 tāfāng** V to collapse, to cave in

**塌台 tātái** V to collapse; to fall from power

**塌下来 tāxiàlái** V to fall down

**塌陷 tāxiàn** V to subside, to sink

**RELATED WORD**

倒塌 1281

---

**1904 搞**    U+641E    TM **18** FM |

**gǎo** V to do; to get, to obtain; to cause; to make; to produce

**搞**市场经济 *to manage the market economy*

给他们**搞**些喝的 *to get them something to drink*

你把事情**搞**糟了。*You have made a mess of things.*

**搞臭 gǎochòu** V to discredit, to put to shame

有人想把傻瓜**搞臭**，但是没有成功。
*Someone tried to slander ShaGua, but he was unsuccessful.*

**搞鬼 gǎoguǐ** V to play tricks

**搞好 gǎohǎo** V to do a good job (of)

**搞垮 gǎokuǎ** V to undermine; to upset

**搞阴谋 gǎoyīnmóu** V to participate in intrigues and conspiracy

傻瓜不聪明，但从不**搞阴谋**。
*ShaGua is not that smart, but he has never been one for intrigue or conspiracy.*

**RELATED WORD**

胡搞 1256

---

**1905 携** 攜    U+643A    TM **18** FM |

**xié** V to carry, to take/bring along; to take/hold (someone/something) by the hand

**携带 xiédài** V to carry, to take/bring along; to guide; to support, to promote

他没有**携带**任何东西。*He didn't bring anything along.*

承蒙**携带**。*Thank you for the promotion.*

**携手 xiéshǒu** V to join hands; to collaborate

**RELATED WORDS**

便携式 865     提携 1554

---

**1906 摘**    U+6458    TM **18** FM |

**zhāi** V to pick, to pluck; to select; to borrow; to extract (from)

**摘编 zhāibiān** V to extract and edit

**摘抄 zhāichāo** V to excerpt

**摘除 zhāichú** V to excise, to remove

**摘录 zhāilù** V·N to extract; to excerpt; extract; excerpt · MW 段、篇

**摘要 zhāiyào** N·V summary; abstract; to summarize; to abstract · MW 段、篇

傻瓜的演讲**摘要**很简明。*The summary of ShaGua's speech is very simple and clear.*

**摘引 zhāiyǐn** V·N to quote; quotation · MW 段、篇

**RELATED WORD**

文摘 70

---

**1907 撒**    U+6492    TM **18** FM |

**sā** V to let go, to release; to lose control of oneself; to let oneself go

**sǎ** V to scatter; to spread; to sprinkle; to spill

**撒旦 sādàn** N Satan

**撒谎 sāhuǎng** V to lie, to tell a lie

**撒娇 sājiāo** V to behave like a spoiled child

傻瓜的孩子都不**撒娇**。*None of ShaGua's kids act spoiled.*

**撒赖 sālài** V to act shamelessly

**撒尿 sāniào** V to urinate

**撒手 sāshǒu** V to let go; to ignore; to give up

**撒野 sāyě** V to throw a fit; to behave atrociously

傻瓜可以容忍孩子**撒野**，但绝对不能**撒谎**。
*ShaGua doesn't mind his kids acting wildly, but he is absolutely opposed to lying.*

**撒播 sǎbō** V to sow (by broadcasting seed)

---

**1908 概**    U+6982    TM **18** FM |

**gài** V·ADJ·ADV·N to generalize; to outline; general, approximate; without exception, categorically; bearing; deportment

**概而论之 gài'érlùnzhī** EXP generally speaking

**概观 gàiguān** N general survey · MW 个

**概况 gàikuàng** N general situation · MW 个

概括 **gàikuò** V·ADJ to generalize; to summarize; brief

傻瓜是个什么样的人，很难简单地**概括**。
*It is very difficult to summarize the kind of person ShaGua is.*

概率 **gàilǜ** N probability

概略 **gàilüè** N·ADJ outline; summary; brief, succinct

你可以**概略**地介绍一下你们的中文课程吗？
*Would you please briefly introduce your Chinese program?*

概论 **gàilùn** N introduction; general discussion · MW 个

概貌 **gàimào** N general picture

我们希望这本词典的例句能够反映傻瓜的**概貌**。 *We hope that the examples in this dictionary can help give a general idea of ShaGua's character.*

概念 **gàiniàn** N concept, notion, idea · MW 个

概要 **gàiyào** N outline; summary · MW 个

**RELATED WORDS**

大概 20          气概 185

---

1909 橱 U+6A71 TM 18 FM |

**chú** N cabinet; closet; wardrobe; case

橱窗 **chúchuāng** N display window; showcase · MW 个

**RELATED WORDS**

书橱 264          衣橱 330          纱橱 639
壁橱 1920

---

1910 隔 U+9694 TM 18 FM |

**gé** V·ADJ to separate, to cut off; to be apart; at/after an interval

隔板 **gébǎn** N separator · MW 块

隔壁 **gébì** N next door

傻瓜的秘书就在**隔壁**。 *ShaGua's secretary is next door.*

隔断 **géduàn** V to break/cut off

隔阂 **géhé** N estrangement (of feeling, thought); misunderstanding · MW 个

傻瓜一般不会跟人产生**隔阂**，除非你老是撒谎。 *It is quite difficult to be cut off or estranged from ShaGua, unless you lie.*

隔火墙 **géhuǒqiáng** N fire wall · MW 道、堵

隔绝 **géjué** V to completely cut off, to isolate

隔离 **gélí** V to keep apart, to segregate; to quarantine

种族**隔离**是一种犯罪。 *Segregation is a criminal act.*

隔热 **gérè** V to insulate from heat

隔声 **géshēng** V to insulate from sound

隔夜 **géyè** ADJ from the previous night

隔音 **géyīn** V to soundproof

**RELATED WORDS**

分隔 173          阻隔 1042

---

1911 随 随 U+968F TM 18 FM |

**suí** V to follow; to comply with; to let (someone) do as he/she likes; to look like, to resemble

随笔 **suíbǐ** N informal essay; casual literary notes · MW 篇

傻瓜不爱写文章，但是喜欢信手写些所谓的"**随笔**"。 *ShaGua hates writing formal papers, but enjoys leisurely writing informal essays.*

随便 **suíbiàn** V·ADJ·CONJ to be free and easy, to do as one wishes; casual; anyhow, no matter

傻瓜不**随便**承诺事情。 *ShaGua does not make commitments carelessly.*

随处 **suíchù** ADV anywhere

随从 **suícóng** V·N to accompany; retinue, entourage · MW 个、帮

傻瓜只有一个兼职秘书，没有任何**随从**。 *ShaGua has only a part-time secretary; he doesn't have an entourage of followers.*

随地 **suídì** ADV anywhere

随和 **suíhe** ADJ amiable; easygoing

傻瓜市长很**随和**。 *As mayor, ShaGua is very easygoing.*

随后 **suíhòu** ADV soon after

随机 **suíjī** ADV randomly; pragmatically, according to the situation

随身 **suíshēn** ADJ (to take) with oneself; (to carry) on one's person

傻瓜总是**随身**带几件工具。 *ShaGua always carries tools with him.*

随时 **suíshí** ADV at any time; whenever necessary

你**随时**都能向傻瓜借工具。 *You can borrow tools from ShaGua at any time.*

随意 **suíyì** ADJ as one wishes; voluntary

傻瓜不**随意**承诺事情。 *ShaGua does not make commitments carelessly.*

**1911 随 suí** (continued)

随员 **suíyuán** [N] attendant · [MW] 个、群

随着 **suízhe** [PREP] along with; following

随着时间的推移, 喜欢傻瓜市长的人越来越多。
*As time goes on, more and more people begin to understand and like ShaGua.*

**RELATED WORDS**

伴随 321     尾随 848     追随 1507
跟随 1784     夫唱妇随 55

---

**1912**  隱     U+9690     TM **18** FM |

**yǐn** [V·ADJ·N] to hide, to conceal; hidden; secret; privacy

隐蔽 **yǐnbì** [V·ADJ] to hide; to take cover; concealed, well hidden

警车隐蔽在树丛后面。 *The police car is hidden behind the bushes.*

隐患 **yǐnhuàn** [N] hidden danger; hidden damage · [MW] 个

隐晦 **yǐnhuì** [ADJ] obscure; veiled

隐居 **yǐnjū** [V] to live in seclusion

隐瞒 **yǐnmán** [V] to hide, to cover up

隐秘 **yǐnmì** [V·ADJ·N] to hide; concealed; secret

隐匿 **yǐnnì** [V] to hide, to cover up; to go into hiding

隐情 **yǐnqíng** [N] subject best avoided, facts one wishes to hide · [MW] 个

隐士 **yǐnshì** [N] recluse; hermit · [MW] 个、名

傻瓜想, 不当市长后就到夏威夷的小岛上隐居, 当一名隐士。 *After resigning from the mayorship, ShaGua considered living in seclusion on a small island in Hawaii.*

隐私 **yǐnsī** [N] privacy; personal matter

不能因为保护隐私而隐瞒了问题。 *We can't conceal problems in the name of protecting privacy.*

隐退 **yǐntuì** [V] to go and live in seclusion; to disappear; to retire

隐喻 **yǐnyù** [N] metaphor · [MW] 个

隐约 **yǐnyuē** [ADJ] indistinct, faint, vague

---

**1913** 瞎     U+778E     TM **18** FM |

**xiā** [V·ADJ·ADV] to go blind; to waste, to spoil; blind; blindly; aimlessly, without a reason

他有一只眼睛是瞎的。 *He was blind in one eye.*

---

傻瓜可能有时会瞎干, 但从来不瞎说话, 也不瞎花钱。 *Sometimes ShaGua may act rashly, but he has never spoken groundlessly nor spent money foolishly.*

瞎扯 **xiāchě** [V] to ramble aimlessly; to talk nonsense

傻瓜太太有时爱与邻居漫天瞎扯。 *Mrs. ShaGua sometimes likes to spend time chatting with her neighbors about everything under the sun.*

傻瓜从不瞎扯。 *ShaGua never talks nonsense.*

瞎闹 **xiānào** [V] to act senselessly; to mess/fool around

瞎说 **xiāshuō** [V] to talk irresponsibly; to talk nonsense

傻瓜从不瞎说别人。 *ShaGua has never talked about others irresponsibly.*

瞎眼 **xiāyǎn** [V] to be blind

瞎指挥 **xiāzhǐhuī** [V] to give arbitrary/contradictory directions

傻瓜有时会自己瞎干, 但不瞎指挥。 *ShaGua may be blind sometimes, but he does not give arbitrary directions.*

瞎子 **xiāzi** [N] blind person · [MW] 个

**RELATED WORD**

抓瞎 406

---

**1914** 瞞 瞞     U+7792     TM **18** FM |

**mán** [V] to hide the truth from; to deceive

不瞒你说 *to speak honestly to you*

瞒哄 **mánhǒng** [V] to deceive

瞒上欺下 **mánshàngqīxià** [V] to deceive one's superiors and bully one's subordinates

傻瓜最不能容忍的是瞒上欺下。 *One of ShaGua's biggest pet peeves is those who deceive those above them and bully those below.*

瞒天过海 **mántiānguòhǎi** [V] to accomplish by trickery (LIT to cross the sea without telling the emperor)

**RELATED WORDS**

欺瞒 1423     隐瞒 1912

---

**1915** 瞧     U+77A7     TM **18** FM |

**qiáo** [V] to look; to see; to watch; to discover

我瞧出来了, 你不喜欢他。 *I see that you don't like him.*

瞧见　qiáojiàn　V　to see, to notice

我瞧见你了！ *I see you!*

**RELATED WORD**

走着瞧　265

---

1916　跑　U+8DD1　TM **18** FM |

**pǎo**　V　to run; to escape; to run around (doing something); to leak; to evaporate (of a liquid)

他跑得很快。 *He runs very fast.*

他跑不掉。 *He can't run away.*

他跑生意。 *He runs around conducting business.*

他被吓跑了。 *He was frightened away.*

跑遍　pǎobiàn　V　to go around; to travel all over

傻瓜跑遍了美国。 *ShaGua has toured America.*

跑步　pǎobù　V　to run; to jog

跑车　pǎochē　N　racing bicycle; race car · MW 辆

跑道　pǎodào　N　running track; racetrack; runway · MW 条、道

跑道上有一辆跑车。 *There is a race car on the racetrack.*

跑江湖　pǎojiānghú　EXP　to wander around; to make a living as a traveling performer

跑龙套　pǎolóngtào　EXP　to play a small role, to be a utility man

傻瓜是市长, 不是一个跑龙套的。 *ShaGua is the mayor, not some common utility man.*

跑马　pǎomǎ　V　to ride a horse

跑腿　pǎotuǐ　V　to run errands · MW 个

傻瓜不需要跑腿。 *ShaGua doesn't need to run any errands.*

跑鞋　pǎoxié　N　running shoes · MW 只、对、双

**RELATED WORDS**

| | | |
|---|---|---|
| 长跑 93 | 奔跑 432 | 起跑 1421 |
| 短跑 1452 | 逃跑 1509 | 赛跑 1813 |
| 慢跑 1882 | 跨栏赛跑 1857 | |

---

1917　疑　U+7591　TM **18** FM |

**yí**　V·N　to doubt; to suspect; to be uncertain; question; query

疑案　yí'àn　N　suspicious case; mystery · MW 个、桩

傻瓜正在查一桩疑案。 *ShaGua is investigating a suspicious case.*

疑点　yídiǎn　N　suspicious/uncertain/unclear point · MW 个、串

这个疑案有一串疑点。 *There are quite a few suspicious points in this suspicious case.*

疑惑　yíhuò　V　to have doubts; to not be convinced

我对傻瓜的演讲有些疑惑。 *I'm not convinced by ShaGua's speech.*

疑惧　yíjù　V　to have misgivings

疑虑　yílǜ　V·N　to doubt; doubt, misgivings

我对傻瓜的能力有些疑虑。 *I have doubts about ShaGua's abilities.*

疑难　yínán　ADJ·N　difficult; problem

解决这个疑案还有些疑难。 *There have been some difficulties in solving this suspicious case.*

疑神疑鬼　yíshényíguǐ　EXP　to be terribly suspicious

疑团　yítuán　N　doubts and suspicions · MW 个

这个疑案还有不少疑团。 *There are still some suspicious points in this case.*

疑问　yíwèn　N　doubt; question · MW 个、串

我对傻瓜的能力没有任何疑问。 *I don't question ShaGua's abilities.*

疑心　yíxīn　V·N　to suspect; suspicion

疑义　yíyì　N　doubt · MW 个

疑云　yíyún　N　misgivings/suspicions clouding one's mind

**RELATED WORDS**

| | | |
|---|---|---|
| 无疑 139 | 可疑 243 | 怀疑 344 |
| 质疑 597 | 狐疑 885 | 猜疑 1594 |
| 置疑 1651 | 嫌疑 1702 | 解疑 1928 |

---

1918　影　U+5F71　TM **18** FM |

**yǐng**　N·V　shadow; reflection; image; photograph; film, movie; shadow play; to hide; to copy

解决这个疑案还没影儿呢。 *There are no leads to help solve this case.*

影集　yǐngjí　N　photo album · MW 本

影剧界　yǐngjùjiè　N　entertainment world

影迷　yǐngmí　N　film buff, movie fan · MW 个、群

影片　yǐngpiàn　N　film, movie · MW 部

影评　yǐngpíng　N　film review · MW 篇

影射　yǐngshè　V　to allude to; to insinuate

傻瓜当市长后, 总是有人用移民问题来影射他。 *Since ShaGua became mayor, some people keep insinuating that ShaGua is no good by bringing up immigration issues.*

**1918 影 yǐng** (continued)

**影响 yǐngxiǎng** V·N to influence; to affect; influence, impact, effect · MW 个

傻瓜在市里很有**影响**力。*ShaGua has strong influence in the city.*

**影像 yǐngxiàng** N image; portrait

**影印 yǐngyìn** V to photocopy

**影院 yǐngyuàn** N movie theater, cinema · MW 间、家

**影子 yǐngzi** N shadow; reflection · MW 个

傻瓜的女儿小时候像**影子**一样老跟着他。*ShaGua's daughter followed him around like a shadow when she was a child.*

**RELATED WORDS**

| | | |
|---|---|---|
| 电影 263 | 电影院 263 | 合影 296 |
| 幻影 475 | 投影 1008 | 阴影 1041 |
| 背影 1380 | 射影 1467 | 泡影 1492 |
| 留影 1582 | 暗影 1676 | 摄影机 1772 |
| 摄影 1772 | 剪影 1816 | 缩影 1927 |
| 立竿见影 125 | 捕风捉影 1400 | |

---

**1919 愿 願** U+613F TM **18** FM 丿

**yuàn** N·V·ADJ desire, wish; vow, promise; to be willing; to want to; honest; sincere

**愿望 yuànwàng** N desire, wish · MW 个

傻瓜心底里有一个连傻瓜太太都不知道的**愿望**。*There is a wish in ShaGua's mind that even Mrs. ShaGua doesn't know.*

**愿意 yuànyì** V to wish; to be willing

**RELATED WORDS**

| | | |
|---|---|---|
| 自愿 305 | 宁愿 336 | 但愿 458 |
| 如愿 464 | 许愿 502 | 志愿者 528 |
| 志愿 528 | 还愿 714 | 宿愿 1480 |
| 情愿 1491 | 祝愿 1516 | 请愿 1632 |
| 遗愿 1829 | | |

---

**1920 壁** U+58C1 TM **18** FM 丿

**bì** N wall; cliff

**壁报 bìbào** N wall newspaper (displayed and read in public places) · MW 篇、版

在傻瓜的市政厅里，你可以看到**壁报**。*You can see bulletins posted in city hall in ShaGua's city.*

**壁橱 bìchú** N built-in cabinet · MW 个

**壁灯 bìdēng** N wall lamp · MW 盏

**壁虎 bìhǔ** N gecko, house lizard · MW 只

**壁画 bìhuà** N mural (painting); fresco · MW 幅

傻瓜的办公室里没有**壁画**。*There are no frescoes in ShaGua's office.*

**壁炉 bìlú** N fireplace · MW 个

**壁纸 bìzhǐ** N wallpaper · MW 张、卷

**RELATED WORDS**

| | | |
|---|---|---|
| 碰壁 1526 | 墙壁 1770 | 隔壁 1910 |

---

**1921 篇** U+7BC7 TM **18** FM 丿

**piān** N·MW writing; sheet of paper; [measure word for articles, chapters, written versions of speeches, etc.]

**篇幅 piānfú** N length (of a piece of writing); space (on the printed page)

文章的**篇幅**太长，读到后面忘了前面。*The paper was so long that when they ended, they had forgotten the beginning.*

**篇目 piānmù** N title; (table of) contents · MW 份

**RELATED WORDS**

| | | |
|---|---|---|
| 千篇一律 19 | 中篇小说 86 | 长篇小说 93 |

---

**1922 箭** U+7BAD TM **18** FM 丿

**jiàn** N arrow

**箭靶 jiànba** N archery target · MW 个

他拉开弓箭，将**箭**头对准**箭靶**。*He is pulling the bow and aiming the arrow at the target.*

**箭杆 jiàngān** N arrow shaft · MW 支

**箭头 jiàntóu** N arrowhead; arrow (sign) · MW 个

**RELATED WORDS**

| | | |
|---|---|---|
| 火箭 72 | 弓箭 250 | 射箭 1467 |
| 核火箭 1026 | 归心似箭 166 | 航天火箭 1717 |

---

**1923 德** U+5FB7 TM **18** FM 丿

**dé** N morality; virtue; heart; mind; kindness

**德才兼备 décáijiānbèi** EXP to have both ability and integrity

**德高望重 dégāowàngzhòng** EXP to have integrity and a good reputation

**德国 Déguó** N Germany

德行 déxíng　N　disgusting/revolting behavior

德育 déyù　N　ethics; ideological and moral education

在中国, 德育教育很难进行。 *Ideological and moral education is very difficult to implement in China.*

德智体 dézhìtǐ　N　virtue, intelligence, and physique

**RELATED WORDS**

| | | |
|---|---|---|
| 以德报怨 101 | 功德 252 | 医德 389 |
| 美德 671 | 品德 1220 | 缺德 1305 |
| 道德 1756 | 仁义道德 64 | 公共道德 103 |

---

1924　饞　饞　　U+998B　TM 18　FM 丿

chán　ADJ　greedy; gluttonous

饞猫 chánmāo　N　cat; glutton · MW 只

饞嘴 chánzuǐ　N　glutton · MW 张

傻瓜太太有一张饞嘴。 *Mrs. ShaGua likes to eat.*

**RELATED WORDS**

| | |
|---|---|
| 眼饞 1570 | 嘴饞 1984 |

---

1925　稳　稳　U+7A33　TM 18　FM 丿

wěn　ADJ　steady; firm; sure, certain; reliable; composed, calm

稳步 wěnbù　ADV　steadily, at a steady pace

稳当 wěndang　ADJ　steady; reliable

稳定 wěndìng　V·ADJ　to stabilize; steady; stable

稳健 wěnjiàn　ADJ　steady; firm

稳妥 wěntuǒ　ADJ　safe; reliable

稳重 wěnzhòng　ADJ　steady (in speech, behavior)

傻瓜很稳健, 也很稳重。 *ShaGua is very reliable and steady.*

**RELATED WORDS**

| | | |
|---|---|---|
| 安稳 487 | 站稳 1189 | 十拿九稳 3 |

---

1926　键　鍵　U+952E　TM 18　FM 丿

jiàn　N　key (of a piano, computer, etc.); (door) key; (door) bolt

键盘 jiànpán　N　keyboard · MW 个

**RELATED WORDS**

| | | |
|---|---|---|
| 关键 224 | 按键 1234 | 琴键 1372 |

---

1927　缩　縮　U+7F29　TM 18　FM 丿

suō　V　to contract, to shrink; to withdraw

衣服缩水了。 *The clothes shrank.*

敌人缩回去了。 *The enemy has withdrawn.*

缩短 suōduǎn　V　to shorten; to cut down, to curtail

缩减 suōjiǎn　V　to reduce; to cut

缩水 suōshuǐ　V　to shrink (of clothing)

缩小 suōxiǎo　V　to reduce, to decrease; to shrink

缩写 suōxiě　N·V　abbreviation; to abridge

缩影 suōyǐng　N　epitome · MW 个、张

**RELATED WORDS**

| | | |
|---|---|---|
| 压缩机 201 | 收缩 282 | 伸缩 457 |
| 畏缩 988 | 浓缩 1168 | 退缩 1508 |

---

1928　解　U+89E3　TM 18　FM 丿

jiě　V·N　to separate, to divide; to untie; to relieve; to dispel; to answer; to explain; to understand; solution

解鞋带儿 *to untie shoelaces*

这个字有了新解。 *This character has a new interpretation.*

这个字的新解很费解。 *The new interpretation of this character is hard to understand.*

jiè　V　to escort

解除 jiěchú　V　to remove, to get rid of

解答 jiědá　V·N　to answer; to explain; resolution · MW 个

傻瓜每周都要解答市民的问题。 *ShaGua answers questions from city residents every week.*

解冻 jiědòng　V　to thaw; to unfreeze (funds); to relax tension (between two countries, parties, etc.); to relax a restriction (on an activity)

这些肉需要解冻。 *This meat needs to thaw.*

中美关系已经解冻。 *The tension between China and the U.S. has been relaxed.*

这个项目还没有解冻。 *The restrictions on this project have not yet been relaxed.*

解毒 jiědú　V　to detoxify; to relieve fever (Chinese medicine)

解法 jiěfǎ　N　solution · MW 个、种

解放 jiěfàng　V·ADJ　to liberate; to emancipate; liberal (as opposed to conservative)

解放军 jiěfàngjūn　N　People's Liberation Army (Chinese Army) · MW 个、队

**1928 解 jiě/jiè** (continued)

**解雇 jiěgù** V   to dismiss, to fire

傻瓜可能会突然被**解雇**。*ShaGua might be suddenly fired someday.*

**解救 jiějiù** V   to save, to rescue

**解决 jiějué** V   to solve; to resolve, to settle

傻瓜太太认为, 没有傻瓜**解决**不了的问题。*Mrs. ShaGua believes that there aren't any problems her husband can't solve.*

**解开 jiěkāi** V   to untie; to undo; to solve (a riddle)

总有一天傻瓜会**解开**那个疑案。*Eventually ShaGua will solve that suspicious case.*

**解渴 jiěkě** V   to quench (one's thirst)

傻瓜总是告诉别人: 啤酒不能**解渴**。*ShaGua always tells others: Beer can't quench your thirst.*

**解码 jiěmǎ** V   to decode

**解闷 jiěmèn** V   to relieve boredom; to amuse oneself

傻瓜太太常常拿傻瓜来**解闷**。*Mrs. ShaGua often makes fun of ShaGua in order to amuse herself.*

**解谜 jiěmí** V   to solve a riddle

**解聘 jiěpìn** V   to dismiss/fire (an employee)

傻瓜可能会突然被**解聘**。*ShaGua might be suddenly fired someday.*

**解剖 jiěpōu** V   to dissect; to analyze; to criticize

**解散 jiěsàn** V   to disband (an organization); to call off (a rally)

**解释 jiěshì** V·N   to explain; to interpret; explanation · MW 个、种

这个字有了新的**解释**。*There is a new interpretation for this character.*

**解手 jiěshǒu** V   to relieve oneself, to use the toilet

**解说 jiěshuō** V   to explain orally; to comment

傻瓜宁愿口头**解说**, 而不愿书面**解释**。*ShaGua would rather give an oral explanation than a written interpretation.*

**解脱 jiětuō** V   to shake off, to free/extricate oneself from

实际上, 对傻瓜来说, 不当市长反而可能是一种**解脱**。*Actually, it may be liberating for ShaGua to quit his job as mayor.*

**解围 jiěwéi** V   to rescue from a siege

**解析 jiěxī** V   to analyze

**解疑 jiěyí** V   to dispel doubts; to remove ambiguities

**解约 jiěyuē** V   to terminate/cancel an agreement / a contract

---

**解职 jiězhí** V   to dismiss from office

傻瓜某天可能会突然被**解职**。*ShaGua might be suddenly dismissed from office someday.*

**RELATED WORDS**

| | | |
|---|---|---|
| 了解 30 | 支解 92 | 分解 173 |
| 劝解 255 | 见解 267 | 曲解 272 |
| 讲解 501 | 和解 644 | 图解 761 |
| 押解 787 | 理解 1200 | 排解 1241 |
| 误解 1354 | 费解 1520 | 离解 1614 |
| 溶解 1744 | 调解 1749 | 递解 1827 |
| 题解 1858 | 土崩瓦解 15 | |

---

**1929 蜜**    U+871C    TM **18** FM 丶

**mì** N·ADJ   honey; [like honey]; sweet

**蜜蜂 mìfēng** N   honeybee; bee · MW 只、群

**蜜糖 mìtáng** N   honey · MW 瓶

**蜜月 mìyuè** N   honeymoon · MW 个

傻瓜的**蜜月**是在哪里度过的? 只有他和傻瓜太太知道。*Where did ShaGua enjoy his honeymoon? Only he and Mrs. ShaGua know.*

**RELATED WORDS**

| | | |
|---|---|---|
| 度蜜月 919 | 甜蜜 1306 | 蜂蜜 1682 |
| 甜言蜜语 1306 | | |

---

**1930 潮**    U+6F6E    TM **18** FM 丶

**cháo** N·ADJ   tide; (social/literary/intellectual) movement; damp, moist; inferior, low-grade

现在是晚**潮**。*It is the evening tide now.*

他领导了当前的思**潮**。*He leads the current intellectual movement.*

不要点了, 鞭炮已经受**潮**了。*Don't try it; the fireworks are damp.*

**潮流 cháoliú** N   tide; (social) trend

我们要顺应历史**潮流**。*We must go along with the current trend.*

**潮湿 cháoshī** ADJ   damp, moist

**潮水 cháoshuǐ** N   tidewater; tide

**潮汐 cháoxī** N   (morning/evening) tide

**RELATED WORDS**

| | | |
|---|---|---|
| 工潮 12 | 大潮 20 | 心潮 232 |
| 低潮 618 | 吸潮器 776 | 受潮 844 |
| 思潮 1214 | 浪潮 1341 | 热潮 1390 |
| 寒潮 1481 | 退潮 1508 | 高潮 1611 |
| 涨潮 1738 | | |

## 1931 遭

U+906D    TM **18** FM ╲

**zāo** V·MW  to encounter, to meet with, to suffer (disaster, misfortune, etc.); [measure word for events]

**遭到 zāodào** V  to suffer, to meet with (misfortune, etc.)

她的大学申请**遭到**拒绝。 *Her application for college admission has been denied.*

**遭劫 zāojié** V  to meet with catastrophe

**遭受 zāoshòu** V  to suffer, to sustain, to undergo

他总是**遭受**各种磨难。 *He suffers assorted disasters all the time.*

**遭殃 zāoyāng** V  to suffer a disaster

**遭遇 zāoyù** V·N  to meet with, to encounter, to experience; bad luck

你和我有共同的**遭遇**。 *You and I have a lot of bad experiences in common.*

## 1932 糊

U+7CCA    TM **18** FM ╲

**hū** V  to plaster

**hú** V·N  to smear, to paste; to be overcooked/burned; porridge

男孩往脸上**糊**番茄酱。 *The boy smeared tomato sauce all over his face.*

把水和水泥搅拌成**糊**状 *to mix water and concrete into a paste*

**浆糊** *paste*

**hù** N  paste

**糊弄** *to fool*

**糊口 húkǒu** V  to make a living; to get by with difficulty

**糊料 húliào** N  thickener

**糊涂 hútu** ADJ  muddled, confused; chaotic

我越学中文越**糊涂**。 *The more Chinese I study, the more confused I become.*

### RELATED WORDS

| | | |
|---|---|---|
| 含糊 592 | 烂糊 702 | 迷糊 1187 |
| 模糊 1673 | 浆糊 1932 | 稀里糊涂 1599 |

## 1933 糖

U+7CD6    TM **18** FM ╲

**táng** N  sugar; candy, sweets

**糖醋 tángcù** N  sweet and sour (dish)

**糖果 tángguǒ** N  candy, sweets · MW 颗、把

**糖浆 tángjiāng** N  syrup · MW 瓶、罐

**糖尿病 tángniàobìng** N  diabetes

**糖水 tángshuǐ** N  syrup · MW 瓶、罐

### RELATED WORDS

| | | |
|---|---|---|
| 白糖 176 | 冰糖 493 | 砂糖 733 |
| 奶糖 878 | 蜜糖 1929 | 口香糖 42 |
| 水果糖 159 | 葡萄糖 1766 | |

## 1934 霉 黴 U+9709 TM **19** FM 一

**méi** N·ADJ·V mold, mildew; moldy, covered with mildew; to grow mildew/mold

**霉病 méibìng** N mildew

**霉菌 méijūn** N mold

**霉烂 méilàn** V to mildew and rot

**霉雨天 méiyǔtiān** N rainy day · MW 个

哎，又是一个**霉雨天**。 *My gosh, another rainy day.*

**RELATED WORDS**

发霉 311  青霉素 740

## 1935 霜 U+971C TM **19** FM 一

**shuāng** N frost

**霜冻 shuāngdòng** N frost · MW 场

**霜花 shuānghuā** N frostwork · MW 朵、片

**霜期 shuāngqī** N frost season · MW 个

**霜叶 shuāngyè** N red leaves; autumn leaves · MW 片

**RELATED WORD**

冰霜 493

## 1936 磅 U+78C5 TM **19** FM 一

**bàng** N·MW·V scale; [measure word for points (unit of typographical measurement) and for pounds (unit of weight)]; to weigh

**磅秤 bàngchèng** N platform scale · MW 个

**RELATED WORD**

过磅 712

## 1937 骗 騙 U+9A97 TM **19** FM 一

**piàn** V to deceive, to fool; to cheat, to swindle

你为什么要**骗**我？ *Why did you deceive me?*

**骗局 piànjú** N fraud, swindle; hoax · MW 个、场

这是你设计的一个大**骗局**。 *This is quite a big scam you've planned.*

**骗钱 piànqián** V to cheat, to swindle, to defraud

**骗取 piànqǔ** V to cheat, to defraud

这个人弄虚作假，**骗取**信任。 *This man worms his way into others' confidence through fraud and deception.*

**骗人 piànrén** V to cheat/defraud other people

他老是**骗人**。 *He is always cheating others.*

**骗术 piànshù** N deceitful trick

**骗子 piànzi** N cheater, swindler · MW 个、伙

**RELATED WORDS**

诈骗 707  受骗 844  欺骗 1423
诱骗 1748

## 1938 醒 U+9192 TM **19** FM 一

**xǐng** V to wake up; to be awake; to become conscious; to sober up; to clear one's mind; to be striking/eye-catching

她早上六点钟就**醒**了。 *She woke up at 6 A.M.*

他酒**醒**了。 *He is sober now.*

我一直很清**醒**。 *I have cleared my mind.*

**醒目 xǐngmù** ADJ eye-catching, attention-getting

我们必须给文章一个**醒目**的标题。 *We must give this article a bold and distinctive headline.*

**醒悟 xǐngwù** V to realize; to wake up to

你应该**醒悟**了。 *You should face the facts.*

**RELATED WORDS**

叫醒 283  苏醒 552  清醒 1495
提醒 1554  睡醒 1571  猛醒 1704

## 1939 飘 飄 U+98D8 TM **19** FM 一

**piāo** V to blow/drift around; to flutter; to wobble; to walk unsteadily

窗外**飘**着小雨。 *Outside the window, it is raining slightly.*

**飘带 piāodài** N ribbon · MW 根、条

**飘荡 piāodàng** V to drift; to float; to wander around; to have no steady profession/lifestyle

小船在大海中飘荡。 *A boat is drifting on the waves in the sea.*

**飘忽 piāohū** V (of clouds) to move swiftly

**飘飘然 piāopiāorán** ADJ floating on air; self-satisfied, smug

**飘然 piāorán** ADJ floating on air; happy and relaxed; swift

**飘洒 piāosǎ** V to drift; to float

**飘扬 piāoyáng** V to flutter; to fly

国旗在迎风飘扬。 *The national flag is fluttering in the wind.*

---

**1940  蔬**  U+852C   TM **19** FM |

**shū** N vegetable

**蔬菜 shūcài** N vegetable · MW 棵

---

**1941  戴**  U+6234   TM **19** FM |

**dài** V to wear; to put on; to adorn oneself (with); to support; to respect

**戴帽子 dàimàozi** V to wear a hat; to pin a label on (someone)

去中国旅游时，男士最好不要戴绿帽子。 *If you are a man, it's best not to wear a green hat when you travel in China. (Wearing a green hat signifies that one has been cuckolded.)*

**戴上 dàishàng** V to put on, to wear (a hat, etc.)

**RELATED WORDS**

拥戴 1014     爱戴 1264     穿戴 1322

---

**1942  撤**  U+64A4   TM **19** FM |

**chè** V to remove, to take away; to move away, to evacuate

把电脑给撤了 *to take the computer away*

**撤兵 chèbīng** V to withdraw troops

**撤除 chèchú** V to remove; to dismantle

警察撤除了路障。 *Police removed the barricades.*

**撤换 chèhuàn** V to dismiss and replace; to recall

**撤回 chèhuí** V to recall

撤回大使 *to recall the ambassador*

**撤离 chèlí** V to leave, to evacuate

---

撤离市中心 *to leave the center of the city*

**撤退 chètuì** V to retreat, to withdraw

我们不能从这里撤退。 *We cannot retreat from here.*

**撤销 chèxiāo** V to cancel; to revoke

我们应该撤销这个声明。 *We should cancel this statement.*

**撤职 chèzhí** V to dismiss (from a job, a position, office)

---

**1943  搬**  U+642C   TM **19** FM |

**bān** V to remove, to take away; to transport, to move; to imitate/copy mindlessly

请你把电视搬去教室。 *Please move this TV to the classroom.*

为什么你喜欢生搬硬套？ *Why do you like to copy others with no discretion or thought?*

**搬家 bānjiā** V to resettle; to move (residence)

**搬救兵 bānjiùbīng** V to call in reinforcements; to ask for help

没有办法，我只好搬救兵啦。 *I have no choice; I must call in reinforcements.*

**搬弄 bānnòng** V to fiddle with; to show off

有些人就是爱搬弄学问。 *Some people just enjoy showing off their academic knowledge.*

**搬弄是非 bānnòngshìfēi** V to sow discord; to tell tales; to make mischief

**搬运 bānyùn** V to carry, to transport

**RELATED WORD**

照搬 1846

---

**1944  赠  赠**  U+8D60   TM **19** FM |

**zèng** V to give (as a gift), to donate

某某敬赠 *compliments of so-and-so*

**赠答 zèngdá** V to present each other with gifts

**赠款 zèngkuǎn** V·N to donate money; grant · MW 笔

**赠品 zèngpǐn** N gift · MW 件

**赠券 zèngquàn** N complimentary ticket; gift coupon · MW 张

**赠送 zèngsòng** V to give (as a gift)

我赠送一只手表给你作纪念。 *I'm giving you a watch as a memento.*

**1944** 赠 **zèng** (continued)

赠言 **zèngyán** N parting words of advice · MW 句

"海内存知己, 天涯若比邻"是我给你的临别赠言。 *"A friend afar brings a distant land near" are the parting words of advice I give you.*

赠与 **zèngyǔ** V to give (as a gift), to donate

**RELATED WORDS**

转赠 1111     捐赠 1552     敬赠 1689

---

**1945** 跪     U+8DEA     TM **19** FM |

**guì** V to kneel

跪拜 **guìbài** V to worship on bended knee

跪倒 **guìdǎo** V to kneel down

**RELATED WORD**

下跪 10

---

**1946** 踢     U+8E22     TM **19** FM |

**tī** V to kick; to play (soccer)

踢皮球 **tīpíqiú** V to kick a ball; to pass the buck

官僚机构办事像**踢皮球**, 你踢给我, 我踢给你。 *Bureaucracies kick matters back and forth like a ball.*

踢踏舞 **tītàwǔ** N tap dance; step dance · MW 个、场

**RELATED WORD**

拳打脚踢 1158

---

**1947** 静     U+9759     TM **19** FM |

**jìng** ADJ·V silent, quiet; still, motionless; to calm down

请静一静。 *Please be quiet!*

静电 **jìngdiàn** N static electricity

静脉 **jìngmài** N vein · MW 根、条

静默 **jìngmò** ADJ·V quiet; to stand in silent tribute

静悄悄 **jìngqiāoqiāo** ADJ silent, very quiet

教室里**静悄悄**的。 *It is so quiet in the classroom.*

静态 **jìngtài** N static state

静止 **jìngzhǐ** V to be motionless/still

生活从来没有**静止**过。 *Life has never stood still.*

静坐 **jìngzuò** V to stage a sit-in; to meditate

**RELATED WORDS**

平静 78     宁静 336     安静 487
冷静 494     肃静 526     幽静 1538
镇静 1872     风平浪静 194

---

**1948** 馒 馒     U+9992     TM **19** FM ノ

**mán** N steamed bread

馒头 **mántou** N steamed bun/bread · MW 个、笼

西方人爱吃烤面包, 中国人喜欢吃蒸**馒头**。 *Westerners love to eat bread, but Chinese like steamed buns.*

---

**1949** 腿     U+817F     TM **19** FM ノ

**tuǐ** N leg (of the body, a table, etc.)

腿脚 **tuǐjiǎo** N mobility (LIT legs and feet)

老年人**腿脚**不方便, 不喜欢住楼上。 *Old people don't like to live on upper floors, because their legs are weak.*

**RELATED WORDS**

大腿 20     火腿 72     伸腿 457
狗腿子 1287     跑腿 1916     二郎腿 2
拖后腿 1396

---

**1950** 鹅 鹅     U+9E45     TM **19** FM ノ

**é** N goose

鹅毛 **émáo** N goose feather · MW 根、团

鹅绒 **éróng** N goose down · MW 团

**RELATED WORDS**

天鹅 25     企鹅 170

---

**1951** 瘤     U+7624     TM **19** FM ㇏

**liú** N tumor; excrescence · MW 个

瘤子 **liúzi** N tumor · MW 个

**RELATED WORD**

肿瘤 1119

## 1952 慈 U+6148 TM 19 FM 丶

**cí** ADJ·V·N kind, loving; merciful; to show compassion; love; mother

**慈爱 cí'ài** ADJ love, affection (toward children)

**慈悲 cíbēi** ADJ mercy; compassion

**慈母 címǔ** N loving mother · MW 位、名

傻瓜是弃婴，他没有享受过**慈母**的**慈爱**。
*ShaGua was abandoned as a baby, so he has never experienced the tenderness of a loving mother.*

**慈善 císhàn** ADJ charitable, benevolent, philanthropic

**慈善家 císhànjiā** N philanthropist · MW 位、名

**慈祥 cíxiáng** ADJ kind and serene, kindly (often of an old person)

**RELATED WORD**

仁慈 64

## 1953 懒 懒 U+61D2 TM 19 FM 丶

**lǎn** ADJ lazy; lethargic

**懒得 lǎnde** V to not feel like (doing something)
我**懒**得理她。*I don't feel like dealing with her.*

**懒惰 lǎnduò** ADJ lazy

**懒汉 lǎnhàn** N lazybones; idler · MW 个、群

**懒散 lǎnsǎn** ADJ lazy; careless
不要这样**懒散**。*Don't be so sluggish.*

**懒洋洋 lǎnyāngyāng** ADJ lazy; lethargic

**RELATED WORD**

偷懒 1591

## 1954 澡 U+6FA1 TM 19 FM 丶

**zǎo** V·N to bathe; bath

**澡盆 zǎopén** N bathtub · MW 个

**澡堂 zǎotáng** N bathhouse; public bath · MW 个、间

在中国，公共**澡堂**也是一个社交场所。
*Public baths are also a place for social contact in China.*

**RELATED WORD**

洗澡 1167

## 1955 激 U+6FC0 TM 19 FM 丶

**jī** V·ADJ to surge; to dash; to catch a chill; to arouse, to excite; touched, moved; fierce; violent

**激变 jībiàn** V to produce a cataclysm

**激动 jīdòng** ADJ·V excited; agitated; to excite

**激发 jīfā** V to arouse

**激奋 jīfèn** ADJ·V exciting; indignant; to be roused to action

**激光 jīguāng** N laser · MW 束、道

**激化 jīhuà** V to intensify, to sharpen

**激活 jīhuó** V to activate
**激活**经济 *to rejuvenate the economy*

**激励 jīlì** V to encourage; to inspire
我们要互相**激励**。*We should encourage one another.*

**激烈 jīliè** ADJ intense, fierce
我们有过一场**激烈**的争论。*We had a heated argument.*

**激流 jīliú** N rapids; torrential current · MW 条

**激怒 jīnù** V to irritate, to provoke; to enrage
不要去**激怒**她。*Don't try to make her angry.*

**激起 jīqǐ** V to arouse
**激起**强烈的反应 *to trigger a strong reaction*

**激情 jīqíng** N passion, enthusiasm
你根本没有学习中文的**激情**。*You don't have any passion for studying Chinese.*

**激素 jīsù** N hormone · MW 种

**激增 jīzēng** V to increase sharply, to shoot up
你的体重**激增**。*You have gained a lot of weight.*

**激战 jīzhàn** V·N to fight fiercely; pitched battle · MW 场

**RELATED WORDS**

过激 712　　　刺激 1050　　　偏激 1587
感激 1860

## 1956 糟 U+7CDF TM 19 FM 丶

**zāo** N·ADJ·V dregs; wretched; messy; rotten; spoiled; to waste; to flavor; to pickle in wine / with grain

她的成绩很**糟**。*Her GPA scores are very poor.*
我把作业弄**糟**了。*I made a mess of my homework.*
**糟**了，我忘了考试了！*Damn, I forgot my exam!*

**1956** 糟 **zāo** (continued)

糟糕 **zāogāo** ADJ how terrible!, too bad!, oh no!

真**糟糕**，我误飞机了！ *Shoot, I missed my plane.*

糟粕 **zāopò** N low point; waste

这是中国传统文化的**糟粕**。 *This is one of the low points of traditional Chinese culture.*

糟蹋 **zāotà** V to waste; to ruin; to rape

不要**糟蹋**纸张。*Don't waste paper.*

**RELATED WORDS**

| 弄糟 251 | 乱糟糟 901 | 乌七八糟 601 |
|---|---|---|
| 乱七八糟 901 | | |

---

**1957** 辫 辫　　U+8FAB　　TM **19** FM 丶

**biàn** N braid; pigtail; plait

辫子 **biànzi** N braid; plait; handle · MW 根、条

**RELATED WORDS**

| 小辫子 61 | 发辫 311 | 抓辫子 406 |
|---|---|---|

---

**1958** 额 额　　U+989D　　TM **19** FM 丶

**é** N forehead; amount, quantity; volume; quota; specified/fixed number

额定 **édìng** ADJ specified/fixed (number)

额头 **étóu** N forehead · MW 个

---

额外 **éwài** ADJ additional

这是你**额外**的工作。 *This is your extra work.*

**RELATED WORDS**

| 巨额 162 | 余额 419 | 金额 420 |
|---|---|---|
| 名额 426 | 份额 449 | 定额 666 |
| 空额 669 | 差额 673 | 面额 721 |
| 缺额 1305 | 总额 1330 | 限额 1417 |
| 超额 1684 | 税额 1705 | 满额 1745 |
| 销售额 1714 | 焦头烂额 1265 | |

---

**1959** 敲　　U+6572　　TM **19** FM 丶

**qiāo** V to knock, to strike; to overcharge; to blackmail

敲边鼓 **qiāobiāngǔ** EXP to back (someone) up (LIT to beat a nearby drum)

敲打 **qiāoda** V to beat; to irritate

老师在用言语**敲打**我们。 *Our teacher used stern language to scold us.*

敲门 **qiāomén** V to knock at the door

敲诈 **qiāozhà** V to extort; to blackmail

你不是在做生意，你是在**敲诈**我们。 *You are not conducting business with us; you are blackmailing us.*

敲竹杠 **qiāozhúgàng** EXP to overcharge (someone) by taking advantage of his/her weakness

**RELATED WORD**

推敲 1242

---

**1960** 噩 · U+5669 · TM **20** · FM 一

è ADJ shocking; upsetting

噩耗 èhào N devastating news; sad news of the death of a loved one · MW 个

---

**1961** 碗 · U+7897 · TM **20** · FM 一

wǎn N bowl; [like a bowl]

**RELATED WORDS**

茶碗 767 瓷碗 1723 丢饭碗 297

---

**1962** 粥 · U+7CA5 · TM **20** · FM 一

zhōu N porridge; gruel

---

**1963** 器 · U+5668 · TM **20** · FM 丨

qì N organ (of the body); weapon; instrument; utensil; talent, aptitude

器材 qìcái N equipment; materials · MW 种

器官 qìguān N organ · MW 个、副

器件 qìjiàn N device; component of an appliance · MW 个

器具 qìjù N instrument; utensil · MW 件、套

器皿 qìmǐn N household utensils · MW 件、套

器械 qìxiè N equipment; instrument · MW 种

器乐 qìyuè N instrumental music · MW 种

器重 qìzhòng V to think highly of, to have high regard for

老师很器重他。The teacher thinks highly of him.

**RELATED WORDS**

| | | |
|---|---|---|
| 木器 40 | 玉器 77 | 凶器 98 |
| 仪器 122 | 石器 144 | 电器 263 |
| 武器 513 | 机器 577 | 脏器 1297 |
| 容器 1320 | 铜器 1712 | 瓷器 1723 |
| 漆器 1746 | 计时器 240 | 计算器 240 |
| 吸潮器 776 | 吸尘器 776 | 助听器 818 |
| 核武器 1026 | 喷雾器 1563 | |

---

**1964** 餐 · U+9910 · TM **20** · FM 丨

cān V·N to eat; to dine; meal; food

餐车 cānchē N dining car; diner · MW 辆

餐巾 cānjīn N table napkin · MW 条、块

餐酒 cānjiǔ N dinner wine · MW 瓶、杯

餐具 cānjù N tableware; table setting · MW 套、件

中餐餐具很简单, 但饭菜花样繁多。
The Chinese table setting is simple, but the foods are wide-ranging.

餐厅 cāntīng N dining hall · MW 个、间

**RELATED WORDS**

| | | |
|---|---|---|
| 午餐 48 | 正餐 76 | 中餐 86 |
| 圣餐 142 | 早餐 268 | 会餐 295 |
| 西餐 352 | 冷餐 494 | 快餐 497 |
| 聚餐 1642 | 野餐 1685 | 晚餐 1779 |
| 自助餐厅 305 | | |

---

**1965** 操 · U+64CD · TM **20** · FM 丨

cāo V·N to hold; to engage in; to speak (a language); exercise; conduct, behavior

我们稳操胜券。We are very sure that we can win.

他重操旧业。He resumed his old business again.

她操一口纯正的汉语。She speaks perfect Chinese.

操场 cāochǎng N playground; playing field · MW 个、片

操持 cāochí V to manage, to handle

爸爸操持生意。My dad manages a business.

操劳 cāoláo V to work hard

终年操劳 to work hard all year round

操练 cāoliàn V to drill; to practice; to exercise

操心 cāoxīn V to worry (about); to be concerned (over/with)

别操心! Don't worry about it!

操行 cāoxíng N (student's) behavior

操纵 cāozòng V to control; to operate (equipment, etc.)

操作 cāozuò V to operate

1965　操　cāo　(continued)

**RELATED WORDS**

出操 258　　　早操 268　　　体操 325
体操馆 325　　　情操 1491　　　健身操 1589

**1966　瞪**　　　U+77AA　　　TM **20** FM |

**dèng** V to stare at; to glare at; to open one's eyes wide

别老**瞪**着我。*Don't stare at me.*

**瞪眼　dèngyǎn** V to open one's eyes wide; to stare at; to get angry at

**RELATED WORDS**

干瞪眼 13　　　目瞪口呆 151

**1967　鞭**　　　U+97AD　　　TM **20** FM |

**biān** N·V whip, lash; to whip

**鞭策　biāncè** V to urge/spur on

老师常常**鞭策**我们。*Our teacher often spurs us on.*

**鞭打　biāndǎ** V to whip

**鞭炮　biānpào** N firecracker · MW 颗、串

**鞭子　biānzi** N whip · MW 条、根

**1968　慰**　　　U+6170　　　TM **20** FM ╱

**wèi** V to comfort, to console

**慰劳　wèiláo** V to show appreciation for (a service, etc.) and present a gift

**慰问　wèiwèn** V to comfort; to convey sympathy/greetings

孩子们, 学习辛苦了, 我们**慰问**你们来了。
*Boys and girls, you have been studying so hard, we have come to honor you.*

**慰唁　wèiyàn** V to console

**RELATED WORDS**

自慰 305　　　安慰 487　　　快慰 497
宽慰 1618

**1969　赞**　赞　U+8D5E　　　TM **20** FM ╱

**zàn** V to assist, to aid; to praise, to compliment

**赞比亚　Zànbǐyà** N Zambia

**赞成　zànchéng** V to agree with; to endorse, to approve

我**赞成**你的意见。*I agree with you.*

三票**赞成**, 两票反对。*Three votes for and two against.*

**赞成**的同学请举手。*All students in favor, please raise your hands.*

**赞歌　zàngē** N song of praise · MW 首

**赞美　zànměi** V to praise; to eulogize

**赞佩　zànpèi** V to admire, to esteem

**赞赏　zànshǎng** V to appreciate; to think highly of

他非常**赞赏**你。*He appreciates your behavior very much.*

**赞叹　zàntàn** V to marvel at; to praise highly

**赞同　zàntóng** V to approve of; to agree with

**赞许　zànxǔ** V to speak favorably of, to praise

**赞扬　zànyáng** V to speak highly of, to praise

**赞助　zànzhù** V to assist, to aid; to sponsor

这个汉语角是我们**赞助**的。*We are sponsoring this Chinese Corner.*

**RELATED WORDS**

参赞 600　　　称赞 1288

**1970　镜**　鏡　U+955C　　　TM **20** FM ╱

**jìng** N mirror; lens

**镜框　jìngkuàng** N eyeglass frames; picture frame · MW 个、副

**镜片　jìngpiàn** N lens; eyeglasses · MW 副、片

我想配一副可以变色的**镜片**。*I want a pair of contacts that change color.*

**镜头　jìngtóu** N camera lens; shot; (movie) scene · MW 个、组

**镜子　jìngzi** N mirror · MW 个

**RELATED WORDS**

风镜 194　　　眼镜 1570　　　墨镜 1843
慢镜头 1882　　　太阳镜 53　　　显微镜 755
望远镜 1622

**1971　躺**　　　U+8EBA　　　TM **20** FM ╱

**tǎng** V to lie; to recline

**躺下　tǎngxià** V to lie down

**躺椅　tǎngyǐ** N deck/lounge/reclining chair · MW 张、把

## 1972 憋    U+618B    TM 20 FM 丶

biē  V  to suppress; to hold (one's breath, etc.);
to stifle; to suffocate; to feel oppressed; to hold
in (urine)

她憋了一肚子火。 *She is filled with pent-up anger.*
教室里太闷, 心里憋得慌。 *The classroom is too
stuffy; I feel suffocated.*

憋不住 biēbùzhù  V  to be unable to hold oneself
back

憋气 biēqì  V  to feel suffocated

## 1973 熟    U+719F    TM 20 FM 丶

shóu/shú  ADJ·ADV  familiar; ripe; cooked;
processed; skilled, experienced; deeply,
thoroughly

苹果熟了。 *The apples are ripe.*
土豆熟了。 *The potatoes are done.*

熟菜 shúcài  N  cooked food ·  MW  道、碟、盘

熟记 shújì  V  to learn by heart, to memorize

熟练 shúliàn  ADJ  skilled, proficient
他是一个熟练的电脑程序员。 *He is a skilled
programmer.*

熟能生巧 shúnéngshēngqiǎo  EXP  practice makes
perfect

熟人 shúrén  N  acquaintance ·  MW  个、位

熟食 shúshí  N  cooked food ·  MW  道、碟、盘

熟睡 shúshuì  V  to sleep soundly, to be fast asleep

熟悉 shúxī  V·ADJ  to know well; familiar (with)
他对学校不太熟悉。 *He is new to the school.*

### RELATED WORDS

早熟 268        成熟 611        烂熟 702
面熟 721        眼熟 1570       性成熟 498
滚瓜烂熟 1819

## 1974 瀑    U+7011    TM 20 FM 丶

pù  N  waterfall

瀑布 pùbù  N  waterfall ·  MW  个

## 1975 遵    U+9075    TM 20 FM 丶

zūn  V  to observe, to follow, to abide by

遵从 zūncóng  V  to defer to; to comply with
在法律问题上, 我们必须遵从律师的忠告。
*Regarding legal issues, we must follow the
lawyer's advice.*

遵命 zūnmìng  V  to obey your commands/
wishes

遵守 zūnshǒu  V  to abide by, to comply with
遵守纪律 *to observe discipline*

遵行 zūnxíng  V  to act on; to follow

遵循 zūnxún  V  to follow, to abide by

遵照 zūnzhào  V  to obey, to comply with
我们必须遵照学校的规定行事。
*We must act in accordance with the school's
policies.*

## 1976 避    U+907F    TM 20 FM 丶

bì  V  to avoid; to escape; to prevent; to repel

避而不见 *to avoid seeing something*

避弹衣 bìdànyī  N  flak jacket ·  MW  件

避风 bìfēng  V  to take shelter from the wind
避风港 *harbor*

避讳 bìhuì  V·N  to avoid (doing/saying something);
taboo on saying the names of emperors, elders,
etc.

避免 bìmiǎn  V  to avoid; to prevent
避免犯错误 *to avoid mistakes*

避难 bìnàn  V  to take refuge; to flee disaster

避暑 bìshǔ  V  to be away for summer vacation

避税 bìshuì  V  to avoid taxes

避嫌 bìxián  V  to avoid arousing suspicion

避孕 bìyùn  V  to use birth control /
contraception

### RELATED WORDS

回避 391         退避 1508        逃避 1509
躲避 1874

## 1977 霞    U+971E   TM **21** FM 一

**xiá** N red sky/clouds; morning/evening glow

霞光 **xiáguāng** N rays of sunlight ·
MW 道、片

**RELATED WORD**

彩霞 1132

## 1978 藏    U+85CF   TM **21** FM |

**cáng** V·N to hide; to collect; to store;
storage area/space

你把钱藏起来了。 *You have hidden the money somewhere.*

**Zàng** N (short name for) Tibet

藏垢纳污 **cánggòunàwū** EXP to shelter evil
people and countenance evil deeds; to harbor
criminals

藏匿 **cángnì** V to conceal; to go into hiding

藏身 **cángshēn** V to hide (oneself)

无处藏身 *no place to hide*

藏书 **cángshū** V·N to collect books;
book collection · MW 部、套

他有很多藏书。 *He has a large collection of books.*

藏族 **Zàngzú** N Tibetan nationality

**RELATED WORDS**

| | | |
|---|---|---|
| 收藏 282 | 西藏 352 | 库藏 482 |
| 冷藏 494 | 珍藏 515 | 矿藏 518 |
| 宝藏 667 | 包藏 836 | 保藏 868 |
| 埋藏 1002 | 暗藏 1676 | 遮藏 1831 |
| 躲藏 1874 | 捉迷藏 1239 | |

## 1979 簿    U+7C3F   TM **21** FM ノ

**bù** N book; register; accounting ledger

簿记 **bùjì** N bookkeeping · MW 本、页

簿子 **bùzi** N notebook · MW 本

**RELATED WORD**

账簿 812

## 1980 籍    U+7C4D   TM **21** FM ノ

**jí** N book; register; native place; nationality

籍贯 **jíguàn** N native place, ancestral home

一般来说，中国人不以自己的出生地，而以父母
的出生地为籍贯。 *In general, Chinese don't
regard their birthplace as their native home,
but their parents' birthplace instead.*

**RELATED WORDS**

| | | |
|---|---|---|
| 入籍 5 | 户籍 129 | 古籍 154 |
| 外籍 218 | 书籍 264 | 典籍 532 |
| 国籍 542 | 学籍 1155 | 祖籍 1190 |
| 原籍 1273 | | |

## 1981 癌    U+764C   TM **21** FM 丶

**ái** N cancer; carcinoma

癌细胞 **áixìbāo** N cancer cell · MW 个

癌症 **áizhèng** N cancer

**RELATED WORDS**

肝癌 650      肺癌 1294

## 1982 爆    U+7206   TM **21** FM 丶

**bào** V to explode, to burst; to emerge,
to crop up; to quick fry/boil

气球爆了。 *The balloon burst.*

爆发 **bàofā** V to erupt (of a volcano); to break out

战争爆发了。 *War broke out.*

爆裂 **bàoliè** V to burst; to crack; to blow out

爆破 **bàopò** V to blow up, to demolish

爆炸 **bàozhà** V to explode, to blow up;
to increase sharply (of population, information,
etc.)

我们处在知识爆炸的时代。 *We are in an epoch
of knowledge explosion.*

爆竹 **bàozhú** N firecracker · MW 颗、串

**RELATED WORDS**

引爆 371      核爆炸 1026

## 1983  邀    U+9080    TM **21** FM ＼

**yāo**  V  to invite; to ask, to request; to seek

**邀功**  **yāogōng**  V  to take all the credit

**邀集**  **yāojí**  V  to invite to a get-together

**邀请**  **yāoqǐng**  V  to invite

给您发出**邀请**  *to send you an invitation*

**RELATED WORDS**

应邀  334        特邀  1094

## 1984 嘴 U+5634 TM **22** FM |

**zuǐ** [N] mouth; [shaped/functioning like a mouth]; words, talk

闭嘴! *Shut up!*
嘴上说说罢了。 *It's just talk.*

嘴巴 **zuǐba** [N] mouth; slap in the face · [MW] 个
他挨了一嘴巴。 *He got a slap in the face.*

嘴笨 **zuǐbèn** [ADJ] inarticulate

嘴馋 **zuǐchán** [ADJ] gluttonous; fond of good food

嘴唇 **zuǐchún** [N] lips · [MW] 片

嘴尖 **zuǐjiān** [ADJ] sharp-tongued
不要嘴尖! *Don't speak so harshly!*

嘴角 **zuǐjiǎo** [N] corner of the mouth

嘴紧 **zuǐjǐn** [ADJ] tight-lipped
他嘴紧得很。 *He is very secretive.*

嘴快 **zuǐkuài** [ADJ] with a loose tongue
她嘴快得很。 *She has a very loose tongue.*

嘴脸 **zuǐliǎn** [N] look, features · [MW] 副、张
丑恶的嘴脸 *ugly features*

嘴皮子 **zuǐpízi** [N] lips; gift of gab

嘴碎 **zuǐsuì** [ADJ] talkative

嘴甜 **zuǐtián** [ADJ] ingratiating; smooth-tongued
她嘴甜得很。 *She talks very sweetly.*

嘴硬 **zuǐyìng** [ADJ] stubborn; reluctant to admit one's mistakes

**RELATED WORDS**

| | | |
|---|---|---|
| 七嘴八舌 34 | 斗嘴 71 | 吵嘴 415 |
| 还嘴 714 | 顶嘴 724 | 贪嘴 827 |
| 亲嘴 908 | 张嘴 1208 | 插嘴 1555 |
| 喷嘴 1563 | 馋嘴 1924 | |

## 1985 擦 U+64E6 TM **22** FM |

**cā** [V] to rub; to wipe (clean); to erase; to apply; to touch lightly, to brush

擦黑板 *to erase the blackboard*
我们擦肩而过。 *We brushed past each other.*

擦光 **cāguāng** [V] to polish, to buff

擦净 **cājìng** [V] to scour

擦亮 **cāliàng** [V] to polish; to be more vigilant

擦伤 **cāshāng** [V] to scrape; to chafe

擦拭 **cāshì** [V] to clean, to wipe clean

---

**1986** 蹲     U+8E72   TM **23** FM |

**dūn** V   to crouch, to squat; to stay

蹲下 **dūnxià** V   to squat down

---

**1987** 警     U+8B66   TM **23** FM |

**jǐng** N·ADJ·V   alarm; emergency; police; vigilant, alert; to be on the alert; to warn

警报 **jǐngbào** N   alarm, warning, alert · MW 阵

拉响了台风**警报**。 *The sirens sounded a typhoon warning.*

警备 **jǐngbèi** N   guard

警察 **jǐngchá** N   police · MW 个、名

警车 **jǐngchē** N   police vehicle · MW 辆

警笛 **jǐngdí** N   police whistle · MW 个、阵

警告 **jǐnggào** V·N   to warn; (disciplinary) warning · MW 个

那个球员已经被裁判两次黄牌**警告**了。 *That player has received two yellow cards from the referee.*

警告处分 *a disciplinary warning*

警棍 **jǐnggùn** N   police baton · MW 根、条

警戒 **jǐngjiè** V   to warn; to keep a close watch on

警句 **jǐngjù** N   aphorism, adage, maxim · MW 个、句

警铃 **jǐnglíng** N   alarm bell · MW 个、阵

警犬 **jǐngquǎn** N   police dog · MW 只、条

警惕 **jǐngtì** V   to be on guard against

你要特别**警惕**这个人。 *You should especially watch out for this person.*

警卫 **jǐngwèi** N·V   (security) guard; bodyguard; to guard · MW 个、名

警钟 **jǐngzhōng** N   alarm bell · MW 个、阵

老师常常给我们敲**警钟**。 *Our teacher often sounds the alarm for us.*

**RELATED WORDS**

| | | |
|---|---|---|
| 火警 72 | 门警 130 | 示警 140 |
| 民警 388 | 告警灯 428 | 告警 428 |
| 法警 686 | 岗警 745 | 报警 1010 |

---

**1988** 繁     U+7E41   TM **23** FM ノ

**fán** ADJ   complicated; numerous; multiple

在许多事情上，我们应该删**繁**就简。 *In many cases, we should simplify by weeding out what is superfluous.*

繁多 **fánduō** ADJ   many; numerous

现在的罚款真是名目**繁多**。 *Nowadays, there are fines for almost anything you can imagine.*

繁华 **fánhuá** ADJ   flourishing; bustling

上海很**繁华**。 *Shanghai is bustling.*

繁忙 **fánmáng** ADJ   busy; bustling

繁荣 **fánróng** ADJ·V   flourishing, prosperous, booming

目前中国的市场很**繁荣**。 *The Chinese market is currently booming.*

繁荣昌盛 **fánróngchāngshèng** EXP   thriving and prosperous

繁琐 **fánsuǒ** ADJ   mired in minor details; overelaborate

繁体字 **fántǐzì** N   original complex (traditional) form of a Chinese character · MW 个

繁殖 **fánzhí** V   to reproduce; to breed

近亲**繁殖** *close breeding*

繁重 **fánzhòng** ADJ   strenuous; heavy (of work, a task); onerous

中国孩子的学习非常**繁重**。 *Chinese students' studies are quite arduous.*

**RELATED WORDS**

| | |
|---|---|
| 纷繁 1102 | 浩繁 1169 |

---

**1989** 翻     U+7FFB   TM **23** FM ノ

**fān** V   to turn over; to cross, to climb over; to multiply; to translate; to search; to fall out, to break up

茶杯被打**翻**了。 *The cup has been knocked over.*

翻案 **fān'àn** V   to overturn a verdict/sentence

谁在闹**翻案**？ *Who is trying to overturn this verdict?*

翻版 **fānbǎn** N   copy; reproduction; reprint · MW 个

**1989 翻 fān** (continued)

他是他舅舅的**翻版**。 *He is a younger version of his uncle.*

**翻覆 fānfù** V to overturn, to turn upside down

**翻滚 fāngǔn** V to roll; to tumble around

**翻脸 fānliǎn** V to fall out; to quarrel

**翻脸不认朋友** *to betray one's friends*

**翻山越岭 fānshānyuèlǐng** V hardships on a journey (LIT to cross mountain after mountain)

**翻身 fānshēn** V to turn over (in bed); to free oneself; to stand up

你别老**翻身**。 *Please stop turning over all the time.*

奴隶**翻身**了。 *The slaves have risen up in rebellion.*

**翻腾 fānténg** V to churn; to think over

**翻新 fānxīn** V to renovate; to retrofit

花样**翻新** *style innovation*

**翻修 fānxiū** V to rebuild; to renovate

**翻修**电脑 *to upgrade a computer*

**翻译 fānyì** V·N to translate; translator; interpreter · MW 个、位、名

请帮我**翻译翻译**。 *Please translate for me.*

**翻阅 fānyuè** V to browse, to look over

**RELATED WORDS**

打翻 289　　　推翻 1242　　　闹翻 1323
滚翻 1819

---

**1990**  鹰　　　U+9E70　　　TM **23** FM 丶

**yīng** N eagle · MW 只

**RELATED WORD**

猫头鹰 1446

---

**1991 颤** 顫　　　U+98A4　　　TM **23** FM 丶

**chàn** V to tremble, to quiver; to vibrate; to shiver, to shake, to shudder

**颤动 chàndòng** V to tremble, to quiver

**颤抖 chàndǒu** V to tremble; to shiver, to shake

他冷得直**颤抖**。 *He is shaking from the cold.*

**颤音 chànyīn** N trill (phonetics)

**颤振 chànzhèn** V to vibrate, to oscillate

**RELATED WORD**

震颤 1839

## 1992 躁 U+8E81 TM **24** FM |

**zào** ADJ rash, impetuous, hot-tempered

躁急 **zàojí** ADJ restless, uneasy

躁狂 **zàokuáng** ADJ manic

**RELATED WORDS**

烦躁 1178 焦躁 1265 急躁 1426
暴躁 1844

## 1993 嚷 U+56B7 TM **24** FM |

**rǎng** V to shout, to yell; to make a racket

嚷嚷 **rǎngrǎng** V to shout, to yell; to argue noisily
你嚷嚷什么？ *What are you yelling for?*

**RELATED WORD**

叫嚷 283

## 1994 蹦 U+8E66 TM **24** FM |

**bèng** V to leap, to jump; to bounce; to hop

蹦蹦跳跳 **bèngbèngtiàotiào** EXP bouncing and
vivacious

## 1995 蠢 U+8822 TM **24** FM ノ

**chǔn** ADJ stupid; foolish; clumsy

蠢材 **chǔncái** N idiot, fool · MW 个

蠢动 **chǔndòng** V to wriggle

蠢货 **chǔnhuò** N blockhead, dunce · MW 个

蠢驴 **chǔnlǘ** N idiot, donkey, ass · MW 头

蠢事 **chǔnshì** N stupidity; folly; lunacy · MW 件
并不是只有蠢材才干蠢事。 *It's not only stupid
people who do stupid things.*

蠢猪 **chǔnzhū** N idiot · MW 头

**RELATED WORD**

愚蠢 1901

## 1996 魔 U+9B54 TM **24** FM ＼

**mó** N·ADJ evil spirit, demon; monster; magic;
mystical; magical

魔法 **mófǎ** N magic; wizardry · MW 个

魔方 **mófāng** N magic square · MW 个

魔怪 **móguài** N demons and monsters · MW 个

魔鬼 **móguǐ** N demon, devil; monster · MW 个

魔窟 **mókū** N den of monsters · MW 个

魔力 **mólì** N magic power; charm · MW 股

魔术 **móshù** N magic
他在变魔术。 *He's performing magic tricks.*

魔王 **mówáng** N prince of the devils · MW 个

魔掌 **mózhǎng** N clutches · MW 个
敌人伸出了魔掌。 *The enemy has expanded his
evil clutches.*

魔爪 **mózhǎo** N claws
斩断敌人的魔爪 *to cut off the enemy's tentacles*

**RELATED WORDS**

入魔 5 妖魔 466 恶魔 1196
着魔 1332

## 1997 露 · U+9732 · TM **25** FM 一

**lòu** V to reveal, to show

**lù** N·V dew; juice; to expose; to reveal, to disclose

露马脚 **lòumǎjiǎo** V to give oneself away

露面 **lòumiàn** V to show one's face; to appear (on public occasions)
我不能露面。*I cannot put in an appearance.*

露头 **lòutóu** V to show one's face
月亮已露头, 她还没来。*The moon has already appeared and she still hasn't shown up.*

露馅儿 **lòuxiànr** V to reveal a secret/surprise, to let the cat out of the bag
不要装傻了, 你的话已露馅儿了。 *Don't be silly, you have already given yourself away.*

露一手 **lòuyīshǒu** V to show off (one's abilities/ skills)

露原形 **lòuyuánxíng** V to reveal/show one's true colors

露光 **lùguāng** V to expose

露水 **lùshuǐ** N dew

露天 **lùtiān** N in the open air; outdoors
这是一个露天电影院。*This is an open-air theater.*

露营 **lùyíng** V to camp out
我们今晚上去露营。*We will go camping tonight.*

**RELATED WORDS**

| | |
|---|---|
| 甘露 95 | 吐露 286 |
| 败露 589 | 泄露 685 |
| 显露 755 | 流露 1493 |
| 裸露 1753 | 透露 1826 |
| 暴露 1844 | 揭露 1851 |
| 抛头露面 1395 | |

## 1998 霸 · U+9738 · TM **25** FM 一

**bà** N·V·ADJ tyrant, despot; feudal chief; bully; to tyrannize, to dominate; to occupy and control; tyrannical; arrogant

霸道 **bàdào** ADJ overbearing; unreasonable
这个人很霸道。*This man is very unreasonable.*

霸权 **bàquán** N hegemony, supremacy

霸占 **bàzhàn** V to forcibly occupy, to seize
霸占别人的财产 *to seize other people's property*

霸主 **bàzhǔ** N overlord · MW 个

**RELATED WORDS**

| | |
|---|---|
| 争霸 595 | 独霸 1095 |
| 恶霸 1196 | 称霸 1288 |

## 1999 嚼 · U+56BC · TM **25** FM 丨

**jiáo/jué** V to chew; to munch
细嚼慢咽 *to chew carefully and swallow slowly*

嚼舌 **jiáoshé** V to gossip; to argue meaninglessly
她喜欢在背后嚼舌。*She likes to gossip behind other people's backs.*

## 2000 赢 赢 · U+8D62 · TM **25** FM 丶

**yíng** V to win; to gain
我赢了比赛。*I have won the game.*

赢得 **yíngdé** V to win; to gain
他赢得荣誉。*He gained honor.*

赢利 **yínglì** V·N to make a profit; profit; gain

赢余 **yíngyú** N profit; surplus

**RELATED WORD**

输赢 1867